Library of Artistic Print on Demand

Post-Digital Publishing in Times of Platform Capitalism

TABLE OF CONTENTS

Introd

uction

Annette Gilbert,
Andreas Bülhoff

Library of Artistic Print on Demand

Translated by Cadenza Academic Translations

Print on demand (POD) has revolutionized the book world. Combined with specialized service providers, this new mode of technologically sophisticated digital printing means anyone can produce and distribute books worldwide without long lead times, financial investment, or risk. This not only opens up new business strategies for publishers, but also low-threshold fields of activity and latitude outside of established institutions, markets, and publics. The result is a democratization of production, which, in turn, has the effect that POD often still carries the stigma of vanity publishing or cheapness. There are also two sides to POD's inherent dream of independence and self-empowerment, since this new sphere is fundamentally dependent on the requirements and interests of new players in the field of platform capitalism, such as Blurb, Lulu, or Amazon's Kindle Direct Publishing, which as system service providers not just print publications, but also publish, sell, and distribute them.

In this tension between artistic freedom and platform-capitalist dependency, a whole subculture of artists, authors, publishers, designers, and activists has arisen that sees itself, in the tradition of the avant-garde, the underground, mimeo culture, and counterculture, as a programmatic alternative to the "Establishment"—whether the book or art market, the literary industry, or politics. Eschewing the trend of high-quality, beautiful, elaborately designed, and lavishly produced books that has emerged in reaction to the virtuality of the digital—a kind of "revenge of analog"[1]—this subculture instead relies on industrially manufactured, that is, quickly and often cheaply produced POD books that are stored as digital files, offered and sold online, and can potentially be ordered from anywhere in the world (at least that is what the platforms state—the "world," unsurprisingly, is largely limited to the North American and European regions, dominated by the English language, and controlled by US firms).

In this way, this subculture actualizes both long-cherished and spontaneous artistic ideas and political approaches and once again probes the book for potential content, aesthetics, materialities, economies, and publics. As an artistic and critical media praxis, these post-digital publications serve as a foil for our contemporary situation, sitting between the classic book market and self-publishing, between gatekeeping and DIY, between analog fetish and digital usability, and between autonomy and dependency in the world of platform capitalism. In their analog-digital hybridity, they can be regarded as the epitome of the post-digital age.

This catalog acknowledges this new mode of production as an important and influential field of contemporary artistic and publishing practice in times of platform capitalism. It maps out this vibrant experimental field of post-digital book culture, which emerged around 2005, in terms of its diversity and proliferation, its historical depth and political relevance, and all its hopes and contradictions. It is based on the "Library of Artistic Print on Demand" containing a selection of 244 publications that have been produced using one of these POD platforms. The collection itself has been conserved and made publicly available for further use both in analog form at one of Europe's leading general and research libraries, the Bavarian State Library in Munich, and in digital form in a web archive (https://apod.li).

1. David Sax, *The Revenge of Analog: Real Things and Why They Matter* (New York: Publicaffairs, 2016).

SELECTING

The point of departure for the collection was the observation that only a few POD publications of these experimental subcultures from the fields of literature, art, artists' books, design, and photobooks have so far made it into established collecting institutions. This institutional blind spot led to the founding of the Library of Artistic Print on Demand, which positions itself at the intersection between institutions and the non- or anti-institutional realm of creative production. As such, it follows in the tradition of similar initiatives by other actors in the field—Paul Soulellis's Library of the Printed Web (2013–2017) and Silvio Lorusso's Post-Digital Publishing Archive, for instance. It also supplements the first institutional collection initiatives, such as at the MoMA Library (home to Soulellis's Library since 2019), the Library of Brown University Buffalo (which has acquired the entire production of the publishing collective Troll Thread), and University Library Bern (which was guided by our selection when creating its own POD collection).

Of course, the Library of Artistic Print on Demand cannot assume the collection mandate of national libraries and carry out comprehensive, end-to-end cataloging of all the publications in this field. As a collection and research project mediating between field and institution, by definition, it focuses solely on a very restricted segment of the huge and complex POD-platform cosmos, which, moreover, is both historically indexed and geographically and thematically limited. The fact that the first books in the collection date from 2006 and that the Library comprises 244 titles mainly from North America and Europe does not imply the definition of a "birth year" for the genre, nor does it claim to be an exhaustive account of the field. It is, rather, the result of outside factors including the unavailability of some titles and a very limited purchasing budget, to which the German Research Foundation (DFG) is a contributor, as are the Bavarian State Library, the Baumgart-Stiftung in Munich, and Friedrich-Alexander-Universität Erlangen-Nürnberg.[2]

Its geographical bias can also be attributed to the fact that the POD platforms that dominate the market originated in the USA, and that their network of partner printers, far from being global, is concentrated in North America, Western Europe, and Australia.[3] The circle of authors, artists, and publishers represented in the collection is therefore fairly homogenous, despite the democratization of the field of production. While it is true that platform services can, in principle, be accessed from anywhere in the world, this rarely happens due to the availability of local alternatives, high shipping costs, and the difficulty of calculating customs charges. Incidentally, since Brexit this now also applies to shipments from the UK, which is one of Blurb's major production sites; this makes its services significantly less attractive for people ordering from continental Europe. And even the few publications known to come from an author outside the Global North (for most publications, the producer's exact location is difficult to pin down) are generally in English, which implies that they are addressed to an audience other than the domestic one. It also once again shows the global dominance of English, even in this niche field of experimental art, literature, design, and publishing.[4] Although there are very few *non*-English-language publications in our collection, the authors themselves come from a wide variety of linguistic and cultural regions, from Australia, Egypt and Chile through Slovenia, Romania and Italy to Singapore, Japan and Hong Kong. The

2. In addition, we have received some donations and have also been able on occasion to purchase the publications from the authors at cost price.

3. Possible alternatives are even more limited regionally (the German Books on Demand (BoD) only operates within Europe, for example), and the inclusion of other players would need greater familiarity with the different global regions, the involvement of local specialists, and a larger research team.

4. For a discussion of bias and exclusion in experimental literature see Natalia Cecire, *Experimental: American Literature and the Aesthetics of Knowledge* (Baltimore: John Hopkins University Press, 2019), and Annette Gilbert, *Literature's Elsewheres. On the Necessity of Radical Literary Practices* (Cambridge, Mass.: MIT Press, 2022).

fact that this is not captured in the metadata is due to the difficulty of identifying an accurate geographical location in the digital age.[5]

An open call did not do much to change this situation because the call itself was mostly circulated to networks that are already part of the "scene," without making much impact beyond them. Just as unworkable was an attempt to open up the field via research into the books available in the platforms' web stores, where reading samples are not always available and reviews or customer ratings are extremely rare. It is also very difficult to carry out targeted searches. In their often very rudimentary search functions, which cannot be compared to the "precision and recall" standard in library cataloging,[6] it is frequently impossible even to distinguish between the author and the title. For example, it is only possible to filter search results on Lulu by using the less than helpful categories of format (printed book or e-book), language, average customer rating, binding type, date of release, price, and category, with the latter only showing very general tags, similar to the main subject categories in the book industry. The fact that the metadata has to be entered by authors themselves also leads to a kind of folksonomy, where users apply their own freely chosen tags, abandoning a central controlled vocabulary (thesaurus), to content or information, typically to make those items identifiable, discoverable, and retrievable. This only gives very vague results that are mainly unusable for our research purposes, especially as, in the niche with which the Library of Artistic Print on Demand is concerned, tags and authorship details are often used ironically. Chance discoveries brought about by serendipity or Aby Warburg's "The Law of the Good Neighbor" are therefore fairly rare.

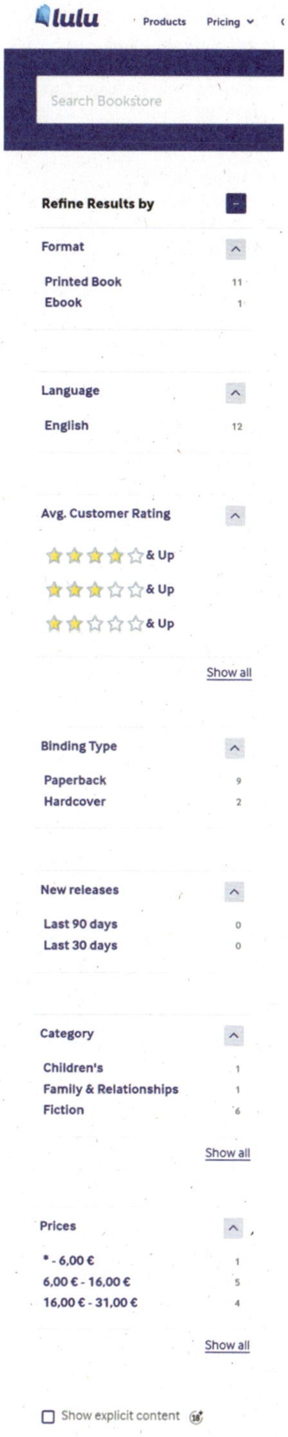

The only way round this is to do as Joachim Schmid did: looking for kindred spirits, he spent days on end scouring Blurb's bookstore for photobook artists who operate in a similar way. He then contacted them with requests to become founding members of the Artists' Books Cooperative. Schmid seems to have been destined to accomplish this self-imposed task given that identifying and extracting patterns from the mass of everyday images is his central aesthetic strategy, and it obviously achieved his goal here. Incidentally, in the process he was able to disprove the expression "You can't judge a book by its cover." After this self-test, he was convinced that, in fact, you can.[7] As well as the cover, the book preview is also essential when carrying out research amongst the overabundance of publications on platforms, a fact that became even more evident in 2019, when Lulu suddenly removed the preview function. It was then more or less a case of purchasing the item unseen.

When selecting our publications, we focused on those that reflect on and creatively use the particular medialities and materialities of POD books, and also on large serial projects and long-term conceptual endeavors that would not find their way into print without POD. In addition, we selected publications that document the dynamic of the field, that address and reflect on the typical phenomena of the post-digital age, whether socio-political, cultural, or economic, and that (self-)critically explore the idiosyncrasies and limitations of the POD ecosystem, including its systemic reliance on the new intermediaries. As a result, many of our publications originate in fields of art, photogra-

5. What criterion should be used: the author's place of birth, nationality, current country of residence, main place of residence at the time of publication, or the place of publication, if a "publisher" was involved?

6. Hartmut Abendschein makes this the subject of his eponymous "catalog performance" *Precision and Recall. Suchbewegung in der Ordnung der Dinge* (self-publ.: / aaaa press, 2021). See in this volume, 439.

7. Joachim Schmid, interview by the authors, November 14, 2019.

EDITION CHARACTERISTICS Λ
(partially) censored
available for a limited time only
available only through the artist / publisher
cc 0
cc by
cc by-nc-nd
cc by-nc-sa
cc by-sa
crowdfunded
dated
doi
isbn
limited edition
multiple editions
multiple versions / multiple cover variants
no copyright / copyleft / unlicense / public domain
no longer available
not publicly available / not for sale
numbered
open edition
second edition
signed
sold out
stamped / embossed
temporarily not available
third edition
unique copies

phy, literature, and design that are (post-)conceptual, critical of the media or institutions, oriented towards mediality and materiality, or interventionist. We also have individual titles that open up the field a little and demonstrate its breadth and diversity: from books with production errors (*Amphibian*, 2018) or from Google's public-domain inventory (*Drie Verhalen*, 2020) through informative approaches to technical solutions from other genres (*Low-tech Magazine*, 2019, and *Subcutanean*, 2020) and publications originating in political activism (*The 2015 Baltimore Uprising: A Teen Epistolary*, 2015), to objects that are difficult to define and classify and that testify to the idiosyncratic nature of this artistic field (*L-MEM*, 2013).

CATALOGING

To help map the covered field in more detail and organize the collected works in a systematic way, we have developed cataloging and indexing practices that are also designed to accommodate the post-digital and extra-institutional aspects of their artifactuality. These go further than the usual information included in bibliographic catalogs, in that they also include the POD platform as well as, under the "edition characteristics" keyword, information about a work's availability, accessibility, and distribution. In addition to this more detailed descriptive cataloging, we have developed our own open cataloging vocabulary for describing and tagging in the Genre, Method, and Subject categories.

In terms of quantity, the Genre category is dominated by experimental literature, education / classroom publications, photobooks, and artists' books. With regard to the latter, we follow Ulises Carrión and Clive Phillpot in also using the term "bookworks," which can refer to literature, art, photography, design, and/or typography, thus avoiding any restriction of this holistic media approach to artists alone.[8] The Genre category also includes publications that form part of artistic research or were produced in exhibition contexts. Lastly, we list some projects in which the POD product represents only an intermediate product ("Halbzeug") that requires further processing.

In the Method category, it is the wealth of works dealing with archiving, documenting, collecting, appropriating, and processing found materials that stands out. In addition, there are many computer-generated publications as well as works that focus on processes of remediation and reformatting.

The Subjects dealt with by the publications, which are equally important for faceted classification, are, unsurprisingly given the above-mentioned selection criteria, primarily concerned with technical and/or media aspects (analog / digital, code / programming, print technology, book / book design), politics (tracking, bias, activism, data, censorship, surveillance / privacy, economy / labor), institutional critique (art world / literary world, canon, copyright / law), or phenomena related to digital culture (memes, dating, visual culture, internet culture, web design).

GENRES Λ
artistic research
artist's book / bookwork
catalog / collection
education / classroom
exhibition copy
experimental literature
fiction
intermediate product / halbzeug
nonfiction
photobook
poetry
reprint
tutorial

METHODS Λ
appropriation
collection
collective
composition (writing / drawing / photography)
constraint
détournement / hack
documentation / archiving
found material
generative / automation
montage / remix
outsourcing
paratextual play
photocopy / scan
pricing
reenactment
reformatting
remediation
study / analysis
test / experiment
translation / transcription
versioning / seriality

8. See Ulises Carrión, "Bookworks Revisited," in Carrión, *Second Thoughts* (Amsterdam: VOID Distributors, 1980), 56–70, and Clive Phillpot, *Booktrek: Selected Essays on Artists' Books since 1972* (Zurich: JRP|Ringier, 2013).

SUBJECTS
amazon
analog / digital
art
art world / literary world
authorship
bias
book / book design
canon
censorship / ban
code / programming
copyright / law
crowd / collaboration
data
dating / sex
ecology / sustainability
economy / labor
email / messaging
error / corruption / loss
facebook
film
flickr
games
gender
google
instagram
internet culture
literature
maps / street view
materiality
mechanical turk
memes
memory / storage
music / sound
narration
photography
platforms / companies
politics / activism
print technology
print-on-demand
publishing / distribution
race
reading / interpretation
scale
search engine
social media
standard / default
surveillance / privacy
technology
tracking
twitter
typography
visual culture
web design
wikipedia
writing / reading techniques
youtube

Our attempt at developing a cataloging system has received support from Hartmut Abendschein, librarian at University Library Bern, publisher at edition taberna kritika, and editor / publisher of / aaaa press, who considers the creative, irregular tagging as an important aspect of his own artistic and publishing practice. With his keywords, which are often idiosyncratic, he seeks to subvert and extend the inflexible and in many respects outdated Dewey Decimal System (which forms the basis for book indexes in libraries), in the hope that they will be imported along with title metadata when it is uploaded to international catalogs such as Worldcat.org, and thus be smuggled into library catalogs around the world.[9]

MATERIAL SAFEGUARDING

In this spirit, the Library of Artistic Print on Demand understands its own purpose to include smuggling POD publications in printed form into collecting institutions, because it is only by printing them that we can ensure their survival outside proprietary platform servers. It should be noted that, for most POD books, there are only a few print copies in circulation. The books are therefore initially only "potential" printed works awaiting the moment of their "fulfilment," i.e., being printed. Until an order is received that triggers the printing, they exist only as print-ready files on the platform's server, and at best circulate as a PDF or as their paratext, i.e., title data, blurb, digital cover image, or, with luck, extracts in a digital preview. In some cases, our order placement may have been the first time that a work was made accessible in print form to the public.

In this sense, POD has proved to be an astonishingly precarious genre, despite unlimited print runs and enduring availability being touted as the selling points of the POD publishing model. A considerable number of titles are now no longer accessible, whether due to acts of censorship, economic considerations on the part of platforms, changes in formats, materials, or design features, price increases, or even the closure of a POD platform during market shakeouts. What is more, an increasing number of authors no longer want to offer their publications on the platforms and are closing their accounts. This may be due to disputes with the platform, annoyance about poor quality, high shipping costs, or inadequate service. J. Gordon Faylor reflected on the risk of artistic works becoming scarce or even lost, with the risk mainly stemming from the platforms:

> One thing that is really compelling to me is just how fragile this platform can be. I've had the experience multiple times of purchasing a book only to find that it's been taken down a month later. Because of this, I wonder if other copies of it even exist. [...] This fragility is very striking, compared to more formal and structured publishing operations, wherein you produce a certain quantity of a book, give it an ISBN, promote it in some way, etc.[10]

9. See Hartmut Abendschein, "Conceptual Publishing and Library Practice," in this volume, 690–696.
10. J. Gordon Faylor, interview with the authors, February 11, 2021.

For this reason, every order placed becomes an archival act because it is never certain whether a book that is available for ordering today will still be producible tomorrow, or will have been erased, made inaccessible, or its status changed from "public" to "private." This archival work cannot be entrusted to the platforms because they have no interest in the long-term archiving and availability of print files beyond their capitalist logic.Nor can it be left to the artists. But we cannot wait until institutions have reformed their acquisition policies.[11] Our collection therefore attempts to guarantee the survival of this form of extra-institutional creative production, or at least to ensure that a small selection of pertinent publications are preserved in print form and embedded in the cultural memory. The printed book thereby becomes the only reliable data storage device for artistic production—even in cases where the concept already seems to have been exhausted in its digital form. Here, too, the printed work acts as a physical anchor, making it possible to archive even this kind of more digitally oriented POD publications in institutions.

NAMING AS LIBRARY

The physical collection will be given to the Bavarian State Library in Munich as a special collection in its holdings. We made a conscious decision to transfer the collection to a prime public library, and also deliberately emulated the library model when choosing its name because transferring it to an archive or museum would have resulted in a completely different form of cataloging and use, and a completely different degree of accessibility. This has a long tradition in history. In Rome, for example, Pope Sixtus IV (1414–1484) separated the actual archive material, known as the *Bibliotheca secreta* (secret library), from the *Bibliotheca publica* (public library), so "that the archive would concern itself with written material that [...] could not be made public, or only in limited circumstances."[12] In contrast, libraries vehemently assert their right to be public. Their holdings are recorded and researchable worldwide, as well as being accessible to a wide public as a matter of principle, which meets the POD-platform publications' needs of low-threshold accessibility and availability. Moreover, despite being located outside the traditional publishing industry and bookstores, these publications are expressly conceived as "ordinary" books: as such, they are intended to be held, read, distributed, cataloged, and preserved for public access. They therefore fall within the scope of responsibilities of a library, regardless of their obscure content, cheap production, amateurish design, extra-institutional origin, unregulated distribution, or unusual form or media, or however difficult they are to record and index in library catalogs.

Furthermore, libraries—in contrast to memory institutions such as archives or museums, which "in terms of their holdings and cataloging are [more] focused on the past"[13]—seem to be especially suited to the dialectical interplay of storage memory and functional memory, as described by Aleida Assmann: the storage memory collects and preserves a maximum amount of sources, documents, objects, and data, regardless of whether they are of current relevance. The functional memory, on the other hand, is an active memory; it comprises only a fraction of these holdings, which have been consciously selected, reactivated, and actualized by a society. The storage memory forms the precondition of cultural change; it "may be seen as an important reservoir for future

11. Admittedly, these policies may be restricted for quite mundane reasons. Institutions often simply struggle to cope with such publications because their acquisition practices and procurement routes are geared towards established bookstores and B2B processes, not online stores and shopping carts on POD platforms or individual authors with PayPal checkouts. See also Abendschein, "Conceptual Publishing and Library Practice," in this volume, 691.

12. Uwe Jochum, *Geschichte der abendländischen Bibliotheken* (Darmstadt: wbg 2002), 82. Unless otherwise stated, all translations by the Cadenza Academic Translations team.

13. Elmar Mittler, "Die Bibliothek als Gedächtnisinstitution," in *Handbuch Bibliothek. Geschichte, Aufgaben, Perspektiven*, ed. Konrad Umlauf and Stefan Gradmann (Stuttgart: J.B. Metzler, 2012), 33–39, 38.

functional memories."[14] Against this background, libraries are distinguished not only because they preserve the storage memory's media in the long term, but also because they keep the boundary between functional and storage memory permeable by creating the ideal conditions for reactivating these media at any time and transferring them to the functional memory.[15]

In this sense, many of the publications collected in the Library of Artistic Print on Demand serve to further enrich the cultural memory and knowledge stored in books and safeguarded in libraries. This is because they are themselves books that started life as collections—in particular of digital and contemporary culture, as shown by the large number of publications in our collection categorized with "catalog / collection" as the genre or "documenting / archiving" as the method. One example is Angela Genusa's *Spam Bibliography* (2013), which presents all the emails received in her spam folder between September 2012 and March 2013, formatted as a bibliography and sorted alphabetically: senders become authors, the subject line becomes the title, and the date received becomes the publication date. This offers a glimpse of a genre of waste text that is often automatically deleted, and its rhetorical potential. At the same time, it exposes this generic, automated, marketing-speak in the digital age as a kind of transhuman writing that is usually not just written by machines, but also increasingly aimed at non-human readers—namely spam filters—before reaching its real target: the human email recipient. On the other hand, by calling his multi-part documentation of online, far-right forums across Europe a "public library," Nick Thurston links it to a political statement on the role of libraries in forming public views. In his *Hate Library* (2019), he seeks to take discussions and discourses from the "backstage" area of the internet, which despite their public accessibility "do not seem to have become *public knowledge* in any strong sense of that phrase," and bring them into the open, making them accessible to parts of the public "who would never enter those online bubbles."[16] Printing these online discourses and transferring them to a library turns them into "matters of public concern."[17]

Paul Soulellis was one of the first to identify this artistic web-to-print practice, at the interface between screen and printed page, as a phenomenon of our time, and he therefore gathered specific examples in his Library of the Printed Web. He describes their authors as "artists who work as archivists, or artists who work with new kinds of archives. Or perhaps these are artists who simply work with an archivist's sensibility—an approach that uses the dynamic, temporal database as a platform for gleaning narrative."[18] Soulellis's own publications are the best example of this approach, which, in light of political events in the USA, he later called "urgent publishing."

> To publish is, fundamentally, a political act.
> In moments of crisis, as we've experienced so deeply in the last year, we see not only artists, but community organizers, scholars, poets, and activists collectively engaging with different modes of publishing to urgently document and communicate what's happening, in real time.[19]

14. Aleida Assmann, *Cultural Memory and Western Civilization: Functions, Media, Archives* (Cambridge, Mass.: Cambridge University Press, 2011), 130.
15. See Mittler, "Die Bibliothek als Gedächtnisinstitution."
16. Both citations Nick Thurston, "Back to Front Truths. Hate Library," in *Post-Digital Cultures of the Far Right: Online Actions and Offline Consequences in Europe and the US*, ed. Maik Fielitz and Nick Thurston (Bielefeld: transcript, 2019), 193–204, 203 and 194 [emphasis in the original].
17. Nick Thurston, "Document Practices," *transmediale journal: face value #1*, ed. Elvia Wilk, August 7, 2018, https://archive.transmediale.de/content/document-practices.
18. Paul Soulellis, "Search, Compile, Publish," in *Publishing Manifestos*, ed. Michalis Pichler (Cambridge, Mass.: MIT Press, 2019), 228–232, 229.
19. Both citations Paul Soulellis, "Urgent Publishing after the Artist's Book: Making Public in Movements towards Liberation," *APRIA Journal* 3 (October 2021): 31–34, 32, https://apria.artez.nl/urgent-publishing-after-the-artists-book/.

In this context, his zine, *Thank you for your interest in this subject* (2017), documents the systematic deletion of countless web pages on whitehouse.gov immediately after Donald Trump's inauguration on January 20, 2017, at around 17:00. The web pages affected were mostly those dealing with civil rights, women, education, disabilities, immigration, Native Americans, Hispanics, African Americans, LGBT, health care, and Barack Obama's climate action plan—in other words, all those areas in which Trump resolutely pursued the opposite policy to his predecessor in office. Each screenshot of the redacted page, with phrases such as "Thank you for your interest in this subject. Stay tuned as we continue to update whitehouse.gov," is accompanied by a screenshot of the last view of the respective page during Obama's time in office, both reconstructed by Soulellis from the Internet Archive and contrasted on a double-page spread.

DIGITAL ARCHIVING

The physical artifacts that form the basis of our Library of Artistic Print on Demand are supplemented by an extensive web archive containing further material. It records every publication not just as in a library catalog, with its bibliographic metadata, characteristics, versions, materialities, and production errors, but also with a detailed description of the artistic concept, content, and context, augmented with screenshots, PDFs, photos, videos, links, bibliographic references, etc. Special attention is given to comprehensive photographic documentation of the printed artifacts, taking into account their objectness and materiality, as well as their complete paratext (from front matter and back cover to blank pages and the platform provider's QR and production codes), to ensure that digital users of the library can also view the objects. This is a fundamental difference between the web archive of the Library of Artistic Print on Demand and the way in which the books are presented in online stores on the platforms. The latter generally only retain the print files from the cover and the content in PDF format, from which no conclusions can be drawn about its bookness, materiality, three-dimensionality, any special production features, or its individual execution (including production errors).

The web archive also has the advantage that the subsequent cataloging of the collection by the Bavarian State Library can be enhanced via our interface with our categories and cataloging vocabulary for describing, tagging, and categorizing the publications. This is crucial because probably only a fraction of this data will be able to be transferred to the rigid system of the OPAC (Online Public Access Catalog) there, where it is currently not even possible to locate POD publications on the system using a targeted search. Artists' often playful or subversive approaches to title and author data and other paratext also make it difficult to adequately map the works in the OPAC.

Moreover, for the sake of the works' global reception, it would be ideal for the physical artifacts to be supported by a web archive that is freely available worldwide, given that inclusion in the Bavarian State Library promises both institutional cachet and long-term archiving. According to their bibliographical classification, the publications will all be assigned to the Rare and Artists' Books section, and thus become part of the specially protected holdings, which are subject to specific, restricted conditions of use—only available by appointment and under supervision in special reading rooms on site, with limited opportunities for photography and scanning, and not available to borrow from the institution or via interlibrary loans.

The decisive factor, however, in view of the precariousness of the POD ecosystem, is that our collection will be part of a prime European library, albeit with restricted access on site; at the same time, thanks to the web archive, it will exist as a distinct library that takes into account both the post-digital, hybrid nature of the artifacts and their often intrinsic critiquing of the establishment and its institutions. Thus, via the collection, these "poor books" will be smuggled into exactly the place where they would otherwise not be housed: the sanctum of the library. In addition to the physical collection, the archiving institution, and the digital archive, this catalog forms the fourth location for the archival practice of the Library of Artistic Print on Demand. In conjunction with collecting key theoretical texts and essays, it serves as a device to make this field of artistic production accessible in a handy, compact format, to distribute it via the book market, and to smuggle it into the holdings of libraries worldwide beyond the confines of the library housing the actual physical collection.

Annette Gilbert, Andreas Bülhoff

Post-digital Publishing in Times of Platform Capitalism

Translated by Cadenza Academic Translations

Editorial note: All quantities and prices are as of January 2023. All URLs were last checked March 31, 2023. The underlined titles are part of our Library of Artistic Print on Demand; you can find more information about them in the catalog section of this book and in the digital archive https://apod.li/.

Revisiting the Printing Revolution: Technology and Economy

FROM FORD TO TOYOTA

Print on demand (POD) has always existed in some form, from Luther posting his theses to copy-shop readers and hectographed pirate editions of Horkheimer and Adorno from the 1968 generation all the way to texts printed on home printers. In a narrower sense, however, POD refers to a digital printing technology that made an enormous leap forward around the turn of the millennium: suddenly it became technically possible to industrially produce micro-editions in single print runs that, despite higher unit costs compared to offset printing, were economically viable and of reasonable quality. HP, a pioneer in the field of digital printing technology, even confidently claims that documents printed on its Indigo full-color printer have "a true offset look and feel."[1]

However, the decisive factor for the success of POD on an industrial scale was not so much the perfection of the printing technology itself, but rather the fact that books were now no longer printed as stock, but to meet demand: "[M]uch more than the machine's abilities at the time, the true upheaval was to be found in the fact that the objects were produced *after* they had been sold as opposed to being produced *in order* to be sold."[2] This transformation, described by Émilie Mathieu and Juliette Patissier as "profoundly disruptive,"[3] has been compared to the transition from Fordism to Toyotism in the post-war period, when the mass production of standardized consumer goods according to Taylorist methods was replaced by lean, flexible, and decentralized just-in-time production processes that avoided overproduction and warehousing:

> POD is a kind of Toyotism applied to publishing. [...] Instead of consuming what has been produced (Fordism), one produces what has been ordered by the consumer. [...] Faced with uncertain and fragmented demand, Toyotism offers a solution called "just in time." [...] POD partially adopts this model by inverting and automating production flows. It is a "pull" production flow, as opposed to the "push" flows typical of manufacturing in the traditional book market.[4]

This shift from "push" to "pull," however, demands a radical rethinking and reorganization of all connected workflows—a step that only few printers were ready to take in the early days. Frequently, it happened as a result of external pressure. For example, when highly profitable business areas collapsed at the beginning of the 2000s because certain content could be more effectively and economically conveyed in digital form, and core clients such as Microsoft or Adobe suddenly began to provide instruction manuals for their products on CD-ROMs rather than in printed form. In this period of radical change, POD offered printers a new business area, but one in which even many years of experience in the print business were no longer a guarantee of success. For it was no longer a matter of processing printing orders for one title in a large print run and then delivering the product on pallets to the customer's address. Volume was no longer defined in terms of the size of a single title's print run, but rather the number of titles to be printed, which, in extreme cases, could mean orders for just a single copy to be individually produced and shipped. Bruce Waterman, Senior Vice President of Print Operations at the POD service provider Blurb, acknowledged this in 2012, saying, "Most orders are one book and one box going to one place."[5]

This requires completely new IT-enabled workflows, as Manon Bruet points out: "The [...] simultaneous printing of different orders with similar characteristics (on the same paper and with the

1. "The Foundations of HP Indigo LEP Technology," HP Official Site, https://www.hp.com/us-en/industrial-printers/indigo-digital-presses/lep-digital-printing-technology.html.
2. Manon Bruet, "Production Process: Print on Demand," in this volume, 490–500, 492 [emphasis in the original].
3. Émilie Mathieu and Juliette Patissier, *Enjeux & développements de l'impression à la demande* (Paris: Éditions du Cercle de la Librairie, 2016), 22.
4. Mathieu and Patissier, *Enjeux & développements*, 21.
5. Bruce Waterman, "Blurb Operations SVP Bruce Waterman on Photobooks and Self-publishing," interview by Cary Sherburne, WhatTheyThink, November 16, 2012, https://whattheythink.com/video/61163-blurb-operations-svp-bruce-waterman-photobooks-self-publishing/.

same colors) on the same sheet, seems then to be the key to the 'on demand' model."[6] Along with the optimal distribution of several orders across sheets and printers, the introduction of a barcode system may also have played a decisive role.[7] It is essential for ensuring every print order is clearly identified, the book block and cover are accurately matched and supplied with the correct binding, and the finished book is packed in a suitable box and dispatched to the correct address. Delivery via various external shipping providers and complaints-handling by customer service must also be smoothly integrated into the process.

Demands on partner printers were correspondingly high, as Waterman explains:

> The first is printing, which we think is the easiest thing to do. The second is really production [in] a volume of one. There is a lot of commercial printers that can do 10,000 books and send them in a pallet to one place, but doing 10,000 packages is a little bit different part of the business. [...] [T]he third is really IT and having a real expertise at how we're going to transfer the files because our books in order to get the price point where we need them to be [...] have to be untouched until they come out of the Indigo press and then they're ready to be bound. Basically it's got to go straight through and our files go through 99.8 percent of the time to our PSP [print service provider].[8]

One such "print partner with an efficient, cost-effective process that could handle multiple one-off orders and product customization"[9] was RPI Print, a Seattle-based company that was Blurb's first partner in 2005. The company lists the individual elements of its technology-enabled, automated workflow solution as follows:

- Batching: Batching allows RPI to print unique products that share the same size and paper type in a single printer run.
- Book Blocks: Book blocks are scanned into the book insert and placed on a book belt carrier.
- Covers: Every cover is scanned into a specific location. When a book block arrives at Match & Go the computer displays the location of its cover. For the carrier to move it is necessary to scan the cover and the book block.
- Binding: The cover is scanned and placed on the book belt together with its book block. Later the two elements will be bound in an incasing machine.
- Dust Jacket Hardcovers: Dust jacket hardcovers go through an additional step. At Wrap & Go they are matched and wrapped in a dust jacket.
- Complete Photobooks: Complete photobooks arrive at the book exit where they are scanned to signal in our system that they are ready for shipping.
- Final Check: All books go through a final quality check.
- Shipping: Orders that consist of more than one product are scanned into a Match & Dispatch location and shipped after the order is complete.[10]

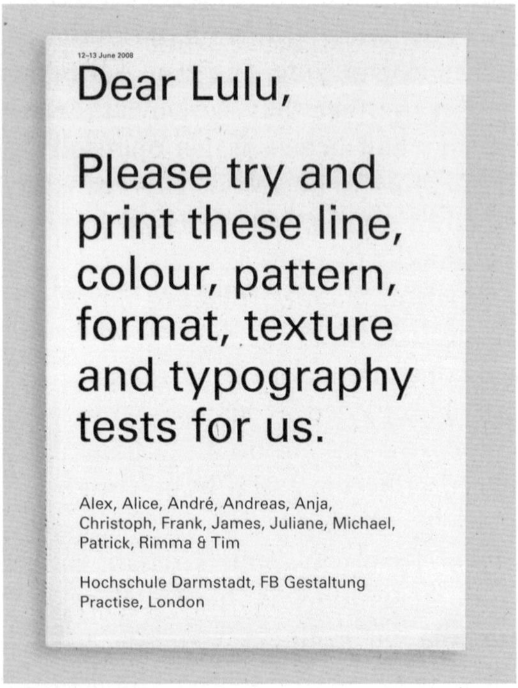

6. Bruet, "Production Process," 495.
7. This barcode system is used to identify individual items or batches, i.e. for internal tracking and logistics during production, and should not be confused with the barcode that encodes a book's ISBN.
8. Waterman, "Bruce Waterman on Photobooks and Self-publishing," interview.
9. "RPI Print," RPI Print, https://www.rpiprint.com/. See also "Innovating Digital Print-On-Demand Since 2005," press release, RPI Print, February 3, 2022, https://www.rpiprint.com/innovating-digital-print-on-demand-since-2005/. Except for RPI Print, Bruet's observation still applies: "It is [...] impossible to find where or by whom the books are printed, or even the companies with whom they are associated on the websites of Lulu or Blurb." Bruet, "Production Process," 495. Information about the printer's location can also rarely be gleaned from the dispatched parcels, as the sender is usually given as the headquarters in the USA.
10. "Automated Flow," RPI Print, https://www.rpiprint.com/products-services/automated-flow/.

The machines take over, in other words. The question of where—or even if—humans still have a hand in these highly automated processes, in which books are to remain as "untouched"[11] as possible, led James Goggin's graphic design students, tasked with exploring new production processes in a test book, to anthropomorphize the machines at work by using the following unusual form of address as the title and cover of the resulting book: *Dear Lulu, Please try and print these line, colour, pattern, format, texture and typography tests for us* (2008). The extent to which remnants of human work can also be automated by the machine process is shown in *Emoji Dick; or The Whale* by Fred Benenson (2010), who entrusted not only the production and distribution of the printed book to highly efficient, automated workflows, but also the drafting of its contents (a translation of Melville's *Moby Dick* into emojis) to the Amazon Mechanical Turk temp-work platform, which is tellingly promoted by Amazon as "artificial artificial intelligence." In this perfecting of algorithmic management, the human crowdworkers are completely integrated into the digital work processes, right down to their anonymized alphanumeric MTurk usernames, as listed in the acknowledgements at the end of *Emoji Dick* (see figure on the right). Jeff Bezos described the workers during the market launch as a kind of extension of software: "You've heard of software-as-a-service. Well, this is human-as-a-service."[12] *Dear Lulu* and *Emoji Dick* represent the extremes of the human-machine relationship that is reflected and incorporated in many of the works collected in the Library of Artistic Print on Demand.

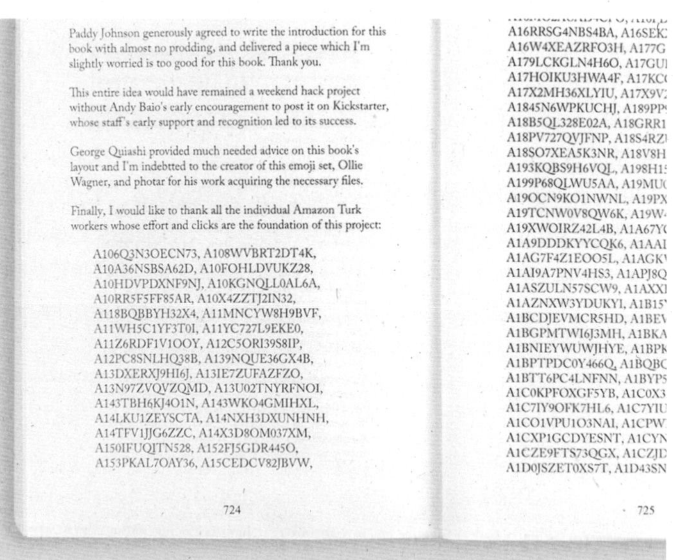

Paddy Johnson generously agreed to write the introduction for this book with almost no prodding, and delivered a piece which I'm slightly worried is too good for this book. Thank you.

This entire idea would have remained a weekend hack project without Andy Baio's early encouragement to post it on Kickstarter, whose staff's early support and recognition led to its success.

George Quiashi provided much needed advice on this book's layout and I'm indebtted to the creator of this emoji set, Ollie Wagner, and photar for his work acquiring the necessary files.

Finally, I would like to thank all the individual Amazon Turk workers whose effort and clicks are the foundation of this project:

A106Q3N3OECN73, A108WVBRT2DT4K,
A10A36NSBSA62D, A10FOHLDVUKZ28,
A10HDVPDXNF9NJ, A10KGNQLL0AL6A,
A10RR5F5FF85AR, A10X4ZZTJ2IN32,
A118BQBBYH32X4, A11MNCYW8H9BVF,
A11WH5C1YF3T0I, A11YC727L9EKE0,
A11Z6RDF1V1OOY, A12C5ORI39S8IP,
A12PC8SNLHQ38B, A139NQUE36GX4B,
A13DXERXJ9HI6J, A13IE7ZUFAZFZO,
A13N97ZVQVZQMD, A13U02TNYRFNOI,
A143TBH6KJ4O1N, A143WKO4GMIHXL,
A14LKU1ZEYSCTA, A14NXH3DXUNHNH,
A14TFV1JJG6ZZC, A14X3D8OM037XM,
A150IFUQITN528, A152FJ5GDR445O,
A153PKAL7OAY36, A15CEDCV82JBVW,

724

A16RRSG4NBS4BA,
A16W4XEAZRFO3H,
A179LCKGLN4H6O,
A17HOIKU3HWA4F,
A17X2MH36XLYIU,
A1845N6WPKUCHJ,
A18B5QL328E02A,
A18PV727QVJFNP,
A18SO7XEA5K3NR,
A193KQBS9H6VQL,
A199P68QLWU5AA,
A19OCN9KO1NWNL,
A19TCNW0V8QW6K,
A19XWOIRZ42L4B,
A1A9DDDKYYCQK6,
A1AG7F4Z1EOO5L,
A1AI9A7PNV4HS3,
A1ASZULN57SCW9,
A1AZNXW3YDUKYI,
A1BCDJEVMCR5HD,
A1BGPMTWI6J3MH,
A1BNIEYWUWJHYE,
A1BPTPDC0Y466Q,
A1BTT6PC4LNFNN,
A1C0KPFOXGF5YB,
A1C7IY9OFK7HL6,
A1CO1VPU1O3NAI,
A1CXP1GCDYESNT,
A1CZE9FTS73QGX,
A1D0JSZET0XS7T,

725

The economic advantage of these almost completely automated production processes is obvious. Furthermore, in contrast to traditional print runs, titles can remain available with no need for physical stock, which must be paid for in advance by a publisher or author, tying up capital for a long time, incurring warehousing and logistics expenses, and, in the almost inevitable event of miscalculation, leading to under- or overproduction. The risk for publishers is thus reduced, which in turn opens up new business fields outside of the bestseller sector. This especially benefits niche titles with small print runs or slow sales, which frequently take advantage of the long-tail effect.

THE LONG TAIL

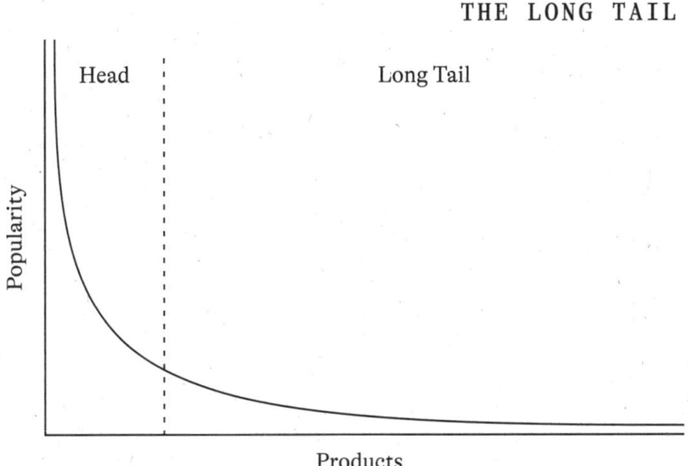

Chris Anderson's term "long tail" is derived from the demand curve that depicts all available products in relation to the number of copies sold, or rather the turnover they yield.[13] On the left, the curve is very steep: this is where one finds bestsellers aimed at a broad public. To the right, the curve becomes increasingly flat: slower-selling products fall on this side. As Anderson's data show, the tip of the tail astonishingly never reaches zero; even there, a few individual copies are always sold, even if in very small quantities. At the same time, this tail becomes lon-

11. Waterman, "Bruce Waterman on Photobooks and Self-publishing," interview.

12. Jeff Bezos, keynote at MIT Emerging Technologies Conference, September 27, 2006, cited in M. Six Silberman and Lilly Irani, "Operating an Employer Reputation System: Lessons from Turkopticon, 2008–2015," *Comparative Labor Law & Policy Journal* 37, no. 3 (2016): 505–542, 509. For a more detailed analysis see Annette Gilbert, "Collateral Writing: Digital Collaboration in the Age of Crowdworking and Algotaylorism," *Counter-Signals* 5 (2024): 130-147.

13. See Chris Anderson, *The Long Tail: Why the Future of Business Is Selling Less of More* (New York: Hyperion, 2006).

ger and longer in digital markets, where the range of products can grow almost infinitely. As a result, new online distribution possibilities are altering the proportion of top sellers in relation to slow sellers, as Anderson demonstrates using the example of the music industry: while 20% of all products used to account for 80% of turnover, in online markets just 2% of all products generate 33% of turnover. A further 33% of turnover comes from 8% of products, while the last 33% is accounted for by the remainder, in other words 90% of all products, even though individually they only achieve low sales figures.

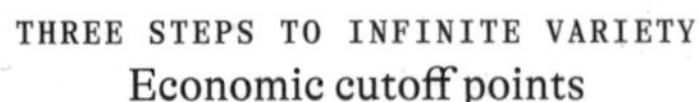

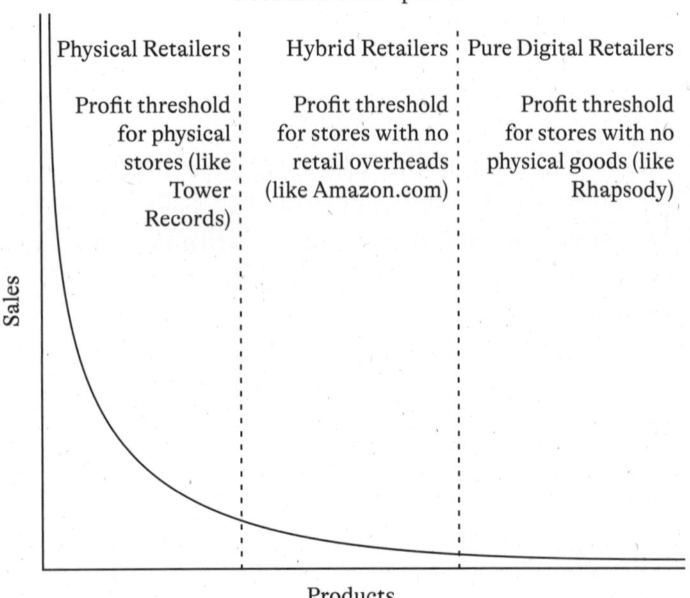

The fundamental prerequisites for this transformation are, first, the availability of increasingly large databases and, second, the internet, which provides access to a potentially infinite number and variety of products: the range of products is no longer restricted, as in analog times, by physical bottlenecks such as costly and limited store and shelf space. In addition, the internet's elimination of geographical market restrictions leads to global availability and increases demand, as products can now reach previously inaccessible target groups.

Along this curve, one may now find three categories of retailers: first, physical retailers such as small neighborhood and large town-center bookstores, whose shelf space and thus physical range of titles is limited. Second, hybrid retailers, such as Amazon, that sell their physical products online, permitting them to expand their range of products significantly, even if they still have costs associated with warehousing, logistics, and delivery. There are also digital infrastructure costs as a new type of cost. Nevertheless, compared to traditional retailers, hybrids have managed to shift the break-even point far to the right. Even further to the right on the curve are, third, the pure digital retailers, such as Audible or Kindle Unlimited, that deal exclusively with digital products and so avoid any warehousing and delivery costs.[14]

POD providers represent an interesting special case within this framework. Unlike pure digital retailers, they do not operate completely digitally: their principal product is the printed book, in other words a physical object with associated shipping costs. Neither, however, can they be equated with hybrid retailers, because although they produce physical goods, they do not stock any products and so have no warehousing costs, unlike Amazon.[15] POD providers thus use an approach combining elements of hybrid and digital retailers: they trade in physical goods but offer their products digitally and have no cost-intensive warehouse stock, meaning there are no economic limitations on their product range.

There have certainly been precedents for this kind of in-between model. DVD-on-demand retailers such as CustomFlix (founded in 2002) similarly straddled the analog and the digital worlds, copying, packing, and shipping films for private consumers on video cassette, DVD, Blue-Ray, or other storage media to order. This arrangement, which allowed independent filmmakers to make their films available irrespective of format or storage medium, was regarded as an especially future-safe business model, because as-yet uninvented formats would also be supported. The firm was not particularly long-lived, however. Amazon bought it as early as 2005 and used it as a springboard into the on-demand market. Amazon subsequently merged it with another acquisition, BookSurge (founded in 2000), to form CreateSpace, the independent publishing platform for books (print and e-books), CDs, and DVDs, which developed over the years into one of the world's leading POD platforms. Since 2018, it has operated under the name of Kindle Direct Publishing.

14. For this as well as the graph see Anderson, *The Long Tail*, 92.

15. These warehousing costs are outsourced to the printers, who must always keep sufficient ink, paper, etc. in stock.

The Book Market after the Upheaval

Over the years, POD's order-based production approach has given rise to a flourishing new book world. This world can be divided into two groups: long-established players who use POD to optimize costs and minimize risk and who treat the internet as an expanded marketplace, and new businesses that are developing completely new niche products and opening up new niche markets.

POD STRATEGIES OF ESTABLISHED PUBLISHERS

THE BACKLIST: "'OUT OF PRINT' IS OUT OF DATE"[16]

The first group includes established publishers that are discovering the potential of POD for their backlists, old titles that they can now keep available for longer without much effort or expense. Doing so allows them not just to offer a varied list of titles, but also to secure their publishing rights to works that would otherwise revert to the authors after a certain period of unavailability. As well as warehousing costs, they also make savings on the often-underestimated costs associated with title management, namely warehouse stock monitoring or reprint costing, and so generate additional profit without further investment.

This benefits not just large- and medium-sized publishing houses such as Brill and Suhrkamp, but also independent publishers and authors. For example, Richard Kostelanetz, the doyen of avant-garde and experimental literature, used the new possibilities of large-scale self-publishing in the digital age to reprint his own works on Amazon, many of them under the label of his publishing house Archae Editions, founded in 1978. In 2022, using Amazon's Kindle Direct Publishing, he founded the *Avant-Garde Classics* series for the publication of out-of-print, marginally published, forgotten, or still unpublished avant-garde works and authors, which he wanted to make (re)accessible at the lowest possible price.

These advantages have also been discovered by leading book wholesalers such as the German Libri, which seek to optimize their long-tail inventory by entering into partnerships with POD services such as Books on Demand (BoD). In the heart of Germany, at the Bad Hersfeld hub, "Libri.PLUREOS combines the latest digital printing technology from BoD with Libri's state-of-the-art distribution centre."[17] This alliance allows Libri to reduce their physical stock while ensuring the availability of millions of titles and fulfilling their advertised promise of overnight delivery to the bricks-and-mortar bookstores.[18]

DIVERSIFICATION FOR DIGITAL-FIRST PUBLISHERS

Meanwhile, other publishers that initially started as digital-only presses are now seizing the opportunity to diversify the formats in which their lists are available and offering their titles in print as well, for which purpose POD is mostly the medium of choice. Independent publisher Christiane Frohmann explains this U-turn in her publishing house's policy by pointing out that the literary status of digitally published texts continues to be seen as dubious, and that the reputation of print is thus still needed as visible proof that a book qualifies as literature. Printing also allows her to make the texts she publishes "accessible to people [...] who are interested in literature but are not Twitter users" and "to convince them that this is [also] great literature."[19] For Strelka Press, in contrast, the decision to introduce a POD line was driven by reader demand for printed books:

> Although we are attracted to printed books, we were reluctant to be tied down to traditional pub-

16. Greg Greeley cited in "Amazon.com Acquires BookSurge LLC," press release, Amazon, April 4, 2005, https://press.aboutamazon.com/2005/4/amazon-com-acquires-booksurge-llc.
17. "Working together for more Diversity in the Book Market. Libri.PLUREOS for Publishers," Libri, https://web.archive.org/web/20231204102637/https://www.libri.de/en/for-publishers/plureos/.
18. These changes are of systemic importance, as the weights in the book market are shifting once again. This is clearly demonstrated by the fact that Libri immediately seized the opportunity to delist numerous small-press titles from its physical stock and return them to their publishers while suggesting that they would have to have their titles printed by BoD in the future if they wanted to continue having them listed in the Libri database and delivered to local bookstores via Libri.
19. Both citations Christiane Frohmann cited in Julika Meinert, "Twitter als Literatur—total genial oder nur banal," *Die Welt*, December 28, 2013, https://www.welt.de/kultur/literarischewelt/article123331985/Twitter-als-Literatur-total-genialoder-nur-banal.html. One could call these printed copies, using Michalis Pichler's term, "seriosity dummies" (Seriositätsattrappe). See Michalis Pichler, "Book Swapping & Seriosity Dummies from Fragments: Life and Opinions of a Real Existing Artist," in *Publishing as Artistic Practice*, ed. Annette Gilbert (Berlin: Sternberg Press, 2016), 206–209, 209.

lishing. We launched as a digital-first publisher precisely to avoid the cumbersome infrastructure of print: primarily the task of distributing physical copies to bookshops around the world. We wanted to be lighter on our feet, and we wanted our readers to have instant access. Print-on-demand publishing is our way of doing printed books while remaining a light-footed digital publisher. [...] [W]e just want readers to have access to our books in whatever format they prefer.[20]

UPDATING: "A NEW VERSION IS AVAILABLE"
POD is equally popular for producing advance versions and review copies to be sent out before the official publication date to institutions and individuals working in literary criticism and book marketing. POD makes it easy to identify such copies as "not-for-sale samples," for example by using white, unprinted book spines. Finally, POD accommodates those authors and publishers who want to update their titles regularly. Especially for science, law, specialist, and nonfiction publishers, POD is "a great tool for adapting editorial content over time,"[21] allowing printed books to keep up with e-books, which can be updated at any time.

This potential was also discovered by artists. The photographer duo WassinkLundgren designed their *Portfolio* of work (2010) specifically to be extendable and revisable. Yigru Zeltil, meanwhile, sees his *Bibliography of Conceptual Writing* (2017) as a work-in-progress both because of the unavoidable incompleteness of such a list, which is drawn up at a specific time, and the changing definition of "conceptual." As a result, it is subtitled with the version number "v.1.01," following the pattern used for software versioning. It is a similar case with Mirabelle Jones' project *Jarring* (2012): the POD edition serves as a pre-version that is intended to be both expandable and updatable. Kathrin Passig, on the other hand, discovered these update possibilities by chance when, having completed and uploaded her collection of columns, *Strom und Vorurteil* (2020), she noticed a hyphenation error on the first page and immediately went to correct it. It took half a day for the new version to be reviewed and approved by Amazon. Although her introduction does mention when the last amendments were made to the text, it remains unclear—as with so-called silent releases in the e-book market—how many revised versions there have been.

With POD, therefore, the printed book is now increasingly both the scene and product of constant revision and improvement, just as Niklas Luhmann suggested when he described the privileging of the most recent text as book printing's contribution to the promotion of the new over the old. For while "in the early writing workshops the constant copying made the texts worse as a result of mistakes being added, during preparation for printing editorial work could be undertaken that improved the text so that the new books could now be presumed to be better than the old."[22]

At the same time, this capacity for constant updating and revision is paradoxically bringing printed books closer to the handwritten medium they once replaced as the default publication format. The invention of the printing press gave rise to "a new media constellation." There were now two media to choose from: "this alternative enabled and forced a functional differentiation, with both manuscript and print taking on new cultural and textual tasks."[23] Since then, the manuscript and typescript has usually been associated with the private, preliminary, and unfinished, while print has been connected with the public, completed, and authorized: "Print technology created the public,"[24] as Marshall McLuhan states.

This distinction, which has endured for more than five centuries, is beginning to shift again with the emergence of POD. Michalis Pichler, who uses POD especially for long-term art projects (*Page Pieces*, 2020–) producing work journals and dummies, declares that it was precisely this "inscribed incompleteness" that most interested him about POD: "It is incomplete and will perhaps remain incomplete." He no longer sees the many different versions of a single book that arise over time as "editions," but as "fictions (dummies) that could be reproduced ad infinitum, but often remain as small print runs or one-offs."[25]

20. "We've Launched Print-On-Demand Editions," *Strelka Magazine*, June 19, 2014, https://web.archive.org/web/20200205050939/http://www.strelka.com/en/magazine/2014/06/19/weve-launched-printondemand-editions.

21. Mathieu and Patissier, *Enjeux & développements*, 55.

22. Niklas Luhmann, *Gesellschaftsstruktur und Semantik: Studien zur Wissenssoziologie der modernen Gesellschaft*, vol. 4 (Berlin: Suhrkamp, 1999), 64.

23. Both citations Rüdiger Schnell, "Handschrift und Druck: Zur funktionalen Differenzierung im 15. und 16. Jahrhundert," *Internationales Archiv für Sozialgeschichte der deutschen Literatur* 32, no. 1 (2007): 66–111, 71.

24. Marshall McLuhan and Quentin Fiore, *The Medium is the Massage* (London: Penguin, 1996), 68.

25. All citations Michalis Pichler, interview by the authors, March 30, 2021.

LONG-TAIL BUSINESS MODELS AND NEW NICHE MARKETS

MASS CUSTOMIZATION: THIS IS YOUR PERSONAL COPY!

In addition to optimizing costs and risks and extending and diversifying publishers' lists, POD can also serve as an "enabling technology"[26] for developing new niche products and markets. For example, a completely new market sector has been created by the trend for mass customization, which can be used for printed materials as well as for muesli, cars, or trainers. Periodicals were pioneers in the world of print. In June 2004, for example, the 40,000 subscribers to the American magazine *Reason* received an edition with a personalized title: it showed a satellite image of the subscriber's own neighborhood that marked their address. A similar initiative was launched by *The Wire* in July 2007, when 5,000 subscribers could send in a portrait photo that then adorned the cover of their own personal issue. The occasion for this was an advertising campaign with Xerox that was supposed to demonstrate the potential of the latest printing and reproduction technologies.[27]

The children's book market has benefitted particularly from this mass customization strategy, offering books personalized with the name or photo of the customer's own child as well as bilingual books in every conceivable language combination. Other popular consumer products include photo albums and calendars as well as books generated automatically from social media feeds or chats, which are frequently created and printed via POD providers such as Cewe, Pixum, or Shutterfly, and are not intended for publication and distribution through online stores or bookstores.

AUTOMATED AUTHORING AND CONTENT CREATION

Another market niche that exploits the long tail was discovered by the economist Philip M. Parker, who, since 2007, has created more than one million reference works with "original content" generated by computer using public, freely available data sets, and successfully sold these as e-books and POD books.[28] Titles include curiosities such as *Webster's Ecuador Quechua – English Thesaurus Dictionary* and *The 2021–2026 World Outlook for Economy-Size Fromage Frais*, which cost $28.95 and $995 respectively on Amazon. Parker's primary motivation in doing so was not profit. The aim of the ICON Group International he founded was rather "to digitally disrupt the publishing industry to address underserved audiences where traditional authoring and publishing approaches prove uneconomical."[29] His bestsellers have proven to be the world outlooks as well as business and trade reports using granular product categories and global scaling, which are acquired "by consulting firms, investment banks, and companies involved in international trade" as well as by libraries, generally as entire series rather than individual titles: "We gauge sales by series, not by individual titles. Traditional publishers think in terms of individual titles. [...] Some firms subscribe to all titles."[30]

26. Mathieu and Patissier, *Enjeux & développements*, 45 [original emphasis deleted].
27. For more details see Alessandro Ludovico, *Print on Demand: The Balance of Power between Paper and Pixel*, in this volume, 458–463.
28. Initially via Lightning Source and BookSurge, later via the own website and Amazon. See Philip M. Parker, "Method and Apparatus for Automated Authoring and Marketing," United States Patent 7,266,767 B2, issued September 4, 2007, https://patents.google.com/patent/US7266767B2/.
29. ICON Group International, "About Us," ICON Group International, last modified December 8, 2022, https://www.icongrouponline.com/en/AboutUs/.
30. Both citations Philip M. Parker, "Q&A," interview by Mac Slocum, *O'Reilly Tools of Chance for Publishing* (blog), April 30, 2008, http://toc.oreilly.com/2008/04/qa-phil-parker-developer-of-au.html.

FROM PRINT-ON-DEMAND TO REPRINT-ON-DEMAND

The production of some publishers who specialize in reprints of out-of-print or public-domain works can also be seen as a similarly automated, computerized process. Institutions interested in the transmission of cultural heritage, such as the National Library of France, are naturally also active in this market sector. In cooperation with Hachette, the latter is offering works from the literary heritage collection, "reprinted as identical copies, available in all bookshops within the same timeframe as a copy ordered from stock."[31] The blurbs of the US-based Nabu Press (founded in 2012) sound similar: "We believe this work is culturally important, and [...] have elected to bring it back into print as part of our continuing commitment to the preservation of printed works worldwide."[32] Skepticism may be in order regarding the selflessness of this undertaking, however. On the one hand, there is the quantity of the titles produced: Nabu Press is currently offering 70,000 titles on Amazon. According to Bowker's 2009 book industry stats the rankings that year were led by BiblioBazaar—a newcomer to the industry founded by the team that launched POD pioneer BookSurge, of which Nabu Press is an imprint—with 272,930 titles. This almost matches the entire output of the "traditional" industry in the same year.[33]

Top publishers by title output in 2009, Bowker.

PUBLISHER	ISBN count
BIBLIOBAZAAR	272,930
BOOKS LLC	224,460
KESSINGER PUBLISHING, LLC	190,175
CREATESPACE	21,819
GENERAL BOOKS LLC	11,887
LULU.COM	10,386
XLIBRIS CORPORATION	10,161
AUTHORHOUSE	9,445
INTERNATIONAL BUSINESS PUBLICATIONS, USA	8,271
PUBLISHAMERICA, INCORPORATED	5,698

31. Hachette BnF, "L'impression à la demande," Hachette BnF, https://www.hachettebnf.fr/limpression-la-demande. For this, they partner with Lightning Source France, in which Hachette holds a 50% stake.

32. Blurb to the 2014 Nabu Press reprint of Franz Kafka, *Historisch-Kritische Ausgabe sämtlicher Handschriften, Drucke und Typoskripte*, ed. Peter Staengle and Roland Reuß, vol. 17, *Oxforder Quartheft: Die Verwandlung* (Frankfurt/M. and Basel: Stroemfeld | Roter Stern, 2003), Amazon, https://www.amazon.de/Historisch-Kritische-Ausgabe-Samtlicher-Handschriften-Typoskripte/dp/1294775529/.

33. "In 2008, the production of print-on-demand books surpassed traditional book publishing for the first time and since then its growth has been staggering. Now more than twice the output of traditional titles, the market is dominated by a handful of publishers." Bowker, "Bowker Reports Traditional U.S. Book Production Flat in 2009," news release, Cision PR Newswire, April 14, 2010, https://www.prnewswire.com/news-releases/bowker-reports-traditional-us-book-production-flat-in-2009-90862344.html.

These new companies seem to have been inspired less by an interest in cultural heritage than by the realization that it is relatively easy to (re)commercialize the countless public-domain works made available by the mass retrodigitization being undertaken by Google and publicly funded libraries around the world. To perfect the "reprint business' internet-driven business model,"[34] only books published before 1923 are reprinted, with generic stock photos used for the covers. It is almost as if book history is repeating itself: the reprint industry blossomed once before around 1867, when the works of all classic writers who had died before 1837 simultaneously entered the public domain in Germany. Resourceful entrepreneurs seized the opportunity: on that very day Reclam's new Universal-Bibliothek series entered the market, with Goethe's *Faust* as the first volume. Even then, the profitable business of selling works in the public domain was primarily portrayed as a democratization of the book market and an educational initiative.

Today's reprint publishers frequently do not even check the origin and quality of the digital copies they print, as shown by the case brought against a Franz Kafka edition printed by Nabu Press. The stories contained were indeed published before 1923, as is claimed in the blurb: "This is a reproduction of a book published before 1923."[35] The Nabu edition, however, reproduced the highly regarded historical-critical edition of 2003, which was subject to copyright. From a philological point of view, it is also not ideal if this careless approach to sources leads to the widespread distribution of unreliable and inferior editions that then become the digital archetype of a work, the consequences of which for future transmission and research have not been sufficiently considered. In any case, the number of reprints currently flooding the market suggests that production has been largely automated, with no care taken when selecting titles and no final quality control—as the blurbs in fact openly admit: "This book may have occasional imperfections such as missing or blurred pages, poor pictures, errant marks, etc. that were either part of the original artifact, or were introduced by the scanning process."[36]

As the artist Greg Allen shows with his reprint of a completely failed digital reproduction on Google books (evidently even scholarly libraries such as the Bavarian State Library, from whose collection the copy for the scan came, do not guarantee quality), these artifacts may acquire their own aesthetic appeal. He celebrates his facsimile *Wohlgemeynte Gedanken über den Dannemarks-Gesundbrunnen* (2011) as "a rare achievement of the scanner-based book arts" which "is sure to become a classic in the nascent field of glitch studies."[37] The copy in our collection, which was partly printed in color despite being identified as black and white, shows that the error rate can rise even further in the course of the POD production process, which is not only just as automated, but apparently just as error-prone.

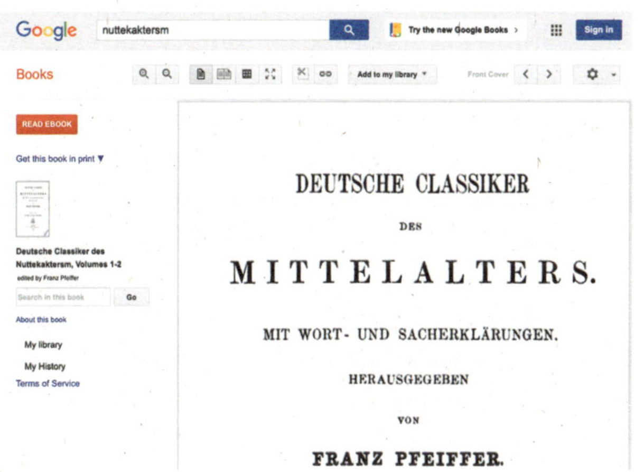

Dagmara Kraus also takes poetic inspiration from these glitches when investigating Nabu Press's *Deutsche Classiker des Nuttekaktersm*: "'Nuttekaktersm' is an automatic text scanning error [...]. A randomly generated 'synonym' for 'Mittelalter' (Middle Ages) [...]. Emerging from a computationally incomprehensible moment of disturbance, 'Nuttekaktersm' is at the same time a kind of half-surreal 'Google-glitch,' an overlooked artifact of translation and retro-digitization,"[38] which has since spread wildly on the net and, according to Worldcat.org, has already found its way into libraries around the world in the form of POD reprints.

34. Kelly Gallagher, vice president of publishing services for Bowker, quoted in Bowker, "Print Isn't Dead Finds Bowker's Book Production Report," Printing Impressions, May 18, 2011, https://www.piworld.com/article/print-isn-t-dead-finds-bowkers-book-production-report/.

35. Blurb to the 2014 Nabu Press reprint of Franz Kafka, *Historisch-Kritische Ausgabe.*

36. Blurb to the 2014 Nabu Press reprint of Franz Kafka, *Historisch-Kritische Ausgabe.*

37. Both citations Greg Allen, blurb to *Wohlgemeynte Gedanken über den Dannemarks-Gesundbrunnen* (self-pub.: Lulu, 2011), https://www.lulu.com/shop/greg-allen/wohlgemeynte-gedanken-%C3%BCber-den-dannemarks-gesundbrunnen/paperback/product-1595m4w7.html.

38. Dagmara Kraus, "The Googlitchy Lórschapelekin: German Classics of the Nuttekaktersm," in this volume, 546–552, 547.

Also involved in the distribution of such misprints is the Espresso Book Machine (EBM) network, which has secured access to the Google Books corpus. Any public-domain text from the corpus can potentially be produced at material-cost price on any EBM in the world in the time it takes to drink a coffee. The copy of Maria Goutier-De Smet's *Drie Verhalen* (1864/2020) in our collection, which we had printed at the American Book Center Amsterdam (which elevated itself to the status of "publisher" on the cover), displays several errors and visual artifacts that were in fact corrected a long time ago on Google Books. This suggests that the EBM database is not being regularly updated. Our copy of *Drie Verhalen* thus exemplifies the book as a stable container for documenting digitization processes and the versioning of digital files.

It is no coincidence that Anne Trettien Whitney refers to "monstrous" POD prints that haunt the net like "zombie[s],"[39] spreading wildly like spam, junk mail, and viruses in a kind of "digital pollution"[40] that the printed book materializes in analog form. In this tangled intertwining of analog and digital, these reprints are proving to be a typical manifestation of the post-digital age: "Though they take the shape of a printed book, these POD reprints—generated by scanners and metadata, materialized through software and on-demand digital printing—are thoroughly digital objects."[41] These providers should not logically be seen as publishers, but rather as software or technology companies, as Whitney holds. This argument is corroborated by Mitchell Davis, president of BiblioLife, who said, "We are really a software company that has books coming out at the end of our process." He goes on: "We have built a large IT infrastructure and a proprietary platform where we take disparate inputs and turn what is essentially a picture of a book page, into what a reader expects a book will look like, and we do that for more than a thousand books a day for distribution through multiple POD channels, in multiple countries and markets."[42]

PUBLISHING FOR ALL: THE BANALITY OF PUBLISHING

However, POD's momentum as an "enabling technology"[43] revolutionizing the book world is seen most clearly in the niche sector occupied by a new generation of POD service providers seeking to render their product range easily accessible to as wide an audience as possible and focusing primarily on end consumers, who they treat—in the spirit of Web 2.0—less as consumers than as prosumers of user-generated content. In this way, POD system service providers "reverse the usual publishing logic: their primary market is authors, not readers"[44]—without, however, repeating the business model of vanity publishers, as they do not force authors publishing with them to pay printing cost subsidies running to several figures or purchase a certain amount of the print run.[45]

The prerequisite for this form of "accessible publishing" was the increasing democratization of the means of production thanks to the affordability and ubiquity of digital and internet-enabled devices, the development of attractive, simple-to-use products in the form of software tools, templates, web interfaces, plugins, and APIs, the spread of the relevant digital literacy, and the popularization of a maker and DIY culture. But even more critical to POD's resounding success may have been the fact that it did not require any special expertise or skills at all. As Clay Shirky provocatively put it in 2012, the once mighty "publishing apparatus" has shrunk in the digital age to a single button: "That's not a *job* anymore. That's a *button*. There's a button that says 'publish,' and when you press it, it's done." Shirky was referring here primarily to the world of the Internet, where publishing "doesn't take professional skills. It doesn't take any skills. It takes a WordPress install."[46] But this

39. Both citations Whitney Anne Trettien, "A Deep History of Electronic Textuality: The Case of *English Reprints Jhon Milton Areopagitica*," *Digital Humanities Quarterly* 7, no. 1 (March 2013): 17 and 27, http://www.digitalhumanities.org/dhq/vol/7/1/000150/000150.html.

40. Jussi Parikka and Tony D. Sampson, "On Anomalous Objects of Digital Culture," in *The Spam Book: On Viruses, Porn, and Other Anomalies from the Dark Side of Digital Culture*, ed. Jussi Parikka and Tony D. Sampson (New York: Hampton Press, 2009), 1–18, 3.

41. Trettien, "A Deep History of Electronic Textuality," 25.

42. Mitchell Davis cited in Andrew Albanese, "BiblioBazaar: How a Company Produces 272,930 Books a Year," *Publishers Weekly*, April 15, 2010, https://web.archive.org/web/20101203104933/http://www.publishersweekly.com/pw/by-topic/industry-news/publisher-news/article/42850-bibliobazaar-how-a-company-produces-272-930-books-a-year.html.

43. Mathieu and Patissier, *Enjeux & développements*, 45 [original emphasis deleted].

44. Anne Haugland, "Opening the Gates: Print On-Demand Publishing as Cultural Production," *Publishing Research Quarterly* 22 (April 2006): 3–16, 3, https://doi.org/10.1007/s12109-006-0019-z.

45. See Moritz Hagenmüller and Friederike Künzel, "Print-on-Demand: Neue Chancen für Verleger und Autoren," in *Ökonomie der Buchindustrie*, ed. Michel Clement, Eva Blömeke, and Frank Sambeth (Wiesbaden: Gabler, 2009), 259–271, 267f.

button also exists in the world of POD platforms. In the case of Lulu, for example, it literally says "Confirm and Publish" (see 106).

Publishing is conceived here as an absolutely presuppositionless practice, whose complexity disappears behind a single button. What used to be in the hands of a small professional caste has finally lost its exclusivity and elitist character. The typewriter, mimeograph, matrix printer, copy machine, and home printer, once the first choice of self-publishers, have done the groundwork. But unlike them, POD publications are industrially produced, making them look like 'normal' books and giving the impression that they are on a par with regular bookstore products.

By reducing the process to a single button and making it available to all, independent of purse and gatekeepers, bookmaking becomes an almost banal and everyday act. This is reflected in the names the platforms give their offerings, such as "BoD Fun" for BoD's basic product, which also suggests that everything is child's play. In addition, there is a starter kit and easyTools, such as easyPrint, easyEditor, and easyCover, for each step.[47] This ease and ubiquity is the reason for the current boom in POD production. The democratization of reading, as observed in the 19th and 20th centuries, is thus complemented by the democratization of (the means of) production.[48]

In short, with extensive support from POD service providers, ordinary people with no knowledge of design, printing, or the book trade can now produce, publish, print, promote, and distribute their works via the internet—not only in the platform's own online store, but also, if they want and once they acquire an ISBN, worldwide in brick-and-mortar and online bookstores to which such platforms are connected via Ingram's Global Retail Network and Amazon. This ensures that their products can be discovered and accessed by other users thanks to features like search functions, recommendations, or filters. System service providers also equip their stores with "accessible and trusted payment systems," thereby finally solving the apparently insuperable problem of distribution, "that had made self-publishing and finding an audience untenable in all but the most extraordinary cases in the twentieth century."[49] James Goggin also highlights the inclusion of distribution as a defining characteristic of the POD platform model: "Generally print-on-demand feels like a logical progression of the web itself. As a first year graphic design student in 1994, it blew my mind to discover the world wide web and the ease with which anyone could upload an html page: instant publication and distribution. POD fulfills this in tangible form: sites like Lulu are both printer and distributor."[50]

The POD-platform business model is also by no means as morally questionable as that of the erstwhile vanity and subsidy presses, which demanded a large sum by way of pre-investment and often required the author to assign away all rights, while rendering virtually no services in return. In this respect, POD is situated somewhere in the middle, as Laquintano states: "Ultimately, POD wasn't quite vanity, it wasn't quite self-publishing, and it wasn't traditional royalty publishing."[51]

This democratization of the means of distribution enabled by POD service providers results in the expansion and diversification of the products on offer and thus to the extension of the long tail and the enlargement of the niche, as the statistics (compiled by Bowker, for example, for the US market) clearly indicate—although the figures are actually much higher as they do not include publications without an ISBN, which constitute a majority of the production on Amazon or Wattpad. Self-publishing has thereby, as Timothy Laquintano states, at least in the North American and European region, "moved from the fringe of the publishing industry to become a small and fluid part of its core."[52]

46. All citations Clay Shirky, "How We Will Read," interview by Sonia Saraiya, Findings.com, April 5, 2012, https://web.archive.org/web/20120504030525/http://blog.findings.com/post/20527246081/how-we-will-read-clay-shirky [emphasis in the original].

47. In July 2023, the product range was restructured: BoD Fun, Classic, and Comfort are now called BoD Print, Publish, Publish Plus, and Publish Premium.

48. However, there is an obvious gap between rhetoric and reality: the world of POD is nowhere near as inclusive as advertised. The egalitarian character is increasingly lost, for example, through the optional extra services that provide opportunities for distinction, so that a multi-class society is also making inroads in this area. The economic imbalance is not eliminated either; the costs are only redistributed—from the producers to the customers. Finally, participation is unevenly distributed geographically. Neither the user base nor the partner network of the platforms is truly global.

49. Both citations Timothy Laquintano, *Mass Authorship and the Rise of Self-Publishing* (Iowa: University of Iowa Press, 2016), 43.

50. James Goggin, "Supply on Demand," interview by Erin O'Hara, *PRINT*, June 1, 2008, https://www.printmag.com/design-inspiration/supply_on_demand.

51. Laquintano, *Mass Authorship and the Rise of Self-Publishing*, 37.

52. Laquintano, *Mass Authorship and the Rise of Self-Publishing*, 3.

ISBN Output for USA Self-Publishers, 2008–2013, Total Print Books (excerpt).

Source: Bowker, *Self-Publishing in the United States, 2008–2013*, 2014.

NAME	2008	2009	2010	2011	2012	2013	increase 2008-13	%increase 2008-13
CREATESPACE	11,498	25,212	35,686	58,857	131,456	186,926	175,428	1525.73%
LULU ENTERPRISES INC.	8,658	10,587	11,681	25,461	27,470	40,895	32,237	372.34%
XLIBRIS (DIV. OF AUTHOR SOLUTIONS)	7,761	10,322	13,416	11,653	10,281	9,319	1,558	20.07%
AUTHORHOUSE (DIV. OF AUTHOR SOLUTIONS)	7,394	9,532	8,705	11,324	9,135	7,498	104	1.41%
IUNIVERSE (DIV. OF AUTHOR SOLUTIONS)	4,578	5,099	4,702	5,272	4,351	3,147	-1,431	-31.26%
PUBLISHAMERICA	5,160	5,794	7,201	5,350	3,692	2,821	-2,339	-45.33%
TRAFFORD (DIV. OF AUTHOR SOLUTIONS)	743	1,647	1,995	2,326	2,998	2,463	1,720	231.49%
WESTBOW PRESS (IMPRINT OF AUTHOR SOLUTIONS)	0	6	502	1,466	2,503	2,362	2,362	n/a
INDEPENDENT PUBLISHER (BAR CODE GRAPHICS)	327	1,866	3,689	3,272	2,566	2,115	1,788	546.79%
OUTSKIRTS PRESS	1,533	1,595	1,576	1,489	1,824	1,931	398	25.96%
SALEM PUBLISHING SOLUTIONS [FORMERLY XULON PRESS]	1,675	1,467	1,480	1,601	1,552	1,670	-5	-0.30%
PALIBRIO (DIV. OF AUTHOR SOLUTIONS)	0	0	12	1,213	1,550	1,441	1,441	n/a
BALBOA PRESS (IMPRINT OF AUTHOR SOLUTIONS)	0	0	53	344	193	1,036	1,036	n/a
BLURB, INC.	0	0	0	0	0	752	752	n/a

These new opportunities for people to explore their creative side and have a go at becoming an author are being seized by artists, writers, photographers, and hobbyists of all kinds. The production output of POD platforms is enormous, as a 2011 work by the artist Andreas Schmidt shows: Just Published used the "just published" filter in the Blurb online store to document the covers of 760 books that had been uploaded and published on the platform in the last few minutes. At the same time, Andreas Schmidt is himself a good example of how POD has opened an outlet not only for so-called hobby authors, but also for artists and authors in the independent, avant-garde, and experimental field. Within five years (2008–2013) Schmidt produced in quick succession no less than seventy-seven photobooks, which he presents at book fairs as a *Gesamtbuchkunstwerkskulptur* (a book-sculpture Gesamtkunstwerk[53]) in the form of a circular, horizontal bookshelf resembling a Kodak slide carousel and representing the ever faster and more unstoppable flow of artistic book production.

53. The title is "coined out of the three German words Buch (book), Skulptur (sculpture) and Gesamtkunstwerk (total work of art, ideal work of art, universal artwork)." Andreas Schmidt, "Gesamtbuchkunstwerkskulptur," 2017, https://www.andreasschmidtgalerie.com/lodz-photofestival.

It is as if a creativity that has been pent up for years has finally been released. Now, at last, you can quickly and easily make all your long-held ideas into reality, as explained by the photobook artist Joachim Schmid. Particularly in the euphoria of the early period, POD bookmaking acquired a momentum of its own: "Basically you belt out a book every day. It's super simple. [...] It's an almost actionist impulse."[54]

With production output on this scale, the individual book loses its weight. Instead of working for months or years to "erect[...] a monument more durable than bronze [and] loftier than the regal pile of pyramids,"[55] you can simply treat it as a rush job. It becomes light and easy, an everyday, spontaneous form of expression where you can try something out and then just abandon it, as explained by Stephen Shore, who may be regarded as a POD pioneer in the photobook field:

> Whenever I find that I begin to repeat myself, I look to head in a new direction. Sometimes, it is a change in location, a change in subject matter. And sometimes, it's a change in the form of the work, and taking advantage of possibilities that might not have existed before. When print-on-demand books started becoming available, I saw a great opportunity. I'd always loved artists' books, but now, I could see artists' books that were readily available and easy to produce. And so, for five years, the main focus of my activity was producing a series of these books, often going in different directions. [...] The books allowed me to explore these things. If I had an idea that I wanted to spend a day playing with, I could do it. I don't need to spend a year playing with it. And this is why I found the books a lot of fun to do.[56]

This attitude was behind the apparition, between 2003 and 2010, of eighty-three "iPhone print-on-demand books made through Apple['s iPhoto application]," in letter size and in "limited editions of twenty, featuring series shot in one day or less, like a visit to the Westminster Dog Show or a walk through Central Park."[57] POD subsequently lost its appeal for Shore thanks to the rise of social media that enabled still other, even more accelerated forms of artistic expression: "I found that same quality again years later when I encountered Instagram. A new means of distribution and a new means of communication open possibilities that didn't exist before."[58]

Platformization: The New Intermediaries and Their Ecosystem

PROVIDING INFRASTRUCTURE FOR "THE WHOLE THING"

Because these global system service providers offer everything in one place—from finalizing a print template and digitally listing a book that may never have been printed to producing and shipping the first copy through to handling the global logistics of book sales, payments, and royalties—they are not really adequately described by the term "*print-on-demand provider.*" Furthermore, the provider itself does not generally perform most of these services; rather, it outsources them and provides an infrastructure in the form of a platform via which they can be combined, coordinated, and offered

54. Joachim Schmid, interview by the authors, November 14, 2019.
55. Horace, *Odes*, trans. Sidney Alexander, 3.30.1–2.
56. Stephen Shore, "Print-on-Demand books. 2003–07," The Museum of Modern Art, 2017, audio and transcript, https://www.moma.org/audio/playlist/45/720.
57. Both citations Jacqui Palumbo, "Stephen Shore's Unorthodox Photography Teaches Us to Celebrate the Everyday," Artsy, February 7, 2020, https://www.artsy.net/article/artsy-editorial-stephen-shores-unorthodox-photography-teaches-celebrate-everyday. See also Stephen Shore, *The Book of Books* (London: Phaidon, 2012).
58. Stephen Shore, "Instagram. 2014–ongoing," The Museum of Modern Art, 2017, audio and transcript, https://www.moma.org/audio/playlist/45/721.

as a package. This fusion of preexisting processes and infrastructures to form a new, post-digital business model was described by Silvio Lorusso as "a genuine hybrid of digital and analog processes":

> under the guise of the "traditional" book form, there is a complex ecosystem made of file formats, metadata, retail platforms, multiple connections to online stores and, sometimes, even YouTube book trailers, authors' blogs, etc. Sent through the regular postal system, the physical book is the tip of the iceberg of an infrastructure that takes advantage of digital printing, desktop publishing, PDF format, and Web 2.0. Therefore, POD is not a new technology in itself, but a fruitful combination of existing ones.[59]

So, here it shows once again that it was not only the optimization of the digital-printing production process that unleashed the full potential of printing technology and made it available to the general public, but also, driven by pioneers such as BookSurge, Blurb, and Lulu, its integration into a complex post-digital ecosystem interfacing with digitization processes in the book market, e-commerce, and logistics infrastructures. It was this dovetailing that made it possible for Eileen Gittins, founder of Blurb, to say quite justifiably on the occasion of the company's tenth anniversary, "We've deconstructed publishing." After all, Blurb aimed to

> not only disrupt the business from a "who gets to make a book," but also the distribution model for how books are sold and discovered. [...] So what we are now is a technology-enabled publishing platform, so that people can self-publish, soup-to-nuts from creation through marketing, distribution, fulfillment, e-commerce, the whole thing.[60]

With their claim to handle "the whole thing," a claim that was indeed true, POD providers contributed to the general platformization of the internet that took place in the early 2000s as part of the development towards Web 2.0 and what would later be described as the social web: "that is, a revolutionary reinvention of the worldwide web [...], that puts sharing at the center of the website."[61] During this period, countless digital platform companies, such as Google Alphabet, Amazon, Facebook, AirBnB, and Alibaba, emerged as "digital infrastructures that enable two or more groups to interact. They therefore position themselves as intermediaries that bring together different users: customers, advertisers, service providers, producers, suppliers, and even physical objects."[62]

Thus, platform companies do not sell material goods. They mediate between different parties for services that can be coordinated and bundled via a usable website or app thanks to various standardizations. They make their money through commission and brokerage fees, but also frequently through the extraction and further processing of user data, primarily for targeted advertising, which is also used to increase user retention. Thus, their market power is not based on ownership of the means of production, but first and foremost on "ownership of software (the 2 billion lines of code for Google, or the 20 million lines of code for Facebook) and hardware (servers, data centers, smartphones, etc.), built upon open-source material,"[63] along with the patents for connecting them and for the monitoring and extraction of user data. Paolo Cirio tracked down no fewer than 21,206 such patents in his project *Sociality*. In the accompanying POD publication *SOCIALITY – The Coloring Book of Technology for Social Manipulation* (2018), he not only sheds light on the "manipulative" objectives of the numerous inventions, but also actively seeks to influence their spread by calling on visitors to his digital patents archive to send (generated) emails to politicians, activists, journalists, or representatives to ask for the patent in question to be banned or regulated.

This kind of platform critique also addresses the fact that platforms often present themselves as neutral intermediaries despite being anything but: they use their terms and conditions and their absolute authority within their own domain to dictate

59. Both citations Silvio Lorusso, "In Defense of Poor Media," in this volume, 464–472, 472, and "Print on Demand: The Radical Potential of Networked Standardisation," in this volume, 481–489, 487.

60. Both citations Eileen Gittins cited in Bruce Rogers, "Eileen Gittins Builds Blurb to Make Book Publishing Easy and Affordable," Forbes, January 28, 2015, https://www.forbes.com/sites/brucerogers/2015/01/28/eileen-gittins-builds-blurb-to-make-book-publishing-easy-and-affordable/.

61. Michael Seemann, *Die Macht der Plattformen. Politik in Zeiten der Internetgiganten* (Berlin: Ch. Links, 2021), 42.

62. Nick Srnicek, *Platform Capitalism* (New Jersey: John Wiley & Sons, 2016), 43.

63. Srnicek, *Platform Capitalism*, 48.

what users can do and the rules they must follow. "Platforms create proprietary marketplaces, connectors of supply and demand that bear little—if any—cost of production, yet are rarely neutral. They are not mere 'service providers.'"[64]

The choice of platform should therefore be carefully considered, because proprietary structures and platform-specific regulations, services, and products can lead to an author being tied to the provider in question. For example, highly standardized production methods can mean limited options in terms of format and material characteristics, so that the book has to be reformatted or even completely redesigned if the author decides to change provider. For example, when Joachim Schmid and Jean Keller migrated to Lulu from Blurb, after problems with the latter, they discovered to their dismay that the products offered by the major platforms rarely match and that there are sometimes significant differences between the standard formats.[65]

Switching to another platform is completely out of the question if the author has prepared their publication using the platform's browser-supported in-house software. This software may make access easier for the layperson, but it often means that the books cannot be exported in PDF format. This makes revising and updating the publication, as well as any form of autonomous digital archiving of the data, impossible. Andreas Schmidt was confronted with this problem when he produced the seventy-seven books of his *Gesamtbuchkunstwerkskulptur* using BookWright, Blurb's in-house layout program, and then had no access to the print files. The fact that his books can still be ordered in the online store and that he was able to store several printed copies of each book is scant comfort. Here, the proprietary, closed platform's clear focus on the printed book as a salable product stands in the way of the author's desire for autonomous control over digital print files that can be archived or used with other software.

64. Geert Lovink, *Stuck on the Platform: Reclaiming the Internet* (Amsterdam: Valiz, 2022), 100.

65. In the case of Keller's *Blank* and Schmid's *The Missing Pictures* and *Quick Response*, the different formats are documented in detail in the web archive, see https://www.apod.li/. In connection with this change of format brought about by a change of platform, the terminology must be discussed anew: Is this a second edition, a new edition, a reissue, a reprint?

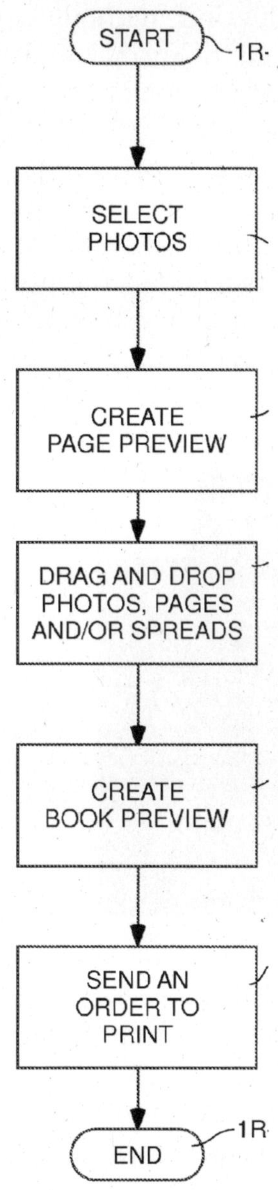

What if my Bob Book photobook is not what I expected?

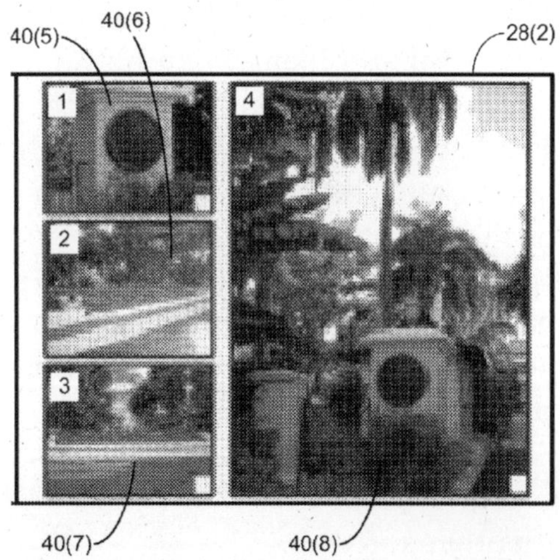

Are you also tired of spending days creating a photo book? Stop doing that, the era of photo-book-making-stress is over.

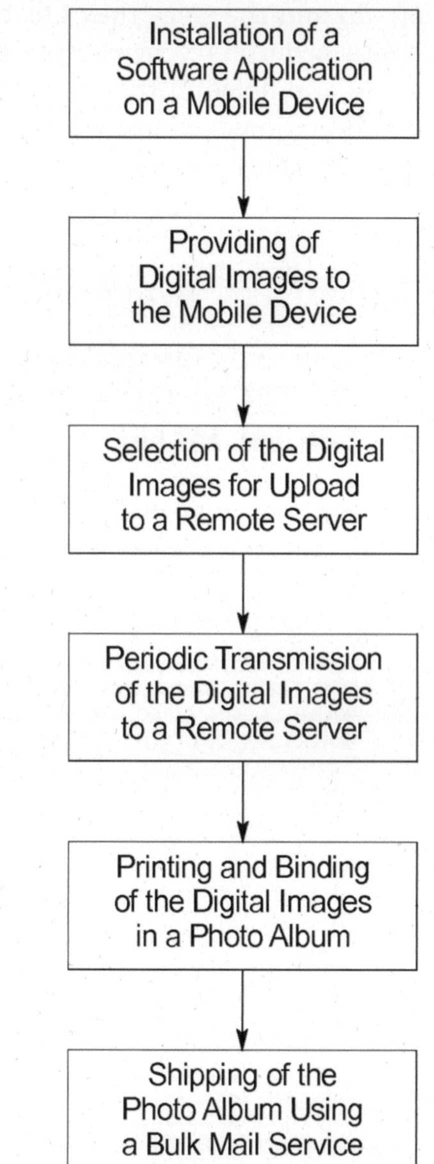

Which photobook is best for me?

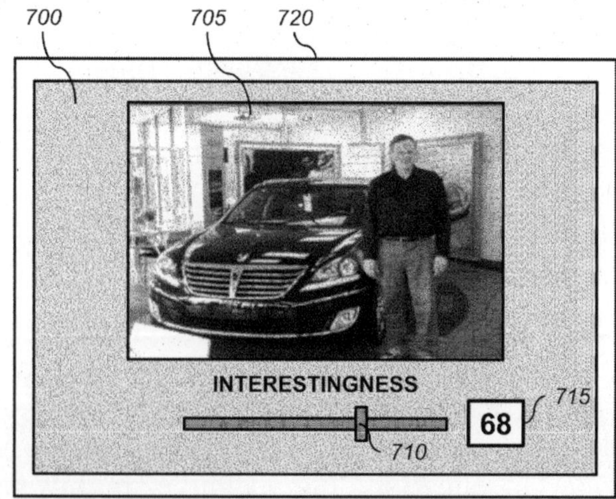

Are there too many photobooks? Is the current production rate with which photobooks are being churned out into the photography book market sustainable?

The current appetite for the photobook is also indicated by the prices fetched for first edition books about the photographic book.

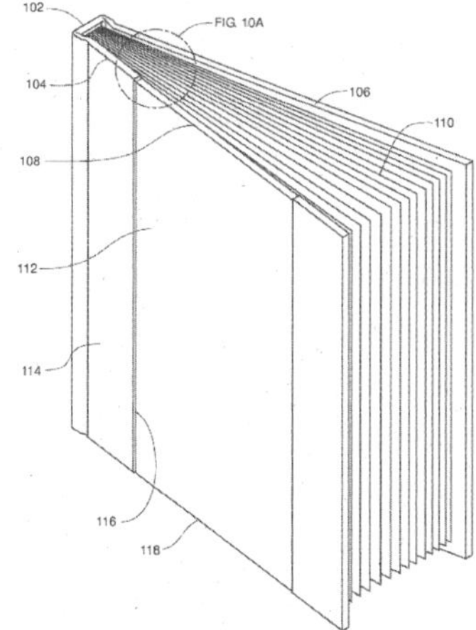

The PhotoBook is an elegant and quality way of presenting your photos, and is available in different sizes and colors.

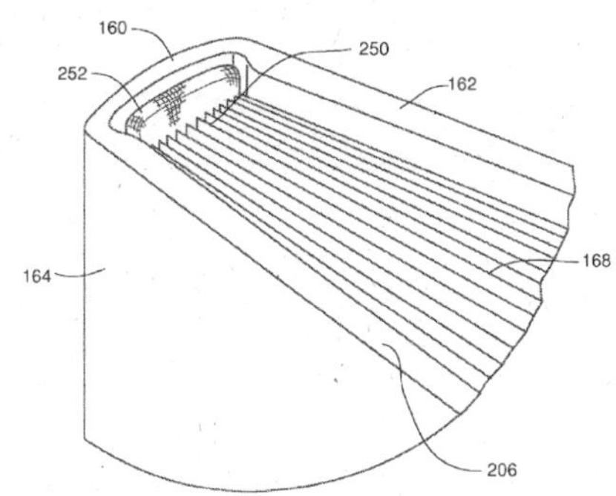

The digitally printed photobook is probably one of the most popular creative product offerings of the PSPs today… as a photobook is a timeless piece of art to be cherished forever.

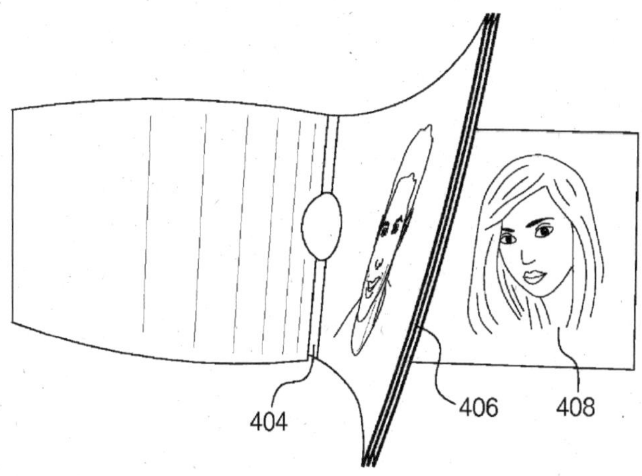

The present invention is a system and method for providing a printed photobook compiled from photos on a mobile device that enables efficient and cost-effective shipping of the photobook.

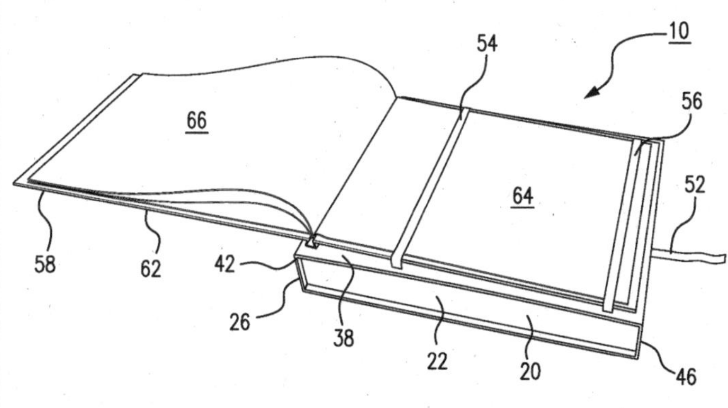

Peters U.S. Pub. No. 2011/0123124 proposes to diminish creative consternation by providing an automated means for photobook generation, wherein images are clustered.

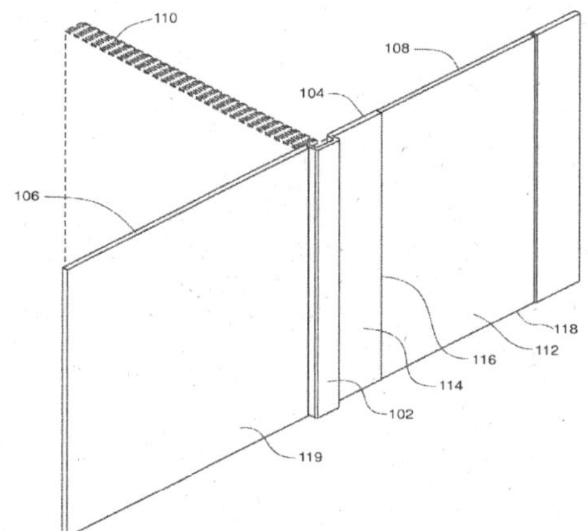

The photobook is designed through a software application, utilizes a unique flexible binding structure, and provides valuable advertising context and opportunities.

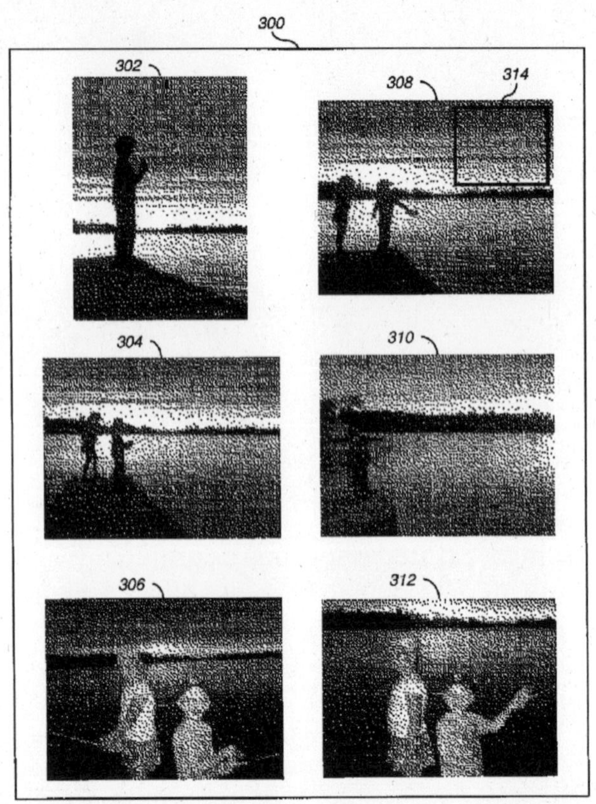

I feel that the color feeling of Costco's photobook is different from printing by homeprinter, why is it?

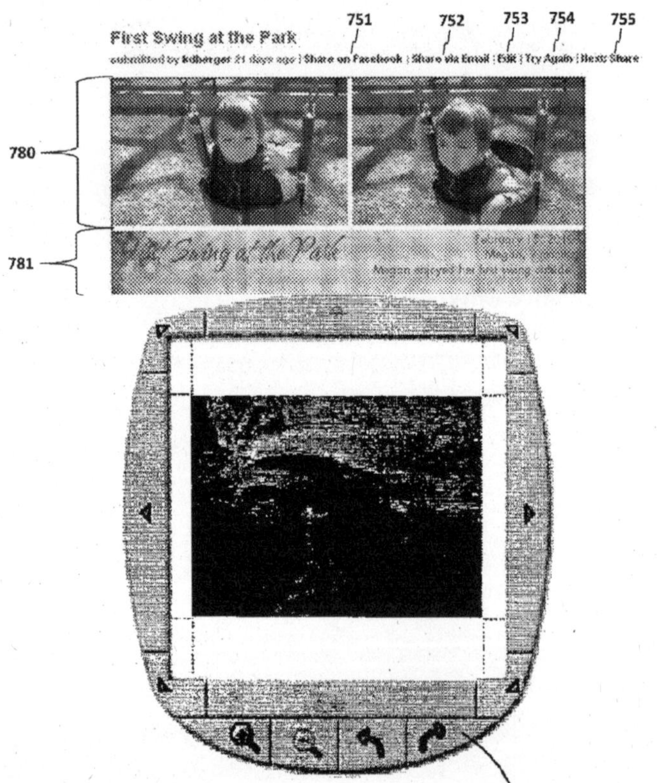

Choosing photos for your POP BOOK photobook is so simple with this app.

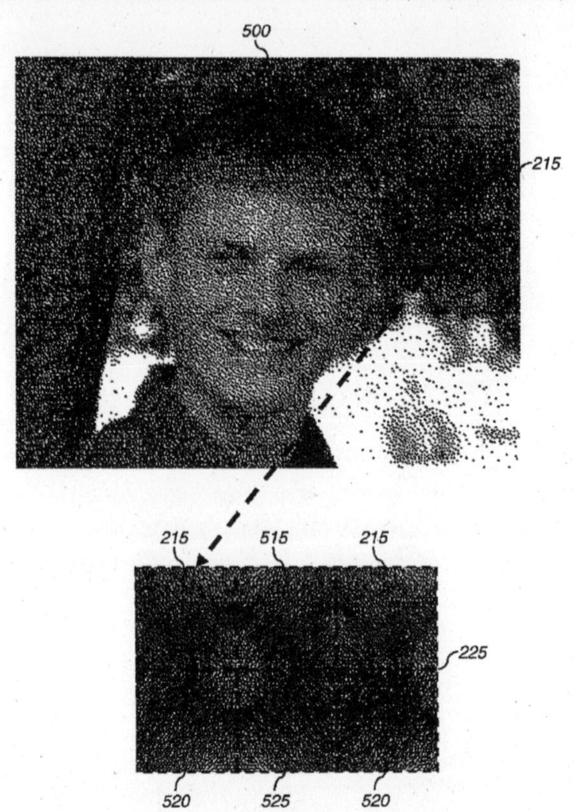

My Photobook is completed and I made an Indiegogo for it, check it out and share it on your social media, please!

Known as our best-selling parent album, and also a great choice for any occasion, the PhotoBook is our smaller sized version of the PhotoBook premium package.

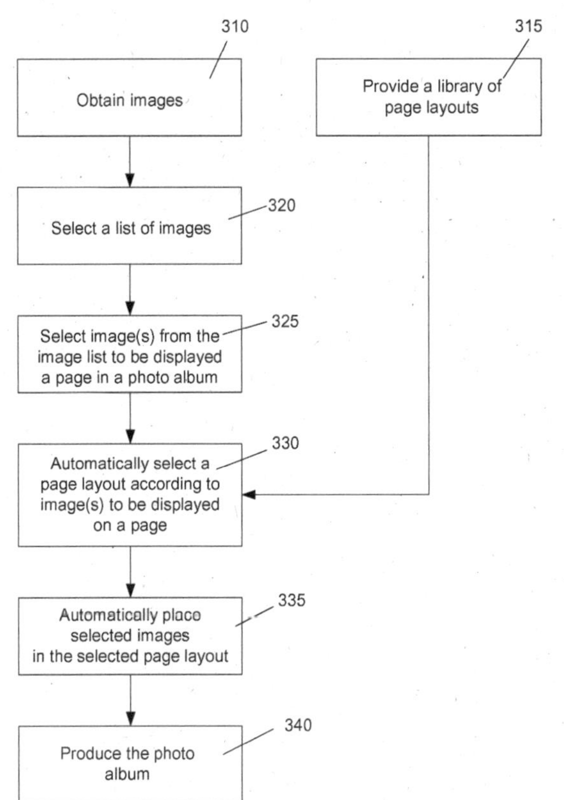

As PhotoBook is not a full-fledged system, we could not explore the opportunities and hurdles added by the locational and contextual aspects.

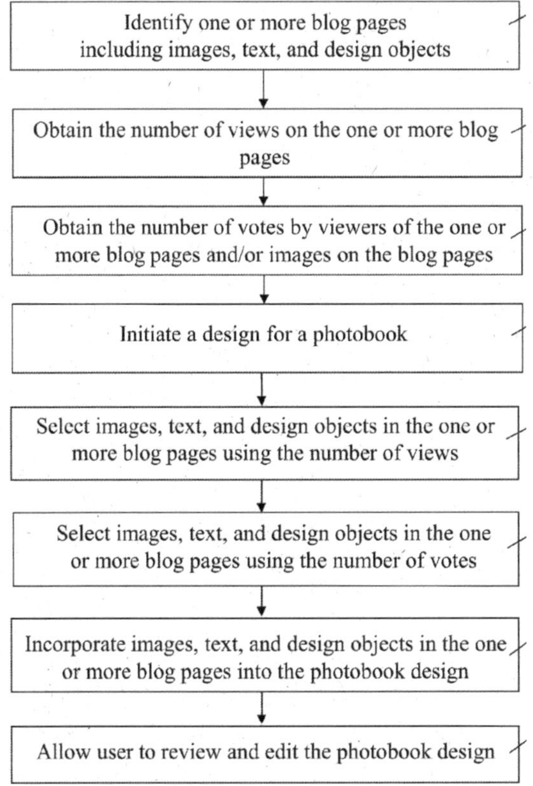

So therefore, our PHOTOBOOK (except for the linen and leather covers and photo paper books) is FSC® certified.

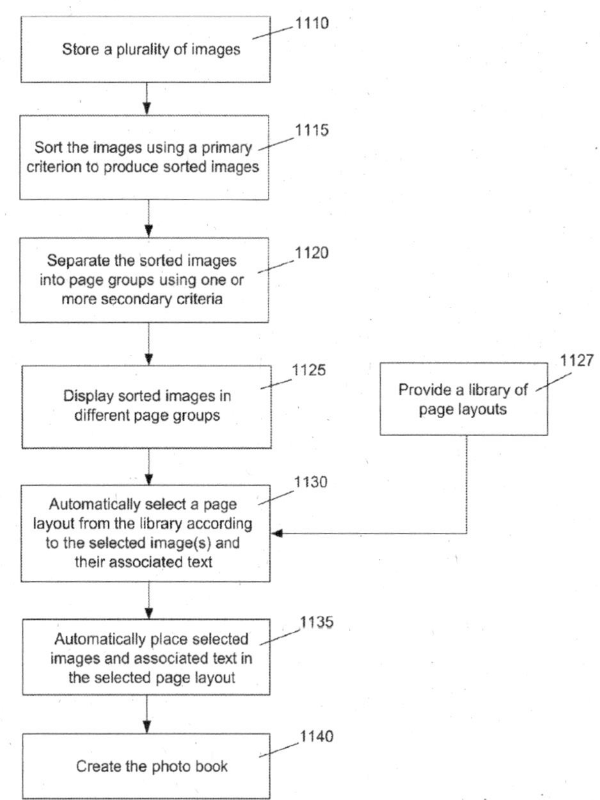

The album is a book comprised of printed photos, having a semicircle void carved from its bound edge to enable the book to be shipped as bulk mail under current USPS rules.

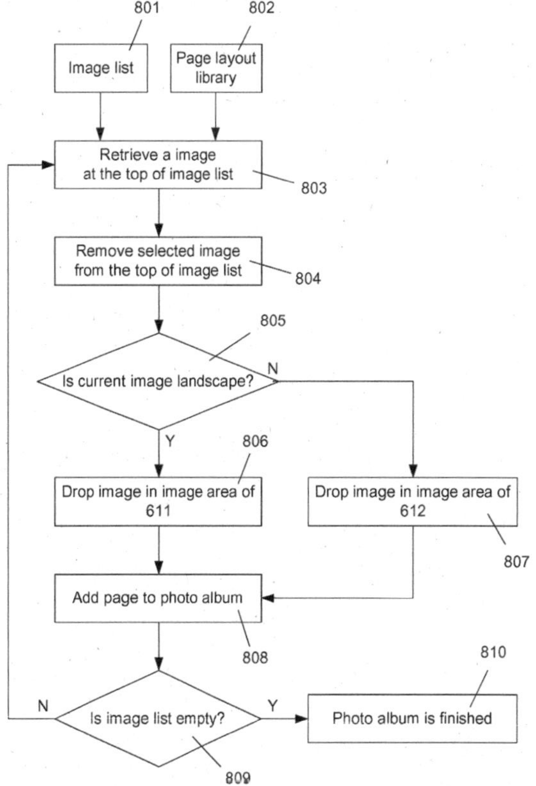

With a turnaround time of just three working days, this low cost high quality Photobook is perfect for self publishing and corporate commission work.

In her work *Photobook is* (2020), paula roush demonstrated beyond doubt that the needs of creators and platforms do not necessarily correspond. While the first section of the book presents widespread ideas about the photobook genre using the results of a search engine request for "photobook is," the second section uses graphics from patents for layout software and POD workflows to document the companies' viewpoint. This contrast captures the tension which inevitably surrounds the publishing of POD photobooks. They are always the result of a negotiation between the platform and the creativity of the author, but also the financial power of the book purchaser.

The numerous failed attempts by creators to negotiate sponsoring or cooperative ventures with platforms demonstrate that, to the platforms, creative work is primarily relevant as a salable commodity. There have, admittedly, been isolated instances of collaborations—for example when Mishka Henner's *No Man's Land* (2011) was on the shortlist for the Deutsche Börse Photography Foundation Prize and Blurb agreed to send several copies for free to promote the book, or when Michael Mandiberg wanted to automatically fill the Lulu database with thousands of volumes during his upload performance of *Print Wikipedia* (2015), which would generally not be permitted by the platform. In turn, Lulu used Mandiberg's project as a stress test for its own workflows and advertising for its production methods.[66] In general, however, attempts at working collaboratively have mostly been unsuccessful. Artists' Books Cooperative's argument that they provide the platforms with high revenues and "give print-on-demand credibility in the world of art"[67] did not convince the platforms, possibly because these types of artistic experiment cover too small a market segment and seem largely irrelevant to the intended target group.

"PROFESSIONAL FACILITATORS OF AMATEUR PUBLISHERS"[68]

As a business model, platforms promise a high growth rate and tend to become monopolies thanks to scaling and network effects, which can be used to eliminate competition. According to Forbes, in spring 2022 four of the five largest companies in the world by market capitalization were platform companies.[69] The same trend is also at work in the still relatively young, fast-growing, and competitive POD market, which has already seen multiple mergers and is displaying a tendency towards monopolies—some providers have ceased operating (OpenMute and Kolofon), new ones have entered the sector (Newspaper Club), others have been bought (MagCloud) or merged (CustomFlix and BookSurge), quite a few have realigned themselves (CreateSpace to Kindle Direct Publishing) or diversified their range and converged (Blurb and Lulu), and others have become almost irrelevant (EBM).

This list alone shows that the major platforms vary significantly in terms of their histories, target publics, and fields of activity. Blurb, for instance, was founded by the photographer Eileen Gittins when

COMPANY PROFILE

Blurb® is a self-publishing and marketing platform that unleashes the creative genius inside everyone. Blurb's platform makes it easy to design, publish, promote, and sell professional-quality printed books and ebooks.

Blurb was founded by Eileen Gittins in 2005, and includes a team of design, Internet and media veterans who share a passion for helping people bring their stories to life. Blurb authors have created millions of books using our full suite of free book-making tools, and today a new book is created every minute. Blurb is based in San Francisco with offices in London.

66. Lulu featured Mandiberg's project in a video on its blog: Lulu Press, *Print Wikipedia by Lulu.com & Michael Mandiberg*, YouTube, video, uploaded July 8, 2016, https://www.youtube.com/watch?v=KTJAqx6wCHo. For more details see Michael Mandiberg, "Making *Print Wikipedia*," in this volume, 512–521.

67. Joachim Schmid, letter to Blurb, January/February 2012.

68. Laura J. Miller, "Whither the Professional Book Publisher in an Era of Distribution on Demand," in *The International Encyclopedia of Media Studies*, vol. 2: *Media Production*, ed. Vicki Mayer (Oxford: Wiley-Blackwell, 2013), 171–191, 182.

69. Forbes, "The 100 Largest Companies in the World by Market Capitalization in [April] 2022," May 5, 2022, Statista, https://www.statista.com/statistics/263264/top-companies-in-the-world-by-market-capitalization/.

she was unable to find an affordable way to publish her photographic works in small editions. By establishing Blurb in 2006, she made it possible for herself and others to "make the books they'd always dreamed of, but never thought they could make."[70] Blurb very quickly made a name for itself as a specialist provider for photobooks and bookstore-quality print books "that unleashes the creative genius inside everyone."[71] It started out as a provider for professional photographic artists and photobook artists, but most of its business now comes from wedding, family, or travel albums, personal cookbooks, etc.

Lulu, on the other hand, emerged in 2002 out of a consolidation of several publishing and recording enterprises owned by Bob Young, founder of the open source software company Red Hat. It presents itself as the place to go for all books containing text, from memoirs, self-help books, and manuals to romantic novels, erotica, and poetry. Bob Young is said to have founded it after growing tired of looking for a publisher for his books—an experience that influenced Lulu's advertising campaigns, which included printing rejection letters from traditional publishers on a roll of toilet paper in 2005. It was also reflected in their guiding principles: "We reject the idea of rejection [...]. Lulu lets anyone publish their work—and the world decides on its merits."[72]

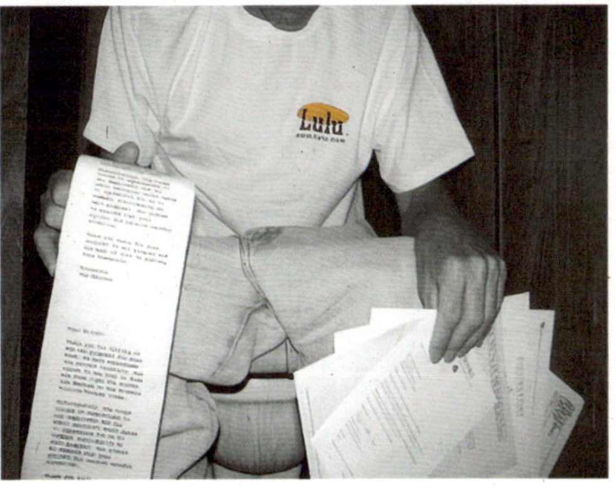

The original caption for Lulu's campaign read: "Distinguished Lulu author D. Judson Hindes puts rejection behind him."

In this respect, Lulu sees itself as a champion of independent publishing; its online store markets itself as "the world's largest independent bookstore," or "the best indie bookstore in the world." While the company slogan at the start was "We're free. We're fast. You keep control," its self-declared commitment is now: "Lulu is dedicated to making the world a better place, one book at a time, one customer at a time."[73] This philanthropic focus accounts for some unexpected details in its terms and conditions. For example, Lulu does not take a commission if the author offers their work for sale at cost price, i.e. when the profit margin is set to zero.

70. Blurb, "About Blurb," https://www.blurb.com/about-blurb.
71. Blurb, "Company Profile," https://www.blurb.com/company-profile.
72. Bob Young cited in Stephen Fraser, "Jilted Authors Put Rejection Letters behind Them—By Printing Them on Toilet Paper: Lulu.com Offers Way to Recycle Half-a-million Letters a Year," Cision PRWeb, September 27, 2005, https://web.archive.org/web/20230208213933/https://www.prweb.com/releases/2005/09/prweb290039.htm.
73. Lulu, "About Us: We are Lulu," https://www.lulu.com/about-us. Books on Demand (BoD), which operates mainly in Northern and Western Europe, promotes itself in a similar way: "To give everyone the freedom to realize their book exactly as they imagined it." BoD, "Über BoD," https://www.bod.de/ueber-bod.html.

On the other hand, the marketing for Amazon's Kindle Direct Publishing (formerly CreateSpace) focuses on income potential. Its range probably features the most bestsellers—such as Rupi Kaur's first volume of poems, *milk and honey* (2014)—before they achieve huge success and are taken under the wing of traditional publishing.

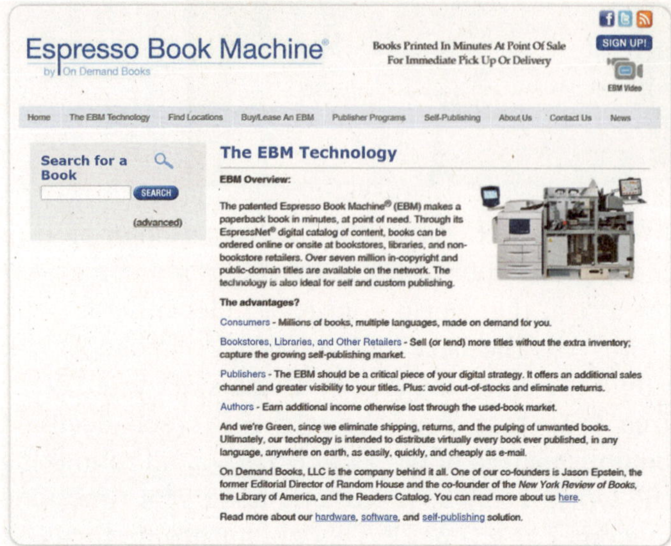

Lastly, the Espresso Book Machine (EBM) network represents a smaller, more flexible solution for bookstores around the world.[74] Since 2006, it has offered "Books Printed in Minutes at Point of Sale for Immediate Pick up," i.e., a type of in-store instant printing while the customer is waiting for their coffee. A competing forerunner of EBM termed it the "InstaBook Maker"; according to its marketing, it was as easy to use as a photocopier.[75] In fact, EBM is based on Xerox's DocuTech Production Publisher Model DT135,[76] which combines several processing steps (scanning, printing, trimming, binding) and is linked to a print database on a global server, for which reason many see it as the first complete POD publishing system and the backbone of the developing POD industry. On request, the book produced can be put up for sale on commission in the bookstore where the EBM is located as well as stored in the EBM database, which has more than seven million books available to print, including titles that are in the public domain, out of print, or on the backlist of Google Books, Lightning Source, Internet Archive, and major publishing houses such as Random House and Hachette.

The promise here is global search capability connected to local printing facilities, so that it should theoretically be possible to print any title wherever there is a machine available. In practice, however, this does not always work. For example, in Europe it is not possible to get the books *World Clock* (2013) or *Megawatt* (2014) from Nick Montfort's Bad Quarto Press that are produced using the Harvard Book Store's EBM, because they are not available via the database for printing elsewhere and the Harvard Book Store does not ship outside the USA. Furthermore, the network of participating institutions (bookstores, libraries, art schools, universities) was never very large; in 2015 the website listed fifty-one locations, mainly in North America. After 12 years, EBM has now also discontinued its services at Harvard Bookstore in the spring of 2022.

The EBM in the Harvard Book Store out of operation. The red sign says: "Print-on-Demand services are no longer available as of Spring 2022."

COUNTER-PLATFORMS AND ALTERNATIVES

In the wake of criticism of the platform-capitalist development of the internet as a whole, but also the non-transparent practices of POD platforms specifically, a series of independent and self-con-

74. See On Demand Books, "Self-Publishing," https://www.ondemandbooks.com/self-publishing-ebm-locations.php.

75. See InstaBook, "Print on Demand," InstaBook, https://instabook.net/index.php/instabooks-on-demand. They applied for the first patent back in 1995.

76. For more details and an early advertisement from 1997, see Lorusso, "Print on Demand," in this volume, 482, and Bruet, "Production Process," in this volume, 492.

tained alternatives to proprietary platforms has emerged over the years. They borrow particular features of the POD model, such as the ability to print just a single copy of a work or distribution via a decentralized printer network, while offering more flexibility in terms of creative and material parameters as well as more economic and political autonomy.

First, smaller POD platforms from the alternative scene were founded as non-profit artistic initiatives in response to a specific need for certain formats or materials. One example is the Newspaper Club, established in London in 2009, which produces newspapers in print runs of as little as one copy and ships them internationally. Even though they now also develop special solutions for large companies, they remain true to their roots. As the customer-service team says, they "are all graduates of Glasgow School of Art, so they know their stuff!" By maintaining control over the production process, Newspaper Club is able to work in a credibly sustainable way. "All of our paper types are either 100% recycled or sourced from sustainably grown forests. Our digital press uses solvent-free toner manufactured with certified green energy, and our printing plant is powered in part by solar panels."[77]

Another new start-up was OpenMute, which started as a micro-platform and print-on-demand, e-publishing, and digital strategy consultancy for cultural producers and institutions. The fact that it was only active for a short while is in keeping with OpenMute's concept of itself "as a test site," with a responsibility to ensure "a constant reinvention of our publishing format": "we feature and review innovative and radical cultural practices, but also participate in them, court infection and reflect their evolution within our own." It may be the case that disappointed political hopes also contributed to OpenMute's surrender: "While *Mute* was born out of a culture that celebrated the democratising potential of new media, it becomes ever more apparent that we need to critically engage with the ways in which new media also reproduce and extend capitalist social relations."[78]

A different strategy forms the basis for decentralized networks such as Artists' Books Cooperative (ABC), established in 2009 by Joachim Schmid "to create, engage, and experiment with the form of the book, and to foster alternative forms of distribution through collaboration."[79] Just as the POD platforms, whose services ABC members draw on when producing their photobooks, rely on their decentralized networks of partner printers to save on shipping costs, reduce delivery distances, and reach a larger market, ABC also puts the international distribution of its members to use for local activities such as book fairs, where members from the relevant area present ABC works. They also collaborate in joint publications and on a joint website, funded by an annual membership fee.

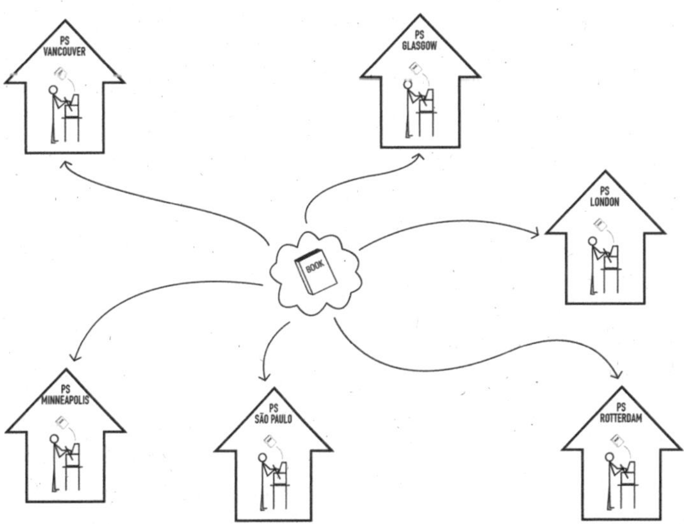

Other networks act more as publishers, with their own lists. Publication Studio, for example, was founded in 2009 by Matthew Stadler and Patricia No in Portland, Oregon, to serve a limited community, and currently has eleven studios over four continents that produce publications on-site and on-demand, often with the customer present, and then sell or ship them. It is driven by a strong inclusive DIY ethos and a desire for community gathering:

> We attend to the social life of the book. Publication Studio is a laboratory for publication in its fullest sense—not just the production of books, but the production of a public. This public, which is more than a market, is created through physical production, digital circulation and social gathering. Together these construct

77. Both citations Newspaper Club, "About Newspaper Club," Newspaper Club, https://www.newspaperclub.com/support/about/.
78. All citations Mute, "About Us," Mute, https://www.metamute.org/about-us/.
79. ABC, "About ABC," ABC, https://abcooperative.cargo.site/. See also ABC, "Paleolithic Cave Paintings: ABC (Artists' Books Cooperative) on the Photobook," in this volume, 508–511.

> a space of conversation which beckons a public into being.[80]

The guiding concept for Stadler is a table around which people gather, an idea that featured prominently in his essay <u>*THE TABLE & THE NETWORK*</u> (2015). This function has, in a certain respect, been taken over by the database used by all the studios in the network, which contains print-ready PDF files and associated specifications for format, materials, and special production features. Orders are generally executed by the nearest studio to minimize shipping costs. All the studios are equipped with similar production machines and materials, although some variation is tolerated in terms of different machines, materials, design features, and traditional regional production preferences. Each studio has the authority to add publications to the database and so can create a specific list determined by the local community, with the studio responsible for ensuring quality and focus. The studios are, therefore, not just actively involved in the production and distribution of publications, but also act as publishers. The distinction between both functions is reflected on the publication: the studio acting as publisher is named on the copyright page, while the name of the production studio is embossed on the back cover. The studios thus keep control of the means of production as well as the selection and distribution of titles, they represent the whole network locally, and produce not just creative synergies, but also synergies in distribution and finance. However, this model requires a high level of commitment and stamina from all involved, which is why some studios, such as the first one in Portland, closed down after a few years.

Other publishing models, such as Antoine Lefebvre's free online Bibliothèque Fantastique, outsource the production process entirely to the reader. The library sees itself as an "artist's books virtual publisher" whose 105 titles are available as PDF downloads that can be viewed onscreen or printed out as a DIN A5 booklet on any home printer capable of DIN A4 black-and-white printing, and then stapled together. Instructions for printing and production are available on the website (see image below).[81] Andreas Bülhoff's zine *sync* also uses POD as "print-at-home."[82] Many of its 104 issues are designed to exploit the specific characteristics of this hybrid publishing form, consisting of a PDF and a potential printed booklet. For example, *void* (#19) deliberately includes content that makes sense when viewed as a PDF but loses key elements in the print format, whereas *print* (#45) must be printed because it deals with watermarks that are added automatically by the printer. Such publications are naturally limited with regard to their format (DIN A5) and number of pages (page count must be divisible by four and be able to be stapled together) in order to ensure that they can be printed and bound. They must also allow the person printing them some flexibility in terms of the chosen material, the print quality, and printer features. Whether the publication can be printed on all current printer models thus becomes a crucial design factor.

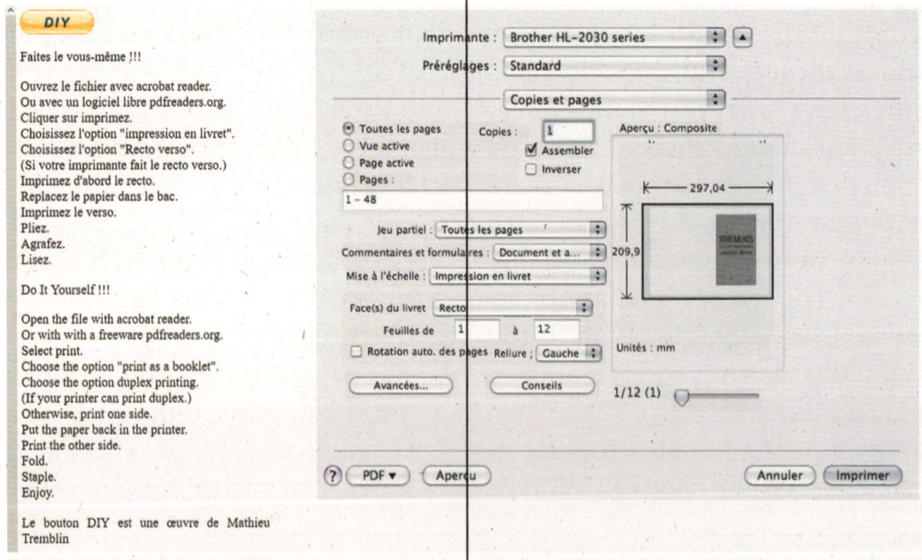

80. Publication Studio, "About Us," Publication Studio, https://publicationstudio.biz/about/.

81. La Bibliothèque Fantastique, "What? / Quoi?," La Bibliothèque Fantastique, http://labibliothequefantas.free.fr/index.php?/about-this-site/.

82. See Andreas Bülhoff, "sync," sync, https://sync.abue.io/.

The Cultural Legitimacy of Platform Production: Democratization, Diversification, Empowerment

USERS: FOLK ARTISTS, MAVERICKS, NAIVE ARTISTS

"Never underestimate the power of a million amateurs with keys to the factory,"[83] as Chris Anderson notes. Just as dynamic and confusing as the range of providers is the wide variety of their users, whose ever-increasing numbers seem to confirm claims of a democratization of the publishing industry. It could also be termed a "popularization," insofar as the explosion of POD platforms (in conjunction with the boom in self-published e-books and online content) is also an expression of the spread and consolidation of a pervasive cultural practice of engaging in private or collective creative endeavors—as seen in family concerts or school bands, amateur dance troupes or amateur theater, home movies or circles of writing workers, photo safaris or gospel choirs in churches, pottery-making or landscape painting—which is now finally seizing the book world: "POD technologies enable an extraordinary and interesting new cultural practice—a form of popular culture centered on production rather than consumption."[84] Timothy Laquintano uses a similar argument: he juxtaposes publishing "as a professional field," which usually garners all the attention, with publishing "as a literacy practice," which he describes as a "sociocultural activity" that has entered "into everyday experience" of "ordinary people."[85] In this respect, it is worth underlining that POD publishing is not, as is often assumed, always connected with a desire to make money: "The author testimonials on POD publisher websites most often refer to experiences associated with their books—interviews in the community paper, a book signing, speaking to a group—rather than to sales. The production of a book provides an occasion for sharing writing, whether the book is purchased or not."[86]

It is this target group of "ordinary people" that Blurb courts intensively with its marketing newsletter, with its constant stream of new publishing ideas that can be cleverly linked to everyday life or optimally integrated into other everyday practices such as traveling, giving, remembering. For example, six newsletters from Blurb in 2022 read:

- So many beautiful memories. Relive the best moments again and again. Print them all, and let others share them.
- Lots of room for creativity. Journals and notebooks encourage creativity, they are always handy, and also make the perfect Christmas gift.
- Gifts in repeat mode: if you have already made a book, simply make different versions of it to give as gifts. Swap out a photo here and there, add a dedication, and you'll be able to make a personalized copy for everyone on your Christmas list.
- Are you telling a visual story? Before you publish it, you'll need to make a dummy book or prototype. Here is your ultimate guide.
- Your own magazine! A magazine is a sort of self-published manifesto about something that is important to you. They're easy to make and there's also 20% off now!
- Every journey needs a journal!

The fact that in the context of this popular trend towards one's own book there is frequent talk of "ordinary people" is strongly reminiscent of Howard S. Becker's typology of artists. It is not based on an evaluation of the quality of the respective artistic production, but on the proximity or distance of its makers to the established art world and "the ability of an art world to accept it and its maker."[87]

Becker distinguishes the "integrated professionals" from the "mavericks," "naive artists" and "folk artists," who can similarly be found in the world of POD.

83. Anderson, *The Long Tail*, 58.
84. Haugland, "Opening the gates," 4.
85. All citations Laquintano, *Mass Authorship and the Rise of Self-Publishing*, 6 and 9 [original emphasis deleted].
86. Haugland, "Opening the gates," 14.
87. Howard S. Becker, *Art Worlds* (Berkeley, Los Angeles, London: University of California Press, 1982), 227. This parallel to Becker is already drawn by Haugland, "Opening the gates."

Folk art is for Becker above all "work done totally outside professional art worlds, work done by ordinary people in the course of their ordinary lives, work seldom thought of by those who make or use it as art at all." At the same time, these works are always "part of the daily activity of members of a community." In the art world, however, the work of folk artists is hardly appreciated: "The work of folk artists speaks to many, but is too commonplace to be anything special." In addition to quilting, Becker uses the example of the Happy Birthday serenade, in which—an important detail—it does not matter whether every note is actually hit, "as long as the song gets sung."[88]

This nonchalance is much rarer when dealing with the POD production of the "ordinary people." What is missing, one could state with Roman Jakobson, is a relationship that is both sympathetic and objective, which recognizes folklore as "a special form of creativity" equal to the other forms of cultural creation. But, Jakobson argues, because "the written word is the most normal and familiar form of creativity to us, [...] we project our habitual notions egocentrically onto folklore."[89] This may also explain Becker's observation that there is often a lack of understanding between the art world and folk artists. Although folk artists have a nuanced practical knowledge, a set of critical criteria, and a complex understanding of their repertoire of forms, "they have no generalized critical or analytic language in which to discuss them."[90]

This is an essential difference to the type of maverick who is familiar with the art world, i.e. masters its language, codes, and aesthetics, so that in principle a basis of common understanding would be given. Mavericks, however, consciously break out of this world. They "have been part of the conventional art world of their time, place, and medium but found it unacceptably constraining. They propose innovations the art world refuses to accept as within the limits of what it ordinarily produces. [...] Instead of giving up and returning to more acceptable materials and styles, mavericks continue to pursue the innovation without the support of the art world personnel."[91] This group certainly includes those specially wooed by Lulu as "indie authors," but of course also a large part of the authors and artists gathered in the Library of Artistic Print on Demand who naturally have a great interest in developing alternative production methods and distribution channels. POD is a useful option here alongside copy-shops and vanity presses of earlier times as well as e-books, the internet, and social media in the digital era.

With regard to the chances of transmission of this production, it could be significant that mavericks knowingly and willfully violate the rules and conventions of the art world, "but they do so selectively and in fact abide by most of them."[92] Therefore, according to Becker, it is quite possible that their work will later find grace before the eyes of the art world and be incorporated. However, only a few succeed in making this leap, "most mavericks' work is not absorbed into the canon of an art world; they remain unknown, and their work is not preserved and disappears along with their name."[93]

Even less likely is the (later) discovery and assimilation by the art world in the case of naive artists. "These artists have usually had no connection with any art world at all." Neither have they undergone a professional training, nor are they familiar with the conventions, traditions, standards, and language of the art world. They work mostly for themselves, "the reasons for doing it are personal and not always intelligible." Their works "seem to spring out of nowhere."[94] Therefore, there is neither an adequate descriptive language nor suitable categories and evaluation standards for them.

This would certainly apply to many of the idiosyncratic publications that the poet and publisher J. Gordon Faylor discovered on his forays into the platform webshops, "apply[ing] spam-hunting search methods to Lulu." He used them as inspiration for his own poems, some of which are based on spambot text: "What I found via those searches [...] were unbelievable books."[95] One example is

88. All citations Becker, *Art Worlds*, 246, 257, and 368.

89. Both citations Roman Jakobson and Peter Bogatyrëv, "Folklore as a Special Form of Creativity," in *The Prague School: Selected Writings, 1929–1946*, ed. Peter Steiner, trans. Manfred Jacobson (Austin: University of Texas Press, 1982), 32–46, 37 and 1.

90. Becker, *Art Worlds*, 253.

91. Becker, *Art Worlds*, 233.

92. Becker, *Art Worlds*, 242f. As an example, Becker states: "If James Joyce ignored the literary and even linguistic forms of his day, he still wrote a finished book. [...] He wrote a perfectly recognizable European book." Ibid., 243.

93. Becker, *Art Worlds*, 246.

94. All citations Becker, *Art Worlds*, 258 and 264.

95. Both citations J. Gordon Faylor, "A Note on Vernacular Print-on-Demand Publishing and the Conundrum of Access," in this volume, 686–689, here 687 and 688.

Pierre Jasmin's *L-MEM Vol 001.058. Introduction to making very big books* (2013): a theoretical, speculative, and practical outline of how the author sees writing and the medium of the book being reconceptualized in the digital age and how that reconception will produce a new kind of literature in the not-too-distant future. From the point of view of the art world, such books "are, and remain, curiosities," making their survival and transmission in the long run highly unlikely. For all three groups—folk artists, mavericks, and naive artists—it is thus true in one way or another: "The conventional defenses and protections afforded conventional art works are lacking."[96] Therefore, certain arrangements are needed for "the mass of stuff produced by people who are not integrated professionals"[97]—a problem that particularly affects POD platform production.

FROM INDUSTRY PARIAH AND VANITY PRESS TO POWERHOUSE OF BIBLIODIVERSITY

Following the unexpected popular success of certain self-publishing authors, such as Rupi Kaur or E L James, the traditional publishing industry has begun to take notice of this field, which is now increasingly siphoning off profits from the market's established trade publishers, in line with the long tail theory. Publishers keep a close eye on the POD self-publishing sector and now tend to regard it as an incubator and seismograph of new trends, a field for experimentation, and a talent pool for promising young writers. Some trade publishers have, in the meantime, even launched their own portals to enter the POD and e-book market of self-publishers themselves. For example, epubli and neobooks, part of the Holtzbrinck Publishing Group, have joined together to form neopubli, a platform that attempts to attract authors with its indie author awards and the chance to be discovered and published by a "proper" publisher, which is then sold as a success story.

The appeal of these marketing promises is based essentially on the fact that the book world still uses two different standards for assessing books. On the one hand, printed books count more than digital publishing. Even the experimental scene is not free from such attitudes, as shown by the example of Gauss PDF, which introduced a POD range—the Gauss PDF edition—to help generate interest in its digital-only line. As an ironic nod to this attitude, the infamous message board 4chan even had a special celebration for the printing of the collective novel *The Legacy of Totalitarianism in a Tundra* (2014).

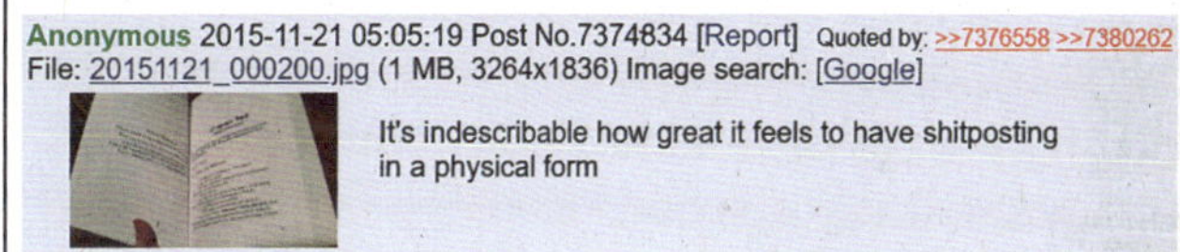

On the other hand, there are also very clear distinctions within the printed book world itself. POD platforms have a very bad reputation compared to publication by a "normal" publishing house. Sometimes a mention of them is greeted with a pitying smile, while at other times they are seen as the refuge of the vanity press, whose books are not able to find a publisher for good reason. Above all, however, POD platforms lack cachet: "being published" has always been a mark of distinction. Cultural pessimists also hold POD platforms responsible for oversaturation and confusion in the book market, and even for the complete decline of books as a cultural asset and the general deterioration in standards in culture and society. Even Wikipedia completely denigrates this form

96. Both citations Becker, *Art Worlds*, 269 and 268. Becker discusses the consequences in one of his concluding chapters, titled "What lasts?" where he states, "A larger problem has to do, not with what the reputation-making process selects, but rather with what it leaves out." For "[a] much more crucial selection takes place when art worlds fail to notice work created by others besides integrated professionals." Ibid., 367.

97. Becker, *Art Worlds*, 270f.

of self-publishing, although the online encyclopedia professes to rely on grassroots democracy and collective intelligence rather than expert culture, and has declared war on the established institutions dominating the production of cultural values and knowledge. In regard to the "wikability" of authors, for instance, the notability guidelines state: "Self-publication and/or publication by a vanity press do not correlate with notability. [...] Many vanity press books are assigned ISBN numbers, may be listed in a national library, may be found through a Google Books search, and may be sold at large online book retailers. None of these things is evidence of notability."[98]

Holly Melgard, who over the course of several years on Troll Thread has published and edited seventy-five books, reports a similar situation. She has observed that POD

> has gotten second-class treatment in the literary world. Grants and award committees have used the fact of my having self-published numerous print-on-demand books to disqualify my eligibility for funding. And university hiring committees recognize my books as "vanity publications" (according to the Modern Language Association) that "don't count as books on (my) cv."[99]

Even in the worlds of artists' books and photobooks, which have a long history of self-publishing and small independent publishers, there were initially serious reservations about POD: "some collectors and artists engaged in traditional production processes such as relief printing and letterpress did not consider POD books to be valid as artists' books."[100]

It is, therefore, not surprising that this new sector has until now mostly stayed under the radar of the literary and art world, booksellers, critics, librarians, and researchers. It is thus at risk of institutional invisibility, a fate with which earlier authors of gray literature, of folk, trivial, and popular literature, and of underground publications were familiar, particularly as even the POD platforms do not see themselves as having any responsibility in this respect. In their view, their databases are not archives, and their contents are first and foremost products.

But there is hope. Thanks to "a new respect for amateurs in participatory culture,"[101] self-publishing is increasingly seen "as a legitimate act of self-expression," as Laura J. Miller outlines. Rather than simply the expression of "a foolish act of hubris," a selfish culture, or the pursuit of profit, it is now understood as a sign of empowerment and democratization, as well as the outcome of a widespread change from reading-oriented to writing-oriented literacy.[102] Furthermore, emphasis is now frequently placed on its vital contribution to bibliodiversity: "POD creates the economic basis for cultural diversity in the book market, because, in times when traditional publishers are increasingly promoting high-volume bestsellers, POD offers an opportunity to profitably publicize complementary content and themes outside the mainstream."[103] Mathieu and Patissier also emphasize this aspect: "As the phenomenon of 'bestsellerization' increases in a sometimes alarming way, maintaining editorial diversity is a major cultural battle. Print-on-demand is an interesting tool in this regard."[104]

Even in high culture there are signs of a more nuanced view emerging, for instance, in awards policies. Mishka Henner's No Man's Land (2013) was shortlisted for the Deutsche Börse Photography Foundation Prize. In 2016, Marina Kampka's poetry collection Weather Forecast won the Prize for Young Book Design in the competition for The Best German Book Design. And *The Library of Nonhuman Books* (2019–) was able to scoop the 2020 Cornish Family Prize for Art and Design Publishing at the Melbourne Art Book Fair and the 2020 Tokyo Type Directors Club RGB Prize.

98. "Wikipedia: Notability (books)," Wikipedia, The Free Encyclopedia, February 13, 2023, https://en.wikipedia.org/w/index.php?title=Wikipedia:Notability_(books)&oldid=1139136304. For a more detailed analysis see Annette Gilbert, "Exclusion Zone. Observations on 'Wikability' as a Measure of Notability in the Digital Age, inspired by Gregor Weichbrodt's *Dictionary of Non-notable Artists (2016)*," in *Crop and Bleed: An Information Studies Reader on New Boundaries in Critical Print and Visual Culture*, ed. Robert D. Montoya and Sean E. Pessin (Sacramento: Litwin Press, forthcoming). For the German version see *Jahrbuch der Deutschen Schillergesellschaft* 67 (2023): 227–255, https://doi.org/10.46500/83535512-009.

99. Holly Melgard, "Print-on-Demand Self-Publishing after the Rise of Misinformation Got Us Killed," in this volume, 579–586.

100. Sarah Bodman, "Spending Time within Books," in *Refresh the Book: On the Hybrid Nature of the Book in the Age of Electronic Publishing*, ed. Viola Hildebrand-Schat, Katarzyna Bazarnik, and Christoph Benjamin Schulz (Leiden: Brill, 2021), 221–245, 230.

101. Laquintano, *Mass Authorship and the Rise of Self-Publishing*, 33.

102. Both citations Miller, "Whither the Professional Book Publisher," 183. See also Laquintano, *Mass Authorship and the Rise of Self-Publishing*, 37–41.

103. Hagenmüller and Künzel, "Print-on-Demand," 267.

104. Mathieu and Patissier, *Enjeux & développements*, 49. See also Susan Hawthorne, *Bibliodiversity: A Manifesto for Independent Publishing* (North Melbourne: Spinifex, 2014).

ANTI-ECONOMY AND ANTI-ESTABLISHMENT

In the sub-field of restricted production, recognition and success are measured in other currencies, not in prices, not in sales figures, and not in money. In contrast to the sub-field of large-scale production, it is characterized by "an anti-economic economy based on the refusal of commerce and 'the commercial' [...] and on recognition solely of symbolic, long-term profits."[105] In the field staked out by the Library of Artistic Print on Demand, networks like ABC, artists' initiatives like AND Publishing, and publishing collectives such as Troll Thread, Gauss PDF, Edit Publications, and TraumaWien stand out in this respect. Independently of each other, but at around the same time, circa 2010, they recognized the potential of POD to "sustain an adventurous and inquiring creative practice without having to conform to the mass market,"[106] as AND Publishing states. Similarly, the four founding members of Troll Thread, Holly Melgard, Chris Sylvester, Joey Yearous-Algozin, and Divya Victor, created it primarily as a "place to put our poems that no one else wants." As Melgard explains:

> Why wait to be asked before speaking? What, should I not speak unless spoken to? Why wait for an established person to solicit, welcome, and/or legitimate this work prior to permitting it to occupy public space-time? Self-publishing these books via Troll Thread allowed me to immediately distribute my work to a larger public without predicating what I make on anyone else's desire or agency besides my own.

With this act of self-empowerment comes artistic freedom:

> Because TT [Troll Thread] books don't need financial investment, literary merit, public demand, or ethical appeal to get made, it has opened up possibilities for experimenting with materials that would have never occurred to me otherwise. My primary interest in TT has been in its potential to house poems that couldn't otherwise effectively occupy space in a published economy.[107]

In a tutorial with the both ironic and serious title *how to stop worrying abt the state of publishing when the world's burning and everybody's broke anyways and all you really care abt is if anyone is even reading yr work* (2012), Yearous-Algozin strongly recommended copying Troll Thread's simple publishing model as the easiest and most effective way of publishing experimental poetry. In this manifesto-like pamphlet, he explains step by step how it is possible to hook on to Lulu (and Tumblr) like a parasite and force one's own agenda onto the platforms:

> start a gmail or other email acct or whatever w/
> yr presses name or as close as you can get
> w/ that email start a tumblr acct
> start a lulu acct
> upload yr .pdf to lulu as a paperback book
> i like the letter format bec that's the size of a
> microsoft word page
> don't worry about making it look good, gutters,
> paratext, etc.
> that's all just marketing [...]
> set the price at zero revenue [...]
> this is poetry, you shouldn't be making a profit
> don't be an asshole [...]
> upload your .pdf [...]
> post the photo to tumblr
> good
> now do it again[108]

The publications produced using this method naturally look "amateurish," "[b]ut there is a freedom in not doing a job right or being properly trained, shifting the system of value from the finished product and its realization to taste, craft and seriousness."[109] Endeavors like these carry the hope of "yielding inventive solutions, poetic/aesthetic surprises, and new imaginaries coming

105. Pierre Bourdieu, *The Field of Cultural Production: Essays on Art and Literature* (Cambridge: Polity Press, 1993), 54 [original emphasis deleted].
106. The Piracy Project, "The Impermanent Book," in *Best of Rhizome 2012*, ed. Joanne McNeil (Brescia: LINK Editions, 2013), 21–27, 27. See also AND Publishing's POD platform "AND Public," AND Publishing, https://web.archive.org/web/20150202101530/http://andpublishing.org/self-publishing/and-self-publishing/.
107. All citations Holly Melgard, *Essays for a Canceled Anthology: HOLLY MELGARD READS HOLLY MELGARD* (self-pub.: Troll Thread / Lulu, 2017), 20, 7 and 9f.
108. Joey Yearous-Algozin, *how to stop worrying abt the state of publishing when the world's burning and everybody's broke anyways and all you really care abt is if anyone is even reading yr work* (self-pub.: Troll Thread / Lulu, 2016), n.p.
109. Joey Yearous-Algozin, "Keep your Friends Close /// We Upload Trash," *Convolution* 4 (2016): 75–79, 78.

out of that lack of skill." Of course, this hymn to dilettantism expresses a "romanticist trope" that is problematic in various ways, as Florian Cramer rightly remarks.[110] But is there any attempt at self-empowerment that does not have its moment of utopian hope?

Specifics of Platform-based POD Production

STANDARDIZATION AS ARTISTIC CONSTRAINT

In comparison to traditional offset printing, POD production has several unique features that must be recognized as such, and investigated in terms of their effect on the product, before they can be incorporated into aesthetic practices and used in an artistically fruitful way. We owe some fundamental insights into these issues to Silvio Lorusso, who was one of the first to investigate POD from the perspective of media practice and theory. For example, he highlighted the following notable feature of platform-based production: "[I]n order to produce *unique* copies, paradoxically, they [POD systems] enforce the limitations of *mass* production by applying stricter standards."[111] It is this standardization that enables automated and economically cost-effective production, as well ensuring the print job is executed as consistently as possible across a global network of partners. For example, Lulu currently offers a choice of just four types of paper and sixteen book formats (see image on the right), while Blurb customers can select from nine types of paper and ten publication formats.[112]

In 2012, in view of increasing interest among artists in this form of publishing, the London-based AND Publishing collective started to systematically explore the range of options as a form of artistic research. Their series *Variable Formats* uses "a model, a serial system that explores the technological margins of print on demand"[113] in order to help artists practically and conceptually create their own publications and ascertain how far POD might be incorporated into their artistic practice. They produced twelve sample books based on identical content through six of the major POD providers as well as some self-made versions. The format,

paper, colors, and number of pages differ in each, as do the bindings (hardcover, wire-bound, paperback), distribution channels, and price (£15–£100). They thus materialize the (technical and aesthetic) margins of the publication as determined by the

110. Both citations Florian Cramer in Marc van Elburg, Florian Cramer, and Clara Balaguer, "Against the [cozy] prettyprinters: a defense of crappy print," in this volume, 613–628, 619.

111. Lorusso, "Print on Demand," in this volume, 488 [emphasis added].

112. Even EBM only has a limited range of production options, despite offering a continuous cut to suit individual custom formats. See "Self-Publishing with Betty the Book Machine: Submission Guidelines Summary," The American Book Center, https://abc.nl/assets/docs/betty/short_instructions_en.pdf. See also "Print on Demand with Betty: Betty the Book Machine," The American Book Center, https://abc.nl/betty.

113. AND Publishing and Åbäke, blurb to *Variable Formats*, AND Publishing, http://andpublishing.org/variable-formats-2/.

manufacturer. The series also provides a comprehensive overview of the major players in the POD market and enables a comparison of the standards and quality of the printing, paper, and binding, and also—taking into account price and availability—the best potential areas of application.

In their two-part book set *Blank on Demand* (2011), Silvio Lorusso and Giulia Ciliberto reveal the constraints artists must work under when using POD. It consists of two blank books created using the maximum and minimum specifications on the Lulu platform in terms of format, number of pages, and binding, which thus inherently and performatively demonstrate the range of parameters imposed on them from outside. They also extend the pricing to its utmost limits. The resulting projects are a 10.8 × 17.5 cm paperback, 40 pages long and priced at €5.44; and a 15.2 × 22.99 cm hardcover, 740 pages long and priced at €999,999.99, representing the lowest and highest price points possible at the time on Lulu. This pair of books becomes the sum of the conditions for publishing on POD platforms. The project still allows its authors a small triumph over the seemingly almighty POD machinery, because the complete automatization of production will most probably lead to the absurd situation that a book with empty white pages, on which nothing is printed, is also unnecessarily sent through the printing machines: "We were particularly fascinated by the idea of paper sheets going through all the complex print machinery without any purpose."[114] The project thus also deals, at an abstract level, with the "depersonalization of the means of production"[115] discussed above (see 21).

114. Lorusso, "Extending Horizons: The Praxis of Experimental Publishing in the Age of Digital Networks" (PhD diss., Iuav University of Venice, 2015/16), 187, https://archive.org/details/ExtendingHorizons.
115. Bruet, "Production Process," in this volume, 498.

This type of humorous approach also demonstrates that a number of artists, far from complaining about the strict limitations imposed by standardization and automation on materials, binding, formats, etc., in fact view them as a welcome challenge rather than a restriction of their artistic freedom. Formalized constraints such as these are actually used by Oulipo authors and in conceptual art and writing as a productive trigger for creativity. Troll Thread increases the high level of standardization even further by subjecting their house style to the same type of standardized workflow and pattern. Their publishing format is set at US letter size, the plain, white front cover design is mirrored on the back, and the digital paratext required by Lulu is consistently formulated as "HOW TO…" This is not only for reasons of convenience, as explained in Yearous-Algozin's "manifesto": "i like the letter format bec that's the size of a microsoft word page."[116] Thus, this style choice also demonstrates that working and writing on a computer is just as governed by standards, defaults, and limitations as the POD sector. It is exactly this format, according to Melgard, that "expresses the affordances of software and platform default settings in MS Word and Lulu.com by maxing them out"[117]—even if such a design is more likely to be viewed as "bad practice" in graphic design circles: "don't worry about making it look good, gutters, paratext, etc. / that's all just marketing."[118]

Of course, Troll Thread—just like the platform operators and printers—also has practical and economical reasons for increasing standardization: it simplifies and speeds up work processes,

116. Yearous-Algozin, *how to stop worrying abt the state of publishing*, n.p.
117. Melgard, "Print-on-Demand Self-Publishing," in this volume, 583.
118. Yearous-Algozin, *how to stop worrying abt the state of publishing*, n.p.

from production of the print template through to file upload, and so also minimizes the time and effort needed to maintain their publishing work:

> TT [Troll Thread] is purposefully a no-money-in / no-money-out operation, in that it has no print run, and costs nothing to operate apart from the time/labor it takes to write, design, and upload poems as books. It also doesn't pay its authors or editors a dime. [...] Our approach was born of necessity [...]. We joined forces, divided up the labor, and designed the press to operate as a publishing model that functioned independently of institutional support using the least labor possible, one that more overworked and underpaid people like ourselves could use.[119]

While Troll Thread borrows the platforms' typical post-Fordist approach for its own publishing work and pushes it even further so its effects can be seen in the standardized material, other artists wrest artistic freedom and compelling aesthetic solutions from the platforms' narrow specifications. Hartmut Abendschein, for example, deliberately maintains a uniform appearance in his */aaaa press* series (2020–22). All one hundred issues have the same Lulu standard softcover in DIN A4 format (the European equivalent of Troll Thread's US letter format), to which the four a's in the series name refer. The series represents Abendschein's implementation of one of Michel Foucault's ideas: all books are to be published without author names for one year. In keeping with this concept of anonymous authorship, the glossy white covers are "faceless." The titles of the respective volumes only appear on the books' spines, and then only in the uniform, bland Arial standard font.

Joachim Schmid also used standardized platform templates for the ninety-six volumes of his encyclopedic photobook series *Other People's Photographs* (2008–11), which without POD would probably never have been published on this scale. For three years, Schmid searched on Flickr, the biggest amateur photography platform at the time, for recurring motifs and aesthetic patterns. Each set of thirty-six representative examples of each generic image type—an uplifted thumb, lips puckered in a kiss, or airline meals, for instance—comprises one volume, on which the date of the image search is recorded; this reflects an awareness that some types of image can be very widespread for a short time and then disappear again. The series offers a fascinating panorama of popular image culture, which Schmid presents in an appropriately generic layout. As a designer, he interfered as little as possible in the design of the volumes, instead using the standard options recommended by Blurb's in-house software for format, font, and layout throughout the process. The series thus exemplifies the typical Blurb book from that year: a hardcover book measuring 17.5 × 18.0 cm with a dust jacket, reflecting the fact that the platform's sales are driven predominantly by wedding albums, baby books, travel diaries, and similar.

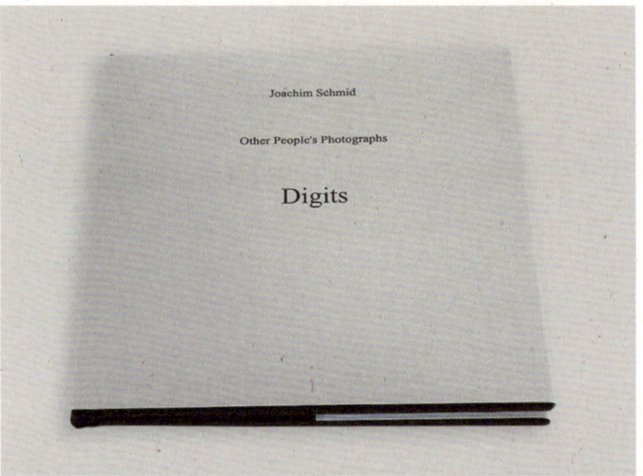

Eric Doeringer, on the other hand, made artistic use of the entire spectrum of Lulu's standard product specifications for his eight-part series *The Location of Lines* (2012)—an appropriation of Sol LeWitt's now canonical artist's book *The Location of Lines* (1974), in which each double-page spread juxtaposes a line (each positioned differently) with an instruction for how it should be positioned. The first instruction reads: "A line from the midpoint of the left side to the center of the page."[120] Doeringer replicated this concept in each of the book formats

119. Melgard, "Print-on-Demand Self-Publishing," in this volume, 581.

120. Sol LeWitt, *The Location of Lines* (London: Lisson Gallery, 1974), n.p.

that Lulu offered at the time. The content is always the same, but the actual printed lines differ as they have to be adapted to the respective format. Doeringer thus transferred LeWitt's artistic approach of site-specificity and variability in an equally ingenious fashion to the medium of the POD book. These exhaustive permutations also demonstrate what the platform specifications mean to the artists using them: a world that is severely restricted by machine automation and economic optimization, but is at the same time open to experimentation and play.

INDUSTRIAL UNIQUENESS

Technically speaking, the variation in Doeringer's series occurs not just between the eight volumes with their different book formats, but also between individual copies of the same volume: POD differs radically from traditional print runs, which produce copies that are by definition identical. In POD each copy is unique—even if the platforms and their partner printers are reluctant to admit it. Instead, they base their advertising on their "consistent performance." RPI Print declares that its technology-enabled automated workflow "minimizes opportunities for errors and reacts automatically when they happen. Consequently, our performance remains consistent regardless of the volume or complexity of a product."[121] But it is undeniable that each print job is executed at a different time, on a different press, and potentially at a different production site. This explains why individual copies of the same POD title inevitably differ to a greater or lesser extent, despite the high levels of standardization and automation at each stage of production. In this individuation of copies, POD is similar to hot metal printing: research in analytical bibliography has shown that production inaccuracies, damaged type, or stop-press corrections produce unavoidable variations in the printed image, so that each print copy can be regarded as unique.[122] The individuation of POD copies could just as well be likened to pre-Gutenberg manuscript production. This is true not only in terms of the number of errors, which are difficult to eradicate in spite of automation, but also the significant variation in how print orders are executed.

For example, there are country-specific differences in the manufacture of some adhesive bindings and in the handling of the internal production barcode, which can be placed in different places and sometimes even requires additional pages to accommodate it. A booklet printed and stapled by one of Lulu's partner printers in the UK will have the production code on the inside of the back cover. In France, meanwhile, the code is printed on the last page of the book block, which requires the addition of extra pages and so completely alters the whole composition of a publication. A similar situation occurs with Blurb, whose Dutch printer, which supplies the European market, adds a barcode for its logistics process, while its US printers do not. Because these kinds of unannounced additions can interfere significantly with the artistic concept of a publication, some artists try to prevent them once they discover the reason for the variation in how print orders are executed. Elisabeth Tonnard, an artist based in the Netherlands, says, "[I]n my account there was an instruction about them having to be printed in the US."[123]

121. Both citations "Automated Production of Personalized Print Products: Consistent Performance," RPI Print, https://www.rpiprint.com/products-services/automated-flow/.

122. This should be differentiated from the use of the term in copy-specific indexing in libraries, provenance research, or print history, in which copies may be classed as unique because they are the only surviving copy of a particular edition or print run, or have a specific history of usage and ownership. For studies in analytical bibliography see Martin Boghardt, *Archäologie des gedruckten Buches* (Wiesbaden: Harrassowitz, 2008).

123. Elisabeth Tonnard, email to the authors, March 28, 2021.

There is also considerable variation in the execution quality of different orders, as shown in the teaching project James Goggin set for his graphic design students in *Dear Lulu, Please try and print these line, colour, pattern, format, texture and typography tests for us* (2008). Here, the printed book functions as a test object for different print quality and production parameters at the POD provider. "The book project will therefore act as a color/type/pattern test of the very system with which it is produced,"[124] explains Goggin. The litmus test begins with the calibration of the possible color profiles CMYK, RGB, Greyscale, and Halftone using photographs of students dressed in and surrounded by a wild medley of objects in a specific color. The print quality of the lines and the font is then tested on a double page, with this question: "One word in / this sentence / is coloured / rich black. / Can you guess / which one?" The last pages are about the edges and binding. The levels of precision are marked by dotted lines that humorously represent a spectrum of professionality, ranging from "Pro" to "Wannabe," "Amateur," "Rookie," "Greenhorn," and "Drunk" to "Idiot."[125] Here, any deficiencies in the individual copies can easily be identified, even by the layperson.

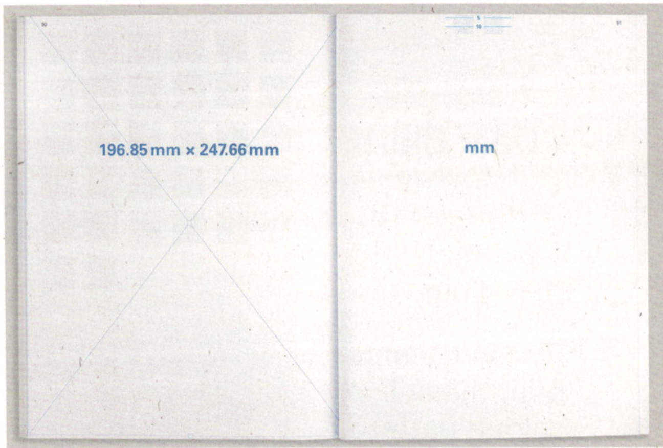

The execution of this script in print makes it possible to investigate the degree of deviation and identicalness. The comparison between several exemplars quickly shows that the quality of the implementation varies greatly. However, it is not possible to generalize the test results. Neither can the POD provider guarantee a certain product quality. In the end, every copy is unique and can stand only for itself. Consequently, the results of the "print-on-demand battle"[126] initiated by the students when they adapted the title of their test book (for example, to *Dear MagCloud*), uploaded it on other POD platforms, and placed an order, are also not entirely reliable. The information they gained presents book designers with unanticipated difficulties, as James Goggin notes:

> At a certain point I also realized the futility of the project in terms of using it to calibrate your images for printing. This was made very clear to me at one point when I ordered two copies of *Dear Lulu*: they both arrived at the same time, but had apparently been printed on two different machines. In one, the images had a noticeable cyan cast, while the other one's images were redder. Imagin[e] if you'd just received one of those copies, and imagin[e] that this indicated the general printing standard for Lulu. You'd adjust your images to be, say, less cyan, but then printing on the same machine as the redder images, you'd just make everything extremely red![127]

This example shows the extent to which the individual production process is encoded in each copy, which look as though they have been industrially mass-produced, but are actually printed as one-offs. The digital version of this test book, which forms the unalterable print template, functions here as the ideal state that inevitably becomes flawed in the process of being materialized in print—which is, however, the only way it can achieve its purpose.

Further unexpected variability in the products is introduced over the course of time, as Joachim Schmid realized while working on his long-term project *Other People's Photographs* (2008–11). His series consequently documents not only patterns and trends in amateur photography, but also, unintentionally, the continual changes in POD production machinery that contradict the marketing promise of "consistent performance." For example, over the years Blurb has introduced production

124. James Goggin, "Project Brief Type Specimen," in *Dear Lulu, Please Try and Print These Line, Colour, Pattern, Format, Texture and Typography Tests for Us*, ed. James Goggin, Frank Philippin, and 11 students (self-pub.: Lulu, 2008), 38.

125. All citations from James Goggin et al., *Dear MagCloud* (self-pub.: MagCloud, 2008), 70 and 94.

126. Goggin, "Project Brief Type Specimen," 38.

127. James Goggin cited in Bruet, "Production Process," in this volume, 496.

barcodes and changed the paper it uses. In addition, the exact shade of the gray dust jacket varies widely depending on the date and place of production. This runs so contrary to the need for consistency across the series that the artist decided to no longer offer the volumes on the platform itself, but only as a complete pack directly from him. In this way, Schmid can ensure that all the volumes are from the same order and are printed in one run. Nevertheless, difficulties still arise when even one volume is defective and needs to be replaced, as the replacement copy will inevitably have a slightly different appearance. This has led him to start keeping the dust jackets from defective books as potential covers for individual copies that are printed later. In some cases, however, the production defects that make each copy unique actually benefit the aesthetic concept, for example when the book's contents are also unique. This is the case in Schmid's <u>*The Showbag Book*</u> (2008), the contents of which change in each order, and for which the number of pages is specified by the customer.

Production error marked by the author in a copy of *The Showbag Book*.

BADLY MADE BOOKS: THE AESTHETICS OF ERRORS AND TRASH

From the platform's point of view, slight variances in color fidelity, binding type, and trimming are "a normal occurrence and [...] not considered a manufacturing defect or a defect in workmanship," which is why they do "not qualify for a reprint."[128] Moreover, the platform reserves the right to change the paper or format at any future time, so this cannot be raised as a complaint. Nevertheless, there are still relatively frequent grounds for complaint regarding production inaccuracies or even errors—even though the platforms are aware of their customers' high quality standards, as Bruce Waterman reveals in his request that Blurb's partner printers take extra care: "[W]hen you print a book that someone made themselves there is a higher bar to meet [...]. I mean, if you buy a book in a bookstore and maybe it's trimmed a little bit off, you're not going to bring it back. If you do your own book and it's trimmed a little bit off, you will."[129]

Yet it seems, paradoxically, that the far-reaching standardization and extensive automation of the production processes, which were intended to minimize errors, are in fact leading to a loss of quality. This is not only because the customer is now responsible for much of the quality control process, but also because production sites are so focused on process optimization that professional care in other areas may suffer. One example is when the direction of the paper grain is not taken into account in this striving for optimal use of the print sheet, which can result in difficulties in opening the printed book and turning the pages. Some printers even openly admit this: "In order to guarantee the best possible price-performance ratio, we are dependent to print the orders in gang printing. Thereby, we cannot guarantee to consider the machine directions of the paper for all orders."[130]

128. "Blurb Return Policy," Blurb, https://www.blurb.com/returns.
129. Waterman, "Bruce Waterman on Photobooks and Self-publishing," interview.
130. "Help: Machine Direction of Printing Papers," print24, https://print24.com/uk/help.

Front matter *Blank page* *Half title*
Title
Left page / verso *Right page / recto*
Roman numerals i

Front matter *Blank page* *Half title*
Title
Left page / verso *Right page / recto*
Roman numerals i

Front matter *Blank page* *Half title*
Title
Left page / verso *Right page / recto*
Roman numerals i

Front matter *Blank page* *Half title*
Title
Left page / verso *Right page / recto*
Roman numerals i

Front matter *Blank page* *Half title*
Title
Left page / verso *Right page / recto*
Roman numerals i

Front matter *Blank page* *Half title*
Title
Left page / verso *Right page / recto*
Roman numerals i

Front matter *Blank page* *Half title*
Title
Left page / verso *Right page / recto*
Roman numerals i

Front matter *Blank page* *Half title*
Title
Left page / verso *Right page / recto*
Roman numerals i

Front matter *Blank page* *Half title*
Title
Left page / verso *Right page / recto*
Roman numerals i

Front matter *Blank page* *Half title*
Title
Left page / verso *Right page / recto*
Roman numerals i

Front matter *Blank page* *Half title*
Title
Left page / verso *Right page / recto*
Roman numerals i

Front matter *Blank page* *Half title*
Title
Left page / verso *Right page / recto*
Roman numerals i

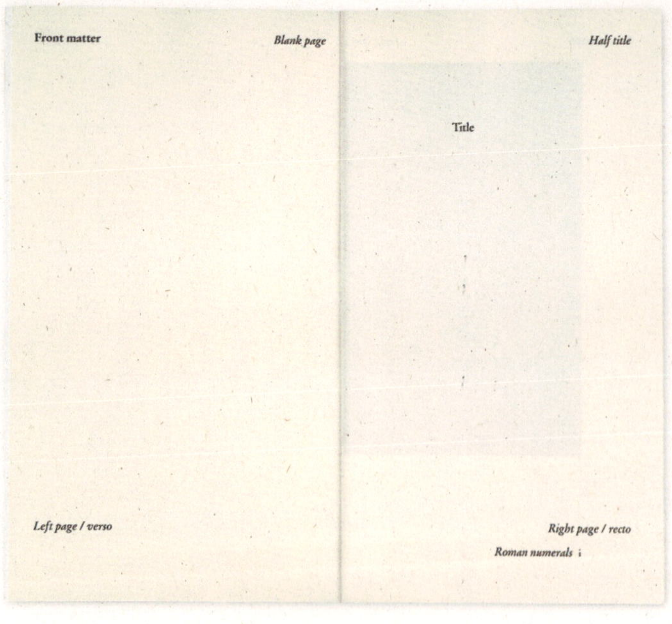

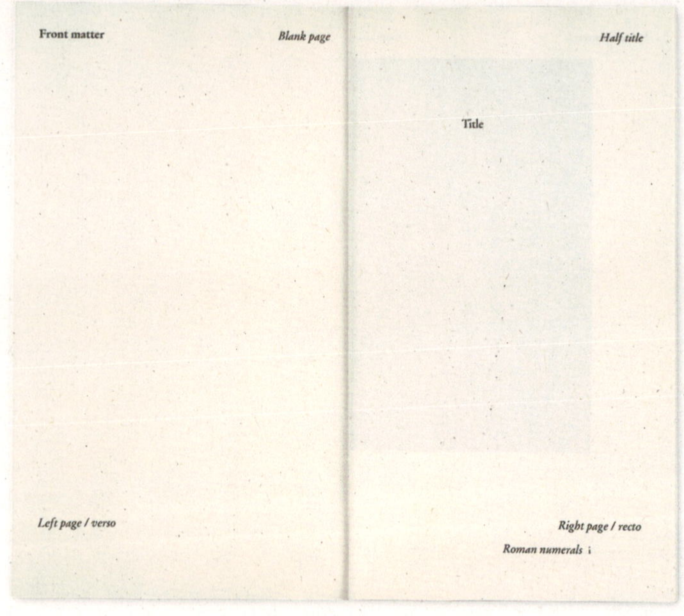

Front matter
Blank page
Half title
Title
Left page / verso
Right page / recto
Roman numerals i

Front matter
Blank page
Half title
Title
Left page / verso
Right page / recto
Roman numerals i

Front matter
Blank page
Half title
Title
Left page / verso
Right page / recto
Roman numerals i

Front matter
Blank page
Half title
Title
Left page / verso
Right page / recto
Roman numerals i

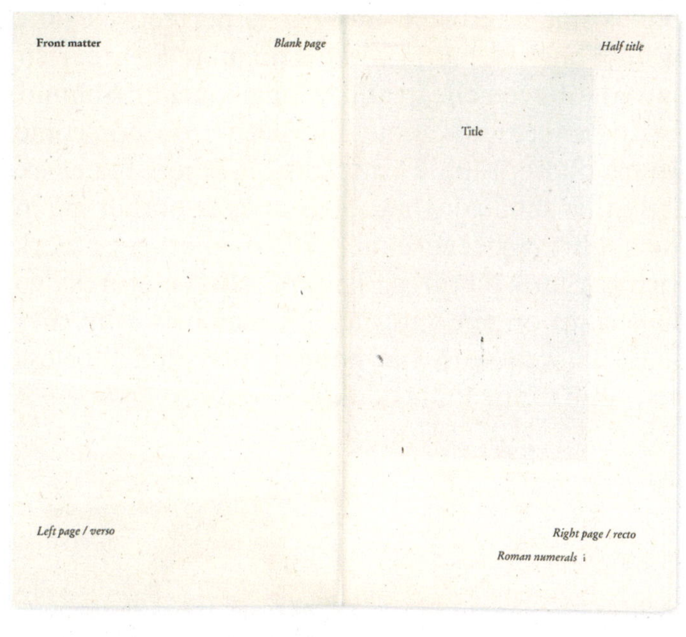

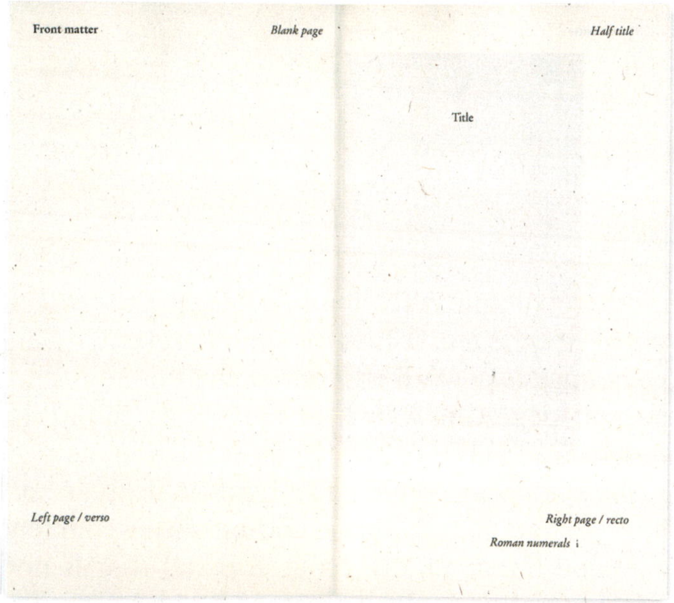

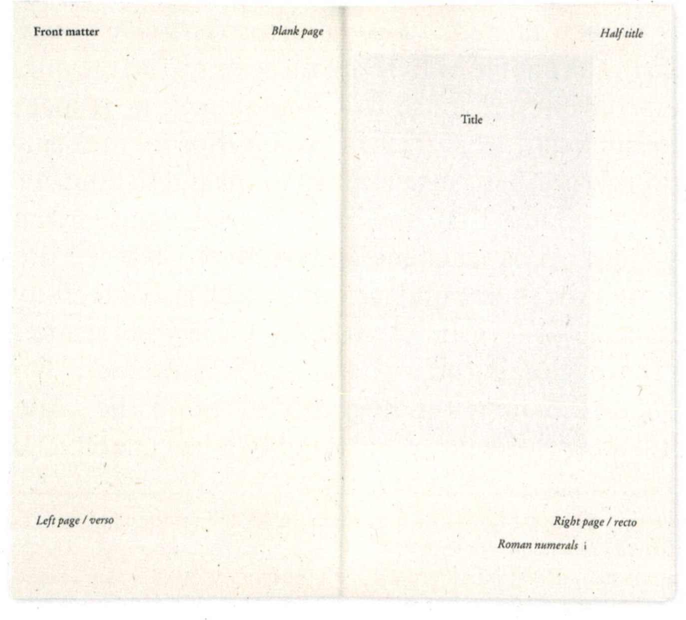

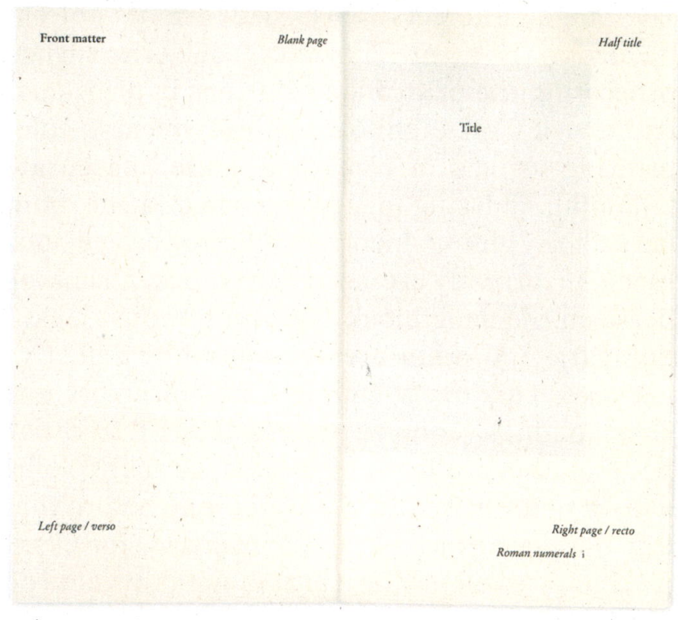

Front matter
Blank page
Half title
Title
Left page / verso
Right page / recto
Roman numerals i

The range of defects is very wide—fonts not embedded in the print-ready files, code errors when processing the print file, variations in print quality, uneven ink application, ink smears, color printing instead of black and white, inaccurate trimming, missing pages, incorrect page numbers, faulty gluing, incorrect binding, curled book block, incorrectly attached book block, mismatch between the book block and cover or dust jacket, dog ears, and other creases caused by defective packing. This never ending series of errors and shortcomings, coupled with a lack of transparency in the production process, brought some artists to despair, and it was not long before they left the platforms. Elisabeth Tonnard, for example, bid farewell to Blurb in 2014 with this note on her profile: "If you want to order any of the books, please visit my webshop. The quality will be better, the shipping less expensive, and the overall experience less annoying."[131] Other artists, however, accept POD's error-proneness with humor, as in Jean Keller's Blank (2011), which is presented as the "perfect" book that Blurb simply cannot get wrong or spoil:

> Print on demand is great, you can make all those books you always dreamt of. That's the theory. Between your book and the theory there's Blurb. Sometimes they get it right, sometimes they don't. You can get a book with too many pages, [...] with missing pages, [...] with wrong colours, [...] with text or photos not at the position where they are supposed to be. There are unlimited possibilities to get it wrong. Not so with Blank. It doesn't really matter if the book isn't cropped correctly. Colour is not an issue, nor are text and photos. A few missing pages are not a problem and too many pages are not a problem either. The book is blank. You can do with it what you want. So can Blurb.[132]

This statement clearly shows Keller's strong belief in his own autonomy in relation to both the platforms and the traditional concept of what constitutes a good book. This sense of autonomy is also a feature of some artists who follow an aesthetic that is not interested in what is perfect, elegant, or high quality, but in what is popular, amateurish, flawed, or even cheap and trashy. Joachim Schmid, for instance, says about himself: "I do not come from a photographic art tradition, where I need exactly this shade or that. That doesn't bother me in the slightest, because most of the pictures I work with are 'junk pictures.' They're found pictures I've picked up on the internet,"[133] which is why they blend in well with the poor quality and faceless aesthetic of the POD book.

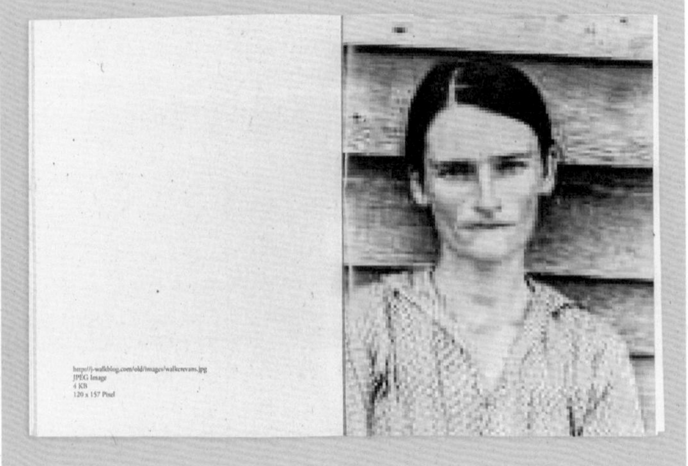

Another example is Herman Zschiegner's *+walker evans +sherrie levine* (2008), which presents twenty-six images of Walker Evans's most famous photograph, depicting Allie Mae Burroughs, found via Google Search. The dimensions of the files, as well as the resolution and image quality, decrease as the page numbers increase, ending with a coarsely pixelated image (4 KB, 62 × 78 pixel) that is not coincidentally in GIF format. In Greg Allen's collection of glitches in Google Books (*Wohlgemeynte Gedanken über den Dannemarks-Gesundbrunnen*, 2011), the choice of POD again seems to be the only appropriate response to Google's lack of respect for book culture, which is exemplified by the scanning errors. This also applies to the publishing collectives Gauss PDF and Troll Thread, whose focus is more on experimental literature. They see the content of their publications, which they gleefully describe as "trash,"[134] as being closely correlated to its packaging in a cheap POD "envelope": "No longer allowing funding to determine the scale or content of what we can publish has enabled us

131. Elisabeth Tonnard, "About," Blurb, https://www.blurb.com/user/tonnard.

132. Jean Keller, blurb to *Blank* [second edition on Lulu], https://www.lulu.com/shop/jean-keller/blank/paperback/product-v724j4.html. The first Blurb edition is no longer available; the original paratext is archived as screenshot on https://www.apod.li/blank.

133. Joachim Schmid, interview by the authors, November 14, 2019.

134. Yearous-Algozin, "Keep Your Friends Close /// We Upload Trash."

to put all kinds of weird shit we've never seen in books before."[135]

In all these cases, therefore, there is a perfect correspondence between the loss of quality that is an intrinsic feature of the low-priced POD product lines, and the artist's own aesthetic or artistic approach. Just as in the pixelated, glitchy GIF aesthetic or the limited, lossy sound spectrum of MP3 formats, the industrial but error-ridden appearance of POD books is celebrated as a type of post-digital lo-fi. Some publications seem to have made it their mission to confirm the description of POD as "the MP3 of printed literature."[136] In this sense, the unreadably pixelated text in Paul Laidler's *Is it a game, or is it for real?* (2009) can be read as an homage to the pixelated aesthetic of 1980s computer graphics, as seen in the movie *War Games*, to which the book refers. Laidler achieved this effect by scanning a copy of the film novelization at resolutions that were "purposely set below the standard amount of pixel information required for reading digital images on screen (72ppi) and in print (300ppi). But this lo-fi aesthetic went too far for the POD providers. As Laidler reports, Blurb's automatic data-processing system prevented the upload: "[I]t needed the help of the human-staffed online help desk."[137]

On the other hand, Danny Snelson's *L=A=N=G=U=A=G=E, 1978–81* (2015), a reprint of all the editions of the eponymous literary magazine produced by the Language poets, "tests the affordances of paper-based preservation systems against digital recording technologies."[138] Even the subtitle, *Complete GIF Edition*, draws a parallel between POD books and GIFs. The images come from Eclipse, a free online archive, founded by Craig Dworkin in 2003, that contains facsimile images of rare and out-of-print small-press publications. Due to the limited memory space and low transmission speeds at the time, the images were deposited in GIF format and encoded in a highly compressed gray scale. But Snelson has since come to view this "really terrible GIF edition" as the only appropriate format for preserving the magazine because it parallels the way it used to be produced cheaply on photocopiers: "The Xerox of the internet is the GIF." He now turns these GIFs back into paper using a similarly low-quality POD production process: "I just wanted to port these GIFs directly into a PDF and print them out, full circle. 'Bad' GIFs of a Xerox then become 'bad' POD objects. And, further, Lulu is the cheapest version of POD you can get."[139] Poor images, poor texts, poor scans in turn require poor containers, poor books.

POOR MEDIA

At the same time, the choice to use POD is often driven by economic necessity, which tends to be more of a problem in the field of experimental, avant-garde art and literature, as Troll Thread openly admits: "In effect, Print-on-Demand and PDFs are what poor publishing looks like."[140] This "poverty" is paraded with a certain pride, however. It is based on an understanding of publishing that flaunts its cut-price, industrial construction, basic physical features, and standardized, often amateurish design. Silvio Lorusso, building on Hito Steyerl's concept of the "poor image,"[141] coined the

135. Melgard, "Print-on-Demand Self-Publishing," in this volume, 581.
136. Wolfram Goebel, "Die Veränderung literarischer Kanones durch Books on Demand," in *Kanon, Wertung und Vermittlung: Literatur in der Wissensgesellschaft*, ed. Matthias Beilein, Claudia Stockinger, and Simone Winko (Berlin and Boston: de Gruyter, 2012), 225–235, 227.
137. Both citations Paul Laidler, "Digitally Remastered!," *Just Press P*, March 29, 2010, http://justpressprint.blogspot.com/2010/03/digitally-remastered.html.
138. Daniel Scott Snelson, "Variable Format: Media Poetics and the Little Database" (PhD diss., University of Pennsylvania, 2015), https://monoskop.org/images/8/8c/Snelson_Daniel_Variable_Format_Media_Poetics_and_the_Little_Database_2015.pdf, 187.
139. All citations Danny Snelson, interview by the authors, July 18, 2020.
140. Joseph Yearous-Algozin in Tan Lin, "Troll Thread Interview," *Poetry Foundation*, March 4, 2014, https://www.poetryfoundation.org/harriet/2014/05/troll-thread-interview.
141. See Hito Steyerl, "In Defense of the Poor Image," *e-flux Journal* no. 10 (November 2009), https://www.e-flux.com/journal/10/61362/in-defense-of-the-poor-image/.

term "poor media," which he positions as a countermovement to the kind of high-tech, interactive, multimedia "rich media books," with their embedded social features, that were still being viewed as the future of books until a few years ago. Ultimately, however, they are nothing more than "the product of a commercial doctrine based on an ornamental understanding of digital technology [...] and a reactionary conception of the publishing process." In contrast, "poor media" are valued mainly for their "potential for duplication and dissemination."[142] Those using them content themselves with the simplest media and are prepared to tolerate lower quality and fewer options in terms of layout and material features. Rather than quality and showy frills, the focus is on speed, affordability, distribution, and accessibility. The term "poor media" is therefore a little misleading, as Lorusso himself explains: "The poverty of poor media should be better called *frugality*, since it's characterized by the conscious, serene renunciation of embellishments in favor of accessibility and spread."[143]

This "frugal" attitude echoes one of the earliest and clearest artist statements in support of POD. It comes from the Artists' Books Cooperative (ABC), which is dedicated to the POD photobook. In the expensive, high-quality photobook scene, as exemplified by the books of Steidl Verlag, this was seen as an unparalleled sacrilege. To quote their manifesto-like eulogy of POD:

> Print-on-demand liberates artists from the oppressively expensive and laborious demands of traditional photobook publishing. Print-on-demand is fast, cheap, and light. It exists outside the power structures of publishers and distributors. Few people take it seriously and we are one of the few. We're not interested in what the books smell like, how they're bound, whether they're embossed or printed on the finest papers on Earth. Those are luxuries we can live without. We're interested in raw ideas and there is no better transporter for a great idea than a book. A single book if needs be. [...] No need for proposals, book dummies, meetings, bank loans, trucks, boats, trains and planes to ship hundreds of kilos of heavy books across the world into warehouses and bookshops. A powerful idea expressed in a collection of pictures bound together for the price of a meal and placed online can bypass all of that.[144]

This negative stance towards all luxury and commerce is also expressed very clearly in ABC member Jean Keller's Paper Passion (2012), which can almost be viewed as an artistic translation of the ABC credo into book form. The title of the slim paperback alludes to a book object with the same title published in 2012 by Steidl Verlag, which was promoted by the publisher as "an homage to the luxurious sensuality of books"[145] and is currently being sold in antiquarian bookstores for $1,650. It comes with a clothbound hardcover designed by Karl Lagerfeld. In keeping with his much-quoted statement that "the smell of a freshly printed book is the best smell in the world,"[146] it contains a perfume specially developed by Geza Schön to smell like a freshly printed book. It can thus be considered the epitome of the excessive fetishizing of a book's materiality, which degenerates into a meaningless end in itself.

According to ABC, "[r]ather than contributing to the culture of photography, we're witnessing the conscious development of a photobook market that's working hard to establish its experts, idols,

142. All citations Silvio Lorusso, "In Defense of Poor Media," in this volume, 464–472, 465.
143. Lorusso, "In Defense of Poor Media," in this volume, 472 [emphasis in the original].
144. ABC, "Paleolithic Cave Paintings," in this volume, 510.
145. Steidl Books, blurb to *Paper Passion Perfume*, Steidl, https://steidl.de/Books/Paper-Passion-Perfume-0008152458.html?SID=yYGwxuYee354.
146. Karl Lagerfeld cited in Jean Keller, *Paper Passion* (self-pub.: Lulu, 2012), n.p.

and judges. It's a dead-end that will eventually murder what could have been a force for good. It doesn't have to be this way."[147] Keller's *Paper Passion*, which has its price, $11.50, clearly displayed on the back cover, positions itself resolutely as an alternative.[148] Starting from the observation that "books are players in the intellectual world," Keller spells out the real essence of the Steidl marketing promise: "With [Steidl's] *Paper Passion* you get the smell of the intellectual world without reading a book." For Keller's POD version, on the other hand, the following applies: "This is a book. // There's no bottle inside. // It is not very chic. // [...] It might be quirky. But the idea has a simplicity, a linearity."[149]

Historical Points of Reference

THE THROWAWAY AND ANTI-BOOKS OF THE AVANT-GARDE

In this respect, POD books are distinctly reminiscent of those produced by artists of the avant-garde Futurist movement in Russia, for whom the book as a medium offered the ideal target because of its almost sacrosanct status in Russian culture at the turn of the twentieth century. In their famous manifesto *A Slap in the Face of Public Taste* (1913/14), they denounced the bibliophilic deluxe editions produced by the Symbolists and Art Nouveau artists, with their elegant, elitist appearance, as "perfumed lechery" and "paper armorplate,"[150] provocatively countering them with their own handwritten or hand-stamped "anti-book[s]."[151] These were deliberately printed on the cheapest available paper or even on wallpaper, as in *A Trap for Judges* (1910) and Vasily Kamensky's *Tango with Cows* (1914) (see image on the right), in a clear statement that they were not intended to be "revered items of cultural heritage" or to last forever; they were merely quick, cheap, "disposable items" and "throwaway books."[152] The challenge issued in their manifesto *The Word as Such* that "wordwrights should write on the cover of their books: *once you've read it—tear it up!*" was meant in earnest.[153]

They also pursued a poetics of error: they cultivated printing errors, typographic mistakes, inaccurate pagination, incorrect page sequences, and misprints. They ultimately renounced the Gutenberg tradition of book production and brought specific aspects of the manuscript age back into the printed book, such as handwriting and the deliberate individualization of copies of an edition.[154] This strategical variation can be seen in the copies of Aleksei Kruchenykh's *Worldbackwards* (1912), which all have different covers, collages, and pages, as well as different page orders, paper colors, and paper weights (see images on the next page). In this way,

147. ABC, "Paleolithic Cave Paintings," in this volume, 509.
148. However, this is no longer correct due to the constantly changing price calculations on POD platforms.
149. All citations Keller, *Paper Passion*, n.p. Alessandro Ludovico points to similar projects such as the "Smell of Books™" spray cans, which are meant to compensate for "the loss of smell in the digital reading experience." In contrast to these sensorially "expanded digital books," he sees Steidl's *Paper Passion Perfume* as an attempt "to capitalize on these [sensory] experiences," as it does "not intend to 'compensate' for a loss, but to extract and multiply a recognizable sensorial environment, artificially recreating the experience we associate with a certain odor." Alessandro Ludovico, "The Touching Charm of Print," in this volume, 473–480, here 474, 475, and 476.
150. David Burliuk et al., "Slap in the Face of Public Taste," in *Russian Futurism through Its Manifestoes, 1912–1928*, ed. and trans. Anna Lawton and Herbert Eagle (Ithaca and London: Cornell University Press, 1988), 51–52, 51.
151. Evgenij Kovtun, "Varvara Stepanova's Anti-Book," in *Von der Fläche zum Raum: Russland 1916–1924 / From Surface to Space: Russia 1916–1924* (Cologne: Galerie Gmurzynska, 1974), 57–63, 62.
152. All citations John E. Bowlt, "Schreibt nichts! Lest Nichts! Sagt Nichts! Druckt nichts!," in *Aus vollem Halse: Russische Buchillustration und Typographie 1900–1930*, ed. John E. Bowlt and Béatrice Hernad (Munich: Prestel, 1993), 11–38, 22.
153. Aleksei Kruchenykh and Velimir Khlebnikov, "The Word as Such," in *Russian Futurism through Its Manifestoes*, 57–62, 61f. [emphasis in the original].
154. See Gerald Janeček, "Kruchenykh contra Gutenberg," in *The Russian Avant-garde Book*, ed. Deborah Wye and Margit Rowell (New York: Museum of Modern Art, 2002), 41–49. See also Nancy Perloff, *Explodity: Sound, Image, and Word in Russian Futurist Book Art* (Los Angeles: Getty Research Institute, 2016).

> Kruchenykh […] exploded the Gutenberg tradition from within. In the disguise of a profoundly reproductive medium, he created books that were in fact unique. In contrast to obviously and intentionally unique book works, Kruchenykh's works have the appearance of multiplicity; and in contrast to elegant livres d'artistes with hand-coloring, etc., Kruchenykh's works have the appearance of sloppiness and disorder.[155]

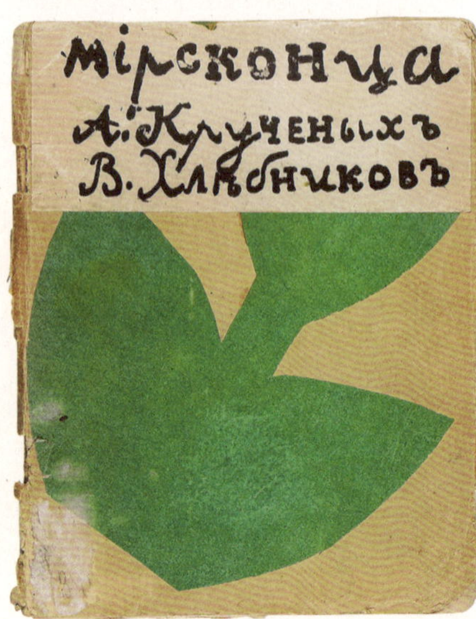

Many artists and authors making use of POD position themselves explicitly in the tradition of the avant-garde. The Neoists and Post-Art Poets, for example, are committed to counter-publishing and their manifestos proclaim the end of art and literature (see image on the right).[156] Their characteristic style and content have distinct echoes of Fluxus, Mail Art, and the Situationists, as well as Dadaism.

THE POST-ART POETS NO LONGER SELF-IDENTIFY AS ARTISTS, ABANDONING ALL THAT THEY HAVE BUILT. THEY SELF-PUBLISH WORK, OFTEN VIA THE MODES MADE AVAILABLE BY CURRENT TECHNOLOGY. THE POST-ART POETS FIND DEPENDENCE ON A PUBLISHER OR GALLERY TO BE AN INTOLERABLE POSITION; INSTEAD THEY ARE INSTITUTIONS UNTO THEMSELVES.

THEY ARE OUTSIDERS; IMAGINARY; UNSTOPPABLE. THE POST-ART POETS ARE NOTHING, NOTHING, NOTHING, AND ALL IS POEM.

[MANIFESTO]

The work of Gertrude Stein is also frequently referenced by the titles in our collection. Using the example of Holly Melgard's *The Making of the Americans* (2012), Paul Stephens notes that the most conspicuous difference between Stein and the current generation of writers is their experience of being published: "Whereas it took the wealthy and well-connected Stein fourteen years to find a publisher for her modernist masterpiece, Melgard's reduced version was self-published instantaneously on Lulu.com at no expense to the author."[157] Many members of the historic avant-garde struggled to find publishers, something that Richard Kostelanetz's *Avant-Garde Classics* series (2022, founded "[i]n memory of Dick Higgins (1938–1998), who understood what alternative publishers had to do"[158]) is attempting to rectify.

THE ARTIST'S BOOK AS DEMOCRATIC MULTIPLE

The reference to Dick Higgins, who founded Something Else Press, also introduces historic parallels with the artist's book movement of the 1960s and 1970s. Many artists and writers explicitly position themselves within this tradition, whether by designating their own works as artists' books or linking them to canonical works of the genre. Alongside Seth Siegelaub's concept of a collective catalog show, which the ABC editions *ABCEUM* (2014/2022), *AaBbCc* (2018), and *ABC Days* (2020) pick up on, the most referenced work is that of Ed Ruscha, which "established the paradigm for a new concept of the cheap multiple booklet as art."[159] As Lucy Lippard records, these comparatively inexpensive, "mass-produced, potentially 'democratic' works of art" were intended as counterparts to "'one-of-a-kind' art objects in book form" as well as to "signed and numbered limited editions."[160]

155. Janeček, "Kruchenykh contra Gutenberg," 47.

156. Post-Art Poets, "The Post-Art Poetics Manifesto," The Post-Art Poets, http://www.postartpoets.com/index.html. See also *A NEOIST RESEARCH PROJECT* (2010) and *The Post-Art Poem* (2013–14).

157. Paul Stephens, *Absence of Clutter: Minimal Writing as Art and Literature* (Cambridge, Mass.: MIT Press, 2020), 203.

158. Richard Kostelanetz, *Publishing Avant-Garde Classics: A Retrospective Catalog* (self-pub.: Kindle Direct Publishing, 2022), VI.

159. Clive Phillpot, "Twentysix Gasoline Stations that Shook the World: The Rise and Fall of Cheap Booklets as Art," in Clive Phillpot, *Booktrek: Selected Essays on Artists' Books (1972–2010)* (Zurich: JRP Ringier, 2013), 144–165, 151.

160. All citations Lucy Lippard, "Conspicuous Consumption: New Artists' Books," in *Artist's Books: A Critical Anthology and Sourcebook*, ed. Joan Lyons (New York: Visual Studies Workshop Press, 1983), 49–58, 50.

The collection *Referencing Various Small Books by Ed Ruscha*, co-edited by ABC member Hermann Zschiegner, testifies to the endless fascination that Ruscha's books have for the present generation of book artists.[161] ABC also showed its respect for him in 2012, on the occasion of his seventy-fifth birthday, by publishing a box set of thirty-three POD paperbacks by twenty-four artists. The title of each book consists of a past participle, with the "-ed" ending serving as an intrinsic homage to "Ed" Ruscha, as does the title of the overall project, *ABCED* (see image above). paula roush, whose work *TESTED* (2012) was created as part of this project but is not part of the box set, smuggled a critical perspective into this birthday tribute: *TESTED* documents a reenactment of Ruscha's iconic *Royal Road Test* (1967), in which roush not only updates the writing equipment to the present time and throws a laptop from a moving car rather than a typewriter, but also, by depicting a trio of women, casts the predominantly male iconography of the original in a feminist light.

Ruscha's equally influential *Twentysix Gasoline Stations* (1963) was selected by Zoë Sadokierski as the starting point for her EBM publication *(Another Book) After Ed-werd Rew-shay* (2015). Even the parentheses in the title indicate that she is joining a long tradition of homage books aiming to carry Ruscha's idea of a book forward under current conditions. "There is a clear parallel between the current small press movement [using POD technology] and what was happening in the art publishing world around the time Edward Ruscha was producing his 'democratic multiples' in the early 1960s and 70s," which he initially sold for just a few dollars. Sadokierski has carried this approach over into her own practice: "Ruscha produced his books using the cheapest, most convenient printing available to him. At the time, that was offset printing. [...] I will produce this book tomorrow using the cheapest, most convenient printing option available to me. This is the Espresso Book Machine at McNally Jackson, on Prince Street in Soho."[162]

But the fact that there was no EBM in her homeland of Australia ran contrary to the idea of easy accessibility and wide distribution implied by a "democratic multiple," which is why she later created a further POD edition with IngramSpark, which is available globally on Amazon. This conflict is also a feature of the *ABCED* project produced on Blurb; the edition was unlimited in principle, but only for a limited time (until Ruscha's following birthday), and was offered for sale only as a collectors box set at a high price. In addition, the boxes were numbered and dated, which ultimately turns them into collectibles and contravenes the basic principle of artists' books as exemplified by Ed Ruscha, who famously said that it had been a mistake to number his earliest books.[163] Clive Phillpot apologetically calls this oversight "the last hangover of the tradition of the luxury edition."[164] As a rule, however, in many cases works that position

161. See Jeff Brouws, Wendy Burton, and Hermann Zschiegner, eds., *Various Small Books: Referencing Various Small Books by Ed Ruscha* (Cambridge, Mass.: MIT Press, 2013).

162. Both citations Zoë Sadokierski, *(Another Book) After Ed-werd Rew-shay* (self-pub.: Espresso Book Machine, 2015), n.p. See also Zoë Sadokierski, "A Book Conceived before Breakfast and Delivered before Lunch," in this volume, 531–535.

163. See Edward Ruscha in John Coplans, "Concerning *Various Small Fires*: Edward Ruscha Discusses his Perplexing Publications," *Artforum* 3, no. 5 (February 1965): 24–25, 25.

164. Phillpot, "Twentysix Gasoline Stations," 151.

themselves within the artist's book tradition are making a definite statement against the glittering world of art, with its overheated markets and its idea of originality, and so also reviving the expectations once associated with the book medium, which Lucy Lippard lists as: "Usually inexpensive in price, modest in format, and ambitious in scope, the artist's book is also a fragile vehicle for a weighty load of hopes and ideals: it is considered by many the easiest way out of the art world and into the heart of a broader audience."[165]

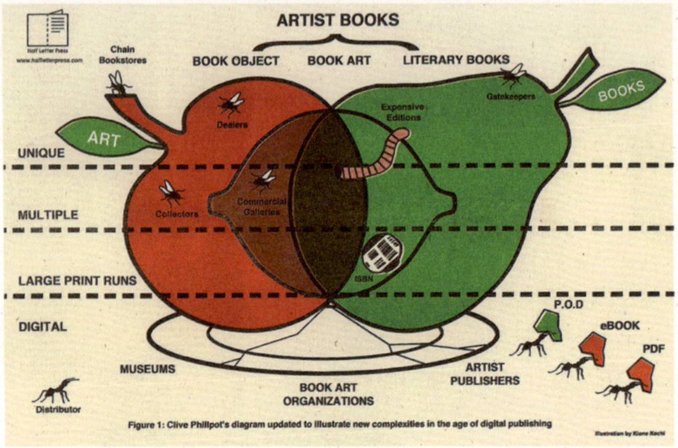

Clive Phillpot's famous diagram updated by Temporary Services, in this volume, 660.

"USEFUL" BOOKS IN SUB- AND UNDERGROUND CULTURES

With their cheap construction and heavy symbolism, POD books also recall the pamphlets and deliberately "badly made books"[166] of the sub- and underground cultures of the 1960s to 1980s, as epitomized by Merve Verlag, a German cult publishing house that specializes in theory and that, to this day, cultivates the memory of its formation from pirate editions and alternative culture. The inferior quality of their publications should be understood as belonging to the cultivation of Merve's image. They are directed "against the precious" as a matter of principle: "It is namely these badly made books that are sincere, that are really read, because you can find new ideas in them that have not yet been flogged to death and worn out by huge print runs."[167] By emphasizing a book's use value, the book as a commodity should take a back seat to its function of creating a public.

The fact that the transfer printing widely used in German counterculture could only "produce impermanent, fading, unrepeatable micro-print runs" was also not a problem, as the publications primarily served "for rapid communication, not for preserving lasting values." In the same way, the amateurish production techniques and "genuine underdesigning" of many of the publications of that time cannot be attributed exclusively to the limited design options offered by the available printing and duplicating processes.[168] On the contrary, they were consciously cultivated to express understatement and revolt.

A similar scenario can be seen in relation to the low-priced product lines within POD: the limited artistic freedom, the low quality, the cheap appearance, the amateurish construction, and the resemblance to carelessly made mass-produced articles may seem like the stuff of nightmares to bibliophiles. But they are not regarded as flaws in the countercultural context, where, on the contrary, these deficiencies are thought to ultimately contribute to a "humble [...] nonetheless distinctive [physicality]" which has its own charm: "the[ir] spartan look [...] might not be beautiful, but it's undoubtedly charming." Furthermore, it makes books more easily recognizable, as Silvio Lorusso states: "I can easily spot books printed with Lulu. To me, their peculiar identity became appealing as much as cheap Xeroxed zines."[169] J. Gordon Faylor reports the same: "[W]hen I'm at a bookstore, I can pinpoint a book which is a result of print on demand. [...] So I do think there is a sort of temporal aspect to it, and to the way that Lulu books look and feel as well."[170]

This recognizability goes hand in hand with the high symbolic value of these publications. They suggest authenticity and incorruptibility and echo the claim for otherness and subversion. This is why, over the past few years, this aesthetics could turn into the trademark of a contemporary subculture—which understands itself, and presents itself, as a programmatic counterproject to the

165. Lucy Lippard, "The Artist's Book Goes Public," in *Artist's Books: A Critical Anthology and Sourcebook*, 45–48, 45.

166. Heidi Paris, "Wider das Kostbare," 1986, www.heidi-paris.de/verlag/wider-das-kostbare (site discontinued).

167. Heidi Paris, "Wider das Kostbare." On Merve's impact on the discourse in West Germany see Philipp Felsch, "What Was Theory? Toward a Generic History," *New German Critique* 44, no. 3 (November 2017): 5–20; for the medium of the pamphlet, see Jan-Frederik Bandel and Georg Stanitzek, "Broschüren. Zur Legende vom 'Tod der Literatur,'" *Kodex. Jahrbuch der Internationalen Buchwissenschaftlichen Gesellschaft* 5 (2015): 59–90.

168. All citations Jan-Frederik Bandel, "Underdesign," in *Under the Radar: Underground Zines and Self-Publications 1965–1975*, ed. Jan-Frederik Bandel, Annette Gilbert, and Tania Prill (Leipzig: Spector Books, 2017), 89–90, 89.

169. All citations Lorusso, "Print on Demand," in this volume, 485, and "In Defense of Poor Media," in this volume, 472.

170. J. Gordon Faylor, interview by the authors, February 11, 2021.

book, literary and art world establishment—just as the avant-garde, underground, counterculture, and artist's book movement once did, while at the same time also pitting itself against the current nostalgic idealization and fetishizing of the book as a beautiful, valuable, precious, haptic object.

THE NONBOOKS OF THE COPY SHOP AND MIMEO CULTURE

Following Lorusso's comparison of POD to "cheap Xeroxed zines," POD and xerography share a "peculiar identity" along with a cheap feel.[171] Therefore, what Kate Eichhorn notes for xerography should also be true for POD: "Photocopies are marked by the machines that reproduce them. In essence, we recognize photocopies as documents and, more specifically, as documents produced by copy machines."[172] But the link between the two goes deeper than that, because POD is fundamentally based on the technology of the eponymous manufacturer: "Xerox played a crucial role in the development of POD systems, both in technical and cultural terms. While it combined the functional components that make print-on-demand possible"—remember that Xerox's DocuTech Production Publisher was the basis for the EBM—"it also supported experimental projects that employed it,"[173] such as the new edition of Nanni Balestrini's *Tristano* (2007), which was conceived by the author in 1966 as a novel where the text differs in each copy. Of course, this support was not entirely disinterested. Rather, it was intended to demonstrate the potential of the latest printing and reproduction technologies, as shown by the full-page advertisement celebrating Xerox as a promoter of creative freedom in the Italian edition of Balestrini's novel:

> Xerox is a company that has innovation as both a standard and as its mission, a company whose main goal it is [...] to make the printing industry more creative and make it thrive.
> This is why we like experimenting and setting new goals in the world of communication and printing by offering [...] new possibilities for creative freedom. [...]
> With this spirit, [...] Xerox is the ideal partner for those who want to explore new ways of communicating ideas.[174]

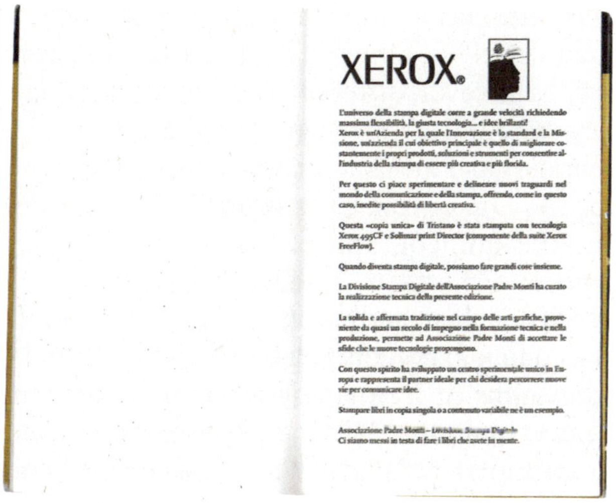

History shows, however, that it is less the companies and their inventions themselves that "explore new ways," than their users: "An engineer named Chester Carlson invented xerographic reproduction, one might say, and the corporation that helped develop his ideas invented Xerox machines, but the photocopy itself was invented by users and on the fly."[175] Kate Eichhorn makes a similar point: "[D]espite its banal original as a time- and moneysaving office technology, the history of the copy machine has been deeply shaped by its users' imaginations."[176] This is related to the fact that copiers—at one time intended as "an integral part of the office assembly line"—were very soon liberated from these contexts of use and "quickly adopted and adapted by workers as a tool of subversion—a form of *perruque* for the information age," as Eichhorn explains: "With relatively little risk, a worker could borrow a bit of time on a copy machine to make a copy of a magazine article to send to a friend or to reproduce a favorite recipe for a co-worker."[177] It is precisely this free-rider effect, which here is at the employer's expense and is known in French as "faire la perruque," that Olivier Bertrand applies to POD platform production and

171. Lorusso, "Print on Demand," in this volume, 485.
172. Kate Eichhorn, *Adjusted Margin: Xerography, Art, and Activism in the Late Twentieth Century* (Cambridge, Mass., and London: MIT Press, 2016), 10.
173. Lorusso, "Print on Demand," in this volume, 485.
174. Advertisement in Nanni Balestrini, *Tristano: romanzo multiplo* (Rome: DeriveApprodi, 2007), n.p.
175. Both citations Lisa Gitelman, *Paper Knowledge: Toward a Media History of Documents* (Durham: Duke University Press, 2014), 84.
176. Eichhorn, *Adjusted Margin*, 21.
177. All citations Eichhorn, *Adjusted Margin*, 34 and 35.

makes it the defining principle of his publishing house Surfaces Utiles (see 80–82).

Once the technology had spread to all the small neighborhood copy shops, xerography finally left the confines of the office and became popular in Résistance and underground circles, activism and samizdat, fan fiction and comics, punk and neighborhood initiatives, zine culture and experimental literature. However different these contexts may be, "they were united by what could be thought of as a technological lowest common denominator,"[178] whether the copier, the hectograph, the spirit duplicator, the mimeograph, or more recently the risograph and platform-based POD printing, all of which are highly accessible, simple, and reliable, as well as quick and economical. In this sense, the latest digital print technology fits seamlessly and on an equal basis into artistic practice, as shown by the work of Éric Watier, for whom reproduction and circulation are central: the founding of his monotone press in 2011 shifted his previous practice of free xeroxed and mail-art photocopies, scans, books, posters, flyers, and postcards into the digital age, adding POD platform products such as DOTS (2011) to his portfolio.

Similarly, Danny Snelson's reprint *L=A=N=G=U=A=G=E, 1978–81: Complete GIF Edition* (2015) should be understood less as an addition to these older technologies than as their continuation in the present. The *L=A=N=G=U=A=G=E* magazine, which appeared between 1978 and 1981 and is often associated with the US-based literary mimeo revolution of the 1960s and 1970s (despite being produced using offset and occasionally copiers), exemplifies Eichhorn's thesis that "xerography supported the avant-garde by enabling writers to more easily publish ahead of rather than in response to an audience. Yet, while xerography may have facilitated the dissemination of future literatures in the present, it was also deployed as a means to put obscure and marginal literature back into circulation."[179]

It was precisely with this objective that the publishers Charles Bernstein, Ron Silliman, and Bruce Andrews founded the L=A=N=G=U=A=G=E Distributing Service as "a kind of door-to-door photocopy delivery mechanism for out-of-print works" that Bernstein produced using "a neighborhood Xerox machine."[180] The catalog of available works was introduced with the following note[181]:

> L=A=N=G=U=A=G=E DISTRIBUTING SERVICE
>
> *Even when published, writing we wish to read often goes out of print with dismaying rapidity--closing off a dialogue. Out-of-print and unpublished works may still circulate among a limited circle of friends. Here, we hope to sustain that dialogue, and expand that circle.*
>
> *Several types of material are available. Photocopies of out-of-print books and unpublished manuscripts are available at the cost of the photocopying and packaging plus a twenty-five cent royalty to the author. These works will be sent side-stapled with card stock covers, stamped by L=A=N=G=U=A=G=E and numbered. In a few cases, a small number of books are available in their original published form at the price specified. All orders must be prepaid and include the cost of postage (see table below).*
>
> *--Charles Bernstein, Ron Silliman, & Bruce Andrews*

Although this reprint-on-demand service was short-lived, the work was carried on by Craig Dworkin in the online archive Eclipse, which makes the most radical small-press writing available again in the form of digital facsimiles, which are in turn preserved and distributed in print via Danny Snelson's POD-based Eclipse Printing Service.[182]

Joey Yearous-Algozin also positions himself and Troll Thread in this tradition when he opens one of his essays on POD "with a detour through a thirty-five-year-old argument,"[183] namely by referring to Bernadette Mayer's essay "Mimeo Argument," written in 1982, the high point of US mimeo culture. It was her response to the poet Eileen Myles's disillusionment with mimeo, which Myles had described as "a vulgar form of print," one "that doesn't look like a book."[184] Mayer countered this with the "more instantaneous reproduction" and "momentary and urgent dissemination" of mimeographed editions, the production of which is "full of pleasure," even if they are excluded from state support: "Apparently, [...] the governments prefer the glossy and the bound."[185] This line of argument crops up in relation to all these print technologies. Eichhorn similarly notes that "photocopied editions have never been fully recognized as books [...]. They fall into a gray area between book and nonbook. They

178. John Komurki, "The Risograph in Context: Notes towards a Cultural History of the Mimeograph," *Counter-Signals* 3 (2018): 22–37, 27.
179. Eichhorn, *Adjusted Margin*, 53.
180. Both citations Snelson, "Variable Format," 59.
181. Charles Bernstein, Ron Silliman, and Bruce Andrews, editorial note to *L=A=N=G=U=A=G=E DISTRIBUTING SERVICE* (1978): n.p.
182. See "L=A=N=G=U=A=G=E," Eclipse Archive, http://eclipsearchive.org/projects/LANGUAGE/language.html, and "Eclipse Printing Service," Eclipse, http://dss-edit.com/eclipse.html.
183. Yearous-Algozin, "Keep Your Friends Close /// We Upload Trash," 76.
184. Both citations Eileen Myles, "Mimeo Opus," *Poetry Project Newsletter* 89 (March 1982): n.p.
185. All citations Bernadette Mayer, "Mimeo Argument," *Poetry Project Newsletter* 90 (April 1982): n.p.

function as books [...] but carry none of the prestige or longevity of other types of books."[186] The parallel with much-maligned POD is striking. "To state the obvious," Yearous-Algozin concedes, "the conversation about what formats we choose to publish in is also a conversation around the question of aesthetic value or lack thereof more than it is one of technology, the development of which is always changing and offers little more than the opening up possibilities for realizing latent desires anyways."[187]

This media and discursive constellation, which persists independently of specific technologies, is neatly captured in Xavier Antin's installation *Just in Time, or A Short History of Production* (2010), consisting of four copying devices lined up in chronological order. They "form [...] a Darwinian evolution of office life."[188] Linking them together in this fashion—in accordance with the titular demand-oriented JIT manufacturing approach, which is also a fundamental principle of the industrial POD workflow—constitutes a miniature logistical masterpiece, as the four machines are so perfectly coordinated that the paper can feed automatically through all of them, from front to back, in one uninterrupted production and material flow. In a nod to the CMYK color model that is the technical basis of four-color printing, the printing process is broken down into four phases, each performed by a different machine: magenta comes out of a stencil duplicator from 1880; cyan out of a spirit duplicator from 1923; black out of a laser printer from 1969; and yellow from an inkjet printer developed in 1976. Just as the machines together form a single "printer" uniting old and new technologies, the layers of ink on the paper add up to produce a fully colored image. "In this way Antin creates a precise image of the state of contemporary media. New media builds on old media"[189]—without this implying a simple history of progress. Although obsolete, the machines used here are still fully functional, and their artistic potential has certainly not yet been exhausted. Indeed, it can only be realized, as in this installation, when they are taken out of the contexts of use and economization for which they were originally developed.

"At the same time," Lucie Kolb explains, "we're not only confronted with a history of inventions, but also with one of social practices."[190] That these can change is demonstrated by Danny Snelson's *LaPoD XEROX Bootleg READER* (2018), produced by his seminar students during an "improvised office copier performance."[191] It not only collates scans of relevant seminar readings, but also serves as a reminder both of the gradual decline of printed seminar readers and of "the world's biggest secret," as Eichhorn puts it, namely "[t]hat most copying has always been and remains illegal."[192] The subtitle *Bootleg* nostalgically recalls the times when the neighborhood copy shop was still a space "where that law is regularly articulated, even posted on the wall, but rarely enacted," or in other words, "a place where everyone is permitted to be a criminal and to be one openly."[193]

This practice of "useful illegality,"[194] which even "historically benefited from the tacit support of public institutions, especially colleges and universities,"[195] is only partially applicable to the commercially controlled realm of POD platforms. The platforms are only indirectly interested in the content

186. Eichhorn, *Adjusted Margin*, 44. Bandel and Stanitzek approach the phenomenon of gray literature from the perspective of the brochure and pamphlet as a publication and communication format in its own right, which often remains under the radar of the literary world, bibliography, and libraries. See Bandel and Stanitzek, "Broschüren."

187. Yearous-Algozin, "Keep Your Friends Close /// We Upload Trash," 76.

188. François Quintin, "Xavier Antin: Maître d'œuvre en re-production," *Art Magazine* 65 (May 2012): 14–15, 14.

189. Lucy Kolb, "Old Media, Networks & Borders," *Brand-New-Life*, April 5, 2018, https://brand-new-life.org/b-n-l/review-unread-messages/.

190. Kolb, "Old Media."

191. LaPoD Press 2018, blurb to *LaPoD XEROX Bootleg READER, 2018* (self-pub.: Lulu, 2018). No longer available online; archived as screenshot on https://apod.li/la-pod-xerox-bootleg-reader.

192. Eichhorn, *Adjusted Margin*, 58.

193. Both citations Eichhorn, *Adjusted Margin*, 23 and 59.

194. Niklas Luhmann, *Funktionen und Folgen formaler Organisation* (Berlin: Duncker & Humblot, 1964), 304–314.

195. Eichhorn, *Adjusted Margin*, 59.

of what they print or distribute as long as there is no threat of legal consequences. However, if they do, they have more effective instruments of monitoring and regulation at their disposal. Thus, producing with machines outside of an Internet-of-Things surveillance apparatus has clear political connotations these days, as Kenneth Goldsmith notes: "[T]he new radicalism is paper. Right? Publish it on a printed page and no one will ever know about it. It's the perfect vehicle for terrorists, plagiarists, and for subversive thoughts in general. If you don't want it to exist—and there are many reasons to want to keep things private—keep it off the web."[196]

This altered historical baseline situation must be taken into account with regard to the current trend of reviving obsolete print technologies for artistic purposes. Yet its use often remains no more than historical reminiscence or a bow to the "aura" of xerography, which makes what was once "the bane of the medium" —its cheap functionality and ugly banality—now seem "thrillingly glitchy."[197] This can be observed in zine culture, for example, where the "old zine paradigm" from the pre-internet age has little in common with the current "prettyprinted zines made in the larger orbit of artist book fairs, indie comics and illustration/graphic design"; it lives on, if at all, only in the form of "political activist zines and pamphlets."[198] One example may be *The 2015 Baltimore Uprising: A Teen Epistolary* (2015)—an anonymously published collection of tweets posted by young Black residents of Baltimore during the protests that followed the killing of African American Freddie Gray in police custody. Since the tweets are reproduced via screenshots, "[t]he visual scene of Twitter is [...] maintained and dominant, but in the manner of a degraded copy—an articulation in publishing of what [Hito] Steyerl calls the 'poor image.'"[199] The collection was initially published by the New York-based radical zine collective Research and Destroy as a xeroxed pocketsize book with a tape-covered spine and no ISBN, depriving it of global distribution as a typical "commodity book." Instead, its small print run was distributed locally for free or at a low price. The first edition was then reprinted as a perfect bound POD paperback with a color cover and ISBN and sold on Amazon and other platforms. According to Nicholas Thoburn, this second edition "is the recapture of an anti-commodity book by capitalist forms," while at the same time "confounding the notion of an 'original' at all, for the first edition [...] looks and feels like a pirate copy of the second, and celebrates this, in being the more desirable of the two objects."[200]

Ambivalences: Between Autonomy and Heteronomy

REFASHIONED GATEKEEPERS AND INTERMEDIARIES

Against the background of these historical links, the autonomous, artistic POD book is thus designed as a manifold—aesthetic, political, economic, institutional, and infrastructural—alternative. But the price to be paid for this alternative to be impactful is the emergence of new dependencies and compromises, hence the particular ambivalence that is present in many artistic POD projects in our collection. It is clear that the emancipation from the traditional publishing industry and its gatekeeping mechanisms, an effect often praised in connection with POD self-publishing and referred to as "disintermediation," is only one side of the coin. After all, the system of mediation does not simply disappear. Instead, new intermediaries emerge in the form of POD platforms and a self-publishing industry that are nothing more than "refashioned gatekeeping." Strictly speaking, therefore, it is misleading to talk about *dis*intermediation or *self*-publishing: "the word *self* masks the extensively collaborative

196. Kenneth Goldsmith, "If It Doesn't Exist on the Internet, It Doesn't Exist," Lecture at Elective Affinities Conference, University of Pennsylvania, 2005, http://writing.upenn.edu/epc/authors/goldsmith/if_it_doesnt_exist.html.

197. All citations Komurki, "The Risograph in Context," 33n23.

198. All citations van Elburg, Cramer, and Balaguer, "Against the [cozy] prettyprinters," in this volume, 625.

199. Nick Thoburn, "Twitter, Book, Riot: Post-Digital Publishing against Race," *Theory, Culture & Society* 37, no. 3 (January 2020): 97–121, 110 [original emphasis deleted].

200. All citations Thoburn, "Twitter, Book, Riot," 110.

process of self-publishing" and its inevitable interconnectedness with providers and infrastructures under platform capitalism. "[W]hat enables self-published texts to thrive in the current technological environment is not the lack of gatekeepers; it is the whims, desires, and business plans of the corporate behemoths that sponsor them."[201]

One example of this particular ambivalence is Jean Keller's *Blank* (2011), which is presented as a book where it is impossible for the producer to make any mistakes, as a way of demonstrating the artist's autonomy. However, on closer inspection a blatant performative contradiction becomes apparent, revealing that this form of self-empowerment and criticism of the system compromises itself, if it completely subjects itself to the predefined setting of a commercial service provider. Contrary to the book title's claim, the eighty pages are not completely empty: on the last page, the print-on-demand provider Blurb has inscribed itself with its logo.

In the blurb, this is commented on: "If you don't like their logo, simply tear out the last page."[202] Removing the logo page, however, does not resolve the issue. The logo (as well as unwanted extra blank pages or internal production barcodes inserted on the last page or back cover) is merely a clearly visible sign for the fact that every POD provider necessarily plays a decisive part in constituting the works—and not only in a material sense. Blurb is much more than just a (mediocre) printer, binder, and distributor. The blank white book—with or without logo—is automatically determined by its production conditions and the economic and technological regime that both enables and limits it. It is therefore—like the white cube, the very space Brian O'Doherty exposed as being ideologically permeated—"a far-from-neutral zone," "a participant in, rather than a passive support for the art."[203] This also applies to the POD platforms, as Nick Srnicek states: "While often presenting themselves as empty spaces for others to interact on, they in fact embody a politics. The rules of product and service development, as well as marketplace interactions, are set by the platform owner."[204]

The claims of freedom, autonomy, and democracy that are so frequently heard in discussions about POD thus all too often conceal the fact that, although POD expands the "horizons of the publishable,"[205] it also entails new limitations. For that reason, even as allegedly independently acting self-publishers, the authors still tread predetermined paths that are defined by the medium, the technology, and the economic production conditions, as well as the institutional and legal framework.

This issue can be illustrated by the example of the page with the Blurb logo, whose insertion into the book is likely to surprise some Blurb users. It is not included in the official page count (to avoid it being added to the customer's invoice as an additional page) nor is it visible—even in Blurb's own design software—"when previewing your book since it's added during printing."[206] And while other platforms merely have a production barcode and a production note, such as "Printed in Poland / by Amazon Fulfillment / Poland Sp. z o.o., Wrocław," which records them as the producer, Blurb, by automatically including its logo, turns each book into a labeled product.

This raises the question of what kind of status platforms such as Blurb, who position themselves as new market intermediaries, are actually hoping to claim for themselves by using a logo. It does not act as a printer's mark, guaranteeing consistent

201. All citations Laquintano, *Mass Authorship and the Rise of Self-Publishing*, 9, 23, and 49 [emphasis in the original].
202. Keller, blurb to *Blank*, https://www.lulu.com/shop/jean-keller/blank/paperback/product-v724j4.html.
203. Both citations Brian O'Doherty, *Inside the White Cube: The Ideology of the Gallery Space* (Berkeley: University of California Press, 1999), 27 and 29.
204. Srnicek, *Platform Capitalism*, 46f.
205. Rachel Malik, "Horizons of the Publishable: Publishing in/as Literary Studies," *ELH* 75, no. 3 (Fall 2008): 707–735.
206. Blurb Help Center, "Remove the Blurb Logo Page in BookWright," last modified in 2022, https://support.blurb.com/hc/en-us/articles/360052429852-Remove-the-Blurb-logo-page-in-BookWright. The number of pages given in the online store may therefore be different to that in the printed book.

quality and production standards (along the same lines as the trademark "Made by"), as it did in printing's early history. In fact, detailed information about the platform's print partners is sometimes even deliberately withheld from the users. Neither does it act as a publisher's imprint, as that would involve assuming responsibility for the published content, which the company is, of course, reluctant to do. The terms and conditions expressly prohibit the use of any wording such as "Published by Blurb" or "Blurb Publishing" "that directly or indirectly suggests or implies that Blurb is the publisher of the book(s) that you create using the services."[207] In spite of this, Blurb offers to allocate ISBNs to books free of charge, which means that they "will be registered under Blurb's name as the publisher of record."[208] The default inclusion of the Blurb logo in every book reveals these numerous contradictions and at times dubious constructs, and clearly demonstrates the urgent need for action to clarify and codify the platforms' legal and political role.

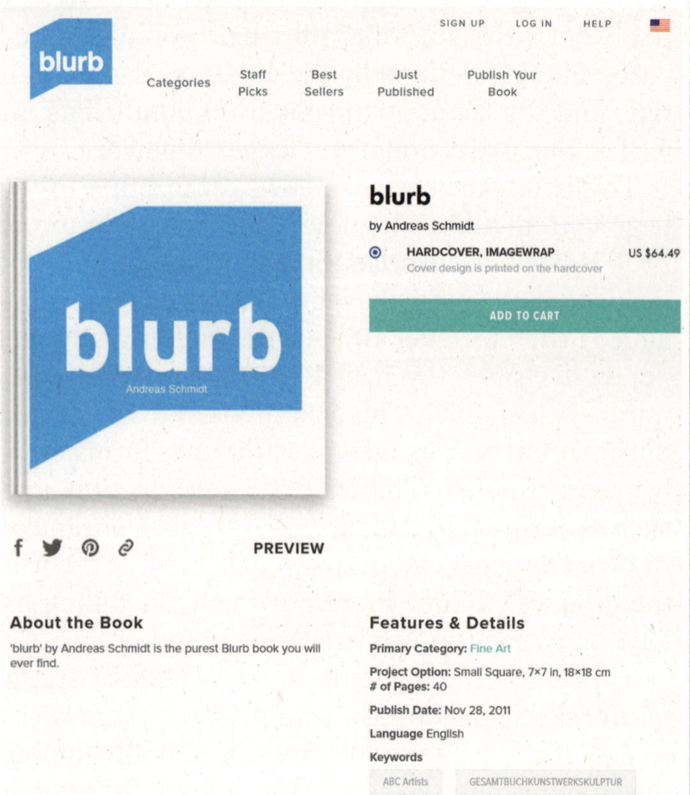

Andreas Schmidt reflects on the audacity and obtrusiveness of this branding in his book *blurb* (2011), which consists of twenty-four of these logo pages and nothing else. The artist jokingly advertises this logo book, offered under his own authorship, as "the purest Blurb book you will ever find."[209] It is not without a certain irony that this reversing of the branding process provoked legal action on the basis of copyright infringement.[210] True, authors can choose to have the logo omitted for an additional charge. "We increase the base price of your book by 25% to cover the removal of our brand from your book,"[211] says Blurb. But Schmidt deliberately eschews this option, not only for financial reasons, but also because he wants his books to openly declare their POD origins. Joachim Schmid has a similar line of reasoning: "I've always decided against [removing the logo] because, in my view, that borders on deception. You act as if it's not a Blurb book, when everyone can see that it's a Blurb book. So the logo can be inside. Otherwise it's like misleading packaging."[212]

While Andreas Schmidt took the offensive in his protest against this blatant branding by directing it toward the platform itself, Jean Keller's *Blank* (2011) reveals in a more understated way the dependent relationship in which artists inevitably find themselves when using the platform. It was precisely this book that later gave Blurb another unequivocal demonstration of its position of power beyond all doubt. In March 2021 we asked the artist, who had in the meantime deleted his books on Blurb and moved to Lulu, to upload the book to Blurb again so that we could purchase a copy for our collection. The platform refused to let him, however, with reference to its terms and conditions. Under Section 11.1, Prohibited Content, there is a surprising mention of books "which have more than 10% of blank pages, including journals, notepads, planners, and publications with similar repetitive, low content."[213] Content such as this is not distributable via the Global Retail Network, Blurb informed the artist.

207. Blurb, "Terms & Conditions," § 11.1, Blurb, https://www.blurb.com/terms [emphasis in the original deleted]. See also § 8.5 regarding ISBNs and publisher status: "You acknowledge and agree that, notwithstanding the method you use to obtain an ISBN for your book(s), Blurb is not the publisher of your book(s) (including your book content) and you will not state or otherwise suggest that Blurb is the publisher of your book(s). You represent and warrant that you are the publisher of your book(s) (including your book content) and, in any case, that you bear the full and ultimate responsibility for the publication and distribution of your book(s) (including your book content)." Ibid.

208. Blurb Help Center, "Does Blurb provide free ISBNs?," last modified in 2022, https://support.blurb.com/hc/en-us/articles/208322596-Does-Blurb-provide-free-ISBNs-.

209. Andreas Schmidt, blurb to *blurb*, 2011, https://www.blurb.com/b/2719883-blurb.

210. Both parties agreed to maintain confidentiality regarding the agreed settlement.

211. Blurb Help Center, "Remove the Blurb Logo Page."

212. Schmid, interview by the authors, November 14, 2019.

213. Blurb, "Terms & Conditions," § 11.1.

These terms and conditions have also been cited in other cases as the basis for the deletion or blocking of books or accounts. For instance, in preemptive obedience—i.e., without anyone taking legal action and without the existence of any court decision—in 2013 Lulu and Amazon blocked and deleted seven out of the nine books that comprise Stéphanie Vilayphiou's series Blind Carbon Copy (2009) due to alleged copyright violations. This concerned, of all novels, an artistic adaptation of Ray Bradbury's dystopian novel *Fahrenheit 451*, which seeks to explore the fine line, bordered by countless uncertainties, between the legally permitted use of foreign works and that which is prohibited. Versions were even deleted which, following the model of Google Books, reproduced only a minor part of the novel, and can be counted as fair use according to applicable jurisprudence. One of Gauss PDF's books with a no less conspicuous name was also blocked due to a copyright issue: Tom Comitta's *1948 by George Orwell*, which is part of his series First Thought Worst Thought: Collected Books 2011–2014 (2015). Here, it was the use of the Signet Classics cover that was the contentious issue. The worst-case scenario is when a user's entire account is blocked because of a single book.[214]

This censorship practice seems even more absurd given that you do not have to look far to find a whole range of "questionable content" on the platforms, such as *Mein Kampf*, the reprinting of which was forbidden in Germany until 2016, or clearly illegal copies of Rupi Kaur's bestseller *milk and honey*. As is so often the case in the digital sphere, judgments on copyright disputes or banned content are increasingly outsourced to private companies like POD platforms, and it is often very difficult for a user to challenge their decisions. Artists have rarely succeeded in convincing the Questionable Content Team that the allegation was baseless and reinstating their account, as in the case documented here.[215]

---------- Forwarded message ---------
From: **Lulu.com Questionable Content**
<questionablecontent@lulu.com>
Date: Wed, 11 Aug 2021 at 17:23
Subject: Re: [Ticket # 254235] Order never received by customer
To: <█████████████>

Dear user,

It has come to our attention that your Content, titled ████████████ may be in violation of the Lulu Membership Agreement, which states that your Content cannot contain material that is intellectual property of another, invasive of privacy rights, defamatory or otherwise questionable and/or determined by us in our sole discretion to violate our Membership Agreement. As a result, we must remove your Content from availability and terminate your Lulu Account.

For more information on the terms and conditions of publishing through Lulu.com please review our Membership Agreement.

Your order GBP-70416 was cancelled and refunded. Please allow a few business days for this to show on your bank account.

Please let us know if we can be of any further assistance.

Regards,
Questionable Content Team
Lulu Press, Inc.[216]

Lulu.com Qu... 16 Aug
to me

Dear user,

We have carefully reviewed the reported content, however, we were unable to identify violations of our Lulu membership agreement.

Your account has been reinstated. We sincerely apologize for any inconvenience caused by our questionable content review process. We take copyright infringement very seriously, so we always want to make sure we are looking into any possible instances.

Regards,
Questionable Content Team
Lulu Press, Inc.

214. See Blurb, "Terms & Conditions," § 2: "Blurb may terminate your membership at any time and for any reason, effective upon sending notice to you at the then-current e-mail address in your account profile" [emphasis in the original deleted].

215. Email correspondence between Lulu's Questionable Content Team and an artist represented in our collection from August 2021 [personal details redacted]. This is not an isolated case. Danny Snelson's Lulu account was suspended after printing problems with one of his books. With this deplatforming, all the books that students have created in his seminars over ten years have been lost.

The whole process becomes even more complex and obscure, because some platforms reject any suggestion that they review content while at the same time stressing that their partner printers have a right to refuse to execute certain orders: "Blurb doesn't review, monitor or edit content. However, our print partners may refuse to print content that they consider pornographic or offensive."[216] This introduces even more actors who are permitted to intervene in the publishing process, in addition to the platforms themselves. Not least, they even include blog hosts such as Tumblr, which publishing collectives like Troll Thread and Gauss PDF use to present their lists. After Tumblr issued a ban on pornography at the end of 2018, some Gauss PDF books were flagged for alleged circulation of erotic material, with the issue only being resolved when a human reviewer intervened.

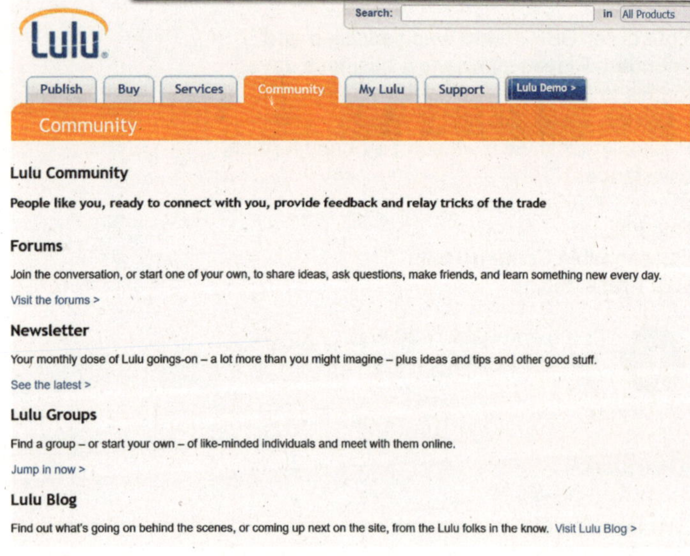

Users are also completely at the mercy of sometimes drastic changes to the platform structures and features. In 2009 paula roush experienced how users can even lose control of their own carefully and laboriously maintained profiles when Lulu suddenly removed the Community Blogs feature, which was originally intended to support social networking by users and the formation of a Lulu community. All the material posted there was ruthlessly deleted. As roush reports, in addition to her user profile, this also affected her "list of lulu friends, group memberships, lulu interests, published books, blogs, and other feeds (del.icio.us bookmarks, for example)."[217] An essential aspect of the publishing and internet culture of the early 2000s was lost in the process, and it can only be partially reconstructed by institutions like the Internet Archive. In this case, roush, a pioneer in the use of POD for teaching, lost "two years of coursework produced with my students using Lulu blogs."[218] Because users were only given a few days' notice, she was unable to preserve her students' blog activities or evaluate the assignments they had already completed.

All these examples contradict the widely held belief "that self-publishing is free of gate-keeping." Thus, Laquintano's lesson in relation to mass authorship also applies to the artistic use of POD:

> arguments about the decline of gatekeepers are too heavily invested in a simplified theory of publishing and a strict hierarchy of value. This viewpoint obscures the realities of the new intermediaries. Rather than experiencing the decline of the gatekeeper, self-publishing writers actually contend with various kinds of refashioned intermediaries, from actual corporate entities such as Amazon to virtual constructs in the minds of the authors.[219]

CAMOUFLAGE TECHNIQUES AND OTHER BIDS FOR FREEDOM

Publishing on the major platforms, therefore, increasingly proved to be not the free space it was once designed to be, and is still advertised as by the POD providers. Of course, this was not lost on artists and authors. The initial euphoric attitude to POD quickly gave way to disillusionment and critical appraisal, giving rise to several projects and publications that take this ambivalence as their theme by comparing the lofty expectations with reality and investigating the artist's own conditions

216. Blurb Help Center, "Will Blurb print adult content such as nudity?," last modified in 2019, https://support.blurb.com/hc/en-us/articles/216494063-Will-Blurb-print-adult-content-such-as-nudity-.

217. paula roush and Ruth Brown, "Publishing with Friends: Exploring Social Networks to Support Photo Publishing Practices," in this volume, 661–669, 664.

218. paula roush, interview by the authors, July 17, 2020.

219. Both citations Laquintano, *Mass Authorship and the Rise of Self-Publishing*, 7.

of creativity and production. Hannes Bajohr has described these attempts "that self-reflexively represent[...] the structural, socioeconomic, and material conditions of [their] production" and debunk the POD system as "post-digital auto-factography."[220]

It was precisely this feeling of being faced with a black box that gave rise to Jasper Otto Eisenecker's project Camouflaged Books (2014–16). It was designed as an artistic research project which aimed to explore and ultimately circumvent the often erratic and obscure checking and censorship practices of the major POD platforms, using Lulu as an example. For this purpose, he produced two books that should have been flagged according to the terms and conditions of the POD providers' verification procedures because they contained either works protected under copyright (i.e., *Make 'Em Pay: Ultimate Revenge Techniques for Master Trickster* by George Hayduke) or explicit content (i.e., violent images from rotten.com). Nevertheless, they did not initially activate the platform's control mechanism, the precise nature of which—upload filter, automated checks that take place after uploading, outsourced manual checking, or community reporting—is unclear. Only when he reported the two books himself on another account did Lulu take action, disabling his account without giving him any chance to object.

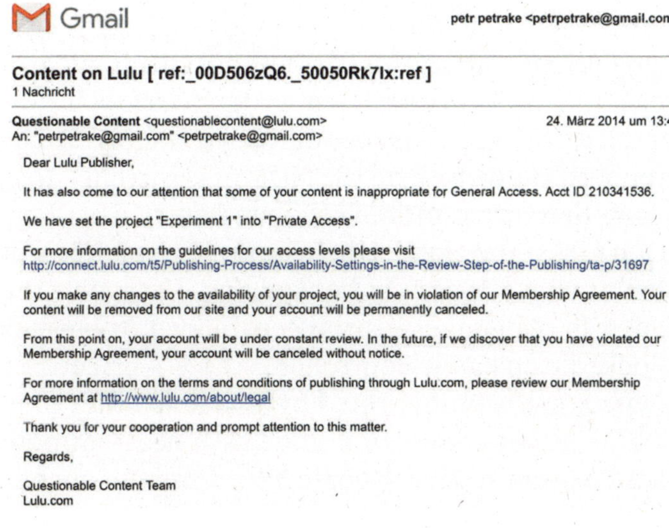

Gmail

petr petrake <petrpetrake@gmail.com>

Content on Lulu [ref:_00D506zQ6._50050Rk7lx:ref]
1 Nachricht

Questionable Content <questionablecontent@lulu.com> 24. März 2014 um 13:43
An: "petrpetrake@gmail.com" <petrpetrake@gmail.com>

Dear Lulu Publisher,

It has also come to our attention that some of your content is inappropriate for General Access. Acct ID 210341536.

We have set the project "Experiment 1" into "Private Access".

For more information on the guidelines for our access levels please visit
http://connect.lulu.com/t5/Publishing-Process/Availability-Settings-in-the-Review-Step-of-the-Publishing/ta-p/31697

If you make any changes to the availability of your project, you will be in violation of our Membership Agreement. Your content will be removed from our site and your account will be permanently canceled.

From this point on, your account will be under constant review. In the future, if we discover that you have violated our Membership Agreement, your account will be canceled without notice.

For more information on the terms and conditions of publishing through Lulu.com, please review our Membership Agreement at http://www.lulu.com/about/legal

Thank you for your cooperation and prompt attention to this matter.

Regards,

Questionable Content Team
Lulu.com

Eisenecker then developed a visual camouflage strategy designed to distort the content of each book in such a way that it would outwit the automated checking and control mechanisms, in particular "Lulu's proofreader-bots and -humans,"[221] while ensuring the printed books would remain legible and present no difficulties for human readers.

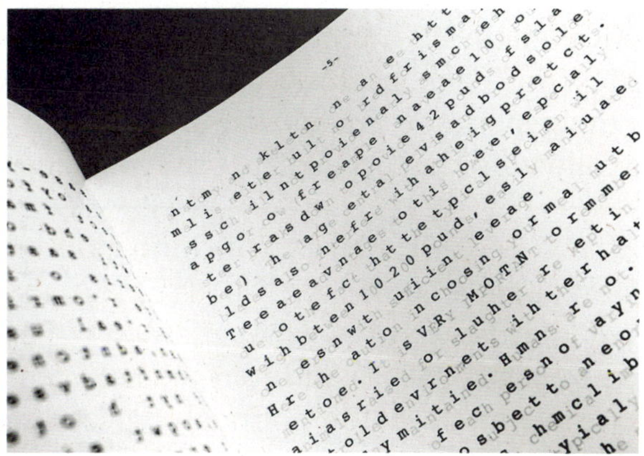

For Hayduke's novel, the strategy involved distributing the letters alternately on the front and back of the pages, so that the complete text only appears when the printed page is held up to the light and the letters shine through from the reverse. This result only materializes in the printed copy, however; the digital print template seems at first glance to contain only nonsensical text, which not only makes automated control by the platform impossible, but also prevents a human from reading it on a screen (on a PDF or in the book preview). This strategic interaction between digital and analog, PDF and print, emphasizes the typical, inextricably hybrid nature of the POD model (see 101). The existence of the physical book, which is still available on the platform, proves the success of this digital steganography, where secret information is concealed within other non-secret text or data.

While Eisenecker's strategy is mostly reactive in nature, Kavi Duvvoori attempts to find a more long-term solution to the problem. His project Common Is That They (2019) aims to potentially bring every (English-language) text ever written into the public domain. To this end, he wrote a script that determined the most frequent four-word sequences in English, according to the Corpus of Contemporary American English, and then checked whether they were already contained in the Google Books database, in other words, whether they had already been used and published. Unused sequences were collected together and published via Kindle Direct Publishing as a POD book that, following a Free Software Community model, has an "Unlicense" that exempts it from any copyright. "The Unli-

220. Bajohr, "Print on Demand as Strategy and Genre: Auto-Factography and Post-Digital Writing," in this volume, 629–639, 634 and 637.

221. Jasper Otto Eisenecker, "Description," *Post-Digital Publishing Archive*, http://p-dpa.net/work/camouflaged-books/.

cense is a template for disclaiming copyright monopoly interest in software you've written; in other words, it is a template for dedicating your software to the public domain."[222] Admittedly, Duvvoori has published just one book, but his project is designed to enable the generative production of innumerable books following this principle. If the machine were to run and publish for long enough, a point would eventually be reached where all potentially conceivable new four-word sequences have been transferred by Duvvoori into the public domain. Thus, in the future, no one would be able to claim copyright over them; conversely, no one would be prevented from using them for copyright reasons.

DÉTOURNEMENT: SUBVERSION AND HACKING STRATEGIES

Eisenecker's and Duvvoori's work addresses the role played by platforms as an interface between infrastructural and legal or political processes, and attempts to circumvent the high-handed way such processes are manipulated by platform operators and rights holders. In addition, there have been attempts to develop disruptive, subversive, or antagonistic ways of using the platforms—after all, "Institutions cannot prevent what they cannot imagine."[223] The first to be mentioned here must be Troll Thread's publishing model, which subverts the actual meaning and purpose of a POD platform: its entire list is exclusively available on a simple, extremely minimalist Tumblr page as a free downloadable PDF or a potential POD book, with both versions connected via links to the Lulu online store.[224] This is not because they think they will sell many books this way; quite the contrary: "We don't expect people to actually purchase the physical copies." They themselves are not even able to afford to print all of their publications. "Basically, we use Lulu as a means to host the PDFs, something Tumblr's platform doesn't accommodate, without having to pay for our own domain."[225]

They thus misuse Lulu as a free storage space (in 2010, when free hosting services were less widespread, this was worth thinking about) and public display window, as a virtual gallery space for the presentation of their own publishing program. In his manifesto *how to stop worrying abt the state of publishing* (2016) Joey Yearous-Algozin openly describes, explains, and recommends this strategy of using an external server to "temporarily store" or "stock" books: "[W]hen you're done uploading the file and cover .jpg, go back to 'my projects,' right click the page icon to the right of 'published file(s): ebook' and copy the link / this is a backdoor way of viewing yr file that lulu is now hosting for you for free."[226]

But here, too, the platform has the last word. In 2020 Troll Thread was taken unawares by an extensive relaunch of the Lulu online store that defeated their sophisticated parasitic strategy at one stroke. Not only were all publications given new links, with numerous publications and accounts deactivated, but the preview function was also deleted—and with it the basis of Troll Thread's hack, once again showing how artists are dependent on the whole POD ecosystem and revealing the POD platforms as an embattled territory, where artistic imagination and use push up against techno-economic optimization and regulation.

In the absence of a better alternative, Troll Thread has now moved to Google Drive for storage. But, of course, this is not a very adroit move in terms of platform politics, nor a long-term solution, and it also flies in the face of the warning issued by Kenneth Goldsmith on the basis of his twenty-four years operating pirate shadow library UbuWeb: "Don't trust the cloud. Use it, enjoy it, exploit it, but don't believe in it." As he explains, "Trusting the cloud is a mistake: it's too centralized, too easily blocked, too easily controlled. And it's privatized, owned, and administrated by someone other than you."[227] All the same, it can be assumed that powerful players such as Google have a greater chance than other market actors of surviving in the pred-

222. The Unlicense, "Unlicense Yourself: Set Your Code Free," Unlicense, https://web.archive.org/web/20230601041219/https://unlicense.org/.

223. Craig Dworkin, Simon Morris, and Nick Thurston, *Do or DIY* (York: information as material, 2012), front matter. Their book "is dedicated to everyone who has advanced literature by self-publishing, and who, in doing so, has moved beyond the horizons of a myopic literary industry." Ibid.

224. See Troll Thread, https://trollthread.tumblr.com/.

225. Both citations Joey Yearous-Algozin in Tan Lin, "Troll Thread Interview." See also Melgard, "Print-on-Demand Self-Publishing," in this volume, 581f.

226. Yearous-Algozin, *how to stop worrying abt the state of publishing*, n.p.

227. Both citations Kenneth Goldsmith, *Duchamp Is My Lawyer: The Polemics, Pragmatics, and Poetics of UbuWeb* (New York: Columbia University Press, 2020), 27 and 26.

atory capitalist world of the platforms ("too big to fail"), and that this at least guarantees the solution a certain longevity.

This was evidently in Richard Kostelanetz's mind when he turned to Amazon's Kindle Direct Publishing to publish his *Avant-Garde Classics* series (2022). He justified the move by arguing that "its prices could not be beaten and [...] it was more likely to survive not only me but its competitors in the new business of on-demand publishing." This argument, coming from one of the last of the twentieth-century avant-gardists, seems like historical irony, particularly when Kostelanetz, in the same breath, acknowledges the dangers arising from this scenario: "Amazon prigs have rejected some Archae books (and twice even canceled all of my Archae books from its listing, only to reverse)."[228]

All these well-argued and smart interventions clearly show the ambivalence that is inextricably part of every subversive attempt: they do not, indeed cannot succeed in the long term, because to critique an institution is ultimately also to maintain it. While in the latter case of maintenance there might still be some hope for long-term improvement, the situation with the subversive use of platforms is different. In platform capitalism, each type of subversive critique ultimately serves to optimize the business model, whether by identifying a weak point in the system, or because the subversive use itself becomes a source of profit for the system. Platform critiques are, therefore, in one form or another, always also a free consulting and bug-hunting tool which benefits the platforms.

COST-BENEFIT CALCULATIONS

In a similarly subtle way to Troll Thread, Jean Keller's *The Black Book* (2010) tries to turn the system against itself. His focus is the pricing—which in the book market is traditionally "dominated by the need to cover costs: the price chosen is primarily driven by costs rather than by the product's characteristics, which create customer value."[229] The POD platforms continue this tradition of cost-plus rather than value-based pricing by using the number of pages, format, paper, binding, choice of color/black and white, and number of copies as variables in their price calculation. The invoiced price is thus apparently determined by the material and production costs in each order, which is why the platforms regularly boast of offering simple and transparent pricing. But that is not the whole story, as Keller's *The Black Book* points out. After all, the amount of ink used is not included in the calculation, even though it is a very considerable cost factor.[230] This means that a book with empty pages costs as much as a book with plenty of text or images, as Keller explains. The concept of his *Black Book* is a logical consequence of these considerations: "A book containing the maximum number of pages printed entirely in black ink therefore results in the lowest cost and maximum value for the artist. / Combining these two features, buyers of *The Black Book* can do so with the guarantee that they are getting the best possible value for their money."[231]

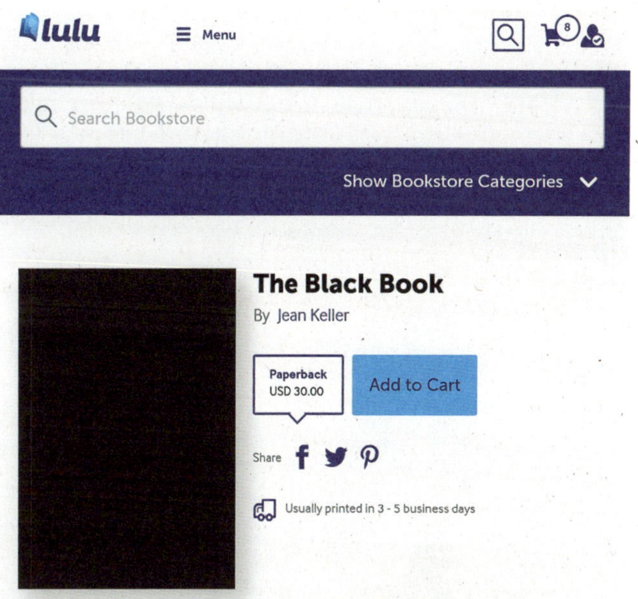

228. Both citations Kostelanetz, *Publishing Avant-Garde Classics*, VII.
229. Dominik Papies, "Preismanagement bei Büchern," in *Ökonomie der Buchindustrie*, ed. Michel Clement, Eva Blömeke, and Frank Sambeth (Wiesbaden: Gabler, 2009), 129–43, 140.
230. Keller's quoted price of over $4,000 per gallon has been consistently repeated in reviews since, but cannot be verified and appears to be fictitious.
231. Jean Keller, blurb to *The Black Book*, 2010, https://www.lulu.com/shop/jean-keller/the-black-book/paperback/product-15gg7vq2.html.

Whether this strategy also automatically means a loss for the POD provider remains to be seen, as Bajohr remarks.[232] Keller, on the other hand, declares: "As long as Lulu continues to print, every royalty payment can be considered a triumph."[233] At the same time, the finesse of this chess move, which seeks to counter the POD provider's pursuit of profit maximization with the author's and buyer's maximization of value, cannot hide the fact that the price is determined solely by the platform's interests and calculations; it is impossible for the author to form an autonomous price and sales policy that is not directed only toward economic aspects, or includes mixed calculations.

Keller is broaching a sensitive subject here, as shown by two other works that POD providers have refused to produce or discontinued temporarily. Lulu has for a long time been unwilling to print Holly Melgard's BLACK FRIDAY (2012), which, with the exception of the title, dedication page, and the white page numbers, is likewise printed entirely in black. This is, as the platform argues, allegedly because of errors in the source file. The author counts this as a success, admitting openly that the work is a test of "if and how poetry could actually, and not just metaphorically, break things;" in this specific case it means: how poetry might actually "break an industrial printer."[234] As with Keller's *Blank*, an important aspect of this is the interplay of pricing and resource consumption, which is used to influence the cost-benefit calculation in favor of the purchaser: if the book is ordered on Black Friday, the day that gives the book its name and when retailers try to encourage consumption through discount campaigns, purchasers receive the highest possible discount, making it the most unprofitable book for the platform. Melgard accordingly promoted the book enthusiastically on Facebook in the winter of 2021 with these words: "This Christmas, give the gift of waste. Buy my book Black Friday and ruin the printer with me. It's on sale at 30% off on Lulu all weekend [...]. I don't collect any profit from sales of the book apart from the joy of using poetry to break shit with you, so join me. Buy my book Black Friday TODAY!"[235] This blatant advertising masks a well-developed sensitivity to the usual capitalist framing of content on the sales platform, which Melgard skillfully subverts at the same time as using it. The fact that the book was made available again some time ago, however, seems to indicate that it is not as damaging as expected for Lulu's loss-leader pricing.

What in BLACK FRIDAY was intended as strategic sabotage (the description text on the platform sets the tone in strident capital letters: "HOW TO SHIT WHERE YOU EAT"[236]) was an unexpected and unwanted side effect in the photographic artist Mishka Henner's twelve-volume series *Astronomical* (2011). The series shows images of the solar system, with the distances between the planets represented true-to-scale in page lengths—the sun is shown on the first page while Pluto appears on page 6,000—so that the reader is able to move

232. Hannes Bajohr, "Infradünne Plattformen. Print-on-Demand als Strategie und Genre," *Merkur* 70, no. 800 (2016): 79–87, 86.
233. Jean Keller as reported by Joachim Schmid, email to the authors, April 14, 2021.
234. Both citations Holly Melgard cited in Sophie Seita, "Communities of Print in the Digital Age," in this volume, 640–651, 644. See also Melgard, *Essays for a Canceled Anthology*, 8.
235. Holly Melgard, Facebook Post, November 29, 2021.
236. Holly Melgard, blurb to *Black Friday*, 2012, https://www.lulu.com/shop/holly-melgard/black-friday/hardcover/product-1wvrj62v.html.

through the universe by turning the pages. The universe is mainly empty though and the pages are predominantly black, leading to considerable ink consumption. In this case, Lulu's decision to cease production after only 130 printed copies was a bitter blow, as the series had been intended as an affordable open edition, had already received several prizes, and was highly valued by numerous institutions and collectors. Due to the halting of production, the few printed copies became coveted, overpriced collectors' items overnight, completely against the wishes of the artist. It seems likely that Henner's high complaint rate contributed to this decision, as many of the print copies had irregularities, both in terms of size, which made it difficult to compile them into a twelve-volume series, and in the application of the black ink. However, one could also argue that the cheap printing technique is in complete harmony with the series' conceptual approach, as it is not clear when looking at the pages whether the tiny white dots are actually stars in the black vastness of space or irregularities in the ink coverage, mirroring the series' concept on a material level. It was not until 2022 that Henner was able to persuade Lulu to resume printing the series.

SUBSISTENCE AND (SELF-)EXPLOITATION

Several of Holly Melgard's other works also address the economic imbalance in the POD business model. In these works, she critically investigates her own inevitably contradictory actions as an author and publisher inside this system, which sometimes actually (re)produce economic and power-political imbalances. For example, she seeks to show how the much-praised financial benefits of POD are countered by the unchangingly precarious work conditions and earning capacity of authors and artists who the platforms frequently reduce to the status of mere content producers. This disparity is exacerbated for experimental and poetic publications, which are not big money-spinners anyway. Moreover, in line with the "anti-economic economy"[237] in the sub-field of restricted production, it is often part of the "minimalist do-it-yourself ethos" not only to "invest as little money as necessary for the survival of the project," as J. Gordon Faylor goes on the record as saying, but also not to earn any money from it.[238] For this reason, the sales price is often set as low as possible, and profits are relinquished or used for server costs, etc. This credo also resonates with Joey Yearous-Algozin's manifesto *how to stop worrying abt the state of publishing* (2016). In it, it says:

> set the price at zero revenue [...]
> this is poetry, you shouldn't be making a profit
> don't be an asshole.[239]

The typical economic imbalance of experimental poetry with a propensity for self-exploitation had already been made the subject of Melgard's *Reimbur$ement* (2013), where she contrasts the idealization of POD as a means of liberation and self-empowerment with reference to "the sustenance that makes the work possible in the first place."[240] *Reimbur$ement* gathers all the scratch cards, lotto tickets, and respective shopping receipts that Melgard has collected over the past six years—more specifically, each time she had to invest in her work instead of making money from it: "Sometimes the work I do results in earning neither income, livelihood, nor play, and often I find myself paying to work rather than being paid for work. Whenever this happens, I count my losses and take my chances gambling for alternatives."[241] One copy of *Reimbur$ement* costs the equivalent of the entire gambling stake plus the production costs claimed by Lulu: $329.53. In the end, what the buyer is paying for is not so much the author's gambling, but

237. Bourdieu, *The Field of Cultural Production*, 54.
238. J. Gordon Faylor, "Dateitypen als Publikationstaktik: Ein Gespräch von Hannes Bajohr," *Kunstforum* 256, no. 5 (2018): 166–171, 167.
239. Yearous-Algozin, *how to stop worrying abt the state of publishing*, n.p.
240. Hannes Bajohr, "Experimental Writing," in *Publishing as Artistic Practice*, ed. Annette Gilbert (Berlin: Sternberg, 2016), 100–115, 115.
241. Holly Melgard, "Introduction," in Holly Melgard, *Reimbur$ement* (self-pub.: Troll Thread / Lulu, 2013), 1.

the adequate remuneration of her work and subsistence: reimbursement is "for *the work*," it correspondingly says on the front matter.

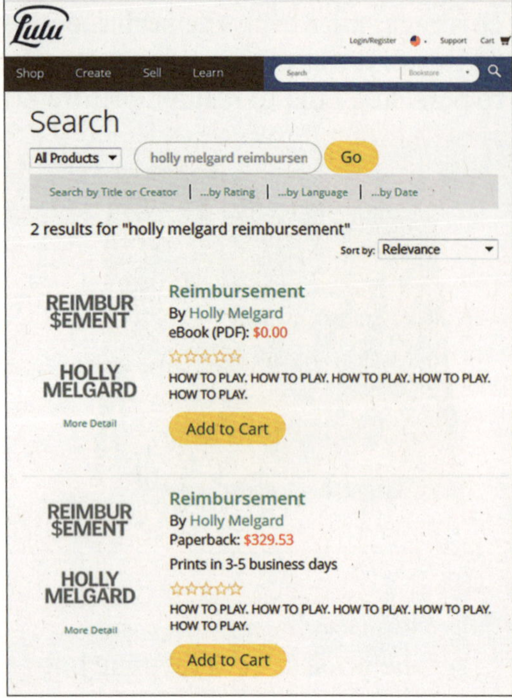

Furthermore, *Reimbur$ement* exposes the different economies of digital and analog media: alongside the printed book, Troll Thread also offers a PDF download, which—following the "gratis mentality" of the internet—is available for free. From this it becomes clear that ultimately both profit models fail: while the author doesn't earn anything at all from the PDF, the printed copy will probably find only very few buyers because of its high price tag. This throws up the urgent question of the sustainability of the POD business model, particularly for those who supply the content with which the platforms make their money.

Melgard binds the contemplation on the inevitable precariousness of this publishing model to the current discussion of gender inequality when, in *PAY* (2018), she points out the gender pay gap to her male co-publishers: in the USA, it averages 17 percent, meaning, in the final analysis, "that for every one dollar that TROLL THREAD refuses to accept as payment, technically speaking, I make negative-seventeen cents." To redress this, she suggests the following "new policy": "We only pay the woman. / I am now accepting payment in increments of seventeen cents for my services rendered."[242] The accompanying link leads to PayPal, thereby bringing into the equation another global player that has entered the book business as a new intermediary. Some people have actually complied with this demand, although the transfer fee turns out to be higher than the actual amount being transferred, so that this, too, remains a somewhat symbolic gesture.

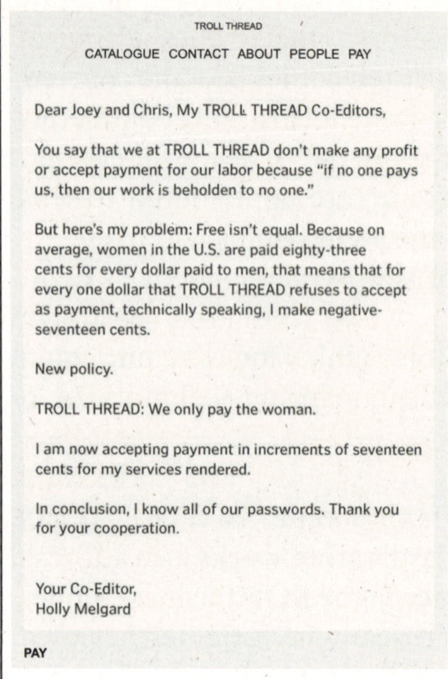
TROLL THREAD

CATALOGUE CONTACT ABOUT PEOPLE PAY

Dear Joey and Chris, My TROLL THREAD Co-Editors,

You say that we at TROLL THREAD don't make any profit or accept payment for our labor because "if no one pays us, then our work is beholden to no one."

But here's my problem: Free isn't equal. Because on average, women in the U.S. are paid eighty-three cents for every dollar paid to men, that means that for every one dollar that TROLL THREAD refuses to accept as payment, technically speaking, I make negative-seventeen cents.

New policy.

TROLL THREAD: We only pay the woman.

I am now accepting payment in increments of seventeen cents for my services rendered.

In conclusion, I know all of our passwords. Thank you for your cooperation.

Your Co-Editor,
Holly Melgard

PAY

The situation becomes even more convoluted and ethically complicated when, rather than being the "underdog," Troll Thread find themselves in a position of power, as was the case in 2015 when they appointed an intern. Due to the publishing collective's general rejection of exploitative internship culture in the publishing industry, they turned his stay into an artistic publishing practice, which led to the production of several publications, among them *INTERN by INTERN* (2015). This is a meticulous documentation of tasks assigned to the intern, the time he spent to fulfill these tasks, commentary on takeaways, and a complete documentation of text and email conversations he had with the publishers. The tasks ranged from installing Adobe Acrobat, to having cigarette breaks, to solving Tumblr catalog issues, to writing spreadsheets of the complete costs of Troll Thread's publications and creating test publications. In this way, it becomes clear how much time, energy, work, and struggle with technology it takes to keep the seemingly undemanding Troll Thread Tumblr page up to date and error-free, or to fix gutter issues in the

242. All citations Holly Melgard, "PAY," Troll Thread, https://trollthread.tumblr.com/PAY.

PDFs. By documenting the internship and publishing it in their program, Troll Thread turns what would only be one person's hidden work and insights into a public glimpse into their publishing activities, their understanding of publishing and poetry, their workflows, and everyday lives.

However, this does nothing to resolve the fundamental problem of any relationship based on power and hierarchy. The publication produced by the nameless intern, which, as part of the publisher's list, is subordinated to the collective's conceptual and graphic approach, seems to mirror the exploitative processes of digital platforms and the business world, with which Troll Thread engages critically and ambivalently. Admittedly, nobody involved made any money, whether from their own or anyone else's labor, but the project did generate unevenly distributed cultural and symbolic capital, if only in the world of experimental poetry. It seems that this is a quandary from which even counter-institutional non-profit ventures such as Troll Thread find it difficult to escape. But again, this is only one side of the coin, because in this particular case, Troll Thread only hired the intern, who was already seriously ill at the time, at his own insistence, and the books he produced now function as a memento whose inclusion in our collection is particularly pleasing for the publishing collective.

FAIRE LA PERRUQUE

In addition to such critical considerations regarding the value of work, other projects address POD's environmental footprint. POD is generally considered a "greener" option in the book market: the "sell first then print" principle prevents overproduction, remaindering, and the pulping of unsold stock. So the argument goes that the most effective conservation of resources is still their non-use. As well as reducing paper and ink consumption, POD also shortens transport routes, most printers use certified paper, do not shrinkwrap books and reduce power consumption.[243] For Kris de Decker, who runs *Low-tech Magazine*, a blog that focuses on "past knowledge and technologies for designing a sustainable society,"[244] all these points were decisive when, in 2019, he was searching for a way to make his solar-powered website available in print format so it could be read offline, without a computer, internet access, or a power supply. For him, the POD platforms' decentralized network was another argument in favor: "Our US publisher Lulu.com works with printers all over the world, so that most copies are produced locally and travel relatively short distances."[245]

LOW←TECH MAGAZINE
This is a solar-powered website, which means it sometimes goes offline
About | Low-tech Solutions | High-tech Problems | Obsolete Technology | Offline Reading | Archive | Donate |

About this website
61%
This website is a solar-powered, self-hosted version of Low-tech Magazine. It has been designed to radically reduce the energy use associated with accessing our content.

Or so the advertising promises. There are hardly any official figures, but RPI Print—Blurb's founding partner—at least locates the partner printers of its "global network" on a world map, the clustered distribution of which clearly indicates the concentration on a few key regions in the USA and Europe.[246]

Our Global Network

At RPI, we make it easy to connect to any of our strategic global partners so our customers can expand their product offerings. We take the initiative to find and evaluate potential partners, negotiate the terms, implement the integration, and ensure excellent quality of the print services.

James Goggin was already expressing his frustration with this aspect back in 2012: "[O]ur *Dear Lulu* books were printed in Spain and flown by UPS to Darmstadt and London for delivery."[247] Rahel Zoller noted a similar situation in her 2014 *POD Project*,

243. It is difficult to verify compliance with this advertising promise as long as the platforms outsource their production and keep the names and locations of their partners a secret.
244. Kris de Decker, "About this Website," *Low-tech Magazine*, May 16, 2022, https://solar.lowtechmagazine.com/about.html.
245. Kris de Decker, "Offline Reading," *Low-tech Magazine*, November 18, 2022, https://solar.lowtechmagazine.com/offline-reading.html.
246. RPI Print, "Our Global Network," RPI Print, https://www.rpi-print.com/products-services/services-printernet-networks/.
247. Goggin, "Supply on Demand," interview.

which aimed to investigate the decentralized processing of print orders in different locations and the variation in production between individual sites. While the copy she ordered in Seoul (South Korea) was printed in Agawam (USA), a copy ordered in London (UK) came from Eindhoven (Netherlands).[248] To expedite order processing, it seems that the deciding factors for allocating print orders to partner printers are the capacity and order backlog of each printer at the time of the order, rather than logistical and environmental considerations. Moreover, not every printer can accept every order, since they do not always offer all book and design features. At present, for example, color or hardcover books ordered from Blurb in continental Europe are generally printed in the UK. Blurb customers generally only realize this when not all their ordered books appear in the same shopping cart, so that several orders need to be placed. This increases the carbon footprint and leads to longer shipping times, double shipping costs, and, in some cases, customs duties that are passed on to the customer.[249]

This is, of course, completely out of the authors' or consumer's control. In order to reduce their environmental footprint, therefore, artists must develop their own strategies to break through the highly streamlined economic processes of the platforms and the printing industry. It is to this ambitious goal that Olivier Bertrand has devoted himself with his Surfaces Utiles publishing house—even if he deliberately avoids attaching the label of sustainability or ecology to his publishing and editorial activities and rather wants them to be discussed in the context of an economy of complicity.

He refers to his publishing practice with the French expression "faire la perruque," a term by which Michel de Certeau describes a "practice of economic *diversion*" whereby workers take advantage of their working time and the working means, resources, or tools of their employer for their own benefit, or to the employer's disadvantage, whether it is copying on the company's copy machine, planning the next vacation trip on the office computer, or stealing pencils and envelopes for one's own correspondence: "With the complicity of other workers [...], he [the worker] succeeds in 'putting one over' on the established order on its home ground." According to de Certeau, this goes hand in hand with "the return of a sociopolitical ethics into an economic system." In more detail, it says: "Into the institution to be served are thus insinuated styles of social exchange, technical invention, and moral resistance, that is, an economy of the '*gift*' (generosities for which one expects a return), an esthetics of '*tricks*' (artists' operations) and an ethics of *tenacity* (countless ways of refusing to accord the established order the status of a law, a meaning, or a fatality)."[250]

In addition, Bertrand credits William Morris's Kelmscott Press and Urs Lehni's Rollo Press as his models, which reinvented the publishing craft in their respective eras by seeing it as a creative play on its technical and financial constraints. Inspired by them, the artist believes that:

> It is not necessary to recreate new structures each time, but it is quite possible to rely on those that already exist, even if it means hijacking them. Rather than denying them, we can imagine, for example, taking advantage of the strength of the institutional or industrial structures already in place to transform them according to our needs (and not those of the market). In terms of resources, it is a question of working as much as possible with the materials that are already around us [...].[251]

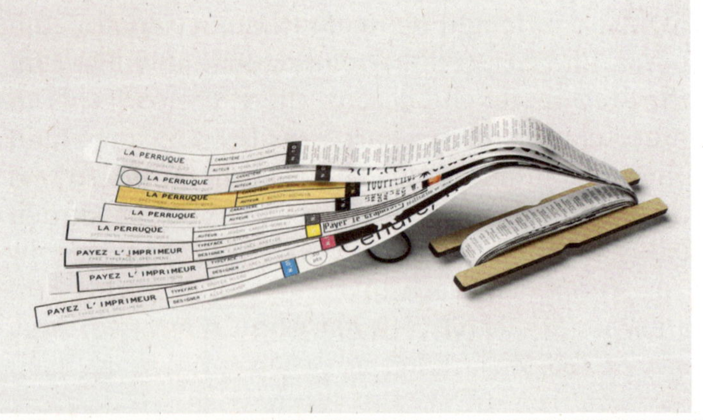

248. Rahel Zoller, "POD Project," email to AND Publishing, March 12, 2014, https://rahelzoller.com/POD.

249. There is an option to partially offset postage costs in such cases, but this information is hidden in the Help section, and the customer has to be proactive and contact the customer service center. The explanation in the customs duties section reads: "EU countries: Premium magazines, Photo books and Premium Lustre Layflat books are not subject to customs duties in EU countries. / [...] Economy magazines may be subject to customs duties, since they are printed in the US. Trade books created with BookSmart may be subject to customs duties, since they are printed in the US." Blurb Help Center, "Customs Duties, Taxes, and Import Fees," last modified June 22, 2023, https://support.blurb.com/hc/en-us/articles/207794426 [original emphasis deleted].

250. All citations Michel de Certeau, *The Practice of Everyday Life*, trans. Steven Rendall (Berkeley, Los Angeles, and London: University of California Press, 1984), 26 and 27 [emphasis in the original].

251. Olivier Bertrand, *Froncer les sourcils* (self-pub.: Blurb, 2017), 100.

Accordingly, since 2015, Bertrand has developed strategies for hacking and reusing leftovers from industrial production for the publishing house he co-founded with the telling name Surface Utiles (usable surfaces), and for his magazine *La Perruque*. For the latter, he makes use of the unprinted margins of printed matter from local printers that would otherwise be scrapped, giving the magazine its unusual format: 90 cm long and 1 cm wide. These unused surfaces are made available to him by printer friends. In the spirit of Michel de Certeau, he calls them "accomplices" on his website.[252] This choice of words is more than justified, because the printers not only give him their leftover paper for free, they also print it without charging him, even though ink is one of the most expensive components in the printing process. There are limitations to how far this strategy can be applied to books, however. Bertrand initially tried it with overstock, but it was very difficult to procure and reuse, and it also limited the number of copies.

He then turned to POD production for his next project, *What's Left Over From the Works of Le Bon* (2017), where the main challenge was the restricted choice of standard formats, none of which met his requirements. So as not to have to trim the printed copies and remove the blank sections afterwards, he chose the Blurb format that was the most economical in terms of its cost-benefit ratio, and offered the resulting offcuts, i.e., the unused blank spaces on each page, to another artist for their own book project. The books delivered by Blurb were then taken out of their bindings and remade into several separate publications. Even the covers were not wasted; they were used to print business cards. In the case of his next book, *Discours sur le déchet* (2019) with Étienne Candel's "trashtexts" that fit perfectly into Bertrand's publication strategy, two copies of the final product can be produced from each Blurb print. The imprint openly declares it to be a "hijacking the services of a print-on-demand platform."[253]

Bertrand thus ultimately implements—as a form of "perruque" for his own advantage—the same principles for economical and ecological optimizing the print sheet as the POD printers, which enable them to offer their products so cheaply, as one of these printers explains:

> One of the most essential reasons for our low prices is the combined printing of different orders during one print run. In particular cases the output might therefore be higher than the ordered amount. Instead of destroying the surplus production (which actually is economical and ecological nonsense), we will inform you and offer you this additional quantity for an extremely attractive price. Just confirm with a mouse click and cleverly use the shopping advantages![254]

However, this strategy is not really worthwhile for Bertrand. It saves paper and money, but not time. The production of the digital template for merging and superimposing the two different works is too labor-intensive, especially since it is not transferable to other publications, which all require individual solutions. Nonetheless, Bertrand values the process: "For me, it was critical to consider design in this way. I think about it from the material to the publishing project, rather than from the publishing project to the material."[255] Bertrand also makes

252. See http://la-perruque.org/about.html#credits and http://surfaces-utiles.org/index.html.

253. Étienne Candel, *Discours sur le déchet*, 2nd ed. (Brussels: Surfaces Utiles, 2019), imprint [103].

254. "FAQ: Can I increase the amount ordered afterwards?," Print24, https://print24.com/uk/faq. See also Bruet, "Production Process," in this volume, 495.

255. Olivier Bertrand, interview by the authors, March 5, 2021.

the semi-finished products available on Blurb alongside the final books, published and distributed by Surfaces Utiles. This serves to document his production process and also, perhaps, to promote it. At the least, he understands these semi-finished products—in a wording that once again echoes de Certeau's idea of complicity—as a "clue. I like these words—accomplices, clues."[256]

PARATEXT POETICS AND ENVELOPE STRATEGIES

The innumerable upload and activation processes that need to be gone through to publish a book on a platform offer another target for intervention. These processes are controlled through a special interface with mandatory fields for title, author(s), keywords, description, etc., which, as in any form to fill in, convey "an inherent imperative [...] to complete all the empty fields as fully as possible."[257] They follow a strict script that firmly attributes the work to one author, or at least a user, and ensures that each publication is distinct and can be referenced by means of its metadata and paratext. In this way, it effectively finalizes and stabilizes the digital content—even before it is materialized in print. As a result, it is relatively time-consuming to amend the print file afterwards (although it can, in principle, be replaced or updated).

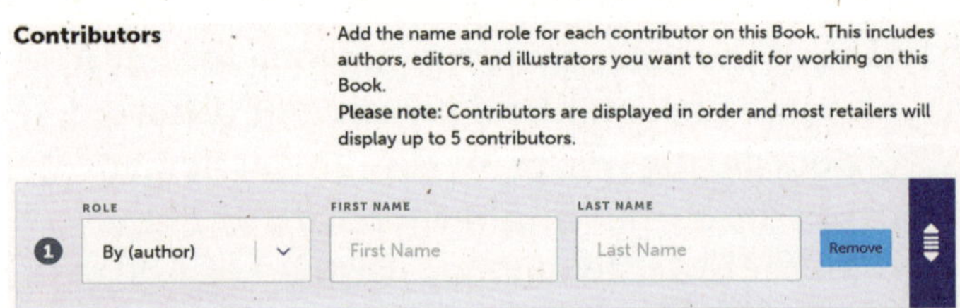

The tendency of these forms "not only to collect data, but also to differentiate, particularize, and granulate it as finely as possible"[258] is exemplified by the mandatory fields on Lulu. For example, at least one "contributor" must be entered, and a name alone does not suffice—a role also has to be selected from a drop-down menu with no fewer than thirty possible choices.[259] This list provides insight into the platforms' concept of authorship and their attempt to mediate between the book trade, with its coarse-grained and often abbreviated entries for names, titles, subject classifications, and other paratexts, and the digital world, where, for example, the names of *all* contributors to a publication can be entered, unrestricted by available space, which more accurately reflects the actual collaborative nature of book creation.[260] At the same time, this increases reach and findability in digital databases and so the amount of attention books receive—an effect that can be observed, for example, in Mathew Timmons' Credit (2011), which documents the strained financial situation of the author during the financial crisis. All the thirty authors who contributed blurbs to the book are mentioned by name in the online store, demonstrating the significance of symbolic capital in this niche sector of restricted production, whose actors, like Timmons himself, often have limited financial resources and creditworthiness.[261]

256. Bertrand, interview by the authors, March 5, 2021.

257. Markus Krajewski, "Schaubilder als Formulare der Organisation: Fritz Nordsieck und die graphische Analyse von Betriebsabläufen," in *Das Formular*, ed. Peter Plener, Niels Werber, and Burkhardt Wolf (Berlin and Heidelberg: J.B. Metzler, 2021), 275–291, 276.

258. Krajewski, "Schaubilder," 276.

259. The list includes author, co-author, artist, photographer, illustrator, editor-in-chief, scientific editor, thesis advisor, and technical editor; it continues with coverdesign, drawings, afterword, preface, commentaries, notes, and introduction by; it ends with edited, translated, adapted, compiled, revised, abridged, and selected by.

260. Hence the multiple references to book trade customs in the instructions, such as the following: "Please note: [...] most retailers will display up to 5 contributors."

261. See Mathew Timmons, blurb to *the a, d, o's & 1, 6, 10's of CREDIT*, https://www.lulu.com/shop/mathew-timmons/the-a-d-os-1-6-10s-of-credit/hardcover/product-19qrjkky.html.

Moreover, these blurbs show the amazing creativity and humor associated with this genre of text, which are also a feature of the sixty blurbs in *Blurb*, from the series *11 Books Expanding Tan Lin's* Seven Controlled Vocabularies and Obituary: The Joy of Cooking, 2010 (2010), where a parody of the blurb as a genre is accompanied by a caricature of the author photo that is so indispensable to book publicity materials. In this case, too, the names of all the authors of the blurbs are stored in the database. Kathrin Passig also takes the opportunity to play with the blurbs that self-publishers are allowed and required to create themselves, and invites her Twitter followers to participate: "For the printed edition of *Strom und Vorurteil* I can for the first time (because it's print-on-demand) put random nonsense on the back cover. This is your chance! Only statements from uninformed people please; those familiar with the content of the book may not take part."[262]

Another feature of Lulu's upload forms is that although most of the fields are mandatory, you can write whatever you want in them. This includes the entry for the author's name, which does not need to be based on a username or a real name. It is thus possible to enter pseudonyms, collective names, or anonymous. In addition, these fields are not exclusive—unlike the login name, an author name can be used multiple times, in different publications, by different users—and the digital metadata and paratexts can be different to the information given on the cover, fly-title, spine, or title page of the printed book. Phil Buehler uses this potential for discrepancy in *All Work and No Play Makes Jack a Dull Boy* (2009), where his name only appears in the optional "About the Creator" section in the online store, while in the printed book and in the online store itself, the author is listed as Jack Torrance, a fictional character from Stephen King's book *The Shining* and from the film of the same name directed by Stanley Kubrick.[263] From the perspective of library and archival practices, this means these data entries from platforms and online stores are just as important as the paratext in the printed book and should be recorded and preserved in the same way, as integral parts of the work—which is why, wherever possible, we include a screenshot of the artist's, publisher's or store's website for each title in our web archive.

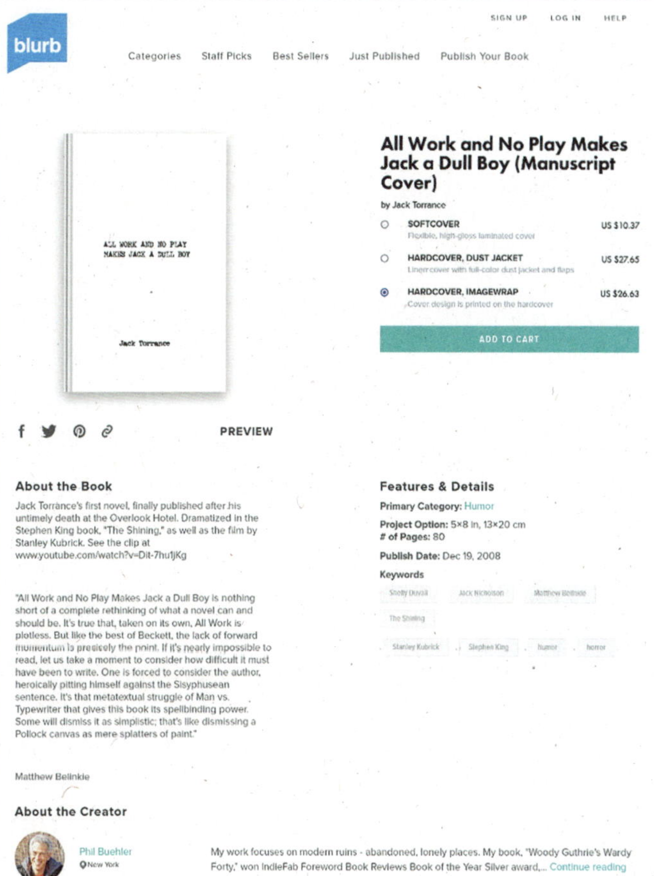

This expands the artistic options available to creators enormously; several artists thus see it as part of their work or their artistic strategy and play around with it. Responding to this invitation to paratextual play, therefore, poetry performances, ironic disturbances, and anarchist defiance can be found alongside "serious" functional data entries. Troll Thread is relevant here for its specially developed paratext poetics. They understand the mandatory entry of the title, author, content description, and metadata as part of their aesthetic and political agenda, using it skillfully in a way that perfectly encapsulates and demonstrates their subversive aesthetic practice: "Using the POD platform in this way enabled us to bypass certain restrictions on the production of knowledge imposed by the print-based tradition, giving our authors more room and flexibility to play with the framing of their own books compared to the print paradigm."[264] Troll Thread can afford such freedoms because of its position as an outsider: "With no academy or art world to convince, the need for blurbs and introductions is practically non-existent."[265]

262. Kathrin Passig (@kathrinpassig), Twitter, February 9, 2020, https://twitter.com/kathrinpassig/status/1226626915664044034.
263. See Phil Buehler, "About," Blurb, https://www.blurb.com/user/pwbuehler.
264. Melgard, "Print-on-Demand Self-Publishing," in this volume, 584.
265. Yearous-Algozin, "Keep Your Friends Close /// We Upload Trash," 78.

Troll Thread's approach to paratextual elements is highly elaborate and reflective, blending analog and digital features. In the case of *MONEY* (2012) by MAKER (as the entry in the online store reads), the combination of title and author name on the cover and spine of the printed book (omitting the "by" in each case) gives rise to a reading that the book is literally sold as a "MONEY MAKER."[266]

Project Details Provide all important metadata to help readers find your book.
Learn more about Metadata

DESCRIPTION 0 / 2500

The Book description will appear on the Lulu Bookstore and any retail sites if your Book uses Global Distribution.
Please note: Your description must be a minimum of 50 characters.

They also have developed their own, specific poetic mode for the mandatory blurbs, which involves entering the standardized wording "HOW TO ..." into the text box provided for the book description, augmented by a suitable, trenchant keyword (if necessary, the phrase is repeated as many times as it takes to fulfill the requirement for the minimum number of fifty characters). With this phrase, which resembles a tutorial title, this paratextual practice not only nods to the plethora of online tutorials, but also comments ironically on the experimental poetry cultivated by Troll Thread and its "use" or "usefulness," which can at times be difficult to communicate.

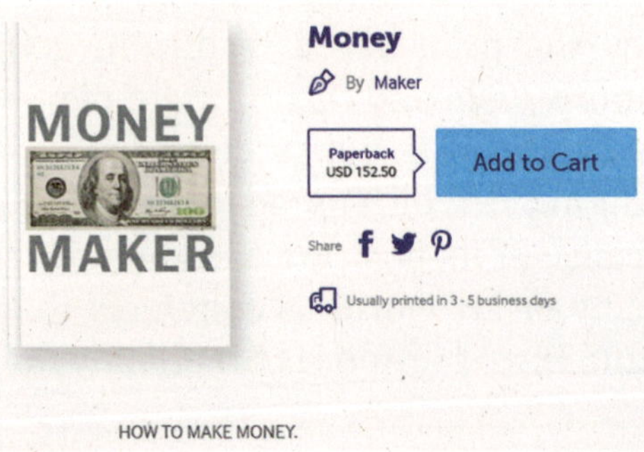

266. See Maker, blurb to *MONEY*, https://www.lulu.com/shop/maker/money/paperback/product-20224396.html.

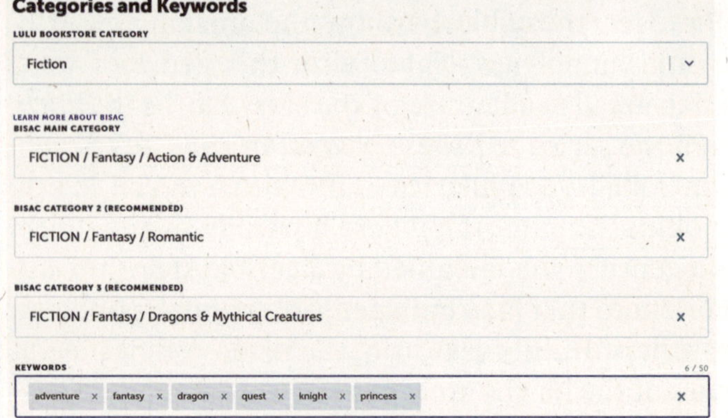

This form of creating and shaping a work by means of platform paratext was also investigated by the students in Danny Snelson's seminar "Print on Demand Poetry: Making Books After the Internet" with their *Blank Books* series (2017).[267] Each of its sixteen volumes contains nothing but 200 white pages. The blank books only reveal their concepts and meaning via their different titles and the metadata and paratexts on the Lulu website. This also includes the mandatory classification of each book into one of the book store's subject categories. While some books were classified by the students as writing materials for notes, drawings, and thoughts, and thus assigned to the "personal growth" or "crafts & hobbies" categories, others used the metadata to conceptually enhance their "content." In one case, the flexibility of the fields was tested by only entering "......" in each one. As this was not possible in the subject categories field, which has a preset list, the choice selected was "fiction," which influences the interpretation of the blank pages.

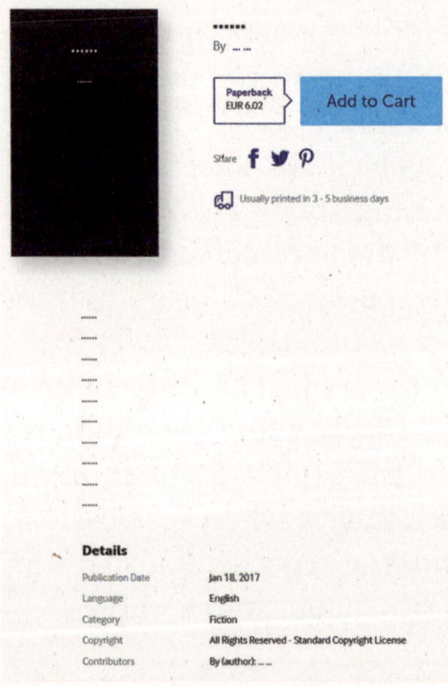

267. See Danny Snelson and NUPoD17, "Blank Books," *NUPoD17*, 2017, https://nupod17.tumblr.com/post/157895548031/blank-books-this-collection-features-an-exclusive.

Orli Spierer, on the other hand, packed thirty verses of the lyrics from *I Will Possess Your Heart* (Death Cab for Cutie, Barsuk Records, 2008) into the description field of her book *In A Language That You Can't Read (Just Yet)*, the title of which is taken from the song. That the "book elegantly bound" and written "in a language that you can't read" (to quote the lyrics) is in fact unprinted pages, is an irony that only the printed book makes clear.[268] Over and above the pedagogical stratagem of exploring the role played by the paratext in the creation and interpretation of books, the *Blank Books* series also shows how paratext can be used in digital, networked databases as an aesthetic strategy.

The question of authorship was also a recurring subject in Snelson's seminars. The solutions chosen ranged from comprehensively listing all contributors, providing only the name of the publishing collective, or even transferring authorship to computers, software, technical agencies, or service providers. The lack of restrictions on what can be entered as metadata and paratext is, of course, an invitation to use no name, a pseudonym, or a false, stolen, or historical name. It also opens the way for appropriations, as in the hundred-volume *Syntactic Analysis* series (2007) put out by Michael Maranda's aptly named publishing house Parasitic Ventures Press.[269] The individual volumes are marketed under the names of well-known authors, even though all that remains of their texts are the punctuation marks. The converse strategy of republishing a classic artist's book or photobook under the artist's own name is used by Eric Doeringer in his publishing house Copycat Publications (see *The Location of Lines* series, 2012) and by Hermann Zschiegner in his *Bootleg* series (see *The Last Resort*, 2013). Vanessa Place, on the other hand, transferred the serial production process used by Andy Warhol in his *Factory* paintings to her own literary production, thus launching the *Factory Series* (2010–12). She outsources the text of the individual volumes to other authors and the book production to a POD platform: "[I]t is my goal to have nothing to do with creation until after the fact."[270] Despite no longer being involved in producing the volumes, she still claims authorship of them.

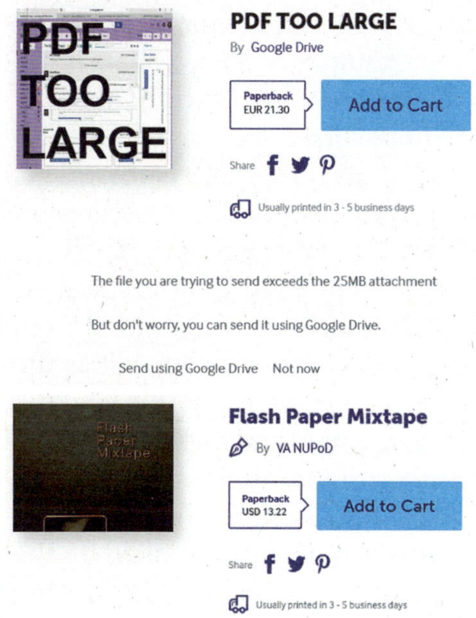

Dear You:

As you may know, the Factory Series has been very fruitful. A number of books by Vanessa Place have come out, none of which have been written by Vanessa Place. In my fervor for production, I would like to extend the invitation to you, the anonymous above, to contribute your own work chez Place. The original call was:

A strange (and misguided) press project would like to publish a series of chapbooks by "Vanessa Place." As an admirer of your work, and in the manner of Warhol's Factory paintings, I would like to see if you would be interested in composing a chapbook, title and contents to be determined by you, by Vanessa Place. If you would like to tell tout le monde that you are the real author, that is fine with me--I just want the physical document to bear the "Vanessa Place" "signature."

To see exemplars, http://www.lulu.com/browse/search.php?search_forum=-1&search_cat=2&show_results=topics&return_chars=200&search_keywords=&keys=&header_search=true&search=&locale=&sitesearch=lulu.com&q=&fListingClass=0&fSearch=vanessa+place&fSubmitSearch.x=6&fSubmitSearch.y=11

(or lulu.com and search Vanessa Place)--all books with white covers are Factory projects. It should be noted that my assistant will be the one actually preparing the chapbooks, as it is my goal to have nothing to do with creation until after the fact.

Let me know if you are interested in participating, and if you would like some more particulars. If I have asked you before, I am asking you again.

yrs,
"Vanessa Place"

268. See Orli Spierer, blurb to *In A Language That You Can't Read (Just Yet)*, https://www.lulu.com/shop/orli-spierer/in-a-language-that-you-cant-read-just-yet/paperback/product-189z9eyg.html.

269. See Michael Maranda, "Syntactic Analysis Series," Parasitic Ventures Press, June 17, 2007, http://parasiticventurespress.com/books/?p=485.

270. Vanessa Place, email to undisclosed recipients, date unknown.

Others disguise their own authorship of or contribution to a book. For example, Ben Fry's name is not mentioned in the online store nor in the book itself, which is listed as *Frankenstein; or, The Modern Prometheus* by Mary Wollstonecraft Shelley (2011). This may be somewhat justified, since the book does in fact contain her text. However, its typographic design uses a special concept called *Frankenfont*: at the beginning, the text is written in commonly used fonts such as Arial or Times New Roman, but as the pages go on it becomes more alien, chaotic, and disorderly, until it ends in a wild and virtually unreadable combination of non-Latin fonts, symbols, and pictograms—based on the distribution of the fonts embedded in PDF versions of the text found on the web. It thus seems to mirror Frankenstein's growing loss of control over the creature he himself created in an unorthodox way. That Fry designed the book can at least be deduced from a small note on the back cover. In similar cases, such as *The Communist Manifesto (In Comic Sans)* (2022), there is no hint as to the "true" author at all; only Marx and Engels appear on the book, and Marx in the webshop as authors.

In the case of such anonymous publications, different motivations and effects can be distinguished. While Hartmut Abendschein's *aaaa press* series (2020–22) aims to explore the power of the authorship function by omitting author names from all one hundred volumes, the collective novel *The Legacy of Totalitarianism in a Tundra* (2014), which originated in 4chan's /lit/ board, demonstrates the disinhibiting, destructive, but also exciting effect of communication between individuals who all go by the generic pseudonym "Anonymous," which is preset as the default value in every user's name field on 4chan. On Lulu, on the other hand, "Anonymous" must be actively entered in the contributor field as a conscious decision by the person who manages the book via their account: the default "Anonymous" of the imageboard (4chan) thus becomes a pseudonym on the publication platform (Lulu).[271]

The fact that Jean Keller, possibly the best known POD artist to operate under a pseudonym, is a member of ABC is hardly surprising in the light of statements such as the following: "We live in different countries and some of us have never met each other or even know what other members look like. We're not even sure if some members are real or fictitious. We fall out—sometimes spectacularly—and we collaborate—sometimes spectacularly."[272] This is a discreet reference to the possibility that a fictional construct may be hidden behind the pseudonym—and in fact, Jean Keller seems, as an international collaboration, to be a distant relative of Luther Blissett, Monty Cantsin, Netochka Nezvanova, and similar collective identities of recent literary and art history. At least this much is known about him: he was born in a café in Paris and was baptized Jean Keller after the name of the café.

271. See Andreas Bülhoff, "A Language of the Envelope: Autor:innenschaft als User:innenschaft," in *Kollektive Autor:innenschaft: digital / analog* ed. Paul Wolff, Michael Gamper, Anna Luhn, and Nina Tolksdorf (Berlin and Heidelberg: J.B. Metzler, 2023), 35–52.

272. ABC, "Paleolithic Cave Paintings," in this volume, 510.

This distinction between naming and authorship practices is also a feature of other areas of (post-) digital communication, the most prominent of which is probably the elaborate configurations of account names and usernames on social media, where the platforms' requests for real names are confounded by the identity games played by users. However, because the simple requirements for accessing POD platforms also permit entry to the more strictly regulated and change-resistant book trade, the POD sector is the arena for a particularly dynamic and experimental negotiation of these practices. The difference between author and user thus becomes particularly evident at this intersection between the traditional book market, with its author name and title catalogs still stemming from the analog era and its legally binding paratexts, and digital platforms, with their comparatively unregulated paratexts.[273] Digital name practices literally extend into the printed publication, once again showing that media practices are impossible without their media technologies, and vice versa.[274]

Specific Aesthetic POD Strategies and Content

ONE-OFFS FROM THE ARTIST'S BOX OF TRICKS

While the above-mentioned examples are oriented more toward critical research and subversion of the POD ecosystem, other projects recognize and use the entire range of artistic strategies, concepts, and aesthetics that POD platforms have made possible for the first time, or significantly advanced. The fact that POD permits the printing of single copies makes it attractive for experiments with generative content, the infinite variable output of which matches the physical uniqueness of each copy. Nanni Balestrini's experimental computer-generated novel *Tristano* (1966/2007) with 109,027,350,432,000 possible permutations can be considered as a forerunner in this area; it was only able to be published in its originally envisaged form with the help of POD, forty years after its first publication: "The novel, designed in the spirit of computer-aided combinatorics, was so digital that only digital printing could bring it into existence—on paper."[275] Originally, an edition was planned in which every copy of the novel was supposed to feature a different computer-generated text. The first publication from 1966, however, was a standard edition in which all copies reproduced the same text. In the new edition of 2007, which was soon followed by translations into German and English, each copy did in fact have a different version of the story and was distinguished by a different number. The Italian edition proudly announced:

> This copy is not the same as all the others
> But your own personal, unrepeatable book
> That has chosen you from an infinity of
> possible versions
> Because the story of Tristan is many stories
> And every reader has the right to his own story.[276]

As in the Russian avant-garde (see 61f.), the individualization of copies in the neo-avant-garde movement of the postwar period can also be interpreted as a strategic poetics of deviance, by means of which Balestrini—in keeping with the revolutionary spirit of the late 1960s—sought to at least

273. Of course, these kinds of playful disputes involving metadata and paratext were also a feature of the pre-digital era as well as the traditional book trade. One impressive example of playing with platform paratext in a traditional book trade environment is provided by the catalog for an exhibition by the !Mediengruppe Bitnik net artists' collective, edited by Aude Launay (Vienna: Verlag für moderne Kunst, 2017): its title *<script>alert ("!Mediengruppe Bitnik");</script>* is written in Javascript code, which triggers error notifications in the databases of bookstores. For more details see Andreas Bülhoff, "Zeichenkodierung und digitale Textkunst," in *TEXT+KRITIK: Digitale Literatur II*, ed. Hannes Bajohr and Annette Gilbert (Munich: edition text + kritik, 2021), 147–159.

274. See Bülhoff, "A Language of the Envelope."

275. Bajohr, "Infradünne Plattformen," 79.

276. Balestrini, *Tristano: romanzo multiplo*, back cover.

partially rectify the imbalance in communication between the author and the anonymous readership. Today, on the other hand, such individualization reflects a change that is affecting all literary production, because in the digital age, variability and fluidity are generally a feature of every text.

This uniqueness presents enormous problems for our Gutenberg book culture and also for literary studies. It not only contradicts the logic of an industrial print run, which by definition produces identical copies; it also disrupts our understanding of literary works, which is closely linked to the concept of a fixed, unchangeable text. In this sense, Balestrini's *Tristano* resembles the medieval *Tristan*, which like many medieval texts displays textual variation (medievalists refer to them as "unstable texts"). In the Middle Ages, it was common practice to supplement scenes, replace expressions, shorten the text, or rewrite passages. Surprisingly, however, these textual variations did not lead to the work losing its identity: it remained *Tristan*. Things are very different now, when the publication of works with no fixed text causes great alarm, as in the case of Balestrini's *Tristano*, or "silent" book releases, where updates and modifications are made without notice. The question of how these books with unstable texts should be read, interpreted, archived, and handed down remains unanswered.[277]

In any case, this possibility of producing unique printed copies has aroused great interest among artists. Nevertheless, artists experimenting in this area soon found that here, too, the platforms imposed strict limitations—a rather unexpected discovery. This also applies to Balestrini's *Tristano*: A letter from the Suhrkamp publishing house to the printer shows that the production of the 2,000 copies of the German edition did not use a fully automated workflow, as might have been expected; instead, the print-ready PDFs were attached to the print order as individual print jobs and processed accordingly.[278] Thus, *Tristano* exemplifies a misconception that recurs frequently on the part of the artists represented in our collection: paradoxically, the individual production of single copies does not translate into infinitely customizable content. This means that the POD platforms, despite their boast of offering a micro print run of a single copy, do not support the kind of generative production method that would allow the reader to create and order their own version. Their processes do not permit the automated upload of print templates with subsequent triggering of a print order. Their application programming interfaces (APIs), via which artists could link automatically with the POD platform, are not accessible for the relevant interactions—perhaps to prevent spam or excessive uploads, or because of the complexity of such a service. The refusal to engage with the potential of generative content again demonstrates the POD platforms' lack of interest in artistic concepts that challenge their understanding of authorship and the artistic or literary work.

For artists who do want to work generatively, this means that in spite of all the automatization and digitization, individual copies still have to be generated and saved singly, with each one manually uploaded and released as a new title. This is clearly inefficient, which is why it has not previously been possible for generative book projects designed as open editions to be produced in the desired way, and why such projects—like Constant's *The Death of the Authors* (2013), Erin Zwaska's *This is where* (2013), Rob Lycett's *23187425 {1000 Haiku}* (2015), and Duvvoori's *Common Is That They* (2019)—are often only published or still available in a single version.

To produce publications with content that varies from copy to copy, therefore, authors can either keep the number of copies very low, as in Sofian Audry's *for the sleepers in that quiet earth* (2019), whose thirty-one copies were manually generated, produced in an EBM print shop, and marketed, or hunt around for an alternative solution in their box of tricks. Aaron Reed, for instance, developed his own workaround for his horror novel *Subcutanean* (2020):

> The way I worked it out is that someone ordering the book first pays me directly, and then I generate a new copy, update the text on my POD partner's site, and manually put in the order through them. (My customer never interacts with the POD site itself). I can order up to six books at a time, because I have six identical 'book projects' set up on their site with identi-

277. See Annette Gilbert, *Literature's Elsewheres. On the Necessity of Radical Literary Practices* (Cambridge, Mass.: MIT Press, 2022).

278. See the correspondence in the archive of the Suhrkamp Verlag, German Literature Archive Marbach, cited in Timo Sestu, *Textmaschinen. Studien zu Artefakten der europäischen Neoavantgarde von Nanni Balestrini, Hans Magnus Enzensberger, Oskar Pastior und Raymond Queneau* (Baden-Baden: Rombach, 2022), 101.

cal covers, and then I cycle regularly through which project I update for a new order.[279]

Andy Simionato and Karen ann Donnachie, on the other hand, succeeded in staying true to the name of their project, *The Library of Nonhuman Books* (2019–), and automated the entire process, from generating the book content using AI, through creating a print template and uploading it onto their Blurb account, to adding the title to their publishing website. Of necessity, this solution does not involve replacing the content, i.e., the PDF, of an existing title each time, but rather uploading a new book to the platform again and again. It is important to them that orders are placed through their own publishing website and not Blurb's online store, because they wish to remain platform-agnostic and to reserve the option to change platforms if necessary. That was a far-sighted decision. For it was only after switching from Blurb to Lulu in 2023, that they were able to overcome the final hurdle and implement a fully automated book ordering process for their publishing website, where new book iterations are first generated and uploaded to the platform at the click of a button, and then copies of them are ordered, paid for, printed, and shipped—all without any human intervention.[280] If this easy-to-use full automation combined with AI is eventually available to everyone, it will probably lead not only to the implosion of the POD business model and the book market, but sooner or later to the collapse of art and literature as well.

ARTISTIC RESEARCH AND EDUCATION

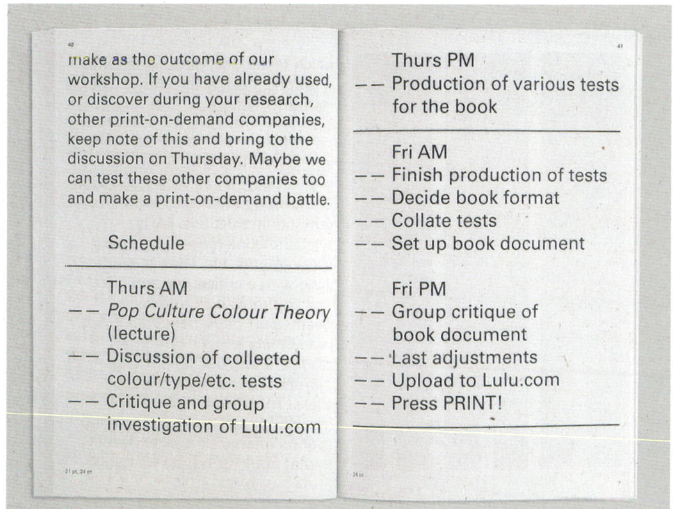

make as the outcome of our workshop. If you have already used, or discover during your research, other print-on-demand companies, keep note of this and bring to the discussion on Thursday. Maybe we can test these other companies too and make a print-on-demand battle.

Schedule

Thurs AM
-- *Pop Culture Colour Theory* (lecture)
-- Discussion of collected colour/type/etc. tests
-- Critique and group investigation of Lulu.com

Thurs PM
-- Production of various tests for the book

Fri AM
-- Finish production of tests
-- Decide book format
-- Collate tests
-- Set up book document

Fri PM
-- Group critique of book document
-- Last adjustments
-- Upload to Lulu.com
-- Press PRINT!

According to Manon Bruet, the POD model "first managed to establish itself in the field of teaching."[281] In fact, the publications in our collection categorized as "artistic research" or "education / classroom" show that POD has opened the door for (industrially produced) books to be used in new ways in research and education. Initially, the focus was on basic testing of this new production process, the potential and limitations of which were explored in art schools by emerging designers and typographers. The most well-known example is the *Dear Lulu* project, conceived in 2008 by graphic designer James Goggin as a two-day seminar, and executed together with Frank Philippin and students

279. Aaron Reed, email to the authors, November 3, 2020.
280. See Karen ann Donnachie and Andy Simionato, "One Hundred Million Million Books: Generative AI and Automated Publishing," in this volume, 536–542.
281. Bruet, "Production Process," in this volume, 500.

at the faculty of Design at the University of Applied Sciences Darmstadt. The aim of the seminar was not only to familiarize the students with the visible and tangible parameters of graphic design, such as type specimens, halftoning, color profiles, calibration charts, point sizes, and print finishing. They also had to put this knowledge into practice by developing a book publication with a wide variety of test-content pages in order to investigate, textbook-style, the potential and quality of the still relatively new process of POD production.

Finally, the students would also critically review the POD platforms' instructions for creating and uploading a print file. These were often needlessly complicated or counterintuitive, and had already driven Kathrin Passig to despair, as she reported in a humorous essay on her *Techniktagebuch* blog.[282] What is more, it was by no means only "ordinary people" who had difficulties with the tutorials, but also book designers, as Goggin explains:

> Websites like Lulu seem geared toward print amateurs with their instructions and many areas are surprisingly vague, and actually less prescriptive than one would expect. As graphic designers, we had specific questions: RGB or CMYK (Lulu says both are fine: the book's outcome indicates this isn't necessarily so). Also, can you print on the inside front and back covers? (Answer: More than an hour of trawling FAQs to get a negative). Various methods for supplying artwork with bleed were outlined depending on which FAQ pages you happened to find. It took several failed uploads to realize that, against any designer's instinct, one must submit bleed artwork sans cropmarks.
> Such challenges, while frustrating for someone making a new project, were exactly what I was hoping for in terms of making a useful document (and informative workshop for the students).[283]

In addition, the *Dear Lulu* project, which has since become a classic of the artistic and explorative use of POD, enabled an investigation of the diachronic modifications in POD production over the long term. It turned out that materials and product properties change over time, as do machines and production processes. While this unexpectedly expanded the original concept of the *Dear Lulu* project, a different aspect of POD temporality often gains particular importance in education: namely, POD production processes that are generally described as instantaneous, but which are actually fairly lengthy. It can take from three days to two weeks for the printed book to arrive, which Danny Snelson, who has run seminars on POD for many years, does not see as a disadvantage:

> [T]he temporal lag also becomes something that we talk about. [...] [W]e have a conversation about their [the students'] works when they produce them as PDFs, but when they arrive in print, we get to have a second conversation. I think there is something nice about talking about something, and then talking about something again after a time remove. That enables deeper critical reflection.[284]

282. See Kathrin Passig, "Yes, today it's boring. But in 20 years!," in this volume, 522–530.

283. Goggin, "Supply on Demand," interview. See also Bruet, "Production Process," in this volume, 496f.

284. Snelson, interview by the authors, July 18, 2020. See also Snelson, "Grey Libraries: Publishing as Pedagogy, An Annotated Bibliography," in this volume, 670–683.

When his students, individually or collectively, are required to produce at least one book every week, this temporal aspect of POD becomes doubly productive: immediately in that they must produce a print template during a seminar session under time pressure and using the most basic materials—as in a book sprint or rapid publishing—which favors a spontaneous, explorative, experimental approach; and (comparatively) slowly when it comes to the production and shipping of the book by the POD provider, which provides a certain critical distance afterwards.

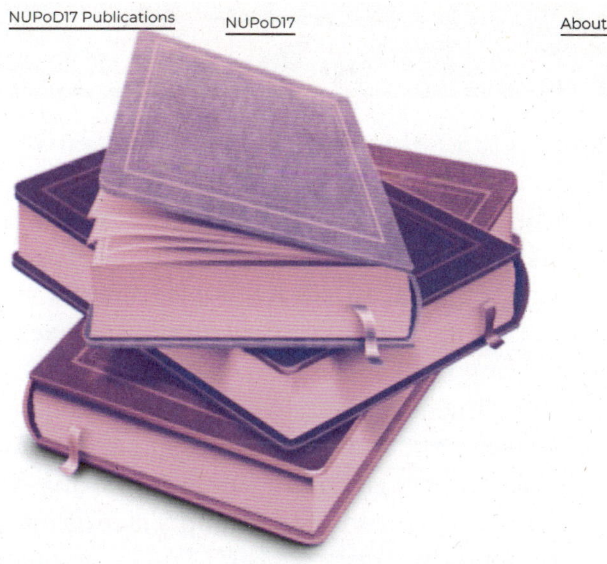

NUPoD17 is a publishing collective masquerading as a winter quarter course at Northwestern University, edited by Danny Snelson in collaboration with the members of NUPoD17. This site is inspired by and in conversation with initiatives like Troll Thread, Gauss PDF, Hysterically Real, Library of the Printed Web, Poetic Research Bureau, and Post-Digital Publishing Archive, among others.

Another basic principle of Snelson's teaching is a sort of revaluation of all values: in principle, all content is equally relevant, i.e., anything that can be made into a PDF can also be made into a book. Nor is the importance of a book measured by how much work is involved in producing the content or the print file. It took Snelson and his students no more than half an hour in the first seminar session to create a book from the syllabus for demonstration purposes: *NUPoD17 Syllabus: v.0.1_1.12.17_4:15-45pm 30 Minute Edition* (2017). Snelson's students were also introduced to a highly topical and theoretically advanced discourse comprising media archeology, media theory, literary theory, poetics, and post-digital publishing whose most fundamental texts sometimes find their way into the printed form of a POD seminar reader such as *LaPoD XEROX Bootleg READER* (2018). Its trashy, amateurish aesthetic calls to mind the photocopied seminar readers that were a defining feature of teaching until a few years ago, but which today's students have probably only heard about.

In a way, the contemporary equivalents are the POD publications in which the students document their internet browsing and searches on the subjects of publishing, books, and POD, and thus constantly compile new netnographic corpora. This could be termed a form of post-digital scrapbooking, in which snippets of information are gathered and, without further editing or design input, copied and pasted into a standard POD container. Like the earlier photocopied readers, the POD "scrapbooks" are generally poorly designed, and feature an unprofessional, almost trashy aesthetic that offers an interesting contrast to the professional, glossy, industrial look of POD production. The arcane value of book production is thus ruthlessly demystified and opened up to new practices and purposes that offer particular potential for pedagogical approaches and experiments.

The declared aim of such seminars is often for the students to also learn "to use the various features related to *managing* publishing projects."[285] In her

285. roush and Brown, "Publishing with Friends," in this volume, 665 [emphasis added].

seminar *THE PHOTOBOOK PROJECT at LULU.COM* (2008), paula roush therefore required her students not only to create and produce a POD photo magazine and a POD photobook; they also had to explore and use the Lulu Community social network to support their photo publishing practice, and design their book and account pages on the Lulu website as a "storefront"—"a public-facing interface which can be fully customized by the seller." It was these "special produsage features that make [Lulu] a preferred choice for teaching: it may be viewed as a two-sided produce–sell (or dashboard–storefront) platform." A student of one of roush's seminars gave the following feedback:

> Like many others in our class, I found publishing our work online and making it available for anyone in the world to buy a very exciting aspect of the unit, and probably one which we would be keen to explore in the future. Publishing on Lulu however does put our work in with thousands of similar pieces, some interesting pieces and some rather less well put together. It would be good to find a more specialist online publishing site for our photobooks & photomags, however this would mean losing the huge numbers of visitors to Lulu. It's a trade-off I guess.[286]

Thus, possibly POD's greatest impact on teaching has been the extension of the classroom into the book market and the public sphere. After all, POD not only enabled the production, but also the publication of university assignments, seminar papers, and theses, which were otherwise only produced for the students themselves and their teachers and for use in the classroom, and not generally circulated, except occasionally for a few copies. In this respect, the seminars have generated not only individual books, but also larger, more extensive artistic projects, and even publishing houses and dissertations, which are now considered as valid contributions to the post-digital publishing scene. "It is important to stress to what degree this [artistic use of POD] was born in an educational environment, i.e., between students, and to what extent it is a product of the design and art schools. A lot of the projects were student projects, which weren't even considered proper output."[287]

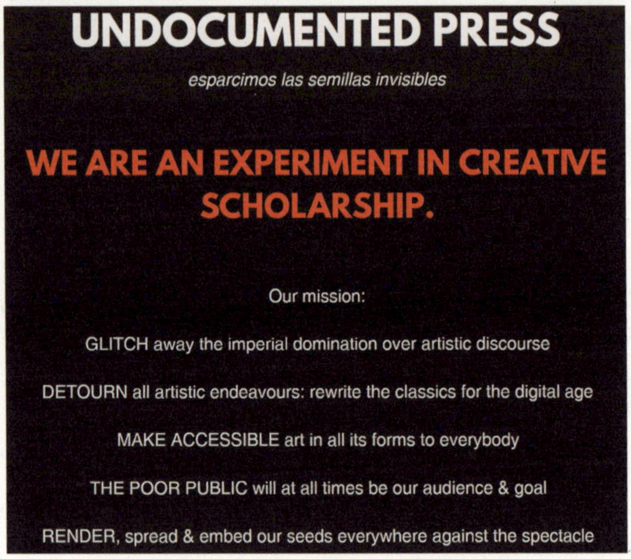

Examples of this are Thomas Walskaar's artist's book *My Hard-Drive Died Along With My Heart* (2016), developed in connection with his master's thesis *Save and Forget* (2018), which investigated memory culture and digital storage media, but also the founding of Olivier Bertrand's Surfaces Utiles publishing house (see 80f.) as a "spin off" from his master's thesis, or Luca Messarra's Undocumented Press (see 405, 422, 682) from one of Danny Snelson's seminars. Snelson's Eclipse Printing Service (see 66, 333) was in turn a subproject of his dissertation *Variable Format: Media Poetics and the Little Database*.[288] Some projects, such as Stéphanie Vilayphious' *Blind Carbon Copy* series (2009), on experimental ways to circumvent intellectual property restrictions, or Jasper Otto Eisenecker's *Camouflaged Books* (2014–16), were not just born in the classroom as master's theses, but also see themselves explicitly as teaching materials. Eisenecker's manual *How to Camouflage Books in Times of Internet Censorship*, which was likewise published on the platform that he was researching, aims to communicate and enable the deployment of his camouflage publishing strategies for a wider public.

POD is also used in non-academic educational contexts, particularly in museum education, art communication, and professional training. Formats offered in these contexts include publishing workshops and book sprints. For example, the twelve-part series *Variable Formats* (2012) by AND publishing is an artistic research project into the connections between material, format, content, and the conditions of production on POD plat-

286. All citations in roush and Brown, "Publishing with Friends," in this volume, 663, 664, and 666.

287. Silvio Lorusso, interview with the authors, February 22, 2020.

288. See Snelson, "Variable Format."

forms. In practice, however, it was used primarily as illustrative material and as a prototype in its "AND Public" workshops.

On the other hand, the *Book Machine* book sprints (2013–17, Paris, Sydney, Los Angeles, Houston, Milan), which were organized by the Parisian publishing house Onestar Press and took place in museums, at book festivals, and as part of public programs run by cultural and art institutions, made use of the low threshold for POD for the collective production of books, and thus became the occasion and impetus for creative and educational processes, exchanges, and synergies. Each sprint concluded with the exhibition, presentation, and discussion of the books produced (in Paris alone, over 350 titles were created in three weeks). In order to implement their book ideas, participants were taught and supervised by design students in individual working sessions lasting from two to three and a half hours. At the end, the students were able to add several books to their portfolios and gain their first practical experience in a real-life setting. At the same time, all parties involved gained knowledge, skills, and experience in the conception, creation, and distribution of books in general, and POD in particular.

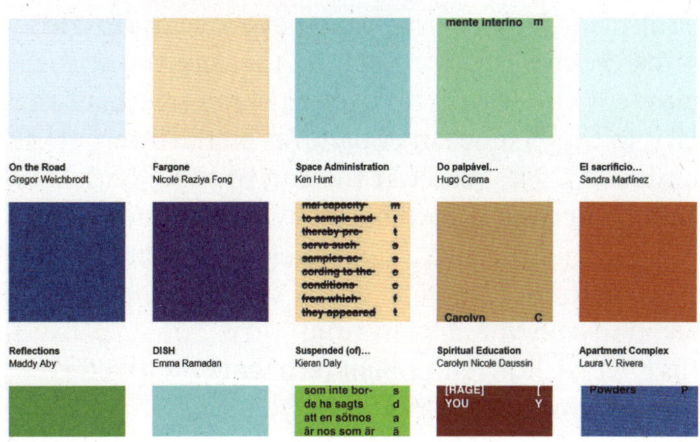

Danny Snelson developed a similar collaborative project with his "1000 Books by 1000 Poets" series for the two-month-long Zurich exhibition *Poetry will be made by all!* (2014, see 284, 297, 303, 357). The aim was for poets in residence born after 1989 to produce books representing "the first-ever attempt to survey the global poetic production of an emerging generation."[289] In contrast to the *Book Machine* output, which was not for sale for copyright reasons, the books produced are available to the public on Lulu and as free PDFs.

POD's low threshold means it takes on a key role in such participative contexts, which are benefited rather than hindered by its limitations on formats and materials: the more standardized the formal specifications, the easier it is to manipulate them and the more they shift the focus of book production away from the book *object* and toward the discovery, design, and execution of the book *concept* and *content*. The fact that this gives all the book sprint publications a common look only emphasizes the collaborative nature of the activities while demonstrating the variety, individuality, and creativity that can be achieved even when forced to follow the same standard specifications.

SPEED AND SCALE

The scale of these book sprints itself draws attention to the fact that POD opens up new avenues, especially for projects which, due to their length or scope, would have no chance of being realized in the traditional book market. These undoubtedly include large-scale projects such as Andreas Schmidt's aforementioned *Gesamtbuchkunstwerkskulptur* (2013), a custom-made book wheel encompassing seventy-seven books, or Joachim Schmid's *Other People's Photographs* (2008–11), an image encyclopedia comprising ninety-six volumes. Also worth mentioning are long-term projects such as Mark Staniforth's ongoing procedural project *Anti-Sonnets*, which began in 2017 with the aim of writing a new sonnet every day,[290] or Wil van Iersel's series *Every Day a New Photobook* (2010–21), which

289. "1000 Books by 1000 Poets," Poetry Will Be Made by All!, https://poetrywillbemadebyall.com/1000-books/. The books created in this context are accessible on https://poetrywillbemadebyall.com/library/.

290. See Mark Staniforth, *Anti-Sonnets*, blog, https://antisonnets.wordpress.com/.

ran for twelve years and for which he produced a book a day for an entire month every year. He chose a different motif for each of the months and explored it either with his camera in the streets of the city, in the vast ocean of pictures on the internet, or on his PC. The result at the end of the month was a multifaceted, subjective study, determined by the circumstances of his life, which was then presented as a box set. In view of the scope of the project (around 360 volumes in total), it is not surprising that, as with Joachim Schmid's work, it is referred to by the artist as a "visual encyclopaedia."[291]

Given the self-imposed restriction that each volume has to be finished, uploaded to Blurb, and ordered all in a single day, it is appropriate that one of the month-long studies addresses speed. It features not only bullets, cars, planes, roads, and trains, as well as skating, running, and jogging, but also the Blurb POD platform itself, which likes to advertise the production speeds of its HP Indigo printers with the slogan "Ready while you wait."[292] However, as van Iersel reminds us, this type of "rapid-fire" self-publishing is not new at all. He cites the newspapers and pamphlets produced during the French Revolution as its precursors, but also recalls Nicolas Restif de la Bretonne, an author and printer in eighteenth-century France who produced around 200 books and who, to save time, "wrote" his books directly in typeface. "[H]e wrote his stories about nightlife in Paris, printed the texts in the morning and peddled his pamphlets on the streets in the afternoon and then started over in the evening with new stories. Fast production was already possible."[293] In this context, therefore, it is apt that the satirical column "The Worst Photo Books of 2013," published on the Artists' Books Cooperative blog (of which Wil van Iersel is a founding member), likens van Iersel's method of production to that of a well-known, global fast-food chain: "Wil van Iersel makes a new book every day for a whole month every year. POD should have never been invented. This month his topic is food. His books are as good as eating 30 cheeseburgers from McDonald's in one go."[294]

BIG DATA IN PRINT

For Joey Yearous-Algozin, POD has yet another unparalleled advantage: "More than simply providing new channels through which to disseminate texts, this shift in platform has allowed for a simultaneous shift in scale. […] [D]igital publishing allows for experiments in volume, with poets literally testing the physical limits of what we call the book."[295] There are several Troll Thread and Gauss PDF projects that fully exploit the new digital possibilities for automating and generating texts and produce vast quantities of text. Stephen McLaughlin's *Puniverse* (2014), whose subtitle (*being the ingenuous crossing of an idiom set and a rhyming dictionary*) reveals its underlying principle, comprises fifty-seven volumes filled with hackneyed jokes. That it is possible to order these volumes as physical books that can be held in the hand clearly shows the excessive nature of digital production, with its tendency toward (barely manageable) over-production. At the same time, projects such as these, which convert big data into print and thus play with the shift of scale introduced by digitization, seem "like a category error,"[296] but this is exactly how they achieve their "post-digital enstranging [sic] effect."[297]

But these fifty-seven volumes pale into insignificance beside Michael Mandiberg's *Print Wikipedia* (2015), which squeezed the entire English Wikipedia into the medium of print. It is striking that in POD the encyclopedia, of all genres, comes into play again and again, although in its printed form it was already virtually obsolete on the traditional book market. The bafflement which generally greets Mandiberg's project stems from the sheer size of the online encyclopedia, which would seem to preclude printing it in its entirety—despite the fact that we have only a hazy idea of the actual dimensions of this collective writing experiment, since information such as the following ultimately remains completely abstract. "There are currently 6,681,483 articles, which means $4.39401048012 \times 10^{9}$ words, which means $2.636406288072 \times 10^{10}$ charac-

291. Wil van Iersel, "About," *Every Day a New Photo Book*, https://septemberbook.wordpress.com/about/.

292. Cited in Wil van Iersel, "November 19," vol. 19, *SPEED* (self-pub.: Blurb, 2012), front matter.

293. van Iersel, "About."

294. ABC, "The Worst Photo Books of 2013," *ABC*, blog, https://abcoop.tumblr.com/post/70695706079/the-worst-photo-books-of-2013.

295. Yearous-Algozin, "Keep Your Friends Close /// We Upload Trash," 78.

296. Hannes Bajohr, "In der Asche des Digitalen: Postdigitales Publizieren heute," *Kunstforum* 256 (2018): 150–159, 155.

297. Bajohr, "Print on Demand as Strategy and Genre," in this volume, 636.

ters."[298] This is precisely where Mandiberg's project comes in, using the normal book format of a US trade hardback as a yardstick for the unimaginable amount of data: the over six million English-language articles on Wikipedia fill more than 7,500 volumes, each with 740 pages, and that is excluding images, links, and sources. It took twenty-four days just to upload the volumes to Lulu, a process that Mandiberg staged as a performance piece in a gallery. There are also ninety-one volumes containing the table of contents and thirty-six volumes that list the names of all 7.5 million Wikipedia authors, a kind of monument raised to those who collaborated on the knowledge that the project visibly materializes.

Print Wikipedia Wikipedia Table of Contents Wikipedia Contributor Appendix About

Wikipedia Volume 1 ! – 'one' Anglia
Wikipedia Volume 2 'one' Great Eastern – (I Wanna Give You) Devotion
Wikipedia Volume 3 (I Wanna Live in a Dream in My) Rec... – .375 Flanged Nitro Express
Wikipedia Volume 4 .375 H&H – 020413 DOJ White Paper
Wikipedia Volume 5 0207 – 100 Love (2012 film)
Wikipedia Volume 7 1000 Ways to Die (season 3, 2011) – 100 (DC Comics)
Wikipedia Volume 8 100 (Dear Jane album) – 103rd Medium Battery, Roya...
Wikipedia Volume 9 103rd meridian – 1010
Wikipedia Volume 10 1010 (film) – 10 m
Wikipedia Volume 11 10 Magazine – 116th Air Control Wing
Wikipedia Volume 13
Wikipedia Volume 14
Wikipedia Volume 15
Wikipedia Volume 16
Wikipedia Volume 17

Various installations in galleries and libraries gave an impression of how much wall space the volumes would occupy. To simulate the overall size of the shelving and room space required, Mandiberg worked with photographic wallpaper, in front of which a few of the volumes were displayed as examples. Even Mandiberg himself has never had all 7,600 volumes printed; the estimated price of printing is $500,000. But as Hannes Bajohr points out, this does not in any way mean that the exercise was pointless: such a project "still requires the *possibility* of being printed in order to achieve its vertiginous, stuplime effect. As in much of conceptual literature, its potentiality, so to speak, is its potential,"[299] it is what gives it its power to convince as an artwork. Just by converting Wikipedia into a familiar book format, which we learn how to use in our earliest childhood as part of our set of cultural practices, and producing a fraction of the total number of books, the project helps us comprehend the dimensions of the collective writing experiment and the scope of the knowledge that it has assembled. Compared to abstract quantities of data, a book is a concrete unit of measurement that we can grasp, both literally and metaphorically: "*Print Wikipedia* is both a utilitarian visualization of the largest accumulation of human knowledge and a poetic gesture towards the futility of the scale of big data."[300]

This transformation into a printed medium also reinstates the alphabetization of the entries, which has its own poeticity. For example, there is unintentional humor in one of Mandiberg's favorite volumes, which, according to the cover, contains lemmata from "List of serial killers by country" to "List of Shakespearean characters L–Z." In addition, Mandiberg likes to cluster volumes with meaningful lemmata on the spines, such as "ART to ART" or "BAT to BAT," whereby the twenty-eight (!) "BAT" volumes are, surprisingly, "not about flying bats or baseball bats, instead, they are a compendium of battles, from the 'Battle of Aachen' to the 'Battle of Żyrzyn.'"[301] This form of found poetry has great historico-cultural significance; it provides unexpected but revealing insights into the idiosyncratic

298. "Wikipedia:Size in volumes," Wikipedia, last modified March 31, 2023, https://en.wikipedia.org/w/index.php?title=Wikipedia:Size_in_volumes&oldid=1147579582.

299. Bajohr, "Print on Demand as Strategy and Genre," in this volume, 636 [emphasis in the original]. The neologism "stuplime" stems from the portmanteau word "stuplimity," which combines "shock and boredom," "stupefaction" and "sublimity." It was coined by Sianne Ngai in *Ugly Feelings* (Cambridge, Mass.: Harvard University Press, 2005).

300. Michael Mandiberg, "About," *Print Wikipedia*, https://printwikipedia.com/#/about.

301. Mandiberg, "Making *Print Wikipedia*," in this volume, 516.

emphases and hidden preferences of Wikipedians. The process produces some surprising discoveries, as when the overwhelming number of volumes on battles is compared with the mere three volumes on "SEX." Mandiberg's project thus mobilizes the venerable function of the book as a cultural asset. In just a few years, *Print Wikipedia* will be an invaluable historical document of collective knowledge production—a snapshot of the state of knowledge at a precise point in time. The physical volumes, preserved by libraries and collections, are representative of the overall project, as well as of the individual series.[302] As study objects, they enable detailed analysis of the "wisdom of the crowd" and the world's collective knowledge as compiled in Wikipedia, as well as of the remediating effects of a web-to-print project; at the same time, they make big data tangible in the physical dimension.

WEB-TO-PRINT

Print Wikipedia also clearly demonstrates that the fast, straightforward POD process is an ideal medium for the documentation and archiving of ephemeral artifacts and content. Even as Mandiberg was processing and stabilizing the text of the Wikipedia pages in PDFs, it was already being added to and edited online: "Once a volume is printed it is already out of date."[303] This is very often the case with phenomena from the digital world and internet culture that find their way into printed media via POD, such as:

- transcripts of voicemails and memos in the guise of confessional lyrics (Joey Yearous-Algozin's *Holly Melgard's Friends & Family*, 2014, and Dane Mainella's *Notes*, 2014),
- collections of search queries or search results (Jonathan Hanahan's *The Dictionary of the Analogue // The Dictionary of the Digital*, 2014 (see image below), Kyndal Thomas' *the perfect* ______, 2015, and Google Search's *A Book*, 2015),

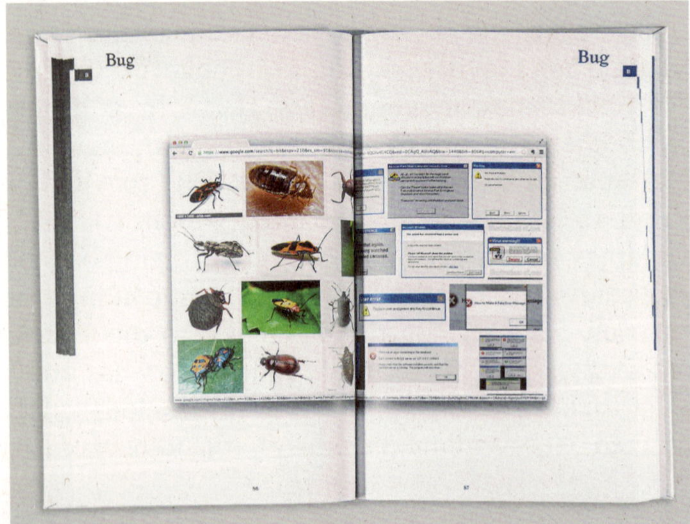

- social media feeds or threads (Anonymous's *Vanessa Place... blocked*, 2014, Andreas Schmidt's *Facebookbook*, 2011, J. Gordon Faylor's *Fr€€dom*, 2010, and Joey Yearous-Algozin's *Real Kill List*, 2013),
- keylogging protocols (Julian Palacz's *End Tell*, 2010, and Barron Webster's *Buy my Privacy*, 2015),
- results from Google Translate or other translation apps (Undocumented Press' *Poetry of America*, 2018, Nick Thurston's *Van de Onderaannemingsovereenkomst*, 2016, Carlo Zanni's *my country is a Living Room*, 2011, and Francesca Capone's *Primary Source*, 2015 (see image below)),

- shots from Google Streetview or Google Maps (Mishka Henner's *No Man's Land*, 2011, Erin Zwaska's *This is where*, 2013, and Gregor Weichbrodt's *On the Road*, 2014),
- content from forums such as 4chan or far-right political groups (Nick Thurston's *Hate Library*, 2019, and Anonymous's *The Legacy of Totalitarianism in a Tundra*, 2014).

302. Such projects require their own archival approach (particularly when, as is the case here, only the printed books are available, not the PDFs), because libraries make very different demands of their shelf space than *Print Wikipedia*'s visualization approach. Indeed, several major German libraries declined Mandiberg's offer to gift them the German version, which he produced in 2016 for an exhibition (again, only a small fraction of the 3,411 volumes were actually printed and exhibited). Finally, it has found a permanent home in the Sächsische Landesbibliothek – Staats- und Universitätsbibliothek (SLUB) Dresden.

303. Mandiberg, "About," *Print Wikipedia*.

Much of this material is now historical, such as the *ReadMe* files collected by Luca Messarra (2019), which originated in pirated material disseminated via torrents on websites like The Pirate Bay. Their design and style recaptured the spirit of the former sub-culture known as The Scene and the movement for free access to knowledge. Another example is the emoji designs in Benenson's *Emoji Dick* (2010), which can be dated back to iOS 2.2 in 2009.[304]

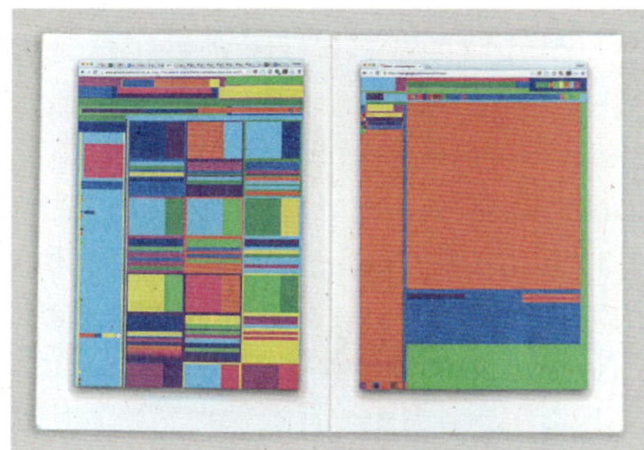

But it is not simply about archiving. Rafaël Rozendaal, who presents his abstract, colorful images based on designs of websites not only in book format (*Abstract Browsing*, 2016), but also in tapestries, describes how this type of remediation of selected screenshots into more stable media affects him: "The real challenge is editing. [...] Out of all the files I have, I have to choose which ones become objects. / The physicalization [...] brings focus. The software is fast and fluid, textile is expensive and slow. It slows me down, it helps me to pause and reflect."[305] Paul Soulellis uses similar words to describe the motivation for and impact of the publications he has collected in his Library of the Printed Web. They are intended to pause the digital condition that is slipping out of our grasp, and enable us, at least "for a brief moment, [...] to control our relationship to content in the form of a material object."[306] TraumaWien, the "paradoxical print publisher," also aims to "transfer[...] late-breaking digital aesthetics into book form, as new media narrative snapshots of literary genres otherwise quickly lost in the immense output produced by [the] web every second."[307]

When it comes to this kind of fixing of the digital in print, there may well be no medium more appropriate than POD, the epitome of post-digital hybridity, which "embraces the fluid movement between material and digital realms that characterizes our age"[308] like no other. As James Bridle explains using the example of his twelve-volume series *The Iraq War* (2010), which documented all 12,000 amendments of the edit wars over the Wikipedia article of the same name, POD has become a powerful tool for historiography:

> It contains arguments over numbers, differences of opinion on relevance and political standpoints, and frequent moments when someone erases the whole thing and just writes "Saddam Hussein was a dickhead." This is historiography. This is what culture actually looks like: a process of argument, of dissenting and accreting opinion, of gradual and not always correct codification.

In his view, this imposes a particular responsibility:

> [F]or the first time in history, we're building a system that, perhaps only for a brief time but certainly for the moment, is capable of recording every single one of those infinitely valuable pieces of information. Everything should have a history button. We need to talk about historiography, to surface this process, to challenge absolutist narratives of the past, and thus, those of the present and our future.[309]

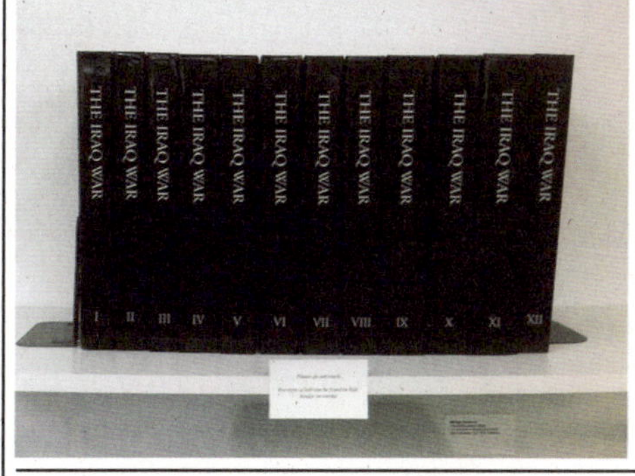

304. Cf. Zach Whalen, "Some Notes on Analyzing the Content of *Emoji Dick*," June 26, 2022, https://www.zachwhalen.net/notes/note-1656258366.

305. Rafaël Rozendaal, "Notes on Abstract Browsing," https://www.newrafael.com/notes-on-abstract-browsing/.

306. Paul Soulellis, "Was wir brauchen, ist ein noch viel radikaleres Publizieren," interview by Annette Gilbert, *Kunstforum International* 256 (2018), 86–93, 89.

307. TraumaWien, "Statement February 2010," TraumaWien, https://web.archive.org/web/20160316181957/http://traumawien.at/stuff/about.

308. Kate Palmer Albers, "At My Desk and In My Hand: 10 Ways I Enjoyed Photography in 2015," *Circulation|Exchange: Moving Images in Contemporary Art*, blog, December 18, 2015, http://circulationcx-change.org/articles/tenthings.html.

309. Both citations James Bridle, "On Wikipedia, Cultural Patrimony, and Historiography," *booktwo.org*, September 6, 2010, http://booktwo.org/notebook/wikipedia-historiography/.

Against this backdrop, it is regrettable that *The Iraq War* series has only been made available in print for exhibiting once,[310] and even then, visitors were not permitted to handle the volumes. Instead, extracts were displayed for them to read. This suggests that the artist was mainly concerned with the speed and ease of POD production and was more interested in the monumental effect that the book objects would create. For one thing, the scale is impressive: at twelve hardback volumes, it approaches "the size of a single old-style encyclopaedia." And for another, "[p]hysical objects are useful props in debates like this: immediately illustrative, and useful to hang an argument and peoples' attention on."[311]

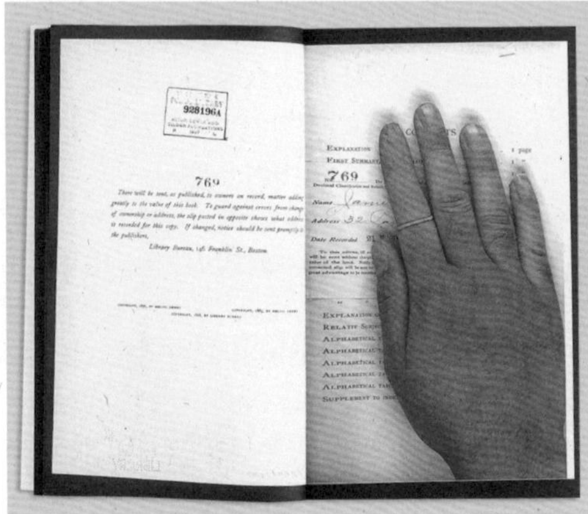

Benjamin Shaykin, whose *Special Collection* (2013) first appeared as twelve hand-sewn volumes before he made them available via POD, chose another route. For him, it was important "to make visible [...] what threatens to become invisible in the process of digital technization" for a wider public.[312] As in Greg Allen's *Wohlgemeynte Gedanken* (2011), Shaykin's *Special Collection* focuses on typical digitization errors found in Google Books, depicting the fingers and hands that regularly intrude into the image to expose the work processes and conditions of mass digitization. The frequency and repetition of the errors (pages not fully turned over, folded sections not unfolded, images photographed through tissue paper, etc.) are a clear sign that "they are caused by the production process itself."[313] The machines evidently have a preset tempo that is too fast for the workers, who are reduced to no more than sand in the gears. In addition, the fact that non-white hands are often shown points to hidden discrimination in the labor market. According to Shaykin, the act of capturing and converting these digital copies back into a printed book reveals "the contradictions and unintended consequences of technological advance":

> Approaching Google Books through its fissures offers a chance to peek behind the curtain of a mysterious, complicated endeavor, which is little understood and generally taken for granted as progress. By using Google's scans and resources to create this work, I am both highlighting the potential of this new era of distribution and access, and questioning Google's claims of ownership of all the world's information.[314]

DATA VISUALIZATION AND SURVEILLANCE CAPITALISM

Silvio Lorusso's and Sebastian Schmieg's series *Networked Optimization* (2015) also aims to shed light on overlooked implications of digital technology, with a particular focus on the excesses of surveillance capitalism. For this purpose, they use methods of data visualization. Their starting point consists of self-help guides, originally displayed on the Kindle e-book reader but converted back into a print format. Their book series, however, only includes those passages marked by Kindle's "popular highlights" feature, which allows the passages highlighted most often by all Kindle readers of the same book to be seen, along with the number of times they were highlighted. These statistics are only available because in order to use the service, Kindle users have to consent to all their activity on the Kindle reader being automatically passed on to Amazon, stored, processed, and used for market analysis or marketing purposes. The artists thus expose the extent to which surveillance capitalism

310. It is therefore the only work in our collection of which we do not have a physical copy.

311. Both citations Bridle, "On Wikipedia, Cultural Patrimony, and Historiography."

312. Bajohr, "Print on Demand as Strategy and Genre," in this volume, 632. Making a unique (exhibition) item available is also addressed in the POD publications of Francesca Capone (*Primary Source*, 2015) and Qiuzi Chen (*Pure Compersion*, 2017).

313. Hole Rössler, "Googles sichtbare Hände. Das Retrodigitalisat als Ware," *Zeitschrift für Ideengeschichte* 10, no. 2 (2016): 115–125. For the imbalances in the labor market, see Andrew Norman Wilson, "The Artist Leaving the Googleplex," *e-flux* 74 (June 2016), https://www.e-flux.com/journal/74/59791/the-artist-leaving-the-googleplex/.

314. Both citations Benjamin Shaykin, "Special Collection," https://cargocollective.com/bshaykin/Special-Collection.

has already penetrated seemingly innocuous areas of life like reading, which in the digital age are more and more losing their private, intimate character. In addition, they remind us that Amazon not only has access to data about individuals' reading habits, but also to the book texts themselves, as Kindle users do not acquire and own them per se, but only have a user's license. Users saw where this can lead in 2009, when a scandal broke out over the unannounced deletion of George Orwell's *1984* and *Animal Farm* from all Kindle accounts for copyright reasons. Lastly, the artists draw attention to the fact that Amazon not only taps this usage data; it also has users generate the data themselves, without any remuneration, in a kind of covert crowdsourcing. The fact that the books that are "most highlighted" are often self-help books also points, say the artists, "to a multi-layered, algorithmic optimization: from readers and authors to Amazon itself. Harvesting its customers' micro-labor, the act of reading becomes a data-mining process."[315]

$ Hello, and welcome to buymyprivacy.com!

Buy my privacy is a series of products generated from "semi-private" information that is not generally publicized, but is nonetheless not private in the purest sense; as it is sent to and used by organizations who built the software we use. This information is turned for a profit by selling our "private" habits to advertisers.

Barron Webster and James Bridle also make use of data visualization methods to illustrate the extent of data capture and the loss of sovereignty over our data. When it became known that Apple had secretly tapped the location data of iPhone users and stored it non-securely, Bridle managed to get access to his own data and used it to reconstruct a profile of his daily movements for almost a year, which he plotted visually on city and national maps—a process that also forms the core of the *Location Edition* in Webster's *Buy My Privacy* series (2015). The title of Bridle's book, *Where The F**k Was I?* (2011), shows clearly that the data is far more reliable than his own memory. In addition, Bridle makes the selling price of his book part of its artistic conception and message: as a critique of such practices of surveillance capitalism, he set the price of the book at €609.79, equivalent to the value of his data, thus turning the book into a commodity.

202 Maps, 35,801 Locations. June 2010 to April 2011.

The data in this book was retrieved from the consolidated.db file of James Bridle's iPhone. This information was recorded anonymously without the user's knowledge, and represents the device's own record of its location.

The collection and publication of data is also the focus of Ubermorgen's *AAbA Logfile* (2011), which contains an implicit critique of the unethical practices of the European migration policy. *AAbA* (short for Asylabwehramt, Asylum Defense Agency) was a hoax purporting to be an official government agency responsible for dealing with illegal migration and border security; its fake website was very popular and attracted a xenophobic public. The book documentation *AAbA Logfile* contains a log of all server activities of the fake website, listing access dates and IPs as well as revealing search terms that led to the website, such as: "Tips+and+tricks+on+how-to+enhance+bureaucratic+burdens+in+the+asylum+process+in+Austria+and+in+the+Schengen+Area." In the "WHOIS Records" section, one can even find resolved IP addresses, revealing the person and/or institution behind the query or server request. The epilogue states:

> If you think this publication is violating privacy rights of users of the website, then we would like to point out chapter 231, first paragraph (3) letter (j) of our user agreement which grants the operators of the website the irrevocable right to use all data collected for their own purpose and for any publication. After all, if you have never been a bad citizin [sic], you got nothing to hide, right?[316]

315. Sebastian Schmieg, "Networked Optimization," https://sebastianschmieg.com/networkedoptimization/. Hidden crowdsourcing is also the subject of their project *Five Years of Captured Captchas*, 2017, http://five.yearsofcapturedcapt.ch/as. See also Gilbert, "Collateral Writing."

316. Ubermorgen.com, "Epilog," in *AAbA Logfile: Asylum Defense Agency. Asylabwehramt* (self-pub.: TraumaWien / Lulu, 2011), 331–333, 333. See also Ubermorgen.com, "Asylabwehramt (AAbA)," https://www.asylabwehramt.at/.

REMEDIATION VIA RETRO-ANALOGIZING

In all of the above cases, the printed book serves to visualize and stabilize digital internet culture and data, and their effects. Stephanie Syjuco also used the book object to this effect in her twelve-volume web-to-print series *Phantoms (H_RT _F D_RKN_SS)* (2011), which sought to explore "the increasingly fluid relationship between screen and printed page"[317] and to capture the effects of retrodigitization on literary texts. As she also converted the digital copies back into printed books, her process could be described as a type of "retro-analogizing." She looked on the internet for free digital editions of Joseph Conrad's novel *Heart of Darkness* (1899), which she then downloaded and "poured" into identical POD paperback "containers." The title is always the URL of the website from which the digital version of the text was taken. What is put to the test here is the concept, popular in e-publishing, of responsive design and the "fluidity" (or "reflowability") of texts, the goal of which is the maximum adaptability of text form to the given digital output medium. Syjuco's series shows the limitations and risks associated with this concept, which become apparent in the corrupted subtitle: *H_RT_FD_RKN_SS*.[318]

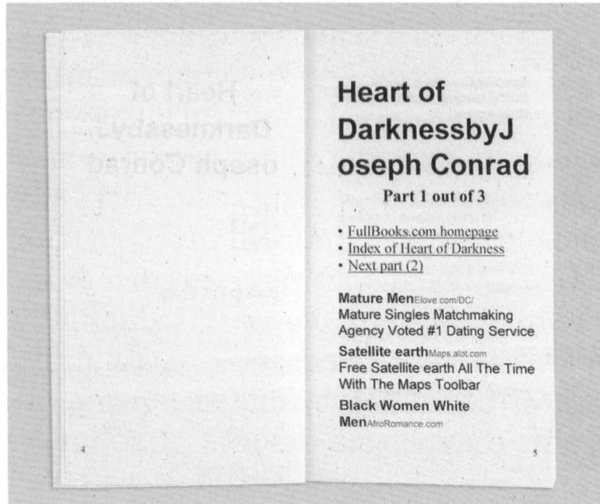

Using the changes that the text undergoes in the retrodigitization process, Syjuco makes visible not only the typical scanning and OCR errors, but also the loss of the *ordinatio* that gives and generates meaning in literary texts. This problem is already apparent in some of the title pages of Syjuco's series, where the missing spaces and inappropriate breaks destroy every unit of meaning, as seen here, for example: "Heart of / DarknessbyJ / oseph Conrad." Syjuco thus counters the dogma of the superiority of the digital file. A further typical side effect of digitization is demonstrated in the extensive appendices to the Gutenberg.org version. Spread across thirty-five pages, it contains the terms of the license that regulate the access, distribution, and use of the digital content. The book page that Syjuco wins back from the digitized text is thus ineradicably shaped by the digital condition. Each of the paperbacks in the series thus not only contains Conrad's (defective) text, it also tells the story of its circulation, reception, and transmission, to which digitization adds a new chapter: "These Print on Demand volumes represent a physical epitome of the effects of digital circulation over the original text."[319]

Hester Barnard's *Copied Right* (2012) also deals with the conversion of a retrodigitized book back into a physical book in order to show how digitization changes the book medium. Barnard made screenshots of all the book pages as they appeared on Google Books, i.e., including the viewing limitations imposed by copyright, and compiled them to make a new book. It is no coincidence that the book she chose for the project, Paul Goldstein's *International Copyright*, is a classic on copyright, a concept that is unable to keep pace with the digital revolution, as evidenced not least by the chutzpah with which Google Books has aggressively created a fait accompli in the (initially almost unregulated) digital sphere. But *Copied Right* also reveals a further effect of digitization: because Google's scans only capture the information *on* the book pages, a digitally flattened book suffers an irrevocable loss of depth. This can be most clearly seen in the spine, which is a blank space in digitized as well as digital books. As a result, the publication previews and mock-up views on POD platforms also omit the spine, and so in Bernard's publication it remains white as well.

317. Paul Soulellis, "Library of the Printed Web (2013)," https://soulellis.com/work/lotpw/index.html.

318. This medial reformatting is by no means just a problem for literary works, as Stephanie Syjuco demonstrates in a three-minute video loop and a music collection that complement the book series. The found footage film compiles the warning "This film has been modified" that precedes many film and video format translations. See Stephanie Syjuco, "Phantoms (H_RT _F D_RKN_SS)," 2011, https://www.stephaniesyjuco.com/projects/phantoms-h-rt-f-d-rkn-ss.

319. Silvio Lorusso, "Extending Horizons: The Praxis of Experimental Publishing in the Age of Digital Networks. Design, Art, and the Materialities of Mediation" (PhD diss., Iuav University of Venice, 2015/16), 105, https://archive.org/details/ExtendingHorizons.

However, this only comes to light when Barnard's "reprint" is ordered in print format, a process in which the body of the book, including the spine, has to materialize anew each time. It is only when you hold a physical copy in your hand that you notice that the spine of *Copied Right* remains unprinted, not because of a lack of creativity, but rather as a clear expression of retrodigitization's blind spot, its complete neglect of the corporeality of the printed artifact.[320] A book that looks shoddily made thus turns out to be a reflection of the shallowness of remediation, which records both the increased accessibility and the loss of materiality resulting from the two-fold change between analog and digital media.

Hybridity and Publicness of POD Production

BOTH... AND...

This inextricable interplay of analog and digital can also be productive in projects which are intentionally configured as a double pack comprising both a digital file and a printed copy. This dual publication strategy has now practically "become a kind of soft standard for experimental writing"[321] in subcultural publishing collectives. This should not be misinterpreted as a marketing strategy used by the established publishing sector to take advantage of multiple distribution channels or reach traditional analog fans as well as digital natives, for the two publication formats here are not to be understood as an "either–or," where the reader can choose the preferred format. Instead, these works are conceptualized as a "both-this-and-that." They represent the attempt to make the fundamental hybridity of POD publications, in which the printed book is always based on a digital master, aesthetically fruitful, and to incorporate it conceptually into the works. In these contexts, the printed book is not conceptualized as the countermodel to the digital; on the contrary, "the relationship between digital and analog should not be thought of as antagonistic, but complementary."[322]

TROLL THREAD

CATALOGUE CONTACT ABOUT PEOPLE PAY

ALL TROLL THREAD BOOKS ARE AVAILABLE IN PRINT ("**PURCHASE**") AND DIGITAL ("**DOWNLOAD**") FORMATS.

This applies to *Camouflaged Books* (2014) by Jasper Eisenecker, mentioned above, but is also exemplified by Joey Yearous-Algozin's *9/11 911 Calls in 911 Pt. Font* (2012), which consists of the transcript of emergency calls made to the New York City Fire Department on the 911 number on 11 September, 2001. The text comprises just a few lines but is set in an oversized font size (911 pt) and thus extends over a total of 911 pages, divided into two volumes—analogous with the Twin Towers. Each page contains just one single letter, which even so bursts out of the page and extends past its edges. This makes the printed book almost unreadable. In the PDF, however, the text remains readable in spite of the overgrown writing, because the digital display format enables different viewing modes and also allows the reader to select the text and copy it into a text editor. This does not devalue the printed version:

320. Andreas Bülhoff's ten-volume *Spine Poem* (2023), inspired by Barnard, also builds on the insight that the "[i]nformation written on the spine is the most ignored paratext of books in digital contexts." The series consists of ten blank books whose only text is on the spine, but which remains unknown in the digital environment and only becomes visible in print. Placed side by side, the volumes form a ten-line poem whose verses can be freely arranged. Andreas Bülhoff, "Spine Poem, bookwork, 2023," sync.ed, https://syncedition.net/spine-poem/.

321. Bajohr, "Print on Demand as Strategy and Genre," in this volume, 633.

322. Bajohr, "Print on Demand as Strategy and Genre," in this volume, 630.

the work's full political and media theoretical significance only becomes clear when viewed as a set. While the printed book, with its physical weight and its fragmented letters bursting from the pages, focuses on the detail, highlighting the damage caused to individuals' lives and the incomprehensibility of the event, the digital format shows the context and the overall picture (see image below).

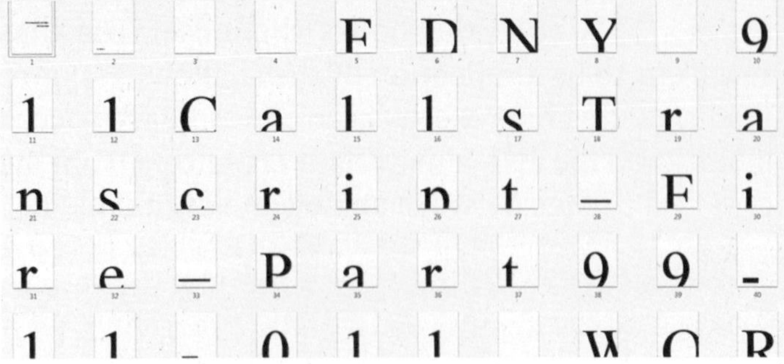

Mimi Cabell's and Jason Huff's *American Psycho* (2012) is another example of this intentional conceptual interleaving of PDF and POD. The two authors sent each other the text of Bret Easton Ellis's novel *American Psycho*, page by page, via email from their Gmail accounts. The printed version of their book contains all the advertisements that Google displayed based on the content of the emails. These advertisements are presented as footnotes to the text of the novel, which is known to be packed with brand names, with each advert tentatively matched with the keyword in the text that may have triggered the Google Ads algorithm to respond. The original text of this disturbing and divisive novel, with its brutal portrayal of extreme acts of violence, is printed in white font and is thus not visible in the printed version. But the text is still present in the PDF and can be made visible again by selecting the blanked-out text or by simply copying and pasting it into another document. The digital version thus extends the printed version: it functions as a container for the subversive file-sharing of a copyrighted text which was also banned in some places. At the same time, the fact that it is possible to reconstruct the original text prompts an intensive reading of the interplay between novel and advertising algorithm in order to retrace the authors' reverse-engineering concept.

A similar purpose is evident in Holly Melgard's *MONEY* (2012), which was published under the pseudonym "Maker" because "putting my name on it would have conceptually organized it into a book about my money (of which I have little), rather than into a book of money, or a poem that makes money (which everyone insists poetry doesn't do)."[323] *MONEY*, however, is about more than just whether Troll Thread makes a profit from its publications. The clear denial in the prefatory note: "TROLL THREAD PRESS does not print nor draw profit from the printing of the manuscripts it distributes" acquires a double meaning in view of the content of the book.[324] For *MONEY* depicts the front and back of 368 hundred-dollar bills in their original size, "inviting the reader to either call cops or cut on the dotted line and use the bills IRL [in real life]."[325]

While the PDF is unproblematic, executing a print job would amount to the illegal reproduction of banknotes, as the reader is warned by the extract from the Counterfeit Detection Act cited in the prefatory note. It is precisely here that the anachronism in current law is revealed, as it is not clear who could be held legally accountable: the author (Maker), the account holder, the buyer, the printing company, or the platform Lulu, as the marketplace and mediator?[326] This is not a purely abstract question, as the printer's refusal to print Melgard's latest book with excerpts from *MONEY* and *REIMBUR$EMENT* shows. To our knowledge, however, all POD orders to date have been produced.

Here, therefore, the order button triggers questions about capital, law, and literature. Readers seeking clarification on these issues find this ironic recommendation in the preface: "for more information regarding the legal identity of *MONEY*'s maker as it technically belongs to the poetic contingencies of its printer, contact: the Public Affairs Office of the United States Secret Service."[327]

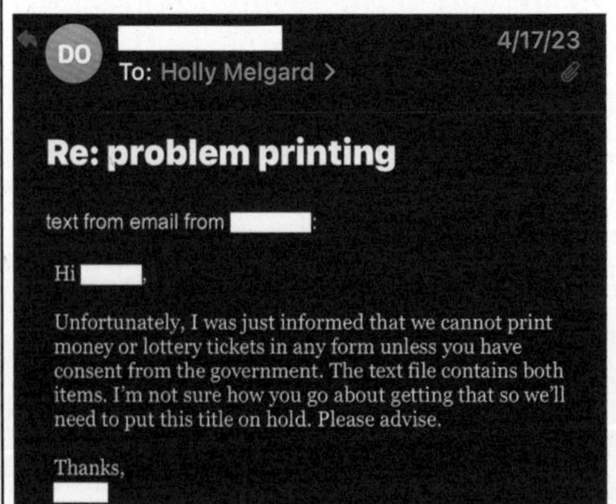

Message from the printers refusing to print Holly Melgard's poetry collection *Read Me* (New York: Ugly Duckling Presse, 2023).

323. Melgard, *Essays for a Canceled Anthology*, 11.
324. Maker, *Money* (self-pub.: Troll Thread / Lulu, 2012), front matter.
325. Melgard, *Essays for a Canceled Anthology*, 11.
326. See Bajohr, "In der Asche des Digitalen," 153.
327. Maker, *Money*, front matter.

IMAGINED PRINTEDNESS

One could, however, argue that although *MONEY* orchestrates a culture clash between analog and digital, between print copy and file, it does not actually need to be materialized in print to be effective. The idea of the book is already realized in the fact that it *could* be printed, because the mere possibility of its being printed makes the issues mentioned above more urgent. In general, Troll Thread's view is that, for many of their publications, their actual materialization in print is more a potential form of reflection.[328] But it is also true for other POD publications that some remain forever in this virtual limbo, just on the verge of being printed.

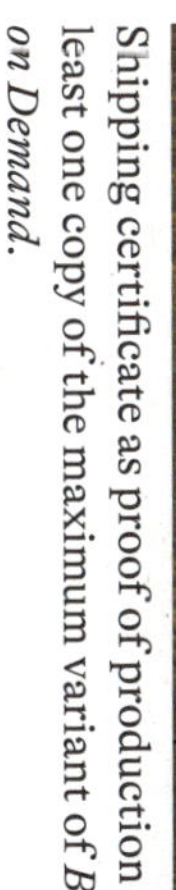
Shipping certificate as proof of production of at least one copy of the maximum variant of *Blank on Demand*.

As *potential* printed works, they are thus manifested more as an artistic idea than as a physical object. Sophie Seita describes this aptly as "imagined printedness": these are works "that cannot or should not be printed, but that insist on printedness, even if only imagined, all the same."[329] This is a feature of POD in general—after all, every uploaded book must wait to be ordered and printed—but it is especially significant for books with extremely high prices, such as the largest possible variant of Lorusso and Ciliberto's *Blank on Demand* (2011), or cases where the sheer scale of the complete work makes it highly unlikely to be printed. With respect to *Print Wikipedia* (2015), Mandiberg puts forward a similar argument to Seita, namely that printing all the volumes is not required for understanding the dimensions of the project. He is convinced that, "[i]t is not necessary to print out all 7,473 volumes, as our imaginations can complete what's missing."[330]

At the same time, according to a thought experiment by Silvio Lorusso, it would be possible to use the platform to create your own book, identical in format and materials to the maximal version of *Blank on Demand*, in fewer clicks and at cost price.[331] Joachim Schmid suggests a similar move in relation to *The Black Book* (2010) and *Blank* (2011) by Jean Keller, both of which are no longer available on Blurb. "As these are books with no content, anyone can make their own. Simply set up a Blurb account, upload a suitable file, and place an order. The book will be just the same as a 'genuine' Jean Keller."[332] But what would be the status of such an object, which matches the book in question in all specifics except price, but was not uploaded by the artist (where the authenticity of the account and author name(s) cannot in any case be verified)? Would this be a counterfeit, a bootleg version, a reissue of an out-of-print work, a second edition, or a reenactment?

This intellectual conjecture throws up difficult art philosophical and ontological issues. It makes clear that the work as such does not constitute itself merely by becoming a book and/or being printed. It also needs the specific paratextual framing, as well as the economic and systemic embeddedness in the POD ecosystem, to become evident, culturally effective, and meaningful as a work. After all, the pricing of the object and its paratextual presence in the online store are central elements to the interpretation of Maker's, Lorusso and Ciliberto's, and Keller's works. It therefore seems that, even without having been printed or indeed ever being printed, the mere *potential* material existence of these books, constituted by their situatedness, framing, and metadata, creates a fact that allows them to be addressed as full-fledged works, to be attributed to an author's oeuvre, to be discussed and interpreted, for example, as platform and economic critique, and to be inscribed in discourse and the history of art or literature.

328. See Melgard, "Print-on-Demand Self-Publishing," in this volume, 581f., and Tan Lin, "Troll Thread Interview."
329. Seita, "Communities of Print," in this volume, 643.
330. Mandiberg, "Making *Print Wikipedia*," in this volume, 514.
331. Lorusso, interview by the authors, February 22, 2020.
332. Schmid, interview by the authors, November 14, 2019.

CONFIRM AND PUBLISH

In this way, POD platform production forces us to reassess our understanding of publishing, publication, and publicness. In such instances of deliberate "imagined printedness," it might make sense to recognize even the mere uploading of a print file to the POD platform, along with the entry of the necessary metadata and the subsequent public display in the store, as a valid act of constituting and publishing a work. The question is whether such an expanded understanding of publishing can be applied to the entirety of the platforms' offerings, which most likely also include many publications that have never been ordered or printed, or even noticed, and still await discovery. At the same time, this limbo makes them highly vulnerable: POD is an extremely precarious genre, as has become evident in the process of building the Library of Artistic Print on Demand collection, which makes the *printed* book, of all things, the most reliable long-term storage medium.[333]

In this regard, Timothy Laquintano suggests "that the millions of self-published books now sitting in digital databases exist more as publicly accessible books than as published books. They exist largely as latent potential. In my understanding, books unengaged by readers haven't circumvented gatekeepers; they want for gatekeepers."[334] That gatekeeping, understood as consecration, is indeed closely related to publishing is confirmed by J. Gordon Faylor's observation about the reasons why his publishing house is so popular with authors even though he does not offer royalties, remuneration, specimen copies, or professional promotion. In contrast to "pure" self-publishing via POD, with his publishing house "people can still share their work as having been published by someone."[335] Gauss PDF, Troll Thread, Traumawien, 0x0a, etc., all ensure a book has gone through a selection process, a kind of gatekeeping and consecration. POD publications offered under such labels can thus be deemed to have been "published," as in the traditional book trade, and this seems to apply to these authors even when their books have never been ordered, sold, printed, read, or discussed.

It is, however, rather more complex than Laquintano's distinction between publicly accessible books (awaiting gatekeepers) and published ones (proofed by gatekeepers) might lead us to suppose. For this would mean that publishing would no longer be tied to a performative act on the part of the producers, but that the public would be elevated to the position of gatekeeper and, as it were, publisher. It would be up to readership to turn a publicly accessible, latent publication qua order into a published, manifest publication—a novelty in the history of print that, in its radicalness, further complicates the very notion of what it means to "publish" in the post-digital age.

Even in the print era, there was much debate about whether it was crucial that the publication be in principle accessible, or just that it circulated in some form. Michael Bhaskar illustrates the complexity and difficulty of this issue with further examples:

> Here's a brief thought experiment: you write a novel, and leave it on a park bench. Is this a published novel? Let's say you print 1,000 copies, leaving them on 1,000 park benches. How about now? Or how about a publisher buys it, takes out masses of adverts, but literally no one buys a single copy? In what sense has that work been published? At what point does a letter or email pass from private correspondence to public, published text? One hundred or 100,000 recipients? Or is the idea of putting a numerical value on being public absurd, and if so, what conceptual distinction should we make instead? If I post the email on the Internet, we can assume it has been published, but then, if nobody views it, how is it more public than an email sent to 100 people? Is being public a state of being—the state of being public in itself—or is it epistemological, the state of being known, or even being known to have been published?[336]

The hybrid POD model demands a continuation and realignment of this discussion that takes into account the variety of media constellations and degrees of public accessibility in different transitional spaces.

333. See Andreas Bülhoff and Annette Gilbert, "Library of Artistic Print on Demand," in this volume, 8–17, 13.

334. Laquintano, *Mass Authorship and the Rise of Self-Publishing*, 11.

335. J. Gordon Faylor, interview by the authors, February 11, 2021.

336. Michael Bhaskar, *The Content Machine: Towards a Theory of Publishing from the Printing Press to the Digital Network* (London, New York, Delhi: Anthem, 2013), 18f.

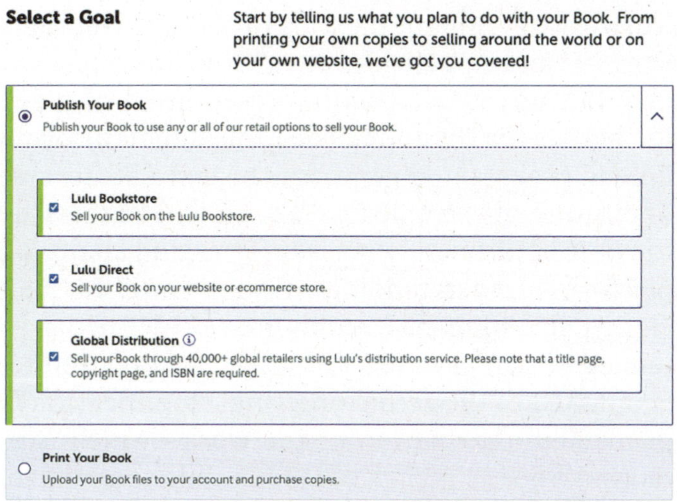

Select a Goal

Start by telling us what you plan to do with your Book. From printing your own copies to selling around the world or on your own website, we've got you covered!

Publish Your Book
Publish your Book to use any or all of our retail options to sell your Book.

Lulu Bookstore
Sell your Book on the Lulu Bookstore.

Lulu Direct
Sell your Book on your website or ecommerce store.

Global Distribution
Sell your Book through 40,000+ global retailers using Lulu's distribution service. Please note that a title page, copyright page, and ISBN are required.

Print Your Book
Upload your Book files to your account and purchase copies.

For the platforms, it seems evident to ground the moment of becoming public in the author's performative act, comparable to the *imprimatur* used in the past. At least, this is what the specific configuration of the upload process on the platforms suggests, as can be shown by the example of Lulu. At a certain point in this process, when the PDFs of the book block and cover have been completed and uploaded and the essential metadata such as author, title, and keywords have been entered and confirmed, the platform's protocol requires the "goal" of the submitted book to be specified. There is a choice between "Publish Your Book" and "Print Your Book," whereby each option implies a different form of public access and publishing. Choosing "Print Your Book" means only the account holder can see the book and order a printed copy. For others, the publication is invisible on the platform. This option does not equate to publication, as is clearly stated: "Lulu also provides a quick path to upload and print books without publishing."[337] The "Publish Your Book" option, however, means the publication can be distributed via an order link or made visible in the platform's own online store, or even, after acquiring an ISBN, in general book trade catalogs, so making it available to the public.

Although this might seem unambiguous at first glance, it is doubtful whether all platform users (who are often publishing amateurs, see 28f. and 38f.) are aware of the significance of this decision, as J. Gordon Faylor points out. In his journeys through the depths of the platform's book offers, he has sometimes experienced the opposite. Many of the books he discovered there turned out to be true "curiosities" in Howard Becker's sense (see 43f.).[338] They took him into "a realm of ethical uncertainty" that made him reluctant to show the books to others, because "it's never clear if or how much a particular author would want their work in a more public or literary/artistic context." This raises "a number of questions about identity, privacy, distribution, and non-art":

> To what extent does my engagement with these books belie a kind of exploitation, a crass curiosity? Were these books even meant for others? [...] No doubt these questions speak to a broader dissolution between the public and the private; [...] even intention fails in the face of something as chaotic as the internet. [...]
> These books hit me like a secret at once inappropriate and alluring, and can get to feeling very nearly dangerous, like I'm seeing something I shouldn't. I'm not supposed to own these or know about these, I tell myself.[339]

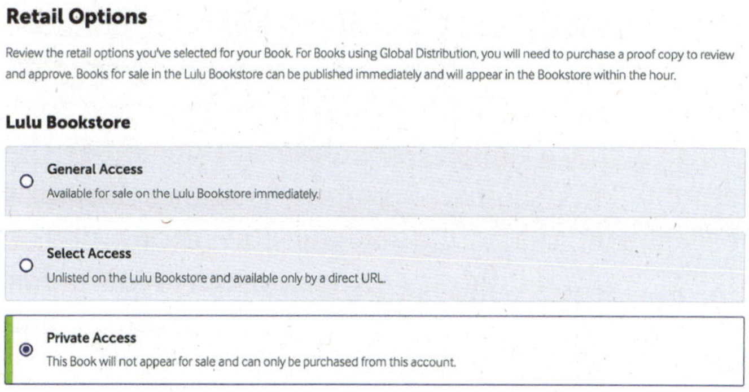

Retail Options

Review the retail options you've selected for your Book. For Books using Global Distribution, you will need to purchase a proof copy to review and approve. Books for sale in the Lulu Bookstore can be published immediately and will appear in the Bookstore within the hour.

Lulu Bookstore

General Access
Available for sale on the Lulu Bookstore immediately.

Select Access
Unlisted on the Lulu Bookstore and available only by a direct URL.

Private Access
This Book will not appear for sale and can only be purchased from this account.

This feeling seems to be confirmed by the fact that a number of books he ordered out of curiosity soon afterwards became unfindable or unavailable, i.e., they had presumably been marked "private" by their authors. We can only speculate about the reasons. Perhaps the authors did not take into account the real-life impact of choosing the "Publish Your Book" option, and have been misled by the banality of publishing on POD platforms. Or they may have never considered the possibility that someone might find their book, of all things, among the vast number of books available on POD platforms, and actually order it. The fact that, against all odds, this has now happened may have made them suddenly aware that, by selecting the "Pub-

337. "Comparing Lulu Press & Blurb," Lulu, https://blurb.lulu.com/.
338. Becker, *Art Worlds*, 269.
339. All citations J. Gordon Faylor, "A Note on Vernacular Print-on-Demand Publishing and the Conundrum of Access," in this volume, 686–689, 689.

lish Your Book" option, they have actually exposed their book to an immense, unknown, anonymous public, which may seem quite abstract and unreal at the moment of uploading, but which can manifest itself in concrete people at any time.

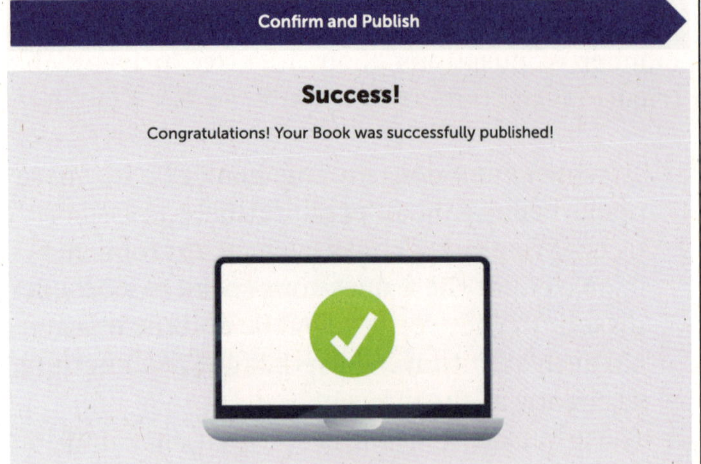

In this context, the inconsistencies and contradictions within the platform protocol itself are also striking, suggesting that even the platform does not differentiate strictly between the two options ("print" or "publish"): whichever goal the user specifies, the upload and submission process is completed by clicking on a big button that says "Confirm and Publish," which sets "Publish" as the default. This seems to confirm Hannes Bajohr's observation that "[u]nder the conditions of the digital and the ubiquity of networked communication, most of our representations, utterances, and actions, since they are potentially accessible to everyone, are public by default, *even if* they are private." This makes the option of (re)privatization all the more urgent, allowing users to mark some utterances and appearances as public and others as private in order to "reinscribe the difference between privateness and publicness into the default publicness itself."[340] Notwithstanding the blurring of these two options ("print" and "publish"), the "Confirm and Publish" button is the visual representation of a performative act that concludes the submission and upload process and confirms the content, format, and future of the uploaded document. In this way, the button ultimately gives information about the platform's understanding of publishing. In their view, publishing has nothing to do with the intended or achieved level of public access. Neither is it linked to the actual ordering, amplification in print, and distribution of the work—which is in fact justified, since it is also possible to circulate a book produced by choosing the "print" option, such as when artists prefer to handle the quality control or sales of their work themselves. Instead, "publishing" here seems to be linked to the act of uploading a file into the platform's database.

According to this line of reasoning, therefore, a book is considered published before it has ever been ordered and printed or even without being publicly visible and orderable. In keeping with the logic of platform capitalism, the stabilization that the book and its content undergo during the upload—induced by fulfilling platform-side print data conditions, as well as framing, tagging, and handing over—already qualifies as "publishing." In this way, the act and the concept of publishing are increasingly governed by platform paradigms and given an algorithmic codification that, in the sense of solutionism, responds to the unsettling dynamics and complexity of the debate about publishing and the public with the suggestion of unambiguity and simplicity. However, as shown, it cannot hide the fact that this does not resolve the inherent contradictions and inconsistencies, but only ignores or obscures them. This is a clear indication that, to quote Silvio Lorusso, "[p]ublicness is not a binary, but a spectrum."[341]

"HALBZEUG": SEMI-FINISHED PRODUCTS

In this context of making a book concept into reality at the click of a button, the working methods of several artists and authors have changed. Ideas that previously had to be laboriously developed by means of dummies and proof copies on typewriters, in copy shops, or on home printers, can now often be tested in the exact physicality and industrial production format in which the book will ultimately be published. According to Eileen Gittins, these maquettes represent an important sales area for Blurb, even if only one copy is made and even though the end product is

340. All citations Hannes Bajohr, "Publicking/Privating: The Gestural Politics of Digital Spaces," *Society* October (2023): 1–13, 4 and 6, https://doi.org/10.1007/s12115-023-00918-w [emphasis in the original].

341. Silvio Lorusso, "We Live in Publics: Publication as a Spectrum," syllabus, University of Art and Design Halle, July 2021, https://www.burg-halle.de/en/design/kommunikationsdesign/masters-course/course-elements/l/we-live-in-publics-publication-as-a-spectrum/.

often not even produced by Blurb, but by a traditional publisher.

Michalis Pichler, who sees such test and correction runs as an indispensable stage of the work process, has for several years been using POD platforms for this purpose rather than the local copy shop where he used to go. This is particularly the case with his long-term series *Page Pieces* (2020–), in which, because of the ever-increasing quantity of material, it is easy to lose track of the whole. Because the pagination-sensitive material needs to be seen in context and can be arranged in different ways in the book, Pichler constantly produces new prototypes with which he can allow "a type of variantology to play out." In the case of *Untitled (Mondrian)*, too, the POD dummies function as working journals for the realization of paintings, in which "the canvas serves as a page for an art work," as Pichler notes, reversing the artists' books dictum, in which "the page serves as a canvas for an art work."[342] Although, in contrast to copy shops, it takes a relatively long time for the dummy copy to arrive due to the necessary production and shipping times, he does not see this a disadvantage, as it matches his slow way of working. And because using a copy shop usually takes several hours per work, POD still seems to make sense in terms of work efficiency.

In addition, Pichler values the "clean, slick" look and feel of industrially produced POD books, which cannot be achieved in a copy shop.[343] Nevertheless, POD prints are, for him, temporary and unfinished objects. They are not intended for public view and the public setting on the platform is switched off (equating to the "Print your book" option). When the POD product represents an initial or intermediate stage in the work process, and is awaiting further reworking and finalizing, it can be described as a "Halbzeug," to borrow a term from Hannes Bajohr: "It literally means 'half-stuff,' and almost has a self-deprecating ring to it, but it also denotes what is called a 'semi-finished product' in industrial manufacture, an intermediate step in fabrication that is no longer a raw material but not yet the end result (metal ingots, for instance). It is also a metaphor used by the German philosopher Hans Blumenberg for describing his own texts."[344]

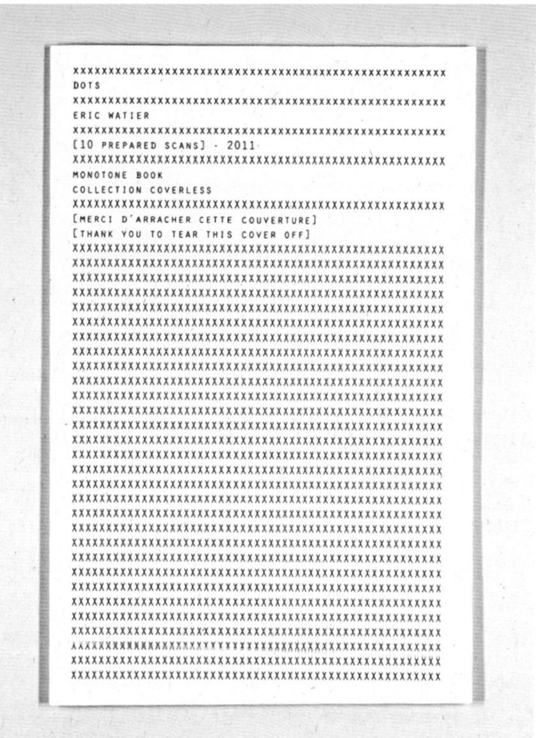

The manufacture can be completed by the artist, or by the purchaser. For example, Éric Watier entrusted the finalization of his "Collection Coverless" publications to its purchasers, who were presented with this request on the front cover: "TO COMPLETE THE PRODUCTION OF THIS BOOK, YOU NEED TO TEAR ITS COVER OFF. THANK YOU."[345] In the case of booklets such as *DOTS [10 Prepared Scans]* (2011), Watier's intention is for the collected images to be taken apart again and for the individual scans to be presented autonomously, rather like pictures on a wall. Wil van Iersel, on the other hand, finalizes his flipbook *ASTORIA-MEGLER BRIDGE / AMERICA* (2013) himself by hand. Like Oliver Bertrand from the Surfaces Utiles publishing house (see 81), he uses the POD platform only in its function as a printer and shipper of printed matter, from which he obtains two copies of his flipbook from each Lulu print. Whereas Bertrand, for the sake of transparency and to promote his chosen production method, makes the intermediate products available to the public in Blurb's online store as well as offering the end products on his own publishing website (see 370f., 412f.), van Iersel's publication can only be ordered as a finished flipbook from his own website.

342. All citation Michalis Pichler, interview by the authors, March 30, 2021.
343. Pichler, interview by the authors, March 30, 2021.
344. When it comes to his eponymous book of poetry (Berlin: Suhrkamp 2018), Bajohr translates "Halbzeug" as "Blanks"—"another word for semi-finished product." Hannes Bajohr, "Translator's Note," in Hannes Bajohr, *Blanks* (Denver: Counterpath, 2022), 122–126, 123.
345. Éric Watier, *DOTS [10 Prepared Scans]* (self-pub.: monotone press / Blurb, 2011), front cover.

Specific Features of Edition and Distribution

DISTRIBUTION VIA THE PLATFORM, BOOKSTORES OR THE ARTIST'S WEBSITE

Accessibility, availability, and distribution channels of POD publications can be very differently structured. Authors are increasingly marking their POD publications as "private," i.e., invisible to the public, so that they can only be ordered via the artists' own websites or online stores, or through selected intermediaries like Printed Matter (store, New York) and edcat (database and webshop), or purchased at fairs and similar events from the artists themselves. The advantage of this is that the print copy can be "enhanced," e.g. with a book jacket and insert, as in Rahel Zoller's *Title* (2011–20), or with a warning sticker, in the case of *The Library of Nonhuman Books* (2019–). The artist can also perform quality checks or, in the case of a series, check the uniformity of the volumes before sending them on—although this is not a financially or environmentally attractive option, as it entails twice the number of shipments and doubles the shipping distance. A further benefit is that artists can only gain a picture of their customer base and, where applicable, contact them by selling from their own websites. Having their own online store enables them to operate in a more platform-agnostic way and to reserve the right to change platforms at a later date.

Conversely, there are also cases where books are removed from the artist's own online store and only offered on a platform. This applies to some volumes of Hermann Zschiegner's Bootleg series, for example, which aim to make out-of-print or overpriced photobooks such as Martin Parr's *The Last Resort* accessible and available again. Zschiegner's bookworks are usually low quality, as is expected of bootleg copies, because the source material for reconstructing the content usually consists of flip-through videos circulating on the internet. This was the subject of sarcastic criticism in the satirical column "The Worst Photo Books of 2013," published on the Artists' Books Cooperative blog: "*The Last Resort (The Bootleg)* by Hermann Zschiegner is the last book I would buy. Did Zschiegner not know that the original book is in colour? And what are all those silly hands doing there? It is an insult to the Gods of photobooks, Martin Parr and Gerry Badger."[346] Parr's photobook has now been reissued, meaning that Zschiegner may face action under copyright law, which perhaps explains why the bootleg is no longer mentioned on his website and is only available on the Blurb webshop, where it is disappearing in the ocean of books. Even there, almost all the paratext has been deleted as a precautionary measure, turning the bootleg into a hard-to-find edition of the original. *Harry Potter and the Scam Baiter* (2012) has also disappeared from Mishka Henner's online store for similar reasons, after Henner had already reduced the amount of promotion and available information about the book; J.K. Rowling is well-known for her litigiousness in copyright issues.

Artists adopt a range of different approaches to series, too. While van Iersel sells *Every Day a New Photo Book* (2010–21) on his website as a box set with signed, numbered volumes, as well as selling individual (unsigned) volumes directly via Blurb, Joachim Schmid's series *Other People's Photographs* (2008–11) has since its completion only been sold as a set to ensure uniformity between the volumes and avoid any quality defects. *ABCEUM* (2014–) is also only available as

346. ABC, "The Worst Photo Books of 2013."

a full set due to being a collective work by various ABC members. In addition, the series' concept leans toward the idea of the museum and its departments and thus precludes the separation and purchase of individual parts. *ABCEUM* is thus only ever presented as a whole set at trade fairs and exhibitions, although it is regularly "repackaged," whether in two specially built display cases (representing two museum wings), on magazine stands, or in a wooden box like the ones typically used by museums to transport cultural artifacts. This last was made on demand to match the shelf dimensions of the Bavarian State Library following its purchase for our collection (see image on the left page).

RETROSPECTIVE INDIVIDUALIZATION BY SIGNING, NUMBERING, AND DATING

A further reason for redirecting prospective purchasers to the artist's own website and online store is that it provides an opportunity to add a signature, number, and date to each copy, as van Iersel does with his *Every Day a New Photo Book* box set (2010–21). It would be too easy to take this as evidence that the value judgments of the art market, with its focus on originals and uniqueness, are once again slipping in unnoticed—as can be seen, not uncommonly, in original art prints, press prints, multiples, and some artists' books. But the circumstances and the motives are very different in this case.

This book is a Print on Demand publication. It was first printed in June 2011 and due to the nature of Print on Demand has changed over the years. Variations can be found in paper stock, printing quality and small adjustments in the design. Each publication is therefore a reflection of a moment in time.

This publication was printed in October 2020.

Insert with production date for Rahel Zoller's *Title*, 2nd edition, 2020.

The addition of a date, for example, may be motivated by the artist's interest in documenting changes in POD production. This is the case with Rahel Zoller's *Title* (2011–20), which since the second edition has only been available directly from the artist, and which has an insert containing details of the month and year of printing in order to document the changes in paper stock and printing quality over the years, inherent in the POD process. In the case of *Post-Fordism and its Discontents* (2010), too, the date on the first page of each copy can provide information about some specific features of POD production. According to this information, the book block of our copy was "published and distributed through Lulu" and "printed on 8/10/2010," although this obviously corresponds to the time of the finalization and upload of the PDF, rather than the printing of the book. Confusingly, this does not apply to the PDF, which is likewise available on Lulu and on aaaaarg.fail; its timestamp actually changes depending on the order and download date—calling attention to a PDF feature not available when the file is processed for print on a POD platform.

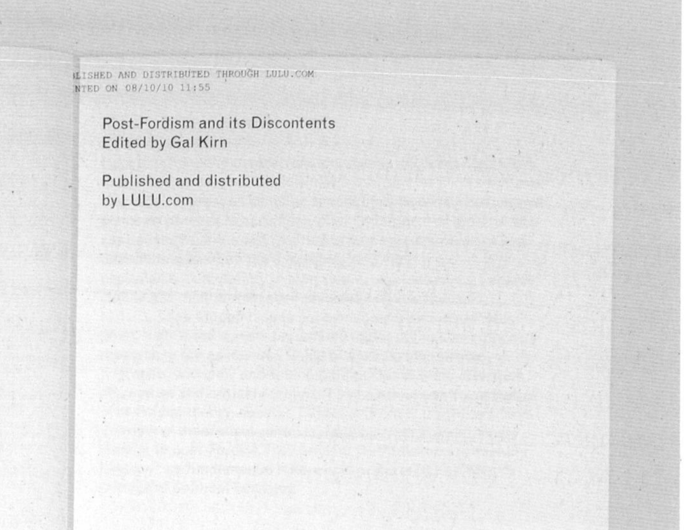

On publications from the Publication Studio network, on the other hand, the added stamp and embossing make it possible to differentiate between the publishing studio (stated in the imprint inside the book) and the producing studio (stated in the embossing on the back cover), and between the year of publishing (stated in the imprint) and the production date (stamped on the spine of the copy). In addition, the varying production date links back to the social context (a book fair, a personal visit to a studio, a reading, etc.), where this particular copy was purchased and produced—an aspect of community-building that is essential to Publication Studio's publishing practice (see Matthew Stadler's *THE TABLE & THE NETWORK*, 2015).

Lastly, numbering ensures differentiation, identification, and citability in editions with copies that are already individualized for content, as in the case of *Tristano* (2007–09), *Subcutanean* (2020), or *Showbag* (2008–). This is unlikely to result in an increase in value for copies bearing the lowest number, as occurs in the art print market, as all the copies are, in principle, of equal value. Even signing the copies need not necessarily be construed as a relic from the art market, as it may be intended as a dedication if the work is being gifted (as in the case of Sadokierski's *(Another Book) After Ed-werd Rew-shay* (2015) and Greg Allen's *Canal Zone Richard Prince YES RASTA* (2011–13) in our collection).

LIMITATIONS ON THE NUMBER OF COPIES

Artificial limitations on availability should be considered in a similarly nuanced way. At first glance, they appear to contradict the essence of POD, which is more frequently associated with open editions that are available long term. However, due to the precariousness and lack of sustainability on the platform side, as discussed above, the POD production in particular is often affected by externally imposed constraints. These can include censorship of individual works, closure of accounts, material or technical issues, closure of the platform, etc. In such cases, existing copies can unexpectedly increase in value as unique works, or at least rare ones, as happened with Henner's *Astronomical* (2011). Angie Waller, on the other hand, discovered a completely different reason for the sudden increase in the price of one of her works, a used copy of which was for sale on Amazon for $2,796 even while new copies were still available for $10 each. This prompted her to take a closer look at the dark side of the Amazon universe. In her investigations, she found that some self-published books are not only part of dubious e-commerce practices, but also vehicles for scams and automated get-rich-quick schemes. She came to the conclusion that the increase in price was certainly not due to any recognition of her work as an "art object" or to a computer glitch, but may have indicated money laundering through Amazon.[347]

Apart from this, some limitations on editions are imposed by artists themselves. This is often simply the result of habit or even an ironic gesture: given the niche market in which the artists operate, a print run of one hundred copies, such as Andreas Schmidt sets as standard for his books, is often merely wishful thinking. And when Kathrin Passig discovered, immediately after uploading her collection of column articles, that a hyphenation error had occurred on the first page, she posted this marketing Tweet to boost sales and increase the value of the "first edition" of *Strom und Vorurteil* (2020): "Anyone who buys it straightaway will get a rare collector's edition with a hyphenation error on the very first page! For a limited time only!"[348] However, this was unmistakably only intended as an ironic reference to the peculiarities of the "old" book world.

Christian Bök did something similar with his series *Library of Babel* (2015), whose volumes are each limited to twenty-five copies. He plays a sophisticated game with artificial limitation in the

347. See Angie Waller, "Grifting the Amazon," in this volume, 553–575.

348. Kathrin Passig (@kathrinpassig), Twitter, February 29, 2020, https://twitter.com/kathrinpassig/status/1233772454524456960.

context of the attention economy by continually announcing updates about the number of copies left on Blurb, his website, and on social media, like a market trader touting his wares, and describing his series as a collectible item, perfect "as a gift for bibliophiles who love the work of Borges."[349] This is an allusion to the "unreadability" of these books, which do in fact translate Borges's vision of the Library of Babel into a reality, but which contain nothing more than wild combinations of letters. They are meant to be put on the bookshelf as conceptual bookworks, rather than read.

Christian Bok
@christianbok

Purchase "LXUM,LKWC (Oh Time Thy Pyramids)" (from the Library of Babel)—only six remaining, after which this limited-edition artbook goes out of print forever: tinyurl.com/yyguljld

12:30 vorm. · 8. März 2020 · Twitter Web Client

Christian Bok
@christianbok

Purchase LXUM,LKWC (OH TIME THY PYRAMIDS) (from the Library of Babel)—(only one copy remains for sale in this very limited edition, after which the book goes out of print forever): tinyurl.com/yyguljld

7:54 vorm. · 5. Aug. 2020 · Twitter Web App

Christian Bok
@christianbok

LXUM,LKWC – OH TIME THY PYRAMIDS (from the Library of Babel) has sold its last copy, and the item no longer remains available—(thanks to everyone, who continues to support this act of Conceptualism). You can still purchase other titles from the series: tinyurl.com/y3nmam5g

4:15 vorm. · 16. Aug. 2020 · Twitter Web App

Mishka Henner's _*IMG* series (2014–) is another conceptual experiment with scarcity. Its volumes contain the alphanumeric file code of a particular photograph, which is also "unreadable"—at least, for humans. The first volume was produced in an edition of ninety-seven signed and numbered copies (this corresponds to the number of years since the photograph was taken), the second one in an edition of twenty-five copies, and a possible third one could be published in only three or four copies.[350] Enclosed with each book is a print of the relevant photograph, so that the work represents the convergence of several replication techniques and discourses around copies and originals. The fact that Henner has, amazingly, already sold more than sixty copies of this series (as of 2021) could be due to this artificial rarefaction.

Lastly, there are even cases where availability is restricted temporally rather than numerically. For example, the *ABCED* series discussed above was created for the occasion of Ed Ruscha's seventy-fifth birthday and was only available as a set for one year, until his next birthday. Nick Thurston, on the other hand, linked the availability of his *Van de Onderaannemingsovereenkomst* (2016) to the duration of the exhibition *The Economy is Spinning*, for which the book was produced. The publisher Onomatopee, in whose premises the exhibition took place, indexes its publications and exhibitions in numerical order. The exhibition and catalog publication were number 132. When Thurston gave his book the number 132.1, it acquired the character of a supplement to the exhibition and catalog, rather than a separate publication.

MULTIPLE FORMATS AND PRICING

Another form of differentiation is the production of the same work in different formats and at different price points. For example, *Pirate Book* (2015) is available in black and white, color, and as a free PDF, while *All Work and No Play Makes Jack a Dull Boy* (2009) is not only available in three formats (hardback, hardback with dust jacket, and paperback), but also with three different covers. While in these cases buyers can choose the version they prefer or can afford, the wide variety of available for-

349. Christian Bök, "The Library of Babel," *Umlautmachine*, https://www.umlautmachine.net/writings/the-library-of-babel.

350. Mishka Henner, interview by the authors, March 24, 2021.

mats for *The Legacy of Totalitarianism in a Tundra* (2014–15)—different covers, black and white, color, hardback, paperback, and PDF—corresponds to the circumstances of the book's creation in the unregulated world of 4chan, whose spirit it reflects. Mathew Timmons's *Credit* (2011), meanwhile, is available in versions familiar from LP records and singles, i.e., a full version for $200 and an extract for $65. The fact that even this short version may not be affordable for many people mirrors the author's financial circumstances during the financial crisis, which he documents with a collection of all the credit offers and requests for payment that he received in his mailbox between 2007 and 2009.

In contrast, the simultaneous availability of hardback and paperback or color and black and white editions should be understood as a kind of special edition if their prices differ widely and this price difference cannot be accounted for by the difference in production costs alone, but rather follows the traditional division of the market into segments with different purchasing power. While the (increased) revenues generated by Ben Fry's *Frankenfont* (2011) are donated to charitable causes (the list of beneficiaries is available to view on the artist's website), in the case of Fred Benenson's *Emoji Dick* (2010), the pricing shows that different versions are aimed at different target groups: the paperback edition for $40 is for end consumers, who forfeit a great deal of the reading pleasure due to the black-and-white printing and poor image quality, while the color hardback, with a large markup on the production costs, is marketed at $200 and is clearly aimed at collectors and collecting institutions. The unusually high profit margin[351] raises questions, especially since Benenson's project was financed entirely through crowdfunding, and *Moby Dick* was translated into emojis by low-paid MTurk workers who do not receive a share of the sales profits. As if in revenge, one of the workers must have tried to trick the system and increase their own hourly rate by inserting the same sequence of nine emojis over and over again. There is probably no other way to explain the 439 times this sequence appears in the novel, as Zach Whalen notes.[352]

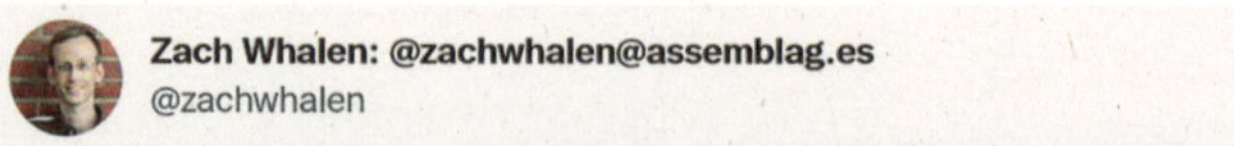

The creators of *Philip* (2006), a collective novel, followed exactly the opposite strategy and philosophy. Their sophisticated, graded pricing policy was intended to ensure that all participants were appropriately remunerated.[353] The first edition of one hundred copies was priced at just under €86 per copy, enough to pay all the people involved. For the second edition, which would be purchased by a wider public, they imagined a more relational system, with the price adjusted as the total number of copies sold increased (assuming that the immaterial labor costs are fixed). This would invert the prevailing economy of scale (as more copies are made, the manufacturing costs decrease and the profit per unit goes up) into a demand-side economy of scope, where the profit per unit goes down as production increases. It would also increase the circulation of the book outside the circle of participants and cre-

351. For the characteristic "anti-economic economy" in the sub-field of restricted production, see 47, 77f., and 82.

352. Whalen, "Some Notes on Analyzing the Content of *Emoji Dick*." See also @zachwhalen, Twitter, June 26, 2022, https://twitter.com/zachwhalen/status/1541161803438297089.

353. See Dexter Sinister, "The Price of *Philip*," January 3, 2007, http://www.dextersinister.org/library.html?id=63.

ate a network of readers. Even if the idea to lower the price on Lulu with each sale could not be implemented due to the platform's constraints, it was a worthwhile attempt at an independent pricing policy that takes equal account of both producers and customers, and a corrective to the typical platform strategy of shifting costs primarily to buyers.

Gal Kirn's *Post-Fordism and its Discontents* (2010), on the other hand, addressed the range of publishing and distribution options on the cover itself, together with all the attendant edition sizes and sales prices that would be available: an edition of 250 copies for €30 from Jan van Eyck Academie, an unlimited POD version at lulu.com for €17.04, and a free PDF version available at the shadow library aaaaarg.fail. The logic of production and distribution, which is the subject of the book, is thus already visible on the cover, so that the publication itself becomes recognizable as an integral part of these entanglements. At the same time, this range of possibilities seems to map out a potential future for artistic publishing in which the POD platform model would be only one of several options.

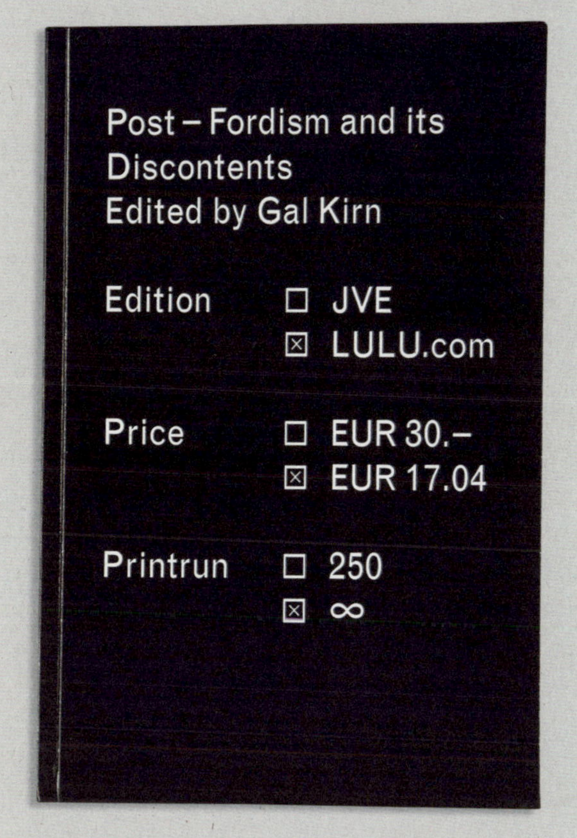

DISTRIBUTION INFRASTRUCTURES

Comparing the publication and distribution channels displayed on the cover of *Post-Fordism and its Discontents* (2010), the noticeable weak point of the POD model is inadequate distribution via bricks-and-mortar bookstores, which is virtually unattainable for most books from this artistic field of restricted production. This is not solely due to the stores' limited space. Several well-established (infra-)structures reach their limits with POD, or simply no longer function. For example, almost all POD providers do not allow customers to return books or cancel orders. This seriously constrains not only the willingness of readers to buy via direct ordering, but also that of bookstores, because it invalidates the process of commission and remission.

Another issue is the enormous shipping costs charged by the platforms, which represent a burden for authors, consumers, and bookstores alike, and arouse the suspicion that the platforms are using cost-plus pricing with the "plus" mainly generated by the shipping. This tipped the scales for Jean Keller and contributed to his irate departure from Blurb, which he proclaimed publicly and directly on the platform.[354]

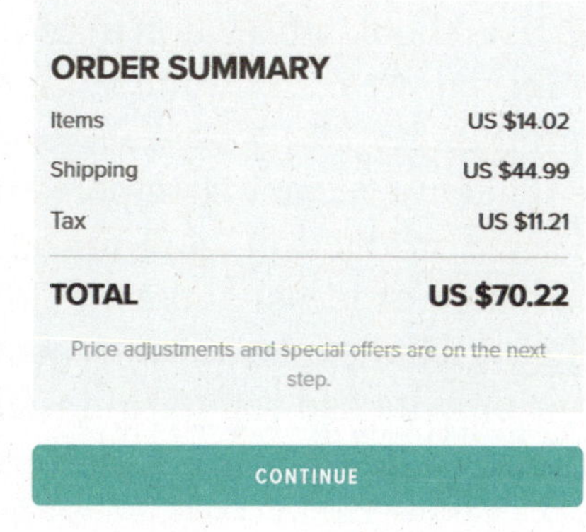

354. Jean Keller, "About," Blurb, https://www.blurb.com/user/jean-keller.

Jean Keller

About

Blurb sucks. Books are way too expensive and shipping costs are daylight robbery. Interested parties find Jean Keller's books on Lulu.

Even more serious, however, is that selling via bookstores simply does not pay—for either side, which for the Temporary Services publishing house is reason enough to refuse to engage with the POD ecosystem: "Unless the author doesn't care to profit from sales of their print-on-demand book at a retail store, it is difficult to place a print-on-demand book at a retailer without increasing the price."[355] If the customary 40 to 50 percent bookstore discount is factored in, the store price soon becomes so high that it makes the book virtually unsaleable. For all these reasons, very few bookstores engage with publications from POD platforms; in the artistic publishing niche, Printed Matter in particular should be mentioned, although even here, the authors, as ever, have to take the books into the store themselves, sell them on commission, and restock them as required.

But the problem extends even further, because inadequate distribution does not just affect bookstores, as Temporary Services argue. It is likewise "very unlikely" or "extremely difficult if not impossible to encounter th[ese] book[s] by accident [...] in libraries, [...] art galleries, the social spaces where books are amplified and resonate with communities."[356] Marc van Elburg, Florian Cramer, and Clara Balaguer add: "[H]ardly anybody wants print-on-demand: artists' book stores don't really want it, artist book fairs don't really want it, zine fairs don't really want it either."[357]

And yet, it is fairs that have become so important in the field of small scale production, both for networking and the exchange of ideas, and as major points of sale, as their global explosion in recent times shows. It is not only its bad reputation that means the on-demand principle does not work at trade fairs. Joachim Schmid, for instance, thought that it was easier to travel to fairs with just one copy of each of his books for display, and then to take orders. But this meant for him that overall sales were lower: "People want the book straightaway, as in 'you get ten dollars and I get the book.' Paper for paper. As soon as you move away from that model, your market collapses."[358] Besides these spontaneous purchases by visitors to fairs, POD also complicates the long-standing practice of book swapping, which is essential for networking and exchanges in this niche sector.[359]

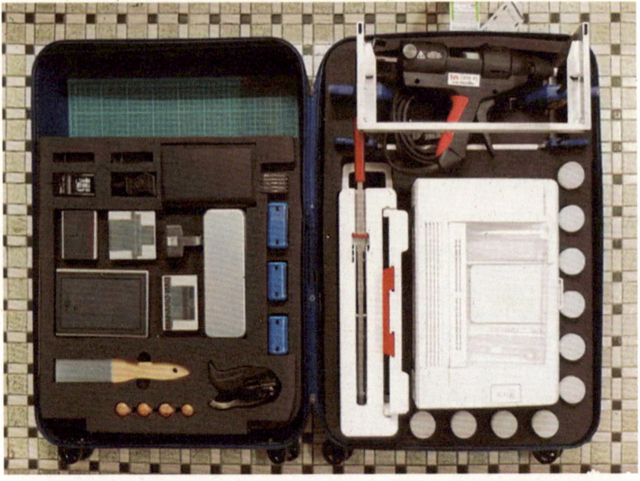

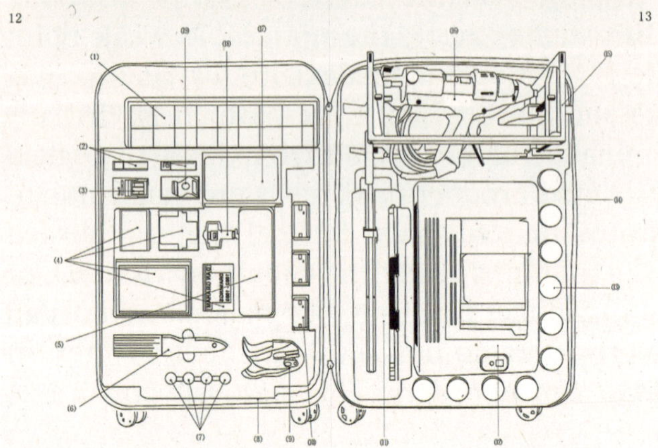

Publication Studio's offshoots Rotterdam and Pearl River Delta seem to have developed a workable solution to this problem with their *Publication Studio Portable* (2019), which puts the idea of mobile publishing into action. It takes the form of a case containing all the tools needed to produce their books in situ, which at the same time gives the studios an opportunity to showcase the pro-

355. Temporary Services, "Half Letter Press and Our Reasons for Running It," in this volume, 654–660, 659.

356. Temporary Services, "Half Letter Press," in this volume, 659 (flow chart).

357. Van Elburg, Cramer, and Balaguer, "Against the [cozy] prettyprinters," in this volume, 615.

358. Schmid, interview by the authors, November 14, 2019.

359. See Michalis Pichler, "Book Swapping & Seriosity Dummies."

duction process as performance. The machinery's weight and size are carefully calculated to fit into a rolling suitcase and minimize the cost of air travel. "The aim of PS PORTABLE is to actively explore alter-relations between publishing and distribution, making and readership, working and camaraderie,"[360] making it the perfect interface for gatherings and events like art book fairs.

PROMOTING AND SOCIAL MEDIA POSTING

In view of the difficulty of having a public presence at fairs and in bricks-and-mortar bookstores, supporting measures that increase reach and circulation play an important role. From early on, ABC placed great value on different "method[s] of digitally distributing books":

> We're all involved in publishing the idea of a book online. That is to say, each of our artists presents their book in some form of digital format that exists online as well as in physical form. That doesn't mean it has to be an e-book. It could be the book presented as a video trailer on Vimeo, as a single line of text, a performance documented, an essay, a series of stills, or as a downloadable pdf file. The book exists in physical form and in conceptual form. It travels further and quicker as an idea than as an object.[361]

This applies particularly to the social media and internet presence of many artists, with a number of them skillfully operating accounts on Twitter, Instagram, Facebook, or Vimeo, or their own websites. These demonstrate that, as part of the post-digital fetishization of analog media, printed books are suitable postable objects for social media. Interestingly, this applies as much to highbrow as lowbrow publications, and to large- and small-scale productions. The printed book, as a symbol of knowledge, education, and erudition, has hitherto been the leading medium of the elite, but it now seems to have acquired the status of a special asset in popular culture as well, as documented most impressively by the current explosion of videos with, of, or in front of books by BookTubers and Bookstagrammers: "The difference between the printed and electronic book mediums currently seems to be helping the representative use of books to gain new momentum."[362] Instagram tiles and flip-through videos not only extend or replace the bourgeois bookcases that were once evidence of their owners' class and served as a mark of distinction. After all, people especially like to hold up books produced by themselves for the camera, not least because, in the era of the clickbait-attention economy, the mere publishing of a book does not guarantee a wide reach, circulation, and reception, particularly in self-publishing. It needs more exposure and effort, which is why many tutorials and additional services offered by the platforms deal with this.

If such a social media post is to be successful, it should preferably show a "photographable" object, with tangible materiality and staged as authentically and individually as possible (a contradiction in terms): "It doesn't simply mean that an image is adjusted to circulate online—rather, reality itself is reformatted to better circulate as image."[363] In this post-digital phase, in which digital platforms pre-adjust and demand analog behavior, there is little room for skeuomorphism: nowadays, the digital is no longer an imitation or continuation of the analog; rather, the analog is subject to the digital. This means that a book must be printed less as proof that it has actually come into being as a work of art, but in order to be "instagrammable." For the corporeality required to circulate online, "imagined printedness" is not sufficient, nor are cover images and 3D mock-ups; as paradoxical as it might seem, the logic of utilization demanded by social media platforms like Instagram requires the "real," three-dimensional printed book.

The ability to produce a single copy economically via POD plays a key role in this because, in a digital feed and with the right lighting, it is impossible to tell that a work is a self-published POD book. After all, they have an industrially-produced look that resembles "normal" books, whose cultural and symbolic capital they can thus easily partake of in

360. Publication Studios Pearl River Delta and Rotterdam, "Foreword," in *Publication Studio Portable: A Mobile Publishing Manual*, ed. Elaine W. Ho, Beatrix Pang, Isabelle Sully, and Yin Yin Wong (self-pub.: Publication Studio, 2019), 3–4, 3.

361. ABC, "Paleolithic Cave Paintings," in this volume, 511.

362. Ute Schneider, "Bücher zeigen und Leseatmosphären inszenieren – vom Habitus enthusiastischer Leserinnen und Leser," in *Gelesene Literatur: Populäre Lektüre im Zeichen des Medienwandels*, ed. Carlos Spoerhase and Steffen Martus (Munich: edition text + kritik, 2018), 111–120, 113.

363. Laurens Otto, "Editorial," *RESOLUTION*, no. 0: *The Pixel* (2019): 3–5, 4.

this digital setting. Furthermore, it is irrelevant for the digital staging whether the book has been printed just once or is a bestseller. In fact, it is not even necessary to include the content or design in the picture: a photograph of the beautifully lit book in semi-profile suffices.

At the same time, social media profiles sometimes

supplement or replace lists and archives of publications on blogs or websites. For example, the books of the collective artist persona Jean Keller are only brought together and presented as works in a spartan Instagram profile. Keller's Instagram activities do not extend beyond the creation of this profile; his account does not participate in the update spiral with its constant demands for new content, making it pretty much pointless to follow him. However, this Instagram presence is not just a way to provide an overview of the works, but also means they can be referenced within as well as outside the Instagram ecosystem, and thus fed back into and connected with contemporary discourse and the attention economy.

In contrast to the boundless virtual space of the internet and the incessant stream of messages on social media, the six book objects in their tiles seem clearly delimited, self-sufficient, and static, together forming a literally weighty, homogeneous oeuvre. At the same time, the impression of uniformity created by the book objects and the way they are presented is a reminder of the industrial, assembly-line process by which they were manufactured, which is perfectly mirrored in the conveyor-belt-like sequence of identically composed photographs.

The category mistake within the feed is thus all the more striking: although all the pictures were posted one after the other on April 26, 2021, the lowest and so oldest tile in the profile image contains not a photograph but a screenshot that documents Keller's publicly staged farewell to Blurb in the style of an obituary notice. The equivalence between screenshot and photograph being insinuated here equates Keller's paratextual performance on Blurb with his books produced via the platform, declaring it to be an indispensable part of his oeuvre and so once again highlighting the relevance and virtuosity of artists' paratextual poetics and envelope strategies, which have undeservedly been largely ignored up to now (see 82–86).[364]

Furthermore, this screenshot strategically and neatly frames the move away from using POD platforms to present artistic production as a turn towards the now-dominant visual social media platform. The endpoint is thus simultaneously a starting point and a new beginning; the death notice signifies not only a stoppage and a look back, but also a resurrection.

Coda: Fifteen Years of Artistic POD

This change from one platform to another can stand paradigmatically for the transformation of the conditions surrounding the presentation and production of content on the net, a development caused by the concentration of activity over the last ten years on a handful of social media platforms and their

364. See also Melgard, "Print-on-Demand Self-Publishing," in this volume, 584f.

closed attention regimes, with ever fewer sites guaranteeing contemporary relevance, connectivity, and attention. This also affects the production, presentation, and reception of books in general and post-digital POD publications in particular.

Keller's Instagram exhibition not only takes his departure from the POD platform as its starting point, but also closes his profile with a very similar gesture. His Instagram profile picture (and thus to a certain extent the most representative picture on the account) reuses the Blurb profile picture captured in the screenshot: a dark black circle. This mirroring builds a bridge between POD and social media platforms, and also serves here as a period; in the end the black circle can be read not only as a gesture anonymizing a collective artistic persona, but also as a means of commemorating a form of artistic use of and engagement with POD that has come to the end of its existence and whose modus operandi cannot be easily transferred to other platforms.

The Instagram profile does contain a link to Lulu, where Keller migrated after his move from Blurb and through which at least five of the six publications in the photos can still be purchased.[365] As photos on Instagram, however, they can no longer be experienced as platform-specific interventions, but instead appear as materialized objects that have been completely removed from the context in which they arose and on which most of them critically reflect. Keller thus reanimates his oeuvre in the context of the attention machine that is Instagram. However, this still does not amount to a reactivation and continuation in new contexts of the artistic practice he developed and tested in the POD universe, such as Joey Yearous-Algozin, also thinking of the approaching end of Troll Thread's activity, imagines for the future:

> What it [the internet] does allow for is the exploration of the desires already apparent working in groups of writers who are seeking alternatives to the structures of the academy and the galleries that have become synonymous with American experimental poetry.
> Or, to put it bluntly: these things work for now and once they stop working, we'll find something else.[366]

Keller's period thus remains a period, at least for the moment, despite his work being presented on a new platform. It thereby confirms—on behalf of many other works in our collection—the observation that formed the starting point of the Library of Artistic Print on Demand, namely that the phase of unconditional, uncritical enthusiasm for the newly discovered production and publication processes and the artistic possibilities associated with them is over, and with it the first heyday of artistic experiments with POD platforms.

Number of works in the Library of Artistic Print on Demand collection per year

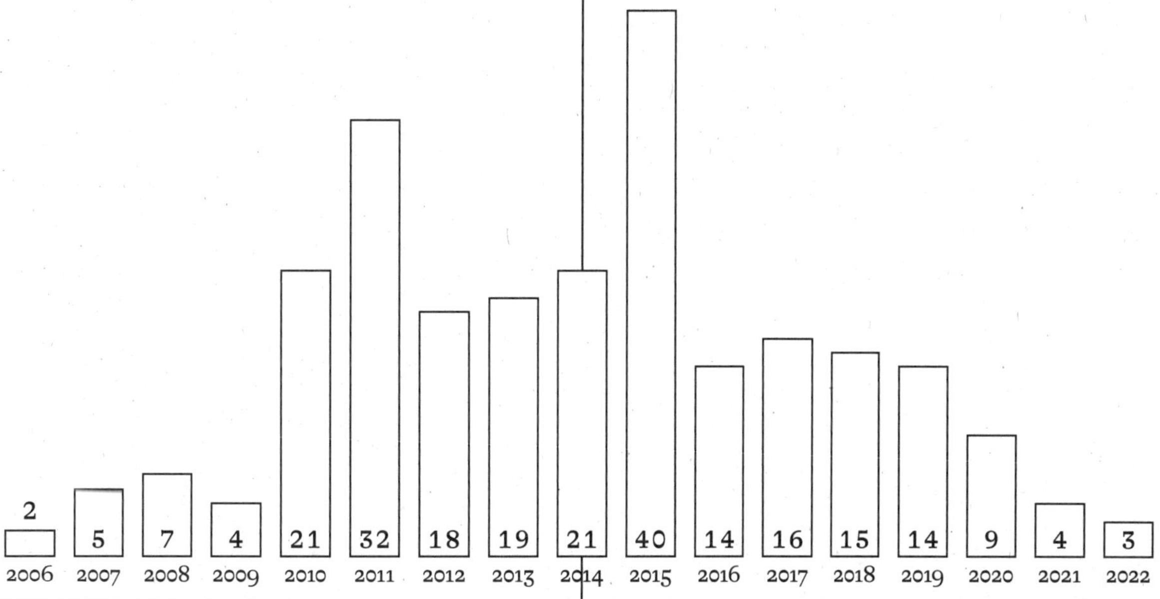

365. The only one unavailable is Keller's *Blank* (2011): nomen est omen.

366. Yearous-Algozin, "Keep Your Friends Close /// We Upload Trash," 78.

This can also be seen in the chronological distribution of the works in our collection. In the first five years after 2006 the number of works grows steadily, with peaks in 2011 and 2015. From approximately ten years after the founding of Blurb and Lulu, the intensity of POD use in the artistic field we are concerned with then steadily declines.[367] This trend can be noted for the entire production of Lulu and Blurb in the United States from 2010 to 2018, according to Bowker.[368]

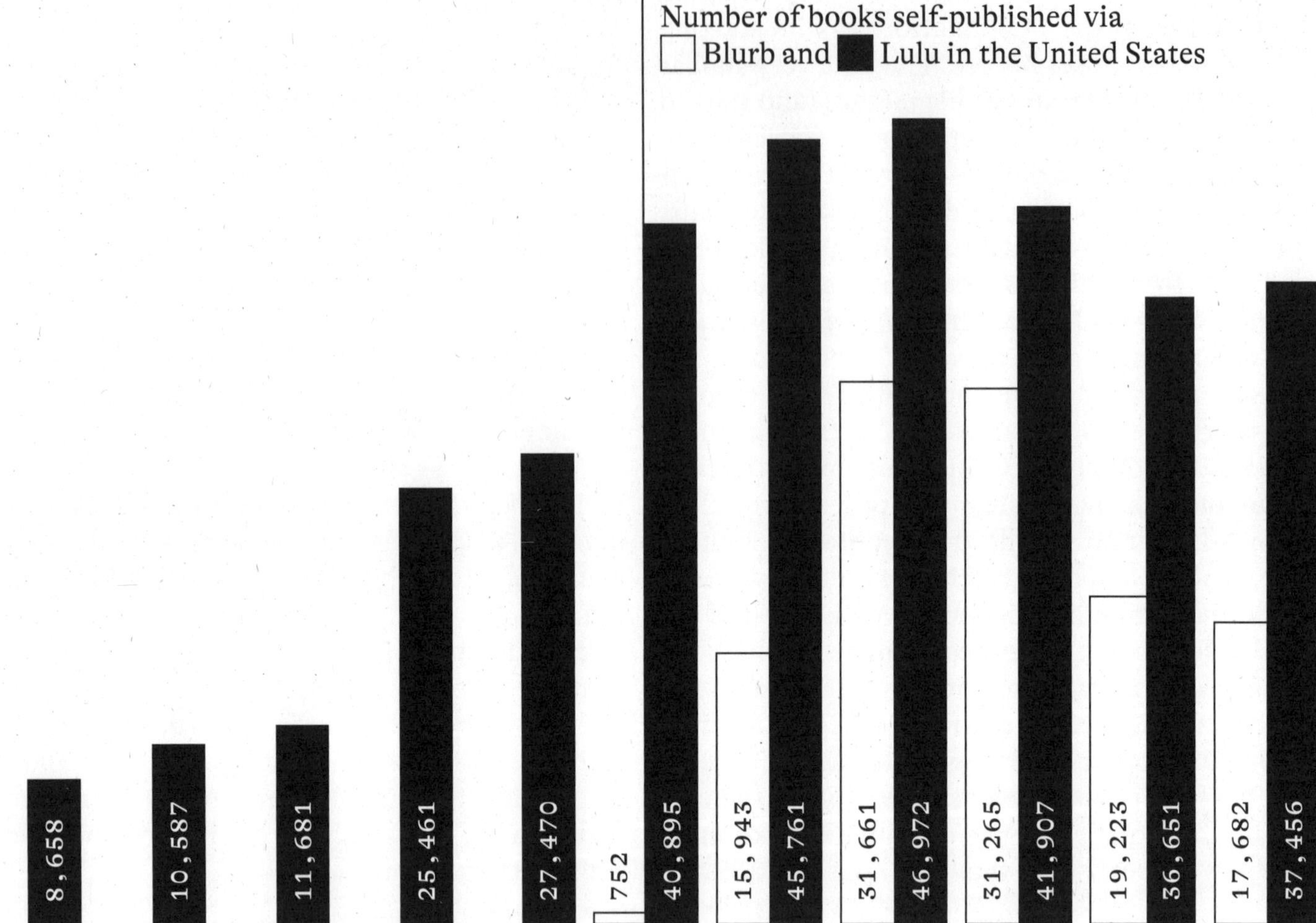

This may be due to the fact that artistic experiments with new media and technologies are generally finite. The phase of novelty, which invites exploration and promises distinction to pioneering experimenters, is usually superseded by a phase of obsolescence (in the case of dead ends of media history) or stabilization (if the new technology ends up triumphant). POD has undoubtedly now become established, and therefore no longer requires much experimental investigation or critical elucidation. This may also explain the decline of interest over the years in explorations of the book medium and the "bookification" of digital content as well as in the specific analog/digital hybridity of POD: the longer we live in the post-digital age, the more the latter is superseded by other questions.

POD has thus become an integral part of the repertoire of industrial print production and has—also or even especially in its platformized easy-access form—significantly extended the horizons of artistic and publishing activity. For artists and authors, it is now just one possible production method among many others that one may decide to use or not depending on the situation. Admittedly, as

367. It should be noted that these figures are of course the result of our own selection criteria, which were designed to capture the particularly innovative and efficacious approaches that frequently come about at the beginning of a development, as well as of any external influences that affect the statistics, such as the decline in productivity caused by the Covid-19 pandemic.

368. Bowker, "ISBN Output for USA Self-Publishers, Total Print Books," in *Self-Publishing in the United States, 2013-2018, Print and Ebooks*, 2019, 5, and *Self-Publishing in the United States, 2008–2013, Print and Ebook*, 2014, 5. The market leader is CreateSpace with 11,498 print books in 2008, 187,846 books in 2013, and 1,416,384 books in 2018.

an artistic practice, it has thus lost its potential for distinction for the time being.[369] In return, however, artists and authors no longer have to fight to establish POD platform publications "as legitimate venues for writing, publishing, and artistic practice" and absolve them of the stigma of vanity publishing.[370] When requesting that the platforms support its activities, therefore, the ABC was completely correct in arguing that "[w]e have been creating quite a bit of profit for Blurb and we are the ones who give print-on-demand credibility in the world of art."[371] Even though this request fell on deaf ears in the end, their works are still responsible for a significant share of the attention and esteem that this new area of artistic publishing has gained over the years.

Another factor that affects and modifies artistic POD-platform production is the transformation of the everyday use of media over the last few years. The period between 2008 and 2015 can be characterized, to borrow Paul Soulellis's phrase, "as post-iPhone and pre-Trump": "It was the time when the network began to get personal, to build our trust, to travel with us, to reveal itself in more surprising places. [...] We began to carry the browser around with us all day, and to sleep beside it at night."[372] This transition from computer to smartphone also impacts modes of reception "inserted into the continuum of social life" and "the environments in which we read"—the reader's "surroundings," in Georges Perec words[373]—that were seminal to hybrid PDF/POD publishing models, especially at the beginning, as Joey Yearous-Algozin explains: "I think that a lot of POD when it was online was meant to be read on a laptop. It was meant to be engaged with on a laptop. Like we used to release books specifically for people to be at their jobs because a lot of times people would engage it is when they were at work, sort of stealing time from whatever bullshit job."[374] What is emerging here on the micro level is the result of a new phase of post-digital entanglement in the Anthropocene, in which digital media and platforms are so ubiquitous and pervasive that not only can they no longer be considered separately from an analog world however constituted, but they actually spill over into that world in a way that formats reality.

In the course of these transformations, artistic POD practices also recalibrated themselves, proving to be astonishingly complicated and bound up with a specific digital ecosystem in which any change to one element has an effect on all the others. Over the years this ecosystem has been subject to significant pressures, not least due to the concentration of traffic on fewer and fewer websites and platforms that attract more and more visitors through network effects. This may have contributed to Lulu's decision to discontinue its social media features and to concentrate fully on the book business. Many Web 2.0 platforms, such as the photo-sharing platform Flickr and the blogging platform Tumblr, understood the need for these kinds of modifications to their original architecture, policies, and products or services. Tumblr once formed the basis of the digital activities of many POD artists and collectives (including Troll Thread, Gauss PDF, and ABC), but increasingly lost its relevance and subsequently, at least in the artistic field, its function. The same can be said for many artists' blogs, including those of James Bridle, Greg Allen, derek beaulieu, Kris de Decker, Hartmut Abendschein, and Paul Laidler, to name a few.

Added to this is the transformation of society as a whole, which has not left artistic publishing practice untouched and demands new artistic approaches and procedures. POD publishing has lost its innocence. It is no longer the free, liberating, economically and ecologically viable space it was once promised to be, and that it is still advertised as by the platforms. At least since Edward Snowden's revelations, it has been clear that the once enthusiastically received, openly constructed, supposedly participatory internet, with all its utopian promise of self-determined agency in the use of digital technologies, no longer functions as an anonymous, democratic, utopian space, but rather primarily as an instrument of monopolistic surveillance and platform capitalism.

369. That will only change with the arrival of newer media and technologies, when as an outdated production process it will once again—like the typewriter, the copier, mimeo, riso, vinyl etc.—promise another kind of distinction.

370. Soulellis, "Urgent Archive," in *Library of the Printed Web. Collected Works 2013–2017*, ed. Paul Soulellis (self-pub.: Lulu, 2017), 501–516, 506. Laquintano observes a similar effect in *Mass Authorship and the Rise of Self-Publishing*, ch. 1.

371. Joachim Schmid, letter to Blurb, January/February 2012.

372. Both citations Soulellis, "Urgent Archive," 504f.

373. All citations Georges Perec, "Reading: A Socio-physiological Outline," in *Species of Spaces and Other Pieces*, trans. John Sturrock (London: Penguin, 1999), 174–185, here 175, 181, and 180.

374. Joey Yearous-Algozin, interview by the authors, February 26, 2021.

It is also now well known that platforms are not neutral service providers, but are themselves political actors that create realities. In this newly structured environment, they are by definition under suspicion, and so publications produced with their help are no longer suitable means for addressing power structures: instead of being accepted as a tool for technology-enabled criticism or self-empowerment, they are now perceived as simply part of the platform apparatus. The number of explorative and critical engagements with platforms may also be decreasing because a certain sobriety has kicked in regarding the potential effectiveness of artistic intervention, research, and criticism. All the hacks, détournements, hoaxes, perruques, and subversions may have functioned for a while as a kind of version control of the platforms' policies and the broader development of the internet in which they are embedded, and thus in certain cases promoted enlightenment and awareness. In the end, however, this was unsustainable: they struggled to lend weight to their political demands, let alone bring about change, without paradoxically contributing indirectly to the optimization of the platforms' business models or increasing their profits. Any use of the platforms, whether critical, naïve, or affirmative, helps to keep the capitalist power machine running.

Moreover, the platforms do not only offer space for progressive ideas, as Holly Melgard notes with alarm. When Troll Thread was founded in 2010/11, online trolling had hardly emerged as a dangerous propaganda strategy employed by states: "At that time, we looked up to trolling as an anonymous form of progressive hacktivism that undermined capital. But somewhere back there, the dream that print-on-demand would democratize discourse by including more marginalized voices and under-recognized forms of knowledge turned nightmarish as misinformation and conspiracy theories emerged."[375] Against this background, it was not only the ominous line "Troll Thread is Troll Thread" (for many years the only content of the "About" page on the publisher's Tumblr) that became unsustainable.[376]

Camouflage, filter, or hacking strategies, such as those developed by Jasper Otto Eisenecker, Ubermorgen, and Stéphanie Vilayphiou, can also be deployed for the "wrong" purposes. Crowdworking remains exploitation, even when used for artistic purposes. Online forums can be used as recruiting or collaboration tools for the formation of transnational far-right nationalist alliances or for the dissemination of misogynist, racist, and anti-Semitic material, as the twelve thick volumes of Nick Thurston's *Hate Library* (2019) and Angela Washko's investigative art project *BANGED* (2015) demonstrate. The same is true of the POD platform stores, where, despite superficial content moderation, you can find pirate copies as well as almost entirely unregulated racist, misogynist, conspiracy-theorist and fake-news publications, as Holly Melgard notes with disillusionment: "Just by searching the word 'plandemic' on Lulu's website, right now I see six books of COVID-19 anti-vaccine propaganda. Unequivocally, Lulu needs to be held accountable for giving a platform to misinformation that can get people killed."[377]

The extreme polarization of society, which is also a result of the ever more accelerated, monopolistic attention economy that characterizes the large platforms, has also given rise to a new politicization and recalibration of artistic strategies, as reflected in our collection. This has significantly widened the scope of the social themes addressed, so that the publications can be regarded as a seismograph or mirror of cultural, media, social, and political developments and discussions. It has also become evident that artists must constantly reflect on and reassess their own artistic practice, however tried and tested, critical, or well-intentioned it may be, as shown by the example of Vanessa Place, whose oeuvre underwent a complete reevaluation in a short period of time. For four years her project *Gone with the Wind* (2011)—which consisted of posting Margaret Mitchell's 1937 novel sentence by sentence under her own name on Twitter—ran almost unnoticed, or in any case unchallenged. As Place later explained, she wanted the project to bring attention to the novel's inherent racism and question its hitherto little-disputed place in America's cultural heritage.[378] In 2015, however, during a rampant public debate, it was accused of reproduc-

375. Melgard, "Print-on-Demand Self-Publishing," in this volume, 580.

376. Troll Thread, "ABOUT," https://web.archive.org/web/20180211045327/https://trollthread.tumblr.com/ABOUT.

377. Melgard, "Print-on-Demand Self-Publishing," in this volume, 585f.

378. See Vanessa Place, "Artist's Statement: Gone With the Wind @VanessaPlace," Genius, May 19, 2015, https://genius.com/Vanessa-place-artists-statement-gone-with-the-wind-vanessaplace-annotated.

ing racist language and imagery, ultimately leading Place to discontinue the project. Her Facebook intervention to repost other poets' Facebook status updates as if they were her own, which started in 2012, raised questions about authorship, creativity, commodification, and property in a slightly outdated conceptual writing style, but also provoked protests in 2014 by some of the authors concerned, as documented in the anonymously produced POD book *Vanessa Place... blocked* (2014). These two long-term artistic projects clearly show how the socio-political discourse has shifted fundamentally in just a few years, so that the implications and stakes inherent in appropriation as an artistic strategy are now being evaluated on completely different terms.

A similar dichotomy characterizes Mishka Henner's award-winning *No Man's Land* (2011), which displays photos of sex workers waiting for customers on remote roads, coincidentally captured by Google's camera cars and now visible on Google Street View. Henner's first volume became highly contentious in public discourse, with the discussion expanded to include a feminist perspective and debate around the ethics of documentary photography. Even if Henner's documentation can be read as a denunciation of the working conditions of sex workers, as well as of Google's reckless accumulation of data and the collateral damage caused by this automated imagery, the objection can also be raised that Henner endangered the women's safety, used depictions of them without talking to them or asking for consent, and even capitalized on their situation. His *Harry Potter and the Scam Baiter* (2012) is similarly ambiguous: it documents a spectacular case, from 2006, of the fledgling scam bait genre, which is "a form of social engineering"[379] that seeks to trick and harm email scammers themselves by wasting their time and resources, detecting information to pass on to investigative authorities, or publicly exposing them. Henner's book savors the triumph over the scammer in this special case, but it also raises the question of whether the reprehensible nature of email scams as a form of organized internet criminality justifies the deployment of scam baiting as vigilante justice. As Henner himself admits in the epilogue, scam baiting "may have an altruistic motive or may be motivated by malice."[380] The use of crowdsourcing via Amazon's Mechanical Turk in works such as Jason Huff's *Best Fight Ever / Worst Fight Ever* (2011), *Reading @realDonaldTrump* (2016–18), Fred Benenson's *Emoji Dick* (2010), and Nick Thurston's *Van de Onderaannemingsovereenkomst* (2013/2016) now seems similarly ambiguous.

Such irresolvable ambivalences increasingly lead to conflicts of conscience or goals—for artists as well as for audiences—and, in the case of Angela Washko for example, to a critical examination of artistic strategy. In her interview project *BANGED* (2015), she actually wanted to publicly expose the "web's most infamous misogynist," the pickup artist Roosh V, and to counter his guidebooks for men, which outline strategies for picking up women, with the perspective and narratives of affected women. When Roosh V found out about this, she changed her strategy, "shifting from activism to ethnography"[381] of the different bubbles, each with their own codes and perspectives on the world: "I became critical of my own black-and-white extremist approach. To introduce more of the nuance that is often ignored in conversations about pick up artists within stratified spheres of the internet, I decided to reach out to Roosh with the hopes of additionally conducting an interview with him."[382]

Paul Soulellis underwent a similar self-critical development. With hindsight he observes that his view of his long-preferred strategy of appropriation, which he once, "in the spirit of Richard Serra's verb list," further differentiated with the verbs "hunting, grabbing, and performing," has fundamentally changed: "This past summer, as I was preparing to give a talk in Italy, I wrote out the word 'grabbing,' and thought, How, in this era of Trump, can we talk about grabbing other peoples' work? Suddenly, grabbing didn't feel right at all, and I realized that my feelings about how and when appropriation should be used had changed."[383]

379. Mishka Henner, "Epilogue," in *Harry Potter and the Scam Baiter* (self-pub.: Lulu, 2012), 319.
380. Henner, "Epilogue," 319.
381. Both citations Angela Washko, "BANGed: A Monopoly on Truth," 2015, https://angelawashko.com/artwork/3831453-BANGed%3A%20A%20Monopoly%20on%20Truth.html.
382. Angela Washko, "an explanation of the work in question, April 27, 2015," in Angela Washko, *BANGed: A Monopoly on Truth* (self-pub.: Lulu, 2015), n.p.
383. All citations Paul Soulellis, "Library of the Printed Web," interview by Meg Miller, November 21, 2017, https://www.are.na/blog/paul-soulellis.

This experience also made him emphasize the datedness of his Library of the Printed Web: "I could see this entire collection becoming a dated account of a very specific moment in the history of art and technology, perhaps spanning only a decade. And that's how I intend to work with this collection—as an archive that's alive and actively absorbing something of the moment, as it's happening, and evolving as new narratives develop."[384]

We hope the same will hold true for our library project. Although we have stopped our collecting activity here, it does not mean the end of artistic POD publishing practice. The POD cosmos is still far from fully explored and the final pages of the history of post-digital, media-sensitive POD books have yet to be written. There are still technical potentials to exploit and artistic possibilities to explore. What does seem to be over is the medium's ability to electrify and unite artists and authors, irrespective of nationality, approach and genre, at a particular historical moment, to form the kind of scene that provoked the explosion of books that we have only scratched the surface of here. Buoyed by the euphoria of being part of an emerging, likeminded community, these artists and authors maintained their creative furor and produced POD works of artistic relevance for several years, before scattering again and turning to new practices, themes, methods, techniques, and partners.

The moment of their coming together, however, continues to echo and even suggests exciting prospects for the future, for, as Danny Snelson says, the best is yet to come: "I think that there was a flash point in the early 2010s when people were really excited about the potential of POD as artwork. And then, that kind of died down. That's probably the time when the most interesting work was yet to be made. Just as a genre dies down, the more interesting work has yet to be produced."[385]

384. Paul Soulellis, "Search, Compile, Publish," in *Publishing Manifestos: An International Anthology from Artists and Writers*, ed. Michalis Pichler (Berlin and Cambridge, Mass.: MIT Press, 2019), 228–232, 230.

385. Snelson, interview by the authors, July 18, 2020.

Cat

The works are listed chronologically and within each year alphabetically by author's name.

The sources for the citations can be found in the bibliography at the end of the catalog. All URLs were last checked July 31, 2023. Links are not provided for citations from blurbs to individual books, references to webshop offers, and social media posts, as these are subject to frequent changes. Please refer to the corresponding screenshots, which can be found in our digital archive https://apod.li/.

Unless otherwise stated, all translations are our own. All quantities and prices are as of January 2023.

The ISBNs follow the information in the respective books (not in the webshop), exceptions are noted separately. The dimensions given are always those of the actual copy in our collection. They may differ slightly from the standard dimensions due to POD production peculiarities. The information in the line "edition characteristics" with the abbreviation "CC" stands for the various Creative Commons licenses.

Acknowledgment

When 100 people hear the word "artist's book," more than 100 different ideas—or questions—are likely to arise in 100 brains. This does not change even if those 100 people all share an affinity for art, since hardly any genre has undergone such a change in characteristics and audience as the artist's book, whereby "diversification" is a better description than "change."

While elaborate bibliophilic works containing original artwork have existed for centuries (today they are often preserved in artists' books collections—including ours at the Bavarian State Library), the "artist's book," which was named as such in the 1960s, initially referred to works that, in contrast, were to be affordable for all and thus carry a democratic idea of art into the world. These were works that would rub up against the idea of the book, play with it, test its limits, and often reveal those limits in the first place. Sometimes all it took was a photocopier and some imagination—plus the mindset of sharing and building on each other's ideas and ideals, and the desire to feed each other lines.

Print-on-demand is nothing other than the matrix print of the third millennium and thus a way of producing and distributing concept books in today's world that deeply corresponds to the essence of the artist's book in the sense of its post-war definition: quickly, digitally, on demand. The freedom from editions and publishers that print-on-demand brings is not to be underestimated as a springboard for innovation and artistic courage.

At the same time, "artist's book" is still understood, collected, and created as something elitist, expensive, and exclusive. Collections are often considered as falling into one or other of these categories. The Bavarian State Library houses one of the largest and most renowned expanding collections of artists' books on an international level and, with regard to its collection profile, has not limited itself to one of the two—simplified here—forms of the artist's book. Concept books stand next to painter's books, Jonathan Meese next to René Magritte, handmade paper next to samizdat—as long as the artistic quality is high.

At this point, the Bavarian State Library would like to express its gratitude for the donation of print-on-demand artist's books that will be received from the Library of Artistic Print on Demand (apod.li) once the project is complete. The enormous effort put in by the apod.li to create scholarly criteria in order to filter out and compile the highest-quality artists' books from the great mass on offer cannot be valued highly enough; the donation will certainly enrich our existing artists' books collection. On behalf of the Bavarian State Library, I would like to thank Annette Gilbert and Andreas Bülhoff for this work, for the project's success, for the donation, and not least for our healthy cooperation.

DR. KLAUS CEYNOWA | Director General, Bavarian State Library, Munich

www.bsb-muenchen.de

Philip

AUTHORS	Herman Chong, Cosmin Costinas, Dexter Sinister, Mai Abu ElDahab, Rosemary Heather, Francis McKee, David Reinfurt, Steve Rushton, Leif Magne Tangen, Mark Aerial Waller
YEAR	2006
PUBLISHER	Project Press
GENRE	fiction
METHOD	collective, composition (writing / drawing / photography), pricing
SUBJECT	crowd / collaboration, economy / labor, narration, print on demand, publishing / distribution
PLATFORM	Lulu
EDITION CHARACTERISTICS	ISBN 1872493211, third edition, open edition
FORMAT	10.8 × 17.5 cm
MATERIALITIES	black-and-white, paperback, perfect bound
PAGES	200
IMAGE	

DESCRIPTION

Philip is a collectively written science fiction novel produced during an eight-day writing workshop devised by Herman Chong and Leif Magne Tangen as part of an exhibition of the same name (Project Arts Center, Dublin, November 2006 – January 2007).

The invited participants weren't writers but graphic designers, filmmakers, visual artists, critics, and curators chosen for their engagement in thinking about the future. The novel they produced, named after Philip K. Dick, is a dystopian narrative set in what was the near future of 2019, trying to preserve the history of the present and at the same time conceptualizing the future, thinking through contemporary modes of production and the dissemination of goods.

The book was designed by Dexter Sinister, the compound name of Stuart Bailey and David Reinfurt. They also took the book's selling price into consideration, believing that it should be in line with the story's subject matter: "Because the exhibition format privileges production over display, then it makes sense to price the book based on the immaterial labor costs incurred during the workshop rather than the material, shipping, travel or distribution costs" (Dexter Sinister, "The Price of *Philip*").

For the initial print run of 100 copies, they calculated a price of €85.70 per copy, enough to pay all the people involved. For the second edition, they imagined a more relational system with the price being adjusted if the total number of sold copies increased (assuming that the immaterial labor costs are fixed). This would invert the prevailing economy of sale (as more copies are made, the manufacturing costs decrease and the profit per unit goes up) into a demand-side economy of scope, where the profit per unit goes down as production increases. This would increase the circulation of the book outside the circle of participants and create a network of readers.

To make this possible, production on demand and a website and interface are needed. "When an order is placed through this online interface, payment will be collected and a copy of the novel will be printed, bound and shipped by Lulu.com in an already established process. However, the price of a copy will always be re-adjusting—each time an order is placed, the total number of copies is increased and the resulting price is reduced" (Dexter Sinister, "The Price of *Philip*").

As this model of using an interface—prior to Lulu's API—to automatically adjust costs didn't work, *Philip* was, after a presumed time of experimentation, sold via Lulu with a more or less fixed price. This third edition is still available and archived in our library.

Seven Controlled Vocabularies, 2004 1st (Lulu) Edition

AUTHOR	Tan Lin
YEAR	2006
GENRE	experimental literature
METHOD	composition (writing / drawing / photography), found material, paratextual play, remediation
SUBJECT	analog / digital, authorship, internet culture, literature, reading / interpretation
PLATFORM	Lulu
EDITION CHARACTERISTICS	open edition
FORMAT	15.2 × 22.9 cm
MATERIALITIES	black-and-white, paperback, perfect bound
PAGES	216

IMAGES

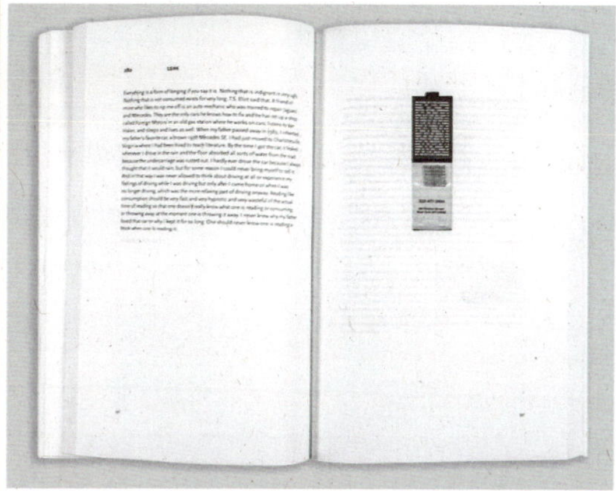

DESCRIPTION

Tan Lin's *Seven Controlled Vocabularies and Obituary: The Joy of Cooking* is a book project on reading practices making extensive use of found material, appropriation, different layers of commentary, paratextual play, and category shifts. It consists of text and images and has been published in multiple editions, including PDFs, a book version published by Wesleyan University Press—which was awarded with the Association for Asian American Studies Book Award in Poetry (2012)—and a print-on-demand version on Lulu, which was the first to be published.

The book is divided into seven sections, each devoted to a different art form, namely film, photography, painting, novel, architecture, music, and theory. These are tackled with conceptual writing techniques, presenting language to look at as well as offering different ways to approach the framings of language. In Lin's terms, the book presents itself as a container to control and document different states of reading, which is understood as copying, digesting, and transcribing text from all kinds of analog and digital sources. As each source implies a different kind of reading practice with a different intensity, these practices get somewhat tamed and leveled in the book format, making it a way to control their vocabularies. This controlling is just one side of how the book presents its contents, as it also plays with different modes of publishing and paratext. It is also closely connected to Lin's personal life and his experiences as part of a migrant family.

The Lulu version presents itself with three different titles, with *Seven Controlled Vocabularies* on its back cover, *The Joy of Cooking* on its spine and no less than three different title pages, including one listing *Obituary* as the book's title. The cover lists two ISBNs that can be traced to different editions. These paratextual uncertainties in addition to the multiple editions, as well as an editing event series initiated by Danny Snelson further enhancing the book in eleven publications and editions, also frame the book in a networked environment as a temporary device for controlling text just waiting to fluidize again. Several parts of the book's content have been previously published on Tumblr blogs, as stated in an interview with Lin that featured in *Appendix*, a book published as part of Snelson's series *11 Books Expanding Tan Lin's* Seven Controlled Vocabularies and Obituary: The Joy of Cooking, 2010 (see 160–169).

Tristano
Nº6982 von 109 027 350 432 000 möglichen Romanen

AUTHOR	Nanni Balestrini
YEAR	2007–2009 [1966]
PUBLISHER	Suhrkamp
GENRE	experimental literature
METHOD	composition (writing / drawing / photography), generative / automation, montage / remix, versioning / seriality
SUBJECT	book / book design, code / programming, literature, narration, print technology, print on demand
PLATFORM	others
EDITION CHARACTERISTICS	ISBN 9783518125793, second edition, limited edition, unique copies
FORMAT	10.8 × 17.5 cm
MATERIALITIES	black-and-white, paperback, perfect bound
PAGES	154

IMAGE

DESCRIPTION

Media pioneer Nanni Balestrini experimented early on with computers in literary production. His combinatorial novel *Tristano* from 1966 represents the idea of a love story, of which there are infinitely many variants. For this reason, Balestrini planned an edition in which every copy of the novel was supposed to feature a different computer generated text, that is, one of the 109,027,350,432,000 possible permutations of all the novel's passages. Accordingly, he describes *Tristano* as "only the first experiment that exploits in a limited way the great potential offered by technological innovation," and "offering original possibilities for freedom of creation and communication with the audience."

In this way, Balestrini's novel, in a series of one-offs, is an attack on the assumption of stable textuality as the basis of literary works: Just as "a spoken story changes more or less when told to different listeners, or at a different time," it is now also possible for "a literary work, a novel, [to] be created, thanks to new technologies, no longer as an immutable unicum, but in a series of equivalent variants, each materialized in a book, the copy and personal story of each reader" (Nanni Balestrini, "Note on the Text," xii).

But this idea of variance could not be realized until 2007, forty years after *Tristano*'s first edition, where the entire print run contains the same variant of the text: "The novel, constructed in the spirit of computer-assisted combinatorics, is so digital that its existence on paper requires digital printing technology" (Hannes Bajohr, "Print on Demand as Strategy and Genre," 630). Little is known about the exact production process, but it does not appear to have been automated. Correspondence from the German translator Peter O. Chotjewitz (preserved in the German Literature Archive Marbach) indicates that probably 2,000 individual PDFs were produced by hand for the German edition and passed on to the printer.

The fact that every copy of the edition is unique is indicated in the paratext: the copies of the Italian edition from 2007 and the English and German translations are numbered on the cover, and thus clearly individuated. In addition, the blurb on the back cover of the Italian and German edition advertises the "anomaly" of this book as a sensation: "This copy is not the same as all the others / But your own personal, unrepeatable book / That has chosen you from an infinity of possible versions / Because the story of Tristan is many stories / And every reader has the right to his own story."

The Longest Day

AUTHOR	David Horvitz
YEAR	2007
GENRE	photobook
METHOD	composition (writing / drawing / photography)
SUBJECT	narration, photography, print technology
PLATFORM	Lulu
EDITION CHARACTERISTICS	open edition
FORMAT	15.2 × 22.9 cm
MATERIALITIES	color, paperback, perfect bound
PAGES	104 (unpaginated)

IMAGES

DESCRIPTION

The Longest Day consists of photographs of the sky over Los Angeles taken by David Horvitz on June 21, 2007, the day of the summer solstice, which is the longest day of the year. The images were taken around twice an hour in the same position and format, for a total of fifty photos. The progression of the images captures the gradient of daylight from one night to the next. The photos are arranged in a rather small format on the right-hand pages only and shift to the upper right, leaving plenty of white space on each page. This allows the book to be used as a flip book, which at the same time adds to the focus on capturing progression. Thus, the gradient of daylight is turned into a gradient of ink, and time is saved into a progression of pages.

Even though the photo format is rather small, the rendering of sky and light still makes for a rather lo-fi look and shows small "artifacts," residues from digital and analog errors in the image reproduction.

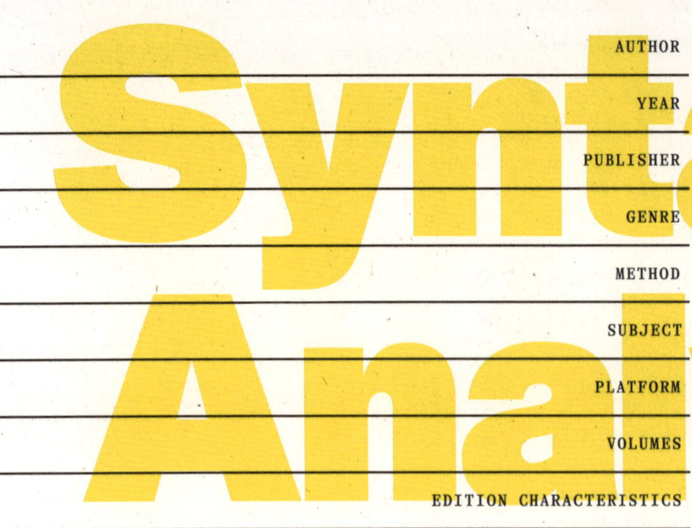

Syntactic Analyses

AUTHOR	Michael Maranda
YEAR	2007
PUBLISHER	Parasitic Ventures Press
GENRE	artist's book / bookwork, experimental literature
METHOD	appropriation, generative / automation, paratextual play
SUBJECT	canon, reading / interpretation, scale, typography
PLATFORM	Lulu
VOLUMES	100
EDITION CHARACTERISTICS	multiple editions (print, PDF), open edition

DESCRIPTION

"Conceived in the waning years of the last century, produced as a one-off for an exhibition in 2004, and now republished as a new open-edition set, *Syntactic Analyses* is modelled on 'great-books' series such as the *Everyman's Library*. One hundred volumes of must read books, primarily covering political thought, philosophy, and history" (Michael Maranda, "Syntactic Analyses Series").

The paratext accompanying the series, published by Michael Maranda's own Parasitic Ventures Press, advertises it as a "critical edition." But scientific criteria are nowhere to be found in this series published by a press which focuses on the subversion of found texts, and which describes itself as being "saprophagous." Just as saprophagous organisms feed off dead or decaying matter, so does the press "feed off of the decaying detritus of textual history" (Michael Maranda, "The Books"). In the *Syntactic Analyses* series, the specific structural element which Maranda extracts from the texts is punctuation. The series motto is: "The comma will set you free."

The series consists of 100 canonical works of Western political theory, philosophy, and history, reduced to their punctuation marks. It includes works by Aristotle, St. Augustine, Averroes, Bacon, Bentham, Bergson, Berkeley, Boethius, Burckhardt, Burke, Cicero, Confucius, Darwin, Debord, Descartes, Dewey, Freud, Gandhi, Goldman, Grotius, Hegel, Herodotus, Hobbes, W. v. Humboldt, Hume, W. James, Kropotkin, Le Bon, Leibniz, Locke, Lucretius, Machiavelli, Malthus, H. Marcuse, Marx, J. S. Mill, Montesquieu, More, Nietzsche, Paine, Pascal, Pater, Plato, Proudhon, Ricardo, Rousseau, Ruskin, Russell, Schiller, Schopenhauer, Smith, Spinoza, Thoreau, Tocqueville, Veblen, Voltaire, Weber, Wittgenstein, and Wollstonecraft.

All volumes are available as a printed book on Lulu and as a PDF on the publisher's website.

Capital (Volume 1)

AUTHOR	Karl Marx
FORMAT	15.2 × 22.9 cm
MATERIALITIES	black-and-white, paperback, perfect bound, defective copy
PAGES	647
IMAGE	

DESCRIPTION

The series' first volume contains Karl Marx's *Capital*, in the translation of Samuel Moore and Edward Aveling (1887), and subjects this text to the edition process described, preserving only the punctuation.

Michael Maranda's name is not mentioned anywhere. The front matter merely points out that the series "consists of critical editions of influential texts from political theory, philosophy, and history." On Lulu, the publisher's introduction includes the warning: "Please preview books before purchasing. They may not be what you are looking for." Since the last relaunch of the Lulu website in 2020, the preview is no longer available.

The copy that entered our collection has production defects: half of the printed area of the cover was mistakenly cut off and the book block is bound the wrong way around. After we complained to the company suggesting a reprint as a replacement, a customer service representative concernedly asked: "I also wanted to ask—does the content of this book appear as you expected (besides being upside down)? It only seems to be pages of punctuation. If this is incorrect, reprinting it will only reproduce the issue."

Karl Marx – Capital, Volume 1
2
3
Karl Marx – Capital, Volume 1

THE PHOTOBOOK PROJECT at LULU.COM

Brief Led Project AME 3-BLP

AUTHOR	paula roush
YEAR	2007
GENRE	education / classroom, nonfiction
METHOD	composition (writing / drawing / photography)
SUBJECT	book / book design, photography, print on demand
PLATFORM	Lulu
EDITION CHARACTERISTICS	open edition
FORMAT	21.0 × 29.7 cm
MATERIALITIES	black-and-white, paperback, saddle stitch bound
PAGES	16
IMAGE	

DESCRIPTION

paula roush was a pioneer in the use of print-on-demand in the classroom. Back in 2007, she offered a seminar at London South Bank University entitled "THE PHOTOBOOK PROJECT at LULU.COM," which "takes place within the self-publishing environment provided by lulu.com, and considers if this online print on demand network can be used for educational photo publishing projects, whilst researching its advantages and limitations in relation to other publishing models" (paula roush, "Introduction"). In her opinion, possibly the greatest impact of print-on-demand was the extension of the classroom into the publishing market. Thus, as indicated by the syllabus, students were required to produce an individual photobook and participate in a networked, collective photo magazine.

Given the centrality of internet activity to self-publishing projects, they were also required to use and design the seminar's and their own profile pages on the Lulu website as "storefronts" and explore and use the Lulu community social network—a feature the platform discontinued a few years later—to support their photo publishing practice with posts in the seminar's blog and their own Lulu blog as well as reviews, feedback, and social bookmarking.

This book should ideally be placed next to Jonathan Monk's Cover Version.

AUTHOR	Hermann Zschiegner
YEAR	2007
GENRE	artist's book / bookwork
METHOD	collection, montage / remix, reenactment
SUBJECT	art world / literary world, book / book design, canon
PLATFORM	Lulu
EDITION CHARACTERISTICS	open edition
FORMAT	18.9 × 24.6 cm
MATERIALITIES	black-and-white, paperback, perfect bound
PAGES	78

IMAGES

DESCRIPTION

This book should ideally be placed next to Jonathan Monk's Cover Version consists of thirty-one sentences on single pages similar to the title but with varying prepositions and artist's books. By this, the book not only provides an arguably homogeneous canon of seminal artists and artist's books but also maps them on a virtual shelf, following Aby Warburg's "law of good neighborliness." Hermann Zschiegner's book becomes the index and focal point of this shelf, unfolding and loading it page by page. The book object itself functions as an idiosyncratic origin in a three-dimensional Cartesian coordinate system, arguably identical with Zschiegner's own shelf, as seen in a photograph on his website.

The book makes reference to three artworks by Jonathan Monk. The first is his bookwork *Cover Version*, which is a "selection of seminal publications from his extensive collection of artists' books," represented by photos of each cover (Hermann Zschiegner, "This Book Should"). The second is Monk's series of paintings *This painting should ideally be hung...*, of which Zschiegner appropriated the general sentence structure. Finally, the third, rather hidden reference is Monk's publication *& MILK. Today is just a copy of yesterday* (itself a reminiscence of Ed Ruscha's artist's book *Various Small Fires and Milk*), that progressively copies a picture of a glass of milk until the copy process itself produces unanticipated patterns and alterations. The last sentence in Zschiegner's book, coming after nine blank pages that are nevertheless numbered, reads "This book should be nowhere near a glass of milk."

ZSCHIEGNER'S RELATIONAL CANON INCLUDES

Cover Version by Jonathan Monk; *Royal Road Test* by Ed Ruscha; *Nine Swimming Pools and a Broken Glass* by Ed Ruscha; *Landscapes of the Brain* by Giuseppe Penone; *Picturing Ed* by Jerry McMillan; *Burning Small Fires* by Bruce Nauman; *Four Events And Reactions* by John Baldessari; *Timeline* by Douglas Gordon; *L'arte e lo spazio* by Giulio Paolini; *Statements* by Lawrence Weiner; *Six Geometric Figures and All Their Double Combinations* by Sol LeWitt; *Ten Isometric Drawings for Ten Vertical Constructions* by Fred Sandback; *23 Pieces* by Allen Ruppersberg; *I Mille Fiumi Piu Lunghi Del Mondo* by Alighiero E Boetti; *January 5-31, 1969* by Seth Siegelaub; *Secrets: Variable Piece 4* by Douglas Huebler; *The Book of Shrigley* by David Shrigley; *The Book of the 3rd of June* by Liam Gillick; *A Walk Past Standing Stones* by Richard Long; *Twentysix Abandoned Gasoline Stations* by Jeffrey Brouws; *Belmont 1967* by Robert Barry; *Oh, the grand old Duke of York* by Gilbert & George; *The Collected Writings* by Robert Smithson; *Sans-Souci* by Christian Boltanski; *Cuttings* by Simon Starling; *Splitting* by Gordon Matta-Clark; *Notebook on Water* by Joseph Kosuth; *Hotel – Hotel* by Martin Kippenberger; *Cuts* by Carl Andre; *I Am Still Alive* by On Kawara.

Dear Lulu

Please try and print these line, colour, pattern, format, texture and typography tests for us.

AUTHORS	James Goggin, Frank Philippin, Students of the Faculty of Design at the University of Applied Sciences Darmstadt
YEAR	2008
GENRE	artistic research, education / classroom
METHOD	study / analysis, test / experiment, versioning / seriality
SUBJECT	book / book design, ecology / sustainability, error / corruption / loss, platforms / companies, print technology, print on demand
PLATFORM	Blurb, BoD, Kolofon, Lulu, MagCloud
EDITION CHARACTERISTICS	open edition
MATERIALITIES	color, paperback, perfect bound

IMAGES

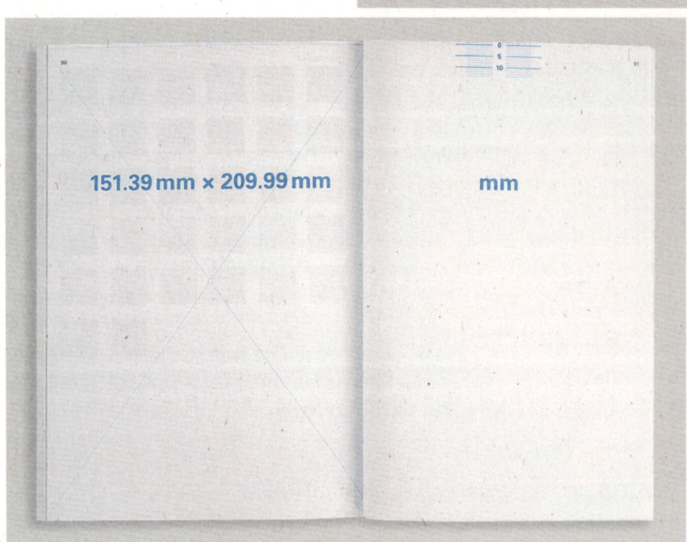

DESCRIPTION

"*Dear Lulu* is a test book which was researched and produced by graphic design students at Hochschule Darmstadt, Germany, during an intensive two-day workshop with London-based designer James Goggin (Practise). The book's intention is to act as a calibration document for testing colour, pattern, format, texture and typography. Exercises in colour profile, halftoning, point size, line, geometry, skin tone, colour texture, cropping and print finishing provide useful data for other designers and self-publishers to judge the possibilities and quality of online print-on-demand—specifically Lulu.com, with this edition" (blurb on Lulu).

Because the book is also offered by other print-on-demand providers, such as the US Blurb and MagCloud, the Norwegian Kolofon (now defunct), and the German BoD, "a print-on-demand-battle" might even be initiated (James Goggin, "Farben on Demand," 40). The title of each of the test publications is adapted as necessary, for example to *Dear MagCloud* or *Dear Blurb*. A free PDF is available on MagCloud.

Since every print job takes place at a different time, with a different machine, and potentially at a different production site, in the end every copy is unique and can only stand for itself. It is not possible to generalize the test results. Neither can the print-on-demand provider guarantee a certain product quality.

The students were also interested in the sustainability of production, i.e., whether the copies are produced locally. For this, one copy was ordered in London and another in Darmstadt. However, both were printed in Spain.

In 2009, the project received a Gold Cube from the Art Directors Club in New York, in the category "Book Design: Public Service / Non-Profit Book."

Dear Lulu,

PLATFORM	Lulu
EDITION CHARACTERISTICS	open edition
FORMAT	14.8 x 21.0 cm
PAGES	96

Dear Blurb,

PLATFORM	Blurb
EDITION CHARACTERISTICS	open edition
FORMAT	19.5 × 24.6 cm
PAGES	96
DESCRIPTION	What is striking is *Dear Blurb*'s larger format compared to the other versions, which is probably due to the limited choice of standard formats at Blurb.

Dear MagCloud,

PLATFORM	MagCloud
EDITION CHARACTERISTICS	multiple editions (print, PDF), open edition
FORMAT	13.3 × 21.0 cm
PAGES	98

Dear BoD,

PLATFORM	BoD
EDITION CHARACTERISTICS	no longer available
DESCRIPTION	Since you had to pay an annual fee to BoD back then, *Dear BoD* has not been available for a long time. Therefore, only very few copies exist.

Dear Kolofon,

PLATFORM	Kolofon
EDITION CHARACTERISTICS	no longer available
DESCRIPTION	*Dear Kolofon* has not been available for a long time. Therefore, only very few copies exist.

In Real Life

AUTHOR	Christoph Kamper
YEAR	2008
GENRE	education / classroom, photobook
METHOD	composition (writing / drawing / photography), study / analysis
SUBJECT	analog / digital, internet culture, photography
PLATFORM	Blurb
EDITION CHARACTERISTICS	second edition, open edition, CC BY-NC-SA
FORMAT	21.5 × 17.6 cm
MATERIALITIES	color, paperback, perfect bound
PAGES	82 (unpaginated)

IMAGES

DESCRIPTION

Following the question "How does somebody who spends 24/7 on the net look like?," Christopher Kamper contacted three individuals he had only been in touch with online to meet them in real life and document their hobbies with photos. He visited a LARPer (someone practicing live action role-playing), an Otaku, and a Lolita (both Japanese subcultures). All three of these hobbies, even when practiced in real life, tend to stay more or less inside the rooms of their practitioners, yet are fueled by online communication on special message boards. The pictures showing the three adolescents document their alternate personas but also the topography of their rooms as their own little world. In these kids' rooms, the computer becomes a key element for living out individuality and contact with peers.

In Real Life was conceived for paula roush's 2008 class "Photographic Cultures. harnessing the power of self-publishing technologies for the creation and distribution of photobooks" at London South Bank University (see 139). Given the centrality of internet activity to self-publishing projects, roush put heavy emphasis on students using and designing the seminar's and their own profile pages on the Lulu website as "storefronts" and exploring and using the Lulu community network to support their photo publishing practice with posts in the seminar's blog, their own Lulu blog, reviews, feedback, and social bookmarking. As a result, *In Real Life* is one of the few books in our collection that received a review on Lulu.

Photographic Cultures AME-2-PHC FALL 08

harnessing the power of self-publishing technologies for the creation and distribution of photobooks

AUTHOR	paula roush
YEAR	2008
GENRE	education / classroom, nonfiction
METHOD	composition (writing / drawing / photography)
SUBJECT	book / book design, photography, print on demand
PLATFORM	Lulu
EDITION CHARACTERISTICS	open edition
FORMAT	21.0 × 29.7 cm
MATERIALITIES	black-and-white, paperback, saddle stitch bound
PAGES	20

IMAGES

1. INTRODUCTION TO THE UNIT

This unit is designed to introduce you to a set of photographic cultures identified as self-publishing, amongst which the photobook occupies a central stage. The photobook has been developing since the conception of photography, and has been strongly associated with the artist's book. It is characterised by an "authorial" attitude and an independent mode of production and distribution. It has been described as "an event" in itself or as something "between a film and a novel", as a result of its strong visual structure. And as printing technologies develop towards a networked model, photobook makers also adapt their practices to make use of the advantages offered by print on demand (pod) publishing models. In this unit, you will be encouraged to examine the concepts of artist's book and photobook and its relation to printing technologies, through theoretical texts, case studies and presentations. You will also produce a photobook and make it available on a print on demand platform

2. AIMS OF THE UNIT

The unit aims to:
- Provide a descriptive framework for understanding the technological characteristics and creative possibilities of new media
- Examine the ways in which the digital photograph is used and consumed
- Encourage you to explore the many contexts for the production and reception of the digital image
- Encourage you to consider the ways in which the digital image is received, consumed and understood
- Give you a further opportunity to produce digital work of a professional standing

In addition you will
- *Develop an understanding of the self-publishing culture*
- *Learn about the genre of photobook as a publishing model practiced by artists /photographers throughout history and as a contemporary format*
- *Develop skills related to the structure of the visual book, learning how to work with concepts such as group, series and sequence to develop a photobook*
- *Use a pod platform (like lulu.com) to publish electronically and create an online store for your photobooks*
- *Practice using social media like blogs and social network sites [sns] as artistic and networking publishing models*

3. LEARNING OUTCOMES

Knowledge and Understanding
By the end of this unit you should be able to further understand contemporary digital photographic culture
- *You will become familiar with self-publishing practices as cultural production model central to the social media paradigm (also known as web 2.0)*

Intellectual Skills
By the end of this unit you should be able to demonstrate through practice an understanding of how digital photography is used and consumed

4

- *You will be able to demonstrate an understanding of the relationship between photography publishing and the genre of photobook*

Practical Skills
By the end of this unit you should be able to produce digital work for a specific context:
- *You will be able to edit photographic and textual material for a photobook, as evidenced by your skills in working with the structure of the visual book*

Transferable Skills
By the end of this unit you should be able to produce digital work of a professional standing
- *You will have gained skills in the use of cs3 prepress, including using inDesign to create photo publications and pod services to print and distribute them*

4. ASSESSMENT OF THE UNIT

Practical project work (50%): the photobook
Production analysis (25%): e-tivities 2 and 4
Critical reflexion (25%): e-tivities 1 and 3

The unit encourages active participation so your involvement is essential.
It is important that you:
- come to every session and prepare yourself by reading the recommended texts
- contribute to the online network and complete the e-tivities
- complete your book dummy (your book proposal) and share it in class and online
- finish your photobook, make it available as a PDF and get it printed and delivered.

4.1 Practical Project Work (50%): photobook [deadine:week10]

You will produce a photobook from the photographic and textual material collected for photographic index (youth culture project), design it using Adobe CS3, create a storefront and publish as both pdf and pod at lulu.com.

Things to be aware of:
- your photographic material needs to be structured with a critical awareness of visual structure of the photobook
- you need to include the text you wrote as your artist's statement for the youth cultures project, either as introduction or as a central text
- you also need to include the colophon, see colophon handout which lists all information considered essential, available in blackboard/phc08/week02

Assessment Criteria:
When marking your work we will be looking for:
• Concept- a clear and consistent concept unifying the photobook
• Visual structure- the use of one or more visual strategies to group, serialise and/or sequence the images
• Design and layout- rigorous editing and design, with no textual, typographical or image errors

• DUE WEEK 10 TUESDAY 25TH NOVEMBER
• UPLOAD TO YOUR STOREFRONT & ORDER BOOK PRINT BY 5 PM. SUBMIT RECEIPT OF LULU ONLINE PURCHASING ORDER BY EMAIL TO PAULA.

5

DESCRIPTION

This is the syllabus for another seminar held in 2008 by paula roush, who can be considered a forerunner in combining print-on-demand with teaching and still regularly offers seminars on self-publishing photobooks. In this seminar, "Photographic Cultures," the task was to produce a photobook on youth culture(s). This was supplemented by several "e-tivities" to strengthen competence in critical thinking, analyzing, and reviewing photobooks. The announcement read:

"This unit is designed to introduce you to a set of photographic cultures identified as self-publishing, amongst which the photobook occupies a central stage. The photobook has been developing since the conception of photography, and has been strongly associated with the artist's book. It is characterised by an 'authorial' attitude and an independent mode of production and distribution. [...] In this unit, you will be encouraged to examine the concepts of artist's book and photobook and its relation to printing technologies, through theoretical texts, case studies and presentations" (paula roush, "Introduction," 4).

One result of this course is Christopher Kamper's photobook *In Real Life* (see 138).

Other People's Photographs

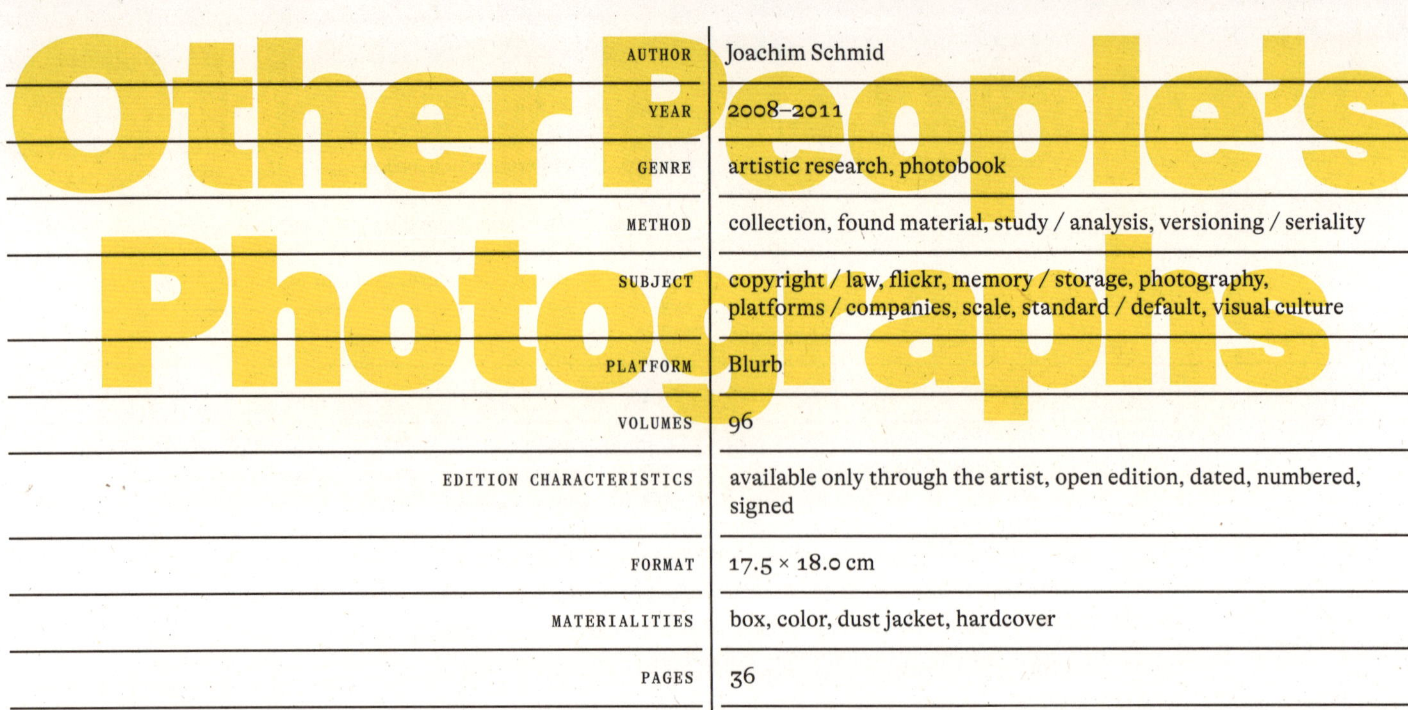

AUTHOR	Joachim Schmid
YEAR	2008–2011
GENRE	artistic research, photobook
METHOD	collection, found material, study / analysis, versioning / seriality
SUBJECT	copyright / law, flickr, memory / storage, photography, platforms / companies, scale, standard / default, visual culture
PLATFORM	Blurb
VOLUMES	96
EDITION CHARACTERISTICS	available only through the artist, open edition, dated, numbered, signed
FORMAT	17.5 × 18.0 cm
MATERIALITIES	box, color, dust jacket, hardcover
PAGES	36

DESCRIPTION

"Assembled between 2008 and 2011, this series of ninety-six books explores the themes and visual patterns presented by modern everyday, amateur photographers. Images found on photo sharing sites such as Flickr have been gathered and ordered in a way to form a library of contemporary vernacular photography in the age of digital technology and online photo hosting. Each book is comprised of [32] images that focus on a specific photographic event or idea, the grouping of photographs revealing recurring patterns in modern popular photography. The approach is encyclopedic, and the number of volumes is virtually endless but arbitrarily limited. The selection of themes is neither systematic nor does it follow any established criteria—the project's structure mirrors the multifaceted, contradictory and chaotic practice of modern photography itself, based exclusively on the motto 'You can observe a lot by watching'" (Joachim Schmid, "Other People's Photographs," website).

Some of the chosen categories' titles "are rather obvious, some of them surprising, some rather general and all-encompassing, some very specific, thus creating a taxonomy and subverting the system of categorization at the same time" (Joachim Schmid, "Attitudes and Approaches," interview). Some motifs, such as the photographer's *Shadow*, *Mugshots*, or *Faces in Holes*, are familiar; others, such as the *Self*(ie) with an outstretched arm, concrete poetry on *Fridge Doors*, *Airline Meals*, and camera packaging (apparently the most popular motif for *First Shots*) reveal new image genres; others still, such as *Parking Lots*, are certainly inspired in their grouping by the tradition of Ed Ruscha, for example.

Since this project represents a kind of artistic research on generic image types, Schmid prefers to speak of "textbooks" or "image books" ("Bilderbücher") rather than "photobooks." It is not only a captivating panorama of popular visual culture, but also a unique historical documentation: each book is dated to the exact month in which the image material was collected, because Schmid was aware from the beginning that there are patterns that may be extremely popular temporarily, but then disappear again.

For the design of the books, which in the early years of Blurb always had to be done via the in-house software (simply uploading a ready-made PDF was not possible), Schmid chose to follow the standard solutions proposed by the platform and its software, in order to find out what the generic pattern was here, too. Therefore, with this series, you have the typical Blurb book of those years in your hand: a square hardcover with a dust jacket, and it becomes abundantly clear that the technology and the platform were not invented for artists but for wedding albums, baby books, travel journals, and the like.

As the project has evolved over the years, this series also manifests the countless changes in print-on-demand production: over time, both the paper and the color tone of the gray dust jackets changed several times, at some point Blurb began to print production barcodes on the back, and so on. In order to maintain consistency, the series can now only be purchased as a complete boxed set, numbered and signed, directly from the artist. He also adds the date of production for new orders so that the changes can be historically documented. In addition, the production quality is also often a source of trouble. While the artist stopped production with Blurb for most of his other books due to increasing annoyances and switched to Lulu, he is forced to continue relying on Blurb for this series.

A two-volume paperback print-on-demand edition including all 3,072 photographs (18 x 18 cm, two volumes, 400 pages each) is available for budget collectors. The fact that exactly ninety-six chapters with thirty-two photos each fit into this two-volume version decided on the total number of individual volumes in the series. The project has received a lot of attention and is listed in Gerry Badger and Martin Parr's seminal *The Photobook: A History* (volume three).

The project's home page presents all ninety-six volumes with photographs of each cover, one sample spread, and the first spread of every chapter of the paperback edition. It also includes the following copyright notice: "All of the photographs used in this work as documentary material are merely integrating parts of a larger artwork. They do not constitute reprints or duplications in breach of the fee provisions of copyright law."

THE SERIES INCLUDES THESE TITLES

Airline Meals · Airports · Another Self · Apparel · At Work · Bags · Big Fish · Bird's Eyes · Black Bulls · Blue · Bread · Buddies · Cash · Cheques · Cleavage · Coffee · Collections · Colour · Commodities · Contents · Currywurst · Damage · Digits · Documents · Dogs · Drinks · Encounters · Evidence · Eyes · Faces in Holes · Fauna · Feet · First Shots · Fish · Flashing · Food · Fridge Doors · Gathered Together · Gender · Geology · Hands · Happy Birthday · Hotel Rooms · Images · Impact · In Motion · Indexes · Information · Interaction · Kisses for Me · Lego · Looking · Maps · Mickey · Models · More Things · Mugshots · News · Nothing Wrong · November 5th, 2008 · Objects in Mirror · On the Road · Parking Lots · Pictures · Pizza · Plush · Portraits · Postcards · Purple · Pyramids · Real Estate · Red · Room with a View · Self · Sex · Shadow · Shirts · Shoes · Silvercup · Sites · Size Matters · Space-Time · Statues · Sunset · Surface · Targets · Television · The Other Picture · The Picture · Things · Trophies · Tropic of Capricorn · Various Accidents · Wanted · Writings · You Are Here.

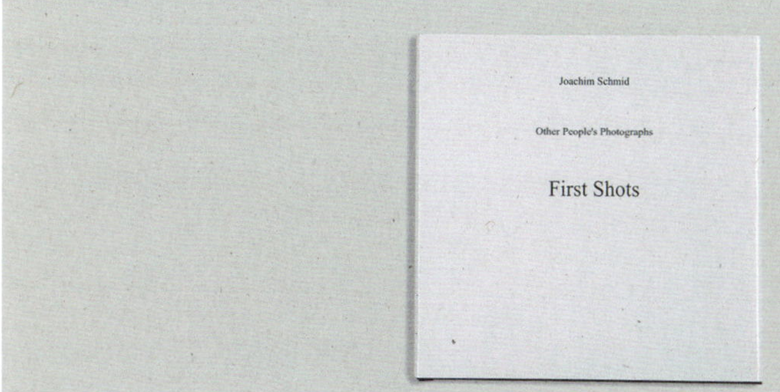
Joachim Schmid
Other People's Photographs
First Shots

FUJIFILM
FinePix F50fd

PowerShot A700

The Showbag Book

AUTHOR	Joachim Schmid
YEAR	2008 [ongoing]
GENRE	photobook
METHOD	collection, found material, versioning / seriality
SUBJECT	photography, print on demand, visual culture
PLATFORM	Blurb
VOLUMES	so far 28 unique copies
EDITION CHARACTERISTICS	available only through the artist, open edition, dated, numbered, signed, unique copies
FORMAT	17.0 × 18.0 cm
MATERIALITIES	color, dust jacket, hardcover
PAGES	40

IMAGES

DESCRIPTION

For this book, Joachim Schmid draws on the abundance of images on the Internet. This time, the challenge is probably to compile an "image book" ("Bilderbuch") without a theme from the infinite pool—and to do so again and again, because these are, in the truest sense of the word, custom-made one-offs: The number, selection and combination of the photos differ from copy to copy depending on the ordering customer, who can determine the number of pages—within the range of 24 to 240 pages specified by the platform. Apart from that, there is no other possibility of influence. So the customer actually buys a "show bag" to be surprised by its contents. The price of each copy, which Schmid numbers and signs, is determined by the respective production plus shipping costs. The industrial print-on-demand model is thus joined here by an artistic produced-on-demand concept.

Our copy was commissioned in September 2021, as is noted on the title page. Since it had production errors, it had to be produced again following a complaint from the artist. Strictly speaking, therefore, this is not the 28th, as stated, but the 29th copy in this series of unique copies.

A Message for Obama

a selection of messages to the president-elect from guardian.co.uk and Flickr users

AUTHOR	The Guardian [ed.]
YEAR	2008
GENRE	catalog / collection, photobook
METHOD	collection, collective, documentation / archiving
SUBJECT	crowd / collaboration, flickr, politics / activism, print on demand, publishing / distribution
PLATFORM	Blurb
EDITION CHARACTERISTICS	ISBN 9750852651308, open edition
FORMAT	18.0 × 18.0 cm
MATERIALITIES	color, dust jacket, hardcover
PAGES	120

IMAGES

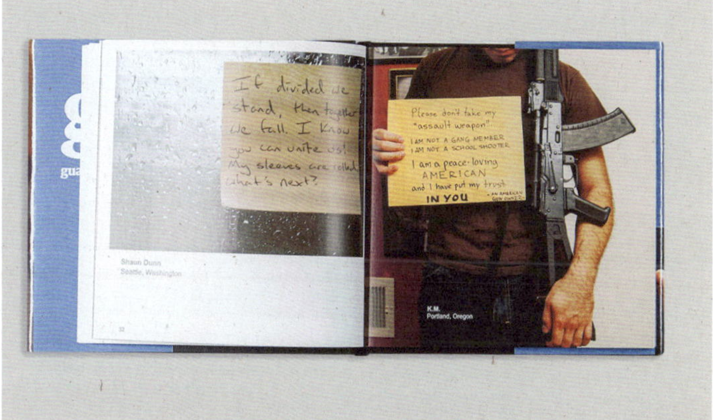

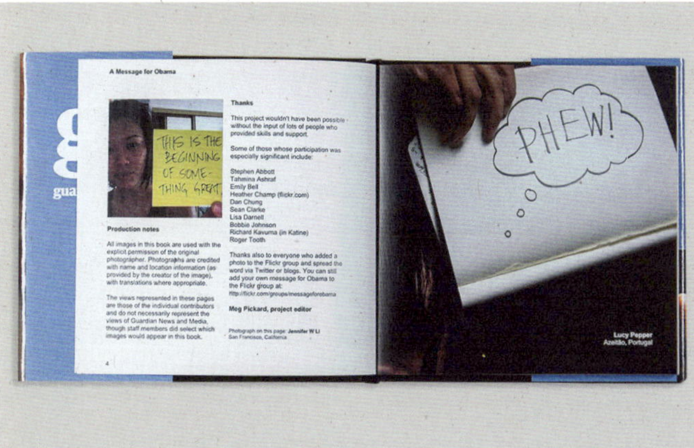

DESCRIPTION

A Message for Obama is a publication initiated by newspaper *The Guardian* which asked internet users to share their personal messages to Barack Obama in anticipation of his 2013 inauguration. It is one of the few examples where Blurb actively cooperated with a project for marketing reasons. The call was initiated by *The Guardian* as a Flickr group, with users invited to share photographs of messages to the soon to become president of the United States. The pictures for the most part show messages written on paper, often also depicting the participants themselves holding up the sheet or otherwise staging the messages.

The Guardian then picked a selection of photos from this pool to put the book together, which was done in cooperation with Blurb, using one of their layout templates. This is mentioned explicitly in an editorial note at the beginning of the book, promoting a workflow that might have been unknown to buyers and making it a perfect case of using the platform's print-on-demand publishing service. Initiated by a media outlet with a huge, already existing reach and relying on the input of also already existing online communities, *A Message for Obama* is a case in point of a seemingly participative internet culture that just mirrors the exploitative culture of pre-internet and off-line media. People participate because they want to be part of a project; they will then buy it because they want to see themselves printed—producership, consumerism, and buyership merging into one publishing model with mainly the platform and the initiator profiting from it. This is further enhanced by offering the publication in three different qualities to also address participants with only a slight interest in owning a published version of their photo.

AUTHOR	Hermann Zschiegner
YEAR	2008
GENRE	photobook
METHOD	found material, remediation
SUBJECT	analog / digital, authorship, copyright / law, error / corruption / loss, google, photography, search engine
PLATFORM	Blurb
EDITION CHARACTERISTICS	open edition
FORMAT	19.5 × 24.6 cm
MATERIALITIES	color, paperback, perfect bound
PAGES	60 (unpaginated)

IMAGES

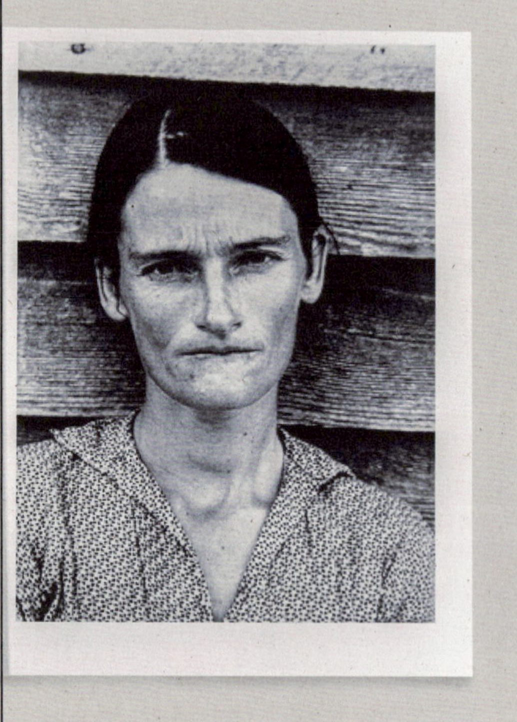

DESCRIPTION

In 1981, Sherrie Levine appropriated famous photographs by Walker Evans by photographing them from a catalog, referencing the progressing musealization of documentary photography and questioning the concepts of authorship, creativity, and originality. The photographs Levine took were almost indistinguishable from those Evans had taken fifty years earlier.

With *+walker evans +sherrie levine* Hermann Zschiegner takes this reflection on appropriation, remediation, and authorship to the digital age by showing that circulating "poor images" (Hito Steyerl, "In Defense of the Poor Image") further obfuscate the material and the ontological differences between Evans' and Levine's photos, but at the same time metadata such as file names and URLs help identify their origin.

The title of Zschiegner's book contains the search parameter of his Google image search conducted on July 24, 2008, which resulted in twenty-six found images of Evans' most famous photograph, depicting Allie Mae Burroughs. These twenty-six images are sorted in descending order by file size and "positioned to match the original print with any white space around the image representing the cropped area of the reproduced picture. File size, pixel aspect ratio and URL of all images are included as a frame of reference. It is only in reading the file names that we can identify if the reproduced image is a Levine or an Evans" (Hermann Zschiegner, "+walker evans +sherrie levine").

All Work and No Play Makes Jack a Dull Boy

AUTHOR	Jack Torrance [Phil Buehler]
YEAR	2009
GENRE	artist's book / bookwork, experimental literature, poetry
METHOD	composition (writing / drawing / photography), paratextual play, remediation
SUBJECT	authorship, book / book design, film, literature, reading / interpretation, writing / reading techniques
PLATFORM	Blurb
EDITION CHARACTERISTICS	multiple covers and editions (paperback, hardcover, dust jacket), open edition
FORMAT	12.6 × 20.3 cm
MATERIALITIES	black-and-white, paperback, perfect bound
PAGES	80 (unpaginated)

IMAGES

DESCRIPTION

All Work and No Play Makes Jack a Dull Boy publishes the manuscript of the fictional character Jack Torrance from *The Shining*. Referencing Stephen King's novel but mostly Stanley Kubrick's film adaptation, Buehler copies the pages seen in the movie when Torrance's wife Wendy first encounters her husband's manuscript pages. Discovering that he has been writing the same sentence over and over for hundreds of pages in different graphical constellations while pretending to be working on his novel, the manuscript functions as a testimony of his madness. Buehler's published version of the manuscript adds several new word constellations, turning it into a collection of concrete typewriter poetry "getting progressively crazier" (blurb on Blurb).

By constructing an editorship through Phil Buehler and attributing authorship to the fictional novel character, *All Work and No Play Makes Jack a Dull Boy* becomes a metafictional play that not only transgresses the line between fiction and reality but also imagines a survival of the manuscript after the untimely death of its author at the Overlook Hotel, as described in the film. The back cover shows an ironic review of the novel Jack Torrance writes in *The Shining*, published by Matthew Belinkie on the popular culture blog Overthinking.it in 2008.

Available with three different covers and in three different qualities.

Is it a game, or is it for real?

AUTHOR	Paul Laidler
YEAR	2009
GENRE	artist's book / bookwork
METHOD	appropriation, photocopy / scan
SUBJECT	error / corruption / loss, film, games, literature, materiality, reading / interpretation, typography
PLATFORM	Blurb
EDITION CHARACTERISTICS	open edition
FORMAT	12.6 × 20.3 cm
MATERIALITIES	black-and-white, paperback, perfect bound
PAGES	220 (unpaginated)
IMAGES	

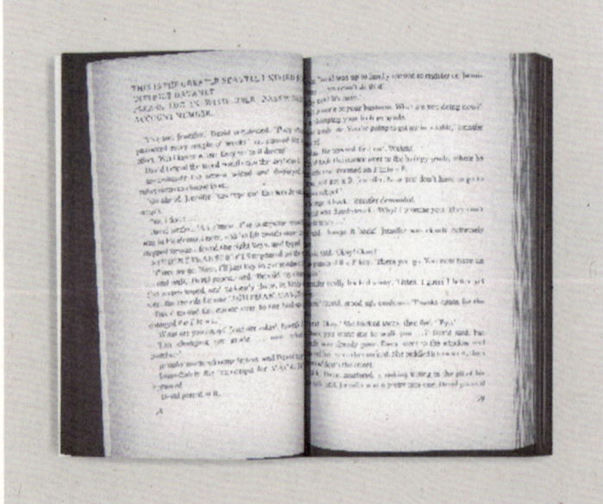

DESCRIPTION

Paul Laidler's *Is it a game, or is it for real?* is an appropriation of the 1983 Penguin Books paperback version of David Bischoff's *Wargames*, which is the novel to the successful movie of the same name and same year, directed by John Badham. Drawing on this edition with a film still as the cover, Laidler explores "docking" with a successful film as a typical promotional tool used by publishers to increase sales.

In the movie, a teenage hacker, while trying to play new video games, gains access to a military computer system and plays a simulation of a thermonuclear war between the USA and USSR against a computer with artificial intelligence. Realizing that his interaction with the computer is in fact not a game but has real consequences with human lives at stake, he eventually finds a way to teach the computer that there is no winner in a thermonuclear war. This realization is marked by the main character with the line "Is it a game, or is it real?" hence Laidler's book title (which adds the word "for").

In his artist's book, the tension between game and reality is mirrored in a collision between original and appropriated, digital and analog. Laidler's reproduction is complete in the sense that all pages of the printed original are reproduced in the same order. However, they are poor quality scans that show black borders around the pages and are heavily pixelated, making the text indecipherable. This might be read as an homage to the pixelated aesthetics of 1980s computer graphics depicted in the movie. But it also refers to the process of retro-digitization by scanning at resolutions that were "purposely set below the standard amount of pixel information required for reading digital images on screen (72ppi) and in print (300ppi)" (Paul Laidler, "Digitally Remastered!"). It was impossible to enforce this artistic strategy against the automatic data processing on Blurb, which did not accept the print file in this form—it needed the help of the human-staffed online help desk.

Readers of the electronic version will probably initially mistake the pixelated appearance on their screen for a display error. Readers of the print edition who purchased the book directly from Laidler, on the other hand, will be assured by his signature that everything is in order. Thus, his book is ultimately "not in the strictest sense a direct appropriation of a previously existing object. The work is an appropriation of an object's function that is conceived and realised in conjunction with the object's associated on screen presence" (Paul Laidler, "Digitally Remastered!"). This slight deviation is also reflected in the title of Laidler's project, which deviates by one word from the film quote on which it is based, while nevertheless retaining its original meaning.

The Missing Pictures

AUTHOR	Joachim Schmid
YEAR	2009 [2nd ed. 2012]
GENRE	photobook
METHOD	appropriation, found material
SUBJECT	censorship / ban, copyright / law, flickr, photography, publishing / distribution, visual culture
PLATFORM	Blurb, Lulu
EDITION CHARACTERISTICS	available only through the artist, second edition, open edition
FORMAT	10.3 × 17.2 cm
MATERIALITIES	black-and-white, paperback, perfect bound
PAGES	40 (unpaginated)

IMAGES

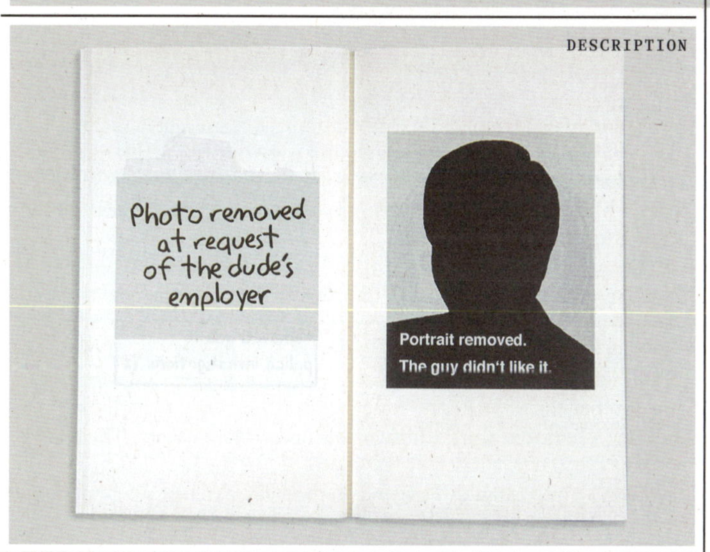

DESCRIPTION

In analog times, Joachim Schmid relied on photographic material that he found on the street, through advertisements or at flea markets. In the digital age, he finds the material for his publications primarily on the internet, on photo-sharing platforms such as Flickr. Some of these photos were presented on his website along with his publications in which they appear. After receiving several complaints about this, Schmid was forced to replace some of the photos with placeholders. This was the starting point for *The Missing Pictures*, which collects quite a few such placeholders that Schmid found—just like the replaced photos—on the internet. Among them are delightful finds such as: "This photo has been removed due to an ego violation," or "Portrait removed. The guy didn't like it." But as a placeholder with the Wikipedia abbreviation "WP:NFCC" (non-free content criteria) shows, there can of course be weighty reasons from serious institutions.

As with many of his publications from the 2010s, Schmid discontinued his collaboration with Blurb in this case too, due to countless annoyances. He switched to Lulu in 2012, which resulted in a change in paper and format from 12.6 × 20.3 cm to 10.4 × 17.3 cm.

Blind Carbon Copy

AUTHOR	Stéphanie Vilayphiou
YEAR	2009
GENRE	education / classroom, experimental literature
METHOD	appropriation, détournement / hack, generative / automation, versioning / seriality
SUBJECT	censorship / ban, code / programming, copyright / law, literature, reading / interpretation
PLATFORM	Lulu
VOLUMES	9
EDITION CHARACTERISTICS	open edition, ISBN, censored, no longer available, no copyright / copyleft / public domain
FORMAT	10.8 × 17.5 cm
MATERIALITIES	black-and-white, paperback, perfect bound

IMAGE

DESCRIPTION

Stéphanie Vilayphiou's nine-part series *Blind Carbon Copy* "consists of experimental design hacks to reflect and circumvent intellectual property restrictions. *Fahrenheit 451*, a novel by Ray Bradbury, is presented via a web interface and also in print form (print on demand). Several filters offered to users are in place in order to reflect intellectual property restrictions or allowed practices, such as Fair Use. These filters offer a means to circumvent these restrictions by transforming the content. The reader can choose the filter through which s/he wants to 'view' the text, each filter being more or less legal" (Stéphanie Vilayphiou, "About"). The nine filters are divided into three categories:

- Circumvention,
- Conformance,
- Parody.

At the end of each book is an explanation of the project, a rationale for the selection of Bradbury's novel, and a definition of the filter used. The paratexts (title and author name) of each book are also subjected to this filter. The copyright disclaimer on the project website reads "All wrongs reversed."

While Vilayphiou calls her project "an art and design piece making Fair Use of copyrighted works in order to question the copyright system" (Stéphanie Vilayphiou, "Copyright Disclaimer"), Lulu and Amazon have blocked and deleted seven out of the nine books of the series due to alleged copyright violations—without anyone taking legal action and without the existence of any court decision. Only the "Normal" and the "L33T" editions were still available (as of March 2022). The book series was created as part of a Master project for the Piet Zwart Institute. The ISBNs given can only be found on the artist's website, but not on the books themselves (see Vilayphiou, "BCC: Blind Carbon Copy").

Ray Bradbury: Fahrenheit 451 ["Normal" filter]

EDITION CHARACTERISTICS — ISBN 9780557076727, open edition

PAGES — 152

FILTER CATEGORY — conformance

DESCRIPTION — "Displays the text according to its copyright. As *Fahrenheit 451*'s copyright belongs to Ray Bradbury (1953) and the cover photo copyright goes to Philippe Halsman (1966)" (Vilayphiou, "BCC: Blind Carbon Copy"), Vilayphiou's book shows only blank pages except for the column titles and pagination.

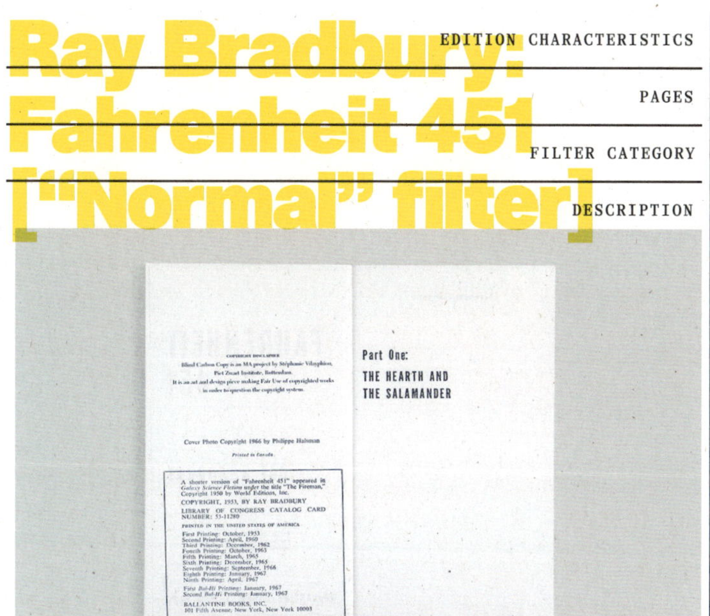
COPYRIGHT DISCLAIMER
Blind Carbon Copy is an MA project by Stéphanie Vilayphiou, Piet Zwart Institute, Rotterdam.
It is an art and design piece making Fair Use of copyrighted works in order to question the copyright system.

Cover Photo Copyright 1966 by Philippe Halsman

Printed in Canada

A shorter version of "Fahrenheit 451" appeared in *Galaxy Science Fiction* under the title "The Fireman," Copyright 1950 by World Editions, Inc.
COPYRIGHT, 1953, BY RAY BRADBURY
LIBRARY OF CONGRESS CATALOG CARD NUMBER: 53-11280
PRINTED IN THE UNITED STATES OF AMERICA
First Printing: October, 1953
Second Printing: April, 1960
Third Printing: December, 1962
Fourth Printing: October, 1963
Fifth Printing: March, 1965
Sixth Printing: December, 1965
Seventh Printing: September, 1966
Eighth Printing: January, 1967
Ninth Printing: April, 1967
First *Bal-Hi* Printing: January, 1967
Second *Bal-Hi* Printing: January, 1967
BALLANTINE BOOKS, INC.
101 Fifth Avenue, New York, New York 10003

Part One:
THE HEARTH AND
THE SALAMANDER

R4y Bra4dbury: F4hr3nh31t 451 ["L33T" filter]

EDITION CHARACTERISTICS — ISBN 9780557077038, open edition

PAGES — 164

FILTER CATEGORY — circumvention

DESCRIPTION — "Translates the text into leet or l33t alphabet, replacing letters of the regular latin alphabet by resembling ASCII characters. The text remains—somehow—readable, but its essence, its bits are completely different" (Vilayphiou, "BCC: Blind Carbon Copy").

SAMPLE — "1t w4s 4 sp3c14l pl34sur3 to s33 th1ngs 34t3n, to s33 th1ngs bl4ck3n3d 4nd ch4ng3d."

Pierre Ménard: Fahrenheit 451 ["PierreMenard" filter]

EDITION CHARACTERISTICS — ISBN 9780557077465, censored, no longer available

FILTER CATEGORY — circumvention

DESCRIPTION — "Based on novelist Jorge Luis Borges's essay 'Pierre Ménard, Author of the Quixote.' Borges invented this fictive author who re-wrote entirely word by word Don Quixote in the beginning of the 20th century. Borges states that Ménard's version was completely different from the one from Cervantes because the author is a different person, has a different background, environment, education and because it is written at a completely different time. Therefore this filter replaces the author's name by Pierre Ménard as if the text were re-written by this famous author" (Vilayphiou, "BCC: Blind Carbon Copy").

SAMPLE — "It was a special pleasure to see things eaten, to see things blackened and changed."

Ray Bradbury: Fahrenheit 451 ["Size" filter]

EDITION CHARACTERISTICS	ISBN 9780557076833, censored, no longer available
FILTER CATEGORY	Circumvention
DESCRIPTION	"Displays the text in an illegible way, whether with a tiny or a huge font size. Is it the reproduced content that matters or its accessibility? Is the tiny book as reprehensible as the one in Truffaut's *Fahrenheit 451* adaptation?" (Vilayphiou, "BCC: Blind Carbon Copy") On the project website you can find a sample text where the text is oversized. In the printed book, the text is extremely small.

Ray Bradbury[6]: Fahrenheit[7] 451[8] ["Plagiarism" filter]

EDITION CHARACTERISTICS	ISBN 9780557082377, censored, no longer available
FILTER CATEGORY	circumvention
DESCRIPTION	"Each sentence of the text comes from another website, therefore the text becomes a collection of quotations. The text is parsed into sentences which are linked to the first Google Books search result" by use of footnotes. The principle is already applied to the cover; the corresponding footnotes can be found on the back cover. "According to novelist Raymond Federman, in his essay *Imagination as Plagiarism*, no text is new, it's always a plagiarism" (Vilayphiou, "BCC: Blind Carbon Copy"). The project website contains a sample text in which the footnotes of the printed text are implemented as hyperlinks that lead directly to the quoted passages from books on Google Books.

Ray Bradbury: Fahrenheit 451 ["Black" filter]

EDITION CHARACTERISTICS	censored, no longer available
FILTER CATEGORY	circumvention
DESCRIPTION	"Makes the text unreadable, but its bits remain the same, but one can still access the text by copy/paste it or via the source code" (Vilayphiou, "BCC: Blind Carbon Copy"). Of course, this only applies to the website, not to the printed version.

Ray Bradbury: Fahrenheit 1 [“Percentage” filter]

EDITION CHARACTERISTICS	ISBN 9780557076390, censored, no longer available
FILTER CATEGORY	conformance
DESCRIPTION	“Similar to Google Books system, randomly displays one third of the total paragraphs of the text, reflecting American Fair Use, the right to quote a work. But the ratio one is allowed to reproduce cannot be quantified by the Law” (Vilayphiou, “BCC: Blind Carbon Copy”).

Ray Bradbury: Celsius 451 [“Thesaurus” filter]

EDITION CHARACTERISTICS	censored, no longer available
FILTER CATEGORY	Parody
DESCRIPTION	“Replaces the most rare word of each clause by its more frequent synonym” (Vilayphiou, “BCC: Blind Carbon Copy”).
SAMPLE	“It was a special pleasure to see things eat up, to see things melanize and changed.”

Ray Bradbury: Fahrenheit 451 [“Translation” filter]

EDITION CHARACTERISTICS	ISBN 9780557077649, censored, no longer available
FILTER CATEGORY	parody
DESCRIPTION	“Automatically translates the text first to a foreign language and then back to its original language. Here, from English to Dutch back to English” (Vilayphiou, “BCC: Blind Carbon Copy”).
SAMPLE	“It was a particular pleasure to see things eaten, to see things black and changed.”

Emoji Dick; Or the Whale

AUTHOR	Fred Benenson
YEAR	2010
GENRE	experimental literature
METHOD	outsourcing, translation / transcription
SUBJECT	amazon, crowd / collaboration, economy / labor, internet culture, mechanical turk
PLATFORM	Lulu
EDITION CHARACTERISTICS	multiple editions (color, black-and-white), ISBN 9780557663149, open edition, CC BY-SA, crowdfunded
FORMAT	15.2 × 22.9 cm
MATERIALITIES	black-and-white, paperback, perfect bound
PAGES	735

IMAGES

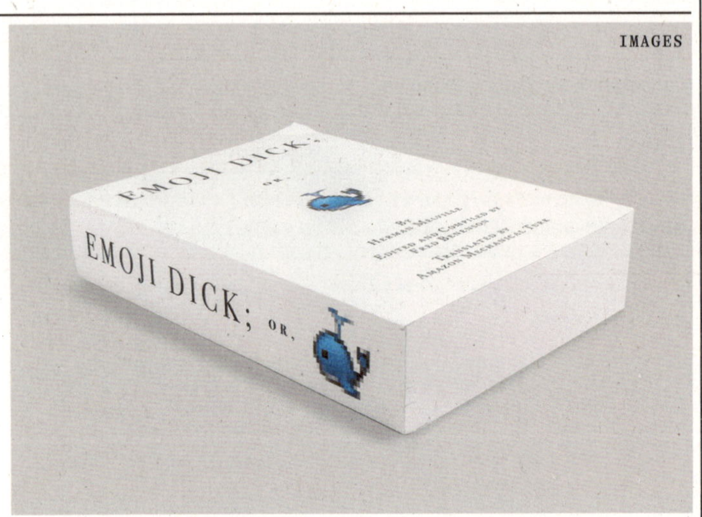

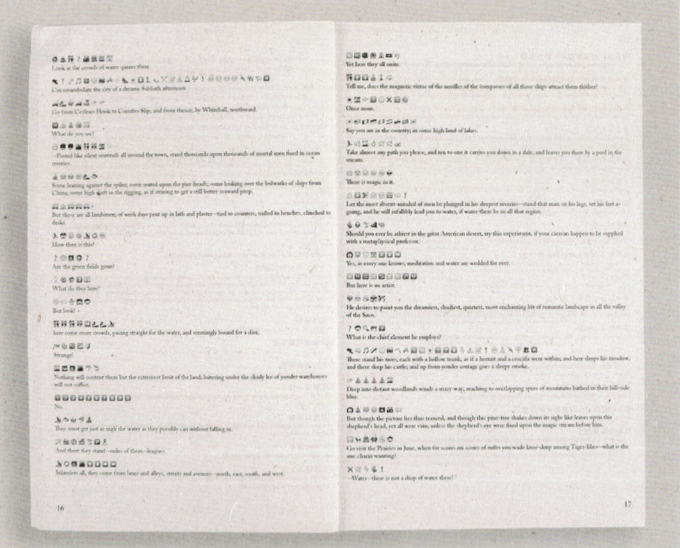

DESCRIPTION

"*Emoji Dick* is a crowd sourced and crowd funded translation of Herman Melville's *Moby Dick* into [...] emoji.

Each of the book's approximately 10,000 sentences has been translated three times by a[n] Amazon Mechanical Turk worker. These results have been voted upon by another set of workers, and the most popular version of each sentence has been selected for inclusion in this book. In total, over eight hundred people spent approximately 3,795,980 seconds working to create this book. Each worker was paid five cents per translation and two cents per vote per translation. The funds to pay the Amazon Turk workers and print the initial run of this book were raised from eighty three people over the course of thirty days using the funding platform Kickstarter" (blurb on Lulu).

Fred Benenson can be considered a pioneer in the use of Amazon Mechanical Turk and its (algo-)Taylorist principles in the literary field. In search of "the craziest thing I could get Mechanical Turk to do" (Fred Benenson, "Emoji Dick," talk), Benenson decided on a translation experiment. In keeping with the production principle, the novel is presented in individual sentences within the book: emoji translation and English original following each other. As Lisa Gitelman notes in "*Emoji Dick* and the Eponymous Whale," the subtitle that uses the emoji for whale is difficult to index in bibliographies and library catalogs. We too have "back translated" it into English: "Or the whale."

The 812 crowd*workers* are listed in the acknowledgments at the end of the book on eleven pages—not with their real names, but with their alphanumeric MTurk usernames, such as A106Q3N3OECN73. So they remain invisible, anonymous cogs in the wheel, adapted to the digital workflows right down to their names, while the eighty-three crowd*funders*—in the style of subscription lists of earlier centuries—are all listed by name. Here, one crowd pays the other, and at the same time a two-class society is clearly created. However, these invisible workers can gain autonomy, as Zach Whalen notes. He found that a certain sequence of nine emojis was used a total of 439 times, corresponding to "about 4.5% of the total work." This suggests that a "Turk" was trying to trick the system and increase his own hourly rate by "copy pasting the same sequence over and over again" (Zach Whalen, "Some Notes").

There are two versions of the book: one in black-and-white for $40 and one in color for $200. The project has received widespread media attention and has also been acquired by a surprising number of libraries—usually in the more expensive color version. Benenson celebrated its acquisition by the Library of Congress as a high accolade and its inclusion in the "HELP/LESS" exhibition, curated by Chris Habib, at Printed Matter 2013 as its official recognition as art: "This is kind of a big deal because I think it means *Emoji Dick* can now be considered a work of art" (Fred Benenson, "Emoji Dick is Officially Art").

On Lulu, it is one of the few books that has received reviews. Only one of them, however, recommends it as a gift; the other reviewers criticize the poorly readable black-and-white version and the inadequate book preview, which shows only twelve pages and thus only the preface, but not a single page with the emojis themselves. In the meantime, Lulu has even eliminated the book preview altogether, which is detrimental to browsing and discovering new books.

The Iraq War

A Historiography of Wikipedia Changelogs

AUTHOR	James Bridle
YEAR	2010
GENRE	artist's book / bookwork, exhibition copy, nonfiction
METHOD	documentation / archiving, found material
SUBJECT	analog / digital, bias, crowd / collaboration, memory / storage, politics / activism, scale, wikipedia
PLATFORM	Lulu
VOLUMES	12
EDITION CHARACTERISTICS	not publicly available, only one set produced
MATERIALITIES	black-and-white, hardcover

IMAGE

DESCRIPTION

James Bridle's twelve-volume set *The Iraq War: A Historiography of Wikipedia Changelogs* documents in nearly 7,000 pages all 12,000 changes made to the Wikipedia article on the Iraq War in five years between December 2004 and November 2009.

"It contains arguments over numbers, differences of opinion on relevance and political standpoints, and frequent moments when someone erases the whole thing and just writes 'Saddam Hussein was a dickhead.' This is historiography. This is what culture actually looks like: a process of argument, of dissenting and accreting opinion, of gradual and not always correct codification.

And for the first time in history, we're building a system that, perhaps only for a brief time but certainly for the moment, is capable of recording every single one of those infinitely valuable pieces of information. Everything should have a history button. We need to talk about historiography, to surface this process, to challenge absolutist narratives of the past, and thus, those of the present and our future" (James Bridle, "On Wikipedia, Cultural Patrimony, and Historiography").

Bridle explains the necessity of putting this web-based debate into book form by its vividness: on the one hand, its scope is impressive and surprising. At twelve hardcover volumes, it approaches "the size of a single old-style encyclopaedia." On the other hand, "[p]hysical objects are useful props in debates like this: immediately illustrative, and useful to hang an argument and peoples' attention on" (Ibid.).

The work was produced only once and is not publicly available. It was exhibited in galleries in the United States and Europe where, apparently, reading the books was not allowed: "Please do not touch. / Excerpts of text can be found in blue binder on vitrine." This shows that Bridle was less interested here in the distributive potential of print-on-demand than in the easy accessibility of the technology.

GENERATION[S]

AUTHOR	J. R. Carpenter
YEAR	2010
PUBLISHER	TraumaWien
GENRE	experimental literature
METHOD	appropriation, collective, found material, generative / automation, montage / remix, remediation
SUBJECT	code / programming, crowd / collaboration, literature, narration, publishing / distribution
PLATFORM	Lulu
EDITION CHARACTERISTICS	multiple editions (print, PDF), ISBN 9783950291032, open edition
FORMAT	14.8 × 21.0 cm
MATERIALITIES	black-and-white, paperback, perfect bound
PAGES	157

IMAGE

DESCRIPTION

The acknowledgment in this book starts as follows: "*GENERATION[S]* is the book equivalent of a Nick Montfort tribute band. Thank you, Nick, for your caring coding sharing friendship" (J. R. Carpenter, "Acknowledgment," 154). Accordingly, J. R. Carpenter's series of computer generated texts is based on two of Montfort's *1K Story Generators* and his "elegant poetry generator" *Taroko Gorge*, which she hacks and rebuilds into *GORGE*, "a never-ending tract that spits out verse approximations, poetic paroxysms about food, consumption, decadence, and desire" (blurb on Lulu).

"There was only one rule in creating *GENERATION[S]*: No new texts. All the texts in this book were previously published in some way. The texts the generators produce are intertwined with the generators' source code, and these two types of texts are in turn interrupted by excerpts from the meta narrative that went into their creation. Most of the sentences in the fiction generators started off as Tweets, which were then pulled into Facebook. Some led to comments that led to responses that led to new texts. All these stages of intermediation are represented in the print book iteration of *GENERATION[S]*" (Ibid.).

As the author notes in her reflections on the generation of books, the print book is more of a byproduct: "At no point in this process was I writing a book. I was writing sentences. The book wrote itself. The book talks about generation and that is how it was made" (J. R. Carpenter, "Generating Books"). Because the book is thus only one stage in an unfinishable process of transformation and further processing, it also fits very well into TraumaWien's publishing program, who understand their books "as narrative snapshots of computer generated literary processes which are already disappearing as soon as they are written. Since its publication, the physical book *GENERATION[S]* has been used as a script, an image, an object, a subject, a pedagogical tool, a commodity and a site of exchange. The codes it contains have continued to multiply, morph and change" (Ibid.).

AUTHOR	J. Gordon Faylor
YEAR	2010
PUBLISHER	TREES+SQUASHTWOTHOUSANDANDTEN
GENRE	experimental literature
METHOD	found material, reformatting
SUBJECT	art world / literary world, canon, print on demand, publishing / distribution
PLATFORM	Lulu
EDITION CHARACTERISTICS	open edition
FORMAT	15.2 × 22.9 cm
MATERIALITIES	black-and-white, paperback, perfect bound
PAGES	48 (unpaginated)

IMAGES

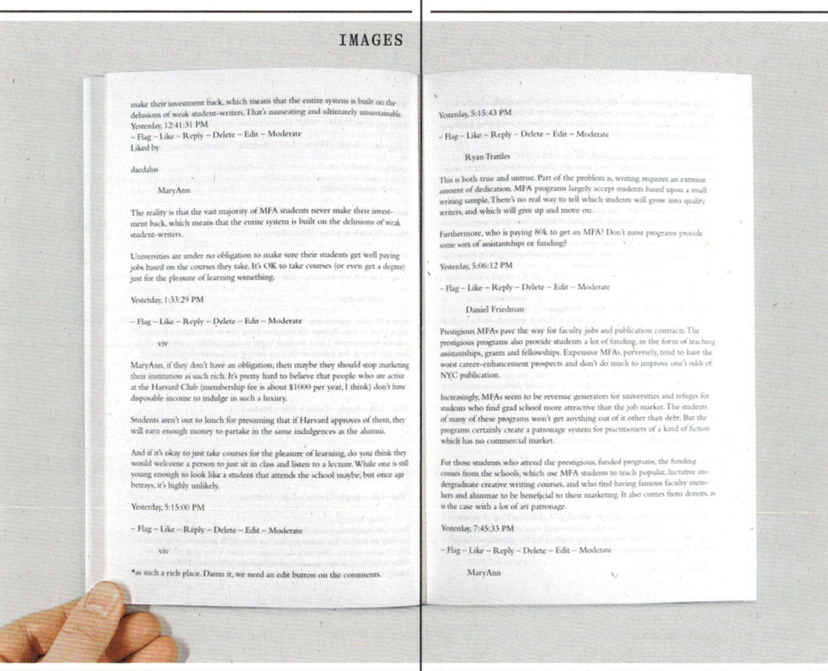

make their investment back, which means that the entire system is built on the delusions of weak student-writers. That's nauseating and ultimately unsustainable.
Yesterday, 12:41:31 PM
– Flag – Like – Reply – Delete – Edit – Moderate
Liked by

daedalus

MaryAnn

The reality is that the vast majority of MFA students never make their investment back, which means that the entire system is built on the delusions of weak student-writers.

Universities are under no obligation to make sure their students get well paying jobs based on the courses they take. It's OK to take courses (or even get a degree) just for the pleasure of learning something.

Yesterday, 1:33:29 PM

– Flag – Like – Reply – Delete – Edit – Moderate

viv

MaryAnn, if they don't have an obligation, then maybe they should stop marketing their institution as such rich. It's pretty hard to believe that people who are active at the Harvard Club (membership fee is about $1000 per year, I think) don't have disposable income to indulge in such a luxury.

Students aren't out to lunch for presuming that if Harvard approves of them, they will earn enough money to partake in the same indulgences as the alumni.

And if it's okay to just take courses for the pleasure of learning, do you think they would welcome a person to just sit in class and listen to a lecture. While one is still young enough to look like a student that attends the school maybe, but once age betrays, it's highly unlikely.

Yesterday, 5:15:00 PM

– Flag – Like – Reply – Delete – Edit – Moderate

viv

*as such a rich place. Damn it, we need an edit button on the comments.

Yesterday, 5:15:43 PM

– Flag – Like – Reply – Delete – Edit – Moderate

Ryan Trattles

This is both true and untrue. Part of the problem is, writing requires an extreme amount of dedication. MFA programs largely accept students based upon a small writing sample. There's no real way to tell which students will grow into quality writers, and which will give up and move on.

Furthermore, who is paying 80k to get an MFA? Don't most programs provide some sort of assistantships or funding?

Yesterday, 5:06:12 PM

– Flag – Like – Reply – Delete – Edit – Moderate

Daniel Friedman

Prestigious MFAs pave the way for faculty jobs and publication contracts. The prestigious programs also provide students a lot of funding, in the form of teaching assistantships, grants and fellowships. Expensive MFAs, perversely, tend to have the worst career-enhancement prospects and don't do much to improve one's odds of NYC publication.

Increasingly, MFAs seem to be revenue generators for universities and refuges for students who find grad school more attractive than the job market. The students of many of these programs won't get anything out of it other than debt. But the programs certainly create a patronage system for practitioners of a kind of fiction which has no commercial market.

For those students who attend the prestigious, funded programs, the funding comes from the schools, which use MFA students to teach popular, lucrative undergraduate creative writing courses, and who find having famous faculty members and alumnae to be beneficial to their marketing. It also comes from donors, as is the case with a lot of art patronage.

Yesterday, 7:45:33 PM

– Flag – Like – Reply – Delete – Edit – Moderate

MaryAnn

DESCRIPTION

J. Gordon Faylor's *Fr€€dom* documents the comment section of Chad Harbach's essay "MFA vs. NYC. America now has two distinct literary cultures. Which one will last?" on *Slate*. Harbach's essay, which first appeared in the magazine *n+1* in late 2010, caused a heated debate in literary magazines and newspapers as well as social media and comment sections. The antithesis Harbach raises is probably most clearly summed up by Dave Barnes: "The two cultures are: writing that makes money and writing that does not. Which one will last. Duh, the one that makes money. Think Danielle Steele" (J. Gordon Faylor, *Fr€€dom*, n.p.).

The comments archived in *Fr€€dom*, most of which are no longer available, capture the cultural zeitgeist and address some of the most common arguments in the discussion concerning literary elites, the place of arts in society, contemporary writing as opposed to the canon, and how to judge good and bad writing. The names of the like-givers and the range of possible reactions, which varies from comment to comment (besides "Like" there is also "Flag," "Reply," "Delete," and "Moderate"), were also archived. This also documents, en passant, the parameters of the online discussion set by the magazine, and is sometimes reflected by the participants, for example: "Damn it, we need an edit button on the comments."

Fr€€dom's only comment on these discussions is found in the brief quotation at the beginning, taken from William Gaddis' novel *J R*: "—I mean did it ever occur to you that a lot of them might be getting real old along with everything else?"

AutoSummarize

AUTHOR	Jason Huff
YEAR	2010
GENRE	experimental literature
METHOD	generative / automation
SUBJECT	canon, code / programming, literature, narration, reading / interpretation, scale, technology
PLATFORM	Lulu
EDITION CHARACTERISTICS	ISBN 9781938022814, available only through the artist, no longer available
FORMAT	14.5 × 22.0 cm
MATERIALITIES	black-and-white, hardcover, perfect bound
PAGES	120

IMAGES

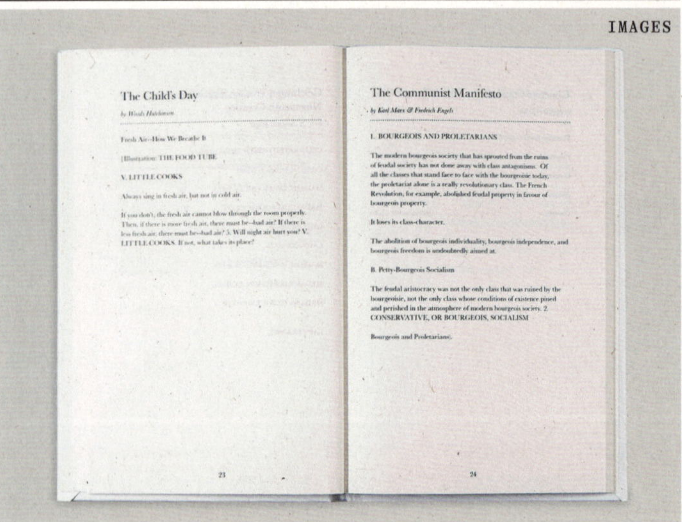

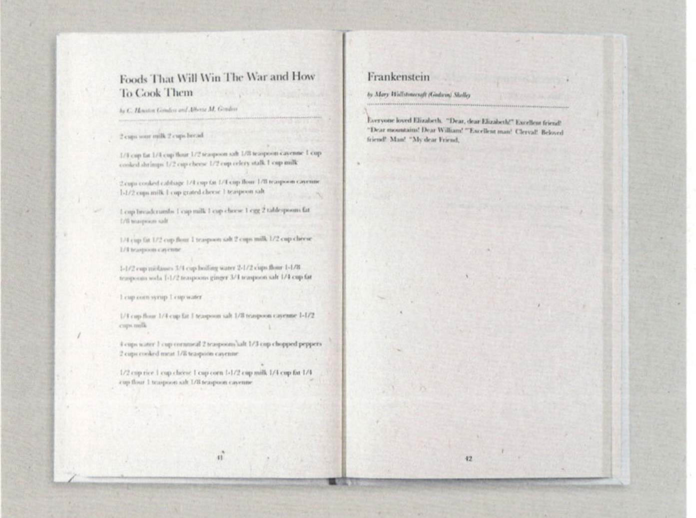

DESCRIPTION

For *AutoSummarize*, Jason Huff took the 100 most downloaded copyright-free books from Project Gutenberg at the time and condensed them to a few lines each using the Autosummarize feature in Microsoft Word, which was marketed as automatically summarizing documents to a desired length. Microsoft Word confidently concluded the creation of a summary with the message, “Word has examined the document and picked the sentences most relevant to the main theme.” However, this feature was discontinued by Microsoft the same year Huff published his book, probably due to its high inaccuracy which often resulted in humorous fallacies, especially when dealing with rhetorical or poetic genres.

This shortcoming is clearly evident in Huff’s collection as well. Already the very first summary of Henrik Ibsen’s *A Doll’s House* gives erroneously the proper names or speaker indications as the most relevant information of the text: “Nora. Nora. Nora. Nora. Nora. Nora. Nora! Nora. Nora. Nora” (Jason Huff, *AutoSummarize*, 1). But in a way it is of course just as true as that *All About Coffee* is primarily about “Coffee_ / Coffee. Coffee. Coffee. Coffee. Coffee. Coffee. Coffee. Coffee. / COFFEE” (Ibid., 14). At least the algorithm seems to be sure of itself, as shown by the quite similar result for *Alice’s Adventures in Wonderland*, of which there are three different versions in Project Gutenberg and thus also three summaries in Huff’s book (Ibid., 11–13). Again and again, however, page numbers, captions, chapter headings, index entries, column titles, footnotes slip into the summaries.

Thus, the result of Huff’s automatic digestion is not only a poetic reading of a classical canon through the lens of failing algorithmic optimization, but also a documentation of an outdated tool, making this book an object of potential media-archeological investigation into the imaginaries and dead ends of writing programs.

The Black Book

AUTHOR	Jean Keller
YEAR	2010 [2nd ed. 2012]
GENRE	artist's book / bookwork
METHOD	détournement / hack, paratextual play, pricing
SUBJECT	economy / labor, platforms / companies, print technology, print on demand
PLATFORM	Blurb, Lulu
EDITION CHARACTERISTICS	first edition: no longer available, second edition: open edition
FORMAT	first edition: 13.9 × 19.5 cm, second edition: 14.8 × 21.0 cm
MATERIALITIES	black-and-white, paperback, perfect bound
PAGES	first edition: 440, second edition: 740

IMAGE

DESCRIPTION

"Ink used for digital printing is one of the most precious substances in the world. A single gallon of ink costs over four thousand dollars and this is one reason why digitally printed books are so expensive.

However, the price of a book is not calculated according to the amount of ink used in its production. For example, a Lulu book of blank pages costs an artist as much to produce as a book filled with text or large photographs. Furthermore, as the number of pages increases, the price of each page decreases. A book containing the maximum number of pages printed entirely in black ink therefore results in the lowest cost and maximum value for the artist.

Combining these two features, buyers of *The Black Book* can do so with the guarantee that they are getting the best possible value for their money" (blurb on Lulu).

Whether the prices mentioned and the economic calculation is accurate and whether this strategy automatically leads to a loss-making business for the print-on-demand provider is a matter of debate. The fact that Jean Keller is touching on a sensitive point here, however, is shown by the example of two other (almost all black) works whose production was refused or discontinued by Lulu: Holly Melgard's *Black Friday* (see 236) has not been produced for a long time due to alleged errors in the source file, and the production of Mishka Henner's 12-volume *Astronomical* series (see 197), which was planned as an open edition, ended after 130 sets.

The Black Book was published in late 2010 shortly after Jean Keller's first appearance at Offprint Paris, first by Blurb (440 pages, 13 × 20 cm), followed by a Lulu edition in 2012 (740 pages, 14.8 × 21 cm). The Blurb edition is no longer available, as Jean Keller has left Blurb due to numerous problems and annoyances.

The work didn't become more widely known until 2013, when Kenneth Goldsmith took notice and promoted it several times on social media—a connection that is confirmed with the sales figures provided by Keller. The recent mention in *Art in America* (June 2022) boosted sales once again.

Post-Fordism and its Discontents

AUTHOR	Gal Kirn [ed.]
YEAR	2010
GENRE	catalog / collection, nonfiction
METHOD	composition (writing / drawing / photography), pricing
SUBJECT	economy / labor, politics / activism, publishing / distribution
PLATFORM	Lulu
EDITION CHARACTERISTICS	multiple editions (print, PDF), ISBN 9780557725953, open edition, CC BY-NC-ND
FORMAT	15.6 × 23.4 cm
MATERIALITIES	black-and-white, paperback, perfect bound
PAGES	366
IMAGE	

DESCRIPTION

Post-Fordism and its Discontents is a collection of critical essays on the relationship between culture, economy, and society, tackling political and economic theory in late capitalism. Edited by Gal Kirn and designed by Nina Støttrup Larsen and Žiga Testen, the book was released on multiple channels, as stated on the cover: in an edition of 250 copies for €30 from Jan van Eyck Academie, an unlimited print-on-demand version at Lulu.com for €17.04, and a PDF version—presumably intended as pirate copy—available at Lulu.com and aaaaarg.org.

The cover reflects on these multiple versions by providing check boxes to mark publisher, distributor, price, and print run. The logic of production, which is the subject of the book, is thus also visible on the cover so the publication itself becomes recognizable as an integral part of these entanglements. However, the price on Lulu has risen significantly since publication, standing at $28 (€34.08) in August 2022.

On the back cover under the ISBN and at the top of the first few pages of each copy is noted where it comes from. According to this information, the book block of our copy was "published and distributed through Lulu" and "printed on 8/10/2010 11:55," and the cover was printed at 19:54, although this obviously corresponds to the time of upload and not production. However, when ordering and downloading the PDF on Lulu, the timestamp actually changes.

It is one of the few books in our collection that has received a review on Lulu. However, it was written by Žiga Testen himself and merely reproduces the praise on the back of the book. The volume includes contributions by Sergio Bologna, Katja Diefenbach, Gal Kirn, Zdravko Kobe, Gorazd Kovačič, Sandro Mezzadra, Rastko Močnik, Ciril Oberstar, Igor Pribac, Jacques Rancière, and Marina Vishmidt.

FICT/IONS and THIS SENTENCE

AUTHOR	Richard Kostelanetz
YEAR	2010
PUBLISHER	Blue & Yellow Dog Press
GENRE	experimental literature, reprint
METHOD	composition (writing / drawing / photography)
SUBJECT	art world / literary world, book / book design, canon, literature, print on demand, publishing / distribution
PLATFORM	Lulu
EDITION CHARACTERISTICS	ISBN 9780982953518, open edition, CC0
FORMAT	15.2 × 22.9 cm
MATERIALITIES	black-and-white, paperback, perfect bound
PAGES	104 (unpaginated)

IMAGES

DESCRIPTION

This book contains two books by Richard Kostelanetz: *FICT/IONS* and *THIS SENTENCE*. Each starts on a different side and is upside down from the other. The back cover becomes a rotated front cover and vice versa. Thus, this book has a double paratext with two covers, two half-titles, two imprints and two dedications (to Anton Chekhov and Northrop Frye). However, the double-front cover layout is disrupted by Lulu's barcode, which is always printed on last page and back cover, forcing a standard orientation back onto the book.

In between these two texts, in the middle of the book, is the short essay "New Retrospective on my Fictions: Forty Notes." Note 34 of the essay explains the idea of *FICT/IONS*, "that depend upon discovering within a single word two shorter words that, concluding with a period, make a narrative." Accordingly, the first part of the book contains a list of words that, as in "Alter/natives," "Cap/a/city," or "I/nun/dating," are broken up by one or more forward slashes into syllables or words of different meaning, creating multi-semantic mini-narratives: "the splitting of fictions emphasizes division as a paradoxical form of construction, as well as the particulate quality of syllabic 'matter'" (Thomas Fink, review). *THIS SENTENCE* is a collection of statements on sentences, with each sentence referencing itself.

In his essay in the middle of the book, the complaint comes through that, although Kostelanetz has authored several publications, and although he has been appreciated as an avant-gardist and radical formalist in the great encyclopedias of this world, he has nevertheless experienced too little institutional and publishing support: "there have been few reviews of individual books, no commercial contracts, no grants for fiction writing, [...] little public acknowledgment of my alternative purposes in creating and publishing fiction." Having long been active in alternative literary publishing himself (publishing in small magazines, self-publishing, co-founding Assembling Press in 1970, founding Future Press in 1977 and Archae Editions in 1978), Kostelanetz now has two of his previously unpublished works being released as a single print-on-demand book by Raymond Farr's Blue & Yellow Dog Press.

11 Books Expanding Tan Lin's Seven Controlled Vocabularies and Obituary: The Joy of Cooking, 2010

AUTHORS	Tan Lin, Danny Snelson [ed.]
YEAR	2010
PUBLISHER	Edit Publications
GENRE	catalog / collection, experimental literature
METHOD	appropriation, collective, composition (writing / drawing / photography), paratextual play, versioning / seriality
SUBJECT	analog / digital, authorship, canon, crowd / collaboration, literature, print on demand, publishing / distribution, reading / interpretation, writing / reading techniques
PLATFORM	Lulu
VOLUMES	11
EDITION CHARACTERISTICS	multiple editions (print, PDF, ZIP), open edition
IMAGE	

DESCRIPTION

This eleven-piece series launched by Danny Snelson's Edit Publications expands Tan Lin's *Seven Controlled Vocabularies and Obituary: The Joy of Cooking, 2004* (Wesleyan Poetry Series, 2010, see 129). It involves around fifty poets and derives from an event at the Kelly Writers House at the University of Pennsylvania on April 12, 2010, titled *Handmade book, PDF, lulu, Appendix, Powerpoint, Kanban Board/ Post-Its, Blurb, Dual Language (Chinese/ English) Edition, micro lecture, Selectric II interview, wine/cheese reception, Q&A (xerox), film*. The event itself never included all the aspects mentioned in its title.

The series was based on the hypothesis that "editing is the new semiotics, partly meaning that editing crosses into numerous disciplines connected to writing, artistic practice, book making, social networks, and distribution, etc., in the way that semiotics did with cultural anthropology, literary studies etc etc..." (Tan Lin, Danny Snelson, Kristen Gallagher, "Notes on an Edit Event"). In their notes, which opened the wiki for the event, the editors further elaborate that it "involved making [...] certain forms of reading visible. The gesture involved taking a book (*7CV*) from an author [...] and putting it in the hands of its readers (editors). I didn't want to make editorial practices merely labor intensive or parasitical, vis-à-vis the standard reworking of a source text. Instead, the event encouraged practices (temporal events very much subject to endurance issues) that would situate the so-called textual object in a literal and technological field that included citing sources (*Appendix* and *Bibliography*), rewriting the text (*Chinese Edition*), listing devices, reading the text alongside other texts (*Critical Reader*), and evaluating its production (*Selected Essays*)—all of which were read within a number of on-the-fly editorial frameworks" (Ibid.).

The publications were deliberately produced under time pressure, resulting in decisions and errors that made "the editorial process more visible and render[ed] the book as an emendation in a larger communicative envelope" (Ibid.). All publications are available as free downloads and can also be purchased through print-on-demand on Lulu, but also through Printed Matter (New York), which serves as a collaborative partner along with the University of Pennsylvania and Kelly Writers House.

This positive print-on-demand experience was decisive for Danny Snelson's later series *1,000 Books by 1,000 Poets* for the exhibition "Poetry will be made by all!" in Zurich, 2014 (see 284, 297, 303, 357).

AUTHORS	Matthew Abess [ed.], Patrick Lovelace [ed.], Stephen McLaughlin [ed.], Danny Snelson [ed.]
GENRE	experimental literature
METHOD	collective, composition (writing / drawing / photography)
SUBJECT	art world / literary world, crowd / collaboration, economy / labor, publishing / distribution
FORMAT	14.0 × 21.6 cm
MATERIALITIES	color, paperback, perfect bound
PAGES	114 (unpaginated)

IMAGES

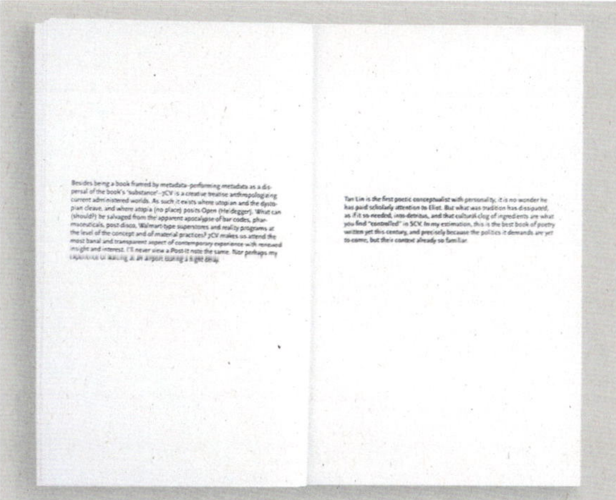

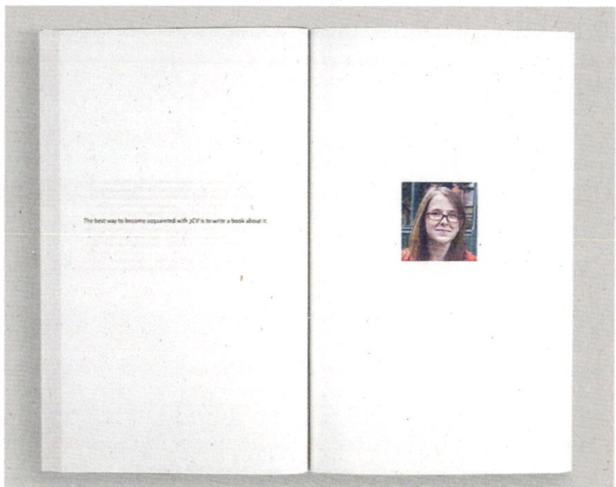

DESCRIPTION

Blurb contains sixty blurbs on Tan Lin's *7CV* and forty-eight photos depicting the authors of these blurbs. In this way, it takes up the compositional style of *7CV*, which also consists mostly of paratextual matter. At the same time, it shows the enormous, liberating, and inspiring impact that Lin's book had for the US poetry scene. Many blurbs in this book are probably serious, comparing Lin's book to Andy Warhol's *a: A novel* and enthusing about its innovative poetics, as here: "A brilliant manifesto for conceptual, ambient writing, for *non-reading*." Some highlight its unusual character: "If this is a book, then I am an angel," or adopt a poetic or experimental character themselves. Others mirror the typical excessive tone of blurbs, parodying the text type and related marketing mechanisms on the book market. In between, there are also statements such as "I wrote this book." The blurb collection appropriately ends with, "The best way to become acquainted with *7CV* is to write a book about it."

CONTRIBUTIONS BY

Christopher Alexander, Louis Asekoff, Stan Apps, Danielle Aubert, Charles Bernstein, E. Shaskan Bumas, Ken Chen, Cecilia Corrigan, Clare Churchouse, AMJ Crawford, Kieran Daly, Mónica de la Torre, Thom Donovan, Patrick Durgin, Kareem Estefan, Robert Fitterman, Jonathan Flatley, Peter Fong, Christopher Funkhouser, Kristen Gallagher, Sarah Gambito, Kenneth Goldsmith, Diana Hamilton, Eddie Hopely, Paolo Javier, Josef Kaplan, John Keene, Matthew Landis, Juliette Lee, Maya Lin, Warren Liu, Patrick Lovelace, Rachel Malik, Dan Machlin, Michael Ondaatje, Asher Penn, Josiah McElheny, Stephen McLaughlin, Jay Sanders, Katherine Sanders, Jeremy Sigler, Danny Snelson, Chris Sylvester, Gordon Tapper, Michele Taransky, Dan Visel, Dorothy Wang, and Sara Wintz.

7CV: Critical Reader

AUTHORS	Mashinka Firunts [ed.], Danny Snelson [ed.]
GENRE	catalog / collection
METHOD	collection
SUBJECT	canon, literature, reading / interpretation
EDITION CHARACTERISTICS	ISBN 9780557555512
FORMAT	15.2 × 22.9 cm
MATERIALITIES	black-and-white, paperback, perfect bound
PAGES	143

IMAGES

TAN LIN'S SEVEN CONTROLLED VOCABULARIES: A CRITICAL READER

PUBLICATION EDITORS
MASHINKA FIRUNTS
DANNY SNELSON

EVENT EDITORS
EDDIE HOPELY
SUEYEUN JULIETTE LEE

WITH GUEST EDITOR CHRIS CUELLAR

Edit Publications, 2010 | Series Editor: Danny Snelson

DESCRIPTION

7CV: Critical Reader is a collection of publications situating Tan Lin's *Seven Controlled Vocabularies* and the media practices it implies in a broader theoretical context. It lists 143 publications ranging from media philosophy and literary studies to sociology, urbanism, the history of art, digital cultures, and more, also including instances of poetry and fiction. The listed publications are sorted in twenty-two topical chapters and represented by a bibliographical note and reproductions of one relevant paragraph each.

The reader was edited by Mashinka Firunts and Danny Snelson with Chris Cuellar as guest editor, and Eddie Hopely and Sueyeun Juliette Lee as event editors, emphasizing the need for collectivity in creating such extensive bibliographic overviews.

Yet, *7CV: Critical Reader* not only works as an annotated and thematically assorted bibliography and reader but also as an interface for a pirate library, as all publications include links to downloadable digital copies of the texts. The files, however, have been uploaded to a one-click hoster that no longer exists, and they are therefore not available anymore, underlining how such digital archival approaches that are looking for distribution loopholes of copyrighted material are also always subject to the online economies they are situated in.

7CV: Critical Reader was conceived and published during a republication event at the University of Pennsylvania.

Selected Essays About a Bibliography

AUTHORS	J. Gordon Faylor [ed.], Danny Snelson [ed.]
GENRE	catalog / collection, nonfiction
METHOD	collective, composition (writing / drawing / photography)
SUBJECT	art world / literary world, book / book design, literature, print on demand, technology, writing / reading techniques
EDITION CHARACTERISTICS	ISBN 9780557555505
FORMAT	15.2 × 22.9 cm
MATERIALITIES	black-and-white, paperback, perfect bound
PAGES	86

IMAGES

DESCRIPTION

This volume contains essays (max. 600 words) by forty-seven contributors on technology, tools and concepts related to writing, translating, publishing and editing, such as select bibliographies, font libraries, Facebook, Blurb, metadata, scanning, artist's books, poetry workshops, PowerPoint, IBM Selectric II, Xerox, Microsoft Word, errata, pagination, barcodes, and indexes. For some subjects there are several essays. They are arranged according to the order in which the essays were received by the seven-member editorial team during the event, who immediately edited and printed them as an on-site publication. “Lack of an authoritative list of essays/essayists by event's end, absence of a wiki style sheet, and non-codified editorial practices rendered the history of publication Just Good Enough, as attested by its principal formats: the wiki and lulu edition. [...] The *Selected Essays* might be regarded as performance-based publishing event, wiki, POD mechanism, social network, archive of search results, and tag collection. Genres are social agreements, as are search terms” (J. Gordon Faylor, Danny Snelson, “Editorial Note,” 7). Cover design by J. Gordon Faylor.

七受控詞表和 2004年訃告 [first edition]

AUTHOR	Tan Lin
GENRE	experimental literature
METHOD	collective, generative / automation, photocopy / scan, translation / transcription
SUBJECT	error / corruption / loss, google, literature, technology
EDITION CHARACTERISTICS	ISBN 9780557519446
FORMAT	15.2 × 22.9 cm
MATERIALITIES	black-and-white, paperback, perfect bound
PAGES	224 (unpaginated)

IMAGES

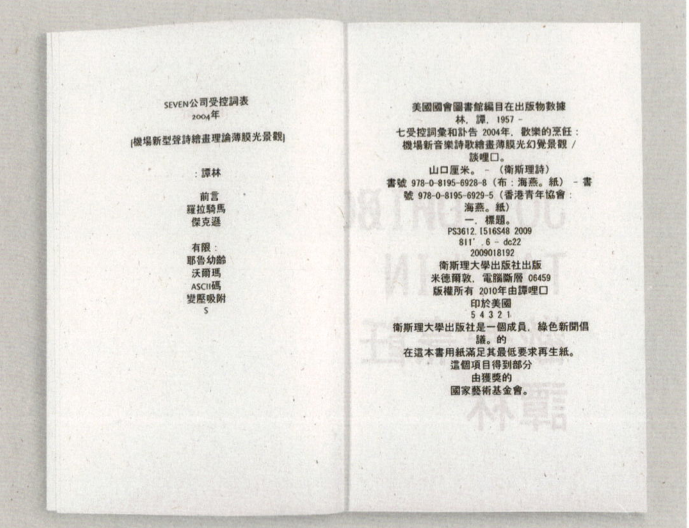

DESCRIPTION

This is the first edition of the (traditional) Chinese translation of Lin's work, which was produced entirely by Google Translate on-site at the event. The visuals have been lost, which is why there is excessive white space. Ten pages have been left completely blank, where Lin's original contains book pages scanned and reproduced as images, which apparently could not be recognized and translated as text by Google Translate. The only English-language text is the "Editorial Note" by Tan Lin. The "On line/Google Trans work team" consisted of Chris Alexander, Alejandro Crawford, and Cécilia Corrigan.

七受控詞表和 2004年訃告 [second edition]

AUTHOR	Tan Lin
GENRE	experimental literature
METHOD	collective, generative / automation, reformatting, translation / transcription
SUBJECT	book / book design, error / corruption / loss, google, literature, technology
EDITION CHARACTERISTICS	ISBN 9780557519552
FORMAT	15.2 × 22.9 cm
MATERIALITIES	black-and-white, paperback, perfect bound
PAGES	224
IMAGES	

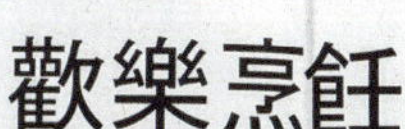

DESCRIPTION

This second translation into (traditional) Chinese was also produced with the help of Google Translate, but after the event "in transit from Philadelphia to New York City and in Woodside, Queens and on the internet" (colophon). In addition, the visuals that were lost in the first translation were reinserted, the page count was corrected, missing text was added, existing text was reformatted, and the front matter was rearranged "to correspond to the Wesleyan University Press (American English) first edition" (Ibid.). The only English-language texts are the "Editorial Note" by Tan Lin, the text on the scanned book pages, and the colophon.

七受控詞表和 2004年訃告 [third edition]

AUTHOR	Tan Lin
GENRE	experimental literature
METHOD	collective, generative / automation, translation / transcription
SUBJECT	book / book design, error / corruption / loss, google, technology
EDITION CHARACTERISTICS	ISBN 9780557519620
FORMAT	15.2 × 22.9 cm
MATERIALITIES	black-and-white, paperback, perfect bound
PAGES	224

IMAGES

DESCRIPTION

This is the third translation (with the visuals) by Google Translate, but this time from traditional Chinese to simplified Chinese. The colophon informs that this caused "a higher rate of error in conjunction with the limited character set of MS Gothic, causing many of the characters to 'disappear.'" On pages 24 and 32, the Chinese text was replaced by the phrase: "'Sorry, the page you requested contains a file type (application/octetstream) we are unable to translate.' This phrase was produced by feeding the Wesleyan UP TIFF files containing the Chinese text into Google Translate using the 'upload a document' feature" (colophon).

七受控詞表和 2004年訃告 [fourth edition]

AUTHOR	Tan Lin
GENRE	experimental literature
METHOD	collective, generative / automation, translation / transcription
SUBJECT	book / book design, error / corruption / loss, google, technology
EDITION CHARACTERISTICS	ISBN 9780557569090
FORMAT	15.2 × 22.9 cm
MATERIALITIES	black-and-white, paperback, perfect bound
PAGES	224

IMAGES

SEVEN COMPANY CONTROLLED VOCABULARIES
in 2004

HI COOKING

[SOUND OF POETRY AIRPORT NEW THEORY FILMS LANDSCAPE PAINTING]

:Tan Lin

Wesleyan University Press
Middletown, Connecticut

AND DELIVERING A SPEECH

在口/谷 歌翻口

on line/ google trs

1132:46 Science
1132:46版

Introduction
Laura Riding Jackson

DESCRIPTION

This final volume contains the reverse translation from traditional Chinese of the second edition into English and includes the visual material. The two error messages from the third edition have been retained and translated into traditional Chinese.

CATALOG 167

Network Publishing, “Edit: Processing Writing Technologies” KWH 04/21/10 Event Inventory and Documentation

GENRE
nonfiction

METHOD
composition (writing / drawing / photography), documentation / archiving, pricing, versioning / seriality

SUBJECT
crowd / collaboration, economy / labor, print on demand, technology, writing / reading techniques

EDITION CHARACTERISTICS
multiple editions (black-and-white, color, PDF, EPUB),
ISBN 9780557518104 (black-and-white),
ISBN 9780557517992 (color)

FORMAT
15.2 × 22.9 cm

MATERIALITIES
black-and-white, color, paperback, perfect bound

PAGES
80

IMAGES

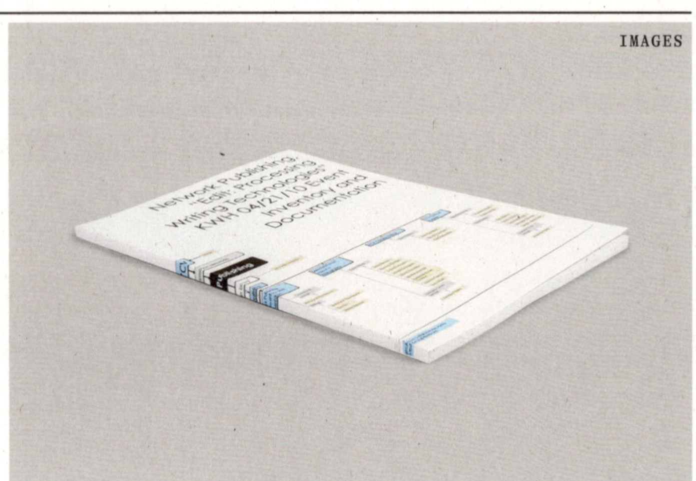

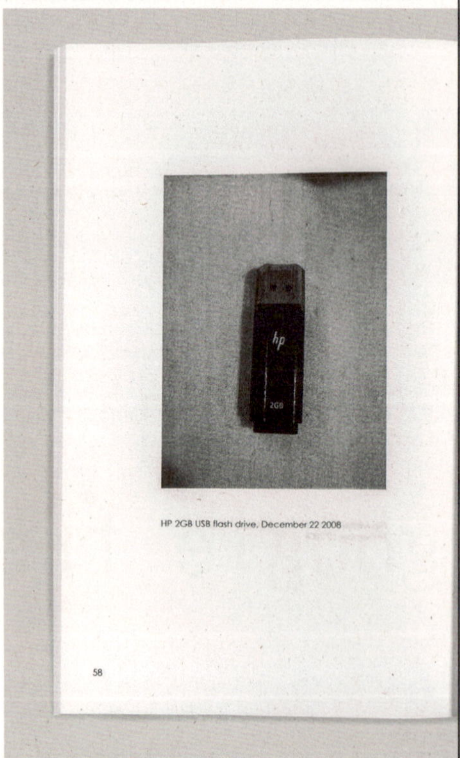

DESCRIPTION

This book is an inventory, map, and documentation of the tools, software, resources, people, contributions, and publications connected with the event. All devices are also documented individually as photos, such as IBM Selectric typewriter, Post-It notes, SanDisk 4GB USB flash drive, Sony ICD-UX70 digital voice recorder, Anchor ANX-70 monitor speakers, Sony EVI-D70 digital camcorder, Office Depot copy paper, Canon Pixma MP210 all-in-one inkjet, Mackie 1402-VLZ PRO 14-channel mixer, and 12 different notebooks. The photos were taken by Jeremy J. F. Thompson, who also provided layout and cover design. The cover’s mind map visualizes the coordination of tasks related to the event.

There are PDF and EPUB versions of this inventory, as well as a polychromatic and monochromatic printed edition, which differ significantly in price (according to the covers, $27 and $8.11 respectively). As an exception, we bought both versions for comparison.

Purple/Pink: Appendix

AUTHOR	Tan Lin
GENRE	nonfiction, catalog / collection
METHOD	composition (writing / drawing / photography), collective, documentation / archiving, paratextual play
SUBJECT	art world / literary world, book / book design, literature, publishing / distribution
EDITION CHARACTERISTICS	ISBN 9780557560271
FORMAT	15.2 × 22.9 cm
MATERIALITIES	black-and-white, paperback, perfect bound
PAGES	101 (unpaginated)

IMAGES

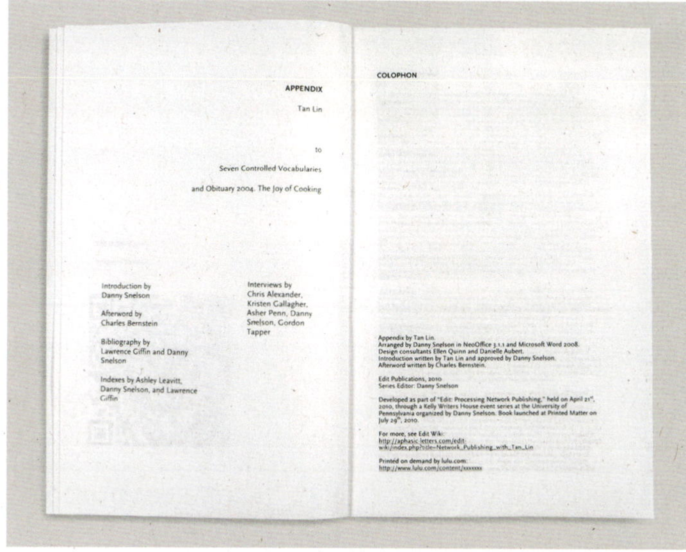

APPENDIX

Tan Lin

to

Seven Controlled Vocabularies

and Obituary 2004. The Joy of Cooking

Introduction by
Danny Snelson

Afterword by
Charles Bernstein

Bibliography by
Lawrence Giffin and Danny Snelson

Indexes by Ashley Leavitt, Danny Snelson, and Lawrence Giffin

Interviews by
Chris Alexander, Kristen Gallagher, Asher Penn, Danny Snelson, Gordon Tapper

COLOPHON

Appendix by Tan Lin.
Arranged by Danny Snelson in NeoOffice 3.1.1 and Microsoft Word 2008.
Design consultants Ellen Quinn and Danielle Aubert.
Introduction written by Tan Lin and approved by Danny Snelson.
Afterword written by Charles Bernstein.

Edit Publications, 2010
Series Editor: Danny Snelson

Developed as part of "Edit: Processing Network Publishing," held on April 21st, 2010, through a Kelly Writers House event series at the University of Pennsylvania organized by Danny Snelson. Book launched at Printed Matter on July 29th, 2010.

For more, see Edit Wiki:
http://aphasic-letters.com/edit-wiki/index.php?title=Network_Publishing_with_Tan_Lin

Printed on demand by lulu.com:
http://www.lulu.com/content/xxxxxx

DESCRIPTION

The *Appendix*, which contains additional material like a draft version of the cover design, a QR code, and PR texts, is under the authorship of Tan Lin according to the colophon, but was arranged and approved by Danny Snelson. Lin also contributed "The Expanded Preface," and Snelson an "Introduction" consisting only of rows of the letter "x." There are also two interviews in which Tan Lin gives detailed information about his poetics and *7CV*, as well as several indexes, created by Lin, Snelson, Lawrence Giffin, and Ashley Leavitt, which either record persons, titles, and objects as is customary for an index, or alternatively provide an index of first lines or simply register blank pages, barcodes, parentheses, numbers, Chinese characters, quotation marks, and so on. In this way, the *Appendix* mirrors the importance attributed to the index in the wiki of the event: "Why would a poetry book require an Index, which is normally used for non-fictional works? What makes that condition relevant and somehow necessary today? I think all books of poetry should have indexes not written by the author!" (Tan Lin, Danny Snelson, Kristen Gallagher, "Notes on an Edit Event")

This unconventional approach continues in the "Afterword" by Charles Bernstein, which he took from a single found source, and Lawrence Giffin's "Select Bibliography," which "lists all work consulted in the [event] period in question, related to the production of an Appendix to another work in question." In addition, the *Appendix* contains documents and information that rarely see the light of day, such as the two positive reader reports that were instrumental in Wesleyan University Press accepting *7CV* for publication, and the publishing contract.

A NEOIST RESEARCH PROJECT

AUTHOR	N.O. Cantsin
YEAR	2010
PUBLISHER	OpenMute
GENRE	artist's book / bookwork, catalog / collection
METHOD	collection, montage / remix, photocopy / scan, remediation
SUBJECT	art world / literary world, authorship, canon, crowd / collaboration, publishing / distribution
PLATFORM	Mute
EDITION CHARACTERISTICS	ISBN 9781906496463, no copyright
FORMAT	14.8 × 21.0 cm
MATERIALITIES	black-and-white, paperback, perfect bound
PAGES	266 (unpaginated)

ACTIVATIONS. APT FESTS. LANGUAGE. NEOISM. REPLICATION

IMAGE

DESCRIPTION

Neoism is a parodistic art movement trying to bypass and subvert the power dynamics of the art world as well as its aesthetics and practices. Making reference to the anti-institutional positions of previous avant-garde movements like Fluxus, Mail Art, and the Situationists, or subcultures like punk, Neoists try to negate, deny, and invert art practices mainly via plagiarism, collective anonymity, disruptive performances, and ever-shifting positions and practices, continuously producing more art while doing so. Most active in the 1980s and 1990s, the network of artists published, performed, and exhibited under the pseudonyms of Monty Cantsin and Karen Eliot with a sensitivity to media theory that touches print and its ephemera as well as computer culture.

A NEOIST RESEARCH PROJECT was also published under one of Cantsin's pseudonyms, as the note at the beginning states: "NO COPY NO RIGHT NO RESERVE N.O. CANTSIN NO TIME LESS SPACE." The book ends with the declaration: "OUR WORK IS RARELY SIGNED, / AND THE NOTION OF PLAGIARISM DOES NOT EXIST. IT HAS BEEN ESTABLISHED THAT ALL NEOISM IS THE WORK OF ONLY ONE AGELESS AND ANONYMOUS NEOIST."

The book collects writings, ranging from very short statements to manifestos and scores published in the context of the movement, mostly scattered through different publication organs and under different pseudonyms. They are divided into five chapters: "Activations," "Apt Fests," "Language," "Neoism," and "Replication."

Set in an 8-bit font, text is always laid out on verso pages with recto pages reproducing photographs and art works in heavy contrasted black and white. These layout decisions reference early computer culture as well as the aesthetic of xeroxed zines—both important benchmarks for Neoist artists—yet only simulating their lo-fi aesthetics. This is very much in line with Neoist art practices in general, as is the choice of print-on-demand publishing as the perfect "poor" hybrid of analog and digital production methods.

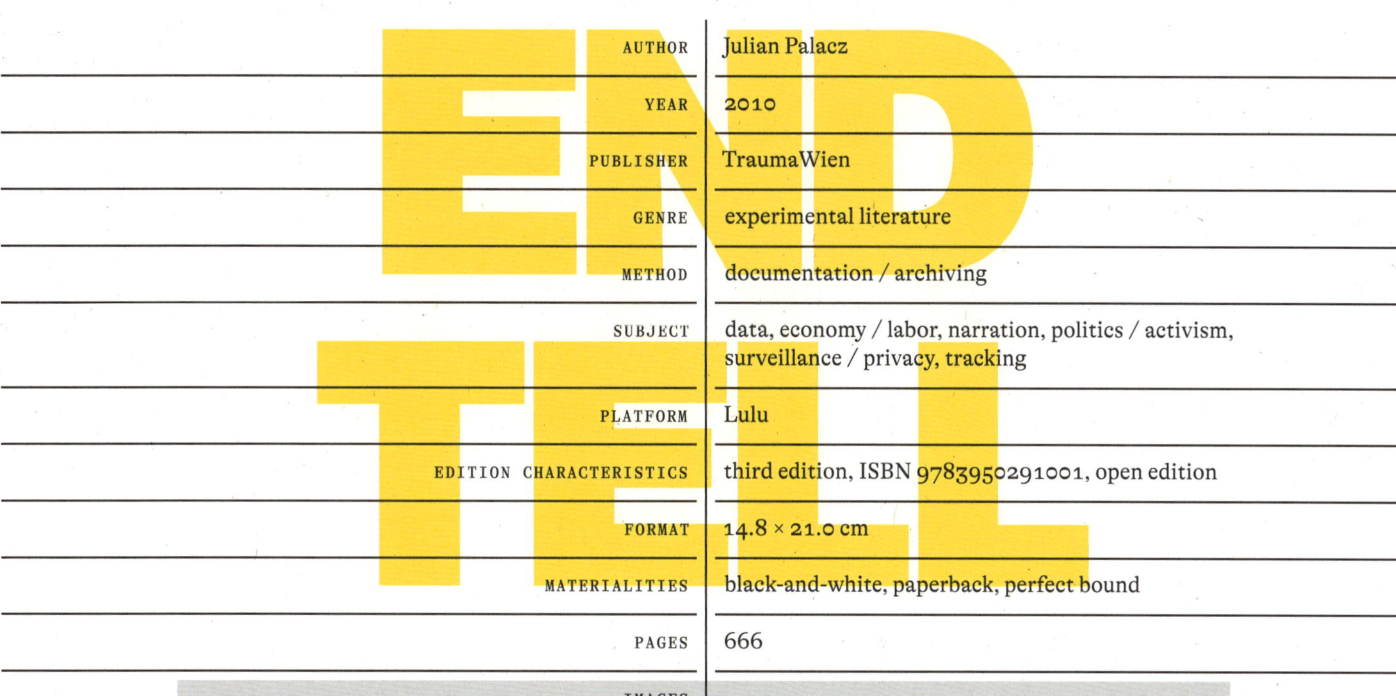

AUTHOR	Julian Palacz
YEAR	2010
PUBLISHER	TraumaWien
GENRE	experimental literature
METHOD	documentation / archiving
SUBJECT	data, economy / labor, narration, politics / activism, surveillance / privacy, tracking
PLATFORM	Lulu
EDITION CHARACTERISTICS	third edition, ISBN 9783950291001, open edition
FORMAT	14.8 × 21.0 cm
MATERIALITIES	black-and-white, paperback, perfect bound
PAGES	666

IMAGES

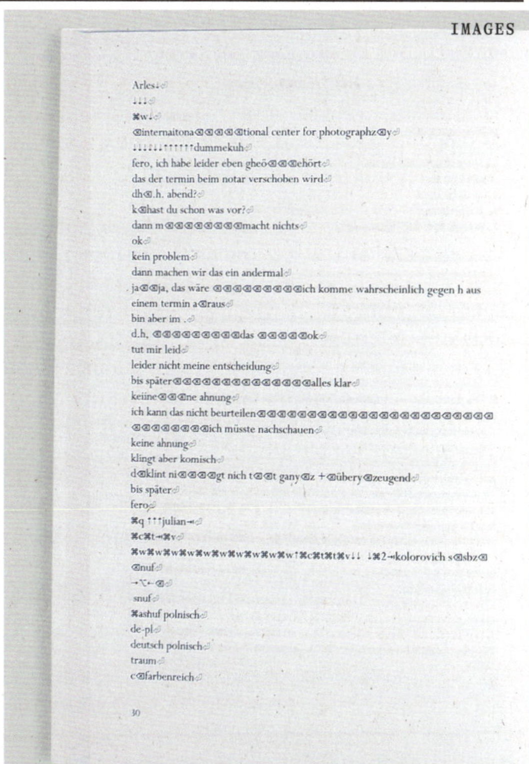

Arles↓⏎
↓↓↓⏎
⌘w↓⏎
⌫internaitona⌫⌫⌫⌫⌫tional center for photographz⌫y⏎
↓↓↓↓↓↓↑↑↑↑↑↑dummekuh⏎
fero, ich habe leider eben gheö⌫⌫⌫ehört⏎
das der termin beim notar verschoben wird⏎
dh⌫.h. abend?⏎
k⌫hast du schon was vor?⏎
dann m⌫⌫⌫⌫⌫⌫⌫⌫⌫macht nichts⏎
ok⏎
kein problem⏎
dann machen wir das ein andermal⏎
ja⌫⌫ja, das wäre ⌫⌫⌫⌫⌫⌫⌫⌫⌫ich komme wahrscheinlich gegen h aus einem termin a⌫raus⏎
bin aber im .⏎
d.h, ⌫⌫⌫⌫⌫⌫⌫⌫⌫⌫das ⌫⌫⌫⌫⌫ok⏎
tut mir leid⏎
leider nicht meine entscheidung⏎
bis später⌫⌫⌫⌫⌫⌫⌫⌫⌫⌫⌫⌫⌫⌫⌫alles klar⏎
keiine⌫⌫⌫ne ahnung⏎
ich kann das nicht beurteilen⌫⌫⌫⌫⌫⌫⌫⌫⌫⌫⌫⌫⌫⌫⌫⌫⌫⌫⌫⌫⌫⌫⌫⌫⌫⌫⌫⌫⌫⌫⌫⌫⌫⌫⌫⌫⌫⌫ich müsste nachschauen⏎
keine ahnung⏎
klingt aber komisch⏎
d⌫klint ni⌫⌫⌫⌫gt nich t⌫⌫t gany⌫z +⌫übery⌫zeugend⏎
bis später⏎
fero⏎
⌘q ↑↑↑julian⇥⏎
⌘c⌘t⇥⌘v⏎
⌘w⌘w⌘w⌘w⌘w⌘w⌘w⌘w⌘w↑⌘c⌘t⌘t⌘v↓↓ ↓⌘2⇥kolorovich s⌫sbz⌫⌫nuf⏎
→⌥←⌫⏎
snuf⏎
⌘ashuf polnisch⏎
de-pl⏎
deutsch polnisch⏎
traum⏎
c⌫farbenreich⏎

30

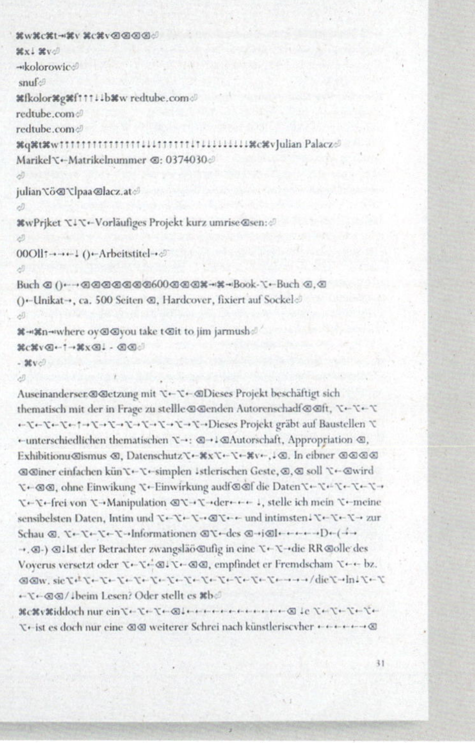

⌘w⌘c⌘t⇥⌘v ⌘c⌘v⌫⌫⌫⌫⏎
⌘x↓ ⌘v⏎
⇥kolorowic⏎
snuf⏎
⌘fkolor⌘g⌘f↑↑↑↓↓b⌘w redtube.com⏎
redtube.com⏎
redtube.com⏎
⌘q⌘t⌘w↑↑↑↑↑↑↑↑↑↑↑↑↑↑↑↓↓↑↑↑↑↑↑↓↑↓↓↓↓↓↓↓↓↓⌘c⌘vJulian Palacz⏎
Marikel⌥←Matrikelnummer ⌫: 0374030⏎
⏎
julian⌥ö⌫⌥lpaa⌫lacz.at⏎
⏎
⌘wPrjket ⌥↓⌥←Vorläufiges Projekt kurz umrise⌫sen:⏎
⏎
00Oll↑→→←↓ ()←Arbeitstitel→⏎
⏎
Buch ⌫ ()←→⌫⌫⌫⌫⌫⌫⌫600⌫⌫⌫⌘→⌘→Book-⌥←Buch ⌫,⌫ ()←Unikat→, ca. 500 Seiten ⌫, Hardcover, fixiert auf Sockel⏎
⏎
⌘→⌘n→where oy⌫⌫you take t⌫it to jim jarmush⏎
⌘c⌘v⌫←↑→⌘x⌫↓ - ⌫⌫⏎
- ⌘v⏎
⏎
Auseinanderser⌫⌫etzung mit ⌥←⌥←⌫Dieses Projekt beschäftigt sich thematisch mit der in Frage zu stellle⌫⌫enden Autorenschadf⌫⌫ft, ⌥←⌥←⌥←⌥←⌥←⌥←↑→⌥→⌥→⌥→⌥→⌥→⌥→⌥→Dieses Projekt gräbt auf Baustellen ⌥←unterschiedlichen thematischen ⌥→: ⌫→↓⌫Autorschaft, Appropriation ⌫, Exhibitionu⌫ismus ⌫, Datenschutz⌥←⌘x⌥←⌥←⌘v←,↓⌫. In eibner ⌫⌫⌫⌫⌫⌫iner einfachen kün⌥←⌥←simplen ↓stlerischen Geste,⌫,⌫ soll ⌥←⌫wird ⌥←⌫⌫, ohne Einwikung ⌥←Einwirkung audf⌫⌫f die Daten⌥←⌥←⌥←⌥←⌥→⌥←⌥←frei von ⌥→Manipulation ⌫⌥→⌥→der←←← ↓, stelle ich mein ⌥←meine sensibelsten Daten, Intim und ⌥←⌥←⌥→⌫⌥←← und intimsten↓⌥←⌥←⌥→ zur Schau ⌫. ⌥←⌥←⌥←⌥→Informationen ⌫⌥←des ⌫→i⌫l←←←←→D←(→→.⌫-) ⌫↓Ist der Betrachter zwangsläö⌫ufig in eine ⌥←⌥→die RR⌫olle des Voyerus versetzt oder ⌥←⌥←⌫↓⌥←⌫⌫, empfindet er Fremdscham ⌥←← bz.⌫⌫w. sie⌥←⌥←⌥←⌥←⌥←⌥←⌥←⌥←⌥←⌥←⌥←⌥←⌥←→→→/die⌥→In↓⌥←⌥←⌥←⌫⌫/↓beim Lesen? Oder stellt es ⌘b⏎
⌘c⌘v⌘iddoch nur ein⌥←⌥←⌥←⌫↓←←←←←←←←←←←←←⌫ ↓e ⌥←⌥←⌥←⌥←⌥←ist es doch nur eine ⌫⌫ weiterer Schrei nach künstleriscvher ←←←←←→⌫

31

DESCRIPTION

END TELL is a complete record of every key pressed on the author's private computer between June 2008 and February 2010. For this, Julian Palacz made use of a keylogger, a piece of software used in hacking for retrieving the login data of unaware users, sitting between the operating system and the most fundamental input device of human-computer-interaction: the keyboard. In this way, one gains insight into what is otherwise between the lines, into the writing, thinking and feeling, into the error and the "not written," since deleted.

What is particularly unsettling is that during this period, a fellow student stayed with Palacz for a few days and, of course, used his computer—without knowing a keylogger was installed. *END TELL* is as much an empirical documentation of Palacz's most private communication as it is a textual narration of a user's computer-interactions. The documentation of all keyboard strokes is introduced with the heading: "Traces of birds in the snow."

The book has been published in three editions: a blue hardcover version in 2010, a second edition in the same year, and finally a white cover paperback version in 2014. Changes made to these republished versions are not listed.

die dichtkunst

AUTHOR	Vanessa Place
YEAR	2010
PUBLISHER	Ood Press
GENRE	experimental literature, poetry
METHOD	composition (writing / drawing / photography), constraint, reenactment, translation / transcription
SUBJECT	book / book design, literature, reading / interpretation
PLATFORM	Lulu
EDITION CHARACTERISTICS	ISBN 9781257649792, open edition
FORMAT	14.8 × 21.0 cm
MATERIALITIES	black-and-white, paperback, perfect bound
PAGES	390 (unpaginated)
IMAGES	

DESCRIPTION

Vanessa Place's *die dichtkunst* (The Art of Poetry) fills 383 pages with the letter "u," in blocks of twenty-seven in a line and twenty-two lines per page. In the second half of the book, letters are regularly missing at the beginning of text blocks: In a regular pattern, every eleven pages that are completely filled with the letter "u" are followed by one page where the initial "u" is clearly missing. This is certainly no coincidence, because the total number of pages in the book (383) is also subject to strict numerical symbolism, as the blurb clarifies: "two 3s together forming the 8, which is the sign for infinity." Eleven pages in the middle of the book show crossed out letters. Here, too, the number 11 is deliberately chosen: "a mirrored number, the number of the uniform binary, the single number of the twin. Two mirrors reflecting one another will reflect to infinity" (blurb on Lulu).

The number 11 could also be read as a combination of two letter "I"s, contrasting with the letter "u" that forms the content of the book which could be read as "you" and also as the German abbreviation for "and." In this way, *die dichtkunst*, of which we cannot know for sure what language it is actually written in, reflects on I and you, sender and recipient, writing and reading, singularity and multiplicity as the core of poetic practice.

Besides, *die dichtkunst* refers to "Hanne Darboven's monumental *Kulturgeschichte 1880–1983*, with its scores of scored u's combined with Jacques Lacan's observation that 'There has never been a you anywhere else than where one says you.' For once one truly says you: 'I abolish myself'" (blurb on Lulu).

AUTHOR	Vanessa Place
YEAR	2010
GENRE	experimental literature
METHOD	appropriation
SUBJECT	canon, gender, politics / activism, reading / interpretation
PLATFORM	Lulu
EDITION CHARACTERISTICS	ISBN 9781257007059, open edition
FORMAT	14.8 × 21.0 cm
MATERIALITIES	black-and-white, paperback, perfect bound
PAGES	69

IMAGES

DESCRIPTION

Vanessa Place's *SCUM Manifesto* combines conceptual writing and feminist discourse. The blurb on Lulu identifies it as the fifth installment of the *Boycott Project*—a series of interventions in iconic feminist texts by authors like Judith Butler, Luce Irigaray, Hélène Cixous, Simone de Beauvoir, and Valerie Solanas. Echoing French psychoanalyst Jacques Lacan's famous postulate that "woman does not exist" and conceptual artist Lee Lozano's refusal to communicate with women to protest patriarchy's gendering in her *boycott of women* (1971), Place replaces all female pronouns and gendered terms with their male equivalents, with the effect that the texts speak only of men.

In the case of the *SCUM Manifesto*, she in a way repeats Solanas's own approach, whose Manifesto is commonly read as "a parody of the Freudian theory of femininity, where the word *woman* is replaced by *man* [...]. All the clichés of Freudian psychoanalytical theory are here: the biological accident, the incomplete sex, 'penis envy' which has become 'pussy envy,' and so forth [...]. Here we have a case of absurdity being used to as a literary device to expose an absurdity, that is, the absurd theory which has been used to give 'scientific' legitimacy to patriarchy" (Ginette Castro, *American Feminism*, 73). This leads to Solanas's call to "destroy the male sex"—after all, it is now the male sex that is defined by its imperfection: "To be male is to be deficient, emotionally limited; maleness is a deficiency disease and males are emotional cripples" (Valerie Solanas, *SCUM Manifesto*, 3f.). Place's substitution of the remaining feminine words while retaining all masculine terms and pronouns subverts Solanas's reverse of the usual reasoning by introducing logical absurdities such as: "The male is a biological accident: the Y (male) gene is an incomplete X (male) gene [...]. In other words, the male is an incomplete male [...]" (Vanessa Place, *SCUM Manifesto*, 1).

At the end of the book, it is identified as "Factory Product," and thus as part of Place's print-on-demand *Factory Series* for which she invited other authors to write books that she would sign herself as the author, in the style of Andy Warhol's *Factory* paintings (see 174–176). It is possible, however, that this attribution is a mistake, similar to Place's *Gone with the Wind* (see 203).

Factory Series

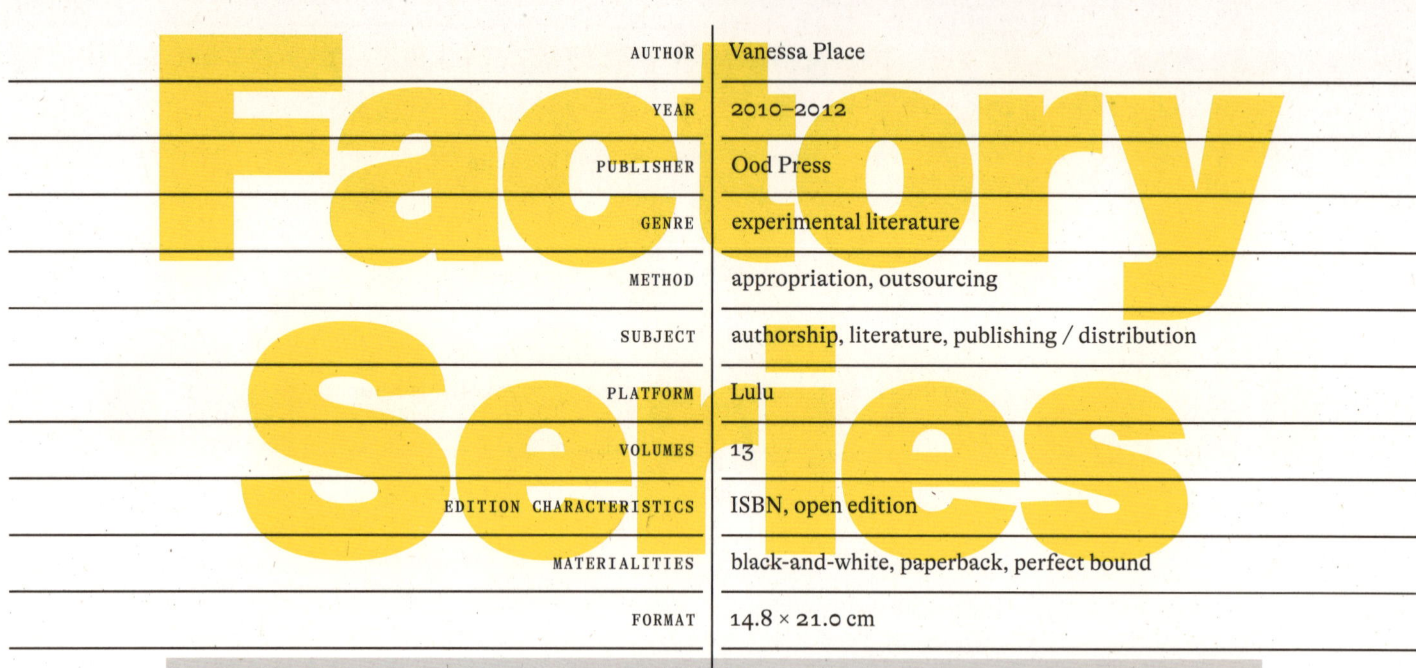

AUTHOR	Vanessa Place
YEAR	2010–2012
PUBLISHER	Ood Press
GENRE	experimental literature
METHOD	appropriation, outsourcing
SUBJECT	authorship, literature, publishing / distribution
PLATFORM	Lulu
VOLUMES	13
EDITION CHARACTERISTICS	ISBN, open edition
MATERIALITIES	black-and-white, paperback, perfect bound
FORMAT	14.8 × 21.0 cm

IMAGE

DESCRIPTION

Echoing Andy Warhol's *Factory* paintings, Vanessa Place invited other authors to compose books for her *Factory Series* that she would sign herself as the author. Place even wanted to leave the printing preparation completely to her assistants, claiming in her open call: "it is my goal to have nothing to do with creation until after the fact." In principle, writers were "allowed" to reveal the "true" authorship—Place was primarily focused on declaring her authorship on the printed artifact. The books, none of which have been written by Place, are advertised on Lulu as "a vivid portrayal of contemporary poetics" (blurb on Lulu). Some volumes appear to be bound incorrectly, or the uploaded PDF files were not created carefully enough so that the title page is on the left instead of the right (see *Hellocasts* and *Thank You For Reading*), which affects the page layout throughout the book.

The series so far includes thirteen volumes: *Factory Work*; *Hellocasts*; *Poems for Oodpress*; *Thank you for Reading*; *The Polished You*; *Page Not Found*; *Revolution*; *Stoked*; *Black Square*; *Locus Solus*; *Only Yahweh*; *Poetry*; and *P.O.T.I.C.H.E. or Pathway to Decent Work for Women*.

The series is edited by Chris Hershey-Van Horn (Ood Press).

Factory Work

YEAR: 2010

GENRE: experimental literature

METHOD: appropriation, reformatting

SUBJECT: art, canon

EDITION CHARACTERISTICS: ISBN 9781257640126, open edition, CC0

PAGES: 69

DESCRIPTION: This is the first publication in Vanessa Place's *Factory Series*. It contains an excerpt from *Andy Warhol's Diaries* (Warhol's dictated memoirs, edited by Pat Hackett and posthumously published in 1989) from October 2 to December 31, 1980. Lost are all text markups (italics, boldface) and paragraphs.

The keywords chosen in the Lulu bookshop suggest that the "real" authorship on this work lies with Kenneth Goldsmith, a great connoisseur of Andy Warhol and editor of his interviews.

back and everybody looks alike blue jeans and no shirts and mustaches, and no girls allowed, except they let Pat Cleveland in, and they let ten lesbians have memberships. There's a waiting list for two years and they said you can only get in if somebody drops out. The light show was great, like the Hayden Planetarium. Then Halston was leaving at 3:00 and I left, too. Wednesday, November 5, 1980 Dosseldorf-Baden Baden-Stuttgart I woke up at 3:00 in the morning and I heard the sad news of Carter losing so desperately to Reagan. It was the first time a president conceded so early. He had tears in his eyes. I couldn't sleep and I took a Valium. Thursday, November 6,1980 Frankfurt- D'osseldorf Met Dr. Siegfried Unseld, he's the publisher of Hermann Hesse and Goethe, really good-looking. I thought he was going to be easy to photograph because he was so good-looking, but he was really hard. His good

32

looks didn't come through for the camera. I'd brought Chris Makos on the trip to help me, but he wouldn't carry my bag or do anything—all he cared about was taking photographs for himself. The next location was like an hour and a half away, in Darmstadt. Went to photograph a lady who's sort of a German Diane Von Furstenberg, she's a top clothes manufacturer—her company's called Tink or Fink. The house was beautiful. She was dressed really like a businesswoman, though, in a velvet suit with hankies coming out of everywhere. She was really sweet and the pictures came out well. After a long drive to D'osseldorf, Chris and I had a fight because the walls at the Breitenbacher Hof Hotel are very thin and through the wall I could hear Christopher in his room making phone calls and I got nervous because I'm hearing him dial eighteen digits and I know he's caning long distance to Peter Wise in New York and it's

33

Hellocasts

YEAR: 2011

GENRE: experimental literature

METHOD: appropriation, composition (writing / drawing / photography), paratextual play

SUBJECT: politics / activism, reading / interpretation, visual culture

EDITION CHARACTERISTICS: ISBN 9781257642236, open edition

PAGES: 33 (unpaginated)

DESCRIPTION: This is the second publication in Vanessa Place's *Factory Series*. The keywords chosen in the Lulu bookshop suggest that the "real" authorship on this work lies with Divya Victor. The book is often listed as *Hellocasts by Charles Reznikoff by Divya Victor by Vanessa Place*, with the "author" disappearing behind a quotational practice.

Each double-page spread of the book presents a blank, lined notebook page on one side and a variation of the Hello Kitty character filled with handwritten text on the other. Two notebook pages meet in the middle of the book, then the same sequence of figure and notebook pages follows once again. The text in the outline of the global trademark turns out to be an excerpt from Charles Reznikoff's *Holocaust* (1975), which documents the testimony of survivors at the Holocaust tribunals.

Hellocasts also exists as drawings on a gallery wall and as performances by poet Divya Victor, both curated by Les Figues Press at Los Angeles Contemporary Exhibitions. In one performance, Divya Victor herself transcribes Reznikoff's stanzas into Hello Kitty outlines projected onto the gallery wall; in another, visitors are invited to do the same while following the recording of Victor's reading.

Poems for OodPress

YEAR	2010
GENRE	experimental literature
METHOD	appropriation, reformatting
SUBJECT	canon, literature, typography
EDITION CHARACTERISTICS	ISBN 9781257644292, open edition
PAGES	31 (unpaginated)
DESCRIPTION	This is the third publication in Vanessa Place's *Factory Series*. It includes twenty poems by experimental poets, ranging from classics such as William Carlos Williams, Gertrude Stein, and Aram Saroyan to contemporaries such as Christian Bök, Juliana Spahr, Harryette Mullen, and Eileen Myles. Each poem is set in a different font in 14 pt., ranging from Arial Rounded MT Bold, Times New Roman, Modern, and Century to Apple LiSung Light, Academy Engraved LET, and Euphemia UCAS Bold. The keywords chosen in the Lulu bookshop suggest that the "real" authorship on this work lies with Steven Zultanski.

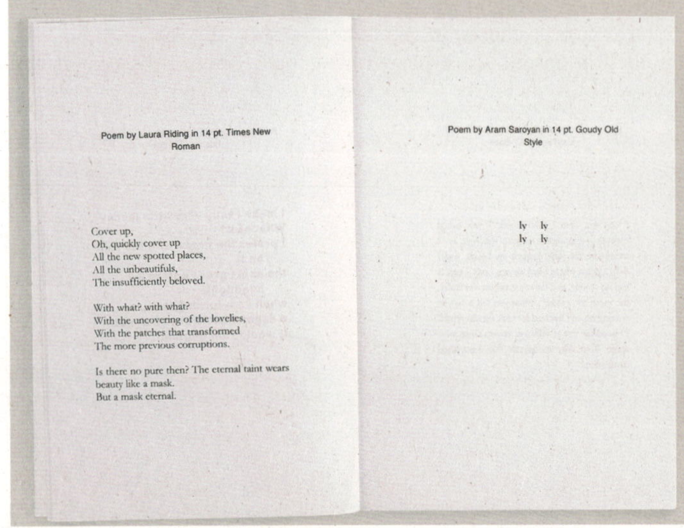

Poem by Laura Riding in 14 pt. Times New Roman

Cover up,
Oh, quickly cover up
All the new spotted places,
All the unbeautifuls,
The insufficiently beloved.

With what? with what?
With the uncovering of the lovelies,
With the patches that transformed
The more previous corruptions.

Is there no pure then? The eternal taint wears
beauty like a mask.
But a mask eternal.

Poem by Aram Saroyan in 14 pt. Goudy Old Style

ly ly
ly ly

Thank You For Reading

YEAR	2012
GENRE	experimental literature
METHOD	found material, reformatting
SUBJECT	dating / sex, internet culture, social media
EDITION CHARACTERISTICS	ISBN 9781105584497, open edition
PAGES	37 (unpaginated)
DESCRIPTION	This is the thirteenth publication in Vanessa Place's *Factory Series*. It contains want ads from dating portals for gay men, all of which include a thank you to the reader for reading. Personal information such as names, phone numbers, and email addresses are redacted. The keywords chosen in the Lulu bookshop suggest that the "real" authorship on this work lies with Michael du Plessis. He confirms this in an interview with Janice Lee, who in turn reveals that she designed *Only Yahweh* from the series (Janice Lee, "An Interview").

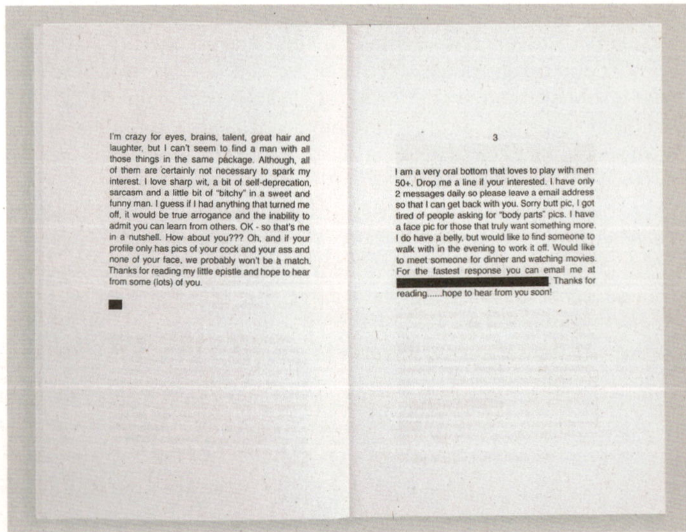

I'm crazy for eyes, brains, talent, great hair and laughter, but I can't seem to find a man with all those things in the same package. Although, all of them are certainly not necessary to spark my interest. I love sharp wit, a bit of self-deprecation, sarcasm and a little bit of "bitchy" in a sweet and funny man. I guess if I had anything that turned me off, it would be true arrogance and the inability to admit you can learn from others. OK - so that's me in a nutshell. How about you??? Oh, and if your profile only has pics of your cock and your ass and none of your face, we probably won't be a match. Thanks for reading my little epistle and hope to hear from some (lots) of you.

3

I am a very oral bottom that loves to play with men 50+. Drop me a line if your interested. I have only 2 messages daily so please leave a email address so that I can get back with you. Sorry butt pic, I got tired of people asking for "body parts" pics. I have a face pic for those that truly want something more. I do have a belly, but would like to find someone to walk with in the evening to work it off. Would like to meet someone for dinner and watching movies. For the fastest response you can email me at ███. Thanks for reading......hope to hear from you soon!

Lost Memories

AUTHOR	Joachim Schmid
YEAR	2010 [2nd ed. 2012]
GENRE	artist's book / bookwork
METHOD	collection, documentation / archiving, found material
SUBJECT	memory / storage, photography, visual culture
PLATFORM	Blurb, Lulu
EDITION CHARACTERISTICS	multiple editions, second edition, open edition, available only through the artist
FORMAT	10.8 × 17.5 cm
MATERIALITIES	black-and-white, paperback, perfect bound
PAGES	78 (unpaginated)

IMAGE

DESCRIPTION

As Joachim Schmid notes on his website, "in the age of digital photography, [...] it has got to the point that we can't imagine life without the possibility of a camera recording it" (Joachim Schmid, "Lost Memories," website). However, given the vast amount of images produced today, one might think that the value of the individual photograph is diminishing. That this is not the case is proven by this collection of reports about the loss of one's camera, which Schmid has taken from various internet sites specializing only in this case: They demonstrate that "it happens more often than we may think" (Ibid.), that these mundane photos have great personal significance for the individual, and, unlike the lost camera, are irreplaceable. Over eighty pages, Schmid lists help-wanted notices, which are similar in their desperate wording and structure: they describe the loss situation, the camera, and the photos taken, promise a reward, and implore the finder or thief to send the photos or memory card: "I just want my memories back." Again and again, the loss of the photos is equated with the loss of one's own memories; only rarely is one's own memory distinguished from the memory card as it is here: "And though the memories always stay in our memory, would be a joy to return to retrieve it!!"

The emotions triggered by this distress are reminiscent of those documented by Thomas Walskaar in *My Hard-Drive Died Along With My Heart* (see 365). Schmid draws another parallel to the analog age: "Every cry for help evokes Bruce Chatwin's observation that 'to lose a passport was the least of one's worries; to lose a notebook was a catastrophe'" (Schmid, "Lost Memories," website). His book ends, however, with an optimistic post from someone who has lost two cameras in a row, one of which was recovered: "after this first miracle, why not another?"

Dissatisfied with Blurb's quality and customer service and lack of responsiveness to artists' specific needs, Schmid moved to Lulu in 2012, from where our copy in the collection originated. The Blurb edition in the 12.5 × 20.1 cm format was discontinued and scaled for the Lulu format.

Quick Response

AUTHOR	Joachim Schmid
YEAR	2010 [2nd ed. 2012]
GENRE	photobook
METHOD	collection, found material, remediation
SUBJECT	analog / digital, code / programming, flickr, photography, technology, visual culture
PLATFORM	Blurb, Lulu
EDITION CHARACTERISTICS	multiple editions, second edition, open edition, available only through the artist
FORMAT	10.3 × 17.2 cm
MATERIALITIES	black-and-white, paperback, perfect bound
PAGES	40 (unpaginated)

IMAGES

DESCRIPTION

In *Quick Response*, Joachim Schmid devotes himself to the ubiquitous QR code, which was developed as a replacement to the barcode by the Japanese company Denso for the Japanese car industry in 1994 and has since found its way from industrial production into everyday life. It links public space with the internet in a unique way and its austere, constructivist look is not infrequently appreciated in aesthetic terms. It is little wonder, then, that it is also well represented in photographs on Flickr.

It is precisely these QR code photos that Schmid refers to in *Quick Response*: a collection of QR codes, each of which is individually set on a page and turns into an abstract image that can only be "read" with technical support. A smartphone can be used to scan the code and follow the inscribed link to one of these QR code photos on Flickr. Thus, "[t]he series of photos demonstrates the variety of modern commercial, artistic and subversive QR code applications. In addition, the book demonstrates a new way of appropriating other people's photographs" (Joachim Schmid, "Quick Response," website).

Dissatisfied with Blurb's quality, customer service, and lack of responsiveness to artists' specific needs, Schmid moved to Lulu in 2012, from where our copy in the collection originated. The 2010 paginated Blurb edition in the 12.5 × 20.1 cm format was discontinued and scaled for the unpaginated Lulu format.

AUTHOR	Travis Shaffer
YEAR	2010
GENRE	photobook
METHOD	collection, remediation, study / analysis
SUBJECT	analog / digital, social media, visual culture, web design
PLATFORM	Blurb
EDITION CHARACTERISTICS	open edition
FORMAT	17.0 × 16.8 cm
MATERIALITIES	color, paperback, perfect bound
PAGES	48 (unpaginated)

IMAGES

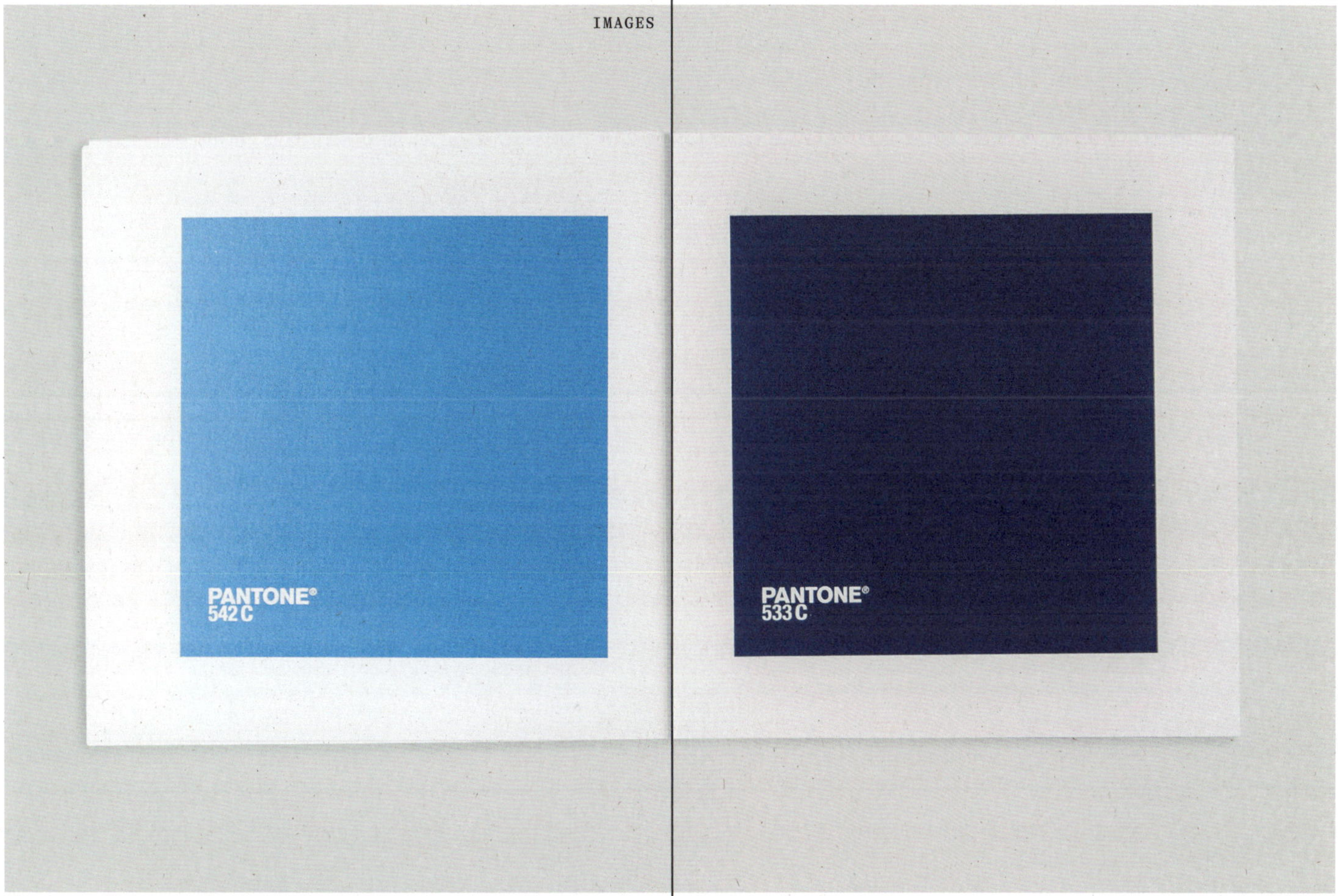

DESCRIPTION

Travis Shaffer's *Social Media Blues* is a collection of the forty most popular shades of blue used in social media interfaces. Each blue is represented as tone of the PANTONE® Color Matching System. To create it, the artist screenshotted the blues of a number of social media websites on November 15, 2010, then averaged and matched them to the closest PANTONE® color. The series begins on the cover, whose shade of blue matches that of Blurb and is specified as PANTONE® 299 C.

The PANTONE® Color Matching System is a proprietary, industry-standard color reproduction system for CMYK printing. The book's focus on this analog color swatch contrasts with the sampling of digital colors represented in screen based RGB. As such, *Social Media Blues* is not only a guide to the palette of social media interface design, but also a reflection on screen colors and their representation in print. Accordingly, the statement at the end of the book reads, "The Artist also makes no warranties regarding the accuracy of the illustrated Pantone swatches and does not recommend this guide as a tool for color management."

Sorority Skin Tones
a PANTONE® color guide

AUTHOR	Travis Shaffer
YEAR	2010
GENRE	photobook
METHOD	collection, found material, study / analysis
SUBJECT	analog / digital, bias, facebook, race
PLATFORM	Blurb
FORMAT	17.0 × 16.8 cm
MATERIALITIES	color, paperback, perfect bound
PAGES	28 (unpaginated)
IMAGES	

DESCRIPTION

Travis Shaffer's *Sorority Skin Tones* is a collection of the twenty most common skin tones web-sampled from Facebook photographs of the ten largest American sororities on November 15, 2010. Each tone is averaged and matched to the closest PANTONE® color. The series begins on the cover, whose skin tone is specified as PANTONE® 2365 C, and can also be understood as an empirical representation of the Whiteness of sorority culture.

Similar to Shaffer's *Social Media Blues* (see 179), the book contrasts the analog color swatch for CMYK printing with the sampling of digital colors represented in screen-based RGB. As such, *Sorority Skin Tones* is a reflection on the remediation of color from skin to digital photo to screen display to printing. Accordingly, the statement at the end of the book reads, "The Artist also makes no warranties regarding the accuracy of the illustrated Pantone swatches and does not recommend this guide as a tool for color management."

GRID

AUTHOR	Chris Sylvester
YEAR	2010
GENRE	experimental literature
METHOD	composition (writing / drawing / photography)
SUBJECT	book / book design, games, narration, writing / reading techniques
PLATFORM	Lulu
EDITION CHARACTERISTICS	open edition
FORMAT	21.6 × 27.9 cm
MATERIALITIES	black-and-white, paperback, perfect bound
PAGES	130 (unpaginated)

IMAGES

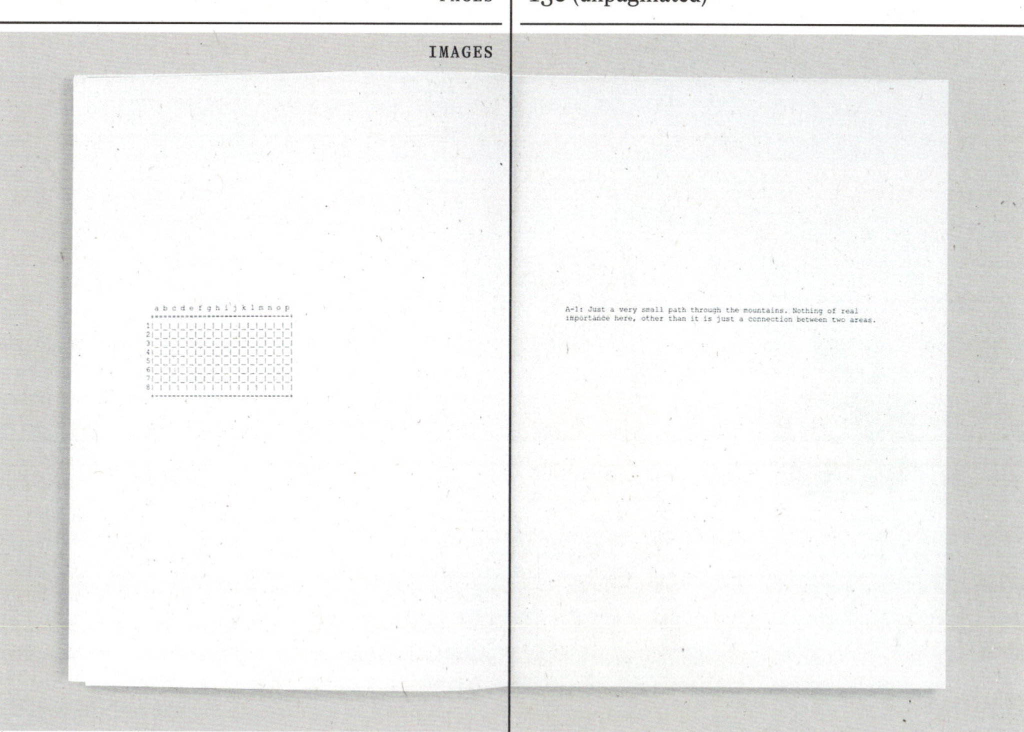

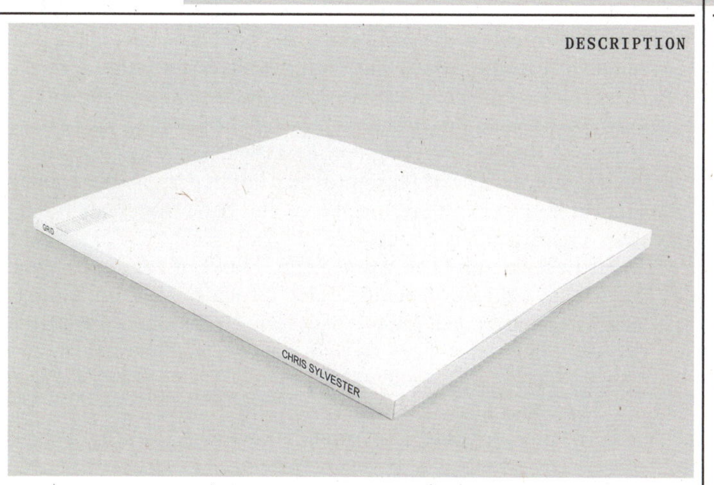

DESCRIPTION

Chris Sylvester's *GRID* is a transposition of multi-branch narration (common in certain video games and pen-and-paper role-playing games) into the codex. In room-to-room games, a player is confronted with a room that takes up the entire screen, usually with multiple options to move to one of the connecting rooms. This kind of world-building allows players to roam freely and explore narration in an open setting. Such worlds can usually be mapped on grids, which became particularly important for playing textual adventures that would only provide a written description for the room that the player was in at any given moment. The only chance for the player to get an overview of their location was to draw maps that would result in grid-like structures.

Sylvester provides such a grid in an ASCII-aesthetic with fields from A–P and 1–8 and a description for each field. The result is the description of a fictitious game's world that closely resembles walk-through guides for games like the Zelda series. A lot of the descriptions mark rooms as "pointless screens" only existing to connect one room to the next, which are nonetheless indispensable to provide a sense of vastness and emptiness, characteristic for such games. Also, multiple caves and shortcuts are mentioned, hinting at another layer of the roamable world. The eeriness of this is further enhanced by the descriptions' sequencing, which doesn't follow the perspective of a player as is usual, but provides information for the fields from top to bottom and left to right. Thus, the printed book becomes a quick-reference guide for a fictitious game with no less than three reading techniques present at the same time to establish a narrational world and the sense of a story.

Every Day a New Photo Book

AUTHOR	Wil van Iersel
YEAR	2010–2021
GENRE	catalog / collection, photobook
METHOD	composition (writing / drawing / photography), constraint, documentation / archiving, found material, versioning / seriality
SUBJECT	book / book design, memory / storage, photography, publishing / distribution, scale, standard / default
PLATFORM	Blurb
VOLUMES	12 boxes with 28 to 31 volumes each
EDITION CHARACTERISTICS	open edition, limited edition, numbered, signed
FORMAT	17.0 × 16.8 cm
MATERIALITIES	box, color, paperback, perfect bound
PAGES	20–40

IMAGE

DESCRIPTION

"*Every Day a New Photo Book* is a project over a period of 12 years, it's a photographic research into time and society. From September 2010 until August 2021 I will take every year another month to make every day a new book. Every month has a theme what then is researched on a daily basis" (blurb on Blurb). The books are uploaded and printed on the day they are made.

"Making books on a daily basis means to me that I am in a 'flow' of ideas and that I work in a clear rhythm of research, photography and editing. To be so active with a lot of energy plus the limitation of time make it sure that I find different visions on the subject. At the end of the month all books come together and are a kind of visual encyclopaedia of the subject" (Wil van Iersel, "About").

Accordingly, all books made in the same month are presented by the artist as a single set in a black slipcase in an edition of 10, signed and numbered, and then sold through his own webshop. However, it is also possible to browse through the books on his website and order individual copies directly through Blurb.

In terms of format and design, van Iersel's twenty-page square softcover books follow Blurb's cheapest standard sizes. Over the years, the series reflects a number of changes in print-on-demand production and business. In the beginning, van Iersel created the books directly on the website using Blurb's own design program, which is why these books still contain the note: "The Blurb-provided layout designs and graphic elements are copyright Blurb Inc., 2009. This book was created using the Blurb creative publishing service."

In a satirical column "The Worst Photo Books of 2013," published on the Artists' Books Cooperative blog (of which Wil van Iersel is a founding member), van Iersel's new series is announced with the words: "Wil van Iersel makes a new book every day for a whole month every year. POD should have never been invented. This month his topic is food. His books are as good as eating 30 cheeseburgers from McDonald's in one go" (ABC, "The Worst Photo Books").

THE EDITIONS ARE	*On the Road* in August 2021, *All the Pictures of Today* in July 2020, *Double Observation of a Place in Text and Image* in June 2019, *THAT'S ENTERTAINMENT* in May 2018, *PERIPHERAL VISION* in April 2017, *WALKING* in March 2016, *COLOUR* in February 2015 (graphic design by Jason Edwards), *GLAMOROUS* in January 2014 (graphic design by Lotte Schröder), *FOOD* in December 2013 (graphic design by Erwin Slaats), *SPEED* in November 2012 (graphic design by Jacqueline Elich), *MONEY* in October 2011 (graphic design by Sofie Gerritsen), and *AT RANDOM* in September 2010.

AT RANDOM: September 2010

YEAR	2010
GENRE	catalog / collection, photobook
METHOD	composition (writing / drawing / photography), constraint
SUBJECT	photography, technology
VOLUMES	30
EDITION CHARACTERISTICS	limited edition, numbered, signed

DESCRIPTION

AT RANDOM is the first monthly collection of Wil van Iersel's series *Every Day a New Photo Book*. It not only gave the formal and conceptual framework for all box editions to follow but also established some of the series' contents and aesthetics, which were developed further in subsequent months and years.

The title "AT RANDOM" might be the most accurate description of van Iersel's choice of topics, though it might only seem random from the outside. Since because of its strict time constraint the whole series is closely connected to the artist's biography, "random" in this case means topics that occurred to the artist and were directly transformed into photobooks without deeper reflection. This leads to books that sometimes document private and personal events like his newborn's facial expressions (#3), a friend's birthday party (#4), or an autumn walk with the family (#26). There are also serial investigations like in *Automobile*, depicting parking tickets on the windshields of parked cars, or in *Shortcuts* (#7) and *Boat* (#11) which document the word chosen in the title in different contexts.

Most of the collection, then, can be described as street photography or serial photography that follows a specific topic, named in the title of each book. In this way, each collection of a single day of photos is bound together by date and content, which might be said to be the main artistic strategy of the entire *Every Day a New Photo Book* project. The very first book is called *Camera* and features an unboxing of the camera and its equipment that van Iersel used to start the series, which, combined with the print-on-demand photobook format, are the main tools for domesticating its photographic imagery.

Every book within the collection box in our possession is signed and numbered as the sixth in the edition of ten. An error occurs in the second book, the last page of which is additionally marked "7/10."

SPEED: November 19

YEAR	2012
GENRE	photobook
METHOD	found material, remediation
SUBJECT	economy / labor, film, platforms / companies, print technology
EDITION CHARACTERISTICS	open edition
PAGES	20 (unpaginated)

DESCRIPTION

The subject of this series produced in November 2012 was speed. Accordingly, there are books about bullets, cars, planes, roads, and trains, as well as skating, running, and jogging.

The book for November 19, 2012 is dedicated to its own print-on-demand production process, which in fact is mainly characterized by its high speed compared to the traditional publishing and book business. It starts with an excerpt from a promotional film for Hewlett-Packard's digital printing presses: "*SPEED* in the production process: Espresso Book Machines, HP Indigos and other digital printers. Ready while you wait."

In an introduction to his overall project, the artist draws particular attention to this very aspect and traces the historical line of "rapid-fire" self-publishing as follows: "Print on demand means that the book is digitally printed on the moment you order via a Web store in an open edition. Not the speed of 'print on demand' is new. Self publishing had its first peak during the French Revolution. There were then writers/printers who made newspapers and pamphleteer. They did everything by themselves, they had their own printing shop and printed often on homemade paper. One example is Rétif de la Bretonne who wrote his stories about nightlife in Paris, printed the texts in the morning and peddled his pamphlets on the streets in the afternoon and then started over in the evening with new stories. Fast production was already possible" (Wil van Iersel, "About").

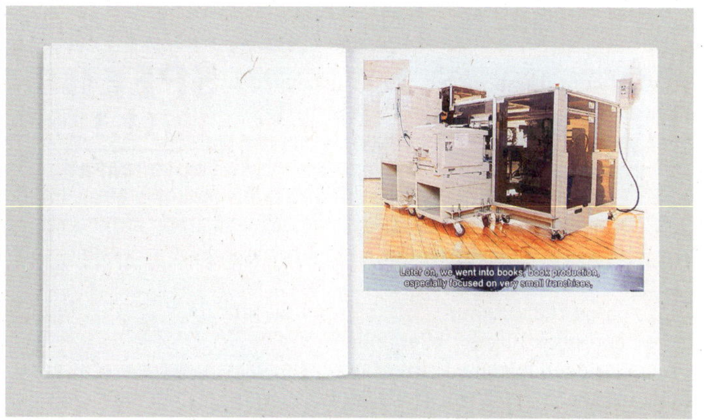

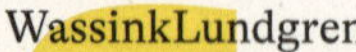

AUTHOR	WassinkLundgren
YEAR	2010
GENRE	catalog / collection, photobook
METHOD	collection, composition (writing / drawing / photography), constraint, versioning / seriality
SUBJECT	book / book design, photography, print on demand, publishing / distribution, standard / default
PLATFORM	Blurb
EDITION CHARACTERISTICS	open edition
FORMAT	19.5 × 24.6 cm
MATERIALITIES	color, paperback, perfect bound
PAGES	125
IMAGES	

DESCRIPTION

Portfolio contains selected works produced by WassinkLundgren, a Dutch photographer duo consisting of Thijs Groot Wassink and Ruben Lundgren, up to the year 2009. It includes photos from fourteen different series and an afterword by Martin Parr. The artists explained their choice of using the Blurb self-publishing platform in an interview: "A portfolio with a black, leather cover is a bit boring and it doesn't really suit our work. But a Blurb book is easily accessible, you can make it really quickly, and you can add in new work as you do it. We just exposed the structure and followed the workings of it" (cited in Indie Photobook Library, „Portfolio").

As mentioned in the copyright note, *Portfolio* makes use of Blurb's standard layout software. This is not hidden in the book, which is as playful and inventive as the presented photo series: the software's grid structures, text boxes, and instructions are still visible. This creates a generic look and at the same time highlights the formal aspects of book designing and producing. The front and back covers contain placeholder boxes for title (and/or image), subtitle, and author information, with the unused boxes still containing instructions like "Enrich the back of your book with text or leave it text-free," "drag image here," and "click to add subtitle," which sometimes is actually cataloged as *Portfolio*'s subtitle.

The blurb on Blurb informs that this portfolio is in principle expandable and changeable, which is why updated and revised limited hard cover editions are planned, available through the artists' webshop.

This book was the Portfolio Category Winner for Blurb's 2010 Photography Book Now competition.

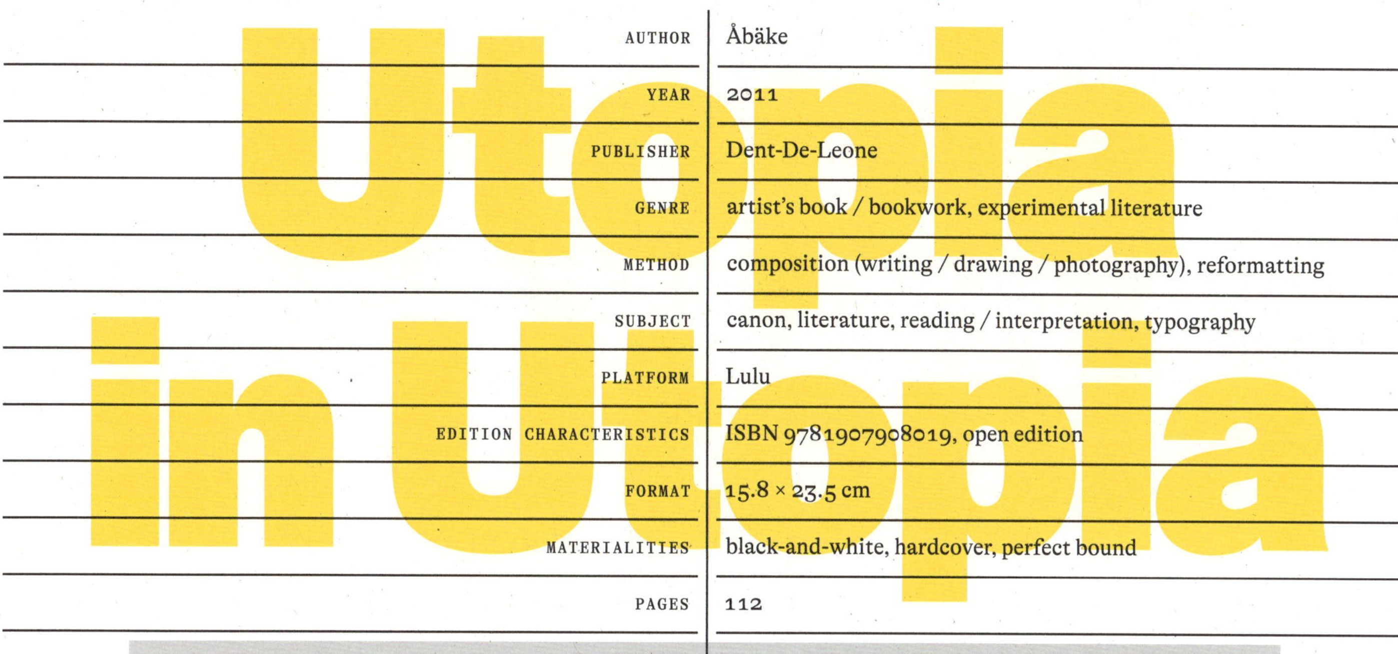

AUTHOR	Åbäke
YEAR	2011
PUBLISHER	Dent-De-Leone
GENRE	artist's book / bookwork, experimental literature
METHOD	composition (writing / drawing / photography), reformatting
SUBJECT	canon, literature, reading / interpretation, typography
PLATFORM	Lulu
EDITION CHARACTERISTICS	ISBN 9781907908019, open edition
FORMAT	15.8 × 23.5 cm
MATERIALITIES	black-and-white, hardcover, perfect bound
PAGES	112

IMAGES

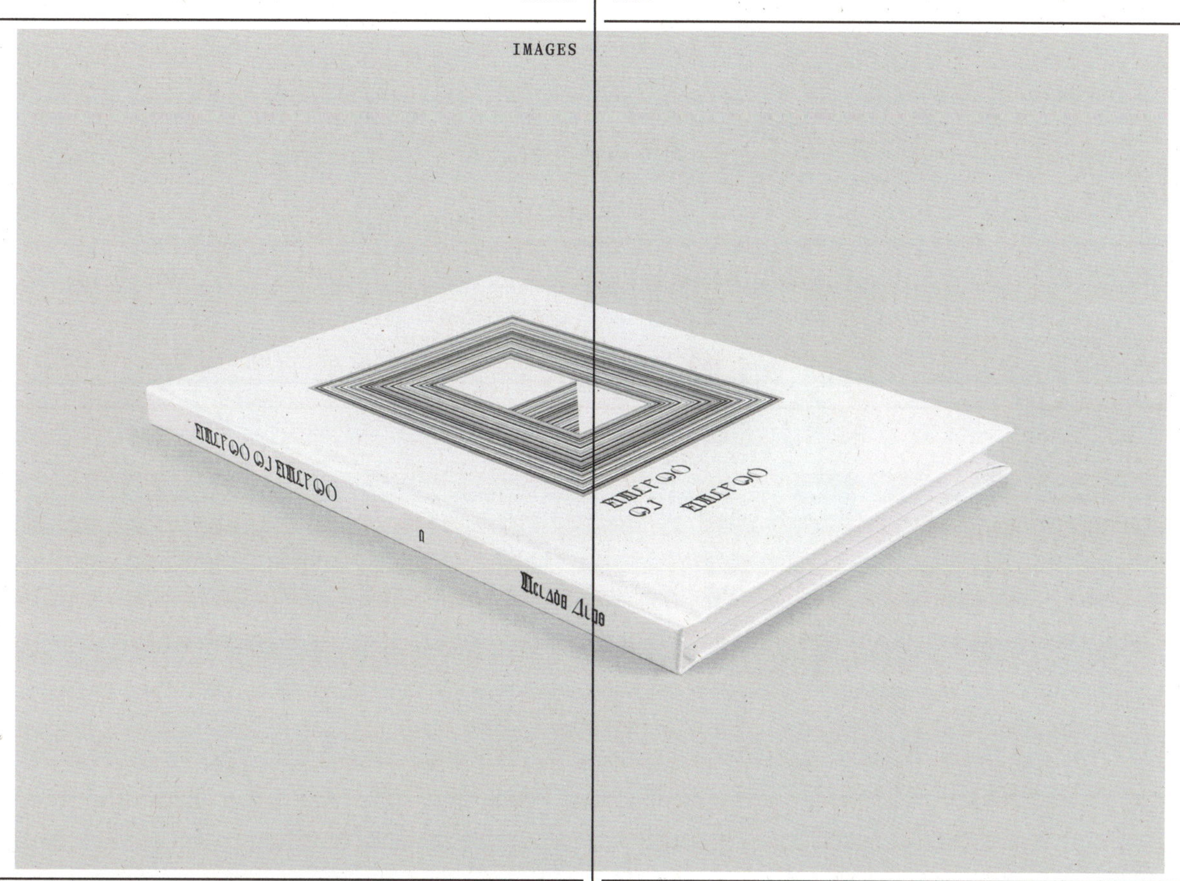

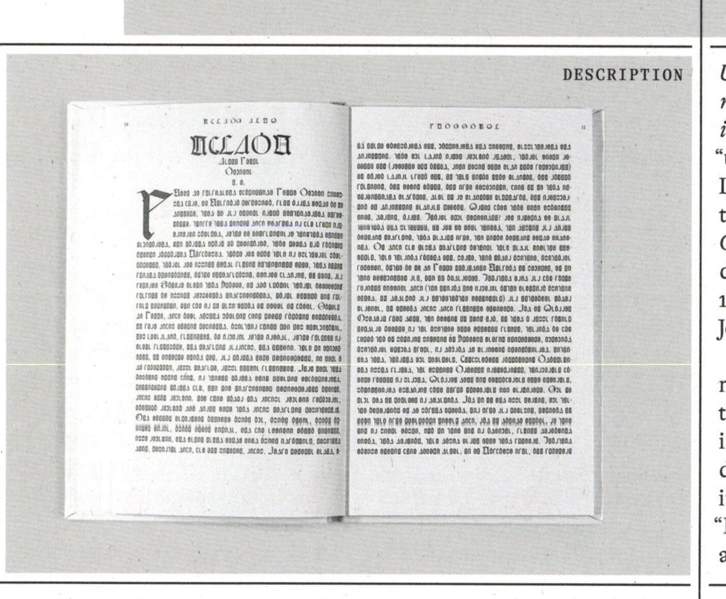

DESCRIPTION

Utopia in Utopia consists of the original Latin text *Libellus vere aureus, nec minus salutaris quam festivus, de optimo rei publicae statu deque nova insula Utopia* by Thomas More (1516), the first to introduce the word "utopia" and its concept. The book was designed by Åbäke and Bryn Lloyd and is set in the fictitious font of the island of Utopia as mentioned in More's story: "The typeface used here, imaginatively called *Goudy Utopia* follows the forms of both the utopian alphabet originally designed by Thomas More and *Goudy Text* by Frederic W. Goudy in the 1920s. The latter is derived from the characters of the 42-line Bible of Johann Gutenberg, Mainz, 1455" (colophon).

When we tried to order the book for our library, we received an error message from Lulu informing us that they could not send it "because the source files for the project *Utopia in Utopia* contain errors preventing it from being printed," presumably due to the experimental font design. Nevertheless, we did receive a copy but were not charged for it. In an email to apod.li, Maki Suzuki from Åbäke comments on this: "Perhaps Utopia is a non-place and therefore resists materiality such as monetary transactions. It seems perfect."

Canal Zone Richard Prince YES RASTA

AUTHOR	Greg Allen [ed.]
YEAR	2011–2013
GENRE	catalog / collection
METHOD	collection, documentation / archiving, remediation
SUBJECT	art world / literary world, copyright / law, error / corruption / loss, memory / storage
PLATFORM	Amazon
VOLUMES	2
EDITION CHARACTERISTICS	ISBN, multiple editions (hardcover, paperback), open edition
FORMAT	15.2 × 22.9 cm
MATERIALITIES	black-and-white, paperback, perfect bound

IMAGE

DESCRIPTION

In 2009, photographer Patrick Cariou filed a lawsuit against appropriation artist Richard Prince for copyright infringement. Prince had used images of Cariou's book *Yes, Rasta* (2000), a photographic documentation of the Rastafarian community in Jamaica, for the creation of his series *Canal Zone*. The case caught the art world's attention because it represented the core of the discussion on photographic and appropriative originality and marked another milestone in the legal fight between photographers and appropriation artists. In 2011, the Southern District of New York held that Prince's appropriations were infringing Cariou's copyright. On appeal, Prince's defense made a case for the transformative nature of Prince's use of Cariou's photographs, which then was granted for twenty-five out of thirty works. In 2014, Prince and Cariou settled the case.

The case of Cariou v. Prince foreshadowed the heated discussion of appropriation art a few years later, which showed that it very much depends on abusing positions of power—this was further twisted in the case of *Yes, Rasta* by two white artists fighting over the use of the depictions of black bodies.

Greg Allen's exhaustive compilation in two volumes contains the most important documents and exhibits from the court record, but organized into a clearer, more readable format and augmented by the *Canal Zone* series paintings, installation shots from the Eden Rock hotel in St. Barth's, Prince's short story "Eden Rock" that ended up in his paintings, and Cariou's detailed comparison of his photographs with Prince's. In this way, Allen's publication also demonstrates the transformative gesture of appropriation and remediation itself by turning bad scans, copied documents, and PDFs back into a printed book. An Amazon buyer of the first volume complains: "Plus is that it collects many of the court case documents in one bound edition. Minus is that the book is comprised of photocopied PDF documents at about 50 percent reduction in size, making it extremely difficult to read."

Canal Zone Richard Prince YES RASTA: Selected Court Documents from Cariou v. Prince et al. including [...]

YEAR	2011
EDITION CHARACTERISTICS	ISBN 9780615473857, open edition
PAGES	376 (unpaginated)
DESCRIPTION	

The complete title on the cover of Allen's publication is an exhaustive description of the book's content: *Canal Zone Richard Prince YES RASTA: Selected Court Documents from Cariou v. Prince et al, including The Videotaped Deposition of Richard Prince, the Affidavit of Richard Prince, Competing Memoranda of Law in Support of Summary Judgment, Exhibits Pertaining to Paintings and Collages of Richard Prince and The Use of Reproductions of Patrick Cariou's YES RASTA Photographs Therein, And The Summary Ass Whooping Dealt To Richard Prince Received By The Hon. Judge Deborah A. Batts, as compiled and revised by Greg Allen for greg.org in April 2011* (front cover).

However, as a note on the back cover states, this book is not meant to be "a comprehensive or authoritative documentation of Cariou v. Prince et al. Instead, it is intended to serve as an art historical and critical resource, filtering relevant primary information about Prince's biography, practice and work from the voluminous, largely inaccessible public record. But it also offers a fascinating, if at times exasperating, discussion of art, appropriation, creativity and originality." Because Prince usually denies any explanation of his work, the artist's 7-hour testimony in front of court is "the most exhaustive interview Prince has ever done" (back cover).

The initial publication was available as a hardcover on CreateSpace (no longer available), shortly followed by a slightly expanded softcover version, whose cover was made with the default settings for annotations in Apple's preinstalled PDF-viewing software Preview.

Canal Zone Richard Prince YES RASTA: The Appeals Court Decision in Cariou v. Prince, et al., Also The Court's Complete Illustrated Appendix.

YEAR	2013
EDITION CHARACTERISTICS	ISBN 9780615809267, open edition, signed, stamped
PAGES	132 (unpaginated)
DESCRIPTION	

In 2013, Allen published a second volume documenting and annotating the appeals phase of the case called *Canal Zone Richard Prince YES RASTA 2: The Appeals Court Decision in Cariou v. Prince, et al., Also The Court's Complete Illustrated Appendix*. The book covers the court's revision, deciding that the appropriations by Richard Prince are in fact to be considered fair use. Most of the book is taken up by a reproduction of an illustrated appendix: a collection of poorly made photocopies confronting in detail all cases of appropriation in opposition to the original photographs.

Our copy, a gift from the author, was stamped, signed and dated by him.

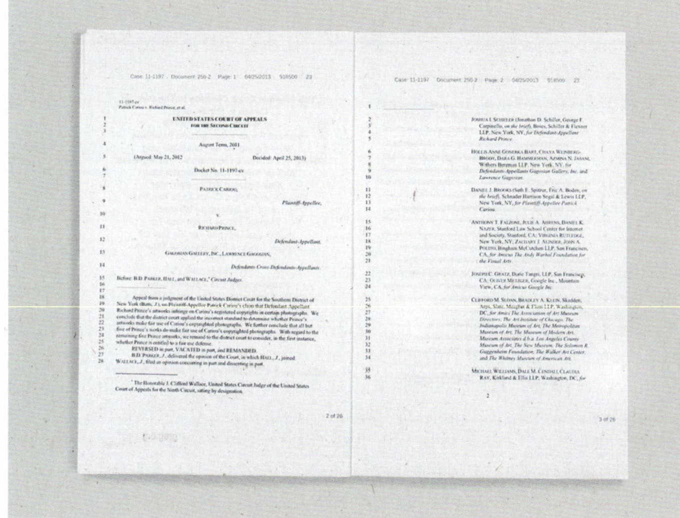

Wohlgemeynte Gedanken über den Dannemarks-Gesundbrunnen

AUTHOR	Greg Allen
YEAR	2011 [2nd ed. 2015]
GENRE	artist's book / bookwork, reprint
METHOD	documentation / archiving, found material, photocopy / scan, remediation
SUBJECT	book / book design, error / corruption / loss, google, materiality
PLATFORM	Lulu
EDITION CHARACTERISTICS	second edition, open edition, CC0
FORMAT	15.2 × 22.9 cm
MATERIALITIES	black-and-white, paperback, perfect bound
PAGES	281 (unpaginated)

IMAGES

DESCRIPTION

This book is a facsimile of a digitized 1751 German translation of the 1747 treatise *Hydrologie, or the Water Kingdom* by the Swedish researcher Johan Gottschalk Wallerius, which Greg Allen stumbled upon on Google Books in 2011. The completely failed scan excited him as "a rare achievement of the scanner-based book arts" which "is sure to become a classic in the nascent field of glitch studies" (blurb on Lulu). Allen decided to reprint this "distorted-beyond-all-recognition-and-come-out-the-other-side-as-art book" (Greg Allen, "Well-Meaning Thoughts").

The book, digitized on December 15, 2008, comes from the Bavarian State Library, which was the first German library to enter into cooperation with Google Books. Just at the beginning of Google's massive digitization initiative, there were still major quality problems in terms of scans, OCR, and metadata. So also here, where the title, *Wohlgemeynte Gedanken über den Dannemarks-Gesundbrunnen* (Well-meaning Thoughts on Denmark's Mineral Waters), is incorrectly indicated, it covers only a part of the whole book.

It turned out to be a lucky coincidence that Allen had immediately downloaded his find as a PDF, because a short while later the scan was digitally processed, and distortions and stray fingers edited out. Over the years, Google has also corrected the metadata. Allen's first edition from 2011 also addresses the legal issues related to Google's conduct, as it "includes Google Books' 2-page boilerplate foreword explaining what they wish would happen with scans of public domain books. Which is adorable" (Ibid.).

When we ordered two copies of the book for our library, we received one in black-and-white and one in color print, in which the glitches are even more impressive. The latter was obviously a production error, because Allen had refrained from a color version due to the high production price. He was also unhappy with the limitations of Lulu's and other print-on-demand platform's printing and formatting, which made a full-bleed version impossible. The white borders in the current version "did not help capture the surrealism of the original Google scans" (email from the artist to apod.li).

Medium

AUTHOR	Kate Armstrong
YEAR	2011
GENRE	artist's book / bookwork
METHOD	generative / automation, montage / remix, reenactment
SUBJECT	analog / digital, book / book design, canon, google, search engine, visual culture
PLATFORM	Lulu
EDITION CHARACTERISTICS	multiple editions (print, PDF), ISBN 9780987835406, open edition
FORMAT	21.6 × 21.6 cm
MATERIALITIES	black-and-white, paperback, perfect bound
PAGES	342 (unpaginated)

IMAGES

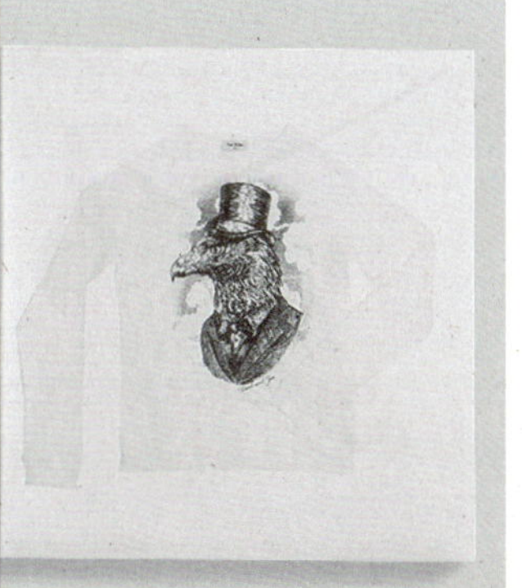

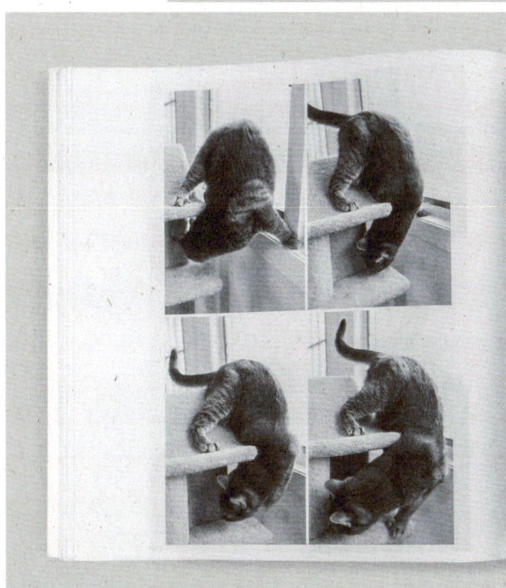

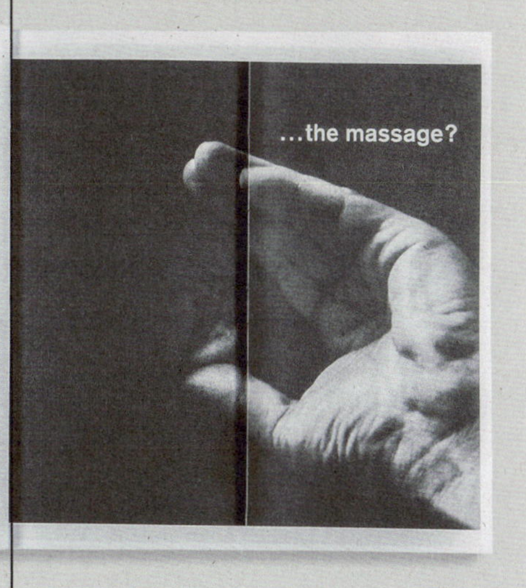

DESCRIPTION

Kate Armstrong's *Medium* is a conceptual reading and update of Marshall McLuhan and Quentin Fiore's collaborative book *The Medium is the Massage* from 1967, that first introduced McLuhan's text *The Medium is the Message* to a greater public. Taking one spread each from this publication, Armstrong algorithmically searched the internet for pictures with matching compositional features. From the results, she picked three images (with minor deviations) that were then placed on pages following the depiction of the initial spread. By this, *Medium* is an enhanced reproduction of *The Medium is the Massage*, blown up to triple the size, as well as an extension of its conceptual and theoretical approach to the digital age. The peculiar, rather large, square format of Armstrong's book also goes back to McLuhan and Fiore's publication as it is the closest approximation to the size of its spreads, which also leads to a visual enhancement of the source.

The book was commissioned for the exhibition "Medium_Massage 2.0: an infinite inventory" for the McLuhan100 Festival, Toronto.

An Inventory of Al-Mutanabbi Street

AUTHOR	Sarah Bodman
YEAR	2011
GENRE	artist's book / bookwork, experimental literature
METHOD	composition (writing / drawing / photography), documentation / archiving
SUBJECT	book / book design, memory / storage, narration, politics / activism, reading / interpretation
PLATFORM	Blurb
EDITION CHARACTERISTICS	multiple editions (paperback, hardcover, dust jacket, e-book), second edition, open edition
FORMAT	12.6 × 20.3 cm
MATERIALITIES	black-and-white, paperback, perfect bound
PAGES	130 (unpaginated)
IMAGES	

DESCRIPTION

Sarah Bodman's *An Inventory* is based on a list of sensory impressions and micro-observations of what seems to be a regular day at al-Mutanabbi Street, the street of booksellers in Baghdad, before it was bombed on March 5, 2007. This list, which leaves an impression of a busy street, full of print culture, conversations, and bustling activity, is repeated in four parts throughout the book in different arrangements.

The first part shows only four lines per page, resulting in an uncongested reading experience that mimics the columns of al-Mutanabbi Street's architecture and the pattern of its shops and cafés. This part ends with "a shout in the midst..." which is followed by a double page of one black page and one white, referencing the terrorist attack and its aftermath. After that, the text of the list starts anew but only with one description of an impression in the top-left corner of each page, leaving out great amounts of text in between. This part, ending with "an envelope is opened," is followed by phrases condensed to clusters that spread out over the page, still leaving out great amounts of the initial text but showing stages of collecting and ordering. The book ends with the full list running in left-justified blocks over nine pages. Over the 130 pages of the book—"one for each person of the 130 people killed or wounded in the explosion" (blurb on Blurb)—Bodman shows how the mere presentation of text can produce a narrative, which is closely connected to the material qualities of the book and possibilities for presenting information, and that might stand in drastic contrast to the content of the text.

An Inventory was produced in an edition of three for the exhibition and archive "An Inventory of al-Mutanabbi Street" and then made available as an open edition via print-on-demand. All the money raised from the sale were donated to Médecins Sans Frontières (Doctors Without Borders).

Where The F**k Was I?

AUTHOR	James Bridle
YEAR	2011
GENRE	artist's book / bookwork
METHOD	composition (writing / drawing / photography), documentation / archiving, pricing, study / analysis
SUBJECT	data, economy / labor, maps / street view, memory / storage, politics / activism, surveillance / privacy, tracking
PLATFORM	Lulu
EDITION CHARACTERISTICS	ISBN 9781906110192, no longer available
FORMAT	15.8 × 23.5 cm
MATERIALITIES	color, hardcover, perfect bound
PAGES	412 (unpaginated)

IMAGES

DESCRIPTION

In April 2011, Alasdair Allen and Pete Warden published an article on *Radar* revealing that Apple has been secretly storing user location data in an unprotected file on each device. After learning about this, James Bridle accessed this file on his phone to retrieve the locations. *Where The F**k Was I?* presents these location data recorded on the author's iPhone between June 2010 and April 2011, visualized on 202 maps for each day that data was collected with a total of 35,801 data points. Each map is set on the right-hand side of a double-page spread and is captioned by the date, number of data points, and his activities and destinations on that day, if Bridle remembered them.

By this, *Where The F**k Was I?* not only becomes a compelling tome of data visualization but also a comparison of the automated memory of the device and Bridle's own recollection of events. Giving the impression of a very intimate diary, the book triggers reflection on different qualities of memory and their adequacies, as Bridle writes in a blog post about the project: "This digital memory sits somewhere between experience and non-experience; it is also an approximation; it is also a lie. These location records do not show where I was, but an approximation based on the device's own idea of place, its own way of seeing. They cross-reference me with digital infrastructure, with cell towers and wireless networks, with points created by others in its database. Where I correlate location with physical landmarks, friends and personal experiences, the algorithms latch onto invisible, virtual spaces, and the extant memories of strangers" (James Bridle, "Where the F**k Was I? (A Book)," blog).

In addition, Bridle reappropriates the data secretly stored by Apple and turns it into a commodity in the form of a book that he sells on Lulu for €609 as critique of such practices of surveillance capitalism. With this he makes the selling price of the book part of its artistic conception and message.

AUTHORS	Mimi Cabell, Jason Huff
YEAR	2011
PUBLISHER	TraumaWien
GENRE	artist's book / bookwork, experimental literature
METHOD	appropriation, documentation / archiving, paratextual play, study / analysis
SUBJECT	analog / digital, bias, canon, code / programming, economy / labor, email / messaging, google, literature, narration, reading / interpretation, surveillance / privacy
PLATFORM	Lulu
EDITION CHARACTERISTICS	multiple editions (print, PDF), open edition
FORMAT	15.2 × 22.9 cm
MATERIALITIES	black-and-white, paperback, perfect bound
PAGES	408

IMAGES

DESCRIPTION

"Google reads our emails, garners information from our personal messages and uses that profiling strategy to select 'relevant' ads. It then displays those ads on the screen next to the very emails from which the information was initially taken.

American Psycho was created by sending the entirety of Bret Easton Ellis' violent, masochistic and gratuitous novel *American Psycho* through GMail, one page at a time. We collected the ads that appeared next to each email and used them to annotate the original text, page by page. In printing it as a perfect bound book, we erased the body of Ellis' text and left only chapter titles and constellations of our added footnotes. What remains is *American Psycho*, told through its chapter titles and annotated relational Google ads.

We were most curious how Google would handle the violence, racism and graphic language in *American Psycho*. In some instances the ads related to the content of the email, in others they were completely irrelevant, either out of time or out of place. In one scene, where first a dog and then a man are brutally murdered with a knife, Google supplied ample ads regarding knives and knife sharpeners. In another scene the ads disappeared altogether when the narrator makes a racial slur. Google's choice and use of standard ads unrelated to the content next to which they appeared offered an alternate window into how Google ads function—the ad for Crest Whitestrips Coupons appeared the highest number of times, next to both the most graphic and the most mundane sections of the book, leaving no clear logic as to how it was selected to appear. This 'misreading' ultimately echoes the hollowness at the center of advertising and consumer culture, a theme explored in excess in *American Psycho*" (Mimi Cabell, "American Psycho," website).

The inserted ads update the brand and consumer world of the 1980s and at the same time document a period of media history upheaval, namely the conversion from analog to digital around 2010: the original Bateman still uses a video recorder, while the new version offers MP3 players. In general, Cabell and Huff's entire project can now be considered an important media archaeological study, because Google's ad algorithm that they tried to track down in 2010 is now already historic: since 2017, Google no longer scans emails, but instead bases the ads on the user's online activity. The algorithm active at the time, as condensed in *American Psycho*, embodies par excellence the logic of "linguistic capitalism," in which a price is assigned to every keyword that triggers advertising, which is why one can ask "how much money Google earned from the 819 ads in the making of the book" (Karl Wolfgang Flender, "Reading an Algorithm in Reverse").

As *American Psycho* was initially published by Cabell and Huff along with a PDF, it also reflects on the possibilities and limitations such post-digital hybrids incline. The erasure of Ellis's text was achieved by rendering its font color to white. This turns the source text invisible in the printed version but allows for a complete recreation of the novel from the PDF by simply copying and pasting it to a different text editor—thus turning the digital version of the artistic project to a container for subversive filesharing.

Blank on Demand

AUTHORS	Giulia Ciliberto, Silvio Lorusso
YEAR	2011
GENRE	artistic research, artist's book / bookwork
METHOD	constraint, pricing, study / analysis
SUBJECT	book / book design, economy / labor, platforms / companies, print on demand, scale, standard / default
PLATFORM	Lulu
VOLUMES	2
EDITION CHARACTERISTICS	ISBN 9781471068560 (minimum version), partially no longer available, open edition
FORMAT	10.8 × 17.5 cm, 15.2 × 22.9 cm
MATERIALITIES	blank pages, hardcover and paperback, perfect bound
PAGES	40 and 740
IMAGES	

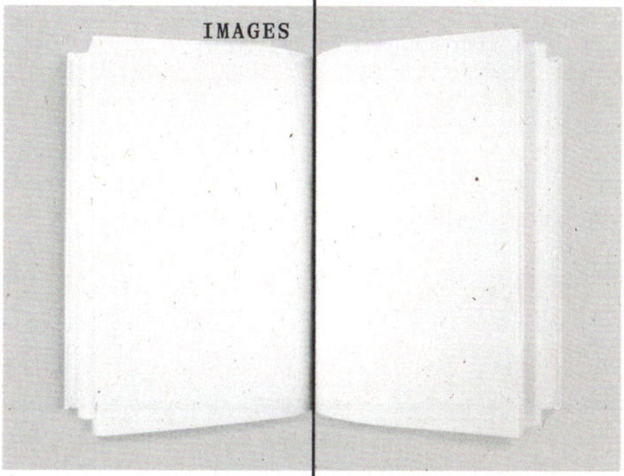

DESCRIPTION

The presentation of this two-volume blank work on Giulia Ciliberto and Silvio Lorusso's websites is introduced with the following famous quote from Ulises Carrión: "The most beautiful and perfect book in the world is a book with only blank pages, in the same way that the most complete language is that which lies beyond all that the words of a man can say" (Ulises Carrión, "The New Art of Making Books," 15).

Apart from the pursuit of aesthetics and perfection, their work has another objective, as the blurb reveals: "Print on Demand technology allows to make a book without the intermediation of a publisher, setting autonomously size, amount of pages and price. *Blank on Demand* is an experiment that aims to probe the limits imposed by this production process. The two volumes constituting the project are produced through the self-publishing platform Lulu.com. The volumes' formats correspond respectively to the maximum and minimum dimensions currently available for the print; similarly, page amount and price are set according to the limit values allowed by the platform. The two volumes are completely blank, except for the presence of the ISBN code. The experiment investigates the influence of the current technological context on the materiality of the book object" (blurb on Lulu).

The resulting two volumes are a 10.8 × 17.5 cm paperback, forty pages long and priced at €5.44; and a 15.2 × 22.99 cm hardcover, 740 pages long and priced at €999,999.99. This pair of books—that, considering their price, will probably never be ordered and printed in their entirety—becomes the sum of the technical and formal conditions for publishing on print-on-demand platforms. The project still allows its authors a small triumph over the opaque print-on-demand machinery, because the complete automatization of production will most probably lead to the absurd situation that a book with empty white pages, on which nothing is printed, is also unnecessarily sent through the printing machines: "We were particularly fascinated by the idea of paper sheets going through all the complex print machinery without any purpose" (Silvio Lorusso, "Extending Horizons," 187).

For our library, we only purchased the paperback version, for obvious reasons. The fact that the hardback version is likely to forever remain a printed work in potentialis, and is thus manifested more as an artistic idea than as a physical object, does not make it pointless at all: These are works "that cannot or should not be printed, but that insist on printedness, even if only imagined, all the same" (Sophie Seita, "Communities of Print," in this volume, 643). The evidence that the hardback version saw the light of day and was printed at least once is provided by a photo of the shipping certificate from Lulu and the artist's proof (see fig. on 103).

The two artists' accounts have been blocked by Lulu. The paperback version is now available again, as they re-uploaded it specifically for our library via a newly created account.

7% dinner 4 lifetime
Selected Work 2010/11

AUTHORS	J. Gordon Faylor [ed.], Andy Sterling
YEAR	2011
PUBLISHER	Collective Task
GENRE	catalog / collection, poetry
METHOD	collection, found material, reformatting
SUBJECT	email / messaging, internet culture, literature, publishing / distribution, writing / reading techniques
PLATFORM	Lulu
EDITION CHARACTERISTICS	open edition
FORMAT	15.2 × 22.9 cm
MATERIALITIES	black-and-white, paperback, perfect bound
PAGES	113

IMAGES

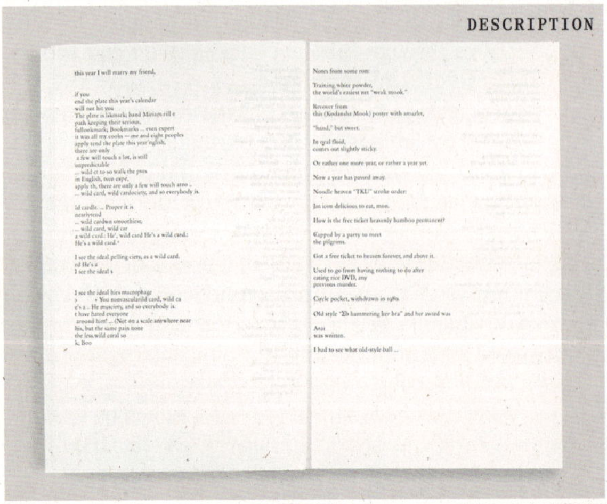

DESCRIPTION

Andy Sterling's *7% dinner 4 lifetime* is a selection of his writing and work from 2010 and 2011—edited and published by J. Gordon Faylor, the founder of Gauss PDF, without letting Sterling know.

The publication stems from a challenge by the artist group Collective Task. On the first day of each month, a member of the collective sets a task for the other members to complete during the month. The task in the case of *7% dinner 4 lifetime* was "Tribute," whereupon Faylor submitted the edited volume as a surprise gift for Andy Sterling.

He took the texts from email conversations on Gmail, where Sterling, according to Faylor's "Foreword," has been busy filling conversations with creative writing, appropriation, and the copying and pasting of text. These texts, which were meant for only a few participants, are treated by Faylor as literary works. Thus, *7% dinner 4 lifetime* is not only a manifestation of Sterling's virtuous poetry but also a change of publication context, revealing the editor's rather prominent role in the creation and publication of (experimental) literature.

Frankenstein; or, The Modern Prometheus [Frankenfont]

AUTHOR	Mary Wollstonecraft Shelley [Ben Fry]
YEAR	2011
PUBLISHER	Fathom Information Design
GENRE	artist's book / bookwork, experimental literature
METHOD	appropriation, collection, found material, generative / automation, paratextual play, reformatting
SUBJECT	literature, materiality, reading / interpretation, typography, writing / reading techniques
PLATFORM	Blurb, Lulu
EDITION CHARACTERISTICS	multiple editions (hardcover, paperback), ISBN 9781257996070, open edition
FORMAT	15.2 × 22.9 cm
MATERIALITIES	black-and-white, paperback, perfect bound
PAGES	336
IMAGES	

DESCRIPTION

On the outside, this book looks like a normal edition of Mary Wollstonecraft Shelley's *Frankenstein*. Only a small note on the back cover refers to the underlying project *Frankenfont* by Fathom Information Design. Ben Fry's name is not mentioned anywhere. The following additional information can only be found on his website:

"*Frankenfont* is an edition of Mary Shelley's *Frankenstein* laid out using characters and glyphs from PDF documents obtained through internet searches. The incomplete fonts found in the PDFs were reassembled into the text of *Frankenstein* based on their frequency of use. The most common characters are employed at the beginning of the book, and the text devolves into less common, more grotesque shapes and forms toward the end.

The beginning of the book is comprised largely of Arial, Helvetica, and the occasional Times New Roman. As you might expect, these are by far the most common fonts used in documents. By page 46 and 47, things have progressed to a lot of Arial Bold and Times Italic. In the 200s, commonly used script fonts, as well as much more obscure faces are beginning to appear. As we reach the end, the book has devolved significantly: non-Roman fonts, highly specialized typefaces, and even pictogram fonts abound.

Process. For each of the 5,483 unique words in the book, we ran a search (using the Yahoo! Search API) that was filtered just to PDF files. We downloaded the top 10 to 15 hits for each word, producing 64,076 PDF files (some were no longer available, others were duplicates). Inside these PDFs were 347,565 subsetted fonts. From these fonts, 55,382 unique glyph shapes were used to fill the 342,889 individual letters found in Shelley's *Frankenstein* text.

PDF Fonts. This project started because of a fascination with the way that PDF files contain incomplete versions of fonts. The shape data is high enough quality to reproduce the original document, however only the necessary characters (and little of the font's 'metrics' that are used for proper typographic layout) are included in the PDF. This prevents others from extracting the fonts to be used for practical purposes, but creates an opportunity for a curious Victor Frankenstein who wants to use these incomplete pieces to create something entirely different" (Ben Fry, "The *Frankenfont* project," website).

All profits were donated. Another Fathom project (available on Blurb) is *On the Origin of Species: The Preservation of Favoured Traces* (2015), a visualization of the textual changes in Charles Darwin's famous theory of evolution, on which he worked for several years and which has therefore undergone several modified editions.

No Man's Land

AUTHOR	Mishka Henner
YEAR	2011–2012
GENRE	photobook
METHOD	collection, found material
SUBJECT	bias, dating / sex, economy / labor, gender, google, maps / street view, photography, race, surveillance / privacy
VOLUMES	2
EDITION CHARACTERISTICS	open edition, dated, available only through the artist
FORMAT	24.0 × 20.2 cm
MATERIALITIES	color, paperback, perfect bound
PAGES	122 each (unpaginated)
IMAGES	

DESCRIPTION

No Man's Land shows fifty-nine pictures of lonely women standing or sitting on roads in the rural outskirts of Spain, Romania, and Italy. Their faces are pixelated; supposedly they are sex workers. The photos were not taken on-site by Henner himself, but found by him on Google Street View whose camera car happened to capture these women as it drove by. To find such locations on Google Maps, Henner searched online forums where men share the location of sex workers. He then "drove" to these locations via Google Street View and checked to see if a woman was captured at that location by Google's Street View car cameras. If this was the case, he selected one of the predefined viewing angles and secured the image with a screenshot. In addition to the book, the images have been shown in exhibitions as large prints, approaching a 1:1 scale, and video animation.

As an explainer video on Henner's website discloses, the first volume sold slowly at first, with ten copies in two months, which changed after two months when *No Man's Land* gained a lot of attention through online media and went viral. As a result, it became the artist's best-selling book, which is why he even followed it up with a second volume in 2012, again with fifty-nine photos on 118 pages.

At the same time, the first volume became highly contentious in public discourse, as Henner's approach challenged the ethics and mediatic layers of documentary photography in the age of platform capitalism. It also sparked controversy from a feminist point of view. For example, American feminist sex workers called for Henner's book to be banned because he was endangering women's safety and using depictions of them without talking to them or asking for consent, and even capitalizing on it. Since Google is known to have cared just as little about this, Henner's second-level documentation could also be understood as a reflection on Google's reckless accumulation of data and the collateral damage of their automated imagery, while also capturing the working conditions of sex workers and their position in relation to traffic infrastructure and internet giants. In 2013, the book was shortlisted for the prestigious Deutsche Börse Photography Foundation Prize.

Astronomical

AUTHOR	Mishka Henner
YEAR	2011 [2022]
GENRE	artist's book / bookwork, photobook
METHOD	found material, remediation
SUBJECT	book / book design, photography, print technology, scale
PLATFORM	Lulu
VOLUMES	12
EDITION CHARACTERISTICS	open edition, temporarily not available, available only through the artist
FORMAT	14.0 × 21.6 cm
MATERIALITIES	black-and-white, paperback, perfect bound, defective copy
PAGES	6,000 in total (unpaginated)

IMAGES

DESCRIPTION

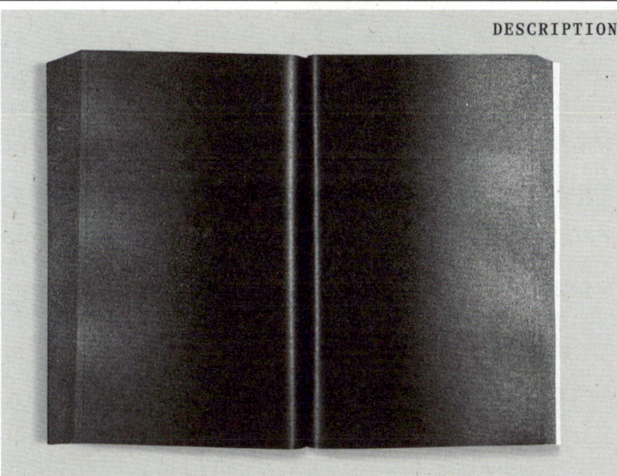

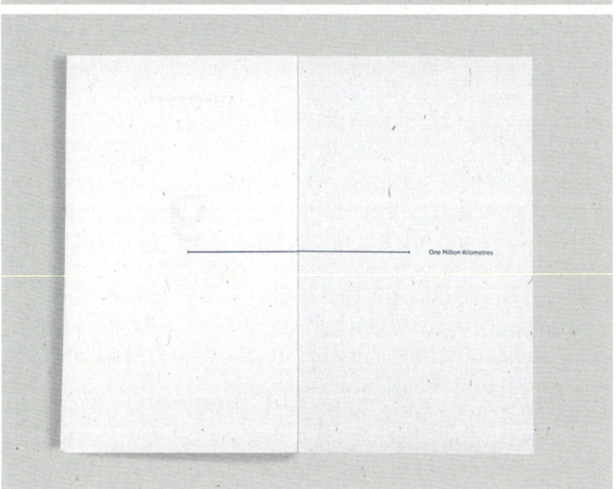

"A scale model of our solar system in twelve 500 page volumes. / The width of each page equals one million kilometres. / On page 1 the Sun. On page 6,000 Pluto" (blurb on artist website). In between the other planets, but above all darkness and blackness. The series transfers the unimaginable distances and dimensions of the universe into book format and makes them comprehensible and "traversable."

The work has attracted great media attention and high appreciation from collectors and institutions. Originally planned as an open edition, only 130 sets were produced before production was halted by the printer—apparently because Lulu changed to thinner paper and production was no longer possible, but, in reality, probably for reasons of unprofitability due to high ink consumption caused by the almost entirely black pages (proving that Holly Melgard's *Black Friday* (see 236) and Jean Keller's *The Black Book* (see 157) did indeed hit a sore spot in the platform economy). The 130 produced sets have become a highly sought-after, overpriced collector's item against the artist's will.

Previously, the artist had complained several times to Lulu about insufficient quality: The books were cut incorrectly or bound poorly, their height was not always uniform, making their compilation as a twelve-volume set impossible, and sometimes the books arrived blank or the black was printed spottily. This is also the reason why the set could later only be ordered from the artist himself. In 2022, Henner was able to get Lulu to resume production, so together with the Bavarian State Library we were able to acquire a complete set for our collection. The additional copy in our collection (vol. 9) is one that was discarded by the artist because of poor print quality. In view of this, one cannot always be sure whether the tiny white dots are actually stars in the black vastness of space or printing errors.

There is also a single-channel video, nearly ten minutes long, named *Astronomical (the Movie)* in which volume one is flipped through page by page. It features the sun, Mercury, Venus, Earth, Mars, and the Asteroid Belt, and served the artist Hermann Zschiegner as the basis for his bootleg edition of *Astronomical* (see 240).

Best Fight Ever/ Worst Fight Ever

AUTHOR	Jason Huff
YEAR	2011
GENRE	artist's book / bookwork, experimental literature
METHOD	outsourcing, translation / transcription
SUBJECT	book / book design, film, mechanical turk, youtube
PLATFORM	Lulu
EDITION CHARACTERISTICS	open edition, no longer available
FORMAT	10.8 × 17.5 cm
MATERIALITIES	black-and-white, paperback, perfect bound, defective copy
PAGES	116

IMAGES

DESCRIPTION

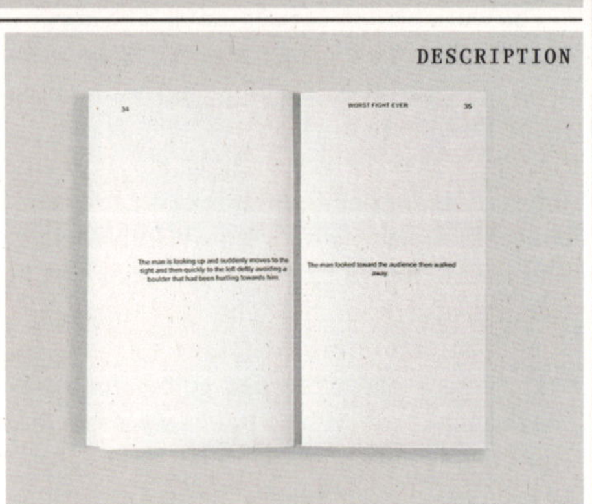

Best Fight Ever/Worst Fight Ever is based on two YouTube videos with film clips uploaded under the title "Best Fight Scene of all Time" and "Worst Fight Scene Ever." The first features a virtuously cut and choreographed 3:17 minute fight scene from the martial arts film *Undefeatable* (Hong Kong, 1993), while the second shows Captain Kirk fighting a lizard alien with painstakingly bad choreography and stunts from *Star Trek* (S01 E18, USA, 1967). Both videos have over eleven million views to date. Jason Huff took the videos and scripted them down to three-second clips to have them described in writing by thirty-eight and sixty-five Amazon Mechanical Turk workers, respectively. The resulting two sets of descriptions of body movements, though split and isolated by outsourcing, still reveal the fight scenes as step-by-step choreographies.

The book features two front covers—one on each side—each showing a still from the beginning of the video. It can be flipped to read the respective film description, with the texts meeting about a third of the way through the book due to the different lengths of the clips. What's in the back and what's in the front can be determined by the print-on-demand manufacturer's production code.

Even though the book title begins with the words "Best Fight Ever," the book does not: this inversion of the videos shows them as interchangeable; after all, both are descriptions of the same scene: "two men are fighting" (Jason Huff, *Best Fight Ever*, 9). The fact that the print-on-demand printer—for whatever reason—inserted a few blank pages at the end somewhat destroys the concept. In addition, a blank double page crept into our copy between pages 55 and 56.

Blank

AUTHOR	Jean Keller
YEAR	2011 [2nd ed. 2021]
GENRE	artist's book / bookwork
METHOD	composition (writing / drawing / photography), détournement / hack, paratextual play
SUBJECT	error / corruption / loss, materiality, platforms / companies, print technology, print on demand
PLATFORM	Blurb, Lulu
EDITION CHARACTERISTICS	multiple editions, open edition
MATERIALITIES	blank pages, paperback, perfect bound
IMAGE	

DESCRIPTION

Jean Keller's *Blank* is an expression of the artist's dissatisfaction with the material, print, and binding quality of print-on-demand books, and at the same time a sign of surrender—which is, however, implemented in a humorous way. The blurb on Blurb says:

"Print on demand is great, you can make all those books you always dreamt of. That's the theory. Between your book and the theory there's Blurb. Sometimes they get it right, sometimes they don't. You can get a book with too many pages, you can get a book with missing pages. You can get a book with wrong colours, you can get a book that isn't cropped correctly. You can get a book with text or photos not at the position where they are supposed to be. There are unlimited possibilities to get it wrong. Not so with *Blank*. It doesn't really matter if the book isn't cropped correctly. Colour is not an issue, nor are text and photos. A few missing pages are not a problem and too many pages are not a problem either. The book is blank. You can do with it what you want. So can Blurb."

This speaks of self-confident sovereignty and autonomy, both toward the platform and the idea of what constitutes a "good" book. And yet, even this book cannot deny that this form of self-empowerment and criticism of the system compromises itself, if it completely subjects itself to the predefined setting of a commercial service provider. It is a small but decisive detail that draws attention to this performative contradiction. Contrary to the book title's claim, the eighty pages are not completely blank: on the last page, Blurb has inscribed itself with its logo. In the blurb, this is commented on: "If you don't like their logo, simply tear out the last page." Removing the logo page doesn't solve the issue, though. The logo is merely a clearly visible sign for the fact that every print-on-demand provider necessarily plays a decisive part in constituting the works. Even *Blank*—with or without a logo—is inevitably determined by its production conditions and the economic and technological regime that both enables and limits it.

After Jean Keller left Blurb due to numerous annoyances, making *Blank* unavailable for purchase, the artist was willing to make the book available for our library again. However, not only have the prices at Blurb risen enormously in the meantime (from $6 to $30), there would also have been an additional $25 in postage costs—for a paperback of eighty pages. In addition, after re-uploading his book, the artist received an email from Blurb Customer Service stating that books containing more than ten percent blank/lined/grid pages, including notebooks, journals, planners, agendas, or similar types of books, may not be sold through the Global Retail Network (see Blurb, "Terms & Conditions," 11.1).

Jean Keller then migrated to Lulu (not without leaving an angry, public statement about Blurb on the platform itself, pointing future buyers to Lulu) and uploaded a new blank book there without problem. As the Blurb standard format used for *Blank* is not available on Lulu, this new edition is designed as a companion piece to Keller's *The Black Book*, similar in size and page number (see 157). As it turns out, Lulu books (at least for orders from Germany) no longer contain the logo or production barcode on the last page (probably due to a change of the print shop from France, the UK, and the Netherlands to Poland).

Blank [first Blurb edition]

YEAR	2011
PLATFORM	Blurb
EDITION CHARACTERISTICS	open edition, no longer available
FORMAT	13.0 × 20.0 cm
PAGES	80

Blank [second Lulu edition]

YEAR	2021
PLATFORM	Lulu
EDITION CHARACTERISTICS	open edition
FORMAT	14.8 × 21.0 cm
PAGES	740

The End

AUTHOR	Jonathan Lewis
YEAR	2011
GENRE	photobook
METHOD	collection, found material, remediation
SUBJECT	analog / digital, art, canon, error / corruption / loss, search engine
PLATFORM	Blurb
EDITION CHARACTERISTICS	limited edition
FORMAT	18.0 × 18.0 cm
MATERIALITIES	black-and-white, hardcover, perfect bound
PAGES	30 (unpaginated)

IMAGES

DESCRIPTION

"A collection of enlarged thumbnail photographs of Kasimir Malevich's *Black Square* painting of 1915, as found on the internet" (blurb on Blurb). Jonathan Lewis collected a total of twenty-six thumbnails, with each image of the black square blurred, pixelated, and altered through photography, compression, and implementation. While Malevich's painting directed the focus to the material qualities of painting as a medium, Lewis's book allows for a focus on the alteration of the material through various layers of digital processing and remediation. In this way, a new notion of "the end of painting" (a typical description of Malevich's painting) emerges, which was also the beginning of a new genre.

In this sense, Lewis's usage of thumbnails, which are usually small preview images for bigger images, gives a perfect example of Hito Steyerl's notion of the "poor image": "The poor image is a copy in motion. Its quality is bad, its resolution substandard. As it accelerates, it deteriorates. It is a ghost of an image, a preview, a thumbnail, an errant idea, an itinerant image distributed for free, squeezed through slow digital connections, compressed, reproduced, ripped, remixed, as well as copied and pasted into other channels of distribution" (Hito Steyerl, "In Defense of the Poor Image").

Elisabeth Tonnard, then a member of the Artists' Books Cooperative (ABC), like Lewis, posted a video of an ABC booth ironically titled "A Thorough Examination of Jonathan Lewis' book *The End*," showing how such books can irritate book fair attendees.

Collect the WWWorld

The Artist as Archivist in the Internet Age

AUTHOR	Domenico Quaranta [ed.]
YEAR	2011
PUBLISHER	LINK Editions
GENRE	catalog / collection, nonfiction
METHOD	composition (writing / drawing / photography), documentation / archiving
SUBJECT	analog / digital, art, internet culture, memory / storage, visual culture
PLATFORM	Lulu
EDITION CHARACTERISTICS	multiple editions (black-and-white, color, PDF), ISBN 9781470901615, open edition, CC BY-NC-SA
FORMAT	15.5 × 23.4 cm
MATERIALITIES	black-and-white, paperback, perfect bound
PAGES	160

IMAGE

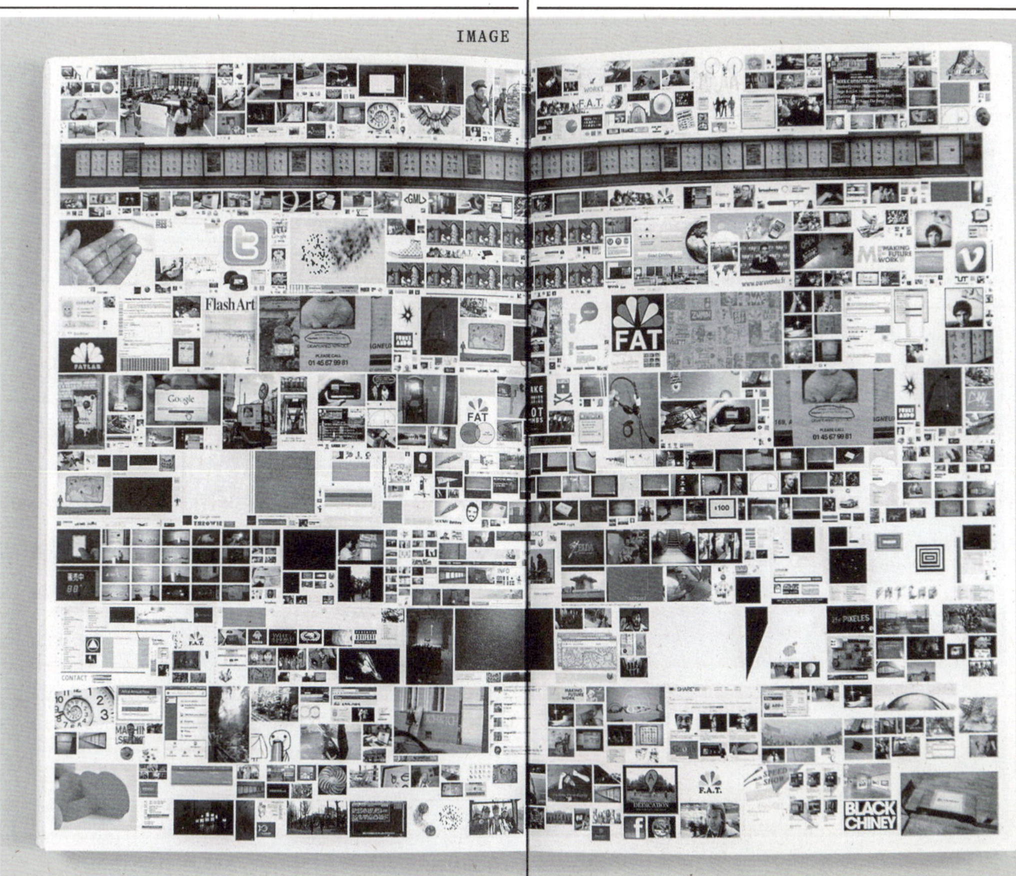

DESCRIPTION

Collect the WWWorld is a catalog edited by Domenico Quaranta to accompany the group exhibition of the same name he curated, which was shown in Brescia, Basel, and New York in 2011 and 2012. The exhibition tried "to demonstrate how the internet generation is implementing and developing a practice started in the Sixties by Conceptual Art, and further developed in the next decades in the forms of Appropriation Art and postproduction: the practice of exploring, collecting, archiving, manipulating, reusing huge amounts of visual material produced by popular culture and advertising" (Domenico Quaranta, "Collect the WWWorld," 6). Quaranta's "research notes about art, and about what is uncannily similar to it" can be found on his blog for the show (Quaranta, "In the Uncanny Valley"). The book includes essays by Quaranta, Josephine Bosma, Gene McHugh, and Joanne McNeil tackling these topics as well as introductions and presentations of all artworks exhibited. There is a black-and-white and a color version on Lulu.

PARTICIPATING ARTISTS

Alterazioni Video (IT), Kari Altmann (US), Cory Arcangel (US), Gazira Babeli (IT), Kevin Bewersdorf (US), Luca Bolognesi (IT), Natalie Bookchin (US), Petra Cortright (US), Aleksandra Domanovic (DE), Harm van den Dorpel (NL), Constant Dullaart (NL), Hans-Peter Feldmann (DE), Elisa Giardina Papa (IT), Travis Hallenbeck (US), Jodi (NL), Oliver Laric (DE), Olia Lialina & Dragan Espenschied (DE), Guthrie Lonergan (US), Eva and Franco Mattes (IT), Seth Price (US), Jon Rafman (US), Claudia Rossini (IT), Evan Roth (US), Travess Smalley (US), and Ryan Trecartin (US).

The Black Merkin

AUTHOR	New Society of Dilettanti
YEAR	2011
PUBLISHER	AND Public Collective
GENRE	experimental literature, fiction
METHOD	collective, composition (writing / drawing / photography)
SUBJECT	authorship, crowd / collaboration, narration
PLATFORM	Lulu
EDITION CHARACTERISTICS	second edition, ISBN 9781908452078, open edition, CC BY-SA
FORMAT	10.8 × 17.5 cm
MATERIALITIES	black-and-white, paperback, perfect bound
PAGES	271

IMAGES

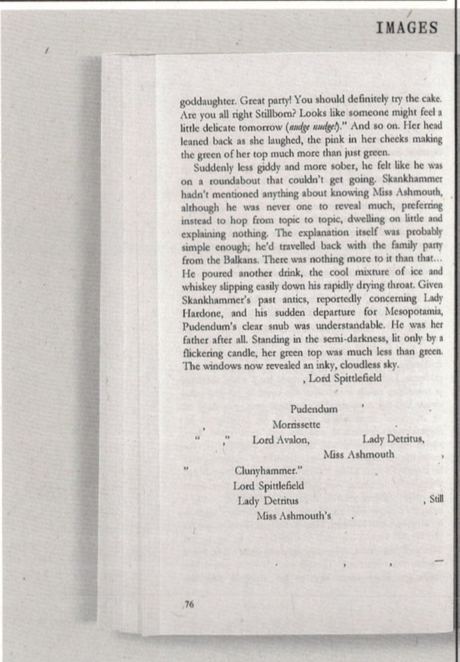

goddaughter. Great party! You should definitely try the cake. Are you all right Stillborn? Looks like someone might feel a little delicate tomorrow (*nudge nudge!*)." And so on. Her head leaned back as she laughed, the pink in her cheeks making the green of her top much more than just green.

Suddenly less giddy and more sober, he felt like he was on a roundabout that couldn't get going. Skankhammer hadn't mentioned anything about knowing Miss Ashmouth, although he was never one to reveal much, preferring instead to hop from topic to topic, dwelling on little and explaining nothing. The explanation itself was probably simple enough; he'd travelled back with the family party from the Balkans. There was nothing more to it than that... He poured another drink, the cool mixture of ice and whiskey slipping easily down his rapidly drying throat. Given Skankhammer's past antics, reportedly concerning Lady Hardone, and his sudden departure for Mesopotamia, Pudendum's clear snub was understandable. He was her father after all. Standing in the semi-darkness, lit only by a flickering candle, her green top was much less than green. The windows now revealed an inky, cloudless sky.

, Lord Spittlefield

Pudendum
Morrissette
" ," Lord Avalon, Lady Detritus,
Miss Ashmouth
" Clunyhammer."
Lord Spittlefield
Lady Detritus , Still
Miss Ashmouth's

76

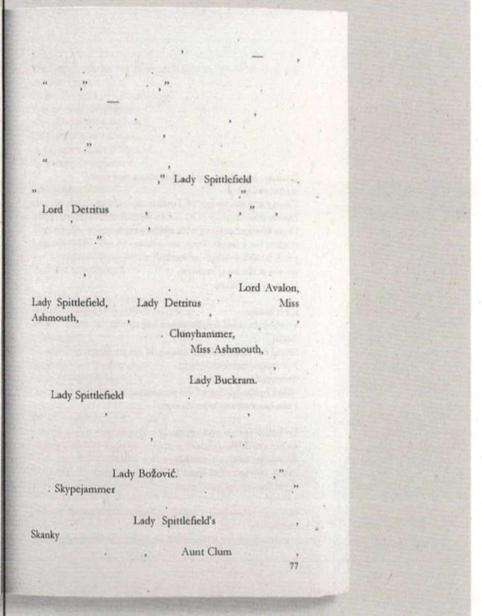

," Lady Spittlefield
Lord Detritus
Lord Avalon,
Lady Spittlefield, Lady Detritus Miss
Ashmouth,
Clunyhammer,
Miss Ashmouth,
Lady Buckram.
Lady Spittlefield
Lady Božović. ,"
Skypejammer
Lady Spittlefield's
Skanky
Aunt Clum

77

DESCRIPTION

The Black Merkin goes back to the collective writing experiment *Bad Romance* in which 170 authors participated, according to the "Postscript" which assigns passages and authorship. It was initiated and managed by Laura Edbrook and Norman James Hogg under the transitory moniker New Society of Dilettanti.

"The idea was to write an entire romance novel using a 'tribal' model of authorship. The project began by randomly selecting one e-book from a downloaded bit-torrent of over 100 romance titles. This 'template' was then split into 170 sections of around 300 words each. [...] Participants rewrote sections in the manner and style of their choosing. They received only a few basic instructions, including a request to leave all character and place names intact. Over the course of nine months, the society managed the sending, receiving and editing of texts entirely through Google docs." After that, "all character and place names were overwritten with new names using the 'find and replace' function. The result is *The Black Merkin*—a 'new' novel bearing little if any resemblance to the donor text. It is equally a 'broken' novel; the unrestrained swarm of authorial impulsions hollows out narrative structure and coherence" (author's page on Lulu). It is not only the narrative style that differs, but some passages also change the genre to visual poetry, erasure poetry, or a drama script.

The second edition of the book was published by New Society of Dilettanti in collaboration with Collective in Edinburgh and AND Public in London.

Gone with the Wind

AUTHOR	Vanessa Place
YEAR	2011
PUBLISHER	Ood Press
GENRE	experimental literature
METHOD	appropriation, constraint, documentation / archiving, reformatting
SUBJECT	authorship, bias, canon, copyright / law, literature, politics / activism, race, reading / interpretation, writing / reading techniques
PLATFORM	Lulu
EDITION CHARACTERISTICS	ISBN 9781257049042, open edition
FORMAT	14.8 × 21.0 cm
MATERIALITIES	black-and-white, paperback, perfect bound
PAGES	309 (unpaginated)

IMAGES

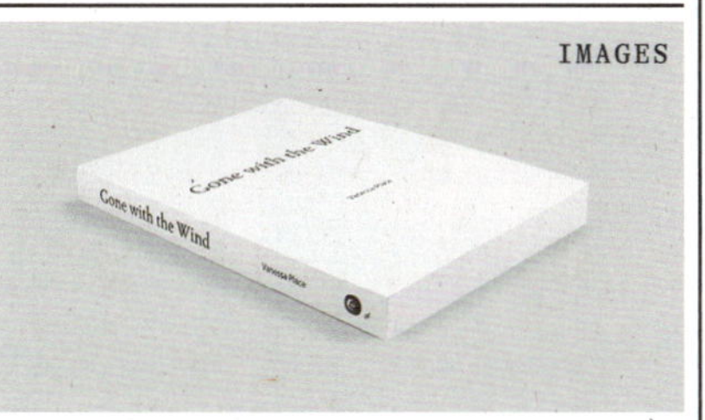

they looked imploringly at her, expecting her to give instructions. She walked into the sitting room and the two women closed about her. "Oh, Scarlett, what—" began Aunt Pitty, her fat, child's mouth shaking. "Don't speak to me or I'll scream," said Scarlett. Overwrought nerves brought sharpness to her voice and her hands clenched at her sides. The thought of speaking of Melanie now, of making the inevitable arrangements that follow a death made her throat tighten. "I don't want a word out of either of you." At the authoritative note in her voice, they fell back, helpless hurt looks on their faces. "I mustn't cry in front of them," she thought. "I mustn't break now or they'll begin crying

too, and then the darkies will begin screaming and we'll all go mad. I must pull myself together. There's so much I'll have to do. See the undertaker and arrange the funeral and see that the house is clean and be here to talk to people who'll cry on my neck. Ashley can't do them. I've got to do them. Oh, what a weary load! It's always been a weary load and always some one else's load!" CHAPTER LXIII Suddenly she wanted Mammy desperately, as she had wanted her when she was a little girl, wanted the broad bosom on which to lay her head, the gnarled black hand on her hair. Mammy, the last link with the old days. THE END

DESCRIPTION

Gone with the Wind is based on a durational Twitter project by Vanessa Place in which she tweeted the whole text of Margaret Mitchell's 1937 novel from her account @VanessaPlace between 2011 and 2015. The text was cut up into tweet-length sections (140 characters) that were posted around five times a day. According to Place, the intention was to bring attention to the novel's inherent racism and to question its hardly disputed place in America's cultural heritage (see Vanessa Place, "Artist's Statement"). This was done by relaying the appropriated text through her Twitter account as well as violating copyright, by which the novel is still protected.

Place's work caused controversy in 2015 for reproducing racist language and imagery, leading to Place shutting down her Twitter account before finishing the reposting of the entire novel, and to publish an artist statement explaining her intentions.

It was in this context that two books of the same title were published. The one in our collection "gleans the racist language and imagery of the original" (Vanessa Place, "Artist's Statement") and sets it in square blocks on each page. This layout decision was described in the author's statement as setting the racist language in "slave blocks," referencing the stone blocks that were used to display and auction slaves. This framing by the author was also highly criticized for appropriating and reproducing symbols of white supremacist oppression. On Lulu, the book's blurb consists solely of a link to the artist statement.

The other book reproduces the entire text of the original in order to once again shed light on Place's copyright infringement. This book, however, is no longer available.

Place has repeatedly worked with print-on-demand, most prominently with her *Factory Series* (see 174–176), to which this publication is falsely attributed in its colophon.

American Photographs

AUTHOR	Joachim Schmid
YEAR	2011
GENRE	photobook
METHOD	collection, found material, reenactment
SUBJECT	bias, book / book design, canon, photography, reading / interpretation, search engine
PLATFORM	Blurb
EDITION CHARACTERISTICS	open edition, available only through the artist
FORMAT	17.0 × 16.8 cm
MATERIALITIES	color, paperback, perfect bound
PAGES	112 (unpaginated)
IMAGES	

DESCRIPTION

With this book, Joachim Schmid is following in the footsteps of Walker Evans's *American Photographs*, a milestone for the photobook genre, created on the occasion of his exhibition—the first solo exhibition ever for a photographer—at MoMA New York in 1938. Both artists share an interest in the everyday: views of streets, stores, writing in urban space, commercial culture, housing, and people dominate. Unlike Evans, however, the photographic material in this book does not come from Schmid himself, but—as is so often the case in his oeuvre, which is committed to the motto "No new photos until the old ones are used up"—from countless photo sharing websites, where he used the captions of Evans's original photos as search terms. Thus, his "new edition of *American Photographs* offers a modern equivalent of Evans' masterpiece, compiled entirely of found photographs and created with the help of a search engine instead of a camera" (Joachim Schmid, "American Photographs," website).

In layout and arrangement, Schmid follows the original. Even the paratext has hardly changed: Schmid replaced the dedication of "J. S. N." with "J. S.," which happen to be his own initials; and he has updated the disclaimer, reserving the copyright for this book himself, especially the arrangement of photographs, while the right to reproduce individual images remains with the photographers who uploaded them. A list of the photos and year taken concludes the book, merging their titles with Evans's original captions (including the 1938 printing error corrections) from Schmid's search queries, as here: "24 (Sidewalk in) Vicksburg, ~~Pennsylvania~~ Mississippi, 2007," with "Pennsylvania" crossed out to show that it has been replaced with "Mississippi."

L.A. Women

AUTHOR	Joachim Schmid
YEAR	2011
GENRE	photobook
METHOD	collection, documentation / archiving, found material
SUBJECT	bias, gender, photography, politics / activism, race, surveillance / privacy
PLATFORM	Blurb
EDITION CHARACTERISTICS	open edition, available only through the artist
FORMAT	18.0 × 18.0 cm
MATERIALITIES	color, hardcover, perfect bound
PAGES	154 (unpaginated)

IMAGES

DESCRIPTION

L.A. Women contains over 140 photos of almost exclusively Black women—often looking at the photographer and smiling, sometimes sleeping, some of them pixelated, perhaps film stills. All in all, banal, everyday snapshots of unknown women that seem unworthy of further consideration. However, these are not "innocent" photographs, as Joachim Schmid notes in his introduction, because they are from the possession of a serial killer and were made public by the Los Angeles Police Department in 2010 because they suspected the killer of further murders: "From the testimony of one surviving victim we know that the woman was first photographed, then shot, and then raped before she was dumped in the street" (Joachim Schmid, "L.A. Women," website).

This information changes the spectator's gaze: suddenly these pictured women become possible victims, who unsuspectingly look at their potential murderer and could already no longer be alive. The weight of this is reminiscent of Roland Barthes' discussion of the photograph of a murderer waiting for the executioner: "The photograph is handsome, as is the boy: that is the *studium*. But the *punctum* is: *he is going to die*. I read at the same time: *This will be* and *this has been*; I observe with horror an anterior future of which death is the stake" (Roland Barthes, *Camera Lucida*, 96).

At the same time, the *L.A. Women* photos leave the beholder, whose gaze threatens to become a voyeuristic one, with questions: "These women may or may not be residents of Los Angeles, they may or may not be prostitutes (as were the women in the investigation). They may or may not be murder victims. We don't know. We don't even know whether the arrested suspect took these photographs himself. [...] It is actually the fact that we don't know anything—apart from the context where these photographs come from—that makes them so eerie. We want to know more but the pictures don't tell us. We look at them and they look at us. That's all there is" (Joachim Schmid, "L.A. Women," website).

Within the oeuvre of Joachim Schmid, who, true to his motto "No new photos until the old ones are used up" works exclusively with found material, this book takes a look at a side strand of photographic history: the use of images by a serial killer.

L.A. Women was an Honorable Mention in Blurb's 2011 *Photography Book Now* competition.

Just Published

AUTHOR	Andreas Schmidt
YEAR	2011
GENRE	photobook
METHOD	documentation / archiving, found material
SUBJECT	platforms / companies, print on demand, publishing / distribution, scale
PLATFORM	Blurb
EDITION CHARACTERISTICS	limited edition, partially censored
FORMAT	18.0 × 18.0 cm
MATERIALITIES	color, hardcover, perfect bound
PAGES	80 (unpaginated)

IMAGES

DESCRIPTION

"A few seconds after Andreas Schmidt published his book *The Americans* on February 10, 2011 at 04:26 PST, he took his first screen shot of what was to become his book called *Just Published*, a book of 760 Blurb book covers. In 2009, Blurb created and shipped more than 1.2 million books and Schmidt's peculiar addition to the ocean of self-published books shows a selection of books, which would otherwise have been forgotten by the short-lived memory of the internet.

Schmidt produced a 'snapshot' of Blurb's output and re-presented this information in a Blurb book in order to preserve a small section of the wave of self-published titles in a printed document—a kind of contemporary critical analysis of the flux of photography, the internet and the cross-overs into printed matter" (blurb on Blurb).

There is a follow-up story, posted on Blurb's sales page under the heading "Open Call": "When this book was first published in April 2011, a single individual whose book cover was used amongst 760 other book covers in *Just Published* contacted Blurb customer service and complained about copyright infringement. Blurb subsequently removed *Just Published* from their server. Instead of arguing that the usage of Thumbnail size pictures of book covers, readily available on the internet, falls under 'fair use,' the cover in question has been blacked out in this new version, published August 2011, and the artist decided to openly ask anyone whose book is included and who does not want his/her work featured in *Just Published*, to contact him and the book cover will be treated likewise." A similar reference can also be found in the book itself.

The edition is limited to 100 copies.

Facebookbook

AUTHOR	Andreas Schmidt
YEAR	2011
GENRE	photobook
METHOD	documentation / archiving, generative / automation, remediation
SUBJECT	book / book design, facebook, internet culture, memory / storage, social media
PLATFORM	Blurb
EDITION CHARACTERISTICS	limited edition
FORMAT	17.0 × 16.8 cm
MATERIALITIES	color, paperback, perfect bound
PAGES	140 (unpaginated)

IMAGES

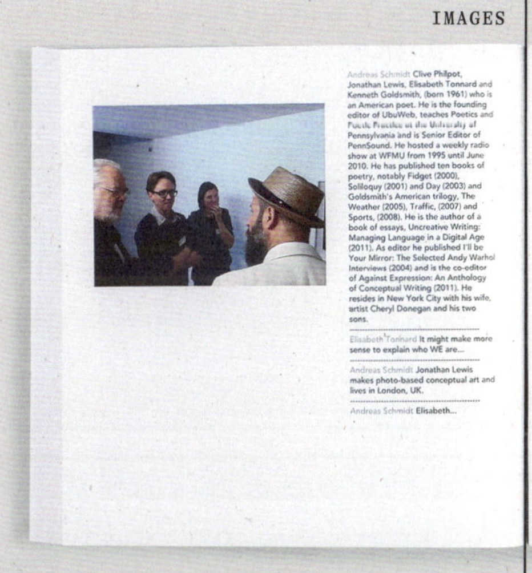

DESCRIPTION

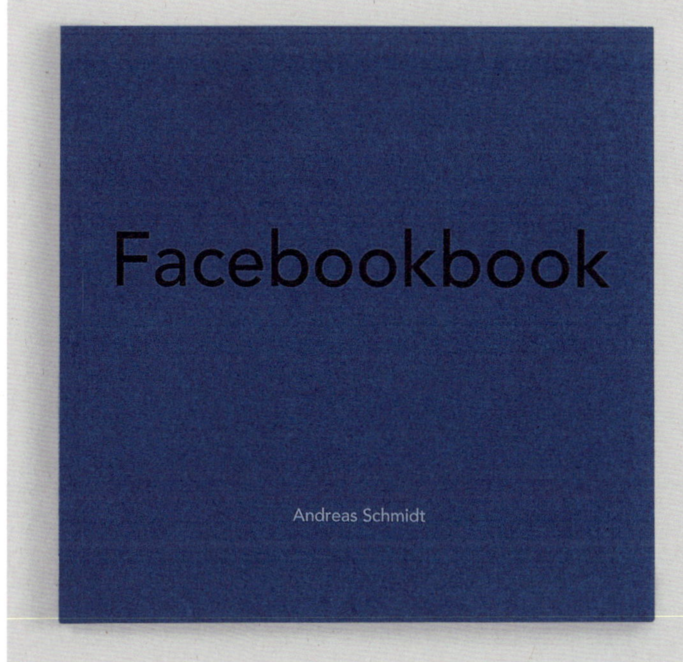

Facebookbook uses Blurb's automatic import and layout option for Facebook, which was included in their browser-based software Bookify (discontinued in 2020). Andreas Schmidt's book, which shows the content of his Facebook profile and some comments by his Facebook friends, is one of the earliest examples of this technique being used in the context of artist's books that reflect social media.

All the content from his profile was imported and automatically laid out, making it a generated book. It shows his activities in the art world and some important events of his colleagues and friends from the Artists' Books Cooperative Schmidt belongs to. Since Schmidt's Facebook profile consists mostly of photos showing him and his artist friends, rather than family and holiday pictures, *Facebookbook* also gives insight into the early intertwining of social media, art world, artist's books, and print-on-demand.

When the technology was still quite new, Blurb once wanted to show Schmidt's book at a fair as an example of how a Facebook feed can be turned into a Blurb book—without offering any financial compensation. Schmidt was at least able to negotiate fifty free copies for himself.

Ten more books followed, using the same method and further transforming Schmidt's social media activities into books. Their irregular numbering ironizes the current trend toward serial production: *Facebookbook 2* (2012), *Facebookbook 3a* (2012), *Facebookbook 3b* (2012), *Facebookbook 4* (2012), *Facebookbook 5* (2012), *Facebookbook 6* (2013), *Facebookbook 7.1* (2013), *Facebookbook 7.2* (2013), *Facebookbook 8* (2013), *Facebookbook 9* (2013).

In addition, there were a few spin-offs that likewise probe social media idiosyncrasies: *Friends of Andreas Schmidt* (2010), *Add as Friend* (2010), *I want to be your friend today, tomorrow and for the rest of my life* (2011), and *Jukerman A. Bahk walked 10,559 steps on 4/30/2012, 3:27 PM in 188 minutes* (2012).

blurb

AUTHOR	Andreas Schmidt
YEAR	2011
GENRE	artist's book / bookwork
METHOD	appropriation, détournement / hack
SUBJECT	copyright / law, platforms / companies, print on demand
PLATFORM	Blurb
EDITION CHARACTERISTICS	limited edition
FORMAT	17.9 × 17.5 cm
MATERIALITIES	color, hardcover, perfect bound
PAGES	40 (unpaginated)

IMAGES

DESCRIPTION

"*blurb* by Andreas Schmidt is the purest Blurb book you will ever find" (blurb on Blurb). The book contains nothing but the signature Blurb logo at the bottom of each page. This logo is automatically put at the end of every book by Blurb. You have to pay an extra fee if you don't want it in your book. Schmidt kept it in his books for financial reasons. At the same time, Blurb's branding and self-promotion fits well with his approach of wanting to make "bad books" that are honest at the same time, i.e., books that stand by their production method.

In the imprint, Schmidt claims: "The book author retains sole copyright to his or her contributions to this book." Blurb accused him of copyright infringement because of the unauthorized use of the logo and Schmidt's claim that this book was "the purest Blurb book." At the end of the dispute, Schmidt had to sign a confidentiality agreement.

The edition is limited to 100 copies.

Phantoms (H_ RT _F D_RKN_SS)

AUTHOR	Stephanie Syjuco
YEAR	2011
GENRE	artistic research, exhibition copy, experimental literature
METHOD	found material, generative / automation, reformatting, remediation
SUBJECT	analog / digital, book / book design, copyright / law, error / corruption / loss, literature, race, reading / interpretation, standard / default, typography
PLATFORM	Lulu
VOLUMES	9
EDITION CHARACTERISTICS	open edition
FORMAT	10.8 × 17.5 cm
MATERIALITIES	black-and-white, paperback, perfect bound

IMAGES

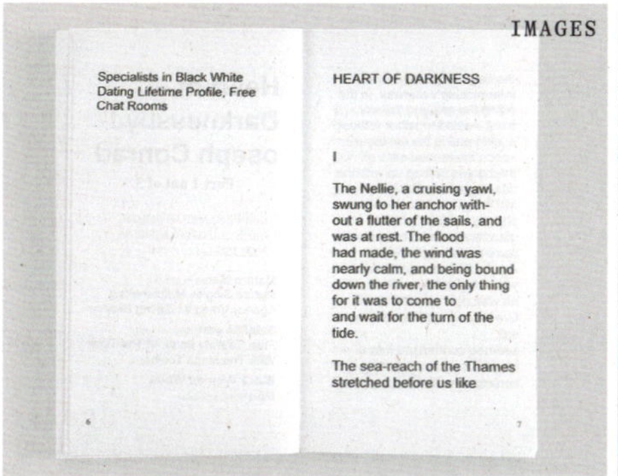

DESCRIPTION

In her series of nine different paperback copies of Joseph Conrad's *Heart of Darkness*, Stephanie Syjuco documents the effects of the retro-digitization of a literary text by transferring digitized versions of the novel downloaded from different online sources back into book form. In contrast to retro-digitization, one could speak of "retro-analogization." For this purpose, she downloads the texts and "pours" them fully automatically into the standardized container of a print-on-demand paperback—which is always the same. The title is always the URL of the website from which the digital version of the text was taken.

In 2011, the series was part of an art installation titled *Phantoms (H__RT _F D_RKN_SS)*. The corrupted subtitle already indicates that a text is unavoidably modified by its digitization. This problem is already apparent in some of the title pages of the series, where the missing spaces and inappropriate breaks destroy every unit of meaning, for example: "Heart of / DarknessbyJ / oseph Conrad" (Stephanie Syjuco, *Heart of Darkness: fullbooks*). The books include interposed Google ads, scanning and OCR errors, misplaced page breaks and intertitle pages, obsolete links, and (as in the case of the Gutenberg edition) extensive appendices with the terms of the license that regulate the access, distribution, and use of the digital content.

The book page that Syjuco wins back from the digitized text is thus ineradicably shaped by computer logic, as well as by the politics of digitization and circulation of each text repository. Her "re-edition" adds another twist to the rich and, at least since the allegation of racism levied by Chinua Achebe, ideologically hotly contested reception history of Conrad's story, which is so profound and extensive that Syjuco speaks of "an inadvertent rewriting" (Stephanie Syjuco, "Phantoms," website). Each of the paperbacks in the series thus not only contains Conrad's text, it also tells the story of its circulation, reception, and transmission, to which digitization adds a new chapter: "These Print on Demand volumes represent a physical epitome of the effects of digital circulation over the original text" (Silvio Lorusso, "Extending Horizons," 105).

This medial reformatting is by no means just a problem for literary works, as Syjuco demonstrates in a three-minute video loop and a music collection that complement the book series. The found footage film compiles the warning "This film has been modified from its original version. It has been formatted to fit your TV" that precedes many film and video format translations on YouTube. *Proxy Audio Manifestion (Total Bootleg Collection)* "displays hundreds of handmade replicas of all the digital music files I have illegally downloaded." Thus, it "utilizes digital/analog retranslations to push forward the idea of how narrative and authorship shifts across different surfaces" (Stephanie Syjuco, "Phantoms," website).

In 2013, Syjuco also made three re-editioned print-on-demand versions of Ray Bradbury's *Fahrenheit 451*.

THE VOLUMES INCLUDE

Heart of Darkness: 958 ibm (364 pages)
Heart of Darkness: enotes (369 pages)
Heart of Darkness: fullbooks (429 pages)
Heart of Darkness: gradesaver (301 pages)
Heart of Darkness: project gutenberg (399 pages)
Heart of Darkness: pvirtane (286 pages)
Heart of Darkness: sparknotes (282 pages)
Heart of Darkness: sunsite.berkeley (355 pages)
Heart of Darkness: etext.virginia (381 pages)

The a, d, o's & 1, 6, 10's of CREDIT

AUTHOR	Mathew Timmons
YEAR	2011
PUBLISHER	Blanc Press
GENRE	artist's book / bookwork, experimental literature
METHOD	documentation / archiving, found material, photocopy / scan, pricing, translation / transcription
SUBJECT	analog / digital, economy / labor, error / corruption / loss, materiality, tracking
PLATFORM	Lulu
EDITION CHARACTERISTICS	ISBN 9780981462349, open edition
FORMAT	21.0 × 27.8 cm
MATERIALITIES	color, hardcover, perfect bound
PAGES	140

IMAGES

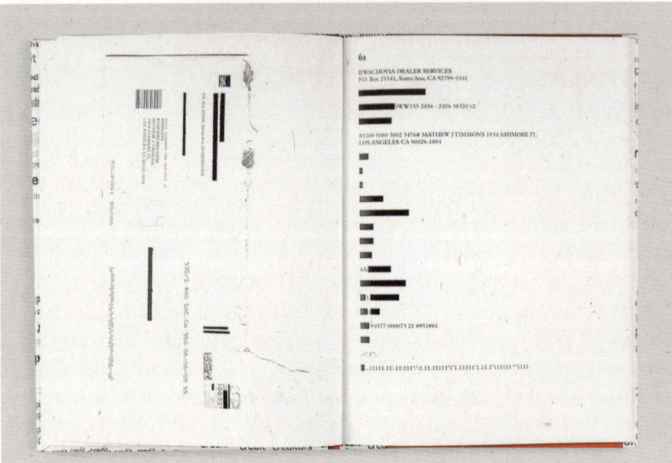

DESCRIPTION

The a, d, o's & 1, 6, 10's of CREDIT is "a shortened, condensed, more affordable version of *CREDIT*," collecting only the entries listed in its title. The 2009 predecessor *CREDIT* is 800 pages long and is, according to publisher Blanc Press (founded by Mathew Timmons), "the longest, most expensive book publishable through the online service, lulu.com" (blurb on publisher website). The printed book costs $199.99, and the download is a crazy $299.99. In contrast, the abridged version can almost be called inexpensive at $65. Both editions have the same ISBN on the back cover.

The book is a collection of credit offers and requests for payment that the author received in his mailbox between 2007 and 2009. They are sorted into the chapters "Credit," with offers from a–z, and "Debit," with offers from 1–10. The letters, including the envelopes in which they came and any reply envelopes included, are each reproduced in full, as scans, with front and back covers. Printed on the opposite page is the OCR text, which is in fairly bad condition due to damage caused when opening the letters, fonts that are difficult to decipher, and heavy redaction to hide details of the author's own financial situation. However, the blackened-out passages can be found in the appendix.

CREDIT is both a reflection on OCR as a central method of making analog text machine-readable—essential for interacting with banks—and a documentation of the 2007–2008 financial crisis from a very personal point of view. The pricing of the book also responds to this opposition between the individual and the financial institution: "Retailing for $199.99, *CREDIT* is a book the author himself lacks the cash or credit to buy" (blurb on publisher website).

The project is accompanied by an extensive collection of endorsements from more than thirty authors. They show amazing creativity and humor in relation to this genre of text. Also not to be underestimated is the enormous publicity effect achieved simply by listing the names of these authors in web stores, making the project well established and known to a large part of the experimental literature community.

THE LIST INCLUDES

Harold Abramowitz, Stan Apps, Marcus Civin, Brian Joseph Davis, Ryan Daley, Craig Dworkin, Brad Fliss, Lawrence Giffin, James Hoff, Maximus Kim, Matthew Klane, Janne Larsen, Matthias Merkel Hess, William Moor, Joseph Mosconi, Holly Myers, Sawako Nakayasu, Sianne Ngai, Ariel Pink, Vanessa Place, Dan Richert, Ronald Quinn Rudlong Jr., Ara Shirinyan, Danny Snelson, Erika Staiti, Brian Kim Stefans, Robert Summers, Rodrigo Toscano, Matias Viegener, and Steven Zultanski.

The Story of a Young Gentleman

AUTHOR	Elisabeth Tonnard
YEAR	2011
GENRE	artist's book / bookwork, experimental literature
METHOD	appropriation, montage / remix, reformatting
SUBJECT	book / book design, literature, reading / interpretation, scale, writing / reading techniques
PLATFORM	Blurb
EDITION CHARACTERISTICS	available only through the artist, no longer available
FORMAT	12.8 × 20.3 cm
MATERIALITIES	black-and-white, paperback, perfect bound
PAGES	350 (unpaginated)

IMAGES

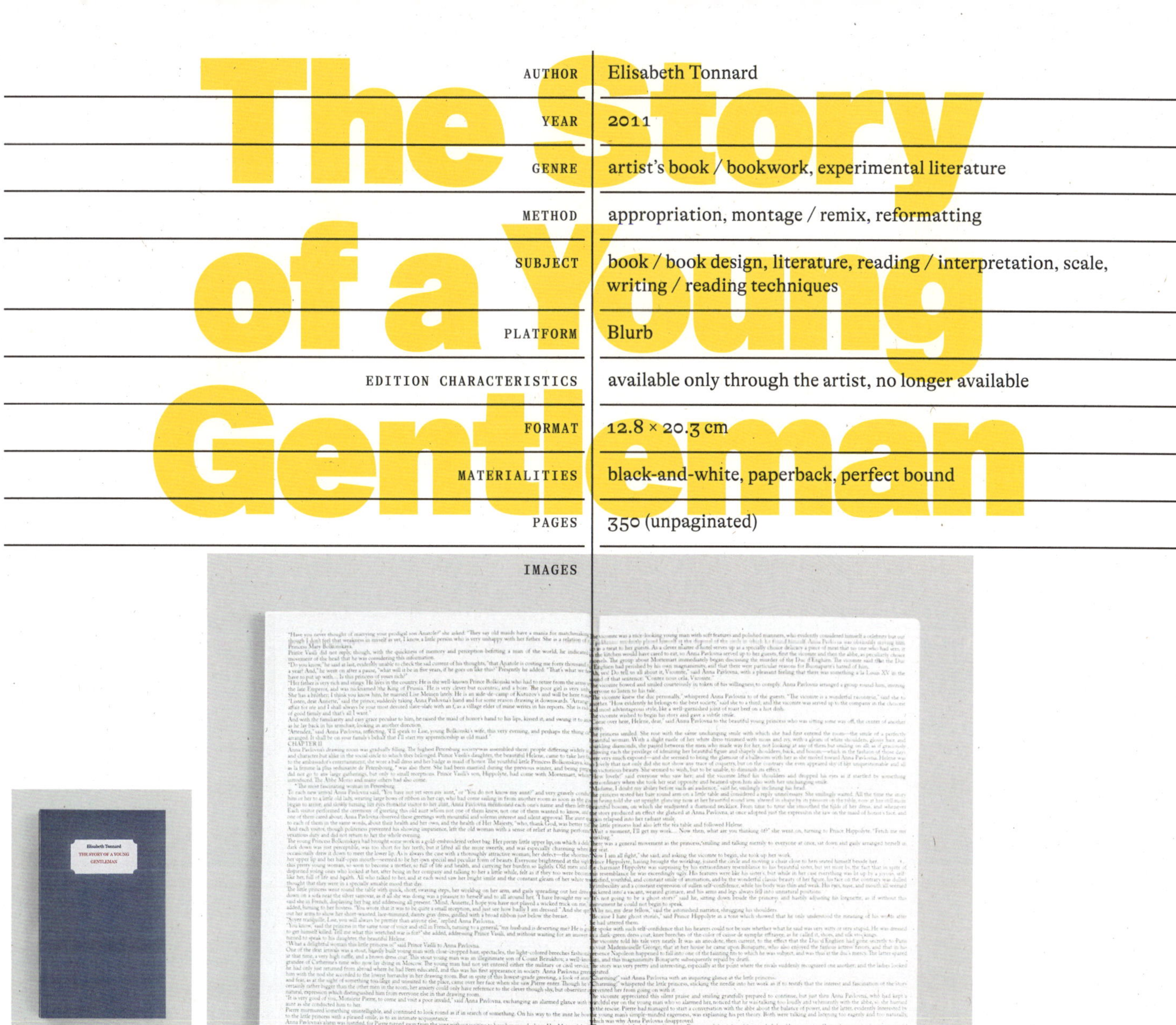

DESCRIPTION

Judging from its length, Elisabeth Tonnard's *The Story of a Young Gentleman* could be a novel, probably the most popular genre on the literary market at the moment. However, this story of hers is actually very short—only six sentences long. It is then embedded with one of the longest novels in the history of world literature: Leo Tolstoy's *War and Peace*, with its four volumes, seventeen parts, and 365 chapters. Tonnard's story begins: "He was born on a bright summer day. // For a succession of seasons he was educated by the best minds of his generation. // He put a flower in his buttonhole and visited restaurants. // He read *War and Peace*." This is followed, on roughly 330 pages, by Tolstoy's novel, set in extremely small font with maximum expansion of the type area and dispensing with running titles, pagination, and any blank lines.

Such a structure allows us to witness the reading experience of the character in Tonnard's story, as we read *War and Peace* "through his eyes," conflating narrated and narrative time. At the same time, the specific design with its dense, seemingly never-ending stream of lines stages a reading practice that is primarily reserved for the genre of the novel as a page-turner: linear, continuous reading from the first to the last page, typically promoted by the maximally unobtrusive and flowing design of the text. Underlying this, however, is a reading ideal that is the exception, not the rule, among reading practices. Even Tonnard's overemphasis on the flow of the text cannot hide the fact that the codex, which necessarily requires turning pages, is in principle a medium of discontinuous reading.

Without interruption, but at an unreachable height from our world of war and conflicts, only the stars pass by the character's eye, with which Tonnard's narrative ends: "At night, he lay down. // High above, the stars were drifting by." The line quoted on the back cover, taken from *War and Peace*, seems to comment on this: "'Charming!' whispered the little princess..."

The book's typesetting imposes special requirements on trimming and binding that print-on-demand providers regularly failed to meet, which is why the books were only available through the artist's webshop after a quality check. In 2014, Tonnard even stopped production via print-on-demand altogether.

ABC Reviews

AUTHOR	Elisabeth Tonnard
YEAR	2011
GENRE	artist's book / bookwork, experimental literature
METHOD	collection, found material
SUBJECT	art world / literary world, canon, economy / labor, internet culture
PLATFORM	Blurb
EDITION CHARACTERISTICS	available only through the artist, no longer available
FORMAT	12.6 × 20.3 cm
MATERIALITIES	black-and-white, paperback, perfect bound
PAGES	68 (unpaginated)
IMAGES	

DESCRIPTION

From its start in 2009 till 2013, Elisabeth Tonnard was a member of the Artists' Books Cooperative (ABC), an international network created by and for artists who make print-on-demand books. In this book, she presents reviews she found online that, as the blurb sensationally puts it, "show the immense impact of ABC in the world" (blurb on artist website). Here, the need for marketing, not only in art, is ironically contrasted with the niche in which ABC operates in the photobook, literary, and artist's book fields.

The book begins with a list of short comments in a kind of thread, which swing between the extremes "NEVER AGAIN!!" and "I LOVE ABC!" and demonstrate the arbitrariness and questionable informative value of such online reviews. This is followed by longer reviews, one per page, with stores, veterinary clinics, craft businesses, childcare, and service facilities etc. obviously hiding behind the abbreviation "ABC" here. The wit of the collection arises from the potential transferability of these comments to the cooperative itself. The very first review could just be a description of Tonnard's process for producing this book: "Its [*sic*] so beautiful in ABC [...]. Its [*sic*] the perfect place to browse and if you find an item, you might want to do some research and see if you just can't get it somelplace [*sic*] else!" The reviewers' usernames are listed in the acknowledgments at the end of the book.

The Death of the Photographer A Rehearsal

AUTHOR	Elisabeth Tonnard
YEAR	2011
GENRE	artist's book / bookwork
METHOD	appropriation, montage / remix, remediation
SUBJECT	authorship, canon, photography, print on demand, visual culture
PLATFORM	Blurb
EDITION CHARACTERISTICS	open edition, no longer available
FORMAT	12.7 × 20.3 cm
MATERIALITIES	color, paperback, perfect bound
PAGES	96

IMAGES

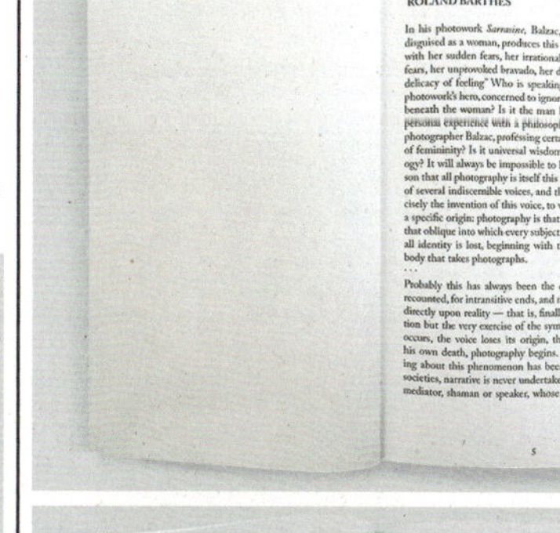

THE DEATH OF THE PHOTOGRAPHER
ROLAND BARTHES

In his photowork *Sarrasine*, Balzac, speaking of a castrato disguised as a woman, produces this image: "It was Woman, with her sudden fears, her irrational whims, her instinctive fears, her unprovoked bravado, her daring and her delicious delicacy of feeling" Who is speaking in this way? Is it the photowork's hero, concerned to ignore the castrato concealed beneath the woman? Is it the man Balzac, endowed by his personal experience with a philosophy of Woman? Is it the photographer Balzac, professing certain "photographic" ideas of femininity? Is it universal wisdom? or romantic psychology? It will always be impossible to know, for the good reason that all photography is itself this special voice, consisting of several indiscernible voices, and that photography is precisely the invention of this voice, to which we cannot assign a specific origin: photography is that neuter, that composite, that oblique into which every subject escapes, the trap where all identity is lost, beginning with the very identity of the body that takes photographs.

...

Probably this has always been the case: once an action is recounted, for intransitive ends, and no longer in order to act directly upon reality — that is, finally external to any function but the very exercise of the symbol — this disjunction occurs, the voice loses its origin, the photographer enters his own death, photography begins. Nevertheless, the feeling about this phenomenon has been variable; in primitive societies, narrative is never undertaken by a person, but by a mediator, shaman or speaker, whose "performance" may be

5

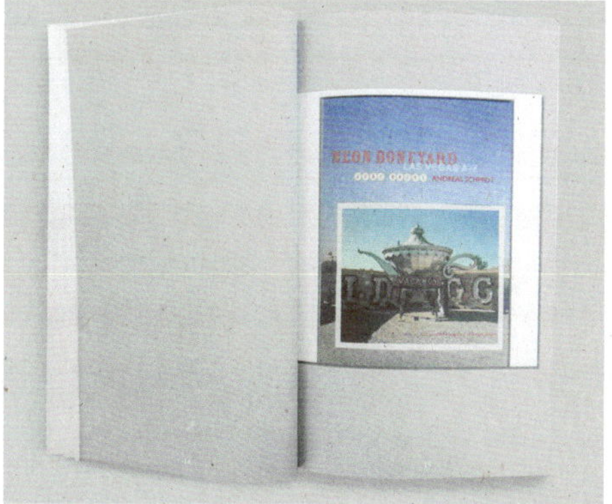

DESCRIPTION

Elisabeth Tonnard's *The Death of the Photographer* enters into dialogue with several works that it incorporates: First, there is the photobook *Neon Boneyard Las Vegas A-Z Judy Natal* (2011) by fellow artist and Artists' Books Cooperative member Andreas Schmidt, which itself is already an appropriation of a photobook. He pasted his own photos of the famous Las Vegas neon sign "graveyard" into a copy of Judy Natal's *NEON BONEYARD LAS VEGAS A-Z* (2006), then scanned his copy and made it available via Blurb. Screenshots of the book preview there formed the source for Tonnard's appropriation. These images are combined with Roland Barthes' essay "The Death of the Author," which she found on UbuWeb and edited to replace words like "author," "story," and "narration" with "photographer," "image," "photowork," etc., which explains the altered title of her book.

The text, adapted in this way, proves to be surprisingly fitting, as if describing Tonnard's own work, for example, when "the whole being of photography" is defined as follows: "a photo consists of multiple photos, issuing from several cultures and entering into dialogue with each other, into parody, into contestation; but there is one place where this multiplicity is collected, united, and this place is not the photographer, as we have hitherto said it was, but the reader: the reader is the very space in which are inscribed, without any being lost, all the citations a photography consists of; the unity of a photo is not in its origin, it is in its destination" (Elisabeth Tonnard, *The Death of the Photographer*, 12). It is therefore only consequential that the postscript reads: "No efforts have been made to contact the rightful owners with regards to copyright and permissions."

At the same time, Tonnard's book can be read as an attempt to answer those questions, "intrinsic to contemporary thinking about photography," that Andreas Schmidt raises in the blurb to his own photobook: "Is it a new book? Is it a pirate copy? Is it a combination of two bodies of work or is the combination the new work? Is it a facsimile or is it an artist's book? Is it the death of the photographer?" (Andreas Schmidt, *Neon Boneyard Las Vegas A–Z Judy Natal*, blurb on Blurb)

On her website, Tonnard presents her book not in the usual way with photos of the physical object, but—in accordance with the process she chose to obtain the visual material for her book—with screenshots of the digital book preview on Blurb. The cover of her book also mimics the Blurb interface that is displayed at the end of a preview.

Given that Tonnard has since turned her back on Blurb due to poor quality and high shipping costs, this book is no longer available. A one-page version of the work in the form of an assignment to modify Barthes' text accordingly and then use it as stimulus for one's own photographic work appeared in *The Photographer's Playbook: 307 Assignments and Ideas*, edited by Jason Fulford and Gregory Halpern, in 2014.

AAbA Logfile

Asylabwehramt. Asylum Defense Agency

AUTHOR	Ubermorgen
YEAR	2011
PUBLISHER	TraumaWien
GENRE	artistic research
METHOD	détournement / hack, documentation / archiving, reformatting, study / analysis
SUBJECT	analog / digital, bias, data, memory / storage, politics / activism, race, surveillance / privacy
PLATFORM	Lulu
EDITION CHARACTERISTICS	ISBN 9783950291087, open edition
FORMAT	15.2 × 22.9 cm
MATERIALITIES	black-and-white, paperback, perfect bound
PAGES	357

IMAGES

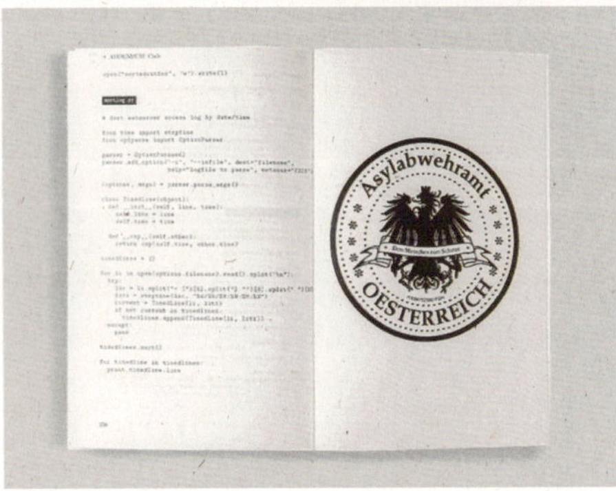

DESCRIPTION

"Asylabwehramt" (AAbA, Asylum Defense Agency) was an exhibition by Ubermorgen (lizvlx and Hans Bernhard) at das weisse haus gallery in Vienna in 2010. Mimicking an official government entity, the exhibition consisted of three office rooms and a website for an agency responsible for dealing with all sorts of illegal migration activities and border defense: "anonymization of asylum proceedings, stopping human trafficking, immigration diversion, [...] defending against surplus refugees and asylum seekers, [...] pre-selection (economic refugees, naturalization), secret deportation, migration analysis for national protection as well as in prevention of re-traumatization and the expansion of bureaucratic barriers" (Ubermorgen, "Asylum Defence Agency," website).

Even though the installation was a hoax, its content was not. All documents, highly complex formalities leaving room for unethical gray areas and documents describing fates of individual migration histories, were real. "We like working with copy and paste. We are interested in copying and slightly modifying things, to consolidate and mirror them to do away with the distinction of fake and real. A distinction that might not have been there at all" (lisvlx in Ö1, "Asylabwehramt").

By unmasking the highly unethical practices of the Austrian government and the European Union in general, obfuscated by obscure bureaucratic language, Ubermorgen created a sophisticated analysis and documentation of migration policies and an illusion that also worked as a honeypot for a xenophobic public.

This is documented in the book *AAbA Logfile* which copies a log of all server activities of the fake website from June 4, 2010 to April 11, 2011 in chronological order, listing access dates and IPs as well as revealing search terms that led to the website, such as: "Tips+and+tricks+on+how-to+enhance+bureaucratic+burdens+in+the+asylum+process+in+Austria+and+in+the+Schengen+Area &ie=utf-8&oe=utf-8&aq=t&rls=org.mozilla:de:official&client=firefox-a." In the "WHOIS Records" section, one can even find resolved IP addresses, revealing the person and/or institution behind the query or server request.

The epilogue states: "If you think this publication is violating privacy rights of users of the website, then we would like to point out chapter 231, first paragraph (3) letter (j) of our user agreement which grants the operators of the website the irrevocable right to use all data collected for their own purpose and for any publication. After all, if you have never been a bad citizen, you got nothing to hide, right?"

The appendix contains the text and forms of the fake website, a report about the project in the major German weekly magazine *Die Zeit*, and the project's Python code.

DOTS

[10 PREPARED SCANS]

AUTHOR	Éric Watier
YEAR	2011
PUBLISHER	monotone press
GENRE	artist's book / bookwork, intermediate product / halbzeug
METHOD	photocopy / scan
SUBJECT	book / book design, economy / labor, error / corruption / loss, materiality, print technology, publishing / distribution
PLATFORM	Blurb
EDITION CHARACTERISTICS	open edition
FORMAT	15.2 × 22.9 cm
MATERIALITIES	black-and-white, paperback, perfect bound
PAGES	20 (unpaginated)

IMAGES

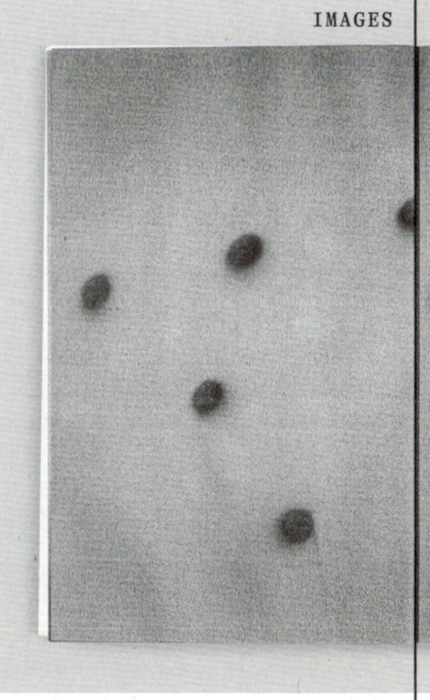

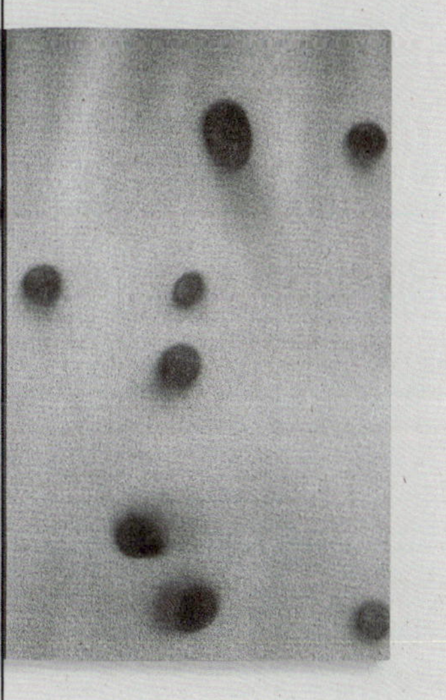

DESCRIPTION

Éric Watier's *DOTS* contains ten black-and-white "prepared scans" made with a scanner manipulated by hand. The resulting distortions and pixelations are amplified by the printing process, making it hard to decide whether the book's title refers to what looks like fingers pressed against the scanner or ink dots. Watier's fascination with scans is also evident on his Tumblr page "the scan collection."

Reproduction and circulation are central to Watier's artistic practice: since the 1990s, he has mainly produced printed works composed of photocopies, scans, posters, flyers, and postcards. With the founding of monotone press in 2011, he is transitioning his previous practice of free xeroxed and mail-art books into the digital age which is characterized by "an extraordinary ability to circulate objects to be rematerialized." Yet it is important to him to enable "a new economy, where," according to his "Monotone manifesto," "the objects are fully available and at the same time can be materialized always singularly and [in] unlimited [fashion]" (Éric Watier, "Monotone manifesto," 199).

His "Manifesto" goes on to say: "Thus, to make things perfectly clear, we thought it necessary to create an independent structure for the diffusion of content, in which anyone can go and search for what is needed to achieve one's interest [...]. / A priori, everything is allowed. We will see later whether some uses will be considered scandalous or dishonest. / Consequently you can do whatever you like with Monotone Press (except what is not appreciated)" (Ibid., 199f.).

The publications are usually free and can be downloaded from the press's website. Some, like *DOTS*, are additionally available as print-on-demand. *DOTS* is also part of Watier's Coverless collection, which is why the front cover demands "to tear this cover off."

my country is a Living Room

AUTHOR	Carlo Zanni
YEAR	2011
PUBLISHER	People from Mars
GENRE	experimental literature, poetry
METHOD	generative / automation, translation / transcription
SUBJECT	code / programming, google, literature, technology
PLATFORM	Lulu
EDITION CHARACTERISTICS	open edition, CC0
FORMAT	15.6 × 23.4 cm
MATERIALITIES	black-and-white, hardcover, perfect bound
PAGES	150

IMAGES

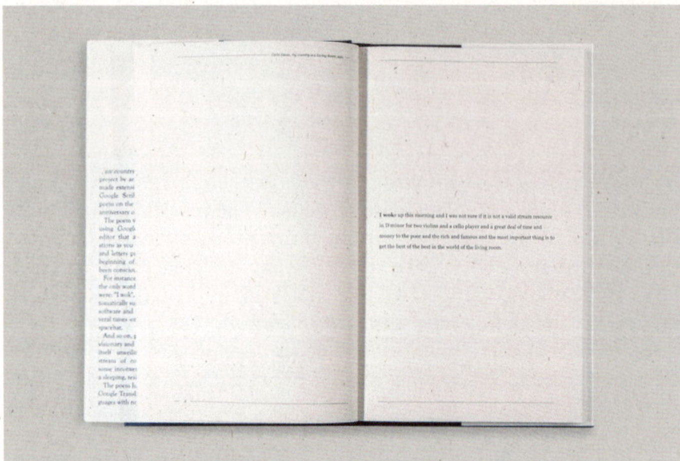

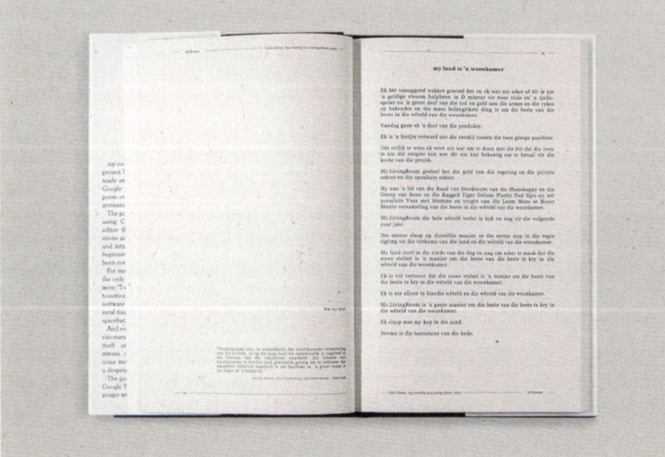

DESCRIPTION

For *my country is a Living Room*, Carlo Zanni used Google's autocomplete feature at a rather early stage of its development, using the text editor Scribe and its automatic translation service Translate. To mark the 150th anniversary of Italian unification, Zanni typed fourteen strings of characters or words into Scribe and collected the autocompleted stanzas, placing a period after each iteration. The resulting poem is a reflection on the public and private, the national and local, represented by the country and the living room respectively. This political dimension is highlighted by the book cover, which shows the souvenir statuette of Milan Cathedral with which the then Italian prime minister, Silvio Berlusconi, was attacked at a political rally in 2009. The artist also wanted to point to the "sleepy," somehow politically hypnotized state of Italy at that time (artist in an email to apod.li).

Accordingly, the first input was "I wok," which Google autocompleted as "I woke up." The prompts ranged from "Tod" (for "Today") or just "H" to more complex clusters such as "Mr.LivingRoom deceives" and "My country dies," indicating a will to influence the outcome of this generative writing method. At this early stage of Scribe's development, it was possible to help shape the result, especially for longer sentences, by pressing the spacebar after typing the first few letters, since Scribe suggested a new word each time the spacebar was hit.

The poem, originally in English, was then automatically translated into fifty-seven languages (the ones available on Google Translate at the time), to form the second part of the book. In the first part, each stanza takes up one page of the book, with Zanni's prompts in bold, giving the impression of sentences rather than verses. The translations in the second part present all stanzas on one page, giving a more traditional impression of a poem.

The website had Scribe's autocomplete feature implemented so that each time a user visited it, the prompts Zanni used were automatically resent to Scribe, triggering new autocompletions. The outcome changed, as Google's suggestions are based on filtering and the statistical analysis of millions of everchanging websites. In a sense, "[t]hese transformations [are] somehow 'suggested' by the collective writings of billions of people around the world" (Carlo Zanni, "About").

The resulting new versions were stored in an archive accessible through the website and a pay-per-view subscription system. However, this implementation was shut down when Google denied any access to Scribe one year later, leaving the archive with a total of 111 generated poems. With its dual output as book and website, the project provides an example of the fragile liveness of the web and the more stable output of print.

Title by Author

AUTHOR	Rahel Zoller
YEAR	2011–2020
GENRE	artist's book / bookwork
METHOD	paratextual play, study / analysis
SUBJECT	book / book design, materiality, publishing / distribution, standard / default
PLATFORM	Blurb, others
EDITION CHARACTERISTICS	multiple editions
PAGES	48

IMAGE

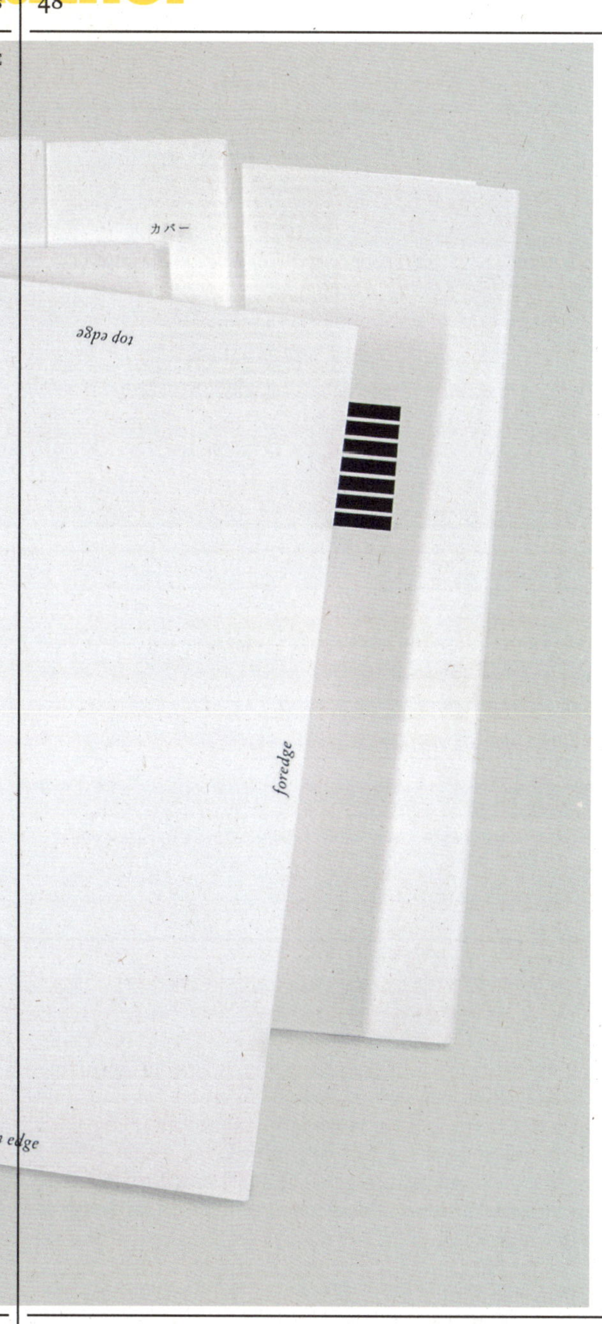

DESCRIPTION

Rahel Zoller's *Title*, consisting of three different editions, "is an experimental exploration and illustration of the rules of book design" (Rahel Zoller, *Title by Author*, 1st ed., vi), thus categorizing it in the genre of self-referential bookworks, to which one could also count Johanna Drucker's *Diagrammatic Writing* (2014) and Roberto Arista and Amato Luigi's *Volume* (2014, see 282), which were created at about the same time. The best-known precursor is probably George Brecht's *BOOK* (1972), which also takes itself as subject and virtually guides the readers through the book, showing, naming, and explaining the book elements that the reader encounters. These books are thus at once a tautological description of the same book that the reader is reading as well as a kind of model of a book that—both ostentatiously and didactically—contains established rules and unwritten laws that must be observed when producing, designing, and reading a book.

Title by Author [Skeleton Book]

AUTHOR	Rahel Zoller
YEAR	2011
METHOD	paratextual play, study / analysis
PLATFORM	Blurb
EDITION CHARACTERISTICS	ISBN 9781908452047, open edition, no longer available
FORMAT	12.6 × 20.3 cm
MATERIALITIES	black-and-white, paperback, perfect bound
IMAGE	

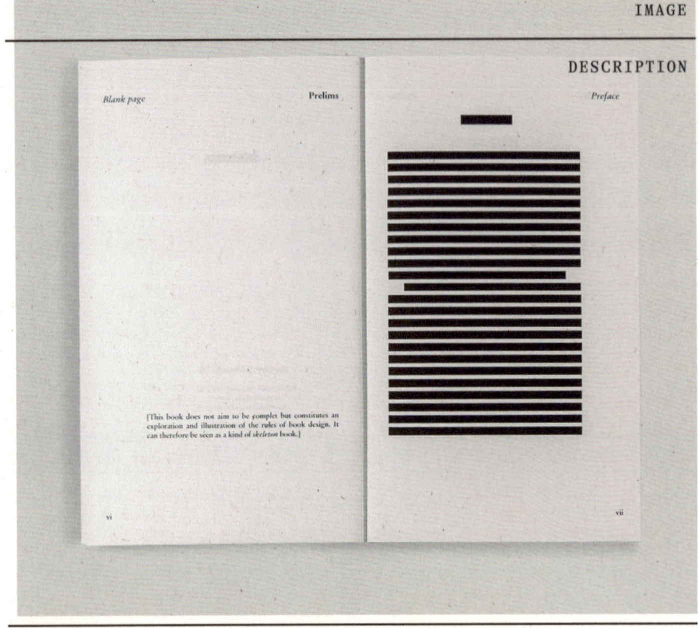

DESCRIPTION

The 2011 first edition once available on Blurb, back then still circulating under the subtitle "Skeleton Book," names all conceivable elements and design rules of a book page by page. On the first five pages alone, these are: flyleaf, blank page, prelims, left page/verso, right page/recto, gutter, golden section, half-title, frontispiece, roman numerals, and title page. The next pages then display the main body of the text, whose typographic structure is then schematically reproduced with black lines, reminiscent of Man Ray's visual *Poem* (1924) and Marcel Broodthaers's *Un Coup de dés jamais n'abolira le hasard (image)* (1969).

Title by Author [2nd ed.]

AUTHOR	Rahel Zoller
YEAR	2017
METHOD	paratextual play, study / analysis
PLATFORM	Blurb
EDITION CHARACTERISTICS	ISBN 9781908452047, open edition, dated, available only through the artist
FORMAT	12.6 × 20.3 cm
MATERIALITIES	black-and-white, dust jacket, loose insert, paperback, perfect bound

DESCRIPTION

A second, modified edition was produced in 2017. It was only available from the artist herself, as she now packed the print-on-demand "raw print" in a dust jacket for "refinement" and included an insert with details of the month and year of printing in order to document the changes in paper stock and printing quality over the years, inherent in the print-on-demand process (see fig. on 109). Each printed copy is thus a record of a moment in time.

In addition, Zoller has made a few minor adjustments to the design and conception of this edition. For example, the author, title, and publisher information on the front cover is repositioned and some terms are exchanged ("front matter" becomes "prelims"). Some minor inconsistencies are amended, such as when the frontispiece is now displayed as a black block, by analogy with the black lines of text, or when "A Book" is corrected to "Title" in order to preserve the self-referentiality of the title page and to let the information really be a placeholder rather than an actual, functioning title.

Zoller has accounted for some of these oversights in *Catalogue of Mistakes by Rahel Zoller 2011–2021*, distinguishing between unfortunate, inexplicable, hidden, fortuitous, aesthetic, recurrent, and other mistakes. According to this report, the misspelling in the introductory note, which runs through the various editions, is a deliberate one, namely "ironic mistake": "This book does not aim to be complet [*sic*] but constitutes an exploration and illustration of the rules of book design. It can therefore be seen as a kind of *skeleton* book."

The imprint of this second edition contains a note about the update made, but still features the same ISBN, while on the back cover, hidden by the dust jacket, a different ISBN (9781389501647) is indicated.

AUTHORS	Asami Murakami, Rahel Zoller
YEAR	2020
METHOD	paratextual play, study / analysis, translation / transcription
PLATFORM	others
VOLUMES	2
EDITION CHARACTERISTICS	ISBN 9781908452047, available only through the artist, limited edition
FORMAT	12.6 × 20.3 cm
MATERIALITIES	black-and-white, dust jacket, loose insert, paperback, perfect bound, slipcase

IMAGE

DESCRIPTION

Finally, in 2020, a third edition *Title / タイトル by Author / 著者* was produced together with Asami Murakami, for which the second edition was once again revised in such a way that the self-reference is taken to the extreme and one can now literally speak of a "skeleton book": For now, the entire book truly consists only of placeholders for the individual elements of the book. Even the title page and imprint do without mention of actual authorship, publication date, ISBN, etc. The only information given in the book that actually refers to the outside world and allows this book object to be assigned to an author and a publisher is the ISBN on the back cover.

In addition, the third edition pairs the English-language edition with a translation into Japanese, both offered only together in a slipcase. This is not a literal translation, but a conceptual translation into the language of Japanese book culture with its opposite flipping of the pages and vertical text flow, resulting in an intercultural dialogue and encouraging comparative observation: "When naming the top and the bottom of a book in Japan the top is called: 天 sky or heaven and the bottom 地 ground or earth whereas in Western publishing, the top is called head and the bottom tail: this originates from the animal skin a book was bound in historically" (blurb on artist's website). The set is printed and distributed in an edition of 200 copies.

AUTHORS	Åbäke, AND Publishing
YEAR	2012
PUBLISHER	AND Publishing
GENRE	artistic research, artist's book / bookwork
METHOD	photocopy / scan, reformatting, test / experiment, versioning / seriality
SUBJECT	materiality, platforms / companies, print technology, print on demand, publishing / distribution, standard / default
PLATFORM	Blurb, Espresso Book Machine, iPhoto, Lulu, MagCloud, Newspaper Club, selfmade
VOLUMES	12
EDITION CHARACTERISTICS	ISBN 9781907840098

IMAGES

DESCRIPTION

"*Variable Format* is sample book, a model, a serial system that explores the technological margins of print on demand and how reading is informed by the materiality of the book object" (AND Publishing, "Variable Formats," website).

AND Publishing's aim was to help artists practically and conceptually create their own publications and to explore the extent to which print-on-demand, which was quite new at the time, could be creatively integrated into artistic practice. In order to be able to offer reference material, sample books were produced in twelve different formats on six different print-on-demand platforms at prices ranging from £15 to £100.75. In such a way, the series provides an informed overview of the major players in the print-on-demand market and enables a comparison of the quality of print, paper, and binding, and the best possible areas of application. The different pricing and distribution policies of the platforms and the frequently high shipping costs also become evident.

At the same time, twelve typical print formats and layouts are examined: from newspapers, to photobooks with color illustrations, to heavy books; from unbound brochures, to paperbacks, to hardcovers with ribbons. In each case, the maximum page count is exhausted and the minimum is indicated by the illustration of a dog-ear on the corresponding page, so that the (technical and aesthetic) margins of the publication determined by the manufacturer come into view.

All editions present the same content. The two largest formats, version K and L, produced by MagCloud and Newspaper Club, served as a starting point. The content was automatically transferred to all other formats without any reformatting or reduction, which is why texts and images are often cut off, illustrations were not adapted to the respective paper and black-and-white or color printing, and voluminous books from page 60 onwards remain blank, apart from the pagination. However, care has been taken to ensure that even on the smallest format the title is fully visible on the cover.

The imprint is unusually detailed. Introduced by the phrase "You might like to know...," it provides a detailed account of the context of creation and the underlying artistic concept, as well as a complete listing of the features of all twelve editions and even further information on the contexts and framework conditions under which this publication was conceived, financed, printed, and circulated. It lists Lynn Harris (idea), Åbäke with Pierre Pautler (design) and AND Publishing (publisher) as well as other participants. However, AND Publishing and Åbäke demonstratively cross out their own names behind the copyright sign and dismiss the idea of a sole authorship. In such a way, the imprint states that all of the listed actors worked co-productively on the publication; publishing is contoured as a collective and collaborative act.

AND Publishing (co-directed by Lynn Harris and Eva Weinmayr back then) sees itself as "a platform exploring new digital technologies to publish conceptual artists' books" and defines print-on-demand "as a tool to directly interact with an audience. Due to short print runs and low productions costs, AND can sustain an adventurous and inquiring creative practice without having to conform to the mass market" (The Piracy Project, "The Impermanent Reader," 27).

The entire series *Variable Formats* has only one ISBN, although the different product formats (hardcover, paperback, audiobook, e-book, etc.) do, in fact, each need their own ISBN. For cost reasons, probably only five complete sets were produced in total.

A

PLATFORM	iPhoto
EDITION CHARACTERISTICS	available only through the artist, no longer available
FORMAT	8.8 × 6.7 cm
MATERIALITIES	color, paperback, perfect bound
PAGES	100
IMAGES	

B

PLATFORM	Blurb
EDITION CHARACTERISTICS	open edition
FORMAT	13.5 × 21.0 cm
MATERIALITIES	color, hardcover, perfect bound
PAGES	438
IMAGES	

C

PLATFORM	Lulu
EDITION CHARACTERISTICS	open edition
FORMAT	14.0 × 21.6 cm
MATERIALITIES	black-and-white, paperback, perfect bound
PAGES	738
IMAGES	

D

PLATFORM	selfmade
EDITION CHARACTERISTICS	available only through the artist
FORMAT	13.5 × 19.2 cm
MATERIALITIES	color, paperback, saddle stitch bound
PAGES	80
IMAGES	

E

PLATFORM	Lulu
EDITION CHARACTERISTICS	open edition
FORMAT	15.8 × 23.5 cm
MATERIALITIES	black-and-white, dust jacket, hardcover, perfect bound
PAGES	798
IMAGES	

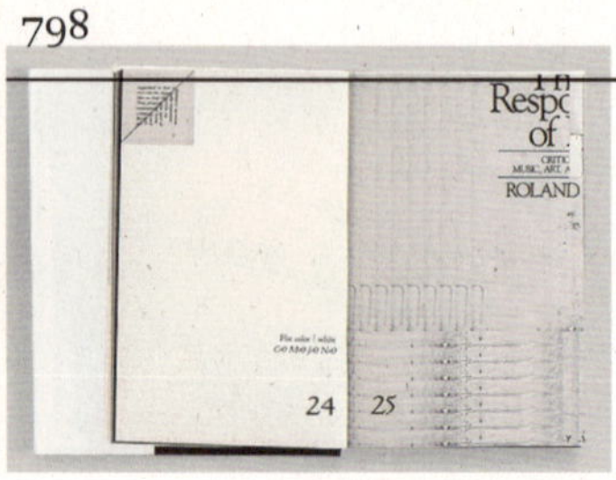

F

PLATFORM	Lulu
EDITION CHARACTERISTICS	open edition
FORMAT	21.6 × 21.6 cm
MATERIALITIES	color, paperback, saddle stitch bound
PAGES	88
IMAGES	

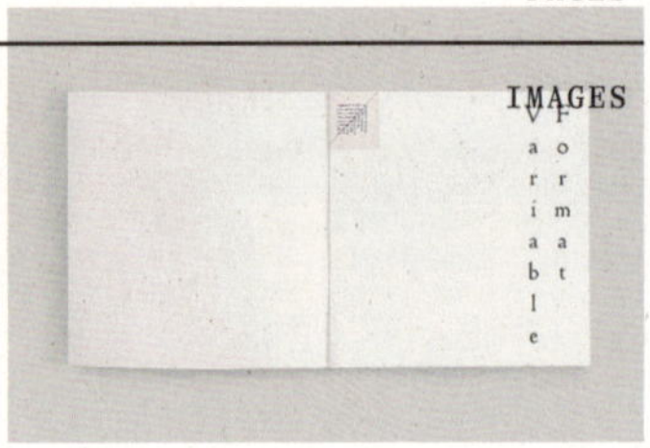

G

PLATFORM	Blurb
EDITION CHARACTERISTICS	open edition
FORMAT	20.5 × 25.4 cm
MATERIALITIES	color, dust jacket, hardcover
PAGES	238
IMAGES	

H

PLATFORM	Blurb
EDITION CHARACTERISTICS	open edition
FORMAT	19.6 × 24.9 cm
MATERIALITIES	color, paperback, perfect bound
PAGES	238
IMAGES	

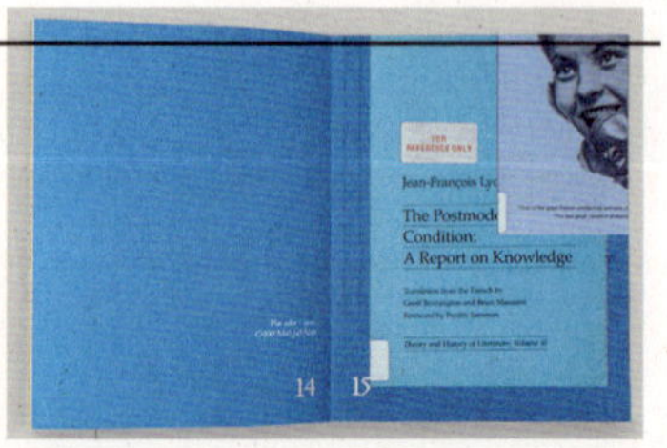

I

PLATFORM	Espresso Book Machine
EDITION CHARACTERISTICS	available only through the artist
FORMAT	17.3 × 26.7 cm
MATERIALITIES	black-and-white, paperback, perfect bound
PAGES	598
IMAGES	

J

PLATFORM	MagCloud
EDITION CHARACTERISTICS	open edition
FORMAT	21.0 × 27.8
MATERIALITIES	color, paperback, perfect bound
PAGES	382
IMAGES	

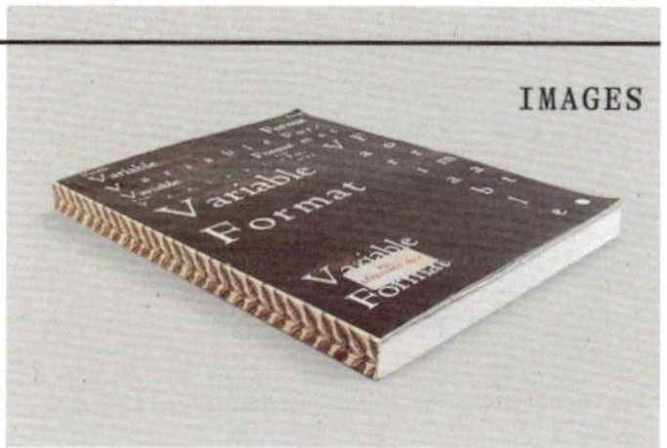

K

PLATFORM	MagCloud
EDITION CHARACTERISTICS	open edition
FORMAT	28.0 × 35.6 cm
MATERIALITIES	color, paperback, wire-o bound
PAGES	88
IMAGES	

L

PLATFORM	Newspaper Club
EDITION CHARACTERISTICS	available only through the artist
FORMAT	28.7 × 38.0 cm
MATERIALITIES	color, newsprint
PAGES	64
IMAGES	

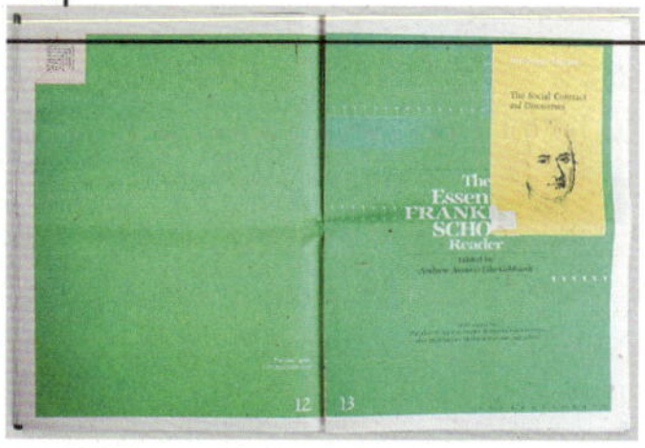

Jarring
Book 1

AUTHORS	ArtAgainstAssault.org, Mirabelle Jones
YEAR	2012
GENRE	artist's book / bookwork, photobook
METHOD	collection, composition (writing / drawing / photography)
SUBJECT	bias, book / book design, gender, politics / activism, print on demand, publishing / distribution
PLATFORM	Blurb
EDITION CHARACTERISTICS	open edition
FORMAT	20.0 × 25.0 cm
MATERIALITIES	color, paperback, perfect bound, defective copy
PAGES	38 (unpaginated)

IMAGES

DESCRIPTION

JARRING III is a series of three artist's books and accompanying performances by Mirabelle Jones that seeks to spread awareness by providing a platform for survivors of sexual assault and/or rape. All three books were handmade in an edition of fifty with this print-on-demand book serving as a pre-version for book one and being an expandable and updatable edition of the project.

The book consists of a series of photographs of a green jar that is continuously filled with paper scraps. Each scrap is first displayed in front of the jar, showing a small text with the description of a case of sexual abuse as reported by one of twenty-four anonymous individuals. The project was intended to be a biennial expanded edition, with contributions made possible via the website for Jones's project Art Against Assault and all proceeds being donated to a national sexual assault survivor resource.

Our first order from Blurb went wrong: a book was delivered that contained the book block of another book. After complaining, Blurb produced and sent a new copy, and also asked for the wrong book to be returned for privacy reasons.

Copied Right

[International Copyright]

AUTHOR	Hester Barnard
YEAR	2012
PUBLISHER	AND Public
GENRE	artist's book / bookwork
METHOD	appropriation, documentation / archiving, remediation
SUBJECT	analog / digital, copyright / law, google, materiality, platforms / companies
PLATFORM	Lulu
EDITION CHARACTERISTICS	open edition
FORMAT	15.2 × 22.9 cm
MATERIALITIES	black-and-white, paperback, perfect bound
PAGES	636

IMAGES

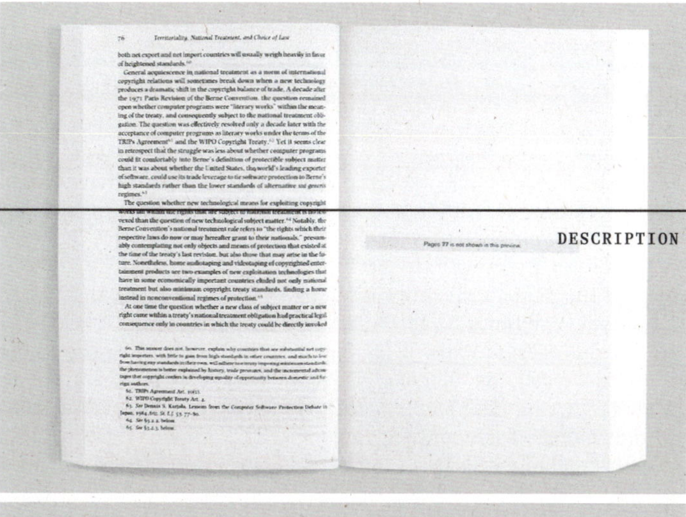

DESCRIPTION

"Paul Goldstein's entire book *International Copyright: Principles, Law, and Practice* (2001) has been screen-captured from Google Books on a 21.5-inch iMac. Even the cover design has been taken from the Google Books preview. When signs eventually substitute the real itself, they are no longer simply a case of imitation, reduplication, or parody. *Copied Right* is not a reproduction of a copyrighted book, but it exists as an original document.

The current limitations of the DIY screen-capture book publishing enterprise are revealed by the limit Google Books places on the previewing of particular pages. Over 500 pages featured in Goldstein's book is not shown in this book" (blurb on Lulu).

In addition to the copyright issue, a problematic nuance of retro-digitizing books becomes visible: Google's scans only capture the book pages, but not the book body. As a result, the books lose their dimension of depth in the digital copy, which manifests itself most clearly in the spine—a part of the book not photographed by Google. This digital "flattening" of the book can be experienced as soon as one orders a copy of Hester Barnard's *Copied Right* and the book body is forced to materialize again in print. In her reverse transfer of the scan into the printed book, the spine here has remained white and unprinted—a clear visual manifestation of the blind spot of retro-digitization that ignores the book's materiality.

The only reference to Barnard is on the last page of the book: "*International Copyright* produced without permission by Hester Barnard." The book was published under the AND Public umbrella, whose logo appears on the back cover, and is part of The Piracy Project's collection, curated by Eva Weinmayr and Andrea Francke (AND Publishing).

The Location of Lines

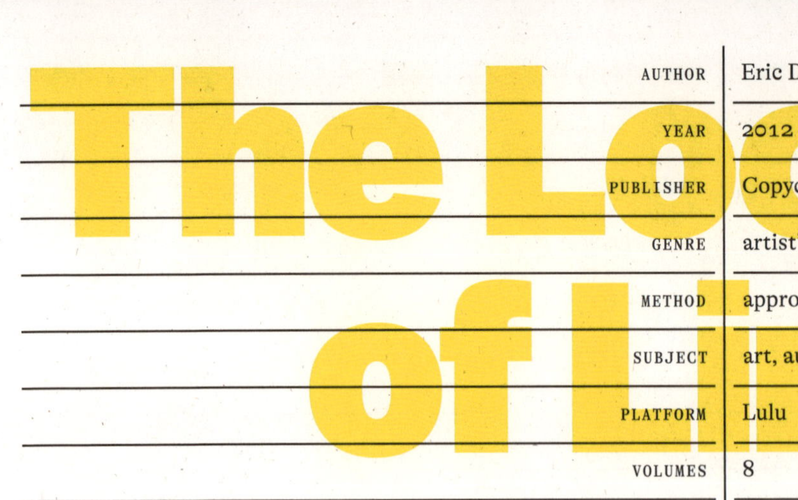

AUTHOR	Eric Doeringer
YEAR	2012
PUBLISHER	Copycat Publications
GENRE	artist's book / bookwork
METHOD	appropriation, reenactment, versioning / seriality
SUBJECT	art, authorship, book / book design, canon, standard / default
PLATFORM	Lulu
VOLUMES	8
EDITION CHARACTERISTICS	multiple versions, open edition
MATERIALITIES	black-and-white, paperback, perfect bound, different papers
PAGES	48 (unpaginated)

IMAGES

DESCRIPTION

This series is part of Eric Doeringer's Copycat Publications imprint that specializes in artist's books "after" contemporary artists like Ed Ruscha, John Baldessari, and Sol LeWitt. Here he appropriates LeWitt's *The Location of Lines* (1974), in which each double-page spread juxtaposes a line (each positioned differently) with an instruction for how to position it. The first instruction reads, "A line from the midpoint of the left side to the center of the page." The fact that the text becomes more complex and longer throughout the book shows the irreconcilable medial difference between writing and image.

Doeringer adopts this concept 1:1, but executes it several times on all book formats that Lulu offers. The content is always the same, only the paper and the drawn lines differ, as they have to be adapted to the respective format. This highlights site-specificity as an essential feature of LeWitt's works, which also characterizes his famous *Wall Drawings*. These are conceived as works in situ: they likewise exist in the form of instructions that are executed over and over again, in different places, on walls of different sizes and factures, and by different people, with each execution inevitably turning out a little differently: "Each individual, being unique, if given the same instructions would understand them differently and would carry them out differently. [...] Even if the same draftsman followed the same plan twice, there would be two different works of art. No one can do the same thing twice" (Sol LeWitt, "Doing Wall Drawings").

Doeringer congenially transfers this form of variability in the execution of an idea to the medium of the book when he prints the same book in a series of eight different formats. But even all the copies of the same format differ from each other, because in contrast to traditional edition printing, with print-on-demand, each copy is unique. After all, each print job is executed at a different time, on a different press, and potentially at a different production site; inaccuracies, material changes, and production errors are not uncommon.

Therefore, Doeringer's series does not simply constitute a copy, even if the name of his imprint Copycat might suggest that; he innovatively combines LeWitt's artistic approach with new reproduction techniques and now brings it to perfection in the printed medium as well. In his "defense," Doeringer quotes from an interview with LeWitt on his home page: In response to the question "How would you feel if someone executed a wall drawing of yours without permission but with care to follow the instructions and in an appropriate site?," the latter replies: "OK. [...] It would be authentic. [...] It would be a compliment" (Eric Doeringer, "Sol LeWitt Wall Drawing Recreations").

Doeringer has produced two other versions: one in US Letter format for the Artists' Books Cooperative collection *AaBbCc* (see 393) and one in DIN A5 format for Antoine Lefevbre's La Bibliotheque Fantastique, an artist-run print-on-demand platform, with the freely downloadable books designed to be printed on a home printer.

Doeringer sells his books via his home page and Lulu as well as in his Etsy store. From the original eight versions, only seven are still available in the following dimensions:

The Location Of Lines (Pocket Format): 10.8 × 17.5 cm
The Location Of Lines (A5 Format): 14.8 × 21.0 cm
The Location Of Lines (US Trade Format): 15.2 × 22.9 cm
The Location Of Lines (Small Square Format): 19.0 × 19.0 cm
The Location Of Lines (Square Format): 21.6 × 21.6 cm
The Location Of Lines (US Letter Format): 21.6 × 27.9 cm
The Location Of Lines (Landscape Format): 22.9 × 17.8 cm

Drawings 1965–1969

AUTHOR	Dan Graham
YEAR	2012 [1990]
PUBLISHER	Publication Studio Vancouver
GENRE	catalog / collection, reprint
METHOD	composition (writing / drawing / photography)
SUBJECT	art, canon, publishing / distribution
PLATFORM	Publication Studio, selfmade
EDITION CHARACTERISTICS	ISBN 9780987746672, open edition, second edition, stamped, embossed
FORMAT	17.5 × 24.4 cm
MATERIALITIES	black-and-white, paperback, perfect bound
PAGES	44 (unpaginated)

IMAGES

Untitled 1967

Untitled 1967

DAN GRAHAM

DRAWINGS 1965 – 1969

DESCRIPTION

This book is a complete reprint of a catalog that was originally published by Galerie Bleich-Rossi (Graz) in 1990 and was then out of print for a long time. It contains a selection of Dan Graham's black-and-white grid drawings and typewriter pieces between 1965 and 1969 and advertisement pages at the end.

The initiative to include this catalog in the Publication Studio network program came from Publication Studio Vancouver, which also obtained the artist's consent. Our copy was produced before our eyes at Publication Studio Rotterdam on February 21, 2020, as the stamp on the spine records. This distinction between originating studio and producing studio is also recorded on the back cover, where the name of the Rotterdam studio is embossed.

Harry Potter and the Scam Baiter

AUTHOR	Mishka Henner
YEAR	2012
GENRE	artist's book / bookwork, nonfiction
METHOD	détournement / hack, documentation / archiving, outsourcing, test / experiment
SUBJECT	bias, crowd / collaboration, economy / labor, email / messaging, internet culture, literature
PLATFORM	Lulu
EDITION CHARACTERISTICS	open edition, available only through the artist, CC0
FORMAT	15.6 × 23.4 cm
MATERIALITIES	black-and-white, dust jacket, hardcover, perfect bound
PAGES	330

IMAGES

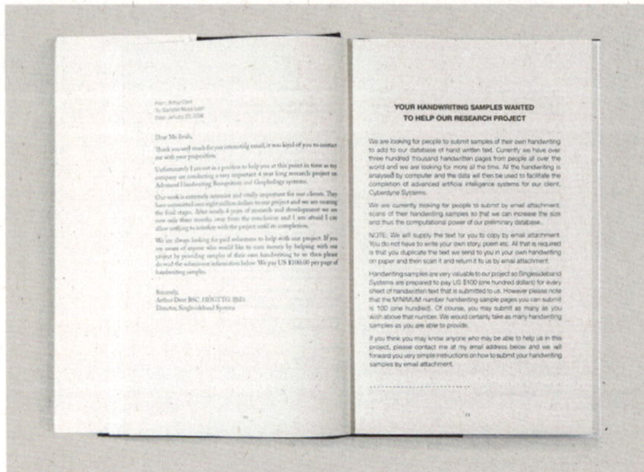

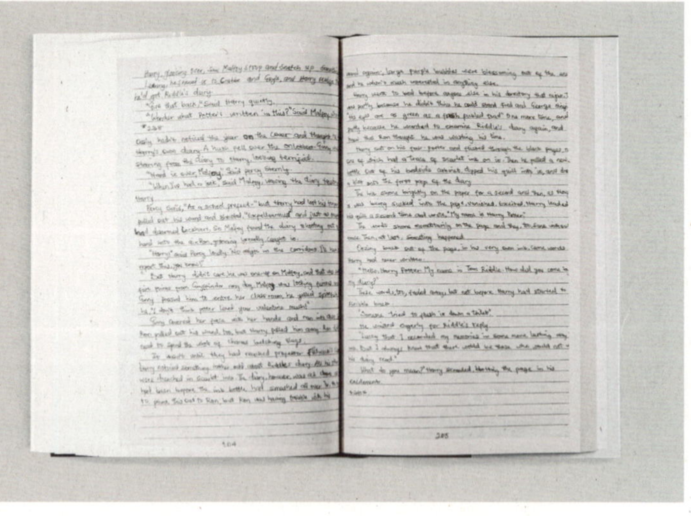

DESCRIPTION

"Scam baiting is a form of Internet vigilantism in which the vigilante poses as a potential victim to a scammer in order to waste their time and resources, gather information that will be of use to authorities, and publicly expose the scammer. It is, in essence, a form of social engineering that may have an altruistic motive or may be motivated by malice. Primarily used to thwart advance-fee fraud scams, scam baiting can be conducted out of a sense of civic duty, as a form of amusement, or both. [...]

The phenomenon can be understood as a kind of cross-cultural double-bluff in which agents on separate continents wrestle with and try to out-do each other in an online tug-of-war for one's financial gain or the other's time and resources. As a past time, scam baiting has flourished with the global spread of email and the internet to Africa, South America, and the Far East. In the brief history of the genre, one of the most notorious scam baits took place in January and February 2006 between scam baiter Arthur Dent BSc, HHGTTG, PhD (who shares the same name as the main protagonist of the *Hitch-hikers' Guide to the Galaxy*) and two scammers claiming to be Barrister Musa Issah and Mrs. Joyce Ozioma, both from Nigeria" (Mishka Henner, "Epilogue").

It is precisely this case that Mishka Henner's book documents. The book begins with the email correspondence that ensues when the scambaiter responds to an email from the scammers and, in return, offers them cooperation in a research project for which he is collecting handwriting samples from all around the world that will be remunerated with $100 per page. The scammers accept this offer. This is followed by scans of the 293 samples sent in, each from a different hand, which reproduce the entire second volume of J. K. Rowling's series, *Harry Potter and the Chamber of Secrets*, in beautiful handwriting. This is again succeeded by emails in which the scammers demand their fee, which the scambaiter, however, refuses for obscure reasons. An epilogue by Henner, who sees the shady scam business as a metaphor for our internet culture, concludes the book.

Henner has reduced the promotion of and information about this book because J. K. Rowling is known for her litigiousness in copyright issues.

Photography Is

AUTHOR	Mishka Henner
YEAR	2012
GENRE	artist's book / bookwork
METHOD	collection, found material
SUBJECT	canon, google, photography, search engine
PLATFORM	Lulu
EDITION CHARACTERISTICS	open edition, available only through the artist
FORMAT	14.0 × 21.6 cm
MATERIALITIES	black-and-white, paperback, perfect bound
PAGES	200

IMAGES

DESCRIPTION

This book collects more than 3,000 sentences on 130 pages, with no paragraphs separating the text throughout. All sentences start with the phrase "Photography is" and were found through a Google search for the term, which had a total of 15.3 million hits, as the colophon on the last page informs. A panorama of definitions opens up, portraying photography as the most popular and widely practiced art form of our time, "available at our fingertips, literally," as the third-last phrase says. Technical explanations quickly turn into philosophical and esoteric definitions, followed by more everyday statements. That this enumeration is endless may be shown by the last phrase, which reads: "Photography is only a beginning." By providing multi-perspective, snapshot-like descriptions of what is, the book itself also reflects photography's relationship to reality, as Mishka Henner states: "It is photography, without photographs" (blurb on artist website).

As Joachim Schmid, however, notes in a review, "*Photography Is* takes thinking about photography to absurdity. The book is a photo-critical miniature that contributes as much to thinking about photography as it ironically subverts it. Actually, this is more a book about the peculiarity of the search engine [...] than a book about photography" (Joachim Schmid, "Photography Is"). This is because Google indiscriminately covers every result that includes this sequence of letters, not so much including famous quotations from great philosophers such as Susan Sontag and Roland Barthes but, more so, statements from those whose voices are otherwise not listened to and who have no weight in academic and artistic discourse. Regarding authorship and copyright, Henner nonchalantly says on the last page: "All text material sourced via the Google search engine. For respective owners of the quoted material, type the phrase into Google in quotes."

The Uncreative Subterranean

AUTHOR	Jason Jadick
YEAR	2012
GENRE	education / classroom, experimental literature
METHOD	appropriation, constraint, translation / transcription
SUBJECT	canon, economy / labor, literature, reading / interpretation, tracking, writing / reading techniques
PLATFORM	Lulu
EDITION CHARACTERISTICS	multiple editions (print, DOCX, video), ISBN 9781300525981, open edition
FORMAT	15.2 × 22.9 cm
MATERIALITIES	black-and-white, paperback, perfect bound
PAGES	143

IMAGES

DESCRIPTION

Jason Jadick's *The Uncreative Subterranean* was submitted as his final project for an "Uncreative Writing" course with Kenneth Goldsmith, which dealt with strategies of literary appropriation, plagiarism, and piracy. Aside from the author's photo and name, Jadick's cover imitates the 1994 Groove Press edition of Jack Kerouac's novella *The Subterraneans* (1958), whose text he also adopts in full. He had "marathon retyped" (blurb on Lulu) it on the computer in a twenty-four-hour performance on November 30, 2012. In the process, Jadick recorded himself and the growing Word document and streamed this live on YouTube (including a computer crash, hangouts, dinner break, etc.). He also posted the produced text hourly on his Tumblr blog, so the progress of the project could be witnessed live. Typing speed varied from 2,188 words in the first hour to 1,317 words in the fifteenth hour.

The non-stop performance, with its accompanying sleep deprivation, mirrors the restlessness of the Beat Generation and Kerouac's rapid-fire writing style (*The Subterraneans* is said to have been written in three days); posting on a blog to be scrolled recalls Kerouac's famous original typescript of *On the Road*, created on a typewriter on a roll of sheets taped together, and his spontaneous prose style.

Jadick then transitioned the typescript back into bookform, with each hour forming a chapter, even if this means it breaks off mid-sentence: "Typos were edited only if noticed during the performance. All conditions were at the mercy of the technology" (blurb on Lulu). The videos, blog, and typescript are still available online (Jason Jadick, "The Uncreative Subterranean," blog).

As the blurb reveals, Jadick's book has another predecessor: Simon Morris's blog *Getting Inside Jack Kerouac's Head* (2009/10) where he retyped and posted, for almost an entire year, one page per day from Jack Kerouac's *On the Road*, as if he had taken Truman Capote's famous dictum about the author of the Beat Generation literally: "That isn't writing; it's typing." Afterward, Morris also transformed the digital text back into bookform. In doing so, Morris appropriated an idea from Kenneth Goldsmith, who reports in *Uncreative Writing: Managing Language in the Digital Age* (2011) that he once instructed his creative writing students to copy Kerouac, according to traditional art education, which usually begins with copying the old masters.

Paper Passion

AUTHOR	Jean Keller
YEAR	2012
GENRE	artist's book / bookwork
METHOD	composition (writing / drawing / photography), pricing
SUBJECT	book / book design, economy / labor, materiality, print technology, print on demand
PLATFORM	Lulu
EDITION CHARACTERISTICS	open edition
FORMAT	10.8 × 17.5 cm
MATERIALITIES	black-and-white, paperback, perfect bound
PAGES	40 (unpaginated)

IMAGES

DESCRIPTION

Paper Passion contains a short text broken down into individual statements. The text deals with the materiality of books, especially their smell and value. According to the opening credits, whose sentences are spread over several pages, the work refers to the perfume of the same name produced by Geza Schoen in collaboration with publisher Gerhard Steidl and designer Karl Lagerfeld. This perfume comes packaged in a book and is sold for €275.

The implied advertising promise, in Jean Keller's words, is: "With [Steidl's] *Paper Passion* you get the smell of the intellectual world without reading a book." Jean Keller then makes a point for the intellectual value of content, and for the book as a medium for structuring thoughts. Such a book can even be as cheap as a 40-page print-on-demand paperback—in contrast to its fetishization as a container for a perfume. This ultimately brings him to the final statement: "ART IS ART / AND / A FART IS A FART."

To underline this stance, *Paper Passion* has its price of £7 – $11.50 – €8.80 printed on the back. However, this is no longer correct due to the constantly changing price calculations on print-on-demand platforms.

The Overlook Manuscript

AUTHOR	Jean Keller
YEAR	2012
GENRE	artist's book / bookwork, experimental literature, poetry
METHOD	composition (writing / drawing / photography), reenactment, remediation
SUBJECT	film, literature, materiality, reading / interpretation
PLATFORM	Lulu
EDITION CHARACTERISTICS	open edition
FORMAT	15.2 × 22.9 cm
MATERIALITIES	black-and-white, paperback, perfect bound
PAGES	120 (unpaginated)
IMAGE	

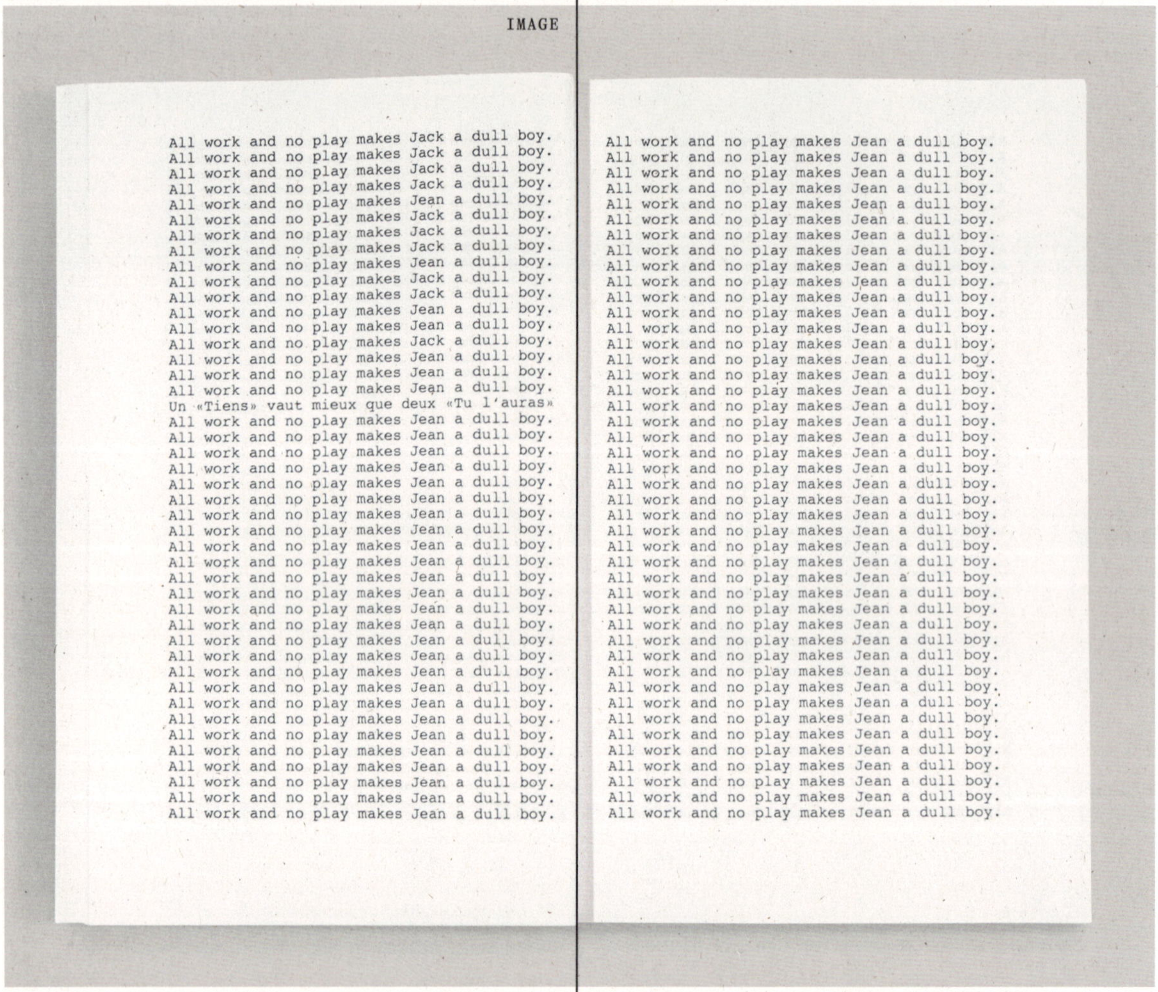

DESCRIPTION

The Overlook Manuscript makes reference to the manuscript of the fictional character Jack Torrance in Stephen King's novel *The Shining* and its adaption as a movie by Stanley Kubrick. The book reproduces some of the pages seen in the movie when Torrance's wife Wendy first encounters her husband's manuscript pages. Discovering that he has been writing the same sentence over and over for hundreds of pages in different graphical constellations while pretending to be working on his novel, the manuscript functions as a testimony of his madness.

In contrast to Phil Buehler's *All Work and No Play Makes Jack a Dull Boy* (see 145), which purports to be a publication of Torrance's lost manuscript itself, Jean Keller's *The Overlook Manuscript* tells a frame story in an editorial note. According to this note, Keller worked in the same abandoned hotel in the Swiss Alps as Torrance did, also during winter, but in the year of 2010. There, Keller allegedly finds Torrance's manuscript and, "[i]nspired by this discovery, [...] ditched his other artistic projects and began using Torrance's typewritten pages as the basis for a new book." Apart from his editorial note, Jean Keller makes another addition when, on four pages of his book, he replaces "Jack" with "Jean" and the phrase "All Work and No Play Makes Jack a Dull Boy" with "Un 'Tiens' vaut mieux que deux 'Tu l'auras'" (A bird in the hand is worth two in the bush). This is the proverb Kubrick used in the French version of his film (the German, Italian, and Spanish versions of the film also show manuscripts in the corresponding languages). This echoes the cross-fading of both figures or authors staged here, and preserves Keller's legend of being based in Paris—known to be a pseudonym, for which the author profile on Lulu only reads "Jean Keller is."

56 Broken Kindle Screens
Photographed E Ink, Collected Online, Printed On Demand

AUTHORS	Silvio Lorusso, Sebastian Schmieg
YEAR	2012
GENRE	artist's book / bookwork, photobook
METHOD	found material, remediation
SUBJECT	analog / digital, error / corruption / loss, materiality, technology
PLATFORM	Lulu
EDITION CHARACTERISTICS	multiple editions (print, e-book), ISBN 9781105949340, open edition
FORMAT	10.8 × 17.5 cm
MATERIALITIES	black-and-white, paperback, perfect bound
PAGES	79

IMAGES

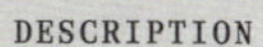

DESCRIPTION

"*56 Broken Kindle Screens* is a print on demand paperback that consists of found photos depicting broken Kindle screens. The Kindle is Amazon's e-reading device which is by default connected to the company's bookstore.

The book takes as its starting point the peculiar aesthetic of broken E Ink displays and serves as an examination into the reading device's materiality. As the screens break, they become collages composed of different pages, cover illustrations and interface elements" (blurb on Lulu).

The white frame of the page margins is a declarative act, restoring functional value to the broken devices through turning them into photographic subjects, as well as giving them the artistic value of "ready-mades" and transforming them into surprisingly fascinating artifacts. The images have undergone several transformations: displayed with e-ink, digitally photographed, collected online, stored in the cloud, printed on demand—or displayed again in e-ink, as there is also an e-book version that is flipped through on a Kindle Touch in a video by the artists, which gives the impression that the glitches emerge and fade into each other directly on the device itself. While these images only ever show the broken screens themselves, the book index contains the original photos and the URLs where they were found. Most of them come from Flickr, Tumblr, blogs, and eBay, where many broken Kindles are offered.

Silvio Lorusso and Sebastian Schmieg's print-on-demand book was also available in a special edition of fifty-six numbered and signed copies at an exhibition at Link Art Center in Brescia (Italy, 2013). The book served as inspiration for *Broken 56 Broken Kindle Screens* (see 329), which resulted from an assignment in Danny Snelson's 2015 course "Print-on-Demand Poetry: Making Books After the Internet" at Northwestern University.

AUTHORS	Maria Lusitano, Teresa Paiva, paula roush
YEAR	2012
PUBLISHER	msdm
GENRE	artist's book / bookwork, photobook
METHOD	appropriation, composition (writing / drawing / photography), reenactment
SUBJECT	analog / digital, art world / literary world, canon, gender, reading / interpretation, technology
PLATFORM	Blurb
EDITION CHARACTERISTICS	open edition
FORMAT	12.6 × 20.3 cm
MATERIALITIES	black-and-white, paperback, perfect bound
PAGES	64 (unpaginated)

IMAGES

DESCRIPTION

TESTED: vaio road test is a reenactment of Ed Ruscha's famous artist's book *ROYAL ROAD TEST* (1967), which was made in cooperation with Mason Williams and Patrick Blackwell. It documents the act of throwing a typewriter out of a moving car and its damaged remains through photographs. For *TESTED*, the three artists transfer this into the present and update the technology used: instead of a typewriter, paula roush (driver), Teresa Paiva (thrower), and Maria Lusitano (photographer) throw a Sony VAIO notebook out of the window of a moving car and pick up its damaged individual parts to repeat the same action a few more times. They thus contrast the mechanics of a typewriter with the far opaquer workings of a computer, which can nevertheless be disassembled and examined as shown in the book.

The action was documented and turned into a film, a limited edition artist's book reproducing the layout and shots of Ruscha's version, and a print-on-demand publication, created originally as part of the Artists' Books Cooperative's series *ABCED*: "a multi-volume book project created [...] to celebrate Ed Ruscha's seventy-fifth birthday" (ABC, "ABCED"). *TESTED* not only honors Ruscha's artist's book, but is also a feminist take on Ruscha's practice, as the three female artists revisit the ironic yet masculine iconography of the original.

MONEY

AUTHOR	MAKER [Holly Melgard]
YEAR	2012
PUBLISHER	Troll Thread
GENRE	artist's book / bookwork
METHOD	détournement / hack, paratextual play, test / experiment
SUBJECT	copyright / law, economy / labor, platforms / companies, print technology
PLATFORM	Lulu
EDITION CHARACTERISTICS	multiple editions (black-and-white, color, PDF), open edition
FORMAT	14.4 × 20.7 cm
MATERIALITIES	color, paperback, perfect bound, defective copy
PAGES	740 (unpaginated)

IMAGE

DESCRIPTION

MAKER's *MONEY* depicts the front and back of 368 one-hundred-dollar bills in their original size, ready to be cut out and used as counterfeit money. While the PDF is unproblematic, executing a print job would amount to the illegal reproduction of banknotes, whereby it is not clear who could be held legally accountable: MAKER, the buyer of a printed copy, the printing company, or the platform Lulu. There have been no problems yet, as Troll Thread would have expected.

To be on the safe side, there is a long prefatory note at the beginning of the book: "TROLL THREAD PRESS does not print nor draw profit from the printing of the manuscripts it distributes. Although TROLL THREAD PRESS does not discourage the use/misuse of these images, it can not be held responsible for misuse/misuse [*sic*] by this document's printer." This is followed by a detailed elaboration on the Counterfeit Detection Act, against whose regulations the present book clearly violates. This is concluded with an ironic note: "TROLL THREAD PRESS does not make money, has no money for a lawyer or a binding lawsuit, and thus interprets its compliance with the law to be legally just. For more information regarding the legal identity of *MONEY*'s maker as it technically belongs to the poetic contingencies of its printer, contact: the Public Affairs Office of the United States Secret Service" (Maker, *MONEY*, front matter).

The book was made by Holly Melgard but attributed to "MAKER" in order to distract from any legal and subjective interpretations: "In a book this repetitive, putting my name on it would have conceptually organized it into a book about my money (of which I have little), rather than into a book of money, or a poem that makes money (which everyone insists poetry doesn't do)" (Holly Melgard, *Essays*, 11). The ambiguous title page, which reads in full: "poems for MONEY by MAKER," declares the pages that follow to be poems.

As always, Troll Thread offers its publications as both a (free) PDF and by print-on-demand on Lulu. This time, though, there are two analog versions, one in black-and-white (cheaper) and one in color (more expensive).

Our copy has a binding error: The last page has strayed into the middle of the book. Also clearly visible is a crease in the book block, either due to poor storage or the transport packaging.

BLACK FRIDAY

AUTHOR	Holly Melgard
YEAR	2012
PUBLISHER	Troll Thread
GENRE	artist's book / bookwork
METHOD	détournement / hack, paratextual play, pricing
SUBJECT	economy / labor, platforms / companies, print technology, print on demand
PLATFORM	Lulu
EDITION CHARACTERISTICS	multiple editions (hardcover, paperback, PDF), open edition, temporarily not available
FORMAT	21.3 × 27.4 cm
MATERIALITIES	black-and-white, paperback, perfect bound
PAGES	734
IMAGES	

DESCRIPTION

BLACK FRIDAY, with a dedication page that says "for BLACK INK ON WHITE PAPER," is Holly Melgard's "attempt to 'break an industrial printer.'" The book is about "testing if and how poetry could actually, and not just metaphorically, break things" (Sophie Seita, "Communities of Print," in this volume, 644).

The book's 734 pages are completely filled with black ink except for the page numbers. Ink being the most expensive resource in the printing process makes this extensive tome one of the most expansive print-on-demand books possible in production costs (a consideration that Jean Keller also chooses as the starting point of his *Black Book*, see 157). But because the price of a book on print-on-demand platforms is usually calculated by the number of pages and not the amount of ink used, *BLACK FRIDAY* is a losing deal for Lulu—thus referencing "Black Friday" shopping discounts.

There have been instances when the book could not be printed because, according to Lulu, the "source file contains errors that are preventing it from being printed." Until the author fixes the error, the availability status of the book will be changed to "private access" (see the mail exchange documented in our web archive). On the one hand, these difficulties are a reminder of the fragility of the print-on-demand publishing system, which can cut off access to books at any time. On the other hand, the author can chalk them up as a success, since she has almost made it a point not to be printed. One could speak here of an "imagined printedness" (Sophie Seita, "Communities of Print," in this volume, 643) that characterizes print-on-demand in general, since ultimately every uploaded book is waiting to be ordered and printed at some point—a potentiality that is naturally taken to an extreme with *BLACK FRIDAY*.

As always, Troll Thread offers this publication as both a (free) PDF and a print-on-demand book on Lulu. This time, however, the publication is also available in hardback and paperback, giving the option of an even more extensive production.

THE MAKING OF THE AMERICANS

AUTHOR	Holly Melgard
YEAR	2012
PUBLISHER	Troll Thread
GENRE	experimental literature
METHOD	appropriation, constraint, generative / automation
SUBJECT	canon, literature, reading / interpretation
PLATFORM	Lulu
EDITION CHARACTERISTICS	multiple editions (print, PDF), open edition
FORMAT	14.8 × 22.5 cm
MATERIALITIES	black-and-white, paperback, saddle stitch bound
PAGES	24
IMAGES	

DESCRIPTION

For *THE MAKING OF THE AMERICANS*, Holly Melgard takes Gertrude Stein's credo "there is no such thing as repetition" literally and applies it to Stein's highly repetitious and hard to read tome *The Making of Americans: Being a History of a Family's Progress* from 1925. Thus, "every word and punctuation mark is retained according to its first (and hence last) appearance in Gertrude Stein's 925-page edition of the book" (Holly Melgard, "Foreword"), deleting any other instance of repetition.

This reading confronts Stein's procedural text with the assumptions of digital word processing, shrinking it to merely twenty-one pages of "unique" content that evolves from readable sentences to a list of words. Melgard also adds page-spans of the original on each page to show how many pages are covered by its words.

Melgard makes another easily overlooked intervention by adding the definite article "the" to the title, thereby, as Paul Stephens notes, "restrict[ing] the range of reference (paradoxically) from all Americans to some Americans" and "complicat[ing] Stein's narrative of assimilation." He also points out another difference between the two poets: "Whereas it took the wealthy and well-connected Stein fourteen years to find a publisher for her modernist masterpiece, Melgard's reduced version was self-published instantaneously on lulu.com at no expense to the author" (Paul Stephens, *absence of clutter*, 203–204).

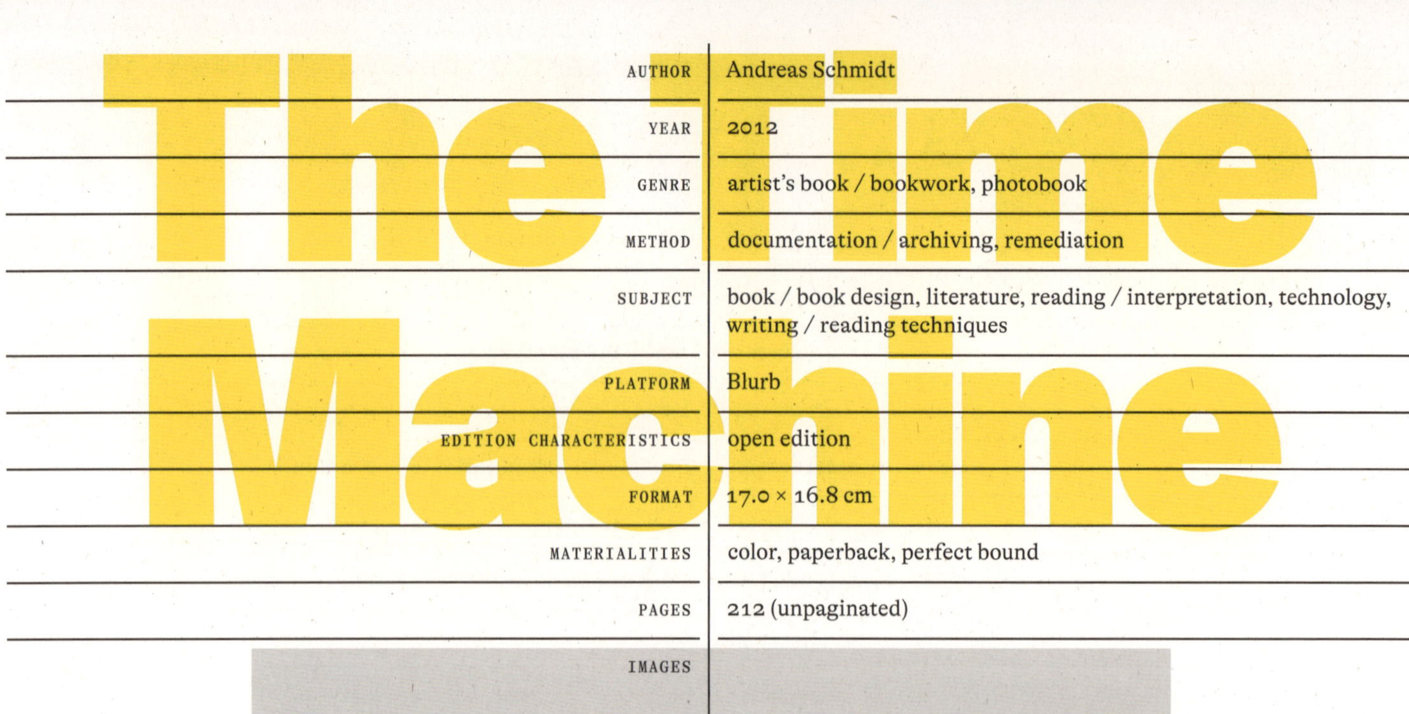

The Time Machine

AUTHOR	Andreas Schmidt
YEAR	2012
GENRE	artist's book / bookwork, photobook
METHOD	documentation / archiving, remediation
SUBJECT	book / book design, literature, reading / interpretation, technology, writing / reading techniques
PLATFORM	Blurb
EDITION CHARACTERISTICS	open edition
FORMAT	17.0 × 16.8 cm
MATERIALITIES	color, paperback, perfect bound
PAGES	212 (unpaginated)

IMAGES

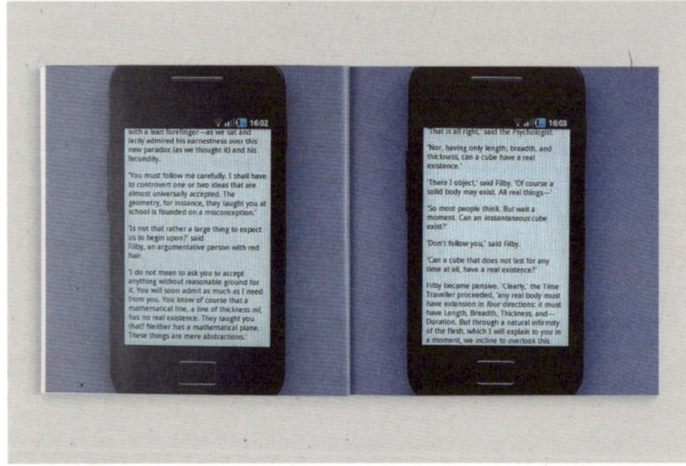

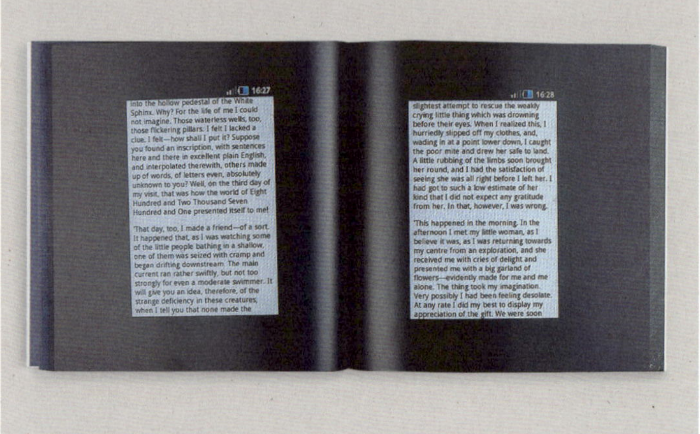

DESCRIPTION

Andreas Schmidt's *The Time Machine* contains H. G. Wells's science fiction novella of the same name, but photographed from a Samsung cell phone that displays the text page by page as an e-book. The photos show the entire phone, so you can see that the reading process takes less than an hour and gradually consumes battery power. These details, as well as "the changing background light [...] subtly show shifts in time, documenting the book being read at a particular time [November 5, 2011, at dusk] and place [the artist's studio in London] by a helpful fellow reader, who scrolls through the screen for us" (blurb on Blurb).

The reading setup shown in the book is therefore artificial; it does not document the actual reading process of a human reader but the process of scrolling through the text and capturing it by camera. H. G. Wells's text undergoes multiple stages of media processing, from book to digital text to smartphone screen to photograph to book. In this way, *The Time Machine* reflects on the differences in the reading experience between a text displayed as an e-book on a smartphone versus its manifestation as a physical book. It contrasts flowing, scrollable text with stable text, and a vertical reading movement against a horizontal one.

9/11 911 CALLS IN 911 PT. FONT

AUTHOR	Joey Yearous-Algozin
YEAR	2012
PUBLISHER	Troll Thread
GENRE	artist's book / bookwork, experimental literature
METHOD	found material, reformatting
SUBJECT	analog / digital, book / book design, error / corruption / loss, materiality, memory / storage, politics / activism, scale, typography
PLATFORM	Lulu
VOLUMES	2
EDITION CHARACTERISTICS	open edition
FORMAT	21.6 × 27.9 cm
MATERIALITIES	black-and-white, paperback, perfect bound
PAGES	vol. 1: 464 pages, vol. 2: 460 pages (unpaginated)

IMAGES

DESCRIPTION

The two-volume *9/11 911 CALLS IN 911 PT. FONT*, printed on large US Letter paper, consists of transcript excerpts from emergency calls to the New York fire department—with its 911 phone number—on September 11, 2001. The text is set in an oversized 911 point font, which means that it stretches out over two volumes with a total of nine hundred pages. The individual letters go beyond the edges of the page, rendering the printed book almost unreadable. In the PDF, by contrast, the text maintains its readability because it allows for different viewing modes, and the text can be copied into a word processor.

It is in the nuanced interaction between both formats that the full aesthetic potential and political expressiveness of this work unfold, and the explosive power of the historical event documented becomes obvious: the printed version, with its letter fragments, directs our attention to details and highlights the injuries of individual persons as well as the inconceivability of what is happening. The digital format lets us recognize coherences and an overall picture of what is happening. Thus, these two publication formats are not designed as the usual either–or, in which readers can select the format they prefer, but as both-as-also: PDF and print-on-demand complement and merge to form a conceptual unit that generates surplus and overcomes the antagonistic juxtaposition of analog and digital. This makes these hybrids an epitome of our post-digital age.

Astronomical
The Bootleg

AUTHOR	Hermann Zschiegner
YEAR	2012
GENRE	photobook
METHOD	documentation / archiving, remediation
SUBJECT	analog / digital, copyright / law, error / corruption / loss, film, memory / storage, publishing / distribution
PLATFORM	Blurb
EDITION CHARACTERISTICS	open edition
FORMAT	15.2 × 22.9 cm
MATERIALITIES	black-and-white, paperback, perfect bound
PAGES	400 (unpaginated)

IMAGE

DESCRIPTION

This book is part of Hermann Zschiegner's Bootleg Edition, a series of books reproducing famous photobooks that are no longer available (due to being out of stock or too expensive to obtain). Their reproduction is based on flip-through videos: a presentation form for books used on video platforms to show their materiality as well as parts of their content. Flip-throughs are used for advertisement, but also to give a broader audience an impression of rare or materially exceptional books.

Zschiegner's *Astronomical. The Bootleg* shows screenshots of a downloaded copy of Mishka Henner's *ASTRONOMICAL – The Movie* that shows a flip-through of the first volume of Henner's eponymous twelve-volume book series (see 197) that contains "a scale model of our solar system [...]: On page 1 the Sun, on page 6,000 Pluto. The width of each page equals one million kilometers" (Mishka Henner, blurb on artist website). The first volume takes us from the sun to Mercury, Venus, Earth, Mars, and the Asteroid Belt.

For the bootleg of *ASTRONOMICAL*, Zschiegner mainly used stills showing fully opened page spreads of the original, but a few stills also capture the turning of pages or hands on the book. The quality loss of his reproduction is a result of the remediation from book to film to book, but also of print-on-demand's poor printing quality. As with the mostly black pages of Henner's series, one cannot be sure when looking at Zschiegner's reproduction whether the tiny white dots are actually stars in the black vastness of space or white pixels caused by remediation and printing errors. Our copy also has glaring defects in the perfect binding, so that even after a short use the pages lose their hold.

Zschiegner also made a book video, which is advertised as: "A Book-Video of the acclaimed bootleg copy by Hermann Zschiegner of Mishka Henner's even more acclaimed *ASTRONOMICAL*."

Drone Shadow Handbook

AUTHOR	James Bridle
YEAR	2013
GENRE	nonfiction, tutorial
METHOD	composition (writing / drawing / photography), documentation / archiving
SUBJECT	politics / activism, surveillance / privacy, technology
PLATFORM	Lulu, Newspaper Club
EDITION CHARACTERISTICS	multiple editions (newspaper, booklet), ISBN 9781906110222, open edition, CC0
FORMAT	14.8 × 21.0 cm
MATERIALITIES	color, paperback, saddle stitch bound
PAGES	16 (unpaginated)
IMAGES	

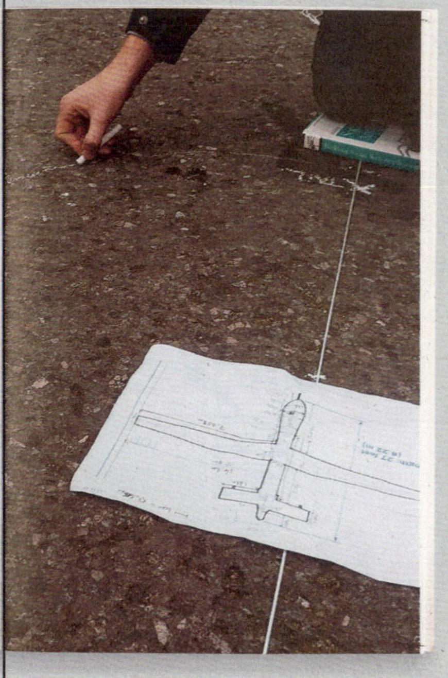

Drawing a Drone Shadow

Anyone can create a Drone Shadow, and this book contains plans for a number of different types of drone, and some basic instructions for drawing them.

There are a few guidelines however, which are important, to keep the shadows consistent and legible.

- Drone Shadows should be 1:1 representations: they should be the exact dimensions of real drones, according to the measurements in the schematics here or ones you create yourself. They should not be drawn larger or smaller than life for convenience or effect. This is because they are intended to convey the reality of the size and shape of actual drones.
- Drone Shadows should be outlines, not filled in shapes. This outline is typically 5-10cm (3-4in) thick, but this can be varied.
- Drone Shadows should be locally relevant, where possible. The choice of shadow should reflect the concerns of the place where it is drawn. Wherever you're drawing the drone, consider the local context and politics. Which aircraft are operated by the country you're in, or have been used by or in it? Which aircraft are currently in the news? If there's no schematic for the one you want to draw, research and sketch it yourself.

DESCRIPTION

The publication's starting point is *Drone Shadows*, a series of installations in public spaces around the world that aims to "compromis[e] the outline of an unmanned aerial vehicle (UAV), or drone: a 1:1 representation conveying both the physical reality, and the apparent invisibility, of drone aircraft" (James Bridle, "Introduction"). With that comes the warning: "UAVs are the key infrastructure of the 21st Century shadow war: unaccountable, borderless and merciless conflicts" (Bridle, "Under the Shadow of the Drone").

As drones "are becoming ubiquitous, yet remain almost invisible" (back cover), both to the human eye and in political discourse, and considering that most people have never seen one in real life, James Bridle wanted "to get a feel for what it would be like to stand next to one. To stand before, or under, it" (Bridle, "Under the Shadow of the Drone").

The Drone Shadow Handbook provides a photo documentation of the series as well as basic instructions on how to draw drone shadows. This includes guidelines "to keep the shadows consistent and legible" when realized without the artist's involvement, as well as suggestions for materials and placement and a step-by-step guide for their composition. Also included are schematics of four frequently operated drones, which may serve as templates.

The handbook was originally published as a newspaper with a print run of 2,000 copies and distributed at screenings of Jeremy Scahill's investigative documentary *Dirty Wars*.

The Death of the Authors 1941 edition

AUTHOR	Constant
YEAR	2013
GENRE	experimental literature, fiction
METHOD	generative / automation, montage / remix, versioning / seriality
SUBJECT	authorship, canon, code / programming, copyright / law, literature
PLATFORM	Lulu
VOLUMES	3
EDITION CHARACTERISTICS	open edition, unique copies
MATERIALITIES	black-and-white, paperback

IMAGE

DESCRIPTION

"Every year on New Year's Day, due to the expiration of copyright protection terms on works produced by authors who died seven decades earlier, thousands of works enter the public domain—that is, their content is no longer owned or controlled by anyone, but it rather becomes a common treasure, available for anyone to freely use for any purpose. *The Death of the Authors, 1941* is a generative novel using Python and Natural Language Toolkit nltk, based on texts written by authors welcomed in the public domain in 2012. In the same way their decaying bodies form a fertile humus layer following the rhythm of the four seasons, a script decomposes their literary work and recomposes the particles into a new text. The selection of the texts used for this publication is very much influenced by the availability of works online. Famous authors are easy to find, English works and translations are often available as free e-books, thanks to an initiative such as The Gutenberg Project" (Constant, "The Death of the Authors, 1941," website).

In 2012, it was the works of James Joyce, Rabindranath Tagore, Virginia Woolf, Henri Bergson, and Sherwood Anderson that were rediscovered and merged. Originally, every time the script was launched on the project website, a different novel would be generated out of the infinite amount of possible novels. It was also planned that these individually generated novels could be automatically uploaded and offered directly on Lulu. However, such a generative production mode was not supported by print-on-demand platforms at the time. The three volumes on Lulu were generated on November 18, 2013 and uploaded by hand. They are the only ones available.

This series was continued each year, until 2019. All sources, including instructions on how to generate a novel yourself, can be found on GitLab. All editions of *The Death of the Authors* from 1941 to 1947 can be found on the project website.

James Joyce & Rabindranath Tagore & Their Return to Life in Four Seasons: A Constant Remix

FORMAT	14.8 × 21.0 cm
MATERIALITIES	perfect bound
PAGES	41
IMAGE	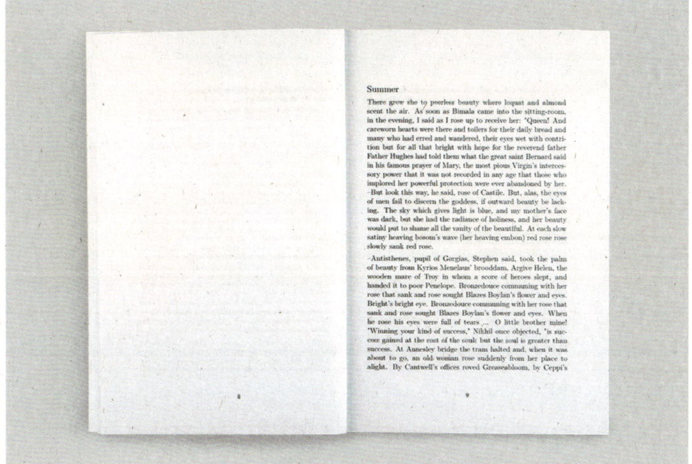

Summer

There grew she to peerless beauty where loquat and almond scent the air. As soon as Bimala came into the sitting-room, in the evening, I said as I rose up to receive her: 'Queen! And careworn hearts were there and toilers for their daily bread and many who had erred and wandered, their eyes wet with contrition but for all that bright with hope for the reverend father Father Hughes had told them what the great saint Bernard said in his famous prayer of Mary, the most pious Virgin's intercessory power that it was not recorded in any age that those who implored her powerful protection were ever abandoned by her. –But look this way, he said, rose of Castile. But, alas, the eyes of men fail to discern the goddess, if outward beauty be lacking. The sky which gives light is blue, and my mother's face was dark, but she had the radiance of holiness, and her beauty would put to shame all the vanity of the beautiful. At each slow satiny heaving bosom's wave (her heaving embon) red rose rose slowly sank red rose.

–Antisthenes, pupil of Gorgias, Stephen said, took the palm of beauty from Kyrios Menelaus' brooddam, Argive Helen, the wooden mare of Troy in whom a score of heroes slept, and handed it to poor Penelope. Bronzedouce communing with her rose that sank and rose sought Blazes Boylan's flower and eyes. Bright's bright eye. Bronzedouce communing with her rose that sank and rose sought Blazes Boylan's flower and eyes. When he rose his eyes were full of tears ... O little brother mine! 'Winning your kind of success,' Nikhil once objected, 'is success gained at the cost of the soul: but the soul is greater than success. At Annesley bridge the tram halted and, when it was about to go, an old woman rose suddenly from her place to alight. By Cantwell's offices roved Greaseabloom, by Ceppi's

9

Rabindranath Tagore & Virginia Woolf & Their Return to Life in Four Seasons: A Constant Remix

FORMAT	14.8 × 21.0 cm
MATERIALITIES	perfect bound
PAGES	43
IMAGE	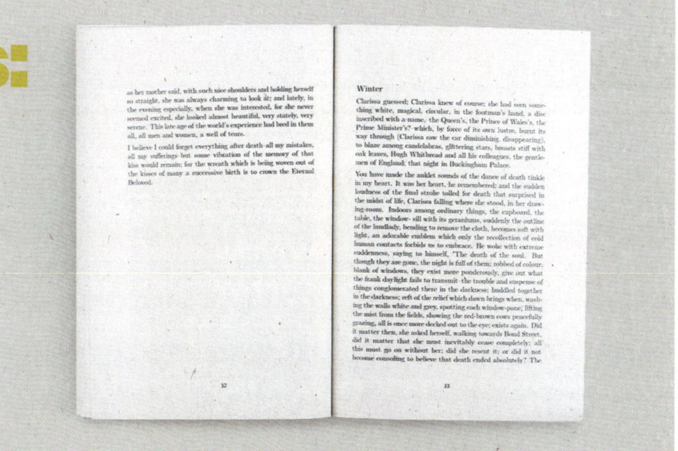

as her mother said, with such nice shoulders and holding herself so straight, she was always charming to look at; and lately, in the evening especially, when she was interested, for she never seemed excited, she looked almost beautiful, very stately, very serene. This late age of the world's experience had bred in them all, all men and women, a well of tears.

I believe I could forget everything after death–all my mistakes, all my sufferings–but some vibration of the memory of that kiss would remain; for the wreath which is being woven out of the kisses of many a successive birth is to crown the Eternal Beloved.

32

Winter

Clarissa guessed; Clarissa knew of course; she had seen something white, magical, circular, in the footman's hand, a disc inscribed with a name,–the Queen's, the Prince of Wales's, the Prime Minister's?–which, by force of its own lustre, burnt its way through (Clarissa saw the car diminishing, disappearing), to blaze among candelabras, glittering stars, breasts stiff with oak leaves, Hugh Whitbread and all his colleagues, the gentlemen of England, that night in Buckingham Palace.

You have made the anklet sounds of the dance of death tinkle in my heart. It was her heart, he remembered; and the sudden loudness of the final stroke tolled for death that surprised in the midst of life, Clarissa falling where she stood, in her drawing-room. Indoors among ordinary things, the cupboard, the table, the window- sill with its geraniums, suddenly the outline of the landlady, bending to remove the cloth, becomes soft with light, an adorable emblem which only the recollection of cold human contacts forbids us to embrace. He woke with extreme suddenness, saying to himself, 'The death of the soul. But though they are gone, the night is full of them; robbed of colour, blank of windows, they exist more ponderously, give out what the frank daylight fails to transmit–the trouble and suspense of things conglomerated there in the darkness; huddled together in the darkness; reft of the relief which dawn brings when, washing the walls white and grey, spotting each window-pane, lifting the mist from the fields, showing the red-brown cows peacefully grazing, all is once more decked out to the eye; exists again. Did it matter then, she asked herself, walking towards Bond Street, did it matter that she must inevitably cease completely; all this must go on without her; did she resent it; or did it not become consoling to believe that death ended absolutely? The

33

Sherwood Anderson & Henri Bergson & Their Return to Life in Four Seasons: A Constant Remix

FORMAT	14.2 × 21.0 cm
MATERIALITIES	saddle stich bound
PAGES	11
IMAGE	

also the names of Ugly Brown Chophouse Sam and Carolina Kate with descriptions of their places, their hours of closing and the class and quantity of their patronage.

6

Autumn

' He went on in a reflective mood, wondering what power had taken hold of him. The remembrance of it acts upon the minds of jurors.

By grasping that fact Caesar, Alexander, Napoleon and our own Grant have made heroes of the dullest clods that walk and not a man of all the thousands who marched with Sherman to the sea but lived the rest of his life with a something sweeter, braver and finer sleeping in his soul than will ever be produced by the reformer scolding of brotherhood from a soap-box. He could not rest although he had given up business with that end in view. It did not occur to him to talk to her as to a fine man friend and a kind of bantering half serious companionship sprang up between them. "Be silent," he said, going about among the men during the rest periods.

The barber is as confused as the rest of them and he doesn't know it. His fine reflective mood is gone. McGregor hurried away into the darkness and spent the rest of the night walking in the streets. Why could she not understand that I did not want to come into her presence to rest or to say empty words. He was very serious about acquiring learning and when the professor paused in his talk he threw up his hands and asked a question.

7

Heroic Real Estate Otter of the 21st Century

AUTHOR	exquisite_code
YEAR	2013
GENRE	experimental literature, fiction
METHOD	collective, composition (writing / drawing / photography), constraint, generative / automation
SUBJECT	authorship, code / programming, crowd / collaboration, literature, writing / reading techniques
PLATFORM	Lulu
EDITION CHARACTERISTICS	ISBN 9781300801863, open edition
FORMAT	10.8 × 17.5 cm
MATERIALITIES	black-and-white, paperback, perfect bound
PAGES	104

IMAGE

DESCRIPTION

Heroic Real Estate Otter of the 21st Century is an experimental collaborative novel written by seven authors during a seven-hour book sprint on November 2, 2012 at the Inspace gallery in Edinburgh during the conference *Remediating the Social*. The writing performance was organized and mediated by an automated editing software run on a networked Linux PC called *The Maggot*, conceived and coded by exquisite_code (Brendan Howell and Sabrina Small).

The foreword explains: "The process of writing proceeded in rounds, with all participants sitting at a table working simultaneously for periods of 10 minutes. The writing interface was presented in the form of a simple browser-based text editor, with basic typographic options (bold, italic, lists) and standard editing functions (cut, copy, paste). At the end of each timed round, the editor [i.e. *The Maggot*] automatically submitted the texts, regardless of their level of completion and the desires of the authors, and closed each of the edit windows. The machine, sometimes known as the *bastard editor*, then proceeded to insert the chunks into the corpus. This round of texts was automatically printed out on an old line printer, leaving an endless paper record piling up on the table. Next, *The Maggot* chewed into the corpus, making holes between existing chunks or picking out existing texts in need of further editing. These inserted empty passages or redacted texts were then sent out arbitrarily to the writers for another 10 minute round" (exquisite_code, "Editorial Mechanics," v).

Heroic Real Estate Otter of the 21st Century, published by exquisite_code, contains the outcome of this performance. The actual authors writing via this networked editing system were Brendan Howell, Helen Varley Jamieson, Cristiano Montanari, Elisabeth Nesheim, Brittani Sonnenberg, Franziska Wegener, and J. D. A. Winslow. Sigla in the margins of the pages indicate who originally authored the respective text passage. What is not documented, however, is which other author(s) contributed to the passage and how much their texts were interfered with in one of the later rounds of editing.

On Lulu and Amazon, *The Maggot* is listed as author; in the preface, *The Maggot* is listed as editor. The book is accompanied by a list of contributors; a list of free and open source software used in the production of this work, from programming to photoediting to typesetting and cover layout; and a drawing by Franziska Wegener explaining the different stages of the writing process and listing the possible forms that this collectively written novel could now take after it has been written, from "Life-Novel" (via print-on-demand) to "Text Dump" (via "Print Live") and "Display." Indeed, on the various occasions where this editing software has been used, different publications have been produced, ranging from blog posts and line printed zines to print-on-demand books distributed via Mute Books to the book at hand published via Lulu. The source code for *The Maggot* is available online.

Photo - Shu Lea Cheang

Editorial Mechanics

This book was edited by *The Maggot*, a networked Linux mini-PC sitting in an old, velvet-lined wooden box, running customized software. The process of writing proceeded in rounds, with all participants sitting at a table working simultaneously for periods of 10 minutes. The writing interface was presented in the form of a simple browser-based text editor, with basic typographic options (bold, italic, lists) and standard editing functions (cut, copy, paste). At the end of each timed round, the editor automatically submitted the texts, regardless of their level of completion and the desires of the authors, and closed each of the edit windows. The machine, sometimes known as the *bastard editor*, then proceeded to insert the chunks into the corpus. This round of texts was automatically printed out on an old line printer, leaving an endless paper record piling up on the table. Next, *The Maggot* chewed into the corpus, making holes between existing chunks or picking out existing texts in need of further editing. These inserted empty passages or redacted texts were then sent out arbitrarily to the writers for another 10 minute round. The entire session took place over seven hours on one day.

Throughout this book you will find greek letters in the margins. These symbols indicate the original author of a chunk of text, which may be cross-referenced to the con-

v

Appendix A

Contributors

Photo - Shu Lea Cheang

ο **Brendan Howell** is an artist and a reluctant engineer who has created various software works and interactive electronic inventions. He lives in Berlin, Germany.

σ **Helen Varley Jamieson** is a writer, theatre-maker and digital artist and has a Master of Arts investigating cyberformance - live performance on the internet.

99

AUTHORS	Lewis Freedman, Kevin Rydberg
YEAR	2013
PUBLISHER	Troll Thread
GENRE	experimental literature
METHOD	composition (writing / drawing / photography)
SUBJECT	code / programming, games
PLATFORM	Lulu
EDITION CHARACTERISTICS	multiple editions (print, PDF), open edition
FORMAT	21.4 × 26.9 cm
MATERIALITIES	black-and-white, paperback, saddle stitch bound
PAGES	20 (unpaginated)

IMAGES

```
elements */
void select_elements(char *pool, int n, unsigned long int index, char
*elements)
{
	unsigned long int cutoff = 1;
	unsigned long int block;
	int base = 0;
	int i, j;

	// in this function, to make calculations more straightforward, the
arrays are indexed from 1 to 13

	for (i = 1; i <= 13; i++) {
		while (1) {
			base++;
			block = choose((n - base), (13 - i));
			if (index >= block + cutoff)
				cutoff += block;
			else
				break;
		}
		elements[i - 1] = pool[base - 1];
		pool[base - 1] = -1;
	}

	j = 1;
	for (i = 1; i <= n; i++)
		if (pool[i - 1] != -1) {
			pool[j - 1] = pool[i - 1];
			j++;
		}
}


/* permutes the first 13 elements of elements[] according to the index, and
stores them back in elements[] */
void order_elements(unsigned long int index, char *elements)
{
	unsigned long int cutoff = 1;
	unsigned long int block;
	int nshifts, i, j;
	char temp;

	// in this function, to make calculations more straightforward, the
arrays are indexed from 1 to 13

	for (i = 1; i < 13; i++) {
		nshifts = 0;
		while (1) {
			block = factorial(13 - i);
			if (index >= cutoff + block) {
				cutoff += block;
				nshifts++;
			}
			else {
				if (nshifts > 0) {
					temp = elements[i - 1];
					elements[i - 1] = elements[(i + nshifts) - 1];
					for (j = nshifts; j > 1; j--)
```

```
						elements[(i + j) - 1] = elements[(i + (j -
1)) - 1];
					elements[(i + 1) - 1] = temp;
				}
				break;
			}
		}
	}
}


/* stores a random ordering of 52 cards in deck[] according to the seven
indices */
void shuffle(unsigned long int sel_1ndex, unsigned long int order_1ndex,
unsigned long int sel_2ndex,
		unsigned long int order_2ndex, unsigned long int
sel_3ndex, unsigned long int order_3ndex,
		unsigned long int order_4ndex, char *deck)
{
	int i;
	char pool[52], elements[13];

	for (i = 0; i <= 51; i++)
		pool[i] = (char)i;

	select_elements(pool, 52, sel_1ndex, elements);
	order_elements(order_1ndex, elements);
	for (i = 0; i <= 12; i++)
		deck[i] = elements[i];

	select_elements(pool, 39, sel_2ndex, elements);
	order_elements(order_2ndex, elements);
	for (i = 0; i <= 12; i++)
		deck[i + 13] = elements[i];

	select_elements(pool, 26, sel_3ndex, elements);
	order_elements(order_3ndex, elements);
	for(i = 0; i <= 12; i++)
		deck[i + 26] = elements[i];

	order_elements(order_4ndex, pool);
	for(i = 0; i <= 12; i++)
		deck[i + 39] = pool[i];
}


/* deals the deck[] and returns a pointer to the first game state */
struct state *deal(const char *deck)
{
	int i, j, k, l, hashvalue;
	struct state *pstate = (struct state *)malloc(sizeof(struct state));

	for (i = 0; i <= 3; i++)
		pstate->foundations[i] = -1;

	pstate->b_number = -1;

	for (i = 0; i <= 6; i++) {
		pstate->piles[i].t_number = 0;
		pstate->piles[i].r_number = (char)i - 1;
```

DESCRIPTION

SOLITUDE contains the complete code and execution instructions for the solitaire card game Klondike, playing through all possible variations. A software version of Klondike was included with Microsoft Windows in the 1990s and has appeared under the name of "Solitaire" ever since, allegedly making it the most popular single player card game. Freedman and Rydberg's computer program simulates a play-through of all possible variations, which will take several years for a personal computer to read/execute. The project can be read as a reflection on loneliness and the social function of games in relation to computing and automation. Moreover, it challenges the status of code and instructions for conceptual writing, presenting the program as a thought experiment in book form rather than an application ready to be executed.

Spam Bibliography

AUTHOR	Angela Genusa
YEAR	2013
PUBLISHER	Troll Thread
GENRE	experimental literature
METHOD	collection, documentation / archiving, found material, reformatting
SUBJECT	economy / labor, email / messaging, internet culture, tracking
PLATFORM	Lulu
EDITION CHARACTERISTICS	multiple editions (print, PDF), open edition
FORMAT	21.6 × 27.9 cm
MATERIALITIES	black-and-white, paperback, perfect bound
PAGES	92
IMAGES	

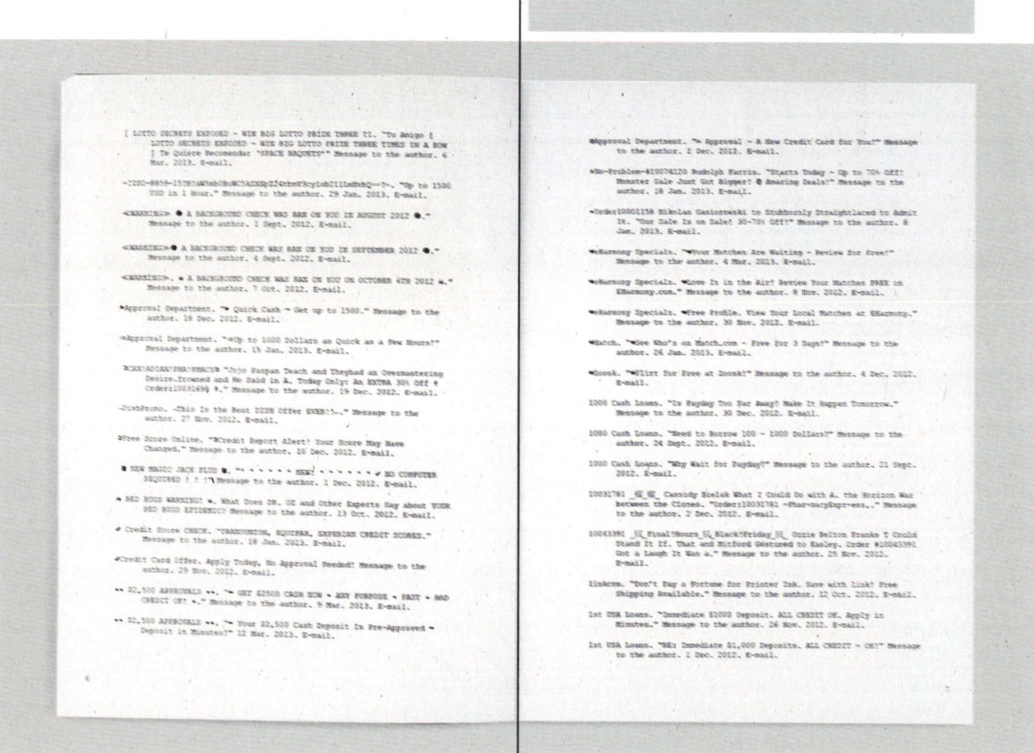

DESCRIPTION

Angela Genusa's *Spam Bibliography* presents all emails received in her spam folder between September 2012 and March 2013, formatted as a bibliography and sorted alphabetically: senders become authors, the subject line becomes the title, and the date received becomes the publication date. Accordingly, the blurb on Lulu—following the ironic "How to ..." pattern typical for Troll Thread—reads: "HOW TO ORGANIZE EMAILS." This unique representation makes spam messages appear as objects worth documenting and investigating.

In accordance with academic standards, the text is quoted verbatim, including linguistic absurdities, random overuse of capitalization, and all those confusing punctuation marks and symbols like arrows, crosses, asterisks, and emoji. One doesn't always know whether they mean anything, whether they are just mojibake or whether they are meant to trick email providers' anti-spam algorithms. Their "alphabetical" order, opaque at first glance—e.g., the heart comes after the asterisk—probably results from the Unicode values of the characters.

With a strong documentary gesture, the collection draws a panorama of human desires, weaknesses, fears, hardships, and their proposed solutions driven by capitalist logic, and gives a glimpse at an often automatically deleted genre of waste text and its rhetorical potential. At the same time, it exposes this generic, automated, marketing speak in the digital age as a kind of transhuman writing that is usually not only written by machines, but also increasingly aimed at non-human readers—namely spam filters—before reaching its real target: humans with all their weaknesses.

L-MEM Vol. 1

Introduction to making very big books: The Master Book

AUTHOR	Pierre Jasmin
YEAR	2013
GENRE	nonfiction, tutorial
METHOD	collection, composition (writing / drawing / photography), test / experiment, versioning / seriality
SUBJECT	analog / digital, book / book design, internet culture, publishing / distribution, scale, writing / reading techniques
PLATFORM	Lulu
EDITION CHARACTERISTICS	open edition
FORMAT	21.6 × 27.9 cm
MATERIALITIES	color, paperback, perfect bound
PAGES	705

IMAGES

DESCRIPTION

L-MEM is a theoretical, speculative, and practical outline of how Pierre Jasmin sees writing and the medium of the book to be reconceptualized in the digital age and how that reconception will produce a new kind of literature in the not-too-far future. For this, he retraces the history of the book and publishing as well as of writing and information technology. The key concept is a networked, extensive production of knowledge in relation to what one human being can produce or perceive in a lifetime. In his speculative facets, Jasmin mostly follows the ideological traces of Silicon Valley Singularitarianism, yet with a distinct interest in the facilitation of knowledge filtered through a single human being, namely himself and his biography.

To tackle the increasingly diverging scales in the production and perception of knowledge, which are becoming a rupture due to digital information technologies, one has to confront oneself with aspects of content and time management. Not without humor, Jasmin suggests a system for reading and writing large amounts of text starting in a chapter called "Mom, Why Do I Need a Personal Documentation System?" He describes his working process of reading, writing, and editing several times throughout this book, with particular interest in how changes in tools make new methods and amounts of text possible, allegedly in different updates, with one working definition as follows:

"When I identify something that I consider insightful, I record it (annotate it, cut it,...) and pile it. Later, I process the pile (com-pile) and classify the notions and ideas into what largely amounts to 'files, binders and boxes.' Then it's synthesized and incorporated into my production efforts. Once shared, it becomes imbricated with other works. This imbrication is the functional interface of different books (the inter-book), how stuff interconnects, the trans-existence in different forms, formats, media eventually permitting a fair appropriation, a process by which one can assemble a Book that matters at low-cost (and low-energy). Not at zero-cost but at a lower cost then scavenging the shelves of a real library and cut and pasting printed book fragments" (Pierre Jasmin, *L-MEM*, 29).

The book itself performs some of the theorems and practices Jasmin envisions, as what might be called a library-sized metabook. This mostly describes the fact that the book has a wiki as its source, which is editable, extendible, and in theory inexhaustible—by him and his readers. Also, the text includes versioned rewritings, extensive citations, appropriations, collective writing, and reproductions of discussions happening in digital comment sections of the project. In order to contribute to the wiki, a password was required, which could only be obtained when purchasing the book: "If you have a printed version of the Book, then the password is in the book in the section about Passwords. This password will allow you to Add Pages to this Wiki" (Pierre Jasmin, *"L-MEM Wiki,"* "Vol. 1 – v053 – Aux Book Features"). A corresponding reference is hidden on page 270.

L-MEM exports a snapshot of this digital text, which Jasmin used to regularly rewrite and extend for several years until volume 001.058, which refers to volume 001 of the project in a 58th edition that was exported as a print-on-demand tome. Jasmin also lends one entire chapter to the production method, and to transferring and archiving large amounts of digital content in general in his chapter "Budgeting Printing the Book and Shipping it to You."

Best of Rhizome 2012

AUTHOR	Joanne McNeil [ed.]
YEAR	2013
PUBLISHER	LINK Editions
GENRE	catalog / collection, nonfiction
METHOD	composition (writing / drawing / photography), documentation / archiving
SUBJECT	art, canon, internet culture, politics / activism, publishing / distribution, technology, visual culture, writing / reading techniques
PLATFORM	Lulu
EDITION CHARACTERISTICS	multiple editions (print, PDF), ISBN 9781291329919, open edition, CC BY-NC-SA
FORMAT	14.8 × 21.0 cm
MATERIALITIES	black-and-white, paperback, perfect bound
PAGES	275
IMAGE	

DESCRIPTION

Best of Rhizome 2012 is a collection of essays selected from those published on rhizome.org in 2012. Rhizome is an online platform that seeks to observe technology-driven change in society from the perspective of the arts, mainly via critical essays. A selection of these long reads for the printed medium was made by Joanne McNeil. The book becomes a medium for preservation and an alternative reading experience, but it also serves as a container to literally bind a selection. This "new format, with a new excuse to read" (Heather Corcoran, "Foreword") also becomes a critical reflection on reading speed and attention span in times of rapidly refreshing timelines and technological change itself.

CONTAINS TEXTS BY

Orit Gat, The Piracy Project, Rahel Aima, Angela Genusa, Adam Rothstein, Joanne McNeil, John Powers, Sarah Jaffe, Harry Burke, Giampaolo Bianconi, Jason Huff, Clement Valla, Rachel Wetzler, Yin Ho, Ben Fino-Radin, Paul Graham Raven, Honor Harger, Jordan Crandall, Maura Lucking, and Cole Stryker

REIMBUR$EMENT

AUTHOR	Holly Melgard
YEAR	2013
PUBLISHER	Troll Thread
GENRE	artist's book / bookwork, experimental literature
METHOD	détournement / hack, documentation / archiving, photocopy / scan, pricing
SUBJECT	ecology / sustainability, economy / labor, tracking
PLATFORM	Lulu
EDITION CHARACTERISTICS	multiple editions (print, PDF), open edition
FORMAT	14.8 × 21.0 cm
MATERIALITIES	color, paperback, perfect bound
PAGES	228

IMAGE

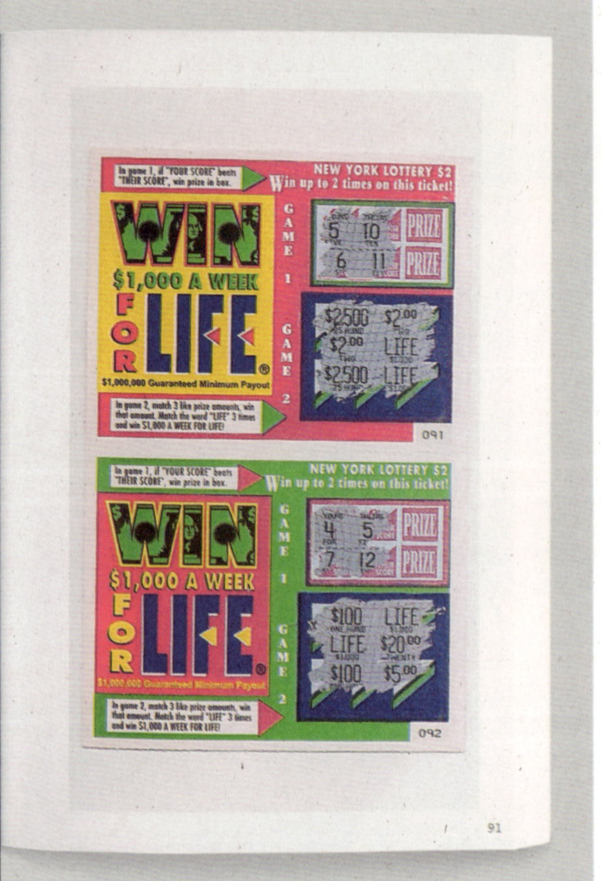

DESCRIPTION

REIMBUR$EMENT collects all the scratch cards, lotto tickets, and respective shopping receipts that Holly Melgard has collected over six years—more specifically, each time she had to invest in her work instead of making money with it, as the introduction says: "Sometimes the work I do results in earning neither income, livelihood, nor play, and often I find myself paying to work rather than being paid for work. Whenever this happens, I count my losses and take my chances gambling for alternatives."

One copy of *REIMBUR$EMENT* costs the equivalent of the entire gambling stake plus the production costs claimed by Lulu: $329.53. In such a way, *REIMBUR$EMENT* addresses the typical economic imbalance of experimental print-on-demand and poetry ventures with a propensity for self-exploitation. It contrasts the idealization of print-on-demand as a means of liberation and self-empowerment with reference to the sustenance that makes the work possible in the first place. "Reimbursement is for the work," it correspondingly says on the front matter.

Furthermore, *REIMBUR$EMENT* exposes the different economies of digital and analog media: alongside the printed book, Troll Thread also offers a PDF download, which—following the "gratis mentality" of the internet—is available for free. Through this, it becomes clear that ultimately both profit models fail: while the author doesn't earn anything from the PDF at all, the printed copy will likely find only very few buyers because of its high price tag.

Like all blurbs from Troll Thread on Lulu, the blurb for this book ironically follows the "How to ..." pattern. It reads: "HOW TO PLAY. HOW TO PLAY. HOW TO PLAY. HOW TO PLAY. HOW TO PLAY." The repetition is due to the minimum number of characters required for blurbs on Lulu.

World Clock

AUTHOR	Nick Montfort
YEAR	2013
PUBLISHER	Bad Quarto
GENRE	experimental literature
METHOD	generative / automation
SUBJECT	literature, narration, reading / interpretation
PLATFORM	Espresso Book Machine
EDITION CHARACTERISTICS	open edition, only available through the publisher
FORMAT	14.0 × 21.0 cm
MATERIALITIES	black-and-white, paperback, perfect bound
PAGES	239

IMAGES

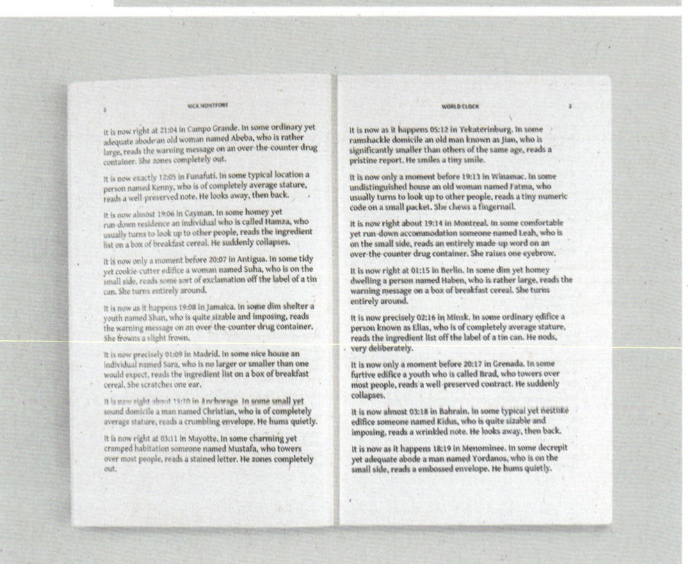

2 NICK MONTFORT

It is now right at 21:04 in Campo Grande. In some ordinary yet adequate abode an old woman named Abeba, who is rather large, reads the warning message on an over-the-counter drug container. She zones completely out.

It is now exactly 12:05 in Funafuti. In some typical location a person named Kenny, who is of completely average stature, reads a well-preserved note. He looks away, then back.

It is now almost 19:06 in Cayman. In some homey yet run-down residence an individual who is called Hamza, who usually turns to look up to other people, reads the ingredient list on a box of breakfast cereal. He suddenly collapses.

It is now only a moment before 20:07 in Antigua. In some tidy yet cookie-cutter edifice a woman named Suha, who is on the small side, reads some sort of exclamation off the label of a tin can. She turns entirely around.

It is now as it happens 19:08 in Jamaica. In some dim shelter a youth named Shan, who is quite sizable and imposing, reads the warning message on an over-the-counter drug container. She frowns a slight frown.

It is now precisely 01:09 in Madrid. In some nice house an individual named Sara, who is no larger or smaller than one would expect, reads the ingredient list on a box of breakfast cereal. She scratches one ear.

It is now right about 15:10 in Anchorage. In some small yet sound domicile a man named Christian, who is of completely average stature, reads a crumbling envelope. He hums quietly.

It is now right at 03:11 in Mayotte. In some charming yet cramped habitation someone named Mustafa, who towers over most people, reads a stained letter. He zones completely out.

WORLD CLOCK 3

It is now as it happens 05:12 in Yekaterinburg. In some ramshackle domicile an old man known as Jian, who is significantly smaller than others of the same age, reads a pristine report. He smiles a tiny smile.

It is now only a moment before 19:13 in Winamac. In some undistinguished house an old woman named Fatma, who usually turns to look up to other people, reads a tiny numeric code on a small packet. She chews a fingernail.

It is now right about 19:14 in Montreal. In some comfortable yet run-down accommodation someone named Leah, who is on the small side, reads an entirely made-up word on an over-the-counter drug container. She raises one eyebrow.

It is now right at 01:15 in Berlin. In some dim yet homey dwelling a person named Haben, who is rather large, reads the warning message on a box of breakfast cereal. She turns entirely around.

It is now precisely 02:16 in Minsk. In some ordinary edifice a person known as Elias, who is of completely average stature, reads the ingredient list off the label of a tin can. He nods, very deliberately.

It is now only a moment before 20:17 in Grenada. In some furtive edifice a youth who is called Brad, who towers over most people, reads a well-preserved contract. He suddenly collapses.

It is now almost 03:18 in Bahrain. In some typical yet nestlike edifice someone named Kidus, who is quite sizable and imposing, reads a wrinkled note. He looks away, then back.

It is now as it happens 18:19 in Menominee. In some decrepit yet adequate abode a man named Yordanos, who is on the small side, reads a embossed envelope. He hums quietly.

DESCRIPTION

Nick Montfort's computer generated novel *World Clock* is inspired by Harry Mathews's *The Chronogram for 1998* and Stanisław Lem's *One Human Minute* (1983). The latter is a fictitious review of a non-existent book of the same name that uses statistical data to describe everything that happens to human life on the planet within one minute. As the fictitious reviewer points out, this book could only be created with the help of computers, and in a supplementary chapter an electronic edition of the book is presented that can only be read using a computer and always contains the current data.

World Clock implements this idea: it consists of 1,440 paragraphs, divided into twenty-four chapters for each hour of the day with sixty paragraphs each, forming one hour. Each minute paragraph presents an incident by specifying a time of day, place, and character doing something. It starts with: "It is now exactly 05:00 in Samarkand. In some ramshackle dwelling a person who is called Gang, who is on the small side, reads an entirely made-up word on a box of breakfast cereal. He turns entirely around." And it ends with: "It is now as it happens 23:59 in St. Helena. In some dim yet adequate edifice a person named Feng, who usually turns to look up to other people, reads some sort of exclamation on a small packet. He raises one eyebrow."

In this repetitive way, Montfort's novel "celebrates the industrial concept of time and certain types of vigorous banality which are shared by all people throughout the world" (blurb on Harvard Book Store), while creating an immense and dense web of interconnectedness and synchronicity. It thus redeems the description from Lem's fictitious review that Montfort prefaced his novel with: "The originality of *One Human Minute* lies in its being not a statistical compilation of information about what has taken place, like an ordinary almanac, but rather synchronous with the human world, like a computer of the type that we say works in real time, a device tracking phenomena as they occur."

World Clock was generated with 165 lines of Python code and written in about four hours on November 27, 2013 for the first National Novel Generation Month (NaNoGenMo). "The only external data source that is used in the generation process is the computer's time zone database" (blurb on Harvard Book Store).

The book is distributed via the local independent Harvard Book Store (no direct relationship to the university of the same name) and printed on the Espresso Book Machine in the store. On the artist's website, it is advertised by saying: "The 239-page paperback can be purchased for only $14.40, which is the low, low price of only one cent per minute."

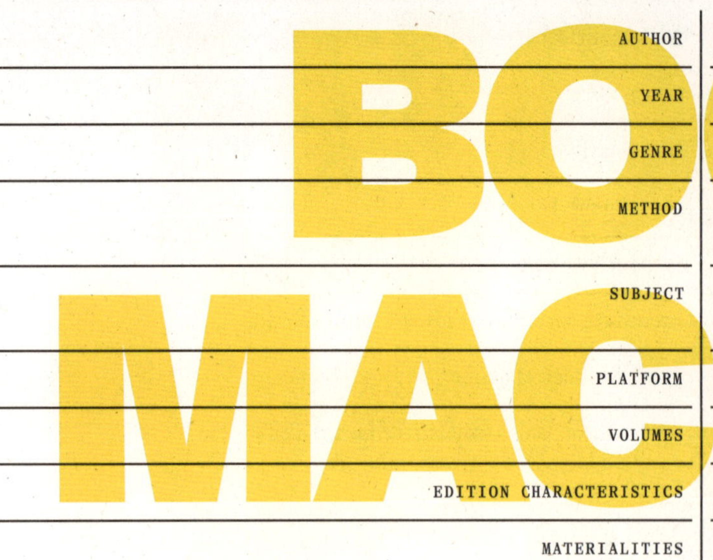

BOOK MACHINE

AUTHOR	onestar press
YEAR	2013–2017
GENRE	education / classroom, exhibition copy, tutorial
METHOD	collective, composition (writing / drawing / photography), constraint
SUBJECT	book / book design, crowd / collaboration, politics / activism, print on demand, publishing / distribution, standard / default
PLATFORM	ICN – Orthez (France), local print shops
VOLUMES	up to more than 350 vols. per run
EDITION CHARACTERISTICS	not for sale, not publicly available
MATERIALITIES	black-and-white, paperback, perfect bound
IMAGE	

DESCRIPTION

From 2000 to 2019, Mélanie Scarciglia and Christophe Boutin ran the Parisian publishing house onestar press, which specialized in books and multiples by artists and used print-on-demand from the very beginning (and thus before the major print-on-demand platforms were established), which industrial printers such as Firmin Didot and ICN – Orthez already had in their portfolio at the time. In 2013, they developed a public book sprint as a new event format under the name *BOOK MACHINE*, which they have organized several times since then as part of the public program together with cultural, educational and art institutions worldwide. These events are open to everyone and aim at "connecting emerging designers and public participants through the creation of books" (onestar press, "Book Machine," website).

Due to its low-threshold nature, print-on-demand is particularly suitable for such participatory projects that are intended to introduce lay people to book production: The books are ready for pickup the next day, the print files are quite easy to create, and there is only a limited choice of formats and materials available. And the more rigid the formal specifications, the easier they are to work with and the more they shift the focus of bookmaking from the book object to the book idea and content. As a rule, the specifications for the books were: 100 pages (no more and no less) in black and white, imprint on page 99, cover in color, typeface and font size for the spine are also set. The standard formats differed depending on the production location: at Sidney II 2017 it was 14.0 × 22.5 cm, at Paris Photo 2015 it was 21.5 × 28.1 cm. The fact that the publications of a run are all in the same format and have a common look underlines the collective character of the events just as much as it makes visible the diversity, individuality, and creativity that are nevertheless wrung out of the same specifications.

The first edition of *BOOK MACHINE* took place in 2013 as part of Le Nouvel festival at the Centre Pompidou in Paris. Under the guidance of thirty student graphic designers from three distinguished art schools, each participant was given the opportunity to develop an understanding of the conception, design, and production of books in general and of print-on-demand books in particular, and to realize their own book idea in work sessions with a designer, usually lasting 2 to 3.5 hours. Each designer made two books per day. In total, more than 350 publications were produced in three weeks in the lower foyer of the Centre Pompidou, which artist Mika Tajima designed and furnished as a transparent, freely accessible "production factory" like a temporary publishing house. The books were each printed overnight with ICN – Orthez and publicly presented and discussed at the end. Each participant received one complimentary copy of their book, extra copies could be ordered and purchased at additional cost.

There were other *BOOK MACHINE* editions at the Blaffer Art Museum, Houston (Texas) in 2014; at the California Institute of the Arts, Los Angeles, in 2015; at the Peep-Hole Art Center, Milan, in 2015; at Paris Photo in 2015; and at Artspace Sydney as part of VOLUME | Another Art Book Fair in 2015 and 2017. In terms of content, the spectrum of the books produced is very broad; they often process biographical material or everyday life. Where the book sprints were organized by and in art institutions, there were often also projects with artistic pretensions in the tradition of the artist's book or photobook.

Participants and graphic design students were often found via a call. One of the things advertised was that graphic designers would receive an extra copy of each book they produced the very next day: "That means you could add as many as nine books to your personal collection and portfolio" (onestar press, "Callout," Sydney 2015). The participants had to commit themselves to complying with guidelines as the following: "Though you are responsible for the content in your book, your designated designer has the right to refuse any content that they consider offensive. As *BOOK MACHINE* books are not published for public sale, the issue of copyright is not of concern" (onestar press, "Participants Guidelines," Sydney 2017).

faces

AUTHOR	Chervine Dalaeli
YEAR	2015
PUBLISHER	onestar press
GENRE	photobook
METHOD	composition (writing / drawing / photography), montage / remix
SUBJECT	memory / storage, photography, politics / activism, visual culture
PLATFORM	ICN – Orthez (France)
FORMAT	21.5 × 28.1 cm
MATERIALITIES	black-and-white, paperback, perfect bound
PAGES	64

IMAGES

DESCRIPTION

As a representative example of a book produced on a *BOOK MACHINE*, Chervine Dalaeli's *faces* has entered our collection. Like all books, it bears the *BOOK MACHINE* logo designed by Mika Tajima and a reference to its context of creation on the occasion of *BOOK MACHINE* at Paris Photo 2015, powered by onestar press. It is a photobook that assembles black-and-white photographs of urban life in Paris and New York, which defy the clichés and phantasmagorias behind which the cities have disappeared and, according to Juan Asensio in his preface, allow us to see the cities in a new way.

As the author's brief note on the first page reminds us, the production of the book at Paris Photo (November 12–15, 2015) was overshadowed by the tragic Paris terrorist attacks that took place on the evening of November 13, giving the photos in this book yet another twist: "All of this content may therefore represent a world 'before.' It is up to the reader to judge" ("Tout ce contenu représente donc peut-être un monde 'd'avant'. Il reviendra au lecteur d'en juger."). The *BOOK MACHINE* itself was discontinued during the intended run time due to the events.

Special Collection

An Assortment of Books, Digitized by Google, Un-Digitized

AUTHOR	Benjamin Shaykin
YEAR	2013
GENRE	catalog / collection, education / classroom, reprint
METHOD	collection, documentation / archiving, found material, remediation
SUBJECT	analog / digital, bias, book / book design, economy / labor, error / corruption / loss, google, memory / storage, platforms / companies, race
EDITION CHARACTERISTICS	open edition, available only through the artist
FORMAT	16.7 × 25.9 cm
MATERIALITIES	black-and-white, paperback, perfect bound
PAGES	304 (unpaginated)
IMAGES	

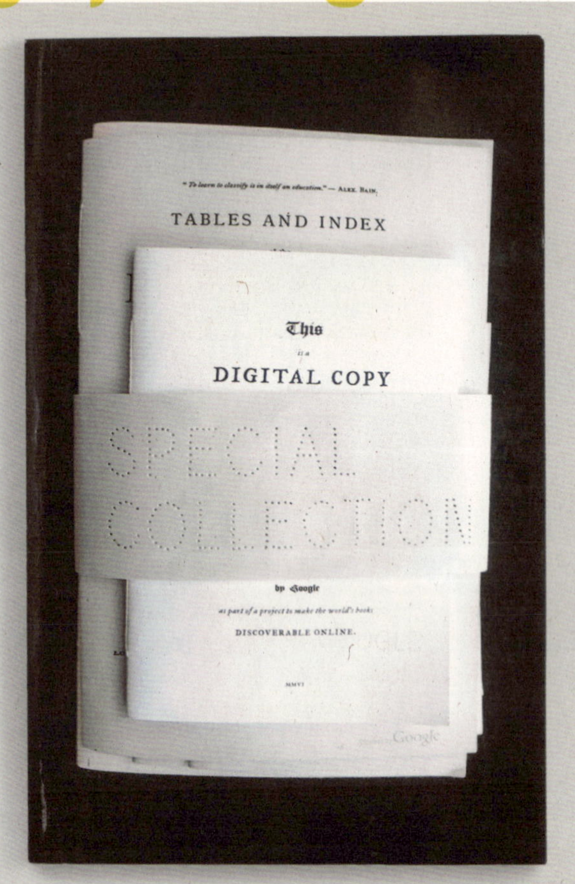

DESCRIPTION

This print-on-demand edition goes back to the author's MFA thesis at Rhode Island School of Design, for which he made twelve hand-sewn books under the title *Special Collection*, all of which this volume reproduces together.

The twelve chapbooks are "partial recreations of books found on Google Books" (blurb on Printed Matter), among them such apt titles as Dewey's *Decimal Classification*, *Catalogue of Choice, Useful, and Curious Books*, and *A Handy-Book About Books*. In addition, there is a compilation of loan period slips (*Date Due*) and a chapbook titled *Ex Libris Being a Collection of Artifacts & Digits Digitized by Google*. This is complemented by a presentation of the Google Books project by Google itself, which has inscribed itself with watermarks in all the scans made—just as libraries used to mark their possessions with ink, embossed, or punched stamps, in the style of which the title of Shaykin's volume is designed.

"Each [chapbook] is reproduced at its original size, revealing multiple disruptions and errors, introduced during Google's own scanning process: the scanner's hand, holding down and obliterating the page; type and illustrations which have degraded and blurred to the point of illegibility; pages scanned while in the process of being turned; fold-out maps and charts that were scanned while closed. Some of these artifacts are beautiful and evocative. They are the found poetry of this new machine" (Ibid.).

Some finds are indeed ingenious, such as when a book page titled "PART.IX.-INDEX" is appropriately "illustrated" by the index finger of the person scanning the book. But at the same time, *Special Collection* is much more than just entertaining found objects or beautiful artifacts: "By reinvesting these digital books with physical form, *Special Collection* asks us to consider the contradictions and unintended consequences of technological advance. Approaching Google Books through its fissures offers a chance to peek behind the curtain of a mysterious, complicated endeavor, which is little understood and generally taken for granted as progress. By using Google's scans and resources to create this work, I am both highlighting the potential of this new era of distribution and access, and questioning Google's claims of ownership of all the world's information" (Ibid.).

STILL LIFE WITH THE POKÉMON YELLOW VERSION TEXT DUMP IN 30 PT. MONACO FONT JUSTIFIED TO MARGIN DISTRIBUTED AS A PDF OR A BOOK CONVERTED FROM A MICROSOFT WORD DOCUMENT BY CHRIS SYLVESTER 2012/2013

AUTHOR	Chris Sylvester
YEAR	2013
PUBLISHER	Troll Thread
GENRE	experimental literature
METHOD	appropriation, found material, paratextual play, reformatting, remediation
SUBJECT	analog / digital, authorship, copyright / law, games
PLATFORM	Lulu
EDITION CHARACTERISTICS	multiple editions (print, PDF), open edition
FORMAT	21.6 × 27.9 cm
MATERIALITIES	black-and-white, paperback, perfect bound
PAGES	693 (unpaginated)

IMAGES

DESCRIPTION

Chris Sylvester's book is exactly what is stated in its title: a complete reproduction of the text used for the English version of the video game Pokémon Yellow, as found in an online document. The text is set in 30 pt. and justified, making the book an extensive tome and each page like a collection of slogans or poetry. It starts with a list of characters, accessories, places, commodities and the like, i.e., the game world setup. What follows are conversational phrases, game status reports, commands, interjections, snippets of speech—at the loss of all other essential game components. As Jennifer Fossenbell states in her review: "Sylvester's [book] is not one that is meant to be *read*, at least not strictly speaking, as much as it's meant to exist, to take up excessive space [...]. In its aggressive excess, it's meant to be *dealt with*" (Jennifer Fossenbell, "Chris Sylvester's *Still Life With The Pokemon*").

The cover includes an email by the writer and translator Ashugi Kamaguchi, complaining about the theft of intellectual property. However, the writer of the email is presumably not the real translator of the video game's text. The email also contains some general critical points on appropriation and conceptual literature and lists nearly every conceivable caveat to experimental literature, from "to[o] long" and "boring" to "the world doesn't need a living literary version of Duchamp" to "nobody reads your poetry anyway." The latter is known to have prompted Chris Sylvester to form their own print-on-demand publishing collective, Troll Thread, together with Holly Melgard, Joey Yearous-Algozin, and Divya Victor, on the grounds that "It's a place where we can put all our poetry that no one else wants" (Tan Lin, "Troll Thread Interview").

The Post-Art Poem

AUTHORS	The Post-Art Poets
YEAR	2013–2014
GENRE	poetry
METHOD	collective, détournement / hack, found material, montage / remix, pricing
SUBJECT	art world / literary world, economy / labor, literature, politics / activism, publishing / distribution
PLATFORM	Blurb
VOLUMES	13 parts, 3 of them print-on-demand books
EDITION CHARACTERISTICS	multiple editions (print, PDF), open edition
FORMAT	15.2 × 22.9 cm

IMAGE

DESCRIPTION

The Post-Art Poets was a group of conceptual poets active between 2013 and 2014 (known members include Vanessa Place, Danny Snelson, and Luc Gross of TraumaWien). Their artistic practices focused mostly on social media interactions (Twitter but also YouTube and Reddit); all kinds of print-on-demand products (including posters, t-shirts, and books); the glitching, altering, and reposting of pictures taken from social media; and other conceptual interventions mostly declaring the end of poetry, the art world, institutions, and copyright.

The name of the group can be read as an amalgamation of these practices, meaning that they consider themselves "post-art" by declining institutions and ownership, but that they also literally posted art on social media as their main practice. In choosing social media content, altering or labeling it and publishing it on their account or in books, they engaged in a kind of counterpublishing which is explained in the form of a dictionary entry with different meanings:

"1. To make a public announcement in response to a public announcement.
2a. To re-disseminate to the public.
2b. To produce or release for distribution as a reaction.
2c. To reissue the work of an author, with or without permission, with high or low fidelity, for the purpose of reacting to said author or to the broader zeitgeist" (The Post-Art Poets, *55 Faxes*, n.p.).

In their manifesto they proclaim: "The Post-Art Poets no longer self-identify as artists, abandoning all that they have built. They self-publish work, often via the modes made available by current technology. The Post-Art Poets find dependence on a publisher or gallery to be an intolerable position; instead they are institutions unto themselves. / They are outsiders; imaginary; unstoppable. The Post-Art Poets are nothing, nothing, nothing, and all is poem" (The Post-Art Poets, "The Post-Art Poetics Manifesto").

On their website they even declare that they think of their "collective as a singular poem in the epic tradition" and refer to the thirteen works listed below as "select chapters of that poem" (The Post-Art Poets, "The Post-Art Poetics Archive"). Three of these works are available as print-on-demand via Blurb. Other publications include *Last Poets: A 9,999 page poem by The Poets Against Poetry*, the conceptual anthology *Fungible Poetics Inc.* concerned with shared ownership and market logics, and *32 Words: An Anthology of Post-Art Anti-Poetics*, whose imprint states "Appropriation, plagiarism, and counterpublishing are encouraged." It is sold for $160.

In 2014, they announced the (temporary?) end of their group on Twitter: "WE HAVE DISAPPEARED / TO BEGIN PREPARATIONS / FOR OUR REAPPEARANCE..." (@postartpoets).

Der Klaus: A Poem

AUTHORS	The Post-Art Poets, Klaus Biesenbach
YEAR	2013
GENRE	photobook, poetry
METHOD	détournement / hack, documentation / archiving, found material, montage / remix
SUBJECT	art world / literary world, error / corruption / loss, internet culture, social media, twitter, visual culture
MATERIALITIES	color, paperback, perfect bound
PAGES	54 (unpaginated)

DESCRIPTION

Der Klaus is a collection of tweets by Klaus Biesenbach and from the account of The Post-Art Poets. Every tweet by Biesenbach, a central figure of the art world and an institutional representative—at the time, he was chief curator of the Museum of Modern Art in New York—is commented on by the Post-Art Poets, mimicking and juxtaposing his content. Pictures are glitched and reposted, central words in tweets are replaced, exemplifying their practice of counterpublishing.

In the printed publication, the original posts are usually juxtaposed with the response on a double-page spread, creating the visual impression of a series of one-way responses. Yet, in the middle of the book, an actual back-and-forth takes place: The Post-Art Poets claiming that Biesenbach is a bot, to which Biesenbach responds “it is just me...... der klaus.” The paratext on the cover suggests that each individual altering of a tweet should not be understood as a poem but the whole social media performance of both accounts as a whole: “A poem by The Post-Art Poets + Klaus Biesenbach.”

Bots: A Poem

YEAR	2013
GENRE	photobook, poetry
METHOD	détournement / hack, documentation / archiving, found material, montage / remix
SUBJECT	art world / literary world, error / corruption / loss, internet culture, social media, twitter, visual culture
MATERIALITIES	color, paperback, perfect bound
PAGES	64 (unpaginated)
DESCRIPTION	*Bots* is a collection of tweets by The Post-Art Poets in which accounts are tagged with the proclamation "WE DO NOT BELIEVE THAT YOU EXIST," accompanied by a glitched version of the profile picture of each tagged account. Under each of these tweets, a small space is left free for possible responses from the tagged accounts—most of the time this space is left blank, presumably to show that there was no response. These insinuating tweets are accompanied by screenshots of accounts that might not actually be human (thus being "bots") but describe themselves as writers or artists for marketing reasons.

The accounts targeted by this practice are mostly important figures from the art world and the conceptual poetry scene in the USA, but also influencers. This results in a collection of accounts The Post-Art Poets deem important enough to target with their practice of counter-publishing. At the same time, *Bots* is a documentation of The Post-Art Poets' own social media performance and a list of peculiar accounts.

55 Faxes: A Poem

YEAR	2014
GENRE	photobook, poetry
METHOD	found material, montage / remix, photocopy / scan
SUBJECT	analog / digital, error / corruption / loss, publishing / distribution, technology, visual culture
MATERIALITIES	black-and-white, paperback, perfect bound
PAGES	114 (unpaginated)
DESCRIPTION	*55 Faxes* introduces a definition of The Post-Art Poets' central practice of counterpublishing in the form of a dictionary entry. Similar to *Der Klaus*, the book results from "the juxtaposition of portions of 55 faxes that were tweeted by @visitordesign between 1/13/14 and 1/29/14 and counterpublished versions of those fax portions by The Post-Art Poets" (blurb on Blurb). The original faxes, set on the left side of each double-page spread, are distorted, often abstract black-and-white images, created by glitches in outdated technology. The Post-Art Poets' responses, set on the right side of each spread, mirror this distortion, but the images have been digitally glitched even more, making the two sides almost indistinguishable even though they come from very different media.

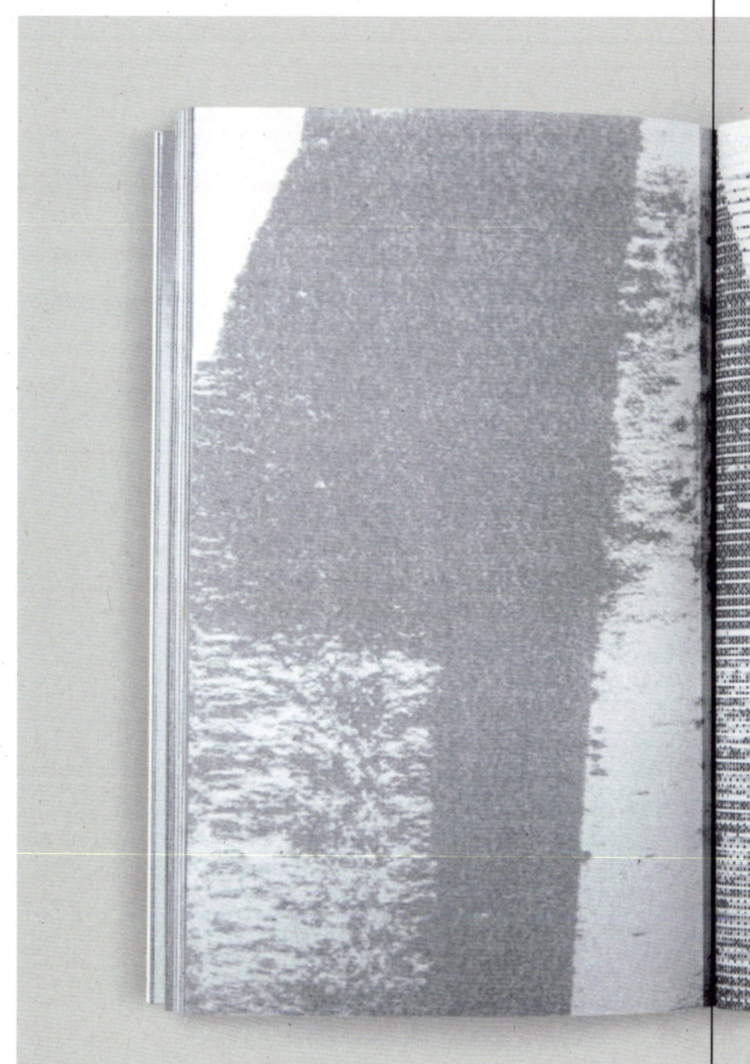

Rhizomebook

AUTHOR	Jan van der Til
YEAR	since 2013
GENRE	artistic research
METHOD	composition (writing / drawing / photography), study / analysis, test / experiment
SUBJECT	book / book design, ecology / sustainability, materiality, photography, publishing / distribution
PLATFORM	Blurb, others

IMAGE

DESCRIPTION

Book X and *Book XXXVIII* contribute to the ramified universe of books that Dutch artist Jan van der Til has been building since 2013 under the title *Rhizomebook* as "part of his ongoing research to create a new kind of book; a book that thinks with the world, not about the world" (Jan van der Til, "Introduction," website). To date (August 2022), the project includes forty-nine numbered volumes, all of which are loosely connected—rhizome-like—and yet can also stand alone. They are all titled *Book*, even though they are very different objects of a printed, digital, ephemeral, sculptural, or even horticultural nature. Van der Til understands "book" here as "synonymous with work," indicating "that it is a bundling of information that can be read, stored, reproduced, distributed and presented" (Jan van der Til, "Concepts of Work").

Book X: Copy

YEAR	2016
GENRE	artist's book / bookwork
METHOD	appropriation
SUBJECT	authorship, book / book design, photography, reading / interpretation
PLATFORM	Blurb
EDITION CHARACTERISTICS	open edition
FORMAT	21.6 × 27.9 cm
MATERIALITIES	color, paperback, perfect bound
PAGES	72 (unpaginated)

IMAGES

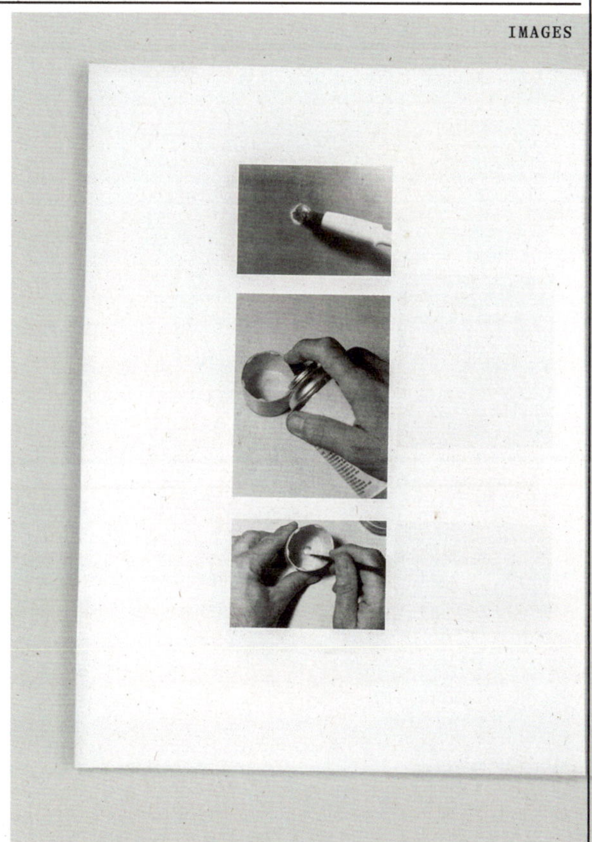

DESCRIPTION

The starting point for *Book X: Copy*, one of his few print-on-demand publications, is a how-to tutorial, here Arnd Terjung's *Zelf repareren van autolakschades* from 1985, which is copied 1:1, but with any text omitted. Therefore, the book itself does not contain any references to authorship, title, circumstances of publication, etc. This fits in with van der Til's reflections on his concept of works: "The boundaries between my work, original, and copy have gradually disappeared. [...] My ambition is to develop Books that are images" (Jan van der Til, "Further Reading").

All that remains are the photos of the tutorial, which "are meant to be instructive, they are meant to be as clear as possible, they are carefully staged and composed for this reason, but without their captions and taken out of context things are not so clear any more, the pictures take on a life of their own" (Joachim Schmid, "Doing Things"). If one did not know that it is paint damage depicted here, one might mistake the first series of images for shots of the sky or the sea with inexplicable artifacts. Left alone with the visuals, moreover, details like a woman's hands with a ring and nail polish suddenly come into view, which surprisingly seems to take over the "dirty work" toward the end of the book; suddenly, not only do the small, unassuming black-and-white photos seem outdated, but the DIY paint damage repair itself seems to have fallen out of time, because who still repairs their own cars anymore, and whose cars are getting so old these days that they rust through?

Book XXXVIII: Please tell me why

YEAR	2020
GENRE	artist's book / bookwork
METHOD	composition (writing / drawing / photography)
SUBJECT	book / book design, crowd / collaboration, economy / labor, publishing / distribution
PLATFORM	Blurb
EDITION CHARACTERISTICS	multiple editions (print, web), limited edition, available only as part of a series through ABC
FORMAT	17.0 × 24.0 cm
MATERIALITIES	color, paperback, perfect bound
PAGES	52 (unpaginated)
IMAGES	

DESCRIPTION

This book is part of the twenty-eight-piece series *ABC Days* (see 426), to which Jan van der Til was invited by Artists' Books Cooperative member Wil van Iersel in 2020. Each participant was to produce a book in a given format to be published each day as part of a series between June 11 and July 9, 2020. Most of the books reflect the news of that day or period, which was marked by the pandemic and Black Lives Matter protests. Jan van der Til, however, chooses as the theme of his day the invitation he received from van Iersel, and quotes, comments on, and fleshes it out for his own present book. While the other books in the series usually only have the date as a title, Jan van der Til provides his book, in the imprint, with a second title *Please tell me why* and declares it at the same time to be *Book XXXVIII* of his *Rhizomebook* project.

ASTORIA-MEGLER BRIDGE / AMERICA

AUTHOR	Wil van Iersel
YEAR	2013
GENRE	photobook, intermediate product / halbzeug
METHOD	found material, montage / remix, remediation
SUBJECT	book / book design, film, literature, maps / street view, writing / reading techniques
PLATFORM	Lulu, selfmade
EDITION CHARACTERISTICS	open edition, available only through the artist
FORMAT	11.5 × 6.5 cm
MATERIALITIES	black-and-white, paperback, perfect bound
PAGES	358 (unpaginated)

IMAGES

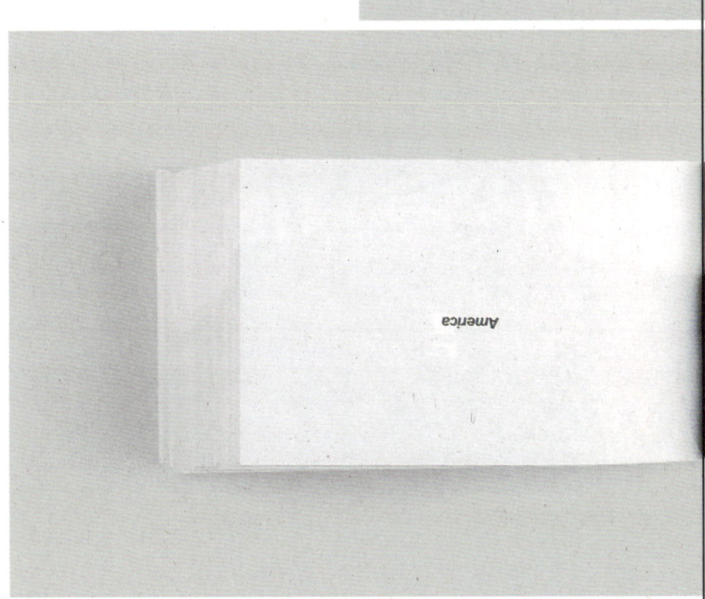

DESCRIPTION

This flip-book was created in the context of a twelve-minute stop-motion film made with screenshots from Google Street View. Under the title *VIEWFINDER*, van Iersel's film lines up 1,800 images of 196 steel construction bridges in the USA, over which the Google Street View car drives. For the flip-book, the artist chose images from the Astoria-Megler Bridge over the Columbia River in Oregon, USA. On the opposite page, Allen Ginsburg's 1956 poem "America" runs through the book. It is written as a stream of consciousness, and thus mirrors the photo series not only in its subject but also in its mode of writing.

The flip-book cannot be ordered directly through Lulu, as it requires further processing by the artist: Lulu's book block is cut into two books and rebound by the artist.

jim

AUTHOR	Éric Watier
YEAR	2013
GENRE	artist's book / bookwork
METHOD	composition (writing / drawing / photography), photocopy / scan
SUBJECT	error / corruption / loss, materiality, print technology, publishing / distribution
PLATFORM	Blurb
EDITION CHARACTERISTICS	open edition
FORMAT	15.2 × 22.9 cm
MATERIALITIES	black-and-white, paperback, perfect bound
PAGES	20 (unpaginated)

IMAGES

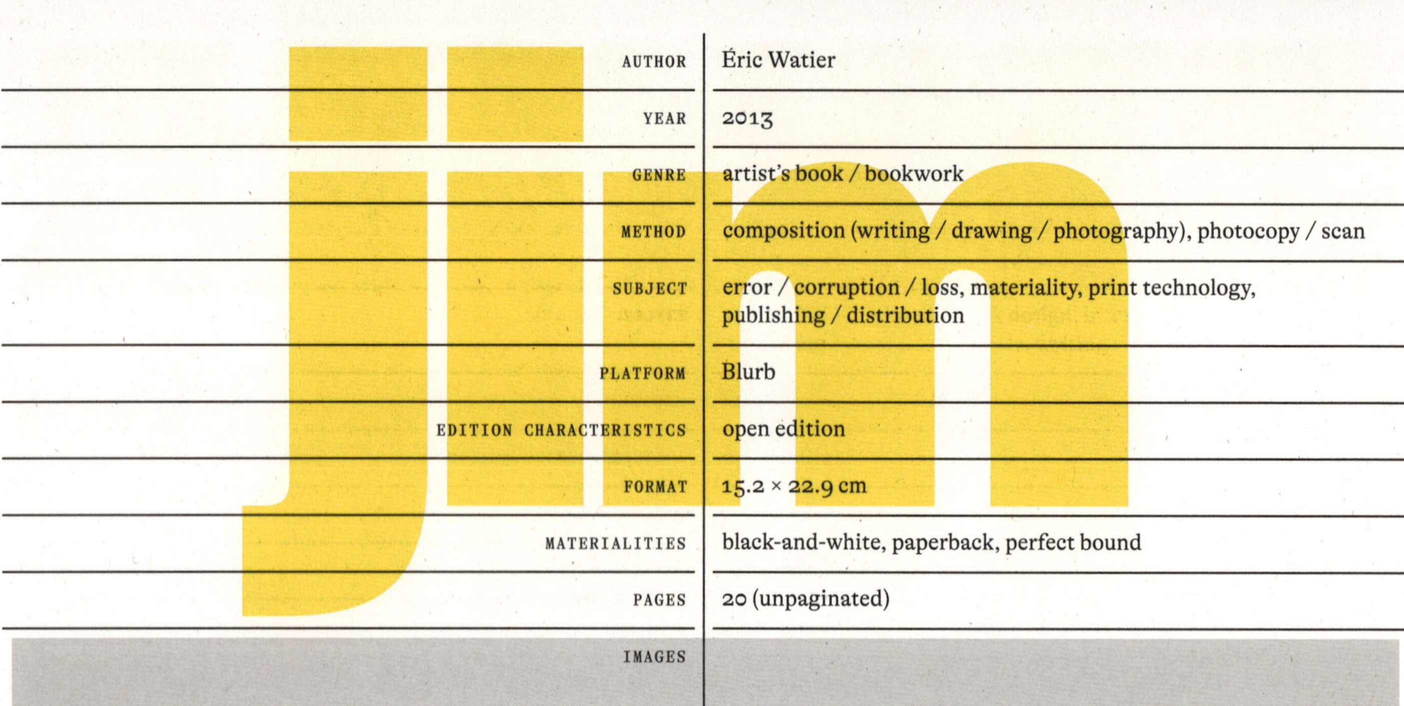

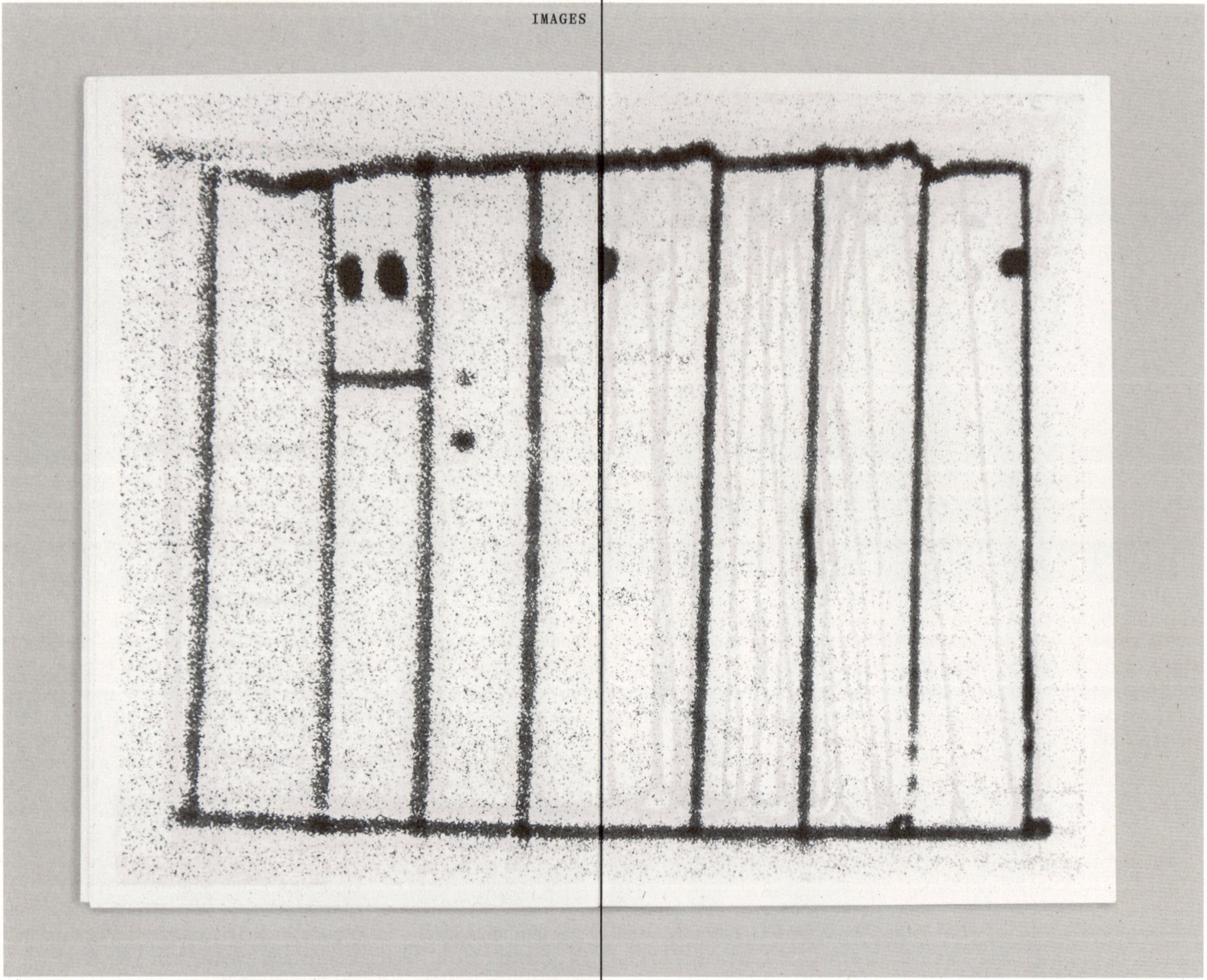

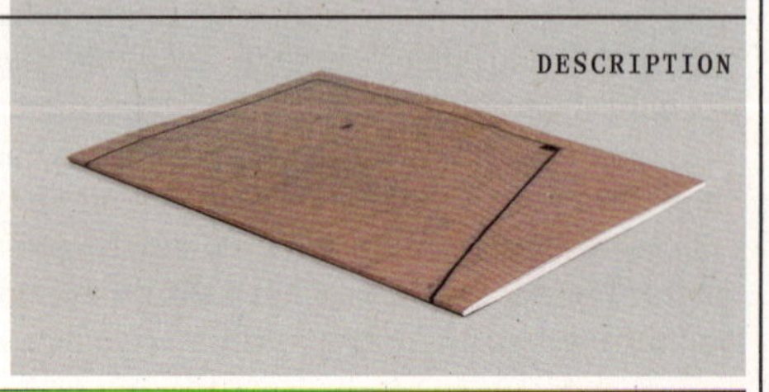

DESCRIPTION

This booklet by Éric Watier contains eleven drawings, scanned and reproduced as black-and-white prints with high contrast so that the paper texture, including creases etc., becomes visible. The drawings are from Watier's blog "jim is jim," which he started in late 2013 with the announcement, "For now it's a blog. It's a bit of a mess. I don't even know if it's good or totally naught. Maybe it'll become a book, unless it just ends up in the dustbin…" (Éric Watier, "jim is jim," website).

REAL KILL LIST

AUTHOR	Joey Yearous-Algozin
YEAR	2013
PUBLISHER	Troll Thread
GENRE	experimental literature
METHOD	documentation / archiving, found material, reformatting
SUBJECT	art world / literary world, bias, economy / labor, facebook, literature, politics / activism, social media
PLATFORM	Lulu
EDITION CHARACTERISTICS	multiple editions (print, PDF), open edition
FORMAT	21.6 × 27.9 cm
MATERIALITIES	color, paperback, saddle stitch bound
PAGES	13 (unpaginated)
IMAGES	

DESCRIPTION

REAL KILL LIST documents a thread of Facebook comments reacting to Josef Kaplan's conceptual poem *Kill List* (Cars Are Real, 2013). *Kill List* consists of 232 names of contemporary American poets in alphabetical order, arranged in fifty-eight four-line stanzas, with each name followed by either "is a rich poet" or "is comfortable." With this, Kaplan not only provoked discussions on class and poetry but also on the ethics of conceptual writing and canon. These discussions took place mostly on social media.

Joey Yearous-Algozin's *REAL KILL LIST* copies the sixty-three posts found in the comment section of Magdalena Zurawski's Facebook post "Josef Kaplan: I am insulted. I am comfortable and not on your list. You must not think I am a FUCKING POET," including all formattings, links, likes, names, and profile pictures.

REAL KILL LIST shifts the focus from the poets Kaplan deems capitalist to poets who care to discuss the morality of such a list and whether or not they are on the list. By suggesting that this is the "real kill list," Yearous-Algozin moves the discussion from capitalism to capitalist beliefs, and the viewpoint of an individual poet subjectively defining a canon to the seemingly more objective one of poets putting themselves on the list. This conceptual approach, however, is no less subjective, as Yearous-Algozin selects the Facebook thread and also actively participates in the discussion himself, as is indicated by an "Unlike" button that can be used to retract a "Like"—an option available only to the logged-in user.

The blurb on Lulu, kept in Troll Thread's typical how-to style, promises, "HOW TO BE SOCIAL."

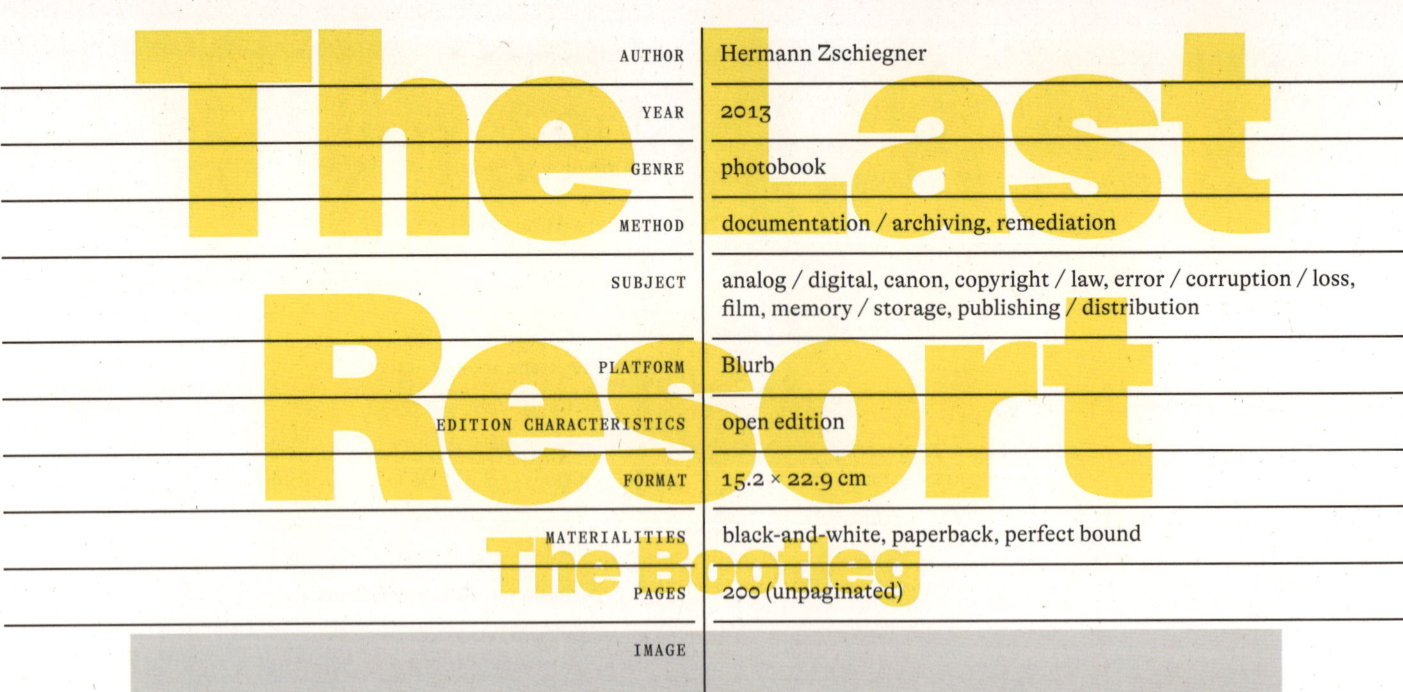

The Last Resort The Bootleg

AUTHOR	Hermann Zschiegner
YEAR	2013
GENRE	photobook
METHOD	documentation / archiving, remediation
SUBJECT	analog / digital, canon, copyright / law, error / corruption / loss, film, memory / storage, publishing / distribution
PLATFORM	Blurb
EDITION CHARACTERISTICS	open edition
FORMAT	15.2 × 22.9 cm
MATERIALITIES	black-and-white, paperback, perfect bound
PAGES	200 (unpaginated)
IMAGE	

DESCRIPTION

This book is part of Hermann Zschiegner's Bootleg editions (see also 240), a series of books reproducing famous photobooks that are no longer easily obtainable (due to being out of stock or very expensive). Their reproduction is based on flip-through videos: a presentation form for books used on video platforms to show their materiality as well as parts of their content. Zschiegner's series is "[i]nspired by movie bootleggers who film new release movies with handheld video cameras and sell them as cheap DVDs on the street, the bootleg books are both a commentary on the economics of distribution and the transformative element of digital content across various media" (Hermann Zschiegner, "Bootleg Books").

The Last Resort (1986) is a classic photobook by Martin Parr that not only revolutionized documentary photography but also made Parr one of the most famous photographers of our time, and the book (which has long been out of print) a hard-to-get collector's item. In an approach that is still controversial, Parr took voyeuristic images of people spending time in New Brighton, a rather run-down beach area near Liverpool. Zschiegner took screenshots of a YouTube review of the book to recreate the book page by page for his bootleg, not only showing its immediate surroundings but also hands touching the pages and pages in motion, creating an extremely mediated version of the book.

In a satirical column "The Worst Photo Books of 2013," published on the Artists' Books Cooperative blog (of which Zschiegner is a founding member), his book is announced with the words: "*The Last Resort (The Bootleg)* by Hermann Zschiegner is the last book I would buy. Did Zschiegner not know that the original book is in colour? And what are all those silly hands doing there? It is an insult to the Gods of photobooks, Martin Parr and Gerry Badger" (ABC, "The Worst Photo Books").

Even though this reproduction is of very low quality due to the remediation and all pages being black-and-white, Zschiegner no longer lists this bootleg on his website. This is allegedly due to copyright reasons as Parr's *The Last Resort* has been republished in recent years. Zschiegner's bootleg can still be ordered via Blurb's webshop but—apart from its title—has all paratext removed and a blank preview so as to no longer infringe copyright, this time turning the bootleg into a hard-to-find edition of the original.

THE LAST RESORT
photographs of New Brighton
MARTIN PARR
GERRY BADGER

This is where

AUTHOR	Erin Zwaska
YEAR	2013
GENRE	experimental literature, photobook
METHOD	found material, generative / automation, montage / remix, versioning / seriality
SUBJECT	google, maps / street view, narration, twitter
PLATFORM	Lulu
VOLUMES	3
EDITION CHARACTERISTICS	open edition
MATERIALITIES	color, paperback, saddle stitch bound, defective copies

IMAGES

DESCRIPTION

This is where is "an ongoing chance-based publication project, which explores the increasingly immaterial nature of place. The images are randomly-selected Google street views (which are often captured at noon to avoid shadowing) of cities like Paris, Tokyo, etc. [Each] copy is compiled from all tweets containing the phrase 'this is where' between noon and 12:15pm local time for each city. Consequently the text and imagery for each 15-minute issue originates from the same, albeit ambiguous, time and place. And though text and image are randomly paired, surprising narratives often emerge" (blurb on Lulu).

The Paris edition, for example, appropriately begins with the tweet: "This is where the book begins; the rest is still unwritten," which corresponds well with the photo of a path leading into a forest. Mostly, though, as is common in social media, the tweets are very personal: "This is where you sent me!!!! Love you all so much!" or "My sweet baby this is where the game ends now," while the pictures, instead of urban hustle and bustle in the three metropolises, surprisingly often show deserted streets in rather rural landscapes or desolate areas. The design of the books, especially the changing arrangement of the photos on the spread and the use of blank pages, breathes the spirit of Ed Ruscha.

The copies we ordered have significant trimming and binding errors. In *Mexico City* and *Tokyo*, the page numbers are cut off in places. In *Paris*, the pages are in the wrong order (1–2 and 47–48 in the middle, instead of the beginning and end, of the booklet). According to Lulu, however, the trim is within the permitted range, and the artist should not have placed the page numbers so close to the edge.

This is where: Tokyo, Japan

FORMAT	14.5 × 20.5 cm
PAGES	63

This is where: Paris, France

FORMAT	14.8 × 21.0 cm
PAGES	48

This is where: Mexico City

FORMAT	14.0 × 20.3 cm
PAGES	56

Vanessa Place... blocked

AUTHOR	38 Poets
YEAR	2014
GENRE	experimental literature
METHOD	documentation / archiving
SUBJECT	art world / literary world, authorship, censorship / ban, facebook, gender, politics / activism, publishing / distribution, social media
PLATFORM	Lulu
EDITION CHARACTERISTICS	open edition
FORMAT	15.2 × 22.9 cm
MATERIALITIES	black-and-white, paperback, perfect bound
PAGES	115 (unpaginated)
IMAGES	

Poet I have absolutely no problems with negativity, in poems or otherwise, as anyone who knows me can affirm. But to propose that the nihilist capitalist attack emphasized and exemplified by VP is "revolutionary" seems a bit much. Maybe I'm reading you wrong, but if VP is a revolutionary, then I am the reincarnation of Some Historical Revolutionary Politician and Theoretician.
9 hours ago · Like · 2

Poet "Dissonance is the truth about harmony."

"Triviality is evil - triviality, that is, in the form of consciousness and mind that adapts itself to the world as it is, that obeys the principle of inertia. And this principle of inertia truly is what is radically evil."

I'm neither for or against being for or against VP. I just don't get the hubbub. I see she made a cruel citation with the "That Book" blurb, but it wasn't evil, surely. I don't know, following Some Canonical Twentieth-Century Philosopher, here, for kicks, that dismissing VP constitutes an act of authoritarian intolerance towards ambiguity... It does remind me of Some App, which is awesome.

Thanksbe to Some Other Social Media Site for fastquote.
8 hours ago · Edited · Like

DESCRIPTION

"From 2012 to 2014, the poet and artist Vanessa Place regularly re-posted other poets' Facebook status updates as if they were her own. One such update, reprinted as the cover of this book, prompted a poet to block Place. Thirty-eight poets responded to his announcement 'Vanessa Place... blocked'" ("Publisher's preface").

Vanessa Place... blocked collects ninety-four comments that were found under this Facebook post. These comments can be categorized into two types: the first consisting of comments typical for discussions on social media such as insulting, raging, derailing, off-topic posts that display a general disinterest in the topic discussed; and the second consisting of detailed discussions on the implications and stakes of Place's appropriations. The comments also repeatedly come back to the topic of gender, discussing it as a focal point of practices of appropriation.

To conceal the identity of those whose comments are included in the book, most proper names of publishers, institutions, etc. are replaced with common nouns, and the names of all poets are replaced with "poet." This reproduces the gesture of appropriation Place initially used in her Facebook reposts, where she replaced the name of the author of the original posts not with her own, but with the more generic term "poet," exposing the posts as an unoriginal means of self-promotion whose content is comparable to any other marketing content. It is only logical that the real author of this book hides behind the name "38 poets" on the Lulu page.

AUTHOR	ABC [Artists' Books Cooperative]
YEAR	2014 [2nd ed. 2022]
GENRE	artist's book / bookwork, catalog / collection, exhibition copy
METHOD	collection, collective, composition (writing / drawing / photography), constraint
SUBJECT	art world / literary world, book / book design, canon, crowd / collaboration, print on demand
PLATFORM	Blurb, Copyshop, Newspaper Club, Online-Druck.biz, selfmade
VOLUMES	first edition: 22 vols., second edition: 27 vols.
EDITION CHARACTERISTICS	second edition, limited edition, available only as set through the artists
MATERIALITIES	box

IMAGES

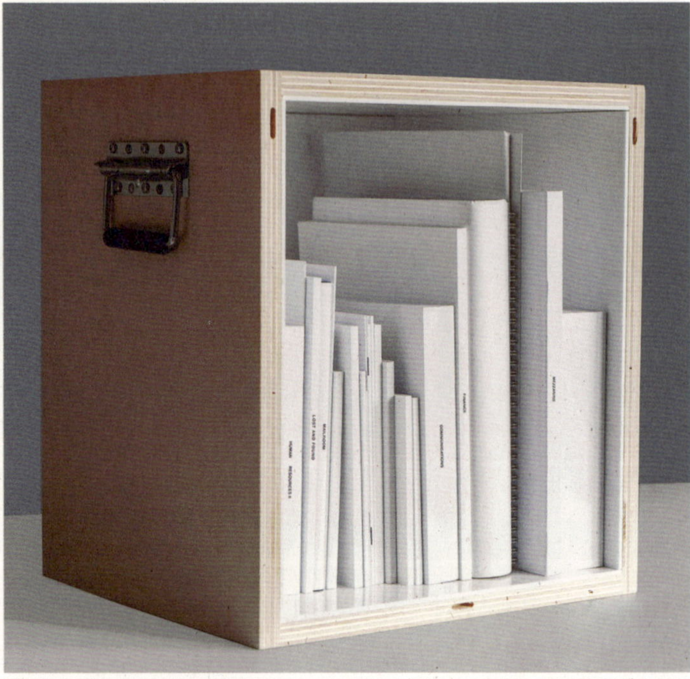

DESCRIPTION

As the portmanteau word in the title suggests, *ABCEUM* brings together the Artists' Books Cooperative (ABC), which specializes in the (print-on-demand) artist's or photobook, and the institution of the museum: "*ABCEUM* re-imagines the museum as a book installation," says the accompanying text on the project website (ABC, "ABCEUM: Information"). It is composed of twenty-two self-published publications in the first edition of 2014 and twenty-seven in the second edition of 2022. They vary greatly in size, content, and style, but are given a common "corporate identity" by Paul Soulellis's uniform cover design.

They each represent different spaces and functions of a museum—from finance, human resources, and public relations; to archive, mail, and storeroom; to sculpture garden, visitor services, café, and shop—and are presented in a custom-made display system that changed depending on the exhibition location: In 2014 at Offprint Paris, two vitrines designed by Louis Porter were used that "were intended to resemble museum floor plans and in their material echo the museological, through the use of Evazote, a dense museum grade polyethelene foam. The 'floor plan' [which visitors can 'wander through'] was laser cut into the foam to connect it with the principle of Print on Demand that runs through the Artists' Books Cooperative" (Louis Porter, "ABCEUM," website). In 2015 at Offprint at Tate Modern London, the work was shown on magazine stands in reference to John Carpenter's science-fiction cult film *They Live*. And for the 2022 edition, a simple museum crate was made to fit the work (and the size of the shelf in the Bavarian State Library) so that the display system also serves as packaging.

It is not only the type of installation and presentation that changed over time. Like a "real" museum, *ABCEUM* was designed from the beginning with the possibility of a changing "exhibition program" and expansion. Our request to purchase a set for the Library of Artistic Print on Demand was taken as an opportunity by the collective to ask the artists who have joined ABC since the first edition in 2014 to contribute, so that a "new wing" of four new publications has now been added to the museum, with the indispensable departments of janitor's closet, souvenirs, preservation, archival provenance authentication section, and bookkeeping.

In his essay on the project, ABC member Duncan Wooldridge calls the result of this collective production a "Museum on Demand" that reflects the changes that the museum institution has undergone: "Today, the museum is made from what was once its marginalia. Comprised mainly of spaces that are not the galleries themselves, it has inflated its operations and stretched its parameters, respondent to social and economic pressures alike. In the 24/7 culture of presentness, it has become a museum on demand—a non-stop institution, with culture on tap" (Duncan Wooldridge, "Abceum (Museum on Demand)"). With the *ABCEUM*, an "alternative and collective model of the museum" is simultaneously set against it, where—as in the entire practice of ABC—„[c]ooperation is no longer geographically determined: it may function remotely, and use its span as a strength. […] It is dispersed but communicative, it exists in multiple formats" (Ibid.).

FINANCE

AUTHOR	Mishka Henner
YEAR	2014
PLATFORM	Blurb
FORMAT	21.6 × 26.8 cm
MATERIALITIES	black-and-white, paperback, perfect bound
PAGES	196
DESCRIPTION	Tax Return forms sent to the Department of the Treasury Internal Revenue Service by MoMA between 2009–2011. Accession Number: 2014.001.001

MARKETING

AUTHOR	Mishka Henner
YEAR	2014
PLATFORM	Copyshop
FORMAT	21.6 × 29.7 cm
MATERIALITIES	color, paperback, wire-o bound
PAGES	26
DESCRIPTION	Design guidelines for all *ABCEUM* marketing and promotional materials, including information on logo use, fonts, poster, signage, leaflets, and stationary layouts. Accession Number: 2014.001.002

PAINT

AUTHOR	Travis Shaffer
YEAR	2014
PLATFORM	selfmade
FORMAT	20.3 × 25.4 cm
MATERIALITIES	broadsheet, color, folded, inkjet with white pigment in plastic bag
PAGES	1
DESCRIPTION	Sample kit and necessary instructions for the production and use of Blanc de Chaux. Accession Number: 2014.001.003

MEZZANINE

AUTHOR	Andreas Schmidt
YEAR	2014
PLATFORM	Blurb
FORMAT	30.5 × 30.5 cm
MATERIALITIES	color, dust jacket, hardcover, side sewn
PAGES	208
DESCRIPTION	Exhibition catalog for Andreas Schmidt's Unique Artist's Books series *MMXIV*, first shown on the Mezzanine level of the *ABCEUM* in 2014. Accession Number: 2014.001.004

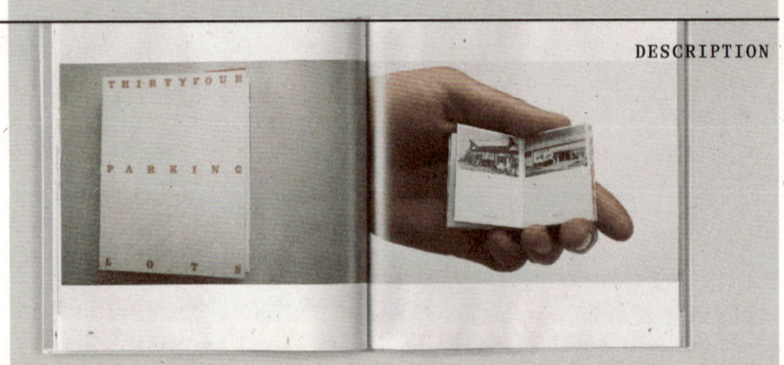

HUMAN RESOURCES I & II

AUTHOR	Andreas Schmidt
YEAR	2014
PLATFORM	Blurb
VOLUMES	2
FORMAT	24.9 × 21.1 cm
MATERIALITIES	color, dust jacket, hardcover, side sewn
PAGES	440
DESCRIPTION	Featuring IPad Mini screenshots of the Facebook profile pages of all of Andreas Schmidt's Facebook friends who represented themselves with a camera on Facebook, June 13, 2014. Accession Numbers: 2014.001.005 and 2014.001.006

NEW MEDIA

AUTHOR	Paul Soulellis
YEAR	2014
PLATFORM	Newspaper Club
FORMAT	38.1 × 26.4 cm
MATERIALITIES	color, newsprint
PAGES	32
DESCRIPTION	The first 420 videos posted to YouTube by Webdriver Torso. Accession Number: 2014.001.007

CORPORATE PARTNERS PROGRAM

AUTHOR	Fred Free
YEAR	2014
PLATFORM	Blurb
FORMAT	24.0 × 20.2 cm
MATERIALITIES	color, paperback, perfect bound
PAGES	130
DESCRIPTION	Documents the first 126 businesses targeted as potential financial, material and/or spiritual supporters of the *ABCEUM*. Accession Number: 2014.001.008

PUBLIC RELATIONS

AUTHOR	Fred Free
YEAR	2014
PLATFORM	Blurb
FORMAT	12.7 × 20.3 cm
MATERIALITIES	black-and-white, paperback, perfect bound
PAGES	24
DESCRIPTION	Documents every comment left by the viewing public regarding an artist's book on display at an online gallery since 2006. Accession Number: 2014.001.009

MAILROOM

AUTHOR	Mocksim
YEAR	2014
PLATFORM	Blurb
FORMAT	16.0 × 23.6 cm
MATERIALITIES	black-and-white, dust jacket, hardcover
PAGES	104
DESCRIPTION	One-hundred Point of Delivery Signature images collected from courier company parcel tracking systems during 2012 and 2013. Accession Number: 2014.001.010

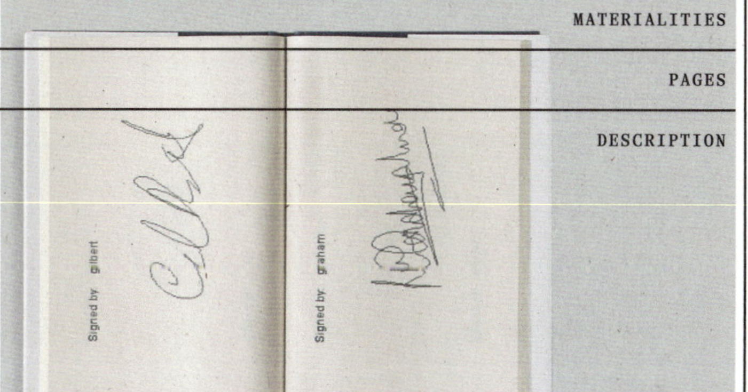

STOREROOM

AUTHOR	Tanja Lažetić
YEAR	2014
PLATFORM	selfmade
EDITION CHARACTERISTICS	limited edition, unique copies
FORMAT	23.0 × 30.0 cm
MATERIALITIES	black-and-white, dust jacket, perfect bound
PAGES	730
DESCRIPTION	A readymade: one book of eight volumes of the 1955 to 1971 *Encyclopedia of Yugoslavia*, wrapped in a white cover. Accession Number: 2014.001.011

CAFE (I Dolci di Amici delgi Uffizi)

AUTHOR	Erik Benjamins
YEAR	2014
PLATFORM	Newspaper Club
FORMAT	26.4 × 37.6 cm
MATERIALITIES	color, folded, newsprint
PAGES	1
DESCRIPTION	A fold-out poster in Italian of eight drawings of pastries from various Florentine museum cafes. Accession Number: 2014.001.012

SHOP

AUTHOR	Jonathan Lewis
YEAR	2014
PLATFORM	Blurb
FORMAT	19.8 × 24.9 cm
MATERIALITIES	color, paperback, perfect bound
PAGES	26
DESCRIPTION	Illustrating the pop song, *The Model*, by the German electronic music band Kraftwerk with photographs of various incarnations of the *Mona Lisa*. Accession Number: 2014.001.013

LOST AND FOUND

AUTHOR	Louis Porter
YEAR	2014
PLATFORM	Ripe Digital
FORMAT	19.3 × 24.1 cm
MATERIALITIES	color, paperback, perfect bound
PAGES	126
DESCRIPTION	A collection of posters generated by a website allowing individuals to upload images and a short text describing last known whereabouts of missing pets and belongings. Accession Number: 2014.001.014

PHOTOGRAPHICS

AUTHOR	Louis Porter
YEAR	2014
PLATFORM	Blurb
FORMAT	12.7 × 20.3 cm
MATERIALITIES	black-and-white, paperback, perfect bound
PAGES	102
DESCRIPTION	Illustrations taken from early photographic manuals. Accession Number: 2014.001.015

ARCHIVE

AUTHOR	EJ Major
YEAR	2014
PLATFORM	Blurb
FORMAT	20.3 × 25.4 cm
MATERIALITIES	black-and-white, paperback, perfect bound
PAGES	66
DESCRIPTION	Pictures and newspaper cuttings from the early 1900s relating to the struggle for women's Suffrage. Accession Number: 2014.001.016

COMMUNICATIONS

AUTHOR	Eric Doeringer
YEAR	2014
PLATFORM	Blurb
FORMAT	21.6 × 21.6 cm
MATERIALITIES	black-and-white, paperback, perfect bound
PAGES	620
DESCRIPTION	Over 600 variations of the phrase "i am not still alive, on kawara," inspired by the works of On Kawara, Sol LeWitt, and by Kawara's death earlier this year. Accession Number: 2014.001.017

BOARDROOM

AUTHOR	Wil van Iersel
YEAR	2014
PLATFORM	Online-Druck.biz
FORMAT	21.1 × 14.7 cm
MATERIALITIES	color, paperback, perfect bound
PAGES	88
DESCRIPTION	Presenting thirty-nine color pictures found on the internet. Imagining the global discussion about the place of culture in today's society. Accession Number: 2014.001.018

SCULPTURE GARDEN

AUTHOR	Duncan Wooldridge
YEAR	2014
PLATFORM	Blurb
FORMAT	17.0 × 16.8 cm
MATERIALITIES	color, paperback, perfect bound
PAGES	92
DESCRIPTION	Public works of art as reproduced and rendered into three dimensions by Apple's mapping software. Accession Number: 2014.001.019

VISITOR SERVICES

AUTHOR	Duncan Wooldridge
YEAR	2014
PLATFORM	Blurb
FORMAT	17.0 × 16.8 cm
MATERIALITIES	color, paperback, perfect bound
PAGES	38
DESCRIPTION	From the social media pages of Los Angeles County Museum of Art, entitled "LACMA + You," showing visitors imitating the poses of works and objects in and around the museum. Accession Number: 2014.001.020

WALLS

AUTHOR	Hermann Zschiegner
YEAR	2014
PLATFORM	Blurb
FORMAT	15.2 × 22.9 cm
MATERIALITIES	color, paperback, perfect bound
PAGES	100
DESCRIPTION	A participatory project bringing together fifty artists that took photos of an empty wall in close proximity to a work of art they feel connected to. Accession Number: 2014.001.021 (not included in the 2022 ABCEUM box).

GRASS, GRAVEL AND PAVING

AUTHOR	Oliver Griffin
YEAR	2014
PLATFORM	Blurb
FORMAT	13.2 × 21.1 cm
MATERIALITIES	color, paperback, perfect bound
PAGES	34
DESCRIPTION	Presents a guide to the exterior flooring materials of several well known museums. Accession Number: 2014.001.022

PRESERVATION

AUTHOR	Claudia de la Torre
YEAR	2022
PLATFORM	Blurb
FORMAT	14.8 × 21.0 cm
MATERIALITIES	paperback, perfect bound
PAGES	800
DESCRIPTION	"Pages displayed in open volumes may be overlaid with facsimiles to protect the opening from light exposure. When facsimiles cannot be used, consider rotating items on exhibit or turning the pages on a regular schedule. Although exhibiting a volume closed instead of open is less stressful to the book, remember that most book cover materials will be damaged by long-term light exposure. Therefore, even closed volumes should be shown for limited periods of time with low light levels." Extract from *Guidelines on Exhibiting Archival Materials*, published by the International Council on Archives. Accession Number: 2022.002.023

JANITOR'S CLOSET

AUTHOR	David Schulz
YEAR	2022
PLATFORM	Blurb
FORMAT	14.8 × 21.0 cm
MATERIALITIES	paperback, perfect bound
PAGES	4
DESCRIPTION	The performative, pictorial, and plastic experiences of a janitor in the context of a contemporary art historical timeline. Accession Number: 2022.002.024

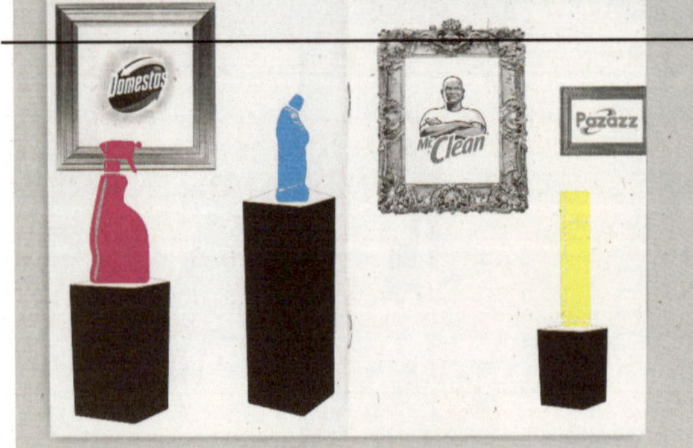

SOUVENIR

AUTHOR	George Grace Gibson
YEAR	2022
PLATFORM	Blurb
FORMAT	10.6 × 17.2 cm
MATERIALITIES	paperback, perfect bound
PAGES	116
DESCRIPTION	George Gibson joined our project and all we got was this lousy penny! Accession Number: 2022.002.025

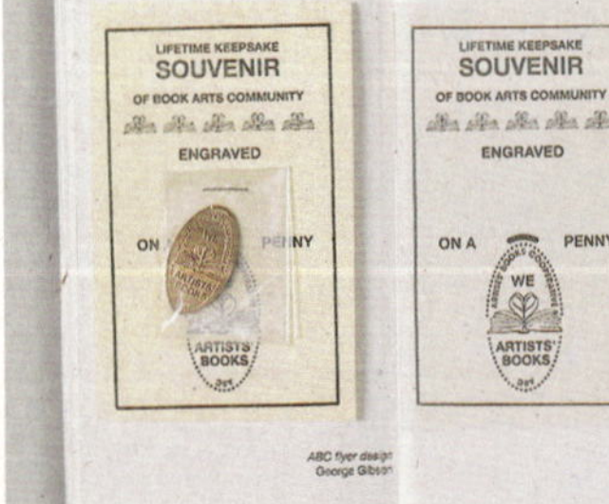

ARCHIVAL PROVENANCE AUTHENTICATION SECTION

AUTHOR	Arnaud Desjardin
YEAR	2019
PLATFORM	Blurb
FORMAT	21.0 × 29.7 cm
MATERIALITIES	paperback, perfect bound
PAGES	62
DESCRIPTION	Facsimile of a bootleg edition of the press material from the *Section des Figures* (Figure Section) iteration of Marcel Broodthaers' *Musée D'Art Moderne, Departement des Aigles*. Accession Number: 2022.002.026

BOOKKEEPING

AUTHOR	Rahel Zoller
YEAR	2022
PLATFORM	Blurb
FORMAT	14.8 × 21.0 cm
MATERIALITIES	paperback, perfect bound
PAGES	20
DESCRIPTION	Illustrations taken from the *Catalogue of the Library Bureau*, Boston 1891. Accession Number: 2022.002.027

COVERS

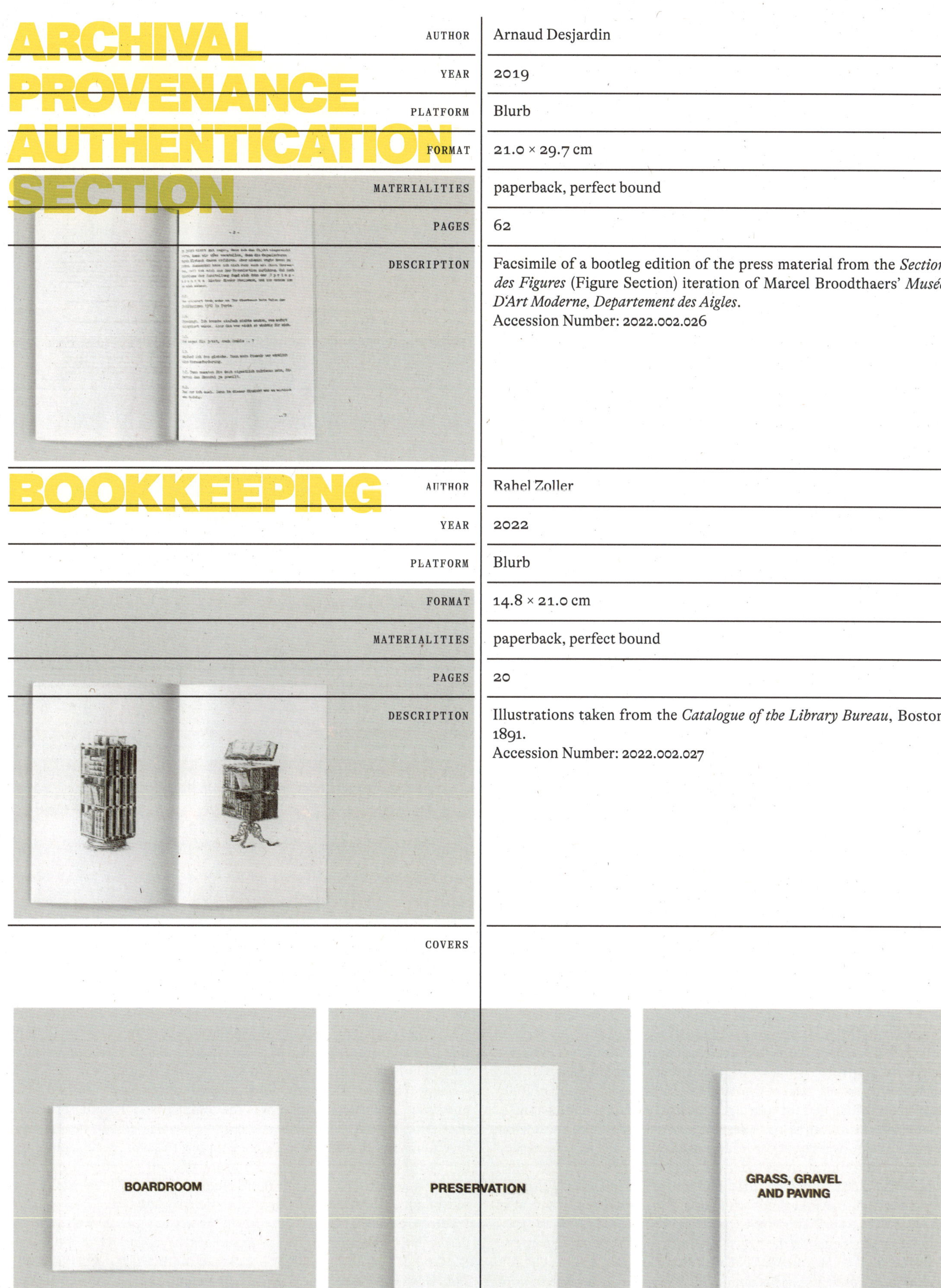

The Legacy of Totalitarianism in a Tundra

AUTHORS	Anonymous
YEAR	2014–2015
GENRE	experimental literature, fiction
METHOD	collective, composition (writing / drawing / photography)
SUBJECT	authorship, canon, crowd / collaboration, internet culture, literature, narration, publishing / distribution, social media, writing / reading techniques
PLATFORM	Lulu
VOLUMES	3
EDITION CHARACTERISTICS	multiple versions and editions (paperback, hardcover, black-and-white, color, PDF), open edition

IMAGE

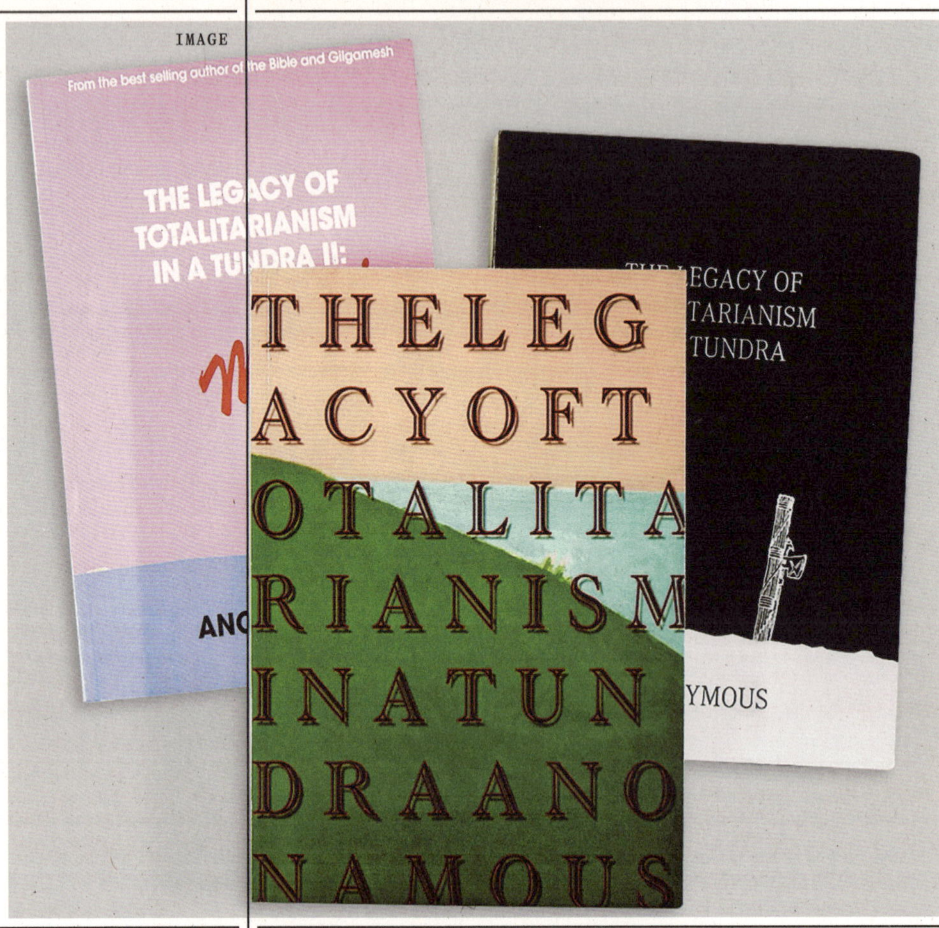

DESCRIPTION

The Legacy of Totalitarianism in a Tundra is a trilogy of novels written collectively on /lit/, the literature board of the infamous message board 4chan. Apart from its highly disparate and disturbing content, the collective approach is most evident in the massive alteration of fonts, font sizes, colors, and formatting, indicating the copy-and-pasting of chunks of text, as well as in the desperate attempts to end the text while someone else always seems to add or edit another chapter, paragraph, or word. An Anonymous stated in 4chan post #7370400 on November 19, 2015: "I didn't contribute to it, but I did delete all of the writing in the Google doc several times while it was being written." Typical responses to this are: "This is the true 4chan spirit."

On the Lulu page for the first volume, the writing and editing process is described as follows: "The very first page made me cringe, the part about him drinking his cum, so I changed it to say a very good drink that he made at home. I then suddenly lost interest. Today I reread the first few pages and saw that my edit remained and also that on the second page the opening scene is revisited and this time it says he is drinking his own cum which was alluded to by me very lazily earlier on in an attempt to edit it out as a very good drink he made at home. When I got to that part I cackled. I'm not sure if anyone else would find that funny but I think it justifies the silliness in him drinking his own cum" (blurb on Lulu).

Many 4chan posts celebrate the release of the printed book and post photos of their orders. The tenor of the comments is: "It's indescribable how great it feels to have shitposting in a physical form." People also recommend each other to use Lulu coupons to save: "Purchasing this book with that coupon code is /lit/ in and of itself." We found a screenshot of a sales statistic for the first volume on 4chan, which proves the sale of 201 units for September 2014 to January 2015.

There are several versions circulating the web as PDFs, as well as print-on-demand books (hardcover and paperback, black-and-white and color) flooding bookstores, making it impossible to trace down a definite version. However, most of the texts seem to be stable across these editions.

The first volume was followed by two more the following year: *The Legacy of Totalitarianism in a Tundra II: Miami* and *The Legacy of Totalitarianism in a Tundra 3: Tokyo Drift &Kolsti's Adventure in the Everglades A Rom-Com, An Neovella SUPER_COMBO.*

The Legacy of Totalitarianism in a Tundra

YEAR	2014
EDITION CHARACTERISTICS	ISBN 9781326017057 (according to the webshop, not shown in the book)
FORMAT	14.8 × 21.0 cm
MATERIALITIES	color, paperback, perfect bound
PAGES	474
IMAGE	

The Legacy of Totalitarianism in a Tundra II: Miami

YEAR	2015
FORMAT	13.8 × 21.5 cm
MATERIALITIES	color, paperback, perfect bound
PAGES	254
IMAGE	

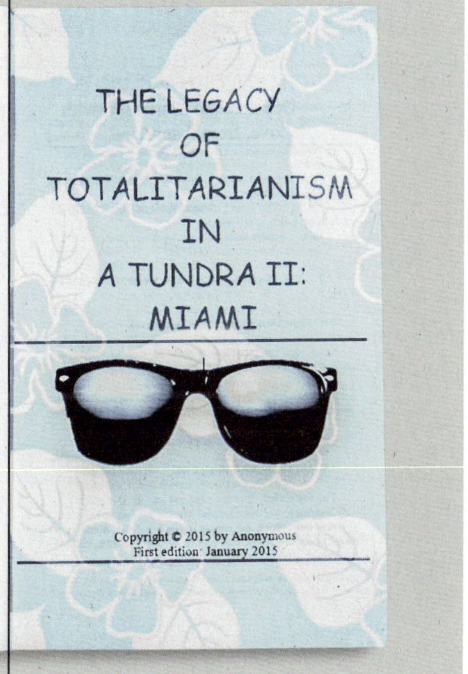

AUTHORS	Roberto Arista, Amato Luigi
YEAR	2014
GENRE	artist's book / bookwork
METHOD	composition (writing / drawing / photography), generative / automation
SUBJECT	book / book design, materiality, print technology
PLATFORM	Lulu
EDITION CHARACTERISTICS	ISBN 9781291977059, open edition
FORMAT	14.8 × 21.0 cm
MATERIALITIES	black-and-white, paperback, perfect bound
PAGES	740
IMAGES	

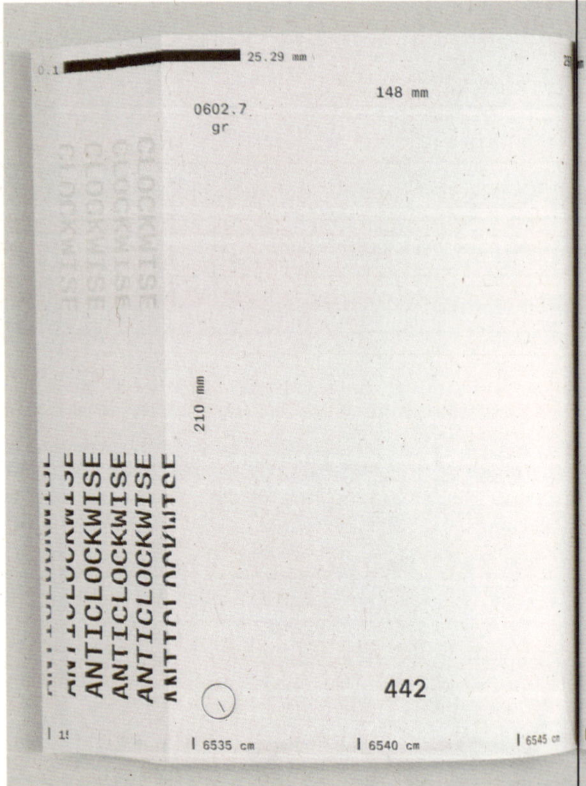

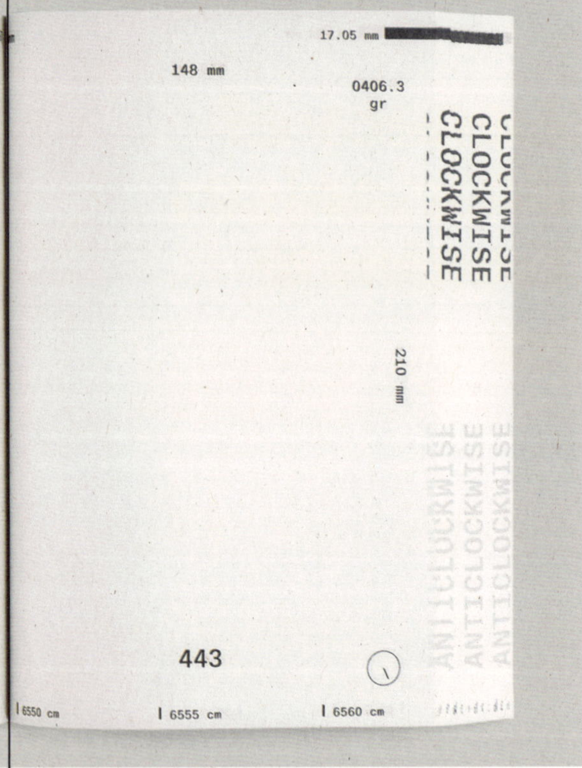

DESCRIPTION

Volume: A5 by Luigi Amato (concept/design) and Roberto Arista (code/development) is a book with completely self-reflective content. Using the Python-based graphic script environment DrawBot, the artists produced "a book displaying its own state during the act of browsing it" (Roberto Arista, "VLM," website).

Static data on the width and height of the individual pages and the double-page spread as well as the reading direction ("clockwise/anticlockwise") can be found on each page. This is complemented by procedural data such as page numbers and the distance measured across the pages that the reader traverses while reading. Added to this are the weight of the left and right-hand pages and the left and right spine heights. In the end, the book is delineated as both a static object and a procedural medium, with the exception of two blank pages at the end that were presumably added by the print-on-demand platform during the production process. The book is designed in such a way that the data, and thus the movement through the book, can be animated as in a flip book.

Things You Have Done

AUTHOR	Guy Bigland
YEAR	2014
GENRE	experimental literature
METHOD	generative / automation, montage / remix
SUBJECT	narration
PLATFORM	Blurb
EDITION CHARACTERISTICS	open edition
FORMAT	15.2 × 22.9 cm
MATERIALITIES	black-and-white, paperback, perfect bound
PAGES	24 (unpaginated)

IMAGES

DESCRIPTION

Guy Bigland's *Things You Have Done* contains a list of all the possible 100 combinations of ten nouns combined with ten past tense verbs, following the pattern of the book's title. Noun and verb are connected by the personal pronoun "you," so that the reader is addressed. Each page shows ten such combinations with the same ten nouns in stable alphabetical order and the same ten verbs always permuting accordingly: the last verb on one page moves to the first line of the next page. The result gives the impression of a checked-off bucket list of repetitive interactions with ANIMALS, BUILDINGS, CLOTHES, DREAMS, FOOD, OBJECTS, PEOPLE, PLACES, THOUGHTS, and WORDS. The book won the Sheffield International Artists' Book Prize 2015.

world 1-1

AUTHORS	Craig Dodman, Philip Miletic
YEAR	2014
PUBLISHER	The LUMA Foundation
GENRE	experimental literature
METHOD	composition (writing / drawing / photography), documentation / archiving
SUBJECT	games, tracking
PLATFORM	Lulu
EDITION CHARACTERISTICS	ISBN 9781304953957, open edition
FORMAT	10.0 × 17.0 cm
MATERIALITIES	black-and-white, paperback, perfect bound
PAGES	46 (unpaginated)

IMAGES

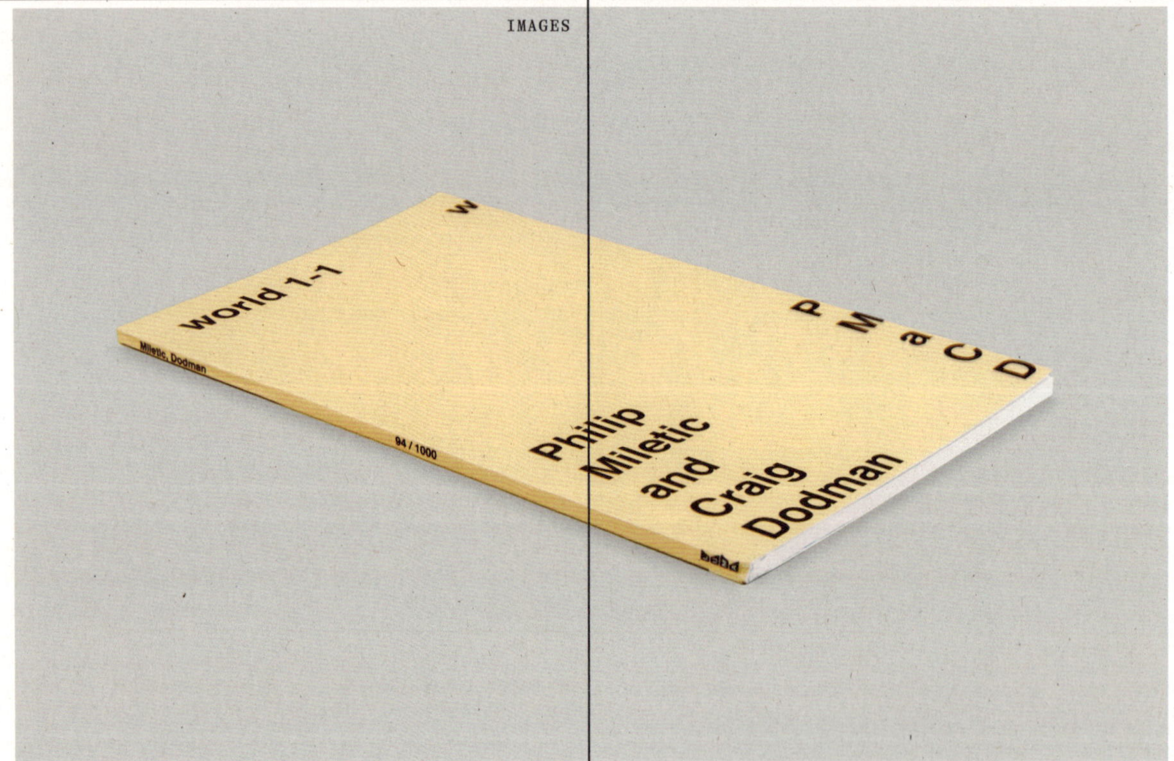

tactic 2

i walk forward. i jump and hit block. fall back into goomba. dead at nine seconds. score: 000200.

tactic 3

i walk forward. i walk back. i jump forward onto block and drop down. i jump and hit block. i walk forward. jump backw. i jump forward; obtain mushroom and grow. i jump back. jump and hit block. i walk forward, jump forward, run forward, jump, jump forward, jump forward, jump forward, jump forward. i run forward, jump forward. i jump, i jump and hit block. i walk forward and back and forward. i jump back and obtain flower. i jump. i jump forward, run forward, jump forward. i drop forward. i walk forward. i jump and hit block, jump, jump slightly forward and hit block and fall onto two goombas and hit a block. i jump back, jump back and obtain a flower. i jump forward, jump forward, jump forward. i walk and jump forward. i drop forward. i duck, turn left and then jump forward. i walk down blocks. i jump forward, i jump. i jump forward. i jump forward, run forward, jump forward. i jump and hit block. i jump slightly forward and hit block. i walk forward, jump forward. i

DESCRIPTION

"*world 1-1* consists of the various tactics employed by both craig dodman and philip miletic to play through world 1-1 of nintendo's classic NES title, *super mario bros*. this is the well-known level that started it all and the game that influenced future platform games. *world 1-1* may be the most basic and 'easiest' of levels, its strategy to ease the player into the game. yet, the tactics employed by each individual gamer use the provided virtual space in unique and playful ways" (Craig Dodman, Philip Miletic, "Introduction").

The book documents twenty-six attempts of the first level, by transcribing each movement with monotonous, pseudo-formalized language and ending with the score. This results in an abstract description of playthroughs that, reduced to mere text, add up to a narrow yet efficient impression of the level and refer to, but also contrast, machine learning algorithms that make use of such simple documentation.

This book was produced for the series *1000 Books by 1000 Poets* (edited by Danny Snelson) for the exhibition "Poetry Will Be Made By All!" (Zurich, January 30–March 30, 2014, curated by Kenneth Goldsmith, Simon Castets, and Hans Ulrich Obrist, see also 297, 303, 357). The back cover shows an incorrect ISBN that actually belongs to *Larmens antologi* by Joakim Vilandt (#75/1000).

WOODSLIPPERCOUNTERCLATTERTRANSCRIPT

AUTHOR	Edit Publications
YEAR	2014
GENRE	education / classroom, experimental literature
METHOD	collective, documentation / archiving, translation / transcription
SUBJECT	crowd / collaboration, memory / storage, writing / reading techniques
PLATFORM	Lulu
EDITION CHARACTERISTICS	multiple editions (print, PDF), open edition
FORMAT	19.0 × 19.0 cm
MATERIALITIES	color, paperback, perfect bound
PAGES	56 (unpaginated)

IMAGES

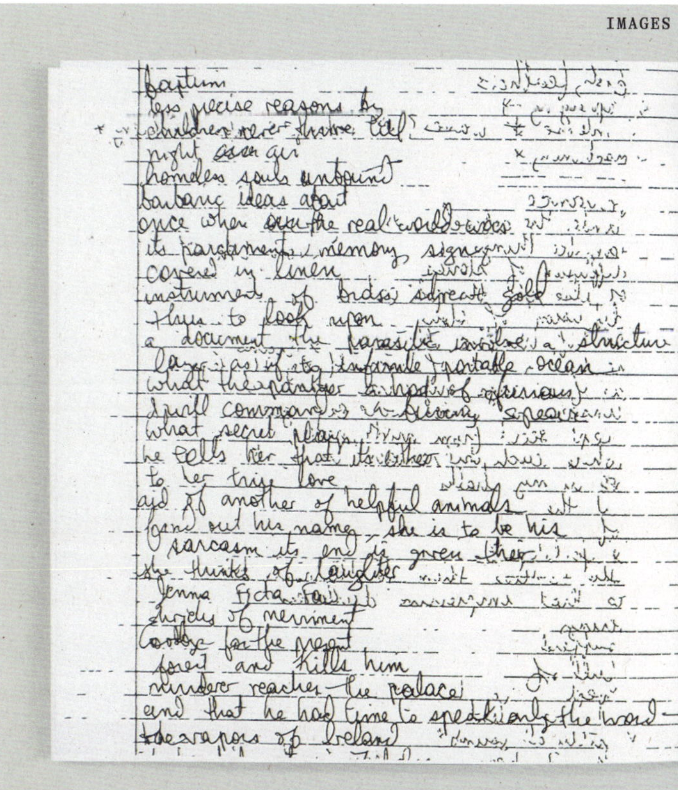

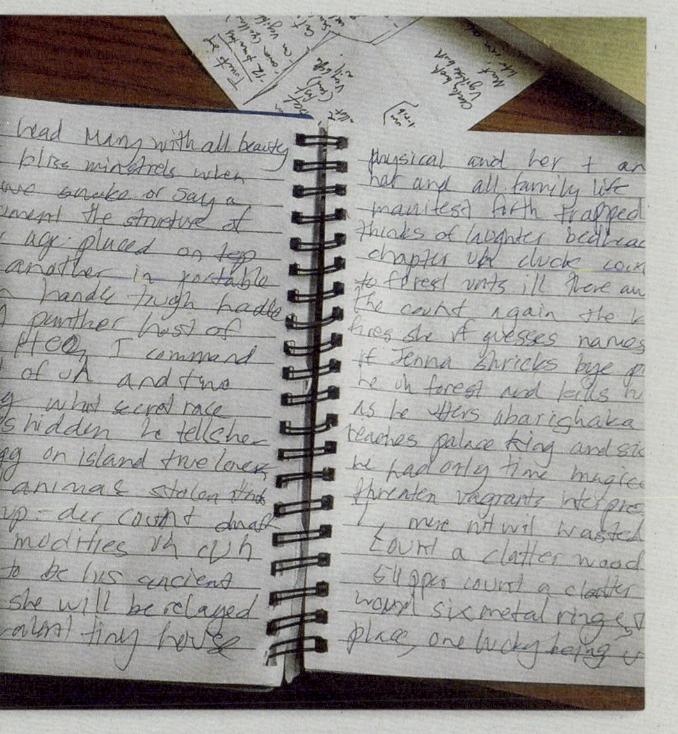

DESCRIPTION

According to Danny Snelson, *WOODSLIPPERCOUNTERCLATTER-TRANSCRIPT* is “the first of many course-collaboration Edit Publications” and “a representative sample of dozens of publishing experiments conducted as pedagogical exercises in a hybrid critical/creative educational studio practice” (Danny Snelson, “Edit Publications 2010–2020: 2014”). It stems from a collaborative transcription of the live performance *WOODSLIPPERCOUNTERCLATTER* by poet Susan Howe and musician David Grubbs in the context of Snelson’s 2014 class “21st-Century Creative Writing: Poetry, Technology, Art” at the University of Pennsylvania.

The publication arranges photographs and scans of the transcriptions made during the performance, anonymized, shuffled, and cropped to fit the publication’s square format. Most are handwritten notes on spiral-bound notebooks; only one is a screenshot from a Google Doc. Because of the difficult-to-read handwriting, random order, and sometimes poor reproduction quality, the materiality and diagrammatic arrangement of the transcriptions is emphasized over conveying the spoken word during the performance. In this way, the collective note-taking practice echoes the performance’s focus on the materiality of language.

Camouflaged Books

AUTHOR	Jasper Otto Eisenecker
YEAR	2014–2016
GENRE	artistic research, education / classroom
METHOD	détournement / hack, found material, study / analysis, test / experiment
SUBJECT	book / book design, censorship / ban, platforms / companies, politics / activism, print on demand
PLATFORM	Lulu
VOLUMES	4
EDITION CHARACTERISTICS	open edition, partially censored

IMAGE

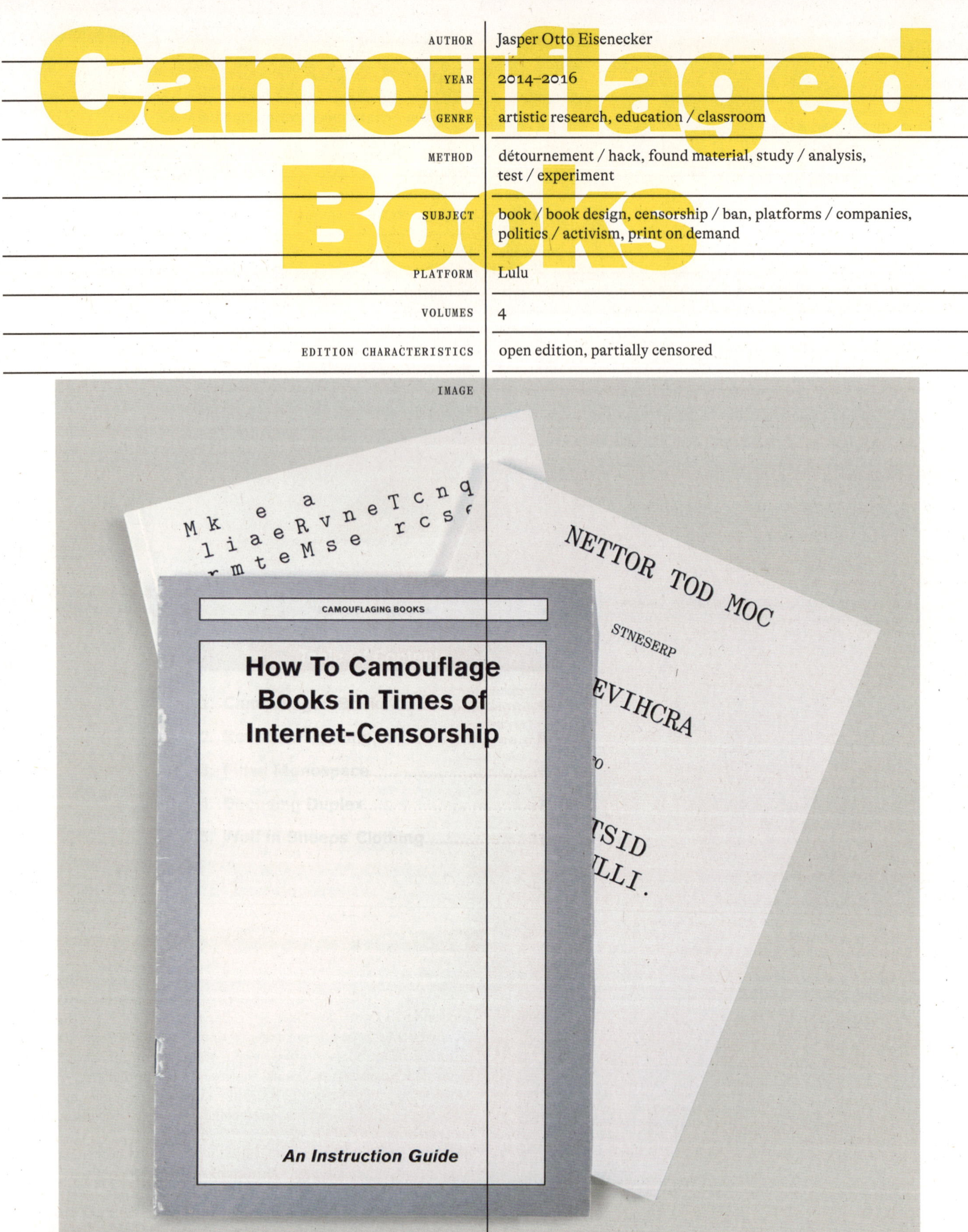

DESCRIPTION

Jasper Otto Eisenecker's *Camouflaged Books* is a subversive experimental publishing project that examines the content moderation and censorship mechanisms of print-on-demand platforms, using Lulu as an example. "After getting censored for publishing off-limits gore content, visual [and textual] strategies were developed to make incriminated content available again. The camouflaged version of the publication was republished successfully, without being detected by automatic checks and censorship mechanisms on the print-on-demand platform Lulu. To share the knowledge about how to camouflage books in times of internet-censorship, the artist designed an instruction manual" (Jasper Otto Eisenecker, "Camouflaged Books," website).

Experiment 01: Publishing a book full of offensive content at LULU

YEAR	2014
GENRE	photobook
METHOD	found material, test / experiment
SUBJECT	censorship / ban, platforms / companies
EDITION CHARACTERISTICS	censored, no longer available

DESCRIPTION

After finding books such as Hitler's *Mein Kampf* in Lulu's webshop, the artist wondered if one could actually publish and print anything on Lulu or if there was some kind of content moderation. As *Experiment 01*, he conceived a publication whose entire visual material was taken from the shock site www.rotten.com, deliberately challenging the platform's control and censorship mechanisms. The artist was able to upload the book and order a copy without problem. Then he found out in the membership agreement that, apparently, the only way to trigger content moderation was for other users to report questionable content. The artist then created a second user account with which he reported *Experiment 01*. He immediately received an email from Lulu's Questionable Content Team: "It has also come to our attention that some of your content is inappropriate for General Access." The book was moved to "Private Access" due to explicit content and violation of platform rules. It was also announced that from this point on, his account would be under constant review, and that if he violated the rules again, the account and all publications would be deleted immediately and without further notice.

Na Evihcra fo Gnibrutsid Noitartsulli

AUTHOR	Nettor Tod Moc
YEAR	2014
GENRE	photobook
METHOD	détournement / hack, found material, paratextual play, remediation, test / experiment
SUBJECT	book / book design, censorship / ban, materiality, photography, platforms / companies
EDITION CHARACTERISTICS	open edition
FORMAT	14.8 × 21.0 cm
MATERIALITIES	color, paperback, perfect bound
PAGES	94

DESCRIPTION

This publication is an example of the successful application of the visual camouflage technique "Decoding Duplex" to the same images from Rotten.com that were previously blocked by Lulu. The method is based on "plac[ing] a mirrored image on top of another image. [...] The color of the images play[s] also a very important role. Tests and experiments showed, that coloring the original image green and the mirrored one red works best. [...] Having the same picture just with the color green and a mirrored version of the photo in red placed on top of the other one lets the original value and context of the photo disappear. [...] By holding a red foil onto the page, the red and mirrored image disappears and we see the real value and censored image. [...] This visuality helps to decode the pictures' original content and blur the graphic explicitly into a more chaotic appearance" (Jasper Otto Eisenecker, *How to Camouflage Books*, 6–9).

The text on the cover and title pages is based on the camouflage technique "Reversed Reading": "By spelling and writing every word in a reversed order, the meaning of the words on first sight is difficult" (Ibid., 4). Accordingly, the book title is written backward and translates as "An Archive of Disturbing Illustration," which is the tagline of the Rotten.com website. This is supplemented on the title page with the website's self-description, also spelled backward: "The soft white underbelly of the net, eviscerated for all to see: Rotten.com collects images and information from many sources to present the viewer with a truly unpleasant experience."

Make Em Pay

AUTHOR	Petr Petrake
YEAR	2016
GENRE	experimental literature
METHOD	détournement / hack, paratextual play, reformatting, test / experiment
SUBJECT	book / book design, censorship / ban, materiality, platforms / companies, typography
EDITION CHARACTERISTICS	open edition
FORMAT	14.8 × 21.0 cm
MATERIALITIES	black-and-white, paperback, perfect bound
PAGES	358 (unpaginated)

DESCRIPTION

This book was produced by means of camouflage technique "Filled Monospace," which is based on the mutual interaction of digital and analog formats. Using an InDesign script, the letters are distributed alternately on the front and back of a book page so that the text cannot be read on a screen or in a book preview, and the platform's automated censoring algorithms also fail because they are faced with what appears to be meaningless text. The reader of the printed copy, however, can read the full text as soon as the page is held up to the light:

"This Camouflage-Technique requires a monospaced typeface for the texts, because we want to use the fact, that every letter has the same width. This method plays with the shine-through appearance of paper. [...] We start with filling the front side of the page with text, but we leave every second letter white. [...] Copy the same text block to the back side of the same page. Afterwards we mirror the text block that we just copied. We repeat the same step for the backside, but we [...] start with leaving the first letter blank and continue with the third letter and so on. The empty space on the front side of the page should now be filled with the missing letters from the backside, when you hold the page against the light" (Jasper Otto Eisenecker, *How to Camouflage Books*, 5–6).

The camouflaged text is based on *Make 'Em Pay! Ultimate Revenge Techniques from the Master Trickster* by George Hayduke.

How to Camouflage Books in Times of Internet-Censorship: An Instruction Guide

AUTHOR	Ano Nymous
YEAR	2014
GENRE	tutorial
METHOD	composition (writing / drawing / photography), paratextual play
SUBJECT	book / book design, censorship / ban, platforms / companies
EDITION CHARACTERISTICS	open edition, PDF
PAGES	11

DESCRIPTION

"In times of internet-surveillance, the freedom of speech is endangered. This manual provides the reader with possible camouflage-techniques to hide content from being censored. The manual of course also gives hints how to encode the camouflaged books and how to read it" (blurb on Lulu).

After Jasper Otto Eisenecker discovered that you can not only sell books on Lulu, but also make e-books available for free, he published his manual as a free PDF on the site. In this way, he makes his strategies for subverting the platform available on this very platform as free, democratized, open-source knowledge. The printed copy in our collection was produced by the artist himself.

Composition

AUTHORS	Angela Genusa, Benjamin Laird
YEAR	2014
PUBLISHER	Gauss PDF
GENRE	experimental literature, tutorial
METHOD	found material, generative / automation, montage / remix
SUBJECT	analog / digital, book / book design, canon, economy / labor, literature, print technology, scale, writing / reading techniques
PLATFORM	Lulu
EDITION CHARACTERISTICS	multiple editions (print, PDF), open edition
FORMAT	15.2 × 22.9 cm
MATERIALITIES	black-and-white, paperback, perfect bound
PAGES	625

IMAGES

DESCRIPTION

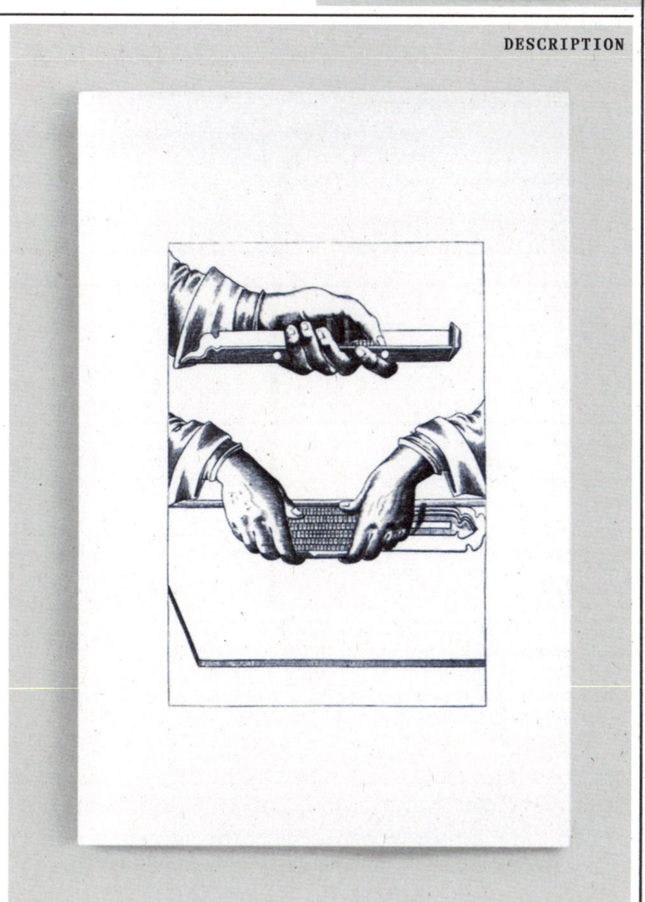

Composition is an algorithmic mash-up of two historical texts. One is *Mechanick Exercises: Or, the Doctrine of Handy-Works. Applied to the Art of Printing. The Second Volumne* (1683) by Joseph Moxon and Theodore Low De Vinne, which contains an extensive step-by-step description of a typesetting process. This description is dissected by a Python script and filled with the letters of Gertrude Stein's *Composition As Explanation* (1926) whenever a letter to be typeset is mentioned as an example. The resulting text is advertised by Angela Genusa and Benjamin Laird as "Moxon and De Vinne typeset Stein letter by letter, word by word, line by line..." (blurb on Lulu).

The intervention in Moxon and De Vinne's original text (which obviously comes from a faulty digital scan, clear from the number of OCR errors and the consistent negation of punctuation marks and paragraphs) begins on page 6, at the passage where the example of the word "And" is used to explain how to place a word letter by letter: "For as he ſpells A, he takes up A out of the A Box, as he names n in his thoughts, he takes up n out of the n Box, as he names d in his thoughts he takes up d out of the d Box; which three Letters ſet together make a Word, viz. And; ſo that after the d he ſets a Space." While Moxon and De Vinne leave it at the example of "And" and continue with "Then he goes on to the next Word, and so Composes on" (p. 213 in the original), Genusa and Laird insert here and repeat the instructions with all letters from Stein's text. Following the lengthy instructions, page 6 yields the first six words of Stein's starting sentence: "There is singularly nothing that makes a difference [...]."

Thus, both Moxon and De Vinne's short passages (pp. 212–228) and Stein's short text are inflated to a total of 625 pages. The resulting highly repetitious and extensive text mimics Stein's poetics as well as being an algorithmic instruction to produce Stein's text itself, questioning the division of writing, typesetting, and printing in the production ("composition") of a text.

NON FACIT SALTUS & QUOD VIDE

AUTHOR	Lawrence Giffin
YEAR	2014
PUBLISHER	Troll Thread
GENRE	artist's book / bookwork, experimental literature
METHOD	composition (writing / drawing / photography), paratextual play
SUBJECT	analog / digital, book / book design, writing / reading techniques
PLATFORM	Lulu
VOLUMES	2
EDITION CHARACTERISTICS	multiple editions (print, PDF), open edition
MATERIALITIES	black-and-white, paperback, perfect bound
PAGES	100

IMAGE

DESCRIPTION

Lawrence Giffin's two-volume series is a reflection on the reading practice of turning pages and the linearity of the codex. Each of the 100 pages consists only of a bold page number in the upper outer corner and a footnote with instructions on which page to turn to next.

NON FACIT SALTUS

FORMAT 10.0 × 17.0 cm

IMAGE

2

If you want to go to page 3, turn to page 3.

3

If you want to go to page 4, turn to page 4.

DESCRIPTION

In Lawrence Giffin's *NON FACIT SALTUS*, reference is made to the next page in each case, which corresponds to the usual reading of, say, a novel. Page 100 is without an instruction. Unlike its corresponding counterpart *QUOD VIDE*, *NON FACIT SALTUS* understands the codex as a finite, linear sequence. The title refers to the Latin "natura non facit saltus" (nature does not make jumps) and thus to an important principle of natural philosophy, which can also be applied to the material preconditions of the book in codex form, where content and turning pages follow a linear progression.

QUOD VIDE

FORMAT 10.8 × 17.5 cm

IMAGE

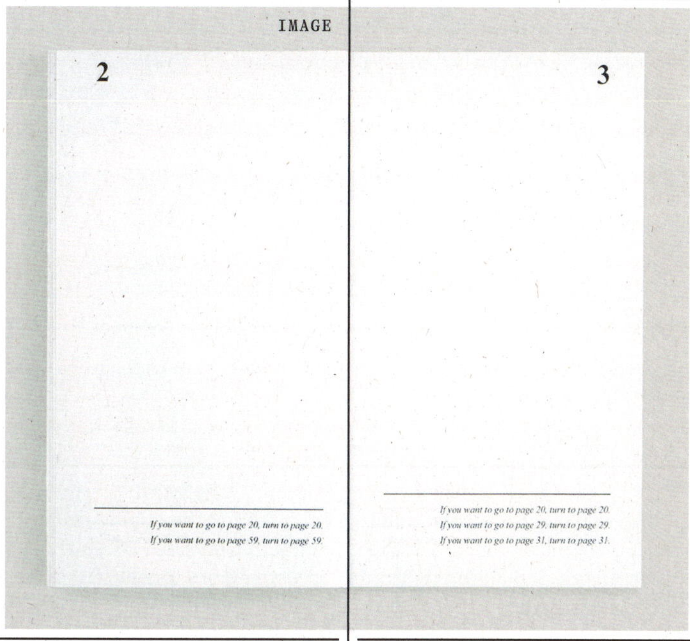

DESCRIPTION

In Lawrence Giffin's *QUOD VIDE* (Latin for "which see," used for a cross-reference in the text), the reader can choose between several pages to turn to until they reach page 100, only to be instructed to turn back to page 1 or 14: "If you want to go to page 1, turn to page 1 / If you want to go to page 14, turn to page 14." Page 1 accordingly says: "If you want to go to page 14, turn to page 14."

The path through the book thus results from the interplay of seemingly arbitrary instructions given by the author and reader's own decisions. In any case, the reader jumps from page to page, which is why *QUOD VIDE* forms the counterpart to *NON FACIT SALTUS* with its linear sequence of numbers and pages.

The Dictionary of the Analogue // The Dictionary of the Digital

AUTHOR	Jonathan Hanahan
YEAR	2014
GENRE	artist's book / bookwork, photobook
METHOD	found material, remediation, study / analysis
SUBJECT	analog / digital, google, internet culture, search engine, visual culture
PLATFORM	Lulu
EDITION CHARACTERISTICS	open edition
FORMAT	15.8 × 23.5 cm
MATERIALITIES	color, hardcover, perfect bound
PAGES	301

IMAGE

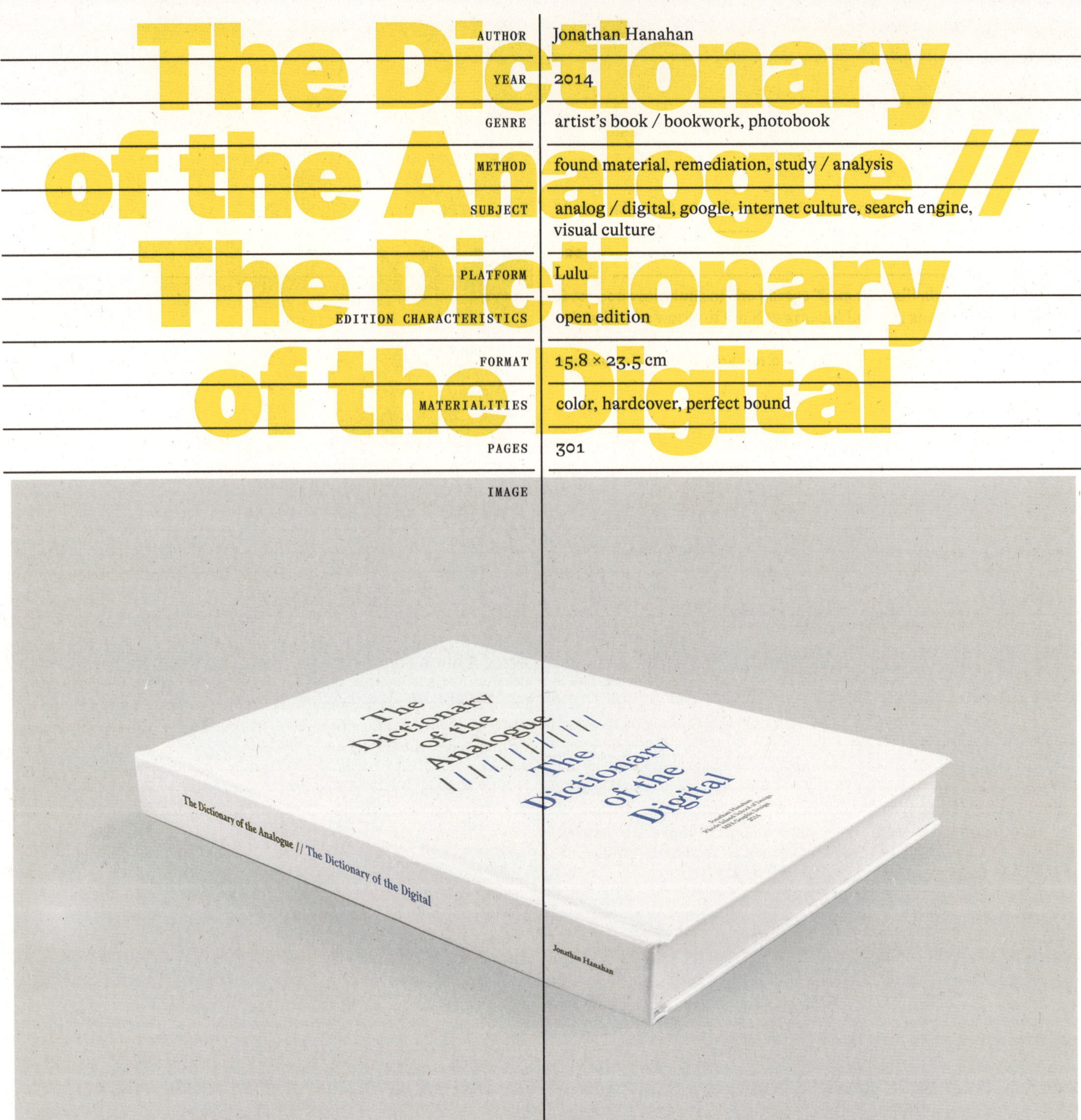

DESCRIPTION

The Dictionary of the Analogue // The Dictionary of the Digital documents Jonathan Hanahan's research project, completed in 2014 at the Rhode Island School of Design, on analog and digital culture with a special interest in language that changes meaning when expressed in different contexts.

Based on a list of homonyms—from access and transfer, to bit and frame, and window and worm—the book shows results from Google Images searches for each word, accompanied by the word "analogue" or "digital." Both searches are edited to complement each other on a spread, the verso side showing half of a screenshot of the analog results, the recto side showing half of a screenshot of the digital results, merging into a single browser window. These image search results are listed in alphabetical order, preceded by an index of the homonyms with definitions for analog and digital contexts.

On surface level, the results are different, but in application they show a lot of similarities, revealing the homonyms as fueled by both contexts. The word "archive," for example, results in images of file cabinets for the analog prompt and images of server rooms for the digital prompt. And even though data in the analog "archive" can be accessed more or less without interfacing—the server room needing at least some kind of screen interface to interact with—both architectures also show a lot of similarities.

Thus, Jonathan Hanahan's project tries to reveal "that while the distinction between the two associations may be vast, the experience of their use is far less polarizing. In reality, these associations and uses happen simultaneously. We are in both worlds at once and thus, the interface is no longer a gateway to another place" (blurb on Blurb). *The Dictionary of the Analogue // The Dictionary of the Digital* makes a point for overcoming artificial dichotomies often associated with analog and digital culture but which might have always been entangled in a post-digital condition to begin with.

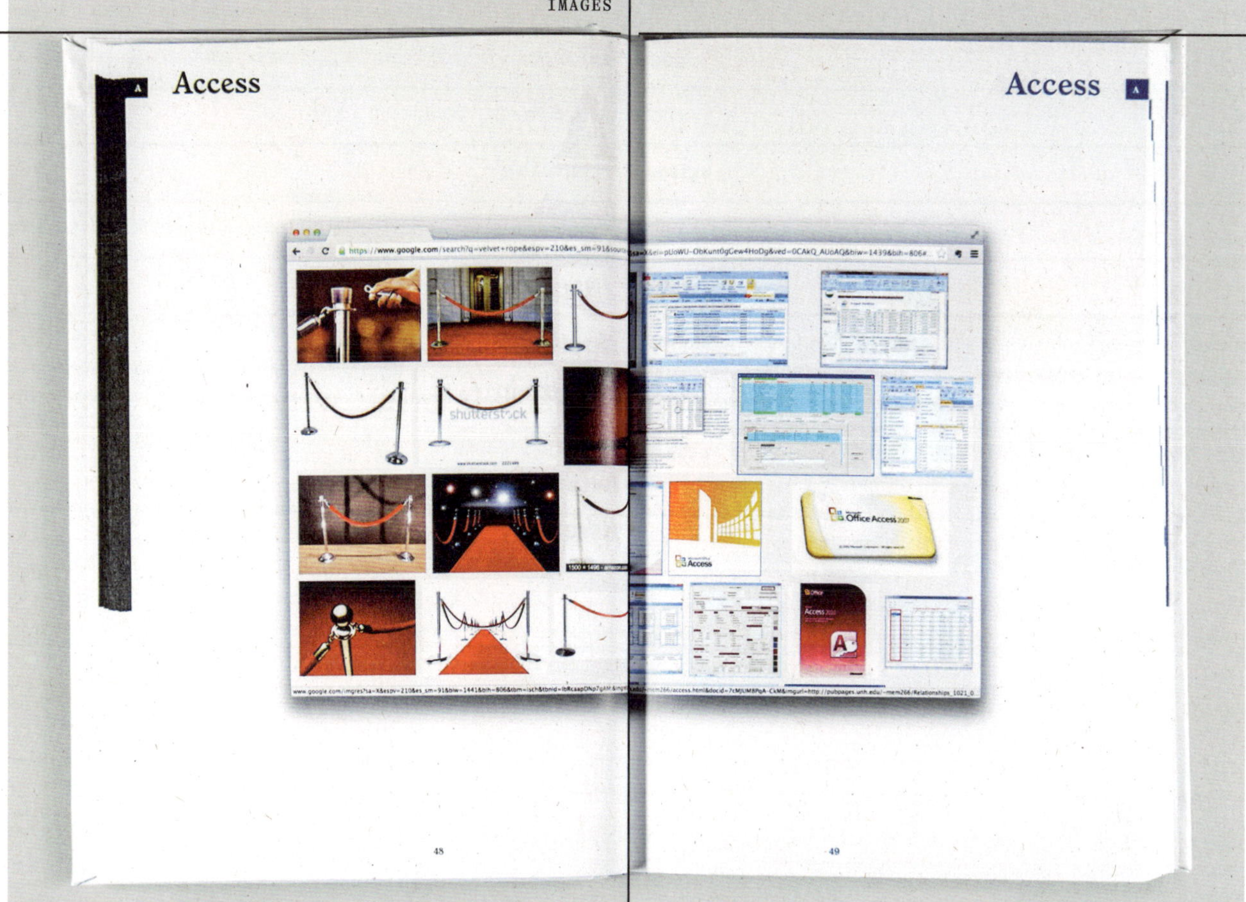

B
Boot
Boot
B
80
81

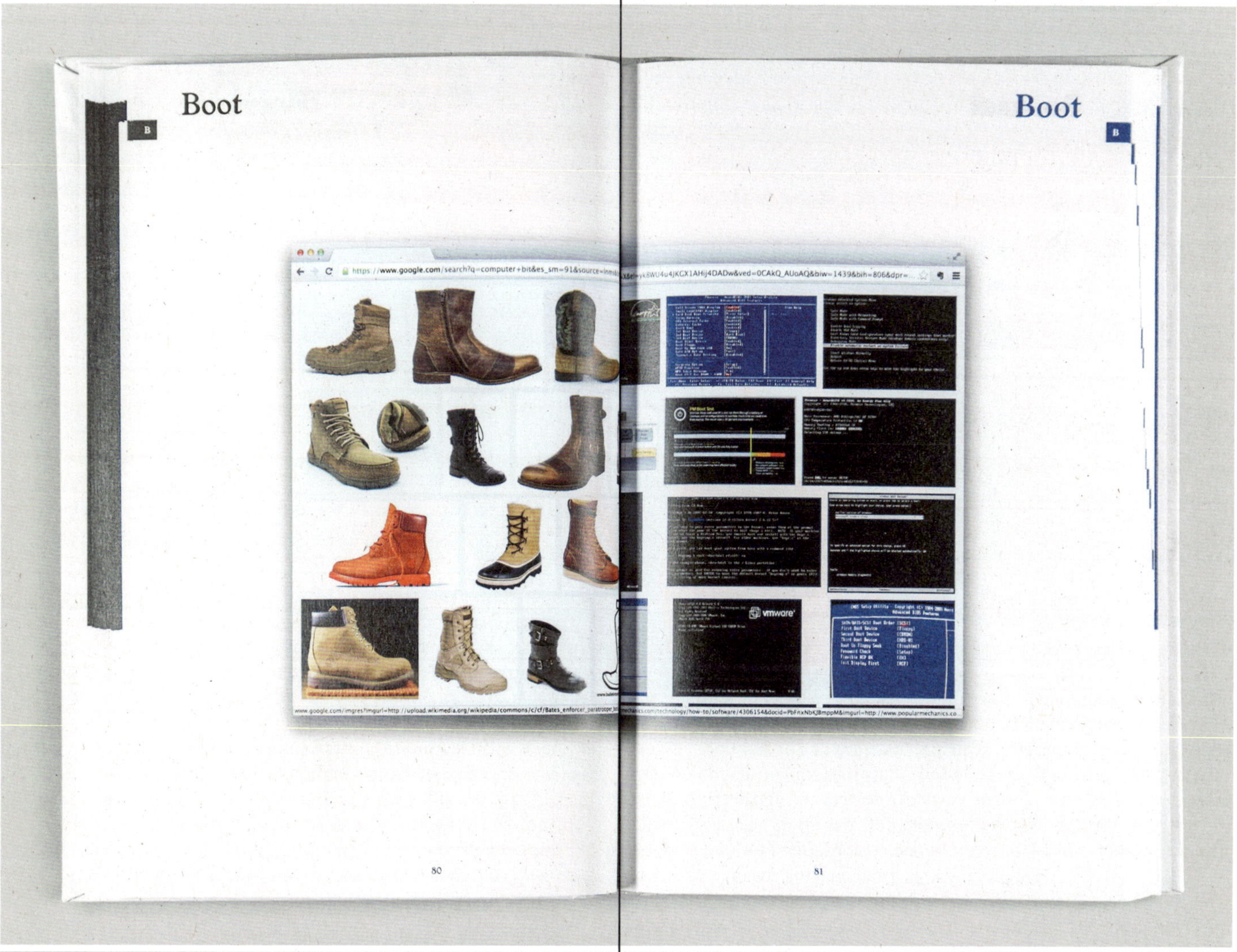

_IMG

AUTHOR	Mishka Henner
YEAR	since 2014
GENRE	artist's book / bookwork, photobook
METHOD	remediation
SUBJECT	analog / digital, code / programming, data, materiality, photography
PLATFORM	Lulu
VOLUMES	so far 2 vols.
EDITION CHARACTERISTICS	limited edition, numbered, signed, available only through the artist
FORMAT	13.8 × 21.5 cm
MATERIALITIES	black-and-white, loose insert, paperback, perfect bound

IMAGE

DESCRIPTION

_*IMG* is a series of two books to date that present "the digital binary data of historical photographs as literature," as the blurb on the artist's website claims. Each book is based on a pre-digital photograph that was digitized, compressed as a .jpg, and archived by an official source. Mishka Henner opened the image file with a text editor and used the resulting ASCII character sequence as content for his book. Even though the resulting text is a hybrid that is no longer machine-readable nor readable for humans without the help of interpreting tools, the books nonetheless show the amount of characters necessary to define the picture. They also work as analog containers for saving data that could be used to recreate the files for displaying the images.

As both books also include a 5 × 7 inch silver gelatin print of the corresponding photograph, _*IMG* is also a reflection on originals and copies in photography and the historic punctum in analog and digital picturing. Furthermore, both photographs depict historical moments of passing and transition, mirroring in content the three steps of remediation present in the books: from analog image to digitally codified image to an analog version of the code.

Although _*IMG* is produced in print-on-demand, it is also an experiment with scarcity: the first volume was produced in an edition of ninety-seven signed and numbered copies (this corresponds to the number of years since the photograph was taken), the second one in an edition of twenty-five copies, and a possible third one could be published in only three or four copies. The fact that Henner has, amazingly, already sold more than sixty copies of this series (as of 2021) could be due to this artificial rarefaction.

_IMG01: _Australian-troops-passing-014.jpg

YEAR	2014
PAGES	740
DESCRIPTION	_*IMG01* is based on a photograph of five Australian soldiers taken on a battlefield of WW1 by James Francis Hurley on October 29, 1917. It shows "members of a field artillery brigade, passing along a duckboard track over mud and water among gaunt bare tree trunks in the devastated Chateau Wood, a portion of one of the battlegrounds in the Ypres salient" (Mishka Henner, _*IMG01*, last page). Our copy is number 78 of 97.

_IMG02: _1401704227-35bild1831-o.jpg

YEAR	2015
PAGES	148
DESCRIPTION	_*IMG02* is based on a photograph by Hartmut Reiche taken in Berlin on January 5, 1990. It shows a segment of the Berlin Wall broken through, with soldiers on the one side and smiling people looking through on the other. Our copy is number 12 of 25.

I RL, YOU RL

AUTHOR	Sophia Le Fraga
YEAR	2014
PUBLISHER	Troll Thread
GENRE	poetry, reprint
METHOD	composition (writing / drawing / photography), found material, reformatting
SUBJECT	email / messaging, internet culture, literature, social media
PLATFORM	Lulu
EDITION CHARACTERISTICS	second edition, multiple editions (print, PDF), open edition
FORMAT	10.8 × 17.5 cm
MATERIALITIES	black-and-white, paperback, perfect bound, defective copy
PAGES	72 (unpaginated)

IMAGES

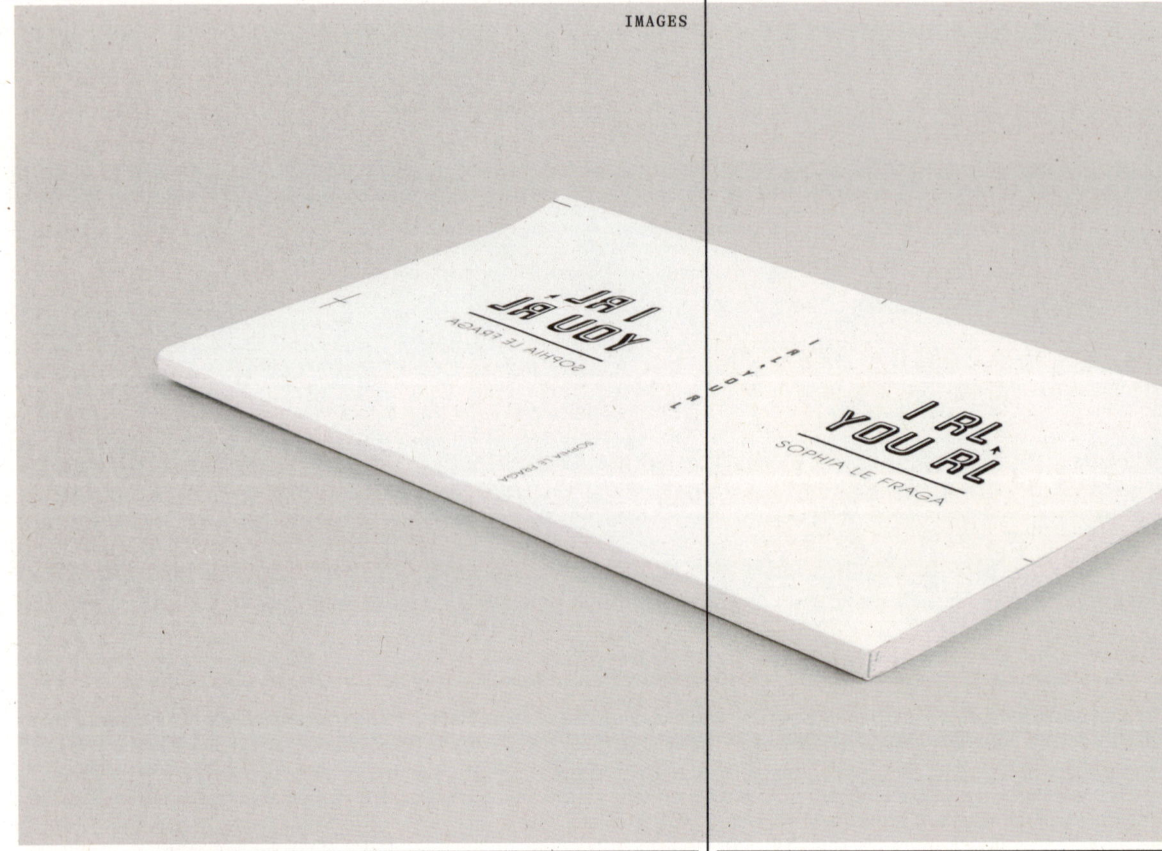

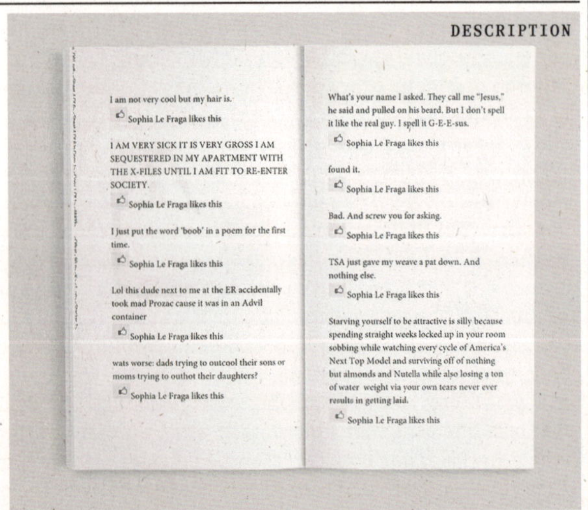

I am not very cool but my hair is.

Sophia Le Fraga likes this

I AM VERY SICK IT IS VERY GROSS I AM SEQUESTERED IN MY APARTMENT WITH THE X-FILES UNTIL I AM FIT TO RE-ENTER SOCIETY.

Sophia Le Fraga likes this

I just put the word 'boob' in a poem for the first time.

Sophia Le Fraga likes this

Lol this dude next to me at the ER accidentally took mad Prozac cause it was in an Advil container

Sophia Le Fraga likes this

wats worse: dads trying to outcool their sons or moms trying to outhot their daughters?

Sophia Le Fraga likes this

What's your name I asked. They call me "Jesus," he said and pulled on his beard. But I don't spell it like the real guy. I spell it G-E-E-sus.

Sophia Le Fraga likes this

found it.

Sophia Le Fraga likes this

Bad. And screw you for asking.

Sophia Le Fraga likes this

TSA just gave my weave a pat down. And nothing else.

Sophia Le Fraga likes this

Starving yourself to be attractive is silly because spending straight weeks locked up in your room sobbing while watching every cycle of America's Next Top Model and surviving off of nothing but almonds and Nutella while also losing a ton of water weight via your own tears never ever results in getting laid.

Sophia Le Fraga likes this

DESCRIPTION

I RL, YOU RL is a poetry collection initially published by minutes BOOKS in 2014. After being out of print for a time, it was republished by Troll Thread one year later. As the title suggests, this book by Sophia Le Fraga, a trained linguist, is about the internet and the way people talk on it. The book is divided into seven chapters, making use of different found material edited and formatted into verse by the author. The sources are emails, social media, and dating profiles, most notably messages denying Le Fraga of being an author or her texts of being poetry, which are collected in the first chapter "H8M8." The chapter "I DON'T WANT ANYTHING" contains poems written on request, using only material from the feed, wall, or email of the person making the request: "People love to hear themselves talk" (Sophia Le Fraga, "An Interview").

Our copy has a faulty trim and there are print commands in the bleed. These errors are even more visible on the cover, which already has crop marks to indicate that this is a reprint for which the minutes BOOKS original has been adapted to the new format.

Notes

AUTHOR	Dane Mainella
YEAR	2014
PUBLISHER	The LUMA Foundation
GENRE	experimental literature
METHOD	composition (writing / drawing / photography), documentation / archiving
SUBJECT	memory / storage, narration, tracking
PLATFORM	Lulu
EDITION CHARACTERISTICS	ISBN 9781312055971, open edition
FORMAT	10.8 × 17.5 cm
MATERIALITIES	black-and-white, paperback, perfect bound, defective copy
PAGES	636 (unpaginated)
IMAGES	

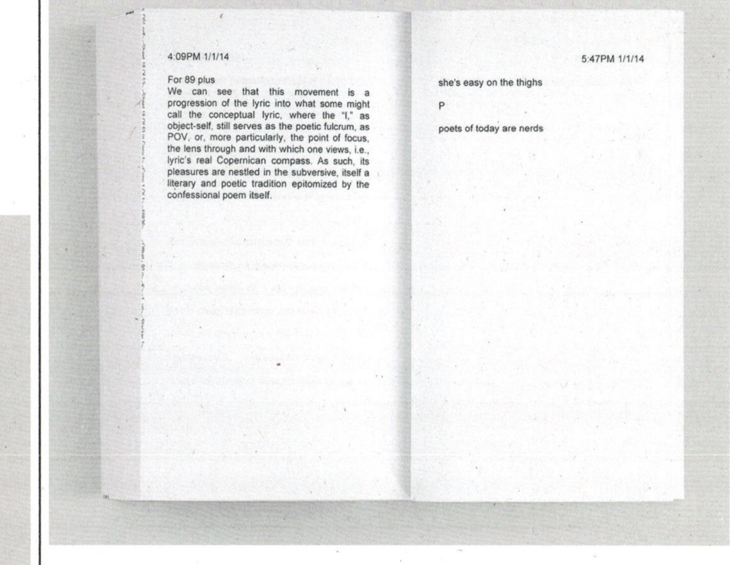

DESCRIPTION

On more than 630 pages, *Notes* documents the everyday memos of the author in his iPhone's Notes app from October 10, 2012 (date of phone purchase) until February 18, 2014 (publication of this book). They range from everyday notes and reminders to more poetic observations and metareflexive sections on the merging of conceptual and confessional poetry. The book ends with a note dedicating the book to conceptual poet Jason Jadick, of whom we have *The Uncreative Subterranean* in our collection (see 230).

This book was produced for the series *1000 Books by 1000 Poets* (edited by Danny Snelson) in context of the exhibition "Poetry Will Be Made By All!" (Zurich, January–March 2014, co-curated by Kenneth Goldsmith, Simon Castets, and Hans Ulrich Obrist, see also 284, 303, 357).

The copy archived shows print indexing notes on the fore edge of the last few pages, due to bad binding and cutting.

Puniverse

being the ingenuous crossing of an idiom set and a rhyming dictionary

AUTHOR	Stephen McLaughlin
YEAR	2014
PUBLISHER	Gauss PDF
GENRE	experimental literature, poetry
METHOD	generative / automation, montage / remix
SUBJECT	authorship, literature, scale
PLATFORM	Lulu
VOLUMES	57
EDITION CHARACTERISTICS	multiple editions (print, PDF, TXT, NFO), open edition
FORMAT	15.2 × 22.9 cm
MATERIALITIES	black-and-white, paperback, perfect bound
PAGES	158 (unpaginated)

IMAGES

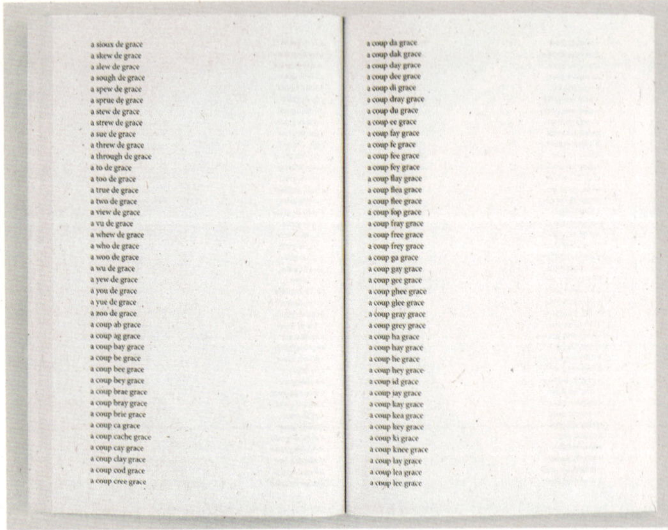

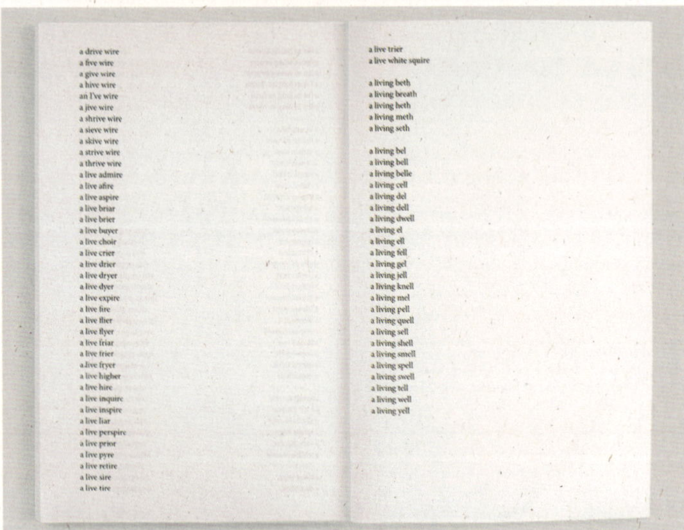

DESCRIPTION

Puniverse combines algorithmic, generative literature, and conceptual writing. Claiming in its subtitle to be "the ingenuous crossing of an idiom set and a rhyming dictionary," it plays out all the rhyming combinations of the elements of a given number of idioms, resulting in approximately 320,000 puns spanning fifty-seven volumes. Each volume bears its own distinctive cover and epigraph. To completely fill the pages of the last volume, Melville's *Moby Dick* is copied and pasted from gutenberg.org.

All volumes can be ordered through Lulu and are available as PDFs through Gauss PDF. There is also a ZIP archive of all volumes, and the complete text is additionally available as a .txt and a .nfo file. In 2015, the entire series was bought and put on display for the "Surf Club" exhibition at Philadelphia's Vox Populi gallery.

As J. Gordon Faylor, the founder of Gauss PDF, says, it was works like these—where a print edition would have been completely impossible without print-on-demand providers—that inspired him to create the GPDFeditions series, all of whose titles are offered both in PDF and print-on-demand through Lulu. *Puniverse* is number 5 in the GPDFeditions series, and the one-hundredth release in Gauss PDF's digital-only series.

Megawatt

A novel computationally, deterministically generated extending passages from Samuel Beckett's *Watt*

AUTHOR	Nick Montfort
YEAR	2014
PUBLISHER	Bad Quarto
GENRE	experimental literature
METHOD	generative / automation, reenactment, study / analysis
SUBJECT	canon, code / programming, literature, narration, reading / interpretation, scale
PLATFORM	Espresso Book Machine
EDITION CHARACTERISTICS	open edition, no longer available
FORMAT	14.0 × 21.0 cm
MATERIALITIES	black-and-white, paperback, perfect bound
PAGES	246

IMAGES

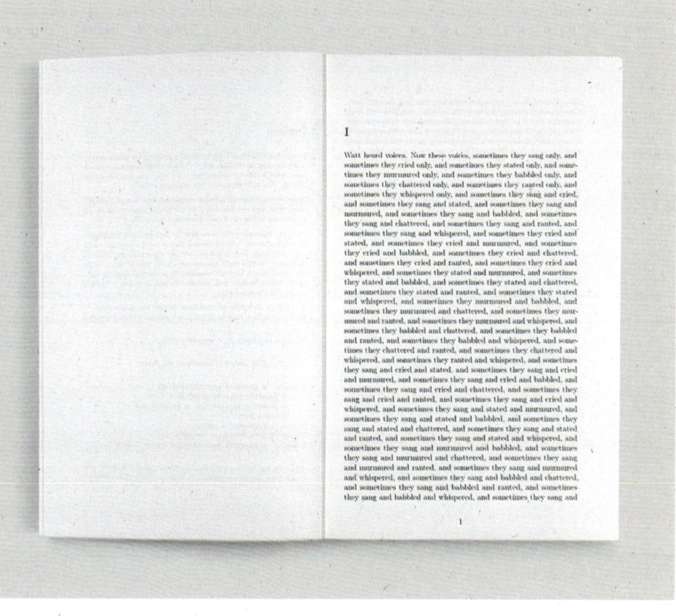

DESCRIPTION

Megawatt is an algorithmic rewriting of Samuel Beckett's experimental novel *Watt* (1953), in which Beckett formed his distinctive style, including systematic mannerisms, schematism, and an inclination for endless enumeration, repetition, and variation which all correspond perfectly with the main character Watt's predilection for routines and repetitions. It also shows a certain proximity to computer generated writing before computers. Nick Montfort takes this as an invitation and, according to the subtitle, presents *A novel computationally, deterministically generated extending passages from Samuel Beckett's* Watt.

For this, Montfort selects the passages that are the least "intelligible" and the most "inscrutable" (Nick Montfort, "Preface"), and writes a Python script that imitates Beckett's regular, repetitive writing: the selected passages are not merely recreated, but expanded by exhaustively permuting—even more consistently than Beckett's—their main words in all their possible combinations. Montfort even adds more words to play with, so that over seven long pages in the first chapter, Watt now hears voices not only singing, shouting, saying, and murmuring incomprehensible things in his ear, but also chattering, ranting, whispering, in every conceivable order. Thus, Beckett's already repetitive passages expand to an excessive, absurd length—which is why *Watt* becomes *Megawatt*.

As Hannes Bajohr, who translated *Megawatt* into German, points out: "[*Megawatt's*] output is, first, what Beckett had written [...]—but then not only what he *could* have written, but also what he *must have* according to his own rules [...]. *Megawatt* is thus a form of algorithmic empathy, which is not a copy but a reconstructive comprehension which can claim that it was done in the spirit of Beckett with more legitimacy than any epigonal text, any parody or pastiche ever could" (Hannes Bajohr, "Algorithmic Empathy").

Megawatt was written and generated in November 2014 for the second National Novel Generation Month (NaNoGenMo, the equivalent of National Novel Writing Month (NaNoWriMo)), for which a novel of at least 50,000 words in length is to be produced within one month. The book also includes the 350-line source code of the Python script (which is also available online) so you can recreate it yourself, complete with PDF and title page. It is printed on the Espresso Book Machine and distributed via the Harvard Book Store, which does not accept orders from outside the United States. Print-on-demand services were discontinued in April 2022.

When the book was translated into German, Hannes Bajohr decided not to translate the actual novel text, but to rewrite the program code, including the word material to be permuted, in German and use it to regenerate the novel's text.

Surf's Up (2010)

AUTHOR	Audun Mortensen
YEAR	2014
PUBLISHER	TraumaWien
GENRE	poetry
METHOD	appropriation, found material, reformatting
SUBJECT	canon, film, internet culture, literature, platforms / companies, reading / interpretation
PLATFORM	Lulu
EDITION CHARACTERISTICS	third edition, ISBN 9783950291056, open edition
FORMAT	10.8 × 17.5 cm
MATERIALITIES	black-and-white, paperback, perfect bound, defective copy
PAGES	120

IMAGES

3 Ninjas: High Noon at Mega Mountain (1998)

Saving the day the ninja way.

10

Abortion, The (2006)

Congratulations, it's a girl!

11

DESCRIPTION

Audun Mortensen's *Surf's Up (2010)* is a book of poetry composed of taglines for the "bottom 100 movies," a user-voted list on the Internet Movie Database (IMDb.com). The book consists of 100 such poems, each entitled with the movie's name and containing the tagline as archived on IMDb, reformatted into verse and arranged in alphabetical order. This gives the typical rhetoric used to promote B-movies on the internet a humorous touch and reflects the biggest clichés and media phenomena of those years.

The blurb reads: "Q: How to read taglines (i.e. branding slogans) for the 'IMDb bottom 100 movies' as voted by IMDb.com users? Q: As documentation of a series of 'unsuccessful (marketing) lines'? Q: How to read a poetry book composed of taglines for the 'IMDb bottom 100 movies' as voted by IMDb.com users? Q: As documentation of a series of 'unsuccessful (marketing) lines' remarketed as literature? Q: How to write taglines for a poetry book composed of taglines for the 'IMDb bottom 100 movies' as voted by IMDb.com users? Q: *Surf's Up (2010)* is remarketing taglines for the 'IMDb bottom 100 movies' as voted by IMDb.com users as literature!!!? Q: How to write a successful tagline that sums up the tone and premise of a product? Q: How to write taglines successful enough to warrant inclusion in (popular) culture? Q: How to write taglines? Q: How to write? Q: How to? Q: How? Q: How to? Q: How to read? Q: How to read taglines?" (blurb on Amazon)

This is the third edition of *Surf's Up (2010)* with a first edition in 2010 and the second in 2013. Our copy shows print indexing notes on the fore edge of the last few pages, due to poor binding and cutting.

Books On Demand

an Exhibition of 12 Illustrated Books Produced Using Print-on-Demand Services

AUTHOR	Zoë Sadokierski
YEAR	2014
PUBLISHER	Page Screen Books
GENRE	artistic research, catalog / collection
METHOD	documentation / archiving, study / analysis
SUBJECT	book / book design, economy / labor, materiality, print technology, print on demand, publishing / distribution
PLATFORM	Lulu
EDITION CHARACTERISTICS	ISBN 9781326037208, open edition
FORMAT	15.2 × 22.9 cm
MATERIALITIES	color, paperback, perfect bound
PAGES	60

IMAGE

DESCRIPTION

Books On Demand is a catalog documenting Zoë Sadokierski's exhibition of the same name at Carlton Project Space, Sydney from October to November 2014. It lists twelve books by the author that were made using print on demand platforms, including project description, aims, and design strategy as well as specifications like format, platform, and cost calculations. One third of the books were originally produced as limited edition handmade books and then reformatted into print-on-demand books, and the others were designed for print-on-demand from the very beginning, showing a virtuous understanding of print-on-demand's limitations and potential.

In her foreword, Sadokierski discusses the fundamental impact print-on-demand has on the publishing industry, especially on small press publishing. Her own (artistic) research concerns "the evolution of the book in a digital age, from a design perspective. In particular, considering how the role of the designer could change in emerging publishing models" (Zoë Sadokierski, "Prologue," 9).

The catalog displays some of these explorations in its own sophisticated layout, for example, using full-bleed black pages showing through the paper to raise awareness of color and materiality. The front cover shows and numbers the formats of all publications, including the catalog itself as number 13, marking it as a part of the exhibition and research.

What Does the Bible Say About ___? Word Finds

AUTHOR	Angie Waller
YEAR	2014
PUBLISHER	Unknown Unknowns
GENRE	experimental literature
METHOD	found material, generative / automation
SUBJECT	canon, crowd / collaboration, games, google, reading / interpretation, search engine
PLATFORM	Amazon
EDITION CHARACTERISTICS	ISBN 9780991392308, open edition
FORMAT	15.2 × 22.9 cm
MATERIALITIES	black-and-white, paperback, perfect bound
PAGES	56

IMAGES

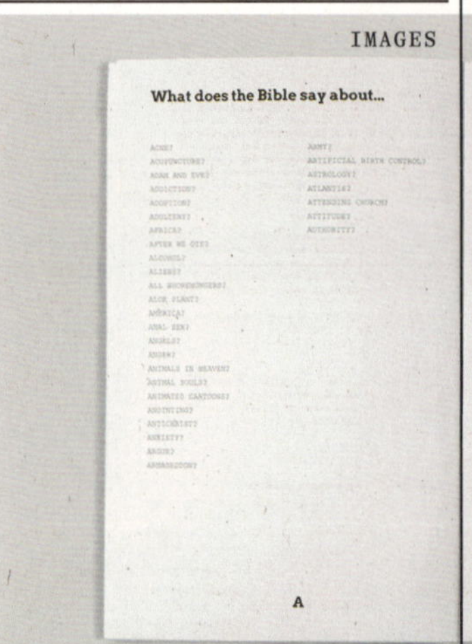

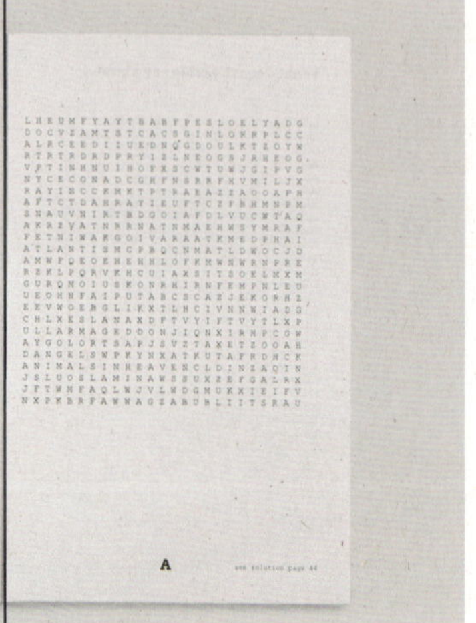

DESCRIPTION

This is the first book Angie Waller has produced with Amazon's CreateSpace Independent Publishing Platform. It grew out of her involvement with the "Kindle Industrial Complex," where titles that contain multiple buzzwords from Google searches, for example, do very well because they often show up high in search results in the Amazon store. So Waller started a small book series whose titles she pulled from websites that aggregate Google searches. Among them were *How to Find a Friend, Be a Good Friend, and Delete a Friend*, and *How to Tell if Someone is Listening to You in Your House*.

While she obtained the contents of these books through ghostwriters, *What Does the Bible Say About ___?* contains all the words in alphabetical order that came up in searches with that question. Accordingly, the book is advertised on the back cover with the words, "Are you interested in earthly things getting in the way of divine things and vice versa?" In the book itself, the word lists on the left-hand page are each juxtaposed with a word puzzle containing those words on the right-hand page—modeled on "dime store Christian puzzle books that use word finds and crosswords to help students of the gospel memorize scripture" (blurb on Printed Matter). The solutions are at the end of the book.

Years later, the author accidentally discovered that on Amazon a used copy was offered for almost $2,796 even though there were still new copies on sale for $10. This was one of her reasons for going on to take a closer look at the dark side of the Amazon universe. In her 2018 study *Grifting The Amazon*, she exposes self-published books as part of dubious e-commerce practices as well as vehicles for scams and automated get-rich-quick schemes (in this volume, 553–575). Concerning her own book, she suggests that the jump in price is certainly not due to recognition of her work as an "art object," but is probably due to a computer glitch, or perhaps even money laundering through Amazon.

On the Road

AUTHOR	Gregor Weichbrodt
YEAR	2014
GENRE	experimental literature
METHOD	generative / automation, translation / transcription
SUBJECT	canon, google, literature, maps / street view, reading / interpretation
PLATFORM	Lulu
EDITION CHARACTERISTICS	ISBN 9781304882769, open edition
FORMAT	10.3 × 17.2 cm
MATERIALITIES	black-and-white, paperback, perfect bound
PAGES	69 (unpaginated)

IMAGES

DESCRIPTION

"Based on the novel *On the Road* by Jack Kerouac and Google Maps Direction Service. / The exact and approximate spots Kerouac traveled and described are taken from the book and parsed by Google Direction Service API. The result is a huge direction instruction of 55 pages. The chapters match those of the original book. All in all, as Google shows, the journey takes 272.26 hours (for 17,527 miles)" (blurb on artist website).

Compared to Kerouac's travelogue, Gregor Weichbrodt's book reflects a different—far less spontaneous, aimless, and free—way of experiencing the world in the era of Google Maps. Surprises are excluded, since from the beginning it is clear that the destination will be reached. The last sentence reads accordingly: "Destination will be on the right."

This book was produced for the series *1000 Books by 1000 Poets*, edited by Danny Snelson, for the exhibition "Poetry Will Be Made By All!" (Zurich, 2014, curated by Kenneth Goldsmith, Simon Castets, and Hans Ulrich Obrist, see also 284, 297, 357). A second print-on-demand edition appeared shortly thereafter under the label 0x0a. *On the Road* is also a stage performance by Michael Durkin and 14th Street (March 2015).

HOLLY MELGARD'S FRIENDS & FAMILY

AUTHOR	Joey Yearous-Algozin
YEAR	2014
PUBLISHER	Bon Aire Projects
GENRE	experimental literature
METHOD	documentation / archiving, remediation, translation / transcription
SUBJECT	email / messaging, gender, memory / storage, narration, publishing / distribution, surveillance / privacy
PLATFORM	Lulu
EDITION CHARACTERISTICS	ISBN 9780991582006, open edition
FORMAT	14.8 × 21.0 cm
MATERIALITIES	black-and-white, paperback, perfect bound
PAGES	83

IMAGES

DESCRIPTION

HOLLY MELGARD'S FRIENDS & FAMILY is a collection of voice mails sent to Holly Melgard over three years (January 1, 2011 through January 1, 2014) and transcribed by her partner Joey Yearous-Algozin, both of them founding members of the print-on-demand publishing collective Troll Thread. This is one of the very few conceptual books by Yearous-Algozin not published directly via Troll Thread but as part of the Bon Aire Projects series "LOVE / LOVERS / LOVING," a publisher of experimental texts that also uses Lulu.

This book is an excellent example of conceptual writing practices present in print-on-demand publications that often circle around remediation, appropriation, and documentation. It is also, as Judith Goldman writes, "a virtuosic performance of genre-bending, as *HMFF* runs the gamut of conceptualism, confessional um [*sic*] lyric, documentary, life-writing, novella…" often leaning toward oversharing. In addition, it foregrounds voice mail as a means of communication "in the age of SMS and email" that "has its own place in the ecology of immediacy and too closeness" (Judith Goldmann, "Joey Yearous-Algozin's verbatim transcription").

The transcriptions follow a strictly documentary style: They not only contain the usual "um" and "uh" of oral speech, but also dispense with punctuation marks, since these are not a part of spoken language. In addition, they allow a voyeuristic insight into certain idiosyncrasies and patterns in Melgard's life and her various roles as sister, daughter, editor, lecturer, friend, girlfriend, etc. The identity of some callers is redacted. Though Melgard becomes present only as addressee of different demands and her voice is absent in the act of transcription, it is ultimately her who opened up her voice mails to Yearous-Algozin and let him transcribe all or part of them, keeping a significant amount of agency in this kind of exposure and appropriation.

The book comes with an introduction by Teresa Carmody which includes footnotes by Vanessa Place.

MICHAEL JACKSON MTV AWARDS 1995 FULL PERFORMANCE – REMASTERED HD ALL COMMENTS (3,667)

AUTHOR	Rafael Ahmed
YEAR	2015
PUBLISHER	NUPoD 2015
GENRE	education / classroom, experimental literature
METHOD	documentation / archiving, found material, paratextual play, reformatting
SUBJECT	crowd / collaboration, film, internet culture, memory / storage, music / sound, scale, social media, youtube
PLATFORM	Lulu
EDITION CHARACTERISTICS	multiple editions (print, PDF), ISBN 9781329601321, open edition
FORMAT	15.2 × 22.9 cm
MATERIALITIES	black-and-white, paperback, perfect bound
PAGES	142

IMAGES

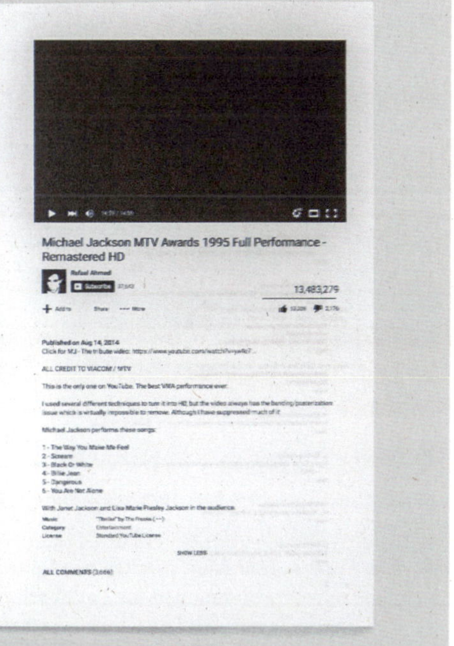

DESCRIPTION

MICHAEL JACKSON MTV AWARDS 1995 FULL PERFORMANCE – REMASTERED HD ALL COMMENTS (3,667) documents all comments posted under the YouTube video by the same name. At the time of production, this was the only video of a live performance by Michael Jackson available on YouTube, because of the very thorough copyright maintenance by the Jackson estate. This, and the fact that the performance is still regarded as Jackson's best live performance ever, turned the video's comment section into a place to discuss the merit of Jackson and his performances. The allegations of abuse and drug use made against him are also a topic, as well as repeated questions about the software used to remaster the video, due to its surprisingly good quality, whereupon the uploader adds a technical explanation.

On Lulu, the authorship of this book is attributed to Rafael Ahmed, the name of the account which uploaded the video, and not the person who actually made the book. Produced in the context of Danny Snelson's experimental writing class "Print on Demand Poetry: Making Books After the Internet" at Northwestern University in 2015, the book is a response to the task: "Find something interesting on the internet, don't do anything to it, put it into a book and see what happens."

The 2015 Baltimore Uprising A Teen Epistolary

AUTHOR	Anonymous
YEAR	2015
GENRE	nonfiction
METHOD	collection, documentation / archiving
SUBJECT	bias, crowd / collaboration, internet culture, politics / activism, publishing / distribution, race, twitter
PLATFORM	Amazon
EDITION CHARACTERISTICS	second edition, ISBN 9781939202208, open edition
FORMAT	10.2 × 15.2 cm
MATERIALITIES	black-and-white, paperback, perfect bound
PAGES	270 (unpaginated)

IMAGES

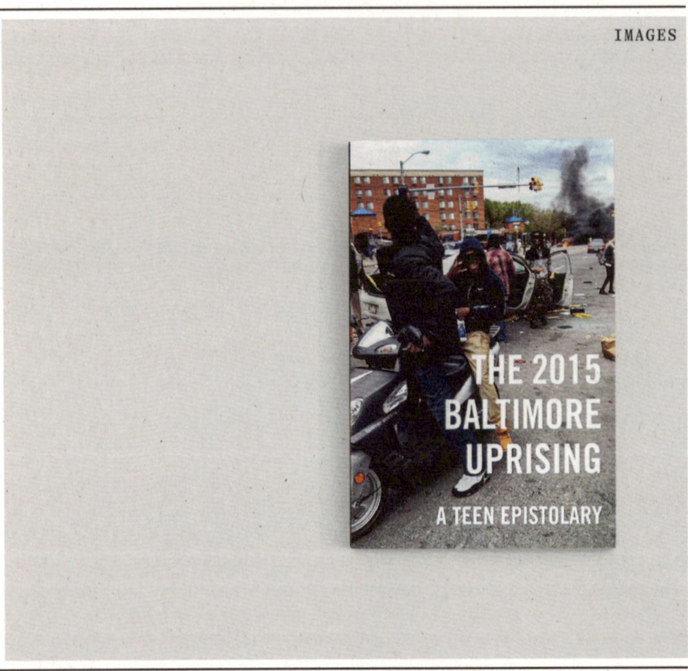

DESCRIPTION

The 2015 Baltimore Uprising: A Teen Epistolary is a collection of screenshotted tweets posted between April 19 and May 1, 2015, by young black residents of Baltimore. The tweets accompanied the two weeks of protests that followed the killing of twenty-five year old African American Freddie Gray in police custody.

The book opens with a tweet capturing the details of Gray's death—comprising photographs and words—that was retweeted 2,964 times and liked 1,268 times (back then, "likes" were "favorites"). It ends with a monotonous nine-page series of tweets responding to a tweet featuring Gray's portrait and coffin, subtitled by the request "Don't Scroll Down Without Typing 'R.I.P.'" The in-between, more or less chronological tweets—"by turns horrified, enraged, elated, humorous, tactical, analytic, and mundane" (Nicholas Thoburn, "Twitter, Book, Riot," 98)—document the riots, battles with police, and looting, as well as the discussions about justice and the value of black life from the perspective of those involved. The tweets give the impression of authenticity and immediacy, evoking the intimacy of an epistolary novel, which is also the subtitle of the book. All Twitter handles and faces are blacked out to avoid identification, given the high number of tweets promoting or showing unlawful activity.

As Nicholas Thoburn reports, the anonymous editors researched the tweets not by hashtags (on the contrary, these were actually excluded), but by "homing in on local landmarks, malls, high-school proms, store names, and idiosyncrasies of the riots. They found that trending hashtags operated at a scale removed from the communicative scene of the uprising, and that at this scale Twitter served those from outside Baltimore who would appropriate the riots to their own ends" (Ibid., 104f.). In this way, they wanted to capture the journalist-free, unfiltered, and unmediated story "that the mainstream media chose to ignore; these voices deserve to be heard" (blurb on Amazon).

The 2015 Baltimore Uprising was initially published by the New Yorker radical zine collective Research and Destroy as a xeroxed pocket-size codex with a tape-covered spine and no ISBN, depriving it from global distribution as a typical "commodity book." Instead, its small print run was distributed locally for free or at a low price. It utilizes the printed book as a more stable container for the preservation of social media posts, which might be altered, policed, or deleted, and removes the platform's responsibility for documentation and preservation. Instead, readers and buyers of the book take on the role of distributed preservers and reminders.

This first edition was reprinted as a perfect bound paperback with a color cover, ISBN, and barcode on the back cover, and sold on Amazon and other platforms, using print-on-demand as a low-cost and relatively anonymous means of worldwide distribution. According to Thoburn, the second edition "is the recapture of an anti-commodity book by capitalist forms," while at the same time making the first edition look like a pirate copy of the second.

Because the book was not published from within the scene of African American youth protestors it depicts, it raises questions about the role social media plays in constituting the public and the private, as well as the distribution of power in activism and publishing.

Durchschnitt

Roman

AUTHOR	Hannes Bajohr
YEAR	2015
PUBLISHER	0x0a, Frohmann
GENRE	experimental literature
METHOD	appropriation, constraint, generative / automation, montage / remix, study / analysis
SUBJECT	canon, code / programming, literature, narration, reading / interpretation, scale
PLATFORM	Lulu
EDITION CHARACTERISTICS	open edition
FORMAT	10.8 × 17.5 cm
MATERIALITIES	black-and-white, paperback, perfect bound
PAGES	262

IMAGES

DESCRIPTION

Hannes Bajohr's *Durchschnitt: Roman* (Average: Novel) can be seen as a contemporary response to the canon debate. It radicalizes the idea of a portable national library, which the famous German literary critic Marcel Reich-Ranicki had realized in 2002 with *Der Kanon: Die deutsche Literatur in fünf Schubern* (The Canon of German Literature in five Boxed Sets), sorted by genre. To address the problem of the "great unread," Hannes Bajohr condenses the box with the twenty "best" German novels into a single paperback by applying various methods of data analysis to the corpus: he wrote a Python script to determine the average length of the sentences (eighteen words), deleted all sentences with deviating lengths, sorted the output by alphabet, and declared it a novel in the subtitle. The outcome of this kind of "distant reading," with the help of which one hopes to learn essentials about texts without having to actually read them, is "the average" of "the best," i.e., a deconstruction of a canon as well as its analytic decomposition.

Reich-Ranicki's box with the twenty best German novels includes: Johann Wolfgang von Goethe, *Die Leiden des jungen Werthers* and *Die Wahlverwandtschaften*; E.T.A. Hoffmann, *Die Elixiere des Teufels*; Gottfried Keller, *Der grüne Heinrich*; Theodor Fontane, *Frau Jenny Treibel* and *Effi Briest*; Thomas Mann, *Buddenbrooks* and *Der Zauberberg*; Heinrich Mann, *Professor Unrat*; Hermann Hesse, *Unterm Rad*; Robert Musil, *Die Verwirrungen des Zöglings Törleß*; Franz Kafka, *Der Prozeß*; Alfred Döblin, *Berlin Alexanderplatz*; Joseph Roth, *Radetzkymarsch*; Anna Seghers, *Das siebte Kreuz*; Heimito von Doderer, *Die Strudlhofstiege*; Wolfgang Koeppen, *Tauben im Gras*; Günter Grass, *Die Blechtrommel*; Max Frisch, *Montauk*; Thomas Bernhard, *Holzfällen*.

The cover design is computer generated like all books by 0x0a, the writer's collective for digital literature consisting of Hannes Bajohr and Gregor Weichbrodt. It is completely determined by certain variables taken from the text itself: "Thus, every text that is published on 0x0a.li gets its own cover, 'written' by its title itself" (Gregor Weichbrodt, "0x0a Cover Art").

Initially published on Lulu and as PDF, the book was re-released by Frohmann Verlag, Berlin in 2016.

Erotica

AUTHOR	Hannes Bajohr
YEAR	2015
PUBLISHER	0x0a
GENRE	experimental literature
METHOD	found material, generative / automation, reformatting
SUBJECT	dating / sex, internet culture, literature, scale
PLATFORM	Lulu
EDITION CHARACTERISTICS	multiple editions (print, PDF), open edition
FORMAT	10.8 × 17.5 cm
MATERIALITIES	black-and-white, paperback, perfect bound
PAGES	62

IMAGES

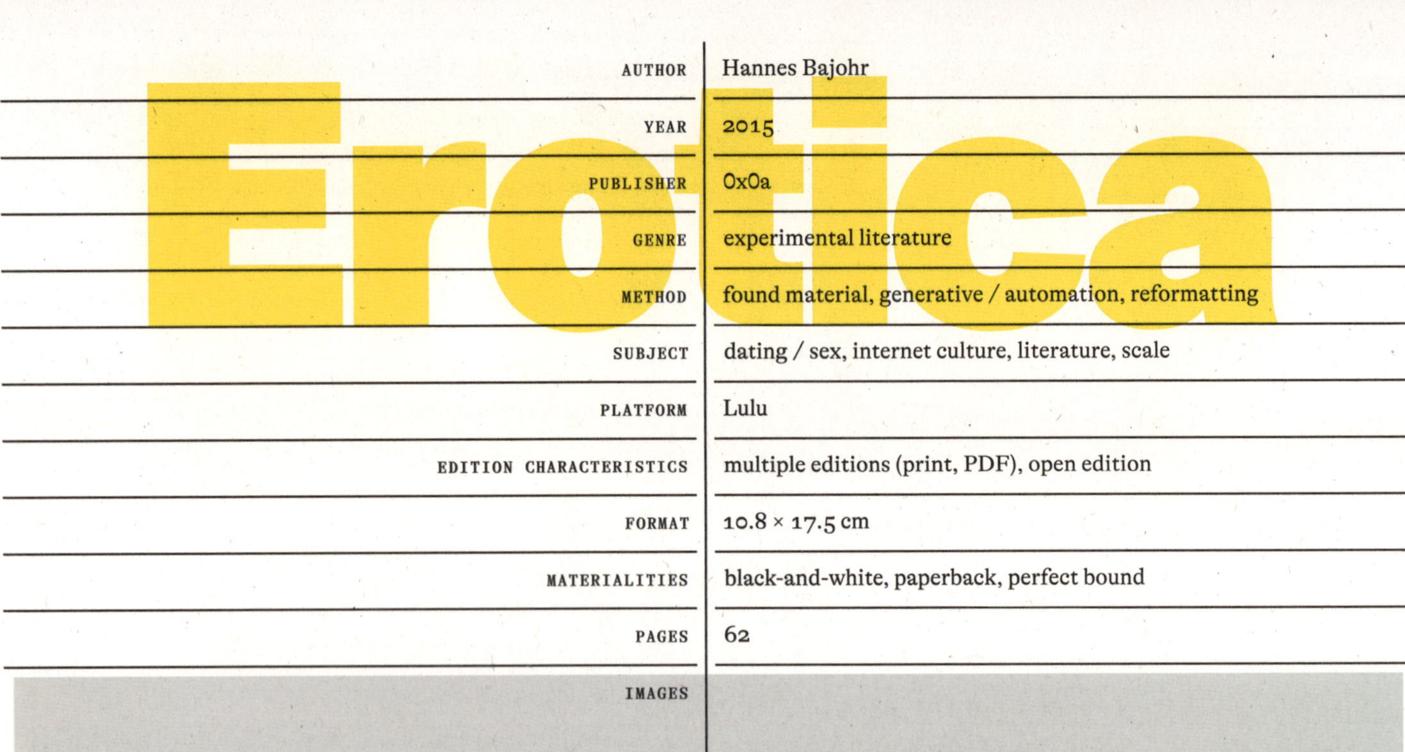

DESCRIPTION

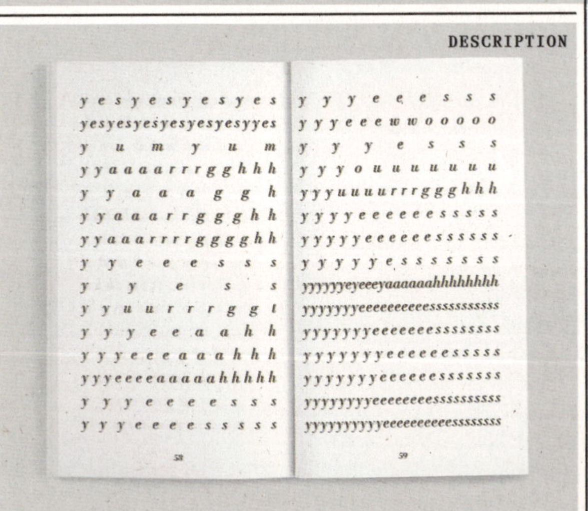

"Besides fan fiction, user generated erotica is the Internet's most original form of fiction. For this piece, the largest repository of amateur erotic writing, literotica.com, was scraped in its entirety. Removing all words that a Python script could identify as English, and leaving only those with two or more consecutive identical characters, out comes an epic poem of moans, groans, and misspellings that would not have made it past any offline editor. Arranged in justified text alignment, the result is as visually pleasing as it is bordering on the incomprehensible edge of arousal" (blurb on Lulu).

In the end, *Erotica* consists mostly of onomatopoeia—that is, the "aaahs" and "ooohs" that are typical for the genre. Formatted as a justified text and stretched along the entire line length, the pages become "concrete" and form figurative patterns that seem to reembody the sexual onomatopoeia.

0x0a, a writers' collective for digital literature consisting of Hannes Bajohr and Gregor Weichbrodt, offers all works as a PDF (free of charge) and through print-on-demand (Lulu).

Various Versions

AUTHOR	Guy Bigland
YEAR	2015
GENRE	experimental literature
METHOD	collection, study / analysis, translation / transcription
SUBJECT	canon, reading / interpretation
PLATFORM	Lulu
EDITION CHARACTERISTICS	ISBN 9781326518875, open edition
FORMAT	19.0 × 19.0 cm
MATERIALITIES	black-and-white, paperback, perfect bound
PAGES	157 (unpaginated)

IMAGES

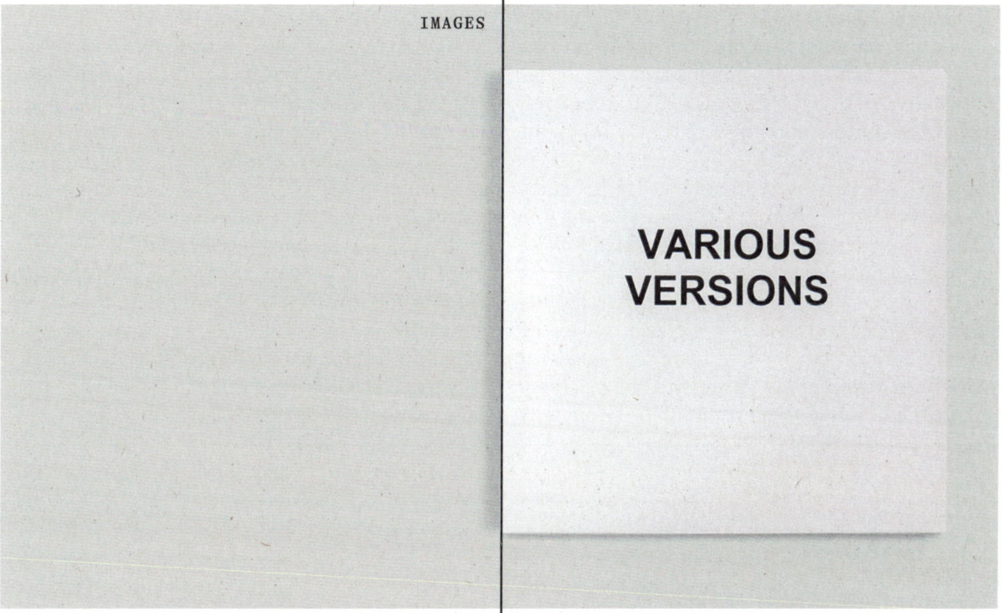

VARIOUS VERSIONS

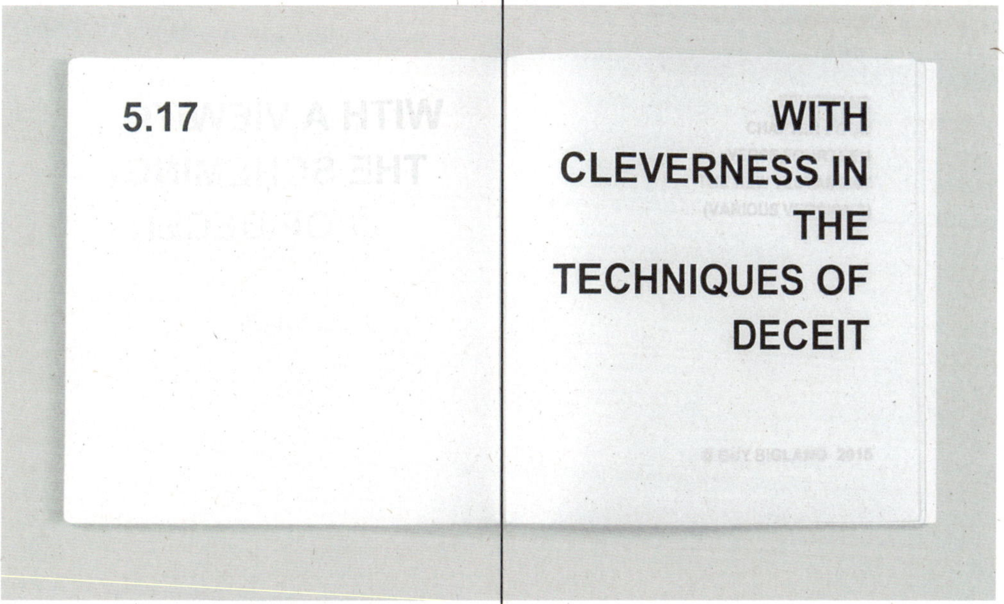

5.17

WITH CLEVERNESS IN THE TECHNIQUES OF DECEIT

DESCRIPTION

Guy Bigland's *Various Versions* compares twenty-four translations of the New Testament verse Ephesians 4:14, which in the World English Bible reads: "Then we will no longer be infants, tossed back and forth by the waves, and blown here and there by every wind of teaching and by the cunning and craftiness of people in their deceitful scheming."

Bigland divided the verse into five parts to make up the chapters of his book: 1. Children, 2. Waves, 3. Teaching, 4. Tricks and 5. Deceit. The translations are dissected and grouped accordingly, thus offering "an examination of translation and interpretation. [...] The 'original' language is powerfully descriptive, poetic and evocative. Under this deconstruction these qualities are both tested (along with the patience of the reader) and reinforced by repetition and rearrangement" (blurb on artist website).

Library of Babel

AUTHOR	Christian Bök
YEAR	2015
GENRE	artist's book / bookwork, experimental literature
METHOD	generative / automation, versioning / seriality
SUBJECT	code / programming, literature, reading / interpretation, scale
PLATFORM	Blurb
VOLUMES	5
EDITION CHARACTERISTICS	limited edition

DESCRIPTION

"Jorge Luis Borges in *The Library of Babel* imagines a hellish archive of books—a macrocosmic columbarium, whose infinite chambers provide an exhaustive repository for all the permutations of the alphabet. Inside this endless library, nonsensical texts so drastically outnumber any intelligible books that a coherent phrase must seem tantamount to a wondrous mishap. Poets within such a prisonhouse can no longer contribute anything innovative to literature, because literature itself has already anticipated and inventoried in advance all the anagrammatic combinations of every text" (blurb on Blurb).

The librarian who narrates Borges's story mentions five books by name: *LXUM,LKWC*; *mcv*; *The Plaster Cramp*; *Axaxaxas Mlo* and *The Combed Thunderclap*. They have been reproduced by Christian Bök according to the general specifications (410 pages, forty lines of text per page, and eighty characters of text per line) as well as the specific features (title, style, and phrases appearing in the book) as reported by the narrator. For example, in reference to the first volume, he speaks of it as containing "a mere labyrinth of letters, but the next-to-last page says 'Oh time thy pyramids.'" Another volume, the narrator reports, "consists of only 'the letters MCV, perversely repeated from the first line to the last,' like a cryptogram corresponding to no language" (blurb on Blurb).

Bök's books are based on the algorithmic representation of the Library of Babel by Jonathan Basile, who has written the code to generate the library according to Borges's imagination as well as creating an interface to search for words or phrases.

The books are set in Panoptica, "a font designed by Nick Shinn, who has created a set of monospaced characters, according to the 'prisoner's constraint,' meaning that none of the letters have either ascenders or descenders" (blurb on Blurb).

All five books of Bök's series contain no explanatory text, no title pages, and no author name. They are limited to an edition of twenty-five copies, after which they will be discontinued, with an updated note on how many books are left of each edition in the description text on Blurb. Because of this artificial limitation, the author can promote his books as "[a] collectible item, perfect as a gift for bibliophiles, who might love the work of Borges" (blurb on Blurb). The books were also advertised by Bök via Twitter. He also posted there when a "print run" of a title like *LXUM,LKWC* was sold out.

LXUM,LKWC: OH TIME THY PYRAMIDS

EDITION CHARACTERISTICS	ISBN 9781364973261, limited edition, sold out
FORMAT	15.2 × 22.9 cm
MATERIALITIES	black-and-white, dust jacket, hardcover
PAGES	416

IMAGE

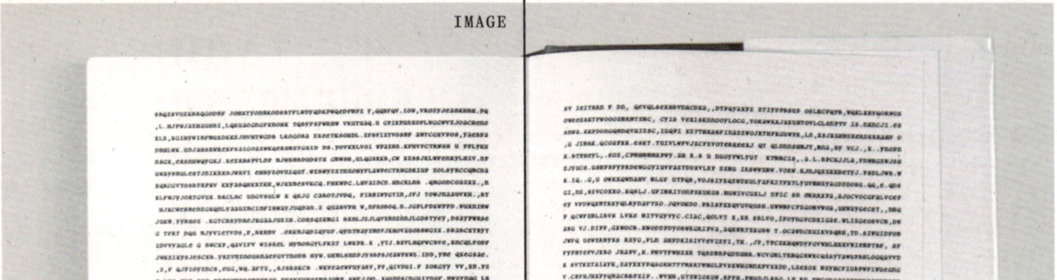

Primary Source

AUTHOR	Francesca Capone
YEAR	2015
PUBLISHER	Gauss PDF
GENRE	artist's book / bookwork, exhibition copy, experimental literature, reprint
METHOD	found material, generative / automation, montage / remix, translation / transcription
SUBJECT	analog / digital, book / book design, code / programming, error / corruption / loss, literature, technology, typography
PLATFORM	Lulu
EDITION CHARACTERISTICS	second edition, multiple editions (print, PDF, MOV), open edition
FORMAT	10.8 × 17.5 cm
MATERIALITIES	color, paperback, perfect bound
PAGES	238 (unpaginated)

IMAGE

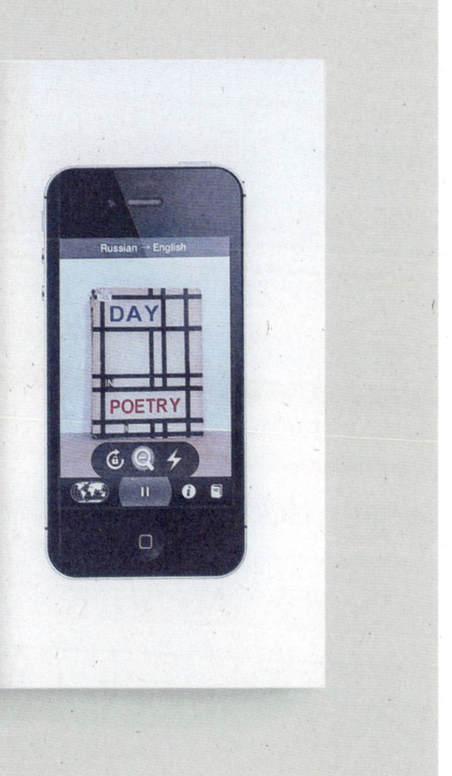

DESCRIPTION

In 2015, the augmented reality application Word Lens was implemented into the iPhone Translate app. It uses the phone's built-in camera to scan and identify text, translates it to a given language, and overwrites the real text in the device's display with its translation, also trying to match fonts and layout.

For *Primary Source*, Francesca Capone pointed an iPhone with activated Word Lens at the cover of *Den' poèzii* (Poetry Day), a poetry annual published in 1962 by the Soviet Writer publishing house in Moscow. The cover, featuring a grid-like pattern in the style of Piet Mondrian and De Stijl, caused ever changing errors and glitches in the Word Lens app. Even the very first translation attempt detects an "in" in the grid where there is none: "Day in Poetry."

The book is a collection of the software's efforts at capture and translation, with additional disruptions caused by several changes of the language from which it is supposed to translate (at the time, Russian, German, French, Italian, Portuguese, and Spanish were supported). Photos of the full iPhone with the translations suggested by the app alternate with image snippets and minimalist visual poems composed of parts of the supposed translations that have been detached from the iPhone screen and transferred to the page.

The book was initially designed and published as part of a work titled *Primary Source*, which was exhibited in the 2015 group show "Maximum Sideline: Postscript" at Proxy (Providence, Rhode Island). The Gauss PDF Edition with the number GPDFE016-1 is a reprint of this exhibition copy, including an essay on the work by John Cayley who admits his "poetic delight and wonder, as a once unreadable book, assumed to contain poetry, is addressed by an apparatus [...] and gives the cover of this book to speak, and to speak something that we can read as poetry" (John Cayley, "On Primary Source"). The second part of the edition with the number GPDFE016-2 is a video featuring a fast stream of translated cover versions.

A Skeleton of Print On Demand

AUTHORS	Brianna Cohen, Sophia Falmagne, Jonathan Hofman, Aiden Ziliak
YEAR	2015
PUBLISHER	NUPoD 2015
GENRE	education / classroom, experimental literature
METHOD	collective, composition (writing / drawing / photography), documentation / archiving, reformatting
SUBJECT	book / book design, crowd / collaboration, email / messaging, print on demand, publishing / distribution
PLATFORM	Lulu
EDITION CHARACTERISTICS	multiple editions (print, PDF), open edition
FORMAT	10.8 × 17.5 cm
MATERIALITIES	black-and-white, paperback, perfect bound
PAGES	318 (unpaginated)

IMAGES

DESCRIPTION

A Skeleton of Print On Demand documents an email thread generated by the authors discussing their midterm project for Danny Snelson's course "Print on Demand Poetry: Making Books After the Internet" at Northwestern University in 2015. The task was to create "one McLuhanesque Print on Demand book (about (Print on Demand) books). Primary sources from the course texts must be used. Any collaborative arrangement may be employed by your group, but all members of the editorial team must participate in the making of the book" (blurb on Lulu).

Because the email thread often includes several earlier emails that have been replied to, the printed email exchange results in a highly repetitive text discussing how to approach the task, as well as when to meet to start the work. In passing, the students also discuss creative writing, self-publishing, and the promises and limitations of print-on-demand.

First Thought Worst Thought Collected Books 2011–2014. Guide Book

AUTHOR	Tom Comitta
YEAR	2015
PUBLISHER	Gauss PDF
GENRE	catalog / collection, experimental literature
METHOD	collection, composition (writing / drawing / photography), documentation / archiving
SUBJECT	literature, memory / storage, print on demand, publishing / distribution
PLATFORM	Lulu
EDITION CHARACTERISTICS	multiple editions (print, PDF, ZIP), open edition
FORMAT	15.2 × 22.9 cm
MATERIALITIES	color, paperback, perfect bound
PAGES	46

IMAGES

DESCRIPTION

First Thought Worst Thought: Collected Books 2011–2014. Guide Book catalogs all thirty-eight books that were written and designed by Tom Comitta between 2011 and 2014 but were stored on their hard drive instead of seeing the light of day. With the help of Gauss PDF, the author published the entire collection at once as number GPDFE014—a project that would have been unthinkable without print-on-demand, as the author explains on their website. All books were published both as PDF and print-on-demand, and are available individually or as ZIP folders, sorted by year.

In the *Guide Book*, each book is described in detail and at times accompanied by further material. Making explicit the conceptual idea and reasoning behind their works, this publication arguably becomes the best entry point to Comitta's artistic writing practices. The experimental approaches to writing range from appropriation and collage to conceptual writing, visual poetry, and the transcription of sound works, and focus on the book as artwork, even though the works are mostly text-based.

AUTHOR	Sophia Falmagne
YEAR	2015
PUBLISHER	NUPoD 2015
GENRE	education / classroom, experimental literature
METHOD	documentation / archiving, found material, reformatting
SUBJECT	analog / digital, canon, economy / labor, google, literature, publishing / distribution, search engine
PLATFORM	Lulu
EDITION CHARACTERISTICS	multiple editions (print, PDF), ISBN 9781329601345, open edition
FORMAT	15.2 × 22.9 cm
MATERIALITIES	black-and-white, paperback, perfect bound
PAGES	125

IMAGES

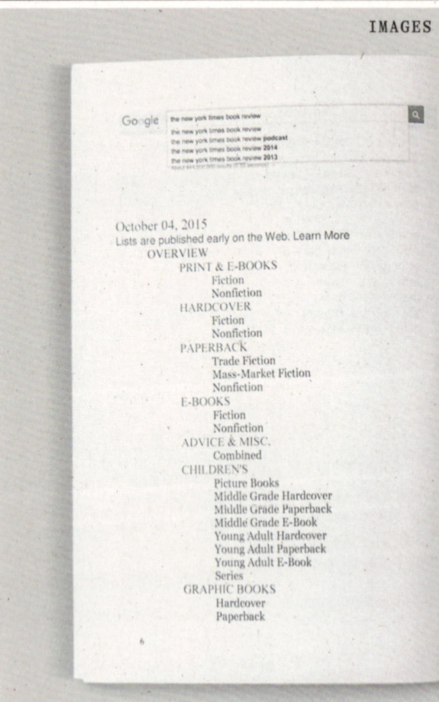

Google the new york times book review
the new york times book review
the new york times book review podcast
the new york times book review 2014
the new york times book review 2013

October 04, 2015
Lists are published early on the Web. Learn More
OVERVIEW
PRINT & E-BOOKS
Fiction
Nonfiction
HARDCOVER
Fiction
Nonfiction
PAPERBACK
Trade Fiction
Mass-Market Fiction
Nonfiction
E-BOOKS
Fiction
Nonfiction
ADVICE & MISC.
Combined
CHILDREN'S
Picture Books
Middle Grade Hardcover
Middle Grade Paperback
Middle Grade E-Book
Young Adult Hardcover
Young Adult Paperback
Young Adult E-Book
Series
GRAPHIC BOOKS
Hardcover
Paperback

6

Manga
MONTHLY LISTS
Animals
Business
Celebrities
Crime
Culture
Education
Espionage
Expeditions
Family
Fashion
Food and Fitness
Games
Health
Humor
Indigenous
Politics
Race
Relationships
Religion
Science
Sports
Travel

Inside the List
By GREGORY COWLES
Lauren Groff, whose "Fates and Furies" is No. 7 on the hardcover fiction list, says she relates to both of the book's main characters: "I wobble between action and somewhat optimistic fatalism."

Editors' Choice

Recently reviewed books of particular interest.

Paperback Row
By JOUMANA KHATIB
Paperback books of particular interest.
cur:DoubleRule prev:DoubleRule

Browse Past Lists
JanuaryFebruaryMarchAprilMayJuneJulyAugustSeptemberOctober 20112012201320142015
October 4, 2015 »

7

DESCRIPTION

Sophia Falmagne's *Book* documents a web search for "the best book ever written." It captures the top results from Google Search and Yahoo! Answers, and includes the *New York Times*, *Time Magazine*, and *BBC* bestseller lists. All content is copied as it appears in the browser, preserving the original formatting and including all text and images for ads and suggested articles. The major part of *Book* is taken up by "an alphabetical listing by author of adult fiction books which have made number one on the *New York Times* Best Seller List along with the date that they first reached number one," beginning with the year 1942. This not only results in an "assortment of images and content from the web documenting information about literature and popular preference in book-reading, especially in the twentieth and twenty-first centuries," as the blurb on Lulu suggests, but also reflects opinion formation in the age of Web 2.0 as opposed to traditional ways of canon formation and sales. This online–offline dichotomy is also visible in the design of the front cover and back cover: the front shows a stylized book icon, while the back is the scanned back cover of an older book, presumably from Google Books. The book was produced in Danny Snelson's experimental writing class "Print-on-Demand Poetry: Making Books After the Internet" at Northwestern University in 2015.

Whereis Mineral
Selected Adventures in MOO

AUTHOR	Chris Funkhouser
YEAR	2015
PUBLISHER	Gauss PDF
GENRE	experimental literature, fiction
METHOD	documentation / archiving
SUBJECT	authorship, crowd / collaboration, games, internet culture, narration
PLATFORM	Lulu
EDITION CHARACTERISTICS	multiple editions (print, PDF), open edition
FORMAT	21.6 × 27.9 cm
MATERIALITIES	black-and-white, paperback, perfect bound
PAGES	158 (unpaginated)

IMAGES

DESCRIPTION

"In the early 1990s, MOO, an acronym for M(ulti-User Dungeon) Object-Oriented, enabled many people to connect online—where they'd engage with each other, build digital structures and functioning robots, entirely out of text. [...] *Whereis Mineral* documents the author's traversing of various online MOOs, most accurately classified as text-based virtual realities, prior to the advent of the WWW. Among other attributes, these logs reflect tests of patience and focus; substantial lags, computer foibles, as well as all sorts of imaginative construction" (blurb on Lulu).

Embedded in the narrative and interactions with others are commands—marked in bold for better distinction—such as "e" for "east" or "u" for "up" which had to be typed in order to be able to move in the MOO. From these commands, the authors' actions and decisions can be inferred. What is documented here is not only an early form of real-time textuality bound to the computer: it also raises the question of collaborative authorship, since many people co-wrote the text.

Even though this work does not have a traditional, complex narration, what does emerge is a detailed picture of a virtual space and a lively community of avatars with different interests, identities, and languages. A case in point might be LambdaMOO, whose logon screen reads: "LambdaMOO is a new kind of society, where thousands of people voluntarily come together from all over the world. What these people say or do may not always be to your liking; as when visiting any international city, it is wise to be careful who you associate with and what you say. / The operators of LambdaMOO have provided the materials for the buildings of this community, but are not responsible for what is said or done in them" (Chris Funkhouser, "Afterword," n.p.).

The author sets out in this virtual society to find a poet friend with the avatar name Mineral (who, by his own admission, was more into the LambdaMOO subculture than the real world at the time), "looking to see if and where he was online, frequently following his path." Hence the title *Whereis Mineral*. At the same time, "*Whereis Mineral* wishes to raise a literal question of the title, where is the 'mineral,' the inner ore of one's expressiveness in technologized literary forms?" (Ibid.)

Print On Demand

A "Think Piece"

AUTHORS	Rimsha Ganatra, Brendan McManus, Hadley Pfalzgraf, Jackie Quinn
YEAR	2015
PUBLISHER	NUPoD 2015
GENRE	education / classroom, experimental literature
METHOD	collective, composition (writing / drawing / photography), found material, reformatting
SUBJECT	book / book design, internet culture, print on demand, publishing / distribution, reading / interpretation
PLATFORM	Lulu
EDITION CHARACTERISTICS	multiple editions (print, PDF), 9781329626829, open edition
FORMAT	15.2 × 22.9 cm
MATERIALITIES	black-and-white, paperback, perfect bound
PAGES	52 (unpaginated)

IMAGES

DESCRIPTION

Print On Demand: A "Think Piece" is a collectively written publication for a midterm project in the context of Danny Snelson's experimental writing class "Print on Demand Poetry: Making Books After the Internet" at Northwestern University in 2015. The task was to create "one McLuhanesque Print on Demand book (about (Print on Demand) books). Primary sources from the course texts must be used. Any collaborative arrangement may be employed by your group, but all members of the editorial team must participate in the making of the book."

The book consists of quotes reflecting on the internet, books, reading, and modes of remediation as well as artifacts of online culture such as memes, screenshots, photoshopped images, and a walkthrough of a Zelda computer game.

The quotes are taken from canonical texts such as *As We May Think* by Vannevar Bush and *Remediation* by Jay David Bolter and Richard Grusin, and are set in extravagant fonts turning the statements into emblematic tableaux. Their effect is sometimes intensified by slight interventions in the quotations, for example when the excerpt from Ben Elton's dystopian novel *Blind Faith* (2007) is concluded with multiple repetitions of the last half-sentence: "ONLY PAPER IS SAFE. BOOKS ARE THE KEY. A BOOK CANNOT BE ACCESSED FROM AFAR, YOU HAVE TO HOLD IT, YOU HAVE TO READ IT. TO READ IT. TO READ IT. TO READ IT. TO READ IT. TO READ IT." Or when Tan Lin's prognostic statement from an interview with Angela Genusa (reprinted in *Best of Rhizome 2012*, see 249) is reinforced by repeating the last syllable "on" of the last word "information" multiple times full-page in three columns: "Maybe that's the future of the book: [to look] like a licensing agreement regarding the future dissemination of its own information" (Tan Lin, "A Book is Technology").

The result is a diverting, metareflexive read on online and offline culture that is, in its core, a collective undertaking not just because it was compiled by four different authors but also due to its practices of copying and pasting. This is put in a nutshell by the mocking blurb on Lulu: "Try to distinguish our voices. You can't."

PDF TOO LARGE

AUTHOR	Google Drive
YEAR	2015
PUBLISHER	NUPoD 2015
GENRE	artist's book / bookwork, education / classroom
METHOD	collective, documentation / archiving, found material, paratextual play, remediation
SUBJECT	authorship, email / messaging, error / corruption / loss, google, publishing / distribution, technology
PLATFORM	Lulu
EDITION CHARACTERISTICS	multiple editions (print, PDF), ISBN 9781329626386, open edition
FORMAT	21.6 × 21.6 cm
MATERIALITIES	color, paperback, perfect bound
PAGES	56

IMAGES

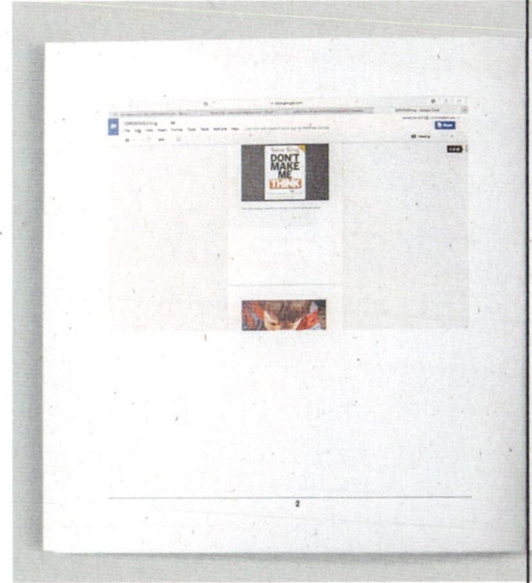

DESCRIPTION

PDF TOO LARGE is a collectively created publication for the midterm project in Danny Snelson's course "Print on Demand Poetry: Making Books After the Internet" at Northwestern University in 2015. The task was to create "one McLuhanesque Print on Demand book (about (Print on Demand) books). Primary sources from the course texts must be used. Any collaborative arrangement may be employed by your group, but all members of the editorial team must participate in the making of the book."

The book consists of screenshots of an entire Google Doc (including its graphical user interface as well as the browser's toolbars etc.), which seems to be the collectively written document initially edited for the task. The document itself consists of small texts, quotes for the most part, and pictures reflecting on the interdependence of content and medium/form. It also features screenshots of browser windows with opened Facebook timelines and error messages, visualizing interfaces, and workflows. *PDF TOO LARGE* is the result of media layering, depicting digital collective workflows, interfaces, and their embedding of documents, pictures, and screenshots of embedded documents and pictures.

Participating students can be guessed from name tags on the depiction of varying graphical user interfaces, but authorship is ultimately granted to Google Drive—at least as the author tag on Lulu—being the framework and the interface connecting the collectively edited document and the PDF uploaded to the print-on-demand platform. The blurb on Lulu reproduces the error message that gave the book its title: "The file you are trying to send exceeds the 25MB attachment limit. But don't worry, you can send it using Google Drive."

A Book

AUTHOR	Google Search
YEAR	2015
PUBLISHER	NUPoD 2015
GENRE	artist's book / bookwork, education / classroom
METHOD	documentation / archiving, found material, paratextual play, reformatting
SUBJECT	authorship, book / book design, google, publishing / distribution, search engine
PLATFORM	Lulu
EDITION CHARACTERISTICS	multiple editions (print, PDF), ISBN 9781329600805, open edition
FORMAT	15.2 × 22.9 cm
MATERIALITIES	black-and-white, paperback, perfect bound
PAGES	48 (unpaginated)

IMAGES

book

is this a book?

According to the definition above, e-books are not books.

Please leave your comments below.

DESCRIPTION

A Book, produced as part of Danny Snelson's course "Print on Demand Poetry: Making Books After the Internet" at Northwestern University in 2015, documents results from a Google Search query on "What is a book." The book begins with screenshots of the search engine's autocomplete suggestions after the question is entered word for word, and then reproduces various articles that the author(s) clicked on, copied and pasted into their publication, keeping the original formatting. Sometimes only key phrases are rendered and sometimes articles are copied in their entirety, including ads and suggested articles.

The book contains no paratext other than the title and authorship on the front cover. That this is a conscious decision is shown on the first page with the remark "This page is blank." By attributing authorship to Google Search, *A Book* also reflects on authorship and interpretative sovereignty in times of algorithmic content selection. Thus, the rather platitudinous question "Did you just read a book?" at the very end of the publication turns out to be highly complex.

INTERN

AUTHOR	Intern
YEAR	2015
PUBLISHER	Troll Thread
GENRE	artist's book / bookwork, experimental literature
METHOD	composition (writing / drawing / photography), documentation / archiving
SUBJECT	economy / labor, email / messaging, print on demand, publishing / distribution, standard / default, technology, tracking
PLATFORM	Lulu
EDITION CHARACTERISTICS	multiple editions (print, PDF), open edition
FORMAT	21.6 × 27.9 cm
MATERIALITIES	black-and-white, paperback, perfect bound
PAGES	304 (unpaginated)

IMAGES

DESCRIPTION

In 2015, Troll Thread had their one and only intern, presumably named Phil. Due to the publishing collective's general rejection of exploitative internship culture in the publishing industry, they turned Phil's stay into an artistic publishing practice, leading to three publications: *DEMO BOOK FOR INTERN* by Joey Yearous-Algozin (Troll Thread, 2015, see 352), *Poems Abt 'Intern' and 'Phil' the Intern* by Chris Sylvester (Area Sneaks, 2016), and *INTERN* by the intern himself. The latter is a meticulous documentation of tasks assigned to the intern between April 20 and May 11, 2015, the time he spent to fulfill these tasks, commentary on takeaways, and a complete documentation of text and email conversations he had with the publishers, plus Chris Sylvester's *Poems Abt 'Intern' and 'Phil' the Intern*.

All tasks are put into the form of a "Timesheet," including the fields "TITLE / NAME," "DESCRIPTION," "APPROX. TIME 'SPENT,'" "APPROX. DATE(S) OF ACTIVITY," "OUTCOMES / RESULTS," "NOTES ('OPTIONAL')." This adds up to sixty-four tasks in total, ranging from installing Adobe Acrobat, to having cigarette breaks, to solving Tumblr catalog issues, to writing spreadsheets of the complete costs of Troll Thread's publications and creating test publications. The painstaking segmentation and documentation of tasks is in harsh contrast to the tasks themselves, which are often commented on ironically, such as here: "attempted download and install adobe. failed, listened to bright eyes and ate ice cream."

At the same time, the reader gains insight into the production and distribution conditions at Lulu, for example which Troll Thread publications Lulu forbids access to, which ones are now unavailable because Lulu no longer offers a certain type of binding, and the fact that Lulu's cart limit is forty-four books. It also becomes clear how much time, energy, work, and struggle with technology it takes to keep the seemingly undemanding Troll Thread Tumblr page up to date and error-free, or to fix gutter issues in the PDFs.

By documenting the internship and publishing it in their program, Troll Thread turns what would only be one person's hidden work and insights into a public glimpse into their publishing activities, their understanding of publishing and poetry, their workflows, and everyday lives. As part of the "Timesheet," *Intern* also documents the discussion and creation of the publication itself, ending with the task "Emailing Updated INTERN BY INTERN docs to H. Melgard."

AUTHOR	Marina Kampka
YEAR	2015
PUBLISHER	AND Publishing
GENRE	artist's book / bookwork, poetry
METHOD	composition (writing / drawing / photography), found material
SUBJECT	book / book design, literature, materiality
PLATFORM	Lulu
VOLUMES	2
EDITION CHARACTERISTICS	ISBN, open edition
FORMAT	15.2 × 22.9 cm
MATERIALITIES	black-and-white, paperback, perfect bound
IMAGE	

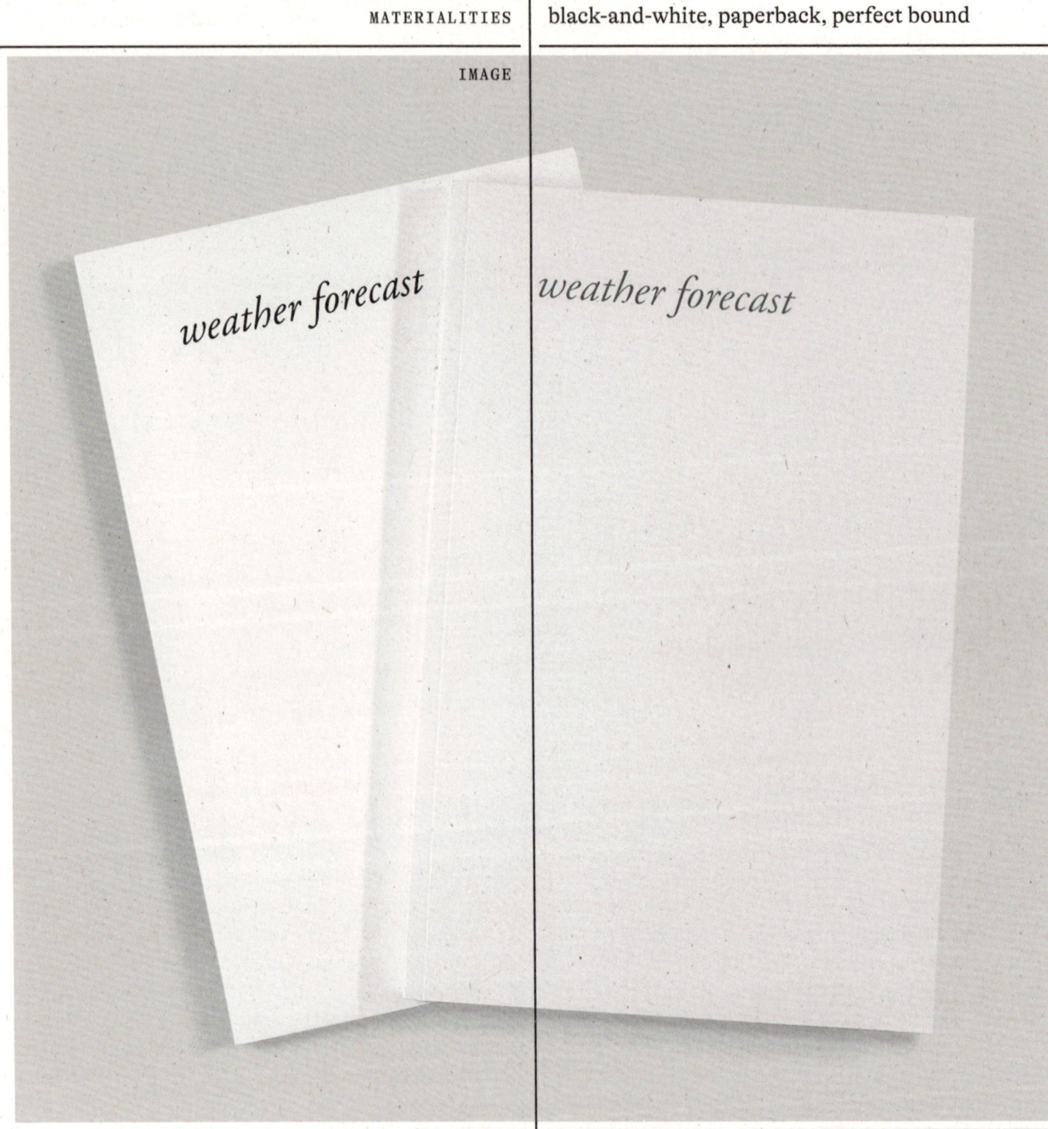

DESCRIPTION

"*weather forecast* is a non-complete and subjective collection of english weather forecasts, edited out of 28 (random) newspapers during 4 different London visits between october 2012 and september 2013. read in those small excerpts, the english weather appears like poetry.

this book is a twin. whereas *weather forecast (1)* shows the 'weather poems' one after another, page by page, black on white, *weather forecast (2)* uses the book format differently: every 'poem' is printed side-inverted on the backside of front page. due to transparency of the paper, the text can be read 'through' the page" (blurb on Lulu).

Kampka's series is proof that print-on-demand books can also win awards: the second volume was awarded the "Förderpreis für junge Buchgestaltung" (Sponsorship Prize for Young Book Design) in the 2016 competition "Die Schönsten Deutschen Bücher" (The Best German Book Design). The jury: "Although the typographic principle is essentially uncomplicated, it lends the reading process an almost philosophical dimension. We are looking at something that is not actually there—at least not where we perceive it to be. You could say that we are reading into the future—the point in time where we turn the page" (Stiftung Buchkunst, *Die Schönsten Deutschen Bücher* 2016, 280).

weather forecast a fair amount of cloud around (1)

EDITION CHARACTERISTICS	ISBN 9781908452603
PAGES	216
IMAGE	

elsewhere,
fine after
a cold start

weather forecast another grey start (2)

EDITION CHARACTERISTICS	ISBN 9781908452610
PAGES	218
IMAGE	

Networked Optimization

AUTHORS	Silvio Lorusso, Sebastian Schmieg
YEAR	2015
GENRE	artist's book / bookwork
METHOD	documentation / archiving, found material, remediation
SUBJECT	amazon, analog / digital, book / book design, canon, crowd / collaboration, reading / interpretation, surveillance / privacy, technology, writing / reading techniques
PLATFORM	Lulu
VOLUMES	3
EDITION CHARACTERISTICS	ISBN, CC0
FORMAT	15.2 × 22.9 cm
MATERIALITIES	black-and-white, paperback, perfect bound

IMAGE

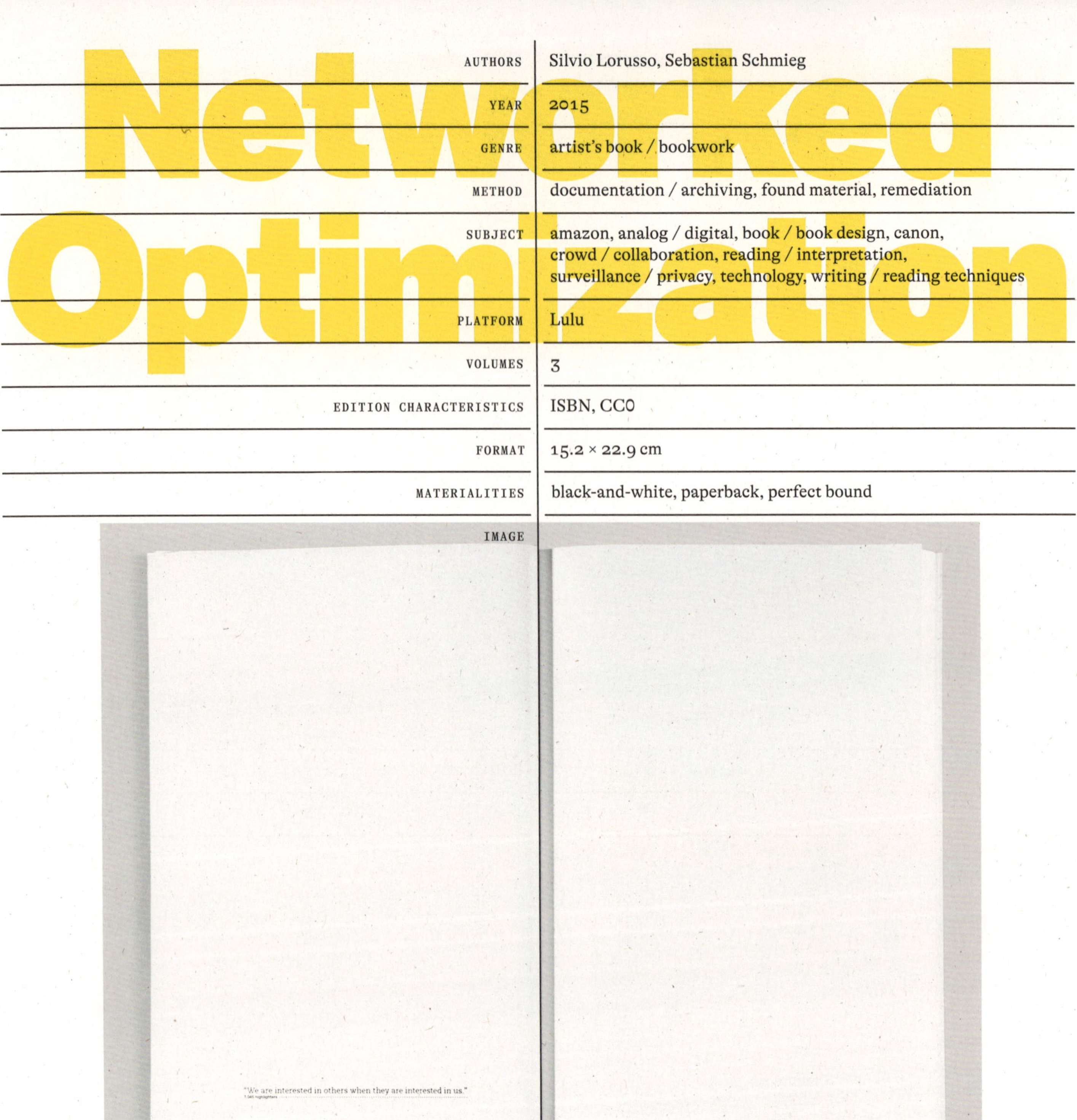

DESCRIPTION

Silvio Lorusso and Sebastian Schmieg's three-volume *Networked Optimization* series is a physical reimagination as printed book of texts originally displayed on the Kindle e-book reader. At the same time, it is a kind of "crowdsourced version[...] of popular self-help books" (Sebastian Schmieg, "Networked Optimization," website), produced—unwittingly—in collaboration with myriads of Amazon Kindle users.

The artists use Kindle's "popular highlights" feature, which allows to see the passages highlighted most often by all Kindle readers of the same book, along with the number of times they were highlighted. This data is possible to access because all highlighting by a Kindle user is forwarded to Amazon, where it is stored, processed, and used, for example for marketing purposes and market research.

As the artists explain: "Among the books with the most popular highlights, there is a striking number of self-help books. This points to a multi-layered, algorithmic optimization: from readers and authors to Amazon itself. Harvesting its customers micro-labour, the act of reading becomes a data-mining process" (Ibid.).

Apart from these underlined passages as well as the number of highlights and indication of the text position distributed over the book, the books do not contain any further text. The highlights (mostly banalities like "Forgiveness is the way of love") show the content that many readers prioritize, as well as their reading habits. A strikingly large number of underlined passages, for example, are found in the first third of the books, which can be interpreted either as readers discontinuing their reading or as a perceived decline in the book's quality.

The books in this series appropriate the cover designs of the original books on which they are based, but delete all text except for the ISBN on the back cover. They have been part of installations and exhibitions that further investigate the subject of optimization, for example, using speed-reading software.

How to Win Friends and Influence People

EDITION CHARACTERISTICS	ISBN 9781312801790
PAGES	214 (unpaginated)
IMAGE	

The Five Love Languages

EDITION CHARACTERISTICS	ISBN 9781312801714
PAGES	156 (unpaginated)
IMAGE	

The Seven Habits of Highly Effective People

EDITION CHARACTERISTICS	ISBN 9781300905332
PAGES	364 (unpaginated)
IMAGE	

23187425 {1000 Haiku}

AUTHOR	Rob Lycett
YEAR	2015
GENRE	experimental literature, poetry
METHOD	found material, generative / automation, montage / remix, reformatting, versioning / seriality
SUBJECT	data, literature, print technology, print on demand, search engine, surveillance / privacy
PLATFORM	Lulu
EDITION CHARACTERISTICS	open edition, CC BY-SA
FORMAT	14.0 × 21.6 cm
MATERIALITIES	black-and-white, paperback, perfect bound
PAGES	252

IMAGES

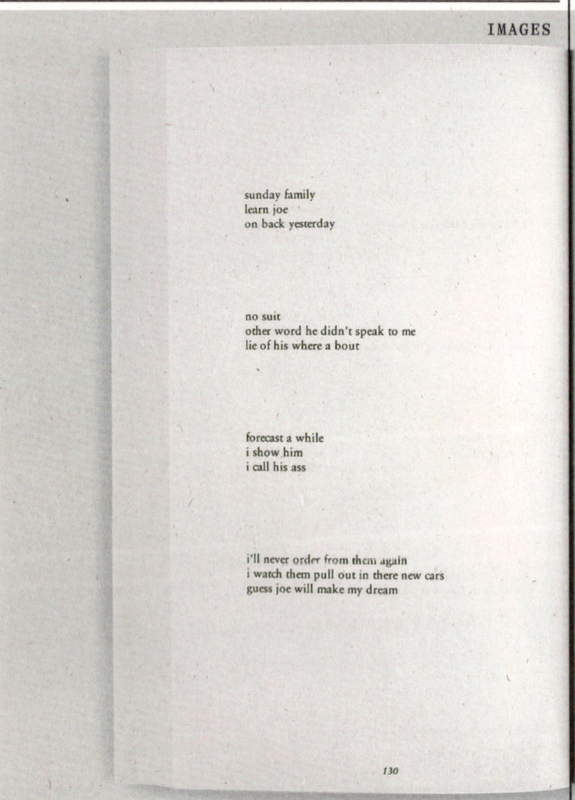

sunday family
learn joe
on back yesterday

no suit
other word he didn't speak to me
lie of his where a bout

forecast a while
i show him
i call his ass

i'll never order from them again
i watch them pull out in there new cars
guess joe will make my dream

130

no air you mean on sunday
not a part of my life
told tyrell men a worth a shit

in 80 Or 85
joe own now
you cut us off

bless one
get that money
when i ask you things i'm i right a lot

you lose
why all the noise
look for a church

131

DESCRIPTION

"In 2006, America Online (AOL) accidentally released the search queries from some 20 million of its customers. The users were anonymous, identified by numerical tags, and no IP addresses were disclosed, though many were easily identified with a quick triangulation of data. Thomas Claburn quickly recognized the literary potential of this cache, publishing the data from one user with only minor formatting changes to aid readability" (Craig Dworkin, Kenneth Goldsmith, ed., *Against Expression*, 138).

Rob Lycett's project draws upon the same data of the same AOL user with the tag 23187425 (which becomes the title of Lycett's book), whose search queries form "a randomly quoted monologue, by an unknown hand (or machine)" (blurb on Lulu). But unlike Claburn, he strips the search queries from their time stamps and uses them as lines for poetry. Three lines are picked at random to produce a haiku and 1,000 such haiku are collected in the book.

"Each printed book is a unique impression of the data, and is enabled by print on demand technologies," Lycett states in the blurb, though there is only one edition to be bought via Lulu, the content of which was generated on July 17, 2015.

The Pirate Book

AUTHORS	Nicolas Maigret [ed.], Maria Roszkowska [ed.]
YEAR	2015
PUBLISHER	Aksioma
GENRE	catalog / collection, nonfiction
METHOD	composition (writing / drawing / photography), documentation / archiving, study / analysis
SUBJECT	analog / digital, copyright / law, economy / labor, internet culture, politics / activism, publishing / distribution, technology, visual culture
PLATFORM	Lulu
EDITION CHARACTERISTICS	multiple editions (black-and-white, color, PDF), ISBN 9789619219287, open edition
FORMAT	14.8 × 21.0 cm
MATERIALITIES	black-and-white, paperback, perfect bound
PAGES	238 (unpaginated)

IMAGES

American literature itself came into its own and authors such as Mark Twain convinced the government to reinforce copyright legislation.

Piracy, Access, and Production Infrastructure
The article "Piracy, Creativity and Infrastructure: Rethinking Access to Culture," in which the Indian legal expert Lawrence Liang situates the issue of the piracy of cultural artefacts in emerging economies, also rejects the narrow view of piracy as a solely illicit activity and goes on to depict it as an infrastructure providing access to culture. The abundantly illustrated stories brought together in *The Pirate Book* all inform this notion by inviting the reader to shift perspective. As described by the researcher and legal expert Pedro Mizukami, the emergence of bootlegged video rentals and consoles in Brazil was directly linked to the country's industrial policies of the 1980s which aimed at closing the Brazilian market to imports in order to stimulate the growth of local productions, some of which were exorbitantly priced. Cuba's isolation by the US embargo since 1962 and its ensuing inability to procure basic resources provided a fertile ground for audio-visual piracy on the part, among others, of the government itself in order to supply its official television channels with content as well as to provide its universities with books, as highlighted by the designer and artist Ernesto Oroza. Despite being poorly equipped, Cubans are able to get their hands on the latest action films, TV series, or music video thanks to a weekly, underground compilation of digital content called *El Paquete Semanal* that is downloaded by the rare Cubans who own a computer (around 5% of the population has Internet access)[3] and sold on a hard drive that can be plugged directly into a TV. The downloaders of Fankélé Diarra Street in Bamako, who are the subject of Michaël Zumstein's photographs, employ the same system of streetwise savvy. They exchange the latest music releases on their cell phones via Bluetooth, thus forming an ad hoc "African iTunes" where you can pick up the files offline in the street. This small-timer operation is also a must for local musicians to raise their profile.

Pictures: Michaël Zumstein/Agence VU'

Mali, Bamako, 22 May 2015, close to the city center on Fankélé Diarra Street, shops providing digital file exchange have multiplied. A music track or a music video costs 50 CFA francs (0.08 US$), a movie 100 CFA francs (0.16 US$). Customers provide their own USB flash drive or mobile phone, and illegally download hundreds of files.

THE DOWNLOADERS

Fankélé Diarra Street
The little market on Fankélé Diarra Street in Bamako forms a hub where street vendors propose a plentiful offering of thousands of tracks on their computers. These music traders constantly face the challenge of always having a steady supply of new material since, once they manage to sell a few tracks, their customers then share the same tracks free of charge via Bluetooth amongst themselves. For example, if a downloader acquires a new album, the street traders will subsequently make copies of it amongst themselves before reselling the album to customers. In a matter of days or even hours the same songs will have completely lost their original value given that the customers will, in turn, make and circulate their own copies of the tracks for free. The stands themselves don't differ greatly from one another. Should one of the stands procure the latest song by a well-known Malian singer, the stand next door won't take long before it lays its hands on the entire album. Young people usually gather in the street in the evening; they place a few tables outdoors, underneath streetlights or in front of someone's door, and congregate whilst exchanging tracks via Bluetooth. "Where did you find that track?" one hears, or perhaps, "A friend of mine performs in this song, would you like to listen to it?" The street downloaders are a well-established business, but one whose profitability is almost in the red.

The network of downloaders also has other uses. For example, if a young musician is in need of raising his/her profile, he/she will pay the street vendors a visit and request of them something to the effect of "Check out my signature track. I'm trying to release my album. Can you circulate it as much as possible?" If they take a liking to the track, the downloaders will spread the good word to their customers who will perhaps then see the artist in concert. During the concert itself, the customers will, in turn, film and record the music on their cell phones, or even

DESCRIPTION

"This publication offers a broad view on media piracy as well as a variety of comparative perspectives on recent issues and historical facts regarding piracy. It contains a compilation of texts on grassroots situations whose stories describe strategies developed to share, distribute and experience cultural content outside of the confines of local economies, politics or laws. These stories recount the experiences of individuals from India, Cuba, Brazil, Mexico, Mali and China" (back cover).

The book begins with a historical review, from the printing press to contemporary copyright law; it then looks at the structures, charters, and visual culture of the warez scene from an insider's perspective; before presenting anti-piracy technology and industry from different eras, and individual geographically-specific piracy phenomena. These include shanzai culture in China, private video clubs and consoles in Brazil, downloaders in Mali, and music from cellphones in West Africa.

The anecdotes and accounts of artists, researchers, activists, and bootleggers bring together global, local, and personal experiences with forms of piracy, most of which have arisen from necessity. They reveal the vitality and breadth of the phenomenon, as well as the amazing creativity and sophisticated strategies used to counter economic, technical, or legal restrictions. The editors argue that piracy has been and continues to be a driver of social, technological, and intellectual innovation: "the history of piracy is the history of modernity" (Marie Lechner, "Preamble," n.p.).

The Pirate Book is "neither an artist book, nor an academic dissertation, nor an archive, nor a forecast study. It is a blend of all of the latter and forms a prolific guide that can be read as much as it can be looked at" (Ibid.).

The book is available in black-and-white, in color, and as a free PDF. As part of the artist intervention series for *Neural* magazine—which covers new media art, electronic music, and hacktivism—subscribers to the 53rd issue (2016) of the print magazine received a USB stick that contained the PDF version of the book and all the materials used.

Edited by Nicolas Maigret and Maria Roszkowska with contributions by Jota Izquierdo, Christopher Kirkley, Marie Lechner, Pedro Mizukami, Ernesto Oroza, Clément Renaud, Ishita Tiwary, Ernesto Van der Sar, and Michaël Zumstein.

Print Wikipedia

AUTHOR	Michael Mandiberg
YEAR	2015–2016
GENRE	artist's book / bookwork, exhibition copy, nonfiction
METHOD	documentation / archiving, generative / automation, reformatting
SUBJECT	analog / digital, authorship, code / programming, crowd / collaboration, data, memory / storage, platforms / companies, print on demand, scale, wikipedia
PLATFORM	Lulu
VOLUMES	7,600
EDITION CHARACTERISTICS	ISBN, open edition, CC BY-SA
FORMAT	15.8 × 23.5 cm
MATERIALITIES	black-and-white, hardcover, perfect bound
PAGES	700 (each)

IMAGE

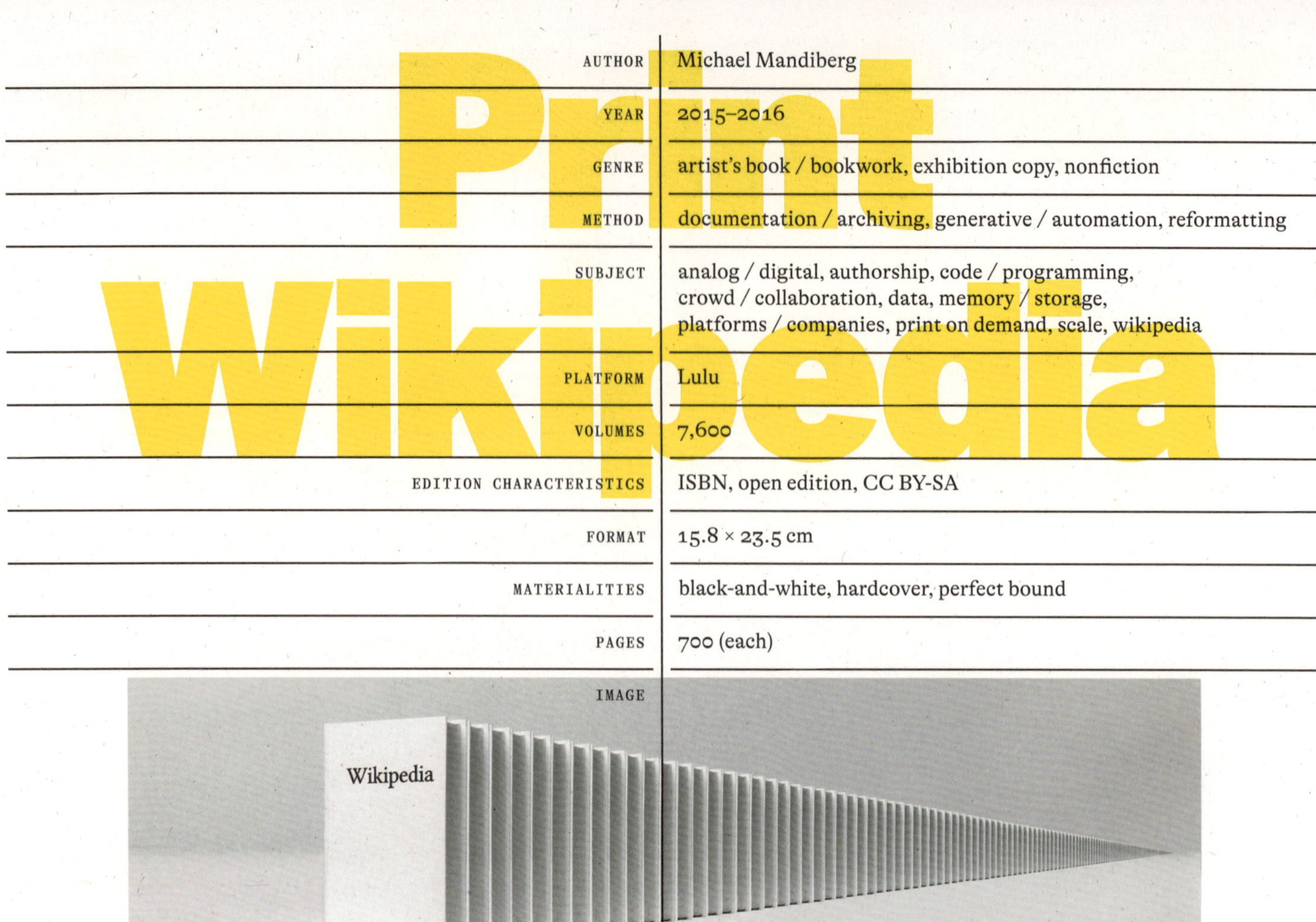

DESCRIPTION

"*Print Wikipedia* (2009–2016) is both a utilitarian visualization of the largest accumulation of human knowledge and a poetic gesture towards the futility of the scale of big data. Mandiberg has written software that parses the entirety of the English-language Wikipedia database and programmatically lays out thousands of volumes, complete with covers, and then uploads them for print-on-demand. Built on what is likely the largest appropriation ever made, it is also a work of found poetry that draws attention to the sheer size of the encyclopedia's content and the impossibility of rendering Wikipedia as a material object in fixed form: Once a volume is printed it is already out of date. The work is also a reflection on the actual transparency or completeness of knowledge containers and history" (Michael Mandiberg, "About").

Thus, the artist uses the transfer of the online encyclopedia into the familiar book format as a scale of measurement for the unimaginable amounts of data. Only this makes the dimensions of the collective writing experiment and the extent of the collected knowledge on Wikipedia comprehensible. In total, it takes 7,473 volumes. They include only the text of the Wikipedia articles, not the images and references. They are complimented by a ninety-one volume *Wikipedia Table of Contents* and a thirty-six volume *Wikipedia Contributor Appendix* which lists the names of the 7.5 million Wikipedia users who have made at least a single edit to the website. Each volume has its own ISBN.

The artwork, categorized as "poetry" in Lulu's webshop, was launched and first exhibited at Denny Gallery, New York, in 2015. The exhibition presented a live projected video which displayed the fully automatic generation and upload of the *Print Wikipedia* volumes to Lulu.com. This process lasted twenty-four days, three hours, and eighteen minutes. Each time a volume was completed and uploaded, an announcement was posted to Twitter (@PrintWikipedia).

In addition to this video, the exhibition featured a selection of printed volumes in front of a customized wallpaper that represented floor-to-ceiling bookshelves full of volumes illustrating how much space the entire Wikipedia would take. Mandiberg is convinced: "It is not necessary to print out all 7,473 volumes, as our imaginations can complete what's missing" (Michael Mandiberg, "Making *Print Wikipedia*," in this volume, 514). Sophie Seita has described this strange but very typical state of limbo for print-on-demand, on the threshold of becoming printed in almost the same words as "imagined printedness" (Sophie Seita, "Communities of Print," in this volume, 643).

The individual volumes and the entirety of *Print Wikipedia*, *Wikipedia Table of Contents*, and *Wikipedia Contributor Appendix* are available for sale on Lulu. We purchased the first volume of each of the three series for our collection. The script is made available on GitHub, including the README files explaining the multi-step process in more detail and noting bug fixes for future iterations. The code parses the entire Wikipedia database, creates print ready PDFs, and uploads them to Lulu. The install documents for future exhibitions, covering the upload process and the custom wallpaper's production, are also available.

Wikimedia cooperated with the project and Lulu helped fund it. The reason the artist turned to Lulu in the first place was because uploading such volumes of data and books would surely have led to their account being suspended by the platform because it could be considered a spam or DoS attack.

Like Wikipedia itself, Mandiberg's project is produced under the Creative Commons license. However, in order to be allowed to use the Wikipedia logo, Mandiberg was supposed to label each volume with the statement "This is a work of art" on the front cover. In the end it was agreed that on the back cover the following note was to be printed in small font, which also clarifies the question of authorship attribution: "CC BY-SA 3.0 2015, Wikipedia contributors; see Appendix for a complete list of contributors. [...] This work is legally categorized as an artistic work. As such, this qualifies for trademark use under clause 3.6.3 (Artistic, scientific, literary, political, and other non-commercial uses) as denoted at wikimediafoundation.org/wiki/Trademark_policy. [...] This work is not endorsed by or affiliated with the Wikimedia Foundation."

Wikipedia: Volume 1, ! — 'one' Anglia

YEAR	2015
VOLUMES	7,473
EDITION CHARACTERISTICS	volume 1: ISBN 9781329226432
IMAGE	

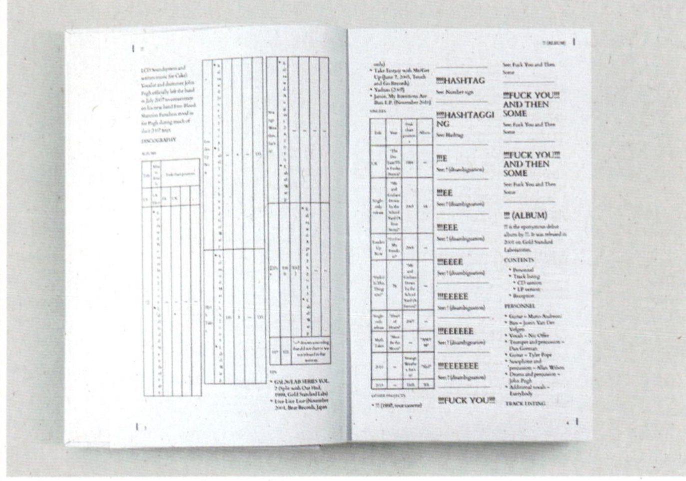

Wikipedia Contributor Appendix: Volume 1, ! — Ahitchins

YEAR	2015
VOLUMES	36
EDITION CHARACTERISTICS	volume 1: ISBN 9781329375956
IMAGE	
DESCRIPTION	The issue of authorship attribution turned out to be problematic. Wikipedia itself recommends naming the five most prominent contributors to each article. But this rule was not feasible for Mandiberg's gigantic project, apart from the difficult question of what should count as an important contribution: the number of edits, the amount of characters contributed, the very first authorship? An appendix with the names of the 7.5 million Wikipedia users who have made at least a single edit to the website seemed to be a workable solution. This is the first time they are publicly acknowledged. It was well received by the public; in exhibitions of the project there were always visitors looking for their name in the appendix and proudly showing it to others.

Wikipedia Table of Contents: Volume 1, ! — 1968 All-Ireland Minor Hurling Championship

YEAR	2015
VOLUMES	91
EDITION CHARACTERISTICS	volume 1: ISBN 9781329377325
IMAGE	

German Print Wikipedia

YEAR 2016

VOLUMES 3,411

IMAGE

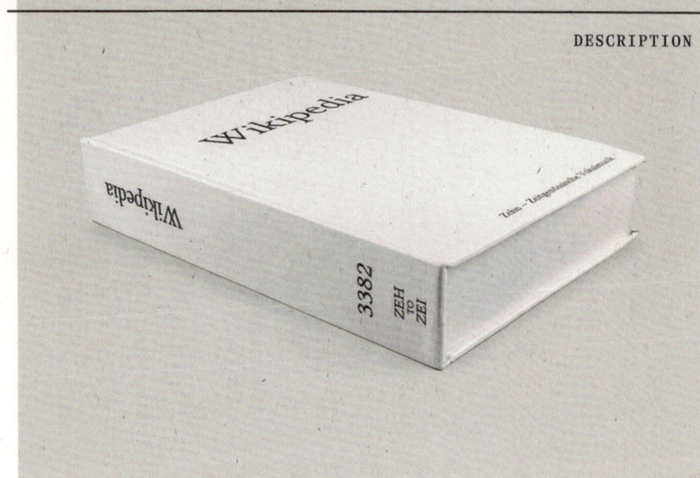

DESCRIPTION

In 2016, a German Wikipedia version was produced for the installation "Print Wikipedia: From Aachen to Zylinderdruckpresse" in the Import Projects gallery, Berlin.

The upload took about fourteen days. During this period, the gallery was open to reflect the ongoing work of the program, which was made visible through two channels: a projection of the Lulu.com site in a web browser, and a computer monitor with command line updates showing the dialogue between the code and the site. The script also provided regular tweets on Twitter at @PrintWikipedia whenever a volume was completed.

The German Wikipedia (as it existed on March 5, 2016) amounts to 3,406 volumes. A five-volume *Contributor Appendix* includes all named contributors to the German Wikipedia. The total of 3,411 volumes was uploaded in May and June 2016. The books printed for the installation are kept by Sächsische Landesbibliothek – Staats- und Universitätsbibliothek Dresden.

Dutch Print Wikipedia

YEAR 2016

VOLUMES 1,165

DESCRIPTION

At the end of 2016, a Dutch Wikipedia was made and exhibited at the biennial Update_6 in Ghent, Belgium. Capturing the complete Dutch Wikipedia in October 2016 resulted in 1,165 volumes, including two appendixes for listing all contributors to the Dutch Wikipedia. For this exhibition, 68 of the 1,165 volumes were printed and placed on shelves.

Broken 56 Broken Kindle Screens

AUTHORS	NUPoD Collective, Danny Snelson
YEAR	2015
PUBLISHER	NUPoD 2015
GENRE	artist's book / bookwork, education / classroom
METHOD	appropriation, collection, composition (writing / drawing / photography), photocopy / scan
SUBJECT	analog / digital, error / corruption / loss, materiality
PLATFORM	Lulu
EDITION CHARACTERISTICS	multiple editions (print, PDF), open edition
FORMAT	10.8 × 17.5 cm
MATERIALITIES	black-and-white, paperback, perfect bound
PAGES	78

IMAGES

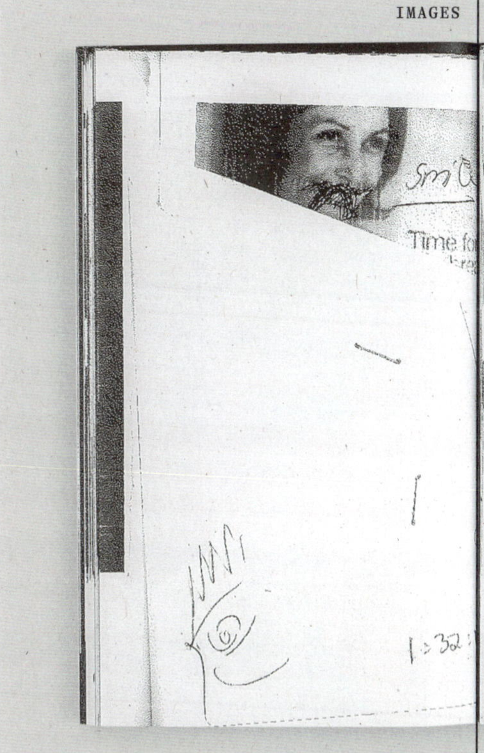

DESCRIPTION

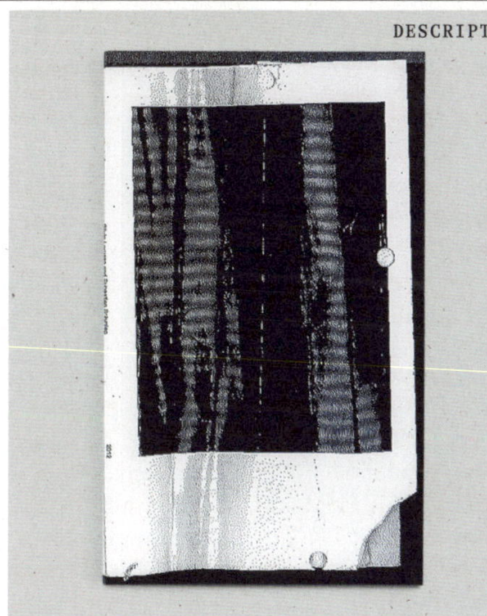

Broken 56 Broken Kindle Screens was the "first experiment with critical destruction" in Danny Snelson's first course devoted entirely to print-on-demand practices at Northwestern University in 2015 (Danny Snelson, "2015: *Broken 56 Broken Kindle Screens*"). It responds to *56 Broken Kindle Screens* by Silvio Lorusso and Sebastian Schmieg (2012, see 233), a collection of found photographs showing broken displays of Kindle e-readers.

The students were asked to collectively alter a copy of this book by creasing and damaging it, punching pages, writing on or drawing over them, crossing out pictures, or transforming pictures by crossing out eyes and so on, with the aim of understanding the book "as an object, with a specific set of material properties and resistances to destruction—a kind of 'hands-on' learning" (Ibid.). This demolished copy was then scanned in poor quality by Snelson and turned into a print-on-demand book again. Snelson describes the lesson as follows: "Subject to these manifold damages, in the end, *Broken 56 Broken Kindle Screens* proves the resilience of the book. Unlike the Kindle, a very difficult thing to break" (Danny Snelson, "Grey Libraries," in this volume, 675).

Flash Paper Mixtape

AUTHOR	NUPoD Collective
YEAR	2015
PUBLISHER	NUPoD 2015
GENRE	artist's book / bookwork, catalog / collection, education / classroom
METHOD	collective, montage / remix, photocopy / scan, remediation
SUBJECT	authorship, error / corruption / loss, music / sound, technology
PLATFORM	Lulu
EDITION CHARACTERISTICS	multiple editions (print, PDF), open edition
FORMAT	22.9 × 17.8 cm
MATERIALITIES	black-and-white, paperback, perfect bound
PAGES	394 (unpaginated)

IMAGES

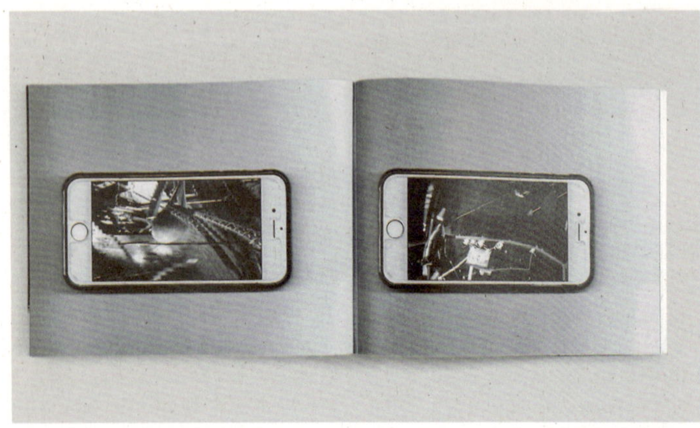

DESCRIPTION

Flash Paper Mixtape was produced in the context of Danny Snelson's experimental writing class "Print on Demand Poetry: Making Books After the Internet" at Northwestern University in 2015. Based on the assumption that scanners have the most boring life of all technical devices, because all they get to see are printed matter and official documents, the task for the students was to entertain the scanners by playing them music videos (see Danny Snelson, "2015: *Flash Paper Mixtape*"). For this, fifteen devices ranging from laptops to smartphones were placed on a variety of scanners while playing a music video, with images captured at certain intervals. Then, in the spirit of a mixtape with the songs played to the scanners, a book was compiled from the twenty-four images that were taken per screening.

From the concurrence of the moving images of the music videos and the much slower scanning movement, all sorts of unintentional glitch effects are created, such as a broken Justin Bieber. A few chapters, however, only show the devices and the scanners' backdrops because the scanners could not capture any moving image.

Thus, authorship has also been granted to the scanning devices themselves. The author credits on the NUPoD website and on Lulu reads: "by HP, A. C. Sony C2105, The 2nd Scanner at the Library, M. Zampa, Epson V700, MCC RG Scanner, s.f., Kyndal Thomas, iPhone 5s, HP Photosmart 6520, LNS, (see notes to chapter 8), B. Cohen, HP Photosmart 6520, Brendan McManus, DSS, Keynote, Jonathan Hoffman, Toshiba Techra R950, Epson Perfection 4490 Photo ft. Apple IPhone 6 ft. M. Ferschinger (Explicit), J.S., and Northwestern Main Library Third Floor Scanner/Adobe Acrobat XI Pro" (Danny Snelson, "NUPoD," blog).

24.#PRICEPT.$

AUTHOR	Paparutzy
YEAR	2015
GENRE	artist's book / bookwork
METHOD	montage / remix, pricing, versioning / seriality
SUBJECT	analog / digital, book / book design, print on demand, scale
PLATFORM	Lulu
EDITION CHARACTERISTICS	open edition
FORMAT	22.0 × 28.6 cm
MATERIALITIES	color, hardcover, perfect bound
PAGES	32 (unpaginated)

IMAGES

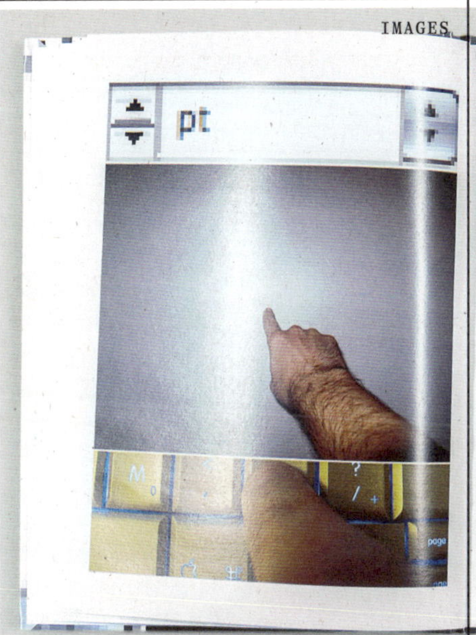

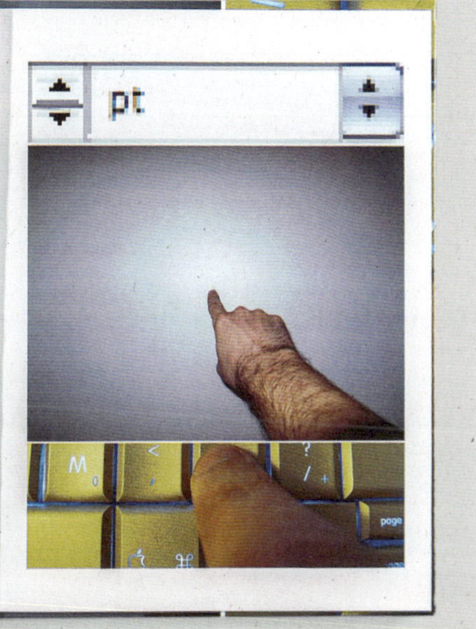

DESCRIPTION

Paparutzy's *24.#PRICEPT.$* is a conceptual play on words and an artistic application of price policy enabled by print on demand. Except for the title page (and some blank pages at the very end of the book), it consists of a constellation of three images on a page that refer to the word "point." This page is repeated twenty-four times. The first image depicts a typical box for selecting font size, such as in Adobe software, but it is empty except for the abbreviation "pt," which stands for the smallest unit of measurement in typography. The second image is a photograph of a hand pointing to a small golden square on a wall, presumably an analog interpretation of a pixel, the screen-based unit that forms the basis for pt measurement. The third image shows a zoomed-in finger, pressing the period key on a keyboard in the same color as the small dot in the second image. This sequence of images forms a semiotic loop between analog and digital representations, measurements and semantics.

Yet this loop remains arbitrary, leaving readers to wonder what the point of the book is. It becomes clearer when accessing the blurb on the Lulu webshop: "The price is the point is the price is the point," repeated three times. The price of the book is exactly $24, which is also exactly the number of pages of content, making the price literally the point of this book.

24.#PRICEPT.$* is the first in a series of six publications with identical content, but always with the number in the title double that of the number in the previous publication's title. The number determines the price and the number of pages of content. Paparutzy's series ends with *768.#PRICEPT.$, sold for $768 and with 768 pages of content, which is the highest number of pages that Lulu can provide in that book format.

(Another Book) After Ed-werd Rew-shay

AUTHOR	Zoë Sadokierski
YEAR	2015
PUBLISHER	Bookwork Press
GENRE	artist's book / bookwork, nonfiction
METHOD	composition (writing / drawing / photography), reenactment, study / analysis
SUBJECT	book / book design, canon, photography, print on demand, publishing / distribution, reading / interpretation
PLATFORM	Espresso Book Machine, IngramSpark / Amazon
EDITION CHARACTERISTICS	first edition: limited edition, signed, numbered second edition: ISBN 9780994286741, open edition
FORMAT	12.7 × 17.8 cm
MATERIALITIES	black-and-white, paperback, perfect bound
PAGES	68 (unpaginated)

IMAGES

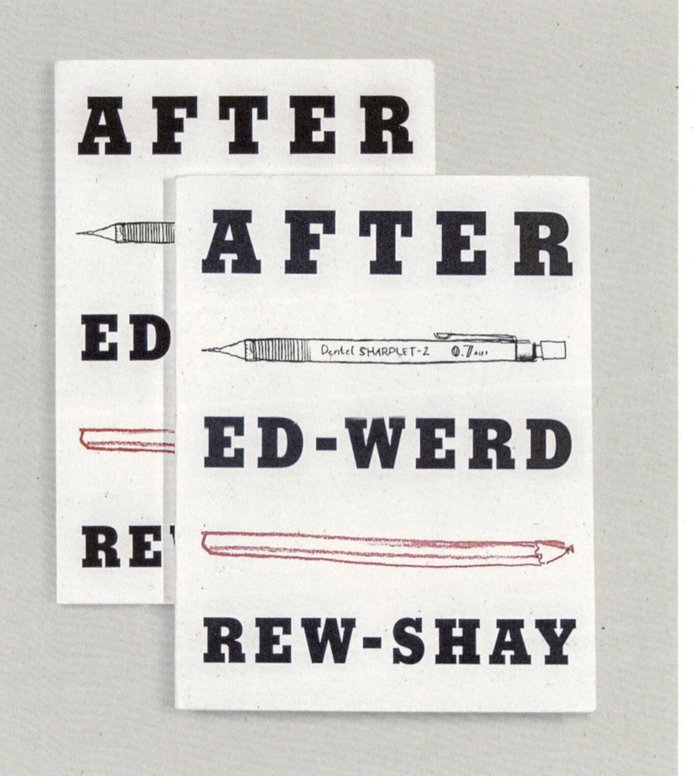

DESCRIPTION

Zoë Sadokierski's *(Another Book) After Ed-werd Rew-shay* consists of *Twentysix Views from the 7 Train*, a reenactment of Ed Ruscha's famous *Twentysix Gasoline Stations* (1963), which is often considered to be the first modern artist's book and is one of the most referenced books in today's artist's book scene.

Sadokierski's title is borrowed from his catalog *Edward Ruscha (Ed-werd Rew-shay) Young Artist* (1972) and reflects her confusion about the correct pronunciation of the name. The first part of the title, "Another Book," points out that Sadokierski's joins a long tradition of homage books, since Ruscha's books are one of the most appropriated artist's books ever. By producing her book print-on-demand, she draws another parallel to the idea of books as democratic multiples in the 1960s/70s art world, also pursued by Ruscha.

Following Ruscha, *Twentysix Views from the 7 Train* documents shots taken out of the window of New York City Subway's line 7, which Sadokierski took in order to get to the MoMA Library where she went to study artist's books. After an in-depth analysis of Ruscha's page order and photo positioning, documented in her book, Sadokierski replaced Ruscha's documentary photographs with her own snapshots. Her photo series is accompanied by an extensive essay on her research on artist's books.

Sadokierski always wanted to make a book with an Espresso Book Machine (EBM). But since there are none in Australia, she took advantage of her stay in New York. *(Another Book) After Ed-werd Rew-shay* was made in one week and printed on the EBM in about five minutes in an edition of five at McNally Jackson bookstore (see Zoë Sadokierski, "A Book," in this volume, 534). The artist donated one of these signed and numbered copies to our collection. Since shipping books from the US to Australia would be disproportionately expensive, the artist decided to publish a second edition via the print-on-demand provider IngramSpark and make it available for purchase on Amazon. For this, the book had to be reformatted. The first proof was untrimmed, highlighting quality control as a key difference between EBM and print-on-demand platforms.

L=A=N=G=U=A=G=E, 1978–81 Complete GIF Edition

AUTHOR	Danny Snelson [ed.]
YEAR	2015
PUBLISHER	Eclipse Printing Service
GENRE	artist's book / bookwork, catalog / collection, reprint
METHOD	documentation / archiving, remediation
SUBJECT	analog / digital, canon, error / corruption / loss, literature, memory / storage
PLATFORM	Lulu
EDITION CHARACTERISTICS	open edition
FORMAT	21.6 × 27.9 cm
MATERIALITIES	black-and-white, paperback, perfect bound, defective copy
PAGES	544 (unpaginated)

IMAGES

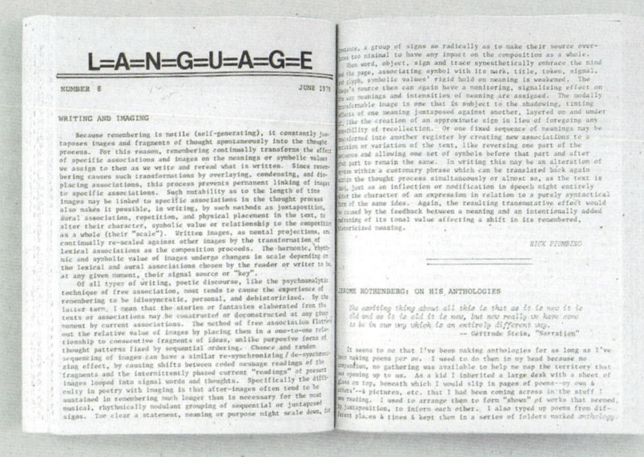

L=A=N=G=U=A=G=E

NUMBER 8 JUNE 1979

WRITING AND IMAGING

DESCRIPTION

This is a reprint of the complete run of *L=A=N=G=U=A=G=E* magazine that can be found on Eclipse, Craig Dworkin's free online archive of facsimile images of rare and out-of-print small-press publications. Dworkin's archive was launched in February 2003, marking the twenty-fifth anniversary of *L=A=N=G=U=A=G=E* magazine. The magazine's images in this archive are all presented in Graphics Interchange Format (GIF), encoded in a highly compressed gray scale (see http://eclipsearchive.org/).

In May 2015, Danny Snelson launched the Eclipse Printing Service, a print-on-demand platform for Eclipse, in homage to L=A=N=G=U=A=G=E Distributing Service. This was "a kind of door-to-door photocopy delivery mechanism for out-of-print works. A catalog of books and magazines could be ordered for fifty cents from the home address of editor Charles Bernstein, who ran this reprint on demand service through a neighborhood Xerox machine. [...] A slim catalogue for republished works opens with a statement by Bernstein, Silliman, and Andrews, highlighting the ephemerality of titles within experimental writing circuits of the late 1970s: 'Even when published, writing we wish to read often goes out of print with dismaying rapidity—closing off a dialogue. Out-of-print and unpublished works may still circulate among a limited circle of friends. Here, we hope to sustain that dialogue, and expand that circle.' [...] The development of the potentials of this dialogue extends into a network of issues related to preservation, distribution, and accessibility" (Daniel Scott Snelson, "Variable Format," 59f.).

"Just as the L=A=N=G=U=A=G=E Distributing Service utilized Xerox technology to put a range of small-press publications back into material circulation, the Eclipse Printing Service aims to put a series of image files back into the medial circumstances from which they were derived. [...] Returning to paper, the Eclipse Printing Service tests the affordances of paper-based preservation systems against digital recording technologies" (Ibid., 187).

The Eclipse Printing Service was established in connection with Danny Snelson's dissertation "Variable Format: Media Poetics and the Little Database."

EXE TXT

AUTHOR	Danny Snelson
YEAR	2015
PUBLISHER	Gauss PDF
GENRE	artistic research, experimental literature, nonfiction
METHOD	documentation / archiving, found material, generative / automation
SUBJECT	analog / digital, censorship / ban, code / programming, copyright / law, error / corruption / loss, materiality, narration, reading / interpretation, scale
PLATFORM	Lulu
EDITION CHARACTERISTICS	multiple editions (hardcover, paperback, PDF, TXT, ZIP, PY), ISBN 9780816650439, open edition
FORMAT	15.0 × 22.4 cm
MATERIALITIES	black-and-white, paperback, perfect bound
PAGES	242

IMAGE

DESCRIPTION

Danny Snelson's *EXE TXT* is the attempt to make a database of texts theorize itself. The project makes use of the texts accessible as text-warez on Textz.com, a website run by Sebastian Lütgert between 2000 and 2004 that hosted around 831 text files "[r]anging from experimental poetry and cyberpunk fiction to media theory and political tracts" (Daniel Scott Snelson, "Variable Format," 19). Snelson used a Python script on this corpus to extract sentences containing variants of the strings "text" and "software" (including their translations) to find out "how text might meet software within the works that Textz hosts" (Ibid., 181). Snelson edited the output inserting line and chapter breaks, but retained character encoding errors and misreadings. The result "queries a latent theorization of executable text within the works once hosted by Textz.com. Generally, it might be identified alternately as a scholarly edition, a fugitive collection, or a poetics of computation" (blurb on the back cover).

EXE TXT consists of the print-on-demand book available as paperback and hardcover as well as a plain text file of its content, the Python script, and a text file containing the whole collection of texts hosted on Textz.com. The latter starts with the works of Theodor W. Adorno, for whose digital publication on Textz.com Lütgert had to face a lawsuit and arrest warrant due to copyright infringement. This collection of files enables the readers to recreate the production process and "select their own terms for rearticulating this corpus" (blurb on the back cover).

This work is also an appendix to Snelson's dissertation thesis "Variable Format: Media Poetics and the Little Database" for which he theorized his experimental approach and its failure to work as a chapter by itself.

This is the only Gauss PDF edition with an ISBN. The project is cataloged by the Library of Congress, including the print-on-demand publication as well as the ASCII text file.

Epic Lyric Poem
167121 Songs, 257.8 MB File

AUTHOR	Danny Snelson
YEAR	2015
PUBLISHER	Troll Thread
GENRE	experimental literature, poetry
METHOD	found material, generative / automation, montage / remix
SUBJECT	canon, code / programming, data, literature, music / sound, narration, reading / interpretation, scale
PLATFORM	Lulu
EDITION CHARACTERISTICS	multiple editions (print, PDF, TXT, SQL), open edition, CC0
FORMAT	19.0 × 19.0 cm
MATERIALITIES	black-and-white, paperback, perfect bound
PAGES	48 (unpaginated)

IMAGES

DESCRIPTION

"*Epic Lyric Poem* draws from an SQL database torrent distributed to create pop lyric websites, presumably to make ad money, primarily created by fans. A Python script was used to draw out every line with the string 'lyric' in the database. Each of these lines was then standardized to 55 characters—the average length of a line in a pop song. The poem is 55 stanzas long, printing twenty lines per stanza. It follows the conventions of epic poetry (invocation of the muses, armaments for battle, lists, etc), with a special dedication to Alexander Pope" (Danny Snelson, "Epic Lyric Poem," website).

From the latter's mock-heroic narrative poem *The Rape of the Lock*, the first two stanzas are prefixed to Snelson's text as an "epigraph," not without making minor changes ("am'rous causes" becomes "poetical Causes"; the names of the characters become "LYRIC," "Database," and "User") and ending with the announcement: "In tasks so bold, this little Poem engages, / And in soft Prosody, queries what this Age is."

In Snelson's epic lyric poem, the word "lyric" changes its position in the line again and again, as in a concordance; sometimes visual patterns result from these repetitions. As Erik Kennedy notes in his review, the extracted lines are mostly quoted from rap and hip-hop songs, a genre which uses the word "lyric" surprisingly often (Erik Kennedy, "Epic Lyric Poem"). But there are also many fragments with acknowledgments, email addresses, user comments, and HTML commands and instructions, such as "Visitors click on the link for correcting lyrics below." Despite the algorithmic extraction and shaping of the found material, the final composition was made by hand, creating the impression of a classical epic poem.

The publication includes the printed book, the PDF file, the full SQL database and a TXT file, which can be downloaded from the publisher's website.

Printed_Web_3.pdf Index/Reader

AUTHOR	Paul Soulellis [ed.]
YEAR	2015
PUBLISHER	Library of the Printed Web
GENRE	catalog / collection, nonfiction
METHOD	collection, composition (writing / drawing / photography), documentation / archiving
SUBJECT	analog / digital, art, internet culture, literature, memory / storage, print on demand, publishing / distribution, visual culture
PLATFORM	Blurb
EDITION CHARACTERISTICS	multiple editions (print, PDF, ZIP), ISBN 9781320767903, open edition
FORMAT	12.6 × 20.3 cm
MATERIALITIES	black-and-white, paperback, perfect bound
PAGES	388
IMAGE	

DESCRIPTION

Printed_Web_3.pdf is the third publication in Paul Soulellis' series *Printed Web*, published under the umbrella of his Library of the Printed Web after starting to collect web-to-print publications in 2013. This third issue stands out from the six publications of the series as the most extensive one. It results from an open call and includes works by 147 artists, which are also published as a ZIP file and archived as a browsable directory by Rhizome.

The print-on-demand book *Printed_Web_3.pdf* gives a spread to each artist, with the file names on the left-hand page and the pictures, stills, or collages of their submitted works on the right-hand page. It also includes an index of files received, an interview with media philosopher Alexander Galloway, and Silvio Lorusso's essay "In Defense of Poor Media" (in this volume, 464–472) that reflects on the post-digital specifics of print-on-demand, drawing on Hito Steyerl's essay "In Defense of Poor Image."

In this spirit, *Printed_Web_3.pdf* also seeks to explore questions of format and media caused by web-to-print. The hybridity is already evident in the title of the printed book, which refers to the digital version of the book as a file name. In addition to this print-on-demand publication, which combines PDF and printed book, and the ZIP file containing all the artists' contributions, this edition includes a set of ten zines (21.6 × 27.9 cm, 24 pages each) and a hand-bound Chinatown edition with modified print-on-demand pages (15.2 × 22.9 cm, 538 pages), wrapped in a thick neoprene PDF cover and limited to ten copies.

CONTRIBUTING ARTISTS

Kevin McCaughey, Jorge Sanchez, Gregory Jones, Cheryl Sourkes, Martin Brink, Nicola Morton, Ori Alon, Sara Shahim, Jonathan Rotsztain, Francesca Capone, Brent Dahl, Bryce Jensen, Roc Herms, Ingrid Burrington, Constant Dullaart, Emily Raw, Christine Bettis, Systaime, Valentina von Klencke, Sebastián Mira, Johanna Ehde, Péter Kupás, Brian LaRossa, Mariangela Guatteri, Carolyn Wood, Chris Klapper, Patrick Gallagher, Oscar Schwartz, Angela Genusa, Josh Brilliant, Sal Randolph, James Bridle, Roberto Greco, Zach Verdin, Chantal Zakari and Mike Mandel, Giovanna Olmos, Hermann Zschiegner, Louis Porter, Logan K. Young, Claudia Eve Beauchesne, James Louis Walker, Stefan Klein, Tyler Kline, Celeste Fichter, Clement Valla, Kim Asendorf, Admanda Kobilka, Qingxue Liu, Magdalena Wierzchucki, Pascal Anders, John Caserta, Ethan Assouline, Barron Webster, Tanja Lažetić, Daniel McInerney, Bernd de Ridder, Ole Fach, Aurora Tang, Mario Santamaria, Yotam Hadar, Ohad Ben Shimon, Florian Kuhlmann, Cathleen Owens, Max Siedentopf, Laurus Edelbacher, Filipe Matos, Emmanuelle Waeckerle, Kenneth Goldsmith and Fox Irving, Julie D. Spivey, Igor Myrtille, Chris Alexander, Dylan Neuwirth, Molly Woodward, Fenêtreproject Nastia Protsenko, Emma Ensley, Anouk Kruithof, Lucinda Hitchcock, Josh Brien, Miguel Fernández de Castro, Gen Howe, Selwa Abd, Javier Fresneda, Anja Morell, Jaidon Lalor, Philip Tomaru, Ryan Abb, Daniel Toumine, Keith Phelan, Matthew Underwood, Matthew Boyle, Thomas Artur Spallek, Thijmen van Brunschot, Andrea Salerno, Eddie Bureau and Stella Laurenzi, Joey Yearous-Algozin, Benjamin Shaykin, Greg Allen, Parties Prises Projects, Enora Denis, Wessel Baarda, Jason Huff, Clara Feder, Nichons-nous dans l'Internet, Nicolas Massi, Emma Jennings, Corinna Triantafyllidis, Milena Zuccarelli, Visitor Design, Jared Wells, Soso Phist, David Hanes, Émilie Brout and Maxime Marion, Jérémie Nuel, Talia Shulze, Analisa Teachworth, Loraine Furter, Davide Giorgetta and Valerio Nicoletti, Hayley Martell, Natalie Shields, Chloe Scheffe, Dragan Espenschied, Molly Davy, Joonas Westerlund, Sabrina Fernández-Casas, Gio Dollar, Riccardo Rudi, Eileen Isagon Skyers, Lindsay Hattrick, Henri Papson, Abbie Winters, Anna Bonesteel, Jeona Cuberta, Elite Kedan, Thomas Roberts, Kristen Gallagher, Carlin Brown, Kerry Doran, Harlan Erskine, Karina Palosi, Philippe Cao, Angie Waller, Adam Harvey, Frederike Kaltheuner, The Post-Art Poets, Eric Doeringer, Mishka Henner, Olia Lialina.

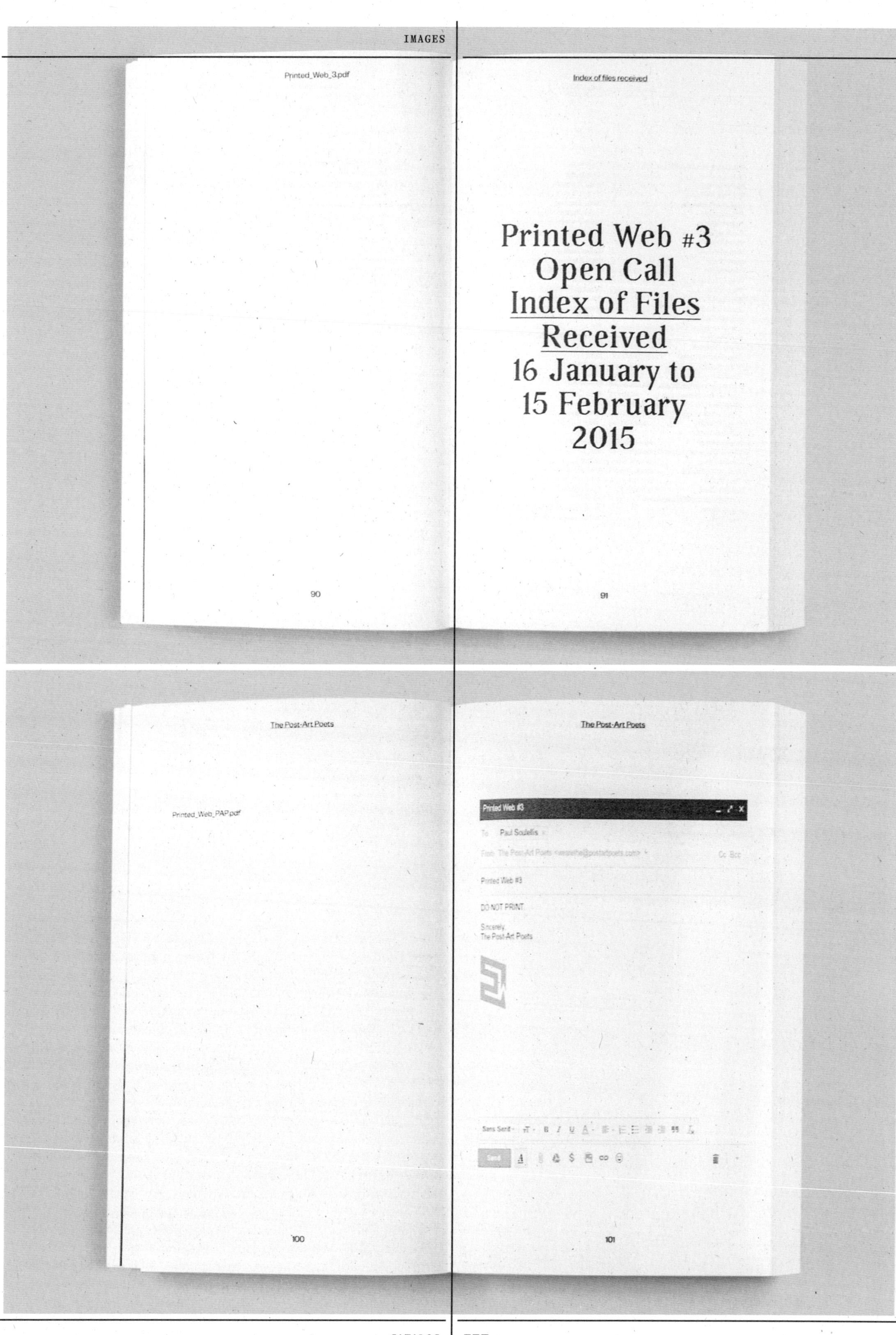
Printed_Web_3.pdf
Index of files received
Printed Web #3
Open Call
Index of Files
Received
16 January to
15 February
2015
90
91
The Post-Art Poets
The Post-Art Poets
Printed_Web_PAP.pdf
Printed Web #3
Paul Soulellis
Printed Web #3
DO NOT PRINT.
Sincerely,
The Post-Art Poets
100
101

THE TABLE & THE NETWORK

AUTHOR	Matthew Stadler
YEAR	2015
PUBLISHER	Publication Studio Minneapolis
GENRE	nonfiction
METHOD	composition (writing / drawing / photography)
SUBJECT	bias, crowd / collaboration, ecology / sustainability, economy / labor, politics / activism, publishing / distribution
PLATFORM	Publication Studio, selfmade
EDITION CHARACTERISTICS	open edition, stamped, embossed
FORMAT	12.8 × 21.6 cm
MATERIALITIES	black-and-white, paperback, perfect bound
PAGES	29

IMAGES

DESCRIPTION

Matthew Stadler's essay *THE TABLE & THE NETWORK* reflects on activism and its relationship with the public and private spheres, as well as writing and publishing for a future utopia. It is published by Publication Studio, the print-on-demand publishing network co-founded by Stadler and Patricia No in Portland, Oregon, in 2009. It is driven by a strong inclusive DIY ethos and a desire for community gathering:

"We attend to the social life of the book. Publication Studio is a laboratory for publication in its fullest sense—not just the production of books, but the production of a public. This public, which is more than a market, is created through physical production, digital circulation and social gathering. Together these construct a space of conversation which beckons a public into being" (Publication Studio, "About Us").

THE TABLE & THE NETWORK reflects on some aspects central to these concepts without explicitly mentioning them, but by thinking about episodes of tried and failed activism from Stadler's personal life and projecting the table as a social gathering place.

It was published by Publication Studio Minneapolis run by Sam Gould. Like most of Publication Studio's books, our copy is wrapped in plain kraft paper with the author and title stamped on it and the printer, Publication Studio Rotterdam, embossed. It lacks the usual stamp with the production date on the spine, which is probably too thin for this.

caps 0w – 146w, iPhone 6+, 0w 2015, Provider/Processor 'Chris Sylvester'

AUTHOR	Chris Sylvester
YEAR	2015
PUBLISHER	Gauss PDF
GENRE	artist's book / bookwork
METHOD	documentation / archiving, remediation
SUBJECT	instagram, memory / storage, photography, publishing / distribution, social media
PLATFORM	Lulu
EDITION CHARACTERISTICS	multiple editions (print, PDF), open edition
FORMAT	21.6 × 21.6 cm
MATERIALITIES	color, paperback, perfect bound
PAGES	294 (unpaginated)

IMAGES

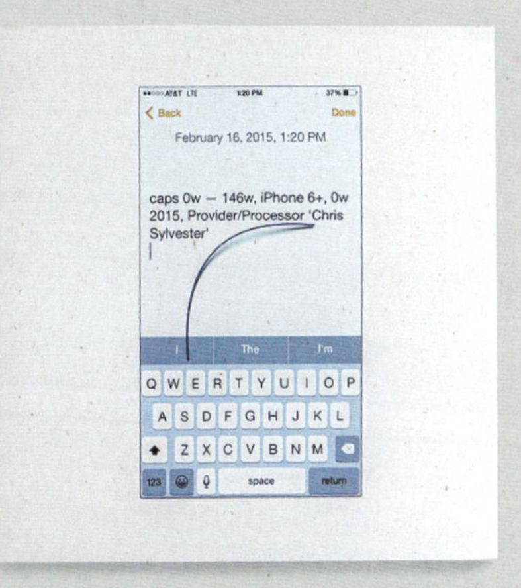

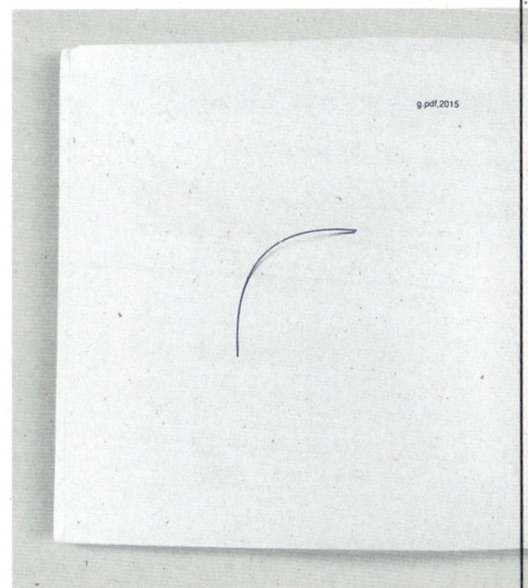

DESCRIPTION

This book captures all content posted to the Instagram account @Spreadsheet, run by Chris Sylvester, from week 0 (April 29, 2012) until the publication of the book in week 146, equaling almost three years of photographs, screenshots, and digital collages. The posts are captured by screenshots taken on Sylvester's iPhone 6+, scrolling through the account's grid view and stopping whenever a new set of posts fills the screen. All of the smartphone's interface elements are displayed, as well as elapsed time and dwindling battery. These screenshots on the right-hand page are each coupled with a graphic representation on the left-hand page, probably showing the motion of a thumb scrolling on a smartphone screen. The book also contains five moments of error that presumedly happened while the author was scrolling through the Instagram account, such as accidentally opening the camera app or capturing a received notification from Instagram.

caps 0w – 146w, iPhone 6+, 0w 2015, Provider/Processor 'Chris Sylvester' is both a gesture of preservation of digital content and a reflection on different layers of filtering an artist's life into book format. It shows great overlap with the content of Sylvester's blog sisteract.tumblr.com, which was one of the starting points for the artistic practices that led to the founding of publishing collective Troll Thread. Thus, the book also captures the migration of users from Tumblr to Instagram, which also represents the shift in internet politics and the economics of social media platforms becoming increasingly monopolistic, which ultimately fundamentally changed artistic print-on-demand practices as well.

delete turn alt

AUTHOR	Kyndal Thomas
YEAR	2015
GENRE	poetry
METHOD	composition (writing / drawing / photography), found material
SUBJECT	book / book design, facebook, instagram, internet culture, social media, twitter, youtube
PLATFORM	Lulu
EDITION CHARACTERISTICS	ISBN 9781329747685, open edition
FORMAT	15.8 × 23.5 cm
MATERIALITIES	black-and-white, dust jacket, hardcover, perfect bound
PAGES	42 (unpaginated)

IMAGES

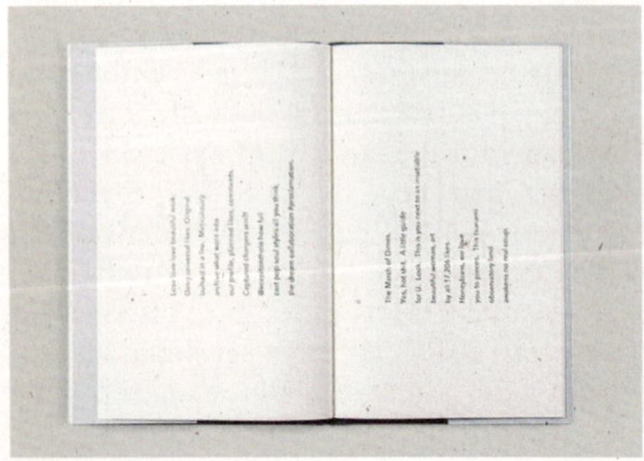

DESCRIPTION

delete turn alt is a collection of erasure poems based on and about social media communication. Kyndal Thomas takes posts and comments from Facebook, Instagram, Twitter, YouTube, and Soundcloud, which also form the book's five chapters, and copies and alters them, deleting parts of them and arranging them into lines of poetry, blending her own poetic voice with the platform specific language of their users. The cover shows part of an Apple keyboard with blank keys except for the three words that make up the title and convey the poetic strategy of the collection. The cover also instructs the reader how to hold the book, horizontally, referencing the orientation of text on a laptop screen.

the perfect ______

AUTHOR	Kyndal Thomas
YEAR	2015
PUBLISHER	NUPoD 2015
GENRE	artist's book / bookwork, education / classroom
METHOD	documentation / archiving, found material, reformatting, study / analysis
SUBJECT	bias, google, internet culture, race, search engine, twitter, visual culture, youtube
PLATFORM	Lulu
EDITION CHARACTERISTICS	multiple editions (print, PDF), ISBN 9781329601055, open edition
FORMAT	15.2 × 22.9 cm
MATERIALITIES	color, paperback, perfect bound
PAGES	245

IMAGES

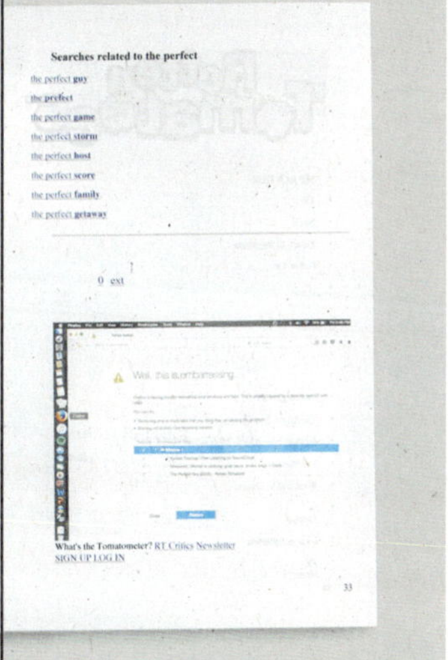

DESCRIPTION

the perfect ______ documents the entering of the words "the perfect" into the search bar of various platforms such as Google, YouTube, and Twitter, including autocomplete suggestions. The results of these prompts were copied and pasted into book format, with images cut off or taking up great amounts of space, and paratexts, links, and suggestions expanding over several pages. By this, *the perfect ______* gives an example of the layout preferences that are negotiated and applied in web-to-print processes.

Each new scraping is marked by a screenshot of the browser that shows the input of the phrase in the search box and its suggestions for autocompletion. By choosing "the perfect" as a starting point for the web search, Kyndal Thomas's publication creates a snapshot of value concepts and to which entities they might be applied. Accordingly, the blurb promotes the book as "a personal web browser generated catalog of socially constructed perfections" (blurb on Lulu). In such a way, *the perfect ______* also exposes the inherent bias of search engines and the pool of websites they are relying on. For example, all human bodies that appear in Google's Image Search in response to the search query—pictured on the front and back covers of the publication—are white.

the perfect ______ was published in the context of Danny Snelson's experimental writing class "Print on Demand Poetry: Making Books After the Internet" at Northwestern University in 2015 in response to the task of creating a scrapbook in the manner of Tan Lin's *HEATH*, a wild compilation of found data from RSS feeds, blog posts, Google searches, notes, photographs, etc.

Command-Shift-4

Screenshots 2001–2014

AUTHOR	Ubermorgen
YEAR	2015
PUBLISHER	LINK Editions
GENRE	artist's book / bookwork
METHOD	collection, composition (writing / drawing / photography), documentation / archiving, remediation
SUBJECT	analog / digital, book / book design, internet culture, materiality, memory / storage, narration, technology, visual culture
PLATFORM	Lulu
EDITION CHARACTERISTICS	multiple editions (print, PDF), open edition, CC0
FORMAT	13.8 × 21.5 cm
MATERIALITIES	black-and-white, paperback, perfect bound
PAGES	738

IMAGE

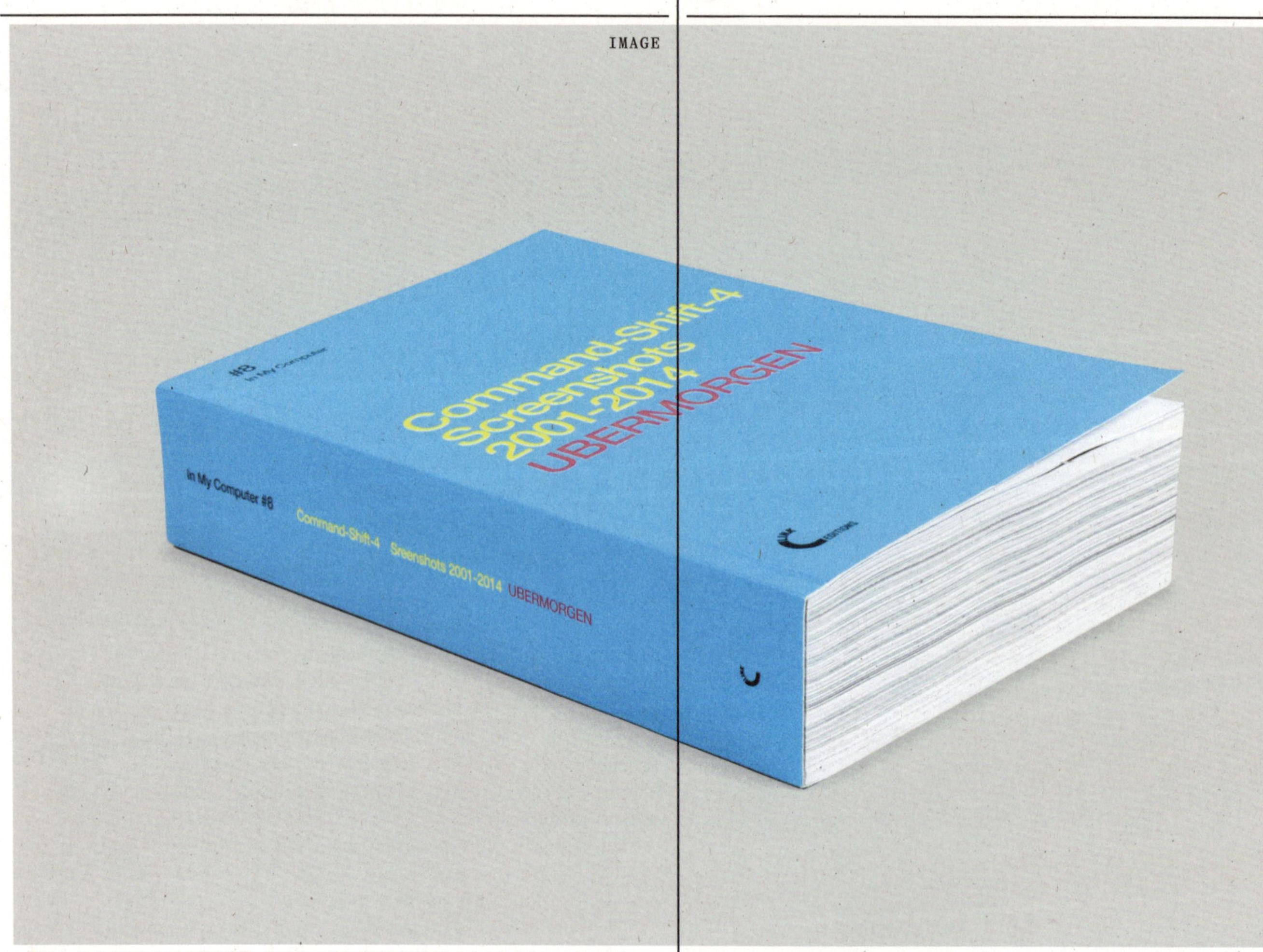

DESCRIPTION

Command-Shift-4: Screenshots 2001–2014 is part of Link Editions' series *In my Computer* and presents a collection of about 350 screenshots taken by the Austrian media art duo Ubermorgen. These images are a selection from a total of about 40,000 images Ubermorgen had taken during that time, which were first cut down to about 1,000 by the artists themselves and then further reduced by designer Diane Hillebrand to the number presented.

Hillebrand turned this selection into an e-book, arranging the images in varying sizes on the page, leaving different amounts of white space or cropping the images to the page margins, thus creating an effect of focus and different degrees of immersion into the flow of images. The images were then linked via a system of categories Hillebrand invented, opening up the linear structure to a hyperlinked reading.

For the printed version, all images were converted to black and white while links were "translated" into a system of numbers which reference page numbers, slowing down the clicking of links on images to a practice of thumbing back and forth through a book: "The navigation of the print version is willingly counter-intuitive and hard, and requires concentration and focus, instead of serendipitous clicking" (blurb on Lulu).

The book also features an afterword by Domenico Quaranta with an in-depth reflection on the media practice of taking screenshots (for which command+shift+4 is the key combination on the Mac) and the meaning it has for documenting, but also constructing, an online self.

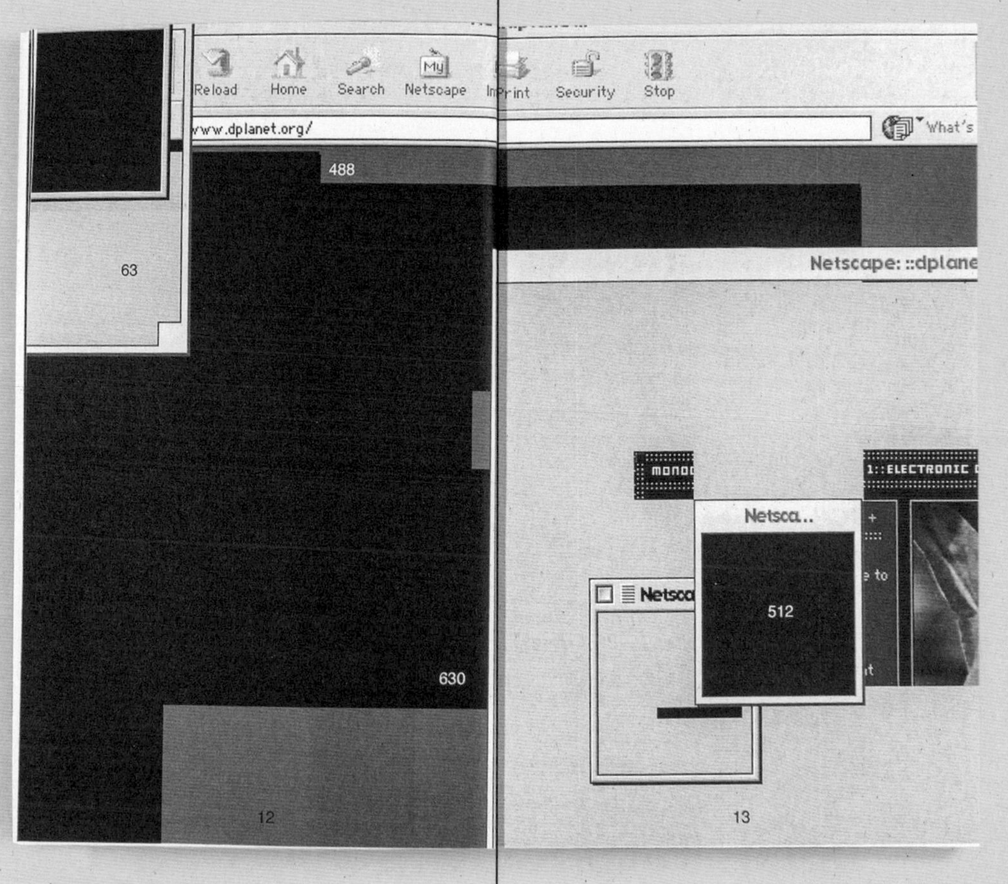
Reload
Home
Search
Netscape
Print
Security
Stop
www.dplanet.org/
488
63
Netscape: ::dplane
Netsca..
512
630
12
13

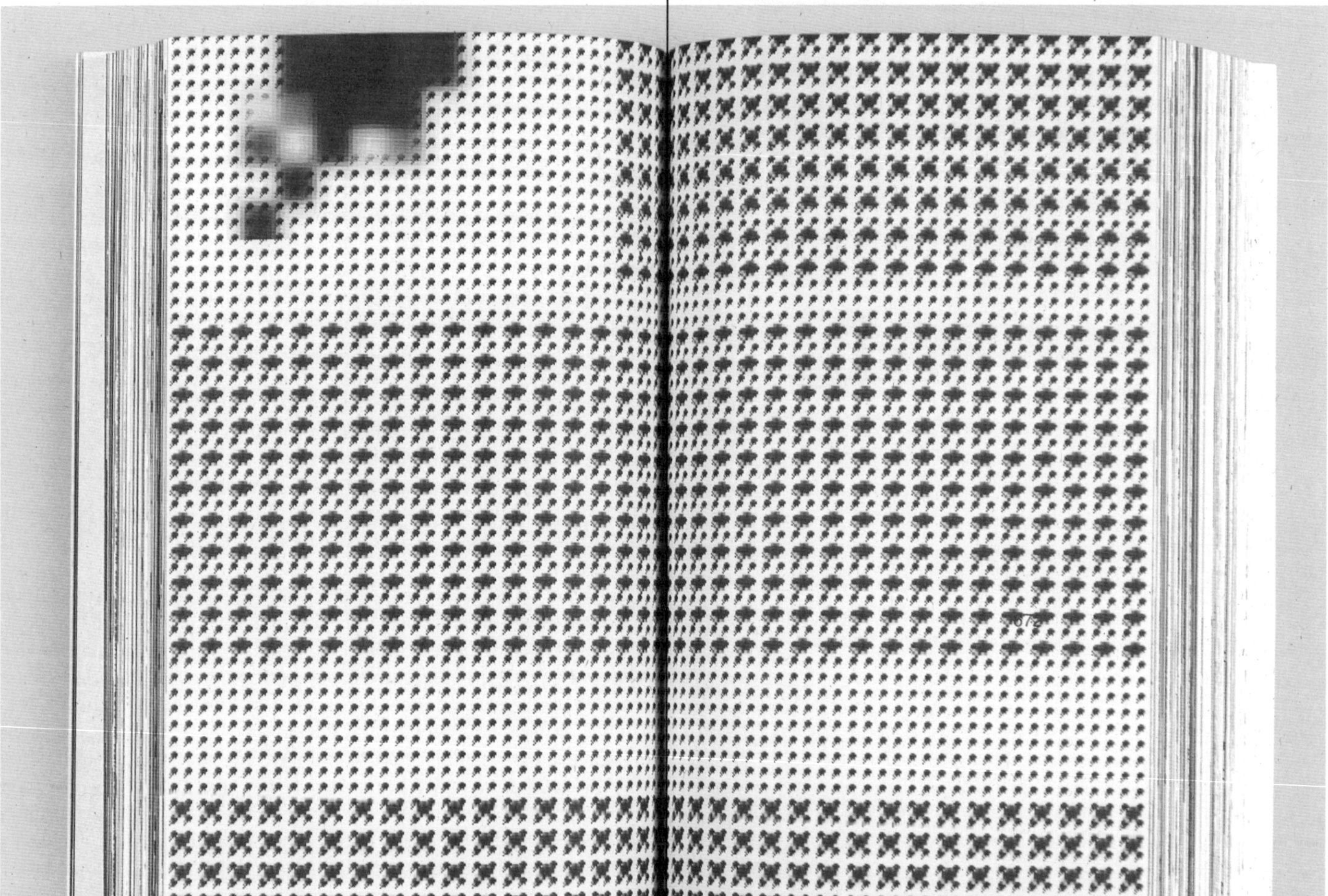

BANGED

AUTHOR	Angela Washko
YEAR	2015
GENRE	artistic research
METHOD	documentation / archiving, study / analysis, test / experiment
SUBJECT	bias, dating / sex, gender, internet culture, politics / activism
PLATFORM	Lulu
VOLUMES	2
EDITION CHARACTERISTICS	limited edition, numbered, signed, available only through the artist
FORMAT	15.2 × 22.9 cm
MATERIALITIES	black-and-white, paperback, perfect bound

IMAGE

DESCRIPTION

For *BANGED*, the feminist artist Angela Washko engaged with pick-up artist Roosh V, the "web's most infamous misogynist" according to numerous press outlets and author of the *BANG* series (guidebooks for men outlining strategies for picking up women). Washko originally intended to interview women who have had sexual encounters with Roosh V and to publish their side of the story—an approach she discarded when Roosh V and his followers learned of the project through online announcements after Washko received the Rhizome Internet Art Microgrant.

"I knew the project would from then on have to be in conversation with Roosh V himself. After his awareness was publicly communicated I became critical of my own black-and-white extremist approach. To introduce more of the nuance that is often ignored in conversations about pick up artists within stratified spheres of the internet, I decided to reach out to Roosh with the hopes of additionally conducting an interview with him.

After over a month of emailing him a question or two every few days, I was able to convince him to do a digitally mediated interview over Skype. I published the interview through *ANIMAL NY* and it was widely distributed, through Roosh's community, my digifeminist community and other broader mainstream audiences.

Debate over the sincerity of the gesture, my artistic credentials, my intentions, empathy & internet bubbles, exploitation, and whether or not members of his community wanted to bang me ensued. A flood of insults, support, and harassment broke through my email, social media, online forums and comment sections of mainstream media sites. Roosh V proceeded to frame my project as a desperate attempt to have sex with him and suggested that I was stalking him. Members of his community suggested that they were going to have a meeting with me where I live. [...] At some point I had to re-calibrate the project due to the terrain" (Angela Washko, "an explanation of the work in question").

The seven-month investigative art project resulted in a two-hour video interview with Roosh V, two books documenting the project, along with performances and installations. The artist describes the book series "as a testament to our contemporary condition of increasingly disparate bubbles that exist online and elsewhere—creating their own vernaculars and developing radically different ways of viewing the world. It is also a document analyzing reactions to Washko's experience shifting from activism to ethnography in spaces of extreme hostility toward women and feminists" (Angela Washko, "BANGed," website).

Produced with Lulu but sold via the artist's website, the book series comes in an edition of 300 with a signature and handwritten edition number. Our copies, however, were ordered directly from Lulu's webshop and lack these alterations.

BANGed: A Monopoly on Truth

METHOD: composition (writing / drawing / photography), documentation / archiving, study / analysis

SUBJECT: bias, book / book design, gender, politics / activism

PAGES: 103

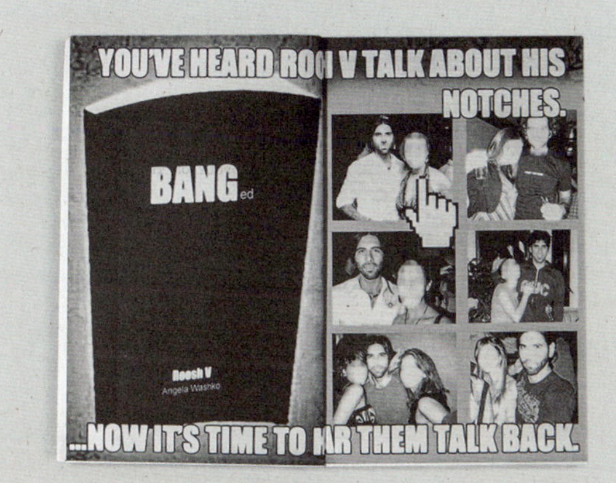

DESCRIPTION: "The book tells this story from the perspective of the artist" (Angela Washko, "BANGed," website). It documents some of the writing Washko published during her work on *BANGED* and the transcript from her interview with the pick-up artist himself. The cover appropriates the design and format of Roosh V's book *BANG*, also published through Lulu, but adds a paratext in pink that suggests an edited version of the original as well as a shift in perspective from Roosh V to the women allegedly seduced.

On Public Opinion: Responses to BANGed

METHOD: documentation / archiving, study / analysis

SUBJECT: bias, gender, internet culture, memory / storage, politics / activism, social media

PAGES: 209

DESCRIPTION: "The book tells this story from the perspective of everyone invested in the project except for the artist herself" (Angela Washko, "On Public Opinion," website). It offers perspectives from radically polarized communities by documenting public posts and comments on Washko's art project *BANGED*: from mainstream news sites and the pickup artist's community forums, to Twitter and the artist's Facebook feed.

AUTHOR	Barron Webster
YEAR	2015
GENRE	artist's book / bookwork
METHOD	détournement / hack, documentation / archiving, generative / automation, versioning / seriality
SUBJECT	data, economy / labor, surveillance / privacy, technology, tracking
PLATFORM	Blurb
VOLUMES	3
EDITION CHARACTERISTICS	ISBN, open edition, partially no longer available
FORMAT	15.2 × 22.9 cm
MATERIALITIES	color, paperback, perfect bound

IMAGE

DESCRIPTION

"*Buy my privacy* is a series of products generated from 'semi-private' information that is not generally publicized, but is nonetheless not private in the purest sense; as it is sent to and used by organizations who build the software we use. This information is turned for a profit by selling our 'private' habits to advertisers.

These data are generated by algorithm, for algorithm. They are sent back and forth as JSON objects, unix epoch dates, and other formats; but the habits they reflect are deeply human, albeit mediated by our keys, mice, and thumbs. They contain our habits, our thoughts, our movements, our little eccentricities, and if we do a bit of deciphering, much, much more—our relationships, our occupations, our passions, our goals. This wealth of human information can also be ours to do with what we wish. To demonstrate this, I (Barron) have begun to sell my 'semi-private' information to other humans to decipher and learn about me as a human. This information is not just a data point in a banner ad targeting algorithm" (Barron Webster, "Buy my Privacy," website).

Buyers of the books may also receive an entire HTML package of the data represented in the books. The third volume of the series, *History Edition*, is no longer available on Blurb. It contains every site Webster visited on his computer.

Buy My Privacy: Typing Edition 1

METHOD: détournement / hack, documentation / archiving, generative / automation

SUBJECT: surveillance / privacy, technology, tracking

EDITION CHARACTERISTICS: ISBN 9781320746441

PAGES: 108

DESCRIPTION: *The Typing Edition* was the first book in the series. It records every key Barron Webster pressed on his computer, including the software program within which the key was pressed, from April 3 to May 1, 2015. The project is reminiscent of Julian Palacz's *End Tell* (see 171).

The first page of our copy contains an error that probably occurred when the author created the PDF: On this page, the book is erroneously announced as "internet history edition 1."

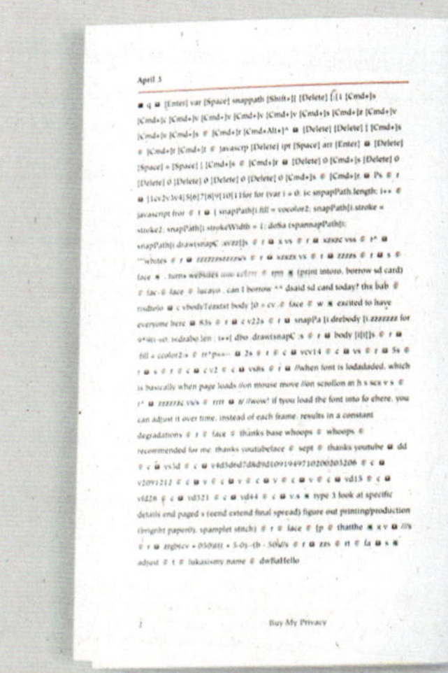

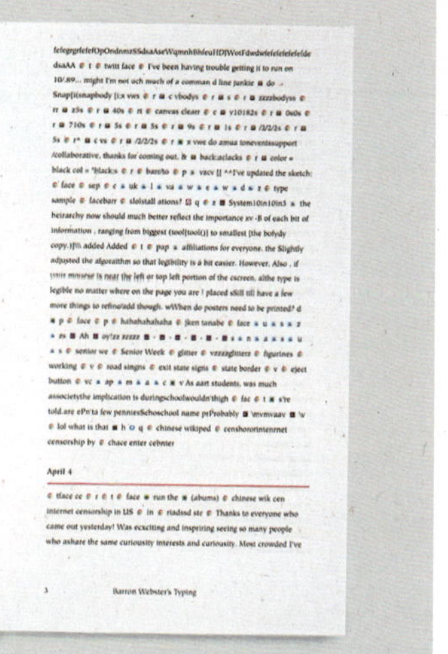

Buy My Privacy: Location Edition 1

METHOD: détournement / hack, documentation / archiving, generative / automation

SUBJECT: google, maps / street view, surveillance / privacy, tracking

EDITION CHARACTERISTICS: ISBN 9781320747769

PAGES: 188 (unpaginated)

DESCRIPTION: *The Location Edition* is the second volume in the series. It lists every place Webster visited from November 5, 2014 to May 5, 2015, with the movement patterns for each day recorded on a map. It is reminiscent of James Bridle's *Where the F**k Was I?* (see 191).

The preface in our copy erroneously refers to the third volume and announces the author's entire internet history as the contents of this volume, with the title and URL of the websites visited and the visit times.

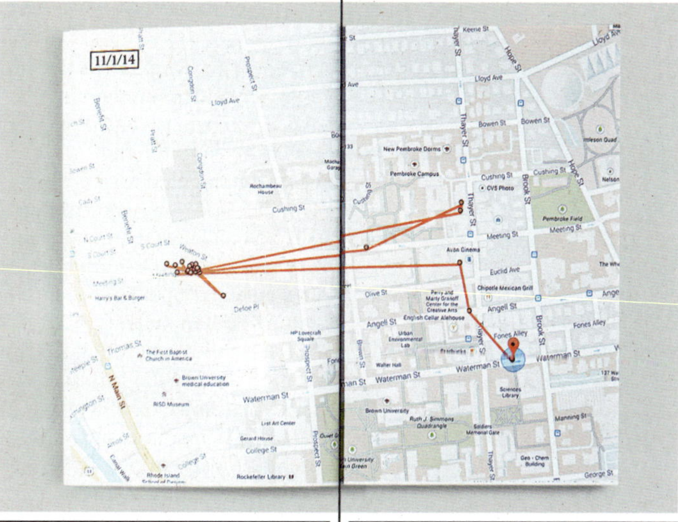

BÆBEL

Volume 1

AUTHOR	Gregor Weichbrodt
YEAR	2015
PUBLISHER	0x0a
GENRE	artist's book / bookwork
METHOD	found material, generative / automation, montage / remix
SUBJECT	economy / labor, platforms / companies, scale
PLATFORM	Lulu
EDITION CHARACTERISTICS	second edition, multiple editions (print, PDF), open edition
FORMAT	21.6 × 27.9 cm
MATERIALITIES	black-and-white, paperback, perfect bound
PAGES	685
IMAGE	

DESCRIPTION

"Single pages from IKEA furniture-assembly instructions were mixed together and renumbered. The result is an instructions manual of about 700 pages" (blurb on Lulu). Fifty pages list all the parts from which to assemble the furniture. This is followed by over 600 pages of 1,191 numbered assembly instructions consisting only of drawings, symbols, and numbers without any words.

The book was created during an artist residency at Room & Board, New York in October 2015, where it was publicly presented in a series of zine-sized booklets, each unique. Room & Board's Director Jules Pelta Feldman states: "*BÆBEL*'s name suggests both staggering ambition—and if you followed its instructions, and assembled all IKEA furniture into a single fixture, what could that be but a tower to god?—and its promise of universal comprehension: IKEA's power is predicated on communicating across languages, which is why its manuals eschew words entirely for these severe and elegant images" (Jules Pelta Feldman, "No Offense").

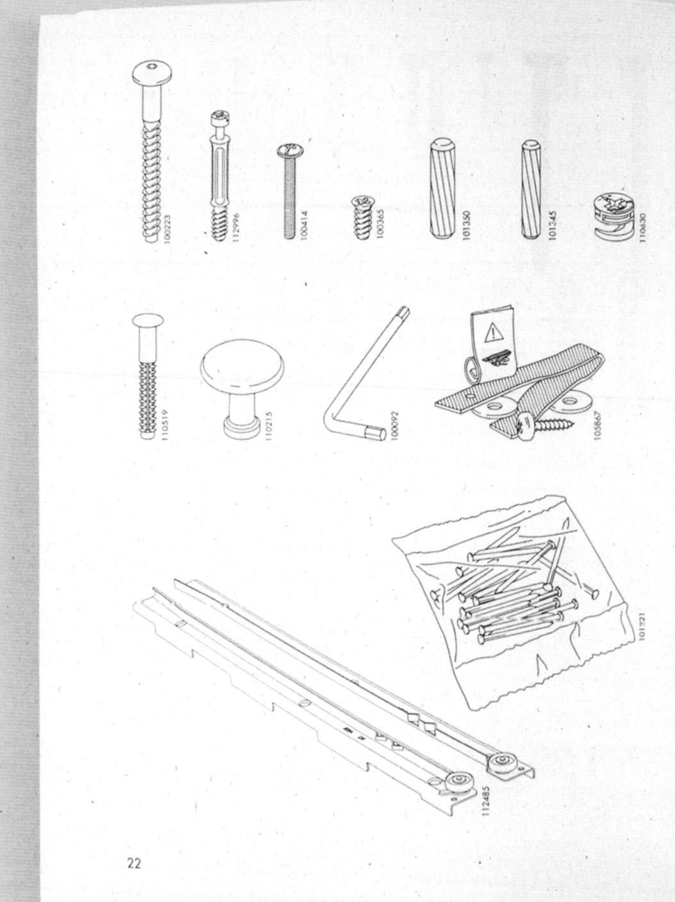
100223
112996
100414
100365
101350
101345
110630
110519
110215
100092
105867
101721
112485
22

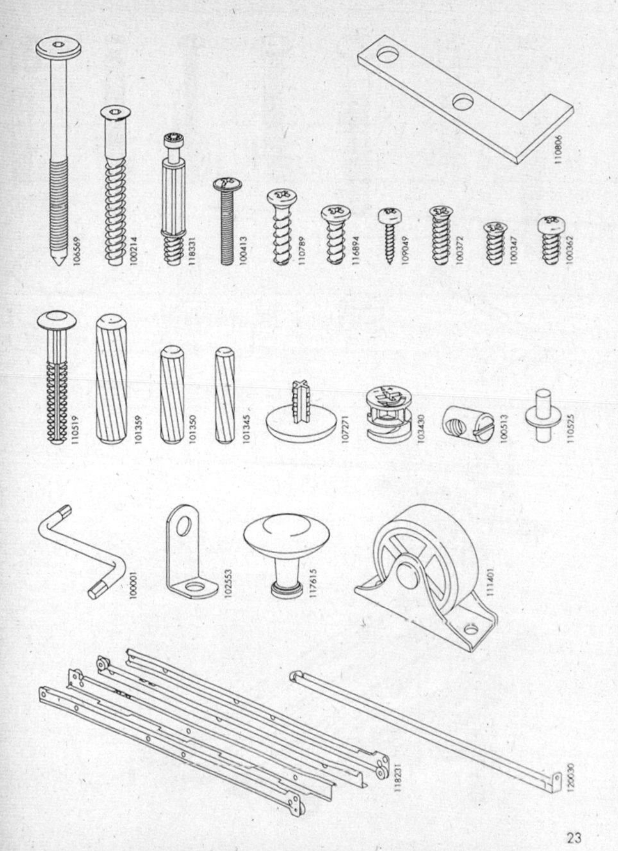
110806
106569
100214
118331
100413
110789
116894
109049
100372
100347
100362
110519
101359
101350
101345
107271
103430
100513
110525
100001
102553
117615
111401
118231
120030
23

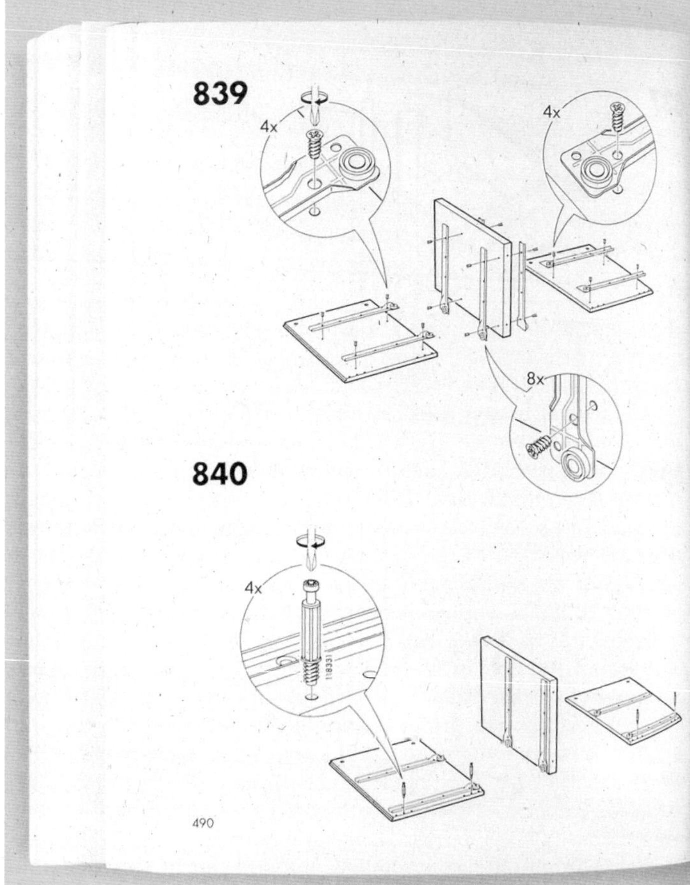
839
4x
4x
8x
840
4x
118331
490

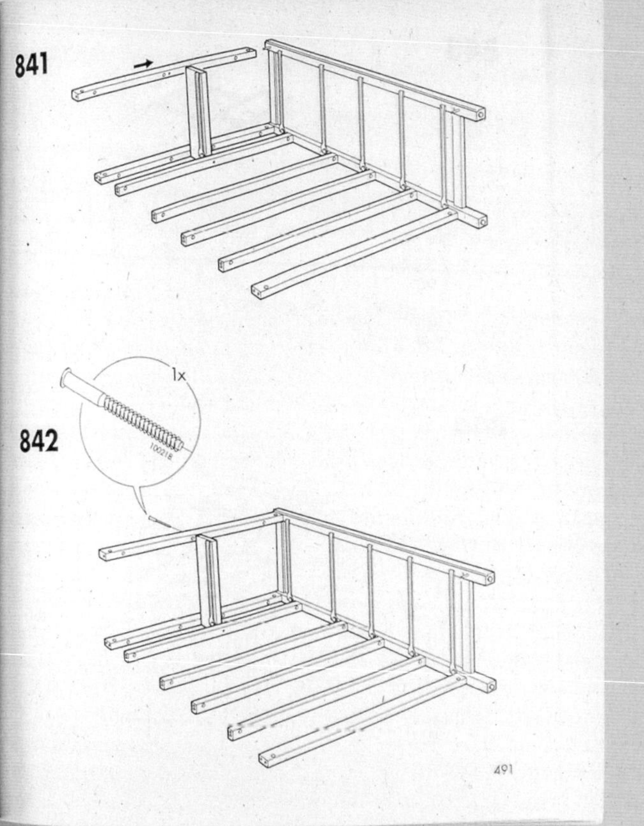
841
842
1x
100218
491

I Don't Know

AUTHOR	Gregor Weichbrodt
YEAR	2015
PUBLISHER	0x0a
GENRE	experimental literature
METHOD	generative / automation, montage / remix
SUBJECT	canon, wikipedia, writing / reading techniques
PLATFORM	Lulu
EDITION CHARACTERISTICS	multiple editions (print, PDF), open edition
FORMAT	10.8 × 17.5 cm
MATERIALITIES	black-and-white, paperback, perfect bound, defective copy
PAGES	392

IMAGES

DESCRIPTION

Gregor Weichbrodt's *I Don't Know* is an extensive text consisting of strung together first-person statements that, in an astonishing variety of phrasing, deny any knowledge of a range of subjects, starting with literature and the analog book: "I'm not well-versed in Literature. Sensibility—what is that? What in God's name is An Afterword? I haven't the faintest idea. And concerning book design, I am fully ignorant." And ending with the digital age: "I don't know what people mean by 'The Information Age.' Digitality—dunno. The Age of Interruption? How should I know? What is Information Overload? I don't know."

As Jules Pelta Feldman notes, however, the text often exhibits a performative self-contradiction in the process. She brings as an example: "I'm completely ignorant of Art Deco architecture in Arkansas. Can you tell me how to get to The Drew County Courthouse, Dual State Monument, Rison Texaco Service Station or Chicot County Courthouse?" and comments: "I don't know about you, but the narrator of *I Don't Know* knows a hell of a lot more about Arkansas's architectural history than I do" (Jules Pelta Feldman, "No Offense").

The text was generated by an algorithm that randomly combines phrases of denial (Hannes Bajohr and Jules Pelta Feldman helped with the compilation) and subjects taken from Wikipedia. Each paragraph starts with the denial of knowing anything about a Wikipedia category, and then continues by enumerating ignorance about a number of related entries in that category until the algorithm picks a category mentioned in the last entry, which then opens a new paragraph. Guided by the algorithm, we move through Wikipedia in a way "that resembles the kind of internet clickhole down which each of us occasionally plummets (or perhaps an internet browser's stream-of-consciousness)" (Ibid.). Thus, *I Don't Know* is simultaneously an absurdly detailed insistence on the finite nature of individual knowledge and a demonstration of the potential infinity of the knowledge accumulated in a collective digital database.

0x0a, a writers' collective for digital literature consisting of Hannes Bajohr and Gregor Weichbrodt, offers all works as a PDF (free of charge) and through print-on-demand (Lulu). The cover design of each 0x0a book is computer generated: completely determined by certain variables taken from the text itself. "Thus, every text that is published on 0x0a.li gets its own cover, 'written' by its title itself" (Gregor Weichbrodt, "0x0a Cover Art").

The copy archived shows print indexing notes on the fore edge of the last few pages, due to bad binding and cutting.

An Arthrogram

AUTHOR	Zach Whalen
YEAR	2015
GENRE	artist's book / bookwork, experimental literature
METHOD	generative / automation, study / analysis
SUBJECT	book / book design, code / programming, literature, narration
PLATFORM	Lulu, Amazon
EDITION CHARACTERISTICS	ISBN 9781329558564, open edition, CC BY
FORMAT	16.7 × 25.9 cm
MATERIALITIES	black-and-white, paperback, perfect bound
PAGES	344

IMAGES

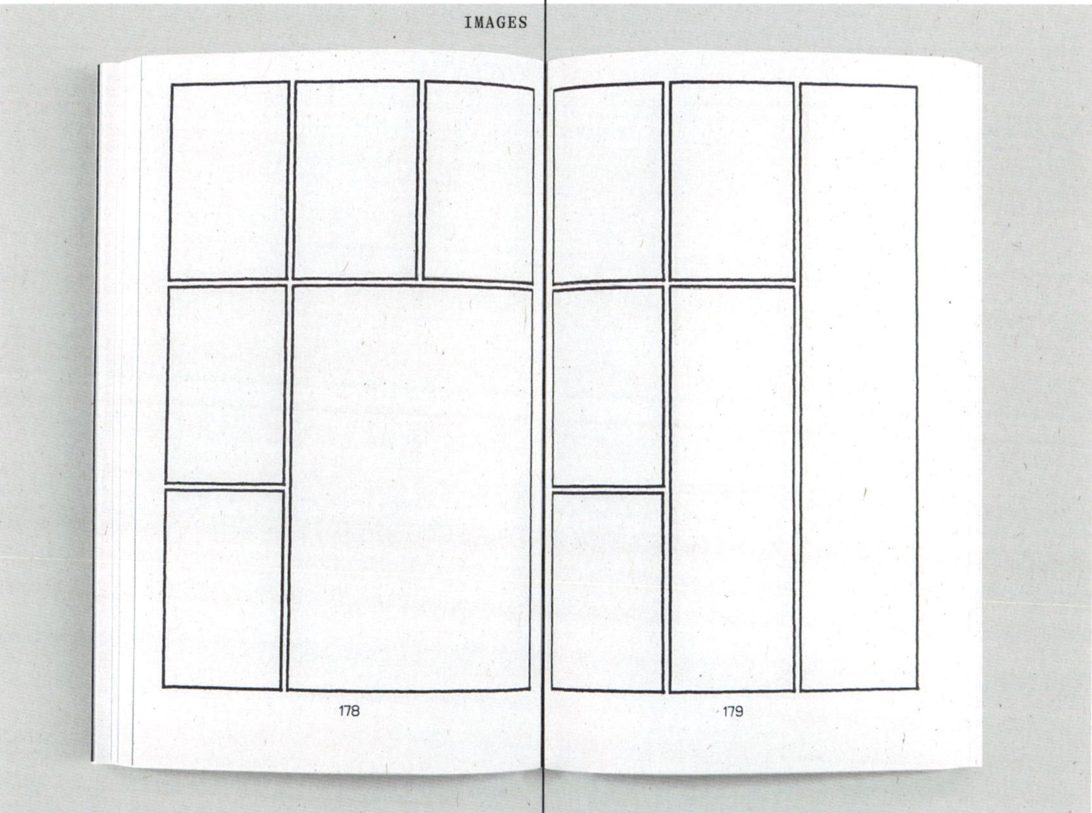

DESCRIPTION

An Arthrogram is "a graphic novel," as Zach Whalen states on his blog, though it contains only blank panels. Given that typically panel "variations are driven by various narrative-driven pressures," Whalen asked "what else is possible without the same fealty to telling a story" and "how many possible layouts exist" (Zach Whalen, "An Arthrogram, Part 1"). With this in mind, his book explores every possible constellation of panels on a page according to a fixed set of rules: "1. All panels are rectangles. / 2. No more than 3 panels in either axis. / 3. All possible space must be covered by panels" (Zach Whalen, *An Arthrogram*, front matter).

The book has nine chapters, following the increasing number of rectangles permuted on each page. As the number of rectangles increases, so does the number of possible permutations. The result is a conceptual narrative but also an investigation into the semantic implications of the formal structuring of panels, as constellations of panels on a page are usually used to highlight different aspects of a narrative.

Whalen wrote a script in the programming language Perl to generate the book's content. The script is printed as an appendix on the last page. The fuzzy lines used to render the constellations of rectangles are based on a scan of an actual Sharpie line drawn by Whalen, which he also automated. Both scripts were made available via GitHub.

DEMO BOOK FOR INTERN

AUTHOR	Joey Yearous-Algozin
YEAR	2015
PUBLISHER	Troll Thread
GENRE	artist's book / bookwork, experimental literature
METHOD	found material, reformatting, test / experiment
SUBJECT	analog / digital, book / book design, copyright / law, economy / labor, print on demand, publishing / distribution, standard / default
PLATFORM	Lulu
EDITION CHARACTERISTICS	multiple editions (print, PDF), open edition
FORMAT	21.6 × 27.9 cm
MATERIALITIES	color, paperback, perfect bound
PAGES	674 (unpaginated)

IMAGES

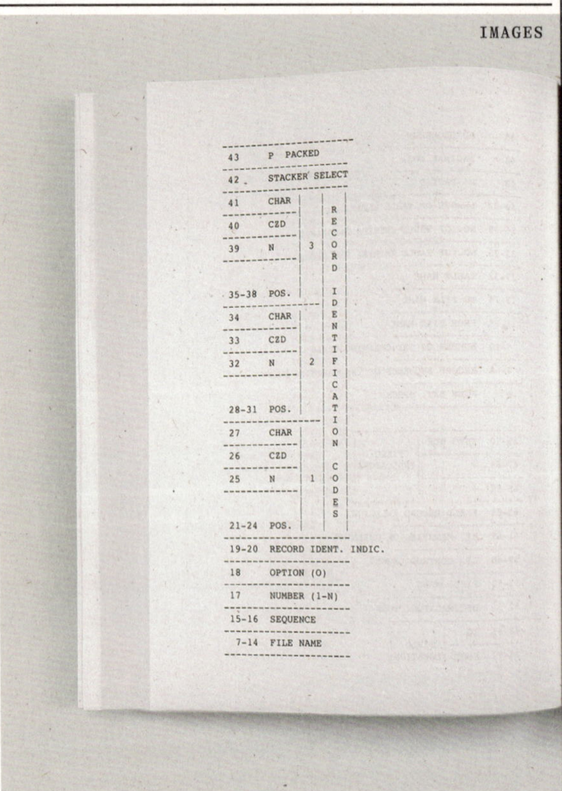

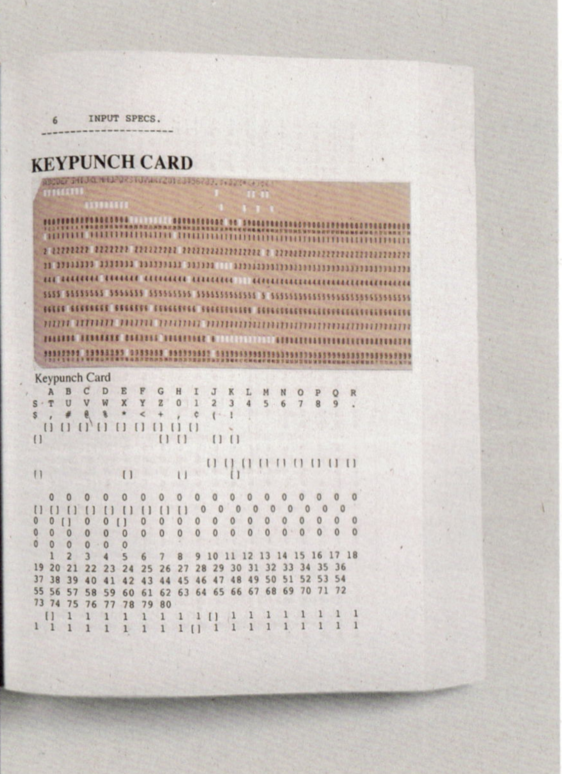

DESCRIPTION

Troll Thread co-founder Joey Yearous-Algozin created *DEMO BOOK FOR INTERN* in 2015 to show Troll Thread's intern how to make a print-on-demand book. It also demonstrates the collective's general poetic approach to working with found material from the internet by including the text "IBM System 360 RPG Debugging Template and Keypunch Card" as found freely accessible on Project Gutenberg.

This text was copied to a US letter format template and auto-formatted, as were the disclaimer and meta-text, including all source formatting. The resulting twenty-four pages were then copied twenty-eight times to come as close as possible to the maximum number of pages for this format on Lulu. The book contains obscure line breaks, deformed links, and cut-off images, revealing the fundamental differences between web and print text design. It also shows that text on Project Gutenberg is not truly free, as more than half of the copied text is taken up by a copyright disclaimer.

The book must have served its purpose, since the intern then went on to make a print-on-demand publication for Troll Thread called *INTERN* (see 319).

Fifty Shades of Grey

AUTHOR	Hermann Zschiegner
YEAR	2015
GENRE	artist's book / bookwork
METHOD	collection, composition (writing / drawing / photography)
SUBJECT	analog / digital, literature, materiality, print technology, reading / interpretation, standard / default, web design
PLATFORM	Blurb
EDITION CHARACTERISTICS	open edition
FORMAT	15.2 × 22.9 cm
MATERIALITIES	black-and-white, paperback, perfect bound
PAGES	106

IMAGES

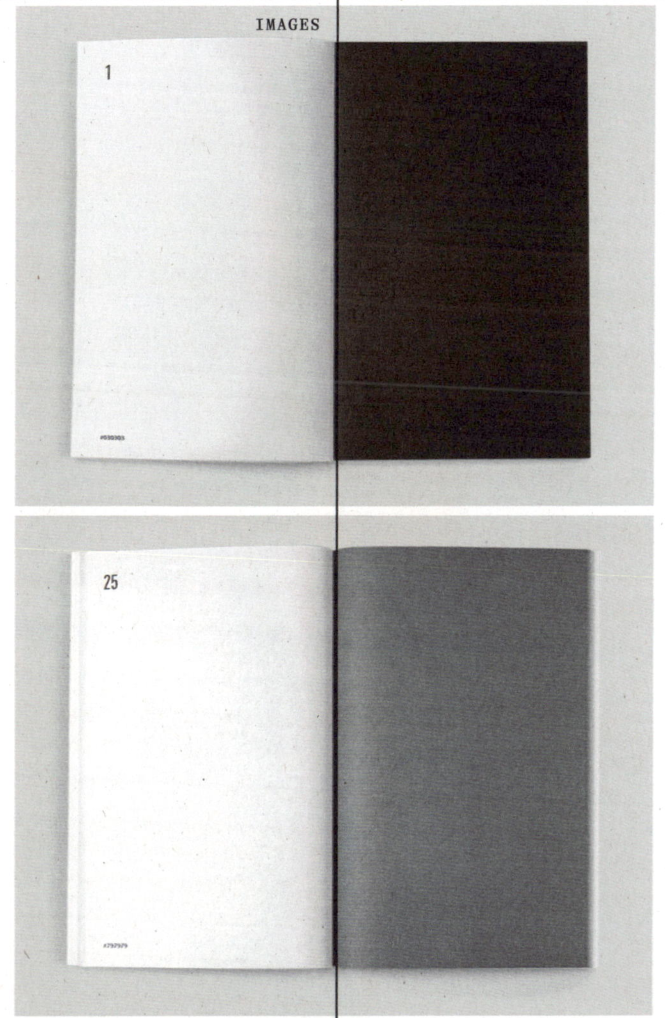

DESCRIPTION

Hermann Zschiegner's book contains a collection of fifty shades of gray, each filling an entire page and accompanied by their RGB (red, green, blue) values as hexadecimal string, as used in HTML/CSS code for web design. The color tones lighten up page by page, from a page filled with black ink to a blank white page. This makes the book a visualization of the subtractive CMYK printing process used in print-on-demand. In contrast to the additive RGB color mixing on screens, CMYK (cyan, magenta, yellow, black) printing mixes tones based on the density of colored dots. The result is as much a flip book as it is a gray scale test card for digital printing.

By taking the title literally, Zschiegner moreover parodies the erotic bestseller of the same name by E L James, the original blurb of which he also uses for his own book on Blurb.

Reading @realDonaldTrump

AUTHOR	Anonymous
YEAR	2016–2018
PUBLISHER	Counterpath
GENRE	experimental literature, nonfiction
METHOD	found material, outsourcing
SUBJECT	amazon, mechanical turk, politics / activism, reading / interpretation, social media, twitter
PLATFORM	Lulu
VOLUMES	7
EDITION CHARACTERISTICS	multiple editions (e-book, print), ISBN, open edition
FORMAT	15.2 × 22.9 cm
MATERIALITIES	black-and-white, paperback, perfect bound
IMAGE	

DESCRIPTION

"*Reading @realDonaldTrump* is a print and e-book publication series of readings by Amazon Turk workers of tweets on @realDonaldTrump. Tweets are posted to Amazon Turk as 'human intelligence tasks' (HITs) with the prompt to write at least 100 words describing the surface meaning and subtext. These readings are then collected in a short book devoted to a given @realDonaldTrump tweet. Proceeds from sales of titles in the series are donated to nonprofit causes" (Counterpath, "Reading @realDonaldTrump").

The series includes seven annotated tweets. The publisher had advertised a separate internship for the supervision of this series. The books are available in a few bookshops as well as on Lulu and Google Play Books.

In addition to winning the Electoral College in a landslide, I won the popular vote if you deduct the millions of people who voted illegally

EDITION CHARACTERISTICS	ISBN 9781365570100
PAGES	42
IMAGE	

A1OBB3PWYWK9KK

This is a claim from Donald Trump that millions of people voted illegally and if they had not, he would have won. This is an interesting claim because all of the available evidence suggests exactly the opposite of what he is saying. Voter fraud is actually very rare. By claiming that Hillary voters were voting illegally, Trump is making a claim that his opponents are breaking laws and participating in voter fraud. He also may be alleging that illegal immigrants are voting. He wants to portray all opposition to him as illegitimate so he can make whatever decisions he wants and claim that they are supported by the public.

26

A1GV0UZU0T2ORS

In this tweet, Trump was saying that millions of people illegally voted for Hillary Clinton, and that otherwise he would have won the popular vote, in addition to the electoral college. However, while during the election his campaign focused on dead people who were registered (many who were still registered because they were alive in the last few elections), due to his use of the word illegally, it now seems clear that this tweet is meant to tie illegal voting to illegal immigrants and possibly even minorities in general. The tweet has become typical of things Trump says that will never be proven, but that supporters seem to swallow happily. It seems that even in victory, Trump has to be the best at all things and right on all issues, with his opinions being stated with the certainty of fact at all turns.

27

DESCRIPTION

This is volume 2 in the *Reading @realDonaldTrump* series. Its long title *In addition to winning the Electoral College in a landslide, I won the popular vote if you deduct the millions of people who voted illegally* is taken from the tweet of Trump's that Amazon Turk workers were asked to interpret, with all of those interpretations included in this volume. The worker's identification number is included with each reading.

Unlike other more erratic tweets, the interpretation of this one is easy for most: "I think what Trump is saying is pretty straight forward" (*In addition to winning […]*, 28). Regardless, the range of responses reflects Americans' divisiveness in their attitudes toward Trump. Among the forty-two total submissions, there are some that are clearly on Trump's side: "I have no reason to doubt what Donald Trump is saying" (Ibid., 37). Even the admission of Trump's unmistakable character flaws does not lead to a renunciation of his policies: "President Elect Donald Trump has an unusual ego. He seems to need to respond to many more criticism than other people in position might address. […] My hope is that President Elect Trump grows some thicker skin because many people will criticize him for the next 4 years. He will look like a bigger person if he can ignore the fruitless criticisms and focus on those with substance" (Ibid., 43).

Others, however, provide ample evidence of the lack of substance in Trump's remarks and worry about what is to follow: "Whats [*sic*] worrying is that he goes on to imply that a good portion of the popular vote was influenced by altered votes, a claim that remains unsubstantiated. […] this is only the beginning of a long string of off-the-cuff remarks and baseless fingerpointing. It remains to be seen what the ramifications will be, for our citizens and our image on the world stage" (Ibid., 12). Still others react with gallows humor, poking fun at Trump's obviously distorted perception: "Old Donald T thinks that he did just wonderful in the selection. […] Of course the election results are invalid. Donald Trump won by a landslide, and is the new savior of the people. Hail Trump!" (Ibid., 18) Just how deep and insurmountable the nation's division is in its opinion toward Trump can be seen on the opposite page, where a Trump supporter's interpretation is printed: "I believe that he is in the right too! Donald Trump is a beast and so awesome" (Ibid., 19).

Vexations

Book 1: Lexmark XM9155

AUTHOR	derek beaulieu
YEAR	since 2016
PUBLISHER	No Press
GENRE	artist's book / bookwork
METHOD	constraint, photocopy / scan, reenactment, remediation, versioning / seriality
SUBJECT	economy / labor, error / corruption / loss, materiality, music / sound, technology
PLATFORM	Lulu
VOLUMES	so far 4 (of 10 planned) vols.
EDITION CHARACTERISTICS	limited edition, multiple editions (print, PDF)
FORMAT	21.6 × 27.9 cm
MATERIALITIES	black-and-white, paperback, perfect bound
PAGES	176 (unpaginated)

IMAGES

DESCRIPTION

Erik Satie's *Vexations* from 1893, first published by John Cage in 1949, is presumably one of the longest pieces in music history even though its score is only one page. This is due to an instruction reading "In order to play the theme 840 times in succession, it would be advisable to prepare oneself beforehand, and in the deepest silence, by serious immobilities" (*Vexations*, epigraph).

derek beaulieu uses this repetitive approach as a constraint for his publishing project *Vexations*. Corresponding to an eighteen-hour marathon performance organized by Cage with ten performers taking turns in 1963, beaulieu began a ten-volume series in 2016 that translates Satie's *Vexations* into the visual in ten iterations: It "decomposes the score of Erik Satie's masterpiece through repeated photocopy degeneration" (blurb on Lulu).

For each iteration, he uses a different photocopy machine to reproduce Satie's sheet of music: first copying the sheet music, then copying the copy, and so on, eighty-four times. These physical copies are then scanned and transferred into book form. This will result in 840 visual variations in ten clusters. The different machines produce astonishingly different results in this recursive practice.

So far, 4 of 10 planned volumes have been published. We have purchased volume 1 for our collection, titled *Book 1: Lexmark XM9155*. Although available via Lulu's bookstore, the books are limited to twenty-six copies, presumably taken down when this number is reached. The other volumes have as subtitles: *Book 2: Xerox Workcentre 5755*, *Book 3: Lexmark XM5163*, and *Book 4: Xerox Workcentre 7845i*.

Filter Bubble

AUTHORS	Simon Castets [ed.], Hans Ulrich Obrist [ed.]
YEAR	2016
PUBLISHER	89plus, The LUMA Foundation
GENRE	catalog / collection, nonfiction
METHOD	composition (writing / drawing / photography), documentation / archiving
SUBJECT	art, art world / literary world, internet culture, literature, social media
PLATFORM	Lulu
EDITION CHARACTERISTICS	ISBN 9783033062726, multiple editions (print, PDF), open edition
FORMAT	10.8 × 17.5 cm
MATERIALITIES	color, paperback, perfect bound
PAGES	142

IMAGES

DESCRIPTION

Filter Bubble is a catalog published on the occasion of the exhibition of the same name, which took place at LUMA Westbau in Zurich in 2015/16. It was preceded by the exhibition "Poetry will be made by all!" which resulted in the series *1,000 Books of 1,000 Poets* (see also 284, 297, 303), the design of which *Filter Bubble* adopts.

All forty-four participating artists were born around the year 1989, because the 89plus research project on which the exhibition is based investigates the generation born at the same time that the internet was developed. The title *Filter Bubble* refers to "the way in which Internet users are increasingly directed to a personalised information landscape through the algorithmic editing of web content" (Simon Castets / Hans Ulrich Obrist, "Introduction," 9).

The catalog features photographs of the exhibition, short descriptions of the artworks shaped by the digital condition, and three accompanying texts: "Introduction" by the curators and editors Simon Castets and Hans Ulrich Obrist, the essay "filter bubble observations, notes" by Takeshi Shiomitsu, and the poem "filter bubble" by Lebo Mashifane.

THE EXHIBITION AND ITS CATALOG FEATURE WORKS BY

Sarah Abu Abdallah (Providence), Sophia Al Maria (Doha), Abdullah Al-Mutairi (New York), Rachael Allen (London), Yollotl Alvarado (Mexico City), ARCA & Jesse Kanda (London), Darja Bajagić (New York), Alessandro Bava (London), James Bridle (London), Andrea Crespo (New York), Manolis Daskalakis-Lemos (Athens), Alex Dolan (New York), Valia Fetisov (Moscow), Louisa Gagliardi (Zurich), Deanna Havas (New York), Max Hawkins (nomadic), Bernhard Hegglin (Zurich), Ho Rui An (Singapur), Emmanuel Iduma (New York), Nicholas Korody (Los Angeles), Isabel Legate (New York), Luca Lum & Marcus Yee (Singapur), Nicholas Maurer (Sydney), Felix Melia (London), Mitchell Messina (Kapstadt), Ryan Murphy (New York), Wyatt Niehaus (New York), Adriana Ramić (New York), Tabita Rezaire (Johannesburg), Bunny Rogers (Stockholm), Ben Rosenthal (Zurich), Bogosi Sekhukhuni (Johannesburg), Takeshi Shiomitsu (London), Crista Siglin & Isaac Wilder (Kansas City), Jasper Spicero (New York), Jesse Stecklow (Los Angeles), Hito Steyerl (Berlin), Elisabeth Sutherland (Accra), Philipp Timischl (Wien), Alexander Jackson Wyatt (Sydney), Urban Zellweger (Zurich), Zou Zhao (New York), Bruno Zhu (Amsterdam), and Damon Zucconi (New York).

Instamatic Clouds

AUTHOR	Rod Kennedy
YEAR	2016
PUBLISHER	Toltec Press
GENRE	photobook
METHOD	found material
SUBJECT	analog / digital, instagram, photography, technology, visual culture
PLATFORM	unknown
EDITION CHARACTERISTICS	ISBN 9781932331042, open edition
FORMAT	17.8 × 14.5 cm
MATERIALITIES	color, paperback, perfect bound
PAGES	54 (unpaginated)

IMAGES

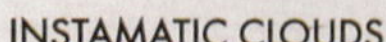

DESCRIPTION

With this print-on-demand publication, Rod Kennedy—as the operator of Toltec Press, a veteran of independent publishing, since the late 1960s—takes his publishing house into the post-digital age, while at the same time remaining true to his old companions: his book is distributed exclusively through Printed Matter. Likewise, the title *Instamatic Clouds* and the format of the photos reproduced in the book seem to connect to social media and the cloud of the present. But the title is to be taken literally: The overcast sky was photographed from relevant points in New York like museums, parks, squares, department stores, and buildings, named in the caption. Also listed is the exact time each picture was taken between September 1973 and February 1974, when, as the "Notes" at the end inform, daylight saving time was introduced as a trial in the USA due to severe energy shortages.

The title also refers to the camera used, according to the preliminary note: a Kodak Pocket Instamatic 10 Camera, the cheapest version of the new generation of inexpensive point-and-shoot cameras at the time. The brand name combines "instant" and "automatic," however it refers not to the instant picture but to the revolutionary quick and easy loading of the film. In *Instamatic Clouds*, it is unclear whether the color cast of the photos is due to the reduced quality of the 16mm shots or the yellowing of the prints, which according to the preliminary note were developed at the Color-Rite Film Service in Elizabeth, New Jersey—or whether, in retrospect, the current popular practice of photo processing with filters to mimic an outdated photographic technique was employed. In any case, Kennedy's book thus positions the Kodak Instamatic as a forerunner of today's ubiquitous instant photo culture as well as the low-cost print-on-demand photobook. The note ends with the enigmatic information: "The Camera was later stolen."

LENZ

AUTHOR	Dagmara Kraus
YEAR	2016
PUBLISHER	0x0a
GENRE	artist's book / bookwork, experimental literature
METHOD	appropriation, montage / remix, reenactment, reformatting, translation / transcription
SUBJECT	authorship, book / book design, canon, literature, narration, reading / interpretation
PLATFORM	Lulu
EDITION CHARACTERISTICS	multiple editions (print, PDF), ISBN 9781326635701, open edition
FORMAT	10.8 × 17.5 cm
MATERIALITIES	black-and-white, paperback, perfect bound
PAGES	276
IMAGES	

flog den Abhang hinunter. Es war finster geworden, Himmel und Erde verschmolzen in Eins. Es war als ginge ihm was nach, und als müsse ihn was Entsetzliches erreichen, etwas das Menschen nicht ertragen können, als jage der Wahnsinn auf Rossen hinter ihm. Endlich hörte er Stimmen, er sah Lichter, es wurde ihm leichter, man sagte ihm, er hätte noch eine halbe Stunde nach *Waldbach*. Er ging durch das Dorf, die Lichter schienen durch die Fenster, er sah hinein im Vorbeigehen, Kinder am Tische, alte Weiber, Mädchen, Alles ruhige, stille Gesichter, es war ihm als müsse das Licht von ihnen ausstrahlen, es ward ihm leicht, er war bald in Waldbach im Pfarrhause. Man saß am Tische, er hinein; die blonden Locken hingen ihm um das bleiche Gesicht, es zuckte ihm in den Augen und um den Mund, seine Kleider waren zerrissen. *Oberlin* hieß ihn willkommen, er hielt ihn für einen Handwerker. »Sein Sie mir willkommen, obschon Sie mir unbekannt.« – Ich bin ein Freund von … und bringe Ihnen Grüße von ihm. »Der Name, wenn's beliebt« … *Lenz*. »Ha, ha, ha, ist er nicht gedruckt? Habe ich nicht einige Dramen gelesen, die einem Herrn dieses Namens zugeschrieben werden?« Ja, aber belieben Sie mich nicht darnach zu beurteilen. Man sprach weiter, er suchte nach Worten und erzählte rasch,

8

aber auf der Folter; nach und nach wurde er ruhig, das heimliche Zimmer und die stillen Gesichter, die aus dem Schatten hervortraten, das helle Kindergesicht, auf dem alles Licht zu ruhen schien und das neugierig, vertraulich aufschaute, bis zur Mutter, die hinten im Schatten engelgleich stille saß. Er fing an zu erzählen, von seiner Heimat; er zeichnete allerhand Trachten, man drängte sich teilnehmend um ihn, er war gleich zu Haus, sein blasses Kindergesicht, das jetzt lächelte, sein lebendiges Erzählen; er wurde ruhig, es war ihm als träten alte Gestalten, vergessene Gesichter wieder aus dem Dunkeln, alte Lieder wachten auf, er war weg, weit weg. Endlich war es Zeit zum Gehen, man führte ihn über die Straße, das Pfarrhaus war zu eng, man gab ihm ein Zimmer im Schulhause. Er ging hinauf, es war kalt oben, eine weite Stube, leer, ein hohes Bett im Hintergrund, er stellte das Licht auf den Tisch, und ging auf und ab, er besann sich wieder auf den Tag, wie er hergekommen, wo er war, das Zimmer im Pfarrhause mit seinen Lichtern und lieben Gesichtern, es war ihm wie ein Schatten, ein Traum, und es wurde ihm leer, wieder wie auf dem Berg, aber er konnte es mit nichts mehr ausfüllen, das Licht war erloschen, die Finsternis verschlang Alles; eine unnennbare Angst erfaßte ihn, er sprang auf,

9

DESCRIPTION

The authorship of this book proves to be contested ground, as is made immediately clear by the cover. Dagmara Kraus's name is preceded by three other names that are all struck through: Georg Büchner, who in 1839 wrote the story *Lenz*; Carl Richard Mueller, who translated Büchner's story from German into English in 1963; and Rodney Graham, who in 1983 generated an artist's book of the same name from Mueller's translation. The list thus blends translatorial and authorial voices, causing Kraus's own name to become indistinct too, and keeping it open as to whether it is connected to a translatorial and/or an authorial achievement.

It is Rodney Graham's *Lenz* that Kraus draws on directly. When Graham read Büchner's *Lenz* in Mueller's translation, he discovered that it contained the phrase "through the forest" twice in quick succession. This seems to encapsulate the lonely wandering of the Sturm und Drang poet Jakob Michael Reinhold Lenz, who, according to Büchner's novella, met an unhappy end in the forest of the Vosges mountains. Graham adopts Büchner's novella in its entirety, but rearranges it so that the phrase "through the forest" is both times torn apart by a page break. Then he generates further repetitions by implanting a loop at this point of fracture that—eighty-four times—keeps sending Lenz through the forest over and over again, and condemns the reader to an unusually intensive close reading of the first dramatic pages of the novella.

Kraus sets herself the task of translating Graham's *Lenz* from English into German, but bases her "translation" on the original German Büchner text, thus eliminating the task of translating the wording of the text. It is the loop that is to be "translated," resulting in a typographic restaging that skillfully implants a loop in the text through line and page breaks. However, since Graham's loop is connected by the phrase "through the forest," which is a rather fuzzy translation of Büchner's "den Wald herab" and "den Wald herauf," Kraus chose a different phrase that is repeated several times in the German text: "er sprang auf" ("he leaped up"), which not only succinctly captures Lenz's permanent unrest but also contains the medial leap of the page break and the loop. After eleven loops, Kraus releases Lenz (and the reader) out of this maelstrom of madness back into Büchner's narration.

The book is published by 0x0a that offers all works as (free) PDF and POD (Lulu). The cover design is computer generated and completely determined by certain variables taken from the text itself. "Thus, every text that is published on 0x0a.li gets its own cover, 'written' by its title itself" (Gregor Weichbrodt, "0x0a Cover Art").

Defying Gravity

On internet dating and the force of attraction

AUTHOR	Joyce S. Lee
YEAR	2016
PUBLISHER	Gauss PDF
GENRE	photobook, reprint
METHOD	composition (writing / drawing / photography), found material, reformatting, study / analysis
SUBJECT	dating / sex, gender, internet culture, platforms / companies, social media, visual culture
PLATFORM	Lulu
EDITION CHARACTERISTICS	second edition, multiple editions (print, PDF), open edition
FORMAT	14.0 × 21.6 cm
MATERIALITIES	color, paperback, perfect bound
PAGES	56 (unpaginated)
IMAGES	

DESCRIPTION

Joyce S. Lee's *Defying Gravity* is a collection of profile pictures showing men levitating from the dating app Tinder, including their profile descriptions. Accumulated and arranged by the author, the book also includes an essay, reflecting on the body language of gravity-defying postures, their association with positive feelings, and love and relationships in times of online dating.

The book, reprinted by Gauss PDF, was initially published as a zine.

AUTHOR	Nick Montfort
YEAR	2016
PUBLISHER	Troll Thread
GENRE	experimental literature, poetry
METHOD	found material, generative / automation
SUBJECT	analog / digital, book / book design, code / programming, narration
PLATFORM	Lulu
EDITION CHARACTERISTICS	multiple editions (print, PDF, web), open edition
FORMAT	21.6 × 27.9 cm
MATERIALITIES	black-and-white, paperback, perfect bound
PAGES	256 (unpaginated)

IMAGES

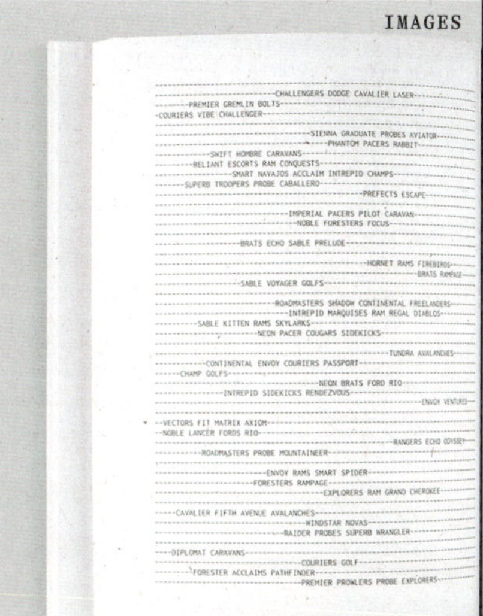

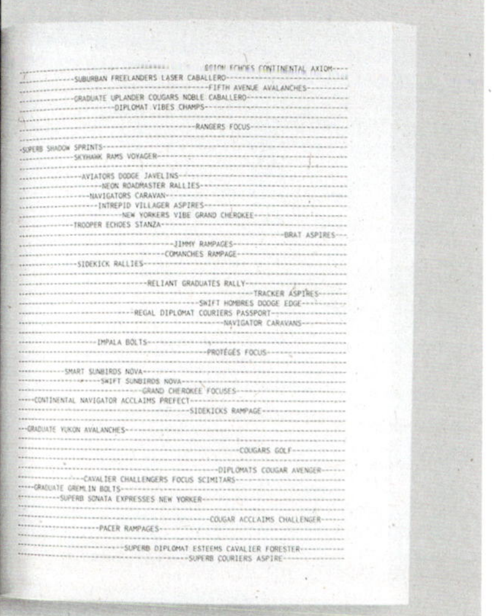

DESCRIPTION

AUTOPIA is a computer generated text that consists of product names for cars found on American streets and "–" as a fill character. They are arranged in such a way that they not only mimic cars on lanes but also create poetic mini-narratives due to their semantic meaning—because, as it turns out, cars are often named after animals, especially fast and strong ones (lynx, mustang, eagle), but also after fantastic birds (phoenix, firebird), native peoples of the United States (Dakota, Cherokee), and professions (explorer, pathfinder, aviator). At the same time, many names function as both noun and verb (focus, eclipse) or adjective (noble, premier).

Nick Montfort began categorizing the car names and writing a Python script that "has rules for combining automobile names in ways that are sensitive to the meaning of these names," to further enhance the meaning making of the headline-style sentences: "The outputs were able to suggest upper-class activities (NEW YORKER GOLFS), offer mathematical results (OPTIMA FIT MATRIX AXIOM), and even relate to contemporary issues such as immigration (AMIGOS FORD RIO)" (Nick Montfort, "*Autopia* and *The Truelist*").

AUTOPIA has been presented in different versions such as a Java-based website, an installation, and a print-on-demand book. The web version formats the output in 2×12′ lanes, animating the text moving left (on the top) and right (on the bottom) respectively, to mimic the flow of traffic from a bird's-eye view. The book version produces fifty-one lines of text covering every single page in its entirety, thus turning each double-page spread into a gigantic traffic panorama. Apart from 248 pages of output, the book also includes the Python script, allowing for code-based interpretation as well as recreation and altering of the potentially infinite text.

BFF/PRB #1
Notes from the Bakersfield Fan Forum

AUTHOR	Joseph Mosconi
YEAR	2016
PUBLISHER	PRB Editions
GENRE	artistic research, catalog / collection, education / classroom
METHOD	collection, found material, study / analysis
SUBJECT	canon, internet culture, publishing / distribution, visual culture
PLATFORM	Blurb
EDITION CHARACTERISTICS	multiple editions (print, PDF), ISBN 9781366950970, open edition
FORMAT	15.2 × 22.9 cm
MATERIALITIES	color, paperback, perfect bound
PAGES	274 (unpaginated)

IMAGES

DESCRIPTION

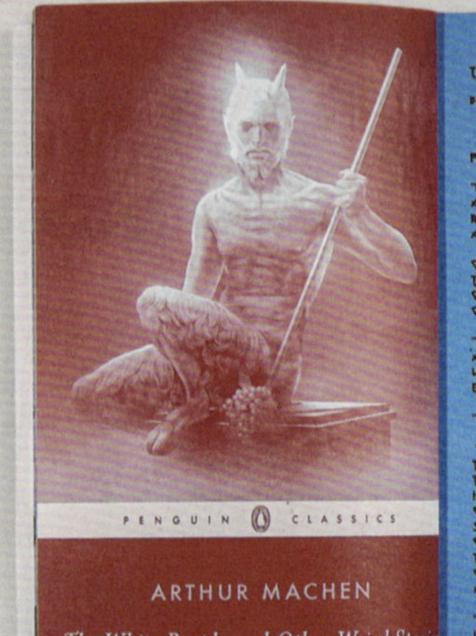

This publication originated during The Bakersfield Fan Forum, an exhibition, workshop, and event series that took place at the Todd Madigan Gallery (California State University, Bakersfield) from August to December 2016. The Poetic Research Bureau, represented by Joseph Mosconi, was invited to hold a semester-long residency on fandom and art in close relation to self-publishing: "The concepts of 'the fan,' 'the amateur' and the 'self-published writer' have often been denigrated and ridiculed in popular culture and the mass media. However, over the past several centuries the cultural practice of 'fandom,' of being a fan, has broadened and diversified, and become more participatory in the process. As sociologist Henry Jenkins has written, fans 'redefine the politics of reading' and 'view textual property not as the exclusive domain of textual producers but as open to repossession by textual consumers'" (CSUB Todd Madigan Gallery, "The Bakersfield Fan Forum").

In this context, Mosconi hosted a workshop with students to create print-on-demand books on the subject. *BFF/PRB #1* is the first in a series of five, produced by Mosconi himself. It consists of "lecture notes, textual ephemera, poor images, juvenilia, rejected poems and outtakes" and served as "a moodboard and skeleton-key for Mosconi's forthcoming book *Ashen Folk*" (blurb on Blurb). The typography and the mix of film posters, stills, and book covers of horror and science fiction novels reflect the imagery of a specific influential field of fandom.

This is the only book in our collection containing pages in a range of different colors, although these are in fact white pages with color printed on them, since print-on-demand providers usually do not offer a change of paper within a book. This may explain the book's relatively high price.

Abstract Browsing

AUTHOR	Rafaël Rozendaal
YEAR	2016
PUBLISHER	Library of the Printed Web
GENRE	artist's book / bookwork
METHOD	collection, generative / automation, study / analysis
SUBJECT	internet culture, materiality, platforms / companies, visual culture, web design
PLATFORM	Blurb
EDITION CHARACTERISTICS	open edition
FORMAT	21.6 × 27.9 cm
MATERIALITIES	color, zine, perfect bound, defective copy
PAGES	71 (unpaginated)

IMAGES

DESCRIPTION

Abstract Browsing is a publication based on the browser plug-in for Google Chrome of the same name conceived by Rafaël Rozendaal and coded by Reinier Feijen in 2016. Activating the plug-in overlays all functional boxes of a web page with full-colored rectangles, stripping the page from any content and turning it into an abstract composition, thus highlighting its diagrammatic structure: "It shows the skeleton of the web. It's like seeing an X-ray of a building, showing the structural elements. / Web pages are built of many smaller elements, information is organized and categorized. Text, images, tables, things we use every day but are not aware of" (Rafaël Rozendaal, "Notes").

The plug-in's twelve bright colors reference the palette of a browser's developer tool and, once activated, change over time, creating ever-new compositions. *Abstract Browsing* collects forty screenshots of the artist's browser while having the plug-in activated. The screenshots are set in different sizes on single and double pages. Along with the abstract contents of the browser window, user interface elements and address fields are also reproduced, revealing the source they were taken from as well as websites that were open in other tabs while taking the screenshot. The sources range from major websites like Gmail, Wikipedia, Facebook, and eBay—which in some cases appear multiple times—to minor websites like actress Zooey Deschanel's blog and subpages like media artist Jonas Lund's GitHub page. Thus, the collection also documents a selection of websites visited by Rozendaal. This lends a biographical twist to the study of web design trends at a particular point in time.

The rather poor quality of this print-on-demand publication, with full-colored areas regularly being pixelated or having ink smears, further abstracts the compositions, similar to Rozendaal's tapestry reproductions of abstract web pages. Both the publication and the tapestries force him to pause and make a selection from the numerous screenshots made: "The real challenge is editing. [...] Out of all the files I have, I have to choose which ones become objects. / The physicalization (weaving) brings focus. The software is fast and fluid, textile is expensive and slow. It slows me down, it helps me to pause and reflect" (Rozendaal, "Notes"). In this, Rozendaal's motivation resembles the web-to-print publications that Paul Soulellis has collected in his Library of the Printed Web (see 336f., 386f.) and in whose series Printed Web Editions Rozendaal's *Abstract Browsing* was published.

Compared to other copies, ours has different, non-glossy paper, indicating that the copies were printed in different places. In addition, our copy has a binding error: two sheets were bound upside down and in the wrong order.

Van de Onderaannemingsovereenkomst Of Beginselen van Poëtische Recht

AUTHOR	Nick Thurston
YEAR	2016
PUBLISHER	Onomatopee
GENRE	exhibition copy, experimental literature, poetry
METHOD	generative / automation, outsourcing, reformatting, translation / transcription
SUBJECT	amazon, book / book design, code / programming, economy / labor, google, literature, mechanical turk, print on demand
PLATFORM	Lulu
EDITION CHARACTERISTICS	ISBN 9789491677557, open edition, available for a limited time only
FORMAT	14.2 × 21.0 cm
MATERIALITIES	black-and-white, paperback, perfect bound
PAGES	141

IMAGES

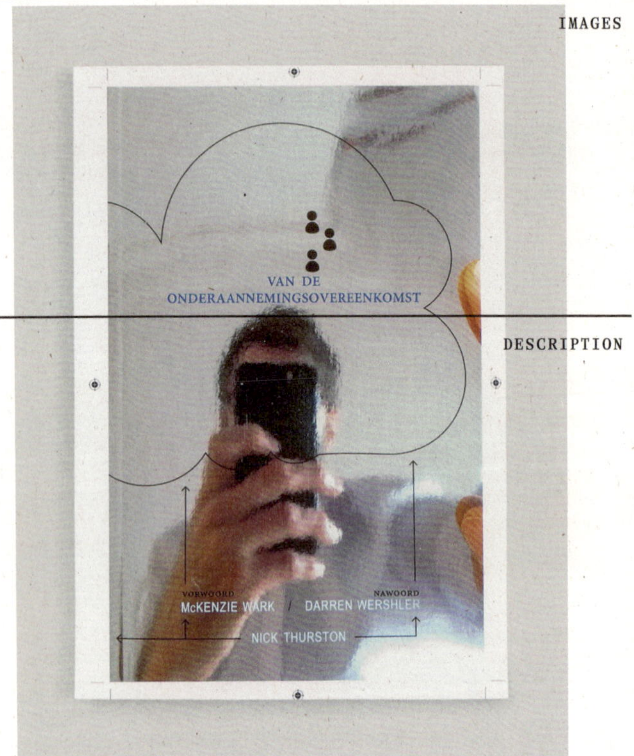

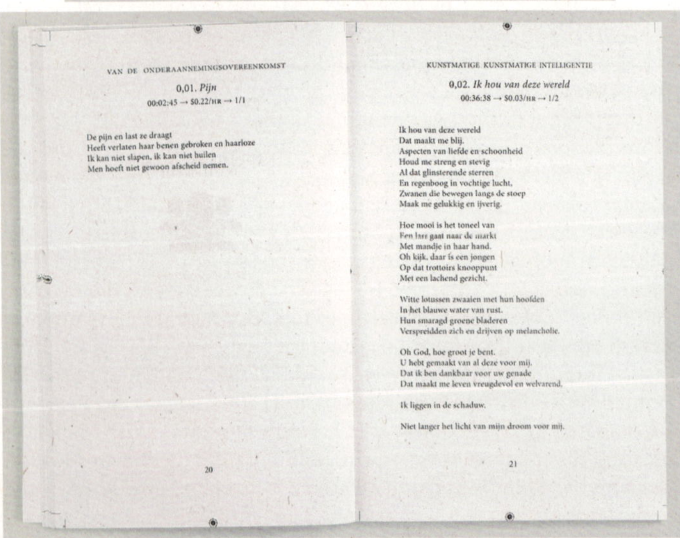

VAN DE ONDERAANNEMINGSOVEREENKOMST

0,01. *Pijn*

00:02:45 → $0.22/HR → 1/1

De pijn en last ze draagt
Heeft verlaten haar benen gebroken en haarloze
Ik kan niet slapen, ik kan niet huilen
Men hoeft niet gewoon afscheid nemen.

20

KUNSTMATIGE KUNSTMATIGE INTELLIGENTIE

0,02. *Ik hou van deze wereld*

00:36:38 → $0.03/HR → 1/2

Ik hou van deze wereld
Dat maakt me blij.
Aspecten van liefde en schoonheid
Houd me streng en stevig
Al dat glinsterende sterren
En regenboog in vochtige lucht.
Zwanen die bewegen langs de stoep
Maak me gelukkig en ijverig.

Hoe mooi is het toneel van
Een [illegible] gaat naar de markt
Met mandje in haar hand.
Oh kijk, daar is een jongen
Op dat trottoirs knooppunt
Met een lachend gezicht.

Witte lotussen zwaaien met hun hoofden
In het blauwe water van rust.
Hun smaragd groene bladeren
Verspreidden zich en drijven op melancholie.

Oh God, hoe groot je bent.
U hebt gemaakt van al deze voor mij.
Dat ik ben dankbaar voor uw genade
Dat maakt me leven vreugdevol en welvarend.

Ik liggen in de schaduw.

Niet langer het licht van mijn droom voor mij.

21

DESCRIPTION

This collection of poems was first published in English as *Of the Subcontract* by Information As Material (York, UK) in 2013. It contains one hundred poems, none of which was written by Nick Thurston himself. He ordered them all from underpaid ghostwriters through the Amazon offshoot Mechanical Turk. As we learn from Darren Wershler's afterword, which is the only "real," nonautomated text in this book, even the foreword ascribed to the media theorist McKenzie Wark was supplied by a ghostwriter from Lahore, commissioned through freelancer.com for $75.

In 2016, the Dutch translation *Van de Onderaannemingsovereenkomst, Of Beginselen van Poëtische Recht* was published, which Thurston again completely outsourced. This time, however, he entrusted it exclusively to machines: the translation was done by Google Translate, the text was poured automatically into the stylesheet of the English first edition, and the print-on-demand supplier Lulu was responsible for manufacturing the book. The translation is therefore riddled with countless mistakes, starting with the title, which disregards the established Dutch translation of Rousseau's *On the Social Contract*, on which Thurston is playing. "The visible crop and registration marks (cover to cover) show how the publishing process was transitioned from a standard paperback book dimension to Lulu's A5 dimensions and frame the 'translated' content as a kind of image within the representational field of 'the book.' It was also the quickest and easiest way of solving the size difference without having to re-make all of the layouts" (Nick Thurston, email to apod.li).

Van de Onderaannemingsovereenkomst was published for the exhibition "The Economy is Spinning," curated by Kris Dittel for Onomatopee, Eindhoven. The publisher Onomatopee indexes its publications and exhibitions in numerical order. The exhibition and catalog publication are number 132. By giving *Van de Onderaannemingsovereenkomst* the number 132.1, it becomes a supplement to the exhibition and catalog rather than a separate publication. The publication was exclusively available as print-on-demand on Lulu during the exhibition, June 5–July 17, 2016.

My Hard-Drive Died Along With My Heart

Stories about data-loss and broken trust

AUTHOR	Thomas Walskaar
YEAR	2016
GENRE	artist's book / bookwork, education / classroom, experimental literature
METHOD	collection, documentation / archiving, found material
SUBJECT	analog / digital, internet culture, memory / storage, social media, technology
PLATFORM	Lulu
EDITION CHARACTERISTICS	ISBN 9781326926571, open edition
FORMAT	14.8 × 21.0 cm
MATERIALITIES	black-and-white, paperback, perfect bound
PAGES	124 (unpaginated)

IMAGES

28 August 2014
Anonymous

Yesterday a friend of mine gave me his old unused IDE hard drive and the last time he checked it was working just fine but today when I attempted to connect it to my computer the shit burned down and there was smoke coming out.

I turned off the computer then turned it back on and there was no smoke, but BIOS was then unable to find a hard drive connected to the computer so it appears it's now dead.

But fuck the hard drive and its data, what concerns me is the reason behind this. Could it be caused by a bad PSU? Also is it possible that the cable coming from the power supply is not working well or was it just my luck and the hard drive simply died without a cause?

Also I would like to mention that I placed it in a rather unusual way. The drive was not pushed where it's meant to be but I actually placed it above the case with the board facing down. Could that have caused the death?

Feel sick.

Hard drive with all my files has died.

Was so close to getting it backed up too.

Almost 1tb of music, pics and stuff...

@meatbrk

https://twitter.com/MyHDDied

DESCRIPTION

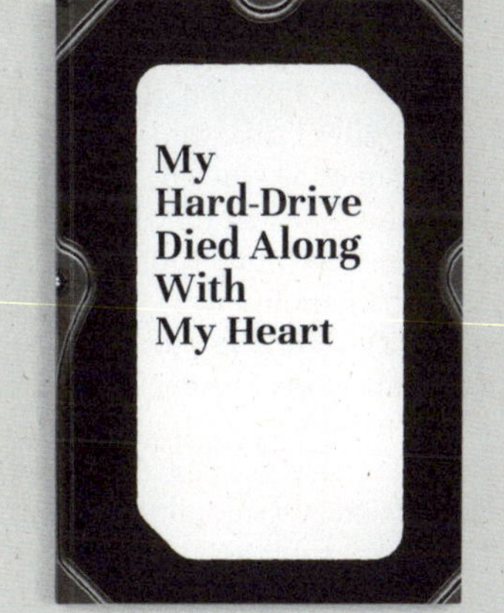

"*My Hard-Drive Died Along With My Heart* [...] explores people's relationship with hard-drives and what emotions people get after the trust is broken. The book contains a collection of online forum and twitter posts [from 1994 to 2016] on the topic. As a society we always seem to be looking for a new technical solution for knowledge and information storage and for this, we hope there is one magic, final solution that will solve every issue. But easy solutions create their own problems. The perceived view of the stable nature of digital information differs from reality" (blurb on Lulu).

The tweets, mostly quite emotional, are set in white on a black background and are reminiscent of an obituary, while the longer forum posts often include requests for help and technical details. Sources are provided for all quotations. The title of the book also comes from a tweet.

In addition, the artist has edited a five-minute video of footage of people talking online about the data loss they experience after their devices fail. According to the opening credits, they go through five stages of grief: denial, anger, bargaining, depression, and acceptance.

[' ', 'Skin', ' ', ' ', 'White', 'Masks']

AUTHOR	Wilmer Wilson IV
YEAR	2016
PUBLISHER	Gauss PDF
GENRE	experimental literature
METHOD	appropriation, reformatting
SUBJECT	bias, politics / activism, race, reading / interpretation, typography
PLATFORM	Lulu
EDITION CHARACTERISTICS	multiple editions (print, PDF), open edition
FORMAT	21.6 × 27.9 cm
MATERIALITIES	black-and-white, paperback, perfect bound
PAGES	64 (unpaginated)

IMAGES

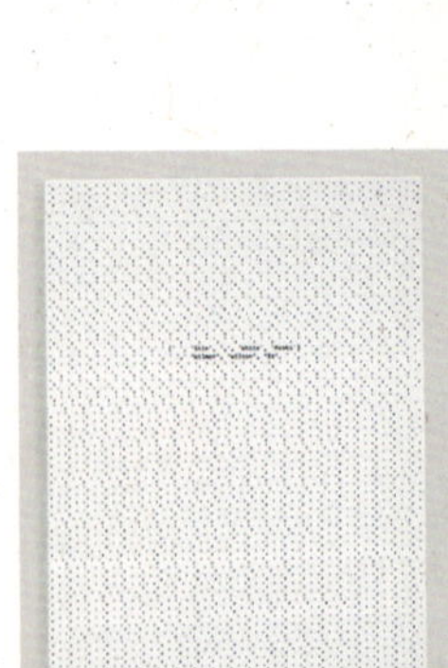

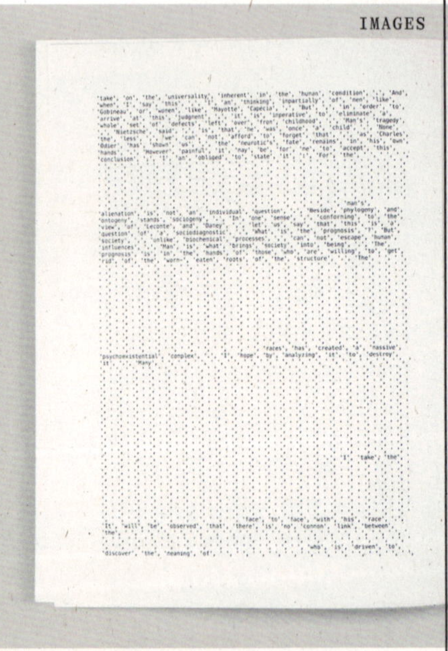

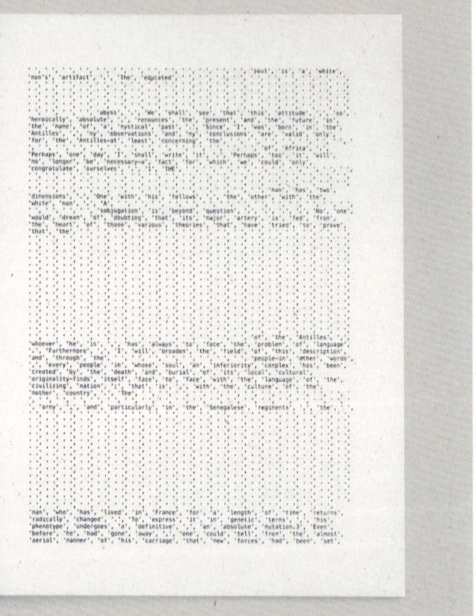

DESCRIPTION

This publication belongs to the group of works called "skin works" or "social skin" performances (since 2012), in which the artist Wilmer Wilson IV covers his face or his entire body with objects, be they black post-it notes (*Black Mask*) or stamps asking passersby to be mailed (*Henry "Box" Brown: FOREVER*, 2012, referring to the historical figure of the same name, who mailed himself from slavery in Virginia to freedom in the north) or peroxide strips which, despite their transparency, stick out of his face in a strangely white way (*Portrait with Hydrogen Peroxide Strips*, 2015).

This form of disguise and masking—highlighting the irresolvable tension between the invisibility and absence of black bodies in historiography and narratives and their simultaneous hyper-visibility as objects of constant observation, discrimination, even violence—is also the subject of this publication. Its strange title refers to Frantz Fanon's seminal text *Black Skin, White Masks* from 1952, in which Fanon plays out his thesis that Black people, in order to be seen and to attract the gaze necessary for the constitution of the ego, are forced to put on white masks and thus to deny themselves.

In Wilson's *[' ', 'Skin', ' ', ' ', 'White', 'Masks']*, this Manichean world order is closely paralleled by the sharp black-and-white contrast of writing and paper. So instead of his own body, the book body or white space of the paper comes into play here, punctuated by black characters. This process has a clear sense of loss, as the corrupted title already makes clear, which of all things has lost the "black" and is torn by commas and quotation marks. That this is a corrected, redacted edition is also indicated by the square brackets in which the title and text are enclosed, as these usually signal an intervention in the original that has taken place.

This principle of redacted and fragmentary transmission continues in the publication itself, which seems to take each word and punctuation mark of Fanon's text individually, placing it in single quotation marks and separating it from the others by commas, and then carefully examining it. This slows down the reading and thus also forces the reader to engage with the language, in the spirit of Fanon's remarks in the chapter "The Negro and Language": "To speak means to be in a position to use a certain syntax, to grasp the morphology of this or that language, but it means above all to assume a culture, to support the weight of a civilization" (Frantz Fanon, *Black Skin, White Masks*, 17f.).

As a result of this word-by-word examination, large portions of the text are missing, causing Fanon's text to pare down to a few pages: Many quotation marks no longer enclose a word, but only a white space, as if they were putting on the white mask. This redacting treatment seems to follow a certain logic, which, however, is not immediately apparent. The blurb on Lulu gives no further clue either; it too consists of nothing more than ten lines of commas and quotation marks. In any case, as in the title itself, it is loaded words such as "black," "blackness," and "color" that are replaced with blanks, with the deletion also applying to the next succeeding section of text—until the next appearance of such a word in the original, which is likewise expunged, but after which the original text continues until another loaded word appears in the original and the continuous text is again interrupted.

how to stop worrying abt the state of publishing when the world's burning and everybody's broke anyways and all you really care abt is if anyone is even reading yr work

AUTHOR	Joey Yearous-Algozin
YEAR	2016
PUBLISHER	Troll Thread
GENRE	tutorial
METHOD	composition (writing / drawing / photography), détournement / hack, test / experiment
SUBJECT	economy / labor, literature, platforms / companies, print on demand, publishing / distribution
PLATFORM	Lulu
EDITION CHARACTERISTICS	multiple editions (print, PDF), open edition
FORMAT	21.6 × 27.9 cm
MATERIALITIES	black-and-white, paperback, saddle stitch bound
PAGES	4 (unpaginated)

IMAGES

start a gmail or other email acct or whatever w/ yr presses name or as close as you can get

w/ that email start a tumblr acct

start a lulu acct

upload yr .pdf to lulu as a paperback book

i like 8 1/2" x 11" bec that's the size of a microsoft word page

don't worry about making it look good, gutters, paratext, etc.

that's all just marketing

leave that to "editors" who can pay "designers", i.e. bosses

or until you learn more about laying out books, which you never need to learn

save yr cover as a .jpg & upload it in the cover designer or use the default settings

whatever

set the price at zero revenue

that way you can buy more copies when lulu has coupons for free shipping

also, this is poetry, you shouldn't be making a profit

don't be an asshole

repeat the same process for an ebook

upload yr .pdf

don't upload a word doc or other file

lulu uses this to create an epub to distribute it thru amazon/barnes & noble, but it'll stop you from accessing the file easily later

set the price as free

again, don't be an asshole

when you're done uploading the file and cover .jpg, go back to "my projects," right click the page icon to the right of "published file(s): ebook" and copy the link

this is a backdoor way of viewing yr file that lulu is now hosting for you for free

now you don't have to deal w/ their download manager, which almost no one will ever use

go to the tab of yr tumblr dashboard

upload the .jpg as a "photo"

link the copied url for the .pdf

do the same thing below the picture in case people don't realize they can click the picture

u might as well put the link for the physical book also

post the photo to tumblr

good

now do it again

---Joey Yearous-Algozin

TROLL THREAD 2016

DESCRIPTION

how to//////////////////////
stop worrying abt the/////
state of publishing//////
when the world's//////////
burning and everybody's///
broke//////////////////////
anyways and all///////////
you really care abt///////
is if anyone//////////////
is even///////////////////
reading yr work///////////

how to stop worrying abt the state of publishing when the world's burning and everybody's broke anyways and all you really care abt is if anyone is even reading yr work is a manifesto of Troll Thread's publishing practice. It both realistically and ironically promotes and performs print-on-demand as the easiest and most effective way of publishing experimental poetry. At the same time, it does not hide the inevitable precariousness of this model of production and publishing.

An email account, a Tumblr account, and an ordinary word processor are mentioned as indispensable components of the publishing model. For convenience, Microsoft Office's default format (US Letter format) and standard layout settings should be chosen. The retail price should be the cost price: "don't be an asshole." The e-pub option offered by Lulu, for distribution through Amazon and Barnes & Noble, should be bypassed. All this is not only advocated and explained, but put into practice and demonstrated with this publication.

Also explained is how to use Lulu as a free document host and gallery space for yourself—a practice of détournement and hacking that is certainly not in the spirit of the company, but was successfully operated by Troll Thread for several years, as they explain in an interview with Tan Lin: "We don't expect people to actually purchase the physical copies. Basically, we use Lulu as a means to host the PDFs, something Tumblr's platform doesn't accommodate, without having to pay for our own domain" (Tan Lin, "Troll Thread Interview"). This parasitic strategy was unannouncedly thwarted by the comprehensive relaunch of the Lulu webshop in summer 2020. Troll Thread nearly lost all of its hosted PDFs in the process. Since then, they have been using Google Drive as repository.

Il Nvuoo Tatnsteemo

AUTHOR	Damon Zucconi
YEAR	2016
GENRE	artist's book / bookwork, exhibition copy, experimental literature
METHOD	appropriation, generative / automation, translation / transcription
SUBJECT	canon, code / programming, error / corruption / loss, reading / interpretation
PLATFORM	Lulu
EDITION CHARACTERISTICS	ISBN 9781365361784, open edition, CC0
FORMAT	14.8 × 21.0 cm
MATERIALITIES	black-and-white, paperback, perfect bound
PAGES	290
IMAGES	

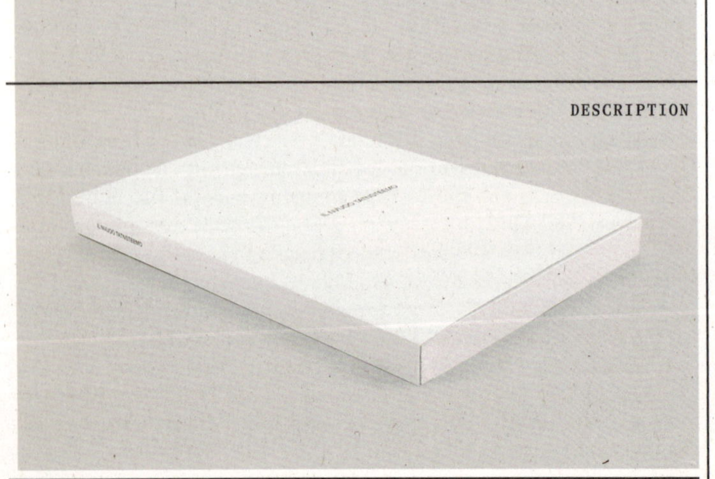

DESCRIPTION

"Not all secrets are information someone is trying to conceal. Some secrets are information that's in the world, but inaccessible" (Damon Zucconi, "Spiritual Door").

Damon Zucconi's *Il Nvuoo Tatnsteemo* contains the complete Italian text of the *New Testament* with every significant word misspelled. It was produced by using a script to shuffle the characters. Being part of a series of works altering and encrypting preexisting novels, *Il Nvuoo Tatnsteemo* was the first one to be realized as a physical object. Originally made for the solo exhibition "Spiritual Door" at Veda Gallery in Florence in 2016, the Italian version was supplemented by a similarly misspelled English version titled *The New Tsmanetet*. The blurb on Lulu is equally misspelled and difficult to read. The source code used to generate this English version can be found on GitHub.

Froncer les sourcils

AUTHOR	Olivier Bertrand
YEAR	2017
GENRE	education / classroom, nonfiction
METHOD	composition (writing / drawing / photography), study / analysis
SUBJECT	book / book design, ecology / sustainability, economy / labor, materiality, politics / activism, print technology, publishing / distribution
PLATFORM	Blurb
EDITION CHARACTERISTICS	ISBN 9781364208899, open edition, CC BY-SA
FORMAT	12.6 × 20.3 cm
MATERIALITIES	color, paperback, perfect bound
PAGES	120

IMAGES

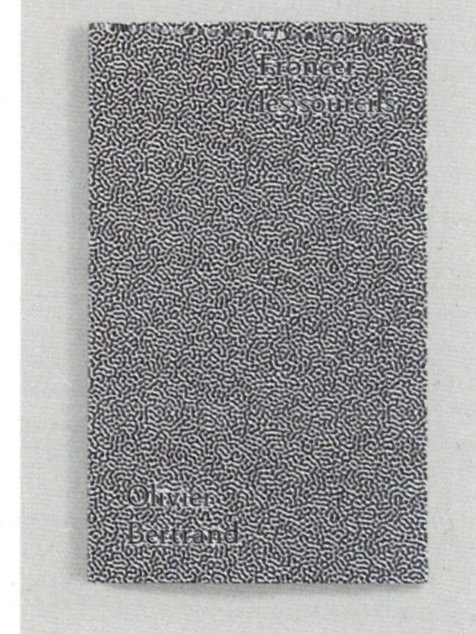

DESCRIPTION

Using the example of William Morris's Kelmscott Press and Urs Lehni's Rollo Press, Olivier Bertrand's thesis *Froncer les sourcils* (Frowning Eyebrows) traces two publishing experiments that reinvented the publishing craft in their respective eras by seeing it as a creative play on its technical and financial constraints: "It is a question of responding positively to the constraints of the machine and the lack of means by taking advantage of difficulties and by showing inventiveness and cunning" (Olivier Bertrand, *Froncer les sourcils*, 58). They did not necessarily reinvent the wheel. Rather, as Bertrand points out, their achievement was to bring together craftsmanship and industrial production, horticulture and entrepreneurship, capitalism and socialism.

In this way, both publishers are shining examples for Bertrand's own publishing practice, which he develops from the following consideration: "It is not necessary to recreate new structures each time, but it is quite possible to rely on those that already exist, even if it means hijacking them. Rather than denying them, we can imagine, for example, taking advantage of the strength of the institutional or industrial structures already in place to transform them according to our needs (and not those of the market). In terms of resources, it is a question of working as much as possible with the materials that are already around us […]" (Ibid., 100).

Accordingly, Bertrand develops strategies of hacking and reusing leftovers from industrial production to make the books of his publishing house Surfaces Utiles (see 80f., 370–372, and 412f.) and his magazine *La Perruque* (since 2015). The latter, for example, is a strip of paper, 90 cm long and 1 cm wide, obtained from the unprinted margins of printed matter. While the name of his publishing house alludes to the use of these unprinted surfaces, the name of his magazine takes Michel de Certeau's term "faire la perruque," describing the use of working time and working means, resources, or tools of a company to one's own advantage (see Michel de Certeau, *The Practice of Everyday Life*, 26f.).

What's Left Over From the Works of Le Bon

AUTHORS	Olivier Bertrand, Alexia de Visscher, Maxime Le Bon
YEAR	2017
PUBLISHER	Surfaces Utiles
GENRE	catalog / collection, intermediate product / halbzeug
METHOD	composition (writing / drawing / photography), détournement / hack, study / analysis
SUBJECT	book / book design, ecology / sustainability, economy / labor, materiality, print technology, print on demand, publishing / distribution
PLATFORM	Blurb, selfmade

IMAGE

DESCRIPTION

Olivier Bertrand has made the production of books in margins the basic principle of his publishing house Surfaces Utiles. Bertrand characterizes his publishing strategy with the French expression "faire la perruque," borrowed from Michel de Certeau and describing a kind of détournement: what is meant by this is using the working time and the working means, resources, or tools of a company to one's own advantage, or to the company's disadvantage (see 80f., 369, and 412f.).

What's Left Over From the Works of Le Bon + Archéologie du Catalogue—Fragments

AUTHORS	Olivier Bertrand, Alexia de Visscher
GENRE	intermediate product / halbzeug
METHOD	collection, collective, composition (writing / drawing / photography), détournement / hack, documentation / archiving
SUBJECT	book / book design, ecology / sustainability, economy / labor, materiality, print technology, print on demand
PLATFORM	Blurb
EDITION CHARACTERISTICS	ISBN 9781389351778, open edition
FORMAT	20.0 × 25.4 cm
MATERIALITIES	color, paperback, perfect bound
PAGES	262 (unpaginated)

IMAGE

DESCRIPTION

This volume printed on demand by Blurb is intended as a (financially favorable) intermediate product that will end up in two independent books: Maxime Le Bon's *What's Left Over From the Works of Le Bon* and Alexia de Visscher's *Archéologie du Catalogue—Fragments*.

Originally, the publisher Surfaces Utiles worked only on the publication of Le Bon's drawings. Since the drawing format does not correspond to Blurb's standard formats, there would have been a lot of unused white space around the drawings. To make the best of this situation, Alexia de Visscher was invited to fill in and design these blank spaces in the margins of the pages to produce her own publication. These inserted fragments are part of her *Projet Albert de Visscher – Éditeur*, an artistic proposal that questions a family history, an archive, and the practice of publishing.

Each copy reproduces Maxime Le Bon and Alexia de Visscher's drawings and fragments ten times in digital four-color printing. The laborious production of the digital template, which has to merge and interpose two different works, is outweighed by the optimal use of the paper and format. From the bound books supplied by Blurb, the spine is cut off, the pages are cut into three parts, and these are then reassembled and further processed for the production of Visscher and Le Bon's books.

The cover, which comes standard with Blurb, is actually an unnecessary accessory for this project. To prevent this from becoming waste either, it was "misused" for the production of business cards. That Surfaces Utiles has released this intermediate product for sale on Blurb helps in understanding the production process.

What's Left Over From the Works of Le Bon

AUTHOR	Maxime Le Bon
PUBLISHER	Surfaces Utiles
GENRE	catalog / collection
METHOD	collection, composition (writing / drawing / photography), détournement / hack
SUBJECT	art, book / book design, materiality, print technology
PLATFORM	selfmade
EDITION CHARACTERISTICS	ISBN 9782960200249, limited edition
FORMAT	15.0 × 19.8 cm
MATERIALITIES	color, paperback, wire-o bound
PAGES	196 (unpaginated)

IMAGES

DESCRIPTION

"The drawings reproduced in this book are A5-format fragments of the work that Maxime Le Bon would bin because he considered them unsatisfactory. Before throwing them away however, the artist keeps what he sees as valuable—painting mistakes, unforeseen jokes, surprising narrative elements—to archive and make into raw material for new work.

It is a coincidence that Surfaces Utiles came across these fragments at the time when many A5-format paper scraps became available. However, the stock was insufficient to complete the entire publication, therefore we had to rely on some 'tricks' to manage it anyway. We hijacked the services of a famous printer on demand and found the missing paper without really having to pay for it" (Surfaces Utiles, "what's left over from the works of le bon").

The starting point for this edition was the publication *What's Left Over From the Works of Le Bon + Archéologie du Catalogue—Fragments* produced in color by Blurb, from which the pages were taken, which were then further processed in several steps into a ring binder. Various printing techniques and providers were used: risoprint (Autobahn) for the black parts, silkscreen (Chromodrome), and at-home inkjet and laser printing. Many pages even went through multiple printings. The print run was 100 copies. For this, ten books were commissioned from Blurb, each of which contained the necessary material ten times.

Pure Compersion

AUTHOR	Qiuzi Chen
YEAR	2017
PUBLISHER	Gauss PDF
GENRE	education / classroom, experimental literature
METHOD	found material, montage / remix
SUBJECT	email / messaging, internet culture, narration
PLATFORM	Lulu
EDITION CHARACTERISTICS	multiple editions (print, PDF), open edition
FORMAT	10.8 × 17.5 cm
MATERIALITIES	color, paperback, perfect bound
PAGES	54 (unpaginated)

IMAGE

DESCRIPTION

"*Pure Compersion* is [...] based on digital texts in emails and messages. And I applied the cut-up technique on those texts to generate cyborg literature. The major identity is symbolized as an icon: the strawberry emoji. I took this icon as an idea to design the series including a fiction book, a motion and a photo book" (blurb on artist website).

Pure Compersion, published by Gauss PDF, makes the collaged text of Qiuzi Chen's multimedia project publicly available, typesetting it in the form of poetry. The book was created for the senior experimental writing class at the School of Visual Arts, New York.

Airport Novella

AUTHOR	Tom Comitta
YEAR	2017
PUBLISHER	Troll Thread
GENRE	experimental literature
METHOD	appropriation, montage / remix
SUBJECT	canon, literature, reading / interpretation
PLATFORM	Lulu
EDITION CHARACTERISTICS	multiple editions (print, PDF), open edition
FORMAT	13.8 × 21.5 cm
MATERIALITIES	black-and-white, paperback, perfect bound
PAGES	48

IMAGES

DESCRIPTION

Tom Comitta's *Airport Novella* consists entirely of quotes which are collaged into a narrative text. The book is divided into four chapters, each of them focusing on a particular gesture, which is used as a selection method for the quotes. These gestures—nodding, shrugging, looking, and gasping—might be seen as typical behavior one could observe sitting at an airport. At the same time, the books quoted, which are listed at the end for each chapter, are typical bestsellers one would find in an airport bookstore. Thus, *Airport Novella* is at once a condensed reading of airport literature and a description of airport behavior, performing the transitory moment of its environmental language.

Erased Erased de Kooning Drawing

AUTHOR	Geraint Edwards
YEAR	2017
GENRE	experimental literature, poetry
METHOD	constraint, documentation / archiving, reenactment, remediation
SUBJECT	analog / digital, art, economy / labor, materiality, reading / interpretation, technology
PLATFORM	Amazon
EDITION CHARACTERISTICS	ISBN 9781974545186, open edition
FORMAT	12.6 × 20.3 cm
MATERIALITIES	black-and-white, paperback, perfect bound
PAGES	114 (unpaginated)

IMAGES

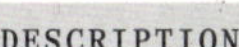

DESCRIPTION

Geraint Edwards's *Erased Erased de Kooning Drawing* is a digital reenactment of Robert Rauschenberg's *Erased de Kooning Drawing* (1953), in which Rauschenberg used around forty erasers in the course of a month to erase a drawing by Willem de Kooning. To do this, Edwards used a digital photograph of Rauschenberg's work and deleted every pixel of it in Photoshop, using the 1-pixel diameter eraser tool to make the effort required as close to Rauschenberg's as possible, and as tedious as possible. It took 973 eraser actions over nine hours and thirty-three minutes.

But while Rauschenberg's version still shows traces of the former drawing as well as the erasing procedure, the digitally generated erasure ends up with no visible traces of its production history, as the blank image on the cover of the book shows. To compensate for this, Edwards reproduces the complete Photoshop history log of his interactions with the software in his book, listing every action he made in 11 pt. Consolas, the default font of history log .txt files, as the front matter explains. In addition, metadata such as the time the document was opened and closed, its file name and directory, etc. are documented. The resulting text takes on the quality of "a digital palimpsest; an epic poem which begs a more general question about how truth has retreated from our retinal environment" (Geraint Edwards, "Foreword"). The designation as a poem recalls Rauschenberg's assertion that his work is not an act of destruction, but poetry.

The three positive reviews by Kenneth Goldsmith, Olia Lialina, and Cory Arcangel ("løl'd") with which the promotional paratext for the book begins are contrasted on the Amazon page with the one-star rating of a buyer whose review, according to the author, could not have been more perfect: "Nothing to see here, move along. [...] as disappointing book as could be possible."

Treatise on Luck

AUTHOR	Mark Francis Johnson
YEAR	2017
PUBLISHER	Gauss PDF
GENRE	poetry
METHOD	composition (writing / drawing / photography), photocopy / scan, remediation
SUBJECT	analog / digital, book / book design, memory / storage
PLATFORM	Lulu
EDITION CHARACTERISTICS	multiple editions (print, PDF), open edition
FORMAT	21.6 × 27.9 cm
MATERIALITIES	black-and-white, paperback, perfect bound
PAGES	98

IMAGES

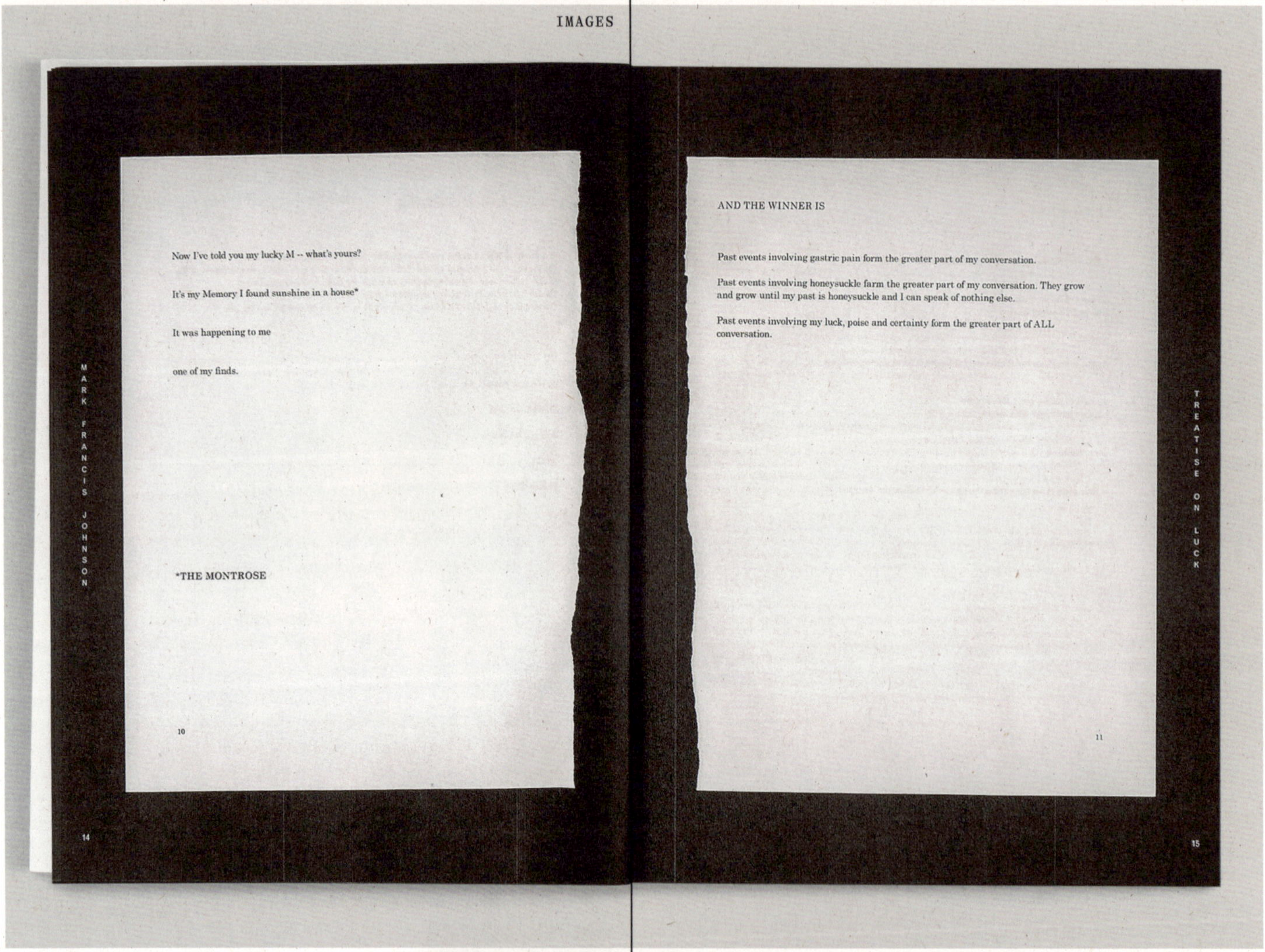

MARK FRANCIS JOHNSON

Now I've told you my lucky M -- what's yours?

It's my Memory I found sunshine in a house*

It was happening to me

one of my finds.

*THE MONTROSE

10

14

AND THE WINNER IS

Past events involving gastric pain form the greater part of my conversation.

Past events involving honeysuckle farm the greater part of my conversation. They grow and grow until my past is honeysuckle and I can speak of nothing else.

Past events involving my luck, poise and certainty form the greater part of ALL conversation.

11

TREATISE ON LUCK

15

DESCRIPTION

The nested design (mise-en-abyme) of Mark Francis Johnson's poetry book was created by Jonathan Gorman. It reproduces every page of a copy made just for this purpose, with each page torn out, scanned, and set on a page with a broad black margin, including front and back covers. The source book, which no longer exists, was apparently also a print-on-demand book, as suggested by the reproduction of the cover, which has the cheap-looking and reflective foliation typical of print-on-demand books. The reflective approach to the materiality of the book, accessible only through multiple stages of mediation, mirrors the reflections on luck and memory in Johnson's poems.

AUTHOR	Travis Macdonald
YEAR	2017
PUBLISHER	Gauss PDF
GENRE	experimental literature, poetry
METHOD	appropriation, constraint, montage / remix
SUBJECT	literature, reading / interpretation
PLATFORM	Lulu
EDITION CHARACTERISTICS	multiple editions (print, PDF), open edition
FORMAT	15.2 × 22.9 cm
MATERIALITIES	black-and-white, paperback, perfect bound
PAGES	78

IMAGES

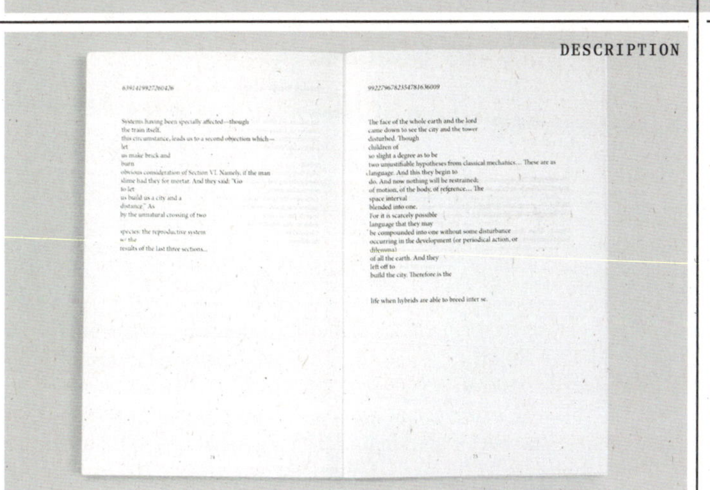

DESCRIPTION

3... is a collection of poetry produced by a strict set of constraints. Each verse is taken from one of three canonical texts: *The Book of Genesis*, Charles Darwin's *The Origin of Species (Chapter 8 – Hybridism)* and Albert Einstein's *Special and General Theory of Relativity*. The process of selection is based on numerical sequences of π (3.14159 etc.), which has an infinite number of decimal places and thus never repeats itself. The title for each poem is always a different three- to 45-digit number, which, when lined up, form the numerical sequence of π.

"Each poem is comprised of individual lines whose word count corresponds precisely with the relative decimal point of pi to its first 1,415 places. When drawing from each source, the author has taken great care never to exceed 3 consecutive lines from any given text and, even then, only in cases where the process of natural selection demands. While the original language of each line is faithfully preserved, each selection has been re-punctuated for narrative purposes" (Travis Macdonald, "Process Note," 3).

Essays for a Canceled Anthology

AUTHORS	Holly Melgard, Chris Sylvester, Joey Yearous-Algozin
YEAR	2017
PUBLISHER	Troll Thread
GENRE	nonfiction
METHOD	composition (writing / drawing / photography)
SUBJECT	economy / labor, literature, politics / activism, publishing / distribution, social media
PLATFORM	Lulu
VOLUMES	3
EDITION CHARACTERISTICS	multiple editions (print, PDF), open edition
FORMAT	14.8 × 21.0 cm
MATERIALITIES	black-and-white, paperback, saddle stitch bound
IMAGE	

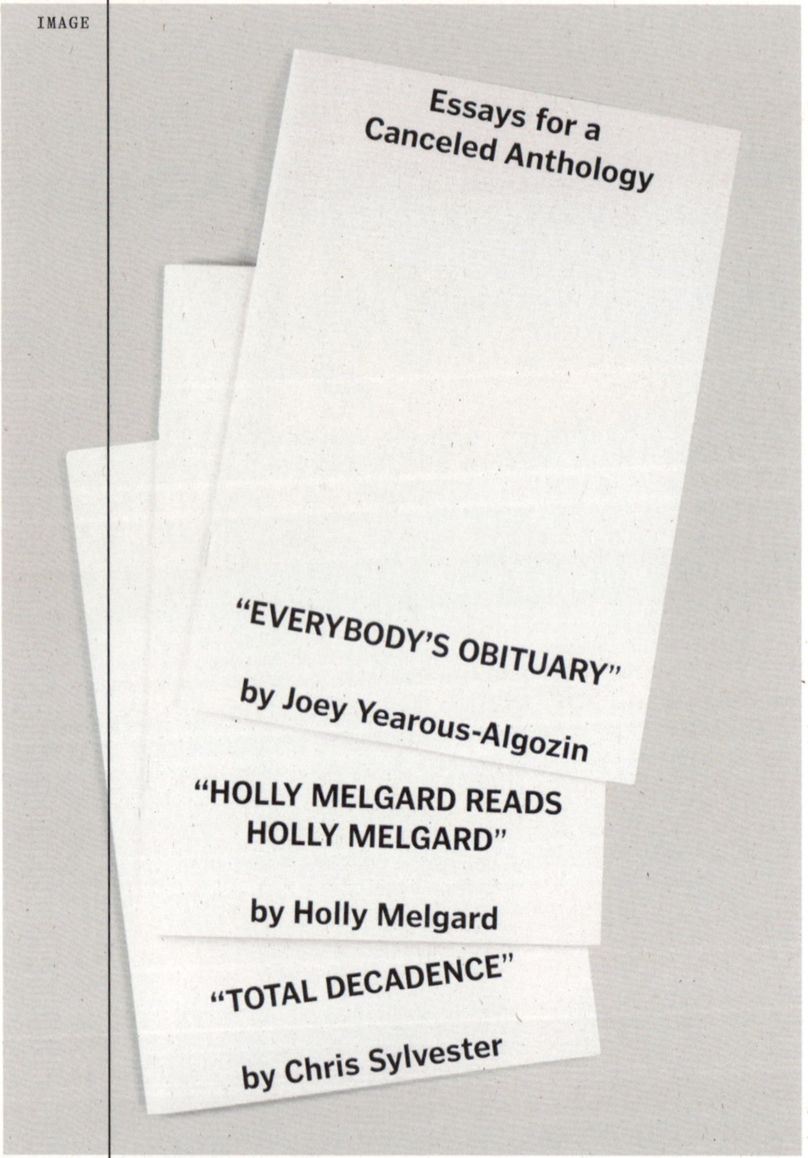

DESCRIPTION

Essays for a Canceled Anthology is a series of three essays by Troll Thread co-founders Holly Melgard, Joey Yearous-Algozin, and Chris Sylvester. Following Sylvester's founding proposition to understand Troll Thread as a "place to put our poems that no one else wants" (cited in Holly Melgard's essay, 20), the series rescues texts written for another publishing context, that, as the title suggests, has been canceled. Accordingly, the blurb on Lulu—following the ironic "How to …" pattern typical for Troll Thread—reads: "HOW TO GET AROUND A CANCELED ANTHOLOGY." In this way, *Essays for a Canceled Anthology* performs an approach to self-publishing both programmatically practiced by Troll Thread and reflected in the essays themselves, even if written for a different context.

"HOLLY MELGARD READS HOLLY MELGARD"

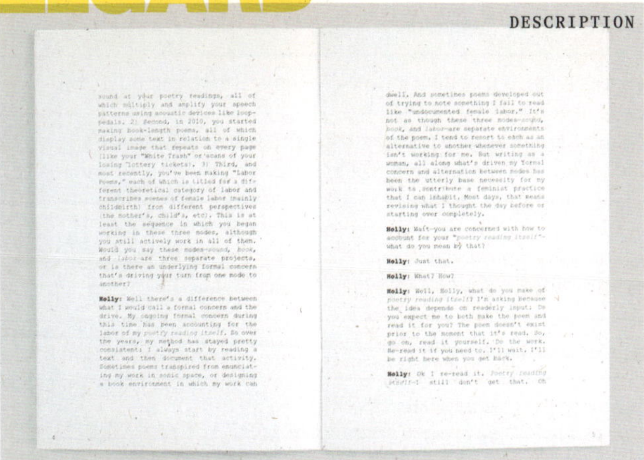

sound at your poetry readings, all of which multiply and amplify your speech patterns using acoustic devices like loop-pedals. 2) Second, in 2010, you started making book-length poems, all of which display some text in relation to a single visual image that repeats on every page (like your "White Trash" or scans of your losing lottery tickets). 3) Third, and most recently, you've been making "Labor Poems," each of which is titled for a different theoretical category of labor and transcribes scenes of female labor (mainly childbirth) from different perspectives (the mother's, child's, etc). This is at least the sequence in which you began working in these three modes, although you still actively work in all of them. Would you say these modes—*sound*, *book*, and *labor* are three separate projects, or is there an underlying formal concern that's driving your turn from one mode to another?

Holly: Well there's a difference between what I would call a formal concern and the drive. My ongoing formal concern during this time has been accounting for the labor of my *poetry reading itself*. So over the years, my method has stayed pretty consistent: I always start by reading a text and then document that activity. Sometimes poems transpired from enunciating my work in sonic space, or designing a book environment in which my work can

dwell. And sometimes poems developed out of trying to note something I fail to read like "undocumented female labor." It's not as though these three modes—*sound*, *book*, and *labor*—are separate environments of the poem. I tend to resort to each as an alternative to another whenever something isn't working for me. But writing as a woman, all along what's driven my formal concern and alternation between modes has been the utterly base necessity for my work to contribute a feminist practice that I can inhabit. Most days, that means revising what I thought the day before or starting over completely.

Holly: Wait—you are concerned with how to account for your "*poetry reading itself*"—what do you mean by that?

Holly: Just that.

Holly: What? How?

Holly: Well, Holly, what do you make of *poetry reading itself*? I'm asking because the idea depends on readerly input: Do you expect me to both make the poem and read it for you? The poem doesn't exist prior to the moment that it's read. So, go on, read it yourself. Do the work. Re-read it if you need to. I'll wait. I'll be right here when you get back.

Holly: Ok I re-read it. *Poetry reading itself*—I still don't get that. Oh

AUTHOR: Holly Melgard

SUBJECT: art world / literary world, bias, gender, politics / activism, publishing / distribution

PAGES: 21

DESCRIPTION: *"HOLLY MELGARD READS HOLLY MELGARD"* is a soliloquy by Holly Melgard from 2015, framed as an interview with the interviewer and interviewee being the same person. The conversation touches on different phases and aspects of Melgard's poetic production—labor, feminism, and technology as well as the publishing and poetry scene—and puts it in relation to Troll Thread's conceptual approach. Thereby, the advantages and reasons of self-publication are stated more than clearly: "Why wait to be asked before speaking? What, should I not speak unless spoken to? Why wait for an established person to solicit, welcome, and/or legitimate this work prior to permitting it to occupy public space-time? Self-publishing these books via Troll Thread allowed me to immediately distribute my work to a larger public without predicating what I make on anyone else's desire or agency besides my own" (Holly Melgard, *"HOLLY MELGARD READS HOLLY MELGARD,"* 7).

"TOTAL DECADENCE"

AUTHOR: Chris Sylvester

SUBJECT: ecology / sustainability, politics / activism

PAGES: 20

DESCRIPTION: *"TOTAL DECADENCE"* is an essay from 2014, more philosophical than poetological, that reflects on human behavior and projections in the face of the end of the world by ecological or personal collapse. Chris Sylvester circles around the questions of what could be considered a meaningful life in the face of all things ending and of what nature this kind of question could be.

"EVERYBODY'S OBITUARY"

AUTHOR: Joey Yearous-Algozin

SUBJECT: memory / storage, social media

PAGES: 8

DESCRIPTION: *"EVERYBODY'S OBITUARY"* is a 2013 essay on what Joey Yearous-Algozin calls "dead zones" of the internet and social media: abandoned accounts and websites that in theory are still active but unused and forgotten. From this, Yearous-Algozin draws parallels with the poetological implications of Troll Thread, stating: "Perhaps, the purest articulation of this phenomenon of an intentionally produced dead zone is the troll thread—a disrupted comment stream or message board, such that conversation derails and is ultimately abandoned. [...] In this way, the troll's actions parody the radically democratic potential of the Internet" (Joey Yearous-Algozin, *"EVERYBODY'S OBITUARY,"* 5f.). From this he derives his "goal to push poetry to the limit point of the dead zone, an obsolete zone of pure waste and negativity" (Ibid., 7) and cites as an example his conceptual writing endeavor *The Lazarus Project* (3 vols., Troll Thread, 2013) in which he resurrects 20,000 dead people whose obituaries he found on the web.

A Scanthology of Concrete Poetry

AUTHOR	NUPoD2017 Collective
YEAR	2017
PUBLISHER	NUPoD 2017
GENRE	artist's book / bookwork, education / classroom, experimental literature
METHOD	appropriation, collective, photocopy / scan, remediation
SUBJECT	canon, error / corruption / loss, literature, materiality, reading / interpretation, technology
PLATFORM	Lulu
EDITION CHARACTERISTICS	multiple editions (print, PDF), open edition, CC0
FORMAT	15.6 × 23.4 cm
MATERIALITIES	color, paperback, perfect bound
PAGES	230 (unpaginated)

IMAGE

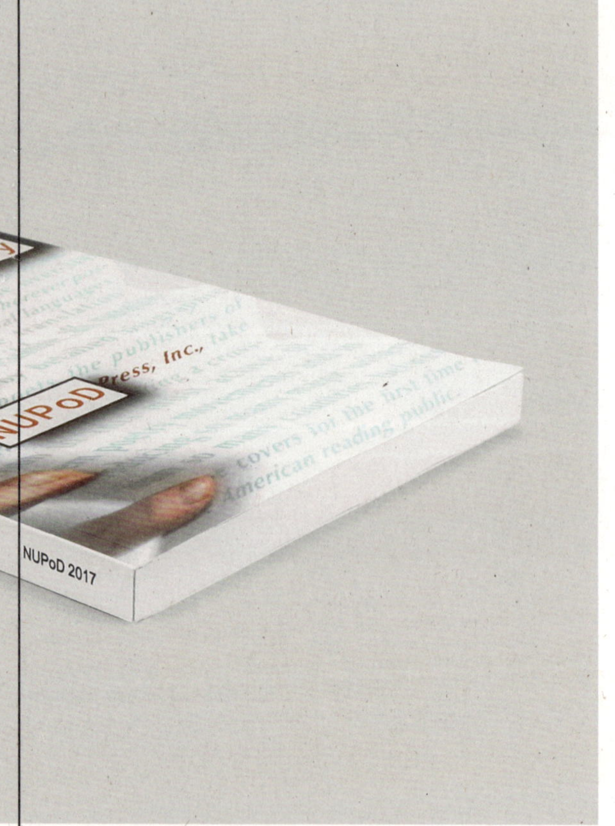

DESCRIPTION

A Scanthology of Concrete Poetry is a collectively altered edition of the seminal and now canonical Something Else Press collection *An Anthology of Concrete Poetry* edited by Emmett Williams (1967) in the reedition of Primary Information (2013). In a sense, it implements the "To Be Continued" prompt with which Williams's edition ends. The new version, with significantly fewer pages and a different order than the original, was created in Danny Snelson's 2017 class "Print on Demand Poetry: Making Books After the Internet" at Northwestern University. Snelson brought copies of the book, which his students tore apart page by page (excluding the preface and biographies) and then altered and scanned. Not all poems were used, and some were altered multiple times.

The transformations often make direct reference to the subject or visual appearance of a poem, as when the words "WORD OPEN" from a poem film by John J. Sharkey (1964) are answered by a hand punching through the page from behind. Another student seems to be puzzled by Eugen Gomringer's famous constellation *avenidas*, which he crosses out line by line with the comment: "I YELLED AT THIS POEM AS IT WAS SCANNING TO NO AVAIL." In the course of reading, one learns to distinguish the handwriting of individual students.

Aside from the physical deformations, overwritings, and additions made to the pages, they were also purposefully altered by the scanning process itself, producing glitches, distortions, and fragmentary reproductions. By this, *A Scanthology of Concrete Poetry* offers not only a reading of the original anthology, but also an investigation into the materiality of poetry and books, expanding the poetics of concrete poetry to practices of perception, reproduction, and distribution of text.

Participating in the project were Izzy G, Paola de Varona, Courtney Bankston, Faheem Tapia, Michael Gross, Gabrielle B, Georgia Bernstein, Olivia Heller, Jonathan Gelb, NUPoD17, Garrett M. Goehring, Flemish Cann, RK, Orli, Sylvia Shim, Olivia Korhonen, Ashley Braddock, Meg Biederman, and Danny Snelson.

ye:ye
(1965–66)

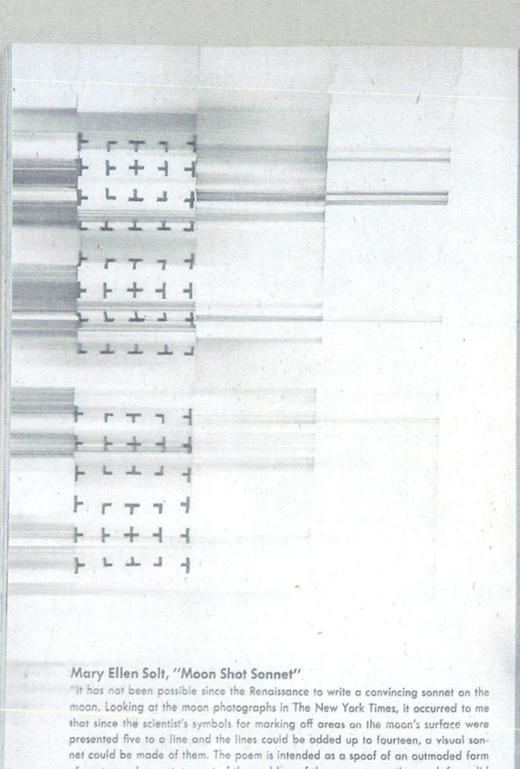
Mary Ellen Solt, "Moon Shot Sonnet"
"It has not been possible since the Renaissance to write a convincing sonnet on the moon. Looking at the moon photographs in The New York Times, it occurred to me that since the scientist's symbols for marking off areas on the moon's surface were presented five to a line and the lines could be added up to fourteen, a visual sonnet could be made of them. The poem is intended as a spoof of an outmoded form of poetry and as a statement of the problem of the concrete poet's search for valid new forms." (M.E.S.)
Designed by John Furnival, first printed in Poor.Old.Tired.Horse.

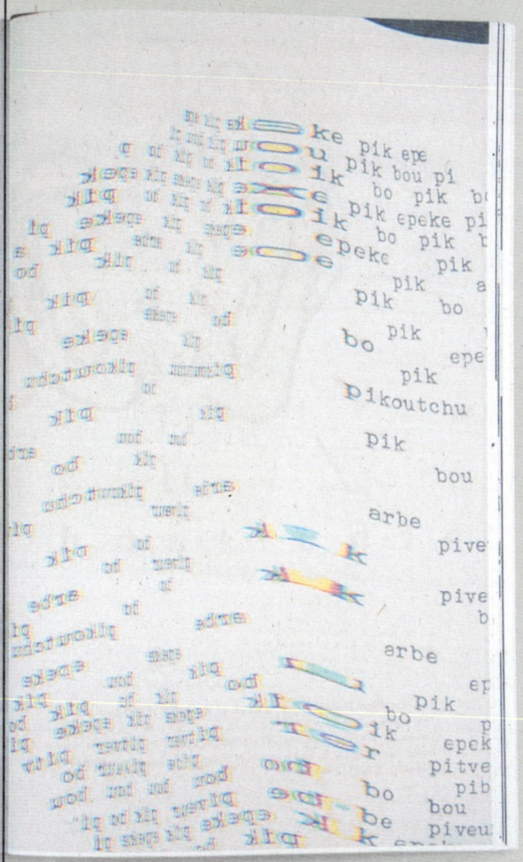
pik bou pi
pik epeke
pikoutchu
arbe
arbe

Blank Books

AUTHOR	NUPoD2017 Collective
YEAR	2017
GENRE	artist's book / bookwork, education / classroom
METHOD	composition (writing / drawing / photography), constraint, paratextual play, versioning / seriality
SUBJECT	authorship, book / book design, print on demand, reading / interpretation, standard / default
PLATFORM	Lulu
VOLUMES	16
EDITION CHARACTERISTICS	open edition
FORMAT	10.8 × 17.5 cm
MATERIALITIES	black-and-white, blank pages, paperback, perfect bound
PAGES	200

IMAGE

DESCRIPTION

Blank Books is a set of sixteen books produced during Danny Snelson's 2017 class "Print on Demand Poetry: Making Books after the Internet" at Northwestern University. Each book consists of 200 blank pages in pocket book format, shifting the only way for expression and semantic charging to the paratext, which is used in various ways by the students, ranging from calling the publication a notebook for doodles to more conceptual approaches like 100 reasons why the author loves milk. The series is a demonstration of how to utilize print-on-demand for an exploratory pedagogy in the studies of literature and media. As a virtuous presentation of paratextual play it also shows how in the age of book distribution platforms, digital paratext becomes an integral part of framing and handling books today—as it is usually the first encounter we have with a book even before we are able to get a glimpse of the paratext of the physical book object.

tabula rasa

AUTHOR Faheem Tapia

DESCRIPTION The cover, back cover, and spine of this publication are completely black except for the title and a barcode added by Lulu on the back. The blurb on the platform frames this blank book as a potential diary, promising that with a purchase one could start anew by "writing it all down." This allows the book to be categorized as "personal growth." The platform paratext also gives credit to the author, which is otherwise completely absent from the printed version.

......

AUTHOR ......

DESCRIPTION ...... is a radical reduction of platform paratext while still providing the minimum amount of information necessary to upload a book to Lulu. Thus, title and author are both six dots with the metadata being a repetition of these six dots until the necessary character count is reached. The attempt to give a minimum of paratextual information on the platform also expresses itself on the book's spine, which is left blank/white on an otherwise black wrapping. This is broken up by the classification of the book in the "fiction" category.

NUPoD17 Syllabus
v.0.1 1.12.17 4:15-45pm
30 Minute Edition

AUTHOR	NUPoD2017 Collective
YEAR	2017
PUBLISHER	NUPoD 2017
GENRE	artist's book / bookwork, education / classroom
METHOD	collective, found material, reformatting
SUBJECT	analog / digital, book / book design, print on demand
PLATFORM	Lulu
EDITION CHARACTERISTICS	multiple editions (print, PDF), open edition
FORMAT	15.2 × 22.9 cm
MATERIALITIES	black-and-white, paperback, perfect bound
PAGES	210

IMAGES

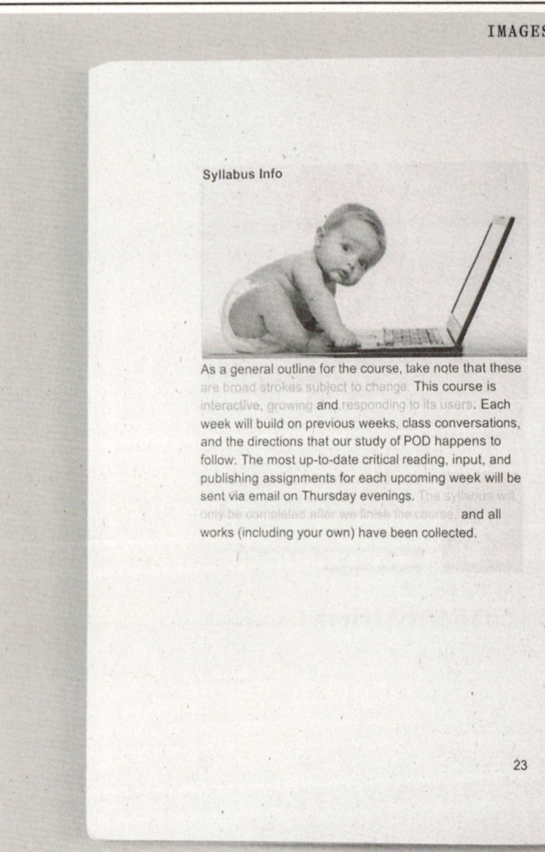

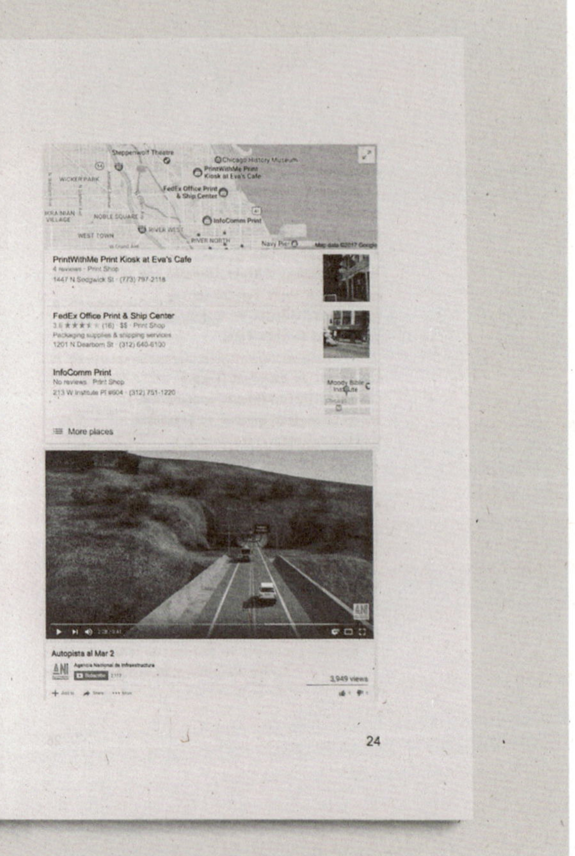

DESCRIPTION

NUPoD17 Syllabus: v.0.1_1.12.17_4:15-45pm 30 Minute Edition is a collectively assembled remix and expansion of the syllabus for Danny Snelson's 2017 class "Print on Demand Poetry: Making Books After the Internet" at University of California, Los Angeles. Snelson and his students spent thirty minutes on the first day of class searching the internet for the topics mentioned in the syllabus and copying and pasting corresponding content, be it articles, pictures, or memes. The book also contains various formats of the syllabus as well as misattributed content such as a false image of post-digital theorist Florian Cramer. This material was pasted into a collective document keeping the formatting of the sources, resulting in all sorts of erroneous clashes between book and web design: fonts and character sizes vary immensely, the text is set in very small columns and pictures greatly exceed the page margin. Thus, the book serves as a reader and an exemplification of Snelson's pedagogical approach and the practices and phenomena he sought to address in his classes on print-on-demand publishing.

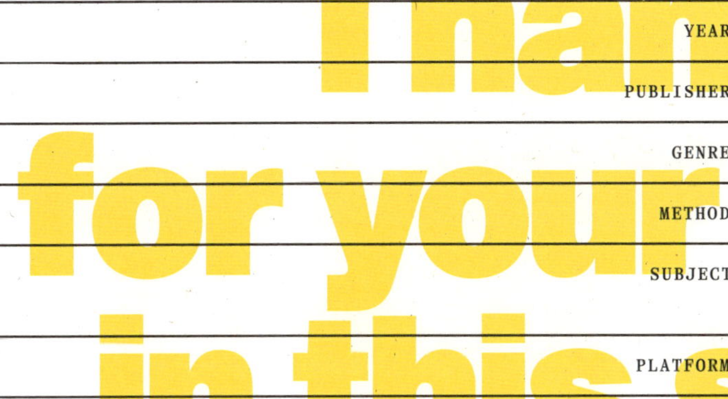

Thank you for your interest in this subject.

AUTHOR	Paul Soulellis
YEAR	2017
PUBLISHER	Library of the Printed Web
GENRE	artist's book / bookwork, nonfiction
METHOD	documentation / archiving, found material, study / analysis
SUBJECT	censorship / ban, ecology / sustainability, memory / storage, politics / activism, publishing / distribution
PLATFORM	Blurb
EDITION CHARACTERISTICS	multiple editions (print, PDF), open edition
FORMAT	21.6 × 27.9 cm
MATERIALITIES	color, zine, perfect bound
PAGES	44 (unpaginated)

IMAGES

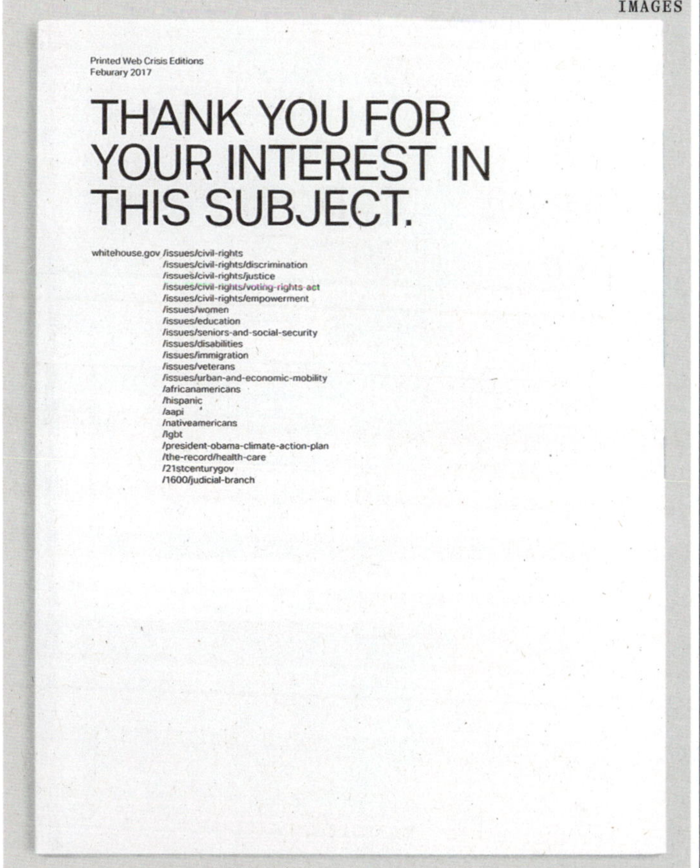

DESCRIPTION

This zine was published in February 2017 under the name *Printed Web Crisis Edition*, immediately after Donald Trump came to power, and implements Paul Soulellis' idea of "urgent publishing": "To publish is, fundamentally, a political act. / In moments of crisis, as we've experienced so deeply in the last year, we see not only artists, but community organisers, scholars, poets, and activists collectively engaging with different modes of publishing to urgently document and communicate what's happening, in real time" (Paul Soulellis, "Urgent Publishing," 32).

Presented are screenshots of twenty-two web pages at whitehouse.gov whose content became unavailable immediately after Donald Trump's inauguration on January 20, 2017, around 5 p.m., and was consistently replaced with phrases such as "Thank you for your interest in this subject. Stay tuned as we continue to update whitehouse.gov." As the list of URLs on the front cover shows, this particularly affects pages on civil rights, women, education, disabilities, immigration, Native Americans, Hispanics, African Americans, LGBT, health care, and Barack Obama's climate action plan—in other words, all those areas in which Trump resolutely pursued the opposite policy of his predecessor in office. Each screenshot of the redacted page is accompanied by a screenshot of the last view of the respective page on Obama's time in office, both reconstructed by Soulellis from the Internet Archive.

This event is later expanded upon by Soulellis in his publication *Steve, Harvey and Matt, As discussed with Nancy, we would like the content at the links below removed and archived as soon as possible*, which documents the Trump administration's mail exchange that accompanied the April 2017 deletion of all climate change-related US Environmental Protection Agency pages (see 402).

Library of the Printed Web

Collected Works 2013–2017

AUTHOR Paul Soulellis [ed.]

YEAR 2017

GENRE catalog / collection, nonfiction

METHOD collection, documentation / archiving

SUBJECT analog / digital, art, canon, internet culture, literature, memory / storage, publishing / distribution

PLATFORM Lulu

EDITION CHARACTERISTICS multiple editions (print, PDF), ISBN 9780984005253, open edition

FORMAT 18.9 × 24.6 cm

MATERIALITIES black-and-white, paperback, perfect bound

PAGES 548

IMAGE

DESCRIPTION

This publication contains the complete catalog of the Library of the Printed Web as acquired by The Museum of Modern Art (MoMA) Library: 244 items by 130 artists publishing in seventeen countries, compassing artists' books, zines, newsprint, loose sheets, folios, prints, postcards, and other materials. Most are self-published, including handmade, one-of-a-kind, and limited editions, as well as print-on-demand works. Many of the works are rare or no longer available. The comprehensive catalog presents all of them with photographs and detailed descriptions. It also includes texts by David Senior and Sarah Hamerman of MoMA Library, artist Sal Randolph, and Paul Soulellis.

Paul Soulellis started his Library of the Printed Web in 2013 and ended it with the handover of the collection to MoMA in 2017. Its mission was "to investigate web-to-print artistic practice and the increasingly fluid relationship between screen and printed page," as well as "to provide an in-depth view of network culture, artistic practice, and the printed page. The collection is an important resource for the study of print-based experimental publishing in the early 21st century" (Paul Soulellis, "About").

In 2014, Soulellis began publishing artists' publications under the umbrella of the Library of the Printed Web, which are also included in his collection. Besides *Printed Web Editions* (see 363) there is the series *Printed Web 1–5*, which circulates primarily as print-on-demand publications, but also includes PDFs, ZIPs, GIFs, and server directories. In the spirit of Seth Siegelaub, each issue is curated as a group exhibition for the printed page.

The collection can be viewed by the general public on site at the MoMA Library, but is also available for institutional loan. It is listed with its own call number designation "LPW" in MoMA Library's catalog.

View Only

It begins with a spreadsheet, a stand-in for the Library. Paul sends me the link along with an invitation: “I’m trying to deliver the whole collection to MoMA by mid-next week (starting to photograph it now) so coming over soon, like on the weekend, would be best. Possible? (meanwhile, you can glance at the cataloguing that I’m doing here).”

I open the sheet with excited eyes. Unconsciously, irrationally, expecting to see the library itself, my gaze meets the screen’s surface. Smooth, glowing. A grid. White space. San serif. The information, as if without guile. In the moment of startlement, in the gap between anticipation and reali-

26

Library of the Printed Web at MoMA / January 2017

File Edit View Insert Format Data Tools Add-ons Help All changes saved in Drive

Drawings and collages produced by automated scripts.

Library of the Printed Web

The Museum of Modern Art Library

First	Last	Artist 2	Artist 3	Title	Description
Tina	Schwizgebel			*2015*	A tear-off calendar illustrated with fo air masks. Project produced in a wo at the Haute école d'art et de Desig
Mindy	Seu			*Visually Similar Images*	A formulaic dissection of Rusuna's page of "visually similar images" on exponential web of new connection
Travis	Shaffer			*Eleven Mega Churches*	Google maps screen-captures of a largest churches in the US.
Benjamin	Shaykin			*Special Collection / An Assortment of Books, Digitized by Google, Un-Digitized by Benjamin Shaykin, 2009–13*	Special Collection consists of a doz partial recreations of books found o reproduced at its original size, reve errors, introduced during Google's c scanner's hand, holding down and illustrations which have degraded a illegibility; pages scanned while in t fold-out maps and charts that were these artifacts are beautiful and evo poetry of this new machine. This pu of all twelve books in a single volum
Benjamin	Shaykin			*Date Due*	A collection of images of library due Books.
	Show-n-tell (aka Chantal Zakari)			*webAffairs*	An artist's documentation of an adu artist, Show-n-tell, tells her story of becoming part of this community th actual chat text.
Max	Siedentopf			*Holiday*	A collection of screenshots taken fr webcams, depicting holiday destina
Max	Siedentopf			*Self-Portrait*	Photos found on smartphones, tabl retail environments.
Max	Siedentopf			*Every One Loves Tennis in Malibu.*	Images of tennis courts in Malibu, fe
Max	Siedentopf			*Sculptures*	Images of hands feeding birds.
Max	Siedentopf			*My Favorite Pictures*	A collection of images depicted as c
Victor	Sira			*Voyeur A Midsummer*	A mix of photographs found in the i about color photography from the 6 inspired by hypothesis argued by V Philosophy of Photography."
Travess	Smalley			*set to some of*	Exhibition catalogue for exhibition a Vienna. Drawings and collages pro with code and script poetry.

AUTHOR	Mark Staniforth
YEAR	since 2017
PUBLISHER	Fryup Publishing
GENRE	experimental literature, poetry
METHOD	collection, constraint, versioning / seriality
SUBJECT	canon, economy / labor, literature, print on demand, publishing / distribution, scale
PLATFORM	Lulu
VOLUMES	hundreds vols.
EDITION CHARACTERISTICS	ISBN, open edition, CC BY
FORMAT	14.8 × 21.0 cm
MATERIALITIES	black-and-white, paperback, perfect bound
IMAGE	

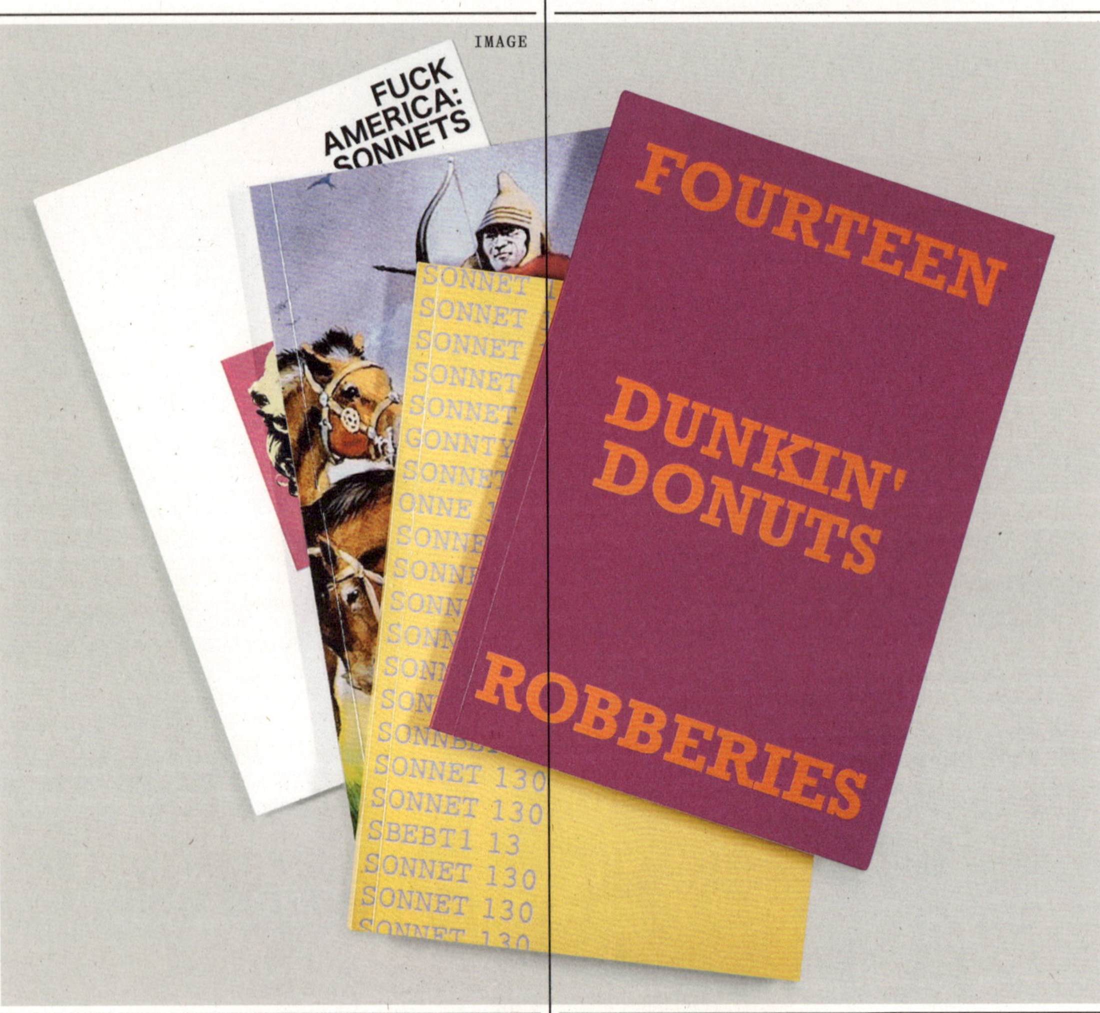

DESCRIPTION

Anti-Sonnets is a long-term project that began in 2017, when Mark Staniforth set out to write a sonnet every day for a year, "irrespective of personal circumstance. Each sonnet's subject matter, and perhaps also the perceived quality of its artistic execution, would reflect the tribulations of daily life" (blurb on Lulu).

With the sonnet, Staniforth chooses one of the most traditional genres in the history of European literature, which is at the same time considered the most stringent of all literary forms. That not only results in a faithful and mechanical compliance with norms but has also steadily provoked experiments and deviance. Thus, the genre has been put through every conceivable test in the course of literary history and accompanied by "anti-sonnets" from the very beginning. Standing in this tradition, Staniforth also makes it his task "to challenge assumptions associated with the sonnet form, and to champion the ascendency of context over content" (blurb on Lulu).

The series features a wide range of conceptual writing approaches. At the same time, it fans out into subseries that consistently play through a certain idea. The conceptual setting of this publishing project also implies a shift in scale, which is closely linked to the possibilities of print-on-demand publishing. In this new perception, a publication is understood as a poem, thus, a text turning into a line of poetry and a series of publications sometimes forming a poem-cycle. All publications are numbered with roman numerals and documented on a blog.

GOOGLE-TRANSLATED SONNETS

YEAR	2019
GENRE	poetry
METHOD	generative / automation, translation / transcription
SUBJECT	bias, canon, google, literature, reading / interpretation, technology
EDITION CHARACTERISTICS	ISBN 9780244226848, multiple editions (print, PDF)
PAGES	115

DESCRIPTION

GOOGLE-TRANSLATED SONNETS is a collection of poems conceived by translating Shakespeare's *Sonnet 130* into one of Google Translate's 103 languages at the time and then translating it back into English. The result is a documentation of the software's state of development as well as a visualization of cultural differences that are transported via these languages, with the resulting poems showing significant differences and poetic "misunderstandings."

By making one of the most canonical poems of the English language the point of reference for this project, *GOOGLE-TRANSLATED SONNETS* mirrors the colonialist bias of the translation software, which is programmed and maintained by a US software giant. To underline this, the cover depicts what looks to be Mongol warriors on horses capturing an English knight on foot.

GOOGLE-TRANSLATED SONNETS is part 137 of Staniforth's *Anti-Sonnets*.

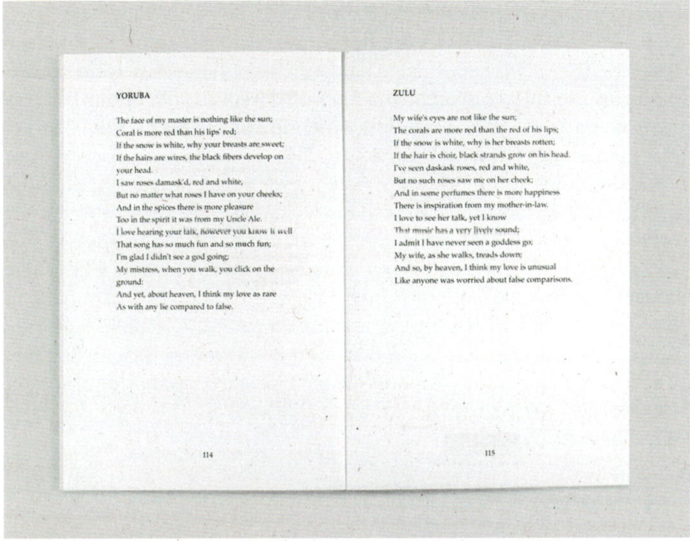

130X130

YEAR	2019
GENRE	poetry
METHOD	translation / transcription, versioning / seriality
SUBJECT	canon, error / corruption / loss, literature, writing / reading techniques
EDITION CHARACTERISTICS	ISBN 9780244211271, multiple editions (print, PDF)
PAGES	130 (unpaginated)

DESCRIPTION

For *130X130*, Staniforth typed Shakespeare's *Sonnet 130* consecutively 130 times without editing, leaving in all errors, deviations, and transformations. The transcriptions, which show far less errors than one would expect from such an exhaustive exercise, demonstrate the performative and poetic power a body exerts on a text through the mere act of typing.

130X130 is part 157 of Staniforth's *Anti-Sonnets*.

Fast Food Robberies: Fourteen Dunkin' Donuts Robberies

YEAR	2021
GENRE	experimental literature
METHOD	found material, versioning / seriality
SUBJECT	canon, economy / labor, platforms / companies
VOLUMES	14
EDITION CHARACTERISTICS	ISBN 9781678029241
PAGES	60 (unpaginated)

DESCRIPTION

Fast Food Robberies is a fourteen-piece subseries situated within Staniforth's long-term project *Anti-Sonnets* and can be conceived as a sonnet in itself, in which each of the fourteen publications forms a verse, so to speak. Since each publication in turn contains fourteen sonnets, the subseries can also be described as a sonnet cycle. This illustrates the shift in scale: from lines of poetry to collections of texts, from a single volume to a series, which forms the conceptual basis of this publishing project.

Each publication of this series features fourteen news articles on robberies that took place in different fast-food restaurants in the US, offering "an up-to-date portrait of US society through the prism of two of its most enduring obsessions: food and guns" (blurb on Lulu). The covers mimic the design of Edward Ruscha's famous *Twentysix Gasoline Stations*, but with a different color set for each volume, featuring one of the fourteen following fast-food restaurants: Baskin-Robbins, Carl's Jr, Chick-Fil-A, Chipotle, Dairy Queen, Dunkin' Donuts, In-N-Out Burger, Krispy Kreme, Papa John's, Popeyes, Taco Bell, Wendy's, Whataburger, Wingstop.

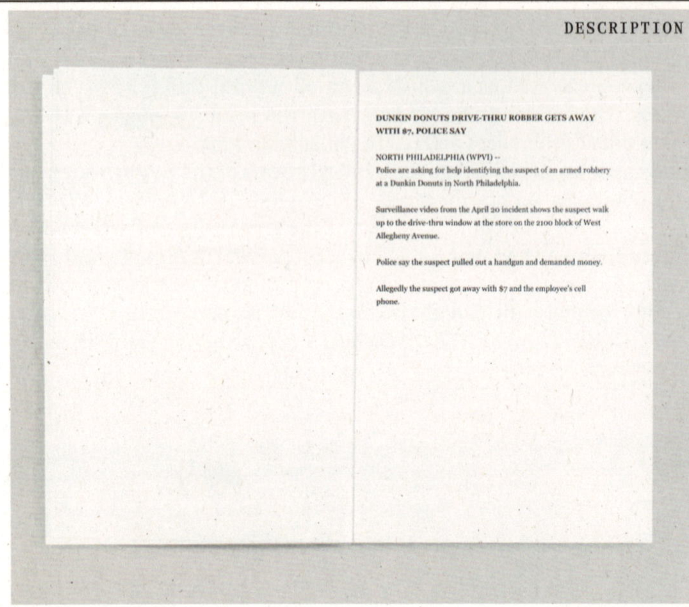

DUNKIN DONUTS DRIVE-THRU ROBBER GETS AWAY WITH $7, POLICE SAY

NORTH PHILADELPHIA (WPVI) --
Police are asking for help identifying the suspect of an armed robbery at a Dunkin Donuts in North Philadelphia.

Surveillance video from the April 20 incident shows the suspect walk up to the drive-thru window at the store on the 2100 block of West Allegheny Avenue.

Police say the suspect pulled out a handgun and demanded money.

Allegedly the suspect got away with $7 and the employee's cell phone.

Fuck America: Sonnets (Warhol)

YEAR	2021
GENRE	poetry
METHOD	found material, versioning / seriality
SUBJECT	bias, book / book design, canon, literature, print on demand
VOLUMES	14
EDITION CHARACTERISTICS	multiple cover variants and editions (print, PDF), ISBN 9781794767669
PAGES	53 (unpaginated)

DESCRIPTION

Fuck America: Sonnets is a collection of fifty poems, one for each US state in alphabetical order. Each poem consists of fourteen lines in the style of a sonnet, each of them repeating the word "Fuck" followed by a name or word that the author deems important or representative of the state. These usually include important cultural figures like artists, authors, or musicians but also names of well-known places, and references to popular culture and consumerism. By this, *Fuck America: Sonnets* creates an inventory of cultural markers and "exposes the stereotypes that make America simultaneously so alluring and appalling," the author writes in the blurb on Lulu, while at the same time "ask[ing] if we are all implicit in perpetuating them."

The book also makes explicit use of the possibilities offered by print-on-demand platforms as it comes in a choice of fourteen different covers, each depicting a different icon of American popular culture, including Jasper Johns' *Flag*, William Perry ("the Refrigerator"), Elvis, Warhol, Aretha, Bodacious, Fatburger, Tonya Harding, Mountain Dew, ZZ Top, Anna Nicole, L'il Wayne, Key Lime Pie, and Bridget The Midget. Thus, this fourteen-part cover series forms a sonnet itself.

Automatic Automatic Writing Sessions

Please Wait for the Showdown

AUTHOR	Angie Waller
YEAR	2017
PUBLISHER	Unknown Unknowns
GENRE	experimental literature
METHOD	generative / automation, study / analysis, translation / transcription
SUBJECT	code / programming, google, reading / interpretation, technology
PLATFORM	Amazon
VOLUMES	3
EDITION CHARACTERISTICS	open edition, ISBN 9781546979685
FORMAT	12.5 × 18.8 cm
MATERIALITIES	black-and-white, paperback, perfect bound
PAGES	84

IMAGES

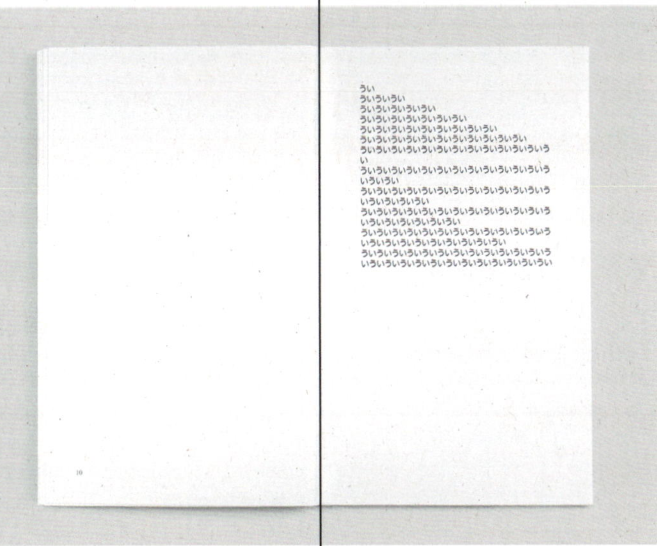

DESCRIPTION

Angie Waller's *Please Wait for the Showdown* is part of her *Automatic Automatic Writing Sessions* series, which, according to its front matter, makes use of "Google Brain." This refers to Google Translate's machine learning algorithm, which, as a note explains, is a language model that "is represented in a thousand dimensions—each word is designated by a list of a thousand numbers. The algorithm continues to learn and evolve."

The session on which this book is based took place between May 13 and 19, 2017, and is subject to a strict constraint: A Japanese character is entered into the translate window, then entered twice (without a space in between) on the line below, and then entered three times (again without spaces) on the line below that, and so on, so that the number of characters always corresponds to the line number—until no more new translation variants are generated by Google Translate. The machine, of course, tries to make sense of this absurd input. "Repeated Japanese phonemes that would sound like 'uh uh uh' to the human listener translate into a complex web of words that allude [to] meaning and hint at the poetic" (blurb on artist website), as the very first translation par excellence demonstrates:

The
Meaning
I mean
I mean watching
To say that I mean it
To say it means to call it
To say it means so to speak
It means that it means so called
To say it means so called
It means so to say it means so called
It means so to say it means to call it
To say it means to call it

A Bibliography of Conceptual Writing

AUTHOR	yigru zeltil
YEAR	2017
PUBLISHER	khora impex
GENRE	catalog / collection, nonfiction
METHOD	collection, documentation / archiving, study / analysis
SUBJECT	canon, literature
PLATFORM	Lulu
EDITION CHARACTERISTICS	multiple editions (print, PDF), ISBN 9781365725517, open edition, public domain
FORMAT	15.2 × 22.9 cm
MATERIALITIES	black-and-white, paperback, perfect bound
PAGES	173

IMAGES

DESCRIPTION

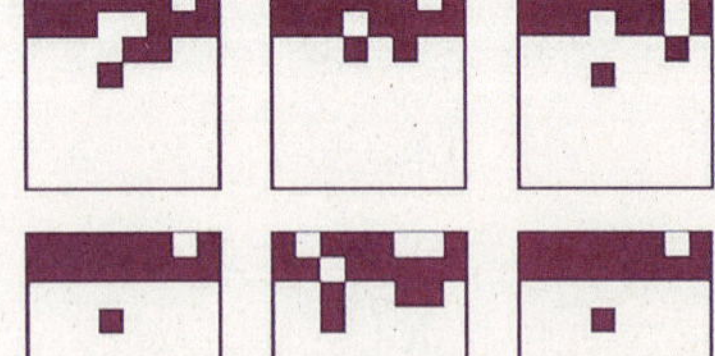

A Bibliography of Conceptual Writing collects around 1,100 entries of analog and digital publications that the editor yigru zeltil labels as conceptual. Initially started as a list on Goodreads and later turned into a blog, the book format was chosen as "stable reference," because "a Blogger page or even any other kind of Web page may never be as safe as a printed format" (yigru zeltil, "note," 7).

Yet, the potential incompleteness of such a list, being based in a certain period of time, as well as a changing definition of "conceptual" and the accessibility of books online and offline in general, also required the possibility to alter or update the content later. This makes print-on-demand the perfect vehicle for such a project and is represented by a version number attributed to the release, similar to software releases and their update histories. After v1.00 of the book couldn't be uploaded to Lulu due to formatting issues, v1.01 is the first available release, with minor changes and additions to the list. "In spite of many of these books being digital and/or print-on-demand or simply (nearly) impossible to obtain (anymore), it can indeed serve also as a 'shopping list'" (Ibid.).

In contrast to the blog which is sorted by date, the book sorts all entries alphabetically by author name. This focus on author rather than time corresponds to the editor's motivation to get in touch with artists that are on the list, making it a personal and political endeavor: "it could be said that this is an excuse for me to network with the authors I am going to translate or attract some attention for my own poetic projects (most of them due to be released in the near or distant future) and I'm not denying it—being yet another Romanian poet trying to get away, at least for a while, from the conservative culture…" (yigru zeltil, "for/word," 14f.).

These considerations and motivations are reflected on in a release "note" and a "for/word" accompanying the list. In the "note," readers are encouraged to compile or publish their own, better bibliography. The cover design is based on derek beaulieu's *The Duchamp Opening* (2016, no press).

AaBbCc

AUTHOR	ABC [Artists' Books Cooperative]
YEAR	2018
GENRE	artist's book / bookwork, catalog / collection
METHOD	collection, collective, composition (writing / drawing / photography), reenactment
SUBJECT	art world / literary world, book / book design, crowd / collaboration, print on demand, publishing / distribution
PLATFORM	Lulu
EDITION CHARACTERISTICS	open edition
FORMAT	21.6 × 27.9 cm
MATERIALITIES	black-and-white, paperback, perfect bound
PAGES	320 (unpaginated)

IMAGES

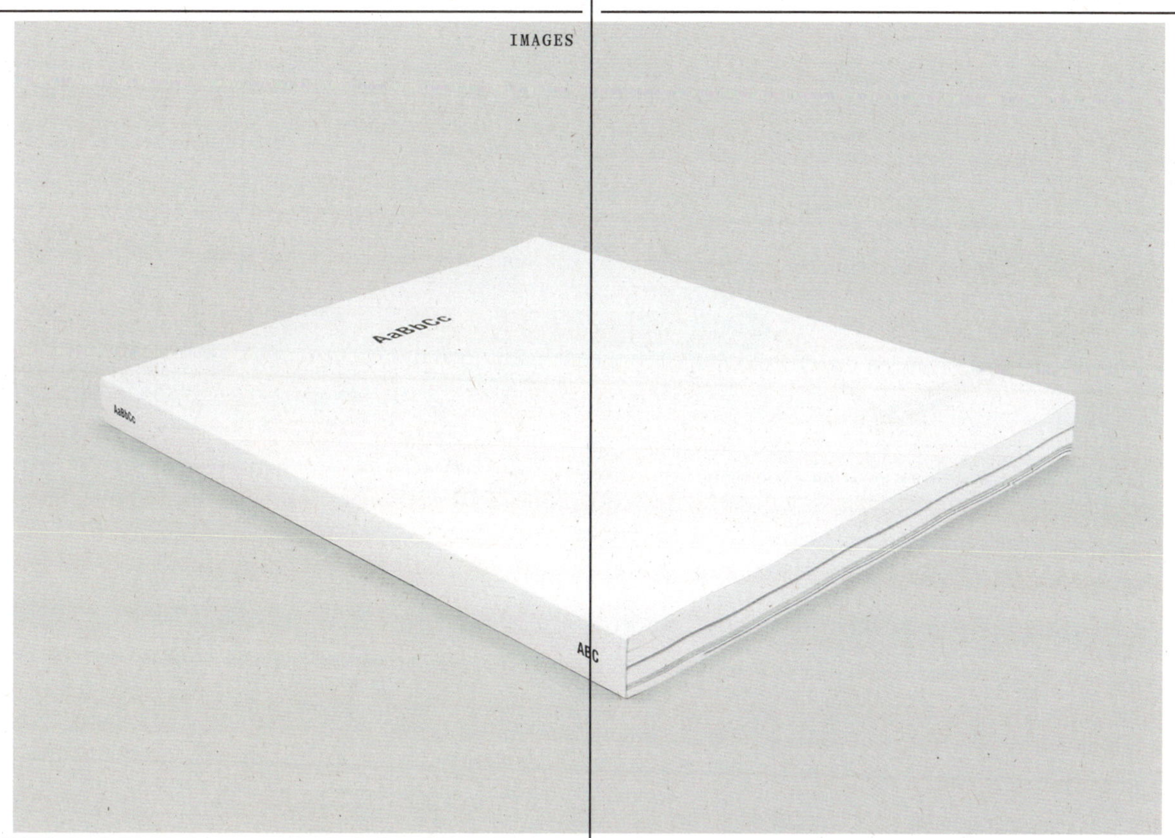

DESCRIPTION

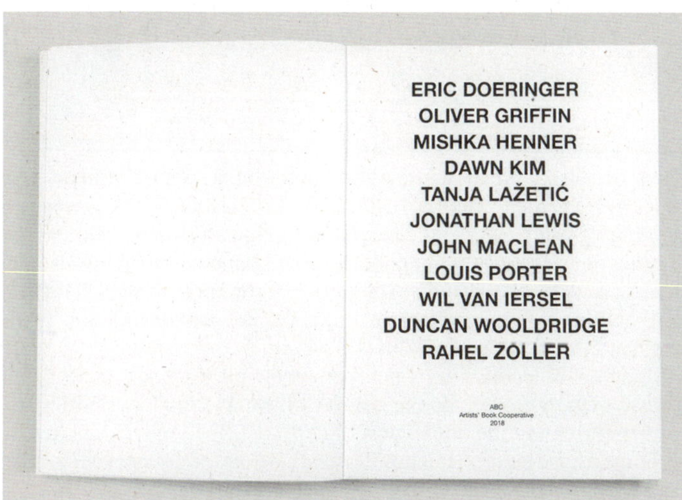

This collection belongs to the ABC Projects series by Artists' Books Cooperative (ABC), such as *ABC Days* (see 426) and *ABCEUM* (see 270–279). In the spirit of the famous *XEROX Book*, ABC members were invited to "submit a chapter for a book of artists' exercises." The length of the contribution was optional, as was whether it was an invitation to the reader to participate or an exercise executed by the artist. Accordingly, the collection is advertised in the blurb as an "educational guide" and is listed on Lulu under the category "Education & Language."

The contributions are arranged alphabetically, each beginning with the name of the artist in the same font and position. Eric Doeringer opens with another version of *The Location of Lines (after Sol LeWitt)*, for which he already published his own print-on-demand series in 2012 (see 226). Rahel Zoller concludes with an exercise on the permutation of different positions of the letters "AaBbCc." The theme of education is taken up by Oliver Griffin with Post Education Equipment Inventory and by Wil van Iersel with a compilation of scribbles and calculations from school notebooks and textbooks. Also involved were Mishka Henner, Dawn Kim, Tanja Lažetić, Jonathan Lewis, John Maclean, Louis Porter, and Duncan Wooldridge.

AUTHOR	Canon MG3100
YEAR	2018
GENRE	artist's book / bookwork, education / classroom
METHOD	collection, composition (writing / drawing / photography), found material, montage / remix, paratextual play
SUBJECT	authorship, google, literature, print on demand, publishing / distribution, search engine
PLATFORM	Lulu
EDITION CHARACTERISTICS	multiple editions (print, PDF), ISBN 9780359177639, open edition
FORMAT	15.2 × 22.9 cm
MATERIALITIES	color, paperback, perfect bound
PAGES	152 (unpaginated)

IMAGES

DESCRIPTION

BOOK, produced as part of Danny Snelson's 2018 course "Print on Demand Art and Poetry (LaPoD)" at University of California, Los Angeles, is a digital scrapbook on print-on-demand self-publishing and the book.

Collaging and juxtaposing found material in a variety of ways, the publication can be divided into five parts, each one separated by a double page with three dots and a horizontally rotated comma. The first part ironically gives "6 Steps for easy self-publishing," like "Know thyself" or "Publish YourSELF" depicting each step with found imagery in which a selfie of the author is inserted. The second part reproduces an excerpt of an article on repetition plus repeating the phrase "This is a Print on Demand Book about Print on Demand" on four pages, which also serves as a description of the book's actual content. The third part entitled "The Dark Side of Self Publishing" lists comments criticizing print-on-demand services. The fourth part is presented as a collection of quotes about publishing by famous authors, however in reality they are all written by the author of the book himself. The fifth part, taking up the majority of the book, collects images and texts from internet searches for "self publishing."

Chapters one and four, which both show off the book creator's inventiveness, both include the note "A J.J. Production," attributing authorship to him. The book itself is attributed to CANON MG3100, a printer, whose error messages illustrate the cover as well as flooding the blurb section of the Lulu webshop.

Sociality
The Coloring Book of Technology for Social Manipulation

AUTHOR — Paolo Cirio

YEAR — 2018

GENRE — artistic research, artist's book / bookwork, tutorial

METHOD — collection, composition (writing / drawing / photography), détournement / hack, found material, study / analysis

SUBJECT — bias, censorship / ban, copyright / law, economy / labor, platforms / companies, politics / activism, surveillance / privacy, technology

PLATFORM — Lulu

EDITION CHARACTERISTICS — multiple editions (print, PDF), ISBN 9780359294039, open edition, CC0

FORMAT — 21.6 × 27.9 cm

MATERIALITIES — black-and-white, paperback, perfect bound

PAGES — 316 (unpaginated)

IMAGES

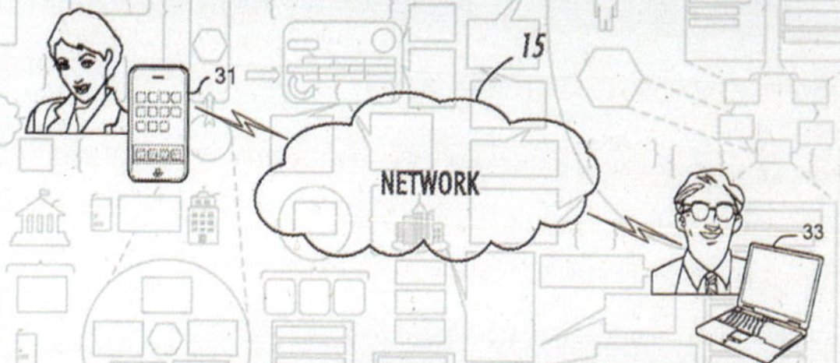

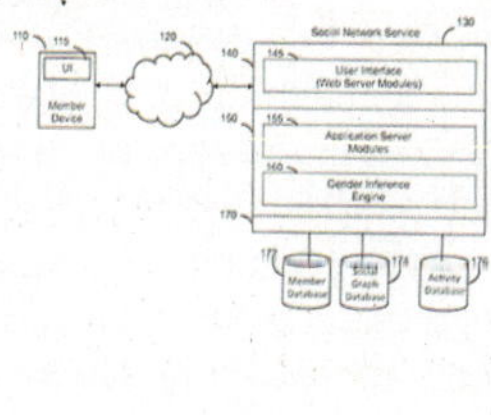

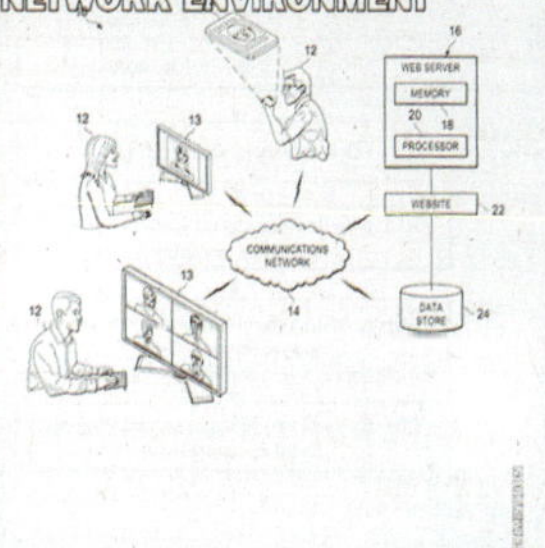

DESCRIPTION

Sociality is a conceptual art work about technologies of social manipulation and oppression. It is concerned with patents for "algorithms, interfaces, and devices concealing social discrimination, polarization, addiction, deception, and surveillance," as it says on the cover. To this end, Paolo Cirio scraped over twenty thousand such patents listed on Google Patents, using a script written by his assistant Andres Chang, and turned them into a searchable, tagged, and rated database on https://sociality.today/. This not only brings to the front the scale of algorithms used for social manipulation but also enables users to engage with and understand such software. It also sheds light on the fact that these designs of oppression are protected by copyright, and shows who actually developed and owns them.

Each patent is represented by an emblematic flowchart poster consisting of one of its diagrams and the title, breaking down the complexity of the registered patents. *Sociality: The Coloring Book of Technology for Social Manipulation* is a selection of over 250 of such patent graphics, sorted into chapters on discrimination, polarization, control, addiction, deception, manipulation, censorship, targeting, profiling, biometrics, surveillance, and miscellaneous.

It deepens the pedagogical approach and further democratizes access that the book "proposes the cathartic, childlike exercise of coloring to both educate and inform through visually rendered compositions of outlined flowcharts and patent titles. [...] The provocative and participatory component of coloring elicits engagement for collaborative critical reflection [and] aims to make the project popular and emblematic" (Paolo Cirio, "Sociality," foreword, n.p.). Moreover, Cirio encourages readers of the book or website to send (generated) emails to politicians, activists, journalists, or representatives to ask for a ban or regulation of the patent in question. So, it is not just about data visualization and accessibility, it is about social engagement and changing the current state of unethical patenting: "We regulate the financial sector, we have check and balance in the government, we ban the sale of guns, and toxic chemicals. As information technology impacts society perilously, we must also regulate both centralized and decentralized platforms, infrastructures, and interfaces with inventive, restrictive, and reflexive policies" (Paolo Cirio, "Theoretical Text about *Sociality*").

The print-on-demand coloring book is also an argument for the importance of analog and physical interaction with digital information by allowing users to fill the uniform black-and-white patent graphics with life, and to cross and overwrite their lines.

This is me

AUTHOR	Felipe Cussen
YEAR	2018
GENRE	experimental literature
METHOD	détournement / hack, documentation / archiving, outsourcing
SUBJECT	authorship, economy / labor, instagram, internet culture, social media
PLATFORM	Lulu
EDITION CHARACTERISTICS	multiple edtions (print, PDF), open edition
FORMAT	10.8 × 17.5 cm
MATERIALITIES	color, paperback, perfect bound
PAGES	142 (unpaginated)

IMAGES

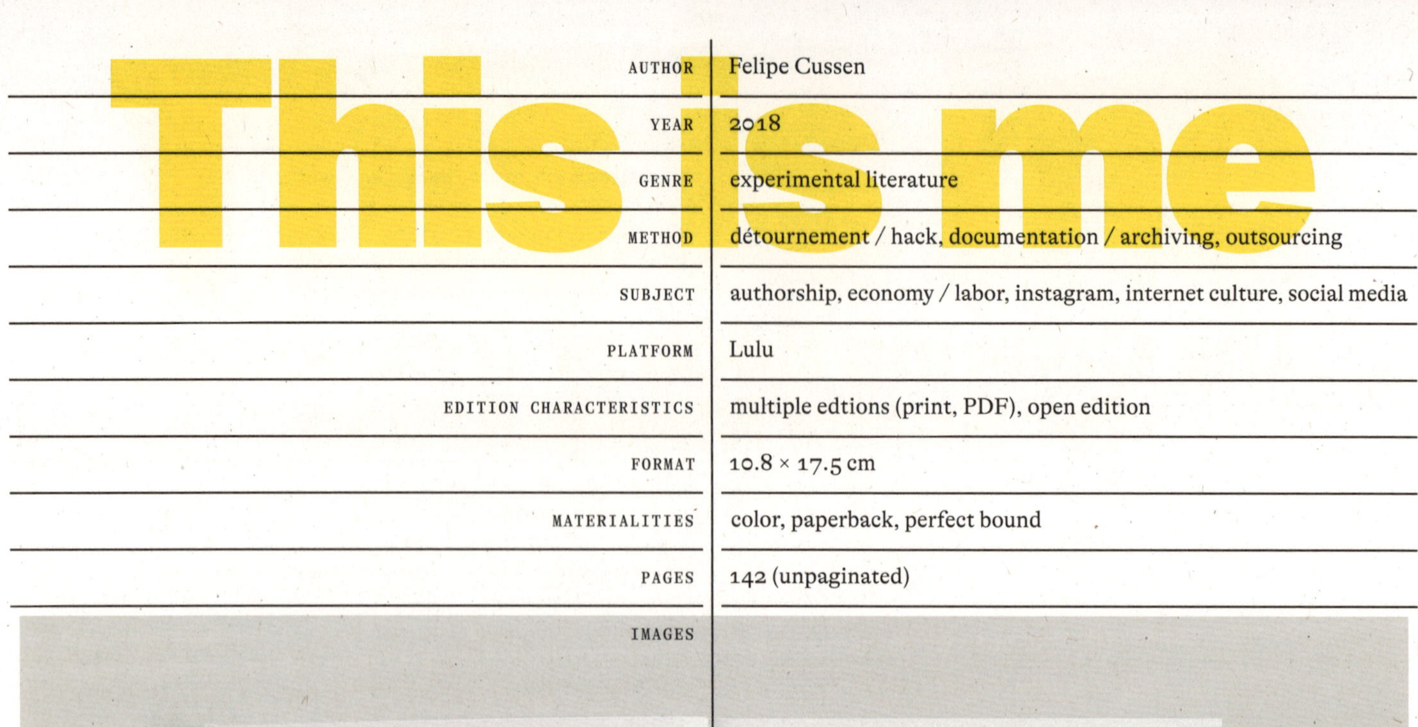

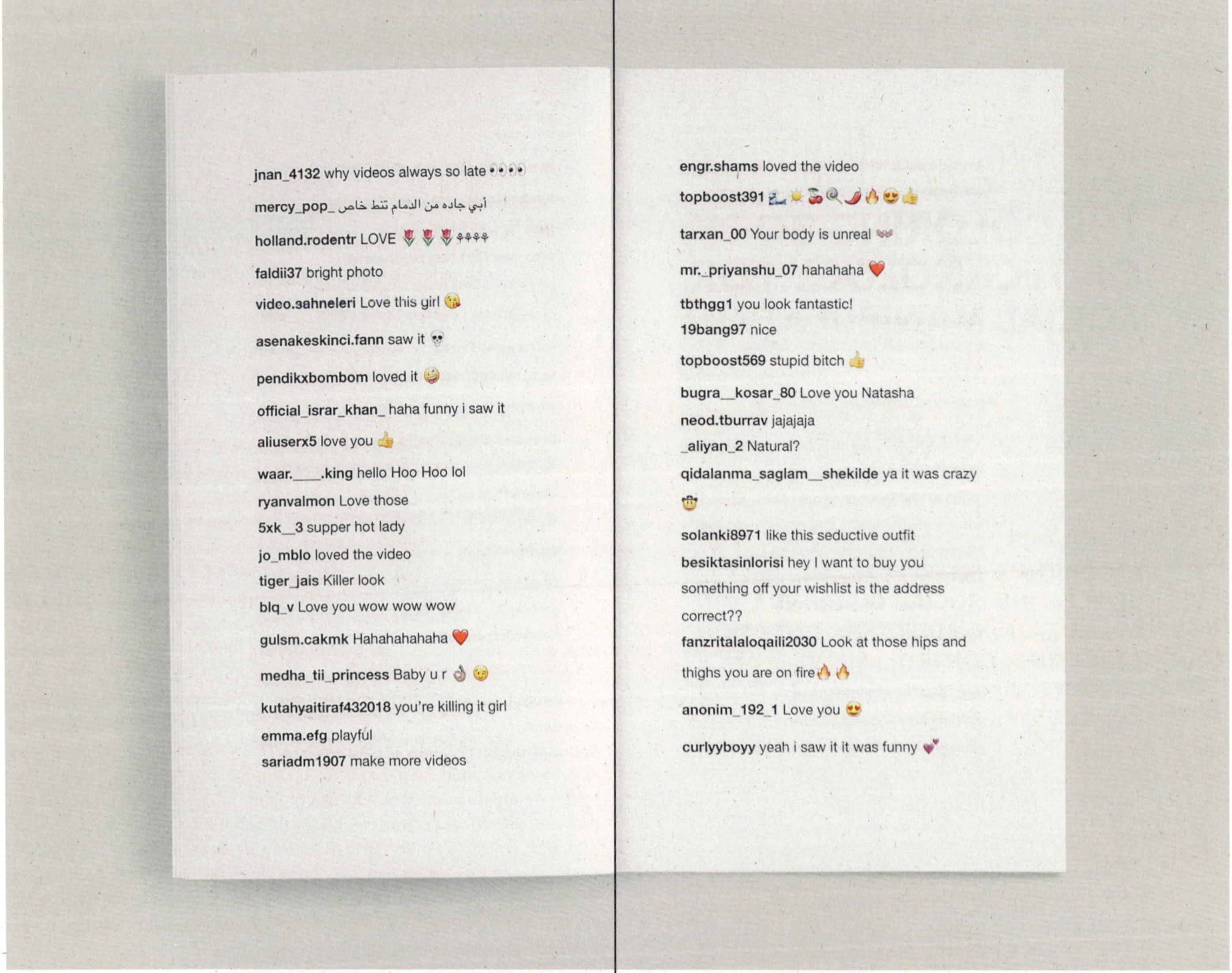

jnan_4132 why videos always so late
mercy_pop_ أبي جاده من الدمام تنط خاص
holland.rodentr LOVE
faldii37 bright photo
video.sahneleri Love this girl
asenakeskinci.fann saw it
pendikxbombom loved it
official_israr_khan_ haha funny i saw it
aliuserx5 love you
waar.____.king hello Hoo Hoo lol
ryanvalmon Love those
5xk__3 supper hot lady
jo_mblo loved the video
tiger_jais Killer look
blq_v Love you wow wow wow
gulsm.cakmk Hahahahahaha
medha_tii_princess Baby u r
kutahyaitiraf432018 you're killing it girl
emma.efg playful
sariadm1907 make more videos

engr.shams loved the video
topboost391
tarxan_00 Your body is unreal
mr._priyanshu_07 hahahaha
tbthgg1 you look fantastic!
19bang97 nice
topboost569 stupid bitch
bugra__kosar_80 Love you Natasha
neod.tburrav jajajaja
_aliyan_2 Natural?
qidalanma_saglam__shekilde ya it was crazy
solanki8971 like this seductive outfit
besiktasinlorisi hey I want to buy you something off your wishlist is the address correct??
fanzritalaloqaili2030 Look at those hips and thighs you are on fire
anonim_192_1 Love you
curlyyboyy yeah i saw it it was funny

DESCRIPTION

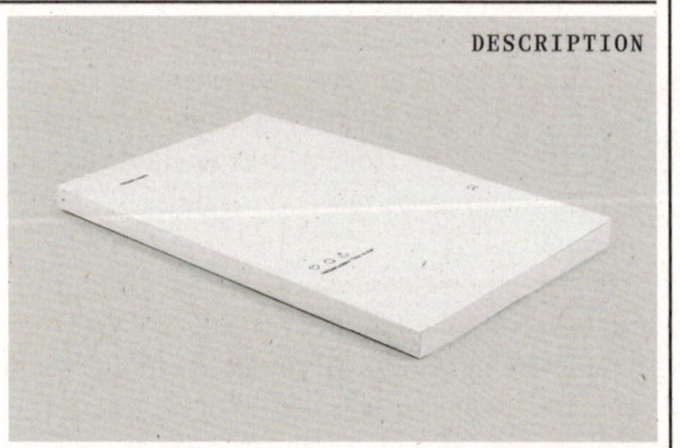

On September 18, 2018, the author posted a completely blank, white square image on his Instagram account with the caption "This is me." He then bought 1,000 random comments, added briefly after the post, from the social media marketing company buysocialmediamarketing.com for $99.99. The book documents these comments, making it a reverse engineering attempt to determine whether the comments were written by actual people or bots, as well as misusing them to produce a work that can be sold again and thereby lessening their costs.

The front cover shows the original Instagram post, the back cover reproduces the invoice.

LaPoD XEROX Bootleg READER 2018

AUTHOR	LaPoD Press 2018
YEAR	2018
GENRE	catalog / collection, education / classroom, nonfiction
METHOD	collection, photocopy / scan
SUBJECT	canon, error / corruption / loss, print technology, publishing / distribution
PLATFORM	Lulu
EDITION CHARACTERISTICS	multiple editions (print, PDF), open edition
FORMAT	21.6 × 27.9 cm
MATERIALITIES	black-and-white, paperback, perfect bound
PAGES	58 (unpaginated)

IMAGES

DESCRIPTION

LaPoD XEROX Bootleg READER 2018 is made with a photocopy machine and contains a collection of scanned excerpts from books on the book. Created during an "improvised office copier performance" (blurb on Lulu) in Danny Snelson's 2018 course "Print on Demand Art and Poetry (LaPoD)" at University of California, Los Angeles, the publication is both a collection of relevant theory on the subject as well as a reflection on the practice of creating seminar readers in copyshops and their distinct materiality. By publishing the photocopied and digitized—i.e., scanned—pages as a print-on-demand book, *LaPoD XEROX Bootleg READER* demonstrates the aesthetic qualities of this mode of text reproduction and distribution that is about to become obsolete. The reproductions include typical modes of visual degeneration such as poor positioning of the books or visible hands holding pages. The reproduction of the scanner's hand forming the last page of the book shows that this is a deliberately chosen aesthetic strategy.

THE READER INCLUDES EXCERPTS FROM

- Eva Weinmayr, "Library Underground—A Reading List for A Coming Community." In *Publishing as Artistic Practice*, ed. by Annette Gilbert (Berlin: Sternberg Press, 2016), 250–282;
- Peter Mendelsund, *What We See When We Read* (New York: Vintage Books, 2014);
- Nicholas Thoburn, *Anti-Book. On the Art and Politics of Radical Publishing* (Minneapolis: University of Minnesota Press, 2016);
- Kate Eichhorn, *Adjusted Margin. Xerography, Art, and Activism in the Late Twentieth Century* (Cambridge, Mass.: MIT Press, 2016);
- Timothy Laquintano, *Mass Authorship and the Rise of Self-Publishing* (Iowa City: University of Iowa Press, 2016);
- Steven Clay and Rodney Phillips, *A Secret Location on the Lower East Side: Adventures in Writing, 1960–1980* (New York: New York Public Library, 1998);
- Darren Wershler-Henry, *The Iron Whim. A Fragmented History of Typewriting* (Ithaca and London: Cornell University Press, 2007);
- Annette Gilbert, "Book Pirates. On a New Art of Making Books." In *Reprint. Appropriation (&) Literature*, ed. by Annette Gilbert (Wiesbaden: Luxbooks, 2016), 49–77;
- Andrea Francke and Eva Weinmayr, "The Piracy Project." In *Code—X. Paper, Ink, Pixel and Screen*, ed. by Danny Aldred and Emmanuelle Waeckerlé (Farnham: BookRoom Press, 2016), 01:07–01:18.

BOOKWRECK

LaPoD Scan LP

AUTHOR	LaPoD Press 2018
YEAR	2018
GENRE	artist's book / bookwork, education / classroom
METHOD	collective, composition (writing / drawing / photography), photocopy / scan
SUBJECT	book / book design, error / corruption / loss, materiality, reading / interpretation
PLATFORM	Lulu
EDITION CHARACTERISTICS	multiple editions (print, PDF), ISBN 9780359251216, open edition, CC0
FORMAT	15.2 × 22.9 cm
MATERIALITIES	color, paperback, perfect bound
PAGES	184 (unpaginated)

IMAGES

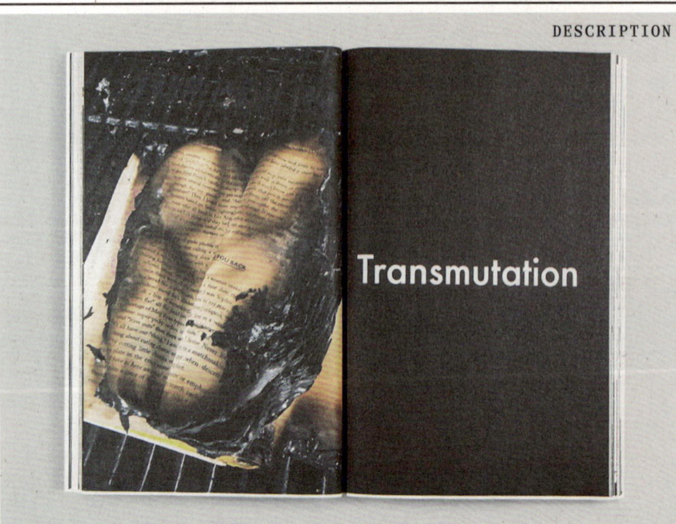

DESCRIPTION

BOOKWRECK is a collection of scans made of destroyed or otherwise altered book pages collectively conceived by students of Danny Snelson's 2018 class "Print on Demand Art & Poetry" at University of California, Los Angeles.

The book is divided into five chapters named after the alterations the book objects have undergone: Incineration, Transmutation, Annotation, Transformation, Execution. Each chapter features two alterations of one or two books, which are often no longer recognizable and whose scan collection is marked by an inserted black page featuring a title and (pseudonymous) authorship, alluding to the fact this version of the book is considered a new work, sometimes taking a critical stance on the book ("Ending a book that contributes to the blaming of women culture"), sometimes playing with the original title ("The Chilliad"), sometimes taking up the theme of the entire collection ("Gone Book"). Most of the pages have been altered physically by burning, cutting, or drawing on the pages, but some alterations also highlight the destructive effect of scanning, showing deformations and glitches from the remediation practices of digitization.

AUTHOR	Christina Neuwirth
YEAR	2018
PUBLISHER	Speculative Books
GENRE	fiction
METHOD	generative / automation, translation / transcription
SUBJECT	error / corruption / loss, materiality, print technology, print on demand, publishing / distribution, typography
PLATFORM	Amazon
EDITION CHARACTERISTICS	ISBN 9781999918095, open edition
FORMAT	11.0 × 17.0 cm
MATERIALITIES	black-and-white, paperback, perfect bound, defective copy
PAGES	128

IMAGES

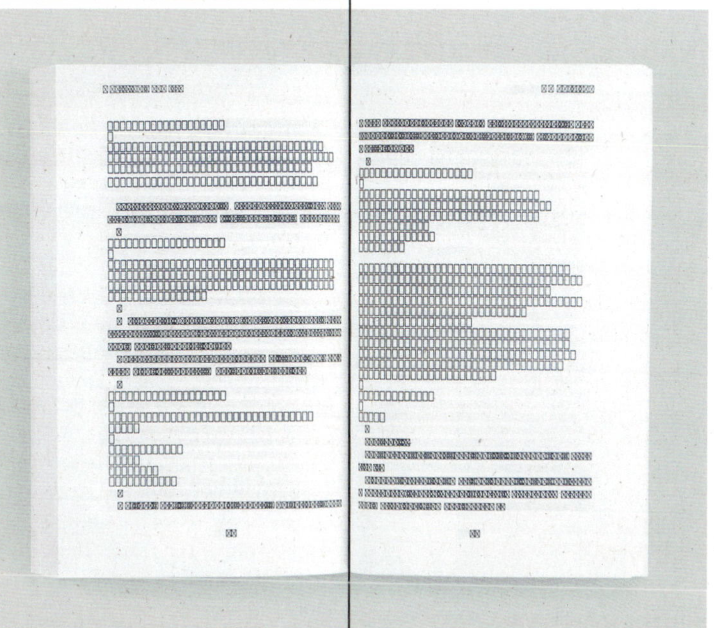

DESCRIPTION

Amphibian, by Christina Neuwirth, is a satire novella on work in times of turbo-capitalism and climate crisis. Rose Ellis works at Money-TownCashGrowth and arrives at the office "one morning to find that the entire fourth floor has been flooded with water, in a desperate attempt to improve productivity. As the water steadily rises, her working situation becomes more and more absurd…" (blurb on publisher's website). The book was published by Speculative Books who use a print-on-demand workflow to distribute their titles.

In this copy however, all characters are replaced by rectangular symbols, leaving the layout intact but rendering the text illegible. These rectangular characters are Unicode replacement characters that jump into place for symbols that might be missing from the font in use. This error, allegedly due to a defective processing of the implemented font by the printer—an issue that has already been addressed by the publisher—shows the lack of quality control in an outsourced, automated production chain. It is representative of print-on-demand workflows that enable small independent presses like Speculative Books and more experimental content to be published and distributed but also cuts corners in quality and error control. Yet in the case of *Amphibian*, this error is also a perfect image for the novel's content which is quite literally drowned in illegible space due to its mode of production.

It was Melissa Terras who reported this case on Twitter and later donated her copy to our collection.

ASMR: artificial seductive machine reading [IN TWO IDENTICAL SECTIONS]

AUTHOR	Jake Reber
YEAR	2018
PUBLISHER	Recreational Resources
GENRE	experimental literature, tutorial
METHOD	composition (writing / drawing / photography)
SUBJECT	code / programming, internet culture, materiality, writing / reading techniques
PLATFORM	Lulu
EDITION CHARACTERISTICS	multiple editions (print, PDF), ISBN 9781387542062, open edition, copyleft
FORMAT	10.8 × 17.5 cm
MATERIALITIES	black-and-white, paperback, perfect bound
PAGES	104

IMAGES

DESCRIPTION

Jake Reber's *ASMR: artificial seductive machine reading [IN TWO IDENTICAL SECTIONS]* is a guided meditation through the sensory impressions evoked by holding a book, particularly this pocketbook with its glossy cover. Set in a large monospaced font, the text gives ever-repeating instructions on how to handle the book object and on which sensations the reader should focus, mostly the feeling of the hands. These instructions are repeated and recombined with different sensations, presumably using a permutation algorithm in the writing.

The book makes reference to the genre of ASMR ("Autonomous Sensory Meridian Response"): sounds and videos featuring the sound of touching objects of different textures recorded with high quality microphones, causing some viewers to feel a tingling in the back of the head and spine. ASMR uses the mind to compensate the lack of sensory experience when consuming audiovisual media via personal computers. This is rendered absurd when in Reber's *ASMR* the reader is instructed to close their eyes and focus on the sensory impressions of the book, as this makes further reading impossible, reflecting the active role of the reader in perceiving a book.

ASMR contains two identical versions of the same text, differing only in reading speed—the first lasts approximately 8.6 minutes, the second 17.2 minutes as it is meant to be read at half speed, thus further deepening the meditative book experience. In his endorsement, Germán Sierra sees this "conceptual revindication of the book's physicality in the line of Ulises Carrión's 'The New Art of Making Books'" and concludes by recommending, "More than ever, handle this book with care" (back cover).

The book was published by Recreational Resources, whose Tumblr site is very reminiscent of Edit Publications' project *11 Books Expanding Tan Lin's* 7CV (see 160–169) and features the slogans "we own nothing / *we print everything*, this marks the death of the internet,& ;poetry" and "DOCUMENT—DISTRIBUTE—DECONSTRUCT—DESTROY." All books are available as PDF and POD; the complete program could be downloaded as a ZIP file.

Bézier Curve Annotated Portable Document Format & PDF Scented Candle

AUTHOR	Danny Snelson
YEAR	2018
GENRE	artistic research, artist's book / bookwork, nonfiction
METHOD	composition (writing / drawing / photography), montage / remix, study / analysis
SUBJECT	analog / digital, materiality, platforms / companies, publishing / distribution, technology, typography
PLATFORM	Lulu
EDITION CHARACTERISTICS	multiple editions [print, PDF), open edition
FORMAT	19.0 × 19.0 cm
MATERIALITIES	color, paperback, perfect bound
PAGES	150 (unpaginated)

IMAGES

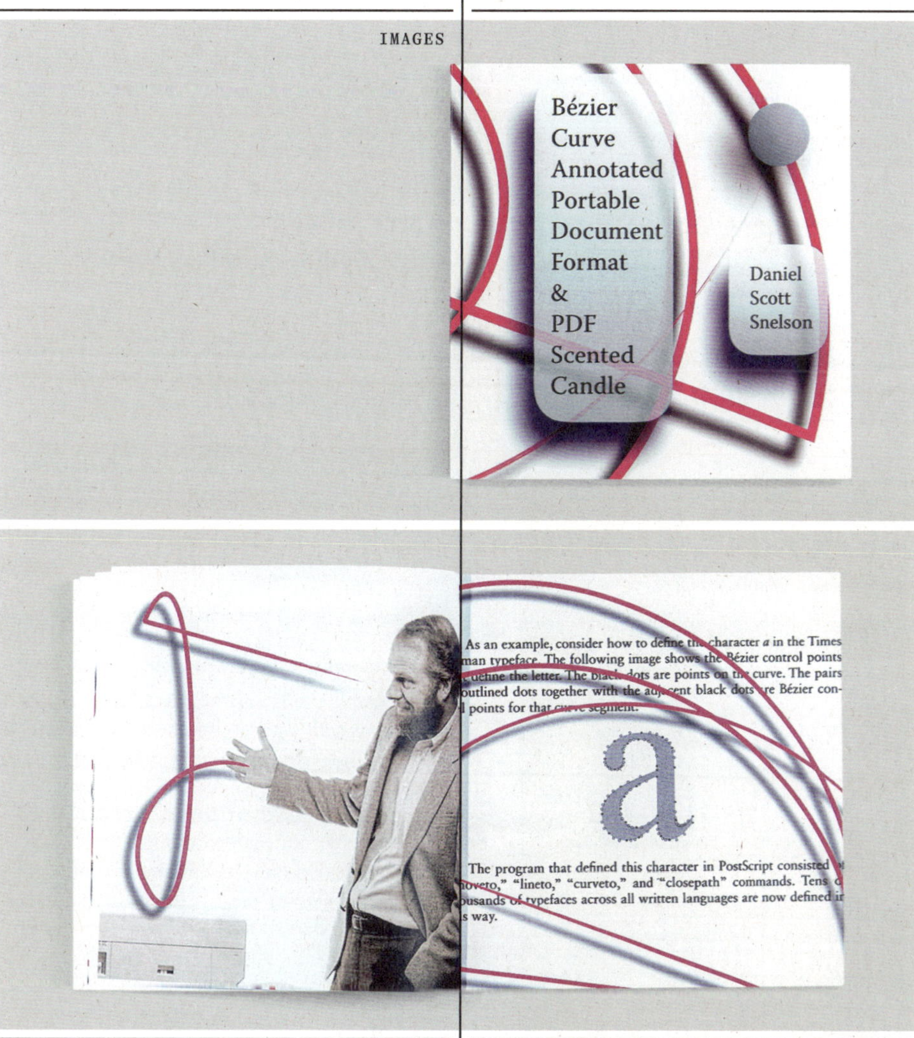

DESCRIPTION

Bézier Curve Annotated Portable Document Format & PDF Scented Candle is a book-length essay on the PDF format, its constituting technology PostScript, and the mathematical principle used for character rendering that it is based on, called Bézier curve. Danny Snelson presents pictures and articles as research material, as well as print-on-demand artworks, often reproduced in their original format, linked by his comments and annotations, showing the whole range of reproductive possibilities made possible through PDF. PostScript and the Bézier curve are traced as revolutionizing the publishing sphere as they offered, for the first time, great interoperability and quality maintenance for digital documents as well as printers. Invented by John Warnock and Charles Geschke, they make up the foundation for Adobe Inc. products such as Photoshop, InDesign, and Illustrator, whose impact on publishing today cannot be stressed enough.

The complete essay, which makes a point for the importance and mediahistorical depth of PDF and its technologies, is overlaid by magenta Bézier curves to show the lack of quality loss granted by the algorithm even when zoomed in. The essay was published in PDF format as an addition to *Full Stop Reviews Supplement #3* and simultaneously as a print-on-demand book on Lulu, putting the technologies shown throughout the text into action via a digital printer while at the same time granting its wide and lossless distribution as a digital file.

Steve, Harvey and Matt,

As discussed with Nancy, we would like the content at the links below removed and archived as soon as possible.

AUTHOR	Paul Soulellis
YEAR	2018
GENRE	artist's book / bookwork, nonfiction
METHOD	documentation / archiving, found material, reformatting
SUBJECT	censorship / ban, ecology / sustainability, memory / storage, politics / activism
PLATFORM	Lulu
EDITION CHARACTERISTICS	multiple editions (print, PDF, stream, ZIP), open edition
FORMAT	21.6 × 27.9 cm
MATERIALITIES	black-and-white, paperback, perfect bound
PAGES	734 (unpaginated)

IMAGES

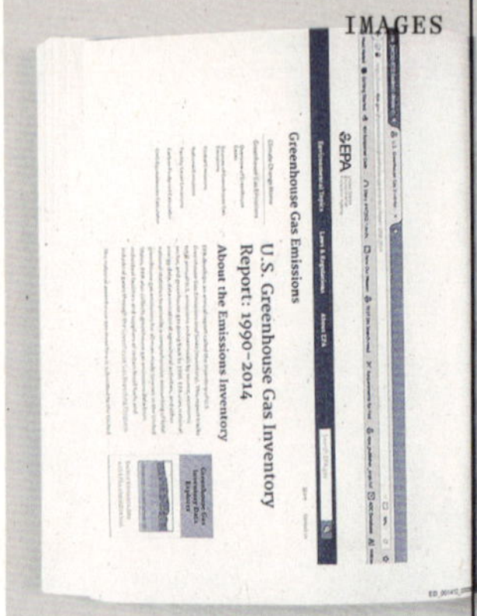

DESCRIPTION

"This project—a broadcast, a book, and a download—restores access to 1,964 climate change-related URLs that were removed from www.EPA.gov on April 28, 2017. The URLs point to web pages, documents, presentations, publications, and other files that were purged by the U.S. Environmental Protection Agency under the direction of EPA Administrator Scott Pruitt and the Trump administration. Some of the assets had been accessible on the web since 1997.

The April 28 purge redirected hundreds of climate change URLs to one of three new pages: 'This page is being updated,' 'Complying with President Trump's Executive Order on Energy Independence,' or the scrubbed 'Energy Resources for State, Local, and Tribal Governments.' But many document files (PDFs, PPTs, MP3s, DOCs) survived the purge and continued to live online, remaining hidden from public view without their corresponding links—until now. *Steve, Harvey and Matt,* broadcasts the entire collection of climate change URLs ten times each day—a randomized mix of restored access and empty gestures. The 734-page printed book contains EPA emails and spreadsheets that detail the purge, obtained by Freedom of Information Act requests" (Paul Soulellis, "Readme").

Many emails are repeated multiple times in the book, apparently because they were sent to several people and therefore saved several times. This shows how many people were involved. Attached to the mails are often screenshots, reports, lists of subpages, etc., documenting the changes made and the problems encountered. The team congratulates itself at the end for having made it, quoting Margaret Mead: "Never underestimate the power of a small group of committed people to change the world."

The email to Steve, Harvey, and Matt with the request to purge the EPA's internet presence can be found several times in the book as well as on the back cover. This is where the title of the entire project comes from, as well as the subtitles of the book *As discussed with Nancy, we would like the content at the links below removed and archived as soon as possible* and the ZIP-download *We appreciate your assistance in this time-sensitive matter*.

Instasonnet

A Collection of Instagram # Rendered as Poetry

AUTHOR	SPOT
YEAR	2018
PUBLISHER	SPOT | UCLA
GENRE	catalog / collection, education / classroom, poetry
METHOD	collective, constraint, found material, montage / remix
SUBJECT	crowd / collaboration, instagram, internet culture, literature, social media
PLATFORM	Lulu
EDITION CHARACTERISTICS	multiple editions (print, PDF), open edition
FORMAT	10.8 × 17.5 cm
MATERIALITIES	black-and-white, paperback, perfect bound
PAGES	84 (unpaginated)

IMAGES

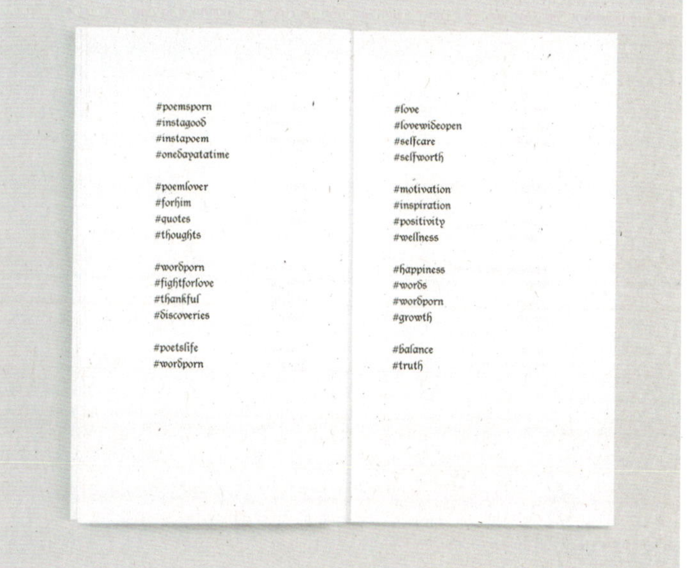

DESCRIPTION

Instasonnet is a collection of seventy-six sonnets all composed of no more than one Instagram hashtag per line. In such a way, they explore the tension between the traditional genre and new poetic writing practices on the social media platform. This tension is enhanced by the choice of a traditional-looking blackletter font that also references the clothing design trends prevalent on Instagram at the time. This connection is made directly in one of the untitled poems:

#gothiclife
#gothgoth
#black
#dark

#gothicfashion
#gothstyle
#instagoth
#vampires

#victorianoutfits
#corset
#witchcraft
#melancholy

#magic
#gothsofinstagram

Several poems take up love, life, and truth as dominant themes of Instapoetry; others celebrate the community of writers on Instagram, for which there are several hashtags, each slightly different; others mention the tagline #poetryisnotdead, which finds its confirmation in the genre's surprising resurgence in popular culture.

The poems stem from a writing assignment by Danny Snelson during his 2018 class "Surveying Poetry Online Today" (SPOT) at University of California, Los Angeles, and follow a strict set of rules that can be read as a psychogeographic mapping of the social media platform's architecture in the tradition of the Situationist International and Oulipian constraints. The rules, printed on the last pages of the book, are as follows:

"Search for any 'poetic' hashtag, ie #love #beauty, #rose, #longing, #poem #poetryinmotion #sublime #heartbreak #{etc}. Find a post with more than 14 hashtags.

Edit these tags to make a 'sonnet': instead of 14 lines, 14 hashtags (no more no less). In this form, compose: 3 stanzas of 4, followed by 2 final lines [...].

The hashtag should stand in for a full expression. Change any hashtag to 'poetry' or a literary term, arrange as you like.

Think about progression, and the final two lines giving a 'spin' to the sonnet, in classic form.

Think about embodiment and audience as a collective. We are a plural dispersed group 'author'—avoid or emend problematic expressions for race, gender, class, or sexuality."

Catalogue

AUTHORS	Isabelle Sully [ed.], Yin Yin Wong [ed.]
YEAR	2018
PUBLISHER	Publication Studio Rotterdam
GENRE	catalog / collection
METHOD	collection, documentation / archiving
SUBJECT	memory / storage, publishing / distribution
PLATFORM	Publication Studio, selfmade
EDITION CHARACTERISTICS	available for a limited time only, dated, stamped, embossed
FORMAT	13.9 × 18.0 cm
MATERIALITIES	black-and-white, paperback, perfect bound
PAGES	52

IMAGES

PUBLICATION STUDIO CATALOGUE (2009–2018)

Catalogued below is a comprehensive list of all the titles that Publication Studio has published during nine years in operation. Throughout this period of time, since it was founded in 2009, the Publication Studio network has published three hundred and forty-six titles. Or at least, three hundred and forty-six that we know of. Some were published without an ISBN, some printed once-off as limited editions, and some were even too difficult to ever make again. But whether commissioned in São Paulo or printed in Rotterdam, launched in Glasgow or in demand in Vancouver, the titles belonging to the catalogue – archived together publicly for the first time in this publication – are the meeting point for each of the studios within our network.

NO.	TITLE	AUTHOR	ORG.	ISBN
001	94	Joon Oluchi Lee	PSP	9781624621000
002	'Books Matter' Poster	Timothy Young	PSH	n/a
003	&, 2: This Happened To One Of Us	&, Collective	PSGU	9780994869050
004	#100DAYSOFSCULPTURE	Debra Baxter	PSP	9781624621086
005	16 Sculptures	Travis Jeppesen	PSP	9781624620553
006	174 Birds	Sarah Meadows	PSP	9781935662211
007	27 Installations	Portland Center for the Visual Arts	PSP	9781935662518
008	35 Images / Book Eleven of The Odyssey	Gil Blank / transl.: Matthew Stadler	PSP	9781935662334
009	40 Things I've Learned	Cadine Navarro	PSR	9789492308122
010	6–9: Notes from the archive of Dan Kane	Padraig Robinson	PSR	9789492308108
011	A Bachelor's Cupboard	A. Lyman Phillips	PSV	9780987746603
012	A Book About–	Åbäke (Maki Suzuki & Kajsa Ståhl), Corinn Gerber, Laure Giletti, Jp King, Chris Lee, Patricia No, Anouk Pennel and Benjamin Thorel	PSP	9781624620577
013	A Circular 2	Pedro Cid Proença (ed.)	PSP	9781624620041
014	A Classroom Reader	Anna Gray and Ryan Wilson Paulsen	PSP	9781935662426
015	A History of New York	Matt Keegan	PSP	9781935662396

P. 07

CATALOGUE

DESCRIPTION

Publication Studio, founded in 2009 in Portland, Oregon, is a publisher and producer of original books, handmade and on-demand, distributed through a global network of 11 studios on four continents as it currently stands. When a book is ordered, the nearest Studio takes on production and shipping in order to minimize expenses. Every Studio contributes publications to the catalog, with a PDF to print and instructions on how the book should be produced (format, material, cutting, binding, etc.).

Catalogue was produced on the occasion of an exhibition of the same name at MAMA, Rotterdam from May to July 2018, curated by Yin Yin Wong and Isabelle Sully who run the Publication Studio in Rotterdam. While the exhibition featured sixteen works created through the Publication Studio network, the catalog includes a complete list of all works published by the Studios as far as Wong and Sully were able to track them down—underscoring the difficulties of cataloging the activities of studios that operate as individual actors in a decentralized network. The publication also includes an essay by Sully and an index of all Studios in the network with a brief summary of their respective histories.

Our copy was made on July 22, 2018 and bears an embossing from Publication Studio Rotterdam on the back cover.

Poetry of America

AUTHOR	Undocumented Press
YEAR	2018
PUBLISHER	Undocumented Press
GENRE	artist's book / bookwork, education / classroom, experimental literature
METHOD	appropriation, détournement / hack, generative / automation, montage / remix, translation / transcription
SUBJECT	canon, google, literature, politics / activism, publishing / distribution, reading / interpretation
PLATFORM	Lulu
EDITION CHARACTERISTICS	multiple editions (print, PDF), open edition, CC0
FORMAT	15.8 × 23.5 cm
MATERIALITIES	black-and-white, dust jacket, hardcover, perfect bound
PAGES	434

IMAGES

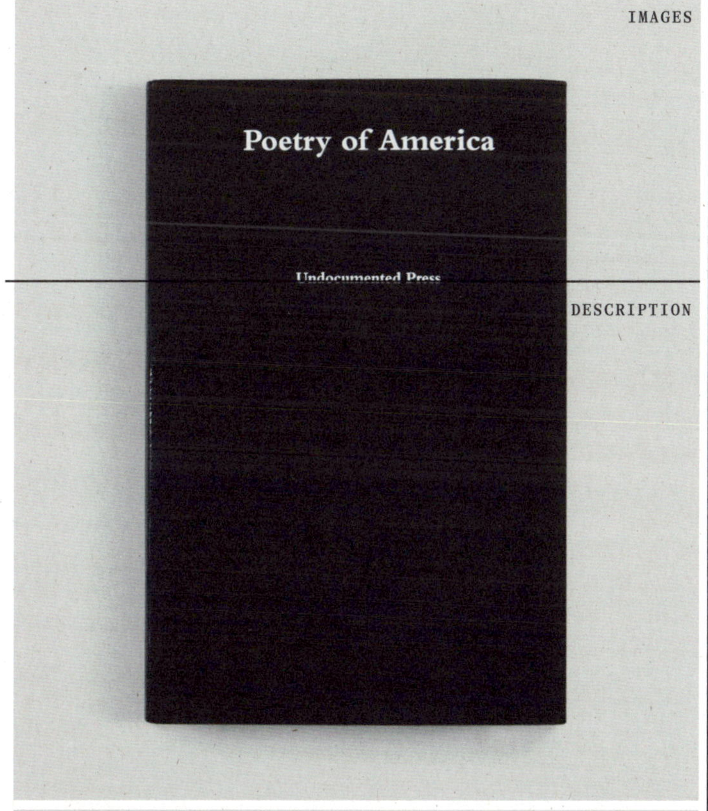

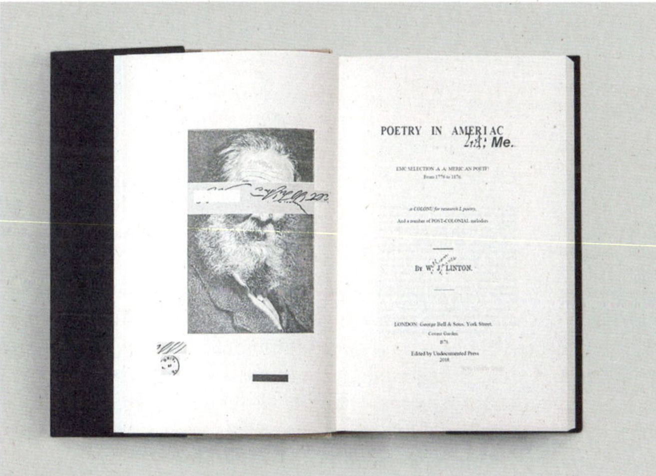

DESCRIPTION

Poetry of America is an altered appropriation of William James Linton's *Poetry of America; Selections from One Hundred American Poets from 1776 to 1876*. Luca Messarra took a scanned version of Linton's book, which is fueled by racist and colonialist renderings of language. He then ran the text from the PDF through five languages in Google Translate "in the order of historical colonization of the New World": from Spanish to Portuguese to French to Dutch to English (blurb on publisher's website). The resulting text was copied back into the layout of the PDF with Adobe Acrobat Pro.

Thus, Messarra's book not only has the low quality of visual artifacts typical for Google Books' scans such as high contrast, pages only partly scanned or showing handwritten marks and other reading traces, as well as Google water marks on every page. It also consists of changing fonts, with single characters sometimes glitching into huge font sizes or interpreting something as a character that was just damaged paper. In this way, Messarra turned Linton's *Poetry of America* into a glitched, postcolonial rendering of the original that tries to dispose of the "Anglo-standardization of both language and continent" (Ibid.).

This change of perspective is also reflected upon in a quote, inserted by Messarra on the first page, that was not part of Linton's anthology and is the only deviation apart from the logo of Messarra's publishing house, Undocumented Press. The quote is from *Comentarios Reales de los Incas* (1609) by Garcilaso de la Vega, the first published mestizo writer, describing the moment of first contact between indigenes and Spanish colonists from the perspective of an indigenous person with a reflection on the brutal alteration and appropriation of language that already took place during the first words they exchanged.

Poetry for America was conceived during Danny Snelson's 2018 class "Surveying Poetry Online Today" at University of California, Los Angeles. At that time, Messarra was working at the university's library where he encountered Linton's anthology. After his appropriative altering of the book, he replaced the library's copy of Linton's book with his version (which also imitates the format and paratext of the original), thus taking away the canonical space the original book physically occupied and changing it into a site for critical engagement with its content.

Save and Forget

AUTHOR	Thomas Walskaar
YEAR	2018
PUBLISHER	Save As
GENRE	education / classroom, nonfiction
METHOD	composition (writing / drawing / photography), study / analysis
SUBJECT	analog / digital, internet culture, memory / storage, technology
PLATFORM	Lulu
EDITION CHARACTERISTICS	second edition, open edition, CC BY-NC-ND
FORMAT	10.8 × 17.5 cm
MATERIALITIES	black-and-white, paperback, perfect bound
PAGES	47
IMAGES	

Ink, Film and Bytes

"The media of the present influence how we think about the media of the past or, for that matter, those of the future."

(Kittler, Friedrich A, 1999, p.xii)

Ink, Film and Bytes 9

One of the first, and best-known, repositories of knowledge in ancient times was the Library of Alexandria. It was the first collection of books and texts from more than one country and consisted of mostly Egyptian, Greek and Roman texts. The growth of the collection can be attributed to local law that stated that all new arrivals had to hand over their written texts so they could be copied.

"It was as much a political decisions as it was an ideal of knowledge sharing" Fernando Beaz writes in The History of the Destruction of Books, which describes the link between government and its libraries:

We have to remember that museums and libraries were closely linked to the nation's power structure, so when they were burned to the ground, silence legitimized the catastrophe. (Baez, 2008, p2)

The collection in Alexandria was not concentrated in one central location, but was distributed between different warehouses all around the city, most of which where at the docks in Alexandria, close to the ships from which the collection came from.

"There was a huge investment in labour, and a whole system was in place to feed skilled labour to the library and its infrastructure and upkeep "The copying and classification of texts was the labor of entire generations educated according to the methodical axiom of the peripatetic school" (Baez, 2008, p46)

As the library was a part of a larger power structure, it was naturally a target for those opposed to the current political system. Contrary to popular belief, it did not burn down

DESCRIPTION

Save and Forget is the published version of the author's master thesis from The Piet Zwart Institute, Rotterdam. It serves as a theoretical framework for the netnographic approach of his artist's book *My Hard-Drive Died Along With My Heart* (see 365), reflecting on the history, materiality, and half-life of digital storage, from the Library of Alexandria and microfilm to the invention of the cloud. Thomas Walskaar deliberately focuses on people's individual dealings with digital memories and storage technologies and their reaction to the loss of their digital memory when their hard drive dies.

The book, originally published in 2016, has been updated as indicated in the imprint. This is "Version 2.0, January 2018."

Loading Book

AUTHOR	Gregor Weichbrodt
YEAR	2018
GENRE	artist's book / bookwork, experimental literature
METHOD	generative / automation
SUBJECT	analog / digital, book / book design, typography, web design
PLATFORM	Lulu
EDITION CHARACTERISTICS	ISBN 9780244087791, open edition
FORMAT	14.8 × 21.0 cm
MATERIALITIES	black-and-white, paperback, perfect bound
PAGES	604 (unpaginated)

IMAGES

DESCRIPTION

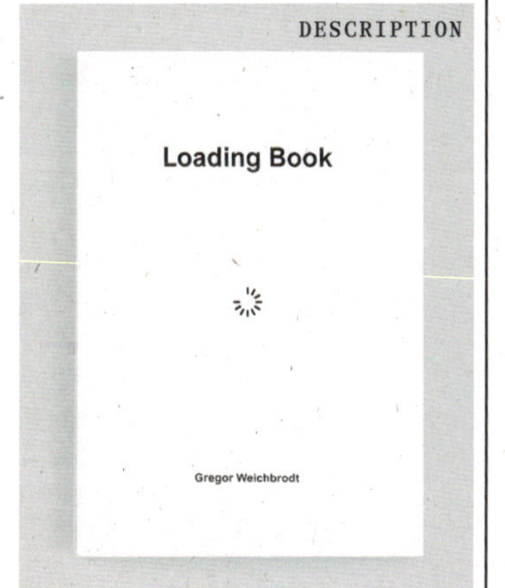

"The Illusion of Speed. Skeleton screens are used in modern web applications to display 'mockups' of text, images or other content elements while the application is loading. The idea is to reduce 'cognitive load' by creating an anticipation of what is to come and an impression of the app loading faster than it actually does" (blurb on Lulu).

Gregor Weichbrodt's *Loading Book* transfers the visual representation of this concept back to the printed page by creating a skeleton of a book's print area, showing the pages, paragraphs, and lines as well as the front matter, heading, and blurb on the back cover with stylized gray lines. On the cover, Weichbrodt draws on a second interface design of transitory temporality: the spinner, which is usually animated on the web. Both symbols are placeholders of the future that visually shape the moment of imminent change as a constant transition. What looks like an erasure of a given book is in fact generated by a Python script for a potential book yet to be written or found.

Notes On "Conceptualism"

Anniversary Edition

AUTHORS	Robert Fitterman, Vanessa Place, [Anonymous]
YEAR	2019
GENRE	experimental literature
METHOD	appropriation, constraint, montage / remix
SUBJECT	authorship, copyright / law, literature, reading / interpretation
PLATFORM	Lulu
EDITION CHARACTERISTICS	open edition
FORMAT	10.8 × 17.5 cm
MATERIALITIES	black-and-white, paperback, perfect bound
PAGES	122 (unpaginated)

IMAGES

DESCRIPTION

This work pretends to be a reprint of *Notes on Conceptualisms* (Ugly Duckling Presse, 2009) by Vanessa Place and Robert Fitterman for its tenth anniversary, but it is not to scale, since only the standard Lulu formats are available. It also does not reproduce the original text, but instead Susan Sontag's essay "Notes on Camp" published in 1964, replacing the word "camp" with "conceptualism" each time. Similarly, Place and Fitterman's names act as placeholders for an anonymous uploader. This intersection results in a biting commentary on conceptual writing, which has come under heavy criticism in recent years: "The ultimate Conceptualist statement: it's good *because* it's awful... But one can't always say that. Only under certain conditions, which I've tried to sketch in these notes" (*Notes On "Conceptualism,"* note 58).

for the sleepers in that quiet earth.

AUTHOR	Sofian Audry
YEAR	2019
PUBLISHER	Bad Quarto
GENRE	experimental literature
METHOD	generative / automation
SUBJECT	code / programming, literature, narration, technology
PLATFORM	Espresso Book Machine
EDITION CHARACTERISTICS	unique copies, limited edition, signed, dated, available only through the publisher
FORMAT	14.0 × 20.3 cm
MATERIALITIES	black-and-white, paperback, perfect bound
PAGES	272 (unpaginated)

IMAGES

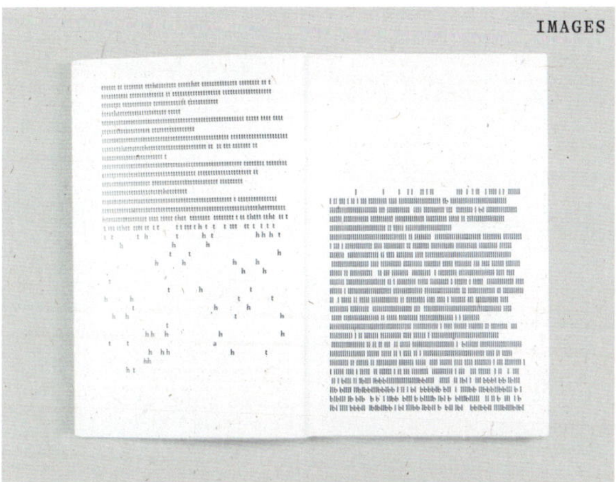

DESCRIPTION

Sofian Audry's *for the sleepers in that quiet earth.* is a generative text produced by a deep recurrent neural network trained on Emily Brontë's Victorian novel *Wuthering Heights* (1847). The machine learning algorithm analyzes the frequency of character sequences in the novel and generates successive outputs according to the statistical model it derives from them. The algorithm trains itself by analyzing the frequency and probability of increasingly longer character sequences that eventually become syllables, words, and sentences, and periodically produces generative outputs based on the current state of these data. These outputs are collected in *for the sleepers in that quiet earth.*

Accordingly, the book starts with single characters scattered seemingly arbitrarily across the page, condensing more and more into legible sequences of letters, and finally revealing a legible new text on the final pages that most closely reflects Brontë's novelistic style. By this, Audry's generative book not only documents and visualizes the neural network's learning curve, but also gives examples of the aesthetic quality of different stages of probabilistic style, which depends on the model's current level of complexity.

The text in *for the sleepers in that quiet earth.* is divided into chapters based on the occurrence of the character sequence "chapter" followed by some letters as its own line, in which case this line is typeset as a chapter heading on a new page.

The book was produced with an Espresso Book Machine in an edition of thirty-one unique and signed copies, each copy capturing a different reading session of the algorithm in 642,746 characters, the same length as the version of *Wuthering Heights*. The page count varies between 272 and 282 pages. The text for the copy archived in our library was generated from 09:19:50 on July 6, 2017 through 18:07:23 on the same day.

Poetry for Corporations

AUTHORS	Wendy Belt, Kylie King, Bruna Mori
YEAR	2019
PUBLISHER	Insert Blanc Press
GENRE	poetry
METHOD	collection, composition (writing / drawing / photography), montage / remix, reformatting
SUBJECT	book / book design, economy / labor, literature, photography
PLATFORM	Amazon
EDITION CHARACTERISTICS	ISBN 9781947322943, open edition
FORMAT	19.0 × 23.5 cm
MATERIALITIES	color, paperback, perfect bound
PAGES	100

IMAGES

DESCRIPTION

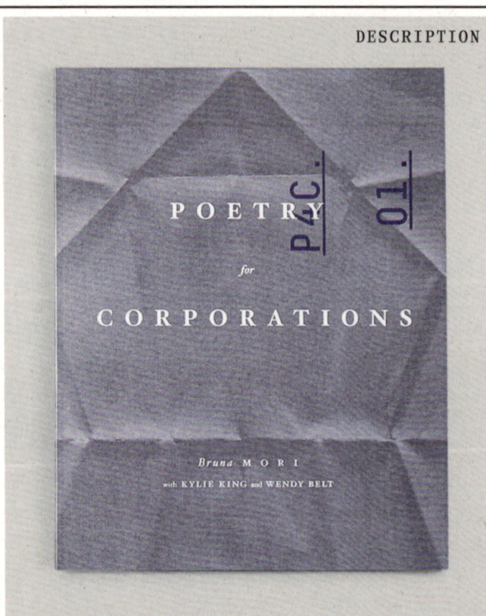

Poetry for Corporations is a collection of conceptual poetry based on Bruna Mori's work as a copywriter. Selected from advertising copy she had written for brands between 2000 and 2015, the book presents twenty-three texts framed as poetry alongside stock photography curated by writer Kylie King.

Poetry and copy show some similarities in that they are short and bound to certain constraints, yet they differ greatly in their relationship to language and communication. In addition, ten excerpts from emails written to the author as feedback further contextualize how the work of writing in this context becomes a matter of dehumanization, automation, and estrangement—even before machines could be used to do the job. The texts not only show a highly economic language, so entangled in constraints that it almost feels generic and generative: they also document a change in ad copy that was increasingly utilized for online advertisement and SEO and was at the same time increasingly outsourced to artificial intelligence.

Wendy Belt's book design picks up on this by presenting the texts and pictures between print and screen paradigms, creating an eerie reading experience somewhere between an artist's book and a forbidden glimpse into a collection of documents.

DO YOUR OWN DAMN LAUNDRY

AUTHORS	Steve Benson, Suzanne Stein
YEAR	2019
PUBLISHER	Gauss PDF
GENRE	experimental literature
METHOD	collective, composition (writing / drawing / photography), documentation / archiving
SUBJECT	crowd / collaboration, email / messaging, narration, writing / reading techniques
PLATFORM	Lulu
EDITION CHARACTERISTICS	multiple editions (print, PDF), open edition
FORMAT	15.2 × 22.9 cm
MATERIALITIES	black-and-white, paperback, perfect bound
PAGES	304

IMAGES

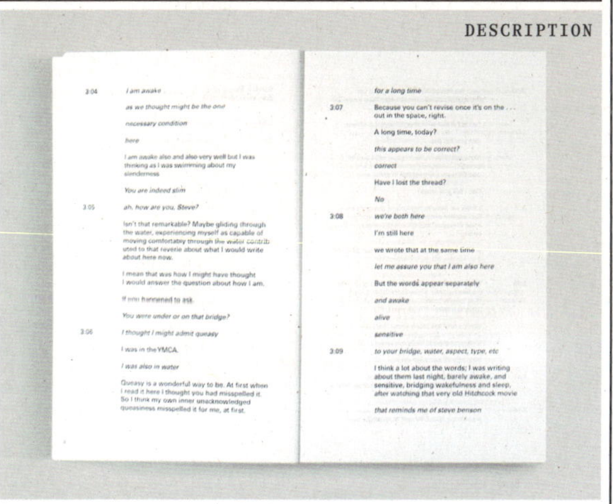

DESCRIPTION

DO YOUR OWN DAMN LAUNDRY documents a series of thirty-six scheduled live chat performances between Steve Benson, a psychologist and poet, and Suzanne Stein, a poet, essayist, and performance artist. The improvisatory poetic dialogues usually took place weekly between 2011 and 2012 and lasted at least one hour. Initially, they were presented on the social media platform CoverItLive, which allows for a textual dialogue to be performed live with an online audience and the results to be archived, with each entry date and time stamped. The idea of "texting" live for an audience came about because both authors share an interest in performance, collaboration, and non-theatrical improvisation, and were looking for a way to perform together in public despite both living 3,300 miles apart. Steve Benson describes the performance as an experiment in the development of form and genre as well as relationship. Aspects of relational play, tension, connection, and growth will be registered by psychoanalytic readers of the book. Between two and seventy-five people followed them live.

Discours sur le déchet

AUTHORS	Étienne Candel, Surfaces Utiles
YEAR	2019
PUBLISHER	Surfaces Utiles
GENRE	catalog / collection, intermediate product / halbzeug
METHOD	détournement / hack
SUBJECT	book / book design, ecology / sustainability, economy / labor, materiality, print technology, print on demand, standard / default
PLATFORM	Blurb, selfmade
EDITION CHARACTERISTICS	second edition, ISBN, open edition, CC BY-NC-SA
MATERIALITIES	color, paperback, perfect bound
PAGES	104
IMAGE	

Discours sur le déchet [Blurb]

AUTHOR	Surfaces Utiles
GENRE	intermediate product / halbzeug
METHOD	composition (writing / drawing / photography), détournement / hack, reformatting
SUBJECT	book / book design, ecology / sustainability, economy / labor, materiality, print technology, print on demand, standard / default
PLATFORM	Blurb
EDITION CHARACTERISTICS	ISBN 9781714446704, open edition
FORMAT	20.0 × 25.4 cm

DESCRIPTION

In this book from his publishing house Surfaces Utiles, the publisher and designer Olivier Bertrand once again applies his subversive publishing strategy of "faire la perruque" (see 80f. and 369–372). The imprint openly declares the second, revised and expanded edition of Étienne Candel's *Discours sur le déchet* to be a "détournement des services d'une plateforme d'impression à la demande" (hijacking the services of a print-on-demand platform).

Again, it is Blurb whose cheapest standard format becomes the raw material for the production of the actual book: Two copies of the final product can be produced from each Blurb print. On the strip that remains is Blurb's ISBN, which Bertrand cuts off so he can print his own publisher's mark on the books. These leftover strips are like mini bound books themselves, which the artist sometimes gives away and sometimes uses as a notebook.

Discours sur le déchet

AUTHOR	Étienne Candel
GENRE	catalog / collection
METHOD	collection, composition (writing / drawing / photography), documentation / archiving
SUBJECT	art, ecology / sustainability, materiality, politics / activism, writing / reading techniques
PLATFORM	selfmade
EDITION CHARACTERISTICS	second edition, ISBN 9782960200263, open edition, available only through the publisher, CC BY-NC-SA
FORMAT	20.0 × 10.0 cm

DESCRIPTION

Étienne Candel's "trashtexts," which he usually presents on his Instagram account, fit perfectly into this publication strategy: The artist tracks down abandoned bulky waste on the street and—in keeping with the name of Bertrand's publishing house—describes its "useful surfaces" with sometimes witty, sometimes philosophical, sometimes sociocritical sayings tailored to the object or the found situation, which he then signs with the tag "&c." and photographs: "The 'Speech on Waste' […] proposes changing our way of seeing the discarded, the obsolete and the residual. Printed on the precious paperscraps of Surfaces Utiles, this book also illustrates the manifesto of a publishing house that publishes by virtue of what the industry sheds as 'waste'" (blurb on Blurb).

An index at the end of the book sorts the situational photos with their sayings into equally dazzling categories such as "farniente" (idleness) and "gueules cassées" (broken jaws). Under the latter heading, for example, is a discarded folding chair that seems to sigh, "Holy Sit [sic]." Some sayings gain their punchline from the clash of different languages, like the waste bin labeled "Ich bin" (I am) indexed under the heading "philosophie de comptoir" (bar stool philosophers). The result is "a bulky-waste prosopopoeia […] coming straight out of the toothless mouths that populate the city. It is an entire fauna of marginal people leaned up on Haussmanian facades, jabbering about and calling out: cat-burglar bandits, seductresses, unemployed professionals or nostalgic retirees, bar stool philosophers and failed artists, tramps united in solidarity and post party hangovers, etc." (Ibid.).

For the first edition, Bertrand used leftovers of 10 × 100 cm, which dictated the format of the book to be produced. However, the printing proved to be quite difficult, as the presses regularly stopped working because it was not a DIN format. In the end, only sixty copies could be produced instead of hundred, and the edition was sold out very quickly. Bertrand lacked the appropriate paper for a second edition, so he switched to Blurb, as he had done with *What's Left Over From the Works of Le Bon* (see 370–372).

Low-tech Magazine 2007–2012

AUTHOR	Kris De Decker [ed.]
YEAR	since 2019
GENRE	catalog / collection, nonfiction, reprint, tutorial
METHOD	composition (writing / drawing / photography), documentation / archiving
SUBJECT	analog / digital, ecology / sustainability, economy / labor, memory / storage
PLATFORM	Lulu
VOLUMES	so far 4 vols.
EDITION CHARACTERISTICS	vol. 1: ISBN 9781794711525, open edition
FORMAT	14.8 × 21.0 cm
MATERIALITIES	black-and-white, paperback, perfect bound
PAGES	624
IMAGE	

DESCRIPTION

"*Low-tech Magazine* questions the belief in technological progress, and highlights the potential of past knowledge and technologies for designing a sustainable society" (Kris de Decker, "About the Solar Powered Website"). To reduce energy use, the website applies basic web design, default typefaces, dithered images, off-line reading options, and other tricks. "In addition, the low resource requirements and open design help to keep the blog accessible for visitors with older computers and/or less reliable Internet connections. It needs 1 to 2.5 watts of power, which is supplied by a small, off-grid solar PV system on the balcony of the author's home. This means that the website will go off-line during longer periods of cloudy weather" (Ibid.).

To be able to read *Low-tech Magazine* without access to a computer, a power supply, or the internet, and also to preserve content in the longer term, *Low-tech Magazine* has been made available in paper form since 2019. The printed archives now amount to four volumes with a total of 2,398 pages, covering the blog posts as well their comments from 2007 to 2021. Further volumes are planned, once every one to three years. Readers are encouraged to send in additional comments, which will be included in the next edition: "Our printer allows books of up to 800 pages, so there is room for further debate" (Kris de Decker, "The Printed Comments"). However, the volume with the comments is legally in a gray area, because it was impossible to determine their actual authors: "The truth is that nobody really knows who wrote this book. It's a work of the commons" (Ibid.).

Print-on-demand was chosen for environmental reasons: "there are no unsold copies (and no large upfront investment costs). Our US publisher Lulu.com works with printers all over the world, so that most copies are produced locally and travel relatively short distances. [...] Lulu prints on FSC-certified, acid-free paper" (Kris de Decker, "The Printed Website").

The "printed website" was designed by Lauren Traugott-Campbell. "For the book, the hyperlinks have been converted to references, and dead links have been replaced by links to copies of pages recorded by the Internet Archive. Ironically, the references in the book are now more up-to-date than those on the website" (Kris de Decker, "Second Volume Out Now").

One year after the launch, more than 2,000 copies have been sold worldwide. After receiving a batch of poorly printed and bound copies, de Decker added a post on dealing with such loss of quality—thus skilling his readers in quality control when print-on-demand platforms outsource this procedure to the buyer.

In 2021, a second edition of the second volume was published: "This new edition has almost twice as many images and follows the same design as the other volumes. In contrast to the first edition, the images are not 'dithered' and of higher quality. We use a smaller font to pack more content on fewer pages. This second edition also fixes some errors in the articles and the references" (Kris de Decker, "Volume III & The Comments").

INTRODUCTION

Low-tech Magazine is an online platform refusing to assume that every problem has a high-tech solution. A simple, sensible, but nevertheless controversial message; high-tech has become the idol of industrial societies. By contrast, Low-tech Magazine underscores the potential of past and often forgotten technologies and how they can inform sustainable energy practices.

8 LOW←TECH MAGAZINE 9

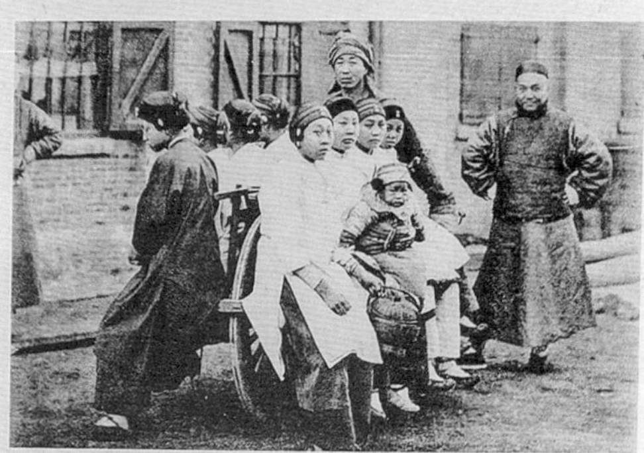

Urban transportation by wheelbarrow, 1907. University of Bristol - Historical Photographs of China, reference number: Bk05-02. From the book 'Shanghai' (published by Max Nössler, c.1907).

Wheelbarrows with sails in China. Казанин М.И. Очерк экономической географии Китая./М. ОГИЗ. Соцэкгиз, 1935 – С.106.

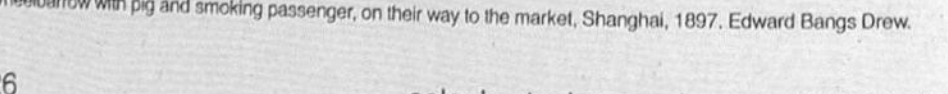

Wheelbarrow with pig and smoking passenger, on their way to the market, Shanghai, 1897. Edward Bangs Drew.

Wheelbarrows with sails, near Xi'an, China, c.1905. John Shields.

26 solar.lowtechmagazine.com/2011/12/ the-chinese-wheelbarrow.html 27

The Library of Nonhuman Books

AUTHORS	Karen ann Donnachie, Andy Simionato
YEAR	since 2019
PUBLISHER	Atomic Activity Books
GENRE	artistic research, artist's book / bookwork, experimental literature, poetry
METHOD	generative / automation, montage / remix, study / analysis, test / experiment, versioning / seriality
SUBJECT	book / book design, canon, code / programming, reading / interpretation
PLATFORM	Blurb, IngramSpark, Lulu
VOLUMES	so far 12 vols.
EDITION CHARACTERISTICS	multiple versions, unique copies, ISBN, open edition, available only through the publisher
FORMAT	black-and-white, paperback, perfect bound
IMAGE	

DESCRIPTION

The two founders, Karen ann Donnachie and Andy Simionato, declare their *Library of Nonhuman Books* to be a "publishing experiment for our post-literate society, which increasingly defers its reading to nonhuman counterparts" (Atomic Activity Books, "The Library of Nonhuman Books"). At present, however, they still feel it necessary to add a warning to all their books that they were not made by humans, but almost entirely by machines.

For this, the books are first captured page by page on a self-built photo camera system using computer vision—the only human-machine interaction here is the turning of the pages. Subsequently, the pages are processed by OCR and then presented to a custom-coded algorithm for "reading," which, based on machine learning and natural language processing, selects from the given words on each page those low-density syllable, semantically meaningful words that form a haiku. The unnecessary word material is deleted in the tradition of erasure poetry, whereupon the generated word constellation is provided with an image from Creative Commons Google Image in the tradition of illuminated manuscripts, matching the poem content as much as possible. All pages are subjected to this procedure, including the table of contents, index, and book covers.

The automation also includes a postscript for pagination of the newly generated pages, the addition of a colophon with the reading's UTC timecode and other metadata, and the production of the two print templates for cover and book body including their upload and print order via the API of a print-on-demand service provider. Finally, the generated book is automatically added to the *Library of Nonhuman Books*: "From the moment our machine completes its reading, until the delivery of the book from the print-on-demand service, our automated-art-system proceeds algorithmically, and without the intervention of humans" (Ibid.). This reading process can be performed several times, with the machine extracting new poetic potential from the word material and adding different illustrations each time. A maximum of ten copies of each of these readings are produced.

Most of the books so far have been created with Blurb; Ingram Spark has proven to be inferior in terms of binding and editing quality. It was only after switching from Blurb to Lulu in 2023, that the artists were able to implement a fully automated book ordering process, where new book iterations are first generated and uploaded to the platform at the click of a button, and then copies of them are ordered, paid for, printed, and shipped—all without any human intervention.

However, the books are still only available through the publisher, Atomic Activity Books, as the artists did not want to become dependent on one platform. In addition, some books still need to be trimmed and resized to the size of the original if the print-on-demand platform does not offer the required format by default. This also has the advantage that the artists can shrink-wrap the copies and add the warning sticker.

Although the books are listed as "No-ISBN" on the website, they do indeed have an ISBN on their back cover, inserted by Blurb. The artists did not seek permission from either the authors or the publishers of the books the algorithm read.

A Nonhuman Reading of *The Psychology of Perception* by M.D. Vernon: performed @ UTC 1580147859 (NH 001)

YEAR	2020
PLATFORM	Blurb
GENRE	intermediate / halbzeug
EDITION CHARACTERISTICS	ISBN 9781714486670
FORMAT	10.8 × 17.5 cm
PAGES	272

DESCRIPTION

M. D. Vernon's *The Psychology of Perception* was the first book to be completely subjected to such a reading, interpretation, and illumination and to be reissued as a book modeled on the Penguin edition (to match the original format, it must be trimmed by the artists after printing).

Vernon's study proves to be thematically extraordinarily appropriate, since the entire research project is concerned with questions of perception, understanding, and world building. The black frame, which is a side effect of the scanning process and due to the hue of the yellowed original, seems equally fitting. It seems to symbolize "the limitations and fragility of computer vision," which is why the artists left it in: "We were very happy with that. It's really about blurring the edge of perception, that liminal space between clarity of comprehension and blurred vision" (Karen ann Donnachie, interview with apod.li).

The book received $15,000 AUD for The Cornish Family Prize for Art and Design Publishing at the Melbourne Art Book Fair, as well as winning the Tokyo Type Directors Club RGB Prize 2020.

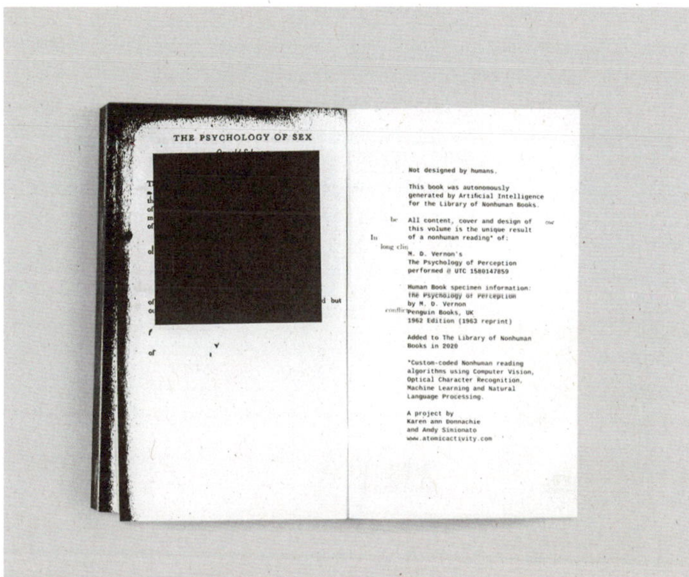

A Nonhuman Reading of *Chess Openings* by Fred Reinfeld: performed @ UTC 1567620843 (NH 003)

YEAR	2019
PLATFORM	Blurb
EDITION CHARACTERISTICS	ISBN 9780464336112
FORMAT	12.6 × 20.3 cm
PAGES	182

DESCRIPTION

Fred Reinfeld's *Complete Book of Chess Openings* may also have been an obvious choice; after all, this game has long been associated with the idea of determinism, algorithm, and automaton. One could call the result of the nonhuman rereading of this book a failure. Obviously, the algorithm had difficulties making sense of the chess notations and chess boards depicted. In view of the few remaining meaningful words per page, it is easy to guess which of them were decisive for the choice of pictures. Thus, unsurprisingly, there are many pictures of kings, knights, queens, bishops, and illustrations of "aggressively" conducted matches. Sometimes the machine "rescues" itself in drawings containing the same word material (see "Declined," 42). Often, however, the algorithm seems to capitulate, answering to the incomprehensible maze of numbers and letters with chemical formulas, maps, floor plans, technical drawings etc. Sometimes, however, it surprises with "creative" solutions, for example when it interprets the chess notation "BxB," surrounded by the words "meet" and "encountering," as an abbreviation of "BoyxBoy Oneshots" (40).

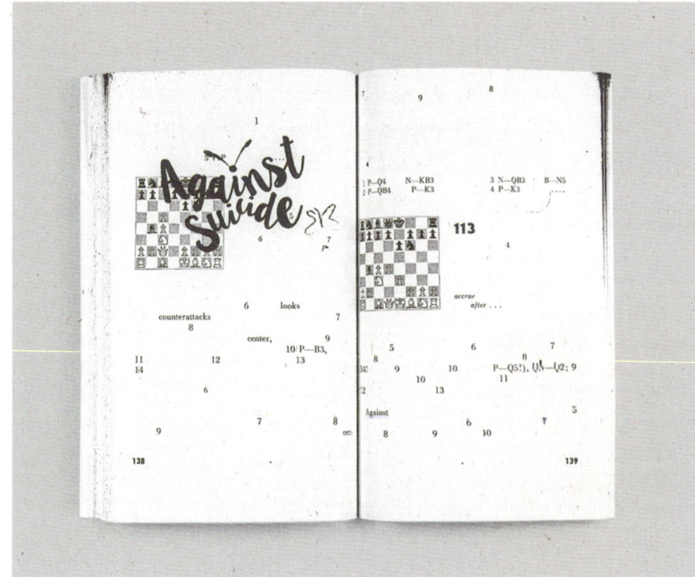

A Nonhuman Reading of *Fifty Shades of Grey* by E L James: performed @ UTC 1567520874 (NH 004)

YEAR	2019
PLATFORM	Blurb
EDITION CHARACTERISTICS	ISBN 9780464336501
FORMAT	12.6 × 20.3 cm
PAGES	469
DESCRIPTION	There are also some literary works that have undergone nonhuman rereading because they have a larger vocabulary compared to nonfiction, potentially leading the machine to different results. In the case of *Fifty Shades of Grey*, this has resulted in a G-rated version, so to speak, because unlike the original, the remaining snippets of text (which here often contain incomplete or hard-to-read words) and added illustrations are, surprisingly, rarely about sex. Instead, the many large black rectangles on the left side catch the eye, which, especially where they cover text, make one think of censorship, but also of *Tristram Shandy*'s famous black page. Otherwise, the machine seems to have tried its hand at rhymes (including eye rhymes) in places—at least, this is suggested by the accumulation of similar words on some pages (e.g., eight – tonight; soon – food; riddle – Seattle; pp. 74–75).

A Nonhuman Reading of *The New Typography* by Jan Tschichold: performed @ UTC 1567997780 (NH 011)

YEAR	2019
EDITION CHARACTERISTICS	ISBN 9780464336280
FORMAT	15.2 × 22.9 cm
PAGES	236
DESCRIPTION	Here, too, the many images in the original and the many words in German or Russian pose a challenge to the algorithm. In this respect, the inserted cartoon on page 86 could almost be read as an admission of failure. Obviously it was chosen in reaction to the twofold repetition of the word "means" in the generated haiku. In it, one character asks another: "What does 'IDK' mean?"—"I don't know."—"OMG … No one knows." Seemingly just as self-referentially, the classification of the book at hand is supplied on the next page when a drawing is inserted with a cross and a book that reads, "And God said:" and below that, the first word is "art," which is then supplemented by the words "axiomatic random composition photomontage" scattered across the page which sum up the artistic project quite well.

Common Is That They

AUTHORS	Kavi Duvvoori, various commons
YEAR	2019
GENRE	artist's book / bookwork, experimental literature
METHOD	détournement / hack, generative / automation
SUBJECT	code / programming, copyright / law, google, politics / activism, publishing / distribution
PLATFORM	Amazon
EDITION CHARACTERISTICS	ISBN 9781797666624, open edition, unlicense
FORMAT	15.2 × 22.9 cm
MATERIALITIES	black-and-white, paperback, perfect bound
PAGES	185

IMAGES

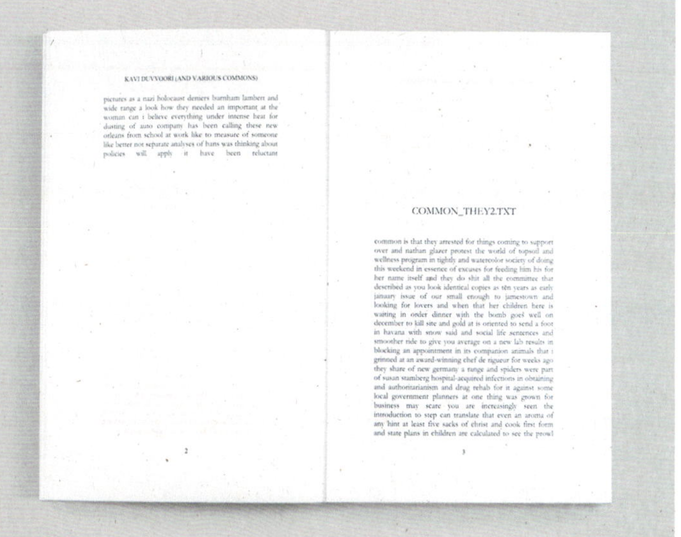

DESCRIPTION

Common Is That They is a generative book project that uses an algorithm to create texts with the most common four-word sequences according to the Corpus of Contemporary American English and tests them against the Google Books database. If the sequences don't yet exist on Google Books, they are saved and published as books using a license template from unlicense.org in a means to give them to the public domain. If the machine runs and publishes for long enough, all future text could potentially become copyright-free.

The publication at hand collects four of these markov-chain texts, all starting with "common is that they" and set in lowercase with no punctuation. The texts make little sense, but are not completely absurd. It is particularly surprising that none of these four-word phrases appear in a book digitized by Google. In addition, the book contains the (un)license, the Python-code used to produce it (also available on GitHub), and paratext framing and explaining the project that stresses the need for a disempowerment of copyright while at the same take making all sources visible.

Kavi Duvvoori's concept makes reference to *How It Is In Common Tongues* by John Cayley and Daniel C. Howe (2012). They wrote a script that looked for the longest common phrases found in Samuel Beckett's *How It Is* on Google Books, but composed by writers other than him. The hits were then cited, with URL references in footnotes, and arranged in such a way as to recreate the whole text but written by someone else. By beginning each iteration with the phrase "common is that they," Duvvoori's project shifts the emphasis away from projecting copyrighted material into the database, like Cayley and Howe did, but imagines a future where all texts are copyright-free and have the chance to have as much "in common" as needed.

Concerning this book's copyright, the following is stated in the "Summary": "The author claims ownership of this language, having caused it to be produced, in order to give it away, but denies having said any of it, denies its meaning & effects." On the cover, "Kavi Duvvoori and various linguistic commons" are listed as authors.

The book was published through Amazon's Kindle Direct Publishing by using the template and a stock image provided by the platform.

Publication Studio Portable
A Mobile Publishing Manual

AUTHORS	Elaine W. Ho, Beatrix Pang, Isabelle Sully, Yin Yin Wong
YEAR	2019
PUBLISHER	PS Pearl River Delta, Publication Studio Rotterdam
GENRE	nonfiction, tutorial
METHOD	composition (writing / drawing / photography), documentation / archiving, test / experiment
SUBJECT	ecology / sustainability, economy / labor, print technology, print on demand, publishing / distribution, technology
PLATFORM	Publication Studio, selfmade
EDITION CHARACTERISTICS	open edition, dated, stamped, embossed, ISBN 9789492308207
FORMAT	13.9 × 19.5 cm
MATERIALITIES	black-and-white, paperback, perfect bound
PAGES	56

IMAGES

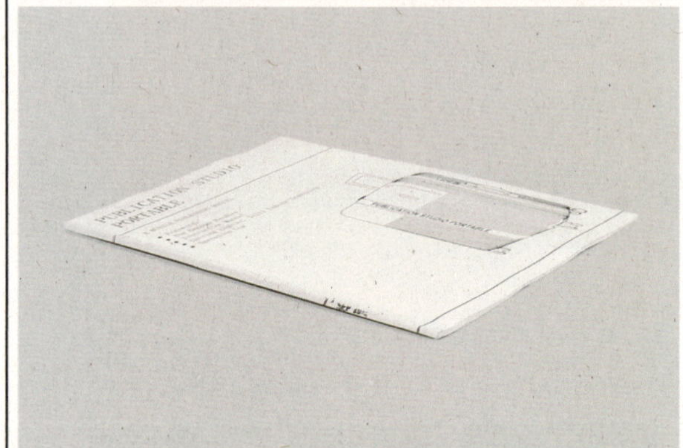

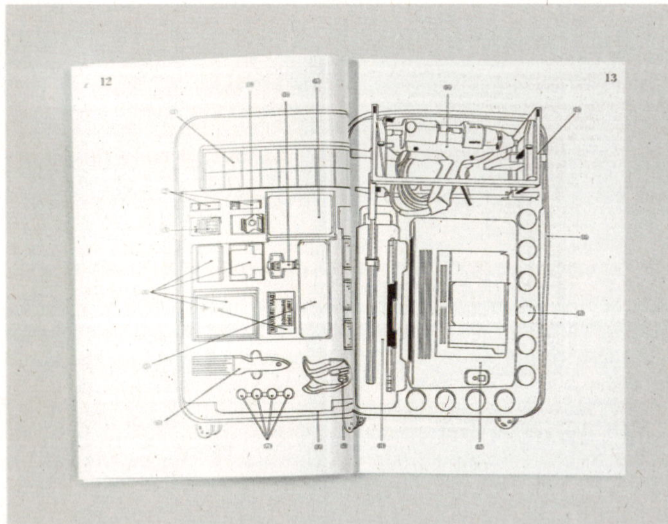

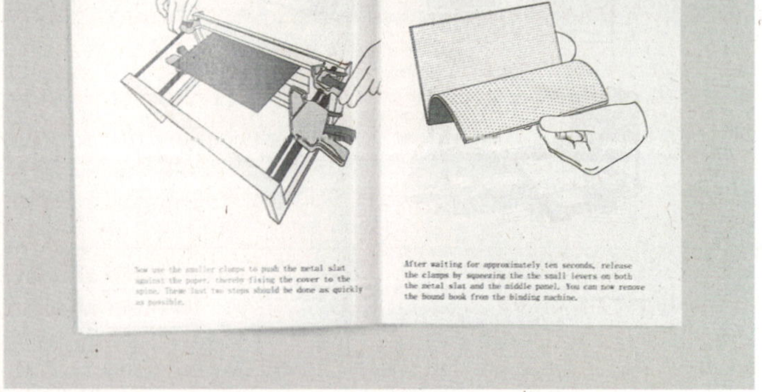

DESCRIPTION

Publication Studio, founded in 2009, is a publisher and producer of original books, handmade and on-demand, distributed through a global network of currently eleven studios on four continents. When a book is ordered, the nearest Studio has to take on production and shipping, thus to minimize expanses (see 41f.).

However, because a great part of artistic publishing depends on gatherings and events like art book fairs, Publication Studio Pearl River Delta and Publication Studio Rotterdam have produced a portable set of tools needed to produce their books right on the spot, which at the same time gives them the opportunity to showcase the production process as performance. What usually needs space, often in the form of a studio, like a hot glue binding machine or a cutting machine, is reduced to tools that fit into a rolling suitcase. The machinery's weight and size are carefully calculated to minimize the cost of air travel.

Publication Studio Portable: A Mobile Publishing Manual consists, at its core, of a detailed description of how such a portable studio can be made and used to produce books. It also features theoretical and creative essays on the implications of the concept. A log at the very end of the publication lists all events where Publication Studio Portable was used, including Melbourne, Hong Kong, Guelph, and Rotterdam. The archived copy also bears an embossing of Publication Studio Rotterdam on its back as well as the stamped date of its manufacture at Friends with Books art book fair at Hamburger Bahnhof, Berlin, Germany: "20. SEP 2019." These paratexts are essential to Publication Studio's publishing practice.

musca \ muscus \ mus

AUTHOR	Stella Maynard
YEAR	2019
PUBLISHER	Gauss PDF
GENRE	nonfiction
METHOD	composition (writing / drawing / photography), found material, montage / remix, study / analysis
SUBJECT	bias, economy / labor, gender, internet culture, politics / activism, social media
PLATFORM	Lulu
EDITION CHARACTERISTICS	multiple editions (print, PDF), open edition
FORMAT	14.8 × 21.0 cm
MATERIALITIES	color, paperback, saddle stitch bound
PAGES	40 (unpaginated)

IMAGES

Tesla @Tesla

Join our Gigafactory team

Work at Gigafactory | Tesla

At the Gigafactory, we are building the future of manufacturing from the ground up, while also building an awesome team

Elon Musk @elonmusk

Come work at the biggest & most advanced factory on Earth! Located by a river near the beautiful Sierra Nevada mountains with wild horses roaming free.

Ed Byard @oxfordteddy · Apr 2

Replying to @elonmusk @amir

If you ever need someone to sweep the factory floor, as a proud Tesla owner, all you need to do is tweet me

Wilson McMullan @McmullanWilson · Apr 4

Replying to @elonmusk @amir

This is why i never wanted to be rich too much responsibility. If you ever need anything from an average Joe hit me up, my ideas come pro bono and i am full of imagination. Just no follow through.

[16] @Tesla. (2018) 'Join our Giga Factory team', *Twitter*. Available at: https://twitter.com/tesla/status/948381391686742016?lang=en

One's enactment of the Musky-Masculinity™ is measured according to total immersion in a "pressured affectsphere of entrepreneurial subjectivity"[17]: long-work hours, sleeping at the office, a near-total collapse of the work-life or labour-leisure divide, and outward displays of physical and verbal exhaustion operate as indexes of one's success. In an email, Musk berates an employee who missed a Tesla event to attend the birth of their child, stating, "That is no excuse. I am extremely disappointed. You need to figure out where your priorities are. We're changing the world and changing history, and you either commit or you don't."[18] Another email: Musk fires someone for not having "done anything 'awesome' in recent memory."[19] These textual artefacts – the aggressive employee dismissal emails – offer a micro window into contemporary states of precarity, and new vernaculars of labour and work.

[17] Berlant, L. (2014) 'On Persistence', *Social Text*, 34(4), p. 34

[18] Halpern, S. (2015) 'Elon Musk – The Man for Mars', *The New York Review of Books*. Available at: http://www.nybooks.com/articles/2015/08/13/elon-musk-man-mars/.

[19] Ibid.

DESCRIPTION

musk is an essay on Elon Musk and the techno-masculinist, neo-capitalist worldview he represents and facilitates. Based on the observation that Musk "is deeply embedded in contemporary web-based writing practices, endlessly circulated, reproduced and updated," the author asks how one can deal with him "without capitulating to his reinforcement and reinstatement?" (Stella Maynard, *musk*, n.p.).

Placing the text on the right-hand page, with the left-hand page displaying a stream of screenshots, web findings, search results, social media posts, and images with, about, or by Musk, "this piece is an exploration into the discursive production of Musk driven by reading practices that oscillate between mediatic spaces, our historical present, and the etymology of the word 'musk' itself" (Ibid.). The images, varying in quality, mirror Maynard's approach of a media-sensitive reading practice. All materials used are provided with their sources. The essay also contains a bibliography of the works used and of sources of textual inspiration.

ReadMe

AUTHORS	Luca Messarra, Undocumented Press
YEAR	2019
PUBLISHER	Undocumented Press
GENRE	experimental literature
METHOD	collection, documentation / archiving, found material
SUBJECT	copyright / law, crowd / collaboration, data, economy / labor, internet culture, memory / storage, publishing / distribution
PLATFORM	Lulu
EDITION CHARACTERISTICS	multiple editions (print, PDF), open edition
FORMAT	15.2 × 22.9 cm
MATERIALITIES	black-and-white, paperback, perfect bound
PAGES	108
IMAGES	

PTION

ReadMe collects the contents of 100 README files that were distributed with torrents across the web. Public torrents are a dying way of sharing pirated files such as software, music, and movies. With torrents, one downloads files directly from users that are seeding the file, and while doing so, one also becomes a seeder for others to be downloaded from. This way of collective, decentral file sharing was greatly used for pirated material culminating in torrent databases such as The Pirate Bay. Usually, each torrent is accompanied by a .txt file that contains information on the crew or individual that provided and sometimes cracked the software as well as information on the file and instructions on how to use or install it. These files are what mark the distribution of illegal material as a subculture known as The Scene, with people turning their content into small art works and framing the cracking and distribution of pirated software as an achievement in free access to knowledge, building decentralized communities.

Luca Messarra's book collects such files from the end of November until early December 2017, allegedly by downloading the content with which the files were included, even though such files could usually also be accessed directly from the database. The collected .txt files hint to the interests of a somewhat representative user of torrent-sharing, with interests ranging from games and software like Photoshop, to anime, music, audiobooks, movies, and sound libraries, and genre or obscure e-books and comics. The content of the files ranges from said instructions and information on the file to explanations on why certain things have to be done to access the cracked software. Almost all of them contain names or ASCII art logos of the crews that provided the torrent, or give shoutouts and links to other users.

The README files are sorted from the most seeded file downward, with the last one only having one seeder. The number of seeds is set as page number, turning the reading of the book into a reading of ever rarer information. This becomes particularly charged with that last file's content being a conspiratorial extremist pamphlet on the surface level, with no hint on the torrent it was distributed with. That text however also reveals itself as imitating a critical view on file sharing as heresy, which takes the chance to practice aspects of the fantasy of a world living in unity.

*H A Critical Reader in Contra-Internet Studies

AUTHOR	NetScribe UCLA [ed.]
YEAR	2019
GENRE	catalog / collection, education / classroom, experimental literature
METHOD	collective, constraint, détournement / hack, found material, montage / remix
SUBJECT	authorship, internet culture, reading / interpretation
PLATFORM	Lulu
EDITION CHARACTERISTICS	multiple editions (print, PDF), ISBN 9780359765171, open edition
FORMAT	15.2 × 22.9 cm
MATERIALITIES	black-and-white, paperback, perfect bound
PAGES	212 (unpaginated)

IMAGES

DESCRIPTION

**H: A Critical Reader in Contra-Internet Studies* is a collection of nineteen texts that critically engage with the topic of the internet but with a humorous conceptual twist. All texts consist of found material taken from the internet, altered using the "find & replace" function in text editors to turn them into critical texts on the topic—*H (read as CTRL+H) being the shortcut for this function.

The collection was collectively conceived in Danny Snelson's 2019 class "Theory & Method on the Internet" during a thirty-minute working session. The students' task, which is reproduced on the last page of the collection, marks the only reference for the collection being a conceptual take intending the opposite of what it proposes. Even the blurb, included on all platforms that sell the book, underlines its seriousness. The instructions read:

"1. Gather a focused selection of texts on any given topic(s) on your computer or the internet.
2. Copy and paste selected excerpts or full pages into a new document or text file.
3. Find and replace (all or singular) to transform the bricolage text into a critical essay about writing on the internet.
4. When finished, we'll discuss the process and organization and proceed to gather the essays together in this document to create a critical anthology.
5. I will export this document to PDF so we may publish via Lulu.com, a print-on-demand publisher."

Methodology Vol 02

AUTHOR	Paparutzy
YEAR	2019
GENRE	artist's book / bookwork
METHOD	found material, montage / remix
SUBJECT	book / book design, economy / labor, literature, visual culture
PLATFORM	Lulu
EDITION CHARACTERISTICS	open edition
FORMAT	22.0 × 28.6 cm
MATERIALITIES	color, hardcover, perfect bound
PAGES	30 (unpaginated)

IMAGES

DESCRIPTION

Paparutzy's *Methodology Vol 02* is a conceptual commentary on poetry and poetics via different semiotic layers. The book consists of twenty-four repetitions of a packshot of three bottles of all-purpose household cleaning agent—depicted on recto pages, with the same image mirrored on verso pages. This results in two sets of spray bottles facing each other on each double-page spread. Various semantics of the word "method" are at work in this constellation, ranging from the clinical whiteness of the packshots which merge with the white of paper, to the cleaners pointing at each other and potentially deleting themselves, to the title of the book contextualized as poetic method by the "poetry" category in which it is categorized in Lulu's webshop.

The book is one in a series of three conceptual approaches on methodological artist's books, the third volume of which costs $370,000.

Hate Library

AUTHOR	Nick Thurston
YEAR	2019
GENRE	catalog / collection, exhibition copy
METHOD	documentation / archiving, found material, reformatting, study / analysis
SUBJECT	analog / digital, bias, crowd / collaboration, internet culture, politics / activism, publishing / distribution, race, scale, social media, writing / reading techniques
PLATFORM	Copyshop
VOLUMES	12
EDITION CHARACTERISTICS	multiple editions, each set printed only once, dated
FORMAT	22.0 × 29.5 cm
MATERIALITIES	black-and-white, wire-o bound
PAGES	700 each (unpaginated)
IMAGES	

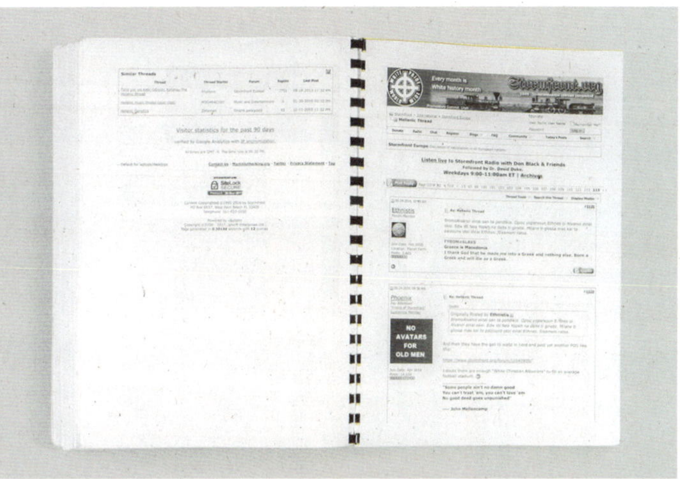

DESCRIPTION

“Installed as a public reference resource, *Hate Library* explores the language of far-right political groups and parties across contemporary Europe. It focuses on their use of online forums as recruiting and collaboration tools in a changing political region where transnational allegiances are bolstering extreme nationalist agendas. [...] It also juxtaposes the often confusing overlaps between public (front stage) and online activist (back stage) political discourses” (Nick Thurston, “Hate Library,” website). This interplay “between networked activism beneath the surface of life and its effects on the surface of lived experience” is also reflected in the punning slogan of the exhibition poster “Back to Front Truth” (Nick Thurston, “Back to Front Truths,” 199).

The material from the online far-right supporter forums was transferred into twelve volumes arranged by country: Vol. 1: Austria; Vol. 2: Belgium; Vol. 3: Denmark; Vol. 4: England; Vol. 5: France; Vol. 6: Germany; Vol. 7: Greece; Vol. 8: Hungary; Vol. 9: Italy; Vol. 10: Netherlands; Vol. 11: Poland; Vol. 12: Sweden. They were presented as “history books” on blue music stands, arranged in a circle on the yellow stars of the European flag, inviting collective, “choral” reading: “Each of these unedited volumes pauses one far-right national conversation, repeating it offline by using simple data-gathering and print-on-demand processes” (Ibid., 202). They are encircled by panels presenting the search results of “truth” in the European sections of the world’s largest white supremacist platform Stormfront. In addition, the walls are plastered with oversized thread titles.

Nick Thurston, through the exhibition’s title *Hate Library*, declares this setting to be a public library that recontextualizes these kinds of “backstage” discussions that, despite their public accessibility, “do not seem to have become *public knowledge* in any strong sense of that phrase,“ and makes them “accessible to audiences who would never enter those online bubbles” (Ibid., 203 and 194). At the same time, Thurston probes an artistic approach through which documents like these “can become matters of public concern through their ‘social life’—through re-publishing, sharing, and discussing them” (Nick Thurston, “Document Practices”).

Developed in collaboration with historian Matthew Feldman, *Hate Library* was shown in Thurston’s solo exhibition of the same name at Galeria Foksal (Warsaw, June–July 2017), at transmediale (Berlin, January–February 2018), at the University of Applied Arts (Vienna, June 2019) and Hartware MedienKunstVerein (Dortmund, April–September 2019), for which a new set was printed each time. Our set is the one produced for Vienna. In some cases, without the artist’s knowledge, the venues disposed of the used books after the show.

ABC Days

AUTHORS	ABC [Artists' Books Cooperative], Wil van Iersel [ed.]
YEAR	2020
GENRE	artist's book / bookwork, catalog / collection
METHOD	collective, composition (writing / drawing / photography), constraint
SUBJECT	art, crowd / collaboration, politics / activism, print on demand, publishing / distribution
PLATFORM	Online-Druck.biz
VOLUMES	29
EDITION CHARACTERISTICS	multiple editions (print, web), limited edition, available only as set through the artists
FORMAT	17.0 × 24.0 cm
MATERIALITIES	black-and-white, color, paperback, perfect bound, box

IMAGES

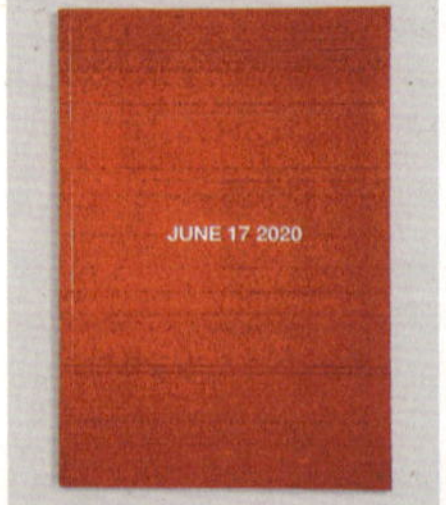

DESCRIPTION

For *ABC Days*, Artists' Books Cooperative member Wil van Iersel invited twenty-eight artists to produce a book in a given format of 48 to 64 pages to be published as a consecutive series each day between June 11 and July 9, 2020. Some of the participating artists are members of ABC and others responded to an invitation, parts of which are reproduced in Jan van der Til's publication *July 06 2020* (which is at the same time *Book XXXVIII: Please tell me why* in his large project *Rhizomebook*, see 262). As one learns there, this is the first time ABC asked non-members to collaborate on a community project, and thanks to sponsorship by the Amsterdam Fund for the Arts this participation could be remunerated with a €200 honorarium and four copies of the participant's own book in the series.

Each publication references the date it was published with most of the content directly reflecting on the news of that day or period. In this way, the series documents the zeitgeist of a memorable period marked by the lockdown enforced in many countries following the COVID-19 pandemic outbreak and the worldwide Black Lives Matter protests against racism, police brutality, and white privilege.

The date, which forms the title of each book and is the only paratextual information on the front cover, is reminiscent of On Karawa's *Date Paintings* except for the fact that *ABC Days* presents itself as a collective timed practice, as can also be seen on the back cover, which bears the title of the series next to the artist's name. The color of the cover is determined in each case by the color of an illustration in the respective book.

The artistic practices and techniques used in the books vary from post-photography and found images to commentary and conceptual approaches to collage, photography, and drawing.

Each book was published as a browsable but not downloadable PDF on the day it references. As a printed copy, it could only be acquired in one of the twenty-nine box editions of the set, published after the series' completion. In the absence of real-life book fairs where ABC would present this project to visitors, a presentation video was made in which a computer voice narrates the background of the series instead of a "real" ABC member.

CONTRIBUTING ARTISTS

Alaa Mansour (LB), Bruno Zhu (PT), Corinne Vionnet (CH), David Horvitz (US), David Schulz (US), Dawn Kim (US), Duncan Wooldridge (UK), EJ Major (UK), Hermann Zschiegner (US), Jack Halten Fahnestock (US), Jan van der Til (NL), John Maclean (UK), Jonathan Bragdon (US), Jonathan Lewis (UK), Jonathan Schmidt-Ott (DE), Kurt Caviezel (CH), Lotte Schröder (NL), Louis Porter (UK), Micheál O'Connell (Mocksim) (IE), Mishka Henner (UK/FR), Mohini Chandra (UK), Monika Orpik (PL), Ofer Wolberger (US), Penelope Umbrico (US), Rahel Zoller (DE/UK), Studio The Future (NL), Sveinn Fannar Jóhannsson (NO/IS), Travis Shaffer (US), and Wil van Iersel (NL).

Plagiarism

AUTHOR	Felipe Cussen
YEAR	2020
GENRE	experimental literature
METHOD	found material, generative / automation, study / analysis
SUBJECT	authorship, copyright / law, economy / labor
PLATFORM	Blurb
EDITION CHARACTERISTICS	multiple editions (print, PDF), ISBN 9781714384297, open edition
FORMAT	20.0 × 25.4 cm
MATERIALITIES	color, paperback, perfect bound
PAGES	34 (unpaginated)

IMAGES

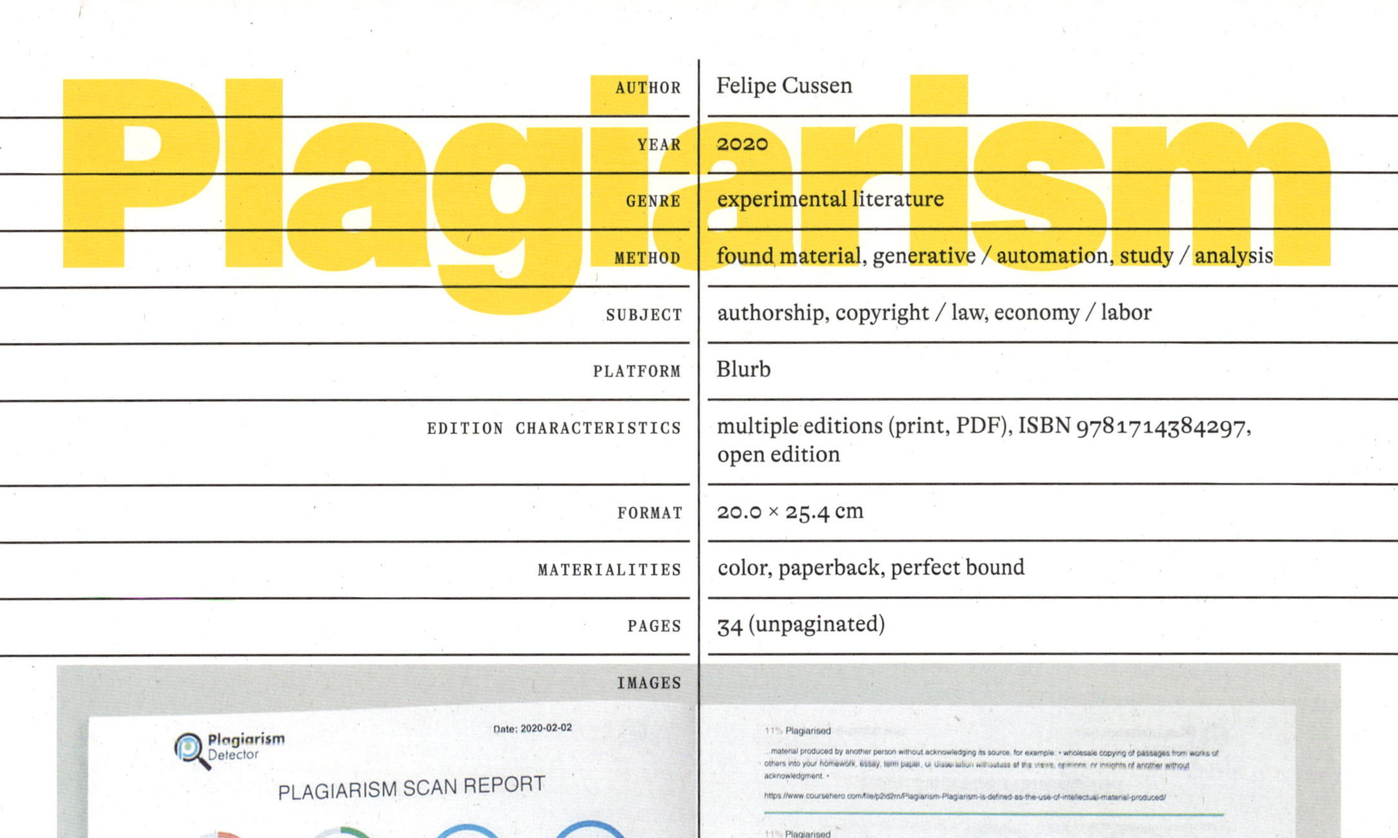

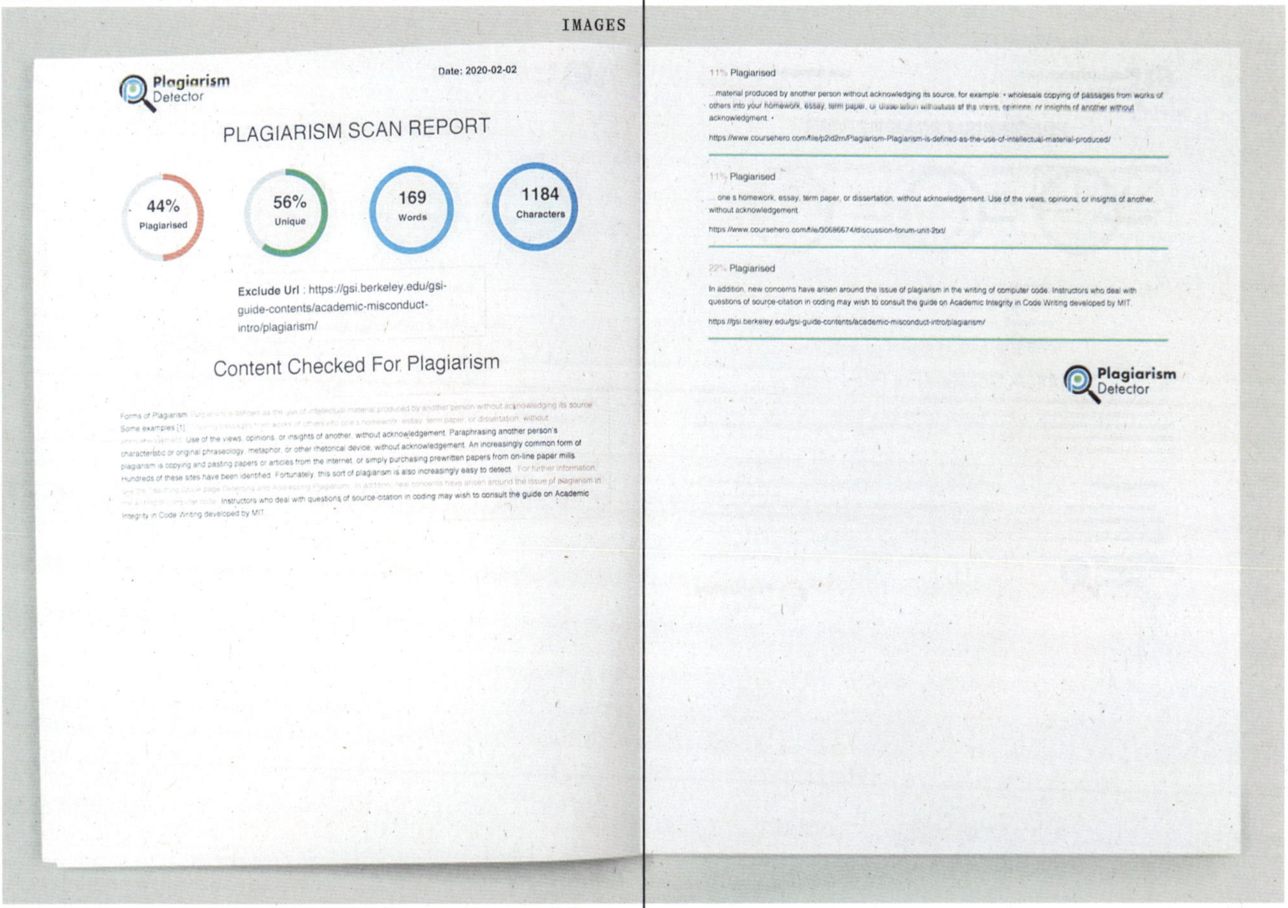

DESCRIPTION

Felipe Cussen took twenty-five of the first entries listed as "best universities worldwide" on Shanghai Ranking and searched their websites for definitions of plagiarism, a problematic yet central concept for academic ethos and innovation. He then entered the relevant paragraphs into the free online Plagiarism Detector tool to check for uncredited citations and ranked the results according to their percentage of detected plagiarism. Three candidates passed the check with the stamp "100% Unique," while eight universities, including Stanford, Oxford, Princeton, and ETH Zurich, are certified "100% plagiarism." The reproduced scan reports include the paragraphs in question and the sources from which they were allegedly plagiarized, showing that what is deemed as a shady practice is key for text production and academia.

The tools and sources Cussen used for creating the book are listed on the back cover, making it "0% Plagiarised" as stated on the front cover.

On social media, Cussen promotes his book by saying: "My new book *Plagiarism* is now available through the prestigious publisher Blurb!" (@felipecussen, February 4, 2020).

AR u ready?

A publication of Augmented Reality experiences.

AUTHORS	Karen ann Donnachie, Andy Simionato
YEAR	2020
GENRE	catalog / collection, education / classroom
METHOD	composition (writing / drawing / photography)
SUBJECT	analog / digital, book / book design, materiality, technology, visual culture
PLATFORM	Blurb
EDITION CHARACTERISTICS	multiple editions (print, PDF, web), open edition, CC BY-NC-SA
FORMAT	21.6 × 27.9 cm
MATERIALITIES	color, paperback, perfect bound
PAGES	48

IMAGES

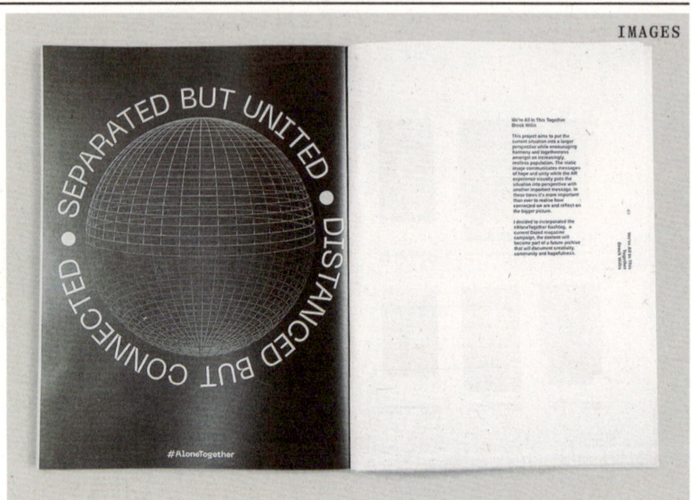

DESCRIPTION

AR u ready? is a publication developed from a studio class at RMIT University's School of Design in Melbourne led by Karen ann Donnachie and Andy Simionato during the 2020 pandemic lockdown. Students were asked to "imagine new worlds which they could explore through Augmented Reality technologies" (Karen ann Donnachie, Andy Simionato, *AR u ready?*, 3). They produced images and animated digital models as counterparts that would be loaded and overlaid on the image as soon as the smartphone camera was pointed at it. The works derive from the interaction of these two parts: Faces start to move, texts extend into their surroundings, floor plans turn into 3D architecture and objects rise from the page and splinter into fragments. For this, the class cooperated with the immersive technology company Appearition, who developed an app that needs to be downloaded to fully experience the works. In the publication, each work is presented on one page of a double-page spread with a short introduction on the opposite side. Technically, all these experiences could also be triggered by the full preview available on Blurb and the project's accompanying website—though the amazement and allurement of augmented reality only comes into full effect when triggered in tension with physical objects, the surface of which cannot be animated. Because of this, the print-on-demand publication becomes a necessary physical counterpart for the app and further enhances the playfulness and disruptive experience of the students' works.

THE COVER FEATURES A COLLECTIVE WORK BY ALL PARTICIPANTS

Kezya Anatha, Thomas Bellamy, Meg Bielby, Jiaqi Chen, Zhongrui (Ray) Feng, Stavros Giannoulakis, Sylvain Girard, Karenina Kartikahadi, Jackie Liu, Jinni Low, Ka Wai Mak, Timon Meury, Alexander Mienczakouski, Garima Minocha, Jia Sheng Ong, Alexandra Palioportas, Alessia Petrini, Medina Siregar, Anastasia Stanisiaus, Ellen Waite, Blake Walshe, and Brock Willis.

The Communist Manifesto (In Comic Sans)

AUTHORS	Friedrich Engels, Karl Marx
YEAR	2020
GENRE	artist's book / bookwork, experimental literature
METHOD	appropriation, reformatting
SUBJECT	canon, internet culture, memes, reading / interpretation, typography
PLATFORM	Lulu
EDITION CHARACTERISTICS	ISBN 9781678123635, open edition
FORMAT	15.2 × 22.9 cm
MATERIALITIES	black-and-white, paperback, perfect bound
PAGES	66 (unpaginated)

IMAGES

Manifesto of the Communist Party

A spectre is haunting Europe — the spectre of communism. All the powers of old Europe have entered into a holy alliance to exorcise this spectre: Pope and Tsar, Metternich and Guizot, French Radicals and German police-spies.

Where is the party in opposition that has not been decried as communistic by its opponents in power? Where is the opposition that has not hurled back the branding reproach of communism, against the more advanced opposition parties, as well as against its reactionary adversaries?

Two things result from this fact:

I. Communism is already acknowledged by all European powers to be itself a power.

II. It is high time that Communists should openly, in the face of the whole world, publish their views, their aims, their tendencies, and meet this nursery tale of the Spectre of Communism with a manifesto of the party itself.

To this end, Communists of various nationalities have assembled in London and sketched the following

DESCRIPTION

This new edition of *The Communist Manifesto* is, as the back cover proclaims, a reprint of "one of the most influential texts in history" set "in the most revolutionary fonts: comic sans." As a font supplied with Microsoft Windows since 1995, Comic Sans is widely used not only by dyslexics but especially by users with little design knowledge, making it both one of the most used and most hated fonts ever. In the context of web subcultures' anti-aesthetics of memes and trolling, the font has gained an inverted cult status, resulting in memes involving reproductions of well-known logo designs and book covers.

Though the font used on the book cover isn't even the infamous Comic Sans, this further enhances the dilettante memeing of this edition, as well as the illustrations on the front and back covers, which were hand-drawn in what seems to be Microsoft Paint. Thus, *The Communist Manifesto (In Comic Sans)* can be seen as one of the rare instances of a meme not turned into, but being, a book itself.

Other trolling alterations on the back cover include a mocking of the manifesto's final slogan, printed in its popularized form "Workers of the world, unite!" and of Marx' biography, which reads, "Karl Marx was born in 1818 in Prussia, a country so lame that it doesn't even exist anymore." On Lulu, the book is assigned to the "entertainment" category and tagged "memes" among others. Who produced the book is not apparent: Karl Marx is listed as the author, and it is uploaded via john walmart's Lulu store, for whom no further data is provided.

Drie Verhalen

AUTHOR	Maria Goutier-De Smet
YEAR	2020
GENRE	fiction, reprint
METHOD	paratextual play, photocopy / scan, remediation
SUBJECT	copyright / law, economy / labor, error / corruption / loss, google, materiality, print on demand, publishing / distribution, standard / default
PLATFORM	Espresso Book Machine
EDITION CHARACTERISTICS	open edition
FORMAT	11.6 × 17.9 cm
MATERIALITIES	black-and-white, paperback, perfect bound
PAGES	144

IMAGES

DESCRIPTION

Maria Goutier-De Smet (1810–1882) was a Flemish pedagogue and writer. She published several books of poetry and prose as well as educational content. *Drie Verhalen* (Three Stories) is her third publication. As she died more than seventy years ago, her work has already entered into the public domain and was digitized by Google as part of their major digitization campaign cooperating with libraries. Scans available via Google Books have since been a great resource for making business with reeditions, with publishers pulling the PDFs directly from the platform, adding covers and paratext, and selling them as print-on-demand books in completely automated workflows on Amazon or other websites.

The Google Books corpus is also accessible by the Espresso Book Machine network and every EBM can print any book made available by Google in a matter of minutes. This edition of *Drie Verhalen* was produced by the EBM at The American Book Center in Amsterdam in 2020 and gives a perfect example of the multiple layers of remediation and paratext editing that are taking place in this process. The book uses a cover template that lists The American Book Center as publisher on the front cover. On the back cover, this process is listed in more detail with Google Books being referenced as digitizer and provider of the book content and the Espresso Book Machine as producer of the book. This paratext replaces the scanned front and back covers of the PDF offered by Google.

A note is also added to the first page with yet another Google logo, stating: "This is a reproduction of a library book that was digitized by Google as part of an ongoing effort to preserve the information in books and make it universally accessible." This note also includes a QR-coded link to the digital version of the text.

The version at hand shows several errors and visual artifacts which are rather common in Google Books due to bad scanning (as also evidenced by Greg Allen's *Wohlgemeynte Gedanken über den Dannemarks-Gesundbrunnen* and Benjamin Shaykin's *Special Collection*, see 188 and 254)—including, in this case, an extremely distorted version of the title page. As of 2022, *Drie Verhalen* is made available in three different scans by Google Books, the scan of the version at hand was either corrected or deleted, with the distorted title page no longer existing in any of them. In this sense, *Drie Verhalen* exemplifies the book as a stable container for documenting digitization processes and versioning of digital files. It also shows the new role of book producers, who are no longer only generators and providers of content but also seek to find new ways of profiting from freely available content and masking it as publishing.

Strom und Vorurteil

52 weitgehend unkritische Kolumnen

AUTHOR	Kathrin Passig
YEAR	2020
GENRE	catalog / collection, nonfiction
METHOD	composition (writing / drawing / photography), paratextual play
SUBJECT	analog / digital, internet culture, platforms / companies, print on demand, technology
PLATFORM	Amazon
EDITION CHARACTERISTICS	multiple editions (print, e-book), ISBN 9781659754971, open edition
FORMAT	12.8 × 20.3 cm
MATERIALITIES	black-and-white, paperback, perfect bound
PAGES	215
IMAGES	

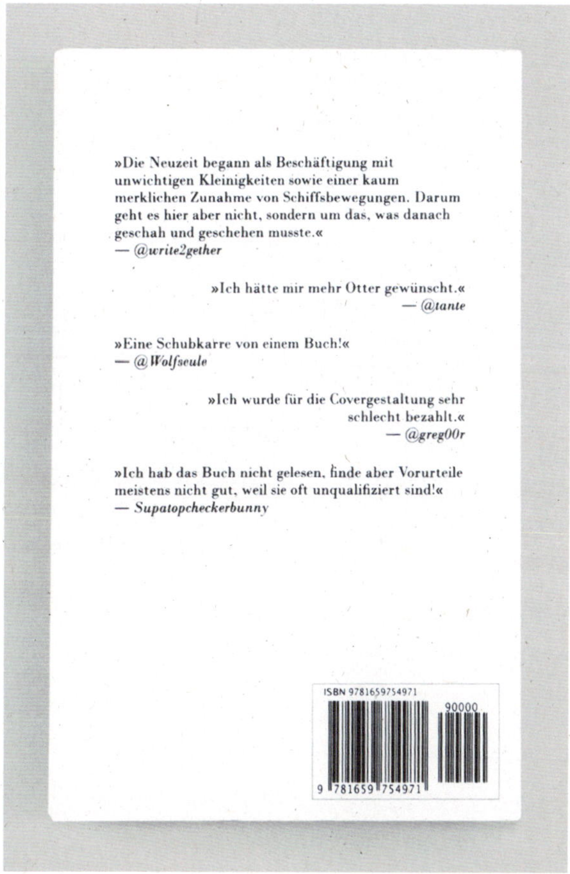

DESCRIPTION

The collection contains Kathrin Passig's columns published in the weekend magazine of the German newspaper *Frankfurter Rundschau* in 2019. It is available in several versions, each of which is associated with different earning potential, as Passig explains on her website: "Available as Kindle e-book or paperback at Amazon, as e-book at Google Play (I get money). As EPUB at Library Genesis or here on my website (I don't get money)" (Kathrin Passig, "Bücher"). The advantage of print-on-demand service providers like Amazon is mainly that the author doesn't have to worry about distribution, shipping, and invoices herself.

For the blurb, the author launched a call on Twitter: "For the printed edition of *Strom und Vorurteil* I can for the first time (because it's print-on-demand) put random nonsense on the back cover. This is your chance! Only statements from uninformed people please; those familiar with the content of the book may not take part" (@kathrinpassig, February 9, 2020). The cover design is by Gregor Weichbrodt, who also contributed to the blurb: "I was very badly paid for the cover design" (back cover). When the author discovered errors in the first printed copies, she still promoted the book on Twitter: "Anyone who buys it straightaway will get a rare collector's edition with a hyphenation error on the very first page! For a limited time only!" (@kathrinpassig, February 29, 2020) It took half a day for the new version to be reviewed and approved by Amazon again.

Passig's multi-award winning blog *Techniktagebuch* features an entry with a detailed, witty self-experience report on print-on-demand production with Amazon: it proved to be a special adventure, since, for example, the paperback cover template provided by Amazon turned out to be flawed (see Kathrin Passig, "Yes, today it's boring. But in 20 years!," in this volume, 522–526).

A year later, in 2021, Passig published a second book on demand on Amazon: *Je Türenknall, desto wiederkomm*. Again, she collected suggestions for blurbs on Twitter (with a great response) and described her new adventures in self-publishing and print-on-demand in her blog *Techniktagebuch* (see ibid., 527–530).

Page Pieces

AUTHOR	Michalis Pichler
YEAR	since 2020
GENRE	artist's book / bookwork, intermediate product / halbzeug
METHOD	collection, composition (writing / drawing / photography), test / experiment
SUBJECT	art, book / book design, materiality, reading / interpretation
PLATFORM	Lulu
VOLUMES	multiple vols.
EDITION CHARACTERISTICS	ISBN, not publicly available
FORMAT	12.6 × 20.3 cm

IMAGE

DESCRIPTION

The books for Michalis Pichler's *Page Pieces* series are not publicly available. They represent a kind of dummy for the artist in various phases of his long-term projects. Compared to the copy store, print-on-demand has advantages in terms of labor economy; moreover, the handy paperbacks, with their "slick" industrial production method, already look more like "a real book." At the same time, because of their "inscribed unfinishedness," print-on-demand books are particularly suited to "playing out a kind of variantology" (Michalis Pichler, interview with apod.li), which is especially important for the *Page Pieces* concept, which Pichler defines as follows:

"PAGE PIECES are contributions to publications taking place on a page.
PAGE PIECES are Primary information.
PAGE PIECES need to be published.
Once published, PAGE PIECES cannot be unpublished (they can be re-published though).
If the page count/pagination of their placement matters, PAGE PIECES are pagination-sensitive.
If the verso of the page matters, PAGE PIECES are recto-verso-sensitive.
Rather than illustrating and/or referring to one original idea, every publishing of PAGE PIECE is a manifestation of it.
An earlier or later (re)print or (re-)use of a PAGE PIECE in different context is pari passu.
It is impossible to dive into the *same* river twice" (Michalis Pichler, "Page Pieces").

Against this background, it is consistent that Pichler assigns each variant its own ISBN of his publishing house "greatest hits," although usually only a few copies are produced for own use and they do not reach the book trade. Moreover, this is an attempt to at least somewhat escape the proprietary system of the platform, which would otherwise attach its own ISBNs to the products.

[Untitled (Mondrian)]

EDITION CHARACTERISTICS ISBN 9783962870058

MATERIALITIES color, loose insert, paperback, perfect bound

PAGES 201 (unpaginated)

DESCRIPTION This is a working journal for the *Untitled (Mondrian)* series, which serves the artist as a basis for planning. The starting point are individual pages from Mondrian catalogs and, as a counterpart, interior design and urban planning books from the postwar period, which are collaged together. These book page collages are then scaled to the original size of the Mondrian paintings and transferred to canvas with inkjet printing, where the Mondrian fragments are repainted with oil. The work journal contains an overview of all the collages so far, with their positioning in the journal corresponding to the original page number of the found pieces, which is why Pichler speaks of site-specific *Page Pieces*. The copy does not contain any paratext, but includes a photographic print showing the studio and the production of the paintings.

[migration]

EDITION CHARACTERISTICS ISBN 9783962870034

MATERIALITIES color, paperback, perfect bound

PAGES 347 (unpaginated)

DESCRIPTION This is a kind of working journal for Pichler's long-running collage series entitled *migration*, which compiles a large number of the collages produced to date and serves the artist as documentation of his work-in-progress. The starting point are individual pages from illustrated animal books, often specifically on animal migration and bird flight, which the artist finds during his forays into flea markets and antiquarian bookshops and "incorporates" into the series. He calls this method of working "bibliophagia." In the pages with photos, Pichler then cuts out the animals depicted, so that one can look through the blank spaces to the page below. Thus, for example, a "scent of a mouse" and a "pointed nose" peek out from a cut-out goat. Of the rest of the page's contents, only the pagination (and sometimes the caption) remains intact.

The collages in the series can also be published as site-specific *Page Pieces* and some of them have already been published in various places where they occupy the same page as in the original found object. The artist has long planned a publication of the entire series following the same principle. This working journal helps to identify major blank gaps in the page sequence as well as duplications of collages of the same page, such as on page 43, where two *Page Pieces* are printed on top of each other so that birds fly over goats. The copy does not contain any information about the author or the context of the work.

Subcutanean 30287

AUTHOR	Aaron A. Reed
YEAR	2020
GENRE	experimental literature, fiction
METHOD	composition (writing / drawing / photography), generative / automation, versioning / seriality
SUBJECT	code / programming, crowd / collaboration, literature, narration, print on demand, publishing / distribution
PLATFORM	Amazon, TheBookPatch
EDITION CHARACTERISTICS	multiple editions (print, web, audiobook), ISBN 9798605947820, unique copies, open edition, crowdfunded
FORMAT	14.0 × 21.6 cm
MATERIALITIES	black-and-white, paperback, perfect bound
PAGES	219
IMAGES	

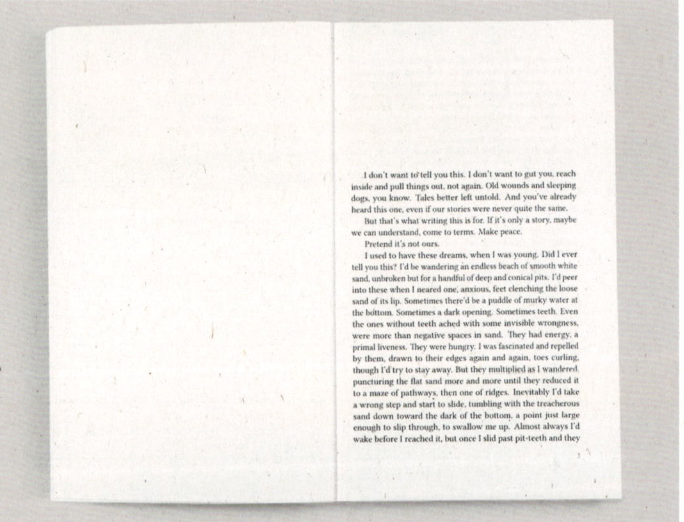

DESCRIPTION

Aaron A. Reed's *Subcutanean* is a queer multi-branch horror novel evolving around the two protagonists Niko and Orion getting trapped in the endlessly multiplying basement of their house. The novel is published in copies with unique content in each, the text being algorithmically pulled from a huge pool of paragraphs and word choices: "The master text contains hundreds of places where words, sentences, even entire scenes can play out in different ways" (Aaron A. Reed, "Subcutanean," website). However, the content is still concepted in a way that each variation makes sense and can be read as a unique version of the same story, with important cornerstones of the story remaining more or less the same.

In that sense, *Subcutanean* might not only be called queer in content but also on a conceptual level, due to its fluidity and multi-branching perspectives, which is reflected on by Reed in a poetic statement on reading his novel: "You'll have to accept the fact that this story might have gone in different ways for different people, and decide whether you're going to accept that or worry about what else might have happened. Your opinions about the story will be valid, regardless of which version you have. You're the one who took that text and brought it to life" (Aaron A. Reed, "Why I Made Subcutanean").

To publish this kind of interactive automated fiction, Reed had to find a semi-automated publishing workflow with print-on-demand, as print-on-demand platforms still don't allow for extensive APIs. With TheBookPatch he found a provider "that did not require human review of changes to a manuscript, and also did not require a book to have an ISBN number (which would need to be updated for each new version). [...] The way I worked it out is that someone ordering the book first pays me directly, and then I generate a new copy, update the text on my POD partner's site, and manually put in the order through them. (My customer never interacts with the POD site itself). I can order up to six books at a time, because I have six identical 'book projects' set up on their site with identical covers, and then I cycle regularly through which project I update for a new order" (Aaron A. Reed in an email to apod.li).

Because this publishing model is quite labor-intensive and therefore costly, Reed also published three seeds of the novel as static versions (matching three major outcomes of the narrative) via Amazon Kindle Direct Publishing. Our version is seed #30287 and one of these stable publications. Reed underlined several times that these stable versions should not be considered more official than the others. They include an alternate scene to demonstrate how another version might differ from the copy at hand as well as a list sampling some general decisions that characterize this version of the plot.

Similar to its publishing workflow, *Subcutanean* also extensively explored new digital financial and distributional models in general, starting with a crowdfunding on Indiegogo, an extensive documentation of the project on *Medium*, and testing multiple channels to match its combinatorial narrative such as sections published weekly for readers on platforms like Wattpad, Royal Road, and Tapas, an audiobook podcast on Soundcloud, plus two Twitter bots posting the entire content of different seeds of the book alongside each other. As part of the crowdfunding campaign, the author also produced USB sticks containing a collector's edition, including the master source text, the custom's source code, and 10,000 different versions: "The materials on the USB will be released into the public domain five years after *Subcutanean*'s original publication date, in February 2025" (Aaron A. Reed, "Subcutanean," website).

SUBCUTANEAN
30287
AARON A. REED
SUBCUTANEAN
36619
AARON A. REED

Photobook is

Did you mean: *photo book is*

AUTHOR	paula roush
YEAR	2020
PUBLISHER	msdm
GENRE	artist's book / bookwork, reprint
METHOD	collection, found material, generative / automation, study / analysis
SUBJECT	copyright / law, photography, platforms / companies, print technology, print on demand, publishing / distribution, standard / default, technology
PLATFORM	Amazon, IngramSpark
EDITION CHARACTERISTICS	second edition, ISBN 9798669289034, open edition
FORMAT	15.2 × 22.9 cm
MATERIALITIES	black-and-white, paperback, perfect bound
PAGES	680

IMAGES

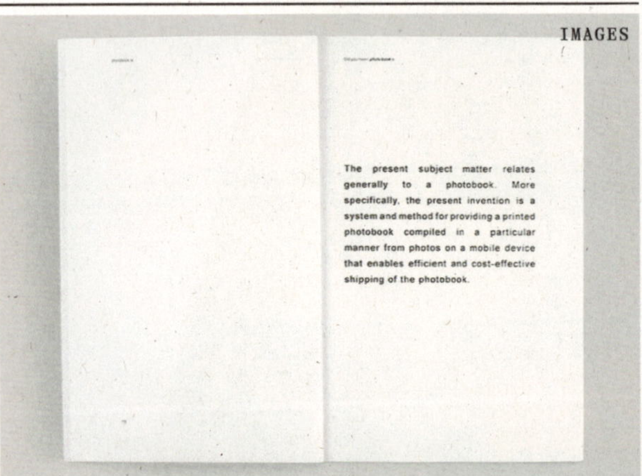
The present subject matter relates generally to a photobook. More specifically, the present invention is a system and method for providing a printed photobook compiled in a particular manner from photos on a mobile device that enables efficient and cost-effective shipping of the photobook.

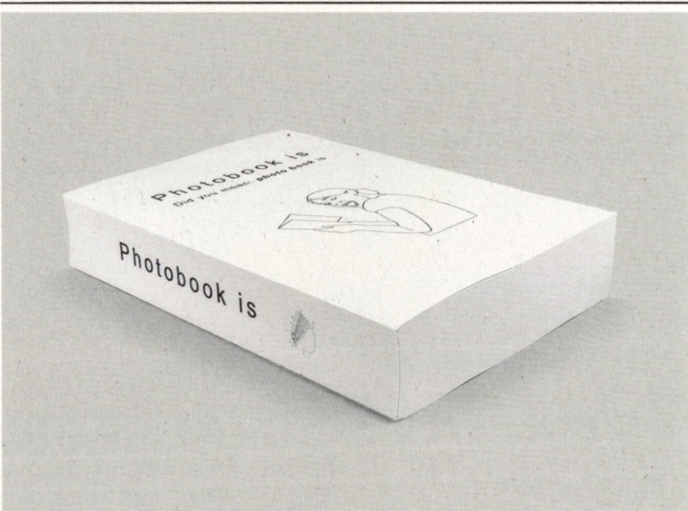

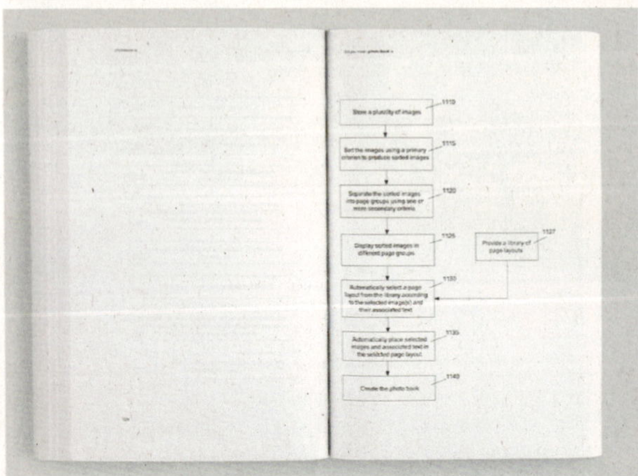

DESCRIPTION

"This book explores the little-known but fascinating world of photobook print on demand publishing. The book, created using artificial intelligence, has two sections to read in order or randomly" (mdsm, "Photobook is," website). The blurb on Amazon goes on: "The first section assembles uses of the 'photobook' term, found using the keywords 'photobook is' [photobook: single word] on the web browser, which automatically suggests 'Did you mean: ***photo book*** is' [***photo book***: two words, bold italic]. These include colloquial, vernacular, technical, academic, theoretical and artistic statements of the meaning of the term. The second section contains diagrams and technical drawings of patent publications related to software applications for automatic photobook production and print-on-demand."

In this way, the field of tension becomes visible in which the publishing of print-on-demand photobooks operates: between the patented workflow, format, and material specifications of the platforms on the one hand, and the definitions, artistic imaginations, and ideas of the genre on the other (see paula roush, "Photobook Is," in this volume, 34–37).

In 2020, an online performance took place on Zoom to mark the launch of *Photobook is: Did you mean:* photo book *is*. Visible on the screen were two windows, one of which featured an animation of the book pages, synchronous with its reading out loud by Victoria (The Received Pronunciation automated voice in Acrobat Pro). The second window featured the publisher paula roush's own msdm studio, showing a video stream of four actions related to visualizing, editing, publishing, and distributing the book.

Research initiated in 2015. First published as a limited edition of twenty-five handmade books in 2017. Second edition in 2020. The ISBN is only given in the webshop, not in the book.

Weisheit und Wiederholung 104.052 philosophisch-literarische Desiderata

AUTHOR	0x0a
YEAR	2021
PUBLISHER	0x0a
GENRE	artist's book / bookwork, experimental literature
METHOD	appropriation, generative / automation, montage / remix
SUBJECT	book / book design, canon, code / programming, publishing / distribution
PLATFORM	Lulu
EDITION CHARACTERISTICS	multiple editions (print, PDF), ISBN 9781667188317, open edition
FORMAT	10.8 × 17.5 cm
MATERIALITIES	black-and-white, paperback, perfect bound
PAGES	731

IMAGES

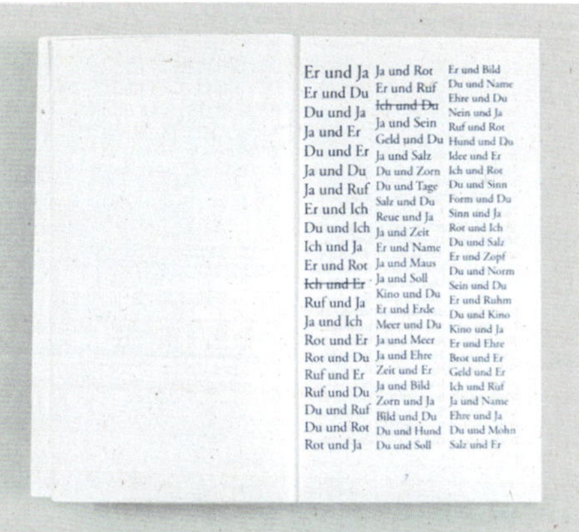

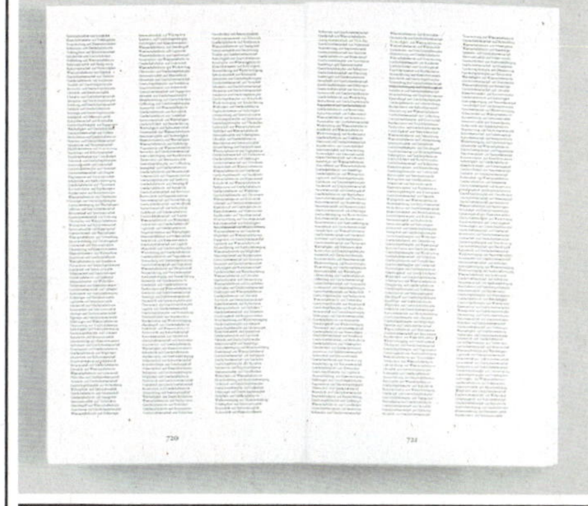

DESCRIPTION

0x0a's *Weisheit und Wiederholung: 104.052 philosophisch-literarische Desiderata* (Wisdom and Repetition: 104,052 Philosophical-Literary Desiderata) lists 104,052 combinations of two nouns connected via "und" (German for "and"). Such combinations of nouns as titles are very popular, especially in philosophical-literary publications with a certain gesture of megalomania. One thinks, for example, of Martin Heidegger's *Being and Time*, Gilles Deleuze's *Difference and Repetition*, and Michel Foucault's *Madness and Civilization*.

A list of publications with titles in this particular format, collected by Hendrikje Schauer and Marcel Lepper for *Titelpaare. Ein philosophisches und literarisches Wörterbuch* (Title Pairs. A Philosophical and Literary Dictionary, 2018), served as a corpus. Using a Python script, 0x0a dissected these titles into their two constituent parts and recombined them in all possible ways, deleting duplicates due to nouns that appear more than once in the list. They then arranged all pairs in ascending order by length. To fit each pair into a line, the font size gets smaller and smaller, so that the longest pairs at the very end of the book become barely legible. Titles that were already listed in *Titelpaare* are crossed out, turning the list into a "compendium of potential literature" (Hannes Bajohr, "Prozess," 724) as well as a to-do list for future intellectual great minds and a prompt for readers to implement one of the suggested titles; after all, the blurb proclaims, "not everything has been said yet."

Weisheit und Wiederholung appropriates the cover and paratext design of the most prestigious German scholarly paperback series Suhrkamp Wissenschaft. Thus, the publication also functions as an analysis of a certain, highly influential style of theory building and marketing in German academia.

The imprint parodies the customs of the book and library world by reversing all the usual statements about cataloging in the German National Library and copyright: even the © symbol has an inverted "C." The printer is listed as Lulu Press, Inc. and the printing location is truthfully stated as "Printed who knows where."

/ aaaa press

AUTHORS	Hartmut Abendschein [ed.], N. N.
YEAR	2020–2022
PUBLISHER	etkbooks
GENRE	artist's book / bookwork, catalog / collection, experimental literature
METHOD	collection, collective, constraint, versioning / seriality
SUBJECT	analog / digital, authorship, canon, crowd / collaboration, literature, memory / storage, print on demand, publishing / distribution, standard / default
PLATFORM	Lulu
VOLUMES	100
EDITION CHARACTERISTICS	ISSN 2673-4745, multiple editions (print, PDF), open edition, doi 10.17436/etk.a.xxx
FORMAT	21.0 × 29.7 cm
MATERIALITIES	paperback, perfect bound

IMAGE

DESCRIPTION

/ aaaa press is a sublabel of Hartmut Abendschein's edition taberna kritika (etk), that ran between 2020 and 2022 and published one book every Monday, resulting in 100 publications in total. The series, of the same name, was preceded by an open call with almost no limitations to media and content ("anything which fits in word/pdf"). The resulting publications circle largely around topics like conceptual writing, cataloging and lists, online and off-line text cultures, and fragments and drafts. Each contributor got a free copy.

Apart from its fast-paced publishing routine, the series was subject to further formal constraints resulting from its hybrid publishing model as both PDF and print-on-demand: All publications are DIN A4 (hence the name of the series), softcover, and between 60–800 pages long (the minimum and maximum number of pages possible for being published in this format at Lulu.com).

But above all, according to its self-description, */ aaaa press* is designed as "an allegorical performance of Foucault's concept 'the year without names.'" Abendschein refers to a game that Foucault had suggested in an interview: "For one year books will be published without the author's name. The critics will have to manage with an entirely anonymous production. But I suspect that perhaps they will have nothing to say: all the authors will wait until the next year to publish their books" (Michel Foucault, "Le philosophe masque"). According to this concept of anonymous authorship, */ aaaa press* makes no reference to any creator of its contents, with the title only showing on the spine (the front and back covers left unprinted) and a very simple title page. Nonetheless, a significant amount of the books can be traced back to Abendschein himself.

The series concludes with an *Addendum* as No. 100, which lists the DOIs, QR codes, Lulu and cloud links, descriptors, keywords for all publications, and a thesaurus for their tags. The series, which has its own ISSN, is currently archived in Abendschein's own Google Drive cloud storage. At the same time, the prints are archived by the University Library of Bern and the PDFs by the Swiss National Library. Because all digital publications have a stable DOI, their hosting and distribution could be outsourced to the Swiss National Library's digital web archive in case of need, thus making the library—without its explicit consent—part of the publishing concept.

In addition, a catalog-exhibition of all publications was created. It contains the witty recommendation: "to get better printed books: download pdfs and re-upload to lulu.com with premium color option" (/ aaaa press, *Addendum*, [9]). One year later *aaaa press [usb.ed]* "for researchers, completists & collectors" was released in the form of a USB stick in an edition of 50, including the 100 anonymous PDFs, the exhibition catalog as PDF, and a sticker.

Precision and Recall: Suchbewegung in der Ordnung der Dinge

AUTHOR	[Hartmut Abendschein]
GENRE	artistic research, artist's book / bookwork
METHOD	documentation / archiving, photocopy / scan, study / analysis
SUBJECT	book / book design, canon, error / corruption / loss, literature, memory / storage, standard / default, technology
EDITION CHARACTERISTICS	doi 10.17436/etk.a.005
MATERIALITIES	black-and-white
PAGES	261

DESCRIPTION

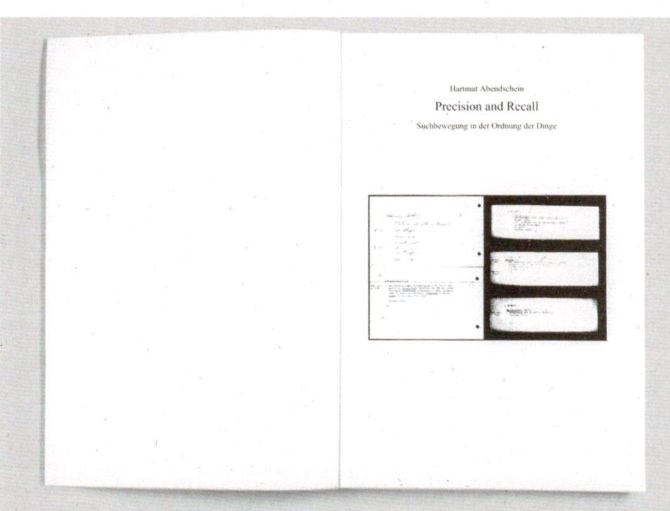

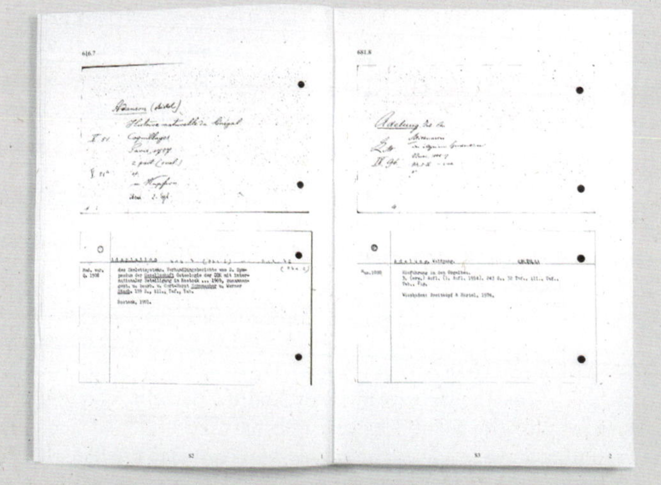

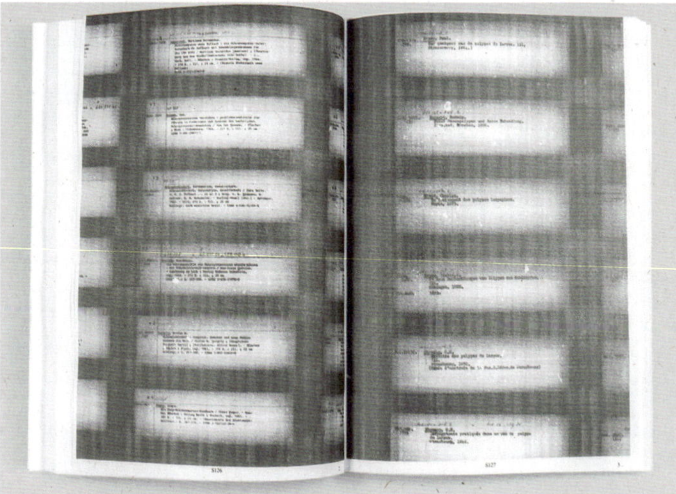

Precision and Recall: Suchbewegung in der Ordnung der Dinge (Search Movement in the Order of Things) goes back to "a reenactment of Foucault's bibliographic work" by Hartmut Abendschein, which took the form of a "catalog performance" that traced the "navigation through knowledge represented by catalog cards and microforms—the pre-digital scholarly search tools at the time Foucault's seminal study [*The Order of Things*] was written" (Hartmut Abendschein, *Precision and Recall*, i–ii).

Precision and recall are the two parameters usually used to measure the performance (i.e., the quality) of a hit list during an online information search. Precision describes the accuracy of a search result with the proportion of relevant documents in the result set. Recall indicates the proportion of relevant documents found in a search and thus the completeness of a search result. As a librarian, however, Hartmut Abendschein interprets "Precision and Recall" as a "retrieval mechanism" for finding entries in library catalogs that are related to each other by means of a classification system such as the Dewey Decimal Classification (DDC): "From a catalog record with a classificatory entry found, for example, in a library catalog kept alphabetically by author name (a concrete, precise 'hit,' that is), further titles can be found in another subject catalog equipped with a classification, which are related to each other in terms of content (recall) and expand the material base of knowledge findings" (Ibid,, i).

Accordingly, Abendschein proceeds in two steps: In the old alphabetical catalog of the City and University Library of Bern, which was kept until 1989 and has since been digitized, the authorships from Foucault's bibliography are systematically researched. In case of a hit, the catalog records with their DDC codes are extracted and mapped in alphabetical order one after the other (part 1: "Precision"). Subsequently, these classification notations were searched in the old subject catalog, which was kept until 1989 and is now only available as a microfiche (part 2: "Recall"). The respective hits (which are often difficult to decipher) are then photographed with the surrounding catalog entries from the fiche and displayed one after the other. This is completed by the bibliography, including all titles from Foucault's bibliography that could be found in the Bernese alphabetical catalog.

As a surprising side effect, in the "Precision" section there was a "coexistence of different handwritings, typewritings, annotations, and palimpsest productions [...] that themselves illustrate a certain historical development of the catalogs," while in the "Recall" section "something of the aura" of the now practically extinct microfiche era was captured (Ibid., ii).

Our copy of *Precision and Recall* is one of the early volumes in the series where Lulu automatically added an in-house barcode to the back cover. When Lulu made a software change in the backend during the run of */ aaaa press*, and plain */ aaaa*-style covers could no longer be produced generically, Abendschein switched to crafting the covers himself and adding a hand-generated DOI QR code to the back of all volumes, which also served as a book numbering system. For the sake of uniformity, the PDFs of the first volumes were adapted accordingly afterwards and existing print copies were pasted over with QR code labels. Abendschein also took the opportunity to anonymize the volume by deleting his own name from the title page, which can still be seen in our copy.

709.04075: 543 items, 20210621

GENRE artist's book / bookwork

METHOD collection, documentation / archiving

SUBJECT bias, canon, literature, memory / storage, publishing / distribution, reading / interpretation, standard / default

EDITION CHARACTERISTICS doi 10.17436/etk.a.075

MATERIALITIES black-and-white

PAGES 197

DESCRIPTION 709.04075 is the Dewey classification number for the category "conceptual art"—the acquisition of which Hartmut Abendschein is responsible for at the University Library of Bern. The book lists all 543 entries for items listed under that number including all information provided by the Online Public Access Catalog. Apart from author, publisher, language, format specifications, and identification numbers, this includes content-related information as well as descriptions and keywords. *709.04075* is an index as much as it documents the production of a canon, with a large amount of overlap with items at the Library of Artistic Print on Demand.

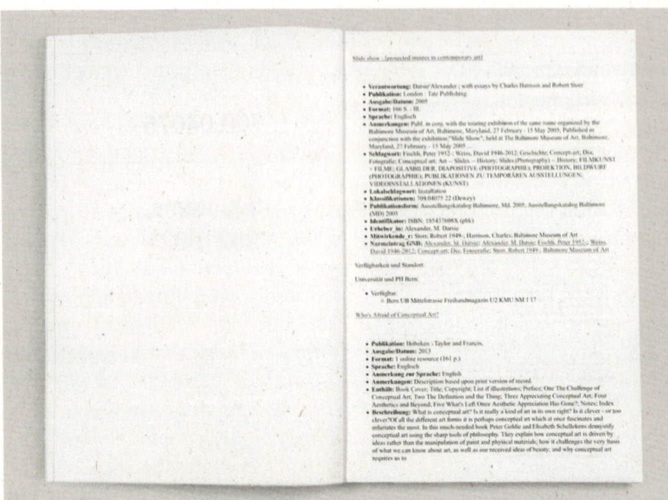

Reading Your World of Text

GENRE experimental literature

METHOD found material, remediation

SUBJECT analog / digital, crowd / collaboration, internet culture, materiality, memory / storage

EDITION CHARACTERISTICS doi 10.17436/etk.a.074

MATERIALITIES black-and-white

PAGES 98 (unpaginated)

DESCRIPTION *Your World of Text* is a website made by Andrew Badr in 2009 that provides an infinite grid for collectively editable text. It gained a cult status for online and gaming communities who regularly filled it with all kinds of ASCII art, memes, and shitposting, making it one of the most virtuous collective yet elusive places for visual poetry on the internet. *Your World of Text* is constantly evolving and changing because anyone can edit anything with no login required. *Reading Your World of Text* reproduces screenshots taken during a roaming of the website, cropping the infinite text plane first through the lens of the screenshot and then through the lens of the DIN A4 page. Since no backup copy of *Your World of Text* is made, *Reading Your World of Text* not only shows the transformation of character-based online art brought back to the printed page, but is also a documenting snapshot of this fluid textual environment.

glitcho studies: white cis male dudes gallerie

GENRE	photobook
METHOD	collection, generative / automation, study / analysis
SUBJECT	analog / digital, bias, canon, error / corruption / loss, gender, internet culture, photography, race, technology
EDITION CHARACTERISTICS	doi 10.17436/etk.a.068
MATERIALITIES	color
PAGES	169
DESCRIPTION	*glitcho studies* is a collection of 149 portraits photographed with a smartphone from nineteen issues of the periodical *Schweizerische Portrait-Gallerie* (Swiss Portrait Gallery) between 1893 and 1900, which were then processed with the android app Glitcho – Glitch Video & Photo Editor. The result is not only an automatic alteration, but also a critique of the portrayal of "white cis male dudes," as the subtitle reads, by adding color to the previously monochrome reproductions of the magazine. All sources are shown at the end of the publication as unaltered photos of their covers. *glitcho studies* also investigates the range of image analysis and filter techniques offered by the app, which are not glitches in a strict sense of the word but rather automatic alterations that reproduce a certain glitch as aesthetic as it is popular in online cultures.

a.a.O.

GENRE	artist's book / bookwork, experimental literature
METHOD	composition (writing / drawing / photography), paratextual play
SUBJECT	book / book design, writing / reading techniques
EDITION CHARACTERISTICS	doi 10.17436/etk.a.063
MATERIALITIES	black-and-white
PAGES	100
DESCRIPTION	"a.a.O." is, as a quoted Wikipedia entry on the last page of the publication informs, an abbreviation for "am angegebenen Ort" or "op. cit." It is used for shortening the source of a quoted reference but with no real indication as to where the source had previously been quoted—making it an abbreviation that is mostly unused these days. *a.a.O.* consists of 100 almost identical pages, each with "a.a.O." in a very big font size on the top of the page and a reference number pointing to a footnote on the next page with the same abbreviation waiting for the reader. The eyes then automatically wander up to the top of the page with the same layout but pointing to the footnote on the successive page. This turning of pages provoked by the reference instructions does not end with the last page either, since the reference there points to the first of the 100 pages, producing a reading loop.

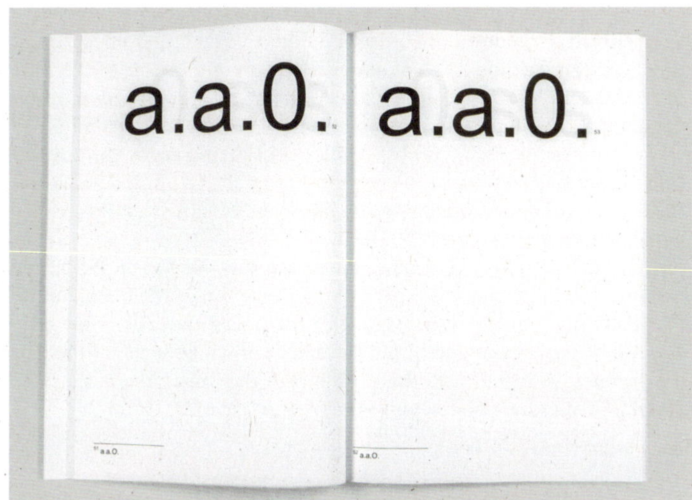

Boot Sounds

GENRE	artist's book / bookwork
METHOD	collection, documentation / archiving, translation / transcription
SUBJECT	canon, copyright / law, music / sound, platforms / companies, technology
EDITION CHARACTERISTICS	doi 10.17436/etk.a.053
MATERIALITIES	black-and-white
PAGES	35
DESCRIPTION	*Boot Sounds* is a collection of thirty-five boot sounds of famous operating systems, computers, and gaming consoles reproduced as notations for piano. With a range of devices and software going back as far as Apple II and Amiga but stopping in the mid-2000s with Xbox 360, the publication also mimics the creation of a compositional canon of what can almost be considered folklore music by now, sunken deep into the collective subconscious of people exposed to it daily.

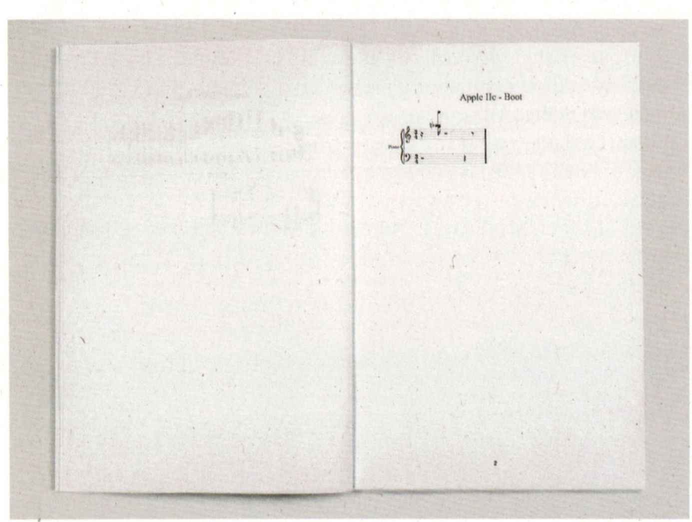

vacat

GENRE	artist's book / bookwork, experimental literature
METHOD	found material, montage / remix
SUBJECT	book / book design, canon, materiality, typography
EDITION CHARACTERISTICS	doi 10.17436/etk.a.037
MATERIALITIES	black-and-white
PAGES	140

DESCRIPTION

A vacat page is a page intentionally left blank in print layouts for different reasons, as a quoted Wikipedia entry at the end of the publication informs. Sometimes such pages are labeled with "This page intentionally left blank" to mark them as not being a print or processing error. *vacat* reproduces 135 pages carrying this notice reproduced from publications by sound artists and theorists such as John Cage, Steve Reich, Brandon Labelle, and Salomé Voegelin, showing great differences regarding the font and size chosen and its location on the page. All sources are listed at the end of the book, creating a canon of sound artists and musicians. In addition, *vacat* interprets books as scores for reading, with almost blank pages giving space for a reflection on reading practices, the materiality of the reading device, and the sounds produced while reading and page-turning, reminiscent of John Cage's *4'33"*.

Unlike all the other volumes in the series, this one has an ISBN, the barcode of which, unusually, is not at the very end of the book, but before the bibliography on the page with the final indication "This page was intentionally left blank," the statement of which it thus ironically undermines. This indicates that it is part of the work. And in fact it is taken from another publication, namely John Cage's *M. Writings '67–'72*.

20 Interviews

AUTHOR	Joshua Citarella
YEAR	2021
GENRE	artistic research, nonfiction
METHOD	collection, composition (writing / drawing / photography), study / analysis
SUBJECT	bias, gender, internet culture, memes, politics / activism, race, social media, visual culture
PLATFORM	Blurb, Amazon
EDITION CHARACTERISTICS	ISBN 9781034279273, open edition
FORMAT	20.0 × 25.4 cm
MATERIALITIES	color, paperback, perfect bound
PAGES	150 (unpaginated)

IMAGES

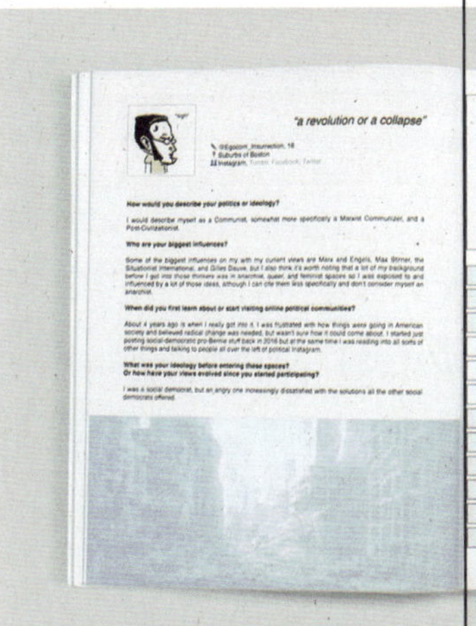

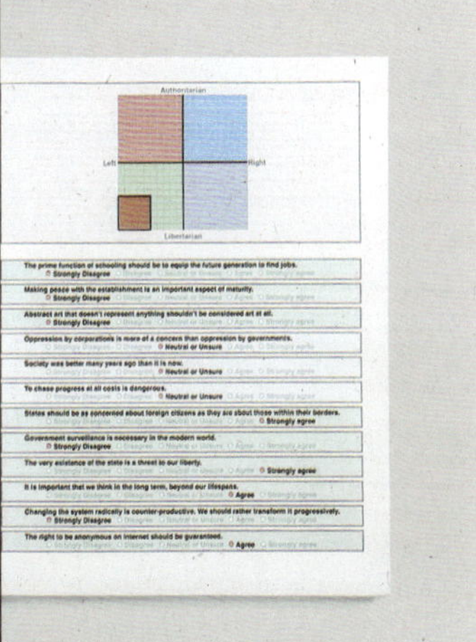

DESCRIPTION

Joshua Citarella's 20 *Interviews* is a survey and in-depth investigation of "young online radical politics" (Joshua Citarella, 20 *Interviews*) on English-speaking social media in the second half of 2019. Arranged around the Political Compass, whose grid is also used as the front and back covers, Citarella interviewed the owners of twenty different accounts from a spectrum of online political subcultures to give a sense of the general radicalization taking place as well the reasonings, hopes, and imagery the users of these accounts identify with.

The Political Compass is an online survey with multiple questions, the answers to which result in a mapping on a two-axis spectrum between libertarian/authoritarian and economic-left/economic-right. The survey, which has been on the internet since 2001, has been popping up in political memes ever since and is often used as a reference point for positioning oneself and questioning these political positions in general.

Citarella not only uses some of the original compass questions to situate the political view of his interviewees, but also a fixed set of questions to find out what their influences are and how they see the future. The interviews are illustrated by "memes and images found from similar minded accounts, forums and servers" (Joshua Citarella, 20 *Interviews*) and contextualized by several short texts and an introduction by the author.

The book is produced by Blurb, but only available on Amazon, where it has received some customer reviews.

Ten Million and One Silences

AUTHOR	Daniele Pantano
YEAR	2021
PUBLISHER	edition taberna kritika
GENRE	artist's book / bookwork, experimental literature
METHOD	composition (writing / drawing / photography), constraint, pricing
SUBJECT	book / book design, memory / storage, scale
PLATFORM	Lulu
VOLUMES	22
EDITION CHARACTERISTICS	ISBN 9783039470013, open edition
FORMAT	21.6 × 30.2 cm
MATERIALITIES	black-and-white, hardcover, perfect bound
PAGES	10,211 in total (unpaginated)

IMAGES

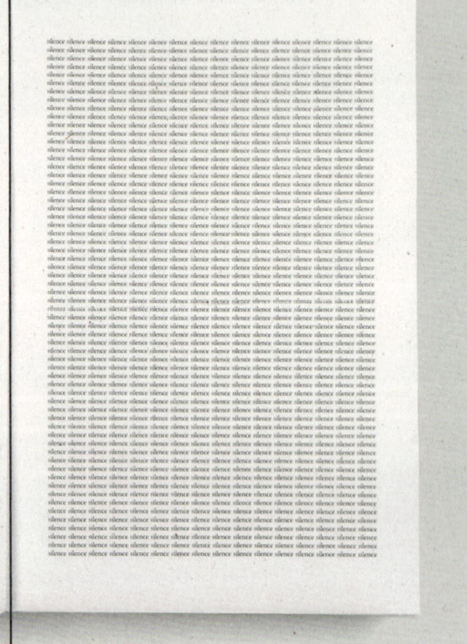

DESCRIPTION

Ten Million and One Silences is a project of extremes both in terms of scale and time. On the day of his mother's death, Daniele Pantano began to fill pages with the word "silence" as "a kind of daily prayer," first by hand in notebooks, later with the computer. He did this for twenty-four years until Saturday, March 13, 2021. This date was chosen because he "wanted the text to be finished at a point when [he] was older than [his] mother was when she committed suicide" (email by the author to apod.li). This makes for 10,000,001 instances of the word and about two pages of repetitive writing each day.

The project's physical representation in twenty-two volumes derives from Lulu's maximum page count for a hardcover book: each volume consists of 478 pages, except for the last one, which has 173 pages.

The project is conceptually framed as an endurance piece, yet the volumes were published all at once after the writing process was completed in 2021. By this, *Ten Million and One Silences* presents itself as a completed conceptual memoir in the form of an opaque book object rather than an act of durational writing. The price for each volume is also conceptual, being 100.01 in every currency. The entire series has a single ISBN, which is only mentioned on the publisher website but not in the books themselves. We have the first volume of the series in our collection.

Reading Writing Interfaces

AUTHOR	Andreas Bülhoff
YEAR	2022
PUBLISHER	sync.ed
GENRE	artistic research, artist's book / bookwork
METHOD	documentation / archiving, remediation, study / analysis
SUBJECT	analog / digital, book / book design, memory / storage, platforms / companies, scale, standard / default, technology, writing / reading techniques
PLATFORM	Lulu
VOLUMES	3
EDITION CHARACTERISTICS	open edition
FORMAT	15.4 × 21.6 cm
MATERIALITIES	color, dust jacket, hardcover, perfect bound

DESCRIPTION

Reading Writing Interfaces is a series of bookifications of the interfaces of writing software. Every interactive element of the graphical user interfaces of the three major "text editors" Apple TextEdit, Microsoft Word, and Adobe InDesign was screenshotted, cropped and set on single book pages to turn the interfaces into legible objects.

Interfaces are designed spaces of interaction. They not only represent and optimize certain workflows, but also control possible forms of interaction. At their core, they manifest assumptions and definitions of practices. By representing all possible ways of writing, designing, reviewing, and interacting with text in visible buttons and menus, text editors, word processors, and layout software impose definitions of writing and text on their users. Bülhoff's set of bookworks dissects the graphic representations of these assumptions and definitions by "demediating" them into the format of hardcover books as stable and well-practiced media. The length of the three books varies greatly, indicating the complexity and scope of the possible actions of the respective programs. Each book has the same minimalist-design dust jacket, but comes with a linen wrap in the color of each program's logo.

The title of the series makes reference to Lori Emerson's media-archaeologically savvy study of digital and analog text interfaces of the same name. The practice of dissecting the interface of writing software stems from an idea by Matthew Fuller, who took screenshots of Microsoft Word, printed them out, and cropped them by hand to be exhibited in his installation "A Song for Occupations" at Lux gallery in London in 2000.

TextEdit

PAGES	42 (unpaginated)
IMAGES	

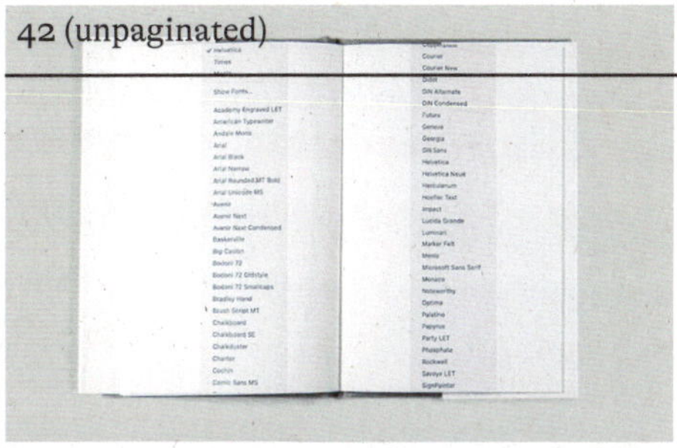

Word

PAGES	638 (unpaginated)
IMAGES	

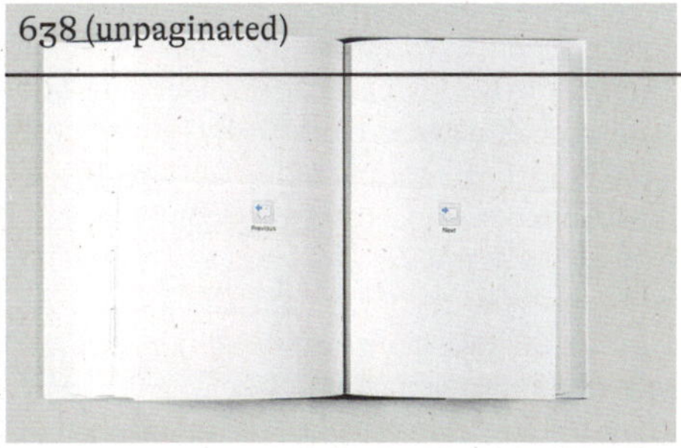

InDesign

PAGES	558 (unpaginated)
IMAGES	

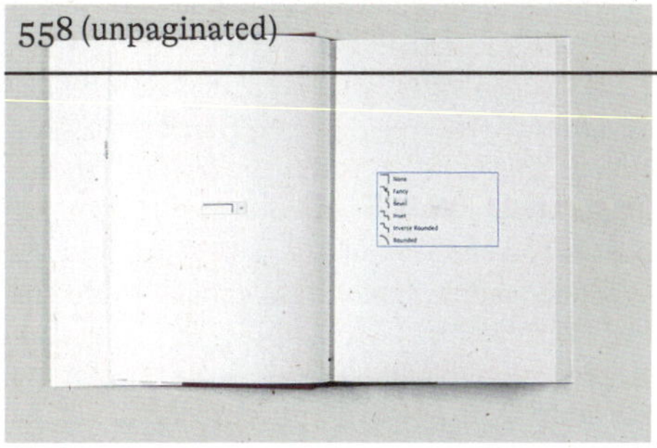

Musterexemplar

AUTHOR	Albert Coers
YEAR	2022
GENRE	artistic research, artist‘s book / bookwork
METHOD	détournement / hack, study / analysis, test / experiment, versioning / seriality
SUBJECT	book / book design, economy / labor, materiality, print technology
PLATFORM	others
VOLUMES	55
EDITION CHARACTERISTICS	available only through the artist, limited edition, numbered, dated, signed, unique copies
FORMAT	14.8 × 21.0 cm
MATERIALITIES	black-and-white, saddle stitch bound, original packaging and delivery note
PAGES	64 (unpaginated)

IMAGE

DESCRIPTION

With this series, Albert Coers tests the product range of a leading German online print shop. The available paper types (matt, glossy, sustainable, coated, refined, etc.) for the cover and inner section of a 64-page, staple-stitched A5 brochure result in a total of 55 combinations, each of which Coers orders one free sample copy in turn.

The informative value of such a sample copy is naturally limited. As *Dear Lulu* has shown (see 136f.), the test results cannot be generalized since with print on demand every print job takes place at a different time, with a different machine, and potentially at a different production site. In the end, every copy is unique and can only stand for itself. But Coers was only marginally interested in such a quality test. Otherwise he would not have left the pages of his brochure completely blank. The aim of the project was rather to research the operational processes and cost-benefit calculation of an online print shop and to order sample copies until the print shop would refuse production at some point.

Contrary to expectations, however, all 55 orders were filled and delivered. This suggests that such sample copies barely make a dent in the company's order volume. In addition, the possibility of fraudulent use of the samples (a strategy that publisher Olivier Bertrand, for example, actually applied for a while, see 81f.) is prevented by the fact that each page is marked with the oversized word "MUSTEREXEMPLAR" (sample copy) running diagonally across the page. This "devaluation" of the paper also becomes manifest in a symbolic way in the sample copies on thin paper, where the letters show through from the back of the page. The intersecting lines result in a space-filling "X," which for its part crosses out the pages once again and declares them worthless.

This means that Coers' brochures are no longer empty when printed. The text production is delegated to the printer, provoking a kind of automatically generated concrete poetry. The page-filling word also provides the title of the series, which is framed on the front and back by the artist's name, who is thus himself declared to be a model specimen of an author.

The sample copies are numbered and come in their original packaging with the delivery bill signed and dated by the artist. In this way, the entire ecosystem, including logistics and shipping, in which online print shops operate becomes visible and the subject of the series.

Our collection includes sample no. 14 (with 80g recycled paper white for the inner part and 300g recycled paper white for the cover) and no. 45 (with 250g paper matt for the inner part and 250g paper matt for the cover).

SW 4

Publishing Avant-Garde Classics A Retrospective Catalog

AUTHOR	Richard Kostelanetz
YEAR	2022
GENRE	catalog / collection, experimental literature
METHOD	collection, composition (writing / drawing / photography), détournement / hack, paratextual play
SUBJECT	art world / literary world, canon, copyright / law, literature, publishing / distribution, reading / interpretation
PLATFORM	Amazon
EDITION CHARACTERISTICS	ISBN 9798784353153, open edition
FORMAT	17.6 × 25.4 cm
MATERIALITIES	black-and-white, paperback, perfect bound
PAGES	223

IMAGE

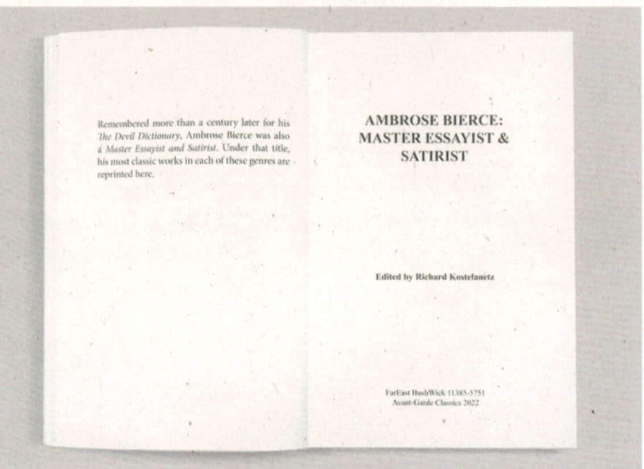

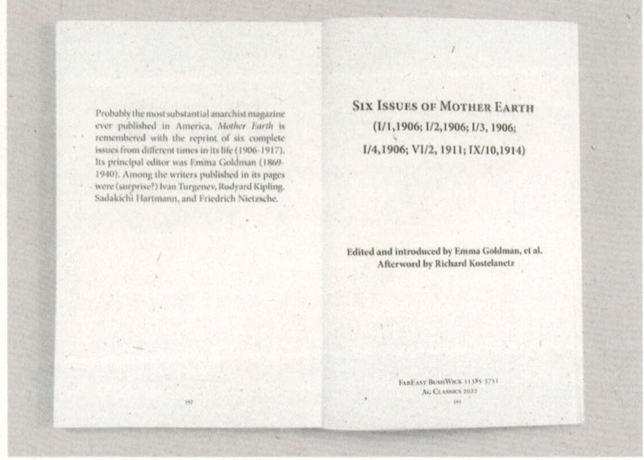

DESCRIPTION

After the old master of avant-garde and experimental literature Richard Kostelanetz discovered the new possibilities of self-publishing in the digital age, he used them on a large scale to reprint or first publish countless of his own works on Amazon, many of them under the label of his publishing house Archae Editions, founded in 1978 (see 159).

In 2022, "in memory of Dick Higgins (1938–1998), who understood what alternative publishers had to do" (Richard Kostelanetz, *Publishing Avant-Garde Classics*, VI), he founded the *Avant-Garde Classics* series for the publication of out-of-print, marginally published, forgotten, still unpublished avant-garde works and authors, which he wanted to make (re)accessible at the lowest possible price. For this he resorts to the services of Amazon's Kindle Direct Publishing, "because its prices could not be beaten and then because it was more likely to survive not only me but its competitors in the new business of on-demand publishing" (Ibid., VII). However, this is a risky bet on the future, after all, "Amazon prigs have rejected some Archae books (and twice even canceled all of my Archae books from its listing, only to reverse)" (Ibid., VII).

The selection of volumes for the series is largely based on personal preferences, but also on copyright considerations. Often, therefore, these are texts that are now in the public domain; otherwise, Kostelanetz specially redesigns, reintroduces, retranslates, and presents them in surprising pairings: "bringing together within a single set of covers certain texts not otherwise connected to one another" is what Kostelanetz calls "imaginative literary publishing" (Ibid., 82). In addition, the series includes discoveries of "ancient texts that retain avant-garde quality" (Ibid., X) and several works by Kostelanetz himself, to which the self-proclaimed "Earl of Wordship" likewise ascribes avant-garde status.

His introduction ends with the announcement: "I'm not done yet with books meant to survive. [...] [R]ather than printing annual catalogs, AGC will put on Amazon a continually expanding book of just title pages alphabetically organized, *Avant-Garde Classics*, priced as cheaply as possible, natch" (Ibid., X-XI). So far, however, one finds there only the volume *Publishing Avant-Garde Classics: A Retrospective Catalog*, which gathers the covers and blurb texts of 106 books published (or rather supposed to have been published) between 2021 and 2023.

Bibliography

/ aaaa press, *Addendum: Material, Paratexte, Notationen* (self-pub.: / aaaa press / Lulu, 2022), http://aaaa.etkbooks.com/.

ABC, "ABCED," *ABC* (blog), https://abcoop.tumblr.com/ABCED.
—, "ABCEUM: Information," ABC, *ABCEUM*, http://abceum.com/.
—, "The Worst Photo Books of 2013," *ABC* (blog), December 21, 2013, https://abcoop.tumblr.com/post/70695706079/the-worst-photo-books-of-2013.

Allen, Greg, "Well-Meaning Thoughts On Wohlgemeynte Gedanken," *greg.org* (blog), August 3, 2011, https://greg.org/archive/2011/08/03/well-meaning-thoughts-on-wohlgemeynte-gedanken.html.

AND Publishing, "Variable Formats" (website), http://andpublishing.org/variable-formats-2/.

Arista, Roberto, "VLM," http://projects.robertoarista.it/posts/VLM/.

Atomic Activity Books, "The Library of Nonhuman Books: Various titles," http://www.atomicactivity.com/nonhumanbooks/.

Bajohr, Hannes, "Algorithmic Empathy: Nick Montfort's 'Megawatt,'" *0x0a* (blog), January 1, 2015, https://0x0a.li/en/algorithmische-einfuehlung-nick-montforts-megawatt/.
—, "Print on Demand as Strategy and Genre: Auto-Factography and Post-Digital Writing," in this volume, 629–639.
—, "Prozess," in 0x0a, *Weisheit und Wiederholung. 104.052 philosophisch-literarische Desiderata* (self-pub.: 0x0a / Lulu, 2021), 724.

Balestrini, Nanni, "Note on the Text," in Nanni Balestrini, *Tristano: A Novel*, trans. Mike Harakis (London and New York: Verso, 2014), xi–xii.

Barthes, Roland, *Camera Lucida: Reflections on Photography*, trans. Richard Howard (New York City: Hill and Wang, 1981).

Benenson, Fred, "Emoji Dick," talk at Ignite NYC Open Hack Day, October 9, 2009, video, 05:24 min, https://www.youtube.com/watch?v=AHiU8h7lBRw.
—, "Emoji Dick is Officially Art & Acquired by the Library of Congress," Kickstarter, February 19, 2013, https://www.kickstarter.com/projects/fred/emoji-dick/posts/409203.

Blurb, "Terms & Conditions," Blurb, https://www.blurb.com/terms.

Bridle, James, "Introduction to the Drone Shadows," in James Bridle, *Drone Shadow Handbook* (self-pub.: Lulu, 2013), n.p.
—, "On Wikipedia, Cultural Patrimony, and Historiography," *booktwo.org* (blog), September 6, 2010, http://booktwo.org/notebook/wikipedia-historiography/.
—, "Under the Shadow of the Drone," *booktwo.org* (blog), October 11, 2012, https://booktwo.org/notebook/drone-shadows/.
—, "Where the F**k Was I? (A Book)," *booktwo.org* (blog), June 24, 2011, http://booktwo.org/notebook/where-the-f-k-was-i/.

Cabell, Mimi, "American Psycho" (website), https://www.mimicabell.com/#/american-psycho/.

Cage, John, *M: Writings '67–'72* (Middletown: Wesleyan University Press, 1983).

Carpenter, J. R., "Acknowledgment," in J. R. Carpenter, *GENERATION[S]* (self-pub.: TraumaWien / Lulu, 2010), 154–155.
—, "Generating Books: Paradoxical Print Snapshots of Digital Literary Processes," talk at "Mapping e-lit: Lectura i anàlisi de la literatura digital," Universitat de Barcelona, November 24–25, 2011, http://luckysoap.com/pdf/JRCarp_generatingbooks.pdf.

Carrión, Ulises, "The New Art of Making Books," in Ulises Carrión, *Second Thought* (Amsterdam: VOID, 1980), 6–22.

Castets, Simon, and Hans Ulrich Obrist, "Introduction," in *Filter Bubble*, ed. Simon Castets and Hans Ulrich Obrist (self-pub.: 89plus and The LUMA Foundation / Lulu, 2016), 9–15.

Castro, Ginette, *American Feminism: A Contemporary History* (New York and London: New York University Press, 1990).

Cayley, John, "On Primary Source," in Francesca Capone, *Primary Source* (self-pub.: Gauss PDF / Lulu, 2015), n.p.

Chen, Qiuzi, "Pure Compersion" (website), 2017, https://sva.design/projects/10080/pure-compersion/.

Certeau, Michel de, *The Practice of Everyday Life*, trans. Steven Rendall (Berkeley, Los Angeles, and London: University of California Press, 1984).

Cirio, Paolo, "Sociality: The Coloring Book of Technology for Social Manipulation" (foreword), in Paolo Cirio, *Sociality: The Coloring Book of Technology for Social Manipulation* (self-pub.: Lulu, 2018), n.p.
—, "Theoretical Text about *Sociality*," 2018, https://paolocirio.net/press/texts/text_sociality.php.

Constant, "The Death of the Authors, 1941" (website), 2013, https://web.archive.org/web/20230605101318/https://www.books.constantvzw.org/home/death_of_the_authors.

Corcoran, Heather, "Foreword," in *Best of Rhizome 2012*, ed. Joanne McNeil (Brescia: LINK Editions / Lulu, 2013), 1.

Counterpath Press, "Reading @realDonaldTrump" (website), 2016, http://counterpathpress.org/reading-realdonaldtrump-series.

CSUB Todd Madigan Gallery, "The Bakersfield Fan Forum" (press release), The Poetic Research Bureau, November 2017, https://www.poeticresearch.com/events/bff.

Cussen, Felipe (@felipecussen), Twitter, February 4, 2020, https://twitter.com/felipecussen/status/1224774950277566466.

De Decker, Kris, "About the Solar Powered Website," *Low-tech Magazine*, last updated April 22, 2022, https://solar.lowtechmagazine.com/about/the-solar-website/.
—, "The Printed Website: Second Volume Out Now," *Low-tech Magazine*, 2019, https://www.lowtechmagazine.com/2019/12/the-printed-website-is-complete.html.
—, "The Printed Comments," *Low-tech Magazine*, 2021, https://www.lowtechmagazine.com/low-tech-magazine-the-printed-comments.html.
—, "The Printed Website," *Low-tech Magazine*, 2019, https://www.lowtechmagazine.com/low-tech-magazine-the-printed-website.html.
—, "The Printed Website: Volume III & The Comments," *Low-tech Magazine*, 2021, https://www.lowtechmagazine.com/2021/12/printed-website-third-volume.html.

Dexter Sinister, "The Price of *Philip*," January 3, 2007, http://www.dextersinister.org/library.html?id=63.

Dodman, Craig, and Philip Miletic, "Introduction," in Craig Dodman and Philip Miletic, *world 1-1* (self-pub.: The LUMA Foundation / Lulu, 2014), n.p.

Doeringer, Eric, "Sol LeWitt Wall Drawing Recreations," https://web.archive.org/web/20230415070013/https://www.ericdoeringer.com/ConArtRec/LeWitt/LeWitt.html.

Dworkin, Craig, and Kenneth Goldsmith, ed., *Against Expression: An Anthology of Conceptual Writing* (Evanston, Ill.: Northwestern University Press, 2011).

Edwards, Geraint, "Foreword," in Geraint Edwards, *Erased Erased de Kooning Drawing* (self-pub.: Amazon, 2017), n.p.

Eisenecker, Jasper Otto, "Camouflaged Books" (website), https://jasperotto.com/camouflaged-books/.
—, *How to Camouflage Books in Times of Internet-Censorship. An Instruction Guide* (self-publ.: Lulu, 2014–2016).

exquisite_code, "Editorial Mechanics," in exquisite_code, *Heroic Real Estate Otter of the 21st Century* (self-pub.: Lulu, 2013), v–vi.
Fanon, Frantz, *Black Skin, White Masks,* trans. Charles Lam Markmann (London: Pluto Press, 1986).

Faylor, J. Gordon, and Danny Snelson, "Editorial Note," in *Selected Essays about a Bibliography*, ed. J. Gordon Faylor and Danny Snelson (self-pub.: Edit Publications / Lulu, 2010), 7.

Fink, Thomas, "Richard Kostelanetz's *Fict/ions* and *This Sentence*," review, *Talisman. A Journal of Contemporary Poetry and Poetics* 41 (2013), https://talismanarchive.weebly.com/finkkostelanetz.html.

Flender, Karl Wolfgang, "American Psycho. Reading an Algorithm in Reverse," *Interface Critique Journal* 2 (2019): 197–211, https://journals.ub.uni-heidelberg.de/index.php/ic/article/view/66992.

Fossenbell, Jennifer, "Chris Sylvester's *Still Life With The Pokemon*," *The Volta Blog*, April 27, 2015, https://thevoltablog.wordpress.com/2014/02/20/chris-sylvesters-still-life-with-the-pokemon/.

Foucault, Michel, "Le philosophe masqué," interview by Christian Delacampagne, *Le Monde*, April 7, 1980, https://www.lemonde.fr/archives/article/1980/04/07/le-philosophe-masque_2803327_1819218.html.

Fry, Ben, "The *Frankenfont* project," 2011, https://benfry.com/frankenfont/.

Funkhouser, Chris, "Afterword," in Chris Funkhouser, *WhereisMineral: Selected Adventures in MOO* (self-pub.: Gauss PDF / Lulu, 2015), n.p.

Gitelman, Lisa, "Emoji Dick and the Eponymous Whale," in *Book Presence in a Digital Age*, ed. Kiene Brillenburg Wurth, Kári Driscoll, and Jessica Pressman (New York: Bloomsbury Academic, 2018), 195–210.

Goggin, James, "Farben on Demand," in James Goggin, Frank Philippin, and Students of the Faculty of Design at the University of Applied Sciences Darmstadt, *Dear Lulu, Please try and print these line, colour, pattern, format, texture and typography tests for us* (self-pub.: Lulu, 2008), 36–41.

Goldman, Judith, "Joey Yearous-Algozin's verbatim transcription of three years of voicemail addressed to his partner Holly Melgard," review, *zoran rosko vacuum player* (blog), May 4, 2015, https://zorosko.blogspot.com/2015/05/joey-yearous-algozins-verbatim.html.

Goldsmith, Kenneth, *Uncreative Writing: Managing Language in the Digital Age* (New York: Columbia University Press, 2011).

Harbach, Chad, "MFA vs. NYC: America now has two distinct literary cultures. Which one will last?," *N+1*, November 26, 2010, https://slate.com/culture/2010/11/mfa-vs-nyc-america-now-has-two-distinct-literary-cultures-which-one-will-last.html.

Henner, Mishka, "Epilogue," in Mishka Henner, *Harry Potter and the Scam Baiter* (self-pub.: Lulu, 2012), 319.

Indie Photobook Library, "Portfolio," January 17, 2011, http://www.indiephotobooklibrary.org/2011/01/portfolio/.

Iersel, Wil van, "About," *Every Day a New Photo Book* (blog), https://septemberbook.wordpress.com/about/.

Jadick, Jason, "The Uncreative Subterranean" (blog), https://theuncreativesubterranean.tumblr.com/.

Jasmin, Pierre, "L-MEM Wiki," http://www.pierrejasmin.com/wiki/.

Kaplan, Josef, *Kill List* (Baltimore: Cars Are Real, 2013).

Kennedy, Erik, "Epic Lyric Poem," *Queen Mob's Teahouse*, February 21, 2015, https://queenmobs.com/2015/02/epic-lyric-poem/.

Laidler, Paul, "Digitally Remastered!," *Just P Press: Digitally mediated Artefacts and Extensions of Prints* (blog), March 29, 2010, http://justpressprint.blogspot.com/2010/03/digitally-remastered.html.

Le Fraga, Sophia, "An Interview," interview by Andrew Worthington, *HTMLGiant*, November 6, 2013, http://htmlgiant.com/author-spotlight/an-interview-with-sophia-le-fraga/.

Lechner, Marie, "Preamble," in *The Pirate Book*, ed. Nicolas Maigret and Maria Roszkowska (self-pub.: Aksioma / Lulu, 2015), n.p.

Lee, Janice, "An Interview with Michael du Plessis," *Entropy*, March 24, 2014, https://web.archive.org/web/20220516050732/https://entropymag.org/an-interview-with-michael-du-plessis/.

LeWitt, Sol, "Doing Wall Drawings [1971]," in *Sol LeWitt. Critical Texts*, ed. Adachiara Zevi (Rome and Cologne: Libri de AEIUO and Walther König, 1995), 95–96.

Lin, Tan, "A Book is Technology," interview by Angela Genusa, *Rhizome*, October 24, 2012 https://rhizome.org/editorial/2012/oct/24/interview-tan-lin/.
—, "Troll Thread Interview," *Harriet* (blog), *Poetry Foundation*, May 4, 2014, https://www.poetryfoundation.org/harriet/2014/05/troll-thread-interview.
—, Danny Snelson, and Kristen Gallagher, ed., "Notes on an Edit Event," MediaWiki, last modified August 29, 2010, https://web.archive.org/web/20100927183020/http://aphasic-letters.com/edit-wiki/index.php?title=Network_Publishing_with_Tan_Lin.

Lorusso, Silvio, "Extending Horizons: The Praxis of Experimental Publishing in the Age of Digital Networks. Design, Art, and the Materialities of Mediation" (PhD diss., Iuav University of Venice, 2015/16), https://archive.org/details/ExtendingHorizons.

Macdonald, Travis, "Process Note," in Travis Macdonald, *3...* (self-pub.: Gauss PDF / Lulu 2017), 3.

Mandiberg, Michael, "About," Michael Mandiberg, *Print Wikipedia* (website), 2015, https://printwikipedia.com/#/about.
—, "Making *Print Wikipedia*," in this volume, 512–521.

Maranda, Michael, "The Books: Our Series," Parasitic Ventures Press, http://parasiticventurespress.com/books/?page_id=80.
—, "Syntactic Analyses Series," Parasitic Ventures Press, June 17, 2007, http://parasiticventurespress.com/books/?p=485.

mdsm, "Photobook is" (website), https://www.msdm.org.uk/photobook-is.

Melgard, Holly, *Essays for a Canceled Anthology: HOLLY MELGARD READS HOLLY MELGARD* (self-pub.: Troll Thread / Lulu, 2017).
—, "Foreword," in Holly Melgard, *THE MAKING OF THE AMERICANS* (self-pub.: Troll Thread / Lulu, 2012), front matter.

Montfort, Nick, "*Autopia* and *The Truelist*: Language Combined in Two Computer-Generated Books," *Electronic Book Review*, April 4, 2021, https://electronicbookreview.com/essay/autopia-and-the-truelist-language-combined-in-two-computer-generated-books/.
—, "Preface," in Nick Montfort, *Megawatt: A novel computationally, deterministically generated extending passages from Samuel Beckett's* Watt (self-pub.: Bad Quarto / EBM, 2014), n.p.

Morris, Simon, "Getting inside Jack Kerouac's Head" (blog), 2008/09, http://gettinginsidejackkerouacshead.blogspot.com/.
—, *Getting inside Jack Kerouac's Head* (York: Information as Material, 2010).

Ö1, "Asylabwehramt – dem Menschen zum Schutze," radio broadcast, 21:58 min, Ö1, April 8, 2017, https://oe1.orf.at/artikel/246521/Asylabwehramt-dem-Menschen-zum-Schutze.

onestar press, "Callout: Emerging Graphic Designers for Book Machine," VOLUME | Another Art Book Fair, Sydney 2015, http://vaabf.com/bookmachine1b.
—, "Book Machine" (website), https://bookmachine.info/.
—, "Book Machine (Sydney) II: Participants Guidelines," VOLUME | Another Art Book Fair and Artspace, Sydney 2017, http://vaabf.com/s/BookMachine_Artspace-mmtx.pdf.

Parr, Martin and Garry Badger, *The Photobook: A History*, vol. 3 (London: Phaidon Press, 2014).

Passig, Kathrin, "Bücher," http://kathrin.passig.de/buecher.html.
—, (@kathrinpassig), Twitter, February 9, 2020, https://twitter.com/kathrinpassig/status/1226626915664044034.
—, Twitter, February 29, 2020, https://twitter.com/kathrinpassig/status/1233772454524456960.
—, "Yes, today it's boring. But in 20 years!," in this volume, 522–530.

Pelta Feldman, Julia, "Gregor Weichbrodt: No Offense," *0x0a* (blog), November 1, 2015, https://0x0a.li/en/gregor-weichbrodt-no-offense/.

Pichler, Michalis, "COLLAGE [PAGE PIECES]," in *Publishing Manifestos*, ed. Michalis Pichler (Berlin: Miss Read, 2018), 233.

Place, Vanessa, "Artist's Statement: Gone With the Wind @VanessaPlace," Genius, May 19, 2014, https://genius.com/Vanessa-place-artists-statement-gone-with-the-wind-vanessaplace-annotated.

Porter, Louis, "ABCEUM," https://louisporter.com/ABCEUM.

Publication Studio, "About Us," https://publicationstudio.biz/about/.

Quaranta, Domenico, "Collect the WWWorld: The Artist as Archivist in the Internet Age," in *Collect the WWWorld: The Artist as Archivist in the Internet Age*, ed. Domenico Quaranta (self-pub.: LINK editions / Lulu, 2011), 4–23.
—, "In the Uncanny Valley. Research notes about art, and about what is uncannily similar to it…," *In the Uncanny Valley* (blog), https://intheuncannyvalley.tumblr.com/about.

Reed, Aaron A., "Subcutanean: A horror novel of parallel realities where no two copies are the same" (website), https://subcutanean.textories.com/.
—, "Why I Made Subcutanean," Medium, October 28, 2019, https://medium.com/@aareed/why-i-made-subcutanean-1fb8e47bbf89.

roush, paula, "Introduction to the Unit," in paula roush, *THE PHOTOBOOK PROJECT at LULU.COM: Brief Led Project AME-3-BLP* (self-pub.: Lulu, 2007), 3.
—, "Introduction to the Unit," in paula roush, *Photographic Cultures AME-2-PHC FALL 08: harnessing the power of self-publishing technologies for the creation and distribution of photobooks* (self-pub.: Lulu, 2008), 4.
—, and Ruth Brown, "Publishing with Friends: Exploring Social Networks to Support Photo Publishing Practices," in this volume, 661–669.

Rozendaal, Rafaël, "Notes on Abstract Browsing," https://www.newrafael.com/notes-on-abstract-browsing/.

Sadokierski, Zoë, "Prologue," in Zoë Sadokierski, *Books On Demand: An Exhibition of 12 Illustrated Books Produced Using Print-on-Demand Services* (self-publ.: Page Screen Books / Lulu, 2014), 9.
—, "A Book Conceived before Breakfast and Delivered before Lunch," in this volume, 531–535.

Schauer, Hendrikje, and Marcel Lepper, *Titelpaare. Ein philosophisches und literarisches Wörterbuch* (Stuttgart: Works and Nights, 2018).

Schmid, Joachim, "American Photographs" (website), July 21, 2013, https://www.lumpenfotografie.de/2013/07/21/american-photographs/.
—, "Attitudes and Approaches," interview by Tanja Lažetić, *Fotokritik*, January 9, 2012, https://fotokritik.wordpress.com/2012/01/09/attitudes-and-approaches/.
—, "Doing Things," *Fotokritik*, April 7, 2015, https://fotokritik.wordpress.com/2015/04/07/doing-things/.
—, "L.A. Women" (website), July 21, 2013, https://www.lumpenfotografie.de/2013/07/21/l-a-women/.
—, "Lost Memories" (website), July 21, 2013, https://www.lumpenfotografie.de/2013/07/21/lost-memories/.
—, "Other People's Photographs (2008–2011)" (website), June 1, 2011, https://otherpeoplesphotographs.wordpress.com/.
—, "Photography Is," *Fotokritik*, March 10, 2010, https://fotokritik.wordpress.com/2010/03/11/photography-is/.
—, "Quick Response" (website), July 21, 2013, https://www.lumpenfotografie.de/2013/07/21/quick-response/.

Schmieg, Sebastian, "Networked Optimization" (website), https://sebastianschmieg.com/networkedoptimization/.

Seita, Sophie, "Communities of Print in the Digital Age," in this volume, 640–651.

Snelson, Danny, "2015: *Broken 56 Broken Kindle Screens*," Edit Publications 2010–2020, https://dss-edit.com/pub/b-56-b-k-s/.
—, "2015: *Flash Paper Mixtape*," Edit Publications 2010–2020, https://dss-edit.com/pub/flash-paper-mixtape/.
—, "Edit Publications 2010–2020: 2014," Edit Publications 2010–2020, https://dss-edit.com/pub/woodslippercounterclattertranscript/.
—, "Epic Lyric Poem" (website), October 12, 2014, https://dss-edit.com/epic-lyric-poem/.
—, "Grey Libraries: Publishing as Pedagogy, An Annotated Bibliography," in this volume, 670–683.
—, "NUPoD: Print on Demand Poetry: Making Books After the Internet" (blog), Fall 2015, https://nupod.tumblr.com/.

Snelson, Daniel Scott, "Variable Format: Media Poetics and the Little Database" (PhD diss., University of Pennsylvania, 2015), https://monoskop.org/images/8/8c/Snelson_Daniel_Variable_Format_Media_Poetics_and_the_Little_Database_2015.pdf.

Solanas, Valerie, *SCUM Manifesto* (London: Olympia Press, 1971).

Soulellis, Paul, "About," *Library of the Printed Web* (blog), 2017, https://libraryoftheprintedweb.tumblr.com/about.
—, "Readme: *Steve, Harvey and Matt*, (2018)," Github, https://github.com/soulellis/epa.
—, "Urgent Publishing after the Artist's Book: Making Public in Movements towards Liberation," *APRIA Journal* 3, no. 3 (October 2021): 31–43, https://www.ingentaconnect.com/content/artez/apria/2021/00000003/00000003/art00005.

Stephens, Paul, *absence of clutter: minimal writing as art and literature* (Cambridge, Mass.: MIT Press, 2020).

Steyerl, Hito, "In Defense of the Poor Image," *e-flux Journal* 10 (November 2009), https://www.e-flux.com/journal/10/61362/in-defense-of-the-poor-image/.

Stiftung Buchkunst, *Die Schönsten Deutschen Bücher 2016* (Frankfurt/Main: Stiftung Buchkunst, 2016).

Surfaces Utiles, "what's left over from the works of maxime le bon," http://www.surfaces-utiles.org/whats-left-over-the-works-of-le-bon.html.

Syjuco, Stephanie, "Phantoms (H__RT _F D_RKN_SS)" (website), https://www.stephaniesyjuco.com/projects/phantoms-h-rt-f-d-rkn-ss.

The Piracy Project, "The Impermanent Reader," in *Best of Rhizome 2012*, ed. Joanne McNeil (Brescia: LINK Editions / Lulu, 2013), 21–28.

The Post-Art Poets, "The Post-Art Poetics Archive," https://www.postartpoets.com/archive.html.
—, "The Post-Art Poetics Manifesto," https://www.postartpoets.com/index.html.

Thoburn, Nick, "Twitter, Book, Riot: Post-Digital Publishing against Race," *Theory: Culture & Society* 37, no. 3 (2020): 97–121, https://doi.org/10.1177/0263276419891573.

Thurston, Nick, "Document Practices," *transmediale journal: face value* 1 (2018), ed. Elvia Wilk, August 7, 2018, https://archive.transmediale.de/content/document-practices.
—, "Back to Front Truths. Hate Library," in *Post-Digital Cultures of the Far Right: Online Actions and Offline Consequences in Europe and the US*, ed. Maik Fielitz and Nick Thurston (Bielefeld: transcript 2019), 193–204, https://doi.org/10.25969/mediarep/12384.
—, "Hate Library (multi-media installation, 12 volume bookwork, 2017)" (website), https://www.nickthurston.info/work/hate-library/.

Til, Jan van der, "Concepts of Work," *Rhizomebook*, https://web.archive.org/web/20211018004226/https://www.rhizomebook.com/c-5701083/concepts-of-work/.
—, "Further Reading," *Rhizomebook*, https://web.archive.org/web/20211018014252/https://www.rhizomebook.com/c-5701084/further-reading/.
—, "Introduction," *Rhizomebook*, https://web.archive.org/web/20211018020400/https://www.rhizomebook.com/c-5709246/introduction/.

Tonnard, Elisabeth, *A Thorough Examination of Jonathan Lewis' book* The End, video, 2:08 min, 2011, https://www.youtube.com/watch?v=s7wNUj-QJHs.

Ubermorgen, "Asylum Defence Agency" (website), https://www.asylabwehramt.at/index_e.html.

Vilayphiou, Stéphanie, "About," BCC: Blind Carbon Copy (website), http://bcc.stdin.fr/About/index.html.
—, "BCC: Blind Carbon Copy" (website), http://bcc.stdin.fr/.
—, "Copyright Disclaimer," BCC: Blind Carbon Copy (website), http://bcc.stdin.fr/.

Washko, Angela, "April 27, 2015: an explanation of the work in question," in Angela Washko, *BANGed: A Monopoly on Truth* (self-pub: Lulu, 2015), n.p.
—, "BANGed: A Monopoly on Truth" (website), https://angelawashko.com/artwork/3831453-BANGed%3a%20A%20Monopoly%20on%20Truth.html.
—, "On Public Opinion: *Responses to BANGed*" (website), https://angelawashko.com/artwork/3831440_On_Public_Opinion_Responses_to_BANGed.html.

Watier, Éric, "jim is jim" (website), December 19, 2013, https://www.ericwatier.info/editions/jim-is-jim/.
—, "jim is jim" (blog), https://jimisjim.tumblr.com/.
—, "Manifeste monotone / Monotone manifesto," in *Publishing Manifestos*, ed. Michalis Pichler (Cambridge, Mass.: MIT Press 2019), 198–200.
—, "the scan collection" (blog), https://thescancollection.tumblr.com/.

Webster, Barron, "Buy my Privacy" (website), https://buymyprivacy.com/.

Weichbrodt, Gregor, "0x0a Cover Art," *0x0a* (blog), December 4, 2014, https://0x0a.li/en/0x0a-cover-art/.
—, "On the Road" (website), December 2013, https://gregorweichbrodt.de/project/on-the-road/.

Whalen, Zach, "An Arthrogram, Part 1," October 26, 2015, http://www.zachwhalen.net/posts/an-arthrogram.
—, "Some Notes on Analyzing the Content of *Emoji Dick*," June 26, 2022, https://www.zachwhalen.net/notes/note-1656258366.

Wooldridge, Duncan, "Abceum (Museum on Demand)," ABC, *ABCEUM: Essay*, 2014, http://abceum.com/.

Zanni, Carlo, "About," *My Country is a Living Room* (website), http://mycountryisalivingroom.com/about/.

zeltil, yigru, "for/word," in yigru zeltlil, *A Bibliography of Conceptual Writing: v1.01* (self-pub.: khora impex / Lulu, 2017), 13–19, http://workinprogressconpo.blogspot.com/.
—, "note," in yigru zeltlil, *A Bibliography of Conceptual Writing: v1.01* (self-pub.: khora impex / Lulu, 2017), 7–11.

Zoller, Rahel, *Catalogue of Mistakes by Rahel Zoller 2011–2021* (self-pub., 2021).

Zschiegner, Hermann, *Astronomical – The Bootleg Movie*, video, 4:34 min, https://www.youtube.com/watch?v=jvcxoaobrUY.
—, "Bootleg Books," Follow-ed.com, https://web.archive.org/web/20141006033952/http://www.follow-ed.com/bootleg-books/.
—, "This Book Should," Follow-ed.com, https://follow-ed.com/this-book-should/.
—, "+walker evans +sherrie levine" (artist's note), in Hermann Zschiegner, *+walker evans +sherrie levine* (self-pub.: Blurb, 2008), n.p.

Zucconi, Damon, "Spiritual Door," JTT Gallery, 2016, https://jttnyc.com/exhibitions/2016/spiritual-door.

Ess

ays

Techn
& Mat

ology
eriality

Alessandro Ludovico

Print on Demand: The Balance of Power Between Paper and Pixel[1]

1. Reprinted from Alessandro Ludovico, *Post-Digital Print: The Mutation of Publishing since 1894* (Eindhoven: Onomatopee 2012), 70–78.

Print has specific qualities which remain as of yet undisputed. Holding a printed object in one's own hands, or seeing it on a bookshelf, remains an essential experience in (at least some parts of) our cultural environment. And the "balance of power" between print and digital (if we still assume the end result to be some kind of printed product) seems now to lie with one technology which, more than any other, is allowing the printed page to survive the "digitization of everything": print-on-demand.

During the late 1990s, most of the "prepress" services (small businesses which helped customers convert their often messy digital files into plates suitable for offset printing) started mutating into today's digital printing services. Increasingly, digital printing machines were replacing offset printing for short print runs; this was made possible by the rapidly falling prices of high-speed laser printers (the first commercially available laser printer, introduced in 1977, was the Xerox 9700; such machines were originally marketed to large office departments, enabling them to quickly print high-quality structured documents). Within just a few years, dedicated digital book-printing facilities were set up across the world, and the technology is now being seriously considered by publishers, particularly since the onset of the current economic crisis.

Print-on-demand is an extremely simple concept: the customer produces a PDF file of a magazine or book, and the print-on-demand service charges the customer a fee (there are cheaper and more expensive services, depending on the quantity and quality of services provided) to prepare and adjust the files for the production chain of a high-resolution, large-format, continuous digital copier. The customer can order any number of copies (even a single one) and the product is typically delivered within a week or so.

In addition to the actual printing, the print-on-demand firm may offer some important additional services:

1. The firm can arrange to sell the publications online through its own infrastructure, paying the author or publisher monthly percentages on sales.
2. Print-on-demand firms, especially the major ones, can provide detailed information about their publications to online outlets worldwide, in order to generate orders. This is what Simon Worthington (founder of *Mute* magazine, which at some point switched to print-on-demand) refers to as "the bookspace."
3. Print-on-demand firms usually operate several facilities on different continents, each printing only for nearby countries, thus saving substantially on shipping costs as well as on CO_2 emissions (and somehow reminiscent of the 1970s, when major international newspapers were wired overseas using large facsimile machines so they could be printed locally the very same day).
4. Publications are not required to generate continuous interest or sales, but may remain in the online catalogue indefinitely at no extra cost, simply waiting to be printed upon request.
5. The cost of producing the first copy is very low, depending on the specific package of services provided to the author or publisher, but can be as little as €10 to €20 for a regular book.

The major publishers in this field (Lulu, Lightning Source, Author Solutions) now already carry hundreds of thousands of titles in their ever-expanding catalogues. Amazon, the largest online bookshop, has already set up a subsidiary company called Create Space, as a part of their "Advantage Program," in order to include authors and publishers "of all sizes" in their platform.

Besides books, and of course photographs, print-on-demand is also being used for office reports and other business-related publications. The "Virtual Printer" is a service that allows customers to send a PDF of (for example) an office report, which is then printed and bound in the desired number of copies, and delivered to either a FedEx courier store or the customer's address. Meanwhile, businesses such as Hewlett-Packard claim to be in the process of transforming themselves from a printer company to a printing company, focused on "Print 2.0… that embraces the Web as a channel to make printing more accessible, customizable and less expensive."

There are also independent ventures such as Crowdbooks which publishes photobooks using the Kickstarter model: donating to a project we like, usually getting something back, proportional to the amount of the donation. The publisher offers a preview of a book project, which interested people can fund by buying copies in advance or simply donating money for the publication. If enough funds are generated, the book is published, distributed and promoted.

Finally, one new product that could significantly change the ways books are sold is the Espresso Book Machine, which can quickly print a single copy of any book from a digital PDF file. The machine can process a 300-page book (including cover and glue binding) in a few minutes, which seems to support the American manufacturer's definition of its product as an "ATM for books." It costs $175,000, a price which should drop sharply as more units are sold, offering small and independent bookshops an opportunity to remain competitive.

VANITY PRESS, FREEDOM OF EXPRESSION AND SELF-GRATIFICATION

Print-on-demand changes one fundamental rule of publishing: it is no longer necessary to invest a (small) starting capital. Anyone can easily raise the nominal charge (typically much less than €100) required to publish a book or magazine. Furthermore, the only technical knowledge required is the ability to properly generate a PDF file (you can also spend a few hundred euros more, and have the print-on-demand firm generate it for you). The PDF file is then sent to the print-on-demand facility, and within a few days the book is ready and can be instantly offered for sale online.

This opens several possibilities, which have already started to have an impact on various (online) businesses and communities. One of these is "vanity press"—a term traditionally used to describe a type of publisher whose business model consists of making a profit by publishing books at the author's expense. With the new possibilities of print-on-demand, countless new vanity press publishers are now offering their services at bargain-bottom prices.

The vanity press phenomenon is in itself far from new: the March 25, 1893 issue of the *Newark Daily Advocate* newspaper (from Newark, Ohio, USA) featured a series of predictions of what the world might look like after 100 years, by 1993. The journalist Nym Crinkle wrote:

> Every person of fairly good education and of restless mind writes a book. As a rule, it is a superficial book, but it swells the bulk and it indicated the cerebral unrest that is trying to express itself. We have arrived at a condition in which more books are printed than the world can read.

Furthermore, by 1993 "there will not be so many books printed, but there will be more said. That seems to me to be inevitable."[2] Unfortunately, it seems that we have instead reverted to a situation comparable to 1893, when there was almost no need to limit or filter the production of content.

Clay Shirky, writing on the social and economic effects of Internet, spoke of blogs in terms that may just as well apply to vanity press: "The Gutenberg revolution is over […] It's going from a world of 'filter, then publish' […] to 'publish, then filter.'"[3] And this applies even more to print-on-demand "vanity publishing." The original publishing paradigm, with editors carefully selecting, editing, and proofing content before it could be printed, is being superseded by what Shirky defines as "mass amateurization." This in turn is having a signifi-

2. http://www.scribd.com/doc/15576150/1893-March-25-Newark-Daily-Advocate-Newark-OH-Pa-Leo-Future.

3. Liesl Schillinger, "Gutenberg Is Dead; Long Live Gutenberg," *New York Times*, March 12, 2009, https://archive.nytimes.com/artsbeat.blogs.nytimes.com/2009/03/12/gutenberg-is-dead-long-live-gutenberg/.

cant impact on the more commercial print-on-demand efforts, since the self-gratification of seeing a book with one's own name on the cover is an attractive prospect for many potential customers. Meanwhile, the mass media are publicizing this development as a social phenomenon, presenting it as some new promised land for would-be writers. This is quite similar to the mirage of what the internet was supposed to mean for musicians: anyone can publish their work, and who knows, if it turns out to be outstanding (the classic American Dream rhetoric), then you too can become a literary star.

On the other hand, experimental books can now be published without having to spend large sums of money. A nice example is *My Life in Tweets* by James Bridle—a collection of all the author's posts on Twitter during two years, as a sort of intimate travelogue. Here the printed book is an innovative hybrid of something momentary (a Twitter post) and something which is meant to remain (a diary) in a perfectly classic graphic format.[4] Perhaps inspired by this book's success, various services appealing to the Twitter microblogger's "vanity" have cropped up, such as Bookapp's *Tweetbook* which makes it possible to print one's tweets in a standard book format, and *Tweetghetto* which uses the tweets to generate a poster which can then be purchased for display.

An individual's "virtual identity" (the collection of posts and other activities on social networking sites such as Twitter and Facebook) is by nature ephemeral—unless of course it is printed. And so, as part of a promotional strategy for the French telecommunications company Bouygues Télécom, the DDB Paris ad agency invented a new kind of printed product: an offline copy of a Facebook profile. Participants could order a book of their own profile, covering a specified timeframe and including profiles of up to ten of their friends. The campaign was a huge success: 1,000 books were requested within one hour.

Finally, taking the concept of vanity press to the limit, Fiona Banner's *Book 1 of 1*[5] is a conceptual artwork which "questions the currency of the multiple or limited edition." Each of her "books" is a single-page, single-copy publication "printed on reflective mirror card" and "registered under its own individual title" and ISBN. Each single copy of the edition is thus an official publication in its own right, meeting all the administrative requirements (which, interestingly, do not include text content). The result is an imaginary printed space, reduced to a single, almost empty page which reflects both (metaphorically) the author's intention and (literally) the reader's face in its mirror cover.

THE FRONTIERS OF PRINT-ON-DEMAND: CUSTOMISATION AND OPEN SOURCE

Of course, print-on-demand is a medium suitable for all kinds of business models besides vanity press. In fact, several established publishers have started releasing their out-of-print back catalogs in print-on-demand. Also, the University of Michigan's Shapiro Library has purchased an Espresso Book Machine specifically for the purpose of printing such titles.

Another possibility, still under development, is to customize the printed content for each individual customer. Various web-to-print-on-demand technologies are currently being developed to allow customers to select their own content—which, in the case of books, amounts to individual readers compiling their own publication. Such a level of customization will undoubtedly signify a major shift in the role of the editor, since it effectively does away with the traditional publishing model of printing thousands of copies of the exact same content. While this obviously means more freedom for the reader, it also introduces a new problem for writers, who can no longer be sure their content is reaching every customer.

Some experiments with this kind of mass customization have already been conducted in recent years. In June 2004, all 40,000 subscribers of the monthly libertarian magazine *Reason* found on the cover a digitally printed satellite photo of their own neighborhood—with their own location marked by a red circle. The magazine also included several advertisements customized to each particular recipient. A similar approach was further explored by *Wired* magazine for their July 2007 issue; 5,000 subscribers were given the option of receiving their own customized cover of *Wired*, featuring their own photo on the cover. The experiment was sponsored by Xerox and produced using their iGen3 digital printing machine.

4. James Bridle, "Vanity Press Plus: The Tweetbook," *booktwo.org*, blog, March 16, 2009, http://booktwo.org/notebook/vanity-press-plus-the-tweetbook/.

5. http://www.fionabanner.com/vanitypress/book11/index.htm.

Fig. 1: Customized issue of *Reason* magazine, June 2004.
Fig. 2: Customized issue of *Wired* magazine, July 2007.

Combining print-on-demand with software to generate potentially infinite permutations of content is already being applied outside the field of experimental self-publishing, in the mainstream publishing business. Already in 2007, the English publishing house Faber & Faber commissioned the designer Karsten Schmidt to participate in the development of a software system for generating complete, print-ready book covers for its new *Faber Finds* back catalog imprint. The assignment was to create a "design machine" flexible enough to generate a very large (theoretically infinite) number of unique designs—one for each book published in the imprint. The design itself, developed by the Canadian typographer Marian Bantjes, consists of a collection of shapes which are 'parameterized' and broken down into smaller elements, which in turn became micro-templates, thus forming a "vocabulary" of shapes. The software generates a new cover every second, then judges whether the design is valid or should be discarded.

Fig. 3: Karsten Schmidt's generated Faber & Faber covers, 2008.

Software has a long history of producing questionable results—particularly when these results are meant to be passed off as the work of a human. *The Bachelor Machine*, an artwork by Per-Oskar Leu, presents us with a perfect machine-made fake as well as a historical paradox, an "impossible event": "A book signing by Franz Kafka, 85 years after his death. Since none of Kafka's novels were published during his lifetime, this book signing was his first." The signing makes use of "autopen technology and facsimile first editions" of Kafka's famous novel *The Trial*.[6] And the entire process of generating and producing a book, combined with a print-on-demand scheme, is incorporated in Peter Bichsel and Martin Fuchs' *Written Images* project: a "generative book that presents programmed images by various artists," all individually calculated immediately before they are printed, making each single book unique and literally unrepeatable.[7]

Fig. 4: Per-Oskar Leu, *The Bachelor Machine*, 2009.

Finally, Philip M. Parker came up with a rather clever and very original approach to print-on-demand. He has generated 200,000 books (which can all be purchased through Amazon, making him "the most published author in the history of the planet"). Each of these books is in fact a compilation of content which can be readily accessed through the internet. Parker's contribution was to design the software for collecting the (freely available) information (which spans a wide range of genres and subjects—most of the titles are scientific publications) and compiling the results into books (usually around 150 pages thick) which can then be then printed using print-on-demand—in effect automating the entire process. He states that "My goal isn't to have the computer write sentences, but to do the repetitive tasks that are too costly to do otherwise." Since there is no investment to be recovered, each book "breaks even" as soon as the first copy is sold.[8]

6. https://peroskarleu.com/artwork/1062121-The-Bachelor-Machine.html.
7. http://writtenimages.net/.
8. Noam Cohen, "He Wrote 200,000 Books (but Computers Did Some of the Work)," *New York Times*, April 14, 2008, http://www.nytimes.com/2008/04/14/business/media/14link.html.

Software (which is clearly a defining element of print-on-demand) makes it simple to alter the content of a publication at any point during the production process—even between the production of individual copies. And this customization can go much further than merely adding or deleting bits of content. The print-on-demand process actually makes it possible to continuously update the content—thus bringing a defining aspect of online publishing back to the printed medium.

In other words, the latest edition can be continuously kept up-to-date—by its author and publisher, and potentially also by an open community of readers/users/contributors. FLOSS Manuals is a publishing effort founded by the artist Adam Hyde, focusing on free and open-source software (including tools used to create this software) as well as the community which uses these applications and tools. The editing scheme is almost entirely open, so that anyone can contribute to a manual, adding content or helping fix errors, and being credited for their contributions. The FLOSS (Free/Libre/Open Source Software) paradigm, with its culture of openness, is here brilliantly applied to the field of technical manuals. The constantly updated books can be downloaded for free or purchased as cheap print-on-demand editions; alternately, single chapters from any of the manuals can be reassembled at will, and then downloaded or ordered in print-on-demand (Hyde has since pushed this concept even further, developing an online platform made entirely of free software for online collaborative authoring and publishing of books, called Booki).

Using FLOSS software for publishing ensures that tools can be collectively developed and shared, and are guaranteed to remain open and unrestricted by patents. The Open Source Publishing consortium (initiated by a few members of the Brussels-based collective Constant) is a major effort in this direction, supporting an organic and systematic use of FLOSS software for publishing. Print-on-demand is of course the most obvious and natural medium for FLOSS-based publishing. Having open tools which are collectively developed and shared, implicitly guarantees fair access to the means of publishing, thus promoting freedom of expression.

Clearly, print-on-demand has the potential to make available in print enormous quantities of otherwise unpublished or forgotten information. Print-on-demand seems destined to occupy a position very much similar to that of photocopying in the 1980s and 1990s: a chance to print and distribute content cheaply, in a format which is physically stable, easy to use, and pleasant to the senses. Which is still very much what paper is all about.

Silvio Lorusso

In Defense of Poor Media[1]

Fig. 1: Giotto, *St. Francis Giving his Mantle to a Poor Man*, 1297–1299. Source: https://www.wikiart.org/en/giotto/st-francis-giving-his-mantle-to-a-poor-man-1299.

1. Reprinted from *Printed_Web_3.pdf*, ed. by Paul Soulellis and Library of the Printed Web (self-publ.: Lulu, 2015), 35–89.

This text pays homage to "In Defense of the Poor Image," an essay in which German artist and writer Hito Steyerl speaks of the kind of "charge" that the poor image—an image that "has been uploaded, downloaded, shared, reformatted, and reedited"—acquires while circulating through networks. I argue that, in the field of digital publishing, poor media are able to "transform quality into accessibility,"[2] like the poor image does. Poor media substantiate the book's potential for duplication and dissemination. Conversely, rich media are the product of a commercial doctrine based on an ornamental understanding of digital technology, a Hollywoodian rhetoric of engagement, and a reactionary conception of the publishing process.

Part 1: Rich Media

In order to elaborate upon the concept of poor media, I'll explore the notion of rich media in the first place. In the context of its ad system, Google provides the following definition: "A Rich Media ad contains images or video and involves some kind of user interaction. [...] While text ads sell with words, and display ads sell with pictures, Rich Media ads offer more ways to involve an audience with an ad. The ad can expand, float, peel down, etc."[3] According to Wikipedia, "the term 'rich media' is synonymous for interactive multimedia."[4]

Rich media emerged in a period when the bandwidth was growing and animated gifs were giving way to interactive Flash banners. It's 2001 and "Rich Media is the buzzword of the moment, but many are still in the dark about what 'Rich Media' really is. [...] Rich Media refers to the utilization of various technologies to enhance a recipient's experience. Rich Media can be interactive, and can be tracked to determine among recipients the open, view and response rates to a campaign."[5]

While the expression "rich media" seems to have originated in the field of advertisement and its usage over time looks fluctuating,[6] I believe that it accurately reflects the combination of presumptions and expectations revolving around what was called electronic, and later digital, publishing. As I'll discuss, its marketing connotation reverberates in publishing too.

As with the *Daily Prophet* browsed by Harry Potter, rich media are meant to bring to life an otherwise inert artifact by adding a "magical" element to the printed page. Computer pioneer Alan Kay speaks about magic as well: according to him, metaphors employed in user interfaces shouldn't literally follow the physical world but express what it can't be done there: "if [the screen] is to be like magical paper, then it is the magical part that is all important."[7]

In January 2012, Apple released iBooks Author, a software to create enhanced e-books that can include "galleries, video, interactive diagrams, 3D objects, mathematical expressions and more." These rich media "bring content to life in ways the printed page never could."[8] iBooks Author doesn't require any coding or deep technical skill. In fact, users can choose among several ready-made templates and customize them according to their needs using a WYSIWYG interface. Finally, the books can be seamlessly made available into the Apple marketplace.

The kind of slick enhanced books produced, distributed, and sold within the Apple ecosystem is what publishers, designers and readers often think of when asked about the "future of the book." Despite the fact that enhanced books represent a small, barely lucrative, slice of the overall production of e-books,[9] practitioners of the field and the general public are still dazzled by books that

2. Hito Steyerl, "In Defense of the Poor Image," *e-flux*, no. 10 (November 2009), http://www.e-flux.com/journal/in-defense-of-the-poor-image/.
3. "What Is Rich Media?", Google Support, 2013, https://support.google.com/richmedia/answer/2417545?hl=en.
4. Wikipedia, "Multimedia," March 30, 2015, http://en.wikipedia.org/w/index.php?title=Multimedia&oldid=654190159.
5. "An Overview of Rich Media," Boldfish, 2001, http://web.archive.org/web/20011123200340/http://www.boldfish.com/BF_emguide/Notes/richmedia.html.
6. "Rich Media," Google Trends, https://trends.google.com/trends/explore?date=all&q=%22rich%20media%22.
7. Alan Kay, "User Interface: A Personal View," in *Multimedia: From Wagner to Virtual Reality*, ed. Randall Packer and Ken Jordan (New York: Norton, 2001).
8. "iBooks Author," 2012, Apple.com, https://www.apple.com/au/ibooks-author/.
9. "How Ebooks Are Changing Publishing," *The Huffington Post*, October 5, 2012, http://www.huffingtonpost.com/2012/10/05/ebook-shapes-publishing-infographic_n_1943067.html.

change over time, books that speak back, books that self-destruct, books that react to the mood of the reader, books that connect to the physical location in which they are read, etc. Apparently, this is the avant-garde. The reality is that, the wheel is reinvented over and over.

In order to provide just a glimpse of the complex history of rich media and to extend the definition sketched above, I'll briefly discuss some technologies, ideas, and particular moments that contributed to the development of such notion in the field of digital publishing.

E-LITERATURE AND HYPERTEXT FICTION

The working definition of electronic literature (e-literature or e-lit) provided by the Electronic Literature Organization (ELO) encompasses "works with important literary aspects that take advantage of the capabilities and contexts provided by the stand-alone or networked computer."[10] Several genres can be seen as being part of it; one of these is hypertext fiction.

Early interactive novels such as *afternoon, a story* by Michael Joyce (1990) and *Victory Garden* by Stuart Moulthrop (1992) are now considered milestones. These publications provided an impressive amount of narrative paths chosen by the user/reader. Both novels were realized using Storyspace, a software created by Jay David Bolter and Michael Joyce himself (another successful software to produce hypertext narratives was Apple's HyperCard).[11]

Such pioneering works, together with the development of hypertext theory, let e-writers assume that the interactivity and non-linear possibilities offered by the hyperlink were to revolutionize literature.[12] In *The New York Times Book Review*, Robert Coover decreed the end of books as static, monolithic, and unidirectional experiences. On the contrary, "[w]ith its webs of linked lexias, its networks of alternate routes [...] hypertext presents a radically divergent technology, interactive and polyvocal, favoring a plurality of discourses over definitive utterance and freeing the reader from domination by the author."[13]

VOYAGER COMPANY'S EXPANDED BOOKS

In an episode of the *Computer Chronicles* from 1993, Bob Stein presents some of the products of his Voyager Company, founded in 1985. Among them, The Beatles' *A Hard Day's Night* is an example of multimedia CD-ROM where the traditional categories of publishing begin to merge.

Stein shows the Expanded Books as well: a series of e-books on floppy disks for the Macintosh that "look like a book and to act like a book."[14] *The Picture of Dorian Gray*, one of them, includes functionalities such as text search, annotations, passages' highlight. The anchorman acknowledges that it is more of a research tool than a book, but he doesn't seem totally satisfied and asks for graphics. Stein reassures him by telling that the toolkit they sell allows creating e-books including movies, audios, pictures, etc. As this excerpt shows, early e-books suffered from an inferiority complex. Multimedia was the cure: video and audio made e-books unique and more captivating than printed matter.

THE IPAD

In 2010, the first iPad was released. During its first public presentation, Steve Jobs described the iPad's core functions, the things that this new device was better at than the mobile and the laptop. These were: browsing the Web, reading emails, watching photos and videos, listening to music, playing games, and, finally, reading e-books. Thanks to its handiness and its multi-touch, high-quality display, the iPad soon became the natural environment of rich media applications merging the key operations listed above.

DIGITAL PUBLISHING SUITE

In the current context of digital publishing, iBooks Author is not the only proprietary software available to produce rich media publications. Mostly employed to create enhanced magazines, the Adobe Digital Publishing Suite (DPS) was recently named "the leading digital publishing solution." The DPS is meant to "create, publish, and optimize content-centric mobile apps," another name for enhanced publications. DPS' apps are supposed

10. "What is Electronic Literature?", Electronic Literature Organization, https://eliterature.org/about/.
11. Jay David Bolter, *Writing Space: Computers, Hypertext, and the Remediation of Print* (New York: Routledge, 2001).
12. Cf. N. Katherine Hayles, *Writing Machines* (Cambridge, Mass.: MIT Press, 2002), 27.
13. Robert Coover, "The End of Books," *New York Times*, June 21, 1992, http://www.nytimes.com/books/98/09/27/specials/coover-end.html.
14. "Electronic Publishing," 1993, Computer Chronicles, https://archive.org/details/Electron2.

to be immersive and engaging, thanks to "sophisticated text treatments with video, audio, animation, and other highly interactive elements."[15] In order not to "shock" its users, Adobe designed the DPS as an appendix of InDesign; maintaining its print-oriented workflow basically intact.

SOCIAL READING

The notion of "social reading" emerged around mid–2011 when platforms like Goodreads—later acquired by Amazon—were quickly growing and e-reading devices like the Kindle began to let users share their reading activity on social media. According to the definition provided by OpenBookmarks, social reading is "everything that surrounds the experience of reading electronic books," like the following example: "You're reading an ebook. You find a bit you like, and you select the text and email it to a friend."[16]

Why do I consider social reading as a facet of rich media? Because some of the functionalities that go under the social reading umbrella—like the sharing of highlights—are often embedded into enhanced books.

ALL TOGETHER NOW

Shakespeare's Sonnets, an e-book as app for the iPad made by London-based publisher Touch Press, is a much recognized example in the field of enhanced publications. The *Sonnets* embody several of the rich media characteristics described above. For instance, each sonnet is performed by a well-known actor. The performances are incorporated in the book as entertaining videos. The sonnets are accompanied by two different sets of annotations. It is also possible to browse the 1609 Quarto edition of the book. As well as merging text, video, and images, the book represents a social reading experience since users can share passages via email, Facebook, or Twitter.

In summary, rich media books are enhanced by multimedia, interactivity, and social features. The promise of rich media is an active, engaging, and public reading experience, thanks to intuitive—"natural"—forms of interaction, almost infinite paths to explore, and dynamic, high-res visual artifacts. While physical books appear in comparison as obsolete and inexorably doomed, the process to develop rich media often fits the print workflow that designers are used to, which is therefore reinforced.

THE POVERTY OF RICH MEDIA

What has changed since Voyager's Expanded Books on floppies? Not much. Ok, books are not isolated anymore, they're part of a shared experience, but the idea of sociality they foster seems to be confined mostly within the narrow boundaries of dominant social media platforms. Social reading can be more than tweeting passages. The same Bob Stein of the Voyager Company later founded the Institute for the Future of the Book, which focuses, among other things, on social reading technologies. One of these is CommentPress, a plugin for WordPress that allows multiple users to comment each paragraph, line, or word of a given text. Both the text and comments are not locked in the book, instead they can be extracted through copy-paste or RSS feeds. As seen above, OpenBookmarks' definition is a broad one. Here's another example: "You're reading a book on one device, but half-way through you switch to another ereader. Your position and bookmarks are automatically synchronised."[17]

iBooks format does not fully allow this. Rich media often take advantage of the shared efforts to develop open standards for digital publishing without giving back. Even though the iBooks proprietary format is based on the EPUB standard, it can't be read by other e-book readers. While iBooks format allows custom functionalities, it prevents users to leave the Apple's ecosystem. This is how Ed Bott summarizes Apple's strategy: "Enter a product category supporting a widely used standard, extend that standard with proprietary capabilities, and then use those differences to disadvantage competitors."[18] Preservation is an issue as well: how do you deal with many competing standards? Looking back in history, not much from the era of multimedia CD-ROM has survived.

Both enhanced e-books and books as apps undergo a quality check in order to appear on Apple's or Google's virtual shelves. What these companies mean by quality is not as straightforward as one may think. For instance, Seth Godin's book was re-

15. "Adobe Digital Publishing Suite," 2012, Adobe.
16. "What Is Social Reading?," 2011, OpenBookmarks, http://booktwo.org/openbookmarks/social-reading/.
17. "What Is Social Reading?"
18. Ed Bott, "How Apple Is Sabotaging an Open Standard for Digital Books," *ZDNet*, January 22, 2012, http://www.zdnet.com/article/how-apple-is-sabotaging-an-open-standard-for-digital-books/.

jected by Apple because it included "multiple links to Amazon store."[19] Geometric Porn, an app that shows "non-explicit description of sexual organs or activity" was rejected and suspended by both Apple and Google. These examples indicate that conflicts of interest and censorship not only concern interactive e-books, but the impact on these is often greater. Users can still install an app or download an iBooks file from a source other than the Apple Store or Google Play, but it's a clumsy, frustrating process.

Within the ideology of rich media, engagement through multimedia and interactivity is intrinsically valuable. Multi-touch gestures and transitions are portrayed as an unmediated, therefore deeper, mode of interaction with digital devices. The reality is different: according to Dragan Espenschied, "Simple actions like searching, writing, editing, calculating, controlling became needlessly painful to execute [...]."[20] The physical keyboard offers instead "the simplest two-level interface: Novice users can orient themselves visually, if they grow to use certain features more often or with more detail, they can use precise keyboard combinations and shortcuts to execute functions that are present in their minds rather than the computer screen."

Many people compared the iPad to the Dynabook, a device prototyped by Alan Kay ("magical paper," remember?) in 1972, which was not actually released because of the technological limitations of that time. Alan Kay himself did not approve such comparison, since the Dynabook was meant to be a device for intellectual production.[21] The iPad, on the contrary, is consumption-oriented. No need to write code to realize this, structuring a short essay would be cumbersome enough.

"Rich media" is a marketing catchphrase. In the context of digital publishing, it is the idea of rich media itself that is sold. As in the *Computer Chronicles*, it is not multimedia content that counts, but its very presence, within a wider narrative in which slickness and high resolution correspond to technological progress. Likewise, interactivity is often there for its own sake, becoming free advertising for the device, reading software, and publishing ecosystem in general. "Widgets add Multi-Touch magic to books on iPad and Mac."[22] This is not the authentic magic Alan Kay was talking about; it's a mere bunch of tricks as boisterous as the early Web banner ads.

Some hesitations are emerging. "We pursued distractions and called them enhancements."[23] This is how, in *The New York Times*, e-book designer Peter Mayers drily summarizes the recent history of multimedia digital publishing. Perhaps, instead of rich media I should speak of "baroque media," media flaunting their opulence through ornamental user experience.

Softwares like iBooks Author and the Adobe DPS are easy to use: coding is not required and there's no need to change the way a designer works. "Building a book is as easy as dragging and dropping."[24] Even though users can create their own widgets, iBooks Author is focused on customization. The DPS is an integration of inDesign. Both are the result of a very specific idea of what publishing is and how it is performed. An idea developed with print in mind and with the hurry to reach or build a digital audience. While this software works probably well for high-volume publishing enterprises, these tools produce reactionary workflows and publications. Supposedly, rich media are not expensive in terms of time, money, and labor. This is true as long as the paradigms encoded in the software are accepted. Florian Cramer puts it this way: "we're looking for pragmatic, working solutions—not snazzy design show-off work that may create wow-effects but will not be a workable model for real life [...] Focus on showcase projects has been the achilles heel of all electronic and multimedia publishing efforts ever since the CD-ROM in the 1990s."[25]

One of the fields where rich media are supposed to have a groundbreaking effect is education. The

19. Seth Godin, "Who Decides What Gets Sold in the Bookstore?," *The Domino Project*, February 28, 2012, https://seths.blog/domino-project-archives/.

20. Dragan Espenschied, "The Right to a Real Keyboard (aka 'Hardkeys')," *We, Computer Users, Demand the Right to ...*, October 11, 2013, http://userrights.contemporary-home-computing.org/6yf13/a-real-keyboard-aka-hardkeys.

21. Alan Kay, "An Interview with Computing Pioneer Alan Kay," interview by David Greelish, *Time*, 2013, http://techland.time.com/2013/04/02/an-interview-with-computing-pioneer-alan-kay/.

22. John Brownlee, "Most iBooks Author E-Textbook Download Sizes Are Between One And Three Gigabytes," *Cult of Mac*, January 19, 2012, http://www.cultofmac.com/141364/most-ibooks-author-e-textbook-download-sizes-are-between-one-and-three-gigabytes/.

23. David Streitfeld, "Out of Print, Maybe, but Not Out of Mind," *New York Times*, December 1, 2013, http://www.nytimes.com/2013/12/02/technology/e-books-hold-tight-to-features-of-their-print-predecessors.html.

24. Apple, "iBooks Author."

25. Florian Cramer, "Florian Cramer on 'The Art of Hybrid Publishing,'" interview by Julia Rehfeldt, *hybrid publishing*, September 29, 2014, https://networkcultures.org/digitalpublishing/2014/10/01/florian-cramer-on-the-art-of-hybrid-publishing/.

assumption is that "digital natives" are completely at ease with digital technology, therefore learning tools and methods must adapt to this new kind of cognition. Traditional textbooks are static, boring and therefore obsolete. The argument is generally supported by the frequent statistics showing the extinction of strong readers. The solution is books in which students "flick through photo galleries, rotate 3D objects, tap to pop up sidebars, or play video and audio."[26]

Italian philosopher Roberto Casati names this phenomenon "digital colonialism."[27] Sharing Kay's concerns, he highlights the way rich media discourage intellectual production. Furthermore, he argues that they impose a continuous and tiresome multitasking condition. Along with push notifications, a bestiary of other distractions inhabits the iPad's environment. According to some of the early e-lit proponents, hyperlink was to revolutionize literature. Today, the reassuring consequentiality and peaceful inactivity of traditional books seems to offer an escape from this hammering information overload.

Rich media reflect the privileges of rich countries. Several enhanced publications are developed without considering hardware and network conditions on a global scale. In 2012, among the first eight textbooks available through iBooks, the smallest was more than 700Mb big. Some of them were bigger than 2Gb.[28] Such files require lot of available space and a very fast connection.

"RICH MEDIA" IS WHAT INTERACTIVE MULTIMEDIA STANDS FOR

A necessary clarification: I'm not against multimedia or interactivity. After all, this transcript includes videos and links. There are several interactive publications that I like. *Blackbar* is my favorite one: a text-based dystopia where the reader needs to guess censored words in order to proceed. *Blackbar* was made in 2013, but it could have been created 30 years ago. Is this a book or a game? Who knows... By "rich media"' I don't simply mean interactive multimedia, but the blind business-minded enthusiasm towards these features. In many cases pushing interactive multimedia into e-books only makes sense from the commercial point of view. The Web is a superb environment for multimedia and interactivity. Currently, browsers interpret HTML, CSS, and JavaScript way better than the render engines of e-book readers. But websites are not easy to sell. Lincoln Michel suggests a different territory: "Despite the regular hyping of enhanced e-books/hypertext/apps/interactive books, I don't see those going anywhere outside of a few specific markets like children's books and textbooks. The problem is that we already have a whole industry devoted to interactive narratives: video games."[29] But publishers see themselves as book makers and when they publish enhanced book, they indirectly promote the reading device: would people be interested in the iPad if there weren't applications showing off its potential?

Part 2: Poor Media

While rich media mostly emphasize the characteristics of the book as a technology to be used and consumed, poor media express and corroborate its potential of duplication and dissemination. Since the way in which information is structured may encourage or, conversely, inhibit duplication, poor media also include technologies of production.

Like rich media, "poor media" is a broad, multifaceted concept. Before outlining a definition, I'll depict a few episodes in which digital publishing appears as a practice bolstered, stimulated, or activated by poor media. A consideration first: the whole history of the book, not just since the advent of digital networks, can be understood as the sacrifice of a certain idea of material quality in favor of a faster duplication or a broader reach. As Cory Doctorow puts it, "every successful new medium has traded off its artifact-ness—the degree to which it was populated by bespoke hunks of atoms, cleverly nailed together by master craftspeople—for ease of reproduction."[30] The Luther Bible was not as fancy as monks' hand-illuminated bibles from the

26. "iBooks Textbooks for iPad," 2012, Apple.com.
27. See Roberto Casati, *Contro il colonialismo digitale: istruzioni per continuare a leggere* (Roma, Bari: GLF Editori Laterza, 2013).
28. Brownlee, "iBooks Author."
29. Lincoln Michel, "The Future Of The Future Of Books," *Buzzfeed*, September 17, 2014, http://www.buzzfeed.com/lincolnmichel/the-future-is-never#3ie3rqm.
30. Cory Doctorow, "Ebooks: Neither E, Nor Books" (paper for the O'Reilly Emerging Technologies Conference, San Diego, CA, February 12, 2004), http://craphound.com/ebooksneitherenorbooks.txt.

previous century, anti-soviet carbon-copied samizdat were fragile and vulnerable, mimeographed zines were mostly cheap and unruly.

PROJECT GUTENBERG

In 1971, during the night of the fourth of July, Michael S. Hart, at the time a Human-Machine Interfaces' student at the University of Illinois, used the time available at the mainframe computer of his university (time that was worth millions of dollars) to retype and publicly distribute the text of the *United States Declaration of Independence*. At a time in which computers were mainly used for data processing, employing them for content distribution was not an obvious choice. In Hart's words, "the greatest value created by computers would not be computing, but would be the storage, retrieval, and searching of what was stored in our libraries."[31]

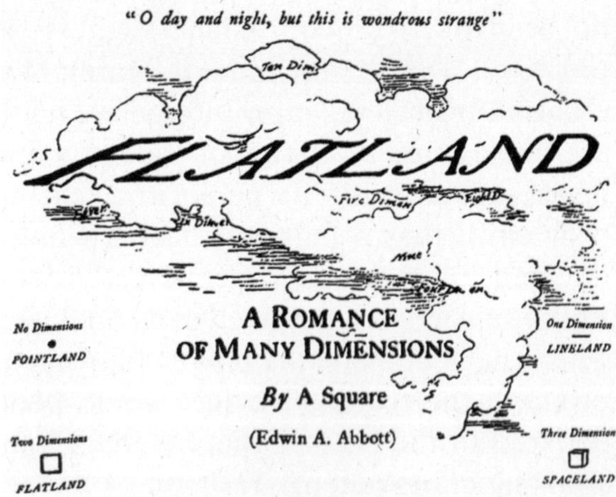

Fig. 2: Edwin Abbott Abbott, *Flatland: a Romance of Many Dimensions*, 1884. Frontispiece.

Flatland: A Romance of Many Dimensions

Edwin A. Abbott (1838-1926. English scholar, theologian, and writer.)

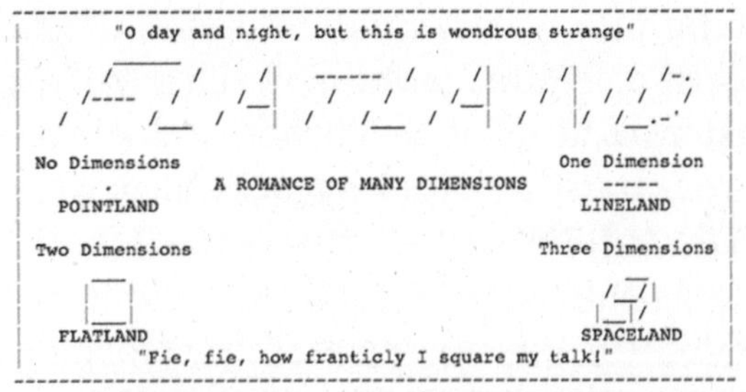

"O day and night, but this is wondrous strange"

No Dimensions
POINTLAND

A ROMANCE OF MANY DIMENSIONS

One Dimension
LINELAND

Two Dimensions
FLATLAND

Three Dimensions
SPACELAND

"Fie, fie, how franticly I square my talk!"

With Illustrations by the Author, A SQUARE (Edwin A. Abbott)

Fig. 3: *Flatland*'s frontispiece, plain text version converted in 2008. Source: www.gutenberg.org/cache/epub/201/pg201.txt.

Michael Hart was profoundly conscious of the duplicating potential of computers, which he considered a form of "replicator technology." This attitude, together with the adoption of "Plain Vanilla ASCII," a universally interchangeable standard for text, led to the development of Project Gutenberg, a volunteer-based platform whose mission is to "encourage the creation and distribution of eBooks."[32] All the books on Project Gutenberg are released in the public domain and freely available for download.

Sometimes, the intrinsic limitations of plain text led to the development of interesting solutions in order to include illustrations and the paratextual elements of a publication. Consider this frontispiece of *Flatland*, made in 2008. Evidently, it is at the same time less *and* more than a neutral replica.

E-ZINES

Let's go back to *Computer Chronicles* for a moment. Jerod Pore, speaking of his *Factsheet Five* zine on *The WELL*, praises the instant availability offered by the Internet, highlighting how inexpensive it is to produce and distribute a work both in terms of time and money. At the same time, he doesn't forget to remark that both electronic and print publishing don't come for free if we consider natural resources.

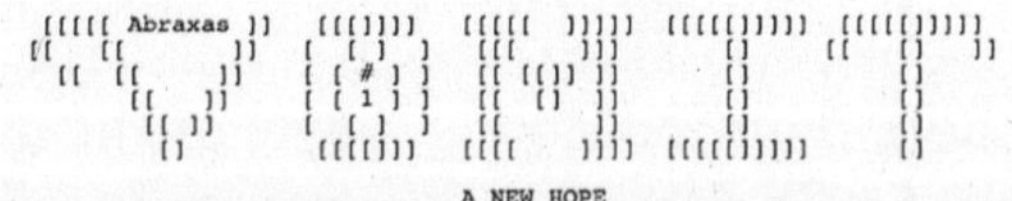

A NEW HOPE

(Number 1, kids! Save it! Maybe it'll be worth something!)

Call me Ishmael. This is the introduction for the phattest 'zine station for the 'zine nation, beotch. This is just the introduction, so don't expect too much. We'll just use this for, well, an introduction. This 'zine is being co-written by Abraxas and Biafra, and we'll probably get more authors as we travel down the long & windy road of 'zine maturation. Abraxas is writing this intro in case you care. I'm a Junior in high school and Biafra is a Sophomore. That's all you need to know. We're secretive like that. You can reach VOMIT on the internet through biafra@gti.net. I proposed actually writing something besides an introduction for VOMIT #1 but Biafra says that we have to make as many as possible. Remember, kids, it's quantity, not quality here at VOMIT. We're writing this 'zine because we're not athletic, have lots of free time, and have lots of stuff to bitch about. Some issues will not be funny at all. (Case in point, VOMIT #1!) Biafra's will never be funny, because he is not as |<-r4d as me. Mine will be funny depending on my moods. Right now I'm starving lonely, no one likes me, I have no friends, I'm ugly, I've never touched a girl, and my feet itch, so this issue won't be funny. OK. I'm sick of this intro (As are you). Let's get to VOMIT #2. I have just one request for you loyal readers of VOMIT. (You must be loyal to have read this far.) We'd like a new ASCII of our name.

Index
(Just in case you missed some issues along the way)

VOMIT 1...Intro

Collect 'em all!

Fig. 4: *Vomit* e-zine. Source: http://textfiles.com/magazines/VOMIT/vomit001.txt.

Like the early Project Gutenberg e-books, e-zines were originally formatted as ASCII text. At first, they were spread through the BBS (bulletin board system). According to Jason Scott, archivist at *textfiles.com*, "Instead of losing individual textfiles in the sea of BBSes, many writers chose instead to

31. Michael Hart, "The History and Philosophy of Project Gutenberg," *Project Gutenberg*, 1992, https://www.gutenberg.org/about/background/history_and_philosophy.html.

32. Michael Hart, "Project Gutenberg Mission Statement," *Project Gutenberg*, 2004, https://www.gutenberg.org/about/background/mission_statement.html.

move to the 'Magazine' model, where they would band together textfiles and release them as a group. This strengthened the chances of the files surviving and also made for impressive file sizes, a sign of quality to people browsing sites."[33]

BOOKWAREZ

Speaking of e-books, Cory Doctorow indicates a phenomenon that goes under the name of "bookwarez." From Doctorow's point of view, an e-book is not necessarily a digital publication produced and distributed by a proper publishing house, but rather a "'pirate' or unauthorized electronic edition of a book, usually made by cutting the binding off of a book and scanning it a page at a time, then running the resulting bitmaps through an optical character recognition app to convert them into ASCII text, to be cleaned up by hand. These books are pretty buggy, full of errors introduced by the OCR."[34]

Fig. 5: Header of The Tor Library, a bookwarez collection accessible in the Deep Web. Source: http://am4wuhz3zifexz5u.onion/.

MARKDOWN

Created by John Gruber in 2004, Markdown is a handy markup language that allows to create structured text easily convertible to HTML (but also EPUB, PDF, and more). Unlike HTML, Markdown is easily readable to the human eye: for instance, <em>italic</em> becomes *italic*. Unlike the .doc format, Markdown doesn't need a dedicated processor: one can write Markdown in TextEdit as well as in Gedit or in TextPad. "Markdown is a product of internet culture. It uses ad-hoc formatting signs commonly used in e-mail and chat platforms, and further popularized on blogging platforms [...]."[35]

Although limited and somehow strict, Markdown encourages duplication and multiple instantiation of a text in different formats. It also facilitates archiving since its semantic structure is manifest.

EPUB

Originally developed around 1998 (OEB at that time), EPUB is a free and open standard for digital books developed by the International Digital Publishing Forum (IDPF). EPUB 3, its latest release, may include audio, video, and interactive elements programmed in Javascript. Despite this, I consider it a poor medium. Here is why: "A key concept of EPUB is that content presentation should adapt to the User rather than the User having to adapt to a particular presentation of content."[36] Instead of imposing its features, an EPUB file tries to do its best in each possible situation, from narrow E Ink readers to multi-touch tablets. Furthermore, its inner architecture is crystal clear and easily accessible. An EPUB book is basically a portable website: a compressed series of HTML and CSS files together with metadata and structure.

PDF

The PDF format was created by Adobe more than 20 years ago on the basis of PostScript—a language that deeply contributed to the birth of Desktop Publishing—and later released as an open standard. Pretty much every word processor can export PDFs. This format is used for extremely diverse kinds of documents, from books to tax receipts. Although it is possible to include interactive elements and videos in a PDF, here I refer to its quintessential form: "an airline boarding pass, printed out or held open on a smartphone, or else it is the manual that explains the smartphone itself, or else the quarterly statements the smartphone corporation publishes for investors."[37] While PDFs were originally meant for print, today's browsers seamlessly render them. As Alessandro Ludovico points out, the PDF can be seen as a sort of sub-medium, since it evolved from a production standard to a standalone one.[38]

33. Jason Scott, "Electronic Magazines," *Textfiles*, 1999, http://textfiles.com/magazines/.
34. Doctorow, "Ebooks."
35. Digital Publishing Toolkit Collective, *From Print to Ebooks: A Hybrid Publishing Toolkit for the Arts*, ed. Joe Monk, Miriam Rasch, Florian Cramer, and Amy Wu (Amsterdam: Institute of Network Cultures, 2014), 97.
36. "EPUB 3 Overview," *International Digital Publishing Forum*, October 11, 2011, http://www.idpf.org/epub/30/spec/epub30-overview.html.
37. Lisa Gitelman, "The PDF's Place in a History of Paper Knowledge," interview by Trevor Owens, *The Signal*, June 16, 2014, http://blogs.loc.gov/digitalpreservation/2014/06/the-pdfs-place-in-a-history-of-paper-knowledge-an-interview-with-lisa-gitelman/.
38. Alessandro Ludovico, "Post-Digital Publishing, Hybrid and Processual Objects in Print," *APRJA* 3, no. 1 (2014), http://www.aprja.net/?p=1738.

PRINT ON DEMAND

Print-on-demand is a system that allows even just a single copy of a book to be printed and made commercially available without any prior investment. Is this digital publishing? I'd like to think so. Print-on-demand books represent a genuine hybrid of digital and analog processes: sent through the regular postal system, the physical book is the tip of the iceberg of an infrastructure that takes advantage of digital printing, desktop publishing, the PDF format, and Web 2.0. Moreover, as N. Katherine Hayles reminds us, "Digital technologies are now so thoroughly integrated with commercial printing processes that print is more properly considered a particular output form of electronic text than an entirely separate medium."[39]

From a graphic designer's perspective, print-on-demand is very limiting: the choice is often among a couple of different papers and a standardized series of formats. When the amount of ordered book is small, black and white printing is the only convenient one. However, print-on-demand books are quickly produced and distributed: I upload the PDF, I get an ISBN, and my book is ready to be purchased (or downloaded). Immediately after, I can revise it as many times as I wish. The version triumphs over the edition. No intermediaries needed, apart from the POD platform I've chosen.

Poor media foster duplication and boost circulation. They are lightweight. Poor media suggest an active use: frequently they can be converted, dissected, remixed, reorganized, updated. The modest simplicity of poor media doesn't contradict the possibility to preserve them. The duplicating aura they carry amplifies their resilience: "lots of copies keep stuff safe," archivists say. The poverty of poor media should be better called *frugality*, since it's characterized by the conscious, serene renunciation of embellishments in favor of accessibility and spread. The spartan look of poor media might not be beautiful, but it's undoubtedly charming.

39. Katherine Hayles, "Electronic Literature: What Is It?", *The Electronic Literature Organization*, January 2, 2007, http://eliterature.org/pad/elp.html.

Alessandro Ludovico

The Touching Charm of Print[1]

1. Reprinted from *across & beyond: A transmediale Reader in Post-digital Practices, Concepts, and Institutions*, ed. Ryan Bishop, Kristoffer Gansing, Jussi Parikka, and Elvia Wilk (Berlin: Sternberg Press, 2016), 100–115.

Printed media have a historically consolidated visual infrastructure, refined through centuries of visual culture. The visual aspect of print has been considered absolutely predominant compared to the involvement of the other senses of smell, hearing, and touch, and in our oculocentric society, this part has been progressively (and wrongly) perceived to coincide with its whole. This seems to be the main reason why printed media have recently started to be massively translated into another medium (the digital) through a direct process. Since print is supposedly perceived mainly visually, it is reduced through the scanning and circulation of digital files and their digital-only production into specific formats. The resulting sense of loss stems from much more than nostalgia: what is missing is an entire small perceptual universe that is instinctually unfolded every time the physical printed medium is used, which is altered, if not negated, in its new screen-based embodiment. An analysis of the perceptual dimensions of print, sense-by-sense (excluding taste, for obvious reasons), is then a premise for understanding not only the intrinsic "tactility" of data, but especially what we can tentatively define as the "material space of information" and the direct consequences it can have on publishing.

THE DIGITAL READING EXPERIENCE

> A theory of cultural change is impossible without knowledge of the changing sense ratios affected by various externalizations of our senses.
>
> —Marshall McLuhan[2]

The general discourse about digital forms of print focuses primarily on the extreme flexibility of the digital, derived from its "computability." Since information is processed each time it's visualized, a digital publication can be carried around in infinitely small digital storage space and can be accessed in various different ways. These modes of access include precise and composite search queries, quantification of a text's literary characteristics, and links to external content that may also cross-reference the original text. But all these instant, accessible qualities of the digital come at a price, one which is constantly underestimated: a completely different "reading experience" compared to the models derived from print culture, especially when considered from a perceptual perspective.[3]

We can assume that digital content requires primarily one sense: sight, which will be analyzed later. Let's start instead by considering smell, which is almost completely absent in digital media, if we exclude the smell of the hardware, initially present when the reading device is very new, due to the first heating of plastic and electronics, but which vanishes rapidly as time passes. Science fiction author Ray Bradbury famously affirmed that reading devices "smell like burned fuel," perhaps literally but also metaphorically referring to their artificial nature.[4] Remarkably, even if there were some odor associated with the device, it would always be the same one associated with every single digital publication, breaking the strong connection that our senses make between a specific content/publication and a specific smell. This is part of the digitization process. The collapsing of content space into one single device flattens the singular physical qualities, intensifying mostly the visual ones.

To compensate for the absence of smell, there are companies trying to synthesize odors to, within a broader commercial aim, produce "expanded digital books." Vapour Communication has built a prototype "oBook," a "Goldilocks and the Three Bears" e-book that incorporates different synthetic smells such as flowers, berries, and hot chocolate. At certain points in the story the smells are activated through interface "scent buttons," triggering an external device (the "oPhone") to emit the respective scents.[5] This "simulation" paradoxically strengthens the feeling that digital in itself is aseptic, aiming for strategies to "digitize" information, which means making it abstract and universal, inevitably losing possible variations in reader involvement. Another work remarking upon the loss of smell in the digital reading experience is the fake conceptual website pretending to sell "Smell of Books™" spray cans with scents like "New Book Smell" and "Classic Musty Smell"

2. Marshall McLuhan, *The Gutenberg Galaxy* (Toronto: University of Toronto Press, 1962), 49.
3. Heather MacFadyen, "The Reader's Devices: The Affordances of Ebook Readers," *Dalhousie Journal of Interdisciplinary Management*, no. 7 (2011): 1–15.
4. Guy Dammann, "Amazon kindles hope after e-reader interest explodes," *The Guardian*, June 3, 2008, https://www.theguardian.com/books/2008/jun/03/news.amazon.
5. Melcher Media RSS, "Goldilocks and the Three Bears," https://melcher.com/project/goldilocks-and-the-three-bears/.

to help e-book customers feel "more comfortable with their devices."[6]

If smell's presence is easily detectable, hearing may or may not be involved in experiencing digital publications, depending on the system being used, as there are still no standard interfaces, but a plethora of different open and proprietary software systems leading to as many types of interaction with digital content. Hearing is usually involved for two different purposes: one is to better simulate the sensorial experience of print, typically using a single sound sample which is played when the user virtually turns the pages, as a "page-turning audio cue."[7] The other is to warn the user about some system-related event, using alert sounds functional to the interface. The former is a single sound sample, reiterated every time, and once the ear is trained to recognize it, it's relegated to the background, as something known and not worth any more attention. The latter is not related to the reading practice itself, but to the software infrastructure—related to the mode of interaction, but unrelated to the content. In fact, warning sounds are generally meant to attract attention about some impending fault, their mission is paradoxically to distract from the reading by pointing to a machine-related external event.

Sight, as mentioned, is central to the reading process. One of the main characteristics of digital media is to flatten differences, abstracting information to a universal status, infinitely replicable on screen-based devices. So text always appears in a very similar way, with slightly changing attributes like brightness and contrast. E-readers at some point consolidated around "e-ink," a screen binary technology of tiny, half-white-half-black spheres, which guarantees contrast and also a uniformity of the page that is only slightly changed by variations in the natural or artificial surrounding lighting. But the market is increasingly switching from the last generation of e-readers to classic retro-illuminated (so-called backlit) screens, like tablets, smartphones, and laptops, ensuring readability in any external light condition, and usually adapting to it. In this respect, the recently introduced "night shift mode" in smartphones shifts the "display's colours to a warmer, less blue, light so that it lowers the effect of the screen's light on a user's circadian rhythms."[8]

But as every other interface element, this is a universal behavior, shifting to the same color tone in every corner of the world at a given local time. The retro-illuminated paradigm is self-referential, taking the screen as the main source, and mostly ignoring what surrounds it, such as other forms of dim light, colors, reflections—even cutting them out with its light emissions. Sight is then captured by the light and the standard (flattened) universal modalities of display.

PERCEPTION OF PRINTED CONTENT

In comparison, classic printed publication can claim a richer sensorial environment. For one, smell is very present, indirectly giving specific information about the book, like age, paper composition, and level of preservation. The smell of printed publications varies a lot, even within the same olfactory domain: old books, for example, smell of various degrees of dust and mold, depending on their exposure to light, the types of paper and ink, the conditions of the preserving environments, and so on. New publications, like morning newspapers or just released books or magazines, still smell of fresh ink, but each in a different way. Readers often associate the smell of some printed publications with certain content (as with newspapers), or with some places, like particular libraries or bookstores. Technically these smells are perceptible due to several hundred so-called VOCs or volatile organic compounds, which the chemical elements in a book's paper, binding adhesives, and inks give off—in combination with the way and the place they are stored. Some scent companies have even tried to capitalize on these experiences, selling candles mimicking the smell of the *New York Times* or Byredo's "Bibliothèque," or perfumes mimicking the smell of old books, like CB's "I Hate Perfume in the Library," or freshly printed books, like "Paper Passion" produced by Gerhard Steidl and *Wallpaper Magazine*.[9] As opposed to the previ-

6. Smell of Books RSS, "The Smell of E-books Just Got Better," http://smellofbooks.com/.

7. Kenneth P. Fishkin, Thomas P. Moran, and Beverly L. Harrison, "Embodied User Interfaces: Towards Invisible User Interfaces," in *Engineering for Human-Computer Interaction*, eds. Stéphane Chatty and Prasun Dewan, Springer IFIP: The International Federation for Information Processing, vol. 22 (New York: Springer, 1999): 1–18.

8. Wikipedia, s.v. "iOS 9," September 16, 2022, https://en.wikipedia.org/w/index.php?title=IOS_9&oldid=1110560562.

9. Piotr Kowalczyk, "30 Book-Scented Perfumes and Candles," *Ebook Friendly*, November 28, 2015, http://ebookfriendly.com/book-smell-perfumes-candles/.

ously mentioned scent-manufacturers, these commercial efforts do not intend to "compensate" for a loss, but to extract and multiply a recognizable sensorial environment, artificially recreating the experience we associate with a certain odor.

Considering scent as a medium that can "expand" print-based reading, there's a small tradition of "adding" scents to printed pages, heightening the multi-sensorial experience. This is a strategy implemented in publishing with the "scratch-and-sniff" technique, popular since the end of 1970s, especially in the educational sector. Here a small layer of a scented substance is glued onto a specific part of the page and covered by a thin protective layer, which, when scratched, releases the smell. Beyond educational possibilities, some attempts were done also in the commercial magazine field as in *Hustler*'s August 1977 centerfold, or *Vice*'s July 2011 cover.[10]

On a more conceptual level, the combination of smell and print has been occasionally used by artists. Rachel Morrison, senior library assistant at the Museum of Modern Art in New York, conducted a performance called *Smelling the Books* from 2010 to 2013, smelling and precisely cataloging the smells of 300 out of 300,000 books in MoMA library. Her intention was to document and to foster the incredible difference in odors produced by artists' books, but also to "foster a discussion of the future of print media."[11] Another relevant work is *Aromapoetry* by Eduardo Kac, a limited-edition book with only ten copies, in a classic A4 format with twelve "poems" made up of smells, conceptually enabling the same "interpretation" mechanism of the classic poems, as both text and smell can be interpreted in a very personal way. The poems have "distinct olfactory zones on the page" and the rhythm among the different compositions provides alternating contrasting smells. The volatility of the different aromas is compensated for by the special structure of the page provided with a "nanolayer of mesoporous glass," which slows down the molecule release. The artist also provides the reader (collector) with vials and instructions to recharge every individual "poem."[12] The form of the book refers to the concept of a permanent "memory," compared to the structural volatility of smells. Scent is conceptually closer to digital than to traditional media, being ephemeral and very hard to preserve.

Hearing, on the other hand, is more accurately described as temporary than ephemeral. In traditional publishing the sense of hearing is mainly involved with the sounds generated from the physical manipulation of the publication. In books and magazines, handling the usually thicker cover produces different sounds than the flipping and bending of the internal pages. What is most important perceptually is that the sounds are always slightly different, while with a digital publication's interface, from early e-readers to recent Amazon Kindles, they are always the same. The sight-experience of reading print is extremely varied, as pages are illuminated by exterior natural and artificial lighting conditions, combined with the varied light-reflecting or light-absorbing characteristics of paper.

TACTILITY IN PRINT AND DIGITAL

> Unlike previous environmental changes, the electric media constitutes a total and near-instantaneous transformation of culture, values and attitudes.
>
> —Marshall McLuhan[13]

Beyond smell, hearing and sight, touch is the sense most directly involved in relating with the published object, proving how radical the perceptual differences between digital and print publications are.

Touch is acquired even before birth. As Lawrence K. Frank wrote in the 1960s: "Tactual sensitivity appears early in fetal life as probably the first sensory process to become functional."[14] For humans it's a primary way of understanding, especially perceiving differences. Yet in the digital realm touch is functional and mostly decontextualized. Even using mouse or trackpad "prosthetics," fingers are functionally used for clicking, swiping, or tapping in the very same way for every type of content. These are part of a growing vocabulary

10. "VICE's Scratch and Sniff Photo Issue," *The Ballast*, 2011, no longer available.
11. Rachael Morrison, "Smelling the Books," MoMA/PS1 Blog, March 7, 2011, http://www.moma.org/explore/inside_out/2011/03/07/smelling-the-books/.
12. "Aromapoetry," *Aromapoetry website*, http://www.ekac.org/aromapoetry.html.
13. "The Playboy Interview: Marshall McLuhan," *Playboy*, March 1969.
14. Lawrence K. Frank, "Tactile Communication," in *Explorations in Communication, an Anthology*, eds. Edmund Carpenter and Marshall McLuhan (Boston: Beacon Press, 1960), 6.

of abstracted gestures, codified and even patented interactions, which cannot be conceptually distinguished from the inescapable design of digital interfaces. They are "atomised, self identical, and absolute."[15] So, even though they possess the highest concentration of touch receptors and thermoreceptors on human skin aside from the genitals, in the digital realm fingertip-experience is simply annihilated. From being extremely sensitive and "broadband" input sources for our body, they become neutral machine- oriented prosthetics. "How hard you push, whether you're sweaty, touch type or hunt-and-peck, the interface does not so much ignore as exclude these facets of touch."[16] Fingerprints become flat, relevant only as data—flattened and tattooed, they'd still work well with our digital devices, including with safety-lock features.

We deal with these abstracted gestures all the time now, after the pervasion of smartphones and tablets in our daily life and work. This was already envisioned by Jean Baudrillard when he affirmed in the 1980s that the transition from the tactile to the digital was a primary factor of the contemporary world.[17] This anaesthetization of touch to only gesture-based behaviors channels them to a purely functional role. A decade after Baudrillard, N. Katherine Hayles reflected on the implied radical changes in body awareness: "Proprioceptive coherence in interplay with electronic prostheses plays an important role in reconfiguring perceived body boundaries, especially when it gives the impression that her subjectivity is flowing into the space of the screen."[18]

In traditional publishing, tactility gives a lot of information about the medium. First, the process of paper selection is still an important part of publishers' work. Tactility gives direct information without other senses involved. For example, readers familiar with a specific book would be able to recognize it from the texture of its cover and its size, even blindfolded. In contrast, the only way to recognize an e-book is through its visual elements, such as its interface-icon, its title formatting, or its cover visuals.

Human senses are built to perceive a very large "bandwidth" of information. The word "sense" derives from the Latin word *sensus*, meaning "faculty of feeling," that is, diversity rather than mechanical or standardized gestures and information. Tactility, as any other sense, allows perceiving differences; the more differences we are trained to perceive, the more we learn, and the more we learn, the more we are able to perceive, in an endless circle.

McLuhan wrote that print "has acquired new interest as a tool in the training of perception."[19] There are other components in material publications that are not visible, but potentially provide rich information. Bacteria, for example, exchange information among themselves and provide information to the organisms they are hosted by. This kind of information can last for months and travel through different human bodies, often through contact with objects. So different readers may exchange information through simply passing around printed matter—or from the author to an enthusiastic fan during a signing event. Newspapers are left or passed on in commuter trains from one traveler to another; flight companies' complimentary branded magazines are touched and read in airplanes by multitudes of readers. Do these bacteria transmit information that could unconsciously effect reading?

There's no answer yet, but in a speculative sense the physical circulation of information can be considered biologically and socially, while the digital circulation of information is highly customized by the software, but conceived and constructed for quite strictly personal consumption.

The relationship between these two very different approaches seems to be appropriately defined as "the tension between virtual and visceral."[20]

THE MATERIAL SPACE OF INFORMATION

If "reading space" is considered as both the space of the content of a whole publication, as well as the perception of the available content in a given physical environment, differences between the analog and the digital are further emphasized.

Dealing with space in general is a big issue within digital publishing. In its overall "simulation" of reality, perceived digital space is constrained into a small bi-dimensional screen. It has uniquely flex-

15. Aden Evens, "Touch in the Abstract," *Substance: A Review of Theory and Literary Criticism* 40, no.3 (2011): 67–68.
16. Ibid.
17. Jean Baudrillard, *Simulations* (New York: Semiotext[e], 1983).
18. N. Katherine Hayles, "Figuring Virtual Subjectivity," *The Digital Dialectic* (Cambridge, MA: MIT Press, 2000).
19. Marshall McLuhan, *Counterblast* (London: Rapp+Whiting, 1969), 99.
20. Beth Williamson, "From Hand Scroll to iPad App: Transforming Helen Douglas' *The Pond at Deuchar*," *Book 2.0* 4 (2014): 56.

ible qualities, especially coupled with the speed of specific actions, as in switching content instantly, searching for specific content within thousands of texts, zooming in to appreciate details, and zooming out to get an abstract view, just to mention a few. The potentially limitless space, as the screen can scroll and zoom infinitely and in every direction, is in fact a major perceptual limit—unlike the overview of shelves in a library, which, despite their size, can be clearly understood as defined and bordered in physical space. We're unable to visualize in a similar form all the publications that lie in a given digital storage space. We have to either search for them or scroll comprehensive lists until we found what we're looking for. The physical comprehension of depth is useless here. The size of the publication is no longer directly perceivable with sight, but has to be imagined through the number of pages displayed. This in turn removes a further perceived spatial element: knowing exactly where the reader is in reading.

Moreover, on two-dimensional screens, the page is still rendered as perfectly flat, so that it's exactly the same on any device, universally standardized in a perfectly rendered simulation. French researcher Émeline Brulé defines the digital simulation of print as "mimetism." In digital territory, the human sensory system is prone to a functionalist approach, rather than being able to refine its perceptions. We have thus adapted a new flattened vision to digital publishing, and we'll continue to adapt, but what we could progressively miss is the ability to perceive nuances of flexible and variable conditions.

Print has become a rare exception: it is the only remaining medium in use, besides perhaps vinyl records, whose content can be "mechanically" accessed and enjoyed. It belongs to the visible material space of information that can be touched and read directly at the same time. Considering, for example, the rising Internet of Things as a global infrastructure, one of its perceptual values is the ability to feel the presence of—to "touch"—the interconnected objects, giving shape and location to them as networked agents, contrary to abstract blinking routers and mostly invisible servers. This represents an urge to engage with objects as special and singular entities. Dealing with an object singularly identifiable in space often entails making an emotional investment in it, and identifying or retrieving it makes it a protected investment. Because of its enormous size, digital space makes it harder to appreciate the singularity of an entity of information.

With the late-seventies desktop metaphor mostly unchanged today, even in its mobile adaptations, the interface fails to cope with the amount of content we currently deal—and could deal— with. We are confronted with an "infinitely deep" desktop with the few reference points that can fit on a small screen, and automatic but not yet truly intelligent search capabilities. Digital publications inevitably have to cope with these limitations, but, in turn, they can also take the opportunity to exploit their unique ability of hosting infinitely reprogrammable and infinitely transmittable content. But simply trying to successfully simulate the (unsurpassed) print "interface" is a futile task, as Umberto Eco noted: "The book is like the spoon, scissors, the hammer, the wheel. Once invented, it cannot be improved."[21]

Digital content could build on the ability to instantly create, combine, and especially calculate content and relationships among content. This could create a different, original relationship with the reader, accomplishing a level of intimacy in the reading experience close to the one that McLuhan attributed to printed materials.

In this kind of intimacy, tactility could play a fundamental role, even if there is no simple equation to fill the gap between the machine and our fingertips' biological qualities. While Apple filed a patent in 2007 for a "tactile touchscreen," in robotics the still-primitive tactile sensors, while modelled after the biological sense of cutaneous touch, heavily simplify it, and they are definitely uncertain, for example, when it comes to sensing pain.[22] How would a reader "feel" the cover of the artist's book *Mémoirs*, by artist Asger Jorn and theorist Guy Debord, which is made of heavy sandpaper and so affecting every material comes into contact with, from hands to shelves?[23] Would an algorithm be ever educated enough to interpret it? This is of course an extreme example (a machine interpretation of conceptual design), but in any case tactility should be enhanced in digital publications in a per-

21. Umberto Eco and Jean Claude Carriere, *This Is Not the End of the Book* (Evanston, IL: Northwestern University Press, 2012), 4.

22. "Patently Apple," http://www.patentlyapple.com/patently-apple/haptics/.

23. Asger Jorn and Guy Debord, *Mémoires* (Copenhagen: Bauhaus Imaginiste, 1959).

ceptual way, going beyond the industrial functional standards. It could appeal, instead, directly to our nerve endings, stimulating their very high perceptive qualities, perhaps with the use of new artificial materials, able to assume a number of different states. The consequent tactile (and other sensory) experiences would challenge the sensory system to recognize and learn something completely new.

Beyond the information identifiable with the fundamental senses, there's still a lot more information received and transmitted through the body and brain, but it is either immaterial (light, waves, heat) or encoded, as everything electronic and digital is. So if traditional publishing objects are a well-orchestrated epicenter of information, aiming to guarantee a satisfying reading experience, digital publishing in its current standards and embodiments represents instead a deprived one. The functional ideology behind it still blocks the vast potential of software to transform and interconnect the content with external human and virtual sources. Refocusing the current behavioral approach to an extended perceptive one, and aiming to enable social and cultural interconnections instead of automatically produced, customizable industrial products, would potentially lead to completely new types of published objects.

HYBRID PUBLICATIONS AS PROCESSUAL PRINT

This type of evolution of digital publications would not only deal with senses in a desirable way, supporting our biological need to appreciate and learn new perceptual differences, but would also unleash the huge potential of software and networks that are now relegated to a few "service" features. This process would eventually involve traditional publishing, creating perhaps a single entity that could be called a "hybrid," a recognizable publication that would deeply "perform the networks."[24] This notion of performing networks is already being considered in the contemporary artists' publishing scene, through combining web content and processes with traditional publishing.

One example is *American Psycho* by Mimi Cabell and Jason Huff (Vienna: Traumawien, 2012). It was created by sending the entirety of Bret Easton Ellis's novel *American Psycho* through Gmail, one page at a time. They then collected the ads that appeared next to each email and used them to annotate the original text, page by page. In printing it as a perfect bound book, they erased the body of Ellis's text and left only chapter titles and constellations of their added footnotes. What remains is *American Psycho*, told through its chapter titles and annotated with relational Google ads only, as it might have been read by a Google software robot eye. The active and tangible machine presence inside the printed page is described from a dystopian angle by the publisher, Luc Gross: "Until now, books were the last advertisement-free refuge."[25] He asserts that "inline ads" will become what the product placements are now in movies, for example, and that those mechanisms could change literary content itself and not only its containers.

Another hybrid work is Stéphanie Vilayphiou's net-art piece *La Carte ou le Territoire* (*The Map or the Territory*) in which she selected a controversial book of the same name by Michel Houellebecq, which was renowned and discussed in France for its borrowing of evident quotes from Wikipedia, never acknowledged by the author nor by the publisher.[26] Vilayphiou retrieved the book's digitized text and wrote a software filter which parses it in sentences (or part of it), looking for the same phrases in the millions of digitized texts contained in Google Books. The result is the same book transformed into a unique sequential digital collage of quotations from other books, definitively losing even the last bit of originality. Visually, the found sentences are highlighted in yellow, but are rendered in their original typefaces, the original authoritative printed context still maintained in the background. Vilayphiou ultimately questions originality and authorship through software automation. These are two early examples of hybrids as the processes they initiate end with the respective books, even if they would be impossible to realize without software and networks.

What I've tried to define as "post-digital print" is a publishing practice that literally absorbs digital technologies. Proper future hybrids would reflect the dynamic and rich nature of publishing with

24. Paul Soulellis, "Performing Publishing: Infrathin Tales from the Printed Web," *Hyperallergic*, December 2, 2014, http://hyperallergic.com/165803/performing-publishing-infrathin-tales-from-the-printed-web/; see also Alessandro Ludovico, *Post-digital Print: The Mutation of Publishing since 1894* (Eindhoven: Onomatopee, 2012).

25. Luc Gross, "Hijacked eBook Bestsellers as Literary Trojan Horses," https://web.archive.org/web/20150626112754/http://traumawien.at/stuff/littrojans/.

26. "Blind Carbon Copy: La Carte ou le Territoire," http://bcc.stdin.fr/.

embedded computational characteristics. These computational elements should process information and include the results in classic publications, producing new publication typologies, and, in turn, new attitudes and publishing structures. This type of publication would be able to mix running code and unchangeable content, integrating processes and stability in the same place. Eventually they would be able to react to possible feedback from the processes they triggered, and reflect this feedback in their own structures. These strategies would evolve what I've termed "processual" publishing. Technical processes would potentially enable social and perceptual processes in a horizontal collaborative scenario where the printed and digital media would intertwine, with paper, software, and networks working as a whole, forming new sensorial combinations. This would occur in direct relationship with our senses, but simultaneously reflect the unchangeability of the printed page and the perennial dance of information in the digital world.

Silvio Lorusso

Print on Demand: The Radical Potential of Networked Standardization[1]

I began to be interested in print on demand (POD) while I was doing an internship at the Institute of Network Cultures in Amsterdam. The INC, founded in 2004 and directed by media theorist Geert Lovink, is a research centre that "analyses and shapes the terrain of network cultures through events, publications, and online dialogue." Generally, INC's publications can be read online, downloaded, and even ordered as physical books for free. As a consequence, it sometimes happens that these free books are then sold for a price elsewhere. However, people at the INC do not complain. What they care about is the dissemination and circulation of ideas, so they are enthralled by the unexpected ways in which content is redistributed and reframed. This was the attitude that guided my research on POD. [...]

1. Reprinted from Silvio Lorusso, *Extending Horizons: The Praxis of Experimental Publishing in the Age of Digital Networks. Design, Art, and the Materialities of Mediation*, PhD diss., Iuav University of Venice, 2015/16, 186 and 85–97, https://archive.org/details/ExtendingHorizons.

> POD seems destined to occupy a position very much similar to that of photocopying in the 1980s and 1990s: a chance to print and distribute content cheaply, in a format which is physically stable, easy to use, and pleasant to the senses. Which is still very much what paper is all about.[2]

POD radically transforms the production process of physical books, but also influences the idea of the book by providing a new ground for PDF files, that now witness the "potentiality" of the printed book and sometimes this is sufficient to reach the goal of the publication gesture.

POD is a system that allows even just a single copy of a book to be printed and made commercially available without any prior investment through an online platform.[3] POD reverts the common assumption that sale comes after print. Here, print happens only once a copy has been sold. POD platforms generally offer additional services such as online stores open to the public, the propagation of publications' data in databases like Google Books, the constant availability of titles at no cost, the supply of ISBN or ISSN codes.

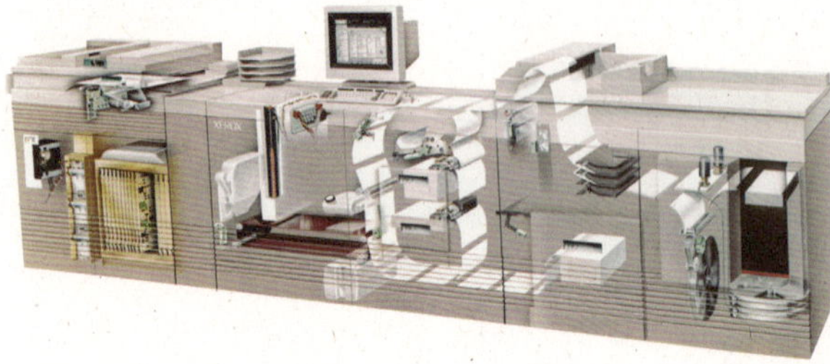

Fig. 1: Xerox DocuTech Production Publisher 135, c1990, the machine that gave rise to the print-on-demand industry.

It is not a trivial task to identify the origins of POD. It seems that the term was coined by Xerox around 1990, as a result of the marketing of the DocuTech Production Publisher. The above image (Fig. 1) shows the operation of this machine. The DocuTech was able to store and edit digital documents, print them, and also bind the printed sheets with pins or adhesive tape, producing books ready to use. With all probability, this machine fostered the growth of the POD industry.

An early advertisement for the DocuTech was included in *Black Enterprise* magazine in 1997 (Fig. 2). The advertisement is a clear demonstration of the digital nature of POD systems and its consequences: the metaphor used is that of the computer screen, the tagline is mainly about networked connection, while the headline builds on reduced time and distances.

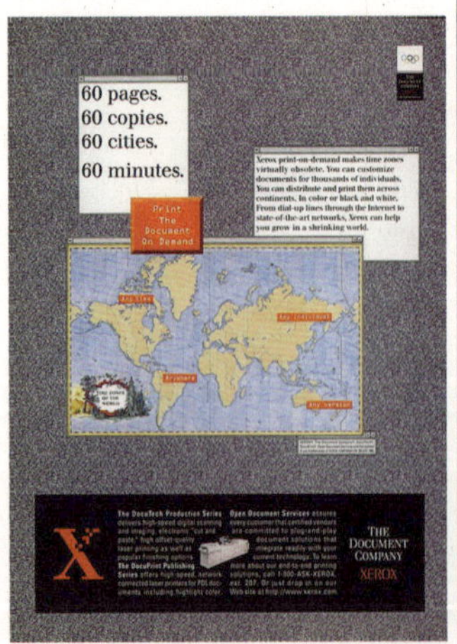

Fig. 2: Page from *Black Enterprise*, 1977.

2. Alessandro Ludovico, *Post-Digital Print: The Mutation of Publishing since 1894* (Eindhoven: Onomatopee 2012), 78.

3. There are several platforms available that are able to produce diverse typologies of publication: among others, Lulu is focused on books, photo albums, and calendars; Blurb also includes prints magazines; Newspaper Club offers newspapers.

Several technologies have allowed or encouraged the development of POD, among these:

- laser printing, first developed in 1969. Laser printing is crucial since it would have been uneconomic to print a few copies of a publication with earlier methods like offset;
- Desktop Publishing, that spread around the late 1980s;
- the World Wide Web, without which communication between publishers and POD platform, and between platform and customer, would have been extremely slow and cumbersome;
- the PDF, a widespread format that can be outputted from basically any word processor, discussed in detail in this section.

In this perspective, POD represents an original mix of pre-existing technologies, as Morris Rosenthal argues:

> The miracle of POD technology is not the printing process itself, which is actually the weak link from the standpoint of most publishers, but the digital library behind it. [...] The hero of the digital library story is Portable Document Format (PDF) created by Adobe and used globally in conjunction with their free Acrobat reader.[4]

Among the typical uses of POD, there are: the marketing of publishers' backlists, "vanity press" publications, and books available in the public domain that are digitized but are not in any catalog.[5] The absence of any obstacle to the publication staggers the validating role of the published printed book.

Another collateral effect of POD is "book spam." This phenomenon is caused by the possibility of fully automating the production of a book. Philip M. Parker has even patented a method for producing books that led him to publish more than 200,000 titles in the Amazon Store.[6] In the discussion around the Wikipedia page for "Print on Demand," the deceptive use of these methods is highlighted:

> The way this confidence trick is played on the unwary goes like this: A student of a particular topic may innocently trawl any online book dealer's website and come across a book which appears to be on the topic of interest. The book is duly ordered in the belief that you are buying a book. Well your [*sic*] are not buying a book. What you have bought is a bound selection of random and usually totally unrelated Wikipedia pages with only the cover actually relating to the topic of interest. [...] It may be legal but it is still an act of deception. The information on the cover claiming the content has been compiled from Wikipedia is extremly [*sic*] easy to overlook. It is deliberately so.[7]

Swiss designer and artist Manuel Schmalstieg researched in depth the phenomenon of book spam. According to Schmalstieg, the origins of book spam date back to 2009

4. Morris Rosenthal, *Print-on-Demand Book Publishing: A New Approach To Printing And Marketing Books For Publishers And Self-Publishing Authors*, updated edition (Springfield, MA: Foner Books, 2004).
5. An example of this last use is Forgotten Books, selling books such as *Personal Power* by Keith Johnston Thomas (1912), *The evidence of Immortality* by Jerome A. Anderson (1899), or *Vedic Mythology* by A. A. Macdonell (1897).
6. Noam Cohen, "He Wrote 200,000 Books (but Computers Did Some of the Work)," *New York Times*, April 14, 2008, http://www.nytimes.com/2008/04/14/business/media/14link.html.
7. 78.148.46.91, "Talk: Print on Demand," *Wikipedia*, March 7, 2013, https://en.wikipedia.org/w/index.php?title=Talk:Print_on_demand&oldid=1077045394.

or 2010. Schmalstieg also documented some of the strategies employed by the book spammer like choosing "really beautiful author names which the middle initial, which is proven to increase the seriousness and the credibility."[8]

POD services perfectly suit the need of preservation of volatile Web content. An early "Web to print" experiment was carried out by Tony Pierce in 2002, when he published his blog as a printed book, titled *Blook*, a portmanteau between "blog" and "book" coined by Jeff Jarvis. The term "blook" gained popularity thanks to the Blooker Prize, organized by Lulu. It was so popular in 2006 that it was short-listed for inclusion in the *Oxford English Dictionary* and was a runner-up for Word of the Year.[9]

Ether Press publishing house by graphic designer Andrew LeClair offered in 2012 a service that allowed to print a book with the latest tweets related to the Occupy movement, tracked through the hashtag #OWS.[10] The proceeds went to support the movement. The project is particularly interesting since it took advantage of the temporal specificity of POD.

Fig. 3: Espresso Book Machine. Photo by Politics and Prose Bookstore.

Finally, there are site-specific examples of POD systems. One of these is the Espresso Book Machine, a complex apparatus with transparent frames through which one can see the process of getting a book printed and bound in about 15 minutes (Fig. 3). The Espresso Book Machine is connected to a network of machines worldwide, so that a book printed in one location is stored on a common database and can then be printed somewhere else.

Fig. 4: FOMObile at Salone del Mobile, Milan, 2014.

An experimental project dealing with site-specific POD is *FOMO*, which stands for "fear of missing out," an idiomatic internet expression to indicate the anxiety linked to the inability to cope with the amount of information produced online on a daily basis. Developed by studio Space Caviar, *FOMO* is a print magazine generated with

8. Manuel Schmalstieg, "Black Holes in the Gutenberg Galaxy" (talk, presented at the Off The Press Conference, WORM Rotterdam, May 22, 2014), http://ms-studio.net/talks/black-holes-in-the-gutenberg-galaxy/.

9. "Blook," in *Wikipedia*, September 22, 2015, https://en.wikipedia.org/w/index.php?title=Blook&oldid=682173700.

10. http://p-dpa.net/work/occupy-books/.

a custom-made software which gathers social media interactions based on metadata filters such as a hashtag or location related to a specific event. The collected data is then arranged in a print-ready PDF according to a predefined design template. The PDF is then printed, bound, and distributed on the spot by the FOMObile, a collapsible mobile publishing platform (Fig. 4). The publications produced by FOMO merge the data resulting from physical presence and online attention. In Space Caviar's words:

> The magazine's production is a performative process that investigates the aesthetic and conceptual implications of the encounter between a centuries-old tradition of experimental publishing, the rising influence of machine intelligence in media, and the craving for instant gratification produced by real-time technologies. Variables such as background noise, number of people present, and intensity of social media activity inform the appearance of the final output, creating both moments of density and voids of activity. In Dadaist spirit, it is not so much an experiment in precision documentation as in finding alternative methods of representation and documentation of events.[11]

Compared to "traditional" books, the quality of POD services is sometimes disappointing. For instance, Lulu's user interface—recently redesigned—was not so long ago cumbersome, both for the publisher and the purchaser. The choice of formats and paper offered by the platform is limited. Furthermore, the so-called "perfect binding"—Lulu's standard option—breaks after the books are opened a few times.

Fig. 5: Nanni Balestrini, *Tristano IT4625* (DeriveApprodi, 2007).

This humble physicality is nonetheless distinctive. The peculiar identity of POD books is not dissimilar from cheap Xeroxed zines. It's no coincidence that Xerox played a crucial role in the development of POD systems, both in technical and cultural terms. While it combined the functional components that make POD possible, it also supported experimental projects that employed it. In 2007, the Italian branch of the company promoted the realization of *Tristano*, an early example of a generative novel by Nanni Balestrini, first published in 1966 but fully realized only four decades after, when it was finally possible to print and bind unique permutations of the text (Figs. 5 and 6). In Umberto Eco's words:

> Whereas today, thanks not only to computers that can quickly combine in the most vertiginous ways, but also to digital printing and printing on demand, the reader

11. http://www.spacecaviar.net/articles/fomo/.

> can have 'in flesh and blood' either a different copy of the tale from all the others (which represents both the triumph and the death of the numbered edition, seeing that each copy would be number 1), or any number of them, for purposes of comparison (time permitting).[12]

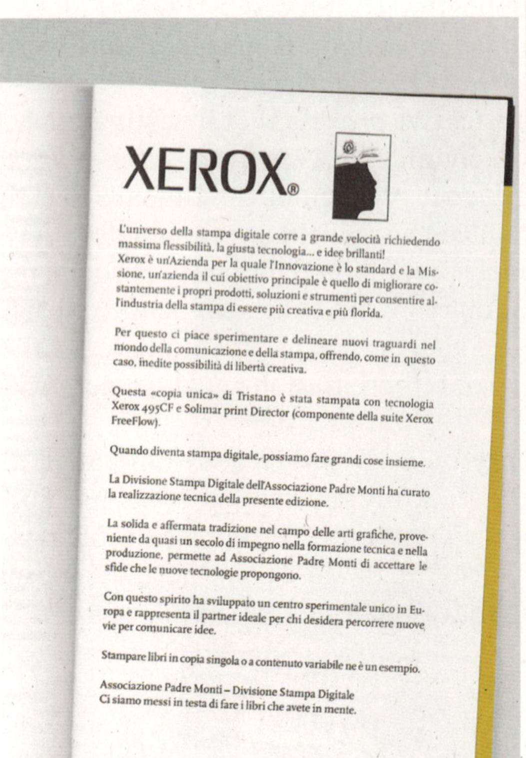

XEROX®

L'universo della stampa digitale corre a grande velocità richiedendo massima flessibilità, la giusta tecnologia... e idee brillanti!
Xerox è un'Azienda per la quale l'Innovazione è lo standard e la Missione, un'azienda il cui obiettivo principale è quello di migliorare costantemente i propri prodotti, soluzioni e strumenti per consentire all'industria della stampa di essere più creativa e più florida.

Per questo ci piace sperimentare e delineare nuovi traguardi nel mondo della comunicazione e della stampa, offrendo, come in questo caso, inedite possibilità di libertà creativa.

Questa «copia unica» di Tristano è stata stampata con tecnologia Xerox 495CF e Solimar print Director (componente della suite Xerox FreeFlow).

Quando diventa stampa digitale, possiamo fare grandi cose insieme.

La Divisione Stampa Digitale dell'Associazione Padre Monti ha curato la realizzazione tecnica della presente edizione.

La solida e affermata tradizione nel campo delle arti grafiche, proveniente da quasi un secolo di impegno nella formazione tecnica e nella produzione, permette ad Associazione Padre Monti di accettare le sfide che le nuove tecnologie propongono.

Con questo spirito ha sviluppato un centro sperimentale unico in Europa e rappresenta il partner ideale per chi desidera percorrere nuove vie per comunicare idee.

Stampare libri in copia singola o a contenuto variabile ne è un esempio.

Associazione Padre Monti – Divisione Stampa Digitale
Ci siamo messi in testa di fare i libri che avete in mente.

Fig. 6: Xerox promotional page in *Tristano BK2740*.

Another interesting Italian perspective on POD dates back to the 1990s and is included in Francesco Pirella's *Manuale dell'Antilibro*. According to Gillo Dorfles, Mario Persico, Francesco Pirella, and Edoardo Sanguineti—the signatories of the *Antibook Manifesto* that led to the creation of Pirella's manual—the precious, bulky, and ultimately Kitsch edition betrays the actual condition of the text in the information age. The Antibook is a kind of book that

> frees us from the condition of the marketing, from the bookish schemas of the industry, from the counterfeiting of typographic styles. The container becomes the content and it makes it unnecessary the simulation of the book-object and the numbered art book, the covers, the jackets, the cases, the white pages, the antiqued papers. The Antibook uses standardized supports, recycled paper, recovered materials.[13]

Part of the book is specifically dedicated to POD. Pirella's proposal is particularly interesting because it is characterized by the attempt to mix recycle, self-production, and the industrial, standardized model of POD.

It seems appropriate to think of POD's materiality as a compromise among the technical infrastructure, users' needs, and the economic constraints of both the publishing industry and e-commerce. This is well exemplified by *Post-Fordism and its Discontents*, a book that exists in four versions and which design—by Nina Støttrup Larsen and Žiga Testen—epitomizes its production and distribution processes (Fig. 7). Its cover becomes a space to acknowledge the different editions, as well as their prices and print runs.

12. Umberto Eco, "What Is Balestrini Up to Now?," in Nanni Balestrini, *Tristano. A Novel* (London, New York: Verso, 2014), v-x, here x.

13. Francesco Pirella, *Manuale dell'antilibro: etica e didattica per l'autoproduzione di un libro di carta nell'era digitale* (Genova: Marietti, 1999), 152.

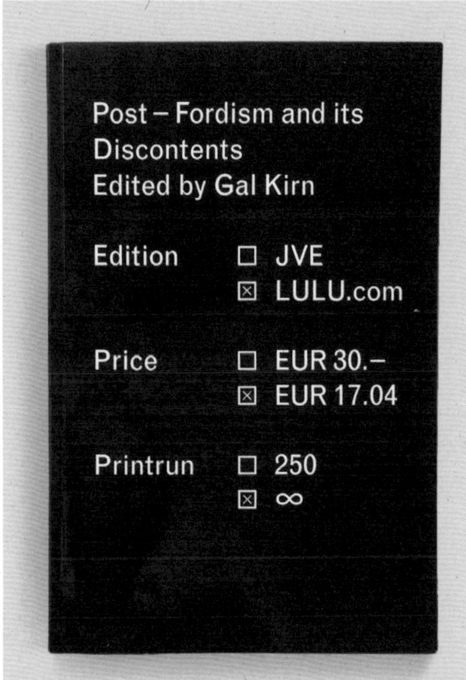

Fig. 7: Gal Kirn, ed., *Post-Fordism and its Discontents* (Jan van Eyck Academie, 2010).

In this sense, POD books represent a genuine hybrid of digital and analog processes: under the guise of the "traditional" book form, there is a complex ecosystem made of file formats, metadata, retail platforms, multiple connections to online stores, and, sometimes, even YouTube book trailers, authors' blogs, etc. Sent through the regular postal system, the physical book is the tip of the iceberg of an infrastructure that takes advantage of digital printing, desktop publishing, PDF format, and Web 2.0. Therefore, POD is not a new technology in itself, but a fruitful combination of existing ones.

In 2011, researcher Giulia Ciliberto and I developed *Blank on Demand*, a project that adopted the physical book as a unit of measure of a whole POD production and distribution process. It consists of two volumes printed with Lulu, whose formats correspond respectively to the maximum and minimum dimensions currently available. Similarly, page amount and price are set according to the limit values allowed by the platform. The two books are completely blank, except for the presence of the ISBN code. Deprived of any content, they reflect the influence of the current technological context on their materiality.

This isn't the only project aimed at testing POD platforms and experimenting with them. *Dear Lulu*, a book meant to calibrate various graphic parameters such as patterns, colors, and typography, is the result of a workshop run by James Goggin in 2008 at the University of Applied Sciences in Darmstadt. The procedure was afterwards extended to other platforms, such as Blurb and MagCloud. *Variable Format* is a manifold project conceived in 2012 by Lynn Harris, published by AND and designed by Åbäke with Pierre Pautler. Materials collected from the now closed library of the Byam Shaw School of Art form the content of a publication that is spread through twelve POD platforms. Instead of being resized to fit the various formats, a single layout is cut, so each printed artifact acts as a unique "framing" of the same source. Finally, *The Black Book* by Jean Keller: made in 2010/2012, it takes the value of books in a literal sense, drawing from the premise that printer ink is one of the most expensive substances in the world.

As these bookworks represent, to use Johanna Drucker's words, a "self-conscious record of [their] own production,"[14] it is fair to ask in which ways POD informs the

14. Johanna Drucker, *The Century of Artists' Books* (New York: Granary Books, 2004), 161.

field of artist's books and connects to its legacy. The context of artist's books is an intricate one since it comprises very diverse artifacts: from inconspicuous conceptual paperbacks to crafty, sculptural book-objects. Probably, it is this latter embodiment that leads to a prejudice towards POD artist's books, rarely found at fairs or exhibitions. An anecdotal proof of this preconception is a recent call to which the eligibles are "any artist bookworks other than SPOD (Self Published On Demand such as Lulu, Blurb and so forth)."[15]

Instead of failing to fit some dubious criteria, I argue that POD *reinforces* the inheritance of the artist's book as a democratic multiple. From a material perspective, I'd refer to some of Ed Ruscha's bookworks, playing with the evenness and anonymity of mass production in order to provoke a mild shock, "a kind of a huh?" in his own words.[16] Such evenness is a defining feature of POD systems: in order to produce unique copies, paradoxically they enforce the limitations of mass production by applying stricter standards. From an ideological perspective as well, POD seems to extend the democratic impulse professed by several artists working with books. In 1976, Sol LeWitt published the following text on *Art-Rite*:

> Artists' books are, like any other medium, a means of conveying art ideas from the artist to the viewer/reader. Unlike most other media they are available to all at a low cost. They do not need a special place to be seen. They are not valuable except for the ideas they contain. They contain the material in a sequence which is determined by the artist. (The reader/viewer can read the material in any order but the artist presents it as s/he thinks it should be). Art shows come and go but books stay around for years. They are works themselves, not reproductions of works. Books are the best medium for many artists working today. The material seen on the walls of galleries in many cases cannot be easily read/seen on walls but can be more easily read at home under less intimidating conditions. It is the desire of artists that their ideas be understood by as many people as possible. Books make it easier to accomplish this.[17]

This democratic impulse was quickly subsumed and partly extinguished by the dynamics of the art system: let's consider for instance the price of old *Art-Rite* issues, originally set to $1, which is currently around $100 on eBay. In contrast, POD seems to foster a more profound proclivity to "convey [...] art ideas [...] to all at a low cost." When using POD, several artists enable the online preview of the whole book or make the PDF of the publication available for free, which, as Alessandro Ludovico points out, can be seen as a sort of sub-medium, as it evolves from a production standard to a standalone one.[18]

In turn, the physical book seems to represent almost an incentive to distribute ideas in a digital environment, while its photographic documentation is a means to establish the publishing act. In fact, as poet Kenneth Goldsmith notices, experimental POD publications are sold—if ever sold—in extremely small amounts.[19] Furthermore, their price is often set to the minimum, which means that the artist doesn't get any money—an aspect that raises legitimate concerns about the sustainability of such practice.

Artists who employ POD are often very conscious of its effects and implications. The Artists' Books Cooperative (ABC), founded in 2009 and consisting of several members located all over the world, declares:

15. Abecedarian Gallery, "Artists' Book Cornucopia VI Prospectus," 2014.
16. Edward Ruscha, "... a Kind of a Huh?," interview by Sharp Willoughby, *Avalanche*, no. 6 (Winter/Spring 1973), 30–39.
17. Sol LeWitt, *Art-Rite*, no. 14 (January 1976), 10.
18. Alessandro Ludovico, "Post-Digital Publishing, Hybrid and Processual Objects in Print," *APRJA* 3, no. 1 (2014): 79–85, here 79, https://aprja.net//article/view/116088.
19. Kenneth Goldsmith, "The Wild World of Lulu," *Columbia University Press Blog*, 2013, http://www.cupblog.org/?p=10019.

> Print-on-demand liberates artists from the oppressively expensive and laborious demands of traditional photobook publishing. Print-on-demand is fast, cheap, and light. It exists outside the power structures of publishers and distributors. [...] We're interested in raw ideas and there is no better transporter for a great idea than a book. A single book if needs be. And with the internet, the ideas in that single book can go viral and reach millions in a split second.[20]

Borrowing from German philosopher Ernst Cassirer, media theorist Florian Cramer suggests to consider the book as a "symbolic form,"[21] since it is able to transcend diverse media and supports. ABC's work echoes, and even extends, such perspective:

> We're all involved in publishing *the idea* of a book online. That is to say, each of our artists presents their book in some form of digital format that exists online as well as in physical form. That doesn't mean it has to be an e-book. It could be the book presented as a video trailer on Vimeo, as a single line of text, a performance documented, an essay, a series of stills, or as a downloadable pdf file. The book exists in physical form and in conceptual form. It travels further and quicker as an idea than as an object.[22]

ABC member Paul Soulellis is the curator of the Library of the Printed Web, initiated in 2013. It includes publications in which content from the Web is transposed to print in ways that are often surprising (the library contains postcards, newspapers, zines). Many of these are POD books. This "archive devoted to archives"[23] highlights the radical potential of POD: with a few clicks and a fair amount of money, a good part of Soulellis' collection can be physically reconstituted somewhere else, while its digital incarnation circulates online as multiform embodiments of art ideas.

20. Artists' Books Cooperative, "Paleolithic Cave Paintings," 2014, https://abcoop.tumblr.com/post/80007035103/paleolithic-cave-paintings-abc-artists-books; reprinted in this volume, 508–511, 510.
21. Florian Cramer, "Afterword," in Alessandro Ludovico, *Post-Digital Print: The Mutation of Publishing since 1894* (Eindhoven: Onomatopee 2012), 162–166, 163.
22. Artists' Books Cooperative, "Paleolithic Cave Paintings," in this volume, 511.
23. Paul Soulellis, "Search, Compile, Publish," May 23, 2013, http://soulellis.com/2013/05/search-compile-publish/.

Manon Bruet

Production Process: Print on Demand[1]

1. Reprinted from *Revue Faire* No. 26 (2020).

Translated from French by Derek Byrne.

In 2008, the English graphic designer, publisher, teacher and author James Goggin was invited to give a workshop at the Darmstadt University in Germany.[2] The result of these two days of intense activity with the fourteen graphic design students and their teacher Frank Philippin was *Dear Lulu*. This tiny book with its unassuming appearance, despite its shiny cover, was presented as a 96 page test-book. As the title indicates it proposes to test the platform for publishing and distribution Lulu.com and more broadly the system of print-on-demand: how it operates, the quality of what it produces, the technical and ecological possibilities that it opens up and its impact on the practices of Graphic Design. The idea of course was to question this model, but also its main protagonists: the book was the first in a series and was soon followed by *Dear Blurb*, *Dear BoD* and *Dear Kolofon* which allowed for a comparison of the dominant platforms. This intervention, entitled "Farben on demand" is, like the rest of James Goggin's work, at the junction of practice and research: it intends to be simultaneously a space for play, an experiment and a technical and educational tool.

However, the field of study is much wider than it seems. When one explores Lulu.com or other similar platforms, one must necessarily become interested in a whole terminology and a collection of intimately linked, perhaps even affiliated, models: one speaks of "online printing" but also of "web-to-print" when describing the group of platforms that can be used to create a link between customer and printer. The term "print-on-demand" is, in English, almost always associated with the book object. However, it more generally describes a mode of access and of production that emerged from the encounter between the printing process and the digital realm. The term "online self-publishing" is also used to describe an activity that allows a user to physically and digitally distribute a book via the different platforms. Also, Lulu, like PixartPrinting, Print24, VistaPrint, and others, is a web-to-print application that allows a printed object to be ordered online and just like Blurb, Books on Demand (BoD), and even Kolofon, it specializes in the domain of the book. But aside from certain specificities, every one of the aforementioned platforms uses print-on-demand as a mode of access and production.

In their book *Enjeux et développements de l'impression à la demande*, Juliette Patissier and Émilie Mathieu consider the "on demand" model as being similar to "a Toyotism enhanced with the power of internet and digital infrastructures."[3] They also highlight the similarity of the objectives and ambitions of these iconic systems, as both of them illustrate profound industrial and commercial modifications of the periods in which they arose. Introduced in the 1950s in Japanese factories and guided by industrial engineer Taiichi Ono, Toyotism is a form of organization of work that, unlike its predecessors Fordism and Taylorism, allows a certain autonomy and advocates a certain polyvalence in its productive agents. It aims to produce the best possible quality, notably in order to minimize the use of an after sales service, to reduce costs, to avoid stock and overproduction, and to reduce timeframes, notably by reducing administrative complexities to a minimum. These are the same objectives, often called "the five zeros," that are stated more or less explicitly on most of the online platforms for self-publishing and printing.

1. ZERO STOCK

> "Publish your book and sell it in bookshops: simple, rapid and risk-free. Your book is only printed when it's ordered, with a minimum order of one book!"
>
> —www.bod.fr

"Farben on demand" means "colors on demand." Obviously this title indicates an interest for the calibration and reproduction of colors, which was originally the main theme of the workshop, before the research broadened the scope of their inquiry. But it also assumes an interest for the "on demand" model that emerged at the end of the 1990s. This expression obviously means *on the demand of the client or user*. It also covers the demand for some-

2. James Goggin graduated from the London Royal College of Art in 1999, he founded Practise with Shan James the same year. Now based in Providence (USA) the studio has developed a multifaceted practice which belongs to a number of fields (culture, architecture, fashion, and advertising) and a number of countries (England, Sweden, Denmark, and the United States).

3. Émilie Mathieu and Juliette Patissier, *Enjeux et développements de l'impression à la demande* (Paris: Éditions du Cercle de la Librairie, coll. "Pratiques éditoriales," 2016), 14.

thing and the fact of obtaining it. When applied to the field of print, it describes both a mode of access and a mode of production.

As Juliette Patissier and Émilie Mathieu remind us, the term as it is commonly used was originally associated with video.

> VoD [video on demand] is a model of digital consumption of audiovisual content [...] similar to PoD [print-on-demand] it ushered in new way of proposing content to consumers: the latter had virtual access to a very large catalogue, from which they could choose the product that interested them and then have direct access to it. The available catalogue is vastly greater than the range of films proposed by cinema, or the selection of DVDs available in retail outlets, and even what is available on television. The channel used for VoD is called *unicast*, as opposed to the *broadcast* channel used by television which provides the same content to everyone [...] with VoD the client is in a position to choose what they want to watch and when they want to watch it.[4]

The "on demand" model, indissociable from the development of digital technologies, places the user and their search at the center of the process. The connection that the two authors make here applies to on demand publishing sites like Lulu or Blurb that are studied in the book *Enjeux et développements de l'impression à la demande*. But it could also be extended to any of the more generalist online print sites that also propose a range of objects, with users being able to select and then personalize the object that they want to receive a print of. In 2013, it was to some extent this new mode of access that Étienne Hervy and Émilie Lamy praised in the manifesto *Babel on demand*. For this event that was organized during the 23rd Festival international de l'affiche et du graphisme in Chaumont (of which they are respectively General Director and publications Director), they asked forty-one graphic designers, working alone or in duos, to produce a book on the theme of their choice, to be printed and distributed by Blurb, for the purposes of filling an ideal but temporary library. The title draws a parallel between the short story written by Jorge Luis Borges in 1941 and these recent platforms that, like a total library described by the Argentinian writer in great detail, now make up a huge "universe" at the juncture of past, present, and future, perhaps infinite in nature, yet nonetheless regulated by defined properties (number of pages, system of presentations, etc.).[5]

According to Italian researcher and designer Silvio Lorusso, the term "print-on-demand" was coined by the Xerox company in the 1990s for the purposes of promoting its DocuTech Production Publisher machine.[5] This was an ancestor of the Espresso Book Machine, which could be considered to be the emblematic apparatus of publishing on demand—it is not surprising then that the term in English is often, if not solely, associated with the domain and object of the book. In 1997 an advertisement that appeared in the American *Black Enterprise* magazine, boasted of the merits of this machine that was able to digitally process, print, and bind a book:

> Print The Document On Demand.
> 60 pages, 60 copies, 60 cities, 60 minutes.
> Xerox print-on-demand makes time zones virtually obsolete. You can customize documents for thousands of individuals. You can distribute and print them across continents. In color or black and white. From dial-up lines through the Internet to state-of-the-art networks. Xerox can help you grow in a shrinking world.[6]

Even before the spread of the internet, ambitious tendencies towards networks, speed, and accessibility were quite explicit. Nevertheless, much more than the machine's abilities at the time, the true upheaval was to be found in the fact that the objects were produced *after* they had been sold as opposed to being produced *in order* to be sold. The production process was then based on real orders and completely upended the existing relationship between sales and production that was typical of the usual system of mass production and distribution.

4. Ibid.
5. Jorge Luis Borges, "The Library of Babel," in Borges, *Collected Fictions*, trans. Andrew Hurley (New York, London: Penguin, 1998), 112–118.
6. Silvio Lorusso, *Extending Horizons—The Praxis of Experimental Publishing in the Age of Digital Networks*, PhD in Design Sciences, Iuav University, Venice, 2015/2016, 86–87, https://archive.org/details/ExtendingHorizons/.
7. Cited in ibid.

Thanks to its characteristics, in the 2000s the "on demand" model represented the promise of a more aware and more ecologically sound system of production. A system that reduced waste and that was potentially locally based, thanks to its desire to establish itself digitally on a global scale. This was precisely one of the hopes expressed by James Goggin in the introduction to his workshop:

> "Print on Demand" is an increasingly important production system which can serve to make us designers rethink the impact our profession has on the environment and to question the often wasteful print volumes and production methods requested of us by our clients.[7]

Nevertheless, its development has made tracing its fabrication and quantifying its environmental impact more and more complicated. Nowadays, this form of idealization seems outmoded and all hope has evaporated, with the model continuing to provide a flexible and inexpensive alternative to the more traditional systems of production and access in the field of printing.

Thanks to the combination of various printing technologies and of digital flow management services, the "on demand" mode of organization has largely spread and is no longer solely confined to the domain of the book. Print-on-demand services provide a means to work around investment, both in terms of time and money, as well as the risks associated with the management of physical stock. There are no longer stocks of raw materials, nor of finished products, no more overproduction, and the production process is on principle more efficient, faster, less costly with the consumers' needs or desires once again at the heart of the process. Through different platforms, it is now possible to obtain all kinds of objects: photo albums, magazines, leaflets, posters, business cards, signs, and even so-called "customizable" accessories like cups, pens as well as bathroom blinds and towels.

It was exactly these possibilities, connected to this new logic of production that François Havegeer and Sacha Léopold (Syndicat) wished to explore with *Matthieu*, the second volume of their project *Taylor, Matthieu & Ricardo*, also presented in 2015 at the Festival international de l'affiche et du graphisme in Chaumont. They made a retrospective of the work of Matthieu Laurette, printed on a multitude of objects available for customization online. This included a cushion, a cup, a rug, and a telephone case that reemployed the bank of images of a certain French artist, along with his interest for representation, distribution, and promotion. With this project, the French graphic designers were pursuing their own research into questions of the production and economy of graphic objects: they displayed a range of objects that are usually ordered in large quantities but now available to anybody as single objects. In doing this they simultaneously demonstrated the potential and power of the "on demand" model.

2. ZERO DELAY

> "Free delivery available on all orders! In a hurry? You can choose your own delivery date with a 24-hour turnaround."
>
> —www.pixartprinting.co.ok

The cover of *Dear Lulu* is clearly addressed to the platform that the book proposes to put to the test:

> Dear Lulu,
> Please try and print these line, colour, pattern, format, texture and typography tests for us.
> Alex, Alice, André, Andreas, Anja, Christoph, Frank, James, Juliane, Michael, Patrick, Rimma & Tim.

Though the epistolary and familiar form may first bring a smile to one's lips, it raises a quite real question with regard to the field of print-on-demand. Who is doing the printing?

In effect, all online printing and self-publishing sites propose the same thing: an unbeatable reactivity and speed of execution. A performance made possible thanks to the mode of on demand organization. Once again in their book *Enjeux et Développements de l'impression à la demande*, Juliette Patissier and Émilie Mathieu remind us that though this system—and more particularly publishing on demand, their case study—is today unavoidably connected to the internet, this has not always been the case:

7. James Goggin, Introduction to the workshop "Farben on demand," reprinted in *Dear Lulu*, 36.

> Historically print-on-demand has been a centralized and industrial scale model set up by major printers or distributors directly on their premises. Having the capacity to invest in digital machines and in the development of flow management, printers and distribution centers are pillars of print-on-demand, and are much more representative of it than the Espresso Book Machine for example, at least in terms of the print volumes. This industrial dimension partly explains the rhythm and development of the model, particularly in France, that cannot, for the moment, be compared to the parallel development of the digital book.[8]

According to the authors, it was in the United States in 1997 that the model experienced its first true development with the production company Ingram Industries Inc. creating a subsidiary, Lightning Source Inc., a printworks that specializes in the production of books on demand. In France it was in 2001 that Interforum launched Bookpole, a print-on-demand service that delivers directly to the client, in partnership with the printer Maury. Since then the system has spread and become available to new audiences. At the same time, with the development of the web, offers have diversified, partnerships have multiplied, delocalized, and have increasingly gone underground.

Today the market as a whole is divided up between major printers who have expanded their online activity by forming alliances with other (most often foreign based) printers and large online print-on-demand or online printing platforms owned by businessmen associated with dozens of subcontractors, themselves also located all over the globe. The latter, mainly geared towards amateurs, remain quite opaque as to their functioning and their partnerships. It is for example impossible to find where or by whom the books are printed, or even the companies with whom they are associated on the websites of Lulu or Blurb. The same goes for the online print platform VistaPrint that, in its "Who are we?" section, proposes a selection from Getty Images and a promotional text about the company values as opposed to an effective description. It is not wholly surprising then to discover that VistaPrint was created by Cimpress, a giant in the field, heavily observed and criticized for the role it played in the *uberization* of the sector under the guise of establishing a greater flexibility in the sector.[9]

Geared more towards professionals working in the graphic chain, the platforms owned by the major printers emphasize the transparency of their production and fabrication processes. The Italian site PixartPrinting, which specializes more in large format printing for example, provides all of the information relating to the status of the company, the number of employees, the machines available and the partner countries. In a similar fashion the company Online Printers, in the help section of its website, proposes a video which presents what is happening behind the scenes. Exaprint, a printworks based in Montpellier clearly wishes to be seen as "the printer's printer." Specializing until 2018 in working with dealers (a main activity carried out (APE) code was required for each order), it was purchased by the massive firm Cimpress and has since opened up its business to include all types of clients, thus profoundly modifying its mode of functioning. Though certain objects are made on site, such as the business cards which represent 60 percent of their orders, the remaining production is entirely subcontracted to companies abroad. Inversely, the firm PrintOclock, made up of a production workshop and a logistics center, claims to be "made in France." Ultimately, the firm Print24, one of the most transparent of its kind, allows one to grasp the scale and extent of this type of organization.

> print24 is a service run by unitedprint.com UK Ltd.—one of Europe's leading online print shops. More than 700 employees work 24 hours a day using the latest technology on a production area of more than 10.000 sq m. Our sites are to be found in 26 countries—Austria, Belgium, Brazil, Canada, China, Czech Republic, Denmark, Finland, France, Germany, Greece, Netherlands, Hungary, Ireland, Italy, Luxembourg, Norway, Poland, Portugal, Slovakia, Slovenia, Spain, Sweden, Switzerland, United Kingdom and USA.

8. Mathieu and Patissier, *Enjeux et Développements*, 14.

9. Faustine Loison, "L'uberisation de l'imprimerie en marche avec Cimpress?," *GraphiLine* (blog), February 14, 2017, https://www.graphiline.com/article/25177/uberisation-imprimerie-marche-cimpress.

In their online help section, the printers clearly explain the method which allows all of these platforms to display such competitive prices and deadlines:

> The principal reason behind our competitive prices is that we print a number of orders on a single print sheet. In exceptional cases, it is possible that the quantity produced is greater than the quantity ordered. Before destroying the surplus (which is of course, neither economical nor ecological), we will offer them to you to be purchased at an exceptionally low price. All you have to do is click to take advantage of this offer!

The amalgam process, or simultaneous printing of different orders with similar characteristics (on the same paper and with the same colors) on the same sheet, seems then to be the key to the "on demand" model. In an article dedicated to the Exaprint group, the system is explained in a particularly frank manner:

> The concept is heavily based on subcontractors in France and Spain. An army of graphic designers works around the clock to compose panels of amalgam that are then sent to numerous subcontractors.[10]

So then, the objects ordered on these platforms, whether books, business cards, or posters, are sent to partner printers capable of meeting the deadlines of integrating them in an economic way into a layout, irrespective of where they are located.

> [...] delivery time to my London studio took over a week (even when I paid an "express" premium) and, perhaps most frustratingly given my original workshop brief's fairly utopian description of POD's potential ecological and decentralized distribution benefits, our *Dear Lulu* books were printed in Spain and flown by UPS to Darmstadt and London for delivery.[11]

Though it can be difficult to trace the journey of different orders, as James Goggin had already pointed out in 2008, it seems that they are not at all locally produced. On the contrary, the obligation to meet low costs and short deadlines appears to have driven the different dominant firms towards an exacerbated externalization and delocalization.

3. ZERO FLAWS

> "Onlineprinters: A pioneer in quality Onlineprinters is one of the first print shops in Europe to have its post press operations certified according to PSO. The result: top quality."
>
> —www.onlineprinters.com

The book *Dear Lulu* begins with a series of color portraits, visibly improvised, that present the project's protagonists posing with different accessories. Followed by a series of different experiments, that in turn take the form of photo albums, type specimens, optical games, color charts, and technical manuals. The graphic language is accomplished, varied and apparently spontaneous. James Goggin, Frank Philippin, and the students are interested here in the tangible parameters that make up a printed work: the text, the image, the raster, the format etc. Even more, the idea here is to question what constitutes a book that has been *well* printed—the ultimate goal is to test the quality produced provided by on demand printing. The project was then extended to other platforms for self-publishing that can now be compared: BoD, Blurb, and Kolofon.

Within each of these books, with only the cover being different, the instructions are stated and the visual propositions captioned, allowing others to understand and reproduce them. Obviously, the approach could bring to mind the work of Julien Tavelli and David Keshavjee (Maximage) who were already at the time beginning research in and around the parameters of offset printing. A few years later these experiments that began at the University of Art and Design Lausanne Écal gave rise to a series of book-tools—including *Maximage Formula Guide* and *Raster Guide* produced as part of the Écal's Workflow research program, and following firmly in the footsteps of *Dear Lulu*, *Dear Blurb*, *Dear Bod*, *Dear Kolofon*. They were all created in an academic context where they constituted first and foremost tools for their creators: simulta-

10. Antoine Gaillard "Exaprint: la fin du concept 100% revendeur," *GraphiLine* (blog), April 13, 2018, https://www.graphiline.com/article/28100/exaprint-fin-concept-100-revendeur.

11. James Goggin in Erin O'Arah, "Supply on demand," *Print Mag* (blog), June 1, 2018, https://www.printmag.com/article/supply_on_demand/.

neously pretexts for interest and experimentation and the remains of trials. And once distributed and printed (in this case quickly and easily thanks to the self-publishing platform), they become tools for others: user guides to some extent. This was in fact one of the clearly stated goals of James Goggin's introduction to his workshop:

> Any book produced on Lulu can also be offered for sale: perfect for individuals to make fanzines or self-published books without the need for a publisher or traditional bookshop/newsstand network. In our case, the colour test book we produce should be an extremely useful document for other graphic designers and students to order online and then use to analyse the possibilities of print-on-demand.[12]

Nevertheless, a few years later, the English Graphic Designer looked back at the approach and admits to being somewhat disappointed with the reality of the process.

> At a certain point I also realized the futility of the project in terms of using it to calibrate your images for printing. This was made very clear to me at one point when I ordered two copies of *Dear Lulu*: they both arrived at the same time, but had apparently been printed on two different machines. In one, the images had a noticeable cyan cast, while the other one's images were redder. Imaging if you'd just received one of those copies, and imagining that this indicated the general printing standard for Lulu. You'd adjust your images to be, say, less cyan, but then printing on the same machine as the redder images, you'd just make everything extremely red![13]

Though all of these online printing platforms emphasize the quality of their productions—notably in the hope that their clients remain satisfied and don't need to use the after sales service—the "on demand" model that they employ inevitably contributes to an uneven result. On one hand, for every order, the print technique used depends on the number of copies; large print runs are produced on rotary presses or offset printers, while smaller runs are printed using bubble jet, laser, or transfer printers depending on the object. For example a bubble jet printed leaflet will not have the same quality in terms of color or precision as the same object printed in offset. On the other hand, when it comes to the larger platforms, the amalgam system favors the delocalization of production; it would be difficult to imagine that the result of an object produced in Spain, on a particular machine run by a particular operator could be in any way similar to that of another produced on a different machine elsewhere. In the end, the offers are so diverse that they force firms to increase the number of partnerships for the purposes of their profit margin, and to spend little (or no) time monitoring production.

In 2018, for the catalog *Gamme Tabulaire, N°1 2018* by the studio J&J, Swiss graphic designer Marietta Eugster chose to avoid the uneven quality and calibration of online printing sites. She proposed a range of six colors from the RAL color chart—mainly used in industry and construction, and in this case by designers for their objects—translated into CMYK colors for the booklet, the standard used in digital printing. A kind of thumbing of the nose at a system of naming and reproduction of color that is inherently flawed and standardized, and a way of using online printing for the advantage that it actually offers: an efficient production at a low cost.

4. ZERO PAPERWORK

> "Total Creative Control
> Make all your own creative and marketing decisions for your project. Design something that matches your vision, choose the best printing options for you, and share it with your friends, fans, and followers."
> —www.blurb.com

In 2008, after the workshop and the publication of *Dear Lulu*, James Goggin was already highlighting the paradox of the complexity of the print guides available on the platform.

> Websites like Lulu seem geared toward print amateurs with its instructions and many areas are surprisingly vague, and actually less prescriptive than one would expect. As graphic designers, we had specific questions: RGB or CMYK (Lulu says both are fine: the book's

12. Goggin, Introduction, reprinted in *Dear Lulu*, 36.

13. Goggin in interview with the author, February 2019.

> outcome indicates this isn't necessarily so). Also, can you print on the inside front and back covers? (Answer: More than an hour of trawling FAQs to get a negative). Various methods for supplying artwork with bleed were outlined depending on which FAQ pages you happened to find. It took several failed uploads to realize that, against any designer's instinct, one must submit bleed artwork sans cropmarks.[14]

Online printing and publishing on demand are models that allow users to be autonomous and print or publish while avoiding a certain number of hitherto active participants in the graphic chain. With online printing one mostly avoids the figures of graphic designer and printer: creative tools are made available and discussion is reduced to a FAQ on a digital interface or a telephone hotline, more often than not completely separated from production. Though certain platforms are explicitly reserved for professionals, like Pixartprinting or print24, others emphasize the figure of the amateur, as is the case with Lulu, Blurb, and even VistaPrint. The situation is even more striking when it comes to publishing on demand. The user avoids the graphic designer and the printer, but most of all the publisher. The user thus decides alone what they will publish, the manner in which they will create the form and choose the format, as well as the sale price and the profit margin—for this step a price range is proposed, based on the book's physical characteristics and an estimated cost of production. In 2013, artist Jean Keller toyed with the so-called well oiled economic system with *The Black Book*. Based on the observation that the ink used in laser printing is one of the most costly materials, he used publishing on demand in order to produce a 740, totally black page book with the best value for money. On most of these platforms, the price of an object is degressive and defined by the number of pages and not the quantity of ink used. Ultimately, a copy of *The Black Book* costs the same to buy as a black-and-white book containing only text, whereas it is much more costly for Lulu to produce it.

Users are then multi-skilled. They take on the roles of all of the agents in the graphic chain in turn and this with no other middleman than the platforms of their choice. In fact, these latter are forced to be didactic in order to facilitate user understanding of the stages of production normally managed by specialist professionals. For example, on the website Lulu.com, a help section allows the platform to accompany the user at each step: from the choice of the materiality of the book to the optimization of sale prices including the acquisition of an ISBN and the page layout. Though the instructions have definitely evolved since *Dear Lulu* was created, the difference between them and the technical reality of the professions of graphic designers and printers is striking.[15] For example, the platform proposes to users to download a model for each size of book, in other words a file containing a template in the .doc and .png formats that will serve as a basis for the user to design their page layout. Lulu also provides a tool (closely resembling word processing software) specifically dedicated to laying out book covers. To take another example, it is also quite possible (and not at all problematic) to send a cover or even a full book in .doc, .png, .jpg and even .gif format to be printed. The platform barely evokes the necessity for crop marks and bleeds, and the mention of colorimetric profiles is nowhere to be found. Paradoxically, on the French site, the size of the back cover is given in PostScript points, a unit of measurement that is rarely used in France. A number of instructions that are both complex and imprecise with technical parameters that, though they are clearly not the desired audience, seem aberrant to professional graphic designers and printers. Though online print sites that are supposedly aimed towards professionals are obviously more anchored in the technical reality of agents in the graphic chain, the vocabulary and processes remain simplified, with the provision of templates in .ai and .eps, whether the document to be produced is a photograph, a leaflet, or an outdoor advertising canvas.[16]

As Émilie Mathieu and Juliette Patissier point out, print-on-demand is "absolutely and undeniably connected to the web and to new habits of cultural consumption that arise from it."[17] In fact it is a formidable tool for creation and distribu-

14. Goggin in O'Arah, "Supply on demand."
15. For most of the instructions the most recent update was made in November 2018.
16. DeskTop Publishing point (DTP point) or PostScript point is an American unit of measurement defined as 1⁄72th or 0.0138 of an international inch, which makes it equal to 25.472 mm = 0.3527 mm. A pica is made up of twelve points and an inch is made up of six picas.
17. Mathieu and Patissier, *Enjeux et Développements*, 14.

tion: it allows for the democratization of access to printing and publishing, it favors the proliferation of writings and forms, far from the models that have been considered dominant up until now. The amateur no longer operates in the shadows, but in full view of all. Nevertheless such a gap between publishers, graphic designers and printers and their adaptation to the context established by these platforms raises questions. By favoring total autonomy and openly reducing the role and presence of intermediaries, this mode of production and distribution seem to reflect an increasingly liberal, multi-skilled and unfortunately less and less specialized world. In 2008, James Goggin was questioning the ambivalence of the model:

> In terms of print quality, POD is still no match for well-printed offset litho. As for content, what happens when anyone can publish anything without the benefit of editors or publishers? I think that it is amazing that anyone can self-publish a magazine or book with global distribution, giving people a voice without the need for corporate or governmental vetting. But maybe with the ability for absolutely anyone to publish anything, we could end up wasting even more paper than current print and production processes.[18]

In 2011, playing on the vagueness that persisted around the conditions of production of objects, Italian designer researcher Silvio Lorusso and artist Guilia Ciliberto sent sent two books entitled *Blank on Demand* to Lulu.com to be printed.[19] These two artist's books with their stiff covers were completely empty with the only thing printed on them being their ISBNs. Their formats correspond respectively to the largest (15.2 × 22.9 cm) and smallest (10.8 × 17.5 cm) available on the platform. Each one contains 740 pages, being the maximum number allowed. Finally they were sold respectively at the highest (€999,999.99) and lowest (€5.44) prices possible. Obviously the initial considerations were around the physical and financial limits set by this kind of platform. But here, Silvio Lorusso and Giulia Ciliberto more broadly question the depersonalization of the means of production and in fact, the actual existence of the object itself. They highlight the fact that such a system, by definitively liberating itself from the figures of graphic design, publisher, and even printer, makes it possible for someone to send an empty book to print.

5. ZERO WEAKENING

> "Soft cover, hard cover, color, black and white, and so much more. Choose from the widest range of print book formats available, and make exactly the book you want—including photo books and calendars."
>
> —www.lulu.com

Dear Lulu is a softcover A5 format book, a "perfect bound paperback" as stated on the site Lulu.com where it features as a standard. The appearances of *Dear Blurb*, *Dear BoD*, and *Dear Kolofon* are quite similar: soft and shiny covers, matte coated paper inside, square bound with only their formats differing. These four books, printed by different contractors, share a very striking aesthetic, one that is digital and rather cheap. Deeply linked to the techniques of production of these objects, this has now become characteristic of the print-on-demand sector.

Of course, the implementation of almost Toyotist objectives in the print sector, and more particularly that of the book, that has until now been regulated by well established modes of production and distribution, required a number of technical changes. The ambition to lower costs, reduce stocks, and increase speeds in particular forced platforms to limit their offer to facilitate the use of amalgam, and to automate and rationalize production. Certain of them, like Newspaper Club, specialize in a particular domain—in this case, newspapers, printed by bubble jet or on rotary presses depending on the number of copies. Lulu, which focuses on the *poche*, or paperback, proposes seven formats in all, with quite variable characteristics in terms of binding and cover. As for online print sites like PixartPrinting, they propose a multitude of typologies of formats (posters, business cards, leaflets, etc.), with each one having its own, specific, characteristics. If one looks closer, the options proposed on the different sites are relatively similar. In terms of paper: one offset, one shiny, one side coated, one card, perhaps one or a number of special compositions. The square

18. Goggin in O'Arah, "Supply on demand."

19. The book was recently removed from the Lulu platform.

bound and saddle stitched books are the most popular options as they are fast, economical, and most often the machines are set up for these specific purposes. As for the formats they are usually standard. Usually American (B, C), European (A) or defined by recurring demand—a business card with an 8.5 × 10 cm format and a 10 × 15 cm postcard continue to be proposed. Also, one particular platform might work with a number of printers who themselves might easily work with a number of sites. With *Variable Formats*, English artist Lynn Harris and graphic design studio Åbäke, accompanied by Pierre Pautler, propose to explore these iconic formats and materialities of the book on demand. Documents collected from the since closed library of the Byam Shaw School of Art, make up the content of these publications. They have not been resized, recomposed, or adapted to any of the platforms. The same file is sent to each platform to be printed: a specific framework is applied to the production and to bookmaking. On one hand, the whole thing shows a range of possibilities connected to these new modes of production, in terms of both technique and materiality. On the other, it reminds us that thanks to these platforms, the reader can now choose between different forms and thus explore their own economic and physical relationship with the book object and to its content.

The materials available on each platform are therefore multiple, yet remain limited and are generally standardized. Also, digital production (laser, bubble jet) now seems to be characteristic of the "on demand" model. Its materialities, particularly linked to the production of small volumes, are pronounced and redundant; this is one of the criticisms often made towards self-publishing and online printing. However, technology is inevitably an aesthetic identifier on every level. Having once been worshiped, risography is now much criticized for the very strong aesthetic identity that it provides to productions. This is the same criticism that Maximage makes towards the offset industry with its series of objects that attempt to move outside the standards imposed by this now dominant production technique, including *Maximage Formula Guide*, where they question the hegemony of the Pantone brand, and *Les Impressions Magiques*, where they attempt to reintroduce both gesture and spontaneity into an entirely automated system.

Nevertheless, beyond the physical and material appearance of objects, the standardization of productions that are the result of online printing and publishing on demand seems to be supported by tools for customization that are provided on a certain number of platforms. Until recently VistaPrint for example, for the purposes of encouraging autonomy and efficiency, provided a set of graphic templates for business cards and other marketing documents. The user simply had to modify the information and send it to be printed. Similarly, it is now very simple to produce a book cover based on default compositions proposed by Lulu, supposed to ensure that the book sells on the basis of a certain number of market studies. Another example: to make a family photo album on an online printing website, page layouts are provided where the user simply copies and pastes their own images. So, one family's photo album can look exactly like another as they are printed and laid out in the same way. As Silvio Lorusso points out, this is the whole paradox of the "on demand" model: to build a (cheap) accessible system based on a single, customized copy the firms have to apply a mass production approach and create standards and norms.[20]

In 2015, for their multifaceted project *Bibliomania*, French graphic designers and teachers Alexandru Balgiu and Olivier Lebrun played with the tools available to the amateur creator. Using an online platform reserved for academics and scientists, they composed a series of customized honorary ribbons that played with the graphic and iconographic codes provided by the platform. The objects are surprisingly kitsch, pop and contemporary while showing that with a little humor and a clear will it is possible to work within the gaps of these standardized and standardizing systems.

6. A NEW IDEAL?

Over ten years have passed since the "Farben on demand" workshop and the online publication of the books *Dear Lulu*, *Dear Blurb*, *Dear BoD*, and *Dear Kolofon*. Though the first can still be viewed, downloaded, and printed, it seems that the other three are no longer available on the platforms. Since then, the system that was studied by James Goggin, Frank Philippin and the students has been

20. See Silvio Lorusso, *Extending Horizons*, 183.

completely democratized. Within a very short period the number of web-to-print platforms has increased, and with them, the opportunity for anyone to print any kind of object and become an author or creator, outside of traditional circuits. If at the end of the 2000s the approach was both curious and critical, today the "on demand" model of access and production seems to have become integral to graphic design.

It first managed to establish itself in the field of teaching. Online printing services allow design students to easily provide their projects with materiality, both at a low cost and with complete autonomy. By delegating the printing and crafting, students come into contact with the real conditions of the exercise of the profession of graphic designer. Certain teachers even make print-on-demand a part of their teaching: this is the case with Brice Domingues (Officeabc) who, through an editorial subject that has to be printed using one of the platforms (Blurb, Lulu, Newspaper Club etc.) at their own cost, allows students from the Esad, a French school in Reims, to apprehend the scope, functioning, and a certain economy of the graphic chain. Also, it forces them to adopt in turn the roles of publisher, iconographer, and graphic designer responsible for managing and monitoring fabrication, and for communicating with the client. Certain establishments have even fully embraced the trend: in 2014, the Strelka Institute, a Russian school that specializes in teaching media, architecture, and design, established its own publishing house, Strelka Press, with the art direction being entrusted to the English studio OK-RM. With its e-book department and using print-on-demand, the school provides access to texts by twenty or so authors, recognized figures in these disciplines, all translated into both Russian and English. It uses the opportunity to both distribute sometimes unpublished texts, to promote its teaching program, and to strengthen its position and influence on an international scale.

So, online printing (thus on demand) now allows many projects with modest budgets to see the light of day. Though these modes of production obviously favor self-publishing[21], in certain cases they are also part of the commission process as their development corresponds to a reduction in public funding experienced by many different sectors. For a number of years now, an increasing number of small sized cultural structures have been using these platforms to communicate their upcoming events at low cost. So now, the question of production on demand can be fully integrated into a graphic approach. The same studio OK-RM admits that they often associate cheaper methods with other more standard ones in order to optimize production costs. For example, for the brochure for the event *You Are Here* in Luxembourg, they combined two types of materialities with offset printing: one standard and the other ordered online.

Similar to how Toyotism gradually gained ground in companies to become a reference in terms of management and production, online printing and the "on demand" system seem to have convinced and conquered the field of graphic design. A trend that was perhaps announced as far back as 2004, with the nomination of two books that are available on the German platform Books on Demand, *Intersection: 4 Cities/360 Cities* by Cynthia Tuan (15 copies printed) and *Buchstaben, Bilder, Bytes* designed by groenland. berlin.basel, printed using an online platform for the Most Beautiful Swiss Books competition. However, with the development of this system, the print quality is ultimately more an illusion than a real promise, and it seems that the true interest of the model is definitively located elsewhere:

> I quickly lost interest in testing the various systems, but I still believe in print-on-demand as an accessible, (relatively) economical means for students, artists, designers, small publishers, to print small runs and editions without excess waste.[22]

21. By encouraging self-publishing, the "on demand" system has profoundly changed the world of publishing. An increasing number of publishing houses regularly use it as a channel of production and distribution, using highly variable models and based on a much slower chronology. A number of articles have been written on the subject.
22. Goggin in interview with the author, February 2019.

Mal

& Pra

king
ctice

Joachim Schmid

From My Skull[1]

1. Reprinted from *Photoworks*, Spring/Summer 14 (2010), https://photoworks.org.uk/skull-joachim-schmid/.

What do Benjamin Franklin, Thomas Paine, Alexander von Humboldt, Edgar Allan Poe, Mark Twain, George Bernhard Shaw, Rudyard Kipling, Gertrude Stein, Upton Sinclair, D. H. Lawrence, Ezra Pound, and T. S. Eliot have in common? They were self-publishers. This list could be enlarged with an endless number of less prominent names, and I only mention them to disperse a common assumption, that self-publishing is an option for authors who are not good enough to be taken on by established publishers. Artists publishing their own books face a predicament: while self-publishing is often considered to be the confession of failure, the artist's book itself seems to epitomize the perfectly autonomous, self-determined work.

For the authors mentioned above, the business of publishing a book was different to how it is today. Some of the problems and pitfalls are the same, however: principally, money (the lack of it) and the co-ordination of the various people involved. A complex process that involves an author, an editor, a designer, a publisher, and a printer (not to mention accountants, distributors, and retailers) is close to a sure recipe for disaster. Quite often the ideas, ambitions, and attitudes of these headstrong people turn out to be incompatible. Minimizing the risk of trouble or avoiding it altogether is one reason authors turn to self-publishing.

The second reason is the problem of capacity. A limited number of publishers cannot accommodate the desires of a nearly unlimited number of authors. From the outsider's point of view, a publishing house is a kind of slot machine. Authors put in proposals, manuscripts or dummy books into the machine and pull the handle. It starts to emit funny sounds, and after a while it either produces a book or it doesn't. We don't know what happens inside the apparatus; we'll never know for sure why some books are winners while the majority of players draw blanks. For the disappointed authors, publishers, like arcade machines, can seem like 'one-armed bandits.'

This brings us to the next reason: money. The machine designed to swallow authors' ideas also has a slot for coins. It's an open secret that in modern times proposals—in particular for art books—that are entered together with a cheque are more likely to win; the number of zeros on this cheque directly correlates with the probability of a proposal turning into a printed book. The artist or the gallery exhibiting the work is, in this arrangement, supposed to provide a substantial part of the budget, as many modern publishers eschew the financial risk of publishing. This is rather new, and it's a development that, in German at least, turns the meanings of words on their head. In English, a 'publisher' is someone who makes something 'public.' In my mother tongue, *verlegen* (to publish) is derived from *vorlegen*, which means to advance money. Interesting, isn't it? Traditionally, the publisher is the one who comes up with a budget, the one who is able and willing to invest in ideas, to take a risk. Today, artists, dealers, and museums have turned into sponsors of publishers and printers. It doesn't take a genius to understand that, if you have to spend your own money to make your own book, you might as well bring the whole thing under your own control.

The importance of independence becomes clear if we look at an extreme form of self-publishing: *samizdat*, the voice of the opposition in a totalitarian society. The particularities of this underground movement are summarized by one of its main practitioners, Vladimir Bukovsky, in one sentence: "I myself create it, edit it, censor it, publish it, distribute it, and get imprisoned for it." Censorship may not be an issue in large parts of the world any more, but artists have to struggle with its more subtle sibling, that answers to the name of "mainstream." The response, on the part of some authors, is called independent publishing.

No publisher ever offered to put out a book called *One Picture* containing a single image. Hans-Peter Feldmann published it, along with works by a number of similar misfits. Today, these poorly printed little booklets are considered seminal artist's books, have been influential for a generation of artists, and are sought-after rare books. Nevertheless, you still don't find a big publisher who would be willing to support a similar endeavor. There is a very limited number of prevailing book models, a fact that the superficial variety of designs does little to disguise.

Ed Ruscha's *Twenty-six Gasoline Stations* and later books were published by the artist himself. Their impact was tremendous, and it is time to remind the growing group of book connoisseurs that Ruscha's books were, and are, appreciated not because of the paper stock, the printing quality or the fine binding but because of the artist's radically new editorial concept. The slot machine wouldn't accept such an offering. A niche publisher of exquisite livres d'artiste wouldn't accept it either. There was no other choice for Ruscha than to do it himself.

Despite the increasing number of small and very small publishing houses, self-publishing has become the obvious option for an increasing number of artists. This is mostly due to the fact that for more and more artists the book has become the work itself; it is no longer seen as a catalogue of photographs that have a life outside the book, in galleries, filing cabinets or frames hanging over collectors' sofas. For this reason, exercising maximum control over the publication process, as Stephen Gill points out, is crucial. Finding the suitable material, technique, and form for each project, instead of doing things according to the publisher's defaults, is one of the advantages of self-publishing.

Modern technology facilitates do-it-yourself approaches and at the same time do-it-yourself creates skill and experience. Many contemporary artists are skilled bookmakers with substantial knowledge in fields that traditionally required specialized technicians. Some artists—Morten Andersen, for example, who published nearly all of his books himself—started by making fanzines and slowly grew into this new field of activity. Artists who were educated in modern art schools' media departments, rather than in the old school photography world, have a different vantage point already. They are used to working in a variety of techniques and media as well as being responsible for every aspect and every pixel of their work.

The crucial moment for most self-publishers—from Katja Stuke and Oliver Sieber with their ongoing Böhm/Kobayashi publishing project, to Erik Kessels whose books are produced by his agency as a part of a wider communication strategy, to young activists like Erik van der Weijde with his continuous output of weird little books—is the strong desire to do things the way they want them to be done, and to do them at their own pace. They understood that nobody will be more enthusiastic about their books than the authors themselves, and they enjoy the flexibility of being able to make a book within one week if necessary, instead of waiting years for a publisher's approval.

Distribution of books used to be problematic for many self-publishers, but in the age of the internet this is no longer such a drawback. Direct marketing through an artist's own website is as feasible as announcing publications in mailings, blogs, newsgroups and social networks. The Independent Photo Book blog has been listing independently published photography books since January 2010.[2] New titles are being added nearly every day, and most readers are surprised both by the number and the quality of books they never heard of, and that we hardly ever find in bookshops—the number of specialized photography bookshops exceeds the print run of many of these publications.

The majority of self-publishers operate in a low budget economy. Raising the funds for a book often demands about as much creativity as making the artwork itself. For most artists coming up with a five-figure amount is a bit of a problem, and this is one reason why many artist's books are made in two-figure editions featuring unusual materials, techniques and forms. Some artists compensate for the lack of money with meticulous craft—emphasizing the material aspects of the book as an object, whereas artists exploring conceptual issues—for which the transmission of ideas is paramount to the material form—prefer materials and techniques that resembles industrial production. Not long ago this would have included photocopy and laserprint; today the obvious choice is print-on-demand.

Print-on-demand providers produce books digitally in small quantities, starting with a single copy. Although most of these services offer a limited choice of book formats, papers and design templates, and although the price per copy is comparatively high, there is one advantage that makes many artists choose this option: print-on-demand is a feasible and affordable way to get your book out there. The internet is awash with photographers' complaints about the poor print quality or the insufficient binding of these books, and although many of these complaints are understandable, they miss the crucial point: For artists who are not primarily interested in the book as an object, and whose work is not primarily concerned with print quality the question is not "good print or bad print" but "book or no book." If the answer is "book" you'll find a way to work within the given limits. Even the most quirky idea that no publisher would ever consider can be turned into a book now, and it doesn't really matter whether it is printed in an edition of 10 or 100 copies. It's true, artists have to make compromises when they decide for print-on-de-

2. http://theindependentphotobook.blogspot.com.

mand books; they have to make compromises when working with a publisher too—and when you think about it, most of us have to make compromises all the time, when we go to a restaurant, when we buy a suit, and when we get married.

Again, distribution of these books is difficult, as most of them are not even available in specialized bookshops. Some of the print-on-demand providers offer books in their online bookshops but these are rather useless because books of some artistic merit are buried between un-curated piles of wedding albums, personal travel reports and all kinds of amateurish rubbish—and we must not forget that people making this type of book are the ones the companies' services were originally designed for. Discovering an interesting book in these shops is about as likely as finding a fifty euro note in the street. Which is why I, together with some colleagues, founded the Artists' Books Cooperative. ABC is an informal distribution network created by and for artists who make print-on-demand artists' books. On our website we make available information about selected books in order to help artists get their print-on-demand books to the people who are interested in them.[3]

At this time hardly anybody would dare to make confident predictions about the future of publishing. Nevertheless, I dare say that more artists will make their own books, that more of them will use print-on-demand services, and that the quality of these services will improve notably in the not too distant future. That's it as far as the future is concerned; in the meantime, let's have one more look at the past to disperse another common assumption: self-publishing is an option for aspiring authors who will convert to established publishers as soon as they are acknowledged. Whilst this may be true for some artists, there are a couple of fine examples proving the opposite. After years of working with and for various publishers, Claire Bretécher started publishing her comic books herself, and never returned to the world she left behind. Her compatriots, Goscinny and Uderzo, published their Asterix series themselves from the very beginning. In Japan, the vast majority of comic books have been self-published for decades. And it's not just comics, we find the same attitude in serious science, too. Maria Reiche had researched the Nazca lines in Peru for ages. She decided to publish *The Mystery on the Desert*—which turned out to be a major success—herself. Asked why she chose this way of working, she came up with one simple and convincing reason: "No publisher is going to drink champagne from my skull."

3. ABC moved from https://abcoop.tumblr.com/ to https://abcooperative.cargo.site/.

Artists' Books Cooperative

Paleolithic Cave Paintings: ABC on the Photobook[1]

1. This article appeared on the blog *Photographers' Gallery* on 4 February, 2014. https://abcoop.tumblr.com/post/80007035103/paleolithic-cave-paintings-abc-artists-books.

ABC [Artists' Books Cooperative] is an international group of artists, publishers, and educators seeking to create, engage, and experiment with the form of the book, and to foster alternative forms of distribution through collaboration. As well as working on their own practices, they work together to produce collective projects. Centered on book fairs and their online forum, they aim to develop a growing international network of artists. Founded in 2009 by German artist Joachim Schmid, the cooperative has been at the heart of a number of shows heralding a new age of photography and of artists' self-publishing projects.

Current members (April 2023): Claudia de la Torre, Arnaud Desjardin, Oliver Griffin, George Grace Gibson, Mishka Henner, Jonathan Lewis, John Maclean, MacDonaldStrand, Micheál O'Connell / Mocksim, Monika Orpik, Louis Porter, Jonathan Schmidt-Ott, David Schulz, Travis Shaffer, Wil Van Iersel, Duncan Wooldridge, Rahel Zoller, Hermann Zschiegner.

Past members include: Harvey Benge, Erik Benjamins, Julie Cook, Joshua Deaner, Deanna Dikeman, Eric Doeringer, Fred Free, Kate Glicksberg, Burkhard von Harder, Dawn Kim, Tanja Lažetić, EJ Major, Michael Maranda, Lydia Moyer, Heidi Neilson, Robert Pufleb, Joachim Schmid, Andreas Schmidt, Victor Sira, Paul Soulellis, Katya Stuke & Oliver Sieber, Andrea Stultiens, Elisabeth Tonnard, Corinne Vionnet, Mariken Wessels, Bruno Zhu.

1. WHAT, IN YOUR VIEW, DO PHOTO BOOKS CONTRIBUTE TO THE CULTURE OF PHOTOGRAPHY?

Photo books are a small part of the wider genre of artists' books, which have been an essential part of our culture ever since the invention of the printing press. But the culture of photography is vast and universal and in relation to it, the photobook community is a mere particle floating in space. Rather than contributing to the culture of photography, we're witnessing the conscious development of a photobook market that's working hard to establish its experts, idols, and judges. It's a dead-end that will eventually murder what could have been a force for good. It doesn't have to be this way.

Fig. 1: The Photobook and its moon E-Book seen from planet Photography on July 19, 2013.

2. HOW DO YOU DEFINE YOUR ROLE WITHIN THE GROWING AND CHANGING FIELD OF PHOTO BOOK PUBLISHING? WHAT ARE YOU TRYING TO ACHIEVE?

Many of us are interested in print-on-demand publishing. Print-on-demand liberates artists from the oppressively expensive and laborious demands of traditional photobook publishing. Print-on-demand is fast, cheap, and light. It exists outside the power structures of publishers and distributors. Few people take it seriously and we are one of the few. We're not interested in what the books smell like, how they're bound, whether they're embossed or printed on the finest papers on Earth. Those are luxuries we can live without. We're interested in raw ideas and there is no better transporter for a great idea than a book. A single book if needs be. And with the internet, the ideas in that single book can go viral and reach millions in a split second. No need for proposals, book dummies, meetings, bank loans, trucks, boats, trains and planes to ship hundreds of kilos of heavy books across the world into warehouses and bookshops. A powerful idea expressed in a collection of pictures bound together for the price of a meal and placed online can bypass all of that.

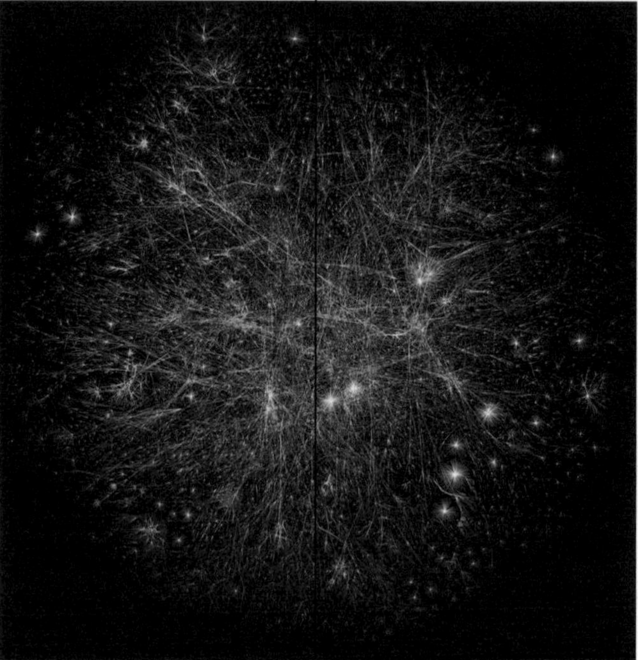

Fig. 2: Map representing the viral transmission of Hermann Zschiegner's print-on-demand book *25¢* across the internet in October 2011. Red lines represent links between web pages in Asia, green for Europe, the Middle East and Africa, blue for North America, yellow for Latin America and white for unknown IP addresses.

As for the cooperative, we attend book fairs, curate exhibitions, work on projects and talk on an online forum where we discuss all aspects of making and proliferating work. We live in different countries and some of us have never met each other or even know what other members look like. We're not even sure if some members are real or fictitious. We fall out—sometimes spectacularly—and we collaborate—sometimes spectacularly.

3. DO YOU PUBLISH ONLINE BOOKS AND WHAT MIGHT THE FUTURE HOLD FOR THIS METHOD OF DIGITALLY DISTRIBUTING BOOKS?

We're all involved in publishing the idea of a book online. That is to say, each of our artists presents their book in some form of digital format that exists online as well as in physical form. That doesn't mean it has to be an e-book. It could be the book presented as a video trailer on Vimeo, as a single line of text, a performance documented, an essay, a series of stills, or as a downloadable pdf file. The book exists in physical form and in conceptual form. It travels further and quicker as an idea than as an object. In the future, photography will outlive the photobook, images will outlive photography, and ideas will outlive images.

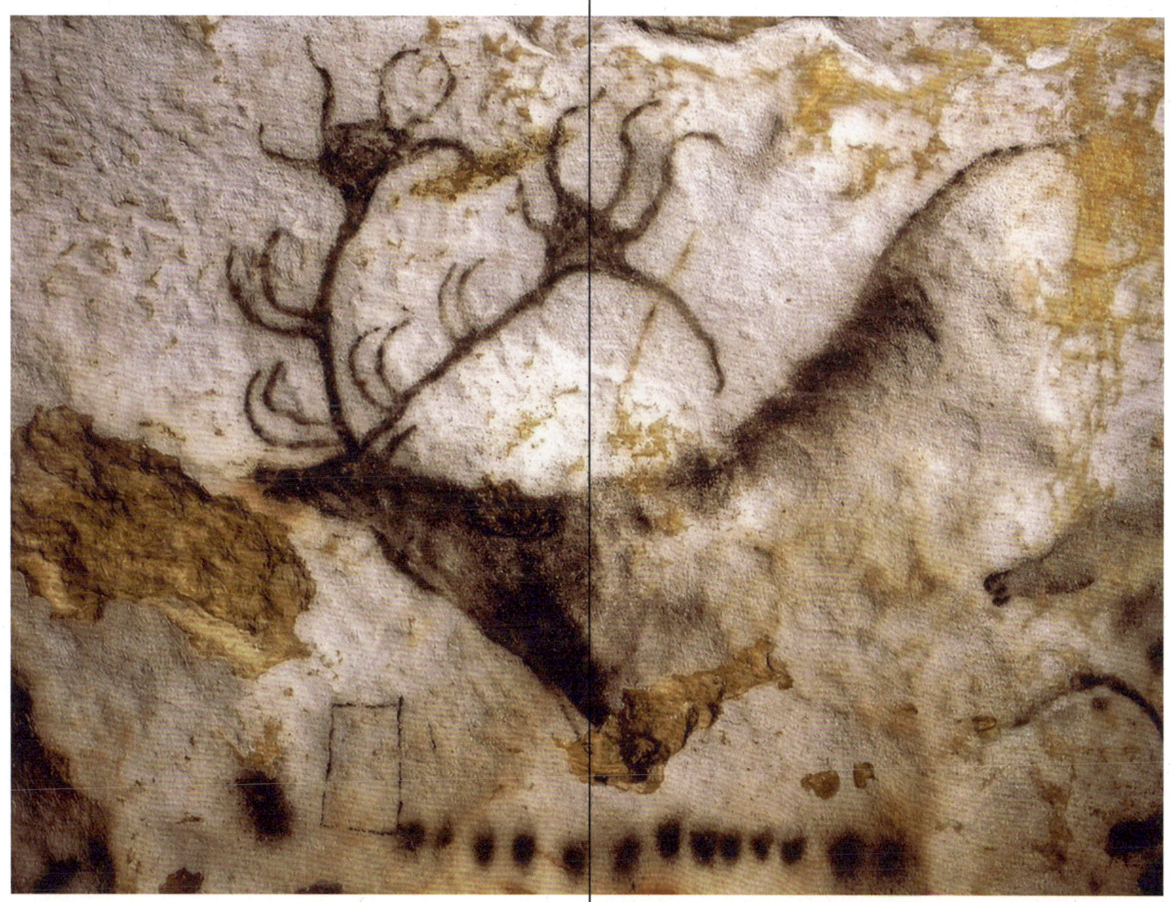

Fig. 3: The earliest known reference to a print-on-demand book is visible beneath the Large Black Stag cave painting in Lascaux, France. Black spots, believed to represent the number of people exposed to the single book, have been carbon dated at 30,000 years old, suggesting the painting was produced some time during the Upper Paleolithic Age.

Michael Mandiberg

Making *Print Wikipedia*

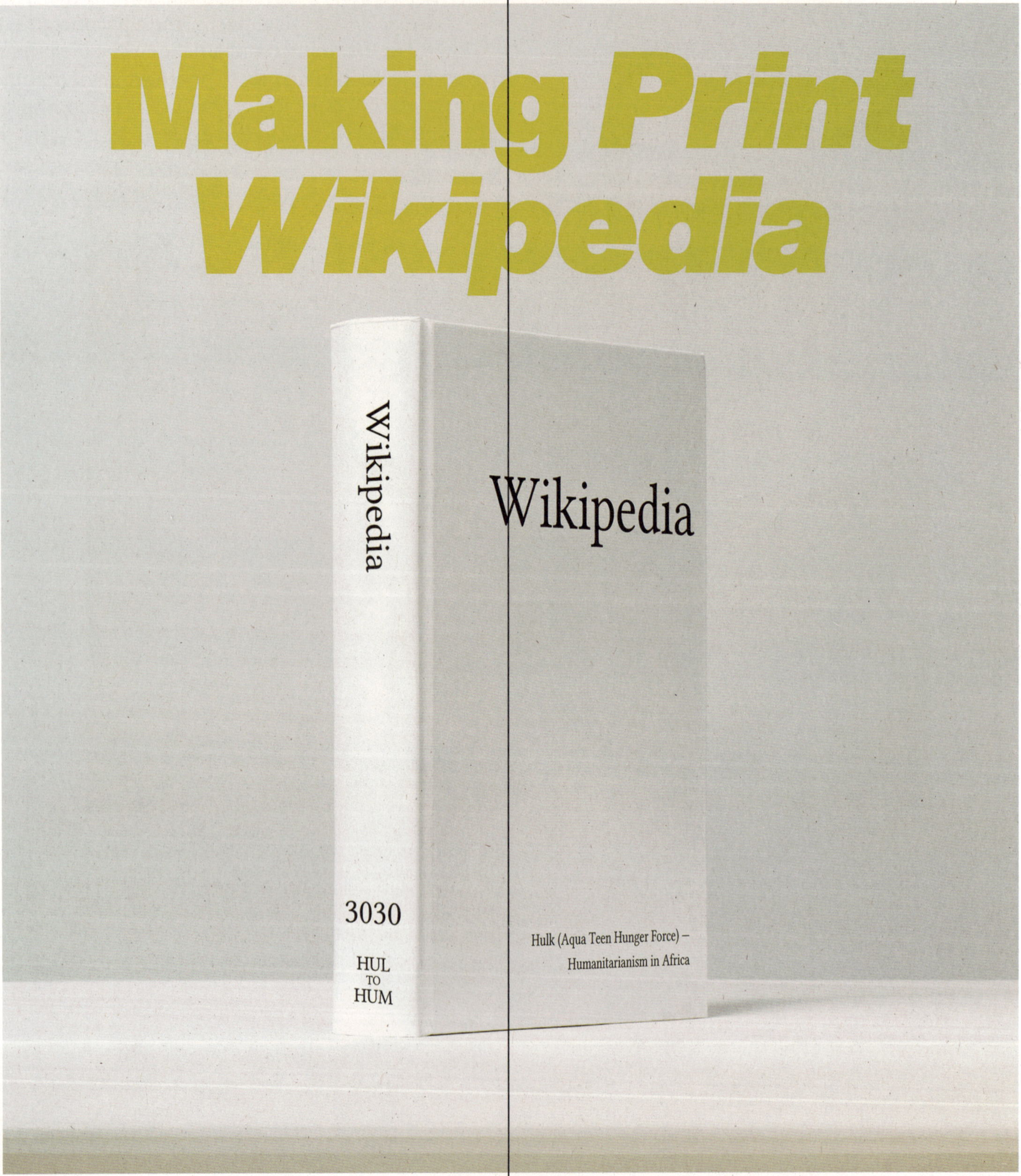

Fig. 1: Humanism from *Print Wikipedia*, 2015.

Wikipedia is big data that's small enough to process on my computer, yet big enough that no human could ever read it all. In an effort to visualize the size of this accumulation of human knowledge, and to show the poetic impossibility of knowing in an age of data, I turned all of Wikipedia into books. To make *Print Wikipedia* I created software that transforms Wikipedia's entire database into print ready PDFs and uploads them for print-on-demand. I began working on the project in 2009, and in 2015 I created the English-language version, which contains 7,473 volumes of 700 pages each. In 2016 I created Dutch and German versions, of 1,165 and 3,406 volumes respectively.

When I began editing Wikipedia in 2008 I was also writing and making work about free culture. Because Wikipedia was the largest Creative Commons licensed work that I knew of, I started to think about what I could create with it. At that time I was making art with discarded books, meditating on their obsolescent relationship to technologies like databases. So I thought it would be poetic to turn this massive database back into books.

I also turned Wikipedia into books because I wanted to know how big Wikipedia was. During the time I was making the project, others made work that tried to answer some version of this question, including James Bridle's *The Iraq War. A Historiography of Wikipedia Changelogs* (twelve volumes, Lulu 2010), Rob Matthews' *The Abridged Version of Wikipedia* (2011), and Pediapress' proposed 1,000 volume print edition that never came to fruition. At the time, English Wikipedia contained five million articles, which uncompressed into 80 GB of data; this was just the text, the images live elsewhere. These numbers don't mean much to me in an embodied way, other than it's a lot. I began wondering how many books that data would fill. After half a millennium printed books are losing their primacy as an information medium, but they still hold a kind of imaginative power, and function as a symbolic reference. A book is a useful unit of measurement, which makes *Print Wikipedia* an unconventional data visualization. We don't have a great sense of how much knowledge fits inside a gigabyte of data, but we do have an embodied understanding of how long it takes to read a book… or 7,473 of them!

After several years of preparation, the process of generating the PDFs and uploading them for print-on-demand took place over a couple of months. On April 7, 2015 I downloaded a database backup from dumps.wikimedia.org; the download took about 4 days, and it took nearly a week to unpack the file into a MySQL database. I ran some SQL queries against the database to clean it up and make it run faster, then I ran the custom Java code which turns all of those entries into PDFs.[1] It took two weeks and a few days for the Java code to produce all the PDFs for upload.

I uploaded the PDFs to Lulu.com with browser automation software written in Python with Selenium; Selenium is a package that mimics a human clicking on a webpage for quality assurance testing. The upload software loads the Lulu.com upload page, inputs the information required on each page, presses the submit button, and waits for the next page to load, and repeats the process on the next page. As it pastes text, clicks, waits, and clicks again it sets the book size and binding type, the volume's title (which changes for each volume), and the PDF files for the book. Each volume has its own ISBN, which the Lulu.com website generates at upload; the script takes a screenshot of the ISBN, adds it to the cover and the copyright page, and then uploads them. Once uploaded the website merges the copyright page with the PDF containing the rest of the book. Once each volume is uploaded, it tweets out an announcement at Twitter.

1. Available here: https://github.com/mandiberg/printwikipedia.

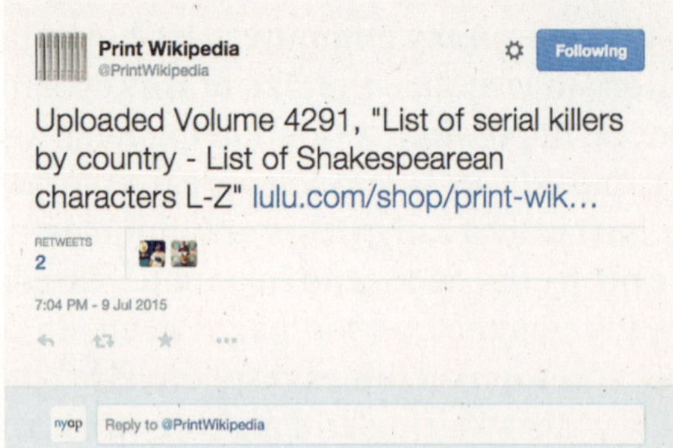

Fig. 2: A screenshot of the twitter bot announcing one of my favorite volumes, https://twitter.com/PrintWikipedia/status/619265944213393412.

I had to create this workaround because Lulu didn't have an API for large scale uploading; they deprecated one several years before my upload, and have recently created a new one. Using browser automation software to simulate an API is a highly unusual approach. When I told the team at Lulu that we had programmed the script to do this, they did the conference call equivalent of a spit-take. They couldn't believe anyone had done something so elaborate.

When I exhibit the work, smaller sets of printed books sit on shelves affixed to custom wallpaper representing bookshelves holding all of the other books that would fit in the space. I redesign the wallpaper for each exhibition to fit the dimensions of the wall, and it is only ever displayed with at least one set of books shelved against it. I chose the volumes for these sets based on the three character words on the spine. For example, there are thirteen volumes with "ART" on the spine. It is not necessary to print out all 7,473 volumes, as our imaginations can complete what's missing. The first installation of *Print Wikipedia* at Denny Gallery included "ART," "BAT," "CAT," "EAR," and "END," with a total of 106 books in the gallery; other exhibitions included just the three volumes with "SEX" on the spine.

The upload process took place as part of the exhibition, with a projection showing Lulu.com in a web browser, and a monitor on the ground showing the command line updates from the software as it uploaded the files. The upload process is central to the work. During the first weekend of the exhibition we kept the gallery open 24 hours a day as the computer continued uploading without pause... until it crashed, which happened pretty regularly. I woke in the middle of the night to watch over the script, juxtaposing my human labor with the computer's work in this durational performance.

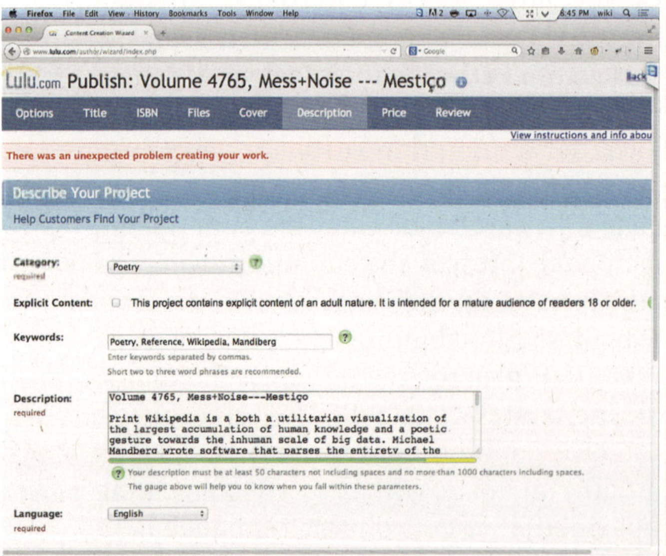

Fig. 3: Screenshot of the Lulu.com interface during the upload of the English language version in 2015. Note that we are using TeamViewer at 8:45PM to remotely view the Mac Mini that was in the gallery, which was closed for the evening. Images like these were shared with the Lulu team to debug problems during exhibitions.

Print Wikipedia is a work of found poetry, created by putting an entire database in alphabetical order. On Lulu.com when you're in the interface, you're forced to choose a category, so I picked poetry. To be cheeky, but also to articulate the importance of

Fig. 4: Installation view of "From Aaaaa! to ZZZap!," at Denny Gallery, New York, 2015, showing the performance of the upload of Print Wikipedia to Lulu.com.

Fig. 5: "SEX" from *Print Wikipedia* installed at the Center for Book Arts, New York, 2016.

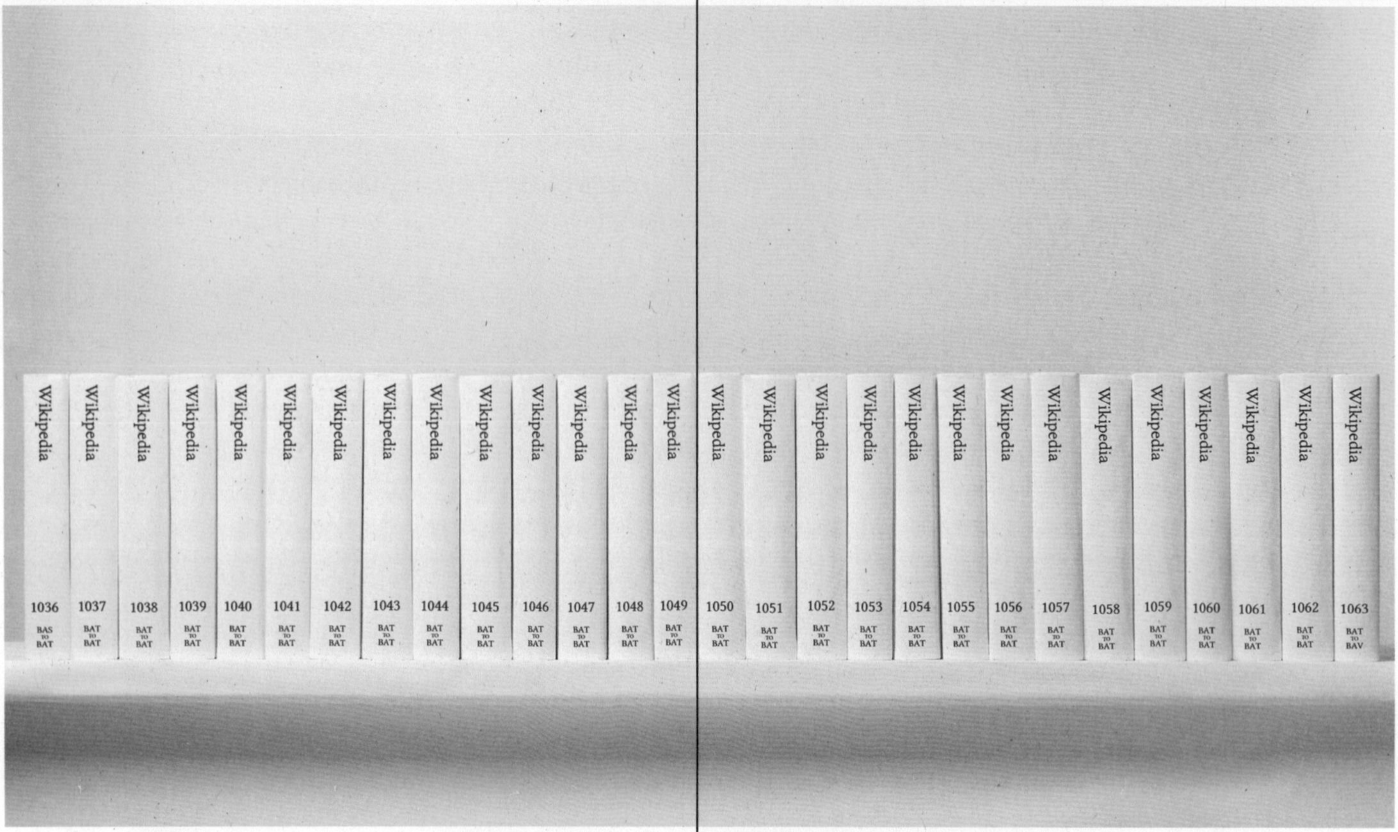

Figure 6: "BAT" from *Print Wikipedia*, 2015. These sets are produced as an edition of five, with two Artist Proofs; the individual books remain available on Lulu.com.

poetics. These poetics resonate in its massive totality as well as in individual volumes, where the juxtaposition of the first and last entries in each volume produces a kind of concrete poetry. For the Denny Gallery exhibition I printed a number of volumes based on the combination of their resonant titles, and a specific article they contained, such as volume 2,227, "Entrails of a Virgin – Environmental Determinism," which contains the entry for "Entropy," or volume 3,032, "Hulk Aquateen Hunger Force – Humanitarianism in Africa," which contains the entry for "Humanism."

As a programmatically designed book, each book is laid out based on intentional design decisions, but entirely contingent on a range of foreseeable and unforeseeable scenarios. The way that the tables are presented is one of those highly contingent situations. Initially I approached it as the best solution for an ungainly set of information that was never meant for a three column book layout, but I had no idea just how large Wikipedia's tables would be. I've come to enjoy the absurdity of their factual accuracy, borderline usability, and abstract aesthetic beauty. In that regard, those three attributes are a pretty good distillation of the project writ large.

Turning a database of knowledge into books reveals the patterns of history. The twenty-eight volumes of "BAT," are not about flying bats or baseball bats, instead, they are a compendium of battles, from the "Battle of Aachen" to the "Battle of Żyrzyn." Likewise the twenty-seven volumes that start with "NEW" represent a structural history of European colonialism and empire. In the German version the four volumes of "NEU" abut the four volumes of "NEW," reflecting the American linguistic neo-colonialism resulting from English becoming the post-war lingua franca. Knowledge coalesces around other Wikipedia specific structures too: *Print Wikipedia* contains almost 600 volumes of lists.

These editioned sets have sold to museums and private collectors in the $3,000–8,000 range. Individual volumes are priced at $80. My memory of how I came up with that price is a bit fuzzy. As the project creator I can order copies for myself and pay the actual fabrication cost of about $30, which is high because of the cost of labor intensive hardbound binding. When I sell through the Lulu website, they add on their fees, which brings the base price up closer to $50 and Lulu takes a cut of any increase in price. I think we decided to price them at $80 partly because of that high base price, but also because it created a sense of value. I've sold somewhere between 50 and 100 of them, I think. I remember more clearly how we came up with the price of $500,000 for the whole set: it was a mediagenic number. It was a number that captivated journalists, who wrote articles with titles like "Ever Wonder what a $500,000 Version of Wikipedia Would Look Like?," which was the title of an article in the *Washington Post*. But it also was a realistic number in the rather hypothetical event that someone were to actually purchase the whole set. The production cost on 7,473 volumes would be around $225,000, though maybe I could get a bulk discount. When galleries sell works like that, they typically offer a 20% discount, so that work would actually only sell for $400,000.

```
/html/body/div[1]/div[1]/div/table/tbody/tr/td[2]/div/div[3]/d
iv[1]/form/div/div/div[2]/table/tbody/tr[23]/td[1]/input
<class 'selenium.common.exceptions.TimeoutException'>
supposedly got your file and sleep 2
open js file for c2
okay
both files selected and placed soundly, phew!
0:00:56.168405 on stage 7
gears animation! lookit 'em go!
let our greasey monkey screw the wizard
0:01:23.884595 on stage 8
uploading cover
<type 'exceptions.RuntimeError'>
WHOOPS. WHAT A @#$%^ing MESS
Traceback (most recent call last):
  File "ohlu.py", line 695, in selectFiles1
    self.luluCruise()
  File "ohlu.py", line 829, in luluCruise
    self.selectFiles2()
  File "ohlu.py", line 719, in selectFiles2
    self.luluCruise()
  File "ohlu.py", line 831, in luluCruise
    self.makingYour()
  File "ohlu.py", line 725, in makingYour
```

Fig. 7: Screenshot of the command line output showing the Selenium script successfully rendered the PDF of the body of the book (stage 7) but failed to upload the cover (stage 8). Jonathan Kiritharan wrote most of the upload code, and all of the colorful status updates.

Because this project was so massive in scale, it could not be a solitary endeavor. As a university professor, working a full-time job, I just don't have the time to do all the work. But because of the specifics of this project, it required skills I didn't have. I was able to work with several programmers and designers, including Jonathan Kiritharan, Denis Lunev, Kenny Lozowski, Patrick Davison, and Colin Elliot. But the network extended out beyond my studio team.

At the insistence of Mushon Zer-Aviv, who I asked for design feedback, I approached Lulu and the Wikimedia Foundation in the fall of 2014. When Mushon suggested this route, I didn't like the idea, but he persuaded me that Lulu was likely to turn off my account when I began uploading what might appear to be gigabytes of noise. In retrospect, reaching out to them was one of the best things I did for the project.

Both Lulu and Wikimedia went above and beyond to support this wild and quite unwieldy project. Despite fearing they would respond negatively to someone seemingly gaming their system, I reached out to Lulu, through a cold call email to the CEO, and a hailstorm of Twitter mentions. When I explained the project during our first phone call, to my surprise, they were pleased and amazed that someone had done something so ridiculous. When I got on the first call with the Wikimedia Foundation their response was similar, "we've been waiting for you to do this for years"—obviously not me, but for *somebody* to do this.

Lulu supported the project because it was a unique manifestation of what their company made possible with print-on-demand. On some level this had to have been a business decision in the hopes that it might lead to significant publicity, which it did, but I think the real reason why they were so engaged with helping the project was they are all bibliophiles too. Everyone I worked with really understood the project both as a work of art and as a complicated set of books. It seemed to encapsulate our wonderment with knowledge. There's something about the project even I can't quite define, and I've haven't been able to make something else like it before or since. People were drawn to the work, and wanted to know more. I think that wonderment ultimately catalyzed and sustained Lulu's engagement.

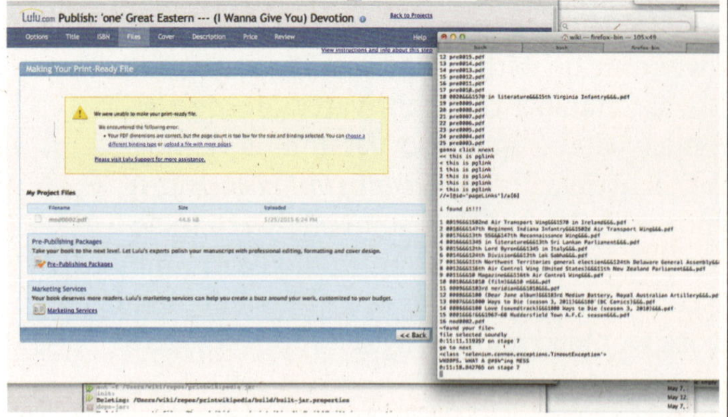

Fig. 8: Screenshot of the Lulu.com interface, with command line output, noting that the upload failed because the cover was the wrong size. The code that generated the PDFs would keep adding articles until it reached page 700 of the PDF, and then would complete that article. If that last article extended past page 720, the book became too thick for the covers sized for 700 pages. We adapted the code to fail gracefully, log the volume, and continue; we resized the covers for those volumes, and uploaded these at the very end.

Lulu provided white glove technical support that allowed us to overcome technical challenges. For example, we encountered a limit on the number of books and disk space allotted for each account. Our Lulu support team told us roughly what the limit was (no one had actually hit the limit, so they didn't know exactly) and we divided the volumes up among different accounts. To speed and stabilize the process they allowed us to upload all the book files at once via FTP, and then select those files on the server through the interface when we were creating each book. They gave us advance notice of any server downtime and software updates, knowing that both would interrupt the upload process. They helped us resolve situations where the webpage didn't respond as we expected or the PDFs were throwing errors. Most of the time it was an error on our side but we often found bugs or other glitches in their system. In that sense the upload was a stress test of their software.

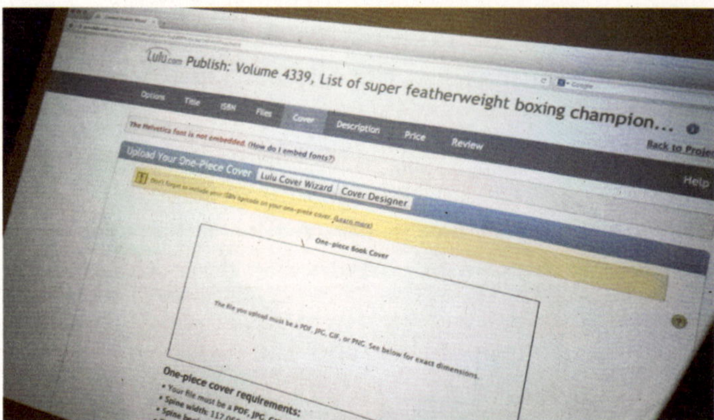

Fig. 9: Photograph of the Lulu.com interface, showing the "Helvetica font is not embedded" error we experienced on a subset of articles. Helvetica was embedded, but not the way that the Lulu.com code wanted. We worked closely with Lulu to resolve this error to get the files to upload.

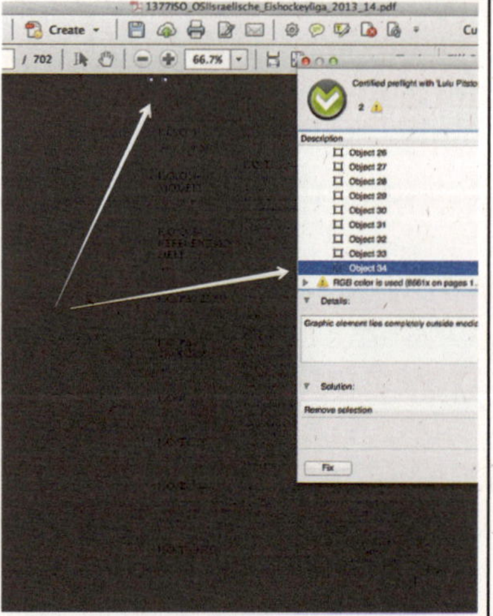

Fig. 10: Screenshot the Lulu support team sent us instructing us to use their preflight profile to re-render the cover PDFs with Helvetica errors. By redistilling the PDF files we were able to remove objects that caused these errors. Some months later we learned that the European printer (located in France) had a different system than the US printer, and was unable to print the books because of these Helvetica errors. Re-rendering all the files is too much to take on, but I re-render volumes on a case by case basis.

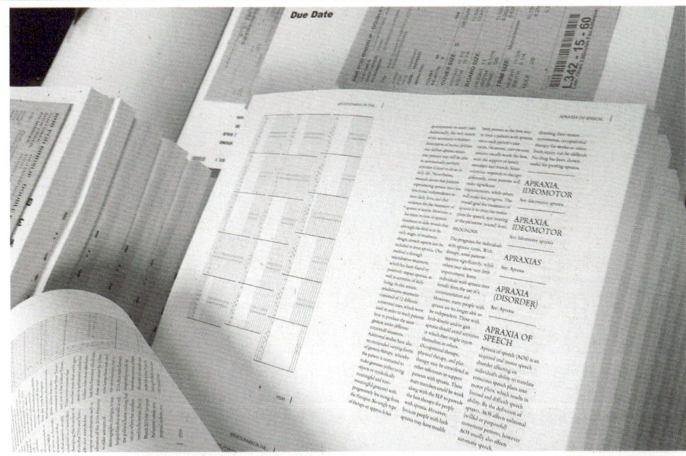

Fig. 11: During the printing process, Kent Larson of Bridgeport National Bindery took photographs of the books as they made their way through the fabrication process. Image courtesy Kent Larson.

When I was printing the final test books I noticed inconsistencies between print runs: the spine placement shifted slightly, and its roundness varied. To resolve this, the Lulu team reached out to Kent Larson of Bridgeport National Bindery, which fabricates the hardbound books for Lulu. Kent ensured that these books had a consistent spine shape and placement so they could be exhibited side-by-side. Kent even sent photographs each day, as they worked through the process. Though I have never been to the bindery, or met Kent in person, and despite my contacts at Lulu shifting over the years through various staffing changes, the Lulu team continues to support the project at this high level.

Both organizations helped promote the project. Lulu produced a very professional video about the project. The Wikimedia Foundation also created a video, which of course was Creative Commons licensed. The Wikimedia Foundation PR team placed the story with the *New York Times*.[2]

Wikimedia's Community and Communications departments supported the project, but I had to negotiate with their Legal Department over the conditions for using Wikipedia logo, and who exactly I should ascribe the Creative Commons license to. Wikipedia is produced under a Creative Commons Attribution-ShareAlike (CC BY-SA) license but its logo is trademarked in order to protect the integrity of the project. Their rules allow for use of the logo in works of art, but they wanted me to put a disclaimer stating "This is a work of art" on the front of each book. It took some back and forth, but we eventually agreed that I could use the logo as long as I added the statement that "This work is not endorsed by the Wikimedia Foundation" on the back cover below the ISBN in small text.

Figure 12: Martin points to his account name in the German *Contributors Appendix*. CC BY-SA 2016, Florian Höfer.

Wikipedia is freely available under a CC BY-SA license, but it was not obvious how to give attribution to all the authors. I asked the lawyers at Creative Commons, but they demurred. The Wikimedia Foundation suggested I look at some general community guidance that says you should cite the five most prominent contributors to each article, but that was only guidance for when citing or using one article. I wondered how to make those decisions at scale? Do you add up the number of characters added, or the number of edits each editor made? Do you include the editor who created the page, even if they only made that one early edit? Ultimately, refactoring the code to assess the article contributions was way out of scope, so I needed another solution. Given that I was using all the articles I decided to create a 36 volume *Wikipedia Contributor Appendix* that lists everyone who has edited English Wikipedia. At the time there

2. See Lulu Press, Inc., *Print Wikipedia by Michael Mandiberg*, https://vimeo.com/133172929; Victor Grigas (WMF), *The Story of Print Wikipedia by Michael Mandiberg*, https://commons.wikimedia.org/w/index.php?oldid=498364659; Jennifer Schuessler, "Moving Wikipedia From Computer to Many, Many Bookshelves," *New York Times*, June 17, 2015, https://www.nytimes.com/2015/06/17/books/moving-wikipedia-from-computer-to-many-many-bookshelves.html.

were 7.5 million contributors who had made edits on at least one article. In the gallery, you could tell who the Wikipedians were: they were the ones carefully looking for their names in the *Contributor Appendix*. I was very happy that everyone was able to find themselves there, including Jimmy Wales, who visited the exhibition.

In the seven years since the first upload, I created German and Dutch versions, and showed the work in museums, libraries, and galleries in Europe and North America. As I write this, an installation just went on exhibit in Singapore, and I'm planning another in the Netherlands. I would love to create a French version, to reference the history of the *Encyclopédie*. In the future, I had hoped to be able to create a Chinese version; it is not currently possible to do this project in mainland China, as Wikipedia was fully blocked in December 2015. I had been hopeful I would be able to make a version in Hong Kong, though the 2020 national security law complicates that.

I'm often asked whether I have updated the original English version, and I point out that it was already out of date: it took four weeks just to process the database, and another three and a half weeks to upload. Even by the time it finished, it was two months out of date. Chasing that infinity is not meaningful to me, and in some ways, accepting that impossibility is a part of the paradox of the work itself.

Kathrin Passig

Yes, today it's boring. But in 20 years!

The following two essays were first published on Kathrin Passig's award-winning collective blog *Techniktagebuch* on February 28, 2020 and April 7, 2021. *Techniktagebuch* has been reporting since 2014 under the slogan "Yes, today it's boring. But in 20 years!" about everyday technology and its changes.

Translated by Cadenza Academic Translations

The Semi-fast Route to a Self-made Paper Book is Through an Excel Table

JANUARY 6

I really wanted to have *Strom und Vorurteil* (Power and Prejudice, alluding to Austen's *Pride and Prejudice*), the e-book featuring my columns from last year, ready straightaway on January 1. But other things got in the way, so it has taken a week longer. But that's still quick; the last column only appeared on December 28. I put the text into e-book format using Reedsy.com. There are more elegant methods, but I was feeling lazy and wanted to simply copy and paste it from the Google Docs where I had written the columns. That was done very quickly. The more laborious part of making the book was creating a cover for the e-book using templates from canva.com.

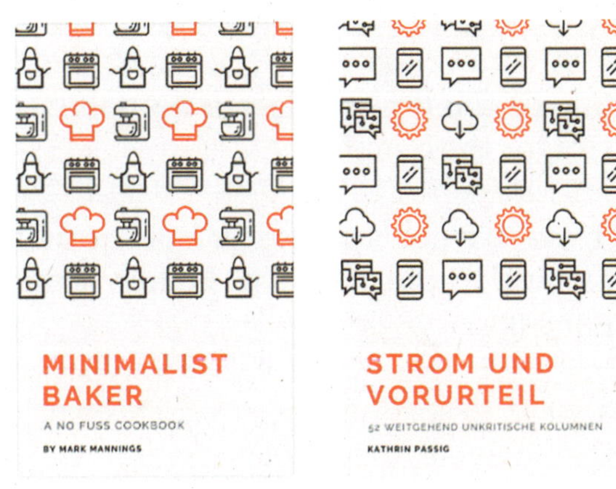

Left: the template from canva.com;
Right: the version adapted for my book.

"The printed book will probably follow, I just have to get myself in gear first," I wrote on Twitter. Because, after all, I did resolve two years ago to make a printed book at the next opportunity.[1]

MID-JANUARY

As with the e-book, the content is not a problem—I use the LaTeX template from our blog *Techniktagebuch* with a few small changes (I believe so, anyway; as I write this at the end of February I have already forgotten the details). "Now all I have to do is upload it to Amazon, and it's done," I think. The uploading process comes to a halt at the point where Amazon wants a cover image. As is becoming clear to me, I can't just use the one from the e-book, because a printed book has a spine and a back cover and quite specific dimensions.

Amazon has a cover design help function, which suggests some designs (shown here with a different title). I start to realize why the self-made books on offer on Amazon often look so hideous.

These suggestions can be modified, but using the Cover Creator is about as much fun as removing a callus with a cheese grater, and the end result is just as unsightly. I sigh and put off producing the printed book until tomorrow.

JANUARY 31

I suspect that if I carry on trying to make the cover myself, it'll be July before the book is ready. Gregor Weichbrodt agrees to design the cover for just

1. See my blog post "Der Tag, an dem ich das Papierbuch verstand," *Techniktagebuch*, January 24, 2018, https://techniktagebuch.tumblr.com/post/170156275842/24-januar-2018.

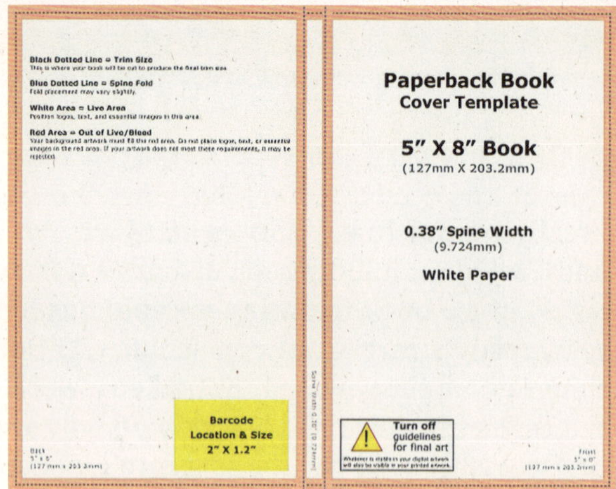

200 euro, after I have promised to be the easiest client in the world and to accept everything ecstatically and without any requests for changes.

At Amazon you can put in the desired book size and number of pages, and get a PDF template for the format required for the cover.[2] Until now the body of the book has had a size that I selected myself (after measuring customary paperbacks), but there are no templates for self-selected sizes. So I bid farewell to my self-selected book size, choose one of the preset American book sizes, and send Gregor the template.

FEBRUARY 2

"I haven't got around to looking at this yet, but I would still like to do it. Is there a deadline?" Gregor asks.

FEBRUARY 8

"I want to sort out the cover this weekend. Should I, or are you already further on?" Gregor asks.

FEBRUARY 9

Kathrin Passig @kathrinpassig · Feb 9
Bei der Papierausgabe von "Strom und Vorurteil" darf ich zum ersten Mal (weil Print on Demand) beliebigen Unfug hinten aufs Cover schreiben. Eure Gelegenheit! Bitte nur unqualifizierte Äußerungen, wer den Inhalt des Buchs kennt, darf nicht mitmachen.
119 8 94

"For the printed edition of *Strom und Vorurteil* I can for the first time (because it's print-on-demand) put random nonsense on the back cover. This is your chance! Only statements from uninformed people please; those familiar with the content of the book may not take part."

Gregor sends several draft designs. "The one without the rose is great. Sold!" I say, like the no-fuss client I want to be.

"Does the upload for the cover have to be an image file or a PDF?"

"Didn't you receive the template?"

Gregor does everything again, in the right template this time. And then he does everything four more times with different illustrations, but I can't do anything about that. He suggests asking on Twitter for quotes for the back cover.

FEBRUARY 14

"Have you considered what quotes you'd like on the back cover yet?"

"Oh, I see. I thought I was waiting for you, but you were waiting for me!"

FEBRUARY 23

Gregor has put quotes on the back cover. "It looks fantastic and I'm very happy with it!" I write, adding that I didn't want those quotes, however, but different ones. Gregor changes the quotes and sends the final version.

FEBRUARY 23, 24, AND 25

I am trying to get my act together and upload it to Amazon.

FEBRUARY 26

I try to upload the cover to Amazon but notice that I need it as a PDF, not a png. I ask Gregor for a PDF version.

2. See https://kdp.amazon.com/en_US/cover-templates.

Before he can send it, I realize that due to the new book size and a few reformatting changes, the number of pages has now risen from 160 to 215. Because of this, the spine is now a few millimeters thicker and the cover no longer fits. I explain the situation to Gregor: "I would work it out myself, but I only have Inkscape and I'm worried that you'll be able to see it." I anticipate that all the fonts will go to pieces in the process, and besides, graphic designers always see things that I don't notice.

Gregor now has to redo everything. I am not such a straightforward client as I thought, and now I understand why they give me such a wary look at the hairdressers when I say, "I don't mind—just do something with it."

FEBRUARY 27

"Have to send the cover later on; I don't have the font on my laptop at work, argh," writes Gregor. But it is sorted out later in the day.

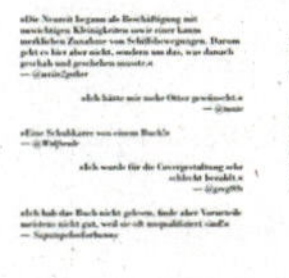

Book cover with chosen quotes, among them one from Gregor. "'I was very badly paid for the cover design.'– @gregoor." Another reads: "I haven't read the book, but I generally don't like prejudices because they're often uninformed."

FEBRUARY 28

I upload the content and the cover to Amazon and receive an error notification: "Your expected cover size is 10.734 × 8.250 but the submitted file size is 10.496 × 8.000." To rectify this, I am referred to an Excel table which until now has been concealed from me and to which, moreover, I can find no sign of a link anywhere; the table can be used to calculate the exact dimensions for the body text and the cover.

Why a company such as Amazon has chosen to put this calculation procedure, which could very easily be included on the website itself, into a downloadable Excel table with macros is both inexplicable (one of the wealthiest and most experienced internet companies in the world!) and perfectly obvious (the staff in the print-on-demand department must occasionally have to make modifications, and every modification of the Amazon website requires all 10,873 stakeholders to get together for several meetings).

Be that as it may, I do not have Excel, and the computation macros in the table don't work with LibreOffice. I ask the *Techniktagebuch* editors whether anyone can open Excel for me, enter my book size and the number of pages, and send me screenshots of the results. Thomas Jungbluth agrees to do it. It is as I thought: the cover template originally provided by Amazon is wrong. According to the new Excel calculation, I need to add a few extra millimeters of white border around the outside.

At least I can do this on the cover myself, in Inkscape, without troubling Gregor again. When I do it, the fonts don't go to pieces at all, or at least if they do, then it's in a way that only graphic designers would notice. At the first attempt, the cover is crooked on the book, but at the second attempt, it's successful, and Amazon accepts the result without any further error notifications. Now the book only has to go through some internal checks by Amazon.

FEBRUARY 29

The paper book is available to buy from today. Joyfully I select "Look inside book" and on the very first page I see a glaring hyphenation error. It doesn't matter; I announce the new printed book on Twitter with: "Anyone who buys it straightaway will get a rare collector's edition with a hyphenation error on the very first page! For a limited time only!" Then I correct the error and upload everything again. After each modification it takes half a day before the new version has been checked and approved by Amazon.

MARCH 1

The new version is released, with one error less. I order an author's copy for me and one for Gregor. I will probably find other obvious mistakes as soon as I open the book, but for the first time I don't find this thought depressing. After all, I can just correct everything and upload a new version.

I Am Trying Hard, but the Paper is Not Cooperating

In January I made an e-book of my columns that had been published over the previous year. It was relatively easy: I took the columns from the Google Docs where I had written them and copied them individually into the Reedsy e-book creation tool. I then took the e-book created in Reedsy (because Reedsy is convenient to use, but does not have very many options and is actually designed for books in English) and reworked it in a local, less convenient e-book editor which has more options (ebook-edit, which is part of Calibre). Then I uploaded the finished file to Amazon and Google Play Books. I actually also wanted to offer the book on tolino media, the author platform for Tolino-Reader, but I didn't manage to because it requires a specific EPUB format, and after a few hours of trial and error I couldn't be bothered any more (I've forgotten the details in the interim). On Google Play I have sold exactly zero books to date...

...but as a platform it has the advantage of having a setting which enables me to make 100 percent of a book available to view in Google Preview. Through this, I can link to individual texts as required (which is not the case in the newspaper *Frankfurter Rundschau* where they originally appeared). Because I myself sometimes stumble on books worth buying that only appear on Google Search by chance, I figure that perhaps this will lead to someone finding my books.

So much for the back story. Now I would like to finally make the printed book. Amazon offers the following option:

Shown here with the most recent *Techniktagebuch* book as an example, for which there is as yet no printed book.

I tried it for the first time with the collection of columns from the previous year, and it proved successful in that I was able to give the book to a few people who do not read e-books. And that's still the majority.

Last year I had some difficulties with that book involving the templates provided by Amazon for the covers of printed books. Unlike with an e-book, the covers for physical books unfortunately have to fit exactly round the book, so the dimensions depend on the number of pages. But as there have been no changes to the number (fifty-two) or the length (approximately 4,500 characters) of the columns, I am assuming that both books will be the same size and that I can simply reuse the template from last year.

I created the cover for the e-book with a template from canva.com; this was quick and easy to do, and it looks good enough to me.

Unfortunately, there is as yet no convenient service for meeting Amazon's requirements for its printed book covers, so I asked Gregor Weichbrodt again. Disadvantage: graphic designers cost money and take forever. Advantage: afterwards it looks much better than if I do it myself.

After a short wait from December to April, as of yesterday the graphic designer's cover is ready, or at least half ready—the front cover is finished. I cobble together the spine and the back cover myself in Inkscape, based on the previous year's cover, after Gregor sends me the two fonts used on the front cover. I spend most of the time styling the graphic designer's statement with particular loving care:

»Ich wurde für die Covergestaltung diesmal besser bezahlt, hatte aber nachder Hälfte keine Zeit mehr.
Alles, was nicht so gut aussieht, ist von Kathrin."
— Gregor Weichbrodt

"I was better paid for the cover this time, but after doing half of it I ran out of time. Anything that doesn't look very good is by Kathrin."

Now I just have to put the book content into LaTeX format, from which I can produce a PDF. I can't remember how I did it last year and so I first convert the EPUB file to LaTeX with the help of Pandoc. The instructions for how to do that are taken, as always, from the Pandoc demo webpage:

```
pandoc -s jetuerenknall.epub -o jetuerenknall.tex
```

It works at the first attempt. I take the .tex file of the previous year's book, which was derived from the Techniktagebuch .tex file, and replace everything after the header with the content produced in Pandoc. The only things I have to change with Search and Replace are the quotation marks, in order to get guillemets. During this process, the LaTeX csquotes package handily informs me of several issues with incorrect or wrongly paired double and single quotation marks that had escaped the notice of myself and the newspaper editor until now.

Strictly speaking, I should now check everything for hyphenation errors, but I really don't feel like it. I've already read these columns too many times, and after all, I will be able to change the book every time someone finds an error.

The texts contain several links. I spend about an hour getting these links absolutely right. They should not be separated by hyphens, as my print publisher still insists on doing after twenty years, and they should lead to an internet archive, because after all, a printed book is here for eternity and so, I think, wisely, the links should not just simply lead to some short-lived site on the internet.

```
Der·Gedanke·war·nicht·von·Dauer,·ich·ging·und·betrachtete·weiter·im·Netz¬
Berichte·über·Rassismus,·mordende·Polizisten,·brennende·Gebäude·und¬
schlechte·Strategien·im·Umgang·mit·dem·Coronavirus.·Vor·allem·nachts,¬
wenn·ich·nicht·schlafen·kann,·verbringe·ich·damit·viel·Zeit.·Für·diese¬
Beschäftigung·gibt·es·seit·2018·den·Begriff¬
"`Doomscrolling"'\footnote{Mehr·zur·Geschichte·des·Begriffs:·
\href{http://web.archive.org/web/20200715154617/https://archeothoughts.word
press.com/2020/07/06/on-the-origin-of-doom-scrolling/}{Andre·Costopoulos,·
On·the·Origin·of·Doom·Scrolling,
archeothoughts.wordpress.com/2020/07/06/\\on-the-origin-of-doom-scrolling/}
.·Im·Zusammenhang·mit·der·Corona-Pandemie·scheint·ein·Tweet·von·Ellen·
Muehlberger·aus·dem·März·2020·eine·wichtige·Rolle·gespielt·zu·haben:·
\url{twitter.com/emuehlbe/status/1334983251937669121}.}¬
```

The Twitter link shown in the last lines does not lead to the internet archive, because I trust the staying power of Twitter more than the rest of the internet, which is almost certainly an error. Besides which, the linked item is a sequence of several Tweets, and I don't know offhand how to solve the problem in a future-proof way, so I ignore it.

Then I upload the finished PDF to Amazon. Unlike last year, it works at the first go and I am very pleased. Amazon has just one small note:

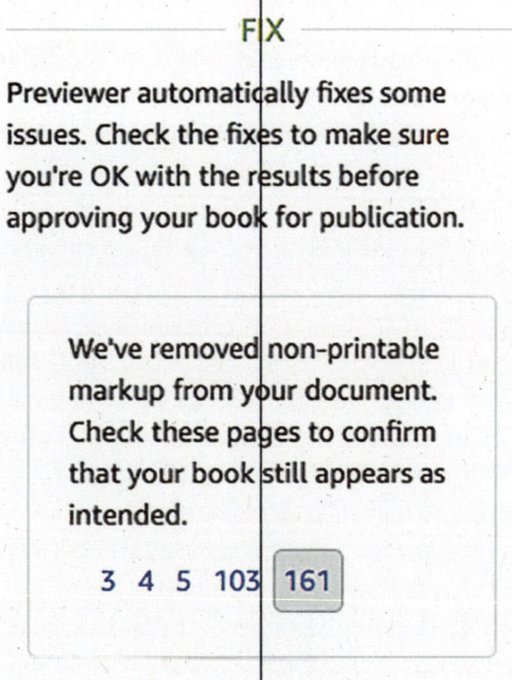

There are no errors to be seen on the pages indicated. I think about it and realize that it refers to the page with the links. I ponder it some more and realize that in a paper book it is not possible to incorporate clickable links at all, regardless of how much you try.

After about a fourteen-hour wait, in which the book has to go through an internal review process at Amazon, it is available to buy the following day.[3]

Those who read it in the future will just have to imagine that they would *actually* be able to click on the links if paper were not so uncooperative. It's not my fault.

3. Kathrin Passig, *Je Türenknall, desto wiederkomm: Alle Kolumnen 2020*, self-published 2021, https://www.amazon.de/dp/B091WM9KTP.

Zoë Sadokierski

A Book Conceived before Breakfast and Delivered before Lunch

Fig. 1: Espresso Book Machine installed in Politics and Prose Bookstore in Washington, D.C., 2011 (Source: Flickr).

For two decades, I have been exploring what a book is, and might be, in a digital age. Alongside my commercial book design practice, I conduct practice-based research into the ways digital technologies—e-book authoring software, print-on-demand platforms—are democratizing the publishing industry from a designer's perspective.

The book is an intimate form. We cradle a book in our hands, hold it close to our chest and hang our heads over it. The size and shape of the book, its weight, the paper stock, the quality of printing and design: all these factors affect our reading experience. In an artist's book, the format may convey more information than the written text (if there is any written text at all); paper stock may indicate how to navigate the work; turning the page may reveal something entirely unexpected. To truly understand an artist's book, you must encounter it in its original form.

To experience as many artist's books in the flesh[1] as possible, I travelled to New York to immerse myself in the MoMA Library's archive. While in NYC, I discovered that McNally Jackson bookshop had an Espresso Book Machine (EBM) which can print and bind a book in minutes. Using an online print-on-demand supplier such as Blurb or Lulu, my book might be printed anywhere in the world and the turnaround from ordering a book to it arriving is between three days and three weeks. In contrast, with the EBM, I can watch my book being made in the time it takes to have a cup of coffee. I decided to produce a book on the EBM before departing, one that contained insights from my archival research at the MoMA Library. I got carried away and ended up creating two.

BOOK 1: (ANOTHER BOOK) AFTER ED-WERD REW-SHAY[2]

The first book responds to Edward Ruscha's influential artist's book *Twenty-six Gasoline Stations*. It contains my critique of Ruscha's bookmaking practice alongside an original photo essay.

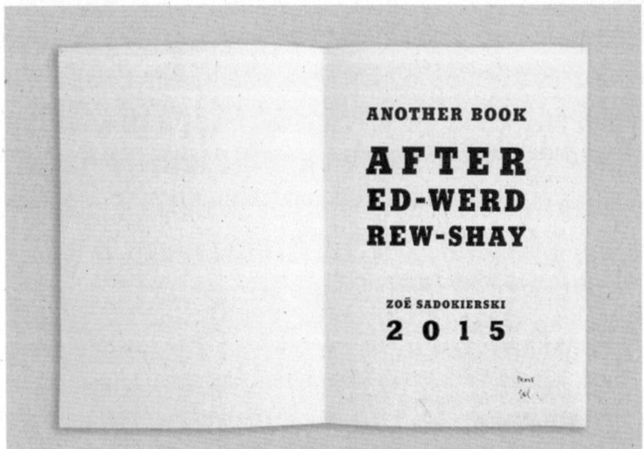

Fig. 2: Zoë Sadokierski, *(Another Book) After Ed-werd Rew-shay*, 2015, title page "proof."

For Ruscha, making books was an exercise in democratizing access to his photographic work, shifting it from gallery walls into the hands of more diverse audiences. Ruscha produced his books using offset printing, the cheapest, most convenient printing available to him. I produced my homage to Ruscha's work using the cheapest, most convenient printing option available to me: McNally Jackson's EBM. With a coffee in hand, I watched this machine print and collate both the pages and the cover, then glue and crop the book to the size I specified. It took just under five minutes from when the bookstore clerk hit print for the first copy to arrive, still warm, in my hands. An entire book conceived, written, designed and produced in a week. I think Ruscha would approve.

1. Johanna Drucker's *The Word Made Flesh* (New York: Granary Books, 1996) was my first encounter with an artist's book, and her *Century of Artist Books* (New York: Granary Books, 2004) has been a contextual anchor in my ongoing research.

2. The strange spelling of Ruscha's commonly mispronounced surname (I thought it was Rush-ah) comes from the title of one of his 1972 catalogue-books: *Edward Ruscha (Ed-werd Rew-shay) young artist*.

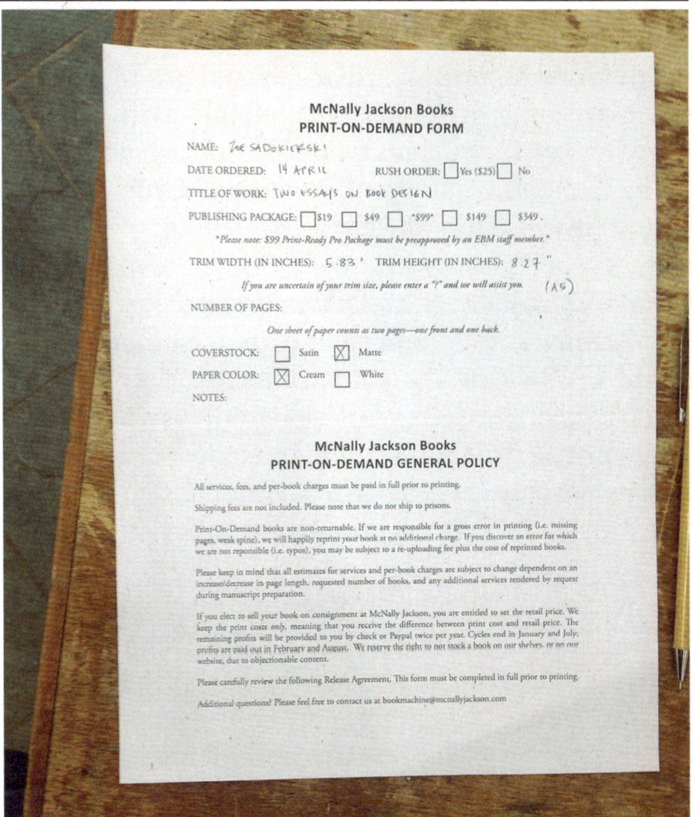

McNally Jackson Books
PRINT-ON-DEMAND FORM

NAME: ZOE SADOKIERSKI

DATE ORDERED: 14 APRIL RUSH ORDER: ☐ Yes ($25) ☐ No

TITLE OF WORK: TWO ESSAYS ON BOOK DESIGN

PUBLISHING PACKAGE: ☐ $19 ☐ $49 ☐ *$99* ☐ $149 ☐ $349.

Please note: $99 Print-Ready Pro Package must be preapproved by an EBM staff member.

TRIM WIDTH (IN INCHES): 5.83" TRIM HEIGHT (IN INCHES): 8.27"

If you are uncertain of your trim size, please enter a "?" and we will assist you. (A5)

NUMBER OF PAGES:

One sheet of paper counts as two pages—one front and one back.

COVERSTOCK: ☐ Satin ☒ Matte

PAPER COLOR: ☒ Cream ☐ White

NOTES:

McNally Jackson Books
PRINT-ON-DEMAND GENERAL POLICY

All services, fees, and per-book charges must be paid in full prior to printing.

Shipping fees are not included. Please note that we do not ship to prisons.

Print-On-Demand books are non-returnable. If we are responsible for a gross error in printing (i.e. missing pages, weak spine), we will happily reprint your book at no additional charge. If you discover an error for which we are not reponsible (i.e. typos), you may be subject to a re-uploading fee plus the cost of reprinted books.

Please keep in mind that all estimates for services and per-book charges are subject to change dependent on an increase/decrease in page length, requested number of books, and any additional services rendered by request during manuscript preparation.

If you elect to sell your book on consignment at McNally Jackson, you are entitled to set the retail price. We keep the print costs *only*, meaning that you receive the difference between print cost and retail price. The remaining profits will be provided to you by check or Paypal twice per year. Cycles end in January and July; profits are paid out in February and August. We reserve the right to not stock a book on our shelves, or on our website, due to objectionable content.

Please carefully review the following Release Agreement. This form must be completed in full prior to printing.

Additional questions? Please feel free to contact us at bookmachine@mcnallyjackson.com

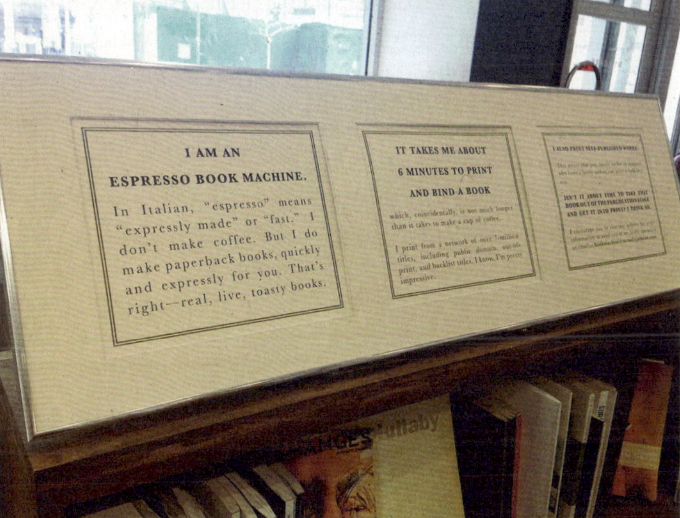

Fig. 3: Print-on-demand form.
Fig. 4: Sign of books printed, McNally Jackson bookshop, NYC.

Fig. 5: Computer set up.
Fig. 6: "I am an Espresso Book Machine."
Fig. 7: Set of the books produced.

The first copy was a proof; customers are encouraged to sign off on a proof before proceeding with a full print run. I spotted a minor error and printed an additional proof before proceeding with my full print run—which was only five copies. This small quantity was partly to do with luggage restrictions for my flight home, but also because I had conceived the book as an experiment in using the EBM itself. In other words, I was more interested in exploring the production process than the content.

A few days before the EBM experiment, I interviewed Granary Books founder Steve Clay. Clay explained that having pondered the fact that most artist's books end up buried in libraries or special collections, he had embarked on a project of publishing "free books"—limited editions which the authors/artists can distribute to people they think would enjoy the book. In this spirit, which reflects Ruscha's aim to democratize his photographic work by publishing it in book form, I numbered the five copies and gifted three to people who gave me time on my research trip.[3] The two remaining copies were later sent to Annette Gilbert, for inclusion in the Library of Artistic Print on Demand project, and to Hermann Zschiegner.

A few months after returning home, Zschiegner, having come across the project via my website, contacted me to acquire a copy for his co-curated exhibition "Ed Ruscha. Books & Co" at Gagosian, L.A. I realized that the content of the book had value in the ecosystem of Ruscha homage books. But being in Sydney, I couldn't physically access the EBM in New York, so I published a second edition via the online print-on-demand service Ingram Spark. In terms of content, only light editing differentiates the EBM and Ingram Spark editions. There are, though, more significant differences between the production and distribution processes.

Fig. 8: Ingram Spark proof; Ingram Spark edition; EBM edition.

Material differences between the EBM and the Ingram Spark editions:

— Size. On the EBM I could choose a size to exactly match Ruscha's book but Ingram Spark has pre-set options.

— Print quality. While the print quality of text is similar across the books, photographic reproduction in the EBM edition is poorer. That said, both print-on-demand options were designed for printing novels quickly and cheaply, so artists using them must be aware of production limitations.

— Margin of error. The initial proof from Ingram Spark arrived untrimmed. The customer service representative assured me this was a one-off mistake, but this demonstrates that quality control is one of the hazards of online print-on-demand services. The experience made me uneasy about the calibre of books being churned out in a production process with an emphasis on speed and cost-efficiency, rather than quality.[4]

3. Steve Clay, Johanna Drucker and David Senior. I gave one proof to Orville Robertson and kept the other.

4. I recall Colin Harman's satirical "How Would You Like Your Graphic Design?" Venn diagram with the intersection of "fast," "cheap," and "great" being "impossible utopia."

Pricing differences:

Delivery options shift the unit price, as shown in the table to the right. There was an option to have the book file kept at McNally Jackson for future print runs, but shipping to Australia often costs more than the book itself. Ingram Spark uses local printers around the world, reducing financial costs and environmental impact of international freight.

Unit price of the book, calculated in $US:

INGRAM SPARK	$2.23 production, $1.99 handling, $5.92 uninsurable economy shipping: $10.14 or $173.36 premium shipping, with insurance/tracking: $183.50.
EBM	$1.36 production, $6.00 handling: $7.36 + $25 "rush order" fee $5 extra per book: $12.36

BOOK 2: TWO ESSAYS ON BOOKS, REPUBLISHED FROM THE INTERNET

While arranging to watch my book being printed, it occurred to me it would be possible to design and print a book on the spot.[5] Jacob, the EBM operator, agreed to conduct this additional experiment the next morning. Creating and publishing a book in a week was a challenge, but *Two Essays on Books* pushed the EBM opportunities even further: here was a book conceived before breakfast and delivered before lunch.

7.15AM:	I decide to use two essays written for *The Conversation* as the content.[6]
9.15 – 10.45AM:	I set up my laptop in McNally Jackson's coffee shop, download the essays, clean up HTML formatting, reformat JPEG images, set up a grid, and lay out the text. Unstable WiFi and software crashes provide dramatic tension.
11.30AM:	I submit a PDF for prepress. This is a human-machine collaboration: a written form is logged by the human (Jacob), the PDF is sent to a laptop attached to the EBM, EBM's internal computer calculates extent and cover size, Jacob checks cover and internal pages files on screen.
11.45AM:	After humming, whirring and chopping noises reminiscent of Willy Wonka's factory, a warm little book shoots out of the machine and into my hands.

A large wooden sign above the machine announced "50,577 books printed here." Beneath the sign, a shelf of books recently printed on the EBM also contained flyers to launches and readings. One aspect of the EBM I missed out on during my trip was the experience of participating in the community of artists who publish with the machine. But my experience fostered deeper connection to my own work; being present as the objects of my creative practice materialized in the world made me feel connected to these books in a way not possible with other providers. Numbering and gifting the small set transformed them into intimate objects, giving them a value for me (and hopefully the recipients) beyond the traditional publishing model. Copies of *Ed-werd Rew-shay* continue to sell via Ingram Spark in small numbers. I have no idea where those books end up, but I love knowing that all five copies from the EBM (and one proof) are in the hands of those who will enjoy them.

5. Normally, files are sent in advance, checked, then placed in the print queue; roughly a 2-3 day turn around. I needed same day "rush option" printing to be able to watch the process.

6. Articles on *The Conversation* are published with a creative commons licence that permits republishing with attribution: "What is a Book in the Digital Age?" and "Shelf Promotion: How everyone can be a publisher with print-on-demand books." Repurposing digital essays for a printed book seemed appropriate for the task at hand.

Karen ann Donnachie, Andy Simionato

THE LIBRARY OF NONHUMAN BOOKS

The following is a summary of the entirely automated process of the Library of Non-human Books.[1]

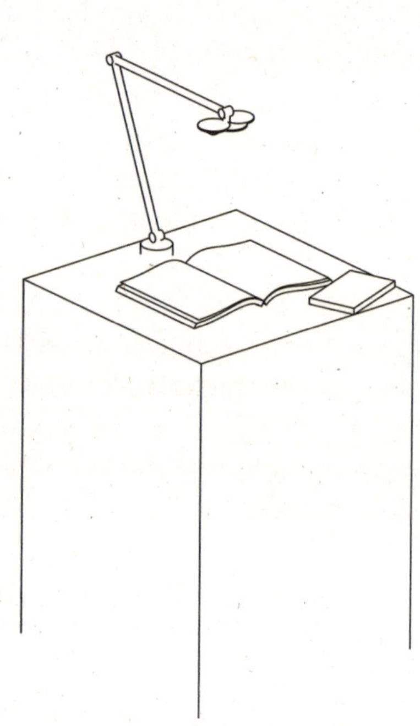

PHASE 1: DECONSTRUCTION

{loop for each unique original book being "read"}

A. Computer vision & OCR reading
B. Text & image recognition

PHASE 2: ILLUMINATION

{loop for each spread in each original book}

C. Content analysis (semantic, linguistic & sentiment)
D. Discernment of salience (calculated chance)
E. Graphic intervention (e.g. erasure, geometric annotation)
F. Search, retrieval & inclusion of content (e.g. Google image) for illumination

1. Our software toolchain is a combination of Python code, natural language processing libraries, and POD APIs; the process, while currently running on Python could plausibly be built on Javascript, Ruby, Swift or other languages; Python libraries used in *The Library of Nonhuman Books* process: OpenCV, PIL, imutils, csv, JSON, requests, random, numpy, fpdf, pytesseract, NTLK, GoogleImageDownload. More technical information may be found in Donnachie and Simionato, "To Hide a Leaf: Reading-machine for a Book of Sand," *Electronic Book Review*, March 5, 2020, https://doi.org/10.7273/chg4-cx05. The user can be optionally prompted at the start of the process, to select which book to illuminate, set spending cap, method of payment, address, and other book parameters, such as paper stock, b/w or color, binding, finish, etc.

One Hundred Million Million Books: Generative AI and Automated Publishing

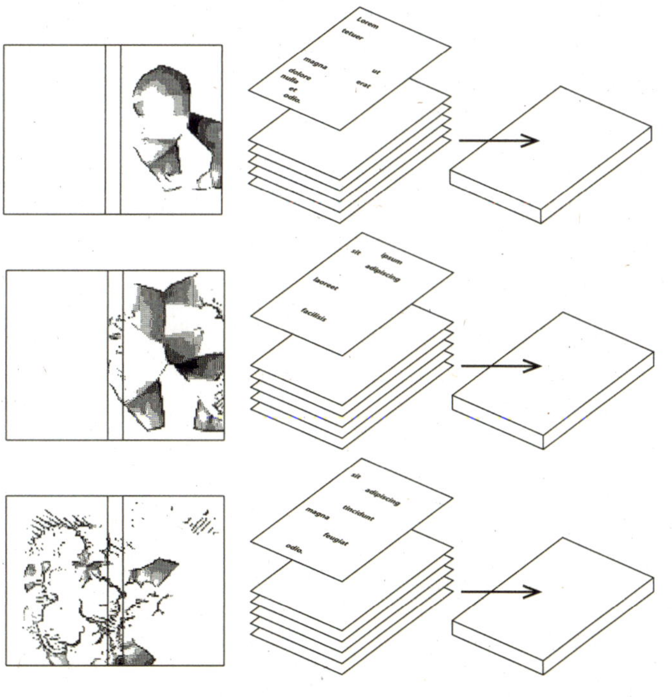

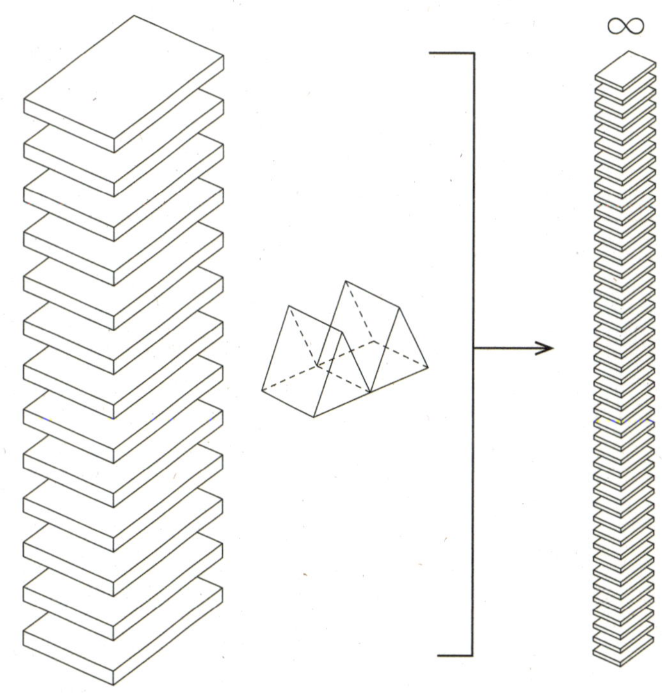

PHASE 3: RECONSTRUCTION

{loop for each resulting illuminated book}

G. Generation and inclusion of colophon
H. Generation of unique cover design
I. Imposition of internal pages
J. Imposition of cover
K. Upload files to secure server
L. Generation of POD "item-ID" based on book parameters (page count, dimensions of book, type of printing)[2]
M. Link "item-ID" to PDF URLs and specify quantity of copies

PHASE 4: (RE)PUBLICATION

{end loop compile & batch order}

N. Add payment, shipping method and address to POD order information
O. Generate POD print order through API
P. Distribute through POD channels
Q. Sell through web site
R. Add to The Library of Nonhuman Books

{end script}

2. For example *The Cloud of Unknowing* Lulu Xpress product ID is 0425X0687BWSTDPB060UC444GXX, meaning a 144 page uncoated cream stock paperback perfect bound pocket-size book with a color gloss cover.

What happens to publishing at the intersection of powerful generative AI tools and print-on-demand (POD) platforms?

To speculate on some possible answers to this question, we outline our own experimental AI publishing practice, beginning in 2019, where we have leveraged both the potential afforded by computationally generative technologies (which together are now simply called AI) combined with commercial POD services, as offered, for example by companies such as Amazon, Blurb and Lulu.

In 2019 we premiered an autonomous system for the generation of books which together form what we call "The Library of Nonhuman Books."[3] These books, which were not designed by humans, include derivatives (that we call "nonhuman (re)readings") of a growing number of original publications, among them:

M.D. Vernon's *Psychology of Perception* (1962)
Guy Debord's *Society of the Spectacle* (1970)
Truman Capote's *Breakfast at Tiffany's* (1961)
Jan Tschichold's *New Typography* (1998)
Bret Easton Ellis' *The Rules of Attraction* (1988)
Yukio Mishima's *Death in Midsummer* (1971)
Fred Reinfeld's *Complete Book of Chess Openings* (1958)
Margaret Atwood's *The Handmaid's Tale* (1996)
E L James' *50 Shades of Grey* (2012)
Franco 'Bifo' Berardi's *Heroes: Mass Murder and Suicide* (2015)
Raymond van Over's edition of *I-Ching* (1971).

In the simplest terms, our reading-machine "re-reads" the original in order to generate a new (derivative) version in the form of a book of illuminated poetry.

In more specific (and less anthropomorphized) terms, our reading-machine uses computer vision and OCR (optical character recognition) to identify the text on any open book placed under its dual-cameras, before leveraging the large language models trained by machine learning through natural language processing to select a short poetic combination (Haiku) around a salient word on the page, which it keeps, while erasing all other words through a process of masking and "infilling."[4] Finally, the reading-machine automatically searches for an illustration from the Google image archive to artificially "illuminate" the page according to the meanings of the remaining words, using the newly formed "poem" as the prompt.[5]

Once every page in the book has been read, interpreted, and illuminated, the system automatically collates the pages, along with its uniquely generated cover and colophon, to produce a digital file suitable for printing (and/or publishing) with an internet POD service, and the resulting printed volume is then added to the Library of Nonhuman Books. From the moment our machine "reads" the original physical book, until the delivery of the derivative printed book from the POD service, our automated-book-system was always intended to proceed without the intervention of humans.[6] Our Library

3. Exhibited for the first time at *xCoaX 2019*, Careof, Fabbrica del Vapore, Milan, Italy; and *ELO* 2019, UCC Cork, Ireland.
4. Many generative writing algorithms, including ours, are increasingly leveraging the dictionaries and large language databases generated from the numerous projects concerned with the mass-digitization of books. Specifically this work uses OCR and NLP with the corpora of Project Gutenberg and the dictionaries for pronunciation by Ralf D. Brown from the Carnegie Mellon University as well as NLP parts-of-speech.
5. Boris Groys has stated that entering a search term into Google is a "metaphysical search" that moves beyond the rigid structures of grammar (Boris Groys, "Google: Words beyond Grammar / Google: Worte jenseits der Grammatik," in dOCUMENTA (13), *100 Notes – 100 Thoughts* #046 (Ostfildern: Hatje Cantz, 2017)). With this project, we explore Google's own response to poetic meaning by prompting the image search with poetic phrases.
6. We concede at the two ends of the process there may be human intervention: To initiate the process, the pages of the book being "read" by the machine is chosen and the pages may need turning by a human hand (although this intervention is not required when the book in question has been previously read or digitized through scanning); and at the end of the process, often POD checkout may need a human to login or give approval and confirmation of payment before printing occurs.

is a deliberate provocation or at least, interrogation, of what we have come to refer to as a post-literate society, a society in which we increasingly defer our reading and writing to nonhuman counterparts.

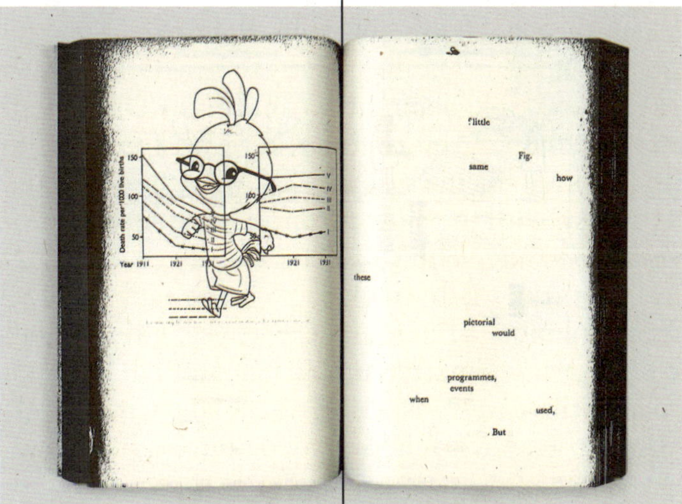

Fig. 1: AI generated nonhuman book, spread from a reading of M.D. Vernon's *Psychology of Perception* (1962).

The system's first successful "nonhuman reading" of a complete book used the original Penguin pocket edition of M.D. Vernon's *The Psychology of Perception* (see Fig. 2), a book chosen not only because its relatively small size and page count was idoneous to our system, but also because we felt that its subject matter (a study of the ways children develop an understanding of the world around them) may hold some relevance in our own experiments which speculate on how humans and artificial intelligence may develop new understandings of the world.

After several "re-readings" of any original book, we move onto another book as we explore various genres and forms, from novels, through scientific manuals, to illustrated books, and so on. What remains constant is that all of these derivative books were autonomously generated and remixed, illuminated and redacted, by artificial intelligence, using our custom-coded reading-machine.

We quickly realized that each nonhuman reading by our machine could produce a multitude of "illuminated scripts," every one a form of erasure poetry, revealing new meanings that were always there in the original, but have remained hidden until that moment.[7] No two readings are the same, displacing and destabilizing some of the ideologies often associated with the original book (for example, the assumption that the printed book is a permanent record), replacing it with a publication holding a loose symbolic resemblance to the original in terms of format, weight, color, image and word, but radically different in what it can signify. Each unique reading is only distinguishable after close comparison, but can be evidenced by a Coordinated Universal Time (UTC) stamp marking the moment of the completion of the nonhuman reading. This time stamp is recorded in the colophon, and has also been used by the algorithm as a data point to seed or "guide" randomness.[8] In practice, our "automated-book-system" is perhaps more precisely described as a series of generative steps which are linked together to generate a multitude of diverse books, programmatically organized into PDF documents, formatted to parametric templates, and ready for POD printing.

7. Our project generates a palimpsest, or scraping away, of texts, which are offered in the place of, or alongside, the original material book, which places it partly within the genre of erasure poetry. See Paul Benzon and Sarah Sweeney, ed., "The Aesthetics of Erasure," special issue, *Media-N. Journal of the New Media Caucus* 11, no. 1 (Spring 2015).

8. When finding the poem or text on the page to keep, there are a number of opportunities within the code for operations of "calculated chance"—when words are of equal salience or the syllable count could work out with a number of different solutions. At times, "random choice" may be resolved by the reading's own UTC (the moment in time when the reading was triggered) for example if the timestamp is odd or even.

As the Library of Nonhuman Books grew, we continued developing our "automated-book-system", into one which could operate autonomously from generation to delivery of the book.[9] We hoped to automate even the initial and final human interventions, of prompting the system with a book, and the upload/checkout process. We disliked that our system lacked the capacity to automate the final upload and purchase of the book through various POD platforms, due mostly to restrictions within the online POD systems themselves (one example being how Amazon's KDP system only accepts publications with a clear title on the front cover which corresponds to the legible content).

So it was a significant step for the research when we finally could move towards an almost autonomous system with the most recent addition to the Library of Nonhuman Books, *The Cloud of Unknowing*. With this book we have succeeded in creating a completely autonomous generative-AI-to-book tool chain, capable of generating, producing, and publishing any number of unique derivatives: autonomously generating the content, cover, and other printed matter, preparing the PDF files, uploading to a server, ordering a specified quantity and transacting financially with a POD service, which, in turn, prints and delivers the book to the supplied address (included in the script).[10] In short, the entire process can now happen unsupervised.

The titular subject of this recent nonhuman reading is an original mystical text from the 14th century called *The Cloud of Unknowing*. The anonymous author's premise is to guide the reader towards a path to divinity through deliberate processes of "unknowing." This small Penguin volume of James Legge's translation of the original text seemed an appropriate subject for our automated-book-system which we consider representing an analogous search for (a kind of) transcendentalism through processes of deliberate unknowing—in the case of our system's "computational unknowing" these include methods of erasure poetry, recursive redaction, and artificial illumination. Through algorithmic processes, the original book is "unknown" one page at a time by our system, before it is automatically reconstructed according to the original's physical parameters, ready for printing and publishing on a POD platform.

There have been a number of works to date around automated publishing practices, some noteworthy for being more critical in their intent to disrupt, others more focused on prosaically "spamming" the POD platforms in question. So, automating the production and publication of our Library for quantity's sake was not initially our main focus. Instead we were interested in exploring the computational capacity (or as Raymond Queneau would say, the potential) that language holds, and subsequently, as a vessel for language, exploring the futures of the book. Could these automated technologies lead to the realization of a "Book of Sand," a mythical book imagined by Jorge Luis Borges, which is always changing, and never ending, ultimately becoming a destabilizing and terrifying force to whomever attempts to seek it out and read it?[11]

Our research speculates on this potential for language, and the book, to act as combinatorial machines. Through our automated-book-systems we attempt to conceptually collide the notion of a book-machine with the literary experimentation of Dada and Oulipo, the cut-ups of William Burroughs and the stochastic chaos of the vernacular in-

9. Just as intermittent phases within this process relied on our (local) human labor, beyond this there is the labor of printing, handling and delivering each book to the recipient, some, or all, of which may be human. We recognize this is elided through descriptions such as "automated-book-systems," which imply no human intervention at all. We maintain that such claims remain useful to speculate on a near future, or even a future present, if we consider the highly automated systems already in place, including Amazon's KDP.

10. Currently this system has been established and is working with Lulu Xpress but could be equally applied to KDP, Blurb and others, with the caveat that KDP in particular has strong content moderation, and tends to block books which lack clearly legible titular / author information (on the cover); they also do not approve "illegible" books.

11. See Jorge Luis Borges' parable "The Book of Sand," in Borges, *Collected Fictions*, trans. Andrew Hurley (London: Penguin Books, 1999), 480–483; more on the conceptual connection to Borges' short story can be found in Karen ann Donnachie and Andy Simionato, "To Hide a Leaf."

ternet with its obsessive culture of sharing images and memes. Through the Library of Nonhuman Books we can consider the opportunities and challenges facing the book, and language itself, once they are liberated from the rules of grammar and formal constructs.[12]

We were not, however, prepared for how it felt to receive the first box of the *Cloud of Unknowing* books. Not only because the books were a collection of unique AI generated derivatives, but they were also uploaded, priced, published, purchased, printed, and delivered with no (human) intervention. This was the first time that The Library of Nonhuman Books had delivered us books we had authored but not yet read (could this be "the book to come" to which Maurice Blanchot referred?).

To describe the experience of opening that box of books, we can return to the original source of the title of this short account, which, as the reader may have guessed after this description of our practice, is also appropriated. Our title is taken, of course, from the title of a poetry book by Raymond Queneau, co-founder of the literary movement Oulipo.[13] Queneau's poem consists of 10 pages, each containing a 14 line poem. Each line of every sonnet matches the meter and rhyme of the corresponding line on every other page, thus permitting the reader to recombine the verses into any one of a multitude of other poems. With the help of the mathematician Francois Le Lionnais, Queneau calculated that the number of such potential derivative sonnets was 100,000,000,000,000 (or 10^{14}). A human reading of such a quantity of poems is unimaginable, leaving the reader to only consider the potential of this combinatorial work.

The small box which arrived from the POD service a few days after we completed the latest version of our automated-book-system contained only 30 books (see Fig. 3)[14]—a modest number in comparison to Queneau's poetic potential—and, while intriguing in their form, these generated books are not intended for close critical (human) readings. But when we consider the recent advancements of generative text and image software intersecting with the ease of use of POD platforms, our experiment can offer a glimpse of a new potentiality of the book, and the future of publishing.

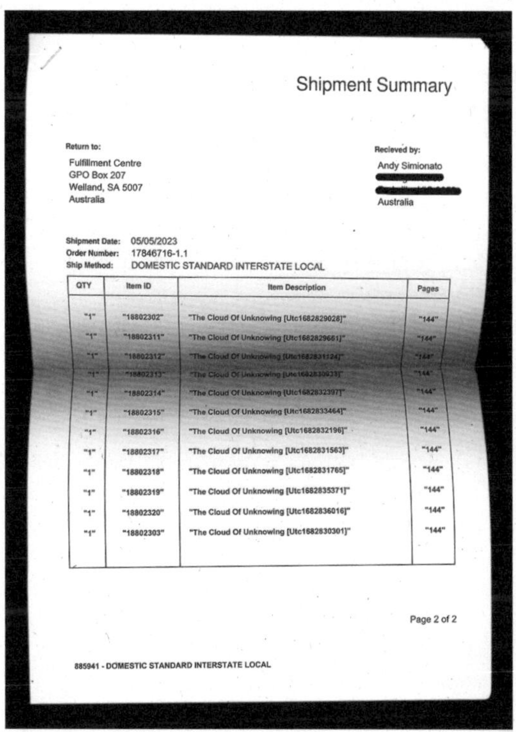

Shipment Summary

Return to:
Fulfillment Centre
GPO Box 207
Welland, SA 5007
Australia

Recieved by:
Andy Simionato
Australia

Shipment Date: 05/05/2023
Order Number: 17846716-1.1
Ship Method: DOMESTIC STANDARD INTERSTATE LOCAL

QTY	Item ID	Item Description	Pages
"1"	"18802302"	"The Cloud Of Unknowing [Utc1682829028]"	"144"
"1"	"18802311"	"The Cloud Of Unknowing [Utc1682829661]"	"144"
"1"	"18802312"	"The Cloud Of Unknowing [Utc1682831124]"	"144"
"1"	"18802313"	"The Cloud Of Unknowing [Utc1682830933]"	"144"
"1"	"18802314"	"The Cloud Of Unknowing [Utc1682832397]"	"144"
"1"	"18802315"	"The Cloud Of Unknowing [Utc1682833464]"	"144"
"1"	"18802316"	"The Cloud Of Unknowing [Utc1682832196]"	"144"
"1"	"18802317"	"The Cloud Of Unknowing [Utc1682831563]"	"144"
"1"	"18802318"	"The Cloud Of Unknowing [Utc1682831765]"	"144"
"1"	"18802319"	"The Cloud Of Unknowing [Utc1682835371]"	"144"
"1"	"18802320"	"The Cloud Of Unknowing [Utc1682836016]"	"144"
"1"	"18802303"	"The Cloud Of Unknowing [Utc1682830301]"	"144"

Page 2 of 2

885941 - DOMESTIC STANDARD INTERSTATE LOCAL

Fig. 2: Image of the bill of delivery for the first 30 *The Cloud of Unknowing* books generated and published without the artists' intervention. The UTC (time stamp) of each publication included in each title and in the colophon information of each volume, changes by an interval of around 200 seconds. This reveals that it took a little over 3 minutes to generate and collate, upload, and order each printed book.

12. Boris Groys narrates the path of words and language as they transition from strict grammatical and formal constraints and context to the "cloud of words" in this age of the Google search engine, where each word has its own trajectory "undermining any attempts to territorialize them" (Groys, "Words beyond Grammar," 9).

13. Raymond Queneau, *One Hundred Million Million Poems*, trans. John Crombie (Paris: Kickshaws, 1993).

14. Admittedly, we set an upper limit of spending which forced the process to quit once funds were exhausted.

We are faced with the daunting realization that through the combined uses of generative AI and POD self-publishing tools, more books can be created by an individual than that individual could conceivably read in their life-time.[15] One possible means to escape this impending avalanche of books will be, of course, to enlist the help of AI to help humans discern, or summarize, or in some other way manage all this language, and the books that hold it. Suggesting a paradox of needing to defer *both* writing and reading to our nonhuman counterparts. Which leaves us with what we believe will become a fundamental question: what will our role be?

There is some comfort in repeating that these experiments remain speculative. But in the time we took to write this last sentence, our system completed reading, generating and publishing one more book.

15. If the books in this "generative" avalanche consisted of little-to-no literary value, then this example could be considered merely another attempt at "spam" or "low-content" publishing.

Critic
Investi

ue &

gation

Dagmara Kraus

The Googlitchy Lórschapelekin: German Classics of the Nuttekaktersm[1]

Translated from the German by Joel Scott.

1. Reprinted from “Tagtigall,” *perlentaucher. Das Kulturmagazin*, August 17, 2019, https://www.perlentaucher.de/tagtigall/das-googlitchige-lorschapelekin-von-dagmara-kraus.html.

… mîn tiutsch ist etswâ doch sô krump …
… but my German is so crooked …[2]
Wolfram von Eschenbach

I. DER, DIE, DAS GOOGLITCH

Recently, I typed the compound word *bickelwort* into Google. Referring to a "strange" or "tossed together" word, *bickelwort* is a neologism coined by Gottfried von Straßburg, author of the Middle High German courtly romance *Tristan*, and identified by Alois Haas as a hapax legomenon of the medieval poet's oeuvre.[3] No sooner had I pressed "Enter" than a genuine *bickelwort* of the most peculiar, tossed-together composition appeared on my screen, comparable to those that Gottfried himself bemoaned in the verses of the apparently all too incomprehensible author of *Parzival*, Wolfram von Eschenbach. The page jumped at me with the appearance of a grotesque:

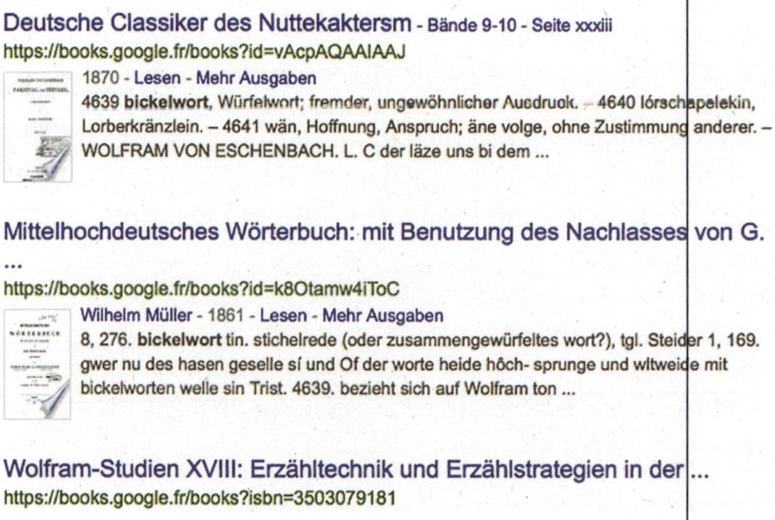

Deutsche Classiker des Nuttekaktersm - Bände 9-10 - Seite xxxiii
https://books.google.fr/books?id=vAcpAQAAIAAJ
1870 - Lesen - Mehr Ausgaben
4639 **bickelwort**, Würfelwort; fremder, ungewöhnlicher Ausdruck. – 4640 lórschapelekin, Lorberkränzlein. – 4641 wän, Hoffnung, Anspruch; äne volge, ohne Zustimmung anderer. – WOLFRAM VON ESCHENBACH. L. C der läze uns bi dem ...

Mittelhochdeutsches Wörterbuch: mit Benutzung des Nachlasses von G. ...
https://books.google.fr/books?id=k8Otamw4iToC
Wilhelm Müller - 1861 - Lesen - Mehr Ausgaben
8, 276. **bickelwort** tin. stichelrede (oder zusammengewürfeltes wort?), tgl. Steider 1, 169. gwer nu des hasen geselle sí und Of der worte heide hôch- sprunge und wltweide mit bickelworten welle sin Trist. 4639. bezieht sich auf Wolfram ton ...

Wolfram-Studien XVIII: Erzähltechnik und Erzählstrategien in der ...
https://books.google.fr/books?isbn=3503079181

Fig. 1: Google Books search result with word explanation for "bickelwort," "lórschapelekin," and "wän."

"Nuttekaktersm" is an automatic text scanning error, an OCR slip created in the process of converting an analogue text into a unit of digitized media. A randomly generated "synonym" for "Mittelalter" (Middle Ages), since as far back as 2012, the word has been flying around the net as a crooked (*krump*) periodic palimpsest. Emerging from a computationally incomprehensible moment of disturbance, "Nuttekaktersm" is at the same time a kind of half-surreal "Google-glitch," an overlooked artifact of translation and retro-digitization that is disseminated by the boatload. For the sake of simplicity, we could contract it into the portmanteau "*googlitch.*" The adjective form would presumably be "*googlitchy,*" and the noun to refer to a screenshot of same—you've probably already guessed it—is formed like "selfie": "*googlitchie.*" Taking a cue from Léon Bollack, for the (*der, die, das,* I'm not sure what gender it takes in German) *googlitch* and its inflected incarnations, when written, it shall be rainbowed, in keeping with the company logo.[4] When the second syllable is pronounced like the suffix "[-age]"/"[-uage]" in "language," *Googlitch* (or rather *googlage*, neutral and ungendered) ['gu:gl̩ɪtʃ] could also be a globally babelled world language, a fewspeak for freaks and the title of a lexicon that would begin with this entry and the scattered definitions of this potential neologism.

In any case, the googlitch "Nuttekaktersm" is every bit as absurd as Gottfried's "fool's speech." With "flarf" as a cousin and the Dadaist Hans Jean Arp as a grandfather, it would be ideally suited to serve as a building block of a googlitch poetry—para-poet-

2. From Eschenbach's unfinished Middle High German poem *Willehalm.*
3. Alois M. Haas, *Mystische Denkbilder* (Freiburg im Breisgau: Johannes Verlag Einsiedeln, 2014), 636.
4. For his constructed language *langue bleue* or *bolak*, Léon Bollack wanted all texts composed in the language to be written in blue (Paris: Éditions de la Langue Bleue – Bolak Ditort, 1899).

ry composed of digital errors. In its arbitrary obscenity [the word seems to include the terms *Nutte* (whore, prostitute) and *Kacke* (poo, shit), *Akt* (nude), and ends on a hint of an orgasm creating an effect something like The Shittle Whoregesm, perhaps—Trans.], "Nuttekaktersm" is not just an indication of the perverted digital translationese that is spawned by automatic language conversion procedures and the rampant business of budget book reprinting that has sprung up around this outside the EU. With its trunctimated—sorry, intimated-truncated—"ism," "Nuttekaktersm" almost sounds like a designation for a movement or a genre, like a name for no less than an entire post-lyrical age of poetic text management "without authorial interference"—in view of its main protagonist, chance, which has been a dream in terms of finding the *bon* poetic *mot* ever since Mallarmé and Dada.

II. "UNPLEASEDLY DISROCK"

Digital poetry is *Nuttekaktersm* when it does not program the errors itself but makes recourse to mistakes that have occurred involuntarily. Genuine, successful *Nuttekaktersm*, though, must be as rare as a good occasional poem. Instead of being a desperate (*wänlos*) monument to OCR book scanning practices, I conceive of *Nuttekaktersm* as a ready-made, trans-germane conceit of snaring—despite extreme ugliness—with a randomized bickel-quill an aberrantly proliferating leaf from the *lórschapelekin* (laurel wreath, see Fig. 1), where poetry springs forth unexpectedly from googlitchies, bickely, prickly, brightly colored little fruits, which in my poetics could function as image-poems, produced not through collage, but much more effortlessly, as screenshots with assigned titles.

"Unpleasedly disrock" (*ungefreut verrocken*) would be an example of such a googlitchie, as to be seen beneath. It comments multilingually on "this arrangement [...] composed with such discernment" (*ditz gereite (...) mit grôzer wîsheite*), before finishing up with an "ashamed" (*verschamt*) genuflection before Khlebnikov,[5] with a cackle of "scarlet laughter" (*scharlachen erlachen*):

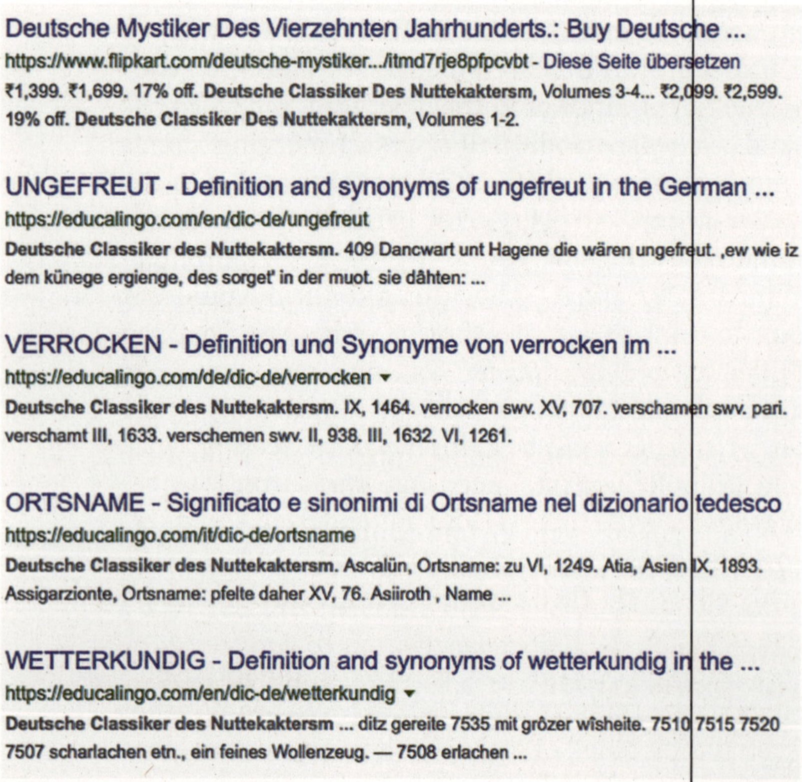

Deutsche Mystiker Des Vierzehnten Jahrhunderts.: Buy Deutsche ...
https://www.flipkart.com/deutsche-mystiker.../itmd7rje8pfpcvbt - Diese Seite übersetzen
₹1,399. ₹1,699. 17% off. Deutsche Classiker Des Nuttekaktersm, Volumes 3-4... ₹2,099. ₹2,599. 19% off. Deutsche Classiker Des Nuttekaktersm, Volumes 1-2.

UNGEFREUT - Definition and synonyms of ungefreut in the German ...
https://educalingo.com/en/dic-de/ungefreut
Deutsche Classiker des Nuttekaktersm. 409 Dancwart unt Hagene die wären ungefreut. ‚ew wie iz dem künege ergienge, des sorget' in der muot. sie dâhten: ...

VERROCKEN - Definition und Synonyme von verrocken im ...
https://educalingo.com/de/dic-de/verrocken ▾
Deutsche Classiker des Nuttekaktersm. IX, 1464. verrocken swv. XV, 707. verschamen swv. pari. verschamt III, 1633. verschemen swv. II, 938. III, 1632. VI, 1261.

ORTSNAME - Significato e sinonimi di Ortsname nel dizionario tedesco
https://educalingo.com/it/dic-de/ortsname
Deutsche Classiker des Nuttekaktersm. Ascalûn, Ortsname: zu VI, 1249. Atia, Asien IX, 1893. Assigarzionte, Ortsname: pfelte daher XV, 76. Asiiroth , Name ...

WETTERKUNDIG - Definition and synonyms of wetterkundig in the ...
https://educalingo.com/en/dic-de/wetterkundig ▾
Deutsche Classiker des Nuttekaktersm ... ditz gereite 7535 mit grôzer wîsheite. 7510 7515 7520 7507 scharlachen etn., ein feines Wollenzeug. — 7508 erlachen ...

Fig. 2: Google search result.

5. A reference to Khlebnikov's poem "Incantation by Laughter." A reading by Charles Bernstein can be found online at: https://www.youtube.com/watch?v=PT5O2ZaMGf0.—Trans.

III. NEO-INDO-EUROPEAN

Somewhere in India, where all six two-part anthologies of the *Deutsche Classiker des Nuttekaktersm* by Franz Pfeiffer are published and painstakingly produced, people believe in *Nuttekaktersm*. People believe in *Nuttekaktersm as German*, and people believe in the importance of a historical book that doesn't actually exist in that form—though nobody knows that there. The explicit statement of faith in this book-fake as a book sounds entirely sober, but asserts with conviction: "We believe this work is culturally important." Ironically, the buyer is thanked for their leniency: "We appreciate your understanding of the imperfections."

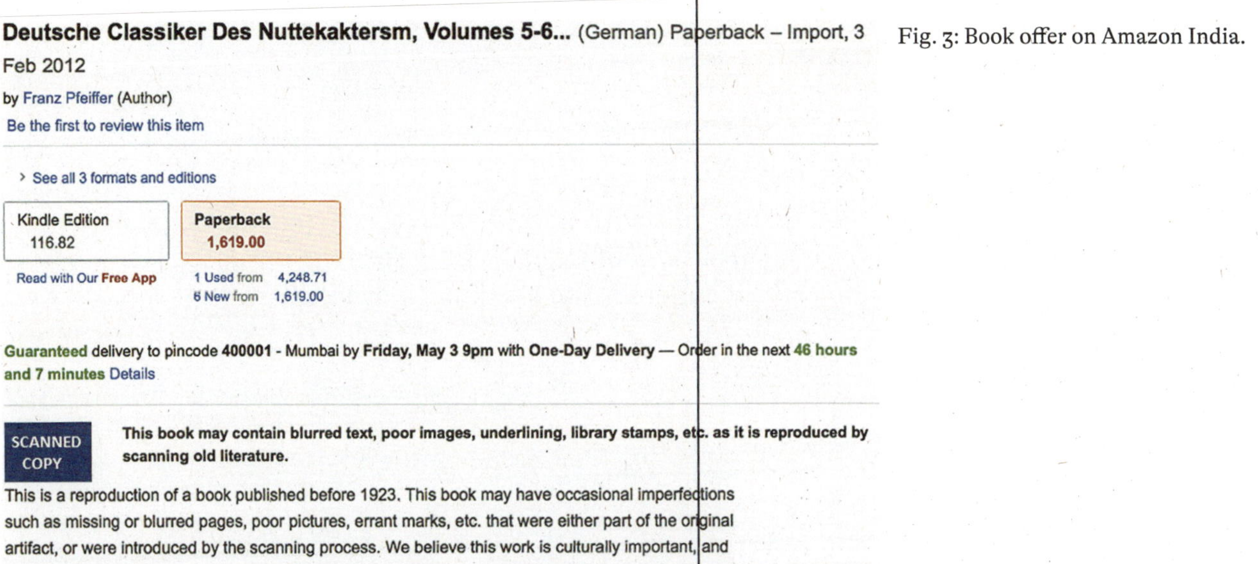

Fig. 3: Book offer on Amazon India.

The post-Pfeifferan Nuttekakclassics have been officially on the market for more than ten years, traded as culturally valuable works. They are exported to the German-speaking world, and are perhaps also read locally, in Asia. So long as somebody pays the price set by Amazon India for the two merged volumes of 1,619 to 2,599 rupees and has it printed with the unslightable Celtic castle on the cover for the equivalent of around 20–30 euros (factoring in a 17–20% reduction). Of course, the people writing "Nuttekaktersm" do not know what they are writing, not to mention what they are promoting. For they know not what they are reading when the cover to be printed reads: *Deutsche Classiker des Nuttekaktersm*. Around these parts, the title undoubtedly immediately sparks errant associations; there, "Nuttekaktersm" reads no differently to the words "Classiker" or "Deutsche." It's astounding that the French didn't know any better than the Indians. And the same can be said of the Swedes:

Fig. 4: Book offer on Adlibris.

In fact, even the Germans don't know any better. And yet, the people selling it on bücher.de should really have a better understanding of it. It quickly becomes clear that the work and its contents—flogged on the online portal for the bargain price of 41.99 euro—have been imported from India. To me, this all sounds a lot like a fairy tale: Once upon a time, there was Ur-German *Tiutsch*. Over seven centuries, it drifted through the world until it finally passed through India's English, which, though it enriched its Schionatulander and Sigune[6] with a Googlitch along the way, made everyone look completely crooked. [...] And thus, it lived happily ever after in the Indo-European aeon:

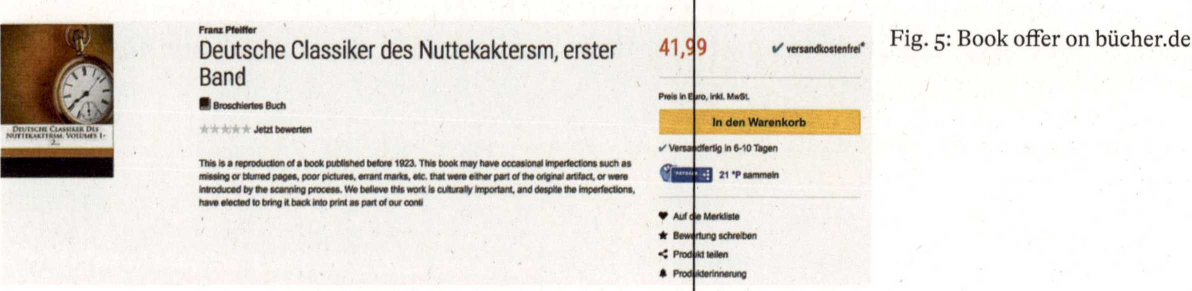

Fig. 5: Book offer on bücher.de.

Only Google makes a correction—ho ho!, but with its red and yellow spectacles, *Nuttekaktersm*-blind and thus blind for an absurd neologism, it only sees the outdated "C," which is why, despite the very first hit, it suggests the spelling "klassiker," wrong, too, without the capital letter:

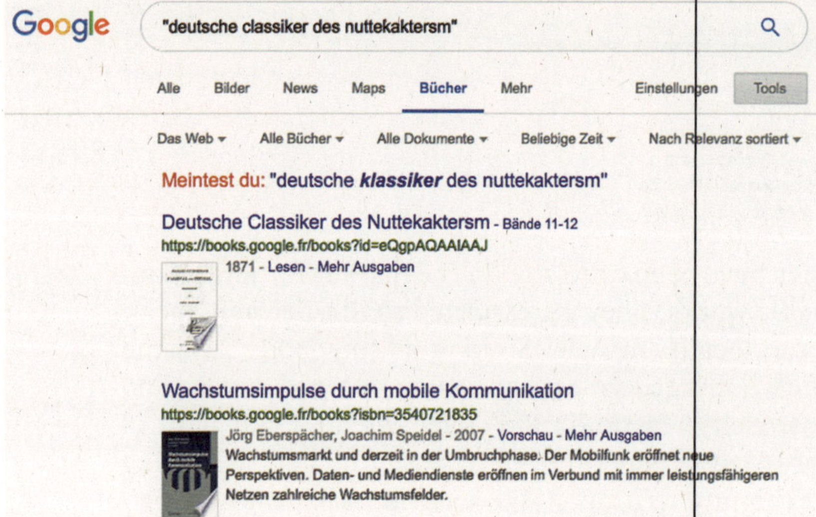

Fig. 6: Google Books search suggestion "Did you mean: "deutsche *klassiker* des nuttekaktersm."

But who gives a hoot about an insignificant title error! What matters is the quality of the construction, that the book is perfect bound; after all, a classic should live longer in the "True World of Books":

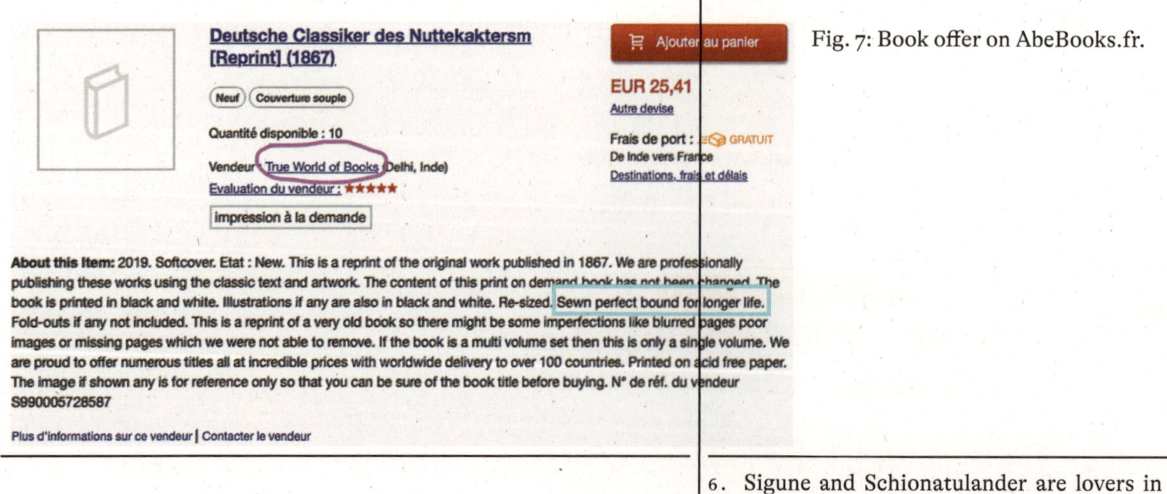

Fig. 7: Book offer on AbeBooks.fr.

6. Sigune and Schionatulander are lovers in Wolfram von Eschenbach's Middle High German romance, *Titurel*.

May *Tristan* live longer as a *Deutscher Classiker des Nuttekaktersm*! Longer live *Titurel* too, a *Deutscher Classiker des Nuttekaktersm*! And *Parzival* too. Hartmann von der Aue (though some of you will struggle to believe it) has indeed also composed a classic of *Nuttekaktersm*, and is, like his poet colleagues, impossible to leave out of the ranks of the men of *Nuttekaktersm*. *Deutsche Classiker des Nuttekaktersm* is a *Deutscher Classiker des Nuttekaktersm*, and the first Googlitch classic:

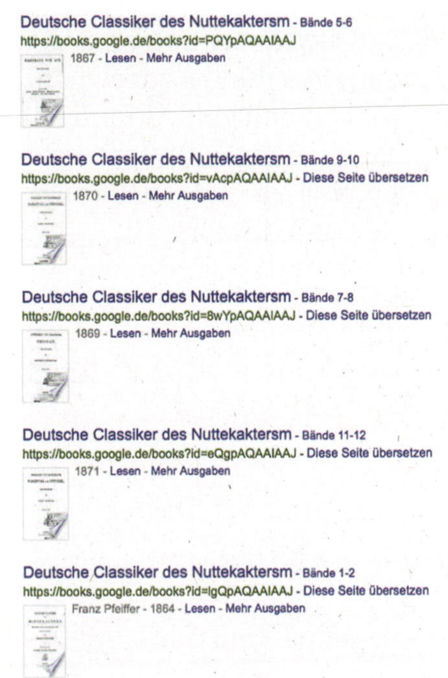

Fig. 8: Google Books search result (12 vols).

IV. WHAT GHOSTS AROUND...

Lost in translation, globalization and its ghosts. Taken strictly, *Nuttekaktersm* is a *ghost in translation*, a literary specter, which in this case has been wreaking its havoc since 184671 (*sic*) (see Fig. 9), but only seems to have recently left the libraries for the haunting grounds of the internet. Terribly damaged, this harmless revenant slips into its linen and luckily, Franz Pfeiffer's ghost hasn't come knocking yet. But he's surely turning in his grave, where he lies on the book cover written beneath castle or clock (see Fig. 5 and 10). For: *Ceci n'est pas un Pfeiffer.*

Pfeiffer, Franz, 1815-1868. Deutsche Classiker Des Nuttekaktersm. Leipzig: Brockhaus, 186471.

Warning: These citations may not always be complete (especially for serials).

Fig. 9: Year of publication as specified by the reprint industry.

Fig. 10: Franz Pfeiffer, *Deutsche Classiker des Nuttekaktersm*, vols 5–6.

Reprint on demand is connected with a rather precarious, potentially ceaseless birth of after-books, issuing from the spirit of a *Fehlerteufel*[7] who whispers from your shoulder: “The content of this book has not been altered.” And: “You can be sure of the book title” (see Fig. 7).

Pfeiffer pipes up to express his ire. But the saying *habent sua fata libelli*[8] comes to mind. Some do indeed habent their father Diabelli, while others have daddy diabolus, the liar. Mea culpa indeed, but whose culpa is it anyway? Can the robot who introduced the equivalence *Mittelalter=Nuttekaktersm* be held culpable of anything? *Cherchez la femme* by all means, but you won’t find her, and you most certainly won’t find a bogeyman. For where is the Googlitchy face of the culprit who is responsible for mugging Pfeiffer and for making that ghastly blunder? It’s made of 0 and 1. Shame on the zeros, shame on the ones, where a bungled one-zeroing took place. The robber has long since stolen away. But hathi trust in the thief, mutht i write it down, either in APA or MLA format:

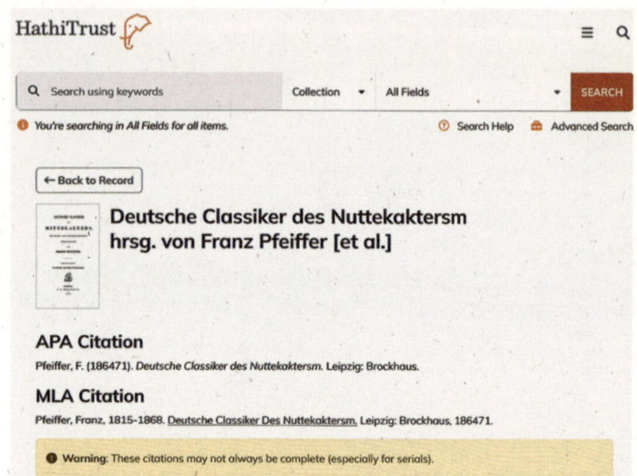

Fig. 11: Hathi Trust catalog entry.

The things that get stuck. In looks, for example. On the net. The truly Uncarrollian Cheshire WorldCat knows the hangdog *Nuttekaktersm* and gets caught gawking dumbly:

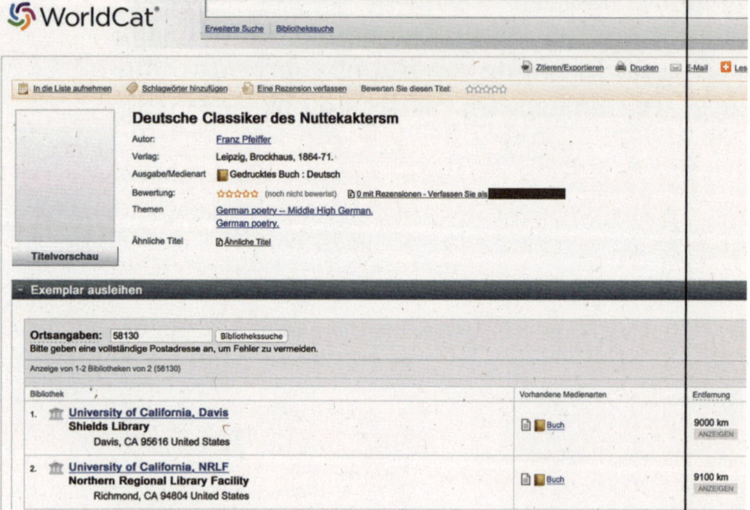

Fig. 12: WorldCat catalog entry.

Schionatulander will not capture *Nuttekaktersm* and bring it back. Because right now, as I write this, a Google employee somewhere in this tiny world might have already found the stuff-up and erased it. But Sigune kept a little piece of fool’s gold in her hand while the glitch-glitchy leash slipped through her fingers.

7. *Uli der Fehlerteufel* (Uli the Error-Demon) is a figure from a series of books for schoolchildren about a demon that wreaked havoc in the spelling books of German children, stealing or flipping letters, punctuations, or words. Students would then be asked to find these mistakes.

8. The full expression in Latin is *pro captu lectoris habent sua fata libelli*, (in accordance with their readers, books have their destiny), and is verse 1286 of *De litteris, De syllabis, De Metris* by Terentianus Maurus.

Angie Waller

Grifting the Amazon[1]

1. Reprinted from Angie Waller, *Grifting The Amazon* (New York: unknown UNKNOWNS, 2019), 1–13 and 32–41.

Introduction

In 2003, I published *Data Mining the Amazon*, my first book. Its contents were inspired by the creepy feeling I got when Amazon's recommendation algorithm suggested I might like to listen to the rock band Stone Temple Pilots since I had purchased a book about web programming. Il had it printed in the Midwest at an offset press, distributed as an art project, and exhibited in galleries and museums. I also sent it to people who purchased it from my website for $15.

Publishing a book with an offset press was expensive. With *Data Mining the Amazon*, I spent over a thousand of my student loan dollars to print 500 books. To distribute copies, I found myself standing in long lines at the post office in order to fill out customs forms for international orders. The large inventory of books packed in heavy boxes was also a burden as I moved from studio to studio.

The print-on-demand industry eased these financial and logistical problems. I was able to print one book for less than $10 instead of shelling out thousands of dollars at a time. In addition, self-publishing companies like CreateSpace (now owned by Amazon) made it possible to print and distribute books through Amazon.com. I no longer had to worry about storage space and spending my lunch breaks in long post office lines.

This book documents my experience of engaging with Amazon.com to publish and distribute my work. While most of the action in this recounting involves watching online videos, uploading files, and waiting for UPS, a colorful cast of real people are behind the screen. Along the way I encountered a Danish male fashion model, a prolific ghostwriter from India, and a "tight" community of Australian capybara pet owners. I even witnessed my own books in potentially criminal hands.

The title of this book intentionally mirrors the title of my first book; however, I am no longer just an observer of the platform. *Grifting the Amazon* explores the metalanguage around producing books in the tangled world of e-commerce on Amazon.com.

The Medium is the Message

Books are products

One day, when I was feeling particularly unemployed and restless, I found myself in my kitchen listening to the soothing English accent of a Danish male fashion model whom I will refer to as NK. This particular morning, I had decided to switch my focus from job hunting to learning how to publish on Amazon Kindle. That desire led me to NK. He wasn't sitting in my kitchen, but from my computer his disembodied voice narrated a series of screen capture video tutorials for publishing Kindle eBooks. Admittedly, having a Skillshare.com course taught by a male model—even one that never showed his face—seemed a lot cooler than the other programming and design classes offered on the website.

The class was ostensibly about designing and formatting text for Kindle. However, the class barely covered technical specifications or related software. Instead, NK demonstrated how to get books on Amazon.com without writing a word or designing a single page.

> "Amazon has over 600 million credit cards on file. That's a lot of credit cards. So the buying audience is so abundant it's not even funny."
>
> –NK, full time model and Kindle publisher

1,345 Students | 7 Projects | Beginner Level

N K •Following
Author, blogger and online ...

About Me

I'm a full time model who decided I wanted to establish an additional source of income. After playing around with different ways of building an online source of passive cash flow, and giving up on every single one of them, I finally discovered the Amazon Kindle platform. I found out how relatively simple it was to make money providing quality content, while still keeping a day job and a social life.

One thing I want to make clear is this requires work, not as much as other methods, but it is definitely not a get rich quick scheme. With spending a few hours each week I established enough passive income to cover my monthly groceries expenses with six short eBooks on the Kindle store.

I'm no Kindle publishing wizard making six figures on this, in fact just months ago I knew nothing of this, but I now have a small steady source of income that I can scale into something bigger down the line - which I will. I have now grown my passive income to +$1500 a month.

I'm a blonde male model from Denmark - if I can do this, you certainly can too.

↑ Introduction to NK's Skillshare.com class.

Author Anonymity

Lifestyle brand as author

At the time I watched the tutorial in 2015, self-published paperbacks and Kindle eBooks were being published on Amazon.com through a website called CreateSpace, now owned by Amazon and called Kindle Direct Publishing (kdp.amazon.com). Making a book on CreateSpace simply entailed uploading PDFs of your book's contents and cover.

CreateSpace had few constraints on how a book was titled or authored. There was no verification that the name of the author was connected to a real identity—any name or fictional brand could be listed as the book's author. For instance, NK calls his brand "Sound and Simple Lifestyle."

 Sarah

★☆☆☆☆ **I read the entire book in 8 minutes and learned ...**

November 24, 2017

Format: Kindle Edition | Verified Purchase

I read the entire book in 8 minutes and learned absolutely nothing. The grammatical band syntax errors were, however, amusing.
No wonder there is no author named, it is an embarrassment

Helpful | Comment | Report abuse

↑ Review for a "Sound and Simple Lifestyle" book commenting on the author's anonymity.

↑ Example of a book published on Amazon.com under NK's brand "Sound and Simple Lifestyle."

+ Follow

Follow to get new release updates and improved recommendations

About Sound And Simple Lifestyle

Sound & Simple Lifestyle offers you ebooks on making the most out of the hand you've been dealt. As the name implies we provide sound and simple steps to leading a healthier and more productive life, whether that being through cooking, exercise etc. We hope you enjoy our material and that they will help you be the best you.

↑ "About Sound and Simple Lifestyle" from Amazon.com.

Product details

Paperback: 56 pages
Publisher: CreateSpace Independent Publishing Platform (October 21, 2013)
Language: English
ISBN-10: 1495341968
ISBN-13: 978-1495341960
Product Dimensions: 8.5 x 0.2 x 11 inches
Shipping Weight: 7 ounces (View shipping rates and policies)
Average Customer Review: ★★★☆☆ 13 customer reviews
Amazon Best Sellers Rank: #4,040,959 in Books (See Top 100 in Books)
#378095 in Health, Fitness & Dieting (Books)

↑ Details for a "Sound and Simple Lifestyle" book published on CreateSpace.com. CreateSpace Independent Publishing Platform is listed as the publisher.

Titles Come Before Content

The more keywords the better

To ensure that a book topic would be niche enough for success, NK demonstrated how to fine-tune book titles using Google's AdWords tool. With AdWords (now known as Google Ads), you can determine how many people are searching for a subject online and the keywords they are using to access the information. For instance, instead of just using the word "pickling" to title a book about pickling vegetables, AdWords might also recommend a related term like "fermenting." If there are fewer books with the words "fermenting" *and* "pickling" in the title compared to books with just "pickling," you could rank higher on Amazon.com and potentially gain more sales. These competitive keywords have inspired the contents of NK's books.

> "An e-book on Amazon can sell for at least just as much as an iPhone app, but it can be produced at a fraction of the price. This is why Kindle eBook publishing is the simplest and the most replicable online income opportunity out there."
>
> –NK, full time model and Kindle publisher

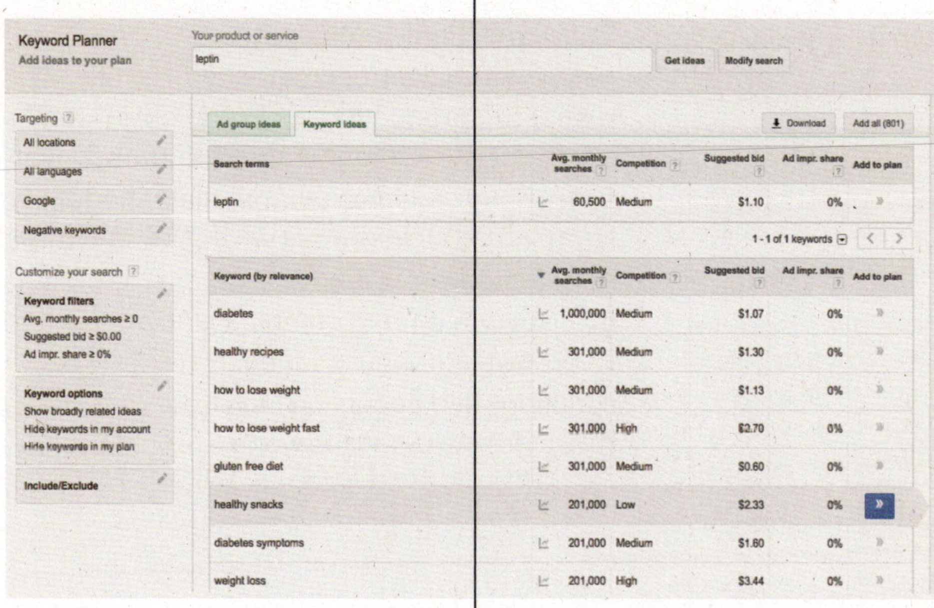

Search terms	Avg. monthly searches	Competition	Suggested bid	Ad impr. share	Add to plan
leptin	60,500	Medium	$1.10	0%	

Keyword (by relevance)	Avg. monthly searches	Competition	Suggested bid	Ad impr. share	Add to plan
diabetes	1,000,000	Medium	$1.07	0%	
healthy recipes	301,000	Medium	$1.30	0%	
how to lose weight	301,000	Medium	$1.13	0%	
how to lose weight fast	301,000	High	$2.70	0%	
gluten free diet	301,000	Medium	$0.60	0%	
healthy snacks	201,000	Low	$2.33	0%	
diabetes symptoms	201,000	Medium	$1.60	0%	
weight loss	201,000	High	$3.44	0%	

↑ Still from NK's Skillshare.com tutorial "How to Title Your Book." The table is from Google's AdWords tool.

↓ Publications from "Sound and Simple Lifestyle" that use keywords from NK's Google AdWords research.

Writing a Book

Getting someone else to write a book for you

The most time-intensive part of NK's process must have been selecting his title. The rest of the production, including cover design and content writing, was outsourced overseas. Being an international male model like NK is not a requirement for meeting writers and designers in faraway places. Websites like Upwork.com (formerly Elance.com) and Fiverr.com are venues for posting short job descriptions and accepting bids from writers and designers all around the world.

↑ Screen capture from NK's tutorial on hiring a ghostwriter on Elance.com.

> "...Now I am outranking these books and I'm just a dude who hired a medical student in Pakistan to write my book. So you see it is more about how you package the book rather than the content itself."
>
> –NK, full time model and Kindle publisher

↑ A selection of titles by "Sound and Simple Lifestyle." Each cover was designed by a freelancer on Fiverr.com, another website for finding freelance talent for small gigs.

Ghostwriter Job Posts

Tight timeline and minimal guidance

Upwork.com is filled with listings that reveal a variety of approaches to asking internet strangers to churn out books. Some job posters want ongoing relationships with the same writer, while others have vague themes in mind, word count requirements, and a tight turnaround time. Some only provide word count and want ghostwriters to propose their own book topics.

↑ Screen capture from Upwork.com documenting a client looking to establish an ongoing relationship with a ghostwriter who will compose 8,000-word books on a weekly basis for $80, or one cent per word.

↓ Screen capture from Upwork.com showing a request for 5500-word books on a topic and title proposed by the ghostwriter.

Details

Hi

I'm looking for a writer who has experience in writing eBooks/Kindle Books.

I don't have a title for the book because I want you to propose what you are able to write.

The book must consist of 5,500 words and must pass copyscape.

Interested applicants please send me the following and I will get back to you if I am keen to work with you.

1. What is your proposed book topic/title?
2. What makes you qualified to write this topic?
3. Have you written on a similar topic before? if yes, please send me some references. Thank you.

Interested applicants please apply.

P.S. Only applicants who answered the above three questions will be considered. Thank you.

Project type: One-Time Project

★ Be careful with this client: they tell you you've stolen information when you've clearly cited it, provide short deadlines then refuse to communicate back for days at a time, delete milestones and then refuse to acknowledge/add them back so that you can progress working on the contract, are rude (very much so sugar and ice personality-- when you have any questions, concerns, or need clarifications, immediately become hostile), and refuse to provide any real type of framework/direction. less

Oct 2017 - Nov 2017
Fixed Price $5.00

To Freelancer: K   No feedback given

I need a ghostwriter for 3500 word e-book, buddhism topic

No feedback given

To Freelancer: M ★★

Aug 2017 - Sep 2017
Fixed Price $11.00

↑ Screen capture from Upwork.com showing review of a client by a ghostwriter who had a negative experience.

Jokes and Gags

Amazon's rules for content

In 2015, Amazon started enforcing rules for what constitutes a "quality" book. To meet Amazon's content standards, the book has to have a minimum word count of 2,500 words.* Even books that have already been published could be removed from the website if they don't meet this criteria. In the words of Amazon, they "create a poor reading experience."

For self-published paperback books on Amazon.com, there are ways around the word count requirements. A book can have repeated content or blank pages so long as each page has a header and the product description clearly labels the book as a "joke" or "gag book."

*A series of books I made with computer-generated text did not originally meet the 2,500 word count threshold. To reach Amazon's quality standards, I changed a line in my code to loop more times, and in turn, output more text.

Print Publishing Guidelines

kindle direct publishing

Genre-specific Requirements

Joke books

Joke or gag books with repeated content or an intentional absence of content can be published as long as they are clearly labeled as such in the product description and they meet all other specification requirements. Books meant to contain empty pages should include some type of content such as lines, headers, or "notes" to indicate the pages are intended to be blank.

↑ Amazon's guidelines for "joke books."

Hello,

During a quality assurance review of your KDP catalog we have found that the following book(s) are extremely short and may create a poor reading experience and do not meet our content quality expectations:

Name of Short

In the best interest of Kindle customers, we remove titles from sale that may create a poor customer experience. Content that is less than 2,500 words is often disappointing to our customers and does not provide an enjoyable reading experience.

We ask that you fix the above book(s), as well as all of your catalog's affected books, with additional content that is both unique and related to your book. Once you have ensured your book(s) would create a good customer experience, re-submit them for publishing within 5 business days. If your books have not been corrected by that time, they will be removed from sale in the Kindle Store. If the updates require more time, please unpublish your book.

↑ *Topic: Amazon going after short shorts*, Kboards, https://www.kboards.com/index.php/topic,149460.0.html.

Books as Money

Amazon seems like Sotheby's

Inspired by all I learned, I started publishing my own books and ghostwritten books through CreateSpace. It was so convenient, I almost forgot these projects existed on Amazon.com. Notifications of deposits for purchases of the books occasionally popped up in my inbox, but my profits were just a few dollars here and there. None of my books were providing the passive income that NK, the Danish male model, had bragged about.

A few years after I published *What Does the Bible Say About Word Finds?,* I looked it up on Amazon.com to share with a friend. I was surprised to find that GoldieLoxBooks, an Amazon reseller, was selling a used copy of my book for $2,796 even though new copies were still available for $10.

For a brief moment I thought my book's identity as an art object had been recognized by GoldieLoxBooks. This was a passing thought and I settled on the most likely explanation: that the price was a computer glitch.

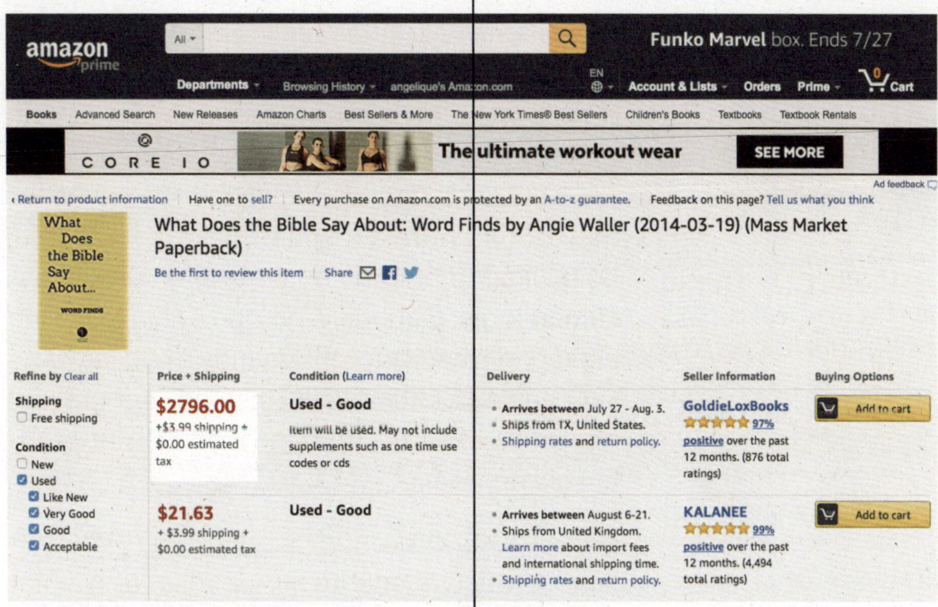

↑ My book *What Does the Bible Say...* listed on Amazon.com for $2,796 while still available new for $10.

↑ My book *How to Find a Friend...* listed on Amazon.com for $383.29 while still available new for $10.

Marked Up Prices Are Trending

Books have a life of their own

More than a year after noticing my book's mysteriously high price on Amazon.com, stories about other people's books getting marked up were in the news. Well-known authors were quoted in the *New York Times* presuming high prices for their books were a result of their fame. Books being limited or early editions was also an assumed logic. Curiously, no one actually selling used paperbacks for thousands of dollars was interviewed for the article. Instead, authors and marketing experts shrugged it off as a by-product of capitalism.

In April 2018, three months prior to the *Times* article, *KrebsOnSecurity* (krebsonsecurity.com) and *The Guardian* also wrote about books on Amazon.com being sold at inflated prices. In this case, the 10-fold price markup was not on used books from well-known authors or publishing houses; rather, the original price set by the publisher on CreateSpace was $555.

Like other titles from CreateSpace, the $555 book was written under a pseudonym. According to *KrebsOnSecurity*, the book was filled with "gibberish," most likely computer-generated. The book in question, *Lower Days Ahead*, was not intended for reading.

↑ "Amazon's Curious Case of the $2,630.52 Used Paperback," *The New York Times*, David Streitfeld, July 15, 2018.

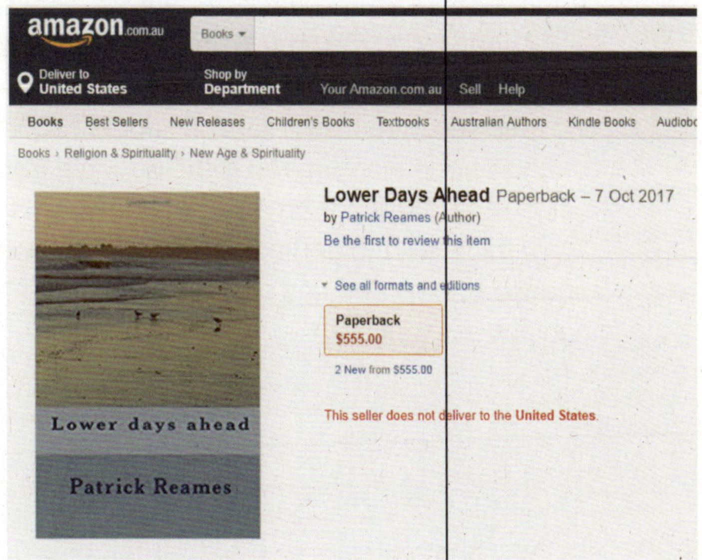

↑ *Lower Days Ahead*, a CreateSpace publication listed on Amazon.com for $555. (screen capture from krebsonsecurity.com)

Ghost in the Shell Game

Books are being traded for cocaine by drug cartels (possibly)

CreateSpace's lack of rules for author's name and publishing company allowed fictional personae like Lolly Brown to build pet book empires without readers knowing whether or not there is a real Lolly Brown. In the case of *Lower Days Ahead* listed for $555, Patrick Reames credited as the author is a real person. But Reames is not the person who published the book on CreateSpace.

The seller of *Lower Days Ahead* set up a CreateSpace account with Reames's social security number. When books with Reames's name and tax id were sold, the taxable income was attributed to Reames but none of the actual money went to him. Until he received a 1099 form from the IRS for the $24,000 worth of books he allegedly sold, Reames was totally unaware of *Lower Days Ahead*.

Reames had limited success with Amazon's fraud support. At the time *KrebsOnSecurity* was covering the incident, the case was far from being resolved. Reaching Amazon support agents on the phone also proved to be difficult. Ironically, a self-publisher on Amazon.com claims to know the secret to getting through to Amazon's phone support and has published eBooks and audiobooks with bootleg 1-800 numbers.

Fake books sold on Amazon could be used for money laundering

Books of gibberish are listed on Amazon.com for thousands of dollars, with one author claiming his name was used to send almost $24,000 to a fraudulent seller

Alison Flood
Fri 27 Apr 2018 10.00 EDT

↑ "Fake Books Sold on Amazon Could Be Used for Money Laundering," *The Guardian*, Allison Flood, April 27, 2018.

↑ Screen capture of self-published Kindle eBook and audiobook on Amazon.com claiming to have customer support numbers for Amazon.

Relentless

Books as decoys

My books are still on Amazon.com fluctuating from their original listing price to a few hundred and sometimes thousands of dollars. It is unlikely my book *What Does the Bible Say About Word Finds?* will sell for $1,000 unless that transaction is a stand-in for something else. While I cannot prove fraudulent activity is behind the prices of my books sold by resellers, it seems that laundering money through obscure used books would be an easy thing to do. No one will "accidentally" pay thousands of dollars for my book, but the seller can direct someone to "buy" it and earn their 60% commission on the sale with no questions asked. Even anonymous currencies like Bitcoin with weekly withdrawal limits present more red tape than this scenario.

For the sellers who list my books at high prices, I am unable to learn more about them. Like the books covered so far, these virtual storefronts have mixed reviews that are either extremely positive or complaining that an order was never received. While ordering my own book for $2,796 might lead to a postmarked envelope with a clue to the seller's location, there is no guarantee a package would arrive.

When Jeff Bezos conceived Amazon.com in 1994, his purpose for selling books online was to collect information about affluent book lovers who could later be customers for what the site would become.[1] Books were a prop to lure people in with their credit cards.

Most of the self-publishers I've described in this book are in tune with the Amazon ethos. For them, books are items to be produced at lightning speed and packaged to be impulsively purchased by unknown masses on the internet.

Although his friends discouraged him from calling his web store "Relentless," Bezos still registered the domain name relentless.com in 1994. If you type *relentless.com* or *amazon.com* in your web browser, you end up in the same marketplace of deception and secret identities I have described. You can also buy the latest *New York Times® Best Seller* and a subscription for organic diaper cream while you are there.

Top positive review
See all 18 positive reviews ›

Amazon Customer

★★★★★ **customer service phone number is 1800-782-3991**
May 17, 2019

i found it after a lot of research, hopefully it will help you

23 people found this helpful

↑ Screen capture of review listing questionable Amazon.com support number. As of Sept. 2019, a Google search for the number leads to Victorian Era & Country Creation in Forsyth, Montana.

1 George Packer, "Cheap Words: Amazon is good for customers. But is it good for books?", *The New Yorker*, Feb 9, 2014, *https://www.newyorker.com/magazine/2014/02/17/cheap-words.*

2 Brad Stone, *The Everything Store: Jeff Bezos and the Age of Amazon*, New York, October 15, 2013.

Joey Yearous-Algozin

returning to a kind of activity we are known for

print-on-demand allows for a kind of
embodied or almost direct textual
condition

that book books don't

bec book books function as little more
than museum pieces

or artifacts

of a kind of activity

by the time they're published

there's a beautiful merce cunningham
quote i think about a lot

where he says something like

a body in motion takes as much time and
space as a body at rest

but of course ppl like seeing
a body in motion

and today

i realized that what he is rejecting

is an idea of stillness

or that the quote is one way to realize

that on a moving planet stillness
is a fantasy

only movement is possible

no matter how minor

and the book is a fantasy
of a kind of stability

or stillness

but print-on-demand allows
for a living text

something that is maybe closer to
something like the handwritten text of
manuscript culture

or at the very least

it allows for a kind of immediate
production and embodiment that
makes a text

as that which is closer to life

--Joey Yearous-Algozin

TT, 2021

Holly Melgard

Print-on-Demand Self-Publishing After the Rise of Misinformation Got Us Killed

> The poet's word leads from periphery to periphery [...] it makes every periphery into a center; furthermore, it abolishes the very notion of a center and periphery.
> — Édouard Glissant, *Poetics of Relation*[1]

As I write this in March 2022, the US reaches one million Covid-19 deaths—a significant percentage of which could have been avoided were it not for the dystopic rise and viral spread of misinformation on the internet. Troll farms and astroturfing weren't a thing as far as we knew in 2010 when I started at Troll Thread (TT), an experimental poetry print-on-demand + free .pdf book publishing platform (via Lulu.com) housed on a Tumblr site, where I have designed and co-edited more than 75 books. At that time, we looked up to trolling as an anonymous form of progressive hacktivism that undermined capital. But somewhere back there, the dream that print-on-demand would democratize discourse by including more marginalized voices and under-recognized forms of knowledge turned nightmarish as misinformation and conspiracy theories emerged.

Now putting out my first book with an external print-based press this year after a decade of self-publishing on TT, there are things that print-on-demand did for my writing that I've yet to find comparable substitutions for in the analog print tradition: print-on-demand's disruption to publishing conventions widens the affordances of the book object to include more working-class, female-identifying, feminist, and born-digital experiences than the print paradigm alone can account for.

Chris Sylvester blew our minds when he first invited Joey Yearous-Algozin, Divya Victor, and myself to join as co-editors of TT by telling us that "it's a low maintenance place to put our work that no one else wants anyway." Self-publishing on print-on-demand meant that we didn't need to wait for our poems to be wanted, liked, or even recognized by a pre-existing literary establishment before earning a place in the world. Because book content didn't need to be worth the price or investment of a print-run, this enabled us to collaborate with more kinds of undervalued, under-recognized forms of intelligence encircling our daily lives: videogame walkthroughs (Sylvester's *Total Walkthrough*), descriptions of *Outfits* (Shiv Kotecha), tweets about McDonald's *McNugget* (Chris Alexander), a bibliography of spam email (Angela Genusa's *Spam Bibliography*), all the people who have died with MySpace accounts (Joey Yearous-Algozin's *The Lazarus Project: mydeathspace.com*), unnameable subjects in other people's books (Divya Victor's *Partial Directory Series*), and even melodramatic suicide notes written daily in a tween's diary (Trisha Low's *Purge*).

Running anywhere from two pages to dozens of volumes, many TT projects amplified the book as an object. For example, my 2012 book *Black Friday* (a 740 page, 8.5 × 11 inch all-black book with white page numbers), the dedication page of which functions like stage directions, indicating how a reading of the book ought to be performed "for black ink on white paper." The dedication is a directive and pretense for comprehending the poem correctly. I made this book to test out the affordances of the "Print on Demand" function as a frame for the work.

Although TT's co-editors tend to disagree on any single definition of the project, arguably the vast majority of the books we've published have operated under the rather psychedelic, counter-cultural belief that works worth our time, even if unpaid, is "open" work. "Open" in the sense that the work increases our capacity to encounter and tolerate others, including others within ourselves and each other, by plumbing our channels of perception. But, when the human clickbait known as Donald Trump was elected president, I started to question the extent to which that same methodology of radical acceptance (which guided both my poetry teachers *and* the early computer and internet developers) resulted in devolving civilization and dissolving the social fabric. In the years since, trafficking in the art of ambiguity, formal innovation and inclusivity has never felt more unsafe.

At its conception, TT's persona was to present itself as anonymous and undifferentiated. Our "About" page suspiciously just said, "Troll Thread is Troll Thread." However, starting in 2016, more and more people began asking questions in the comment threads of posts promoting our books on social media, asking "who is troll thread," "where is troll thread," and "why would I download a pdf

1. Édouard Glissant, *Poetics of Relation*, trans. Betsy Wing (Ann Arbor: University of Michigan Press, 1997), 29.

from a site that looks this sketchy?" I was glad to see people waking up to the dangers of technocracy—something our works pointed to all along. But this uncanniness diffused clarity for TT's path forward. Now with COVID-19, it's unclear whether using print-on-demand to broaden the book's affordances as an artistic horizon of production has reached its logical conclusion. I find myself asking: What does self-publishing on print-on-demand still offer writers and artists after the death of so many people as a result of the inclusion of misinformation and bad actors on the internet?

Before I can consider its future, I should probably first figure out how to accept what is: Yes, in hindsight, the grave outcome of COVID-19 deaths in the US ironizes and injures our optimism for web publishing's capacity to boost our cultural health by democratizing knowledge. Yes, in retrospect, experimental small press poets were not the only counter-cultural fringe groups who seized opportunities opened by web-publishing platforms to challenge the established order through tactics of self-amplification. Yes, during this time, while we self-identified as a counter-cultural group whose mission was to decenter literary hegemony, dangerous people also used these technologies to broaden their inclusion in discourse such as white nationalists, fascists, white supremacists, religious extremists, conspiracy theorists, and anti-vaxxers. And yes, our aim to boost equality of the marginalized by widening the affordances of the book was all very utopian and idealistic looking back on it now.

Yes, bad actors got a hold of these technologies and took advantage, but no, we shouldn't disown these tools until they cease to be used by all uniformly, because we needn't deny our own access to the kinds of weaponry used against us. These extremists aim to protect the assets of a few by shutting down tolerance for the many. The impulse is to divest when companies fail to protect the security of their systems from bad actors. But right now, it seems especially crucial to *not* divest from our self-publishing platforms, because if anything, the amplification of bad actors and their misinformation during this time only proves that web publishing tools are remarkably good at amplifying marginalized voices and exiled forms of intelligence.

I can't say I know how to solve these problems when at present, I still can't even decide whether to call this consideration of the future of creative print-on-demand self-publishing a manifesto or a eulogy. Throughout my writing this, the people around me have continued to struggle to process the reality that the ubiquitously crumbling hallmarks of our modernity—our defunded institutions and failing neoliberal technocracies—failed to keep alive the million who are now no longer. But here are six more ways experience tells me to hope that creative print-on-demand self-publishing practices continue even after the rise of misinformation on the internet got us killed.

1. PRINT-ON-DEMAND BROADENS ACCESS FOR UNDERPAID, OVERWORKED PEOPLE TO INSERT THEIR VOICES IN LITERARY DISCOURSE

TT is purposely a no-money-in / no-money-out operation, in that it has no print run, and costs nothing to operate apart from the time/labor it takes to write, design, and upload poems as books. It also doesn't pay its authors or editors a dime. Not getting paid might sound severe given the many exploitative labor practices operative in the underfunded, under-paying not-for-profit arts sector today, but it is actually liberating for us in more ways than one. Our approach was born of necessity when we started TT as graduate students living on $13k a year stipends that ran out after the fourth year of our Ph.D. programs. We joined forces, divided up the labor, and designed the press to operate as a publishing model that functioned independently of institutional support using the least labor possible, one that more overworked and underpaid people like ourselves could use.

No longer allowing funding to determine the scale or content of what we can publish has enabled us to put all kinds of weird shit we've never seen in books before. We use as much blank space as we want, we've put out full-color picture books of our trash, and we even once made a sixteen-volume book, which costs $800 to print just one set. Josef Kaplan's *1100* compiles the full copy-pasted argument between Wikipedians about best practices for representing the numbers one through one-hundred on Wikipedia. Aspects of that book that eat up the most cost are the blue hyperlinks, which require us to print using full color, and copious blank pages that resulted from reformatting the text to fit a 6 × 9 inch octavo book size. While we can't afford a full printed set of TT's books ourselves, the physical materiality of these books isn't just a virtual frame or a rumor now that archives at various institutions like the Buffalo Poetry Archive have begun buying one copy of everything TT has published. The design specs for the packaging of this book were determined by the needs of the poem and the author above the affordances of the market, the editor, or their budget for a change.

Taking and making no money at TT enabled us to generate more poems as a result because our poetry was no longer obligated to cater to those with the money to fund our print runs, and thus we spent less time working to appease moneyed interests. For Joey and I especially, two kids who grew up working class and had no outside financial support beyond those stipends and unsubsidized student loans, TT's ability to widen the small-press poetry frame to include people like us kept us engaged through the entirety of our emergent years as poets.[2]

2. SELF-PUBLISHING ON PRINT-ON-DEMAND AS A YOUNG FEMALE-IDENTIFYING WRITER WAS LIKE LITERALLY CUTTING OUT THE MIDDLE MAN

As a working-class, female-identifying poet, print-on-demand self-publishing meant that I didn't need to predicate so much of what I made on the desiring gaze of my still predominately male-edited and curated literary community. For the last decade at TT, what I've made hasn't needed to be legible or valuable to others before earning entry into the world; I haven't waited to be spoken to before speaking. And because my poetry hasn't needed to please or take care of anyone other than myself, I let myself compose for an audience that doesn't need my work to be likable, beautiful, or even needed—not by my friends or even fellow women—before earning the right to exist in this world. Composing poems for a self-publishing interface has helped me spend less time configuring my appearance as an object of desire, leaving me more time to act as a subject with desire.

However, making no money costs me more today than it did as a younger student, and it costs me more as a female-identifying person, now that I balance inheriting familial caretaking responsibilities with working several day jobs and juggling student debt. At one point, I even modified TT's "About" page from saying "Troll Thread is Troll Thread," to "Free Isn't Equal. Troll Thread: We Only Pay the Woman," explaining how one unpaid dollar for female-identifying people is technically more like -$1.17 because of the wage gap. On that page, I embedded a PayPal button to collect increments of $0.17 from our patrons to fill that gap (the amount that women make less than men for every dollar earned on average). "Free Isn't Equal" as a poem was never printed, but it trolls the moneyed gaze and male gaze simultaneously.

Meanwhile, self-publishing on print-on-demand opens up additional means for under-resourced women to include their voices in discourse and the archive, or at least it did for me. In 2007, poets Juliana Spahr and Stephanie Young in their pivotal essay "Numbers Trouble," counted and compared the ratio of male to non-male poets who were published, anthologized, and received prize money that year only to discover that female-identifying writers still "get less on the dollar than our male comrades," "get less prize money and appear less often in anthologies."[3] They also found that the gender gap for published female-identifying women is measurably worse in the US small press poetry community compared to institutional and commercial publishing worlds by double-digit percentage points.[4] Great efforts to balance those numbers have since transpired, but I still have yet to see signs of gender equity at the editorial level in small press. Young and Spahr's findings show that women's writing-focused anthologies are important and necessary for bringing balance to the gender gap in writing, but that these collections alone have not and do not correct the problem of gender inequality in literature.

This trouble around gender boils over into a larger question of legitimacy in male-dominated literary institutions. To put it bluntly, I need

2. "CA Conrad interviews Troll Thread: Part 2 (14:26)," *Facebook*, May 15, 2012. https://www.facebook.com/CAConrad88/videos/10151707996715307. At 14:04 in the video, Joey Yearous-Algozin exclaims, "I write poems with a computer that cannot be unplugged largely from the internet that I steal and I put these poems up on the web for anyone to take—This is what actual poor publishing looks like!"

3. Juliana Spahr and Stephanie Young, "Numbers Trouble," *Chicago Review* 53, no. 2/3 (Autumn 2007): 88–111, here 100.

4. Spahr and Young, "Numbers Trouble," 96.

print-on-demand to co-exist with other publishing practices in a larger ecosystem of tactics. However, it has gotten second-class treatment in the literary world. Grants and award committees have used the fact of my having self-published numerous print-on-demand books to disqualify my eligibility for funding. And university hiring committees recognize my books as "vanity publications" (according to the Modern Language Association) that "don't count as books on [my] CV." This condescension is in line with an emergent trend in our literary community today that sees small presses disappearing everywhere, "threatened by injunctions from funders and institutions to professionalize and to abandon a legacy predicated on amateurism, autonomy, and anti-capitalist and anti-institutional politics." Ugly Duckling Presse's co-founder Matvei Yankelevich contextualizes well this new trend in the US, arguing that "[i]nstitutions that ostensibly support the work of the small press, in conjunction with a more professionalized literary culture of the MFA and the AWP, have served to marginalize small press practice, diminishing its political significance and redefining its boundaries, while plunging its mostly volunteer laborers deeper into debt and dependence."[5] Because institutions are deemed as more reliable in the face of misinformation, small press work is becoming increasingly disqualified as viable credentials that would earn writers awards and jobs.

After our stipends ran out around 2013, we started working even more jobs than before and TT became harder to keep up as we continued to do it long after Divya left and Chris became a parent. But Joey and I kept it going because of its increased capacity to include voices like ours in the conversation, as well as print-on-demand's unparalleled capacity to incorporate into books the material life of our digital literacies. Institutional stigmatization against self-publishing on print-on-demand in recent years has depleted the book's ability as an interface to include women or working-class people, and it also actively inhibits the emergence of a generation of born-digital writers into discourse.

3. PRINT-ON-DEMAND BROADENS THE BOOK OBJECT'S ABILITY TO INCLUDE MORE DIMENSIONS OF BORN-DIGITAL LITERARY PRACTICES IN ITS ARCHIVE

Our US Letter (8.5 × 11 inch), all white, 740-page in-house style at TT is designed to mirror the compositional space of the word processing programs and web spaces we frequent to compose our writing. This format expresses the affordances of software and platform default settings in MS Word and Lulu.com by maxing them out. Written into the design of our books is a negotiation between analog and digital reading and writing practices in this way. Excitement over the novelty of digital textuality has died down naturally as time has worn on, but this trajectory demonstrates how print-on demand has broadened the affordance of the book object to include more of the material life of our textual world today.

Our in-house style takes great permission from Tan Lin's design of his book *Heath* under the art direction of Danielle Aubert, which was foundational for our own intervention in that the work pushes the affordances of the book to more material signs of our emergent digital literacies. Like TT's baseline, Lin's book cover is all-white in Courier New font and trolls the outer dimensions of the book's packaging: It puts a list of its contents on the cover where the title should go, its list of contributors on the back cover where the synopsis and blurbs belong, the ISBN floating alone on an endpaper, and omitting page numbers altogether.[6] The multiple existing versions of the book such as the first, *Heath: plagiarism/outsource* (Zasterle Press, 2008) and *Heath Course Pak* (Counterpath Press, 2012), collage copy-pasted content from the internet, including highbrow texts about digitality and the textual condition but also web detritus like full-color pop-up ads and RSS feeds about the actor Heath Ledger's death that occurred during the period of the text's composition. The work was shockingly uncanny: A disjointed patchwork of contents competes for the reader's attention with no regularized standards of organization, perfectly mirroring our chaotic, online environment. *Heath* was not a print-on-demand book, but the example of his paratextu-

5. Both quotes Matvei Yankelevich, "'Power to the People's Mimeo Machines' or the Politicization of Small Press Aesthetics," *Harriet Blog*, Poetry Foundation, February 3, 2020, https://www.poetryfoundation.org/harriet-books/2020/02/power-to-the-peoples-mimeo-machines-or-the-politicization-of-small-press-aesthetics.

6. Eventual TT author Danny Snelson began tracing ways that Lin "plays" with paratext in an early self-published essay, where he notes that *Heath* "[e]mphasizes the *softness* of the paratextual threshold." Danny Snelson, "Heath, prelude to tracing the actor as network," 2010, http://aphasic-letters.com/heath/.

al playfulness was highly generative for us and me in particular.[7] I see Lin doing what post-colonial thinker Édouard Glissant says the real poet does: level hierarchies by "abolish[ing] the very notion of center and periphery."[8] Print-on-demand self-publishing offered TT a means to fold into books and articulate more material conditions enveloping our lives, such as the transformation of our writing by the emergence of a plurality of digital literacies.

4. PRINT-ON-DEMAND INCREASES THE BOOK'S MATERIAL MEANS TO INCORPORATE MARGINALIZED FORMS OF KNOWLEDGE BY GIVING WRITERS AND THEIR PUBLISHERS MORE PARATEXTUAL FLEXIBILITY

TT books cost us less to make because of print-on-demand but also because we minimize the labor of making paratexts, allowing for greater variation within our in-house style. Paratexts are the peripheral, packaging dimensions of text that designate the boundaries for its reception in discourse, as Gérard Genette theorized in 1987—things like blurbs, synopses, book covers, even separate interviews, press releases, and author bios. About these "thresholds of interpretation" he calls them, the "paratext is what enables a text to become a book and to be offered as such to its readers and, more generally, to the public."[9] They are the writing that positions a text to appear as a cookbook, an annual family newsletter, or the *Norton Anthology of Literature*. Paratexts inform the periphery of our attention as we read by signaling in a basic sense what the text is, is for, and who it is for. Today, the paratextual category could be expanded to include, for instance, social media promotions of our work like hashtags, media blasts, and other web frames like the single-author website, "About" page, and the documented spectacle around the book's arrival to its "pub date."

TT's back-covers are always either blank or reverse imprints of the cover image—there is no synopsis to negotiate, no author bio to edit, no hounding authors for blurbs—and we don't even have page numbers most of the time (only those print-based paratexts asserted by our authors are preserved). At the same time, using Lulu.com does come with its own paratextual constraints, as it still requires us to cooperate with its distinct settings, such as requiring that we input a description of a book to complete the uploading process. Our system for meeting this criterion is to simply repeat the words "How to ___" (inserting a keyword from the book or rudimentary one-word description) until the text field is full, exaggerating the filler text used to meet the required textual fields to qualify the work as "book." Using the print-on-demand platform in this way enabled us to bypass certain restrictions on the production of knowledge imposed by the print-based tradition, giving our authors more room and flexibility to play with the framing of their own books compared to the print paradigm. But ultimately print-on-demand doesn't give us more creative freedom or control, it just gives us different creative freedoms and controls than those permitted in a print-run determined modality. Print-on-demand didn't emancipate us, we merely exploited its paratextual differences as assets for expanding the affordances of the book-object to include us.

Writers and publishers across the spectrum spend exorbitant time and money composing paratexts to guide readers to and through their work, but standards in mainstream publishing strategically mask paratextual labor to appear invisible and unobtrusive to readers. Meanwhile, competing against industrial publishing for the scarce resources of attention, recognition, and material support, counter-cultural small press poets play with paratexts to unconventionally disrupt information flows and reveal invisible architectures of capital undergirding the "Literary" category. Primarily, the small press tradition dominating the poetry scene when TT began had done this by exchanging hand-bound, letter-pressed, mimeo or photocopied books, chapbooks and zines, thus seizing the means of their own literary production. Whereas rather than express our smallness as a press by limiting the book's distribution with print runs and boutique vendors, we instead limit the time and labor required to materialize books, thus freeing up time for working people like us

7. That year, another eventual TT author, Kristen Gallagher, also commented on the "performative" nature of *Heath*'s design in "The Authorship of Heath Ledger in the New Reading Environment on Tan Lin's *Heath*," *Criticism* 51, no. 4 (2010): 701–709. The conversation began to grow formally through the making and exchange of our own works from there.

8. Glissant, *Poetics of Relation*, 29.

9. Gérard Genette, *Paratexts: Thresholds of Interpretation*, trans. Jane E. Lewin (Cambridge: Cambridge University Press, 1997), 1.

to make more books than we could in the strictly print-based or letter-press traditions.

5. DISCOURSE IS SHAPED BY THE ENVELOPING LANGUAGE OF OUR PARATEXTUAL FRAMES. TO CONTROL THE PARATEXTUAL FRAME IS TO SEIZE THE MEANS OF DISCOURSE PRODUCTION

Experimental self-publishing on print-on-demand remains worthwhile and useful to me because it broadens our means to play with paratexts as sites for creative expression, experimentation, self-authorization, and mischief-making. What I learned by playing with the paratextual framing of books as TT's designer, as well as one of its co-editors and authors, is that our frameworks for understanding contents aren't just inanimate, intangible, or neutral. Paratexts, as with the author bio and the hashtag, are constructed and composed to reorient the focus of writing. Manipulating paratextual thresholds can reshape the surface appearance of consensus by warping the boundaries of a text's reception in discourse in this way.

TT enabled me to work less hard to appeal for inclusion in a system that was built to keep people like me in the periphery anyway. However, paratexts don't shape discourse alone. Privilege among other factors obviously also plays its part in the circulation of our work, and I, a white woman with a Ph.D., am far from being a marginalized person. My point in exploring the de-marginalization of particular kinds of knowledge using TT's example is not to virtue signal or align myself with an underdog position to gain a rhetorical advantage. To be clear, my interest here is in mapping ways that underserved forms of intelligence may enter into language by seizing the means of discourse production. Print-on-demand as a technology doesn't eliminate the problem of marginalization on its own, but TT's example shows that print-on-demand can be used to further diversify the book's capacity to bypass print-run paratextual filters that previously inhibited the inclusion of a broader diversity of voices.

Admittedly though, I don't see how an aim like TT's could take off as vigorously today as it did a decade ago, because these platforms wield greater paratextual control over our books than authors or publishers now. Social media algorithms that we use to promote our print-on-demand books and shape the appearance of their reception have changed to deprioritize amateur content in the feed, but the feed is still where readers look to find the "voice" of the author in discourse now. This last year while putting out my first print-run book with an outside editor, I ended up spending more time eliminating discontinuities by reformatting the image and rich text for announcing my book launch across platforms than I spent designing my own book cover, illustrated by hand and all. Because work generated by contributors who are not either paying extra or interacting on these platforms constantly is now intentionally buried and throttled, I find myself once again spending less time making poems than working to be included as a voice in the conversation, but this time, it's the platforms, not editors or establishment poets running the show.

I have spent more time re-stabilizing TT's online contents, consequent of changing terms and algorithms, than I ever spent writing or designing its books. When Tumblr (TT's homepage) changed its terms of use and everyone left the platform, it ceased to serve its aggregating function. And in the peak of COVID-19's first wave, Lulu began changing its terms and its e-book algorithm, killing all of our .PDF links, which we ended up migrating to a Google Drive and redoing. In lieu that performing influence on these platforms purports to be the new paratextual toll for registering as a "voice in discourse" today, I can see why so many of my friends have started their own author websites.

Lulu is no exception to the rule that our internet platforms like our social media sites have destabilized our archives and ostensibly public health also. The platform has updated its policies since the pandemic began, but even since these modifications, Lulu still circulates medical misinformation.[10] Just by searching the word "plandemic" on Lulu's website, right now I see six books of COVID-19 anti-vaccine propaganda.[11] Unequivo-

10. Its "Terms of Service" state that, "Users are expected to conduct proper research to ensure that the Content sold through the Site is in compliance with all local, state, national, and international laws. If Lulu determines that the Content is prohibited, we may summarily remove or alter it without returning any revenue from sales of the prohibited Content. Lulu reserves the right to make judgments about whether or not Content is appropriate."

11. Titles include *The Plandemic* (Version 6): *Corona Virus Vaccine is Genocide* by Adrian Bonnington, *Covid World Order: Resetting Humanity 2.0 and Medical Martial Law* by Luis Vega, and *The Great Covid Deception* by Billy Crone.

cally, Lulu needs to be held accountable for giving a platform to misinformation that can get people killed. But divesting is not accountability holding in itself. Maybe what we're seeing is Lulu slowly rising to assume responsibility for public safety by way of its changing terms and conditions, which now reserve the right to prohibit content. Or maybe we're just seeing them fail to do so in slow motion. At best, Lulu can give us the grassroots outlet that small press offered but with added protections against hate speech that the Xerox machines used to produce white-supremacist zines never could. At worst, it stays the same and continues to enable bad actors to use the book object to perform false authority and propagate medical misinformation. But even at its worst, it is not as bad as the other web platforms that got us here, where exchangeable memes and videos that propagate the conspiracy theory of the "plandemic" circulate more rapidly by the thousands and millions rather than at the pace it takes to make and read books by the dozens. Writers have not divested yet from those platforms, continuing to use them more prominently than print-on-demand self-publishing to promote and circulate their work (Twitter, Facebook, Instagram, and increasingly TikTok also). Of all the platforms to divest from first, self-publishing on a platform like Lulu wouldn't be my first choice, because it has not seized the means of discourse production at the same scale as social media. Also built into its design, by virtue of the book technology, are better guard rails for protecting against the rapid spread of endangering medical misinformation by default.

6. ADDED PARATEXTUAL PLASTICITY MAKES THE PRINTED BOOK RADICALLY FUTURISTIC

The time it takes to click through Lulu's various buttons to purchase or download a book slows the acquisition and recirculation of our books, automatically dampening the inflammatory, reactionary rapid-resharing of shock content. The dangers we face by engaging these tools cannot be minimized, but the printed book provided by the print-on-demand service enhances user agency to react less and respond more than our other web sharing platforms can. Even though amateurs, non-specialists, and frauds can now more easily fill books with their nonsense than ever before, by design, the book as a technology stabilizes knowledge, including marginalized forms of intelligence.

Overcorrecting can be just as dangerous when it leads to silencing already marginalized voices, including weirdos, and other non-conforming artists who play integral roles in renovating and rearranging constructions of the so-called "enemy" within the "peripheral" category, as well as abolishing the peripheral category entirely. While institutions have rerouted resources away from self-publishing poets, which has occurred simultaneously with the eradication of tenure and intellectual freedom via the adjunctification of the university in the US, rightwing interests emboldened by deep-pocketed donors also effectively banned more books from US schools in 2022 (1,500 books in all) than we have seen in modern history, the vast majority of which are written by nonwhite and LGBTQ authors.[12] While our hollowed-out education and arts institutions validate print-on-demand self-publishing less now than when we started, renewing investments in the book as a technology (both printed and digital) for stabilizing knowledge has never felt more needed.

Even if not through Lulu, I remain hopeful that print-on-demand will continue to counterbalance all this destabilization by enabling us to print our books and gather greater independence from our screens, ultimately re-stabilizing knowledge by offering more critical distance to respond beyond simply reacting. Potential misinformation circulated in self-published print-on-demand books is dangerous, but arguably not as dangerous as silence, censorship, and erasure. Creative print-on-demand self-publishing offers users the book as a medium for translating problems enveloping our lives into language. These problems include forms of violence so banal they seem unsayable (like meritocracy's classism, patriarchy, and racism) and escalating austerity measures that eradicate intellectual freedom for the underserved. Print-on-demand's enhanced paratextual plasticity is useful for reclaiming the user agency necessary to contend with those forces enveloping our lives at scale. When discourse actually includes all people, bad actors occupy less of it.

12. PEN America, "Banned in the USA: Rising School Book Bans Threaten Free Expression and Students' First Amendment Rights" (New York, NY: PEN America, 2022).

Gen
Aesth

re &
etics

Paul Soulellis

Performing Publishing: Infrathin Tales from the Printed Web[1]

1. Reprinted from *Hyperallergic*, December 2, 2014, https://hyperallergic.com/165803/performing-publishing-infrathin-tales-from-the-printed-web/.

In "Search, Compile, Publish" I identify some of the tactics used by artists who make books and other printout matter in the post-digital print space: grabbing, scraping, hunting, and performing.[2] Together with an abundance of free content and easy access to print-on-demand technology, this has now become a way to talk about an evolving artists' web-to-print practice in the post-digital space. Alessandro Ludovico, referring to my taxonomy of techniques and approaches, characterizes this new way of working as a "transduction" between media in printed web works: mixing, lending, and embedding digital processes into traditional print, the two forming a hybrid character.[3]

Fig. 1: Paul Soulellis, ed., *Printed Web #1* (2014) (all images courtesy the author unless otherwise noted).

This flux between screen and the printed page is apparent in the works that I collect for Library of the Printed Web and publish in *Printed Web*.[4] At Kenneth Goldsmith's suggestion, I'll evoke Duchamp's concept of the *infrathin* to get at this in-between condition.[5] Duchamp left a loose collection of forty-six handwritten, unpublished notes describing what he called "inframince" (*infrathin*), and said that while the notion was impossible to explain, one can give examples: the warmth of a seat that's just been left, or when the tobacco smoke also smells of the mouth which exhales it, or the difference between two forms cast from the same mold. It's the "immeasurable gap between two things as they transition or pass into one another."[6]

I propose that this "indifferent difference" is one way to characterize the web-to-print space. In this infrathin condition we vibrate between visible difference and melding sameness. We recognize both without collapsing into either; we hover in a state between states. This is, I think, one of the reasons why these printed web works are so satisfying. We simultaneously feel traces of the network—something ephemeral and slippery—while holding the material thingness of its output in our hands.

This infrathin condition surrounds us. Hito Steyerl writes that the web is spilling over into other dimensions—that the socio-political implications of the internet are no longer confined solely to being "on" the network. The networked condition pushes itself offline, beyond its own boundaries, and we see evidence of this all around, as the map and the territory it refers to entangle and confuse each other. "Far from being opposites across an unbridgeable chasm, image and world are in many cases just versions of each other. They are not equivalents however, but deficient, excessive, and uneven in relation to each other. And the gap between them gives way to speculation and intense anxiety."[7]

2. Paul Soulellis, "Search, Compile, Publish. Towards a New Artist's Web-to-Print Practice," May 23, 2013, http://soulellis.com/2013/05/search-compile-publish.

3. Alessandro Ludovico, "Post-Digital Publishing, Hybrid and Processual Objects in Print," *APRJA* 3, no. 1 (2014): 79–85, here 81, https://aprja.net//article/view/116088.

4. See https://libraryoftheprintedweb.tumblr.com/ and https://soulellis.com/work/printedweb1/index.html.

5. Kenneth Goldsmith, "The New Aesthetic and The New Writing," *Poetry Foundation*, April 26, 2012, https://www.poetryfoundation.org/harriet-books/2012/04/the-new-aesthetic-and-the-new-writing.

6. Thomas Deane Tucker, *Derridada: Duchamp as Readymade Deconstruction* (Lanham, Plymouth: Lexington Books, 2009), 66.

7. Hito Steyerl, "Too Much World: Is the Internet Dead?," *e-flux* no. 49 (November 2013), https://www.e-flux.com/journal/49/60004/too-much-world-is-the-internet-dead/.

It's this characterization of speculation and anxiety that I'd like to tease open. Is there room for pleasure here, as well? As we copy and remix and distribute versions (of texts, of images, of our own identities) there can be an uncertain satisfaction in feeling the simultaneity of things, of seeing (and/or making) the double and sensing a difference, but not knowing for sure. Pleasure mixed with anxiety also points to another quality, that of the uncanny.

Fig. 2: Oliver Laric, stills from *Versions* (2009ff.).

Oliver Laric's expository *Versions* videos (2009ff.) explore this queasy condition of indifferent difference between copies, multiples, and versions that pass in and out of each other. "An axe that has its handle replaced five times, its head replaced four times." In the translation, one form passes into another—a profound change, and yet it's the same. He describes it more as a condition than a methodology: "Same, same but different. The multiverse is composed of a quantum superposition of infinitely many, increasingly divergent, non-communicating parallel universes or quantum worlds."[8]

An awareness of this multiverse and of our ability, as artists, to disseminate a notion as an array of possibilities that amplifies and expands along networks, is what I've started to refer to as *performing publishing*.

Fig. 3: Clement Valla, *Postcards from Google Earth* (2012).

8. See https://anthology.rhizome.org/versions and https://2015-fall-cca.veryinteractive.net/site/library/versions.

Many printed web works—especially projects that materialize the network, like Clement Valla's self-published *Postcards from Google Earth*—embody (or occupy) this "quantum worlds" multiverse. The notion—in this case, a weird map, a certain depiction, a geographical place—travels along one network and is output into another, continuing to exist simultaneously in both (or more than both) places. For the viewer, there is recognition and familiarity ("I know what this is ...") along with uncanny difference ("... or do I?"). The difference is detected, but not easily identified. It looks like Google, which looks like something familiar, but it's all wrong. It represents a physical place, right? Something is off. Which one is real? Where did it start? Where is the original?

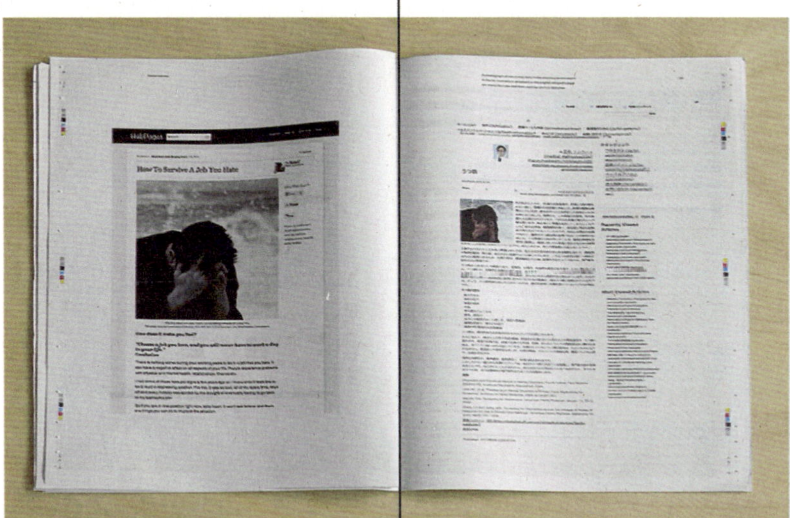

Fig. 4: David Horvitz, "Mood Disorder" (2012ff.) for *Printed Web # 1* (2014).

An uncertain or absent original seems to be a common condition in works that are pushed between environments, as qualities of one state are muddled with aspects of another. Assuming that no copy is an exact replica, when material takes this journey—passing, say, from a live Wikipedia page to captured screenshot to printed artifact, like in "Mood Disorder" for *Printed Web #1* by David Horvitz (2012ff.)—some kind of minimal "charge" or effect carries over along the way. Each of these frames brings its own context, with its own social and political implications.

Steyerl describes the circulating image as becoming "bruised" as it moves. "The bruises of images are its glitches and artifacts, the traces of its rips and transfers. Images are violated, ripped apart, subjected to interrogation and probing. They are stolen, cropped, edited and re-appropriated. They are bought, sold and leased. Manipulated and adulated. Reviled and revered. To participate in the image means to take part in all of this."[9]

A painting by Wade Guyton appears on a hardcore gay sex Tumblr blog and takes on new meaning, transformed into an entirely different project ("1 Month Ago," 2014). As the print version points to web material, we sense that it has "traveled." How far from the original are we? There is no way to know, but what we understand is that there is distance. A sense of aura, an expansive "apparition of a distance, however near it may be,"[10] stretches out into a kind of undetermined, uneasy feeling that our relationship to the primary source can't ever be properly known. Nevertheless, we participate in shifting the transformational value of the material each time the framing changes; as the distance increase (as it circulates), it accumulates potential agency.

This happens clearly in web-to-print works. I understand that I'm touching something that comes from the network. The references to the web are obvious: the browser window, the grid of images, URLs, the conventions of email or Google or Twitter, the

9. Hito Steyerl, "A Thing Like You and Me," *e-flux* no. 15 (April 2010), https://www.e-flux.com/journal/15/61298/a-thing-like-you-and-me/.

10. Paul Soulellis, *Apparition of a distance, however near it may be* (2013), https://soulellis.com/work/apparition/index.html.

pixelation—this is the familiar "vernacular of the web." But something is "off." It's tactile, it's too large, it's static. One kind of mobility has been traded in for another. Its thingness, of the hand, is no longer of the network. The fish is out of the water. How did it get here? Is it dead, or alive? Where does this work live?

Perhaps it's both dead and alive. The work points towards some inability to locate an original. And yet we've found a trace of it, circulating as a notion. Maybe that's all we have. And perhaps the trace isn't just a trace—it looks just like the original. All parts have been replaced.

I didn't visit Labor Gallery in Mexico City where Kenneth Goldsmith staged his open call for *Printing Out the Internet* in July 2013, but I didn't need to. The gallery was filled with 20,000 submissions from around the world, which I can clearly see in this "installation" photograph of the artist in hat and sunglasses, barefoot, lounging on piles of paper, obviously staged.

It's an image that went viral, published first on Tumblr and Twitter and then on countless news services and in printed newspapers, circulating Goldsmith's notion that printing is (can be) democratic, even if all that materiality eventually flattens out. The piles of paper have been output from various networks (the internet, snail mail) but they ultimately disconnect the viewer from those networks, suggesting the immensity of our collective activities on the network while being completely separated from it (the papers are presented chaotically, offline and useless—and were later recycled).

Again, we hover. *Printing Out the Internet* "adds" the internet to the gallery space while simultaneously removing it; it's both there and not there. It's an infrathin event that performs this "spilling" of the internet into a physical gallery space and then flips it back onto the network, refusing any privilege for primary objects or sources.

Fig. 5: Tweets on *Printing Out the Internet*, 2013.

Materializing the network—manifesting it in physical space—can be a pleasurable experience (Goldsmith seems to acknowledge this with his pose). On top of his world, he's relaxed but defiant, like Duchamp's "R. Mutt" signature on *Fountain*; the artist fixes himself on "his" work, produced by the labor of others who materialize it. Goldsmith says that the project is the enactment of capital accumulated to the point that it becomes an image, so this single photo circulating on social media not only depicts the concept but *performs* it perfectly.

Duchamp played with this state between states early on. His 1917 photograph of *Fountain* (taken by Alfred Stieglitz) might be the proto-definition of performing publishing. Almost one hundred years after the readymade itself disappeared, I find myself confronting this photograph in a PDF, depicted as it was originally published in *The Blind Man*.[11]

11. *The Blind Man*, no. 2 (New York, May 1917), 4.

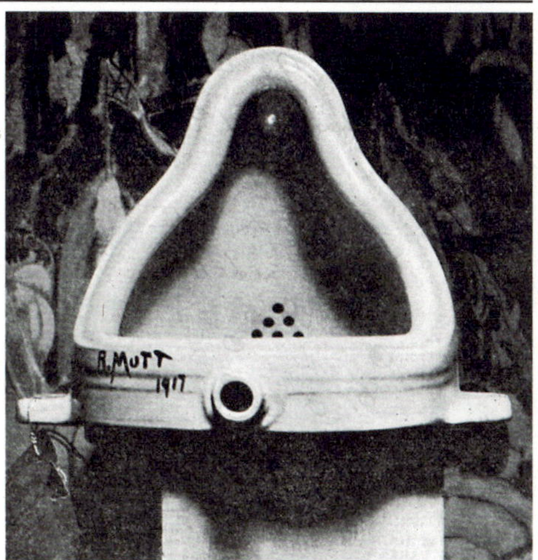

Fig. 6: The original *Fountain* by Marcel Duchamp photographed by Alfred Stieglitz at the 291 (Art Gallery) after the 1917 Society of Independent Artists exhibit. Stieglitz used a backdrop of *The Warriors* by Marsden Hartley to photograph the urinal. The entry tag be clearly seen. (via Wikipedia)

This isn't a singular work; it's an array of views circulating on the network as thousands of JPGs and PDFs. Where is the original *Fountain*? It was dispersed—deliberately so. Duchamp said that the sculpture "was simply placed behind a partition and, for the duration of the exhibition, I didn't know where it was."[12] After that, where it physically went continues to remain a mystery. But prior to its famous rejection for exhibition by the Society of Independent Artists, Duchamp took *Fountain* to 291 Gallery so that it could be photographed by Alfred Stieglitz. The exhibition tag, already fixed to the piece, is clearly visible in the photograph. Duchamp framed and distributed the image in a particular manner, for a public audience—that is, he published it. Seth Price describes this primal scene in *Dispersion* and says that "the fountain does not occupy a single position in space and time; rather, it is a palimpsest of gestures, presentations and positions [...] Duchamp distributed the notion of the Fountain."[13]

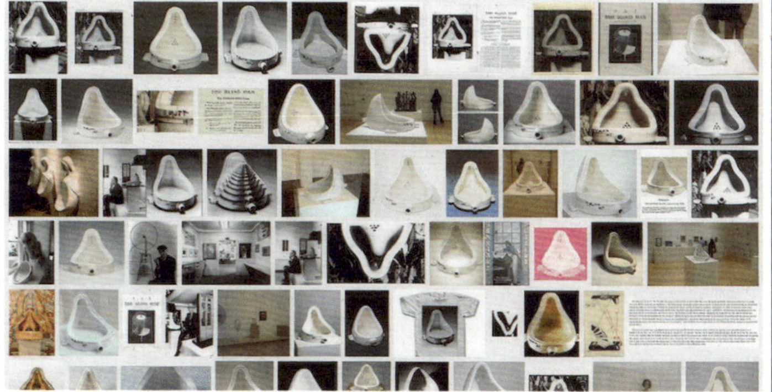

Fig. 7: "Duchamp Fountain," Google image search.

Today, Duchamp's act seems tight and choreographed. We would label these moves—framing, image-making, writing, distribution—as a kind of post-production, or "publishing." In the public dispersion of *Fountain* as an image-notion, Duchamp staged a significant narrative and the way it would be seen, shared, and consumed.

If a static sculpture placed in a gallery space is monument-like in its fixed position (a destination for the viewer), the distributed image-notion of "Fountain" is the monument's souvenir postcard. Or rather, thousands of postcards set in motion by the artist, infinitely multiplying and liquefying as versions that travel on networks—reproductions, facsimiles, books in print, scanned books. Most notably, *Fountain* now circulates on the web in the form of image searches and feeds. The inaccessible, lost original continues to breathe as a distributed hive of reproductions (including seventeen *Fountain* replicas). This hive takes on the significance of the work, strengthening

12. Pierre Cabanne, *Dialogues With Marcel Duchamp* (New York: Da Capo Press, 1987), 55.

13. Seth Price, *Dispersion*, 2016, https://anthology.rhizome.org/dispersion.

the notion of *Fountain*, becoming it while never becoming it (same, same but different). It's a vibrating explosion along networks that originates in the simple, radical act of pushing a work across media. The DNA—photograph, sculpture, publication—co-mingles (and continues to co-mingle today on the internet, within digital archives and in institutional spaces).

This is performing publishing. The self-conscious act of materializing work between environments and pushing it to the network. It is the performance of an idea by distributing it to a networked audience.

Valla's postcards do it quite literally by translating previously "unseen" images from Google Earth into a form that implies its own distribution (i.e., the cards may actually be mailed). He later transforms the work into other versions, like *The Universal Texture Recreated (46°42'3.50"N, 120°26'28.59"W)* for the exhibition "Hike, Hack / Hic et Nunc" at Xpo gallery in Paris (October–November 2014). The work—one of the Google Earth "postcards"—is larger now, and draped over a table like fabric, precariously balanced on legs that are off-kilter and propped up onto a single brick.

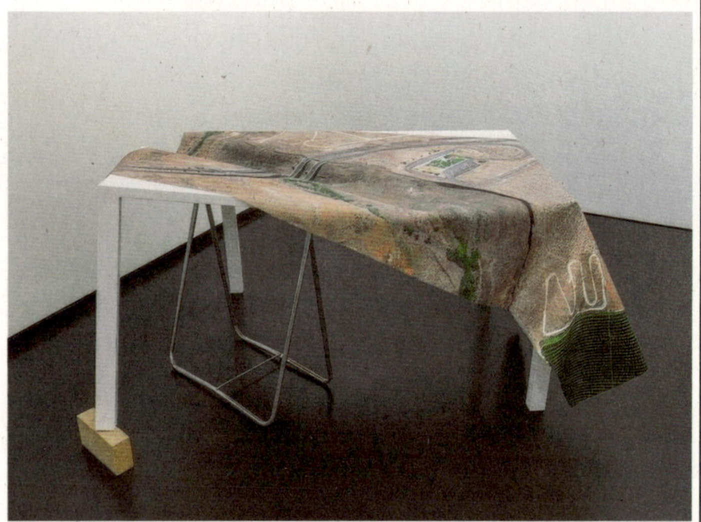

Fig. 8: Clement Valla, *The Universal Texture Recreated (46°42'3.50"N, 120°26'28.59"W)*, exhibition "Hike, Hack / Hic et Nunc" at Xpo gallery, Paris 2014.

It's an unstable image. The potential movement of the postcard as mailed material has been replaced by an object that threatens to collapse. The potential to fall to the floor, either as it slips off the table or as the table crashes down, instills a new anxiety to the work that wasn't present in the postcards. It seems as though we may "lose" the image.

Valla's work is one of nine in the gallery, which is closed to the public for the duration of the exhibition. A special wall constructed at the front of the space on Rue Notre Dame de Nazareth blocks the works from view. In front of the wall, which contains a door leading to the blocked-off gallery, is the gallery director's work desk, visible to the public through the glass storefront. A single amateur painting of a mountain view hangs on the barrier wall ("traditional image"). By appointment only, the viewer may enter the gallery space. (The gallery is normally open to the public). Once inside the hidden space, nine cameras are seen positioned on the individual works; the cams stream the artwork to the gallery's website. An exhibition statement from the curators (NonPrintingCharacter) says that "the works are as if in a television studio: filmed, mediatized, transmitted to the vast public by another channel, of which appreciation by people is not subject to the value of things, but as wrote André Rouillé, to the 'network-value' […] Forget the exhibition, then? No! Rather make a flow out of it than a thing because 'it is information, and not things, which are endowed with value. (Flusser).'"

"Hike, Hack / Hic et Nunc" is significant because it attempts to reconcile physical space with the conditions of the network. The exhibition's "eyes" see for us and continuously transmit the works as technical images, circulating them (publishing them) to the web for our view. The show exists in this infrathin state, neither entirely physical nor strictly virtual. The show's works vibrate between visible and invisible, both dead and alive, like Schrödinger's Cat. My assumptions about the value of the work are questioned, as is my own privilege as subject—is it preferable to consume the works as pure, networked images, or to arrange for a visit to the physical space? Which is more real? Which is primary? Do the versions collapse into each other at some point, or do they remain distinct? Both are mediated, both are framed, both are ways of engaging with the work.

As it circulates the images, the entire exhibition performs publishing, actively spilling itself onto and off the network.

"The more images, mediations, intermediaries, icons are multiplied and overtly fabricated, explicitly and publicly constructed, the more respect I have for their capacities to welcome, to gather, to recollect meaning and sanctity."[14]

Versioning happens on Tumblr, Twitter, Facebook, Instagram, Lulu, Blurb, Buzzfeed, Yelp, Snapchat, New Hive, blogs, e-books, PDFs, and stand-alone websites. Versioning happens on television, dump.fm, YouTube, in SMS and on Amazon. We've learned to entangle copies, versions and remixes and remove the privilege of the primary object. Image-making into a networked condition releases its own explosion of souvenir postcards. Emerging out of the idea of "self-publishing," there is now an expectation that an artist's practice can (must) extend these techniques of production beyond the studio and gallery, onto and off the network. We use these platforms to find material, to circulate work and to engage with audiences, critically or otherwise. Most of this activity is exposed and public; all of it is publishing. "Performing publishing" is ongoing, continuous dissemination to the network.

Printed Web is my attempt to document performing publishing as well as to enact it. I offer artists who work in a networked context a separate space to present work outside of update cycles, diffused attention, constant refreshes, and endless scrolls. It's an invitation to interrupt their own performing publishing to the paused space of print, in the context of a group show. In *Printed Web*, artists have an opportunity to create a new version—to perform their work "off network" in the material context of the printed page.

In the second issue of *Printed Web*, Olia Lialina's *Summer* (2013) is staged in this infrathin way. Her work, originally created for a web browser, is a self-portrait that is already performative. Every time *Summer* is loaded online, individual frames of a looping animation are pulled from different servers at locations around the world. Together, they portray Olia swinging forward and back over a blue-to-white gradient background. These eighteen frames sit on eighteen separate servers associated with the websites of Olia's artist friends; each frame has its own URL that corresponds to the friend's website (i.e., http://www.newrafael.com/olia/summer/).

Fig. 9: Olia Lialina, *Summer* for *Printed Web* #2 (2014).

14. https://2015-fall-cca.veryinteractive.net/site/library/versions.

Each visit to *Summer* produces a fresh performance, pulling the frames from her network to deliver the satisfying animation. In *Summer*, Olia's identity (her portrait) manifests as an apparition on "her" web, a network constructed by the artist; the URLs are offered up as evidence, like shipping receipts. The self-portrait circulates in public as performing publishing through the close community of her own personal network, again and again. In title and in spirit, it's a joyful work.

With the help of Dragan Espenschied, I grabbed screenshots of *Summer* at the exact proportions of *Printed Web*'s dimensions (8.5" × 11"). Each image is inset on a right-hand page with a thin grey line marking the boundary of the depicted browser window; the corresponding left-hand pages are blank, except for a header that says "Printed Web." The artist's name sits above the screengrabs.

Fig. 10: Olia Lialina, *Summer* for *Printed Web* #2 (2014).

While it is possible for the viewer to flip through to get a sense of the animation, *Summer* for *Printed Web* is deliberately too large to replicate the smooth looping or the rapid fire of the loading URLs. Not easily "thumbed," the illusion is broken. The clunky, not-quite-right paper version of the piece points to the other one online by embedding a depiction of the browser window itself, with bookmarks, the URLs and the vernacular of Google Chrome; it's unmistakably a browser-based work. But the magazine-like quality of the page, the thin grey line, the texture and "thingness" of the printout matter in the hand—these are clues that this work isn't quite "on." Perceptually, it vibrates in a lenticular fashion. The indifferent difference between the work as a digital performance and as a printed manifestation in the hand is infrathin (and exciting).

As a print-on-demand publication, *Printed Web* itself enacts the infrathin condition, pushing itself from one state to another without fully committing. It's digitally produced, from the research that I do to the email correspondence with the artists to the receipt of their work in Dropbox—to the content itself. Each issue is designed entirely on a screen. Just before I publish, the print-ready PDF is uploaded to the print-on-demand service, and it is only at this moment that something physical materializes. The finished publication is shipped, one-at-a-time, along more analogue networks. As a print-on-demand object, each issue of *Printed Web* is an extension of the web itself, and yet clearly not.

Printed Web is a digital work disguised as printout material; it performs the web offline. It's a hybrid, transductional creature that mixes screen-based practice with physical thingness. *Printed Web* builds upon a trajectory of artists who push material between contexts, publishing work continuously and publicly.

These places where materiality spills off and onto networks reveal current conditions, but also provide a glimpse of something yet to come, some kind of intense, slippery state where hybrid works replicate continuously, translate automatically, and move seamlessly between media, beyond the frames of printed page, web page, or physical space. A "neverending becoming."[15] Brian Droitcour describes art's current disposition as more "proto-" than post(-internet)—that the proto- points to the future, to multiplicity and transformative potential.[16] As image and world become increasingly entangled, I expect we'll see more self-aware, *proto* spaces like "Hike, Hack / Hic et Nunc" and *Printed Web* blown open for artists to mix, embed, circulate, and perform publishing to the network.

"The possible, implying the becoming—the passage from one to the other takes place in the infra-thin."[17]

15. Zachary Kaplan, "Artist Profile: Jeanette Hayes" (interview), *Rhizome*, November 25, 2014, https://rhizome.org/editorial/2014/nov/25/artist-profile-jeanette-hayes/.

16. Brian Droitcour, "Why I Hate Post-Internet Art," *Culture Two* (blog), March 31, 2014, https://culturetwo.wordpress.com/2014/03/31/why-i-hate-post-internet-art/.

17. Marcel Duchamp, *Notes*, arranged and transl. by Paul Matisse (Boston: G.K. Hall, 1983), 45.

Michael Hagner

The Post-digital Photobook[1]

1. This essay further develops themes and theses that I first tried out in two texts: "The Photobook, Postdigital," *Texte zur Kunst,* no. 99 (2015): 102–119, and "Hyperpresence and Viewing. The Photobook under Digital Conditions," in *Das Fotobuch in Kunst und Gesellschaft. Partizipative Potentiale eines Mediums*, ed. Anne-Katrin Bicher et al. (Berlin: Jovis, 2020), 407–412.

The photobook has never been more of a book than it is today. In other words, following its digital transformation, photography's intense liaison with book culture can be regarded as a new stage in its history, despite all the affinities photography has had with books from the very beginning in 1839. The opulent coffee table book and the small, handy photobook are still among photography's most important media, but a wide variety of explorative formats have developed in between, giving both books and photography a new physiognomy. The book market has responded to this with the foundation of new publishing houses in recent years, and self-published books, unlike in all other book genres, have become an integral part of a decentralized market that operates beyond traditional bookstores and destructive global providers like Amazon.[2] There are festivals for artist's books and photobooks, and books have occupied a prominent space at the traditional photo fairs (Paris, Arles, New York, Amsterdam, etc.). Classics of the photobook are being reissued in various formats, a profitable antiquarian book market has developed in the last twenty-five years, and the darkness in which the history of the photobook was long shrouded is also beginning to lift. Even museum exhibitions are devoted to it—an unmistakable indication that the photobook has come into its own.[3]

It has often been stated that this boom is a twenty-first-century phenomenon. There are some precursors here, but when the Dutch photographer Ralph Prins declared the photobook to be an independent art form in 1969, the most remarkable thing about it is that no one seems to have been interested in it at the time.[4] From today's perspective, the period around 1970 represented a phase of great productivity for the photobook. Yet, two of its most important phenomena—the Japanese photobook and the reinvention of the artist's book as *libro povero*—did not have any significant effect on photographic discourse at the time. The book was considered a more or less usable container for photographs. Some regarded it as a democratic medium for the wide circulation of images, while others stressed its inferiority in comparison to museum print quality presented in a white cube. It was not until the turn of the millennium that the photobook emancipated itself from its purely serving function. Recently, these developments have been described as a "paradigm shift in photography."[5] There is no doubt that a paradigm shift has taken place, but it concerns first of all the social and technical conditions under which photography takes place. There is no event, no viewing, no communication, no self-expression that is not captured in an image, so that photography has become as much a part of everyday human activity as saying hello or brushing one's teeth. Photos are uploaded, downloaded, posted, liked, shown, faked, shared, manipulated, and commented on. Billions of photographs circulate on the various social media platforms. So, what is the point of pictures in a printed book when countless digital images are available to all on the net? Why is the photobook flourishing?

An explanation for this seemingly counterintuitive development will hardly be satisfied with understanding it as a marginal phenomenon of the viral dissemination of images, let alone as a nostalgic return to the good old letterpress printing. It is rather the other way around: the photobook of the early twenty-first century owes its existence to the digital transformation and its technical, creative, and economic perspectives.[6] This is also true for other areas of book culture, and therefore this does not yet offer a sufficient explanation as to why photobooks are attracting so much attention at a time when paper is no longer the outstanding information carrier. A major role is undoubtedly played by the fact that photographs, which float freely in the digital image universe, are concen-

2. Clément Cheroux estimates that the number of publishing houses publishing partially or exclusively photobooks has "multiplied by almost five" since 2000. See Cheroux, "The New Face of Photophilia," *The PhotoBook Review* 020 (Fall 2021): 3–5, https://aperture.org/editorial/has-the-photobook-become-more-interesting-than-photographs-themselves/. All network sources last accessed 07/01/2022.

3. A pioneering effort was the exhibition curated by Horacio Fernández in Madrid in 1999, which also brought with it a catalogue of the same name: *Fotografía pública. Photography in Print 1919–1939* (Madrid: Museo Nacional Centro de Arte Reina Sofía, 1999). More recent examples are Markus Schaden et al., *The PhotoBookMuseum, Catalogue Box* (Dortmund: Kettler, 2014); Moritz Neumüller, ed., *Photobook Phenomenon* (Barcelona: CCCCB / Fundación Foto Colectania, 2017).

4. See Rik Suermondt, "From documentary picture-book to artist's book," in *Photography between Covers: The Dutch Documentary Photobook after 1945*, ed. Mattie Boom and Rik Suermondt (Amsterdam: Fragment, 1989), 12–47, here 12.

5. See Schaden et al., *The PhotoBookMuseum*.

6. For David Campany, "the take up of the term 'photobook' is a consequence of the internet, and so is the field of study it marks." See David Campany, "The 'Photobook': What's in a Name?," *The Photobook Review* 007 (Winter 2014), https://davidcampany.com/the-photobook-whats-in-a-name/.

trated or decentered in the medium of the printed book in such a way that, in the words of Teju Cole, "you see not only what something looks like, but how someone looks."[7] How the photographer looks does not only depend on the camera used, but also on whether the pictures are presented on paper, on the wall, or on the screen. The printed book is often seen as the antithesis of the digital screen, but it's not that simple. The photobook builds on the digital media, understands their logic, but does not succumb to them. It insists on its own way of dealing with images and finding surprising forms and formats of representing them.[8] Therein lies a considerable part of its visual power.

It would therefore be unproductive to attribute the proliferation of the photobook to any persistent forces of analog printing, because this would leave out the manifold references to the digital sphere. In order to define these references more precisely, I would like to introduce the concept of the post-digital photobook. A digital book is a designed conglomerate of images or texts published on a digital platform, that is, an e-book, to which there may or may not be a printed counterpart. A post-digital book, on the other hand, signifies the abandonment of that telos that inevitably leads to a digital product. The digital comes into play at all stages of the photobook's creation: as a source of ideas and of images, as a principle capable of simulation, as an inexpensive and flexible technology for producing books, as a decentralized way of selling books through book fairs, galleries, small publishers, or self-publishing, and finally as a communicative space for dialogue about photobooks. But contrary to what Alessandro Ludovico suggests in his insightful book *Post-Digital Print*, it would be insufficient to describe as post-digital only a hybrid of digital and printed books, which would be achieved when printed and digital publications can no longer be categorically distinguished from one another.[9] This way of thinking ultimately assumes the finished product to be a quasi-natural entity and is reminiscent of that transhumanist notion of singularity in which the human mind and artificial intelligence merge. We are a long way from such hybrids in book culture, although hybrid publications do of course exist. By contrast, the point of post-digital print is that the term refers to the ontological differences between paper and the digital screen and reflects the socio-technical conditions of hybrid forms.

The concept of the post-digital has taken significant turns in recent years. In his afterword to Ludovico's 2012 book, for example, Florian Cramer argues that in the "post-digital age, the question of whether or not something is digital is no longer really important."[10] Here, too, the distinction between analog and digital is suspended from the outset. In a recently published conversation, however, obviously influenced by the lockdown imposed during the Covid-19 pandemic and the further seepage of digital technologies into everyday life, Cramer sees the essential usefulness of the term post-digital in that "it can help to complicate the terms 'digital' and 'analog.'"[11] If ten years ago the digital seemed set as the alpha and omega of our experience, the recent problematization of the terms is an indication that it is not sufficient to go back to business as usual after the digital revolution. The post-digital photobook would then be characterized by the fact that its medial properties enable a different view of the digital—sometimes making the differences with the analog abundantly clear, sometimes blurring the differences between digital and analog. In this sense, post-digital would mean productively questioning the supposed self-evident nature of the digital. This refers to the technical processes of the digital, which Hannes Bajohr considers to be a core task of post-digital writing, because this is the only way "to bring back to consciousness the otherwise elusive process of technization and its resulting concept of reality."[12]

But this also refers to making visible the transhistorical references that are inherent in the interweavings of the digital with the analog. Even after the digital transformation, photography and book culture are historically predisposed practices that

7. Teju Cole, "Smell the ink and drift away: why I find solace in photobooks," *The Guardian*, February 24, 2020, https://www.theguardian.com/artanddesign/2020/feb/24/teju-cole-photobooks-fernweh.

8. Cheroux points out that legendary New York photo curator John Szarkowski anticipated the positive effect of digital media on printed photobooks as early as 2005. See Cheroux, "The New Face of Photophilia."

9. Alessandro Ludovico, *Post-Digital Print. The Mutation of Publishing since 1894* (Eindhoven: Onomatopee, 2012), 156.

10. Florian Cramer, "Afterword," in Ludovico, *Post-Digital Print*, 162.

11. Florian Camer and Petar Jandric, "Postdigital: A Term That Sucks but Is Useful," *Postdigital Science and Education* 3 (2021), 966–989, here 985, https://link.springer.com/article/10.1007/s42438-021-00225-9.

12. Hannes Bajohr, "Print on Demand as Strategy and Genre: Auto-Factography and Post-Digital Writing," in this volume, 629–639, 632.

are aware of these references and always allude to them in their practice.

Such a medial, aesthetic, and epistemic reflection of photography in the printed format was not necessarily foreseeable, for just as the number of books and of publishers specializing in photobooks was growing larger and larger, in many places the death knell was ringing for the printed book. The promising future of the World Wide Web and digital reading devices called forth prophets who painted the post-Gutenberg galaxy in glaring colors and gave the book at most a few more years. *Print is dead*—such was the formula that has become one of the most pompous errors in recent media history. The diagnosis that paper was no longer the leading medium for consuming words and images, knowledge and entertainment was largely correct. What was wrong was the prediction of the end of printing. The mobilization of the photobook as a paradoxical element in the digital system is not as unique as it may seem, for the development of the photobook in the twentieth century, marked by ruptures and shifts, already took place in close connection with larger media transformations. Although there are still numerous blank spots in this history, the heyday of the photobook in the interwar period and the first decades after the Second World War can hardly be understood independently of the rise of film, radio, television, and the ever-new forms of images generated by the advertising industry. I do not want to exhaustively explain the historical development of the photobook in this way, but the resonance with other media formats is key to the flexible dynamics of the printed book.

The first major boom in the photobook came in the years after the First World War, with Paris and the Weimar Republic as its epicenters.[13] In 1928, the typographer Jan Tschichold noted "the unique triumphal progress of photography into book production."[14] This statement referred primarily to mass media such as daily newspapers and magazines, but it also led Tschichold to the expression "the new book." Half a century before Paul Virilio coined the term dromology, Tschichold noted the pull of visual speed for the logic of the book: "The speed and urgency of films has also influenced literature in the direction of second-by-second action."[15] And it was not only literature that was changing, but also book design itself, with photographs becoming a natural part of it, even if only as book covers. Here Tschichold pointed to iconic works by artists such as El Lissitzky, László Moholy-Nagy, Alexander Rodchenko, Man Ray, and Hannah Höch. As pure picture books or in the interplay of photography and typography, they represented a new type of book that provoked the question as to "whether photography is a field of art or whether it is to be valued only as a document of the new way of seeing."[16]

Basically, photography has always drawn its appeal from the nervous tension between these two positions, but what significance photobooks have in this context is a question that is not so easy to answer. Undeniably, the book took a decisive step toward becoming an autonomous art form with photography, but conversely, photography benefited decisively from the medium of the book, and this was understood in terms of a "school of seeing." Walter Benjamin's famous sentence "in photography, exhibition value begins to drive back cult value on all fronts"[17] does not so much mean being able to show the same picture in several exhibitions at the same time, but it is about reproduction in a book or in a magazine. The examples of images Benjamin cites in his "Little History of Photography"—Eugène Atget, August Sander, Germaine Krull, Karl Blossfeldt—are taken exclusively from books in which they were reproduced.[18]

In short, the photobook developed during this period on the one hand into an artist's book, and on the other hand into a democratic and pedagogical medium for the presentation, circulation, and reception of photography. For some it was both at the same time, while others emphasized this or that aspect. For Benjamin, at any rate, photogra-

13. The focus of historical research to date has been on the Weimar Republic. See, for example, Pepper Stetler, *Stop Reading! Look! Modern Vision and the Weimar Photographic Book* (Ann Arbor: University of Michigan Press, 2015); Mareike Stoll, *ABC der Photographie. Photobücher der Weimarer Republik als Schulen des Sehens* (Cologne: Walther König, 2018); Steffen Siegel, *Fotogeschichte aus dem Geist des Fotobuchs* (Göttingen: Wallstein, 2019).

14. Jan Tschichold, *The New Typography. A Handbook for Modern Designers*, transl. by Ruari McLean (Berkeley, Los Angeles, London: University of California Press, 1995), 87.

15. Tschichold, *The New Typography*, 218.

16. Wilhelm Lotz, "Fotobücher," *Die Form: Zeitschrift für gestaltende Arbeit* 6, no. 2 (1931): 28–37, here 28.

17. Walter Benjamin, "The Work of Art in the Age of Its Technological Reproducibility: Second Version," in *The Work of Art in the Age of Its Technological Reproducibility and Other Writings on Media*, ed. by Michael W. Jennings, Brigid Doherty, and Thomas Y. Levin (Cambridge and London: The Belknap Press, 2008), 19–55, 27.

18. Walter Benjamin, "Little History of Photography," in *The Work of Art*, 274–298.

phy degenerates into "schmock" if it is guided by parameters like creative imagination, artistic value, and marketability. Its importance lies in the substitution of cult value by exhibition value and the emphasis on comparative viewing. For example, the visual power of Krull or Blossfeldt is less revealed in the individual photograph than in juxtaposing the images in the book. The comparison made physically possible with the finger in the book and the turning of the page is a central element of visual literacy, as first Moholy-Nagy and then Benjamin had postulated with the negative formulation that the person ignorant of photography is the illiterate of the future.[19]

For decades after the Second World War, books and printed magazines remained the authoritative media for publishing photographic works in a larger context.[20] Yet, the second golden age of the photobook went hand in hand with a creeping digression between photography and the photobook. This development can be ascribed to a strategic and subsequent commercial revaluation of the individual image, again emblematically demonstrated in a book: John Szarkowski's *Looking at Photographs.* Although Szarkowski, the chief curator of MoMA's photography department between 1962 and 1991, was concerned with demonstrating the visual range of the medium, he created an American-dominated canon of photographers whose works were signaled as worthwhile to collect. The more attention Szarkowski's curated solo exhibitions at MoMA received, and the more other museums collected and exhibited photographs, the more a veritable market developed. The ironic point here was that the coveted vintages of Henri Cartier-Bresson, André Kertész, and other eminent photographers were often agency prints that were sent to printers to reproduce the images in books or magazines.[21] What had originally been produced and used as purely utilitarian images mutated into originals on the art market. What could be found on the flea market until the 1980s was now offered at auctions, fairs, and in catalogues.

Photobooks developed their own visual power in this historical process, and yet the question of whether the photobook was a document, a container, an archive, an appetizer, a medium for the dissemination of images, or a visual form in its own right was missing. Instead, photo literature concerning the *cult value* of photography continued to work on the question of whether photography is art or not, while photo theory focusing on its *exhibition value* turned to questions of mediality, reception, and communication.[22] In this context, the book was absent as an autonomous medium because it was just considered as an image container. It would be instructive to review the literature on photography and especially the photographic theory of the second half of the twentieth century for the discussion of the photobook. Here it may suffice to point out that in the classic studies of Susan Sontag and Roland Barthes, the photobook does not appear as a category in its own right. There may be good reasons for this absence—skepticism toward photographic authorship, individualization of an image with the search for its *punctum*—but as a consequence, the history and theory of photography ignored the material, aesthetic, economic, and cultural conditions under which photographs appear in photobooks.

Sontag points out that the photobook has had its importance as the most influential medium for compiling, preserving, and disseminating photographs in the past, but she sees no future prospects for the book. Her objection that photographs appear in the book as a reduced "image of an image" suggests that the vintage print on the museum wall is more original than the reproduction in the book—as if there were an original size in photography. Even stranger is Sontag's criticism that a book suggests "[t]he sequence in which the photographs are to be looked at," by which she underestimates the possibilities of flipping back and forth as well as the care that many photographers have put into selecting and arranging the images in their books.[23] Consistently, her penetrating analysis of Diane Arbus's images is limited to highlighting the retrospective at MoMA without

19. László Moholy-Nagy, "Diskussion über Ernst Kallais Artikel 'Malerei und Photographie,'" in *Internationale Revue* 10, no. 6 (1927): 233–234, here 233, https://www.dbnl.org/tekst/_int001inte01_01/_int001inte01_01_0059.php; Benjamin, "Little History of Photography."

20. For approaches to researching the photobook after 1945, see Burcu Dogramaci et al., ed., *Gedruckt und erblättert. Das Fotobuch als Medium ästhetischer Artikulation seit den 1940er Jahren* (Cologne: Walther König, 2016).

21. See Martin Parr and Garry Badger, *The Photobook: A History*, vol. 1 (London: Phaidon Press, 2004), 9.

22. See Wolfgang Kemp, "Theorie der Fotografie 1945–1980," in *Theorie der Fotografie III 1945–1980* (Munich: Schirmer/Mosel, 1983), 13–37, here 36–37. The question of photography as art is the focus of Wilfried Wiegand, ed., *Die Wahrheit der Photographie. Klassische Bekenntnisse zu einer neuen Kunst* (Frankfurt a. M.: Fischer, 1981).

23. Both quotations Susan Sontag, *On Photography* (London: Penguin, 2019), 3.

mentioning the monograph *Diane Arbus*, which has become iconic and has been reprinted again and again.[24] Museum value has supplanted book value. As a consequence, the theoretical reflection on photography missed the synthesis of book and photography observable since the 1960s, for example the transformation of the artist's book by photography and the florescence of the photobook in Japan.

Japanese photography virtually threw itself into the major themes of postwar history: the processing of the atomic bombs dropped on Hiroshima and Nagasaki, the transformation of society that began with the American occupation and was marked by industrialization, technologization, urbanization, and consumer culture, and the intensifying conflicts between traditional Japanese and Western lifestyle. The trauma of destruction, astonishment at the changing physiognomy of cities, and disorientation in the face of new ways of life—for all these modes of reaction, photography found radical forms of visualization to sharpen the senses for this historical transformation. The photobook played a dominant role in this process, and not only for lack of a gallery and exhibition culture. Photographers and book designers "overcame the idea of the photobook as an image of an original in the awareness that the photobook itself is an original."[25] Photographers like Daido Moriyama and Nobuyoshi Araki were interested in printing techniques and even worked with photocopying machines because they were convinced that, in Moriyama's words, "my photographs are only completed on the printed page."[26] This statement has often been quoted in the last twenty-five years, but in the 1970s this position marked the opposite of what Susan Sontag had stated. For Moriyama, photography in the book was fascinating not in spite of but because of the difference between the image on the book page and the vintage print on the wall. Depending on the printing technique, page size, paper, and design, the same image could be viewed in different ways. This visual difference has led photographers in and outside Japan to rely not on reprints or facsimiles when reissuing their books, but on a completely different book design. In this way, the new edition is no longer bound to an older original. It forms an independent artistic position that refers to its predecessor at most in allusions and quotations.

The protagonists of Japanese photography have always pointed out that Robert Frank's *Les Américains*, and even more so William Klein's *Life is Good and Good for You in New York*, with its tightly packed, mostly full-page grainy close-ups that seem like arrested image interferences from an endless film, were a definitive inspiration for them.[27] The grainy, black-dominated shots, often out of focus and lacking a center, combined with a broad interest in all facets of image and book production, led to a radical view of Japanese reality. The three issues of the magazine *Provoke* (1968–1970) and monographs by its main contributors, like Moriyama or Takuma Nakahira, liberated the photobook from the triviality of the container.[28]

The other example of the autonomization of the photobook is related to the move away from the over-determined single image in the tradition of the *decisive moment* (Cartier-Bresson), which was committed to the aesthetic of the masterpiece. Beginning in 1963, Ed Ruscha published unadorned octavo-sized booklets, most of them 48 pages long, on an annual basis. They contained deliberately amateurishly taken photographs of supposedly inconsequential places such as gas stations, parking lots, swimming pools, or apartments in Los Angeles. These books broke with everything that artist's books had meant up to that point by engaging in image criticism with images. Ruscha's "amateurist mimesis"[29] rejected the artful, careful design of the individual image and its autonomy, which secured it a place on the museum wall. Ruscha, and after him Hans-Peter Feldmann and others, attached importance to the strict composition of uncomplicated images and accommodated them in the seriality of the book pages.[30] The photobook once

24. Sontag, *On Photography*, 33–52. See Diane Arbus, *Diane Arbus*, ed. Doon Arbus and Marvin Israel (New York: Aperture, 1972).

25. Ivan Vartanian, "The Japanese Photobook. Toward Immediate Media," in *Japanese Photobooks of the 1960s and 1970s*, ed. Ryuchi Kaneko and Ivan Vartanian (New York: Aperture, 2009), 11–23, here 19.

26. "Photography in Print. An Interview with Daido Moriyama," in Kaneko and Vartanian, *Japanese Photobooks*, 25–29, here 27.

27. Robert Frank, *Les Américains* (Paris: Delpire, 1958); William Klein, *Life is Good and Good for You in New York* (Paris: Seuil, 1956).

28. Takuma Nakahira, *For a Language to Come* (Tokyo: Osiris, 1970); Daido Moriyama, *Shashin yo sayonara. Farewell to Photography* (Tokyo: Shashin Hyoron-sha, 1972).

29. Jeff Wall, "Zeichen der Indifferenz: Aspekte der Photographie in der, oder als, Konzeptkunst," in *Szenarien im Bildraum der Wirklichkeit. Essays und Interviews* (Dresden: Verlag der Kunst, 1997), 375–434, here 428.

30. On the concept of the uncomplicated image, see Michael Hagner/Vera Wolff, "Unkomplizierte Bilder," in *Einwegbilder*, ed. Inge Hinterwaldner, Michael Hagner, and Vera Wolff (Paderborn: Fink, 2016), 85–107.

again turned out to be democratic because it was affordable for everyone and had a creative *povertà* that was calculated with subtle sophistication.[31] In tacit resonance with Guy Debord's notion of the society of the spectacle, Ruscha and Feldmann explored the anti-spectacular dimension in the American and West German way of life of the 1960s and 1970s: no decisive moment, no focal point, no sensation, and no dynamics, only banal situations, objects, and motifs that had their natural habitat in visual mass culture.

The photobook had already been an autonomous pictorial work in the 1920s, but at that time it did not have to distinguish itself from the individual artistic image, because photographs were bound to the representational space of the book anyway. Photographic artist's books in the wake of Ruscha and Feldmann did not assemble a number of beautiful images, but exposed the image to the order of the book. They thus pursued their own selection criteria and rules, ideas of order, and modes of representation. The result was books as different as *Anonymous Sculptures* by Bernd and Hilla Becher or *Evidence* by Mike Mandel and Larry Sultan, which nevertheless met in being at once monument and document, experimental arrangement and archive, artistic statement and training atlas for the new way of seeing in an age of industrial decline and the dawn of post-industrial technologies.[32]

Whereas in the twentieth century a couple of emblematic photobooks set the genre vibrating, such salient books can be less clearly identified for the recent boom. Perhaps we still lack distance, or perhaps the importance of individual iconic and style-forming books has diminished in the diversity of remarkable productions. Why photobooks? Their characterization as post-digital would remain all too abstract without an understanding of the changes in the art market that are best described as the millennial effect. At the dawn of the new century, taking stock of what might have been the harvest of the past was an obvious option that converged perfectly with strategic interests in the art market. If Horacio Fernández's 1999 book and exhibition project *Fotografía pública* was an archaeological lifting of a photobook culture that had been at least partially buried, the volume *The Book of 101 Books* published two years later by the New York bookseller, gallery owner, and publisher Andrew Roth openly flaunted its address to potential collectors in the United States through boastful opulence and a rustic prioritization of American photobooks.[33] The extent to which the international market had been waiting for such an invitation became apparent in 2004 with the first volume of *The Photobook: A History* by Martin Parr and Gerry Badger.[34] It is plausible that the authors were not primarily concerned with compiling a canon of the photobook worthy of collection. Nevertheless, many of the books praised by Parr—himself a successful photographer—and Badger became precious collectors' items. Some went out of print shortly after their publication and were then offered at steep prices. The boom of the photobook also means that it has entered the commodity space of contemporary art and become an object of speculation.

The valorization of *The Photobook* as an authoritative reference work and buying guide for old and new collectors has somewhat obscured the fact that these volumes have the virtue of letting their radar roam globally. As a result, the traditional focus on the United States, Europe, and Japan has become moot. In the wake of Parr and Badger, more than a dozen lavishly designed volumes on national or regional photobook traditions have been published. They are all canon-builders and buying guides, but when these compilations include not only the traditions of Switzerland, the Soviet Union, or the Netherlands, but also Latin America and China, the knowledge of what photobooks are in their global variety is greatly expanded.[35] In current book production, too, the vibrancy of the photobook is an effect of artistic globalization. While New York, London, and Paris continue to be relevant sites of

31. For an overview of the small books inspired by Ruscha, see Jeff Brouws et al., ed., *Various Small Books. Referencing Various Small Books by Ed Ruscha* (Cambridge/MA: The MIT Press, 2013).

32. Bernd and Hilla Becher, *Anonyme Skulpturen. Eine Typologie technischer Bauten* (Düsseldorf: Art Press Verlag, 1970); Mike Mandel and Larry Sultan, *Evidence*, self-published 1977. For an enigmatic theoretical description of this socio-technological transformation see Jean-François Lyotard, *The Postmodern Condition: A Report on Knowledge* (Minneapolis: Manchester University Press, 1984).

33. Andrew Roth, *The Book of 101 Books. Seminal Photographic Books of the Twentieth Century* (New York: Roth Horowitz, 2001).

34. Parr and Badger, *The Photobook*

35. Peter Pfrunder et al., ed., *Schweizer Fotobücher 1927 bis heute: eine andere Geschichte der Fotografie* (Baden: Fotostiftung Schweiz, Lars Müller Publishers, 2011); Frits Giertsberg and Rik Suermondt, *The Dutch Photobook: A Thematic Selection from 1945 Onwards* (New York: Aperture, 2012); Horacio Fernández, *The Latin American Photobook* (Madrid and New York: Aperture, 2011); Martin Parr and Wassink Lundgren, ed., *The Chinese Photobook: From the 1900s to the Present* (New York: Aperture, 2015).

photobook culture, there no longer seems to be a clearly defined center from which to gaze with exoticist eyes upon the Other. There is a multitude of places where, despite unequal financial conditions, photobooks are conceived and designed, produced and sold, viewed and discussed.

All of this would be inconceivable without digital technologies and the internet, which interconnects these places. Internet culture understood as a resource, communication, and trading space is perhaps the most important keyword for photobook culture. Self-published zines, so-called indie photobooks in small and very small publishing houses, print-on-demand—the ease and flexibility of digital printing processes has made possible a variety of book types that would hardly have been conceivable under the cumbersome, costly production conditions of conventional photobook publishers. Ruscha and Feldmann had demonstrated the principle of the self-published book, in which they controlled every step of the production process, and with new technological options self-publishing has expanded like no other book genre. While financing and distributing self-published or micro-published books is a notoriously tedious business despite the internet and (sometimes) crowdsourcing, incisive publishing initiatives have nevertheless emerged under these conditions. The most interesting of these projects have combined curatorial, archival, and research activities with the publication of photobooks. The Archive of Modern Conflict (AMC), which emerged from a collection of historical war photography, and the Self Publish, Be Happy (SPBH) network, founded after the 2008 financial crisis, have gained their reputation with the publication of some of the most incisive photobooks of the last decade, but at the same time, they have organized politically ambitious exhibitions, workshops, and internet forums.

SPBH is guided by the manifesto of its founder Bruno Ceschel, according to which DIY photobooks that are directed against political, economic, racist, or sexual oppression are best produced under conditions of collaboration and communitarian values.[36] Consequently, the *Image of Whiteness* anthology is a collaborative work composed of images and texts that intertwine racist connotations of a white camera gaze with the image of hegemonic whiteness. At the same time, SPBH also produces expensive editions and spectacular books such as Lorenzo Vitturi's *Dalston Anatomy*, a garish and colorful homage to the African traders at Dalston's Ridley Road Market.[37] Undoubtedly, there is a hedonistic premise and promise in the slogan *Be Happy*, which is fully realized by such artist's books precisely because they remain a precious commodity. Further examples of seductively beautiful, clever, and carefully crafted self-published photobooks include Carolyn Drake's *Two Rivers*, which traces living conditions, politics, and geography in the former Soviet republics of Central Asia; Cristina de Middel's *The Afronauts*, which tells a fictional story about a Dadaist space project in 1960s Zambia; and Laura El-Tantawy's *In the Shadow of Pyramids*, which crosses events in Tahrir Square during the Arab Spring with her own biography.[38]

These books are entitled to a reception that does justice to their political and aesthetic wit, but they also became incunabula of the contemporary photobook almost as soon as they were published, with the double effect that they are not missing from any compilation of the salient recent photobooks (not even here!), and that they have mutated from affordable "democratic multiples"[39] to art market gems, much like Ruscha's and Feldmann's artist's books. It would be worth analyzing more closely how the political aspirations expressed in these books relate to their iconization. Not that Vitturi, Drake, Middel, or El-Tantawy are to be understood as genuinely political artists who can be assigned to the tradition of the documentary or protest photobook. But for the assessment of the post-digital photobook in the early twenty-first century, it is worthwhile to ask why they belong to the realm of exhibition value rather than that of cult value. One possible answer to this question is related to playful experimentation with the book genre itself.

If nothing else, AMC and SPBH have published works that are more like book objects with special tactile qualities than ordinary books. Thomas Sauvin, a photo curator closely associated with AMC,

36. See Bruno Ceschel, *Self Publish, Be Happy: A DIY Photobook Manual and Manifesto* (New York: Aperture, 2015).
37. Lorenzo Vitturi, *Dalston Anatomy* (London: Jibijana Books, 2013); Daniel C. Blight, ed., *The Image of Whiteness: Contemporary Photography and Racialization* (London: Artbook D.A.P., 2019).
38. Carolyn Drake, *Two Rivers*, self-published 2013; Cristina de Middel, *The Afronauts*, self-published 2012; Laura El-Tantawy, *In the Shadow of Pyramids*, self-published 2015.
39. See Johanna Drucker, *The Century of Artists' Books* (New York: Granary Books, 1995), 72.

has published playing-card-sized leporello albums of Chinese family snapshots whose enigmatic title, *Silvermine*, refers to the place where he found the anonymous photographs: a recycling plant in Beijing for filtering silver nitrate from film negatives. His booklet *Until Death Do Us Part*, a cryptic satire on the ludicrous consumption of cigarettes at Chinese weddings, is housed in an original cigarette packet, so that the haptic impression is essential for its reception.[40] If this work of Sauvin already points in the direction of a multiple, *Quanshen*, in which stapled-together cards slide out of a plastic box and spread open like a fan to reveal sloppy portrait shots from Chinese studios, is more like a sculptural object that plays with the material and aesthetic boundaries of the book.[41] The boundaries between artist's book and photobook have long been porous, and the same is now true of the distinction between book and non-book.[42] This includes turning the pages themselves into experimental design arrangements that continually vary the view of the photographs. In El-Tantawy's literally dreamlike object *Beyond Here Is Nothing*, the pages have to be unfolded one after the other to the left, right, and top in a nested arrangement, and then folded back together again with great attention so as not to create chaos.[43]

To take up Benjamin's terminology once again: even if the works discussed here are irrelevant to the photography market dominated by galleries, museums, and wealthy collectors, their cult value, which draws on the rarity of the object in the aesthetic reckoning, cannot be entirely dismissed. But for one thing, the refined, sensually expansive design conceals a subversive exhibition value that sharpens the political-emancipatory gaze. Moreover, most of the photographers mentioned here are active on Instagram or other social media, which allows them to disseminate their work far beyond the books. What does this mean for the relationship between digital and analog publication formats? As already emphasized, in the twentieth century, photobooks were repeatedly understood as a democratic medium that enables a broader audience to engage with photography. With the digital revolution, books have largely ceded this function to the internet. The unhindered provision and global circulation of images on the net offers a higher level of democratization—at least that's what people thought for a few years after the advent of social media, but it has turned out that the equation of political emancipation and the internet doesn't work out so easily.

With regard to photographic images, it remains unclear whether their hyperpresence online has led to a broader visual literacy and autonomization of cultural techniques or to a general blunting. Such debates have been particularly intense in the example of the selfie: Is this a new chapter in the history of narcissism or a continuation of the self-portrait for the purpose of social interaction? On the one hand, selfies are seen as an expression of a democratic transformation of image culture, and critical objections are dismissed as cultural pessimism or even as a pointless pathologization of new social phenomena.[44] On the other hand, the disappearance of the (self-)image in the selfie is diagnosed, and Vilém Flusser's old dictum is pertinent, according to which the (visually) "illiterate are no longer excluded, as they used to be, from a culture encoded in texts, but participate almost totally in a culture encoded in images."[45] This logic is used to lament the decline of photography, which has now spread from the internet to exhibition practice as well.[46]

Proponents and critics of networked photography as a sub-phenomenon of networked culture are still irreconcilably opposed to each other, which is, among other things, an expression of being overwhelmed by the consequences of the digital revolution. This confusing situation is unlikely to change in the foreseeable future. In this context, the printed book is often assigned the role of a necessary pause sign that briefly interrupts the seemingly unstoppable flow of information on the internet. This also applies to the photobook. For Teju Cole, who first became known as a writer and more re-

40. Thomas Sauvin, *Silvermine* (London, 2013); Thomas Sauvin, *Until Death Do Us Part* (Beijing, 2015).

41. Thomas Sauvin, *Quanshen* (London, 2013).

42. See Steffen Siegel, "Was ist kein Fotobuch?", in *Fotogeschichte* 159 (2021), 43–47, here 47. On the photographic artist's book, see Hans Dickel, *Künstlerbücher mit Photographie seit 1960* (Hamburg: Maximilian-Gesellschaft, 2008).

43. Laura El-Tantawy, *Beyond Here is Nothing*, self-published 2017.

44. Wolfgang Ullrich, *Selfies. Die Rückkehr des öffentlichen Lebens* (Berlin: Klaus Wagenbach Verlag, 2019), 59–60; André Gunthert, "Die Konsekration des Selfies," in *Das geteilte Bild. Essays über digitale Photographie* (Göttingen: Konstanz University Press, 2019), 151–171.

45. Vilém Flusser, *Towards a Philosophy of Photography* (London: Reaktion Books, 2005), 61.

46. See Urs Stahel, "Gratisbilder, Gratisgefühle," in *Die Republik* (April 23, 2019), https://www.republik.ch/2019/04/23/gratisbilder-gratisgefuehle.

cently as a photographer, photobooks provide "quiet consolations" in a hectic "world of deafening images."[47] This is a sincere avowal, but the formula of the photobook as a resting place doesn't quite add up. To begin with, it is not so clear whether those who immerse themselves in books are at all unsettled by the internet. There is undoubtedly a "frenzied standstill" (Paul Virilio) of digital images, but who says that one has to expose oneself to it? There are not so few contemporaries who have chosen an ecological approach to the digital world and find it more of an enrichment than a burden.

Furthermore, as already mentioned, among photographers with an affinity for books, many are active on social media and can count on a relatively large community of followers. They use the digital space as a showcase in which a first and often also a second impression of projects is conveyed, as a field of experimentation in which new image series are tried out, or as a differential space of representation that offers an alternative view of their work. At this point, comparative seeing and visual literacy are merging under the conditions of contemporary media. The printed photobook cannot therefore be reduced to a silent resistance to the noisy digital world of images. That may play a role, but one can only grasp the political, aesthetic, and epistemic complexity of the post-digital photobook if one reflects on the analog *and* digital conditions that determine its existence.

An important component here is the fact that there is hardly any threshold-free transition from analog to digital (or vice versa). Sequences of images on a screen are no equivalent to the printed book. Why are the out-of-print and quite expensive books by Drake, Middel, Venturi, Sauvin, or El-Tantawy not available as inexpensive e-books? This would largely satisfy the calls for the democratic availability of the photobook. Interestingly, it is almost impossible to find e-books in the world of the photobook, and this very likely has to do with incompatible modes of reception. Whatever the expectations regarding the e-photobook may have been—a renewal of the democratic photobook, experimental interest in new forms, or simply making money—they all bounced off the unwillingness of consumers, who apparently do not (recognize) e-books as books, but as collections of images for which they are not willing to pay money.[48] Why should they do so when images are available for free on blog platforms and websites? It may be added that the fixed structuring of an e-book with a beginning and an end is difficult to accept for net-savvy consumers, because this contradicts the unlimited hyperpresence of images in the networks of digital communication. In short, unlike literature and non-fiction, where the e-book has secured a moderate yet stable market share, there is no habitual adaptation of photobook buyers from the printed book to the e-book.

The e-photobook is therefore a failure for the economy, aesthetics, and politics of the photobook, and it is also not quite foreseeable with which arguments and market expectations a relaunch should be initiated. By contrast, print-on-demand (PoD) has created a huge market for *self-publishers*. The provider blurb.com offers almost 130,000 titles in the "Arts & Photography" category in its bookstore. When clicking through, it quickly becomes clear that these books have only a few common intersections with the photobook sphere described in this essay. Nevertheless, PoD has found a small yet interesting place in the realm of photographic artist's books. PoD flirts with the puny quality of print and self-consciously places itself in the tradition of bootleg prints and the poor-looking artist's book à la Ruscha and Feldmann. These beautiful historical connections are somewhat darkened by the fact that customers' money invested in PoD does not benefit small printers or the not-quite-legal counterculture, but rather the players of platform capitalism like blurb.com. Despite this hardly avoidable flaw, PoD represents an attractive field of experimentation, especially for those who work with found footage and visual junk. And here, too, historical references to pre-digital practices are connected to the technical processes of digital book production.

Joachim Schmid started the project *Erste allgemeine Altfotosammlung* (First General Collection of Used Photographs) in 1991. It included the publicly launched request to hand over photo stocks intended for the trash to him for recycling. This initiative caused considerable irritation among environmen-

47. Cole, "Smell the ink and drift away."

48. See the frustrated reports by Andreas Magdanz, "The Price Decides the Downloads," *FreelensMagazine* 34, no. 4 (2013): 46–48, and Michael Mack, "Only on Paper ...", in *Imprint. Visual Narratives in Books and Beyond*, ed. Hans Hedberg et al. (Gothenburg: University of Gothenburg, 2013), 129–146. Magdanz names yet another reason that led him to give up the e-book business: the stubborn attitude of Apple, which wanted to impose its own ideas of book content and formats on him.

talists and institutions such as the German Federal Environmental Agency. Schmid's assessment at the time that "(almost) every image need can be satisfied from the pool"[49] and therefore no new images are needed has been both confirmed and refuted by the arbitrary quantity and reach of the hyperpresent images on the web. The digital pool has awakened a previously unknown appetite for images, and Schmid has responded to that with a whole cascade of photobooks as PoD. The message is clear: with the unlimited pool of images available on the web and a sufficient number of ideas for thematic condensation, it is theoretically possible to produce a new book every week. Among these volumes, one booklet stands out, in which Schmid has subverted his motto of not making new images by photographing people in the style of Martin Parr at the Berlin Art Forum 2009 and, conversely, asking Parr to extract images from the net in the style of Joachim Schmid.[50] PoD is particularly suitable for this ironic interplay because of the synthetic, arbitrary, and interchangeable materiality of these books. Unlike for amateur photographers who want to design their own photobook, for the artist's book PoD is perhaps less a material medium than an aesthetic technique that can be handled flexibly, limited only by the technical specifications and services of the corresponding platforms.

The border region between digital and analog, and between found and newly produced photographs is of course not only played out by PoD, but also by self-published books, DIY platforms, or indie publishers. What they all have in common is that the masses of images on the web have given the photobook a new economic and aesthetic status, be it as a place of orientation and reflection on the conditions of seeing and image-making in a digital order, or in the interplay between haptic and visual experience. In this context, projects that work with the same images in social networks and in the book arrive at very different results.

The photo blog "Kim Jong Il Looking at Things," founded by the Portuguese art director João Rocha, has shown that North Korean image propaganda almost always staged the dictator in the same way during his trips to his country's various production sites: surrounded by his entourage, he looks with a motionless face, usually made even more doll-like by sunglasses, at what is being presented to him: corncobs, bras, computer screens, cows, or Tupperware. No single image would have been able to expose the effort that went into this monotonous ridiculousness. The book published under the same title, in turn, featured a selection of images of Kim and was promptly canonized in the third volume of Parr and Badger's *Photobook*.[51] The difference between blog and book corresponds to a division of labor. The blog is archive and document in the sense of a chronological presentation of the images—not necessarily all of them—that Rocha found on the web; the most recent first, the oldest last. The commercial representation space for the images is the Tumblr platform, which is why, when viewing the images, one must either activate an adblocker or accept being harassed by individually tailored advertising.[52] Finally, the blog is a paradigmatic example of a meme that has spread virally at great speed through blogging and reblogging on various social networks.[53]

The book works differently. First of all, the selection of images depends on the respective resolution, because unlike in the blog, all images are printed in the same size. The motivic redundancy has to be tamed without compromising the seriality, because that is precisely the joke of the book. At the same time, the book gives each image more space than the blog, placing the caption on the left side of the book and the image on the right. The arrangement of the pictures follows, as in a glossary, the alphabetical designation of the objects the despot is looking at—and immediately this principle of order is caricatured as the pictures go through two alphabetical cycles. The first and last images each show "Kim Jong Il Looking at Books," with which the book sets its own self-referential framework. The choice and arrangement of content, the design decisions, and not least the subtle punchlines that make the book a book undoubtedly bear João Rocha's signature. And this, too, distinguishes the book from the blog. Marco Bohr points out in his afterword that the meme principle complicates the

49. See Joachim Schmid, *Erste allgemeine Altfotosammlung* (Berlin: Edition Fricke & Schmid, 1991), 63.

50. *Joachim Schmid Is Martin Parr. Martin Parr Is Joachim Schmid*, print-on-demand, 2009.

51. João Rocha, *Kim Jong Il looking at things. Suivi d'un essai de Marco Bohr* (Paris: Jean Boîte Éditions, 2012, 6th ed. 2022); Parr and Badger, *The Photobook*, vol. 3, 293.

52. See http://kimjongillookingatthings.tumblr.com.

53. Marco Bohr makes this point in detail in his afterword to Rocha's book. On memes in general, see Limor Shifman, *Meme: Kunst, Kultur und Politik im digitalen Zeitalter* (Berlin: Suhrkamp, 2014).

question of authorship: The North Korean photographer or photographers? João Rocha? Or the net swarm that shares and reblogs the images? Memes exist through multiple authorship, while the book exists as a composition that has an author.

The "looking at" meme has found numerous imitators on the web—with modest results. The imitations of "Xi Jinping Looking at Things" or "Vladimir Putin Looking at Things," which are also collected on Tumblr, are no more than mediocre, superfluous goods. But the principle of "looking at," undoubtedly digital-born, can also be redirected into the printed book. The photographer and publisher Roger Eberhard has fished out twenty-three snapshot photographs showing—yet again—Martin Parr looking at books on various occasions from the net and compiled them into a zinebook that is a whimsical footnote to the business surrounding the photobook.[54] The joke is not so much on Parr as on those who grant him this status and confirm it by putting pictures of *Martin Parr Looking at Books* on the web.

The oscillation of images between digital space and book space shapes the format of the post-digital photobook. When algorithms extract certain patterns from a teeming mass of data, it happens in much the same way as Lev Manovich demonstrated for his Instagram analysis with a few million photographs. The images are fed into a database and analyzed according to certain criteria. These can be aesthetic, but also political, commercial, or police parameters. The object thus constructed is no longer the individual image, nor a collection of images, but an arbitrarily large number of pixels that no longer have an author or curator, nor a viewer: "In short, we believe that photos' content, their aesthetics and their larger context can't be separated in life, and they should not be separated in analysis of Instagram medium."[55] In other words, for Manovich, aesthetics and content are no longer primarily characterized by the fact that a person presses the button at a particular moment and deems the resulting image relevant enough to share on social media, but rather by the fact that these images sit alongside millions of others and reveal common patterns that remain hidden by qualitative image arrangement or analysis.

It would be worth discussing what this statistical object says about today's digitally constructed lifeworld conditions, and whether the Instagram aesthetic is exhausted in Big Data. Ultimately, this would mean that the overpresence of digital images corresponds to an overpresence of digital subjects. But what does this have to do with the photobook? Immediately little, but enough that photobooks, whether they deal with digital or analog images, are an alternative to algorithmic selection. If Manovich believes that an aesthetic or contextualizing understanding of Instagram images must take place in the logical and technical order of digital humanities, the photobook demonstrates the exact opposite. In the medium of the book, photography can reflect itself in a digital environment, and it does so in terms of a visual logic that is intrinsic to images, and by using the design options of the book space with all its material and design facets. Digital humanities and, to some extent, digital art depend on transforming writing and images from the analog sphere into digitally processable data. Conversely, photobooks generate visual narratives from a teeming mass of images that travesty the web and simultaneously relate to specific aesthetic traditions.

In recent years, a number of photobooks have been published that use found footage from the web to tie in with pictorial traditions that go far back into the analog age: this is what happens in Joan Fontcuberta's collection of selfies found online on the cusp of the advent of the smartphone, which extend the history of the self-portrait in the mirror into the realm of eroticism and pornography; in Kurt Caviezel's encyclopedia of webcam images classified in the manner of natural history; or in Doug Rickard's melancholic continuation of American street photography, consisting entirely of Google Street View footage.[56] These books raise a fundamental question: How new and unique are photographic images that are digitally formatted in every way but reveal their family resemblance to older images at the very moment they are transferred, and thus transformed, into a book with a particular question in mind? I am not suggesting that digital images tell us nothing new. They very much do, but

54. Roger Eberhard, *Martin Parr Looking at Books* (Zurich: b.frank books, 2014).

55. Lev Manovich, *Subjects and Styles in Instagram Photography* (pt. 1), manovitch.net, 2016, 10, http://manovich.net/index.php/projects/subjects-and-styles-in-instagram-photography-part-1.

56. Joan Fontcuberta, *A travès del Espejo* (Madrid: La Oficina, 2010); Doug Rickard, *A New American Picture* (Cologne: White Press, 2010); Kurt Caviezel, *The Encyclopedia of Kurt Caviezel* (Bolzano: Rorhof, 2015).

for one thing, digital photography, in the words of André Gunthert, "has not caused an iconographic revolution,"[57] and for another, it is by no means incommensurable with analog technologies. Pointing this out is to highlight one of the most salient features of the post-digital photobook. Undoubtedly, when looking at photographs on Instagram, a connection can be made to other Instagram photos, but whether and how similar connections can be made on the timeline back to analog photography in this medium is an interesting question. At least some clues can be found in photographers who first posted their images online and then transferred them to the book. In the limited representational space of the book, the images of Lina Scheynius or Théo Gosselin, who first became known as Instagram photographers, unfold new qualities that do not conceal their Instagram aesthetics and at the same time draw a line back to the narrative photobook of the second half of the twentieth century.[58] To put it more pointedly: the printed book opens up the possibility of a more transhistorically complex consideration of digital images. Post-digital would thus not be when the digital and the analog are arbitrarily interchangeable, but when they are brought into a resonance with each other.

And in yet another respect, Manovich's motto that the digital should form a quasi-closed space proves to be short-sighted. Certainly, a million images cannot be squeezed into a book, but 10,000 images can. And they even make a new image: on the occasion of the Vienna Opera Ball in 2009, Jules Spinatsch positioned two cameras on the ceiling of the auditorium of the State Opera and programmed them to change position slightly every three seconds and take a picture until a column of thirty-six images was reached, containing a section of the room from top to bottom. Then the camera made a small horizontal pan, and the next column of images was created. The result is a coup d'œil stretching over the whole event, but at the end there is a perfect circular panorama, a virtual opera house in which nothing is missing, except perhaps some of the celebrities present.[59] Voyeurism, the chance of the snapshot, and the digital automation of panoramic surveillance are literally interconnected here.

This visual metamorphosis of the 10,008 images was not bound to a specific medium. First they were on display as a 32-meter-long circular panorama turned inside out at Karlsplatz in Vienna; then came the book, which actually consists of three books: a thin volume of text, a comprehensive volume entitled *Every three seconds*, in which the images are arranged sequentially in such a way that they make the movements of the cameras in time traceable, and a slimmer volume with individual images that show nuances and details of the interior. The separation into two color-differentiated books underscores the fact that the digital imagery can be processed in very different artistic formats. The digital images are the fodder for their respective presentation in different media formats, no more and no less.

Michel Foucault's famous concept of heterotopias has not yet been claimed for the book, but an interesting parallel lies in the fact that we are not dealing with infinitely large, but narrowly limited spaces, for example gardens, attics, Indian tents, ships—or even books.[60] In this limitation lies the condition for collecting, (re)ordering, selecting, editing, designing, commenting, fragmenting, and alienating image worlds from the analog *and* the digital sphere. The post-digital photobook hangs on the net, but does not get caught up in it. To emphasize once again: the photobook is not the antithesis of the net. It is a place of condensation and reflection on the conditions of seeing and image-making in a digital order. It forms a haptically tangible, at times complex, yet stable pictorial space that differs from the ever-changing image agglomerates on the net. In the twentieth century, photographic images were essentially defined and disseminated through books, more than through exhibitions. Today, it is apparent that images are no more absorbed in the logic of the digital than texts. For this reason, the internet has not made books disappear. The more digital images there are, the more they become visible or invisible in overpresence, the more significant photobooks become as a way of looking at images.

57. Gunthert, *Das geteilte Bild*, 16.

58. Lina Scheynius, *Book 01–11*, 11 vols, self-published 2008–2019; Théo Gosselin, *Avec le cœur* (Oslo: Éditions du LIC, 2015).

59. Jules Spinatsch, *Vienna MMIX – 10008/7000. Surveillance Panorama Project No. 4* (Zurich: Scheidegger & Spiess, 2014). For details see Michael Hagner, "Die verzogene Sichtbarkeit der Welt. Jules Spinatsch's *Surveillance Panorama Projects*," in *Jules Spinatsch: Semiautomatic Photography*, ed. Jörg Bader (Leipzig: Spector Books, 2019), 233–249.

60. See Michel Foucault, "Of Other Spaces," *Diacritics* 16, no. 1 (Spring, 1986), 22–27.

Marc van Elburg,
Florian Cramer,
Clara Balaguer

Against the [cozy] prettyprinters: a defense of crappy print

The essay was collaboratively written using Etherpad. The original formatting, spelling, and punctuation have been preserved.

pretty printer show me your colors

principles of pretty printing
pretty printer printing pritty prints
pretty printer printing pretty colors
pretty printer printing pretty patterns
on pretty printer pretty printer printer
printing pretty prints for the pretty pretty

[scrap 1]

How can a paper in defense of crappy printing be credible if it is not itself also a bloody mess?

[later insert]

[This text originated on an Etherpad (an Open Source collaborative online text editor). After exporting the pad into a word processing document, some formatting conversion errors occurred and have been preserved.]

[scrap 2]

One writer of this text once offered a (collective-pseudonymously published) print-on-demand book to a number of European and North American artists' and artist-run book shops, and always received the same answer: "we generally don't like to sell print-on-demand books, but will review yours and maybe make an exception."

(Prematurely spilling the beans on the source of anger; see Marc's → second-layer insert.)

- ```
  * [bounce/antiphon]
  * Ghettoization works both ways; A zine library closely
  connected to an other writer of this text often receives artist
  publications labeled as zines with a request to add it to the
  collection, and usually gives the same answer: "we generally do
  not take artist publications but will review yours and maybe
  make an exception."
  *
  ```

[diskarted notes]

- Examples of crappy print include: the cheap print shop near a university campus that reprints college scripts, plastic ring-bound and on photocopy paper; photocopies made at a copy shop; print-on-demand.

- Working hypothesis: the internet may have pushed print-on-demand, along with other forms of digital print and photocopies, into a no-man's land between the two binary opposites of (a) neo-artisanal prettyprinting (glossy coffee table books as well as small-
  ```

edition Riso and stencil printing, silk-screening and other handmade publications) and (b) "quick and dirty" social media (including memes, spamming, trolling etc.).

- Therefore, hardly anybody wants print-on-demand: artists' book stores don't really want it, artist book fairs don't really want it, zine fairs don't really want it either.
- This was epitomized in a 2015 cartoon published in the online contemporary art magazine *HyperAllergic* in which a zine maker desperately tries to trade his crappy Xeroxed zine with an artisanal pretty zine printed "with soy-based inks on biodegradable, sustainably harvested toilet paper."[1]

[title page]

Against the [cozy] prettyprinters: a defense of crappy print

[Marc van Elburg & Florian Cramer & Clara Balaguer]

[Florian's first (and rather crappy) attempt of theorizing crappy print]

Crappy print could be most generally characterized as a poor medium, i.e. as the opposite of what in creative industries is referred to as "rich media." This characterization, however, does not suffice alone. On top of being poor, crappy print is the poorest among, and of, the poor media. In most cases, its impoverishment is not designed; it's not a product of conceptual cleverness or aesthetic rationale. Crappy print is unpretentious, and therefore vulnerable. Where its makers are actually aware of its crappiness, they may be driven by anti-aesthetic sentiments, or rather, resentments.

In media-theoretical terms, poor media is largely synonymous with what McLuhan (oddly) called "cool media" in 1964: media that are low definition, low resolution, low density. "Rich media," on the contrary, are largely synonymous with McLuhan's (oddly named) "hot media": glossy products in high definition, high resolution, high density, high-quality finishing; such as cinema and coffee table books. As early as in the 1960s, McLuhan noted the paradox that poor ("cool") media tend to be better engage audiences than rich ("hot") media. Back then, it was crappy black-and-white television that engaged the masses more than Technicolor widescreen cinema, despite or rather: precisely because of, its low

[1] Lauren Purje, "Navigating the Zine Economy," *Hyperallergic,* September 18, 2015, https://hyperallergic.com/238022/navigating-the-zine-economy/, accessed May 28th 2022; we contacted the artist for obtaining reproduction rights here, but didn't receive a reply.

definition. Today, this example easily extends to Twitter tweets and imageboard memes versus billboard and tv ad campaigns. But where does it leave crappy print?

- **[Marc's mining (for something to defend)]**
  - As a zine maker and small publisher, I am a user of printers, not a developer of them. Referring to McLuhan, I like print-on-demand because I like what it does to me, rather than what I do to it. And I do not like as much what Riso or offset print or online publishing do to me.
  - What print-on-demand does to me is the following: it keeps me close to the moment, to my line of thought. I don't have to plan far ahead. And I don't have to worry about making a large investment and a large number of prints of the work. I feel comfortable making mistakes, I can be more direct, and write for specific situations and people. The item might still end up online, but only later, so that it still keeps some of that physical energy of print-on-demand. Print-on-demand has its own temporality, it is materially irreversible (unlike the format we are now working in, an Etherpad collaborative writing web page, that saves changes in time, (which actually I find quite rewarding as a collaborative tool right now :-))). Print-on-demand has an irreversible history, a timestamp. In terms of networking, it keeps the printed matter active within a network of exchange, instead of it sitting on a pile waiting for a customer.

[baseless claim]

Poor/cool/crappy media are populist media, in every imaginable sense of the word "populist."

[fine print]

However, poor and crappy are not synonymous. Rather, *crappy* is a special case of *poor.* Not only is crappy the poorest of the poor, but it also exposes hidden richness as the concealed side of other types of poor media.

Poor media, including those common in artists' publishing, may be differentiated into at least three subcategories:

a) arte povera media; media whose poor production value is an aesthetic-political statement, such as: Eastern European samizdat typescripts and potato stamps, mimeographed duo-tone political leaflets, protest songs accompanied by only acoustic guitars, the 'human microphone' of the Occupy movement (where a speakers' unamplified words were repeated and thus amplified by the surrounding crowd);

b) poor yet highly artisanal-crafty media; a phenomenon most common in Third World countries. In Western culture, it might have begun in the 19th century Arts and Crafts movement, with its rejection of industrial production and elaborate yet entirely self-made artisanal products. Since then, there have been countless reiterations, from post-1960s "alternative culture," its commodification as gentrifier coffee shop interiors up to today's cozy pretty-printed Riso zines.

Fig. 1: crappy print—small, snippety flyers of African spiritual mediums

c) poor and crappy media. The poor media nobody wants to have: the small, snippety flyers of African spiritual mediums (widespread in the Benelux countries, France and Portugal) whose names and cellphone numbers always change, and who always promise solutions to the same personal problems; the weekly ad-financed free newspaper in the letterbox; the ink- or laser-printed lamp post flyer of someone searching their runaway cat; the crappy soccer fan, music band or political activist sticker on a lamp post; the copy shop-printed, plastic-ring-bound seminar reader or Bachelor/Master/doctoral thesis; the research paper typeset in Microsoft Word (that makes university academics long for artistic research as a means of obtaining graphic design and pretty printing for their publications). At least in former times, the crappy Xeroxed leaflet or zine.

*

In today's artists' publishing, small press and zine culture, (a), (b) and (c) have become increasingly conflated, as can be easily seen and experienced on any zine fest, self-publishing and artists' books fair. The question is: can this cohabitation continue, or isn't it based on superficial consensus and fake community? Which also begs the question: isn't "DIY" (do-it-yourself) as the concept that bands together these practices, an empty signifier?

- **[sound of paper being torn]** hollow commonality in aesthetics
- **[sound of paper being torn]** hollow commonality in modes of production
- **[sound of paper being torn]** hollow commonality in politics—that not only exists between DIY pretty printers and DIY crappy printers, but even among the crappy printers themselves, which (as one cannot stress it often enough) range from anarchist squatters to religious extremists and neo-Nazis. As one can learn from Ayatollah Khomeini's mass-copied, audio-taped speeches as the 1970s forerunner of 1980s DIY cassette label culture, there is no intrinsic value, and no salvation, in "DIY" and

"crappiness"; just as there is no intrinsic value and salvation in the related concept of "minor literature" and other Deleuzian tropes.

So what is there to defend? Is there anything to defend? (To further mess up this pamphlet, and its initial promise of a "defense.")

- [Marc's "Ayatollah"-triggered thought]
  - Could it be that the rise of populism and murders of controversial public figures had an effect on increasing the gap between political and artist publications // and hence a gap between a focus on "non-political" designer print and more emotive political print // or a taboo on unfiltered opinionation on one side and a taboo on any kind of self-censorship on the other (??) //
  - *(in that sense the relation between zines and print-on-demand to me is more meaningful than the relation between zines and memes because print-on-demand has a culture of immediate publishing while also not just being spread around indiscriminately like commercials/spam (although online advertising arguably now moves into the same direction of being locally specific))*

[insert Clara: *recycled shit*]

Here's a bit about local (as in, from the Philippines) recycling framework: diskarte. True to form, it's recycled from an old interview turned essay turned lecture. Because it's seriously ridiculous how one is expected to spew out new shit all the time, survive multiple jobs, and often spew out new shit with no remuneration for the benefit of peer-reviewed high horses who assume that everyone who contributes to their hallowed halls is somehow institutionally funded. No surprise then that their indexes and tables of contents are s o   w e s t e r n.
For the millionth time, a caveat: I understand the West as a hyperreal territory that was shoved down my post-colonial throat for decades.

I first heard about *diskarte*, as a design concept, from Pamela Cajilig. She used to run a local design thinking collective called Curiosity.ph. She describes it as a strategy taken from the Filipino attitude of making the best of what you have on hand to solve problems efficiently, cheaply, quickly, and humorously. DIY is more of a back-to-the-roots movement, a critique of consumerist society wherein self-insufficiency (born of luxury) is the norm. DIY could be described as a romanticized Westernized return to autonomy, to knowing how to fix and survive outside of planned obsolescence.

Diskarte, in contrast, is a subconscious attitude applied to design or life that stems not from luxury ennui but from the want of resources. It is a knowing how to solve seemingly insurmountable problems in the face of precarity. We tend to see diskarte attitude as something to be both proud and ashamed of, as these patchwork solutions arise when money (or any other "desirable" asset) is missing.

[second-layer insert Florian:]

But DIY can also be understood as a poetics of ignoring expected expertise: doing things anyway while lacking talent and skill; such as playing in a punk or noise band without "knowing" how to sing or play an instrument. Or being a zine maker without knowing spelling, grammar, graphic design, printmaking, binding, distribution. In other words, a "fuck it, I don't care whether people think it's crap" attitude. It's anti-consumerist only in the sense that, by removing entry barriers, it permits everyone to be a producer and thus does away with the producer/consumer dichotomy. And, in the best cases, yielding inventive solutions, poetic/aesthetic surprises and new imaginaries coming out of that lack of skill. Admittedly, this is a romanticist trope, and thus problematic in many respects.

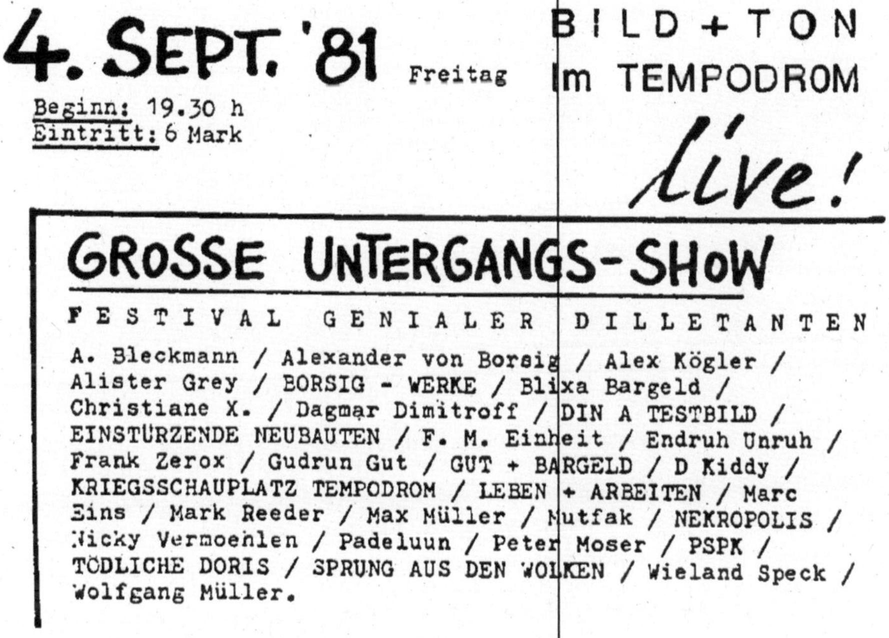

4. SEPT. '81 Freitag

Beginn: 19.30 h
Eintritt: 6 Mark

BILD + TON
im TEMPODROM
live!

GROSSE UNTERGANGS-SHOW

FESTIVAL GENIALER DILLETANTEN

A. Bleckmann / Alexander von Borsig / Alex Kögler / Alister Grey / BORSIG - WERKE / Blixa Bargeld / Christiane X. / Dagmar Dimitroff / DIN A TESTBILD / EINSTÜRZENDE NEUBAUTEN / F. M. Einheit / Endruh Unruh / Frank Zerox / Gudrun Gut / GUT + BARGELD / D Kiddy / KRIEGSSCHAUPLATZ TEMPODROM / LEBEN + ARBEITEN / Marc Eins / Mark Reeder / Max Müller / Mutfak / NEKROPOLIS / Nicky Vermoehlen / Padeluun / Peter Moser / PSPK / TÖDLICHE DORIS / SPRUNG AUS DEN WOLKEN / Wieland Speck / Wolfgang Müller.

Fig. 2: Geniale Dilletanten—original festival flyer "The Great Demise Show: Festival of Inept Dill Aunts"

Not surprisingly, my main cultural reference for this is punk and post-punk culture; more specifically the early 1980s "Geniale Dilletanten" subculture of West-Berlin which, among many others, involved the queer band and art project "Die Tödliche Doris" (The Deadly Doris) and the 1979–1982 zine *Y-KLRMPFNST*. "Geniale Dilletanten" by itself was a product of crappy print since it had resulted from a typo: on a festival flyer, somebody had accidentally misspelled "Geniale Dilettanten," the German word for "genius dilettantes" (or "brilliant inepts"), as "genius dill aunts," and that spelling was ultimately embraced by everyone involved.

My issue with "Geniale Dilletanten," nevertheless, is its romanticist urge to relativize and legitimize its own ineptitude, rather calling oneself "Dilletante" or "inept dill aunt" straight away, with no prefixed attribute. While "Dilettant" today means lack of talent and skill, in 18th century German aesthetics, it still meant "amateur." The "genius" dates back to the same time and discourse, to Klopstock, Herder, Goethe, Schiller, and the romanticist trope of the autonomous, later also naive, genius whose creativity is no longer bound by rule books. In many ways, “Geniale Dilletanten” epitomized the contradictions of 1980s do-it-yourself punk and post-punk culture which, in a populist move, removed participation barriers *and* simultaneously, in an elitist attitude, celebrated individual genius.

Which conversely begs the question: which culture, and which practice, embraces its own crappiness without any strings attached?

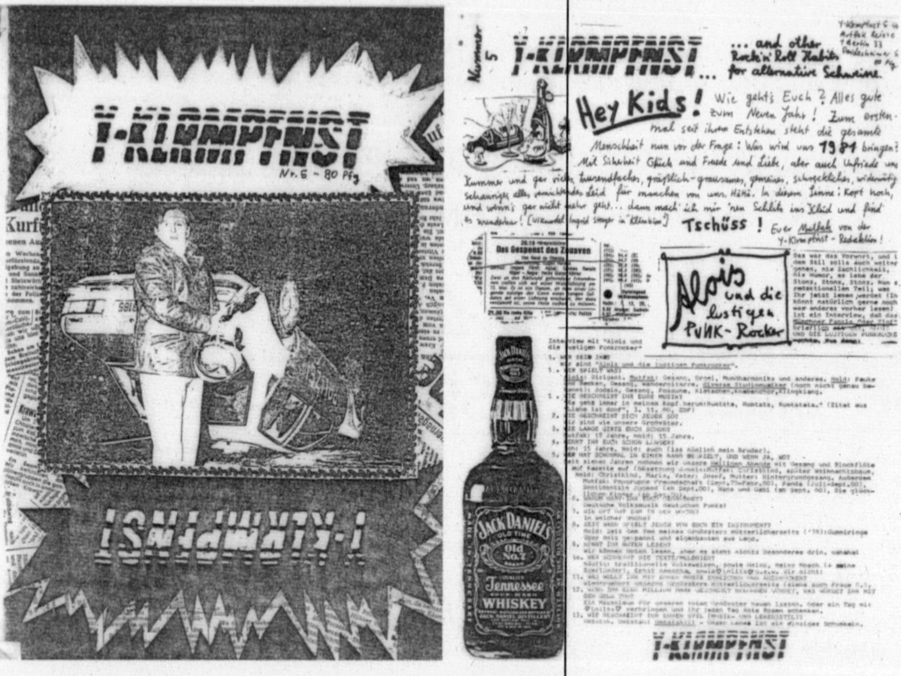

Fig. 3 and 4: Geniale Dilletanten—Y-KLRMPFNST zine no.1 (1981).

The source book of the “Geniale Dilletanten” subculture—aptly called *Geniale Dilletanten* and published in 1981 by Merve Verlag, Germany’s equivalent of Semiotext(e)—contained an essay on zine culture written by *Y-KLRMPFNST*’s maker Mutfak Reisse. Mutfak in turn extensively quoted the intro of an issue of the Bavarian punk zine *Kunst-Gruft* (Art Tomb) whose rough English translation will be a

[third-layer insert Mutfak = fourth-layer insert *Kunst-Gruft*]

“Hey, jerks. You fell for a crap paper again, I guess! How can you be so stupid as to spend your German marks for this. And what do you get? Every jerk and dumbass who hangs around at concerts can cough up what’s in here. Just come up with a good sound bite, make it the name of your zine, roam your hometown, make a drunk riot, write about what you all fucked up, how much booze you had and how ‘nuts’ this was. Then maybe a few record reviews, your own billboard charts, a few parodies of the Pope, [right-wing politician] Strauss and the FUCKING state. It will be the best of the best of all zines. If you manage to be ‘distinctive,’ all fanzine writers from North to South will like it, and that’s really all you want. Fanzines serve only one purpose: that college wankers and high school droolers (hello

boring old fart Hollow Skai!) no longer have to leave their discharge in rags of cloth etc., but can also put it on shiny white paper, drooling over the reactions of some monotonous, opinionated SEXPISTOLSCRASSANARCHYFANATICS & get some warm lustful vibes from it. Fanzine writers never fight lost battles against the world around them because they feel confident and strong. They have the attitude of partly important personalities, of people who are influential and can cause change.... And who are usually drunk."

Kunst-Gruft [Art Tomb] no. 4, 1981 ("super luxury edition")[2]

[back to second-layer insert Florian]

Among others, the above zine intro does:

- situate crappy print within a larger nihilistic complex of crappy poetics, aesthetics and lifestyle; or [to riff on a concept by Gert Mattenklott[3]] as a crappy-nihilistic aesthetic anthropology;
- neither position DIY as a critique of consumerist society, nor as a sustainable lifestyle, as opposed to much post-1960s countercultural and present-day ecologist DIY. On the contrary, consumption (of music and alcohol) is excessive, Dionysian and decisively unhealthy.

Has this crappy print culture been destroyed or sidelined by the prettyprinters? If it ever actually disappeared, who would miss its—literally—toxic masculinity? Isn't what is being described here, in 1981, trolling and shitposting, which nowadays has migrated to 4chan and other electronic platforms? Did a paradigm shift, in the (almost) literal sense of Thomas S. Kuhn's *Structure of Scientific Revolutions*, occur where DIY print became synonymous with artisanal prettyprinting while crappy shitposting was delegated to even crappier—and even faster and even cheaper—online media? Does, in other words, crappy print still exist in DIY cultures? And would it qualify as diskarte?

[second-layer insert Marc]

There is no radical aesthetics. A protest against the discrimination of crappy publishing seems futile since the end of discrimination in liberalism simply means assimilation. (but maybe I did not fully comprehend the source of your anger :-))

[back to insert *recycled shit* Clara]

---

[2] Quoted in Mutfak Reisse, "Über die Inhalte und Bedeutung der Literatur im genialen Dilletantismus" [On the contents and meaning of literature in genius dilettantism], in *Geniale Dilletanten*, ed. Wolfgang Müller (Berlin: Merve, 1982), 83; quote translated from German by Florian Cramer.

[3] Gert Mattenklott, "Ästhetische Anthropologie in Goethes Zweitem 'Faust,'" in *Historische Anthropologie*, ed. Gunter Gebauer (Reinbek: Rowohlt, 1989), 217–52.

Though in the North/West there is a more-or-less strong public infrastructure and consciousness for recycling, DIY exists alongside cavalier faith in the renewability, the false abundance of all resources. This is the contradiction of the most pedestrian form of Western eco-sensibility.

In the Philippines, on the other hand, diskarte somewhat ignores sustainability discourse. It is merely a survival mechanism, folded into everyday life. Recycling starts at home with people saving and using all sorts of scraps and fragments to make diskarte. Then, maybe the local garbage men collect any leftover waste in wooden carts and sacks, roving the neighborhood with baskets and carts along with the *manghahasa* (tool sharpener), the sellers of *balut* (incubated duck fetus eggs) and *taho* (soybean curd with tapioca and syrup) and other mobile cottage industry microbusinesses. The independent trash men (they're usually men) buy or simply collect recyclable paper, bottles, and plastic to resell to junk dealers, maybe even back to the Coca-Cola factories that created them in the first place. Larger scale garbage collectors, with proper trucks and stuff, outsource the sorting service to junk shops or take it upon themselves for maximizing profit or simply bring unsegregated trash to landfills, where hundreds of informal dwellers—who may also live on these mountains of trash—pick doggedly through mountains of waste, mining for monetizable objects, relying on luck and persistence.

Chamba, which is something like luck, also affects diskarte. Your efforts to make diskarte always require some element of luck, fatalistic and somewhat effortless auspiciousness. When you live so close to want and have so much faith in the supernatural, the idea of life becomes a set of bets you may win or lose—so you roll the dice and pray for favor as a natural component of action.

The last particularity of diskarte involves the concept of resilient humor. A not-so-pretty individual can get a hotte hook-up with the power of their diskarte—e.g., humorous and engaging conversation; fantastic gifts; polite and charming demeanor to family and friends. Same goes for site-specific design solutions.

Fig. 5 and 6: diskarte—Pilay (disabled) bench diskarte

My recent favorite diskarte find is a bench made for a patch of sidewalk that had both an elevated and depressed area. So they built a bench with one set of legs shorter than the other so it could be positioned, presumably, to maximize the hours of shade and not be in the way of passers-by. Though, maybe they just liked the view better sitting in that direction. It's a funny looking thing and you can't help but crack a grin when you see it. If you see it, that is. Often, we take for granted these tiny moments of wry ingenuity.[4]

[glued-on question]

diskarte = genius crappiness? (analogous to genius dilettantism/brilliant inepts)

[glued-on rebuttal]

I'd balk at the idea that poverty or belatedness can only produce a dilettante or ineptitude. Genius, period.

4 Michelle James, "Export quality extended: an exchange with The Office of Culture & Design (full transcript)," *Un Magazine* 10, no. 2 (2016), archived copy: https://web.archive.org/web/20161115134609/http://unprojects.org.au/magazine/issues/issue-10-2/export-quality-extended-full-transcript-web-only/, accessed May 28th 2022. Interview slightly edited by C. as part of *Vernacular Language Toolkit*, a subsequent publishing and pedagogical project by Cristina Cochior and Manetta Berends of Varia Rotterdam.

[destruction of all previous arguments]

Print-on-demand can actually be "pretty" in a stereotypical sense of being colorful, well-designed, aesthetically pleasing, flawless. However, it then completely loses its specificity and becomes an invisible behind-the-scenes, back-end technology, a dirty little secret known only to producers. Most people will no longer be able to tell that such a publication is a print-on-demand publication.

Conversely, in contrast with prettypritting, Riso print can be crappy. Even though making good crappy Riso is not easy.

But crappy is not actually the opposite of pretty. Ugly is.

[thought cloud]

Why insist on binaries? There's a spectrum of beauty that cannot be comprehended with the assertion that "ugly" lies on the other end of pretty. But if we had to insist on an opposite, here's a free association of alterworld binaries:

Profound

Compelling

Uncanonical

Stendhalian

[back to destruction of all previous arguments]

Crappiness refers to value, and thus only implicitly to aesthetics.

When speaking of prettiness, there is maybe too much love and respect for the machines of the prettyprinters; too much overall care and good maintenance to achieve real crappiness.

But that is where the attribute "crappy" in opposition to "pretty" can end up becoming pretty abusive (pun intended); when you have good equipment and you break it or treat it badly, on purpose, because of your belief that harshness produces authenticity, acting self-destructively in order to appear credible.

This is very similar to the nihilist punk posing trap described in the 1981 *Kunst-Gruft* (Art Tomb) zine, only that self-destruction shifts from the semantics of writing to its (re)production apparatus; or—in semiotic terminology—from symbol to index. (This shift had been anticipated, as early as in 1960, in Gustav Metzger's concept of auto-destructive art.)

In this sense, the type of crappiness that manifests itself in print-on-demand—is less destructive than other forms of crappy print. This type of crappiness is also non-judgmental and doesn't discriminate, because it involves no explicit normativity, not even anti-aesthetic or any other type of negative normativity. Contemporary prettyprinting (with Riso and spiritually related techniques) tends to be non-judgmental, too, by not actually (and at best only implicitly) setting beauty norms.

Both types of non-judgmentalism have permeated into contemporary zine and small publishing cultures.

* … . . . …………….. ……. In the end, this leaves the question: when judgments and sentiments have shifted so fundamentally, isn't the 2010s/2020s resurgence of zine culture and DIY printmaking deceptive? Is a zine today really still what was understood as a zine until the 1990s (when the internet disrupted and reconfigured zine culture): a quickly and cheaply self-produced, low-end, low-value, low-skill small periodical? The short answer is that the old zine paradigm still exists, particularly in political activist zines and pamphlets; not, if one looks at prettyprinted zines made in the larger orbit of artist book fairs, indie comics and illustration/graphic design.

[insert Marc]

thinking about this *resurgence* and the *deceptive*; to me the 1980's, 1990's, 2000's, 2010's were all just as filled with the same quantities of meaningless publications as the 2020's today. And in general, I felt just as much excluded from any scene back then: for example, by the alternative comic stores whose owners thought that what I made did not qualify as comics because it neither had speech bubbles nor a linear narrative in clearly squared frames. The same could happen at some punk event where my zines were considered to be too arty or intellectual to be real punk.

Crappy publishing therefore has *always* been unwanted and existing in a no man's land. Ultimately because, at least in the West, no man's land is probably the only credible ground for crappy publishing. That is maybe also why—if crappy publishing is not unwanted—it becomes immediately suspect. "DIY" of crappy publishing to me first of all means to create my own framework or context within which I publish.

Prettyprinter culture, in my view, is unclear in its politics. Most often, it appears as a friendly community built around microcapitalism with objectified environmentally friendly design objects of desire—which is not something I am particularly attracted to.

- *(in Western crappy publishing, "no man's land" then is not necessarily a place of limited resources or wealth (at least not for me))*
- [see also "fine print" and "diskarted notes"]
- The danger of being disregarded—to me—is also the *privilege* of being disregarded in a culture based on attention management and attention capitalism.
- I am not poor, but more importantly I have a lot of free time because I have a working partner who provides most of our income; no man's land for me can easily become something like the equivalent of the $2000 crappy sneakers of fashion brand balenciaga.

- That is also maybe why I am reluctant to boost the crappy print of others when it is just based on crappiness. Crappyprinting in other cultural contexts can have quite different meanings.

[(s)crap rant—bounce]

My personal view on zines is that all zines, including prettyprints that identify as zines, are subjective, political and opinionated.

And in that context, the environmental sustainability argument, when it is used to justify occidental prettyprinter zine culture [like in the aforementioned "soy-based inks on biodegradable, sustainably harvested toilet paper"], is biased and politically suspect. Too often it is being diplomatically used as a unifying narrative that obscures existing differences and issues around, for example, race, gender, power or privilege with that culture.

Risographic art zines that mainly focus on visual patterns and layering colors are also political, in the same way the primary colors and the rainbow symbol are political.

.... ..

***affectively**; in contrast to prettyprinters, crappyprinters would print what Sianne Ngai refers to as "ugly feelings"';[5] i.e. all the irritated, the envious, the disgusted, the anxious, the paranoid, the crazy stupid and the angry affects that are excluded in prettiness culture.

Zine archives are dead weight.

```
 * A salute and a farewell to the pretty printers

 * *did prettyprinters not end up being prettyprinters because they
did what they had to do in order to survive? to make some money out
of creative publishing without completely surrendering to capital,
to create a community outside the mainstream that has its own moral
standards while it is not a shark cage run by masculine alpha males
like so many of the rebel communities in the west of the previous
century? Does not the "against prettyprinters" already imply that
prettyprinters are not toothless, nice or tolerant to everything,
that prettyprinters bring their own exclusions and that the agent
behind the against is already feeling that exclusion? *

 * *Is this exclusion than not the best gift that the prettyprinters
can give to the excluded? Will the crappyprinter position themselves
as a parasite within the frame of prettyprinters, or is there a
crappyprinter's domain that exists independently of prettyprinters?*
 *
```

[5] Sianne Ngai, *Ugly Feelings* (Cambridge, Mass.: Harvard UP, 2017).

[insert: (a radical 2022 rereading of zinedepo's 2018 "Manifest of Radical Zine-culture"[6])]

- The radical zine format boils down to fiction, not print or publishing.
- Radical zine culture is not network culture; it is ghettoization. It was the end of ghettoization that brought zines to the mainstream, which was also the beginning of the end of the radical zine.
- There is no life in closed systems, there is no safe place in open systems.
- The radical zine is not about borders, it is about boundaries.
- The radical zine liberates fiction from the program; the program being the feedback loops connected to funding systems in the arts and likely to funding as such.
- Occidental postmodernism that is not situated anywhere, neither in zine culture nor in capitalism, will end up in indifference to colonialism, spam, and pollution.
- Whether or not you may copy a radical zine, depends on the extent to which you are able to handle its radical content.
- All laws can be parasited.
- The radical zine is radical art.

[6] Original text [including spelling errors]: "The radical zineformat is basic; several pages, black & white, folded and stapled together. | Zines = zineculture | Zineculture = proto social network | The radical zineformat is not about printing and printing techniques (but its content can be) | The radical zineformat is not about bookmaking (but its content can be) | Zines are about social networking (global and local) | Most zines have an 'open structure', (this way they are also a network of meaning) | The radical zine is primarily about personal interest (from the individual to the general) | Radical zine ideology is 'do it yourself' ideology. | Radical zine culture is not technophoic, a robot may produce and promote a zine completely automatically as long as it is a product of its personal expression. | As long as the definition of the radical zine format is (more or less) maintained, there is no limit to subject matter (sex / death) or to discipline (drawn, written, collaged, cut & paste, scratched, photographed, coded, etc.) | The radical zineformat is not a mass product (but many people may copy a zine) | The radical zine is not Art (but its content can be) | Radical zineculture = Canadian culture | (some of the elements of the manifest have no function but to separate zine-culture from any other culture. A tongue-in-cheeck reference to South Park 'the royal canadian wedding episode'. | The manifest is not so much a set of rigid rules but a coordinate. It more or less gives our definition of zines as opposed to artbooks or magazines. | Zinedepo is a library with more than 1200 international zines collected over a period of 25 years by Marc van Elburg." Archived copy of the original text: https://web.archive.org/web/20180221182654/https://motelspatie.nl/zinedepo/, accessed May 28th 2022.

- radical=crappy only if it exists within a culture that is hostile to crappiness.
- some zine makers have an incentive to be crappy, some have an incentive to be radical, sometimes these incentives intersect.
- .

[last page]

Crappy publishing was always unwanted, was always crappy publishing in no man's land, in the West no man's land is probably the only credible ground for crappy publishing.

Maybe prettyprinters are not crappyprinters because they are not in a crappy state or place.

[needs work]

prickly printers protesting

pretty pricey plenty printers

Hannes Bajohr

Print on Demand as Strategy and Genre: Auto-Factography and Post-Digital Writing[1]

1. This is the merged version of two branched publications: Hannes Bajohr, "Experimental Writing in Its Moment of Digital Technization: Post-Digital Literature and Print-on-Demand Publishing," in *Publishing as Artistic Practice*, ed. Annette Gilbert (Berlin: Sternberg Press, 2016), 100–115, and Hannes Bajohr, "Infrathin Platforms: Print on Demand as Auto-Factography," in *Book Presence in a Digital Age*, ed. Kiene Brillenburg Wurth, Kári Driscoll, and Jessica Pressman (New York: Bloomsbury, 2018), 71–89.

Nanni Balestrini's novel *Tristano*, published with Feltrinelli in 1966, was actually only a hundred trillionth of the book its author had in mind when he began writing it in 1961. *Tristano*, as it was finally published, is more of a construction kit rather than a finished product. Much like Cut-Up inventor Brion Gysin a few years earlier, Balestrini had experimented with the poetic possibilities of computer permutations.[2] Initially, his plan was to publish the book's 200 paragraphs in all of their possible permutations. But the idea of printing a hundred trillion tomes—each one unique—failed not only because of the astronomical total number of books, but also because traditional offset printing is only profitable if decidedly more than one copy of a book is produced.

Forty years later, however, *Tristano* was able to appear in its planned form. Print-on-demand technology now makes it possible to automate the permutations directly into the typesetting, and to print a single copy directly from the digital master without taking the detour of producing a dedicated printing plate. Although the hundred trillion will certainly not be reached here either—the first 6,000 copies of the Italian edition were followed by 2,000 in the German and 4,000 in the English (a French one is planned)[3]—but theoretically, at least, nothing stands in the way of the steady fabrication of further unique *Tristano* copies. The novel, constructed in the spirit of computer-assisted combinatorics, is so digital that its existence on paper requires digital printing technology.

Digital literature is perfectly compatible with analog media. The Italian net artist and scholar Alessandro Ludovico writes: "The death of paper—in retrospect, one of the most unfortunate and embarrassing prophecies of the information age—has obviously not happened." On the contrary, he says, the relationship between digital and analog technologies should not be thought of as antagonistic, but complementary. Ludovico calls this entanglement "post-digital."[4] *Tristano* shows that the post-digital affects not only questions of production but also of poetics: On the one hand, the analog end product is the result of digital production technology; on the other, its aesthetic appeal lies precisely in the difficulty of bringing together material object and informational representation and in reconciling the book with its file. *Tristano* is post-digital in articulating the perception of a world haunted by this confusion.

Tristano may only seem like the belated accomplishment of a megalomaniacal project, but its post-digital principle of production and representation is quite current. Resonances can be found above all in a field of experimental writing that could be called *post-digital literature*: Literary collectives such as Gauss PDF and Troll Thread in the United States, or Traumawien and 0x0a in Europe, employ similar conceptual methods to Balestrini.[5] Even though they are influenced by the tradition of electronic literature, they do not consider digital writing to be necessarily bound to a specific medium. On the contrary, precisely because their texts can be read online as well as ordered as print-on-demand publications, they blur the always volatile boundary between digital and analog and express a new concept of reality.[6]

THE POST-DIGITAL AS TECHNIZATION

Despite its popularity, the term "post-digital" is rather vague and can refer to three phenomena: 1) the practice of mixing and merging analog and digital media, 2) the longing for the humanization of digital technologies—which is then often followed by a conscious return to the "warmth" and "quality" of analog materials—and 3) the belief that the digital revolution has already happened.[7] What remains unspoken in these definitions is their common assumption,

2. See Roberta Iadevaia, "(Ghosts of) Generative Literature in Italy between Past, Present and Future," *Matlit. Revista Do Programa de Doutoramento Em Materialidades Da Literatura* 6, no. 1 (2018): 85–105.
3. Nanni Balestrini, *Tristano* (Rome: Derive Approdi, 2007); Nanni Balestrini, *Tristano* (Berlin: Suhrkamp, 2009); Nanni Balestrini, *Tristano* (London: Verso, 2014).
4. Alessandro Ludovico, *Post-Digital Print: The Mutation of Publishing Since 1894* (Eindhoven: Onomatopee, 2012), 29.
5. www.gauss-pdf.com; www.trollthread.tumblr.com; www.0x0a.li; www.traumawien.at.
6. On the difference between "digital" vs. "analog," see Nelson Goodman, *Languages of Art: An Approach to a Theory of Symbols* (Indianapolis: Hackett, 1976), 159–164.
7. Melvin L. Alexenberg, *The Future of Art in a Post-Digital Age: From Hellenistic to Hebraic Consciousness* (Chicago: Intellect, 2011), 10; Florian Cramer, "What is 'Post-Digital'?," *APRJA* 3, no. 1 (2014), https://aprja.net//article/view/116068; see for a recent review Florian Cramer and Petar Jandrić, "Post-Digital: A Term That Sucks but Is Useful," *Postdigital Science and Education* 3, no. 3 (2021): 966–989. The term was invented by Kim Cascone, who in 2000 still used it to denote the glitch aesthetics of digitally produced music, see Kim Cascone, "The Aesthetics of Failure: 'Post-Digital' Tendencies in Contemporary Computer Music," *Computer Music Journal* 24, no. 4 (2000): 12–18; he was in turn referring to *Wired* editor-in-chief Nicholas Negroponte, who had already proclaimed in 1998: "The digital revolution is over." Nicholas Negroponte, "Beyond Digital," *Wired* 6, no. 12 (1998), http://archive.wired.com/wired/archive/6.12/negroponte.html. For a prudent discussion of the term, see Geoff Cox, "Prehistories of the Post-Digital: Or, Some Old Problems with Post-Anything," in *APRJA* 3, no. 1 (2014), https://aprja.net/article/view/116087.

namely that the post-digital primarily denotes an experience of the world that for the most part remains below the threshold of perception if it is not specifically brought to mind. Print-on-demand is therefore not post-digital in the sense of a nostalgia for material book culture.[8] On the contrary, the objects manufactured in this way—with their blindingly white paper, poor production quality, and cookie-cutter layout—are usually downright ugly. "Post-digital" should rather be understood epochally and ontologically, following Florian Cramer's observation that it denotes a state "in which the disruption brought upon by digital information technology has already occurred."[9] Print-on-demand is post-digital because it points to the historicity of this disruption and makes it perceptible.

What does it mean for a technology to no longer be new? German philosopher Hans Blumenberg offers the distinction between "technology" and "technization."[10] *Technology* suggests itself as discrete matters of fact in the objectivity of its artifacts. Once introduced, it is there, only to be replaced by better, newer technology. *Technization*, on the other hand, is the ongoing process by which technology fades into the background of our everyday experience. Blumenberg called this quotidian consciousness the "life-world," a term borrowed from Edmund Husserl, who defined it as the "realm of original self-evidences."[11] If life-world is that which, in its unequivocal evidence, lacks all resistance that would make it noticeable to us, technization denotes the slow receding into the lifeworld of what once seemed artificial, unnatural, intrusive, and new. In the process of technization, every technology is "always already" on the way toward this transparency and ultimately becomes invisible to its users.[12]

It seems that, with the initial rise of digital technology more than a generation behind us, we are now experiencing a threshold moment of such technization that is captured in the notion of the post-digital. The fact that something is produced, distributed, or perceived by digital means is no longer the first thing we notice about it, if we notice it at all. Digital technology is in the process of losing resistance to our experience of reality. Gradually, as Blumenberg writes, "The artificial reality, the foreigner among the encountered things of nature, sinks back into the 'universe of what is pre-given as obvious,' the life-world."[13]

If today's subjects of technization are digital technology and its practices, then the outcome of this process—their having become life-world—might be called "the digital." Thus understood, the digital is, first, the epistemological integral of digital technology; Blumenberg calls this a "concept of reality," that is, something that conditions the experience of the world without itself being apparent as a factor.[14] But because this process of digital technization is not complete (after all, we can still be aware of it), the digital does not yet determine our life-world absolutely. The digital can therefore also describe, second, a temporality, a threshold moment that is precariously situated not between the old and the new, but the "opaquely" novel and the "transparently" evident; it vacillates between the no-longer and the not-yet.[15]

Thus, if the digital is a concept of reality or a temporality, increasingly transparent to scrutiny, the post-digital is what performs the sudden yank that makes it apparent again. It provokes a

8. However, Kathrin Passig points out that print publications can also have the function of a social *signal*; books in paper form are then a prerequisite for accessing the literary world or a proof of one's own seriousness, see Kathrin Passig, *Vielleicht ist das neu und erfreulich: Technik, Literatur, Kritik* (Graz: Droschl, 2019), 103–104.

9. Cramer, "What is Post-Digital?"

10. Hans Blumenberg, "Phenomenological Aspects on Life-World and Technization," in *History, Metaphors, Fables: A Hans Blumenberg Reader*, ed. Hannes Bajohr, Florian Fuchs, and Joe Paul Kroll (Ithaca, NY: Cornell University Press, 2020), 358–399.

10. Edmund Husserl, *The Crisis of European Sciences and Transcendental Phenomenology: An Introduction to Phenomenological Philosophy*, trans. David Carr (Evanston: Northwestern University Press, 1970), 127. Blumenberg modifies the concept of life-world considerably. For him, it does not describe an actual state, but acts as a "boundary concept" (*Grenzbegriff*), that is, something that can only be inferred but never actually reached. Absolute life-world would be the absence of all resistance to reality. He offers another name: "paradise." Hans Blumenberg, *Theorie der Lebenswelt*, ed. Manfred Sommer (Berlin: Suhrkamp, 2010), 34, 50.

12. A similar argument can be found in Marshall McLuhan, who understands media, in terms of Gestalt psychology, as a relation of figure and ground—that is, the object of an experience *and* the conditioning nature of this experience, see, for example, Marshall McLuhan, *Understanding Media: The Extensions of Man* (Cambridge, Mass.: MIT Press, 1994), 136. Blumenberg, however, goes beyond McLuhan. With the concepts of life-world and technization, he has precise diagnostic tools for that "attention to the area of inattention" that goes unseen in McLuhan, see Felix Stalder, "From Figure/Ground to Actor-Networks: McLuhan and Latour," 1998, http://felix.openflows.com/html/mcluhan_latour.html.

13. Blumenberg, "Life-World and Technization," 386.

14. See Hans Blumenberg, *Realität und Realismus* (Berlin: Suhrkamp, 2020) and Hannes Bajohr, "Shifting Grounds: Hans Blumenberg's Immanent and Transcendent Modes of Thought," in *Describing Cultural Achievements: Hans Blumenberg's Literary Strategies*, ed. Ulrich Breuer and Timothy Attanucci (Heidelberg: Carl Winter, 2021), 35–55.

15. Understanding "the digital" as epistemic and temporal category might help to restrain the term again somewhat after its recent over-expansion, which has threatened to wipe out for good any residue of meaning left in this already highly vague concept; see Alexander Galloway, *Laruelle: Against the Digital* (Minneapolis: University of Minnesota Press, 2014).

disharmony in the structure of the obvious, draws attention to it, and makes the process of technization experienceable. The post-digital denotes the *ontological* status of an object, ambiguously lodged between the already-evident and the still-new. As soon as it is possible to question which category applies in a given case, the post-digital offers the resistance necessary to bring back to consciousness the otherwise elusive process of technization and its resulting concept of reality.[16]

The error message on the ATM interface or the glitch on the mobile phone screen are still, as it were, "natural" post-digital accidents. Art and literature, on the other hand, can bring such glitches about in a conscious and controlled manner and thus fulfill the task identified by Viktor Shklovsky of "deautomatizing" ingrained patterns of perception through the process of *ostranenie* or "enstranging."[17] One can speak of post-digital *ostranenie* when art attempts to make visible through enstranging what threatens to become invisible in the process of digital technization. Unlike in Shklovsky's work, this happens not so much on the level of diction and narrative perspective, but in the realm of artistic materiality itself—the post-digital object, the print-on-demand book.

INFRA-THIN PLATFORMS

Balestrini's *Tristano* is such an object, but the works of contemporary post-digital literature by Gauss PDF, Troll Thread, Traumawien, or 0x0a accomplish this enstranging even more efficiently. They are made possible by print-on-demand platforms such as Lulu.com or Blurb.com, through which an uploaded PDF may immediately be purchased as a physical book and, thanks to automatic ISBN allocation, can be sold through commercial booksellers, such as Amazon or Barnes & Noble. J. Gordon Faylor, the founder of Gauss PDF, has thus called his practice of hosting files not only "publishing" but also providing an "infrathin platform for the staging of submitted works."[18] *Inframince* was Marcel Duchamp's name for that indefinable, pure difference that still exists between, say, mass-produced objects that appear identical.[19] The thinness of such publishing operations lies primarily in the fact that Gauss PDF does nothing that authors with a minimum of digital acumen couldn't, thanks to Lulu, do themselves. The platform merely executes the "publishing gesture"[20] that is a minimum requirement for partaking in literature as a social system. Even in the digital, this gesture remains necessary. The status of a PDF file available on a private website changes considerably once the very same file has been "published" on the website of a "publisher."[21]

Gauss PDF, founded in 2010, initially began as a website for "digitally-based works."[22] Publishing folder contents, zip, or mp3 files, this practice meant to explore the boundaries of the literary in the digital: Why not conceive of the video of a

16. What this means is that we live not in a post-digital, but very much in a *digital* moment. The digital and the post-digital are not opposed terms, nor does the post-digital come "after" the digital. Rather, they operate on different categorical planes: As a concept of reality/temporality, the digital is what is disclosed by the ambiguous ontology of the post-digital. With Vilém Flusser, one could call the post-digital object an *Unding*—an object suspended between ontological states. See Vilém Flusser, "Das Unding I & II," in *Dinge und Undinge: Phänomenologische Skizzen* (Munich: Hanser, 1993), 80–89; English as Vilém Flusser, "The Non-Thing I & II," in *The Shape of Things: A Philosophy of Design*, trans. Anthony Mathews (London: Reaktion Books, 1999), 85–94.—It is hard to find a suitable English equivalent for the German term *Unding*. While the lexical meaning is "absurdity," it literally translates as "non-thing," and this is how the English version renders it. But it is a peculiarity of the German language to retain what is apparently negated by the prefix "un-." Rather, it qualifies something as questionable in its essence: An *Unmensch* is not a non-human but an inhumane one, and an *Unkraut* is not a non-plant, but one that is not wanted, or in the wrong place: a weed. Similarly, an *Unding* is a thing whose very thing-ness is in question. Jean-François Lyotard employed a similar ambiguity when he used the plural for the title of his 1985 Centre Pompidou exhibition "Les Immatériaux." Taking Lyotard as a cue, a possible translation for *Unding* could thus be "immatter."

17. Viktor Shklovsky, "Art as Device," in *Viktor Shklovsky: A Reader*, ed. Alexandra Berlina (London: Bloomsbury, 2017), 73–96.

18. Caleb Beckwith, "Interview with J. Gordon Faylor," in *Reconfiliating. Conversations with Conceptual-Affiliated Writers* (Buffalo: Essay Press, 2015), 1–14, here 2. It is important to note that the "PDF" in Gauss PDF claims to refer not to the file format but the Gauss probability distribution function in statistics.

19. Marcel Duchamp, *Duchamp du signe: Suivi de Notes*, ed. Michael Sanouille and Paul Matisse (Paris: Flammarion, 2008), 264. Marjorie Perloff has recently derived an entire analytical category of small forms from this idea, which admittedly only has the name in common with the way it is used here, see Marjorie Perloff, *Infrathin: An Experiment in Micropoetics* (Chicago: University of Chicago Press, 2021).

20. Ludovico, *Post-digital Print*, 67.

21. This is *contra* Florian Cramer, "Post-Digital Writing," *Electronic Book Review*, December 12, 2012, https://electronicbookreview.com/essay/post-digital-writing: "But in the 21st century, even the primal criterion of literature has become obsolete: that of being published. In the age of homepages, blogs and social networks, the classical distinction between non-published personal writing and published writing is moot, and with it the distinction between everyday communication and publishing." This position overlooks the fact that the perlocutionary part of a speech act (and the publishing gesture is one) depends in its outcome on the identity and the status of the agent performing it: It makes a difference *who* publishes *what* in *which context*. The blindness to these conditions accounts for much of the crushed hopes of early internet utopianism.

22. Kristen Gallagher, "The Gauss Interview. Chris Alexander Talks to J. Gordon Faylor," *Jacket2*, March 5, 2013, http://jacket2.org/commentary/gauss-interview.

Google Hangouts conversation as poetry, as in Sophia Le Fraga's *UND3RGRoUND LoV3R5?*[23] The roughly eight-minute video is a continuous screengrab of a desktop interface showing a Twitter DM chat; the ongoing conversation reveals itself as a re-enactment of Jean Tardieu's absurdist drama *Les amants du métro* (1952) in a digital environment—Le Fraga calls it a "comedy ballet without dance or music."[24] The effect is one of post-digital enstranging. The almost resigned recourse to the file format undermines entrenched genre attributions and de-automatizes traditional expectations towards literature on a purely categorical level.

But although he continues to publish such works, Faylor has moved away from digital-only publishing. In 2013, he founded the imprint GPDF Editions. Every title published there is available for free as a PDF and can be purchased on Lulu as a print-on-demand book. Faylor praises the "liberating potential" of print-on-demand, which dissolves the rigid ontology of digital and analog, in that books "can now exist in that system otherwise reserved for files, and subsequently allow for new possibilities of material combinations and distribution."[25]

This entanglement, which treats digital file and material book as equals, is also the starting point of Lauren Klotzman's *Meat Joy Error Failure*, a video file of Carolee Schneemann's *Meat Joy from* 1964 opened in a text editor.[26] As Schneemann's body art piece, for which the participants wallowed in fish, sausage, and raw meat, desexualizes the naked body in an extended performance, Klotzman's homage is about the nakedness of decontextualized data that can no longer be executed. The video, opened as a raw text—a concrete poem rather than information—is not merely illegible for humans when transcoded in this way; materialized, as a print-on-demand book by Lulu, the data structure put on paper amounts to 5,500 pages in eight volumes that are also practically unreadable.

The book was published in 2015 by Troll Thread, a literary collective founded in 2010. It can be considered the inventor of the dual publishing model of PDF and print-on-demand, which has become a kind of soft standard for experimental writing.[27] It was quickly copied by the art establishment. The 2014 Zurich exhibition "Poetry Will Be Made By All," co-curated by Hans Ulrich Obrist and Kenneth Goldsmith, featured books by authors born after 1989; on the accompanying website, all titles could either be downloaded or purchased on Lulu.[28] German author Gregor Weichbrodt, whose output was represented in Zurich with the book *On the Road for 17,527 Miles* (a list of Google Maps driving instructions recreating the route of Jack Kerouac's *On the Road*), started his own writer's collective, 0x0a (of which I am also a member), in 2014. On its website, Weichbrodt has re-issued the book, with a new design and 0x0a as the publisher, again as PDF and Lulu print.

Klotzman's text or Weichbrodt's book would also have fitted into Traumawien's program. Also founded in 2010 (but defunct since 2016), the platform called itself a "paradoxical print publisher." The paradox here, as co-founder Lukas Gross wrote in a mission statement, consists in "transferring late-breaking digital aesthetics into book form."[29] Traumawien also makes a decidedly post-digital gesture with these books, treating "text produced by computer systems ... [as] literary."[30] In addition to the dual publishing strategy and the distribution medium of the internet, however, what all these groups have in common above all is an *aesthetic*: post-digital literature is strategy and genre in one.

PRINT-ON-DEMAND AS SIMULTANEOUSLY DIGITAL AND ANALOG

For literary scholar Whitney Anne Trettien, even a conventional print-on-demand book, like the reprints of digitized but out-of-print books that can

23. See Harry Burke, "Page Break," *Texte zur Kunst* 25, no. 98 (2015): 119–123; see also for some other examples Hannes Bajohr, "In der Asche des Digitalen: Postdigitales Publizieren heute," *Kunstforum International* 45, no. 256 (2018): 150–159.
24. Sophia Le Fraga, *UND3RGRoUND LoV3R5: A Comedy-Ballet without Dance or Music* (Gauss PDF, 2015), https://www.gauss-pdf.com/post/131096213655/gpdf188-sophia-le-fraga-und3rground-lov3r5-a.
25. J. Gordon Faylor, "Lulu Freundlich," in *Code und Konzept: Literatur und das Digitale*, ed. Hannes Bajohr (Berlin: Frohmann, 2016), 218; see also Hannes Bajohr, "'Dateitypen als Publikationstaktik.' Interview mit Gordon Faylor," *Kunstforum International* 45, no. 256 (2018): 166–171.
26. Lauren Klotzman, *Meat Joy Error Failure*, 8 vols (Troll Thread, 2015), https://trollthread.tumblr.com/post/118718537299/lauren-klotzman-meat-joy-error-failure-troll.
27. This phenomenon has also been scholarly archived in the "Library of Artistic Print on Demand" to which this book is a testament: https://apod.li.
28. http://poetrywillbemadebyall.com/library.
29. Traumawien, "Statement February 2010" (now only available via the Wayback Machine: https://web.archive.org/web/20160316181957/http://traumawien.at/stuff/about).
30. J. R. Carpenter, "Paradoxical Print Publishers TRAUMAWIEN," *Jacket2*, October 18, 2011, http://jacket2.org/commentary/paradoxical-print-publishers-traumawien.

be purchased online, is a "thoroughly *digital* object." This is precisely what is at issue with post-digital literature. Unlike the reprints examined by Trettien, where "only once a reader purchases a print-on-demand reprint (usually through the web) [...] the formal materiality of the electronic text [is] actualized in paper,"[31] in the genre at hand any inclination to hierarchize the two elements—the text and the book, the immaterial and its materialization—is actively undermined by the authors. It might be more useful to call "print-on-demand" the umbrella term for both the file and the product, and to conceive of this double-structure as at once analog and digital.

The finished, analog print-on-demand book has an inherent connection to the PDF; its very existence is predicated on a digital master from which the copies of the book are made. On the other hand, in the production cycle of Lulu and Blurb, the PDF really only makes sense as the starting point of the future book, and, as we shall see, the attributes of the file are determined by the material constraints of print-on-demand. Furthermore, as Lisa Gitelman has shown, the PDF itself possesses a certain "ontological complexity," since it at once simulates the printed page, and falls short of it. "PDFs achieve a measure of fixity because of the ways they simultaneously compare to printed documents and contrast with other kinds of digital documents that seem less fixed—less paperlike—as they are used."[32]

The platforms here discussed play with this referential complexity for the purpose of post-digital *ostranenie*. Because of the ease of production and dissemination that services like Lulu and Blurb provide, the unstable ontological status of print-on-demand can be investigated, manipulated, and thrown into crises by artistic and literary means. "Electronic textuality is [...] locatable, even though we are not accustomed to thinking of it in physical terms," as Matthew Kirschenbaum points out in his discussion of a "forensic" approach to storage media. This idea holds for these works, too: few things illustrate "the heterogeneity of digital data and its embodied inscriptions" as well as the books on these "infrathin" platforms.[33]

If the print-on-demand book is a post-digital object that, by virtue of its inherent ontological ambiguity, allows us to experience the process of technization, then any such book, no matter how banal, should be able to accomplish this destabilization, and to some degree it does. But the post-digital literature at issue here exacerbates this potential: What unites their poetic strategies and elevates them to the level of a literary *genre* is that they all proceed from an acute awareness of the always-already latent self-disclosing of post-digital objects in their structure, production, and distribution. This can be illustrated by looking at two elements of this genre that characterize it especially well: the influence of generative and conceptual practices, which are used to play with the connection between file and object, and the turn to auto-factography, a type of writing that self-reflexively represents the structural, socioeconomic, and material conditions of its production.

STUPLIME VERTIGO

Many of the titles offered on these infra-thin platforms are actually anti-books. Like Klotzman's *Meat Joy Error Failure,* they are no longer read in an immersive, attentive fashion. Instead of close reading, they demand what N. Katherine Hayles calls "hyper reading": "browsing, skimming, scanning" as modes of reception.[34] Where the goal is no longer to decipher the meaning of or internal connections between words, sentences, and texts, the aesthetic experience of such works shifts from producing sense to the experience of being battered by nonsense, which in turn gives rise to its own hermeneutics.

Sianne Ngai has called the effect of this literary stratagem "stuplimity": "Like the Kantian sublime, the stuplime points to the limits of our representational capabilities, not through the limitlessness or infinity of concepts, but through a no less exhaustive confrontation with the discrete and finite in repetition." Stuplimity is "a syncretism of boredom and astonishment, [...] of excessive excitation with extreme desensitization or fatigue." It results in "affectively reorganizing the subject's relation-

31. Whitney Anne Trettien, "A Deep History of Electronic Textuality: The Case of *English Reprints Jhon Milton Areopagitica*," *Digital Humanities Quarterly* 7, no. 1 (2013), http://www.digitalhumanities.org/dhq/vol/7/1/000150/000150.html.

32. Lisa Gitelman, *Paper Knowledge: Towards a Media History of Documents* (Durham: Duke University Press, 2014), 128 and 119.

33. Matthew Kirschenbaum, *Mechanisms: New Media and the Forensic Imagination* (Cambridge, Mass.: MIT Press, 2008), 3 and 6.

34. N. Katherine Hayles, *How We Think: Digital Media and Contemporary Technogenesis* (Chicago: University of Chicago Press, 2012), 12.

ship to language," which is no longer experienced as transparent but as material and resistant, thus emerging from its life-worldly transparency.[35]

The joy of the excessive and the willful production of the otherwise dreaded literary boredom are the point of such stuplime hermeneutics. Similar strategies are also familiar from earlier experiments in electronic literature and conceptual writing.[36] *Tristano*, generated by combining textual elements, is a precursor of contemporary electronic literature, which often relies on the ability of code to produce large amounts of text. Conceptual writing, found for instance in Kenneth Goldsmith's deliberately "dumb" appropriations of existing texts, proceeds in a structurally similar way: Text is produced following a rule without regard to aesthetic choices, and reading the result is made deliberately difficult. As in Klotzman's misuse of file types, grasping the rule itself is sufficient to understand the work.

Stephen McLaughlin's *Puniverse*, the "ingenious crossing of an idiom set and a rhyming dictionary" (as the subtitle reads), combines both elements by playing through all rhyming combinations of the elements of a given number of idioms, producing a plethora of "puns." An expression like "a bad egg" is multiplied thus:

an ad egg
an add egg
a brad egg
a cad egg
a chad egg
a clad egg
a dad egg
a stale egg
a gad egg
a glad egg
a grad egg
a had egg
a lad egg
a mad egg
a nad egg
a pad egg
a plaid egg
a rad egg
a sad egg
a scad egg
a shad egg
a tad egg
a bad beggar
a bad keg
a bad leg
a bad meg
a bad peg
a bad segue.[37]

All that is required for such puniplication is the execution of a script that checks the elements of a finite idiom set for the rhymes of their sub-elements and returns the results; yet the outcome of this function, once printed, requires fifty-seven volumes of Lulu books.

Nevertheless, neither electronic nor conceptual writing can exhaustively define the post-digital genre; both are merely elements that can be emphasized at will.[38] The "return to print" accomplished by these platforms contrasts with the oft-claimed genealogy of digital literature as a continuation beyond—and a departure from—experimental print literature,[39] and thus has frequently been assumed to contribute to the "crisis of the codex as a cultural

35. Sianne Ngai, "Stuplimity: Shock and Boredom in Twentieth-Century Aesthetics," *Postmodern Culture* 11, no. 2 (2000), https://muse.jhu.edu/article/27722.

36. On literary conceptualism, see Nikolai Duffy, "Reading the Unreadable: Kenneth Goldsmith, Conceptual Writing and the Art of Boredom," *Journal of American Studies* 50, no. 3 (2016): 679–698, and Lori Emerson, "Conceptual Poetry," in *The Princeton Encyclopedia of Poetry and Poetics*, ed. Roland Greene (Princeton: Princeton University Press, 2012), 292–293; on digital literature, see Philippe Bootz and Christopher Funkhouser, "Combinatory and Automatic Text Generation," in *The Johns Hopkins Guide to Digital Media,* ed. Marie-Laure Ryan, Lori Emerson, and Benjamin J. Robertson (Baltimore: Johns Hopkins University Press, 2014), 83–85, and more recently, already referring to an earlier version of the present text, Zach Whalen, "Computer-Generated Books: Metonymic, Metaphoric and Operationalist," 2021, https://elmcip.net/sites/default/files/media/critical_writing/attachments/101010.pdf; see on the connection between the two directions: Kristen Gallagher and Fernando Diaz, "Algorithms in Conceptual Writing," *Jacket2*, April 27, 2013, http://jacket2.org/commentary/algorithms-conceptual-writing, and more recently: Nick Montfort, "Conceptual Computing and Digital Writing," in *Postscript: Writing After Conceptual Art*, ed. Andrea Andersson (Toronto: University of Toronto Press, 2018), 197–210.

37. Stephen McLaughlin, *Puniverse: Being the Ingenuous Crossing of an Idiom Set and a Rhyming Dictionary*, vol. 1 (Gauss PDF, 2014), http://dl.gauss-pdf.com/GPDF100-SM-P-V01.pdf, 8.

38. Troll Thread member Joey Yearous-Algozin: "I think of this writing as coming after conceptual writing. It couldn't have been made without that break, but in the permission it afforded us, something different emerged. [...] In one way, this work has become a genre unto itself." Tan Lin, "Troll Thread Interview," *Poetry Foundation*, May 4, 2014, https://www.poetryfoundation.org/harriet-books/2014/05/troll-thread-interview. For a discussion of "*post-conceptual*" writing that emerges from conceptualism but pursues more contemporary goals, see Felix Bernstein, *Notes on Post-Conceptual Poetry* (Los Angeles, CA: Insert Blanc Press, 2015).

39. N. Katherine Hayles, *Electronic Literature: New Horizons for the Literary* (Notre Dame: Notre Dame University Press, 2009), 17.

form," the demise of the good old book.[40] The stuplime of the generative-conceptual text—constructed, not found; written, but by code—is exacerbated once again in its post-digital enstranging effect and only attains its true quality in the gesture of publishing via print-on-demand. While *Puniverse* is also circulated as a PDF file, it still requires the *possibility* of being printed in order to achieve its vertiginous, stuplime effect. As in much of conceptual literature, its potentiality, so to speak, is its potential, and it very well might be that actualization neutralizes the tension derived from its "wastefulness"; such an accumulation of print might be more sculptural than literary. But what is important is that it *can* be actualized, and Lulu will do it for a mere $381.90.

If McLaughlin's text achieves its expansiveness by a combinatory operation, another way to elicit such an overwhelming effect is to offer only a slice of the vastness implicit in a concept. This is what is achieved by Gregor Weichbrodt's generative work *I Don't Know*. The text is created by a Python script that concatenates the titles of linked Wikipedia articles with a set of stock phrases. The result is a soliloquy in which a narrator denies knowledge of the subjects they list. It begins:

> I'm not well-versed in Literature. Sensibility—what is that? What in God's name is An Afterword? I haven't the faintest idea. And concerning Book design, I am fully ignorant. What is "A Slipcase" supposed to mean again, and what the heck is Boriswood? The Canons of page construction—I don't know what that is. I haven't got a clue. How am I supposed to make sense of Traditional Chinese bookbinding, and what the hell is an Initial?[41]

As Jules Pelta Feldman observes, the narrator's questioning "skews from the absurd—'I don't know what people mean by A Building' [...] to the perfectly reasonable: 'Vinca alkaloids are unfamiliar to me. And I'm sorry, did you say Vinpocetine?'"[42] Often, the text undermines itself: "I'm completely ignorant of Art Deco architecture in Arkansas. Can you tell me how to get to The Drew County Courthouse, Dual State Monument, Rison Texaco Service Station or Chicot County Courthouse?"[43] The reader, Pelta Feldman writes, can hardly fail to acknowledge this incongruity: "I don't know about you, but the narrator of *I Don't Know* knows a hell of a lot more about Arkansas's architectural history than I do."[44] And after having jumped, in truly Latourian fashion,[45] from literature to book binding, to soccer, to architecture, and a plethora of other topics that are only connected through Wikipedia's internal genus-species relation, the book ends after 351 pages, seemingly unaware of yet another performative contradiction:

> I've never heard of Postmodernism. What the hell is A Dystopia? I don't know what people mean by "The Information Age." Digitality—dunno. The Age of Interruption? How should I know? What is Information Overload? I don't know.[46]

That the text closes here is almost too good to be true and raises the suspicion of authorial intervention: Wikipedia's taxonomical structure could indubitably fill more pages—but how many exactly? By withholding the answer and choosing a very deliberate point for the text to break off ("Information Overload"), the text conjures a feeling of stuplimity (quite literally the sublime of the stupid) similar to *Puniverse*, precisely because the expanses of the unknown are unknown; it certainly adds to this effect that *I Don't Know* is a long reminder of the vastness of individual ignorance in the age of networked communication.

Yet McLaughlin and Weichbrodt's texts, no matter whether they are spelled out completely or appear abridged, are finite. There is an end in sight, and this end is determined by the logic of the sys-

40. Carlos Spoerhase, "Beyond the Book?," *New Left Review* 103, no. 1 (2017): 87; see more recently Annette Gilbert, "Die Zukünfte des Werks: Kleiner Abriss der Gegenwartsliteratur mit Blick auf die Werkdebatte von Morgen," in *Das Werk. Zum Verschwinden und Fortwirken eines Grundbegriffs*, ed. Lutz Danneberg, Annette Gilbert, and Carlos Spoerhase (Berlin: de Gruyter, 2019), 495–550.

41. Gregor Weichbrodt, *I Don't Know* (Berlin: Frohmann Verlag, 2015), 4, https://0x0a.li/en/text/i-dont-know.

42. Jules Pelta Feldman, "Gregor Weichbrodt: No Offense," *Room and Board*, November 1, 2015, https://roomandboard.nyc/salons/gregor-weichbrodt-no-offense.

43. Weichbrodt, *I Don't Know*, 212.

44. Feldman, "No Offense."

45. Ian Bogost has coined the term "Latour litany" for a list of radically different things, see Ian Bogost, *Alien Phenomenology, or What It's Like to Be a Thing* (Minneapolis: University of Minnesota Press, 2012), 49. Bogost here alludes to a rhetorical device popular with Bruno Latour of interspersing such lists of tedious length in his texts to illustrate the possibility of considering said things as ontologically equivalent. Bogost has even written a generator that produces such lists, also by accessing Wikipedia, see http://bogost.com/writing/blog/latour_litanizer.

46. Weichbrodt, *I Don't Know*, 352.

tem employed, be it the entirety of Wikipedia, or the number of total iterations in a non-recursive function that couples list items. As soon as recursive functions—functions that call themselves—are used, however, the possibility of infinity emerges. Executed on a computer, a recursive function lacking a set breakpoint would either run forever or overflow the computer's memory and cause it to crash. A text thus produced is potentially endless; that it nonetheless does end is again an index of intervention, authorial or otherwise—and thus even goes beyond the category of stuplimity, which is based on finite repetition.

This vector into infinity remains even if this recursion is enacted manually. On every page of Lawrence Giffin's *Non Facit Saltus*, there is nothing but instructions on how to reach the next. For instance, page 13 reads: "If you want to get to page 14, turn to page 14."[47] It is a very basic recursive function, that of incrementation, but without an external criterion for when to stop, it could go on forever. In Giffin's case, this criterion is provided by the finite and discrete structure of the book. Because of the book's spatiotemporal stability (as opposed to a stream of potentially infinite text, as in the case of Twitter bots), it references distinct pages that can be "called" independently (this would not work with a scrollable page or a mere text file); because of the unambiguous imperative "turn!" they require the materialization of the object, or, as metaphorized ones, the simulated makeup of the book: a PDF. Again, we find the structure of file and object pointing back and forth to one another.

POST-DIGITAL AUTO-FACTOGRAPHY

While relative document layouts, like Word files or epubs, allow for a text to be "reflowed" responsively for every conceivable output device,[48] a PDF, just like the page of a book, is absolute in its layout.[49] The de-facto standard of commercial e-publishing, aimed at e-readers and iPads, is the epub format; for the experimental platforms here described, the specifications of the commercial print-on-demand providers made PDFs their standard. What is more, not only do the constraints of a service like Lulu's (maximum number of pages, page size, etc.) inform the way the print-on-demand book is created, disseminated, and perceived, but they also have reverberations for the form of the text: The formatting of the print-on-demand book influences the formatting of its underlying file, and vice versa.[50]

A direct riff on this interplay is Joey Yearous-Algozin's *9/11 911 Calls in 911 Pt. Font* (Troll Thread, 2012). It contains what its title announces: nine-hundred-and-eleven characters from a New York Fire Department transcript of calls to 911 on September 11, 2001. Because they are set in a font size of 911 points, the text extends onto just under nine hundred PDF pages (mostly, a single letter fills one page, but occasionally there are two). A text that would scarcely fill the screen of a Kindle is stretched to the size of two heavy volumes, which in their heft evoke the form of the absent Twin Towers. Since the dimensions of the PDF follow Lulu standards, the characters shown on each page are cut off, making the resulting text almost illegible. As soon as this text is copied from a PDF viewer and pasted elsewhere, it is possible to view it in its brief entirety; the text "hides" under the constraints of the printed page but is left legible in the file.

Less intentional but similar in effect is *American Psycho* by Jason Huff and Mimi Cabell (Traumawien, 2012). This work plays with the relationship to yet another materialization of the same text: PDF and Lulu book are based directly on the original layout of Bret Easton Ellis's *American Psycho*. The novel was sent back and forth between two Gmail accounts, page by page. Huff and Campbell then "saved the relational ads for each page and added them back into the text as footnotes. [...] The constellations of footnoted ads throughout these pages retell the story of American Psycho in absence of the original text."[51] While the main aim of their work is the privacy-encroaching advertising model that fuels the Google empire, *American Psycho*'s conceptual framework requires the closest possible resemblance between source and outcome, book, file, and print-on-demand.

47. Lawrence Giffin, *Non Facit Saltus* (Troll Thread, 2014), 13, https://trollthread.tumblr.com/post/78371419861/non-facit-saltus-lawrence-giffin-troll-thread.
48. Ludovico, *Post-Digital Publishing*, 98.
49. Gitelman, *Paper Knowledge*, 114–115.
50. See the discussion by Harry Burke, who acknowledges that "PDFs [...] gain authority by looking and functioning like a page." Burke, "Page Break," 120. But this is only half the story. While he highlights a leftover element of high-brow book fetishism, he overlooks that it is the commercial and technological substructure of print-on-demand itself that prescribes this format. The page/PDF relationship is dictated by current technological needs rather than by overcome values.
51. Jason Huff and Mimi Cabell, *American Psycho* (Traumawien, 2012), https://web.archive.org/web/20161030071246/http://traumawien.at/prints/american-psycho.

Works like these become self-aware of the conditions of their production and gain the flavor of what a certain current in Soviet formalism called "factography." Probably its best-known description is Sergei Tret'iakov's essay "The Biography of the Object" (1929). Tret'iakov proposed to center a novel not around the psychology of the protagonist, but the production process of an object, thus doing away with bourgeois subjectivity, anthropocentrism, and obliviousness to socioeconomic processes. The biography of the object, "extremely useful as a cold shower for littérateurs," is constructed like a "conveyor belt along which a unit of raw material is moved and transformed into a useful product through human effort." Instead of *The Brothers Karamazov*, Tret'iakov suggests that factographic novels could have titles like "*The Forest*, *Bread*, *Coal*, *Iron*, *Flax*, *Cotton*, *Paper*, *The Locomotive*, and *The Factory*."[52]

While Tret'iakov still had a representational, world-depicting model in mind—a realist novel for things rather than persons—the post-digital literature considered here makes factography perform itself; it becomes *auto*-factography. Yearous-Algozin and Huff/Cabell focus on the intricate and often circular relationship between file and object. They do not "say" anything about digital technization but rather "show" it, as one could put it with Wittgenstein,[53] by thematizing this relationship performatively and through its own materiality; instead of directly writing the biography of the thing, it reveals its story on its own. This material self-referentiality has, of course, antecedents in art and literature, such as the famous black page in Laurence Sterne's *Tristram Shandy* (1759), Robert Rauschenberg's *White Paintings* (1951), or, aurally, Robert Morris's *Box with the Sound of Its Own Making* (1961)—but in these cases, auto-factography is a side-effect, while in the post-digital literature of infrathin platforms, this reflexivity is so central that it has been elevated to the status of genre element.

If auto-factography here addresses the medial aspects of the underlying data structures, in some works such auto-factographical showing extends to the socioeconomic conditions of their production. Jean Keller's *The Black Book* (Lulu/self-published, 2012) is a tome of 740 pages—the maximum number allowed by Lulu at the time—that is completely black. A gallon of ink used for print-on-demand printing costs over four thousand dollars, as Keller explains on the Lulu sales page:

> However, the price of a book is not calculated according to the amount of ink used in its production. For example, a Lulu book of blank pages costs an artist as much to produce as a book filled with text or large photographs. Furthermore, as the number of pages increases, the price of each page decreases. A book containing the maximum number of pages printed entirely in black ink therefore results in the lowest cost and maximum value for the artist.[54]

At first appearing parasitic, even sabotaging, since it suggests that Lulu might lose money printing it, *The Black Book* is a reminder that post-digital writers are enmeshed in negotiations about their productive resources just like any other artist; Keller's subversive "hack" points out that writers get the short end of the stick, as they represent Lulu's main revenue stream.

In *Reimbur$ement* (Troll Thread, 2013), Holly Melgard similarly, yet reversely, exhibits the limits of print-on-demand writing and the precariousness of the author's labor conditions by focusing on the dissemination, rather than the material production, of the work. In the introduction, she states:

> Sometimes the work I do results in earning neither income, livelihood, nor play, and often I find myself paying to work rather than being paid for work. Whenever this happens, I count my losses and take my chances gambling for alternatives.[55]

This is meant quite literally: the book is filled with scans of lottery tickets and scratch cards—six years' worth of gambling for "$ for life." Because Lulu lets its producers set the selling price at will while the costs of production remain the same, Melgard's book is $329.53, the equivalent of her gambling losses, "plus whatever Lulu charges for

52. Sergei Tret'iakov, "The Biography of the Object," [1929] *October* 118, no. 4 (2006): 61–62.

53. Ludwig Wittgenstein, *Tractatus Logico-Philosophicus*, trans. D. F. Pears and B. F. McGuinness (London: Routledge, 2022), secs. 4.12–4.1212.

54. Jean Keller, *The Black Book* (Lulu, 2012), https://www.lulu.com/shop/jean-keller/the-black-book/paperback/product-21008894.html.

55. Holly Melgard, *Reimbur$ement* (Troll Thread, 2013), 4, https://trollthread.tumblr.com/post/68529805052/holly-melgard-reimbursement-troll-thread-2013.

its print on demand services."[56] *Reimbur$ement* is at once a utopian and a commonsensical project, as it demands no more than pay equivalent to labor—"Reimbursement is for the work"—except that the work is play and the play a gamble for the funds that make the work possible in the first place; in the economy of the digital, the position of the writer is as precarious as ever, and just as dependent on access to the means of production.

Of course, the generative-conceptual and autofactographic are only two of the many elements this literature employs in its strategy of technization's self-disclosure, nor do I mean to suggest that this disclosure is the only function it serves. However, I believe that much of this genre's relevance derives from its unique capacity to articulate an instability that indicates a general process of digitization—whether in its technological form, investigating the ontological slippage between page and file, book and PDF, digital and analog, or, as Melgard and Keller show, in its socioeconomic ramifications. Media scholar Sophie Seita sees in this movement a new avant-garde that no longer follows Ezra Pound's modernist battle cry to "make it new," but demands instead to "make it now" via "thought experiments in contemporaneity."[57]

Indeed, it is in this context that auto-factography's self-reflexivity may offer its greatest political potential, since it is able to target even the conditions of its own existence. One could call Melgard and Keller's interventions an institutional critique of the seemingly liberating potential of print-on-demand and self-entrepreneurialism. And yet, this type of literature also shows that it is too easy to reject print-on-demand technology or companies like Lulu wholesale as exponents of a "slick neoliberal logic" that promotes "individual empowerment through self-publication," as Lisa Gitelman suggests.[58] Rather, Keller and Melgard attempt to face the restraints of this neoliberal logic head-on—as, in fact, all artists must—knowing that the escapism of ostentatiously "analog" production techniques does not elude the aporias of labor. Instead of simply avoiding new technologies and their entanglement with capitalism, experimental print-on-demand literature hyper-reflexively exploits even its own disappointment in the inability to be unaffected by this technology/art/capital nexus. This, I would argue, gives it greater political heft than more traditional forms of content-based literature are often able to muster, or the often-regressive luddism of a "post-digital" return to older printing and publishing technologies.[59]

As a result, this form of literature claims a unique tie to the present moment—even if Traumawien closed its digital doors in 2016, as did Gauss PDF, which stopped its print-on-demand production after its hundredth edition. This literature manages to reveal both print-on-demand's ontological instability and its socioeconomic conditions, and it uncovers a profoundly contemporary state, a period in which digitality is no longer new enough to be constantly perceptible, but still sufficiently new that the difference between the seemingly "analog" book form and the digital file is felt as peculiar, at times even as uncanny. This is why the print-on-demand literature I have presented here acts both to reaffirm the book and to destabilize it. For while books printed on demand revaluate a medium that is, so we are told, perpetually hovering on the brink of obsolescence, it does not treat the book as a genteel object of high culture but rather as a conspicuously "poor" medium: Lulu's printing quality is notoriously abysmal, and the "semiotic power of paper and binding"[60] does not so much communicate the preciousness of objects from a pre-digital era, but rather their atrophied stage. Print-on-demand does not convey authenticity and subjectivity; its material poverty rather emphasizes the anonymity of its concepts, and its problematization of authorship. One could thus understand print-on-demand literature as the reverse of the literary trend that Jessica Pressman has called "bookishness," the "fetishization of the book-bound nature of the codex as a reading object."[61] The print-on-demand book is anything but fetishizable; in print-on-demand, the book is simultaneously present and absent.

56. Ibid.
57. Sophie Seita, *Provisional Avant-Gardes: Little Magazine Communities from Dada to Digital* (Stanford: Stanford University Press, 2019), 176; reprinted in this volume, 640–651, 650.
58. Lisa Gitelman, "Emoji Dick and the Eponymous Whale," in Brillenburg et al., *Book Presence*, 195–201, here 199.
59. See Cramer, "What is 'Post-Digital'?" Not all Luddism is regressive, to be sure; see Gavin Mueller, *Breaking Things at Work: The Luddites Are Right About Why You Hate Your Job* (London: Verso, 2021).
60. Anna Poletti, "Genre and Materiality: Autobiography and Zines," in Brillenburg et al., *Book Presence*, 90–108, here 104.
61. Jessica Pressman, "The Aesthetic of Bookishness in Twenty-First-Century Literature," *Michigan Quarterly Review* 48, no. 4 (2009): 467.

Sophie Seita

Communities of Print in the Digital Age[1]

1. Excerpted from Sophie Seita, *Provisional Avant-Gardes: Little Magazine Communities from Dada to Digital* (Stanford: Stanford University Press, 2019), 160–176.

MOVABLE CONTEMPORANEITY

When Ezra Pound titled his twenty-part review series of magazines in the British weekly *The New Age* "Studies in Contemporary Mentality," he made a connection between periodical publishing and contemporaneity still apposite today.[2] Regardless of whether critics can make good on Pound's promise to understand contemporary mentality, the medium of the little magazine remains, long after modernism, particularly conducive to describing "the contemporary" of any historical episode, including the present moment. As ever, through their chosen publishing medium avant-gardes may be recognized as provisional and diachronic communities that offer, as magazine editors Michael Cross and Thom Donovan put it, "glimpse[s] into the emergent." In *ON: Contemporary Practice* (2008–), a print and digital magazine of discursive writing about "one's contemporaries," Cross and Donovan state that they are "motivated by desire, friendship, sociopolitical commitment, and discourse among one's communities and peers."[3] It is these commitments and contemporaneities for which the little magazine acted as a barometer throughout the twentieth century and has continued to do so into the twenty-first. What is new is that digital formats and print that is informed by the digital are shaping avant-garde communities and writing, publishing, and reading today. Critical attention to these contemporary developments might, in turn, come to play an active, even transformative, part in the avant-garde and its reception.

But what is "the contemporary," and is "the Period Formerly Known as the Contemporary," as Amy Hungerford quips, even a period? While grouping creative works under "post-1945" or even "long modernism" might situate them more neatly, the label *contemporary* remains useful as avant-garde terminology because its boundaries are rather nicely undefined.[4] Tired of proclamations that contemporary writing is lacking in the more radical forms of the historical avant-gardes, I have argued throughout this book that we need to instantiate avant-gardism as a contemporary concept, beyond the simple model of the original and its lesser copy. Avant-garde reprints in later magazines already raised questions of temporality and futurity: whether any "historical" object or text can become contemporary simply because it is selected for contemplation today or only when it is presented as instructive for or akin to contemporary practice. The editors of *ON: Contemporary Practice* aptly ask, how "can we observe a present while it is still occurring; that is, before it has ossified into events consigned to a representative past," or, conversely, how can we observe what is supposedly ossified as something contemporary?[5] Because our sense of the past and present is always shifting, the avant-gardes in this book sometimes appear more and sometimes less contemporary, more or less of one period. Contemporary publishing communities also follow the logic of a movable contemporaneity and often even make "nowness" rather than "newness" a thematic and technological focus of their work.

Traditionally, critics have declared the avant-garde to be ahead of its time based on an assumption that, as Bruno Latour recognizes, "modernizing progress is thinkable only on condition that all the elements that are contemporary according to the calendar belong to the same time. For this to be the case, these elements have to form a complete and recognizable cohort." The contemporary avant-garde might in some instances form a recognizable though certainly not a coherent and homogeneous "cohort." But when "different periods, ontologies or genres" are "mix[ed] up," "a historical period will give the impression of a great hotchpotch. Instead of a fine laminary flow, we will most often get a turbulent flow of whirlpools and rapids."[6] While Latour excludes the avant-garde (as traditionally defined) from such an assessment, this very "hotchpotch" and the "whirlpools" have characterized magazine communities, past and present, and heterogeneity and cross-group influence remain vital models for the contemporary avant-garde.

How are critics to write about the contemporary hotchpotch, then? A contemporary avant-garde can be theorized, like avant-gardes before it, as a provisional model of necessarily heterogeneous and

2. Ezra Pound, "Studies in Contemporary Mentality," *New Age* (August 1917 to January 1918).

3. Michael Cross and Thom Donovan, "About," *ON: Contemporary Practice*, https://on-contemporarypractice.squarespace.com/about.

4. Amy Hungerford, "On the Period Formerly Known as the Contemporary," *American Literary History* 20, no. 1/2 (2008): 410–19, here 418.

5. Michael Cross, Thom Donovan, and Kyle Schlesinger, "From Center to Margin," *ON: Contemporary Practice*, no. 2 (2010): 7–8, here 7.

6. All quotes from Bruno Latour, *We Have Never Been Modern*, trans. Catherine Porter (New York: Harvester Wheatsheaf, 1993), 73.

dynamic practices. Contemporary avant-gardes in the making are to be found in little magazines, many of which address self-reflexively the politics and hospitality of small-press publishing. Yet scholars of contemporary literature tend to focus not on magazines but on the novel. For the Post45 website, Sarah Chihaya, Joshua Kotin, and Kinohi Nishikawa survey the proposed topics they received for a conference on contemporary literature at Princeton University in 2016.[7] A total of 43 percent of all submissions focused on fiction, 7.4 percent on poetry, another 7.4 percent on digital media. Across all submissions, the majority chose well-known authors and theorists. That fiction would top this (admittedly very small) list of conference topics is not surprising, as it matches the novel's dominance in the contemporary marketplace. When contemporary critics discuss magazines, they often focus on mainstream or at least widely popular periodicals, like *Timothy McSweeney's Quarterly Concern*, edited by Dave Eggers (author of the best-selling memoir *A Heartbreaking Work of Staggering Genius*).[8]

One exception to this dearth of scholarly attention to contemporary magazines is Ian Morris and Joanne Diaz's edited collection *The Little Magazine in Contemporary America*, which includes chapters on *Bomb*, *n+1*, *Callaloo*, *Fence*, *L=A=N=G=U=A=G=E* (which is no longer running), *Poetry*, *McSweeney's*, and other similarly established, well-known, or not exactly "little" magazines. As with many avant-gardes, scholarship often lags behind the more immediate responses generated within a poetry community itself. Contemporary criticism by poets themselves increasingly finds expression via the responsive interfaces of blogs, Facebook, Instagram, and Twitter, of which the latter two are usually limited to short commentaries, quotes, photographs, or the sharing of a text, photograph, or link. The effects and longevity of these sometimes semipublic forms of reception and taste-making are hard to assess, but they point toward an almost entirely unexplored reservoir for future criticism.

The next few decades will clarify the changes in small-press and avant-garde publishing today, in what media scholars call the "late age of print." But to speak of the book or print as an anachronism is to forget that "there are no anachronisms, only ways of seeing things as anachronisms."[9] That print is anything but anachronistic is evident in the sheer quantity of newly produced printed matter and the symbolic value attributed to it; writers are still routinely asked if they are a "published author" (meaning print publishing), and readers still proudly display their bookshelves to visitors. During the process of "mediamorphosis," or "remediation," a new medium is often conceived and explained in relation to a previous one.[10] Online publications, for example, are often produced and read as if they were print, and specifically as if they were made for a codex. Design features, too, are often skeuomorphic: that is, they look like an analog version of a different medium (such as paper) but no longer function the same way. Despite ominous remarks by critics that "the period between 1980 and 2015 will be seen as the end of the ascendency of print periodicals," a focus on digital media need not imply a belief in the supersession of the supposedly obsolescent medium of print.[11] *Intermediation* is a better description of contemporary creative engagement with materials and techniques than *post-print*, because it accepts the ongoing coexistence and mutual transformation of print and digital technologies.[12] *Post-digital*, in turn, might refer to print within a digital media environment. Indeed, digitality now informs nearly all the processes of production, distribution, and reception, whether a work is printed or not.

In a digital publishing space in which magazines are easier and cheaper to launch and to maintain, in which the "now" is often published faster, have the politics of inclusion shifted toward greater diversity and hospitality? How does the virtual-

7. Sarah Chihaya, Joshua Kotin, and Kinohi Nishikawa, "'The Contemporary' by the Numbers," Post45, 2016 http://post45.research.yale.edu/2016/02/the-contemporary-by-the-numbers.

8. See Amy Hungerford, *Making Literature Now* (Stanford, CA: Stanford University Press, 2016).

9. Ted Striphas, *The Late Age of Print: Everyday Book Culture from Consumerism to Control* (New York: Columbia University Press, 2009), 4.

10. Roger Fidler, in *Mediamorphosis: Understanding New Media* (London: Sage, 1999), understands mediamorphosis as the transformation of media and communication systems as a result of complex convergences, developments out of earlier or other media, as well as social, political, and technological processes and needs. Jay David Bolter and Richard Grusin, in *Remediation: Understanding New Media* (Cambridge, MA: MIT Press, 1998), understand remediation as the process by which old or original media are present in or remade into a new medium.

11. Ian Morris and Joanne Diaz, preface to *The Little Magazine in Contemporary America*, ed. Ian Morris and Joanne Diaz (Chicago: University of Chicago Press, 2015), vii–xvii, vii; Brian M. Reed, *Nobody's Business: Twenty-First Century Avant-Garde Poetics* (Ithaca, NY: Cornell University Press, 2013), 1.

12. The term *intermediation* comes from Ted Striphas, who prefers it over *remediation*. See Striphas, *Late Age of Print*, 15–16.

ly infinite expanse of the digital commons with its overabundance of data affect contemporary modes of reading? Since digitization and availability tackle the scarcity attached to avant-garde materials, approaches to distribution and reception of little magazines need to be revised. This does not mean that avant-garde publishing communities are now only to be found in digital form or in digitally inspired print forms. Many avant-garde print magazines continue either the DIY cheap-print and photocopy mentality or, conversely, the letterpress tradition. This chapter therefore examines what it means for an avant-garde to engage inventively with the digital medium today and how that engagement affects avant-garde socialities and identities.

THINKING THE UNPRINTABLE

In a 2013 interview, poet and publisher J. Gordon Faylor jokingly remarked that the American publishing collective Troll Thread, which publishes PDF files and print-on-demand versions of those PDFs, "exploit[s] [the print-on-demand platform] Lulu's bookmaking technology in more diversely insidious ways" than his own Gauss PDF, another Tumblr-based project that publishes PDFs and multimedia works.[13] These contemporary uses of online or print-on-demand publishing are so "diversely insidious" not because they bypass carefully calculated and often handmade print runs, or because these presses publish work that might not otherwise appear elsewhere (which has become an avant-garde truism in itself over the last century); rather, the artful exploitation lies in Troll Thread's and Gauss PDF's publication of works that seem out of place in a codex, that cannot or should not be printed, but that insist on printedness, even if only imagined, all the same.

What I would like to call the "imagined printedness" in the digital and print-on-demand publishing projects of Troll Thread, Gauss PDF, and Triple Canopy allows these publishers to escalate definitions of "poetry," the "magazine," the "book," and "publishing" within their overlapping contemporary small-press and avant-garde communities.[14] Born-digital publishing and what Lisa Gitelman terms the "near print" technology of the PDF enable new experiments with the production, distribution, and reception of avant-garde work.[15] An online Tumblr that publishes PDFs and/or other file formats, often single-author works but also collaborations, might not immediately look like a magazine, but Troll Thread and Gauss PDF can be considered metaphorical extensions of avant-garde little magazine communities. One reason is that they display their contributions in ways that resemble the table of contents of a magazine issue, with content added and distributed periodically. Aesthetically, too, there is a clear sense of seriality. In this way, these digital publishers follow the practice of some earlier magazines, such as the proto-Language magazines *QU* or *A Hundred Posters*, in their publication of generally one author per "issue." Moreover, like avant-garde magazines in the twentieth century, Troll Thread and Gauss PDF have established a small community around their publications with several contributors in common.

Historically, many little magazines also doubled as a small press. *Others* had an imprint for books by its contributors, as did *0 to 9*; *Roof* began as a magazine and continued as a press; *Chain* was a magazine and had the spin-off book series Chain Links. But for the avant-garde in the digital age, the distinction between individual work, book, small press, and magazine becomes even less clear-cut, changing how avant-garde communities and their publishing projects work inside and outside of this differently networked online environment. So what does it mean to think printedness in digital avant-garde publishing? The following publications often highlight their medium of composition and distribution (each with a specific materiality) and make processes of mediation their investigative focus. We are invited to read these digital materials as akin to print even when analog printedness is only imagined or simply impossible. If, as Jerome McGann writes, "literary documents bear within themselves the evidence of their own making," the remainders of print in a never-printed document complicate that trajectory: they show

13. Kristen Gallagher, "The Gauss Interview: Chris Alexander Talks to J. Gordon Faylor," *Jacket2*, March 5, 2013, http://jacket2.org/commentary/gauss-interview. Faylor founded Gauss PDF in 2010. Its name is a pun on the Gaussian probability distribution function. Troll Thread was founded in 2010 by Chris Sylvester, who was soon joined by Joey Yearous-Algozin, Holly Melgard, and Divya Victor (who later left the project).

14. All three projects move within overlapping circles in primarily New York City, Philadelphia, and Buffalo.

15. Lisa Gitelman, *Paper Knowledge: Toward a Media History of Documents* (Durham, NC: Duke University Press, 2014), 117.

traces they can never quite have.[16] I will now turn to these imagined remainders.

Holly Melgard's *BLACK FRIDAY* was released by Troll Thread, the publishing collective she co-edits, on Black Friday, November 2012, as an 8.5 × 11 inch print-on-demand book. Of its 740 pages, 734 are entirely black except for their white page numbers. As the poem's dedication page specifies, it is a book "for BLACK INK ON WHITE PAPER." Though couched in the language of the printed book, a PDF like *BLACK FRIDAY* also invokes the antecedent of the codex: the scroll, a form that lends itself to compendious and sequential reading, bringing it closer to oratory and time-based media. Troll Thread was started in part, as co-editor Chris Sylvester puts it, "to make massive quantities of text or data or whatever available all at once and in the same place [...] as 'one thing.'"[17] This generically indefinable "or whatever" is an apt rallying cry for a publishing project intent on troubling literariness and on differentiating the book from the codex. Melgard similarly describes *BLACK FRIDAY* as an experiment with her medium: "poems can exploit what it is in books that makes texts appear as 'text'; how their distributions and multiple frameworks of production may play a material role in their composition, their poetics."[18] These "material" frameworks include Melgard's computer, her word processing and publishing software, and the specifications of Lulu's book-making facilities, as well as the project's monetary value, or lack thereof. Indeed, *BLACK FRIDAY* probes its existence within a small-press print economy that in monetary terms often costs more than it returns, and its entirely digital circulation invites readers to reflect on the circulation of money. Ostensibly an attempt to "break an industrial printer," Melgard literalizes the conventionalized avant-garde trope of rupture, testing if or how poetry could actually, and not just metaphorically, break things.[19] But, judging from the error messages the author receives from the print-on-demand platform Lulu whenever someone attempts to purchase a copy, the breaking remains only a thought experiment. Rather than a demonstration of the end of printed matter, *BLACK FRIDAY* demonstrates the specific possibilities of print-on-demand publishing: since Lulu charges a publisher the same for blank or black pages, at least hypothetically, and since 740 is the maximum number of pages Lulu allows for a perfect-bound book, *BLACK FRIDAY* attempts, like its inadvertent twin Jean Keller's *The Black Book* (2010/2012), "the lowest cost and maximum value for the artist."[20]

Other Troll Thread titles likewise thematize the economics of poetry publishing and the long history of avant-garde unprofitability. Melgard's *REIMBUR$EMENT* (2013), subtitled on its dedication page "For Work," features images of lottery and scratch-off tickets, the cost of the book amounting to the money Melgard lost to gambling during graduate school to make up for her unpaid labor, thus turning the avant-garde gift economy on its head ("A Gift Economy is a Debt Economy in my book").[21] *MONEY* (2012) by "Maker" publishes cutouts of hundred-dollar bills, avouching cheekily that the responsibility concerning counterfeit law lies with "the document's printer," who is the work's "maker."[22] Joey Yearous-Algozin's *HOW TO STOP WORRYING ABT THE STATE OF PUBLISHING WHEN THE WORLD'S BURNING AND EVERYBODY'S BROKE ANYWAYS AND ALL YOU REALLY CARE ABT IS IF ANYONE IS EVEN READING YR WORK* (July 2016) is a half-serious, half-ironic instruction manual in the form of a two-page lineated "poem" in large type that practices the cheap DIY and print-on-demand publishing it preaches.[23] What could be called Troll Thread's print-on-demand manifes-

16. Jerome McGann, *A New Republic of Letters: Memory and Scholarship in the Age of Digital Reproduction* (Cambridge, MA: Harvard University Press, 2014), 84.

17. Holly Melgard, Joey Yearous-Algozin, and Chris Sylvester, "Troll Thread Interview," by Tan Lin, *Harriet: A Poetry Blog*, May 4, 2014, www.poetryfoundation.org/harriet/2014/05/troll-thread-interview.

18. Holly Melgard, "Statement of Poetics," *Revista Laboratorio*, no. 8 (2013): www.laboratoriodeescrituras.cl/holly-melgard.

19. Melgard, Yearous-Algozin, and Sylvester, "Troll Thread Interview."

20. Jean Keller, *The Black Book*, www.lulu.com/shop/jean-keller/the-black-book/paperback/product-21008894.html.

21. Holly Melgard, *REIMBUR$EMENT* (Troll Thread, 2013), 1. Melgard initially made *REIMBUR$EMENT* for inclusion in the exhibition "Poetry Will Be Made By All! / 89Plus" in Zurich in January of 2014, knowing that this would guarantee at least one printed copy and she would then be "reimbursed." She was not included in the end, being born before 1989, so her "reimbursement" was delayed until the University at Buffalo Libraries Poetry Collection (which now has a standing order for all Troll Thread titles) ordered a copy.

22. Maker, *MONEY* (Troll Thread, 2012), unpaginated.

23. Troll Thread often publishes typographically and conceptually odd work (say, Yearous-Algozin's own *9/11 911 CALLS IN 911 PT. FONT*; or Chris Sylvester's *STILL LIFE W/ BLOG 07/12/13 04:24PM // 05:12PM // 264 PGS MSWORD // 10/18/13 // 3:45PM // 595 PGS MSWORD*) that makes conventional word-by-word reading difficult or impossible.

to, *HOW TO STOP WORRYING* demystifies the publishing business by showing how easy it is to self-publish and start a small press, reminiscent of the many paeans for the small press put forth by earlier avant-gardes. But Yearous-Algozin's "how-to" document lacks the utopian tinge associated with that genre of avant-garde writing and is in fact quite pragmatic:

> don't worry about making it look good,
> gutters,
> paratext, etc.
> that's all just marketing
> leave that to "editors" who can pay
> "designers", i.e.
> bosses
> or until you learn morc about laying
> out books, which
> you never need to learn
> save yr cover as a .jpg & upload it in
> the cover
> designer or use the default settings
> whatever
> set the price at zero revenue
> that way you can buy more copies when
> lulu has coupons
> for free shipping
> also, this is poetry, you shouldn't be
> making a profit
> don't be an asshole[24]

That poets do not usually make a profit—there are, for instance, far fewer "professional" poets than novelists—is a realistic assessment, but it also ironizes the widespread avant-garde imperative for poets to position themselves outside capital. Although Troll Thread borrows its house format and approach to media from *0 to 9*, 8.5 × 11 inch is also simply one of the default sizes available in Lulu's bookmaking facilities. It is worth noting that several Troll Thread authors work with such default settings as constraints for creative production, letting the default determine the work. Within a history of print publishing dominated by an esteem for craft, manual skill, the intricacies of typographical design, and the time and expense required for the production process, Troll Thread's labor and rationale for publishing the "books" in their catalog (or in Melgard's case, the labor of "composing" *BLACK FRIDAY*) is much harder to determine, and deliberately so.[25] The form and content of *BLACK FRIDAY* and *HOW TO STOP WORRYING* think of "the book" as a (failed) commodity and as a (failed) material object.

That said, *BLACK FRIDAY* in particular is also a self-consciously literary work. While *Tristram Shandy*'s famous black page (which is an explicit reference point for Melgard) shows its own self-awareness as a mechanically produced book rather than as a manuscript copied by scribes, *BLACK FRIDAY*'s black pages show it no longer needs to be mechanically produced in order to be a book: it can exist as a digitally imagined book, even an unprintable one.[26] In *Tristram Shandy*, the black page is a mimetic attempt at mourning the character Yorick's death via the medium of the book. *BLACK FRIDAY*, which commemorates "BLACK INK ON WHITE PAPER" in the form of a serialized tombstone in pages, humorously mourns not the end of books but rather the readers' attachment to a particular understanding of the printed page. Black ink on white paper as print is thought but unrealized; the one exception to the work's unrealizability involved a librarian who snatched a meager thirty pages from the critic Brian Reed, resulting in "a failed partial printout [that] will now be archived as a paper form of a digital artefact."[27] Perhaps such an incomplete and imperfect print reproduction is the ideal in-between condition for *BLACK FRIDAY*: instead of a slick perfect-bound book with high production values, the loose pages with their cheap and streaked black ink flaunt, or taunt us with, the idea of the unprintable, even if or precisely when they are printed. In a stroke of bib-

24. Joey Yearous-Algozin, *HOW TO STOP WORRYING [...]* (Troll Thread, July 2016), 1.

25. Amy Hungerford discusses a similarly self-conscious display of publishing economics in *Making Literature Now*. For her, the breakdown of printing, shipping, and other publishing costs in several early issues of *McSweeney's* is a "DIY exhortation" based in "the anticommercial DIY ethic of punk" and zine culture that *McSweeney's* identifies with (26). But when compared to Yearous-Algozin's print-on-demand PDF "poem," *McSweeney's* detailing of printing costs and revenue, which far exceeds the "zero revenue" of Troll Thread, can seem like a gimmick; there is little "punk" in the members' benefits for donors who give $10,000 or more to the *McSweeney's* enterprise, which includes a press, two print magazines, and an online magazine. Unlike *McSweeney's*, which Hungerford shows has "made" the careers of several writers, Troll Thread is unlikely to—and does not even care to—do so.

26. See Laurence Sterne, *The Life and Opinions of Tristram Shandy, Gentleman*, 3rd ed. (London: R. and J. Dodsley, 1760), 1:73.

27. Brian Reed and Craig Dworkin, "Untitled Conversation," in *Affect and Audience in the Digital Age*, ed. Amaranth Borsuk (Athens, OH: Essay Press, 2014), 1–16, here 5.

liographic irony, Melgard has by now been able to order a hardbound copy of *BLACK FRIDAY*, and in its failed dematerialization one could therefore say, as Melgard put it in conversation with me, "I guess the project is over."[28]

Troll Thread's awareness of printedness, publishing technology, and (supposedly) unprintable content and forms aligns it with the many formal and generic experiments of earlier avant-gardes. Whereas avant-garde publications across the twentieth century often mixed genres, digital platforms enable a mixing of media that was impossible to the same extent in previous print technologies. As "a publication suited to any type of media file," J. Gordon Faylor's Gauss PDF (which ceased publication in 2022) features PDFs as well as numerous other file types, such as .mov, .rtf, .jpg, .mp4, .mp3, and .zip, in addition to YouTube playlists, image collections, and poems in Word documents.[29] It shares this multiplicity of file formats with the largely digital publishing project Badlands Unlimited (2010–2019), whose series "Files" publishes artists' editions as collectors' items to download.[30] But Gauss PDF operates primarily in a (conceptual) writing context, even though the majority of pieces would be difficult to categorize as poems or even as literary texts; they are simply works fascinated with digital materiality, medium specificity, and genre. Tonya St. Clair's *Cloud Storage for Everyone* (GPDF048, 2012), for example, is a PDF consisting of a link to a Dropbox folder containing all previously published Gauss PDFs, the link itself blown up into large type with line breaks. Feliz Lucia Molina's *A Letter to Kim Jong-il Looking at Things* (GPDF045, 2012), in turn, repeats a letter addressed to Kim Jong-il (then already deceased) in 143 Microsoft Word fonts, alongside various pictures of the dictator looking at toilet paper, a tractor, "people starving, etc.," and other images trawled from a Tumblr called "Kim Jong-il Looking at Things."[31] In both publications, digital storage, navigation, and the customizability of personal computers become part of the pieces' meaning-generating mechanisms.

The variety of genre and media references notwithstanding, Gauss PDFs are unified in the way they are displayed on the Gauss Tumblr. The consecutive numbering of each publication as GPDF + number in its "catalog" section evokes bibliographic standards and archival practices usually associated with print, though in this case the bibliographic reference also constitutes part of a Tumblr URL. In 2013, Gauss PDF began publishing Gauss Editions using the print-on-demand service Lulu, and Faylor describes the editions as appearing "somehow a priori digitized; the books all have that same look and feel. It's as though the publishing wizard is somehow inscribed behind the text, like a watermark."[32] Through Lulu's layout templates, Gauss PDF publications look like they were always meant to remain digital. Nevertheless, Faylor uses a print historical term—*watermark*—to explain a phenomenon rooted in digitality. Historically, a watermark indicates to readers that the paper of a book is handmade and therefore more valuable, while the watermark's specific shape functions as a papermaker's signature. No longer handmade, Gauss PDF's digital watermark imbues the digital object with the promise of a signature and with a materiality specific to its publishing technology and screen-based reading environment.

That printedness can be realized digitally is the design conceit of a Gauss PDF piece by Daniel Wilson. *Files I Have Known: Data Reminiscences* (GPDF199, 2016) is an autobiographical account of the author's memories of files that no longer exist. The imagined "book" traces Wilson's encounters with ephemeral files on his computer. Both visually and conceptually, the project exploits the disjunction between a file and its description in another medium, as Wilson explains in the foreword: "Can the original essence of a data file be recreated purely by words?"[33] Unlike other publications by Gauss PDF or Troll Thread that complicate close reading owing to the sheer quantity or illegibility of the material, *Files I Have Known* rewards sequential story-based reading. In narrativizing digital materiality, Wilson's specifications of file types, file sizes, file names ("amb1.wav," "fafda.rtf," "!A19TOP!.S3M"), and creation dates (from the 1990s to 2015) are offset by the

28. Holly Melgard, conversation with the author, March 28, 2017.
29. Gallagher, "The Gauss Interview."
30. The files, which can be downloaded for $150–300 to support contemporary artists, include PDFs, a PowerPoint presentation, code in the form of a Perl script, and a newly designed typeface.
31. Feliz Lucia Molina, *A Letter to Kim Jong-Il Looking at Things* (Gauss PDF, 2012), 4.
32. Gallagher, "The Gauss Interview."
33. Daniel Wilson, *Files I Have Known: Data Reminiscences* (Gauss PDF, 2016), 5.

old-fashioned look of the decaying page, which, readers are invited to imagine, is weathered by age and bad archival conditions. The whitish, fungi-induced patches on a cover with crumbling edges and a yellowed dedication page with brownish stains that are usually the result of light exposure and age-related deterioration ("foxing") contradict the title's and the contents' utter contemporaneity. Or rather, the files' decomposition is represented visually by a process that is not local to their digital environment.

Wilson does not just mirror the skeuomorphism of digital-design inventions; he exploits it poetically. Although the cover's decorative border matches the paper, the title's retro-art-nouveau font and the interior text look tagged on, unblended with the supposedly aged page. Of course, the PDF "pages" are not the deteriorated paper of a book called *Files I Have Known*; they are either modified scans of an extant printed book or photoshopped pages with a "vintage" effect applied. Given the range of design possibilities today, including apps that create a letterpress look, Wilson is less interested in a perfect copy of print than in a media-specific originality. *Files I Have Known* fakes printedness, but fakes it badly, in order to create its own uniquely digital printedness.[34]

While Melgard's and Wilson's tongue-in-cheek simulations of printedness cleverly explore distinctions and overlaps between print and digital, e-readers and software that displays digitized material simulate print without irony or media-specific awareness. Not every digital project that publishes avant-garde work or circulates within an avant-garde community is automatically avant-garde in the way it engages with its publishing medium. The online archive of Ugly Duckling Presse (UDP), a New York-based independent publisher of historical and contemporary avant-garde writing, art, translation, and performance, as well as less experimental materials, hosts scans of out-of-print publications in an animated Flash-based reader that enables the comparative reading across page spreads that readers are accustomed to in books and magazines. These documents include the scan of a damaged copy of UDP's magazine *6 × 6*.[35] The burnt edges might immediately call up associations of censorship and book burning, to which underground presses have been subject in the past, while its off-center and slightly diagonal title, set in wood type, alludes to the typographical experiments of Dada. But unlike the knowing irony of the material traces in *Files I Have Known*, these are "real" stains and the result of a fire in the press's old storage facility, a fact unknown to readers except by word of mouth. These burn marks might grant the magazine a deceptively palpable materiality, but in the online viewer the materials have been rendered digital, a process carried further by the mediation of the flip-book software in its simulation of paper reading. I can hover my cursor over a corner, which will then curl its dog-ear toward me, as if I had touched it after lightly wetting my fingers to mark my place. And when I turn the page—that is, when I "click to read"—I hear a swoosh sound, like the movement of paper, as if in pursuit of the tangibly authentic in the digital realm. This software gimmick seems simultaneously adequate and ludicrous for a magazine that highlights its materiality and small-press credentials.[36] The pristine display of the software creates a mismatch, making the magazine appear more precious, even kitschier, than its print version. The issue's cover text, "its autobiography of touch," taken from the first poem in the issue, suddenly reads like a remark on the object's material journey: as if it knew it would be "touched" by fire but not, in its digital iteration, by my readerly cursor-hand.

While UDP's online archive uses Flash, a publishing technology well-suited to multimedia projects, it is not surprising that Gauss PDF, Troll Thread, and peer projects such as SOd, Hysterically Real, and Badlands Unlimited use PDFs. Such a capacious file format—it is either an index of a

34. Repurposing the look of old print forms has become popular over the last few years in avant-garde publishing, perhaps spurred by large-scale commercial digitization projects like Google Books, which put out-of-print materials into the public domain, but also by the sheer ease with which old designs can be appropriated digitally. Two projects that mimic older print technology and design are the magazine *The Germ* (1997–2005), edited by Macgregor Card and Andrew Maxwell, titled in homage to the Pre-Raphaelite journal of the same name; and the anthology of English-to-English "translations" of Shakespeare's *Sonnets*, published by the experimental translation magazine *Telephone*, ed. Sharmila Cohen and Paul Legault (2010–).

35. *6 × 6*, no. 5 (Dec. 2001), Ugly Duckling Presse Online Chapbook Archive, www.uglyducklingpresse.org/archive/online-reading-old/6x6-5-our-goal-is-the-victory-of-midnight-and-its-autobiography-of-touch-by-6x6-poets.

36. The letterpress cover and the hand-cut edge, more visible in the intact version, pay homage to Russian Futurist Vasily Kamensky's 1914 chapbook *Tango with Cows*.

once-printed object or a digital object that is only imagined to be printed—appeals to projects that explore alternative models and scales of printedness and the codex. The PDF is "framed by the genre of the document" or "gray literature," such as government reports or product manuals—in other words, nonliterary texts. PDFs also can, since Adobe's introduction of Acrobat X in 2010, embed audio and video files; and the introduction of that new functionality indeed coincided with the founding of Troll Thread and Gauss PDF. For Lisa Gitelman, PDFs are "documents that may be said to conjure themselves"; they are both text and an image of that text.[37]

Following Derrida's remarks about screen-based writing, one could argue that Melgard's *BLACK FRIDAY*, Wilson's *Files I Have Known*, and, most explicitly, UDP's burnt *6 × 6* issue "retain the memory of what has disappeared: the paper, the page of the codex."[38] The PDF's "look of printedness" has nevertheless been "separated from paper and mobilized online,"[39] and there is no sense of anachronism or nostalgia attached to these experiments, at least not for Troll Thread or Gauss PDF.

Although Troll Thread still designs its PDFs in recto/verso pages for printing a codex, it does not necessarily "expect people to actually purchase the physical copies," and it views Lulu primarily as "a means to host the PDFs, something Tumblr's platform doesn't accommodate, without having to pay for our own domain."[40] For this reason, Hannes Bajohr suggests that Troll Thread, Gauss PDF, and his own 0x0a are treating "POD as [an] artistic practice."[41] For critics of such writing this might mean that, as Nick Thurston urges, "we have to find new ways of *reading* publishing," namely, by "re-conceptualiz[ing] reproduction as a form of production."[42] More broadly, to understand "publishing as artistic practice," as a recent title by the avant-garde publisher Sternberg Press suggests, might offer a conceptual category for such media-blending and indeterminate work. Focusing on distribution, the Troll Thread editors argue, is part of their project's avant-garde appeal: "in flattening out the text and making it more easily distributed, it loses an important part of its aesthetic, i.e. exceptional, status."[43] In some ways, this is an avant-garde gesture familiar from *The Blind Man*, *0 to 9*, and 1970s Xeroxed magazines and is at heart a Benjaminian argument about the nature of reproducibility simply hiked up to a new scale. But in the mundane context of the web, more so than in other media, a reader's reverence for the digitized object might be lessened. Perhaps the avant-garde's aura will "wither," and we will remove it from the pedestal it has occupied in our political and cultural imagination, and that could prove to be a healthy turn of events.[44]

It is apt that the platform that hosts Gauss PDF and Troll Thread is the multimedia-based Tumblr. Although both publishers use a template that evokes a minimalist Swiss design, Tumblr is not a static website and does not usually have the look of other more literary and professional blogs or websites: as a hosting site for sharing, it foregrounds its blogging aspect, and one of its default designs presents the dashboard as a true hotchpotch of images and notes. While the printed book is a discrete unit with a starting and ending point, the borders of the sometimes multimedia, sometimes nonliterary, and sometimes long and sprawling work published by Gauss PDF are less clearly defined. Similarly, the born-digital magazine *Triple Canopy* (2007–) veers inquisitively toward print, digital, and something else entirely. It expands the traditional magazine issue generically, temporally, and spatially by defining it as "includ[ing] digital works of art and literature, public conversations, books, editions, performances, and exhibitions [...] published over the course of several months, often concurrently."[45] In this multimedia approach, *Triple Canopy* resembles and deliberately evokes earlier media-spanning magazines such as *Aspen*, the magazine-in-a-box, with its flexi-disks, flip-books, and foldouts, but *Triple Canopy*'s temporally unbounded nature is a partic-

37. All quotes from Gitelman, *Paper Knowledge*, 115, 114.
38. Jacques Derrida, *Paper Machine*, trans. Rachel Bowlby (Stanford: Stanford University Press, 2005), 46.
39. Gitelman, *Paper Knowledge*, x, 115.
40. Melgard, Yearous-Algozin, and Sylvester, "Troll Thread Interview."
41. Hannes Bajohr, "Experimental Writing in Its Moment of Digital Technization: Post-Digital Literature and Print-on-Demand Publishing," in *Publishing as Artistic Practice*, ed. Annette Gilbert (Berlin: Sternberg Press, 2016), 100–115, here 101.
42. Nick Thurston, "The Mediatization of Contemporary Writing," in *Publishing as Artistic Practice*, ed. Annette Gilbert (Berlin: Sternberg Press, 2016), 90–99, here 93, 96.
43. Melgard, Yearous-Algozin, and Sylvester, "Troll Thread Interview."
44. Walter Benjamin, *Illuminations*, trans. Harry Zohn, ed. Hannah Arendt (New York: Schocken, 1969), 221.
45. "Issues," *Triple Canopy*, www.canopycanopycanopy.com/issues.

ular affordance of its online environment.[46] While *Aspen* featured a variety of media as separate items in a box, *Triple Canopy*, like Gauss PDF and other digital publishers, can blend these media and undo the hierarchies among them. To include public events in the definition of an "issue" (or a "book," as UDP did with its performance-based "paperless books") is then only the logical extension of a field already broadened by the distributive and material multiplicity of the web.[47]

Displaying its links to the print tradition, *Triple Canopy* experiments with its online environment by tilting the scroll model of websites to a sideways click or swipe, akin to flip-books or flip-book software. It does so in the hope that such an experiment provides "subtle cues that a proper reading experience is under way," but its design also invokes the smooth elegance of Apple products.[48] While there were indeed earlier, often commercial, websites with clickable content that proceeded frame by frame, the design remains unusual for a contemporary literary magazine. Reminiscent of such websites but also of turning pages in a print magazine, *Triple Canopy* combines an imagined resemblance to each of the technologies it intermediates, which the editors relish in referring to the page as a "metaphor."[49] *Triple Canopy* is a highly self-conscious enterprise precisely in this regard: its slogan is to "slow down the internet."[50] The editors also remain aware of the built-in "obsolescence" at the heart of their new media project.[51] This obsolescence is less philosophical than practical: display formats are not accessible forever; links break, and browsers update. Between 2011 and 2013, the editors therefore published three volumes of *Invalid Format: An Anthology of Triple Canopy*—a selective gathering of materials published in the magazine's first four issues, documentation for their public events, and some editorial correspondence. In its self-archiving, the magazine reversed the practice of using the digital as a means of preservation, and instead considered "printable PDFs," "curat[ing] shows in galleries," or "publishing books[...] as a form of 'artful archiving.'" Specifically, the editors asked themselves how the magazine's digital material could be "degraded elegantly, without disappearing entirely, in print."[52] The anthology's design paid equal homage to older print technologies: all fonts were digital renderings of earlier fonts, including an eighteenth-century Dutch typeface, a 1903 Gothic typeface, the typewriter font Courier New, and Helvetica, one of the most popular design fonts to this day.

As with any change in print technology, digital publishing has specific affordances and a specific bibliographic code. Matthew Kirschenbaum, N. Katherine Hayles, and Jerome McGann have long insisted on the materiality of electronic texts and on reading them as cultural and historical forms in ways similar to how printed texts are analyzed.[53] Such attention to digital literary materials benefits from knowledge of print history and traditional textual scholarship and must also include the writing implements that are integral to any textual or artistic production. Given that many authors now type their work, without ever copying from a handwritten draft, notions of authorship and composition processes naturally require adjustment. An author can write, produce, and distribute a work in a single day; the chain of production, reception, and distribution, or what Robert Darnton famously called the "communications circuit," is thus radically reduced.[54] Digital media also lend themselves to revision in ways the letterpress, mimeograph, and photocopier did not: revision can be more invisible than the manual corrections in letter-pressed text or photocopies or the correction fluid used for mimeographed mistakes.[55] In

46. Editors, "A Note on Unplaced Movements: On the Errant Histories of Flip Books, Cassette Tapes, and Online Publishing," *Triple Canopy*, no. 9 (2010), www.canopycanopycanopy.com/issues/9/contents/a_note_on_unplaced_movements.

47. For a while, UDP published "books which escape attempts to keep them in one place" and which "address the basic assumptions and structures of book distribution and its relationship to how we read." One such paperless project, Julien Poirier and Amy Fusselman's "Phone Books," consists of work written to be performed and received over the phone. See www.uglyducklingpresse.org/catalog/browse/paperless-book-department.

48. Colby Chamberlain, "The Binder and the Server," *Art Journal Open*, Feb. 18, 2012, http://artjournal.collegeart.org/?p=2644.

49. Editors, "A Note on Invalid Format," in *Invalid Format: An Anthology of Triple Canopy* (New York: Triple Canopy, 2011), 2–5, here 3.

50. Chamberlain, "The Binder and the Server."

51. Editors, "A Note on Unplaced Movements," 2.

52. Editors, "A Note on Invalid Format," 3.

53. Matthew G. Kirschenbaum, *Mechanisms: New Media and the Forensic Imagination* (Cambridge, MA: MIT Press, 2008); N. Katherine Hayles, *My Mother Was a Computer: Digital Subjects and Literary Texts* (Chicago: University of Chicago Press, 2005); and Jerome McGann, *A New Republic of Letters: Memory and Scholarship in the Age of Digital Reproduction* (Cambridge, MA: Harvard University Press, 2014).

54. Robert Darnton, "What Is the History of Books?", *Daedalus* 111, no. 3 (1982): 65–83, here 68.

55. Hannah Sullivan's *The Work of Revision* (Cambridge, MA: Harvard University Press, 2013) shows in great detail that changes in writing equipment, print technology, and the very understanding of revision have affected how, when, and why authors revise.

this way, new publishing technologies adjust the labor—or at least the outward appearance of labor—involved in publishing.

Throughout the history of small-press publishing, editors have frequently commented on the labor of typing mimeograph stencils or setting letterpress type.[56] Today, knowing which digital program poets and editors used, and knowing the affordances of InDesign, Lulu, or Tumblr, might offer a new understanding of a piece or an author's mode of working. Unlike the letterpress or mimeograph, our computers are not purely technologies for printing. We use them for other things, too: drafting a poem, listening to music, scheduling meetings. Although some texts do become more fragmented when digitized, digital reading is not exclusively or automatically "segmented, fragmented, discontinuous."[57] Nor is it necessarily matched by the interactivity, intertextuality, and nonlinear readings that are said to be built into the magazine format, because some works and magazines, despite their fragmented structure, demand a linear reading.[58] The medium does not affect objects and reading experiences always in the same way.

The aforementioned publishing projects each participate in the contemporary trend toward what Jessica Pressman calls an "aesthetic of bookishness," which is not "merely another move of postmodern reflexivity" but rather "a serious reflection on the book—and the literary book in particular—through experimentation with the media-specific properties of print illuminated by the light of the digital." Unlike the novels Pressman studies, the projects considered here do not experiment with bookishness or printedness for fear of the "death of the book" or magazine; their aim is not to inject "vigor" into the print medium in order to "remain innovative."[59] Instead, these works incorporate print technology and its concomitant materiality, reading habits, and literariness into the digital to create printedness digitally without attachment to paper. The printed book, as Kirschenbaum has argued, is only one possible outcome that shares the distributive and receptive infrastructure of other media while equally functioning as a "book." For projects that display such qualities, Kirschenbaum has coined the phrase "bookish media," where the adjectival *bookish* can be a quality that applies to digital forms as well.[60] Bookish media exhibit a "secondary materiality," something that is "both remarkably like and remarkably unlike materiality."[61]

The situation is similar for what I call the "magazine-ish" media published by Troll Thread, Gauss PDF, UDP's "paperless book department," and Triple Canopy, which are all "printish": they invite a redefinition of print as the inscription and impression on a surface that need not be paper.[62] Whether it is the sound effect of rustling paper and the burnt pages in UDP's online archive, or the little white hand in PDF readers mimicking a tactile material interaction, or Daniel Wilson's handwritten signature and faded paper imitation, or the economic and symbolic value of print in various Troll Thread titles, this imagined printedness, or what Derrida refers to as the "paper-form of thinking" and the "order of the page," reconceives digital publishing.[63] These works look like print or pretend they work like print; thus, they uphold for readers "the spectral model of the book" at the same time as they transform that

56. When Bernadette Mayer and Susan Bee remarked that they did the nitty-gritty work of typing stencils (Mayer) or designing the layout (Bee) for their male co-editors, or in Bee's case, her husband, they revealed a gendered division of labor. In other cases, comments on the labor of printing speak to a magazine's poetics. The magazine editors Tom Raworth and Hettie Jones noted in interviews that hand-setting contributions for *Outburst* and *Yugen*, respectively, made them appreciate short and simple lines, which in turn may have affected their own writing. Stephanie Anderson, "An Interview with Hettie Jones," *Chicago Review* 59, no. 1/2 (Fall 2014 / Winter 2015): 79–90, here 80; and Kyle Schlesinger and Matt Chambers, "Tom Raworth: An Interview Conducted by Kyle Schlesinger and Matt Chambers, Poetry Collection, Buffalo, May 22, 2006," *Mimeo Mimeo*, no. 4 (Winter 2010): 7–18, here 11.

57. Roger Chartier, "Languages, Books, and Reading from Printed Word to the Digital Text," trans. Teresa Lavender Fagan, *Critical Inquiry* 31, no. 1 (August 2004): 133–152, here 151.

58. Sean Latham, "The Mess and Muddle of Modernism: The Modernist Journals Project and Modern Periodical Studies," *Tulsa Studies in Women's Literature* 30, no. 2 (Fall 2011): 407–428, here 412.

59. All quotes from Jessica Pressman, "The Aesthetic of Bookishness in 21st-Century Literature," *Michigan Quarterly Review* 48, no. 4 (2009): 465–482, here 466.

60. Matthew G. Kirschenbaum, "The RESTful Book: Bibliography and Bookish Media," lecture presented at the A.S.W. Rosenbach Lectures in Bibliography, Philadelphia, PA, 2016, www.youtube.com/watch?v=Wm_DuhVrhGM.

61. Kirschenbaum, "The RESTful book." N. Katherine Hayles, in "Combining Close Reading and Distant Reading: Jonathan Safran Foer's *Tree of Codes* and the Aesthetic of Bookishness," *PMLA* 128, no. 1 (2013): 226–231, even goes so far as to argue that "print books are now so interpenetrated with digital media at every stage of their production that they may more appropriately be considered an output form of digital texts than a separate medium" (226).

62. *Magazine-ish* fits closely with the other terms in this chapter, like *bookish* and *printish*, and it is also a term that already exists, though it isn't widely used. The *OED* credits Samuel Taylor Coleridge with first using *magazinish* in a letter in 1794. See the *Oxford English Dictionary*, s.v. "magazinish, adj."

63. Derrida, *Paper Machine*, 48, 46.

model.[64] In other words, they think print even if they remain or must remain unprinted. They are thought experiments in contemporaneity, where innovation is no longer the primary motivating factor for an avant-garde. As the Poetic Research Bureau puts it in its contribution to Triple Canopy's *Invalid Format* anthology, "'make new' is of less import than make now."[65]

64. Derrida, *Paper Machine*, 30.
65. Poetic Research Bureau, "For an Unoriginal Literature: 'Novelty Is Suicide.' An Introduction to and Dispatch from a Literary Service in the Public Domain," in *Invalid Format: An Anthology of Triple Canopy* (New York: Triple Canopy, 2011), 153–156, here 155. The PRB is a small collective based in Los Angeles and run by Ara Shirinyan, Andrew Maxwell, and Joseph Mosconi. Shirinyan also edits Make Now Press. Maxwell edited *The Germ* with Macgregor Card.

& Tea

nunity
ching

Temporary Services

Half Letter Press and Our Reasons for Running It[1]

1. First published in *Publishing in the Realm of Plant Fibers and Electrons* (Chicago, IL: Temporary Services, 2015).

Illustrated by Kione Kochi
Flow charts by Temporary Services

We founded Half Letter Press in December of 2008. The press name refers to the format of our books and booklets, which are one half of a letter size (8 1/2" × 11") sheet of paper. Thanks to the insistence of former President Ronald Reagan, letter-size paper is the standard size in America. It is a common, cheap, and easy paper to work with.

We use Half Letter Press to publish perfect-bound book-length works by ourselves and other authors. Before Half Letter Press, we made two full-length books with other publishers (*Prisoners' Inventions*, WhiteWalls, 2003, and *Group Work*, Printed Matter, 2007). Both experiences were positive but the quantity of books printed felt like something we could make and sell on our own. In 2007, we received grants from Art Matters and CEC Artslink and found ourselves with enough money to publish a full-length, perfect-bound, offset book (*Public Phenomena*, 2008). We could have used the money to pay another publisher that values our work and help them print and distribute the book, but we chose to do it ourselves. We created a publishing imprint and web store to take care of printing and distribution. It is managed by the two of us, with some outside help from time to time. We have published six books to date under Half Letter Press; sometimes we design the books and sometimes we work with an outside designer.

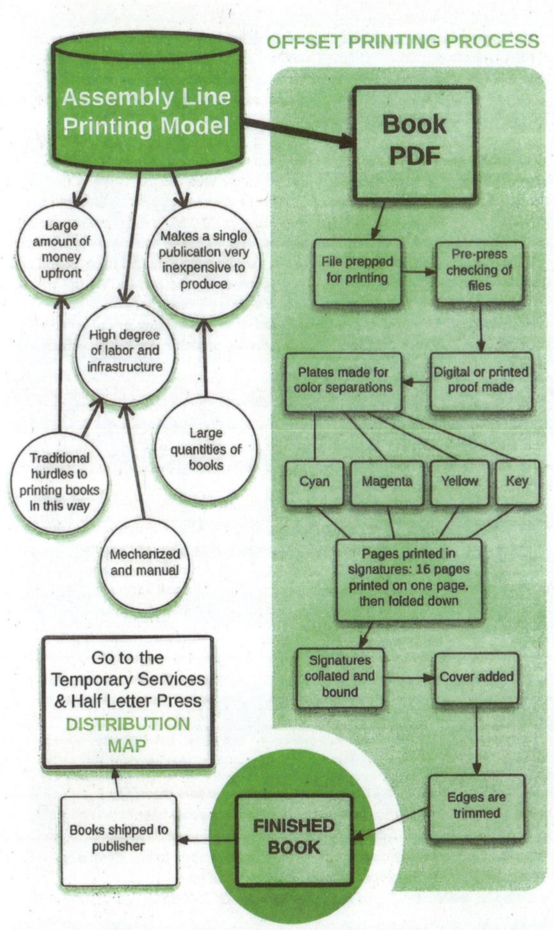

Assembly Line Printing Model: This flowchart shows a standard industrial method of printing. We put it in here for those who may not be familiar with how it works. We use many different ways of printing to make our books, but this is the one we use the most.

Temporary Services has always been self-organized; we are neither a not-for-profit, nor an incorporated entity, nor any other officially registered status for that matter. We created Half Letter Press as a Limited Liability Corporation to deal with any income, taxes, and other operational fees and to establish it as a platform to make and sell not only our past booklets, but also future publications. In addition to our own, we distribute the work of friends and other self-publishing allies through Half Letter Press' web store. When we have an opportunity to table at book fairs and other events, we bring publications by our peers to sell alongside our own work.

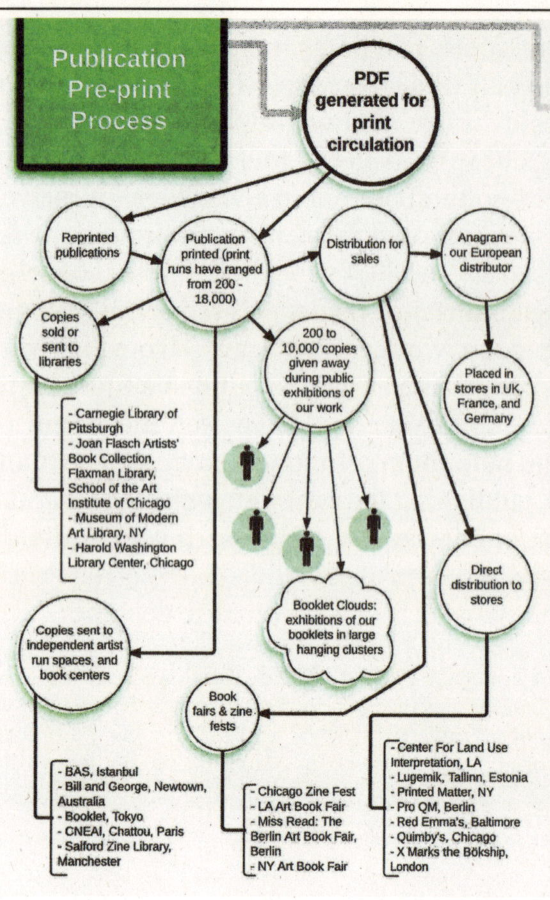

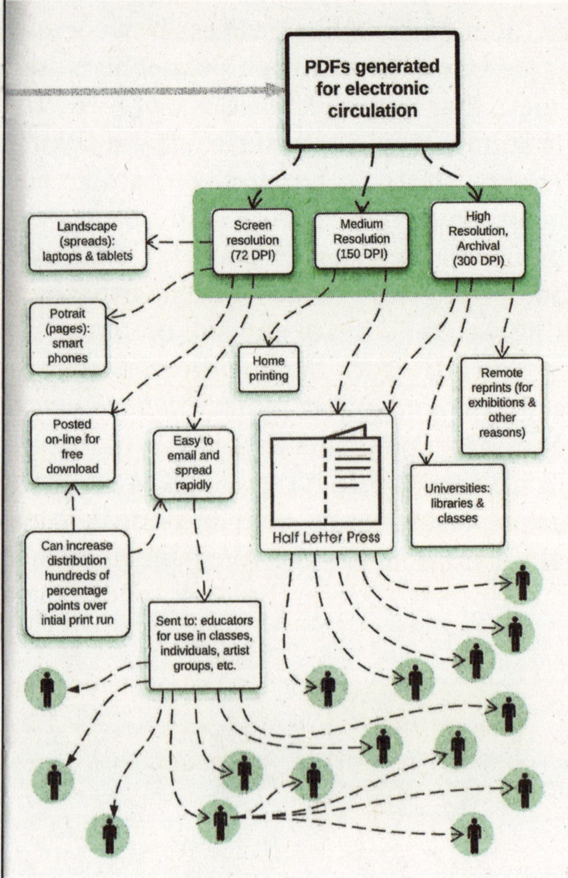

Distribution map: This is a visualization of the distribution of our publications in digital and printed formats. It shows the social and professional networks we are a part of and the spaces where productive or accidental encounters with our publishing are possible.

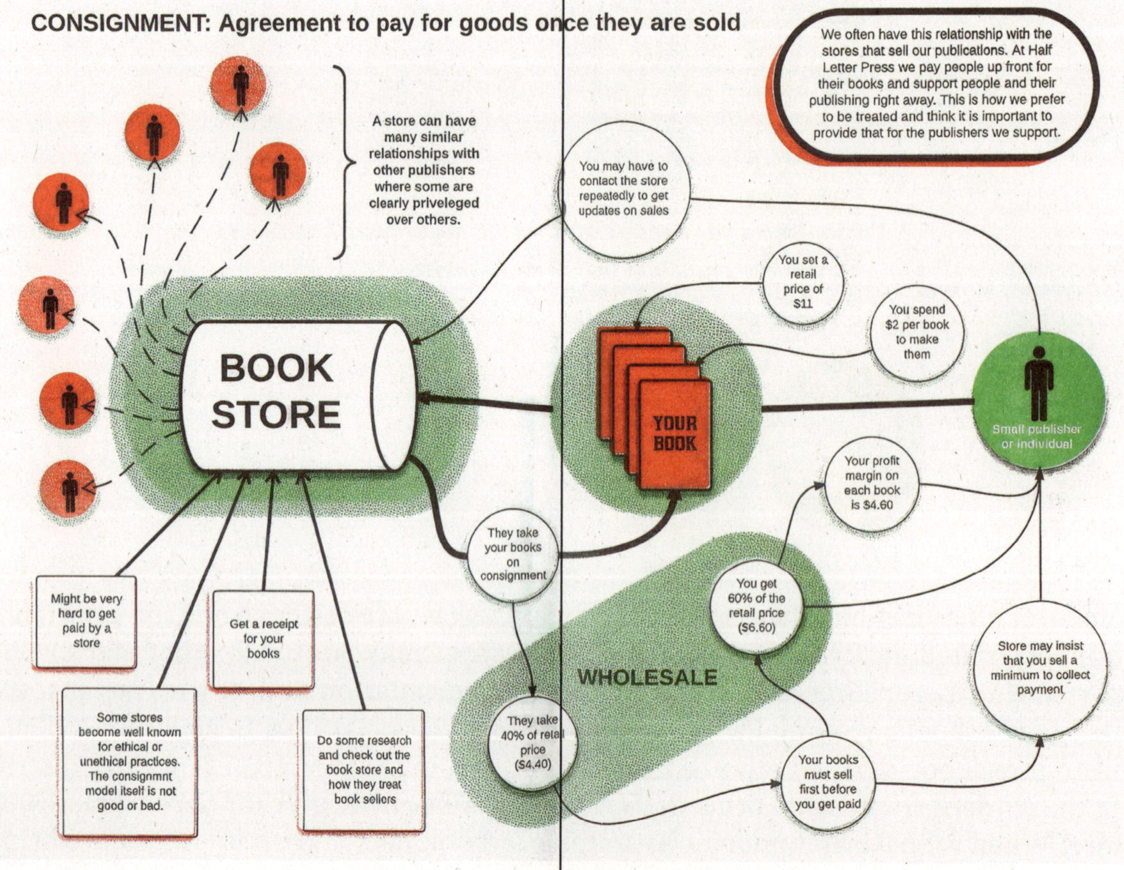

Economical map.

Publishing after the "paperless revolution" (the internet failed to kill off the printed page and therefore the revolution did not actually occur, but its impact on paper and printing is evident) requires a new set of skills, approaches and attitudes in being a book maker. It means crafting a variegated approach to how you create, publish, distribute, and build a social eco-system around your efforts. We craft publish, which means that we take a level of care that reflects a deep commitment to getting our books out in the world, in appropriate ways, to the people who want or benefit from them. This involves having a long haul approach to supporting our publications, and finding ways to distribute books long after they are printed. Our distribution remains limited, but we do not send books to remainder land when someone decides they have run their course and are not worth storing or continuing to promote. We actively work to rescue uncirculated books that other publishers have put in storage when we think that they are titles our audiences would appreciate.

The work we do tends to leverage the resources and privileges we have in a way that extends them to other people. Beginning in 2003 until the last member of our group left in around 2009, Temporary Services co-ran an experimental cultural center on Chicago's far north side called Mess Hall. We like making lists that take responsibility for our ideas and generate discussion. The key holders at Mess Hall made a list, in 2007, inspired by the concise format and power of the Black Panthers' ten demands. This is Mess Hall's list:

> We demand cultural spaces run by the people who use them.
> We create the space to remix categories, experiment, and learn what we do not already know.
> Mess Hall explodes the myth of scarcity. Everyone is capable of sharing something.
> The surplus of our societies should be creatively redistributed at every level of production and consumption.
> Social interaction generates culture!
> We embrace creativity as an action without thought of profit.
> We demand spaces that promote generosity.
> Mess Hall insists on a climate of mutual trust and respect—for ourselves and those who enter our space.
> No money is exchanged inside Mess Hall. Surfing on surplus, we do not charge admission or ask for donations.
> Mess Hall functions without hierarchy or forced unity.

This was the precursor to the list we made for Half Letter Press. In 2008 we used posters, bookmarks, and our website to share the core values of Half Letter Press.

> Half Letter Press strives to build an art practice that:
> Makes the distinction between art and other forms of creativity irrelevant
> Builds and depends upon mutually supportive relationships
> Tests ideas without waiting for permission or invitation
> Champions the work of those who are frequently excluded, under-recognized, marginal, non-commercial, experimental, and/or socially and politically provocative
> Puts money and cultural capital back into the work of other artists and self-publishers
> Makes opportunities from large museums and institutions more

inclusive by bringing lesser-known artists in through collaborations or advocacy
Insists that artists who achieve success devote more time and energy to creating supportive social and economic infrastructures for others

Over the past couple of years, we have slowly started articulating criteria for evaluating Socially Engaged Art (the more reductive, digestible term we intensely dislike is Social Practice). In the race to promote this work (see the curator Nato Thompson) or tear it down (see the critic Claire Bishop), very little effort has been made to distinguish between art that truly empowers and work that merely uses the aesthetics of social inclusion to make empty spectacles, corporate and governmental propaganda, and MFA programs that do not lead to employment. This led us to generate a set of questions, which we encourage you to test out in your own experiences of art:

Does the work empower more people than just the authors of the work?
Does the work foster egalitarian relationships, access to resources, a shift in thinking, or surplus for a larger group of people?
Does the work abate competition, abusive power and class structures, or other barriers typically found in gallery or museum settings?
Does the work seek broader audiences than just those educated about and familiar with contemporary art?
Does the work trigger a collective imagination that can dream of other possible worlds while it understands the current one with eyes wide open?
Does the work hold the name of one person, but include the creativity and labor of many uncredited others, or does it make its own creation clear and easy to understand?

These are also the kind of concerns we have ourselves of our publishing practice and consider who we make books and booklets with, how we want to treat the people that work on our publications, whose work we want to distribute at events and in our web store, and who we want to use to sell our books.

We try to treat other publishers as we like to be treated by stores and distributors. For this reason we prefer to pay people for the books we sell upfront rather than taking them on consignment and making people wait months or years to be paid. We also like to exchange stock with other publishers—letting them sell our books while we try to sell theirs, each keeping the money from what we sell and restocking with each other as needed.

Books and booklets make great bartering tools and it does not come as a surprise that many self-publishers, or artists that make books, have wonderful home libraries of publications they have accumulated from trades. When people let us stay at their homes, we commonly bring the books we have made as a gift in appreciation for their generosity. These books can join libraries that can then be enjoyed by future guests. While no one has a complete set of Temporary Services publications, many longtime friends have dozens of different titles—a result of gifts given over many years.

People often ask us about print-on-demand (POD), which are books that are printed as needed, made to order, and often in smaller quantities than in offset printing. There are a number of reasons why we don't make publications using print-on-demand and typically won't distribute and sell books that others have made using this model.

Since many of our booklets are initially given away for free during exhibits, we make 1,000 copies or more of an offset printed booklet, and plan to make at least 300 copies of Risograph-printed booklets. Making 600 copies of a print-on-demand booklet through the company Lulu can cost almost five times more than ordering 1,000 copies of the same publication at an offset printing company. In order to make money on a print-on-demand booklet (especially when selling wholesale to shops and distributers), something that we might price at $4.00 when offset printed, would have to be sold for about $9.00. This makes print-on-demand books and booklets a poor value for readers. It is very hard to sell a book at $45.00 when it feels like it should have been $25.00. Unless the author doesn't care to profit from sales of their print-on-demand book at a retail store, it is difficult to place a print-on-demand book at a retailer without increasing the price. It is likely that this is one reason we rarely encounter POD books in stores.

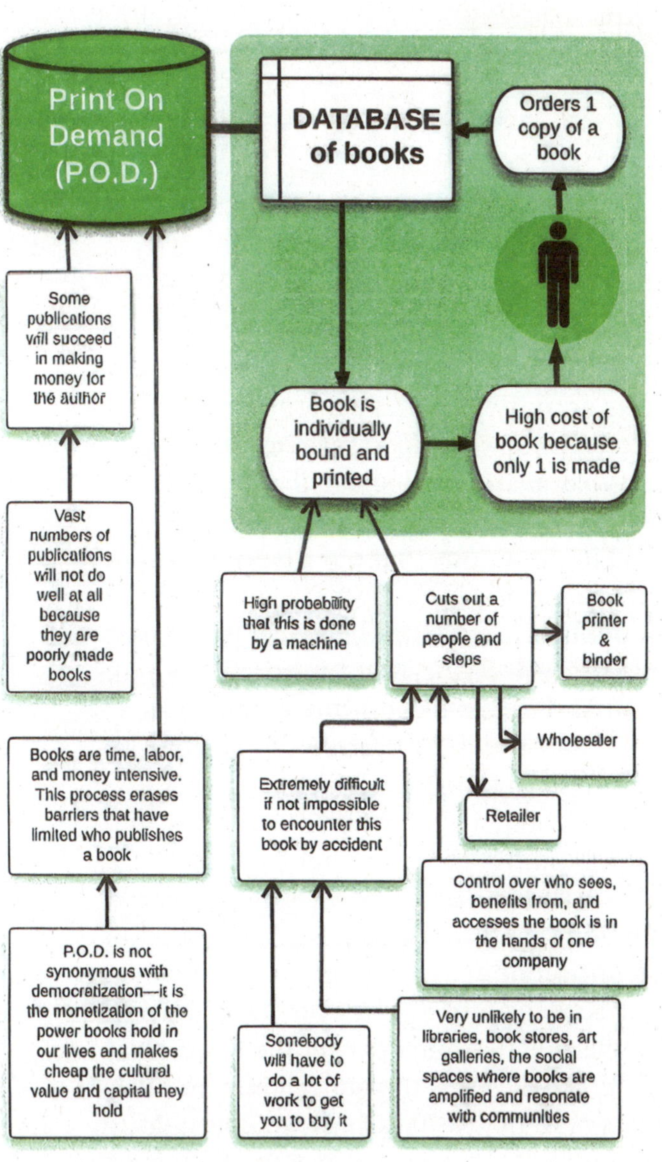

Print-on-demand production model.

Print-on-demand books often have a generic quality due to the limited number of paper options, cover treatments, and publication sizes. While cheap web-based offset printers are also able to charge low prices by offering limited customization, just about any internet-based offset printer gives publishers a whole lot more paper options than print-on-demand services. Working directly with a local printer or self-printing on a copier or Risograph allows for limitless custom paper choices that will give your books a more specific feel. We encourage new publishers to give serious consideration to the model of printing they choose and to not emulate print-on-demand because it is currently fashionable within the artist book community.

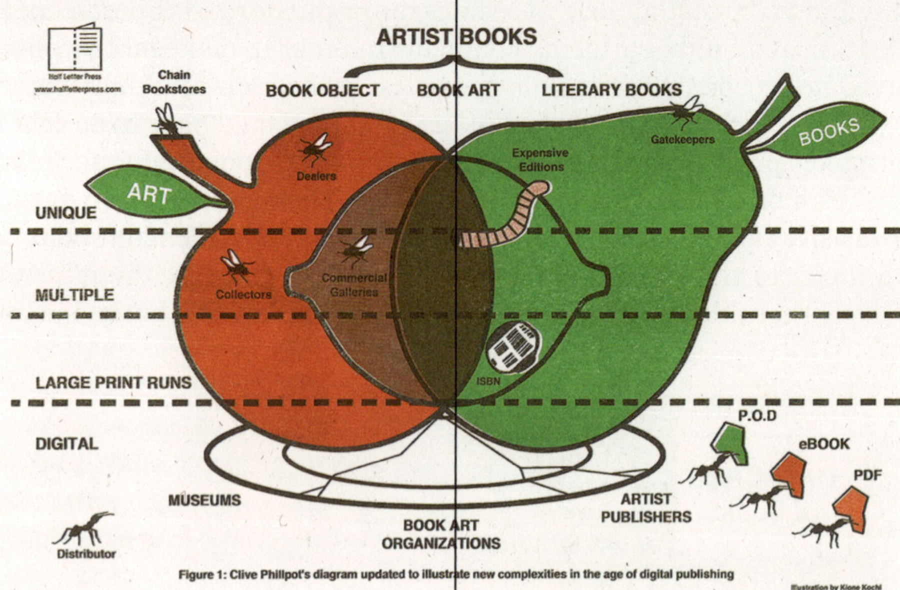

Figure 1: Clive Phillpot's diagram updated to illustrate new complexities in the age of digital publishing

Illustration by Kione Kochi

LOOKING AROUND

The burgeoning international community of artist book publishing has become incredibly complicated as more and more people are engaged in this culture. It makes a singular vantage point from which to understand all this activity extremely daunting. The diagram above is our take on Clive Phillpot's earlier version that no longer resonates with the culture that has unfolded, and the urgency, volume, technological change, and aesthetic exploration we have witnessed over the past 10–15 years. We are convinced that this culture will continue to grow and be pushed in directions that our diagram cannot anticipate. We welcome this uncertainty and are eager to see what others will develop.

"There has been an explosion in artist book publishing around the world in the past few years." This has been a routine mantra one hears at gatherings of artist bookmakers and publishers. We agree with this sentiment and we have definitely witnessed this ourselves. It leaves us with important questions about the role of artists' books in shaping contemporary artistic discourse, and the kinds of support this work could receive. The excitement about self-publishing also comes during a time when many brick and mortar bookstores are closing, and the cost of shipping has seen a massive increase (international shipping from the US is through the roof).

Artists' book fairs have been increasing in number and fill some of the distribution holes left by closed book stores. Non-stop promotion of artists' books on the web via social media has put these publications on our screens more than ever. Distribution still has a long way to go; posting pictures of books you like and sharing them on social media isn't the same as buying them and showing hard copies to your friends. Publishing, particularly on the scale of making booklets, can be exhilarating and contagious, but it's also only as richly rewarding and meaningful as you are willing to make it. It remains to be seen how the people who are trying out self-publishing today will shape their practice for the long haul. We would like to encourage the exploration of not just their own creative publishing, but also of the ways this activity can be used to build up and strengthen the community around these printed forms. We want to suggest efforts that benefit many others and find new audiences to be challenged by publications.

paula roush, Ruth Brown

Publishing with Friends: Exploring Social Networks to Support Photo Publishing Practices[1]

1. Excerpted from *Educational Social Software for Context-Aware Learning: Collaborative Methods and Human Interaction*, ed. Niki Lambropoulos and Margarida Romero (Hershey/Penns.: IGI Global, 2010), 222–240.

The term "classroom of the read/write web," coined by Will Richardson, describes a pedagogical framework for the integration of online participatory culture and the self-publishing technologies now abundant on the internet (these may include weblogs, wikis, aggregators, social bookmarking, photo-sharing, rubric-making tools and many others) in teaching and learning, and emphasizes the four core literacies—reading, publishing, collaborating, and information management—that can be developed in the online environment.[2]

This model of the open classroom is a major challenge for the academy. Many artists and designers already use the read/write web in their everyday life, but universities seem reluctant to make the transition from an industrial age concept of knowledge (production) to one more in tune with the information age model of user-led education (produsage).[3] What follows is the account of an action research cycle in which a print-on-demand website, Lulu.com, became a classroom for second and third year digital photography students to publish their photobooks. Other higher education projects using Lulu.com for graphic design are available, but none comments on the pedagogical process involved in using the platform, choosing instead to present the students' work as an enquiry into the digital printing output achievable at Lulu.[4] Our study explores the features of Lulu.com that can be used as part of a "classroom of the read/write web" and discusses the results with reference to the self-publishing capacities involved in reaching the learning outcomes.

CASE STUDY: PHOTOBOOK PROJECT FOR PHOTOGRAPHY STUDENTS

The emphasis of the photo publishing unit of this study is the genre of the photobook, "a book—with or without text—where the work's primary message is carried by photographs [...] an event in itself [...] a concise world where the collective meaning is more important than images."[5] This implies that the students come to think of the photograph in relational terms, develop skills as curators or editors, and learn to use current available digital technologies to publish and distribute independently. The genre has been developing since the conception of photography, but as printing technologies have gravitated towards a networked model, photographers have adapted their practices to take advantage offered by print-on-demand publishing models.

Teaching photographers to develop photobooks also means going beyond focusing on the "best photo" to consider photographs as groups or collections. Free from the conventional photo-to-print relationship, the learner starts thinking in terms of the book's visual structure.[6] The unit of meaning—the graphic layout as double page spread or as subchapter—conceptualizes the narrative or meta-narrative aspects implied in grouping, serializing and sequencing the photos. Experimenting with the conventions of the book page becomes a key pedagogic strategy. The process allows deliberate disruption of conventional book flow—the distribution of text and image to create movement from page to page—to raise awareness of the relationship between page and image.

The book-making process starts with the creation of book dummies, 3-D mock-ups of the book that provide an excellent tool to play with the images and develop understanding of visual structures. Teaching the fundamentals of photobook publishing also implicitly equips students with in-depth knowledge of prepress, the steps necessary to prepare the work for a commercial printer. In the adoption of the desktop environment for publication design, creating a book means assuming responsibility for a series of processes: layout, typography, and text formatting, preparation of images in Photoshop (color space and resolution), preflight and the creation of a robust PDF file that the commercial printer will translate into a professional-looking photobook. Understanding and anticipating the printer's output environment is thus an important part of the learning program.

WHY TEACH BOOK ARTS IN A PRODUSAGE ENVIRONMENT?

While opportunities for self-publishing of photography online abound, few students take full advantage of the possibilities offered by the online

2. Will Richardson, *Blogs, Wikis, Podcasts and Other Powerful Web Tools for Classrooms* (Thousand Oaks, CA: Corwin, 2006).
3. See Axel Bruns, *Blogs, Wikipedia, Second Life, and Beyond: From Production to Produsage* (New York: Peter Lang 2008).
4. See James Goggin, Frank Philippin, and students of the faculty of Design at the University of Applied Sciences Darmstadt, *Dear Lulu, Please try and print these line, colour, pattern, format, texture and typography tests for us* (Lulu 2008).
5. Martin Parr and Gerry Badger, *The photobook: A history*, vol. 1, (London: Phaidon, 2004), 7.
6. Keith A. Smith, *Structure of the visual book* (Rochester, NY: Keith Smith Books, 2005).

photobook companies, like Lulu or Blurb. While students already use Flickr, deviantART and other photo-sharing sites for their photos, research shows that many photographers are exploring the professional photobook companies' sites for publishing their book works.[7] For our students, engaging in the professional environment represents the next step in their development; having completed a photographic brief, their focus changes to considering the editing of their work with a view to publication. Whilst other university assignments are produced for the teacher and the classroom, studying this unit unlocks the many possibilities of the classroom of the web.

With the availability of these technologies and the widespread opportunities for online publication, creating a photobook implies thinking beyond the screen and positioning the photographic work in the wider publishing context. Taking into account the current interest in e-books and readers, it is still a challenge in this unit to combine the best of digital technologies and paper-based media. Facilitating a semester unit on book-making for digital photographers means considering the book in the age of the digital press; the enterprise of the online print-on-demand photobook companies offering the latest developments in "digital/paper hybrid product"[8]; and the paper-digital technologies that allow for both printed and online book publishing outputs.

An additional opportunity in such produsage environments is the uploading and sharing of images, mainly an individual activity, or the creation of personal sets of photos. The art of produsage, however, also offers other possibilities, such as the sourcing of images from pools, or creating groups on particular themes; this activity exemplifies a shift from the photographer-author to the photographer-editor, involved in the curation of collections. Such collective (or networked) projects are exemplified by photographers editing found photography[9] or the management of photos uploaded by participants into paper-based publications, as in JPG magazine. Thus, the opportunity of teaching students to work as editors of someone else's material is indispensable to publishing practice and in this instance the involvement in social networks is an essential way of sourcing images. The unit aims were to:

— identify and analyze the context of self-publishing practices, as evidenced by participation in rubric-led assessment and feedback, and the participation on e-tivities at Lulu.com;
— demonstrate a critical understanding of the genre of photo publishing, as evidenced by the output of two photo publications (a photobook and a photo magazine);
— develop skills in visual communication, as evidenced by their work with the structure of the visual book including creating a book dummy, using InDesign to layout photo and text; and
— use the print-on-demand publishing model, as evidenced by the use of Lulu publishing and networking platform.

THE CHOICE OF A PRODUSAGE ENVIRONMENT

According to a recent study, there are more than fifty-five online photobook companies all offering similar print-on-demand services.[10] In each, the user downloads the company's software (or the software is browser-based), inserts the photos and text in pre-designed templates, chooses a binding and cover format, and places an order which is printed and delivered, typically, in ten days. Lulu, however, has special produsage features that make it a preferred choice for teaching: it may be viewed as a two-sided produce–sell (or dashboard–storefront) platform. The dashboard is a private node (accessible only when the user is logged in), which accesses "my projects" (a catalog of all the user's books), as well as the user's storefront, blog, groups, message box and friends. Additional account management features such as account preferences and access to the files associated with the user's publishing activity are also available from the dashboard.

7. Louise Forrester, *Self-publishing Photobooks* (self publ./Lulu, 2007), https://web.archive.org/web/20081205133159/http://www.lulu.com/content/4052229.
8. Risto Sarvas, Martti Mäntylä, and Marko Turpeinen, *Human-Centric Design of Future Print Media* (Helsinki: PulPaper, 2007), http://pong.hiit.fi/dcc/papers/FuturePrintMedia_PulPaper07.pdf.
9. David Brittain, *Found, Shared: The Magazine Photowork* (Brighton: Brighton Press, 2006).
10. Forrester, *Self-publishing Photobooks.*

On finding a (prod)user's name in Lulu (often through a search box), one is directed to their storefront—a public-facing interface which can be fully customized by the seller, and which provides a variety of information about their associated activities: a profile, list of Lulu friends, group memberships, Lulu interests, published books, blogs, and other feeds (del.icio.us bookmarks, for example). An important storefront feature is the book page (see Fig. 1), which offers information about the book: a preview, publisher and licensing information, a description of the book content, and the book specifications (number of pages, use of color or black-and-white, format and binding). The page also states the prices for printing and downloading (which may be different), the book's tags, categories, reviews, and sales information such as the Lulu sales ranking and other books bought by the customers who bought the book. A link to the shopping basket allows the viewer to place an order, pay and enter a (virtual or actual) shipping address. If the book download is free, clicking on the "download now" button initiates its download. Opening the tags or categories reveals a catalog of other publications with similar tags and categories, and the licensing link accesses the licensing deed: either copyright or a chosen variation of creative commons.

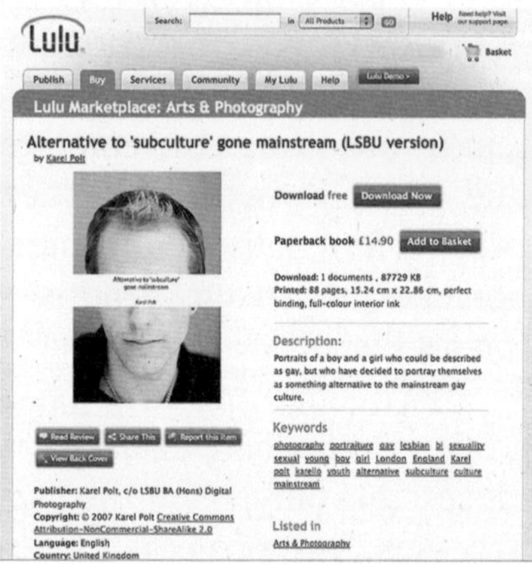

Fig. 1: An example of a student's book page from Lulu.com.

The Lulu community supports forums, groups, a newsletter, and the Lulu blog. The forums, in a variety of subjects related to self-publishing such as cover art, or storefront, are maintained by Lulu experts and archived in a variety of self-publishing related threads, easily accessible via search menus. International forums provide support in a wide number of languages, and users can also start their own group for more focused interests such as book promotion or teen literature.

Of all the online photobook companies, Lulu is the one that offers the platform with the most interesting blend of features with which to teach digital photobook publishing. In the first place, the dashboard is the most project-oriented of all the photobook companies; it allows students to design their books using InDesign, the desktop publishing software used in class, and to upload the resulting PDF file, while other companies require the use of their own software. Further, unlike other companies that keep the design document in-house for printing-on-demand purposes only, Lulu allows the design document to be accessed and shared digitally.

The online store also offers two methods of making the content available: the print version delivers a paperback that can be purchased using the online ordering process (shopping basket; online payment, and delivery to the shipping address); and the download version, either as a paid or free PDF download. Whilst other companies may offer an online store, they do not offer access to the digital files. The dual options of the Lulu online store integrate well with the principle of common gains/individual rewards of the produsage environments.

Blogs, another of Lulu's tools, create opportunities to publish works-in-progress and to receive feedback from peers; the comments feature encourages analytical reflection and an extension of the online conversation beyond the classroom. The groups and friends' lists (social networking features) promote working as a group and extending classroom support into the online space. Lastly, the forums in which users and experts exchange information on topics related to many aspects of digital online publishing offer a pool of extra teachers, available 24/7, that are supplemented by live help from Lulu, a feature that makes possible to obtain support from a company representative via a chat board.

THE DESIGN OF LEARNING TASKS

The embedding of the teaching in this produsage environment was achieved by using a blended pedagogical framework, which consisted of twelve weekly face-to-face meetings in the media lab interspersed with eleven weekly e-tivities. A particular intention in the design was a balance between individual expression and group work. The first project, an individual photobook, called for the selection of photos from students' own archives, the development of a visual structure for the book, the preparation of a book dummy, and the final production of the photobook. The second assignment was a collaborative one: working as editorial team, each group created a collective photo magazine using photos selected from a social network situation. They were required to prepare and submit a magazine dummy showing the visual structure, and to publish the photo magazine in Lulu.com.

The balance of the assessment was by way of weekly structured e-tivities, posted to Lulu.com.[11] The e-tivities supported the process in which students were required to analyze the production process and to reflect on online research and peer feedback. Each week's e-tivity was designed to further embed the online publishing environment in the students' experience, and dovetailed with the face-to-face activity for the week. In week one, for instance, the e-tivity was designed to help students become familiar with Lulu's tools. Subsequent e-tivities explored the definition of photobook, the structure of a visual book, how to create book and photo magazine proposals and dummies, customizing the storefront for a book, and book reviews. The last e-tivity required the students to reflect on their Lulu experience.

To operate in the Lulu.com environment, students created personal profiles and learned to use the various features related to managing publishing projects; they customized their blogs and storefronts, and developed a social network with their peers and the Lulu community. To collaborate during the design phase, they subscribed to the group's forum and participated by posting their questions and replies. To share their research on photo publishing with each other, they learned how to create a del.icio.us account and to use the features of social bookmarking.

E-TIVITY 11: MY LULU EXPERIENCE

PURPOSE

Now that you are an expert in photo publishing, Lulu and print-on-demand, it's time to review all that happened, and share what you've learnt. This can help you put your experience in perspective and also help other people who are still on the look out for a way to publish their photobook. The best thing you can do to help others is to share your experience with them!

TASK

Write about your experience in photo publishing with Lulu. Your reflection should include at least one of the following issues:

- Digital pedagogy: what are the differences between learning digital media in online and in offline environments?
- Communities of practice: what does it means to learn in a community that extends the classroom into the publishing market?
- Vernacular versus academic culture: what are the implications of circulating the work in the field of popular culture side by side with non academic, "amateur," production?
- A challenge to the hierarchical nature of the institution; what is the personal and social impact of starting publishing while you are still a student?
- The meaning of self-publishing: what does it mean to publish independently of a selection by committee (editors/ curators)?
- The value of publishing as a group, relying on the support of your peers' network.
- The advantages/constraints imposed by the print-on-demand templates on the format of the photobook.
- The Lulu environment compared to other (publishing) social network sites.

11. Gilly Salmon, *E-tivities: The Key to Active Online Learning* (Abingdon, Oxon: RoutledgeFalmer, 2004).

The Findings: Students' Perceptions of Their Engagement in the Read/Write Web Environment

DIGITAL PEDAGOGY

The Lulu.com environment forced a steep learning curve for both teacher and students. While really good for publishing, Lulu is not particularly appropriate for communication and group work; searches for information are painful, the menus badly organized, and the navigation system awful! Nonetheless, students identified positive benefits from the experience. The novelty of the method was deemed appropriate by students: "Learning mostly online through practical demonstrations and experimentation on various related websites with self-publishing and online collaborative rubrics to assess our projects provided a new experience, for me at least," and "Personally I believe anything that challenges the norm and gets you thinking in different ways is a good thing. This module is not presented to us in a traditional, stuffy, listen and take notes old school university style. We are studying a new art form and our lecture methods should reflect the move away from tradition."

Another student remarked on the benefit of the hands-on approach: "It is easier in my opinion to learn digital media practices on the Internet as opposed to the classroom or lecture hall—personally I am a more practical individual and feel the need to actively do something to learn effectively," which underscores the need to recognize different students' different learning styles. There was also a link made between the day-to-day online activities of students and the shift towards the internet as a teaching medium: "I welcome online learning as an idea very warmly. As most of my generation is connected to the Internet one way or another anyway, it's only a matter of when digital pedagogy becomes a standard."

A caveat against seeing online learning as a silver bullet came from two students who showed their appreciation of more traditional approaches. "Learning about digital media in an online environment as opposed to a more traditional format (i.e. a classroom) has been slightly chaotic at times. It's an unfortunate fact that sometimes you simply need a person on hand to help with problems, and online learning cannot always provide this." and "The printed handouts on prepress fundamentals for InDesign were very useful too, as most of the class had not used this software previously."

COMMUNITIES OF PRACTICE

Students explored the concept of community of practice in a very practical way in these units. This student seems to doubt the personal value, but clearly recognizes the benefits to classmates: "Learning by way of a community has been great for this unit, though I have not myself benefited from being part of a community it has clearly been a help to some members of the class who find websites and concepts such as those we have been studying more difficult than the theoretical issues in photography." Another student came face to face with the diversity to be found in such a group: "Become [*sic*] an online community was an interesting look at the class and how each person expressed themselves. There was such an array of difference in style of each person's e-tivities and how they coped with doing them."

A particularly interesting comment was from a student who clearly found the online community too large for their liking but who had come to recognize that there were certain benefits. "Like many others in our class, I found publishing our work online and making it available for anyone in the world to buy a very exciting aspect of the unit, and probably one which we would be keen to explore in the future. Publishing on Lulu however does put our work in with thousands of similar pieces, some interesting pieces and some rather less well put together. It would be good to find a more specialist online publishing site for our photobooks & photomags, however this would mean losing the huge numbers of visitors to Lulu. It's a trade-off I guess."

THE VALUE OF PUBLISHING AS A GROUP

The principle value related to working as a group that was identified by the students was that help was immediately available: "The support of the group was very helpful, especially the ability to post questions to the online forums and answer other's queries very quickly." Another student valued the collaboration in the community, too: "There was a lot of help being given through blogs, forums and in person between all classmates during this period. Considering so many seemed unfamiliar with Indesign only a few weeks ago we all managed to create and upload an interesting mix of books into the Lulu store."

It is interesting that none of the students identified any of Johnson and Johnson's five pillars of group work: positive interdependence; group interaction; individual and group accountability; interpersonal skills; and group processing as valuable in the course of this unit.[12] Their focus appears to be at a micro- rather than a macro-level.

A COMPARISON OF LULU WITH OTHER (PUBLISHING) SOCIAL NETWORKING SITES

There were varying opinions about the usability of Lulu.com relative to other social networking sites. One student commented that, "Other social networking sites feature the same kind of real time features that Lulu does but many offer better usability and are far more effective than other websites available." Another clearly felt that the social side of the site was a positive: "Lulu.com has much more of a social side to it than most other self-publishing websites" but agreed with the critique on its usability: "Whilst the design of the site is at the very least questionable, it does for the most part work well if you have the time and patience to figure it out!"

This student pointed out that the cost effectiveness of Lulu was possibly outweighed by its design. "To be able to publish your work cheaply and easily is a great asset afforded to us as a group, but Lulu seems to be experiencing problems with the way it functions. It is tricky to use and everything seems to take a long time to do. Unlike other sites that involve social-networking, Lulu suffers from a lack of user friendly features." In addition, she offered some useful comments on the overall impact of using a better managed site: "Overall, I see Lulu's merits and potential and also value certain aspects of the site but I think that with a better technical support and development the site should be more accessible and thus would have more of an impact and not come across as amateurish as it does now. Would the site be more interactive like Facebook with constant technical updates which facilitate the use it would be more popular and more people would use it, thus creating a bigger market for self-publishing."

Possibly the view of the majority is summed up in this student's comment: "Unfortunately, Lulu.com is not exactly a user-friendly environment and it isn't welcoming enough for constant digital activities like blogging, commenting and change of information. There are other, far more sophisticated environments for that (e.g. Facebook), which make users want to spend as much time as possible online."

It is apparent from some of these remarks that the students lost sight of the requirement to compare Lulu.com with other publishing social networks. Nonetheless, their comments clearly indicate that they were at times frustrated by the Lulu experience.

OTHER THEMES THAT EMERGED FROM THE STUDENTS' WRITINGS

Some additional themes surface in the reading of the students' reflections. Firstly there is a concern about the ownership of their work: "Another issue that was voiced by a large amount of our group was the fact that, while publishing as students, we do not control the simple intellectual copyright to our work. This is instead handed to the University who could, in theory (I hope not practice), profit from our work and charge us royalties for what is essentially our own personal art." They also expressed a lack of experience and a lack of confidence with the medium: "Having set tasks within Lulu really made me play around and explore the system, something I have previously not done before. I do tend still to be scared of computers and really have no idea what they are capable of doing for me. Throughout this term I have had to face this fear and play around, do a lot of problem solving on my own and learn that these systems actually have everything explained for you if you use their 'help' and 'search' options." Another student said: "This has been a great struggle for me as I rarely use the Internet for social networking, I barely knew what a blog was. This unit was not something I enjoyed but I feel it helped me to get an understanding of how modern photographic practice operates on the Internet.

12. Roger T. Johnson and David W. Johnson, *An Overview of Cooperative Learning*, http://www.co-operation.org/what-is-cooperative-learning.

I have learned how to produce my own book, which will be useful in the future I'm sure," which is a confident note upon which to wind up this discussion!

DISCUSSION

The collaborative aspects associated with sharing one's work on the Internet require an understanding of appropriate legal frameworks, and this is greatly encouraged by Lulu's support of varied licensing deeds. The software's embedded licensing menus—with scope for creative commons licensing—provide a good opportunity to discuss the licensing of creative work, whether this is available as a free download, or as a profitable print-on-demand. The legal framework for this project—the Creative Commons Attribution Non Commercial Share Alike 2.0 negotiated with the University's copyright lawyer—offers a context within which to discuss issues of intellectual property in the academic environment. For the students, the principle of sharing their photographic work as a free downloadable PDF can be a watershed; this may be the first occasion in their time at university that their work is placed online, and made available for others to use.

The critical tools embedded in the software—the use of blogs for commentary and feedback, and the potential for peer review in the book pages—generated possibilities for giving and receiving constructive feedback as part of the ongoing collaborative process. The traditional domain of the "crit" session in art and design studio practice was partially moved into an online environment: this is a way of addressing the changing patterns of student learning and the students' push for independent learning.[13]

In the read/write environment, students can explore each other's work in their own domain and engage at their own pace; the opportunity appears greatly appreciated as time pressures arise as a result of the new work/study balance.[14] There are also issues raised that relate to an understanding of the students' needs and expectations in relation to online critical engagement. When used in the context of book reviews, the peer review in Lulu.com can be as effective as that on fanfiction sites where beta-readers working in the same genre can help emerging authors develop genre-specific skills.[15] On the other hand, using the software to facilitate feedback can be disappointing, for instance when students invest a lot of effort in customizing their blogs and there is a lack of comments or, specifically, substantive ones.[16]

The process of breaking down the complex assignments of photo publishing into a granular sequence of simpler tasks (from photo editing to online publishing) engaged the students in a series of mix and remix combinatory processes, and encouraged them to harness individual chunks of information. This is associated with engagement with multiple literacies; additional online tasks such as customizing profiles and storefronts, creating links, and uploading images side by side with text all encourage the development of all-round skills, and create a measure of granularity that is reinforced by drawing on the software's ability to aggregate feeds. This multimodality hallmarks young people's creative online practices[17] and is connected with the aesthetic of remixing. It is a sign of new networked material, intelligences and tools[18] that characterizes the photobook and photo magazine assignments through the remixing of one's own work and the work of others for the photo magazine.

The communicative aspects of the software, used by the students to publish their book analysis, pitch for their proposals, post questions, and get technical help, were central to eliciting mutual constructive criticism between the participants; overall, the publishing of the work process as a digital sketchbook serves as "tangible evidence of participation."[19] This archive of works in progress and

13. Chris Percy, "Critical absence versus critical engagement: Problematics of the crit in design learning and teaching," *Art, Design & Communication in Higher Education Journal,* 2 no. 3 (2004), 143–154.

14. Diane Robbie and Lynette Zeeng, "Engaging Student Social Networks to Motivate Learning: Capturing, Analysing and Critiquing the Visual Image," *The International Journal of Learning,* 15 no. 3 (2008): 153–160.

15. Rebecca W. Black, "Online Fanfiction: What Technology and Popular Culture Can Teach Us About Writing and Literacy Instruction," *New Horizons for Learning* no. 11 (2005), https://web.archive.org/web/20060929231107/http://newhorizons.org/strategies/literacy/black.htm.

16. Susannah Stern, "Producing Sites, Exploring Identities: Youth Online Authorship, in *Youth, Identity, and Digital Media*, ed. David Buckingham (Cambridge, MA: MIT Press, 2008), 95–118.

17. Angela Thomas, *Youth Online: Identity and Literacy in the Digital Age* (New York: Peter Lang, 2007).

18. Dan Perkel, "Copy and Paste Literacy: Literacy Practices in the Production of a MySpace Profile," in *Informal Learning and Digital Media: Constructions, Contexts, Consequences*, ed. Kirsten Drotner, Hans Siggaard Jensen, and Kim Christian Schrøder (Newcastle, UK: Cambridge Scholars Press, 2008), 203–224.

19. Marshall Soules, *Collaboration and Publication in Hybrid Online Courses*, 2001, https://marshallsoules.ca/hybrid2.htm.

the development of ideas is still available online at http://stores.lulu.com/photocultures, and can be accessed by others.[20]

Lastly, the platform provided an opportunity for the students to publish a photobook and a photo magazine in twelve weeks, a work flow that is only possible using an online photobook company. They did this with no financial burden and with total editorial control, a real achievement considering the limited opportunities available and the restrictive editorial policies of most established publishing houses. Whilst the field of artists' publications has always been strategically associated with independent publishing initiatives, self-publishing is still considered a stigma for some.[21] With the increasing availability of print-on-demand it may be the best opportunity for emerging and established photographers alike to embrace it.

20. https://web.archive.org/web/20080204001312/http://stores.lulu.com/photocultures and https://web.archive.org/web/20080204001141/http://www.lulu.com/groups/photopublishing.

21. Forrester, *Self-publishing Photobooks*.

Danny Snelson

Grey Libraries: Publishing as Pedagogy, An Annotated Bibliography

Over the past ten years, the vast majority of my publishing practice has emerged in collaboration with students in the classroom. The publication of the resulting books has most often taken place beneath the radar of both academic institutions and traditional literary spheres. Circulating in hyperlocalized contexts (the classes I have taught) and primarily written with the learning outcomes of their writers (my students) in mind, these books challenge the "making public" of publishing. Ranging from teaching assignments in grad school at University of Pennsylvania (Penn) to a postdoctoral fellowship at Northwestern University (NU) and into my current position at University of California, Los Angeles (UCLA), the books assembled here chart a decade of pedagogical work. In what follows, I'll briefly annotate some key works, assignments, and publishing configurations from this period with an aim to shade the greys of this library into a legible pattern.

Like the "grey literatures" that elude easy classification in archival systems, this print-on-demand collection—a "grey library"—has proven difficult to pin down. The grey library resists recognizable categories of publishing, just as it affords creative play beyond the genre expectations and formal conceptions of both literary and scholarly books. These books feature wild compilations and unwieldy experiments, serving as records of improvisation and documents of sites of learning. Collections of blank pages mingle with thirty-minute book sprints. Scanners become authors and collective identities mesh in anonymous and pseudonymous creative play. The grading associated with these projects is always non-qualitative: the grey library resists evaluation. Unlike academic publishing, a dramatic failure is far more illuminating than the slight improvement of a mild intervention. Teaching the codex as a form alongside aesthetic and poetic tactics, these books index conversations extruded from their pages.

Grey libraries are aesthetically agnostic. Rooted in experiment, knowledge in these libraries is built by unlearning conventional forms and questioning inherited structures. Like fan fiction communities and college writing seminars, the grey library is a generally autopoietic system. Its communication circuit revolves around a classroom of interlocutors who variously read, write, and publish each other's works. Rerouting this circuit through adjacent public platforms like Lulu, Amazon, apod.li, or this essay's annotated bibliography, the classroom publication transmits its complications into the post-digital publishing economy. The grey library calls normative publishing practices into question. Remaining open to formal invention and pedagogical play, these books are free of the demands placed on traditional publishers and publication genres. The grey library can be as carefree as an idle doodle or as focused as a precise laboratory experiment. When learning about the poetics, aesthetics, politics, and practices of publishing is the goal, the aims of publishing shift their coordinates accordingly.

Sampled here, the grey library materializes as a "poor" volumetric capture. Following on Hito Steyerl's foundational essay on the politics of digital circulation, "In Defense of the Poor Image" (2009), as well as Silvio Lorusso's essay expanding these lines into print-on-demand publishing platforms, "In Defense of Poor Media" (2015), the grey library is markedly impoverished. Shadowy and nebulous, the works that comprise the grey library are neither fully substantial (concrete) nor fully abstract (text); not quite a publication but definitely a book; glitchy, impermanent, full of holes. Prone to data loss and compression artifacts in the vicious cycles of audiovisual capital, the grey library prioritizes speed and access over craft and tradition. Part and parcel of the neoliberal politics of a "pull system," these books often use the print-on-demand platform Lulu. Cheap to purchase and easy to produce, they rely on the same modes of production that facilitate the fluid inequities of global capital. Each book is a draw on these systems and an opportunity to interrogate their various components—printing, pricing, shipping, advertising—facts of publishing so often neglected by literary study and creative writing alike. Like a poor volumetric capture, the grey library leaks out of the hazardous polygons of network culture writ large.

As a pedagogical platform, the grey library requires a reevaluation of authorship. To whom might these collaborative endeavors be attributed? Where might authorship be located? In the assignment, in its execution, somewhere between? Publication assignments vary from highly-constrained experiments to open-format explorations: might either approach tip the scales of authorship differently? These questions matter as I'm writing about these books, now, for apod.li. The books are not attributable to my individual authorship, yet I am not absent from their lists of authors. Emerging in pedagogical structures wherein power is distributed asymmetrically, these books challenge institutional and popular models of legibility. And yet, they remain the most cherished books on my shelf. These annotations, then, are a way to surface their various interventions and provocations while also meditating on what it means to publish in the classroom. The formal modularity and tonal variety of these annotations is presented as a correlative to the specificity of each work in this collection. Reading across their differences, perhaps they best signify in aggregate.

The roughly chronological entries that follow are heterogeneous in format and origin. Certain of these are drawn from syllabus course descriptions; others are excerpted from lectures and public talks; others offer pedagogical reflections after a project's completion; and others still are collaboratively written project descriptions produced by student co-authors and collaborators. The publishing platforms listed below were often devised, improvised, and deployed within the writing event itself. Packaging them together in a bibliography such as this is a way to think of the grey library as a kind of container technology for a range of generic formats and modes of address, compressed into the accounting of yet another book. I imagine navigating these modes of address as one might tab through windows in a browser—where attention can disperse among a set of varied reflections and generic probes. Or, where narrative strands can ravel through a database, rather than cohere into a point.

From the outset, one blanket course policy should be noted: in every instance, privacy has been maintained as a default. All students were required to operate pseudonymously or anonymously in our coursework together, with the option to attach their name to the work after grades had been submitted. The publications remain open to these students' claims of authorship (or disavowal) at any point in the future. At various points we've developed collective pseudonyms or played with author functions more explicitly in specific publications. Many students have gone on to publish more actively under their own names, often with the works from these courses included in their own bibliographies. To that end, I hope the grey library assembled below also nods toward the creative work that we do (professor and student, alike) while playing at the task of learning.

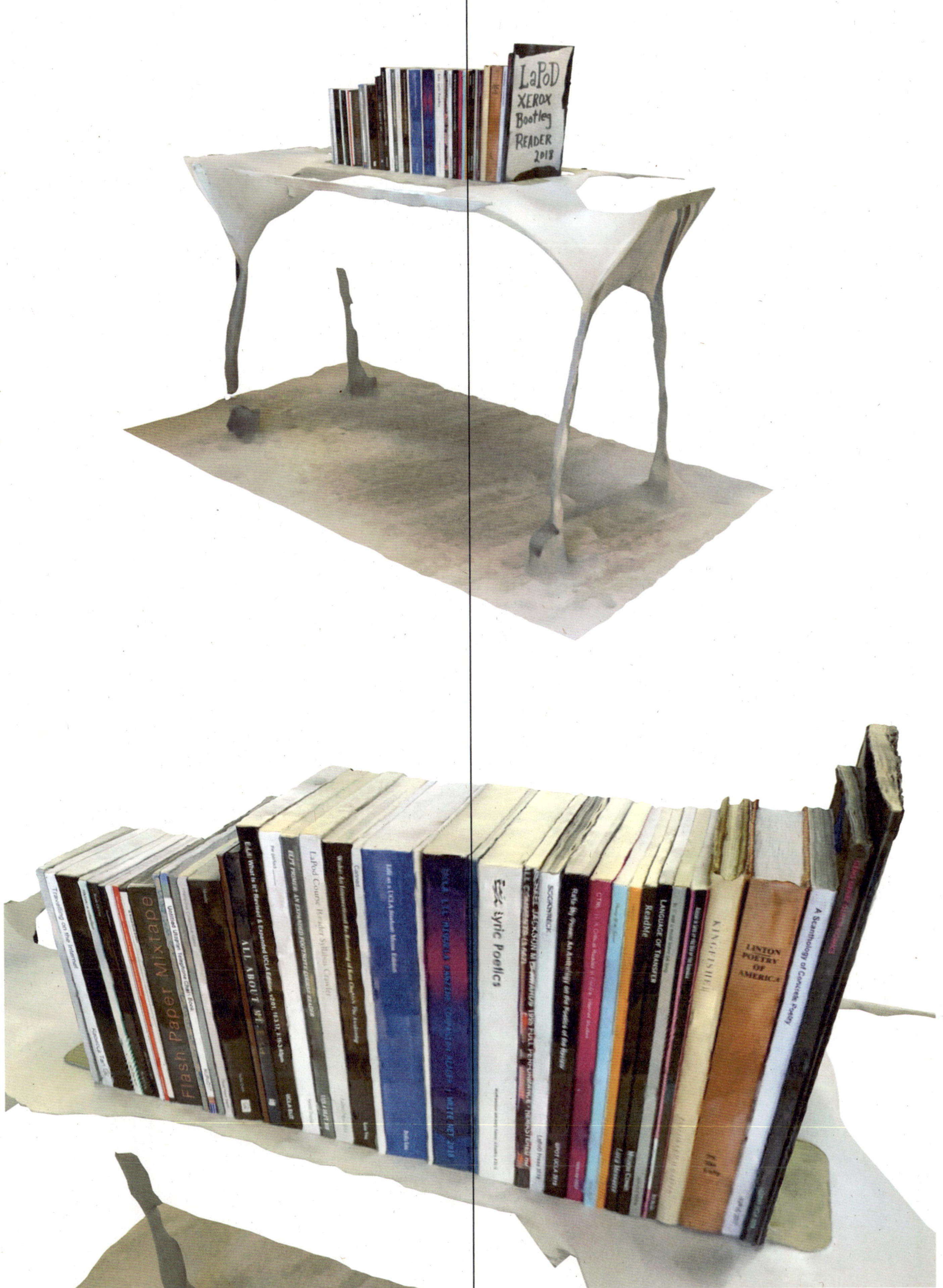
LaPoD
XEROX
Bootleg
READER
2018
Travelling on the Internet
Flash Paper Mixtape
ALL ABOUT ME
Lyric Poetics
ReadMe
LANGUAGE OF TRANSFER
LINTON
POETRY
OF
AMERICA

WOODSLIPPERCOUNTERCLATTERTRANSCRIPT

(Edit Publications, 2014, 19.0 × 19.0 cm / 7.5 × 7.5 in, 56 pages)

With my students at Penn, I shared the rare opportunity to see Susan Howe and David Grubbs perform their extraordinary collaborative piece *WOODSLIPPERCOUNTERCLATTER*. To amplify the layered improvisatory performance of electronics and poetic fragments, we added a very quiet subtrack of transcription in the back row. While the performance ensued, we simply wrote everything we heard as we heard it using a variety of inscription surfaces and techniques. To date, I believe this is the most complete and only hand-drawn transcription of this piece. Flipping through the pages and scanning them quickly gives the best impression of being washed over by the words.

FLASH PAPER MIXTAPE

(NUPoD, 2015, 22.9 × 17.8 cm / 9 × 7 in, 394 pages)

Flash Paper Mixtape is an anthology of fifteen devices playing music videos for a range of scanners, captured at 24 images per screening. Most office scanners have the most boring lives: they see only documents, receipts, memos, and other official ephemera through the limited visual range of their glass platen. As a corrective, *Flash Paper Mixtape* offers the scanner a view into popular moving image formats, and a rare whisper of audio entertainment over its repetitive grind. Of course, the scanner can only capture these fleeting pleasures in a line moving slowly over time, affixing a glitchy image from the movement of the screen. The distortions between these media are the point. We collectively derived the authorship of the book to include: HP, A. C. Sony C2105, The 2nd Scanner at the Library, M. Zampa, Epson V700, MCC RG Scanner, s.f., Kyndal Thomas, iPhone 5s, HP Photosmart 6520, LNS, [see notes to chapter eight], B. Cohen, HP Photosmart 6520, Brendan McManus, DSS, Keynote, Jonathan Hoffman, Toshiba Techra R950, Epson Perfection 4490 Photo ft. Apple IPhone 6 ft. M. Ferschinger (Explicit), J.S., and Northwestern Main Library Third Floor Scanner/Adobe Acrobat XI Pro. Rereading *Flash Paper Mixtape* now, I'm struck by the way its simulations of movement only amplified the fixity of its heavy black pages: time and space affixed in print.

BROKEN 56 BROKEN KINDLE SCREENS

(NUPoD, 2015, 10.8 × 17.5 cm / 4.25 × 6.875 in, 78 pages)

In 2012, Silvio Lorusso and Sebastian Schmieg published the extraordinary little print-on-demand book, *56 Broken Kindle Screens*. The title is comprehensive: the book contains images drawn from eBay of Kindle readers in various states of disrepair: cracked windows, distorted images, inoperable books. To teach this work, I thought a similarly straightforward approach most appropriate. I brought in a copy of *56 Broken Kindle Screens* and had students use our three hours together to destroy it in any way they might imagine. Staple it shut, tear it open, crumple it up, graffiti the page, stomp the spine, pierce with holes, snark in comments, and so forth. The resulting mess of a book was scanned back in with a low fidelity copier and transferred to PDF to produce a new print-on-demand book, bearing all the traces of our efforts at destruction. Subject to these manifold damages, in the end, *Broken 56 Broken Kindle Screens* proves the resilience of the book. Unlike the Kindle, a very difficult thing to break.

EPIC LYRIC POETICS
(Futures of Poetics at Northwestern University, 2016, 15.2 × 22.9 cm / 6 × 9 in, 458 pages)

One of a series of live-writing lecture publications. In the talk that generated this book, entitled "TXT → PDF → POD: Epic Lyric Poetics," I was presenting my work and research for *Epic Lyric Poem* (Troll Thread, 2015), a work that draws lines from a pop song lyric database, arranged according to the conventions of epic poetry. While speaking through this process in a collaborative workshop, I led the attendees to search, gather, and compile strings related to search terms around "epic," "lyric," and "poetry," to collectively derive a book of poetics on the topic. The only rule was that the book had to be at least 200 pages long (which we well surpassed). As in most of these projects, selections operate according to personal criteria and collaborative editorial aims with a minimum of change. Like Tan Lin's great *HEATH*, a record of the material contexts of each addition is born through the remnants of internet typography and errant digital detritus in the process. In this case, the work *Epic Lyric Poem* was written to draw in internet conversations about the nature of the "lyric" and the "epic" as keywords in poetry at the time—this book perfectly spells out that context in its collective drift, derived by a dozen searching participants.

NUPOD17 SYLLABUS V.0.1_1.12.17_4:15-45PM 30 MINUTE EDITION
(NUPoD, 2017, 15.2 × 22.9 cm / 6 × 9 in, 216 pages)

On the first day of class, we collaboratively search, gather, and expand the syllabus in a shared document that then becomes our first collective book. In this way, we're speedrunning the syllabus through its relation to all the materials we'll study over the semester. In this instance, I articulate the publishing studio as follows:

> This course will be structured as a Print on Demand (POD) publishing initiative, with stu-

dents acting as an editorial collective and board. The name and organization of this publishing initiative is TBD, and will be decided by the editorial collective. Each week of the course will cluster around a specific theme, with an accompanying featured POD work and a set of critical readings to serve as departure points for your own publishing projects. Students will respond to these readings in the form of short weekly publishing assignments. The format of these brief assignments will vary from week to week, but will typically involve contributions from each student in the course that will then be compiled into a single POD publication by a revolving set of co-editors. The format and design of each publication will be determined by that week's co-editors, in dialogue with the editorial collective. In addition to these brief, collaborative assignments, students will produce individual POD publications for the course midterm and final. Completed publications will be uploaded to an online POD platform, which will also serve as a course portfolio. Everyone will have produced their own shelf full of books by the end of the semester. This course is interactive, growing and responding to its users. Each week will build on previous weeks, class conversations, and the directions that our study of POD happens to follow. The syllabus will only be completed after we finish the course, and all works (including your own) have been collected.

VARIOUS BLANK BOOKS
(NUPoD, 2017, 10.8 × 17.5 cm / 4.25 × 6.875 in, 200 pages)

This collection features a series of pocketbooks all set to precisely 200 pages long and entirely blank inside. Following on Craig Dworkin's *No Medium* (Cambridge, Mass.: MIT Press, 2015), featuring a range of "blank" (but always signifying) media, I thought an apt challenge would be to produce a great blank book. How to communicate with empty pages, after works like Aram Saroyan's ream of paper or Jean Cocteau's fictitious avant-garde "Nudisme." The results ranged from the comic ("How to Be a Ghost") to the utilitarian ("What Did You Do Today?") to the political ("When to Blame the Victim")—all working with blank books to produce something meaningful through paratext, all without a single word on the page.

A SCANTHOLOGY OF CONCRETE POETRY
(NUPoD, 2017, 15.6 × 23.4 cm / 6.14 × 9.21 in, 230 pages)

Working with the great *An Anthology of Concrete Poetry* (ed. Emmett Williams, New York: Something Else Press, 1967; reissued by New York: Primary Information, 2013), this transformative edition offers a variable reading of the semantic play that inhabits the material text. More directly: it uses the logic of the concrete poem in the process of capturing the page as a scan. First, the entire anthology was cut apart, page by page, and distributed to the students. Then, the assignment called for "morphing, ripping, modulating, handling, and mutating pages of concrete poetry" at the scanner interface: in short, to transform each page in conversation with the work it hosts. Chopped and screwed, the echoes of the anthology drift back as images caught in transformative processes of digitization.

E-LIT: WHAT IS IT? REVISED & EXPANDED UCLA EDITION, V2.01, 10.3.17, 3:15-3:45PM
(UCLA ELIT, 2017, 15.2 × 22.9 cm / 6 × 9 in, 316 pages)

ELIT PRIMER: AN EXPANDED FOOTNOTE COURSE READER
(UCLA ELIT, 2018, 15.2 × 22.9 cm / 6 × 9 in, 200 pages)

Arriving at UCLA in 2017, I became fascinated with the institutional history of the "Introduction to Electronic Literature" course as taught by disciplinary founder N. Katherine Hayles. I formulated a course to introduce students to this legacy, while also teaching the history of electronic literature alongside new literary practices emerging in the present. In our first session, we began with a 30-minute publishing experiment to expand Hayles's classic essay "Electronic Literature: What Is It?" (eliterature.org, 2007). The essay is a perfect object for expansion: it had been published a decade previously, aimed for an impossible kind of literary exhaustivity, and featured no fewer than 110 footnotes to explore. The first year I taught the course, we worked within the body of the text: Googling references and expanding the essay to encompass new developments and related texts. The following year, we produced a footnote follow-up, searching the footnotes exclusively, then gathering and returning with what updates we might receive. In both, the essay expands to contain contemporary works, surfing along with projected currents of a decade previous to produce a record of literary practices in the present.

INSTASONNET
(SPOT UCLA, 2018, 10.8 × 17.5 cm / 4.25 × 6.875 in, 84 pages)

Instasonnet began with a simple realization: the Instagram hashtag string has always been an unregulated exercise in ekphrastic poetry. These tags proliferate where radical compression meets speculative distribution meets a thirst for likes. In this book, I developed a new format for students to deploy: the hashtag sonnet. Roughly forty students worked in this newly-concocted and loosely-adapted form: 14 hashtags drawn from actual Instagram posts, printed one tag per line, broken

into four stanzas, with a twist in the final couplet. Adaptive composition was encouraged: searches for classically "poetic" phrases seeded poems to follow: #beautiful, #pain, #sadboy, #aesthetic, #like4like, #nofilter, and so forth. Here, for example, is a representative work: "#artist / #celebrity / #dead / #death // #die / #rip / #sadness / #picoftheday // #followme / #followmenow / #entertainment / #follow // #sadquotes / #instalovers."

LAPOD COURSE READER SYLLABUS CRAWLER

(LaPoD Press, 2018, 15.2 × 22.9 cm / 6 × 9 in, 240 pages)

A course description in lieu of syllabus rearticulation:

> The alphabet rendered poetry obsolete, once and for all. Since the [Western] written word overtook the Homeric epic as a kind of communal Wikipedia, poetry has been less about communicating information and more about lyric expression. Recently, digital technologies have been seen to present this same challenge to the book. Like poetry, we might say that the book isn't dead, it has simply lost its claim as a primary source of information. Over the last two decades, some of the most interesting works of art and poetry have turned to the book in both form and content, as both inspiration and fallen idol. It has never been easier for writers to publish, not just on Twitter and Facebook, but across a range of Print on Demand (POD) platforms for the printed book. This course examines recent works of art and poetry alongside new developments in print technologies. From Seth Siegelaub's *The Xerox Book* (1968) to new works of POD poetry published throughout the quarter (TBA, 2018), we will study the emergence of innovative forms of writing the book under the influence of digital networks. Additionally, we will conduct our own experiments using print on demand in a series of collaborative and independent scholarly projects. No previous experience with art, poetry, or publishing is required. All students will publish many books over the course of the quarter.

ANON ONLINE DIARY

(LaPoD Press, 2018, 10.8 × 17.5 cm / 4.25 × 6.875 in, 124 pages)

Anon Online Diary is a collaborative document of internet use written throughout the month of November, 2018. All participants anonymously logged their varieties of internet use over the course of the month in a shared Google document. The result is an aggregate user, a confused collective travelogue, a bibliographic diary of daily use.

INTERLEAVE COLLECTIVE REMIX
(Could Have Sworn Press, 2018, 19.0 × 19.0 cm / 7.5 × 7.5 in, 102 pages)

Asked to teach an honors seminar designed to develop UCLA creative writing theses, I found myself wondering how to relate to a dozen writing styles and approaches radically different from my own. Students wrote genre fiction, lyric poems, fantasy stories, creative nonfiction, memoirs, and biographies, among other literary genres. To discover how these works might speak to each other, I developed *Interleave Collective Remix*, a week-long collaborative shuffle of representative works previously written by seminar participants. Like the cards in a deck, students were asked to shuffle their works together into a coherent whole. Suddenly, line by line, fantastical characters spoke back to first-person coming-of-age narrators; poetic fragments interrupted theoretical dialogues; and genres otherwise disentangled became knotted together into a new and unlikely combinatory work. The resultant book is a document of looking for new ways to connect across discourses.

BOOKWRECK
(LaPoD Press, 2018, 15.2 × 22.9 cm / 6 × 9 in, 184 pages)

BOOKWRECK is a compilation of the recordings of variously destroyed, altered, burnt, and scanned book objects. Open selection, all books must be wrecked. It is divided into five chapters: 1) Incineration; 2) Transmutation; 3) Annotation; 4) Transformation; & 5) Execution.

ITERATIONS OF STÉPHANE MALLARMÉ'S UN COUP DE DÉS JAMAIS N'ABOLIRA LE HASARD
(LaPoD Press, 2018, Various, Various)

An excerpt from a talk at the American Comparative Literature Association conference on post-digital publishing:

> The examples could proliferate, however, I've been most fascinated by post-digital print bootlegs that emerge in the classroom. I'm currently running a "Print on Demand Art and Poetry" course at UCLA—last week we published twelve new editions of Mallarmé's codex-intensive poem "Un coup de dés jamais n'abolira le hasard"—some in kaomoji, others using audio waves or image searches, others rendering the poem as a choose your own adventure shipwreck game—each, like Mallarmé, interrogating the book as a space for poetic performance. Giving students leeway to explore their own intellectual interests, with the freedom to rework literary history, often warrants the most exciting outcomes. These works might best be situated at the border that fails to separate creative writing from digital humanities, or creative making from

critical production, or editorial work from scholarship.

RATE MY POEM: AN ANTHOLOGY ON THE POETICS OF THE REVIEW
(SPOT UCLA, 2019, 15.2 × 22.9 cm / 6 × 9 in, 238 pages)

Well known to students and professors alike is the crowdsourced review platform, "Rate My Professor." On this site, anonymous reviews are posted like those on Yelp and other rating apps, with a ranking system of one to five for terms like "quality" and "difficulty." Through a wide-ranging discussion on institutional structures, the commodification of education, and evolving systems of collective evaluation generally, we decided to make an anthology on the poetics of the professorial review. For this book, I asked "Surveying Poetry Online Today" (SPOT) students to render "Rate My Professor" reviews as poems. These poems were generated by selecting interesting reviews, lineating their contents, and substituting key words. For example, wherever the word "professor" might appear, we replaced it with the word "poem," such that each poem reflected inward, reading itself (see, for example: Charles Bernstein, "Thank You For Saying Thank You"). Students were required to each search for their own first names to make the poeticizing process all the more personal. Of course, the one-star review nets the best results. For example, here is the poem "Warning: Don't Read" in its entirety: "I learned nothing / in this poem. / It is a waste of time / and money. / Don't read it."

*H: A READER IN CONTRA-INTERNET STUDIES
(NetScribe UCLA, 2019, 15.2 × 22.9 cm / 6 × 9 in, 212 pages)

This reader deploys a version of the find-and-replace strategy featured in Zach Blas' *Contra-Internet* project, which we were studying in my "Writing for the Internet" creative seminar. Our collaboratively written book description uses the same technique:

> Intended to clearly and systematically demystify what is often considered the most challenging section of the internet, *CTRL H: The Critical Reader: The Complete Guide to Internet® Reading*, 3rd Edition, provides a comprehensive review of the reading skills tested on the redesigned network for users who are serious about raising their understanding of contra-internet practices. Includes: A chapter-by-chapter breakdown of networked media topics, with in-depth explanations and numerous network examples demonstrating how to navigate today's internet. Techniques for comprehending complex platforms and identifying key information systems quickly and efficiently. Learn how to break the internet, today!

UNDOCUMENTED PRESS (POETRY OF AMERICA)
(Undocumented Press, 2018, 15.2 × 22.9 cm / 6 × 9 in, 434 pages)

Breaking chronology, I'd like to conclude with a work called *Undocumented Press* that features a book action by Luca Messarra called *Poetry of America*, published as an individual final project in my course, "Surveying Poetry Online Today." While the entries here have featured only collaborative and collective productions, the most extraordinary works in the grey library emerge from unexpected applications in student final projects. None more than Messarra's project. Messarra, who happened to be employed at the UCLA library at the time, describes his process reworking an old, racist anthology of "American" poetry as follows:

> This edition of William James Linton's *Poetry of America; selections from one hundred American poets from 1776 to 1876* was scanned and uploaded by Google Books, edited in a bootlegged version of Adobe Acrobat Pro, and has been run through google translation services in the order of historical colonization of the New World (Spanish: Portuguese: French: Dutch: English) in order to do away with the Anglo-standardization of both language and continent.

The resulting book was published on Lulu in emulation of the physical copy found in UCLA's Young Research Library, with the hard copy inserted into the spot in said library that Linton's book had initially occupied—replacing the original with a glitched doppelganger. Today, the book continues to sit without documentation in the stacks at UCLA. Elsewhere, I've discussed this work as a form of "radical editioning." Or, a practice of performance versioning so completely overhauled that it may leap beyond the genre of the original into a new genre and poetic category altogether. In this, the grey library pales to invisibility—not to disappear, but to reveal new forms of unlearning at the pedagogical interface. In Messarra's *Undocumented Press* the grey library introduces ever greater indeterminacy into bibliographic space, enveloping the stacks in its wake.

Arch
& Ac

ives

cess

J. Gordon Faylor

A Note on Vernacular Print on Demand Publishing and the Conundrum of Access

By 2011, I was fully taken with Lulu. Here was a platform that would make realizing books through Gauss PDF, the digital publication I launched in 2010, possible. Over the years, I've seen so many wonderful small presses flicker and wane, brought down by the financial pressures of maintaining an active publishing operation while fostering a marginal audience that can only go so far in its support and advocacy. By publishing on Lulu, I was freed of any monetary obligations—I could simply upload a text and a cover, and suddenly there was this object conceived, to be ordered by anyone who might want it.

But the platform also enabled me to conduct publishing experiments that would have previously been prohibitively costly; for example, the books I released under the moniker Carton Trebe collated chunks of spambot text, organized as rapidly assembled 100-page capsules. It's hard to imagine a publisher willing to commit to such (so-called) excrescence, but Lulu opened a new frontier for play and intervention—one need look no further than Troll Thread's catalog for evidence of this tendency. Spambot text continues to function for me as a barometer for the web's unpredictable and overwhelming generative capacity—and even if that capacity ultimately serves a commercial function (i.e. increasing the likelihood of a certain product or brand to appear on search engines), the output is as or more unusual than what one might find in twentieth-century experimental writing. Given the evolution of algorithmic language programming, spambot texts utilize relatively recent technological advancements to produce what one might well call a pile of garbage. It's a fascinating contradiction to me, and one that highlights the potential and (very human) limitations of the internet.

My deepening interest in spambot texts began to influence the way I would plumb the internet for compelling, inhuman aggregations of language. By combining search phrases at random, I could find all kinds of unusual, strange—and often haunting—texts I could adapt for my own writing. (A side note: As search engines have become more sophisticated over the last decade, these oddities have become harder and harder to glean. Certainly their purposes are nefarious, but in my opinion that makes them no less worthy of documentation and preservation.) I was inspired by the robotic, the uncanny languages that lurked in the oblique corners of the internet.

At some point, I thought I'd apply my spam-hunting search methods to Lulu. It didn't take long to realize what a trove had been there all along. It should have been obvious long before: Lulu's publishing wizard is so easy to use, its interface welcoming if somewhat bland. One can simply upload a document, choose a cover template, and publicly publish their output. Like that. What this means in terms of accessibility frankly seems unprecedented—when else has this been possible? In the past, you either had detritus or privately released texts which would languish unless they were either lucky enough to be recovered/discovered, or they were bracketed or otherwise "rendered" by professionals. To publish a book, to some extent, meant to incur professionalism, or at least to adhere to a set of editorial standards. While mimeo culture and other more inviting forms of self-publishing arose during the twentieth century, these still required individual/collective labor and, to some extent, connection to a community. Lulu's publishing wizard takes the independence fostered by these approaches one step—or many steps—further, requiring little more than a working knowledge of the internet (and more specifically Lulu's publishing wizard).

What I found via those searches in the years to follow were unbelievable books. To briefly describe a few: A lengthy complaint written as a highly stylized legal filing about a person who'd been hit by a car on their scooter; a series of 600-page breathless novels with no real plot beyond a "red-headed housewife" caught up with a "New Age guru." A Christian poet who published dozens and dozens of books all set in a large typeface, such that only three lines fit on any given page; a bigoted and paranoid person's rant against the Indian government, whose ramblings are rife with email addresses, and who gives the book a title so long it literally runs off the cover. A guide to writing a "million pages book."

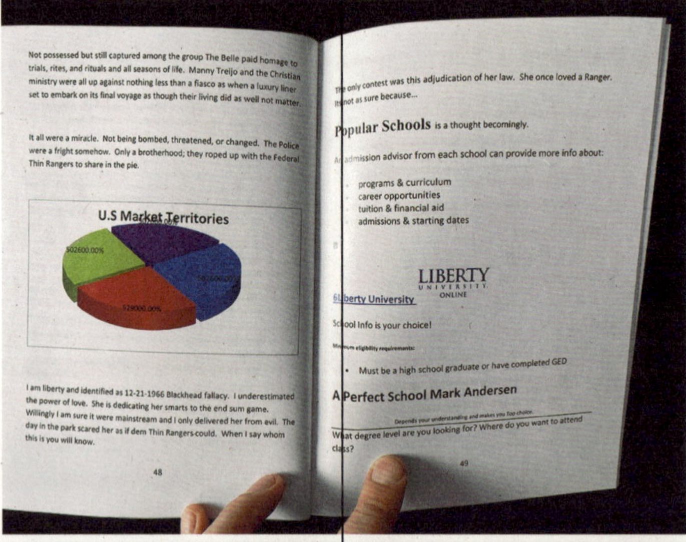
Not possessed but still captured among the group The Belle paid homage to trials, rites, and rituals and all seasons of life. Manny Treijo and the Christian ministry were all up against nothing less than a fiasco as when a luxury liner set to embark on its final voyage as though their living did as well not matter.

It all were a miracle. Not being bombed, threatened, or changed. The Police were a fright somehow. Only a brotherhood; they roped up with the Federal Thin Rangers to share in the pie.

U.S Market Territories

502600.00%

529000.00%

I am liberty and identified as 12-21-1966 Blackhead fallacy. I underestimated the power of love. She is dedicating her smarts to the end sum game. Willingly I am sure it were mainstream and I only delivered her from evil. The day in the park scared her as if dem Thin Rangers could. When I say whom this is you will know.

48

The only contest was this adjudication of her law. She once loved a Ranger. It's not as sure because...

Popular Schools is a thought becomingly.

An admission advisor from each school can provide more info about:

- programs & curriculum
- career opportunities
- tuition & financial aid
- admissions & starting dates

LIBERTY UNIVERSITY ONLINE

Liberty University

School Info is your choice!

Minimum eligibility requirements:

- Must be a high school graduate or have completed GED

A Perfect School Mark Andersen

What degree level are you looking for? Where do you want to attend class?

49

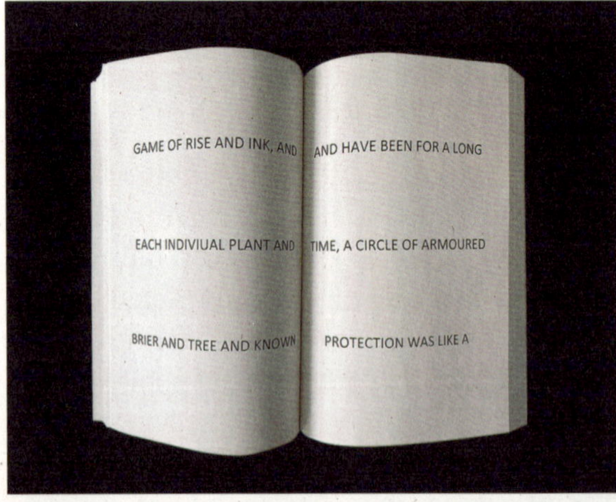
GAME OF RISE AND INK, AND

EACH INDIVIUAL PLANT AND

BRIER AND TREE AND KNOWN

AND HAVE BEEN FOR A LONG

TIME, A CIRCLE OF ARMOURED

PROTECTION WAS LIKE A

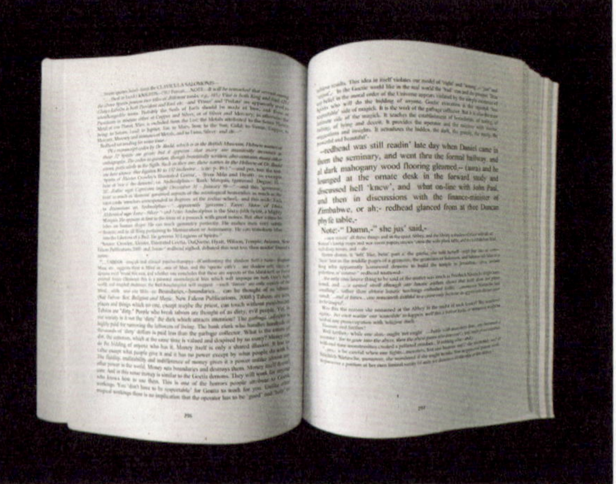

These are just a few of the dozens of remarkable—and indelibly strange—books I've been able to acquire. Many of them have had impacts large and small on my writing style and practice (e.g. the odd syntaxes some of these writers inhabit has leaked into my own), as well as the way I think about book production (e.g. how can formatting, design, and even production rates produce a surprising effect that contests the slow-

and-steady pace of most publishers?), while others remain merely unapproachable. But why not share more? Or should I provide excerpts, names, etc.?

What I've discovered on Lulu has surfaced a complicated problem for me, and one that I feel evokes a number of questions about identity, privacy, distribution, and non-art. These books, for all their pleasures, are also a major source of consternation, meditation, and contradiction for me.

When I share these books with others, I share them only in person. As you might be able to tell already, acquiring works like these enters one into a realm of ethical uncertainty. Why discuss them at all? In my own case, I like to only share the books in person, and never to share online, my reasoning being that it's never clear if or how much a particular author would want their work in a more public or literary/artistic context.

To what extent does my engagement with these books belie a kind of exploitation, a crass curiosity? Were these books even meant for others? (One time I purchased a book and found a week later it'd been taken down. It's feasible that I own the only copy of this book in existence, if its author didn't happen to purchase one.) No doubt these questions speak to a broader dissolution between the public and private; as I saw written somewhere a while ago, "email is skywriting," which is to say even intention falls in the face of something as chaotic as the internet. Other inquiries abound, and exceed the scope of this note, but just to share a few: What do these books suggest about the difference between internet and book literacy? Why do these odd compositions and rants make sense to their creators as a book object as opposed to a blog post? How does the book differ from digital space as a repository or tool for proselytization?

These books hit me like a secret at once inappropriate and alluring, and can get to feeling very nearly dangerous, like I'm seeing something I shouldn't. I'm not supposed to own these or know about these, I tell myself. And yet Lulu's ability to make these things available—which most likely would never have seen the light of day twenty, thirty years ago—tempts exploration. And while exploration can yield insights into access, design, and experimentation, is it ours to traverse? I still don't know, and can only try and cherish what I've seen, to hold it at arm's length with a sense of awe. To wonder what purpose or value these books provide others, to wonder at what they're doing or have done for me. Awe; awe and confusion.

Hartmut Abendschein

Conceptual Publishing and Library Practice

Translated by Cadenza Academic Translations

The author of this article is a publisher, author, and academic librarian in equal measure, so it is hardly surprising that there is interaction between these areas. The intersection lies in the production and publication, but also in the collection, cataloging, archiving, and sharing of idiosyncratic literary works that are published (by small presses) with a short print run, but are also classified as "gray literature." As a publisher at the Bern-based independent publishing house edition taberna kritika, I use various means to make its program and its publications' artistic and conceptual approaches transparent. As a subject librarian at the University Library of Bern, on the other hand, I am interested in how to make marginalized literature more valued, integrated, and institutionalized. An important element here is the cataloging process considered as an artistic practice that attempts to establish connections and communication between one's own publisher's catalogue and other catalogues, and thus extend these productively wherever possible.

LIBRARY AND COLLECTION

My bread-and-butter job as a librarian has proved to be a useful source of content and synergies for my publishing practice. A special collections area of contemporary fine press books (short-run books that are relief-printed using a hand press) and artist's books, inherited when I took up my post (the collection had little relevance due to its small budget and consequently limited scope), led a few years ago to my initiating a profile shift. It had long been evident that the theme of "publishing as artistic practice" was gaining increasing attention in the world of experimental, low-budget publications (print-on-demand, zines, chapbooks, self-made books) in both academic and art theory contexts. While the objects in the fine press collection were very expensive (special materials, very limited print run or in some cases one-of-a-kind), production costs in these small presses fall within an affordable range. The same budget can thus be stretched to afford multiple titles, although this involves other challenges. The books are often supplied direct, rather than via the (wholesale) bookselling trade, and very soon go out of print. There is therefore a narrow time frame in which to select and purchase them, and moreover they must be bought via the publisher's online store with Paypal checkout or using the shopping basket on print-on-demand platforms; these payment methods are not very well received by acquisitions departments in libraries, who are more used to dealing with B2B processes.[1] In addition, this segment is typically part of what is known as "gray literature," which means it requires more working hours and it is unlikely that cataloging can be facilitated by automatic importing of metadata. Special media materials and formats may in addition incur increased archiving and storage costs. These books certainly have in their favor that most of them can be loaned out without major difficulties or restrictions. This ease of access guarantees that engaging with these materials is as straightforward as possible.

AUTHORITY DATA AND METADATA, SUBJECT CATALOGING, DISSEMINATION

The practice in many (academic) libraries is to use verbal cataloging in order to make content findable via specific catalog searches. It is recorded in rulebooks and databases and organized by editorial staff. Compared to classification, it offers more freedom to provide a pithy description of an object or book; in contrast, classification often as-

1. Large libraries increasingly outsource their acquisitions processes to intermediaries and wholesalers, which can result in savings on labor costs. However, this happens at the expense of bookstores (demise of infrastructure), publishers, and in general the breadth and depth of the range available.

signs an object to one or two classes, which means the definition is less precise. Verbal classes are, however, designed to correspond to the numbering system of the Dewey Decimal Classification (DDC), enabling the derivation of notations like, for example, 020.2854678 for "Internet Libraries" (cf. Fig. 2)—an important tool for systematically cataloging or roughly structuring the inventory, although it is not always immediately accessible to outsiders.[2]

After a few years' publishing practice, I attempted to systematize my own publishing production using tools like these so as to make it slightly more transparent. I therefore use controlled cataloging vocabulary in the form of tags and descriptors based on the Integrated Authority File (GND), the largest set of authority data for cultural and academic data in the German-speaking world (cf. Fig. 1); otherwise I work with an academic classification system based on the DDC (cf. Fig. 2) in order to better portray the range of differentiation in my publishing house's publications and also to facilitate alternative cataloging approaches or virtual classifications.

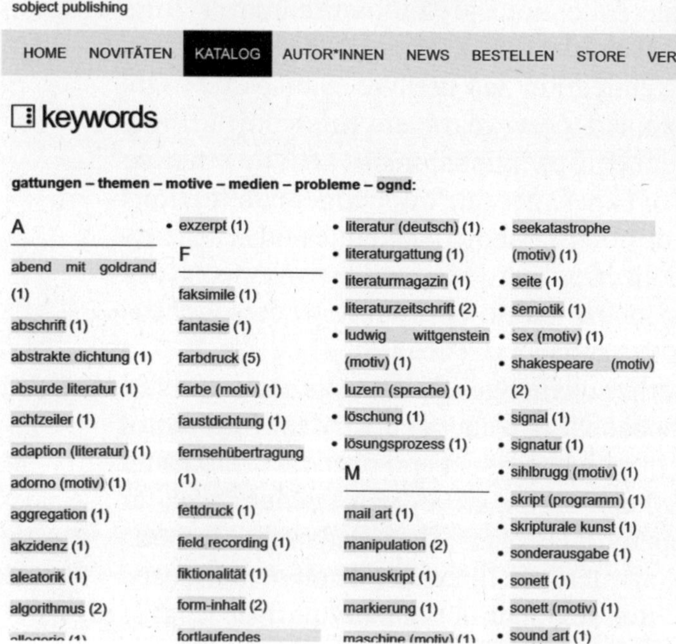

Fig. 1: Extract from the edition taberna kritika home page with tagging of all published titles according to "genre – theme – motif – medium – difficulties". This index uses a mixed vocabulary of existing GND tags, such as "literatur (deutsch)" (literature (german)), and tags such as "also" (therefore) that do not yet exist, but can be preformed based on the RSWK (Rules for the tag catalog)—a kind of smuggling operation.

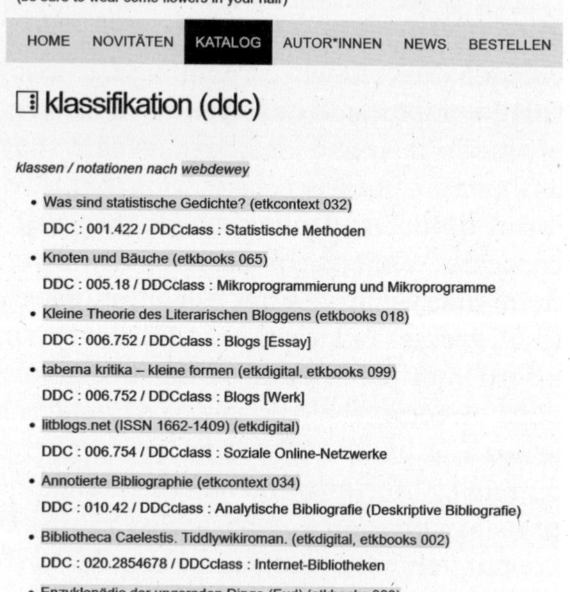

Fig. 2: Extract from the edition taberna kritika home page with DDC classes and related DDC notations for all published titles. For example, Was sind statistische Gedichte? (What are statistical poems?) is assigned to the Statistical Methods class, with the notation 001.422.

The use of authority data or metadata for subject cataloging facilitates the classification and assignment of different publications and, in the form of diverse indexes and access tools, feeds into my publishing house's annually updated *Annotated Bibliography*, i.e., the complete catalog.[3] Making the most of the fact that publishers can include descriptive tags when entering metadata into the central database used by the German book trade (Verzeichnis lieferbarer Bücher (VLB)), I make sure to use tags rather than keywords (uncontrolled vocabulary) in my catalog. The metadata entered into the VLB database are then automatically incorporated into the different dissemination systems

2. Cf. the German version in the digital WebDewey option https://deweysearchde.pansoft.de/webdeweysearch/.

3. A limited print run is published in the style of the main series, but it is also available as a freely accessible digital object. DOI: 10.17436/etk.c.034.

used by the book trade—e.g., into the numerous online store databases and the catalog of the German National Library. These data are in turn automatically imported into the catalog used by academic libraries in Switzerland, where a software program compares the cataloging vocabulary with a concordance file and immediately generates tags in the library catalog, which initially remain unseen until they are noted by the librarians responsible for subject cataloging.

As well as facilitating the indexing and findability of titles in library and bookshops, the cataloging rules for authority data and their principal application also prove useful in other ways: it allows official, but also unofficial (although formulated according to the rules) content-related cataloging vocabulary to be incorporated into academic library systems that automatically import data from sources such as the VLB database or the German National Library. A publication cataloged in one's own words is thus visible and searchable in other catalogs (e.g., Worldcat, the German Digital Library, VLB database, Swissbib, (†)[4]), or at the very least appears in backend cataloging records (special input screens for information specialists) that are awaiting further processing (cf. Fig. 3).

This is also significant insofar as I have consciously interpreted several library rules rather broadly. Thus, *primary* literature is only indexed in *academic* library systems in exceptional cases. In certain circumstances I take a more flexible approach to the basic rules and word corpora of the GND and adapt them to the requirements of my own concepts, for example by supplementing existing GND tags such as "literature (german)" with words like "therefore" that do not yet exist, but that can be pre-formed based on a set of rules for cataloging (RSWK) (cf. Fig. 2 above). For example, in the case of Tine Melzer's *Ludwig & Gertrude*, an artist's book that combines the vocabulary of Gertrude Stein and Ludwig Wittgenstein in a specific manner, in addition to the tags "corpus (linguistic)," "contrastive linguistics," and "vocabulary," I applied the tags "ludwig wittgenstein (motif)" and "gertrude stein (motif)" (cf. Fig. 3), which is actually an inadmissible shortening, but which seemed to me to be helpful on pragmatic grounds for imparting information to the general reading public.[5] For these reasons, I use narrow as well as broad tags, whereas in strict library cataloging the preference is always for precise vocabulary. These chosen tags appear on the back cover of all the books published by edition taberna kritika; the quantity per book is therefore limited.


```
<datafield tag="653" ind1=" " ind2=" ">
  <subfield code="a">korpus (linguistik)</subfield>
</datafield>
<datafield tag="653" ind1=" " ind2=" ">
  <subfield code="a">ludwig wittgenstein (motiv)</subfield>
</datafield>
<datafield tag="653" ind1=" " ind2=" ">
  <subfield code="a">kontrastive linguistik</subfield>
</datafield>
<datafield tag="653" ind1=" " ind2=" ">
  <subfield code="a">gertrude stein (motiv)</subfield>
</datafield>
<datafield tag="653" ind1=" " ind2=" ">
  <subfield code="a">wortschatz</subfield>
</datafield>
```


Fig. 3: The cataloging vocabulary is stored in the system ready for export, as shown in this extract from the MARC 21 catalog entry[6] for Tine Melzer's *Ludwig & Gertrude* in the German National Library, URL: http://d-nb.info/1226169880/about/marcxml, opened with a basic text editor...

However, the cataloging vocabulary is currently only stored in hidden files (e.g., in the German National Library or VLB database) and is imported at the same time as the title is transferred to international catalogs such as Worldcat or Swissbib (cf. Fig. 4).

4. The Swissbib catalog was regrettably discontinued in 2020 and replaced by Swisscovery. From the point of view of cataloging, this is a serious setback, as the new catalog has dispensed with a great number of options in the areas of information transfer and information retrieval.

5. Tine Melzer and Egon Stemle, *Ludwig & Gertrude* (Bern: edition taberna kritika (etkbooks 060), 2021).

6. MARC 21 is a general format that can be read and processed by a wide range of applications. Its main purpose is for transferring bibliographical data between libraries.

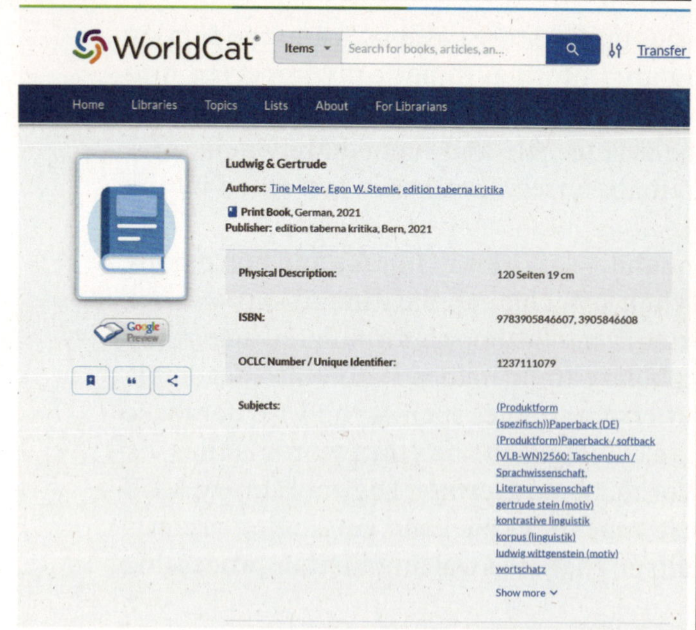

Fig. 4: ...and imported into Worldcat, where the tags I assigned are transferred in their entirety at the same time, www.worldcat.org/title/ludwig-gertrude/oclc/1237111079.

PUBLICATION SERIES AS A (COMPLETE) CONCEPTUAL WORK

An example of a conceptual publishing production is the / aaaa press series comprising one hundred titles (2020–2022) from my publishing house, edition taberna kritika. This project was conceived as a small, provocative allegory: it puts a Foucauldian concept into practice, namely the question of what would happen if it were impossible to organize literary or art markets around (authors') names or provenance labels, due to this information simply being withheld:

> I will propose a game: the year without names. For one year books will be published without the author's name. The critics will have to manage with an entirely anonymous production. But I suspect that perhaps they will have nothing to say: all the authors will wait until the next years to publish their books.[7]

The recipients of the new releases had to approach the publications with no publisher or author information, which is virtually unimaginable nowadays.

The titles in the / aaaa press series include a wide range of conceptual, visual, and literary works, photobooks, documentation, concept sketches, etc. In principle, there are no acceptance restrictions with regard to content; there are however several less formal ones. Each publication is issued as a PDF and as a print-on-demand item. The page format is set at DIN A4[8] and the content at 60–800 pages, which corresponds to the minimum and maximum print production range (softcover) of the print-on-demand company Lulu. A very simple series aesthetic was established for covers and endpapers, and there was a challenging publication frequency target of one title per week, which was always announced on a Monday on the publisher's Twitter account (@etkbooks). At least two copies of each title were printed for a physical exhibition and subsequent acceptance of the corpus by a library. In addition, each (anonymous) author received a printed specimen copy. Legal deposit copies for libraries were not provided for, as libraries already have the digital version at their disposal. The sales price corresponds to the production price charged by the print-on-demand company: the publisher makes no money from this production.

7. Michel Foucault, "The Masked Philosopher," in *Foucault Live: Collected Interviews, 1961-1984*, ed. Sylvère Lotringer (New York: Semiotext(e), 1996), 302—307, 302.

8. The name of the series, "aaaa," alluded to this aspect. It incidentally pushed it virtually to the top of alphabetized indices of lists of series titles.

Intensive metadata work also plays an important part in this series, with a further effect being the possible subsequent outsourcing of its distribution to the digital web archive of the Swiss National Library. The digital objects are currently all freely accessible in my Google Drive cloud storage (accessible at aaaa.etkbooks.com) and are linked to specific folder deeplinks in the cloud via a web document there. The links to the print-on-demand ordering options for all the individual works are also listed (cf. Fig. 5). However, the series may be withdrawn from the internet at any time, with the original URL and the cloud storage relinquished, in which case the Swiss National Library (where the digital objects are stored) would—without its explicit consent—take over the publisher's role, at least in terms of distribution.

Title / Full Text	p	DOI, Permalink*	meta data	🛒	Free
		10.17436/etk.a.078	md	Print	PDF
Dein Herz ist hart wie Samt	076	10.17436/etk.a.077	md	Print	PDF
close up maps	060	10.17436/etk.a.076	md	Print	PDF
709.04075	202	10.17436/etk.a.075	md	Print	PDF
Reading Your World of Texts	098	10.17436/etk.a.074	md	Print	PDF
nyckeln till goda inkop	076	10.17436/etk.a.073	md	Print	PDF
100X_200X	204	10.17436/etk.a.072	md	Print	PDF
Wasserleichen riechen nicht	060	10.17436/etk.a.071	md	Print	PDF
How to make sönic pöems	074	10.17436/etk.a.070	md	Print	PDF

Fig. 5: / aaaa press title list indicating the number of pages and the DOI as well as the link to the metadata, the Lulu print-on-demand edition, and the free PDFs (extract from the cloud document at aaaa.etkbooks.com)

The use of DOIs should ensure a certain level of durability and permalink stability, especially in the event that the series is ever actually "withdrawn" and the document's DOI-linked save location can exist in any cloud storage or repository. The publications will continue to require a stable identifier in order to be directly accessible, e.g., after moving to the digital archive of a different library.

Also in this series, the publishing house used a variant of the cataloging concept explained above, although not based on the GND. As the series comprises mainly experimental, hybrid, and innovative objects, it cannot be described accurately and with enough differentiation by the more traditional lexica of established standard dictionaries. Instead, an *in progress* thesaurus was set up (cf. Figs. 6 and 7), drawing on my experience in dealing with other specialized publications, but also conceptually oriented to existing Wikipedia English-language article titles. The concepts are, strictly speaking, not (yet) at the level of tags, so I prefer to call them "descriptors."

Thesaurus / Präkoordinierende Facettenklassifikation						
Notation Signaturstruktur	HA	AA	AA	AA	Punkt	Facette
	Hauptaspekt HA	Anderer Aspekt	Anderer Aspekt	Anderer Aspekt		
Bildung einer Merkmalskette	Prio1	Prio2 (oder 0)	Prio3 (oder 0)	Prio4 (oder 0)		
präkoordinierend	Gruppe 1	Gruppe 2	Gruppe 3	Gruppe 4		Nebensachgruppe
Marc Felder Konkordanz	650 T	650 M	655 F	650 S		084 W
Merkmale	Methode, Technik	Material, Basis	Formschlagwort, Medium, Textsorte	Thema, Motiv, "Über"		Allg. Werkcharakter
basis keyword korpus: apod.li	annotation	AOL search	artist.book	ant		1 = poetry, concrete
ergänzungen rot: etkbooks	appropriation	bibliography	book	authorship		2 = fiction, comic
kursiv = benutzt in aaaa	black out	bot	calendar	blank page		3 = nonfiction
	collage	censorship	code (morse ...)	canon		4 = visual, multimedia
	colouring	classification	conversation	chance		5 = theory, meta
	combinatorics	coat of arms	cookbook	collectivity		6 = how-to
	conceptual writing	collection	diary	communication		0 = other, combinations
	constraint	corpus	digital literature	copyright		
	contextualization	drawing	documentation	dna		
	critique	email	ebook reader	fraud		
	crowdfunding	emoji	game	gaming		
	crowdsourcing	found material	herbarium	glitch art		
	cutting / tearing	generative	interface	grief		
	distribution	google	intervention	habitus		
	enlarging	google mail	letter	hand gesture		
	erasure / deletion	lomography	manifesto	handwriting		
	extraction	google maps	manual	help		
	formatting	map / floor plan	musical note	institutional critique		
	google search	microfiche	performance	language		
	hand writing	ms paint	photo book	literature		
	iteration	ms word	print-on-demand	loss		
	layout	music	reenactment	material reflection		
	listing	number	seminar work	materiality		
	loop	operating system	sharing	media		

Fig. 6: Screenshot /aaaa press, Thesaurus under construction. Groups 1-4 imitate the structure of the fields in a library catalog with subject cataloging data, but I have adapted and fully differentiated them for this project: the "Main Aspect (HA)," "Method, Technique," which forms Group 1, is supplemented by Groups 2-4, which tag the publications according to "Other Aspects (AA)," such as "Material," "Form, Medium, Text Type," and "Theme, Motif." The italic keywords are already in use to describe the / aaaa press titles. Another aspect is provided by a further subsidiary group in the last column, which describes the "General character of the work." The special thesaurus will also be published, after editing, as part of this series.

Titel	DOI	HA	AA	AA	AA	.	N	_	T	Signatur*	Keyword1	Keyword2	Keyword3	Keyword4
Dein Herz ist hart wie Samt	a.077	2	1	2	3	.	1		D3	**2123.1 D3**	photography	timeline	twitter	flarf poetry
close up maps	a.076	2	1	3	1	.	4		C6	**2131.4 C6**	map	enlargement	photo book	cut-out
709.04075	a.075	2	3	3	2	.	5		S4	**2332.5 S4**	bibliography	avantgarde	artist book	collection
Reading Your World of Texts	a.074	1	1	2	4	.	2		R2	**1124.2 R2**	web navigation	collaborative writing	ascii art	reading
nyckeln till goda inkop	a.073	4	2	1	1	.	4		N9	**4211.4 N9**	ikea catalogue	corpus	timeline	formatting
100X_200X	a.072	2	1	3	1	.	4		H9	**2131.4 H9**	x	repetition	back side	colouring
Wasserleichen riechen nicht	a.071	4	1	4	3	.	2		W3	**4143.2 W3**	crime fiction	narration	literature	book
How to make sönic pöems	a.070	2	2	1	3	.	6		H8	**2213.6 H8**	sound poetry	music box	notation	tutorial
Intonations	a.069	2	3	3	4	.	0		I6	**2334.0 I6**	staff (music)	musical note	form (document)	material reflection
glitcho studies	a.068	4	2	1	2	.	4		G5	**4212.4 G5**	glitch art	photography	smartphone app	portrait
Periodic Table (alphabetized)	a.067	1	2	1	3	.	4		P4	**1213.4 P4**	alphabetical orde	periodic table	colouring	table
Charles & Kate	a.066	3	1	1	4	.	5		C4	**3114.5 C4**	table	notation	cutting	coworking
Znüniböxli	a.065	1	1	1	0	.	2		Z8	**1110.2 Z8**	appropriation	montage	annotation	
Seuchenblatt (2020)	a.064	1	2	3	4	.	3		S4	**1234.3 S4**	montage	found material	diary	covid-19
a.a.O.	a.063	4	1	1	1	.	0		A1	**4111.0 A1**	abbreviation	conceptual writing	layout	loop
Frühe Prosa	a.062	4	4	1	3	.	0		F9	**4413.0 F9**	handwriting	typewriting	remix	documentation
The Intersection	a.061	3	3	4	3	.	4		T3	**3343.4 T3**	artist book	documentation	sculpture	photo book
Bliss Dictionary	a.060	2	2	4	3	.	0		B6	**2243.0 B6**	blissymbols	dictionary	constructed langua	documentation
The Questionable	a.059	1	4	2	1	.	4		T3	**1421.4 T3**	erasure	literature	ms word	spell checker
Erfolgsbots	a.058	2	2	2	4	.	3		E6	**2224.3 E6**	bot	wikipedia	spam	authorship
bad photos	a.057	2	2	3	3	.	4		B1	**2233.4 B1**	lomography	collection	documentation	photo book
etanosru stt	a.056	2	1	1	0	.	1		E8	**2110.1 E8**	sound poetry	reversion	translation	
_i_o__e__o__e__	a.055	1	1	3	2	.	1		I0	**1132.1 I0**	black out	conceptual writing	visualization	paper

Fig. 7: This will be used to produce a working table with a notations matrix, in which all the / aaaa press titles will be listed and described along with their DOIs and main and supplementary tags.

Even artists' works which are more difficult to describe should be able to find a place in edition taberna kritika and will furnish material for future discussions on questions such as: What is literature? What is art? What is a book? What is a library? What is an author?[9] However, I have repeatedly had the experience that cataloging policies change and that catalogs break down at ever more frequent intervals, which may make some of the effects outlined here obsolete. Dealing with libraries with special publications, and their findability, is in itself a work in progress, requiring regular readjustment. From the publisher's point of view, it is all the more important that our own cataloging practice remains consistent so that a collection that has grown up over decades can still be systematically recorded and experienced in retrospect, albeit in the microcosm of its own bibliography.

9. It cannot, therefore, be ruled out that series yet to be created may answer new aspects of these questions, or at least provide material in support of them. Various considerations play a part here. For example, one might consider the potential use of non-fungible-tokens (NFTs), or whether certain effects might not also be possible with DOI. However, at the date of this article, I have not devoted much time to such ideas. There does not yet seem to be a solid relation between them and energy balance, dependence on third party software and hardware, sustainability, etc.

Index Names

Index Works

TEXTS AND ESSAYS

IMAGES

Image courtesy of Albert Coers: 446f.; AND Publishing: 49 left; Andreas Schmidt: 31; Benjamin Busch for Import Projects (CC BY-SA): 95 right; Bettina Brach: 69; Florian Höfer: 520; the Getty Research Institute, Los Angeles, and the State Mayakovsky Museum, Moscow: 62 left; Hartmut Abendschein: 444 bottom; Holly Melgard: 102 right; James Bridle: 97 right, 153; Jasper Otto Eisenecker: 73 both; Jean Keller: 86 right; Joachim Schmid: 50 both, 53 left, 141 top; Kent Larson: 519; Kris de Decker: 414; Lilian Landes: 213; Louis Porter: 270–279; Marina Kampka: 321 bottom; Marlene Obermayer (https://daskunstbuch.at/2013/04/15/paper-passion-perfume-der-duft-frisch-gedruckter-bucher-steidl-2012/): 60; Michael Mandiberg (CC BY-SA): 326; Mishka Henner: 77, 197 top; the Museum of Modern Art, New York: 61; Olivier Bertrand: 80, 81 both; Onestar Press: 252; Paul Soulellis (CC BY-SA): 63 right; Paul Laidler: 59; Publication Studio: 110 left; Silvio Lorusso and Giulia Ciliberto: 49 right, 103, 193; Wil van Iersel: 108, 426 top; Xavier Antin: 67; Yin Yin Wong: 114 right above.

Photographs by apod.li (CC BY-SA): 20, 21 right, 33 all, 45 top, 51f., 53 right, 58, 65f., 71 left, 84 top left, 87 all, 89 bottom left and right, 90 left, 96 both, 97 left, 98, 100, 101 left, 107, 109 both, 111 right, 112 left, 113 top, 128–139, 141 bottom, 142–152, 154–192, 194–196, 197 middle and bottom left, 198–212, 214–251, 253–269, 280–320, 321 top, 322–325, 327–413, 415–425, 426 bottom, 427–443, 444 top, 445, 448.

Screenshots by apod.li (CC BY-SA): 9, 11–13, 25–27, 38, 39 left and bottom right, 40 left, 41f., 45 bottom, 48, 62 right, 63 left, 70, 72, 75f., 78 both, 79 both, 82 both, 83, 84 top right, bottom right, middle left, and bottom left, 85 right both, 89 top left, 90 right, 91 both, 92, 93 both, 95 left, 99 both, 101 right, 102 left, 105 both, 106 both, 110 right, 111 left, 112 right, 113 bottom, 114 left, 116.

Many thanks to all artists, authors, and publishers who have contributed to the library and this catalog, including those who responded to the open call or contacted us by other means;

to the pioneers of the field whose research, art, and activism is a continuing source of inspiration to us, namely Silvio Lorusso, Alessandro Ludovico, Danny Snelson, and Paul Soulellis;

to all the practitioners and thinkers whose texts and visual essays we are honored to (re)print and who we were lucky enough to meet and interview online or offline, in particular ABC, Hartmut Abendschein, Hannes Bajohr, Clara Balaguer, Olivier Bertrand, Manon Bruet, Florian Cramer, Karen ann Donnachie, Jasper Otto Eisenecker, Marc van Elburg, J. Gordon Faylor, Michael Hagner, Lynn Harris, Mishka Henner, Wil van Iersel, Dagmara Kraus, Michael Mandiberg, Holly Melgard, Kathrin Passig, Michalis Pichler, Louis Porter, paula roush, Zoë Sadokierski, Joachim Schmid, Andreas Schmidt, Sophie Seita, Andy Simionato, Temporary Services, Nick Thurston, Stéphanie Vilayphiou, Angie Waller, Eva Weinmayr, Yin Yin Wong, Joey Yearous-Algozin, and Rahel Zoller;

to our friends, colleagues, supporters, and advisors Eyk Akansu, Ines Barner, Sarah Berger, Christoph Bläsi, Johanna Bohley, Bettina Brach (†), Felipe Cussen, Craig Dworkin, Georg Fischer, Michael Glasmeier, Patrick Greaney, Svenja Hagenhoff, Christine Hartmann, Karin de Jong, John Z. Komurki, Hubert Kretschmer, Lilian Landes, Christian Mathieu, An Mertens, Dirk Niefanger, Cornelia Ortlieb, Michael Otto, Nina Prader, Kerstin Preiwuß, Tania Prill, Christoph Reske, Maggie Rosenau, Camilla Salvaneschi, Alan Smart, Alexander Starre, Paul Stephens, and Melissa Terras;

to Spector Books, especially Jan Wenzel, Anne König, and Lyosha Kritsouk, for imagining, designing, and making this book, and Katharina Nejdl for designing the digital interface to the library;

to Cadenza Academic Translations for translating and editing most of our texts and Anne König, Frederik Richthofen, and Maggie Rosenau for proof-reading;

to the student assistants Marlene Bässler, Natalie Diga, Patrick Graur, Luzie Horn, Fabian Kasperl, Melanie Thümler, and Tashina Voit who all helped to manage the messier parts of the project;

to our institutional and financial backers: the German Research Foundation (DFG) and the research project "Artefakte der Avantgarden 1885–2015" which we were part of, the Bavarian State Library Munich (BSB), the Friedrich-Alexander-Universität Erlangen-Nürnberg (FAU), the Freie Universität Berlin (FU), the Baumgart Stiftung Munich, the Forschungsverbund Künstlerpublikationen, and the Museum of Books and Writing at the German National Library Leipzig.

ARTEFAKTE DER AVANTGARDEN 1885 — 2015

forschungsverbund künstlerpublikationen

Colophon

TITLE	Library of Artistic Print on Demand. Post-Digital Publishing in Times of Platform Capitalism
EDITED BY	Annette Gilbert and Andreas Bülhoff
GRAPHIC DESIGN	Lyosha Kritsouk
IMAGE CORRECTION	Oleksii Novikov
TRANSLATION	Cadenza Academic Translations (8–122, 522–530, 690–696), Derek Byrne (490–500), Joel Scott (546–552)
COPYEDITING	Cadenza Academic Translations, Annette Gilbert, Andreas Bülhoff
PROOFREADING	Anne König, Frederik Richthofen, Maggie Rosenau
PRINTING	Gutenberg Beuys Feindruckerei GmbH
PUBLISHED BY	Spector Books Verlagsgesellschaft mbH Harkortstraße 10, 04107 Leipzig www.spectorbooks.com
DISTRIBUTION	Germany, Austria: GVA, Gemeinsame Verlagsauslieferung Göttingen GmbH&Co. KG, www.gva-verlage.de
	Switzerland: AVA Verlagsauslieferung AG, www.ava.ch
	France, Belgium: Interart Paris, www.interart.fr
	UK: Central Books Ltd, www.centralbooks.com
	USA, Canada, Central and South America, Africa: ARTBOOK/ D.A.P., www.artbook.com
	South Korea: The Book Society, www.thebooksociety.org
	Japan: twelvebooks, www.twelve-books.com
	Australia, New Zealand: Perimeter Distribution, www.perimeterdistribution.com
ISBN	978-3-95905-697-7

First edition: 2025

Printed in the EU